DORLING KINDERSLEY
ULTIMATE VISUAL DICTIONARY OF SCIENCE

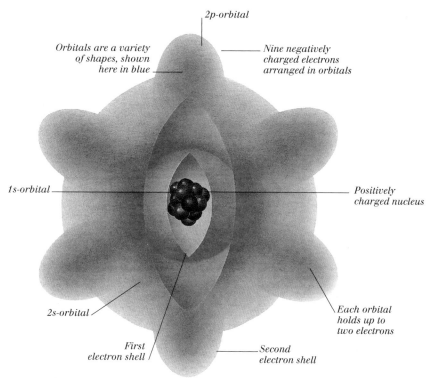

2p-orbital

Orbitals are a variety of shapes, shown here in blue

Nine negatively charged electrons arranged in orbitals

1s-orbital

Positively charged nucleus

2s-orbital

Each orbital holds up to two electrons

First electron shell

Second electron shell

ANATOMY OF A FLUORINE ATOM

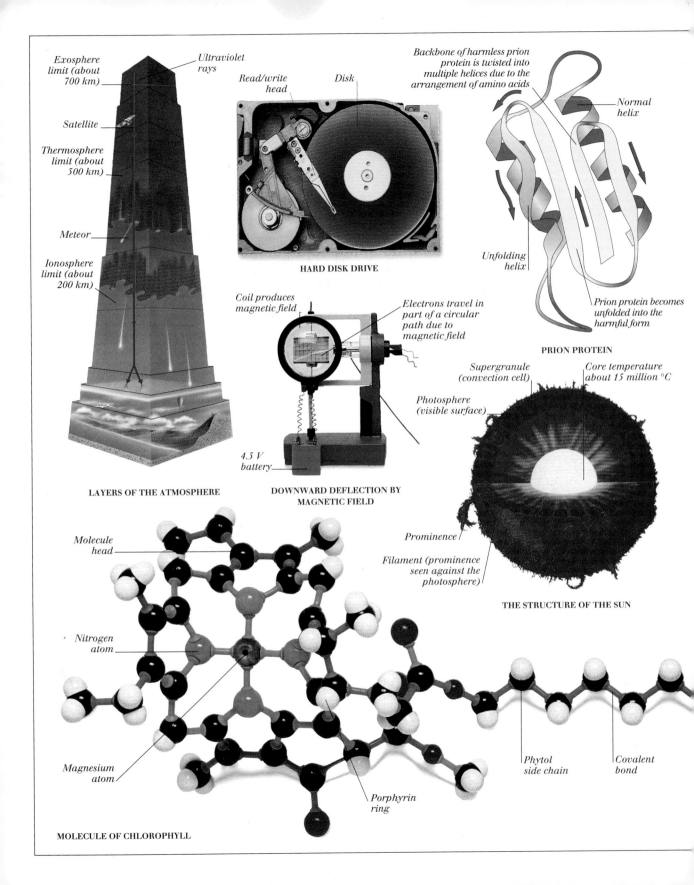

Exosphere limit (about 700 km)

Ultraviolet rays

Read/write head

Disk

Backbone of harmless prion protein is twisted into multiple helices due to the arrangement of amino acids

Normal helix

Satellite

Thermosphere limit (about 500 km)

Meteor

Ionosphere limit (about 200 km)

HARD DISK DRIVE

Unfolding helix

Prion protein becomes unfolded into the harmful form

PRION PROTEIN

Coil produces magnetic field

Electrons travel in part of a circular path due to magnetic field

Supergranule (convection cell)

Core temperature about 15 million °C

Photosphere (visible surface)

4.5 V battery

LAYERS OF THE ATMOSPHERE

DOWNWARD DEFLECTION BY MAGNETIC FIELD

Prominence

Filament (prominence seen against the photosphere)

THE STRUCTURE OF THE SUN

Molecule head

Nitrogen atom

Magnesium atom

Phytol side chain

Covalent bond

Porphyrin ring

MOLECULE OF CHLOROPHYLL

DORLING KINDERSLEY

ULTIMATE VISUAL DICTIONARY OF SCIENCE

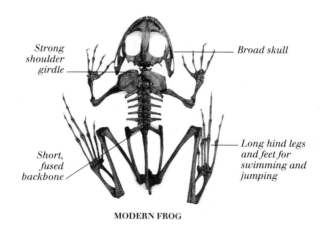

Strong shoulder girdle

Broad skull

Short, fused backbone

Long hind legs and feet for swimming and jumping

MODERN FROG

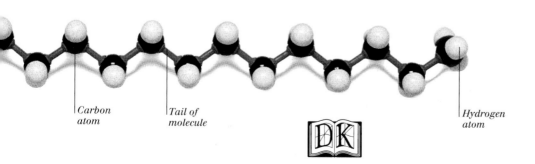

Carbon atom

Tail of molecule

Hydrogen atom

DK PUBLISHING, INC.

A DK PUBLISHING BOOK

DESIGNERS JOANNE LONG, CLAIRE NAYLOR
SENIOR ART EDITOR HEATHER McCARRY
DEPUTY ART DIRECTOR TINA VAUGHAN

EDITOR LARA MAIKLEM
US EDITOR WILLIAM LACH
PROJECT EDITOR MIKE FYLNN
SENIOR EDITORS GEOFFREY STALKER, CHRISTINE WINTERS
SENIOR MANAGING EDITOR SEAN MOORE

SENIOR CONSULTANT EDITOR JACK CHALLONER
HUMAN ANATOMY AND LIFE SCIENCES CONSULTANT RICHARD WALKER
EARTH SCIENCES CONSULTANTS PETER DOYLE, JOHN FARNDON
MEDICAL SCIENCE CONSULTANTS STEVE PARKER, DR ROBERT M YOUNGSON

PICTURE RESEARCHERS SARAH MACKAY, MAUREEN SHEERIN

PRODUCTION MANAGER SARAH COLTMAN

**PRINTED CIRCUIT BOARD
FROM A COMPUTER**

FIRST AMERICAN EDITION, 1998
2 4 6 8 10 9 7 5 3 1

PUBLISHED IN THE UNITED STATES BY DK PUBLISHING, INC.
95 MADISON AVENUE, NEW YORK, NEW YORK 10016

VISIT US ON THE WORLD WIDE WEB AT http://www.dk.com

LIBRARY OF CONGRESS CATALOGING-IN-PUBLICATION DATA

Ultimate visual dictionary of science. -- 1st Amer. ed.
        p.   cm.
    Includes index
    ISBN 0-7894-3512-8
    1. Science--Dictionaries.   2. Picture Dictionaries, English
Q125.U43   1998
503--dc21   98-11900
                                                          CIP

REPRODUCED BY COLOURSCAN, SINGAPORE
PRINTED IN ITALY

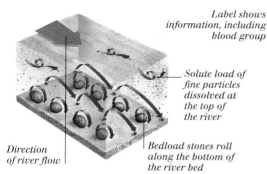

Label shows information, including blood group

Solute load of fine particles dissolved at the top of the river

Direction of river flow

Bedload stones roll along the bottom of the river bed

TRANSPORTATION OF LOAD

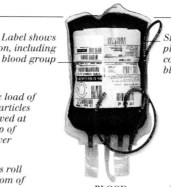

Sterile plastic bag contains blood

BLOOD TRANSFUSION

Outer mantle of liquid hydrogen

Core of rock and ice about 30,000 km in diameter

Equator swept by winds of up to 1,800 km/h

Radial spokes

Cloud-top temperature about -180 °C

THE STRUCTURE OF SATURN

CONTENTS

INTRODUCTION 6

PHYSICS 12

CHEMISTRY 64

LIFE SCIENCES AND ECOLOGY 118

HUMAN ANATOMY 176

MEDICAL SCIENCE 234

EARTH SCIENCES 264

ASTRONOMY AND ASTROPHYSICS 294

ELECTRONICS AND COMPUTER SCIENCE 334

MATHEMATICS 356

USEFUL DATA 374

BIOGRAPHIES 394

GLOSSARY 398

INDEX 414

Gyroscope precesses

Bearing

Spinning wheel

Metal guard

Axis

Plastic stand

GYROSCOPE

Pectoralis major

Trapezius

Cephalic vein

Deltoid

Basilic vein

Medial epicondyle of humerus

ANTERIOR VIEW OF SUPERFICIAL MUSCLES

0°/360°

Acute angle (less than 90°)

45°

Right angle (90°)

240°

130°

Complete circle

ANGLES

Reflex angle (greater than 180°)

Adaxial (upper) surface of lamina (blade)

Lateral branch of adventitious root

Abaxial (lower) surface of lamina (blade)

Rhizome

WATER HYACINTH
(Eichhornia crassipes)

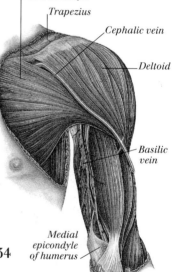

Ammonia dissolves very readily

Round-bottomed flask

Partial vacuum forms

Clamp

Valve

Air pressure on water pushes it up the tube

Water with indicator solution

Glass dish

AMMONIA FOUNTAIN

Introduction

*T*HE ULTIMATE VISUAL DICTIONARY OF SCIENCE *is* the definitive reference book for the major sciences. Its unique style allows you to browse the thematic sections at your leisure or to use it as a quick-reference visual dictionary. Two spreads at the beginning of the book introduce science and discuss its nature, history, and practice. The main part of the book is divided into nine themed sections, each one covering a major scientific discipline. These sections begin with a table of contents listing the key entries, followed by a historical spread that puts the subject into its developmental context. Throughout the book you will find some words in **bold** typeface: these are words that you will find defined in the glossary. Bold words on the historical spreads are the names of important scientific figures featured in the "Biographies" (pp. 394-397). A 20-page "Useful Data" section at the back of the book contains essential scientific formulas, symbols, and charts. The book ends with a glossary and an extensive index.

Subjects featured:

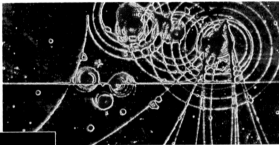

Physics

Physics is perhaps the most fundamental scientific discipline. It concerns matter and energy, and its theories can be applied in every other scientific discipline, often creating a new subdiscipline such as astrophysics or medical physics.

Chemistry

The science of chemistry is concerned with chemical elements, the compounds they form, and the way elements and compounds react together to make new substances. It is important in several other scientific disciplines, in particular life sciences. Biochemistry, for example, examines the compounds and reactions involved in the processes of life.

Life sciences and ecology

This section concentrates on biology, looking at the forms and functions of living organisms. It begins with consideration of the microscopic scale of cells, the building blocks of all living things, and ends with ecology, the study of how plants and animals interact with each other and their environment.

Human anatomy

Anatomy is the study of the structure of living organisms. The investigation of human anatomy and internal parts is particularly essential to medical science. This section also includes human physiology, which deals with the functions of the various systems of the human body.

Medical science

Modern science gives us a sophisticated understanding of the human body. This enables medical professionals to provide accurate and effective diagnoses and treatments, which often involves drawing on other scientific disciplines such as physics and chemistry. The medical science section of this book includes modern diagnostic techniques and emergency care.

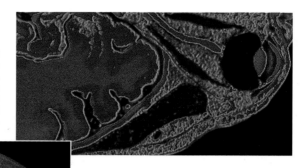

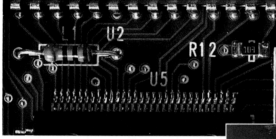

Earth sciences

The main branches of Earth sciences are geology (the study of the origin, structure, and composition of the Earth), oceanography (the study of the oceans), and meteorology (the study of the atmosphere and how it affects weather and climate).

Astronomy and astrophysics

Astronomy – the study of the universe beyond Earth's atmosphere – is the oldest science. Astrophysics is a branch of astronomy that attempts to understand the physical processes underlying the existence and behavior of planets, stars, and galaxies. Cosmology – the study of the origins and destiny of the universe – is an important part of astronomy.

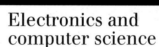

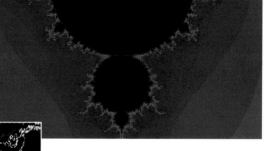

Electronics and computer science

All electronic devices are made up of simple electronic components, such as transistors, connected together to form electronic circuits. This section examines the main types of components and electronic circuits and outlines the function of the modern computer.

Mathematics

Numbers and shapes are fundamental to all sciences and to society at large. Mathematics is the science of numbers and shapes. This section of the book explains some of the key features of mathematics, including areas of modern mathematics, such as chaos theory and fractals.

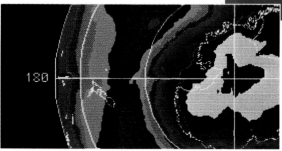

Useful data

It is essential for a science reference book to include scientific formulas, symbols, and charts. The information contained in this section reinforces and extends the information found in the main body of the book.

What is science?

T HE WORD "SCIENCE" comes from the Latin *scientia*, meaning knowledge. Science is both the systematic method by which human beings attempt to discover truth about the world, and the theories that result from this method. The main "natural sciences" are physics, chemistry, life sciences (biology), earth sciences, and astronomy. All of these – except life sciences – are called physical sciences. Subjects such as anatomy and medicine – and usually ecology – are considered parts of life science. Mathematics is not strictly a natural science, because it does not deal with matter and energy directly; it examines more abstract concepts, such as numbers. However, mathematics is important because it is used to describe the behavior of matter and energy in all the sciences.

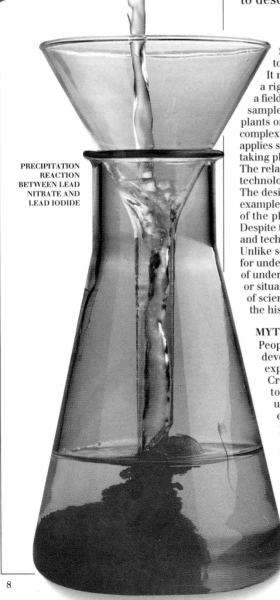

PRECIPITATION REACTION BETWEEN LEAD NITRATE AND LEAD IODIDE

SCIENCE AND TECHNOLOGY

Scientists rely on technology to carry out their experiments. It may be as simple as a quadrat – a rigid square thrown at random in a field in order to take a representative sample and estimate populations of plants or animals. Or it may be very complex, such as a supercomputer that applies statistics to millions of collisions taking place in particle accelerators. The relationship between science and technology works the other way, too. The design of a car's transmission, for example, requires a good understanding of the physics of simple machines. Despite this close relationship, science and technology are not the same thing. Unlike science, technology is not a quest for understanding – it is the application of understanding to a particular problem or situation. To discover the true nature of science, we need to briefly outline the history of scientific thought.

MYTHICAL WORLD VIEW

People in ancient civilizations developed stories – myths – to explain the world around them. Creation myths which attempted to explain the origin of the universe were common, for example. Most myths were probably never intended to be believed. However, in the absence of other explanations, they often were. These myths were handed down from

PRECIPITATION REACTION

The precipitation reaction between lead nitrate and lead iodide, shown here, is caused by a rearrangement of atoms and molecules. Science has proved the existence of atoms.

generation to generation as folktales, and some persist today in many cultures and religions. The roots of the scientific approach to understanding the world are generally thought to be in ancient Greece, where natural philosophers began to reject the mythical worldview and replace it with logical reasoning.

ARISTOTLE AND DEDUCTION

The ancient Greek approach to understanding natural phenomena is typified by the writings of Aristotle (384 – 322 BC). Like others of his time, Aristotle used a process known as deduction, which seeks explanations for natural phenomena by applying logical arguments. An example of this comes from Aristotle's *Physics*. It was assumed that some types of matter, such as smoke, have the quality of "lightness," while others, such as stone, have the quality of "heaviness." (The truth of why things float or sink is not as simple as this.) Applying logic to this assumption, it seemed to Aristotle that all matter naturally moves either upward or downward. He therefore claimed that any matter that neither falls nor rises upward, such as the stars and the planets, must be made of something fundamentally different from matter on Earth. The problem with this deductive process was that flawed assumptions led to incorrect conclusions. Aristotle and his contemporaries saw no need to test their assumptions, or explanations, and this is what sets the process of deduction apart from true science.

THE SCIENTIFIC REVOLUTION

The explanations given by the ancient Greek natural philosophers were adhered to across Europe and the Arab world during the Middle Ages –

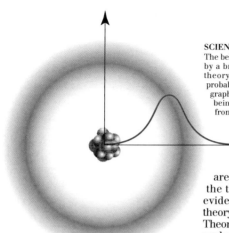

LOCATION OF AN ELECTRON AT DIFFERENT DISTANCES FROM AN ATOMIC NUCLEUS

SCIENCE AND REALITY
The behavior of electrons can be predicted by a branch of physics known as quantum theory, which uses the mathematics of probability. The curve shown here is a graph of the probability of an electron being located at different distances from an atomic nucleus.

are the theory of gravitation and the theory of evolution. The more evidence in favor of a particular theory, the more strongly it is held onto. Theories can be refined or completely replaced in the light of observations that do not support them.

THE LAWS OF NATURE
A scientific law is different from a scientific theory. A law is a mathematical relationship that describes how something behaves. (The law of conservation of mass states that no mass is lost or gained during a chemical reaction.) It is derived from painstaking measurements and other observations, and a theory may be formulated to explain the observed law. In the case of the conversion of mass, one plausible theory is that matter consists of particles that join in particular ways, and a chemical reaction is simply a change in the arrangement of the particles. Discovering the laws of nature and formulating theories to account for them can explain, in ever greater detail, only how – but not why – things happen. However, the methodical efforts of the scientific community – together with the inspirational work of many individuals – have led to a deep understanding of the natural world.

there was little original scientific thought during this period. In Renaissance Europe in the 15th and 16th centuries, there was a reawakening of the spirit of curiosity shown by the ancient Greeks. People began to question many of the untested ideas of the ancients, because new observations of the world were at odds with them. For example, Aristotle and his contemporaries had reasoned that the Earth lies at the center of the universe. During the Renaissance, several astronomers showed that this idea was not consistent with the observed motions of the planets and the Moon and the Sun. A new idea – that the Earth is in orbit around the Sun – was put forward in 1543 by Nicolaus Copernicus (1473 - 1543). There were also several other major challenges to the accepted ideas of the time. It was a period of rapid discovery, a scientific revolution.

SCIENTIFIC METHOD
Recognizing the importance of observation – empiricism – is one of the major features of the scientific method. Another is the testing of suggested explanations by performing experiments. An experiment is an observation under carefully controlled conditions. So, for example, the hypothesis (idea) that all objects on the Earth fall at the same rate in the absence of air, can be tested by setting up suitable apparatus and observing the results. The proof of this hypothesis would support the current theory about how objects fall. A theory is a general explanation of a group of related phenomena. Examples

NATURAL LAWS
The forces acting on a weight on a slope can be measured – here they are measured using a newton meter. If this process is repeated for steeper or shallower slopes, a relationship between the force and the angle of the slope arises. A law can be formulated from this, and a theory to explain the law may follow.

MEASURING THE FORCES ACTING ON A WEIGHT ON A SLOPE WITH A NEWTON METER

The practice of science

S INCE THE SCIENTIFIC REVOLUTION of 17th- and 18th-century Europe (see pp. 8-9), science has had an ever increasing impact on our everyday lives. The proportion of the population engaged in scientific or technological activity has increased dramatically since that time, too. The number of regularly published scientific journals in the world stood at about 10 in 1750. By 1900, there were about 10,000, and there are now over 40,000. Science is carried out by professionals as well as amateurs, and by groups as well as individuals. They all communicate their ideas between themselves, to their funding agencies, and to the world in general.

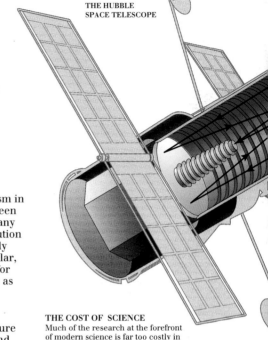

THE HUBBLE
SPACE TELESCOPE

BECOMING A SCIENTIST
Scientists need to be up-to-date with the latest developments in their field of interest. For this reason, most professional scientists have a university degree and are members of professional societies. The first such societies were formed in Europe during the 17th century. Since that time, the number of people worldwide engaged in scientific activity has increased enormously. The amount and detail of scientific understanding have also increased, with the result that most scientists can be experts in only a very tiny part of their subject. Scientific

societies encourage professionalism in science and communication between scientists. There are, however, many amateur scientists whose contribution in certain fields of science is highly valuable. In astronomy, in particular, amateurs have been responsible for many important discoveries, such as finding new comets.

LABORATORIES
The word "laboratory" may conjure up images of wooden benches and countless bottles of chemicals. Some laboratories – particularly those devoted to chemistry – are indeed something like this, but are today also equipped with high-tech devices, such as infrared spectrometers, which can accurately identify a substance by analysis of the infrared radiation it emits. They are safe, clean, and efficient places. However, many laboratories are not like the popular image at all. A laboratory is defined as the place where a scientist carries out his or her experiments. So, a geologist sometimes considers his or her laboratory to be, say, a rock face. A biologist or medical researcher may have a field laboratory, with equipment installed in a tent or temporary building. Fixed laboratories are well-equipped rooms, usually in universities or industrial research buildings. For

THE COST OF SCIENCE
Much of the research at the forefront of modern science is far too costly in time and money for any individual to undertake. The development of the *Hubble Space Telescope*, for example, has cost billions of dollars, and has involved thousands of scientists from many countries.

those engaged in theoretical science, their computers or even their own minds can be thought of as their laboratory.

FUNDING
Science is often expensive. A space-probe mission to Mars, for example, costs many millions of dollars, which may have to be paid by just one organization. The effort to produce a map of all human genes – known as the human genome project – is a lengthy and costly procedure that involves thousands of scientists in several different countries. There are two reasons commonly put forward to justify the huge amounts of

ELECTRONIC COMPONENTS

SCIENCE AND SOCIETY
Electronics is an area of scientific research that has had a huge effect on society. The subject began with the discovery of the electron in 1897. Less than a century later, the technology of electronics enabled the development of computers, television sets, and digital wristwatches, and has made possible international digital communication and trade.

WELWITSCHIA
(*Welwitschia mirabilis*)

money spent on scientific research. First, scientific progress brings technological advances. For example, without advances in medical science, diseases such as cholera would still claim millions of victims every year. The other reason often put forward to justify spending public money on science is a more philosophical one. Human beings are inquisitive creatures, and science provides answers to some fundamental questions – about our own origins, our place in space, the history of our planet, and so on. The money needed to carry out science comes from a variety of different sources. Much of the pure scientific research that goes on is government-funded and is based in universities. Some universities are partly funded by industries or wealthy individuals. Research laboratories in large companies tend to carry out applied science (technology), because most large companies are in the business of applying scientific knowledge to the development of new commercial devices or processes.

COMMUNICATING SCIENCE

There are many ways in which scientific ideas are communicated and as many methods for doing so. Scientists in the same field of research clearly need to communicate with one another to ensure that they do not duplicate on another's work and to ensure that others are aware of of potentially useful findings. Scientific journals and electronic mail (e-mail) are conduits for

much of this communication. Researchers also need to communicate with the agencies who give grants – if those in charge of funding do not recognize the importance or quality of a piece of scientific research, they may cancel funding for it. New discoveries in one field must often be communicated clearly to scientists in different but related fields. New discoveries in organic chemistry may benefit scientists working on research in other areas, for example. The progress of science must also be communicated effectively to governments and to the public at large. Finally, accumulated scientific knowledge must be passed on from generation to generation, and so school and college education have a role to play in communicating scientific ideas.

RECOGNITION

Many scientists pursue their work for the sake of their own curiosity and passion for their subject, or because of a desire to make a useful contribution to science. They are further encouraged by the possibility of recognition in the event of a great discovery or good scientific practice. Many different prizes are awarded each year by organizations across the world. The most famous are the Nobel Prizes, first awarded in 1901. They are given out yearly in six areas of human achievement, three of which are sciences (physics, chemistry, and physiology or medicine). In some cases, scientists who have made truly great contributions become household names, such as Albert Einstein (1879 – 1955) and Isaac Newton (1642–1727).

INTERNATIONAL SYSTEMS

The plant below is identified by all botanists as *Welwitschia mirabilis*. This binomial (two-part) classification is an internationally recognized system. Another well-known system is the SI (Système Internationale), which enables all scientists to use clearly defined standard measurements, such as the meter, in their work.

PUBLIC UNDERSTANDING OF SCIENCE

Most people have heard of viruses, even if they do not understand how they work. A virus is shown here entering a living cell (top), reproducing (middle), and leaving the cell with its replicas (bottom). Scientific knowledge such as this can filter through to the public in school science lessons or via the media.

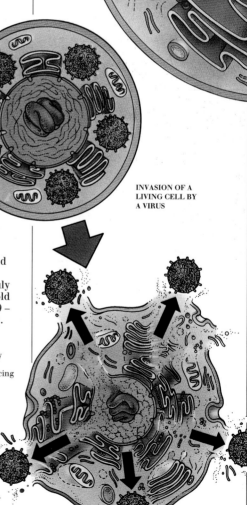

INVASION OF A LIVING CELL BY A VIRUS

Particle tracks following the collision between two protons

PHYSICS

DISCOVERING PHYSICS 14

MATTER AND ENERGY 16

MEASUREMENT AND EXPERIMENT 18

FORCES 1 20

FORCES 2 22

FRICTION 24

SIMPLE MACHINES 26

CIRCULAR MOTION 28

WAVES AND OSCILLATIONS 30

HEAT AND TEMPERATURE 32

SOLIDS 34

LIQUIDS 36

GASES 38

ELECTRICITY AND MAGNETISM 40

ELECTRIC CIRCUITS 42

ELECTROMAGNETISM 44

GENERATING ELECTRICITY 46

ELECTROMAGNETIC RADIATION 48

COLOR 50

REFLECTION AND REFRACTION 52

WAVE BEHAVIOR 54

ELECTRONS 56

NUCLEAR PHYSICS 58

PARTICLE PHYSICS 60

MODERN PHYSICS 62

Discovering physics

THE WORD "PHYSICS" derives from the Greek word for natural philosophy, *physikos*, and the early physicists were, in fact, often called natural philosophers. To a physicist, the world consists of matter and energy. Physicists spend much of their time formulating and testing theories, a process that calls for a great deal of experimentation. The study of physics encompasses the areas of force and motion, light, sound, electricity, magnetism, and the structure of matter.

ANCIENT GREECE
The study of physics is generally considered to have begun in ancient Greece, where philosophers rejected purely mythological explanations of physical phenomena and began to look for physical causes. However, Greek physics was based on reasoning, with little emphasis on experimentation. For example, early Greek philosophers reasoned that matter must be made of tiny, indivisible parts (atoms), but saw no need to establish experimental proof for the theory. Nevertheless, several areas of physics thrived in ancient Greece: mechanics (force and motion) and optics (the behavior of light) in particular. The most notable contributions to ancient Greek physics were made by **Aristotle**, whose ideas would influence physics for 2,000 years, despite the fact that many of them were fundamentally flawed.

MIDDLE AGES
When the first universities were founded in Europe in the 12th and 13th centuries, Greek physics was the basis of the study of the natural world. The ideas of the ancient Greeks had been preserved by Muslim academics, who had learned of them from Greek philosophers who journeyed to the East. In the universities, the ideas of Aristotle were accepted but gradually altered. For example, Aristotle's views on force and motion were developed into the "impetus" theory – an idea similar to the modern concept of momentum – in the 14th century.

RENAISSANCE
In the 15th, 16th, and 17th centuries, experimentation became the norm. Inevitably, there was conflict between those who believed the views of Aristotle, and those who accepted the new ideas arising from experimentation. The most famous example of this conflict is the story of Italian physicist **Galileo Galilei**. Persecuted for his ideas by the Roman Catholic Church, Galileo established new laws of motion, including proof that objects accelerate as they fall. The French philosopher **René Descartes** helped to place physics on a new track by concentrating on the idea that all natural phenomena could be explained by considering particles of matter in motion. This was called the "mechanical" or "mechanistic" philosophy, and it enabled physicists to develop new theories.

NEWTONIAN PHYSICS
Isaac Newton made huge contributions to mechanics, optics, and gravitation, as well as to mathematics. In particular, his ideas about motion developed the mechanistic philosophy into a precise framework, called Newtonian physics. This view held that all of the phenomena of the Universe could be explained by particles and forces and was summarized by Newton's own Laws of Motion. Newton's theory of gravitation made an undeniable link between the motion of falling objects on the Earth and the motions of planets around the Sun. In optics, Newton identified white light as consisting of a spectrum of colors, and he investigated the effects of interference. He also explained many optical effects in terms of light behaving as particles, a view challenged by many physicists, who believed that light was the result of a wave motion. Experiments during the 18th century put the wave theory of light onto a firm footing.

NATURAL FORCES
Whether particles or waves, light was seen as one of a set of separate "natural forces." Others included heat, electricity, and magnetism. During the 18th and 19th centuries, progress was made toward realizing the links between these forces, which were seen as "imponderable fluids" that flowed between substances. Temperature, for example, was seen as the concentration of particles of "heat fluid," called "caloric." The modern interpretation of heat, as the random motion of particles, was not widely believed until later, when it was realized that friction could generate endless amounts of heat. This could not be explained by the idea that heat is a fluid contained within an object. As the connection between

GALILEO'S CLOCK
The Italian scientist Galileo Galilei noticed that, although the distance a pendulum swings may vary, the time taken for each swing remains constant. He exploited this idea in his design for a pendulum clock. The clock shown here was built in 1833, based on Galileo's drawings.

motion and heat was established, so other natural phenomena were linked, in particular electricity and magnetism. In 1820, **Hans Christian Oersted** showed that an electric current produces magnetism. Electromagnetism was studied by many experimenters, in particular Michael Faraday.

ENERGY AND ELECTRO-MAGNETIC RADIATION

In the 1840s, **James Joule** established the "mechanical equivalent of heat": the amount of heat generated by a particular amount of mechanical work. The conversion was always consistent, and a similar result when producing heat from electric current led to the definition of energy. It was soon realized that light, heat, sound, electricity, magnetism, and motion all possessed energy, and that energy could be transferred from object to object, but neither created nor destroyed. This "unified" view of the world was further established in the 1860s, when **James Clerk Maxwell** proved that light was related to electricity and magnetism. The idea led to the discovery of other forms of electromagnetic radiation: radio waves (1888), X rays (1896), and gamma rays (named in 1903). Also around this time came the first evidence of an inner structure to the atom. The electron was discovered in 1897, and in 1899 its mass was found to be less than that of an atom. New models of the atom arose, in line with quantum physics, which, along with relativity, would reshape forever the physicist's view of the world.

MODERN PHYSICS

Albert Einstein developed his theories of relativity to make sense of space and time. Newtonian physics relied on the assumptions that space and time were absolute, assumptions that

FARADAY'S RING
Michael Faraday explored the relationship between electricity and magnetism, producing the world's first transformer.

work very well in most situations. But Newtonian physics was only an approximation to any real explanation. Einstein's relativity showed that time and space could not be absolute. This demanded a completely new outlook on the laws of physics. Einstein was also involved in the development of quantum physics, which studies the world of very small particles and very small amounts of energy. Quantum physics challenged the wave theory of light and led to the conclusion that light and other forms of electromagnetic radiation act as both particles and waves. It enabled the structure and behavior of atoms, light, and electrons to be understood and also predicted their behavior with incredible accuracy.

GRAND UNIFIED THEORY

In the 1920s, showers of subatomic particles – produced by cosmic rays that enter the atmosphere – were detected using airborne photographic plates. This led to the study of particle physics, using huge particle accelerators. In the middle of the 20th century, forces began to be understood in terms of the exchange of subatomic particles and were unified into just four fundamental interactions: gravitation, electromagnetism, the strong nuclear force, and the weak interaction. The "holy grail" of physics is a grand unified theory (GUT) that would unify all the four forces as one "superforce" and describe and explain all the laws of nature.

NEUTRON DETECTOR
Inside this apparatus, particles from a radioactive source struck a beryllium target. Neutrons were given off but could be detected only when they "knocked" protons from a piece of paraffin wax. The protons were then detected with a Geiger counter.

TIMELINE OF DISCOVERIES

	400 BC	**Democritus** concludes that matter consists of indivisible particles
Flotation principle discovered by **Archimedes**, who also studies principles of levers	260 BC	
	1600	**William Gilbert** claims that the core of the Earth is a giant magnet
Galileo Galilei founds the science of mechanics	1638	
	1643	Air pressure discovered and measured by **Evangelista Torricelli**
Isaac Newton publishes *Mathematical Principles*, in which he formulates the laws of motion and gravitation	1665	
	1701	Joseph Sauveur suggests term "acoustics" for science of sound
Battery invented by **Alessandro Volta**	1799	
	1800	Infrared waves discovered by **William Herschel**
Atomic theory of matter proposed by **John Dalton**	1803	
	1819	Hans Christian Oersted discovers electromagnetism
Electromagnetic rotation, discovered by Michael Faraday	1821	
	1831	Electromagnetic induction discovered by Michael Faraday
Relationship between heat, power, and work formulated by James Joule	1843	
	1846	Laws of thermodynamics developed by **William Kelvin**
Dmitri Mendeleyev devises the periodic table, which classifies elements into groups by atomic weight	1869	
	1888	Existence of radio waves demonstrated by **Heinrich Hertz**
X rays discovered by **Wilhelm Röntgen**	1896	
	1897	Electron discovered by **Joseph Thomson**
Quantum theory proposed by **Max Planck**	1900	
	1905	**Albert Einstein** publishes his special theory of relativity
Atomic nucleus discovered by physicist **Ernest Rutherford**	1911	
	1913	Electron shells around nucleus of atom proposed by Niels Bohr
Albert Einstein publishes his general theory of relativity	1915	
	1919	Ernest Rutherford converts nitrogen nuclei into oxygen nuclei
First particle accelerator built by **John Cockcroft** and **Ernest Walton**	1932	
	1938	Nuclear fission discovered by **Otto Hahn** and **Fritz Strassmann**
First nuclear reactor built by **Enrico Fermi**	1942	
	1964	Existence of quarks proposed by **Murray Gell-Mann**
Chaos theory developed by American mathematicians	1980s	
	1986	Superconductors, substances with extremely low resistances to electricity, are developed

Matter and energy

PHYSICS IS THE STUDY OF MATTER AND ENERGY. Matter is anything that occupies space. All matter consists of countless tiny particles, called **atoms** (see pp. 72-73) and **molecules**. These particles are in constant motion, a fact that explains a phenomenon known as **Brownian motion**. The existence of these particles also explains **evaporation** and the formation of **crystals** (see pp. 34-35). Energy is not matter, but it affects the behavior of matter. Everything that happens requires energy, and energy comes in many forms, such as heat, light, electrical, and potential energy. The standard unit for measuring energy is the joule (J). Each form of energy can change into other forms. For example, electrical energy used to make an electric motor turn becomes **kinetic energy** and heat energy (see pp. 32-33). The total amount of energy never changes; it can only be transferred from one form to another, not created or destroyed. This is known as the **Principle of the Conservation of Energy**, and can be illustrated using a **Sankey Diagram** (see opposite).

PARTICLES IN MOTION

BROWNIAN MOTION
When observed through a microscope, smoke particles are seen to move about randomly. This motion is caused by the air molecules around the smoke particles.

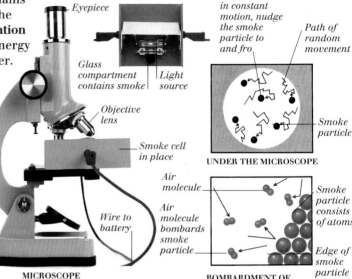

SMOKE CELL

Eyepiece

Glass compartment contains smoke

Light source

Objective lens

Smoke cell in place

Wire to battery

MICROSCOPE

MATTER AS PARTICLES

Air molecules in constant motion, nudge the smoke particle to and fro

Path of random movement

Smoke particle

UNDER THE MICROSCOPE

Air molecule

Air molecule bombards smoke particle

Smoke particle consists of atoms

Edge of smoke particle

BOMBARDMENT OF SMOKE PARTICLE

DISSOLVING

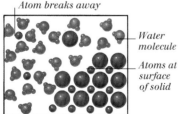

Glass beaker

Solid dissolves to form a solution

Water

Solid potassium permanganate

EVAPORATION

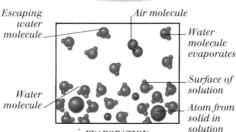

Heated liquid evaporates

Glass beaker

Dissolved solid does not evaporate

Solution is heated

CRYSTALLIZATION

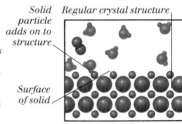

Glass beaker

Water has evaporated

Purple crystals of potassium permanganate remain behind

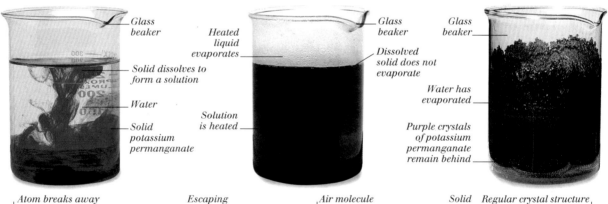

Atom breaks away

Water molecule

Atoms at surface of solid

DISSOLVING
The particles of a solid are held together in a rigid structure. When a solid dissolves into a liquid, its particles break away from this structure and mix evenly in the liquid, forming a **solution**.

Escaping water molecule

Air molecule

Water molecule evaporates

Water molecule

Surface of solution

Atom from solid in solution

EVAPORATION
When they are heated, most liquids **evaporate**. This means that the atoms or molecules of which they are made break free from the body of the liquid to become gas particles.

Solid particle adds on to structure

Regular crystal structure

Surface of solid

CRYSTALLIZATION
When all of the liquid in a solution has evaporated, the solid is left behind. The particles of the solid normally arrange in a regular structure, called a crystal.

THE CONSERVATION OF ENERGY

Sun

Energy radiates into space

Radiation is made in the Sun's core during nuclear reactions and is the source of most of the Earth's energy

PHOTOVOLTAIC CELL
A transfer of energy, from electromagnetic radiation to electrical energy, takes place in a photovoltaic cell, or solar cell. When no sunlight falls on it, it can supply no electricity.

Solar cell

Silicon crystal

Wire from cell to motor

Motor

ELECTRIC MOTOR
Inside an electric motor, electrical energy becomes the energy of movement, also known as kinetic or mechanical energy.

The faster the motor turns, the more energy it has

Motor's spindle turns gears

Worm gear

Crown wheel

String winds around shaft

At each energy transfer some energy is "lost" as heat

ENERGY TRANSFER

SANKEY DIAGRAM
This Sankey diagram shows the energy transfers in an electric motor.

Width of the arrow here shows how much energy is available

0.31 J of electrical energy supplied each second

0.1 J of kinetic energy

Arrowhead shows where energy is transferred

0.21 J wasted as heat in the motor

POTENTIAL ENERGY
As the motor turns, it winds a string around a shaft via a set of gears. The string lifts a 0.1 kilogram mass against **gravity**. The kinetic energy transfers to potential, or stored energy. If the string is broken, the energy will be released, and the mass will fall, gaining kinetic energy.

0.1 kg mass lifted to 1 m

Mass has potential energy of 1 J

String lifts 0.1 kg mass

1 kg mass lifted to 0.9 m

Mass has potential energy of 0.9 J

0.1 kg mass lifted to 0.8 m

Mass has potential energy of 0.8 J

0.1 kg mass

ENERGY TRANSFERS IN A CAR

A car's energy comes from burning gasoline in the engine. This includes the electrical energy in its battery, the **potential energy** stored as it climbs a hill, and any heat generated in the brakes or the engine. The arrows show energy transfer.

Gasoline (chemical energy)

Climbing a hill (potential energy)

Car stereo (electrical to sound energy)

Heat energy generated in engine

Car battery (electrical energy)

Headlight (electrical to light energy)

Kinetic energy greater at higher speed

Braking (heat energy)

Measurement and experiment

THE SCIENCE OF PHYSICS IS BASED on the formulation and testing of theories. Experiments are designed to test theories and involve making measurements – of **mass**, length, time, or other quantities. In order to compare the results of various experiments, it is important that there are agreed standard units. The kilogram (kg), the meter (m), and the second (s) are the fundamental units of a system called **SI units** (Système International). Physicists use a variety of instruments for making measurements. Some, like the Vernier callipers, traveling microscopes, and thermometers, are common to many laboratories, while others will be made for a particular experiment. The results of measurements are interpreted in many ways, but most often as graphs. Graphs provide a way of illustrating the relationship between two measurements involved in an experiment. For example, in an experiment to investigate falling objects, a graph can show the relationship between the duration and the height of the fall.

MASS AND WEIGHT

Mass is the amount of matter in an object, and is measured in kilograms. **Gravitational force** gives the mass its **weight**. Weight is a force, and is measured in newtons (see pp.10-11), using a newton meter like the one shown on the right. It is common to speak of weight being measured in kilograms, but in physics this is not correct.

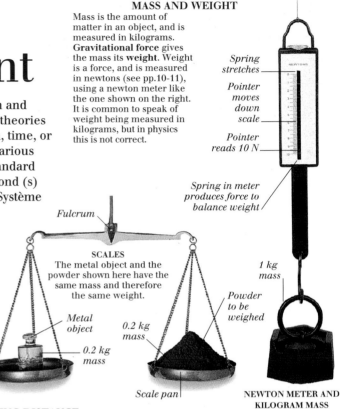

Spring stretches

Pointer moves down scale

Pointer reads 10 N

Spring in meter produces force to balance weight

1 kg mass

NEWTON METER AND KILOGRAM MASS

Fulcrum

SCALES
The metal object and the powder shown here have the same mass and therefore the same weight.

Metal object

0.2 kg mass

Powder to be weighed

0.2 kg mass

Scale pan

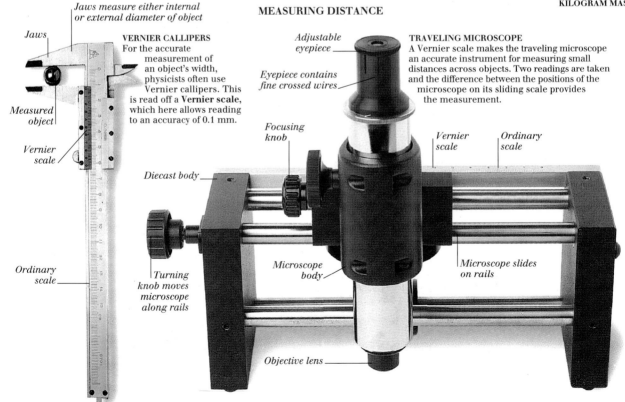

Jaws measure either internal or external diameter of object

Jaws

VERNIER CALLIPERS
For the accurate measurement of an object's width, physicists often use Vernier callipers. This is read off a **Vernier scale**, which here allows reading to an accuracy of 0.1 mm.

Measured object

Vernier scale

Ordinary scale

MEASURING DISTANCE

Adjustable eyepiece

Eyepiece contains fine crossed wires

TRAVELING MICROSCOPE
A Vernier scale makes the traveling microscope an accurate instrument for measuring small distances across objects. Two readings are taken and the difference between the positions of the microscope on its sliding scale provides the measurement.

Focusing knob

Vernier scale

Ordinary scale

Diecast body

Turning knob moves microscope along rails

Microscope body

Microscope slides on rails

Objective lens

THERMOMETERS

There are two types of thermometers commonly used in modern physics. The mercury thermometer has a glass bulb containing mercury that expands as the temperature rises, while the digital thermometer contains an electronic probe and has a digital readout.

DIGITAL THERMOMETER

Mercury column

Electronic probe

Digital (LCD) readout

Plastic case contains electronics

Glass tube

MERCURY THERMOMETER

Scale

Mercury bulb

Human body temperature (37°C)

Glass tube

MAGNIFIED VIEW OF MERCURY THERMOMETER

Glass bulb

INTERPRETING DATA

TABLE OF RESULTS FOR A FREEFALL EXPERIMENT

A steel ball is dropped from a variety of heights and the duration of each fall is timed. The results of these measurements are entered into a table.

HEIGHT (m)	0	0.05	0.10	0.15	0.20	0.25	0.30	0.35	0.40	0.45	0.50
TIME (s)	0	0.10	0.14	0.17	0.21	0.22	0.24	0.26	0.27	0.30	0.31

RESULTS OF A FREEFALL EXPERIMENT IN GRAPH FORM

A **graph** allows us to visually identify the relationship between the time and the height of the fall. There is an element of uncertainty or error in every result obtained, so each is plotted on the graph as a short range of values forming an **error bar** instead of a point. The curve is drawn so that it passes through all the bars.

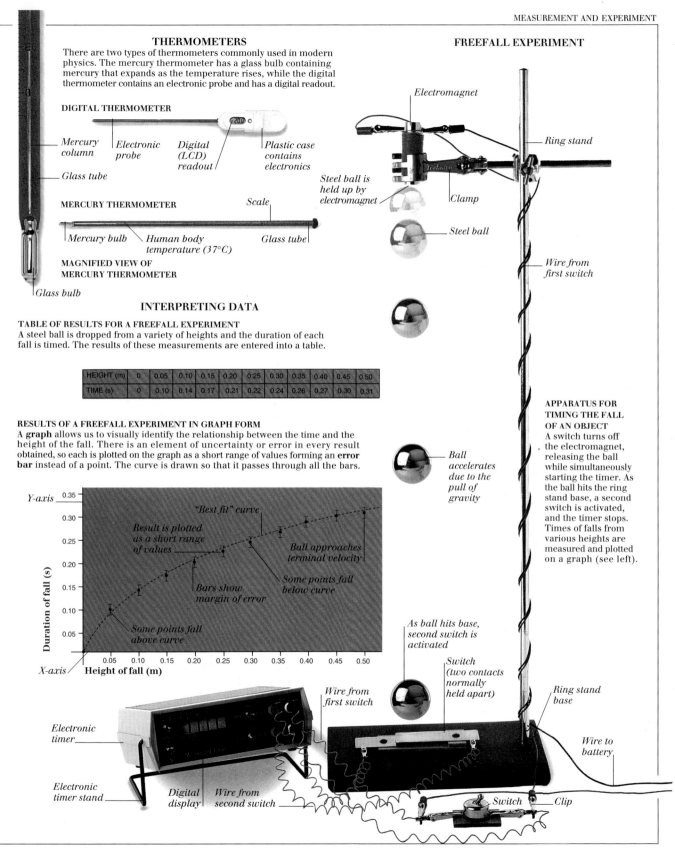

Y-axis

"Best fit" curve

Result is plotted as a short range of values

Ball approaches terminal velocity

Bars show margin of error

Some points fall below curve

Duration of fall (s)

Some points fall above curve

X-axis

Height of fall (m)

FREEFALL EXPERIMENT

Electromagnet

Ring stand

Steel ball is held up by electromagnet

Clamp

Steel ball

Wire from first switch

Ball accelerates due to the pull of gravity

APPARATUS FOR TIMING THE FALL OF AN OBJECT

A switch turns off the electromagnet, releasing the ball while simultaneously starting the timer. As the ball hits the ring stand base, a second switch is activated, and the timer stops. Times of falls from various heights are measured and plotted on a graph (see left).

As ball hits base, second switch is activated

Switch (two contacts normally held apart)

Ring stand base

Wire to battery

Wire from first switch

Electronic timer

Electronic timer stand

Digital display

Wire from second switch

Switch

Clip

19

Forces 1

A FORCE IS A PUSH OR PULL, and can be large or small. The usual unit of force is the newton (N), and can be measured using a **newton meter** (see pp. 18-19). Force can be applied to objects at a distance or by making contact. **Gravity** (see pp. 22-23) and **electromagnetism** (see pp. 44-45) are examples of forces that can act at a distance. When more than one force acts on an object, the combined force is called the **resultant**. The resultant of several forces depends on their size and direction. The object is in **equilibrium** if the forces on an object are balanced with no overall resultant. An object on a solid flat surface will be in equilibrium, because the surface produces a **reaction** force to balance the object's **weight**. If the surface slopes, the object's weight is no longer completely canceled by the reaction force and part of the weight, called a **component**, remains, pulling the object toward the bottom of the slope. Forces can cause rotation as well as straight line motion. If an object is free to rotate about a certain point, then a force can have a turning effect, known as a **moment**.

REACTION FORCES

FORCES ON A LEVEL SURFACE
A table provides a force called a reaction, which exactly balances the weight of an object placed upon it. The resultant force is zero, so the object does not fall through the table.

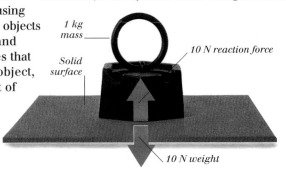

1 kg mass

10 N reaction force

Solid surface

10 N weight

RESULTANT FORCE
A 1 kg **mass** has a weight of 10 N. Here, this weight is supported by two lengths of wire. Each wire carries a force that pulls against the other at an angle. The combination or resultant of these forces is 10 N vertically upward and exactly balances the weight. The force carried by each wire is measured by newton meters.

Wire

Newton meters held at an angle

Resultant upward force of 10 N exactly balances 10 N weight

Reading 5.8 N

Reading 5.8 N

Force acts at an angle

Force acts at an angle

THE METER READINGS
Between them, the two wires support a weight of 10 N, so why is the reading on each newton meter more than 5 N? As well as pulling upward, the wires are pulling sideways against each other, so the overall force showing on each meter is 5.8 N.

1 kg mass

10 N weight

FORCES ON A SHALLOW SLOPE
Gravity acts downward on the 1 kg mass shown. The slope provides a reaction force that acts upward, perpendicular to the slope and counteracts some of the weight. All that remains of the weight is a force acting down the slope.

Reaction force produced by slope

Newton meter

1 kg mass

2.4 N force down slope

2.4 N will stop mass from sliding

Shallow slope

10 N weight

Part of weight acting into slope

FORCES ON A STEEP SLOPE
As the slope is made steeper, the reaction force of the slope decreases, and the force pulling the mass down the slope – which is measured by the newton meter – increases. This force can pull objects downhill.

Reaction force produced by slope

Newton meter

1 kg mass

6 N force down slope

6 N force will stop mass from sliding

Part of weight acting into slope

Steep slope

Weight 10 N

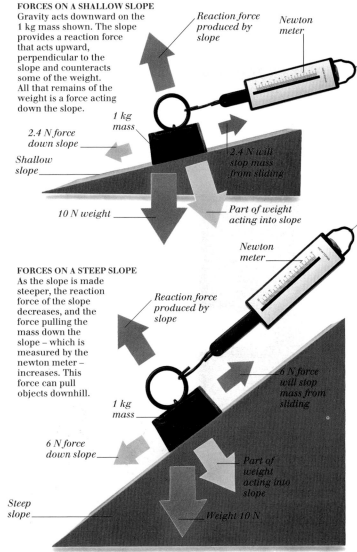

TURNING FORCES

TURNING FORCES AROUND A PIVOT

A force acting on an object that is free to rotate will have a turning effect, or turning force, also known as a moment. The moment of a force is equal to the size of the force multiplied by the distance of the force from the turning point around which it acts (see p. 378). It is measured in newton meters (Nm) or joules (J). The mass below exerts a weight of 10 N downward on a pivoted beam. The newton meter – twice as far from the pivot – measures 5 N, the upward force needed to stop the beam turning. The clockwise moment created by the weight and counterclockwise moment created by the upward pull on the newton meter are equal, and the object is therefore in equilibrium.

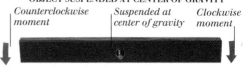

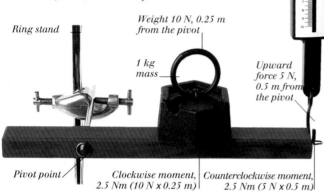

Ring stand

Weight 10 N, 0.25 m from the pivot

1 kg mass

Newton meter

Reading 5 N

Upward force 5 N, 0.5 m from the pivot

Pivot point

Clockwise moment, 2.5 Nm (10 N x 0.25 m)

Counterclockwise moment, 2.5 Nm (5 N x 0.5 m)

OBJECT SUSPENDED AT CENTER OF GRAVITY

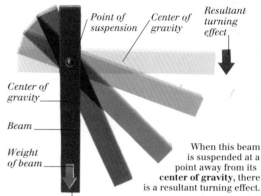

Counterclockwise moment

Suspended at center of gravity

Clockwise moment

The weight of the beam above is spread along its length. The moments are balanced if the object is suspended at its center of gravity.

OBJECT SUSPENDED AWAY FROM CENTER OF GRAVITY

Point of suspension

Center of gravity

Resultant turning effect

Center of gravity

Beam

Weight of beam

When this beam is suspended at a point away from its **center of gravity**, there is a resultant turning effect.

The beam turns until the center of gravity is under the point of suspension

PRESSURE

Why can a thumbtack be pushed into a wall, and yet a building will not sink into the ground? Forces can act over large or small areas. A force acting over a large area will exert less **pressure** than the same force acting over a small area. The pressure exerted on an area can be figured out simply by dividing the applied force by the area over which it acts (see p. 378). Pressure is normally measured in newtons per square meter (Nm^{-2}) or pascals (Pa). A thumbtack concentrates force to produce high pressure, whereas the foundations of a building spread the load to reduce pressure. Gases also exert pressure (see pp. 38-39).

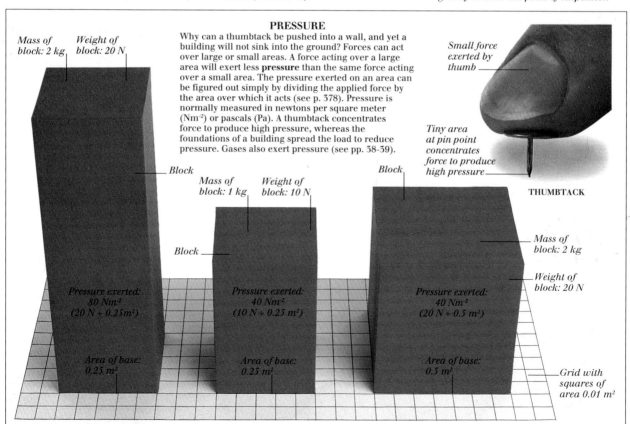

Mass of block: 2 kg

Weight of block: 20 N

Block

Mass of block: 1 kg

Weight of block: 10 N

Block

Block

Pressure exerted: 80 Nm² (20 N ÷ 0.25m²)

Pressure exerted: 40 Nm² (10 N ÷ 0.25 m²)

Pressure exerted: 40 Nm² (20 N ÷ 0.5 m²)

Area of base: 0.25 m²

Area of base: 0.25 m²

Area of base: 0.5 m²

Small force exerted by thumb

Tiny area at pin point concentrates force to produce high pressure

THUMBTACK

Mass of block: 2 kg

Weight of block: 20 N

Grid with squares of area 0.01 m²

Forces 2

WHEN THE FORCES ON AN OBJECT do not cancel each other out, they will change the motion of the object. The object's speed, direction of motion, or both will change. The rules governing the way forces change the motion of objects were first figured out by Sir Isaac Newton. They have become known as Newton's Laws. The greater the mass of an object, the greater the force needed to change its motion. This resistance to change in motion is called **inertia**. The **speed** of an object is usually measured in meters per second (ms^{-1}). **Velocity** is the speed of an object in a particular direction. **Acceleration**, which only occurs when a force is applied, is the rate of change in speed. It is measured in meters per second per second, or meters per second squared (ms^{-2}). One particular force keeps the Moon in orbit around the Earth and the Earth in orbit around the Sun. This is the force of **gravity** or **gravitation**; its effects can be felt over great distances.

NEWTON'S SECOND LAW IN ACTION

Trucks have a greater mass than cars. According to Newton's second law (see right) a large mass requires a larger force to produce a given acceleration. This is why a truck needs to have a larger engine than a car.

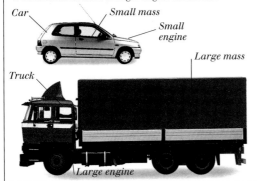

Car *Small mass*
Small engine
Large mass
Truck
Large engine

NEWTON'S LAWS

NEWTON'S FIRST LAW

When no force acts on an object, it will remain in a state of rest or continue its uniform motion in a straight line.

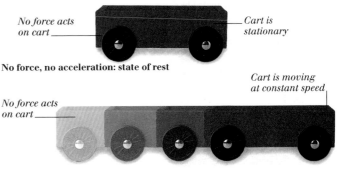

No force acts on cart   *Cart is stationary*

No force, no acceleration: state of rest

Cart is moving at constant speed
No force acts on cart

No force, no acceleration: uniform motion

NEWTON'S SECOND LAW

When a force acts on an object, the motion of the object will change. This change in motion is called acceleration and is equal to the size of the force divided by the mass of the object on which it acts (see p. 378).

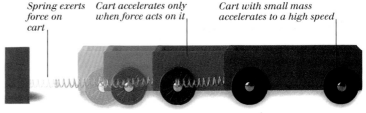

Spring exerts force on cart   *Cart accelerates only when force acts on it*   *Cart with small mass accelerates to a high speed*

Force acts on small mass: large acceleration

Mass on cart
Same force acts on heavier cart   *Cart with large mass accelerates to a low speed*

Same force acts on large mass: small acceleration

NEWTON'S THIRD LAW

If one object exerts a force on another, an equal and opposite force, called the reaction force, is applied by the second to the first.

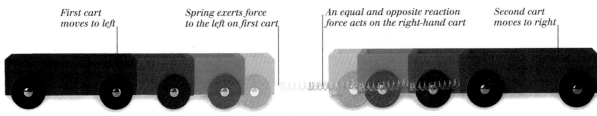

First cart moves to left   *Spring exerts force to the left on first cart*   *An equal and opposite reaction force acts on the right-hand cart*   *Second cart moves to right*

Action and reaction

FORCE AND MOTION

In the images below, each row of balls is a record of the motion of one ball, photographed once each second beside a ruler. This shows how far the ball moved during that second and each subsequent second, giving a visual representation of speed and acceleration.

SPEED

Speed is the distance an object travels in a set amount of time. It is calculated by dividing distance covered by time taken (see p. 378). In physics, speed is measured in meters per second (ms^{-1}).

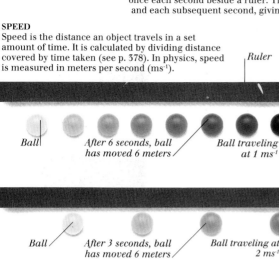

Ruler

Ball
After 6 seconds, ball has moved 6 meters
Ball traveling at 1 ms^{-1}

Ball
After 3 seconds, ball has moved 6 meters
Ball traveling at 2 ms^{-1}

ACCELERATION

Acceleration is the rate that the speed of an object changes. It is calculated by dividing the change in speed by the time it took for that change (see p. 378). It is measured in meters per second per second (ms^{-2}).

Ruler

Ball accelerating at 1 ms^{-2}
After 2 seconds, the ball is moving at 2 ms^{-1}
After 4 seconds, the ball is moving at 4 ms^{-1}

MOMENTUM

The momentum of an object is equal to its mass multiplied by its velocity (see p. 378). Momentum is measured in kilogram meters per second ($kgms^{-1}$). The two balls below have the same momentum.

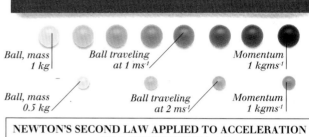

Ruler

Ball, mass 1 kg
Ball traveling at 1 ms^{-1}
Momentum 1 $kgms^{-1}$

Ball, mass 0.5 kg
Ball traveling at 2 ms^{-1}
Momentum 1 $kgms^{-1}$

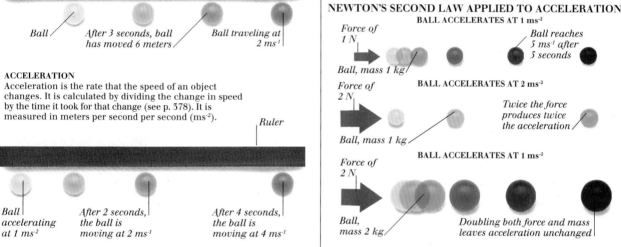

NEWTON'S SECOND LAW APPLIED TO ACCELERATION

BALL ACCELERATES AT 1 ms^{-2}

Force of 1 N

Ball reaches 5 ms^{-1} after 5 seconds

Ball, mass 1 kg

BALL ACCELERATES AT 2 ms^{-2}

Force of 2 N

Twice the force produces twice the acceleration

Ball, mass 1 kg

BALL ACCELERATES AT 1 ms^{-2}

Force of 2 N

Ball, mass 2 kg

Doubling both force and mass leaves acceleration unchanged

GRAVITATIONAL FORCE

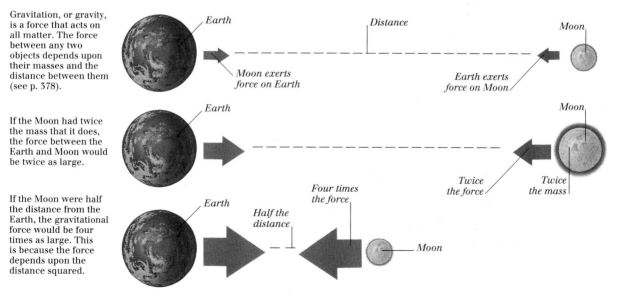

Gravitation, or gravity, is a force that acts on all matter. The force between any two objects depends upon their masses and the distance between them (see p. 378).

Earth
Distance
Moon
Moon exerts force on Earth
Earth exerts force on Moon

If the Moon had twice the mass that it does, the force between the Earth and Moon would be twice as large.

Earth
Moon
Twice the force
Twice the mass

If the Moon were half the distance from the Earth, the gravitational force would be four times as large. This is because the force depends upon the distance squared.

Earth
Half the distance
Four times the force
Moon

Friction

FRICTION IS A FORCE THAT SLOWS DOWN or prevents motion. A familiar form of friction is air resistance, which limits the speed at which objects can move through the air. Between touching surfaces, the amount of friction depends on the nature of the surfaces and the force or forces pushing them together. It is the joining or bonding of the **atoms** at each of the surfaces that causes the friction. When you try to pull an object along a table, the object will not move until the **limiting friction** supplied by these bonds has been overcome. Friction can be reduced in two main ways: by lubrication or by the use of rollers. Lubrication involves the presence of a **fluid** between two surfaces; fluid keeps the surfaces apart, allowing them to move smoothly past one another. Rollers actually use friction to grip the surfaces and produce rotation. Instead of sliding against one another, the surfaces produce turning forces, which cause each roller to roll. This leaves very little friction to oppose motion.

AIR RESISTANCE

Air resistance is a type of friction that occurs when an object moves through the air. The faster an object moves, the greater the air resistance. Falling objects accelerate to a speed called **terminal velocity**, at which the air resistance exactly balances the object's weight. At this speed, there is no **resultant force** and so no further acceleration can occur.

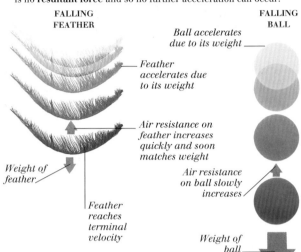

FALLING FEATHER

FALLING BALL

Ball accelerates due to its weight

Feather accelerates due to its weight

Air resistance on feather increases quickly and soon matches weight

Air resistance on ball slowly increases

Weight of feather

Feather reaches terminal velocity

Weight of ball

Terminal velocity of ball much higher than feather's

FRICTION BETWEEN SURFACES

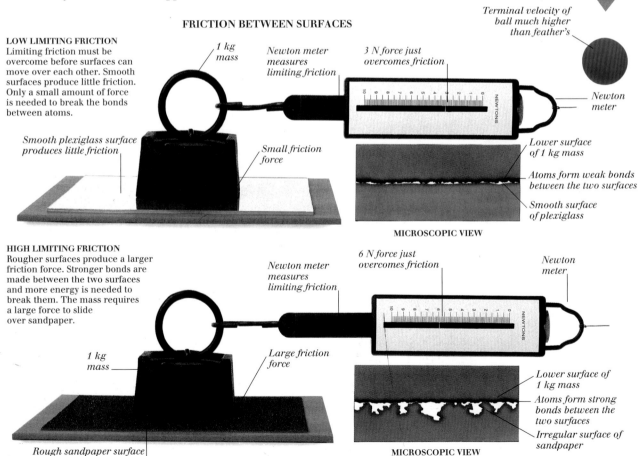

LOW LIMITING FRICTION
Limiting friction must be overcome before surfaces can move over each other. Smooth surfaces produce little friction. Only a small amount of force is needed to break the bonds between atoms.

1 kg mass

Newton meter measures limiting friction

3 N force just overcomes friction

Newton meter

Smooth plexiglass surface produces little friction

Small friction force

Lower surface of 1 kg mass

Atoms form weak bonds between the two surfaces

Smooth surface of plexiglass

MICROSCOPIC VIEW

HIGH LIMITING FRICTION
Rougher surfaces produce a larger friction force. Stronger bonds are made between the two surfaces and more energy is needed to break them. The mass requires a large force to slide over sandpaper.

6 N force just overcomes friction

Newton meter measures limiting friction

Newton meter

1 kg mass

Large friction force

Lower surface of 1 kg mass

Atoms form strong bonds between the two surfaces

Irregular surface of sandpaper

Rough sandpaper surface produces large friction

MICROSCOPIC VIEW

MOTORCYCLE BRAKE

Friction is put to good use in the disk brakes of a motorcycle. The friction force between disk and brake pad slows down the rotation of the wheel, reducing the vehicle's speed. In doing so, it converts the **kinetic energy** of the vehicle into heat (see p. 17).

Piston

Caliper unit

Brake pad (inside caliper unit)

Metal brake disk

BALL BEARINGS

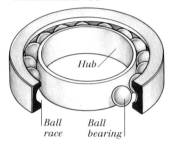

Bearings are a type of roller used to reduce friction between moving machine parts such as a wheel and its axle. As a wheel turns on its axle, the balls roll around inside the bearing, drastically reducing the friction between wheel and axle.

Hub

Ball race

Ball bearing

LUBRICATION

The presence of oil or another fluid between two surfaces keeps the surfaces apart. Because fluids (liquids or gases) flow, they allow movement between surfaces. Here, a lubricated kilogram mass slides down a slope, while an unlubricated one is prevented from moving by friction.

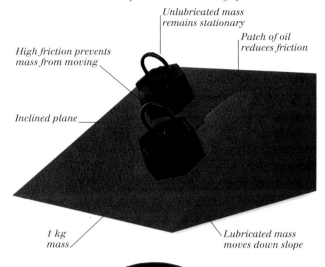

Unlubricated mass remains stationary

Patch of oil reduces friction

High friction prevents mass from moving

Inclined plane

1 kg mass

Lubricated mass moves down slope

ROLLERS

THE ACTION OF A ROLLER ON A SLOPE
Friction causes the roller to grip the slope so that it turns. If there were no friction, the roller would simply slide down the slope.

Roller

Force down the slope

Shallow slope

Frictional force

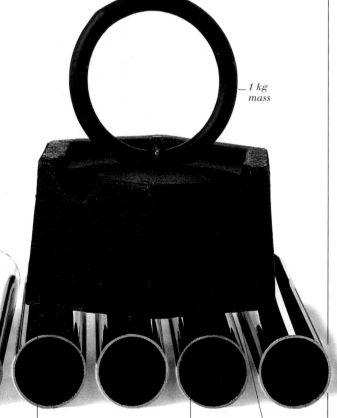

1 kg mass

Steel roller

Flat surface

Friction forces between surfaces create a turning force that turns the rollers

Mass moves smoothly over surface

Underside of 1 kg mass

USING ROLLERS TO AVOID FRICTION
Rollers placed between two surfaces keep the surfaces apart. The rollers allow the underside of the kilogram mass to move freely over the ground. An object placed on rollers will move smoothly if pushed or pulled.

Simple machines

IN PHYSICS, A MACHINE IS ANY DEVICE that can be used to transmit a **force** (see pp. 20-21) and, in doing so, change its size or direction. When using a simple pulley, a type of machine, a person can lift a load by pulling downward on the rope. By using several pulleys connected together as a block and tackle, the size of the force can be changed too, so that a heavy load can be lifted using a small force. Other simple machines include the inclined plane, the lever, the screw, and the wheel and axle. All of these machines illustrate the concept of **work**. Work is the amount of energy expended when a force is moved through a distance. The force applied to a machine is called the effort, while the force it overcomes is called the load. The effort is often smaller than the load, for a small effort can overcome a heavy load if the effort is moved through a larger distance. The machine is then said to give a mechanical advantage. Although the effort will be smaller when using a machine, the amount of work done, or energy used, will be equal to or greater than that without the machine.

Ax handle

AN INCLINED PLANE
The force needed to drag an object up a slope is less than that needed to lift it vertically. However, the distance moved by the object is greater when pulled up the slope than if it were lifted vertically.

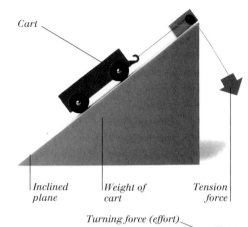

Cart

Inclined plane *Weight of cart* *Tension force*

SCREW
A screw is like an inclined plane wrapped around a shaft. The force that turns the screw is converted to a larger one, which moves a shorter distance and drives the screw in.

Turning force (effort)

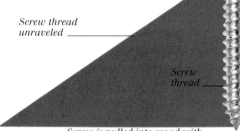

Screw thread unraveled

Screw thread

Screw is pulled into wood with force greater than the effort

WEDGE
The ax is a wedge. The applied force moves a long way into the wood, producing a larger force, which pushes the wood apart a short distance.

Metal ax blade

Small force applied

Block of wood

Large force produced

Wood splits apart

CORKSCREW
The corkscrew is a clever combination of several different machines. The screw pulls its way into the cork, turned by a wheel and axle. The cork is lifted by a pair of class one levers (see opposite).

Handle and shaft form a wheel and axle

Class one lever

Cork

Neck of bottle

Screw

PULLEYS

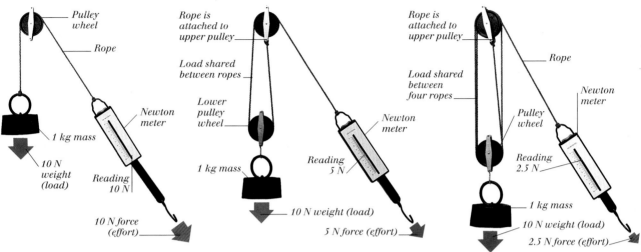

SIMPLE PULLEY
A simple pulley changes the direction of a force but not its size. Here a one kg mass, weighing ten newtons, is lifted by a ten newton force. The mass and the other end of the rope move through the same distance.

DOUBLE PULLEY
A double pulley will lift a one kg mass with only a five newton effort, because the force in the rope doubles up as the rope does. However, pulling the rope by one meter raises the mass by only half a meter.

QUADRUPLE PULLEY
Lifting a one kg mass with a quadruple pulley, in which the rope goes over four pulley wheels, feels almost effortless. However, pulling the rope by one meter lifts the mass by only one quarter of a meter.

THREE CLASSES OF LEVERS

CLASS ONE LEVER
In a class one lever, the **fulcrum** (pivot point) is between the effort and the load. The load is larger than the effort, but it moves through a smaller distance.

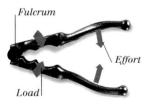

CLASS TWO LEVER
In a class two lever, the load is between the fulcrum and effort. Here again, the load is greater than the effort, and it moves through a smaller distance.

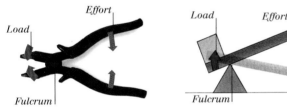

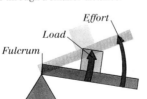

CLASS THREE LEVER
In a class three lever, the effort is between the fulcrum and the load. In this case, the load is less than the effort, but it moves through a greater distance.

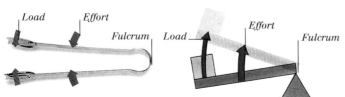

WHEEL AND AXLE
As the pedal and chainwheel of a bicycle turn through one revolution, the pedal moves farther than the links of the chain. For this reason, the force applied to the chain is greater than the force applied to the pedal. The steering wheel of a car is another example of a wheel and axle.

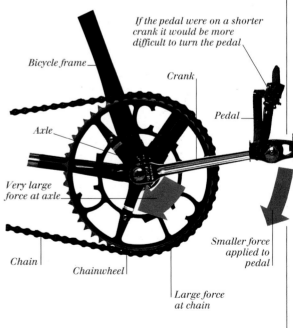

Circular motion

WHEN AN OBJECT MOVES IN A CIRCLE, its direction is continuously changing. Any change in direction requires a **force** (see pp. 22-23). The force required to maintain circular motion is called **centripetal force**. The size of this force depends on the size of the circle, and the mass and speed of the object (see p. 378). The centripetal force that keeps an object whirling around on the end of a string is caused by **tension** (see pp. 34-35) in the string. When the centripetal force ceases – for example, if the string breaks – the object flies off in a straight line, since no force is acting upon it. **Gravity** (see pp. 20-21) is the centripetal force that keeps planets such as the Earth in orbit. Without this centripetal force, the Earth would move in a straight line through space. On a smaller scale, without friction to provide centripetal force, a motorcyclist could not steer around a bend. Spinning, a form of circular motion, gives **gyroscopes** stability.

CENTRIPETAL FORCE

In the experiment below, centripetal force is provided by tension in a length of string, which keeps a 1 kg mass moving in a circle. The mass can move freely as it floats like a hovercraft on the jets of air supplied from beneath it. When the circle is twice as large, half the force is needed. However, moving twice as fast requires four times the force (see p. 378).

CONTROL EXPERIMENT

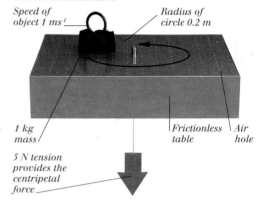

Speed of object 1 ms^{-1}

Radius of circle 0.2 m

1 kg mass

Frictionless table

Air hole

5 N tension provides the centripetal force

TWICE THE SPEED, FOUR TIMES THE FORCE

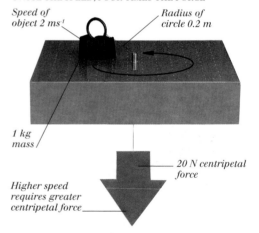

Speed of object 2 ms^{-1}

Radius of circle 0.2 m

1 kg mass

20 N centripetal force

Higher speed requires greater centripetal force

TWICE THE RADIUS, HALF THE FORCE

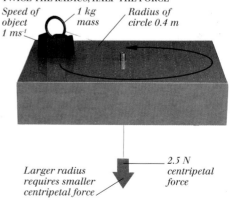

Speed of object 1 ms^{-1}

1 kg mass

Radius of circle 0.4 m

2.5 N centripetal force

Larger radius requires smaller centripetal force

MOTION IN A CIRCLE

ASPECTS OF CIRCULAR MOTION

The force that continuously changes the direction of an object moving in a circle is called centripetal force. It is directed toward the center of the circle. The smaller the radius of the circle, the larger the force needed.

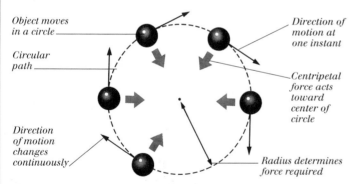

Object moves in a circle

Circular path

Direction of motion changes continuously

Direction of motion at one instant

Centripetal force acts toward center of circle

Radius determines force required

HAMMER THROWER

Tension in muscles provides the centripetal force needed to whirl a hammer round in a circle. When the thrower releases the chain, no force acts upon the hammer, and it moves off in a straight line.

Hammer thrower

Chain

Hammer

Hammer moves in a circle

Hammer moves in a straight line

Chain is released

Thrower moves in a circle

PLANETARY ORBITS

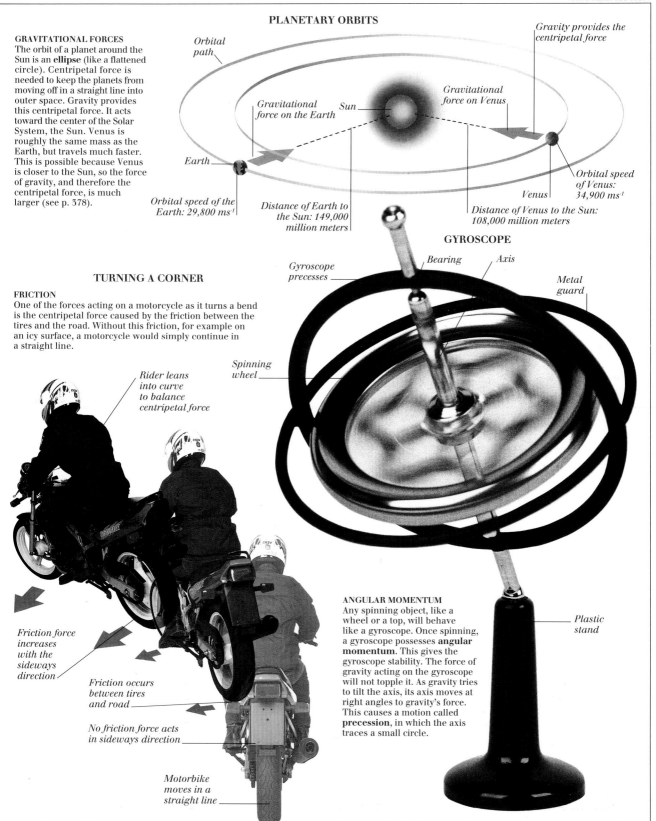

GRAVITATIONAL FORCES
The orbit of a planet around the Sun is an **ellipse** (like a flattened circle). Centripetal force is needed to keep the planets from moving off in a straight line into outer space. Gravity provides this centripetal force. It acts toward the center of the Solar System, the Sun. Venus is roughly the same mass as the Earth, but travels much faster. This is possible because Venus is closer to the Sun, so the force of gravity, and therefore the centripetal force, is much larger (see p. 378).

Orbital path

Gravitational force on the Earth

Sun

Gravitational force on Venus

Gravity provides the centripetal force

Earth

Venus

Orbital speed of the Earth: 29,800 ms⁻¹

Distance of Earth to the Sun: 149,000 million meters

Distance of Venus to the Sun: 108,000 million meters

Orbital speed of Venus: 34,900 ms⁻¹

GYROSCOPE

Gyroscope precesses

Bearing

Axis

Metal guard

Spinning wheel

TURNING A CORNER

FRICTION
One of the forces acting on a motorcycle as it turns a bend is the centripetal force caused by the friction between the tires and the road. Without this friction, for example on an icy surface, a motorcycle would simply continue in a straight line.

Rider leans into curve to balance centripetal force

Friction force increases with the sideways direction

Friction occurs between tires and road

No friction force acts in sideways direction

Motorbike moves in a straight line

ANGULAR MOMENTUM
Any spinning object, like a wheel or a top, will behave like a gyroscope. Once spinning, a gyroscope possesses **angular momentum**. This gives the gyroscope stability. The force of gravity acting on the gyroscope will not topple it. As gravity tries to tilt the axis, its axis moves at right angles to gravity's force. This causes a motion called **precession**, in which the axis traces a small circle.

Plastic stand

Waves and oscillations

AN OSCILLATION IS ANY MOTION BACK AND FORTH, such as that of a pendulum. When that motion travels through matter or space, it becomes a wave. An oscillation, or vibration, occurs when a force acts that pulls a displaced object back to its **equilibrium** position, and the size of this force increases with the size of the **displacement**. A **mass** on a spring, for example, is acted upon by two forces: **gravity** and the **tension** (see pp. 38-39) in the spring. At the point of equilibrium, the **resultant** (see pp. 20-21) of these forces is zero: they cancel each other out. At all other points, the resultant force acts in a direction that restores the object to its equilibrium position. This results in the object moving back and forth, or oscillating, about that position. Vibration is very common and results in the phenomenon of sound. In air, the vibrations that cause sound are transmitted as a wave between air molecules; many other substances transmit sound in a similar way.

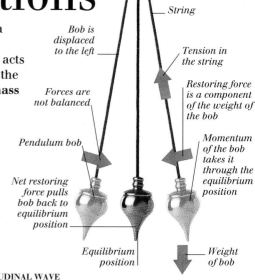

PENDULUM

String

Bob is displaced to the left

Tension in the string

Forces are not balanced

Restoring force is a component of the weight of the bob

Pendulum bob

Momentum of the bob takes it through the equilibrium position

Net restoring force pulls bob back to equilibrium position

Equilibrium position

Weight of bob

WAVES IN SPRINGS

TRANSVERSE WAVE

Energy travels along spring

Spring

Wavelength

Amplitude

LONGITUDINAL WAVE

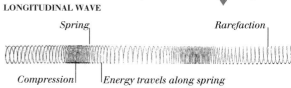

Spring

Rarefaction

Compression

Energy travels along spring

OSCILLATION

MOTION OF MASS ON SPRING

The first mass shown (below left) is in equilibrium. The two forces acting on it – its **weight** and the tension in the spring – exactly cancel each other out. The mass is given an initial downward push. Once the mass is displaced downward (below center), the tension in the spring exceeds the weight. The resultant upward force accelerates the mass back up toward its original position, by which time it has momentum, carrying it farther upward. When the weight exceeds the tension in the spring (below right), the mass is pulled down again. This cycle repeats.

MOTION OF MASS ON SPRING, MASS SEEN IN ISOLATION

Wave nature of motion becomes apparent

Mass

Appears as transverse wave

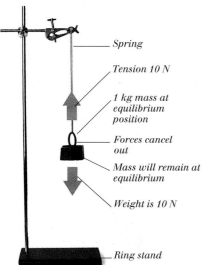

Spring

Tension 10 N

1 kg mass at equilibrium position

Forces cancel out

Mass will remain at equilibrium

Weight is 10 N

Ring stand

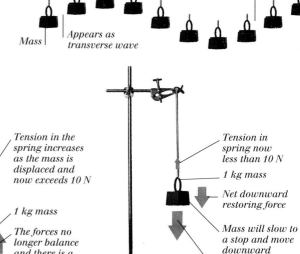

Tension in the spring increases as the mass is displaced and now exceeds 10 N

1 kg mass

The forces no longer balance and there is a net upward restoring force

Weight 10 N

Ring stand

Tension in spring now less than 10 N

1 kg mass

Net downward restoring force

Mass will slow to a stop and move downward

Weight 10 N

Ring stand

SOUND AS VIBRATION OF THE AIR

PROPAGATION OF SOUND

A vibrating object, such as the tuning fork shown here, causes variations in pressure in the surrounding air. Areas of high and low **pressure**, known as **compressions** and **rarefactions**, propagate (move) through the air as sound waves. The sound waves meet a microphone and create electrical oscillations displayed on an oscilloscope.

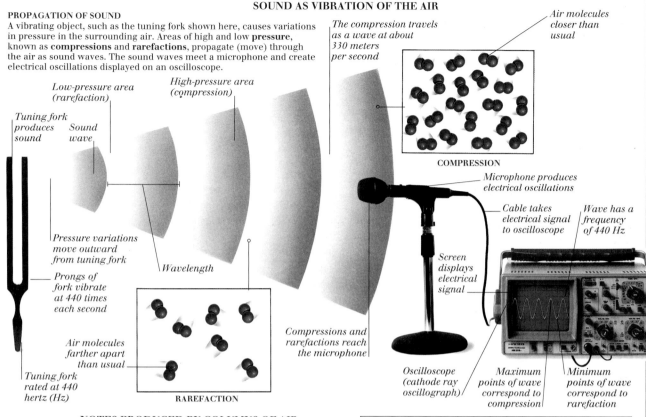

The compression travels as a wave at about 330 meters per second

Air molecules closer than usual

COMPRESSION

Low-pressure area (rarefaction)

High-pressure area (compression)

Tuning fork produces sound

Sound wave

Pressure variations move outward from tuning fork

Wavelength

Prongs of fork vibrate at 440 times each second

Air molecules farther apart than usual

RAREFACTION

Tuning fork rated at 440 hertz (Hz)

Microphone produces electrical oscillations

Cable takes electrical signal to oscilloscope

Wave has a frequency of 440 Hz

Screen displays electrical signal

Compressions and rarefactions reach the microphone

Oscilloscope (cathode ray oscillograph)

Maximum points of wave correspond to compression

Minimum points of wave correspond to rarefaction

NOTES PRODUCED BY COLUMNS OF AIR

FREQUENCY AND WAVELENGTH

The distance between each compression of a sound wave is called its **wavelength**. Sound waves with a short wavelength have a high **frequency** and sound high-pitched. The frequency of a note is the number of vibrations each second and is measured in hertz (Hz). The columns of air in these jars produce different notes when air is blown over them.

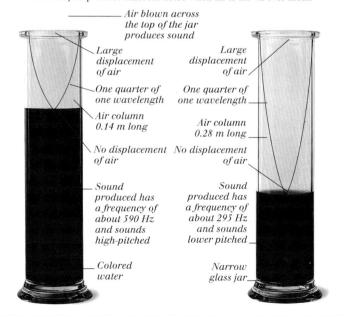

Air blown across the top of the jar produces sound

Large displacement of air

One quarter of one wavelength

Air column 0.14 m long

No displacement of air

Sound produced has a frequency of about 590 Hz and sounds high-pitched

Colored water

Large displacement of air

One quarter of one wavelength

Air column 0.28 m long

No displacement of air

Sound produced has a frequency of about 295 Hz and sounds lower pitched

Narrow glass jar

LOUDSPEAKER

A changing electrical signal is fed to the voice coil of a loudspeaker, which lies within the **magnetic field** of a **permanent magnet**. The signal in the coil causes it to behave like an **electromagnet** (see pp. 44-45), making it push against the field of the permanent magnet. The speaker cone is then pushed in and out by the coil in time with the signal.

If the signal is from a sound recording, the original sound will be reproduced

Collar

Voice coil

Speaker cone is pushed in and out to produce sound

Permanent magnet

Terminal

Heat and temperature

HEAT IS A FORM OF ENERGY (see pp. 16-17). This energy is the **kinetic energy** of the **atoms** and **molecules** that make up all matter. The temperature of a substance is related to the average kinetic energy of its particles. Units of temperature include the degree **Celsius**(°C), the degree **Fahrenheit** (°F), and the **Kelvin** (K). Some examples of equivalent values are shown below. The lowest possible temperature is called absolute zero (zero K). At this temperature, atoms and molecules have their lowest energy. The **state** of a **substance** is determined by its temperature and most substances can exist as a solid (see pp. 34-35), a liquid (see pp. 36-37), or a gas (see pp. 38-39). If two substances at different temperatures make contact, their particles will share their energy. This results in a heat transfer by conduction, until the temperatures are equal. This process can melt a solid, in which case the heat transferred is called **latent heat**. Heat can also be transferred by **radiation**, in which heat energy becomes electromagnetic radiation (see pp. 48-49), and does not need a material medium to transfer heat.

RANGE OF TEMPERATURES

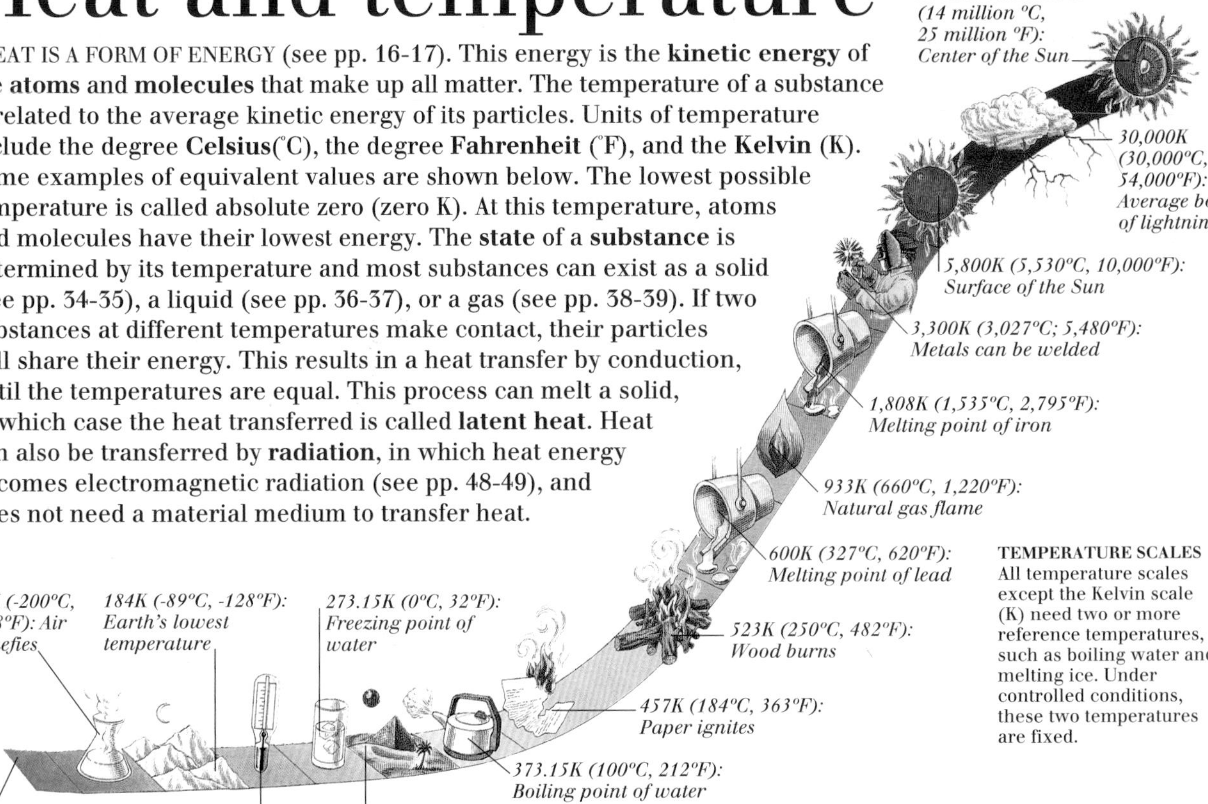

About 14 million K (14 million °C, 25 million °F): Center of the Sun

30,000K (30,000°C, 54,000°F): Average bolt of lightning

5,800K (5,530°C, 10,000°F): Surface of the Sun

3,300K (3,027°C; 5,480°F): Metals can be welded

1,808K (1,535°C, 2,795°F): Melting point of iron

933K (660°C, 1,220°F): Natural gas flame

600K (327°C, 620°F): Melting point of lead

523K (250°C, 482°F): Wood burns

457K (184°C, 363°F): Paper ignites

373.15K (100°C, 212°F): Boiling point of water

331K (58°C, 136°F): Earth's highest temperature

273.15K (0°C, 32°F): Freezing point of water

234K (-39°C, -38.2°F): Freezing point of mercury

184K (-89°C, -128°F): Earth's lowest temperature

73K (-200°C, -328°F): Air liquefies

0K (-273.15°C, -459.67°F): Absolute zero

TEMPERATURE SCALES

All temperature scales except the Kelvin scale (K) need two or more reference temperatures, such as boiling water and melting ice. Under controlled conditions, these two temperatures are fixed.

STATES OF MATTER

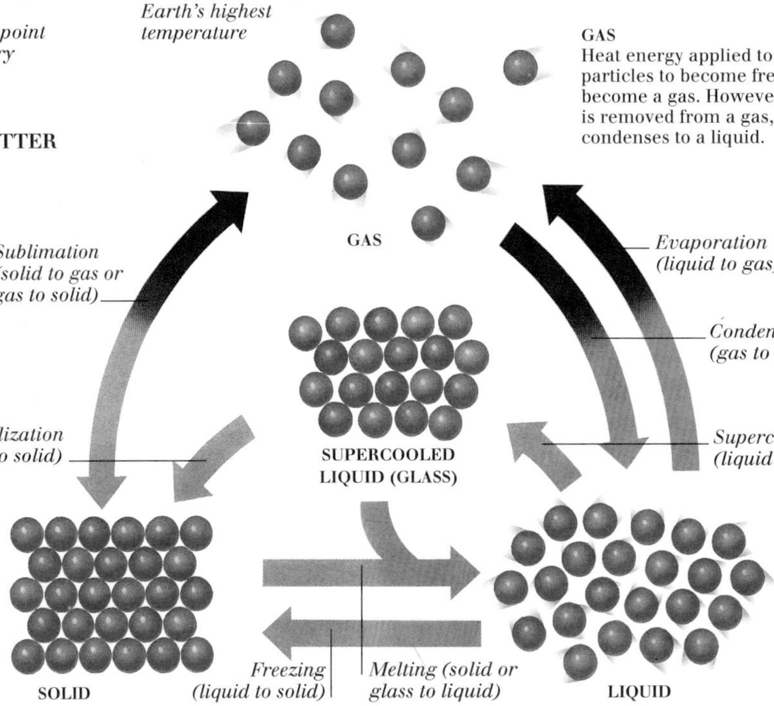

SUPERCOOLED LIQUID
The particles of a **supercooled liquid** are in fixed positions, like those of a solid, but they are disordered and cannot be called a true solid. Supercooled liquids flow very slowly and have no definite melting point.

SOLID
The particles of a solid normally have no motion relative to each other, as they are only free to vibrate about a fixed position. An input of energy breaks the bonds between particles, and the solid melts.

GAS
Heat energy applied to a liquid allows particles to become free of each other and become a gas. However if enough energy is removed from a gas, by cooling, it condenses to a liquid.

LIQUID
Particles in a liquid do not occupy fixed positions like those in a solid, but neither are they completely free, as in a gas. The particles move over one another, allowing a liquid to flow.

GAS

Sublimation (solid to gas or gas to solid)

Evaporation (liquid to gas)

Condensation (gas to liquid)

Supercooling (liquid to glass)

Crystallization (glass to solid)

SUPERCOOLED LIQUID (GLASS)

SOLID

Freezing (liquid to solid)

Melting (solid or glass to liquid)

LIQUID

EQUALIZATION OF TEMPERATURES

OBJECTS AT DIFFERENT TEMPERATURES
The particles of objects at different temperatures have different kinetic energies. The colors of the blocks below are an indication of their temperature.

TRANSFER OF HEAT
When two objects at different temperatures are brought into contact, a transfer of kinetic energy takes place in the form of heat. Here, the hot and cold blocks are touching.

EQUAL TEMPERATURES
Eventually, the average kinetic energies of particles in two touching objects become equal. The temperatures of the two objects are then said to be equal, as shown by the blocks below.

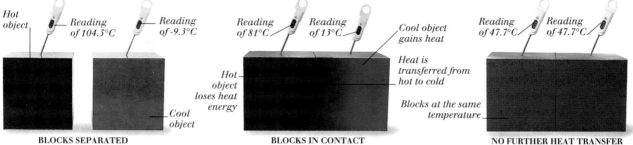

Hot object — *Reading of 104.5°C* *Reading of -9.3°C*

Cool object

BLOCKS SEPARATED

Reading of 81°C *Reading of 13°C* *Cool object gains heat*

Hot object loses heat energy

Heat is transferred from hot to cold

BLOCKS IN CONTACT

Reading of 47.7°C *Reading of 47.7°C*

Blocks at the same temperature

NO FURTHER HEAT TRANSFER

Atoms in hot block have high energy

Atoms in cool block vibrate a little

Atoms in hot object lose kinetic energy

MOLECULAR VIEW

Atoms in cool object gain kinetic energy

MOLECULAR VIEW

No further net heat transfer

The kinetic energy is shared

MOLECULAR VIEW

LATENT HEAT

HEATING A SUBSTANCE
Heat transferred from a hot flame to a cooler substance can cause the substance to melt. The temperature of the substance (here, naphthalene) rises with the transfer of more energy, until it reaches the **melting point**.

Thermometer reads 80.5°C

Temperature stays the same during melting

Beaker

Gauze

Liquid naphthalene

Solid naphthalene

Bunsen burner *Hot flame*

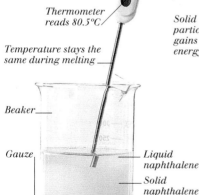

MELTING A SUBSTANCE
At the melting point, the supplied energy must break the attraction between all the particles, melting all the solid, before the temperature will rise again. This extra supplied energy is called **latent heat**.

Liquid particle

Solid particle gains energy

MELTING

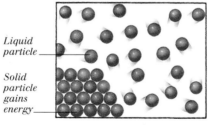

Temperature increases after melting

During melting, no temperature increase

Temperature rises as solid is heated

Temperature

Time

GRAPH TO SHOW MELTING

TRANSFER OF HEAT BY RADIATION
An object at room temperature produces radiation – called **infrared radiation**. A hot object, such as the lamp below, produces a lot of infrared. This radiation can heat up other objects. The hot object cools as it loses energy as radiation.

Metal block at room temperature

Thermometer reads 18.7°C

COOL OBJECT

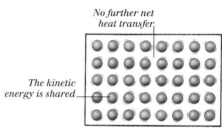

Desk lamp

Temperature of filament about 2,500K

Thermometer reads 31°C

Radiation absorbed by particles in the block

Radiation travels through space

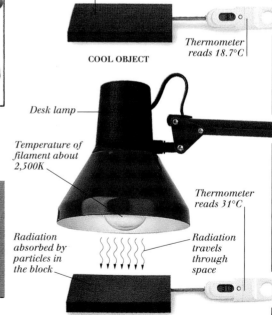

RADIATION

Solids

THE ATOMS OF A SOLID ARE CLOSELY PACKED, giving it a greater **density** than most liquids and all gases. A solid's rigidity derives from the strong attraction between its atoms. A force pulling on a solid moves these atoms farther apart, creating an opposing force called **tension**. If a force pushes on a solid, the atoms move closer together, creating **compression**. Temperature (see pp. 32-33) can also affect the nature of a solid. When the temperature of a solid increases, its particles gain **kinetic energy** and vibrate more vigorously, resulting in **thermal expansion**. Most solids are **crystals**, in which atoms are arranged in one of seven regular, repeating patterns (see below). **Amorphous solids**, such as glass, are not composed of crystals and can be molded into any shape. When the atoms of a solid move apart, the length of the solid increases. The extent of this increase depends on the applied force, and on the thickness of the material, and is known as **elasticity**.

STEEL RAILS

The expansion of a solid with an increase in temperature (see below) would cause rails to buckle badly in hot weather. To prevent this, rails are made in sections. The gap between the two sections allows each section to expand without buckling.

Train can pass smoothly over diagonal joint

Expansion joint

THERMAL EXPANSION

EXPERIMENT TO SHOW THERMAL EXPANSION
When a substance is heated, its atoms gain kinetic energy. In a solid, this results in the atoms vibrating more vigorously about their fixed positions. As a result, solids expand when heated. Below, a thin steel rod is heated by a gas flame, and the resulting expansion is measured using a **micrometer**.

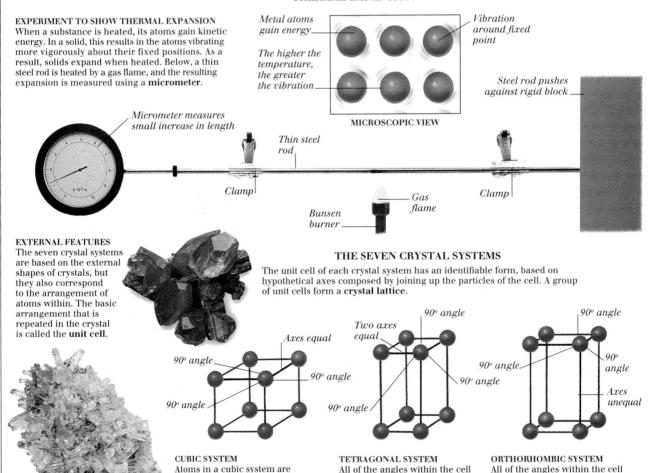

Metal atoms gain energy

The higher the temperature, the greater the vibration

Vibration around fixed point

MICROSCOPIC VIEW

Steel rod pushes against rigid block

Micrometer measures small increase in length

Thin steel rod

Clamp

Gas flame

Clamp

Bunsen burner

EXTERNAL FEATURES
The seven crystal systems are based on the external shapes of crystals, but they also correspond to the arrangement of atoms within. The basic arrangement that is repeated in the crystal is called the **unit cell**.

THE SEVEN CRYSTAL SYSTEMS

The unit cell of each crystal system has an identifiable form, based on hypothetical axes composed by joining up the particles of the cell. A group of unit cells form a **crystal lattice**.

Axes equal

90° angle

90° angle

90° angle

Two axes equal

90° angle

90° angle

90° angle

90° angle

90° angle

90° angle

90° angle

Axes unequal

CUBIC SYSTEM
Atoms in a cubic system are equally spaced, and the angle between each axis of the repeating cell is always 90°.

TETRAGONAL SYSTEM
All of the angles within the cell are 90°, and of the three axes (shown in black), two are the same length.

ORTHORHOMBIC SYSTEM
All of the angles within the cell are 90°, but none of the three axes (shown in black) is equal in length.

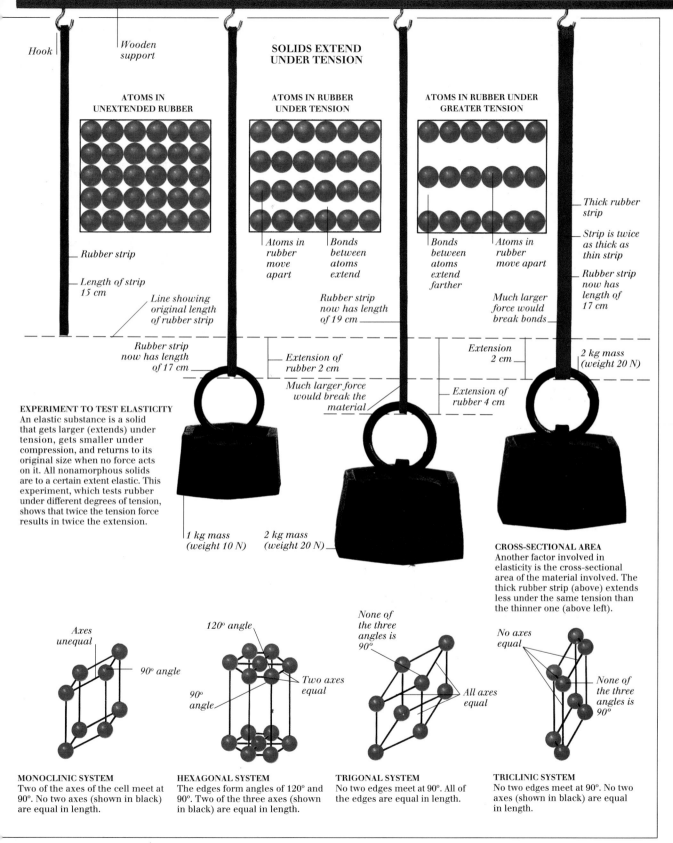

Hook

Wooden support

SOLIDS EXTEND UNDER TENSION

ATOMS IN UNEXTENDED RUBBER

ATOMS IN RUBBER UNDER TENSION

ATOMS IN RUBBER UNDER GREATER TENSION

Atoms in rubber move apart

Bonds between atoms extend

Bonds between atoms extend farther

Atoms in rubber move apart

Thick rubber strip

Strip is twice as thick as thin strip

Rubber strip now has length of 17 cm

Rubber strip

Length of strip 15 cm

Line showing original length of rubber strip

Rubber strip now has length of 19 cm

Much larger force would break bonds

Rubber strip now has length of 17 cm

Extension of rubber 2 cm

Extension 2 cm

2 kg mass (weight 20 N)

Much larger force would break the material

Extension of rubber 4 cm

EXPERIMENT TO TEST ELASTICITY
An elastic substance is a solid that gets larger (extends) under tension, gets smaller under compression, and returns to its original size when no force acts on it. All nonamorphous solids are to a certain extent elastic. This experiment, which tests rubber under different degrees of tension, shows that twice the tension force results in twice the extension.

1 kg mass (weight 10 N)

2 kg mass (weight 20 N)

CROSS-SECTIONAL AREA
Another factor involved in elasticity is the cross-sectional area of the material involved. The thick rubber strip (above) extends less under the same tension than the thinner one (above left).

Axes unequal

90° angle

120° angle

90° angle

Two axes equal

None of the three angles is 90°

All axes equal

No axes equal

None of the three angles is 90°

MONOCLINIC SYSTEM
Two of the axes of the cell meet at 90°. No two axes (shown in black) are equal in length.

HEXAGONAL SYSTEM
The edges form angles of 120° and 90°. Two of the three axes (shown in black) are equal in length.

TRIGONAL SYSTEM
No two edges meet at 90°. All of the edges are equal in length.

TRICLINIC SYSTEM
No two edges meet at 90°. No two axes (shown in black) are equal in length.

Liquids

UNLIKE SOLIDS, LIQUIDS CAN FLOW. Their particles move almost independently of each other but are not as free as the particles of a gas. Forces of attraction called **cohesive** forces act between the particles of a liquid. These forces create **surface tension**, which pulls liquid drops into a spherical shape. If the surface tension of water is reduced, by dissolving soap in it, then pockets of air can stretch the surface into a thin film, forming a bubble. Forces of attraction between liquid particles and adjoining matter are called **adhesive** forces. The balance between cohesive and adhesive forces causes **capillary action**, and the formation of a **meniscus** curve at the boundary between a liquid and its container. Liquids exert pressure on any object immersed in them; the pressure acts in all directions and increases with depth, creating **upthrust** on an immersed object. If the upthrust is large enough, the object will float.

LIQUID DROPS AND BUBBLES

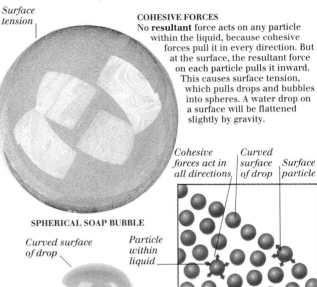

Surface tension

COHESIVE FORCES
No **resultant** force acts on any particle within the liquid, because cohesive forces pull it in every direction. But at the surface, the resultant force on each particle pulls it inward. This causes surface tension, which pulls drops and bubbles into spheres. A water drop on a surface will be flattened slightly by gravity.

SPHERICAL SOAP BUBBLE

Curved surface of drop

WATER DROP ON A SURFACE

Cohesive forces act in all directions | *Curved surface of drop* | *Surface particle*

Particle within liquid

SURFACE TENSION

LIQUIDS IN TUBES

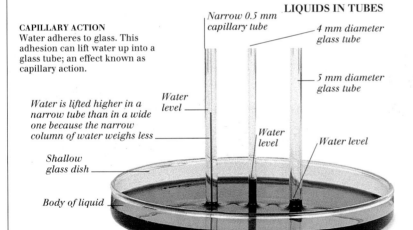

CAPILLARY ACTION
Water adheres to glass. This adhesion can lift water up into a glass tube; an effect known as capillary action.

Narrow 0.5 mm capillary tube

4 mm diameter glass tube

5 mm diameter glass tube

Water level

Water is lifted higher in a narrow tube than in a wide one because the narrow column of water weighs less

Water level

Water level

Shallow glass dish

Body of liquid

Wall of glass tube

MOLECULAR VIEW
Capillary action is caused by adhesive and cohesive forces between particles of glass and water. Here, water molecules adhere to glass and the adhesive force lifts the edge of the water up the glass. The cohesive forces between water molecules means that this lifted edge also raises water molecules lying farther out from the edge of the glass.

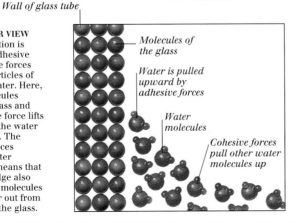

Molecules of the glass

Water is pulled upward by adhesive forces

Water molecules

Cohesive forces pull other water molecules up

MENISCUS
Where a liquid meets a solid surface, a curve called a meniscus forms. The shape of the meniscus depends on the balance between cohesive and adhesive forces.

DOWNWARD MENISCUS

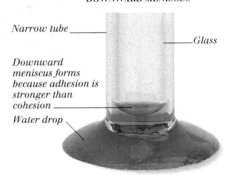

Narrow tube

Glass

Downward meniscus forms because adhesion is stronger than cohesion

Water drop

UPWARD MENISCUS

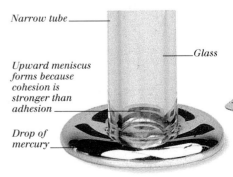

Narrow tube

Glass

Upward meniscus forms because cohesion is stronger than adhesion

Drop of mercury

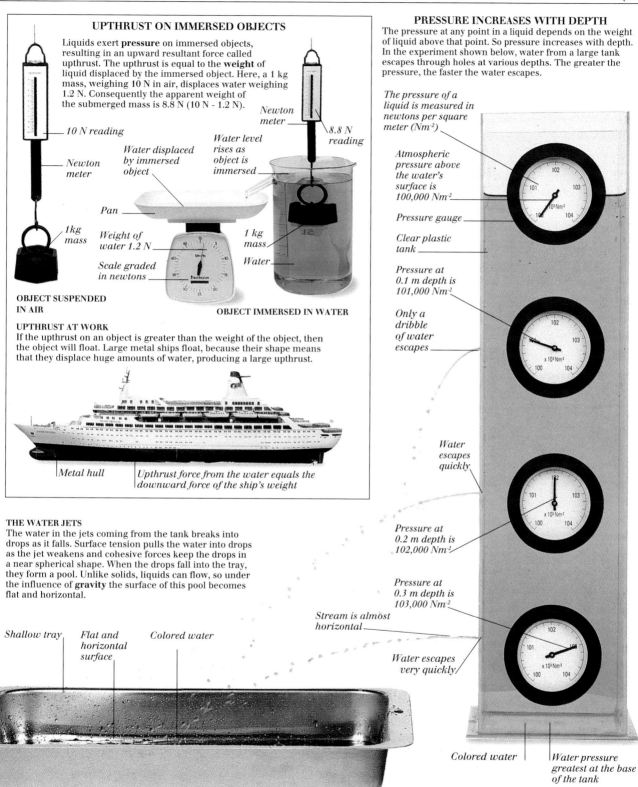

UPTHRUST ON IMMERSED OBJECTS

Liquids exert **pressure** on immersed objects, resulting in an upward resultant force called upthrust. The upthrust is equal to the **weight** of liquid displaced by the immersed object. Here, a 1 kg mass, weighing 10 N in air, displaces water weighing 1.2 N. Consequently the apparent weight of the submerged mass is 8.8 N (10 N - 1.2 N).

Newton meter

8.8 N reading

10 N reading

Newton meter

Water displaced by immersed object

Water level rises as object is immersed

Pan

1kg mass

Weight of water 1.2 N

1 kg mass

Scale graded in newtons

Water

OBJECT SUSPENDED IN AIR

OBJECT IMMERSED IN WATER

UPTHRUST AT WORK

If the upthrust on an object is greater than the weight of the object, then the object will float. Large metal ships float, because their shape means that they displace huge amounts of water, producing a large upthrust.

Metal hull

Upthrust force from the water equals the downward force of the ship's weight

THE WATER JETS

The water in the jets coming from the tank breaks into drops as it falls. Surface tension pulls the water into drops as the jet weakens and cohesive forces keep the drops in a near spherical shape. When the drops fall into the tray, they form a pool. Unlike solids, liquids can flow, so under the influence of **gravity** the surface of this pool becomes flat and horizontal.

Shallow tray

Flat and horizontal surface

Colored water

PRESSURE INCREASES WITH DEPTH

The pressure at any point in a liquid depends on the weight of liquid above that point. So pressure increases with depth. In the experiment shown below, water from a large tank escapes through holes at various depths. The greater the pressure, the faster the water escapes.

The pressure of a liquid is measured in newtons per square meter (Nm^{-2})

Atmospheric pressure above the water's surface is 100,000 Nm^{-2}

Pressure gauge

Clear plastic tank

Pressure at 0.1 m depth is 101,000 Nm^{-2}

Only a dribble of water escapes

Water escapes quickly

Pressure at 0.2 m depth is 102,000 Nm^{-2}

Pressure at 0.3 m depth is 103,000 Nm^{-2}

Stream is almost horizontal

Water escapes very quickly

Colored water

Water pressure greatest at the base of the tank

Gases

A GAS COMPRISES INDEPENDENT PARTICLES – **atoms** or **molecules** – in random motion. This means that a gas will fill any container into which it is placed. If two different gases are allowed to meet, the particles of the gases will mix together. This process is known as **diffusion**. Imagine a fixed mass of gas – that is, a fixed number of gas particles. It will occupy a particular amount of space, or **volume**, often confined by a container. The particles of the gas will be in constant, random motion. The higher the **temperature** of the gas (see pp. 32-33), the faster the particles move. The bombardment of particles against the sides of the container produces **pressure** (see pp. 20-21). Three simple laws describe the predictable behavior of gases. They are Boyle's Law, the Pressure Law, and Charles' Law. Each of the gas laws describes a relationship between the pressure, volume, and temperature of a gas.

BOYLE'S LAW
The volume of a **mass** of gas at a fixed temperature will change in relation to the pressure. If the pressure on a gas increases, its volume will decrease. The apparatus on the left is used to illustrate Boyle's Law. A foot pump is used to push a column of oil up a sealed tube, reducing the volume occupied by the gas in the top part of the tube.

DIFFUSION
The random movement of gas particles ensures that any two gases sharing the same container will totally mix. This is diffusion. In the experiment below, the lower gas jar contains bromine, the top one air.

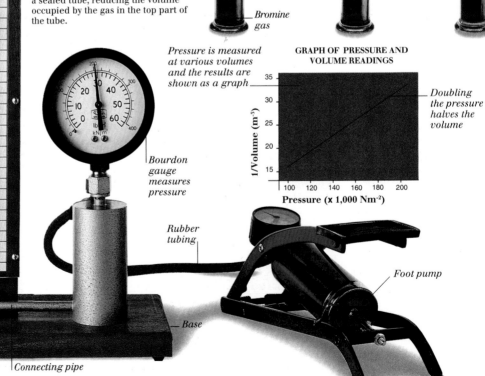

Clear plexiglass shield

Closed glass tube

Thick tube wall withstands pressure

Volume of trapped air

Column of oil

After each pressure change, apparatus is allowed to revert to room temperature

Random motion leads to random mixing of the molecules

Air

Slip separating air from bromine is removed

Some air moves into the bromine and mixes with it

Bromine gas

Random motion of the molecules leads to the complete mixing of air and bromine

Some bromine moves into the air and mixes with it

Pressure is measured at various volumes and the results are shown as a graph

Bourdon gauge measures pressure

Rubber tubing

Foot pump

Base

Connecting pipe

GRAPH OF PRESSURE AND VOLUME READINGS

Doubling the pressure halves the volume

1/Volume (m^{-3})

Pressure (x 1,000 Nm^{-2})

PRESSURE LAW

The pressure exerted by a gas at constant volume increases as the temperature of the gas rises. The apparatus shown is used to verify the Pressure Law. A mass of gas is heated in a water bath, and the pressure of the gas measured. When plotted as points on a graph, the results lie on a straight line.

CHARLES' LAW

The volume of a mass of gas at a fixed pressure depends on its temperature. The higher the temperature, the greater the volume. The apparatus shown is used to illustrate Charles' Law. The volume of a gas sample in the glass bulb is noted at various temperatures. A graph shows the results.

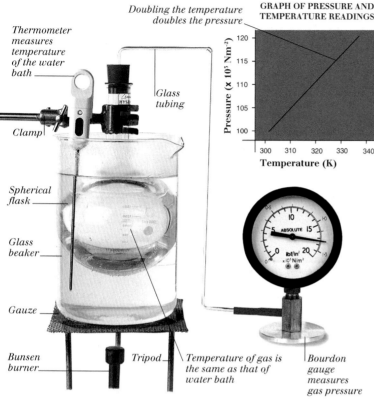

Doubling the temperature doubles the pressure

GRAPH OF PRESSURE AND TEMPERATURE READINGS

Thermometer measures temperature of the water bath

Glass tubing

Clamp

Spherical flask

Glass beaker

Gauze

Bunsen burner

Tripod

Temperature of gas is the same as that of water bath

Bourdon gauge measures gas pressure

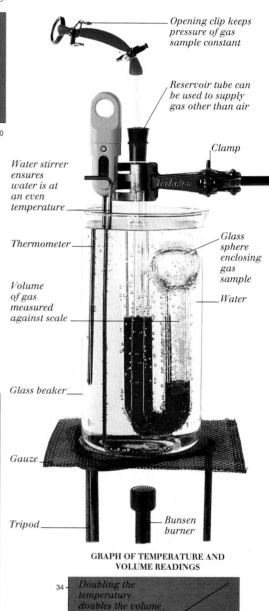

Opening clip keeps pressure of gas sample constant

Reservoir tube can be used to supply gas other than air

Clamp

Water stirrer ensures water is at an even temperature

Thermometer

Volume of gas measured against scale

Glass sphere enclosing gas sample

Water

Glass beaker

Gauze

Tripod

Bunsen burner

GRAPH OF TEMPERATURE AND VOLUME READINGS

Doubling the temperature doubles the volume

HOT-AIR BALLOON – CHARLES' LAW IN ACTION

The air in the envelope of a hot-air balloon is heated by a gas burner. As its temperature rises, the gas expands in accordance with Charles' Law. The envelope is open at the bottom, so some hot air escapes. Because air has mass (and therefore **weight**), the balloon weighs less once some air has escaped, although its volume is still large. The pressure of the air outside the envelope produces an **upthrust,** which (if enough air has been lost from the envelope) will be great enough to lift the balloon.

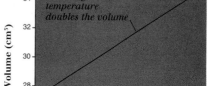

Envelope

Hot air escapes

Gas burner

Basket

Electricity and magnetism

ALL ELECTRICAL EFFECTS ARE CAUSED by **electric charges**. There are two types of electric charges, positive and negative. These charges exert **electrostatic** forces on each other. An **electric field** is the region in which these forces have effect. In atoms, **protons** (see pp. 56-57) carry positive charge, while **electrons** carry negative charge. **Atoms** are normally neutral, having equal numbers of each charge, but an atom can gain or lose electrons, for example by being rubbed. It then becomes a charged atom, or **ion**. Ions can be produced continuously by a Van de Graaff generator. Ions in a charged object may cause another nearby object to become charged. This process is called **induction**. Electricity has many similarities with magnetism (see pp. 44-45). For example, the lines of the electric field between charges (see right) take the same form as lines of magnetic force (see opposite), so magnetic fields are equivalent to electric fields. Iron consists of small magnetized regions called **domains**. If the magnetic directions of the domains in a piece of iron line up, the iron becomes magnetized.

ELECTRIC FIELDS AND FORCES

Charges of the same type repel, while charges of a different type attract. One way to think of an electric field is as a set of lines of force, as illustrated below.

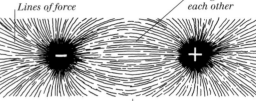

Lines of force

Charges attract each other

TWO DIFFERENT CHARGES

Electric field

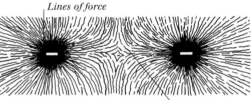

Lines of force

TWO SIMILAR CHARGES

Charges repel each other

STATIC ELECTRICITY

GOLD LEAF ELECTROSCOPE

A polyethylene rod can gain extra electrons when it is rubbed. Touching the charged rod to the top of an electroscope causes electrons to move into the electroscope. The electrons in the central strip and in the gold leaf repel each other, and the leaf lifts.

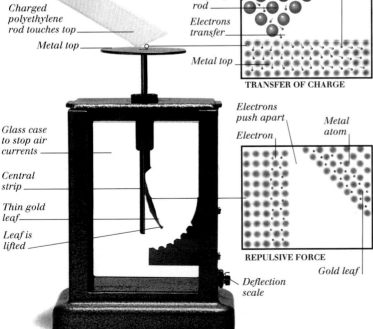

Charged polyethylene rod touches top

Metal top

Glass case to stop air currents

Central strip

Thin gold leaf

Leaf is lifted

Electrons pushed by extra electrons in rod

Metal atoms

Polyethylene rod

Electrons transfer

Metal top

TRANSFER OF CHARGE

Electrons push apart

Metal atom

Electron

REPULSIVE FORCE

Gold leaf

Deflection scale

INDUCTION

When a charged object is brought near to other materials, such as paper, electrostatic forces cause a displacement of charge within that material. This is called induction. Negative charges in the paper are displaced, so the edge of the paper nearest the rod becomes positively charged and clings to the negatively charged rod.

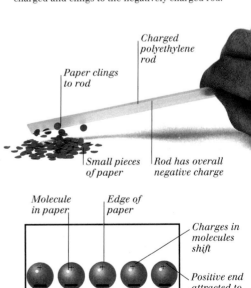

Charged polyethylene rod

Paper clings to rod

Small pieces of paper

Rod has overall negative charge

Molecule in paper

Edge of paper

Charges in molecules shift

Positive end attracted to rod

Positively charged end of molecule

INDUCTION IN PAPER

VAN DE GRAAFF GENERATOR

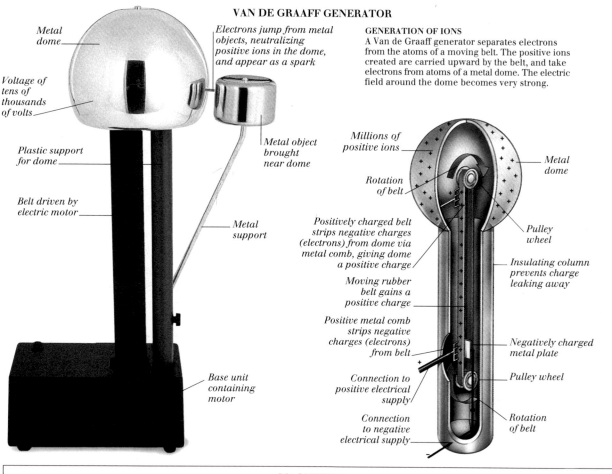

Metal dome

Electrons jump from metal objects, neutralizing positive ions in the dome, and appear as a spark

Voltage of tens of thousands of volts

Plastic support for dome

Belt driven by electric motor

Metal object brought near dome

Metal support

Base unit containing motor

GENERATION OF IONS

A Van de Graaff generator separates electrons from the atoms of a moving belt. The positive ions created are carried upward by the belt, and take electrons from atoms of a metal dome. The electric field around the dome becomes very strong.

Millions of positive ions

Metal dome

Rotation of belt

Pulley wheel

Positively charged belt strips negative charges (electrons) from dome via metal comb, giving dome a positive charge

Moving rubber belt gains a positive charge

Insulating column prevents charge leaking away

Positive metal comb strips negative charges (electrons) from belt

Negatively charged metal plate

Connection to positive electrical supply

Pulley wheel

Connection to negative electrical supply

Rotation of belt

MAGNETISM

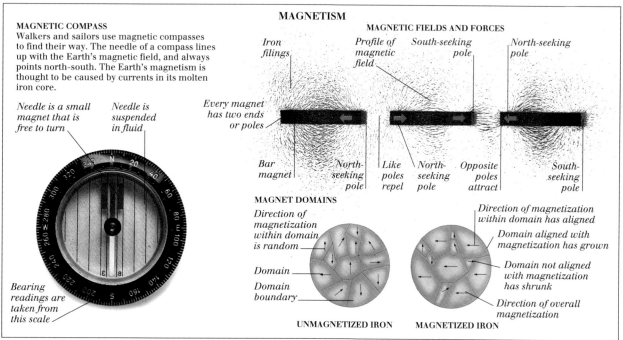

MAGNETIC COMPASS

Walkers and sailors use magnetic compasses to find their way. The needle of a compass lines up with the Earth's magnetic field, and always points north-south. The Earth's magnetism is thought to be caused by currents in its molten iron core.

Needle is a small magnet that is free to turn

Needle is suspended in fluid

Bearing readings are taken from this scale

MAGNETIC FIELDS AND FORCES

Iron filings

Profile of magnetic field

South-seeking pole

North-seeking pole

Every magnet has two ends or poles

Bar magnet

North-seeking pole

Like poles repel

North-seeking pole

Opposite poles attract

South-seeking pole

MAGNET DOMAINS

Direction of magnetization within domain is random

Domain

Domain boundary

Direction of magnetization within domain has aligned

Domain aligned with magnetization has grown

Domain not aligned with magnetization has shrunk

Direction of overall magnetization

UNMAGNETIZED IRON   **MAGNETIZED IRON**

Electric circuits

AN ELECTRIC CIRCUIT IS SIMPLY THE COURSE along which an **electric current** flows. **Electrons** carry negative charge and can be moved around a circuit by **electrostatic forces** (see pp. 40-41). A circuit usually consists of a **conductive** material, such as a metal, where the electrons are held very loosely to their atoms, thus making movement possible. The strength of the electrostatic force is the **voltage** and is measured in volts (V). The resulting movement of electric charge is called an electric current, and is measured in amps (A). The higher the voltage, the greater the current will be. But the current also depends on the thickness, length, temperature, and nature of the material that conducts it. The **resistance** of a material is the extent to which it opposes the flow of electric current, and is measured in ohms (Ω). Good conductors have a low resistance, which means that a small voltage will produce a large current. In batteries, the dissolving of a metal **electrode** causes the freeing of electrons, resulting in their movement to another electrode and the formation of a current.

ELECTRIC CURRENT
Regions of positive or negative charge, such as those at the terminals of a battery, force electrons through a conductor. The electrons move from negative charge toward positive. Originally, current was thought to flow from positive to negative. This is so-called "conventional current."

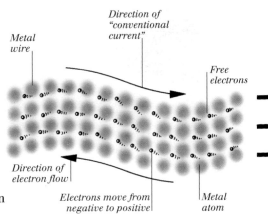

Metal wire

Direction of "conventional current"

Free electrons

Direction of electron flow

Electrons move from negative to positive

Metal atom

RESISTANCE

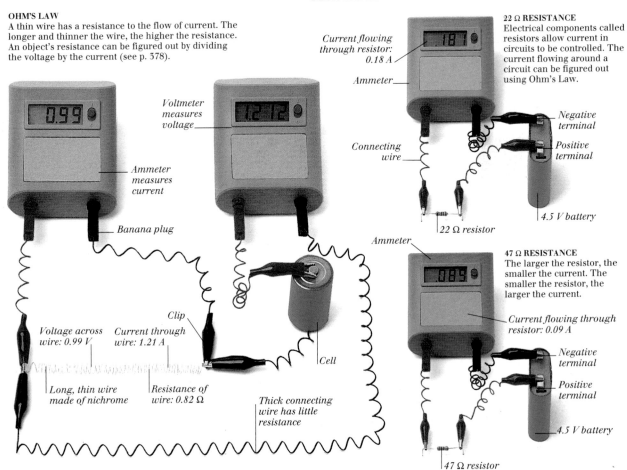

OHM'S LAW
A thin wire has a resistance to the flow of current. The longer and thinner the wire, the higher the resistance. An object's resistance can be figured out by dividing the voltage by the current (see p. 378).

Voltmeter measures voltage

Ammeter measures current

Banana plug

Clip

Cell

Voltage across wire: 0.99 V

Current through wire: 1.21 A

Long, thin wire made of nichrome

Resistance of wire: 0.82 Ω

Thick connecting wire has little resistance

Current flowing through resistor: 0.18 A

Ammeter

Connecting wire

22 Ω RESISTANCE
Electrical components called resistors allow current in circuits to be controlled. The current flowing around a circuit can be figured out using Ohm's Law.

Negative terminal

Positive terminal

4.5 V battery

22 Ω resistor

Ammeter

47 Ω RESISTANCE
The larger the resistor, the smaller the current. The smaller the resistor, the larger the current.

Current flowing through resistor: 0.09 A

Negative terminal

Positive terminal

4.5 V battery

47 Ω resistor

WORKING ELECTRIC CIRCUIT

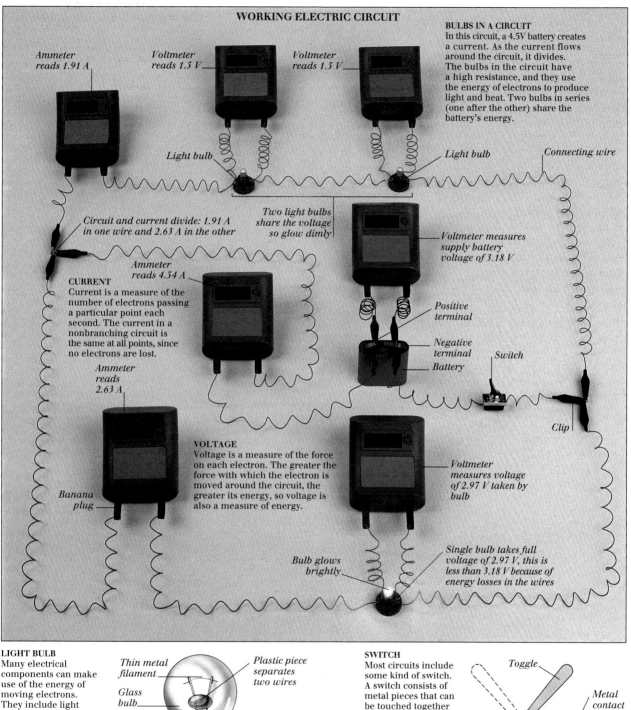

Ammeter reads 1.91 A

Voltmeter reads 1.5 V

Voltmeter reads 1.5 V

BULBS IN A CIRCUIT
In this circuit, a 4.5V battery creates a current. As the current flows around the circuit, it divides. The bulbs in the circuit have a high resistance, and they use the energy of electrons to produce light and heat. Two bulbs in series (one after the other) share the battery's energy.

Light bulb

Light bulb

Connecting wire

Circuit and current divide: 1.91 A in one wire and 2.63 A in the other

Two light bulbs share the voltage so glow dimly

Voltmeter measures supply battery voltage of 3.18 V

CURRENT
Current is a measure of the number of electrons passing a particular point each second. The current in a nonbranching circuit is the same at all points, since no electrons are lost.

Ammeter reads 4.54 A

Positive terminal

Negative terminal

Battery

Switch

Ammeter reads 2.63 A

Clip

VOLTAGE
Voltage is a measure of the force on each electron. The greater the force with which the electron is moved around the circuit, the greater its energy, so voltage is also a measure of energy.

Voltmeter measures voltage of 2.97 V taken by bulb

Banana plug

Bulb glows brightly

Single bulb takes full voltage of 2.97 V, this is less than 3.18 V because of energy losses in the wires

LIGHT BULB
Many electrical components can make use of the energy of moving electrons. They include light bulbs. When current flows through the bulb, a filament inside glows as it gets hot.

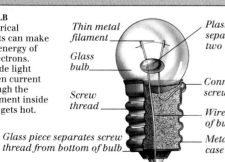

Thin metal filament

Glass bulb

Screw thread

Plastic piece separates two wires

Connection to screw thread

Wire from bottom of bulb

Metal case

Glass piece separates screw thread from bottom of bulb

SWITCH
Most circuits include some kind of switch. A switch consists of metal pieces that can be touched together so that a current can flow, or held apart so that it cannot.

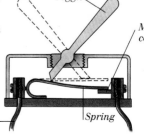

Toggle

Metal contact

Connecting wire

Spring

Electromagnetism

ANY ELECTRIC CURRENT WILL PRODUCE magnetism that affects iron filings and a compass needle in the same way as an ordinary, "permanent" magnet. The arrangement of "force lines" around a wire carrying an electric current – its **magnetic field** – is circular. The magnetic effect of electric current is increased by making the current-carrying wire into a coil. When a coil is wrapped around an iron bar, it is called an **electromagnet**. The magnetic field produced by the coil magnetizes the iron bar, strengthening the overall effect. A field like that of a bar magnet (see p. 41) is formed by the magnetic fields of the wires in the coil. The strength of the magnetism produced depends on the number of coils and the size of the current flowing in the wires. A huge number of machines and appliances exploit the connection between electricity and magnetism, including electric motors. Electromagnetic coils and permanent magnets are arranged inside an electric motor so that the forces of electromagnetism create rotation of a central spindle. This principle can be used on a large scale to generate immense forces.

MAGNETIC FIELD AROUND A CURRENT-CARRYING WIRE

The magnetic field produced by a current in a single wire is circular. Here, iron filings sprinkled around a current-carrying wire are made to line up by the magnetic field.

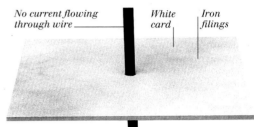

No current flowing through wire   *White card*   *Iron filings*

NO CURRENT THROUGH WIRE

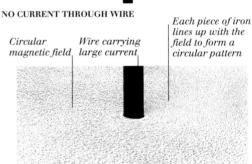

Circular magnetic field   *Wire carrying large current*   *Each piece of iron lines up with the field to form a circular pattern*

CURRENT THROUGH WIRE

ELECTROMAGNETISM AFFECTING A COMPASS NEEDLE

A compass needle is a small magnet that is free to swivel around. It normally points north-south, in line with the Earth's magnetic field. But when a current flows in an adjacent wire, the needle swings around to line up with the field created by the current.

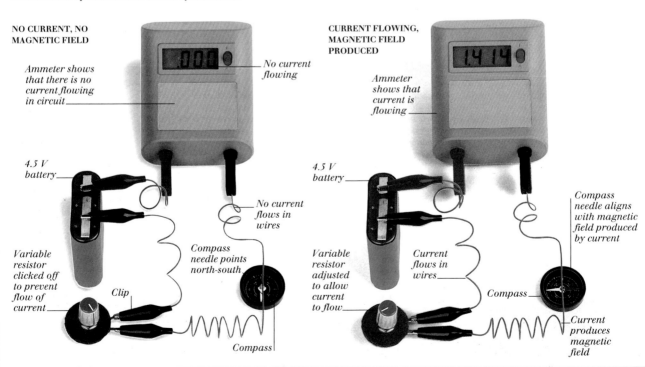

NO CURRENT, NO MAGNETIC FIELD

Ammeter shows that there is no current flowing in circuit

No current flowing

4.5 V battery

No current flows in wires

Variable resistor clicked off to prevent flow of current

Clip

Compass needle points north-south

Compass

CURRENT FLOWING, MAGNETIC FIELD PRODUCED

Ammeter shows that current is flowing

4.5 V battery

Variable resistor adjusted to allow current to flow

Current flows in wires

Compass

Compass needle aligns with magnetic field produced by current

Current produces magnetic field

ELECTROMAGNETS

THE STRENGTH OF AN ELECTROMAGNET

An electromagnet is a coil of wire wrapped around an iron bar. It behaves like a permanent magnet, except that it can be turned off. Here, the size of the magnetic force produced by an electromagnet is measured by the number of paper clips it can lift. The strength of an electromagnet depends on the number of turns in the coil and the current flowing through the wire.

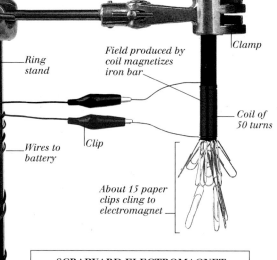

Ring stand

Field produced by coil magnetizes iron bar

Clamp

Coil of 50 turns

Wires to battery

Clip

About 15 paper clips cling to electromagnet

SCRAPYARD ELECTROMAGNET

An electromagnetic crane picks up scrap metal using a powerful electromagnet. The electromagnet is switched on, scrap metal containing iron clings to it, and can be moved around. The metal is dropped by switching the magnet off.

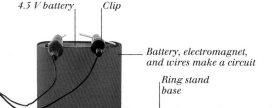

4.5 V battery

Clip

Battery, electromagnet, and wires make a circuit

Ring stand base

A SOLENOID

The magnetic field around a coil of current-carrying wire resembles that around an ordinary bar magnet. The fields of each individual wire add up to give the overall pattern. A coil like this, with no iron bar at its core, is called a **solenoid**.

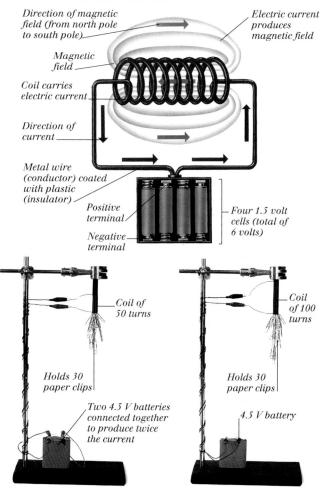

Direction of magnetic field (from north pole to south pole)

Electric current produces magnetic field

Magnetic field

Coil carries electric current

Direction of current

Metal wire (conductor) coated with plastic (insulator)

Positive terminal

Negative terminal

Four 1.5 volt cells (total of 6 volts)

Coil of 50 turns

Holds 30 paper clips

Two 4.5 V batteries connected together to produce twice the current

EFFECT OF DOUBLING CURRENT

Coil of 100 turns

Holds 30 paper clips

4.5 V battery

EFFECT OF DOUBLING NUMBER OF TURNS ON COIL

ELECTRIC MOTORS

Inside the motor, an electric current is sent through a series of wire coils one by one, providing a magnetic field around each coil, one after the other. The magnetism of the coils interacts with the magnetic fields of permanent magnets placed around them. The push and pull of this interaction turns the motor. As the rotor turns, a new coil is activated and the motion continues.

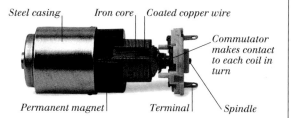

Steel casing

Iron core

Coated copper wire

Commutator makes contact to each coil in turn

Permanent magnet

Terminal

Spindle

Generating electricity

THERE ARE MANY WAYS TO GENERATE electricity. The most common is to use coils of wire and magnets in a **generator**. Whenever a wire and magnet are moved relative to each other, a **voltage** is produced. In a generator, the wire is wound into a coil. The more turns in the coil and the faster the coil moves, the greater the voltage. The coils or magnets spin around at high speed, turned by water pressure, the wind, or, most commonly, by steam pressure. The steam is usually generated by burning coal or oil, a process that creates pollution. Renewable sources of electricity – such as hydroelectric power, wind power, solar energy, and geothermal power – produce only heat as pollution. In a generator, the **kinetic energy** of a spinning object is converted into electrical energy. A solar cell converts the energy of sunlight directly into electrical energy, using layers of **semiconductors**.

GENERATOR

Inside a generator, you will find coils of wire and magnets (or electromagnets). In the generator shown below, electromagnets spin rapidly inside stationary coils of wire. A voltage is then produced in the coils.

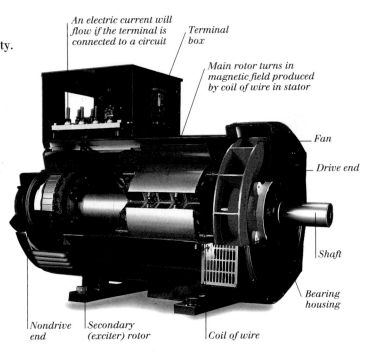

An electric current will flow if the terminal is connected to a circuit

Terminal box

Main rotor turns in magnetic field produced by coil of wire in stator

Fan

Drive end

Shaft

Bearing housing

Nondrive end

Secondary (exciter) rotor

Coil of wire

WATER POWER

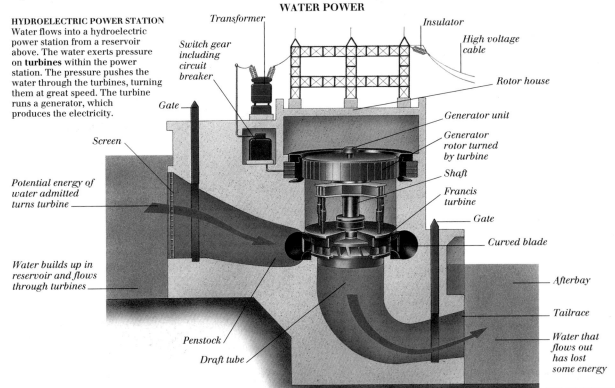

HYDROELECTRIC POWER STATION
Water flows into a hydroelectric power station from a reservoir above. The water exerts pressure on **turbines** within the power station. The pressure pushes the water through the turbines, turning them at great speed. The turbine runs a generator, which produces the electricity.

Transformer

Switch gear including circuit breaker

Gate

Screen

Potential energy of water admitted turns turbine

Water builds up in reservoir and flows through turbines

Penstock

Draft tube

Insulator

High voltage cable

Rotor house

Generator unit

Generator rotor turned by turbine

Shaft

Francis turbine

Gate

Curved blade

Afterbay

Tailrace

Water that flows out has lost some energy

WIND POWER

WIND TURBINE
Energy from the wind is converted to electricity by wind turbines. The rotating turbine blades are connected to a generator, which produces a voltage. The faster the wind blows and the larger the blades, the greater the energy available.

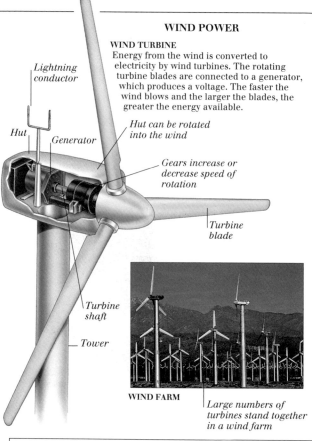

Lightning conductor

Hut

Generator

Hut can be rotated into the wind

Gears increase or decrease speed of rotation

Turbine blade

Turbine shaft

Tower

WIND FARM

Large numbers of turbines stand together in a wind farm

OTHER SOURCES
Two further examples of renewable sources are tidal power and geothermal power. The tides are a result of the gravitational pull of the Moon. Geothermal heat is produced by the disintegration of radioactive atoms in the Earth's core.

Excess hot water carried away to heat homes

Steam turns turbine to produce electricity

Steam emerges

Water pumped underground becomes very hot

GEOTHERMAL POWER
Water pumped underground is turned into high-pressure steam by geothermal heat. The steam returns to the surface under pressure and turns turbines.

Tidewater

Barrier

Turbines in barrier turn to produce electricity

TIDAL POWER STATION
Seawater is held back by a barrage as it rises and falls. When there is a difference in height between the water on either side of the barrage, the water escapes through tunnels, turning turbines.

SOLAR ENERGY
The energy of sunlight produces electricity in solar cells by causing **electrons** to leave the **atoms** in a semiconductor. Each electron leaves behind a gap, or **hole**. Other electrons move into the hole, leaving holes in their atoms. This process continues all the way around a circuit. The moving chain of electrons is an electric current.

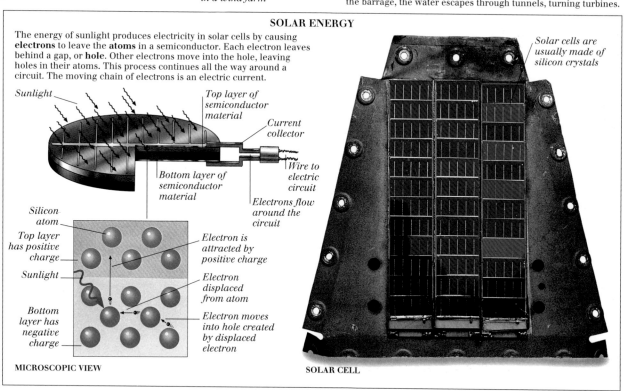

Sunlight

Top layer of semiconductor material

Current collector

Bottom layer of semiconductor material

Wire to electric circuit

Electrons flow around the circuit

Silicon atom

Top layer has positive charge

Sunlight

Bottom layer has negative charge

Electron is attracted by positive charge

Electron displaced from atom

Electron moves into hole created by displaced electron

MICROSCOPIC VIEW

Solar cells are usually made of silicon crystals

SOLAR CELL

Electromagnetic radiation

Electricity and magnetism are directly related
(see pp. 44-47): a changing **electric field** will produce
a changing **magnetic field**, and vice versa. Whenever
an electric charge, such as that carried by an **electron**,
accelerates, it gives out energy in the form of electromagnetic
radiation. For example, electrons moving up and down a radio
antenna produce a type of radiation known as radio waves.
Electromagnetic radiation consists of oscillating electric and
magnetic fields. There is a wide range of different types of
electromagnetic radiation, called the electromagnetic spectrum,
extending from low-energy radio waves to high-energy, short-
wavelength gamma rays. This includes visible light and X rays.
Electromagnetic radiation can be seen as both a wave motion
(see pp. 30-31) or as a stream of particles called **photons**
(see pp. 56-57). Both interpretations are useful, as they each provide
a means for predicting the behavior of electromagnetic radiation.

RADIATION AS PARTICLES AND WAVES

OSCILLATING FIELDS
All electromagnetic radiation has behavior typical
of waves, such as **diffraction** and **interference**.
It can be thought of as a combination of changing
electric and magnetic fields.

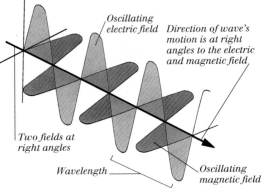

*Oscillating
electric field*

*Direction of wave's
motion is at right
angles to the electric
and magnetic field*

*Two fields at
right angles*

Wavelength

*Oscillating
magnetic field*

PHOTONS
All electromagnetic radiation also has behavior
typical of particles. For example, its energy comes
in individual bundles called photons.

RADIO WAVES

PRODUCTION OF RADIO WAVES
The **electric current** in a radio antenna changes
direction rapidly and produces a changing
magnetic field around the antenna. This
magnetic field produces an electric field, which
in turn produces a magnetic field, and so on.

Antenna

*Radiation
spreads in all
directions*

*Magnetic
field*

*Magnetic field produced
by electric current*

*One section of
the radiation*

*Electric
field*

*Electric circuit
called an oscillator
produces electric
current which
changes direction*

*Changing
magnetic
field*

*Electric field produced by
changing magnetic field*

Direction of wave

*One
wavelength*

*Oscillating
magnetic field*

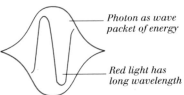

*Photon as wave
packet of energy*

*Red light has
long wavelength*

PHOTON OF RED LIGHT

*Blue photon has
about twice the
energy of red
photon; the shorter
the wavelength,
the higher the
energy*

*Blue light has
shorter wavelength:
waves are more
tightly packed*

PHOTON OF BLUE LIGHT

THE ELECTROMAGNETIC SPECTRUM

	Long-wave radio	Medium-wave radio	Short-wave radio	Very high-frequency (VHF) radio		Microwaves				Infrared radiation
WAVELENGTH (METERS)	10^4 10^3	10^2	10	1	10^{-1}	10^{-2}	10^{-3}	10^{-4}	10^{-5}	
ENERGY (JOULES)	10^{-28} 10^{-27}	10^{-26}	10^{-25}	10^{-24}	10^{-23}	10^{-22}	10^{-21}	10^{-20}	10	

THE WHITE LIGHT SPECTRUM

Human eyes can detect a range of wavelengths of electromagnetic radiation, from "red light" to "blue light." When all of the wavelengths within that range are perceived together, they produce the sensation of white light.

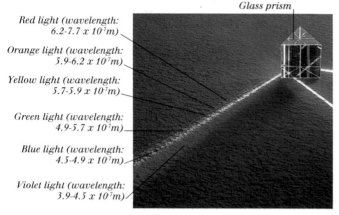

Glass prism

Red light (wavelength: 6.2-$7.7 \times 10^{7}m$)

Orange light (wavelength: 5.9-$6.2 \times 10^{7}m$)

Yellow light (wavelength: 5.7-$5.9 \times 10^{7}m$)

Green light (wavelength: 4.9-$5.7 \times 10^{7}m$)

Blue light (wavelength: 4.5-$4.9 \times 10^{7}m$)

Violet light (wavelength: 3.9-$4.5 \times 10^{7}m$)

X RAYS

PRODUCTION OF X RAYS

Near the high-energy end of the electromagnetic spectrum come X rays. In an X-ray tube, electrons are accelerated by a strong electric field. They then hit a metal target, and their kinetic energy is turned into electromagnetic radiation.

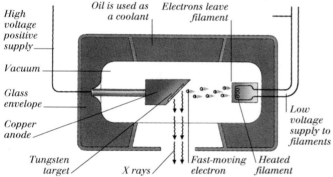

High voltage positive supply

Oil is used as a coolant

Electrons leave filament

Vacuum

Glass envelope

Copper anode

Low voltage supply to filaments

Tungsten target

X rays

Fast-moving electron

Heated filament

X-RAY PHOTOGRAPH

The main use for X rays is in medical photography. Radiation from an X-ray tube does not pass through bone, so when an image is recorded on paper sensitive to X rays, an image of the bone remains. Thus fractures can be investigated without the need for surgery.

Bones can be examined for fractures without the need for surgery

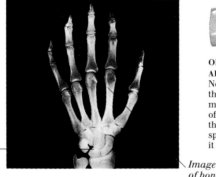

Image of bone

RADIATION FROM HOT OBJECTS

The **atoms** of a solid vibrate (see pp. 32-33). Atoms contain electric charges in the form of **protons** and electrons. Because they vibrate, these charges produce a range of electromagnetic radiation. The rate of vibration – and therefore the wavelengths of radiation produced – depends on **temperature**, as this steel bar shows.

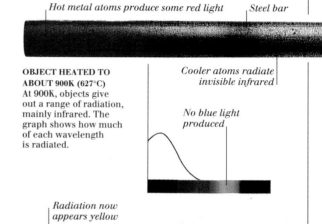

Hot metal atoms produce some red light

Steel bar

OBJECT HEATED TO ABOUT 900K (627°C)

At 900K, objects give out a range of radiation, mainly infrared. The graph shows how much of each wavelength is radiated.

Cooler atoms radiate invisible infrared

No blue light produced

Radiation now appears yellow

OBJECT HEATED TO ABOUT 1,500K (1,227°C)

As the metal atoms vibrate more vigorously, the radiation has more energy. It therefore includes more of the visible spectrum.

More of the spectrum is radiated

Radiation now appears white

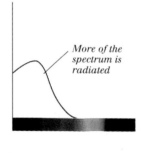

OBJECT HEATED TO ABOUT 1,800K (1,527°C)

Near its melting point, the bar produces even more light. The range of light now includes the entire visible spectrum. This is why it looks bright white.

The complete visible spectrum is radiated

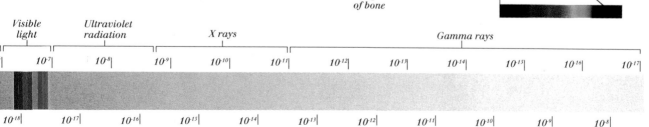

Visible light

Ultraviolet radiation

X rays

Gamma rays

| 10^{7} | 10^{8} | 10^{9} | 10^{10} | 10^{11} | 10^{12} | 10^{13} | 10^{14} | 10^{15} | 10^{16} | 10^{17} |

| 10^{18} | 10^{17} | 10^{16} | 10^{15} | 10^{14} | 10^{13} | 10^{12} | 10^{11} | 10^{10} | 10^{9} | 10^{8} |

Color

THE HUMAN EYE CAN PERCEIVE ONLY a small section of the **electromagnetic spectrum** (see pp. 48-49). We call this section "visible light." Different colors across the spectrum of visible light correspond to different **wavelengths** of light. Our eyes contain cells called **cones**, which are sensitive to these different wavelengths and allow us to see in color. Three different types of cones are affected by light in the red, green, and blue parts of the spectrum. These correspond to the **primary colors**. Different light sources give out different parts of the spectrum, which appear as different colors. When combined, colored lights appear as different colors. This is called the **additive process**. Adding primary light sources in the correct proportions can produce the sensation of other colors in our eyes. When light hits a **pigment** in an object, only some colors are reflected. Which colors are **reflected** and which **absorbed** depends on the pigment. This is the **subtractive process**. Looking at a colored object in colored light may make it appear different. This is because pigments can only reflect colors that are present in the incoming light.

CONE SENSITIVITY

Sensitivity of green cone peaks in the green part of the spectrum

Sensitivity of blue cone peaks in the blue part of the spectrum

Sensitivity of red cone peaks in the red part of the spectrum

Red and blue sensitivity does not overlap

White light (visible) spectrum

COLOR VISION
There are three different types of cone in the normal human eye, each sensitive to a different part of the spectrum. White light stimulates all three types of cone cells.

SOURCES OF LIGHT

BRIGHT FILAMENT LAMP

This spectrum shows which colors are produced

All colors of light together combine to produce white

BRIGHT FILAMENT LAMP
With a high **electric current**, the whole spectrum of visible light is produced (see p. 49).

LED produces colors in the green part of the spectrum

LED appears green

GREEN LED
An LED (light-emitting diode) is made of a **semiconductor**, and produces certain colors of light.

GREEN LED

DIM FILAMENT LAMP

Red, yellow, and green light combine to produce orange

Lamp appears orange | *No blue light produced*

DIM FILAMENT LAMP
With a smaller current, the **temperature** of the **filament** (see pp. 42-43) is low.

Two colors of light very close together in the orange part of the spectrum are produced

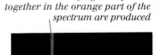

Lamp appears orange

SODIUM LAMP
In a sodium lamp, an electric current excites electrons in sodium vapor, giving them extra energy. The electrons give the energy out as light.

SODIUM LAMP

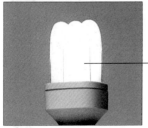

FLUORESCENT LAMP

Lamp produces certain colors in each part of the spectrum

All three types of cones are stimulated and lamp appears white

FLUORESCENT LAMP
In a **fluorescent** lamp, chemicals called **phosphors** produce colors in many parts of the spectrum.

Only certain colors characteristic of neon are produced

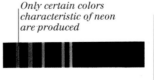

Lamp appears orange

NEON TUBE
In a similar way to a sodium lamp, a neon discharge lamp produces a characteristic orange glow.

NEON TUBE

ADDITIVE PROCESS

Adding red, green, and blue light in the correct proportions can create the illusion of any other color. These three colors are called primary colors. A color made from adding any two primary colors alone is called a secondary color.

BLUE LIGHT (PRIMARY)
Primary blue light stimulates the blue cone

MAGENTA (SECONDARY)
Primary red and primary blue combine to appear as magenta

CYAN (SECONDARY)
Primary green and primary blue combine to appear as cyan

WHITE LIGHT
All the primary colors together stimulate all types of cones and appear white

GREEN LIGHT (PRIMARY)
Primary green light stimulates the green cone

RED LIGHT (PRIMARY)
Primary red light stimulates the red cone

PRIMARY COLORS FOR THE ADDITIVE PROCESS

YELLOW (SECONDARY)
Primary red and primary green combine to appear as yellow

SUBTRACTIVE PROCESS

These three filters contain pigments that absorb some of the colors in the white light passing through them from a light beneath. By mixing primary pigments together, all colors except true white can be produced.

The primary pigment colors are different to the primary light colors

CYAN FILTER (PRIMARY)
A primary cyan filter will absorb all light except blue and green

BLUE (SECONDARY)
Magenta and cyan filters together only allow blue light through

GREEN (SECONDARY)
Cyan and yellow filters together only allow green light through

BLACK (NO COLOR)
Where all three filters overlap, they absorb all colors and appear black

YELLOW FILTER (PRIMARY)
A primary yellow filter will absorb all light except red and green

MAGENTA FILTER (PRIMARY)
A primary magenta filter will absorb all light except red and blue

COMBINING PRIMARY COLORED FILTERS FOR THE SUBTRACTIVE PROCESS

RED (SECONDARY)
Magenta and yellow filters together only allow red light through

COLORED OBJECTS IN COLORED LIGHT

Green pot appears green

White pot reflects all colors

IN WHITE LIGHT
The green pot only reflects the green part of the spectrum, absorbing the other colors.

Green pot appears black

White pot reflects the blue light and appears blue

IN BLUE LIGHT
When only blue light is available, the green pigment can reflect no green light and appears black.

Blue pot appears black

Red pot appears red

Green pot appears black

IN RED LIGHT
When only red light is available, the green pigment can reflect no green light and appears black.

Blue pot appears black

Red pot appears black

White pot appears green

IN GREEN LIGHT
When only green light is available, the green pigment reflects green light and appears green.

Reflection and refraction

LIGHT IS A FORM OF **electromagnetic radiation** (see pp. 48-49). In free space, it travels in a straight line at 300 million meters per second. When a beam of light meets an object, a proportion of the rays may be reflected. Some light may also be absorbed and some transmitted. Without reflection, we would only be able to see objects that give out their own light. Light always reflects from a surface at the same angle at which it strikes it. Thus parallel rays of light meeting a very flat surface will remain parallel when reflected. A beam of light reflecting from an irregular surface will scatter in all directions. Light that passes through an object will be **refracted**, or bent. The angle of refraction depends on the angle at which the light meets the object, and on the material from which the object is made. **Lenses** and mirrors can cause light rays to **diverge** or **converge**. When light rays converge, they can reach a point of focus. For this reason, lenses and mirrors can form images. This is useful in binoculars and other optical instruments.

SEEING BY REFLECTED LIGHT

Light travels out from a source and hits objects such as this plant. The plant reflects some of this light, a proportion of which will enter our eyes.

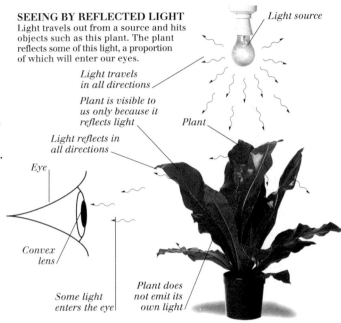

Light source

Light travels in all directions

Plant is visible to us only because it reflects light

Plant

Light reflects in all directions

Eye

Convex lens

Some light enters the eye

Plant does not emit its own light

REFLECTING AND REFRACTING

The illustrations below show what happens when parallel beams of light reflect regularly and irregularly and when they refract.

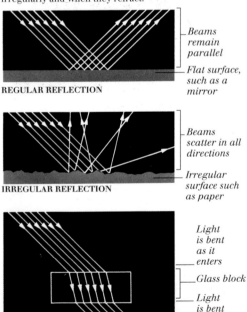

Beams remain parallel

Flat surface, such as a mirror

REGULAR REFLECTION

Beams scatter in all directions

Irregular surface such as paper

IRREGULAR REFLECTION

Light is bent as it enters

Glass block

Light is bent as it leaves

REFRACTION IN A GLASS BLOCK

TOTAL INTERNAL REFLECTION

When light moves from one medium to another, for example from glass to air, some of the light will normally be reflected. When the light striking the boundary reaches a certain angle – the **critical angle** – all of the light reflects back. This is called **total internal reflection**. It is put to use in binoculars, where the light path is folded by prisms so that it can be contained within a compact case.

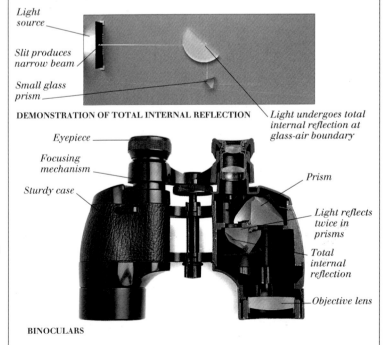

Light source

Slit produces narrow beam

Small glass prism

DEMONSTRATION OF TOTAL INTERNAL REFLECTION

Light undergoes total internal reflection at glass-air boundary

Eyepiece

Focusing mechanism

Sturdy case

Prism

Light reflects twice in prisms

Total internal reflection

Objective lens

BINOCULARS

LENSES AND MIRRORS

The images below show how beams of light from a bulb are affected by **concave** and **convex** mirrors and lenses. Convex lenses and mirrors have surfaces that curve outward at the center, while concave lenses curve inward and are thicker at the edges.

CONCAVE LENS (BENDS LIGHT OUTWARD)

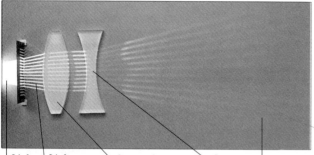

Light source | Light rays travel out in straight lines | Convex lens bends diverging rays into parallel beams | Concave lens | Light rays diverge

CONVEX LENS (BENDS LIGHT INWARD)

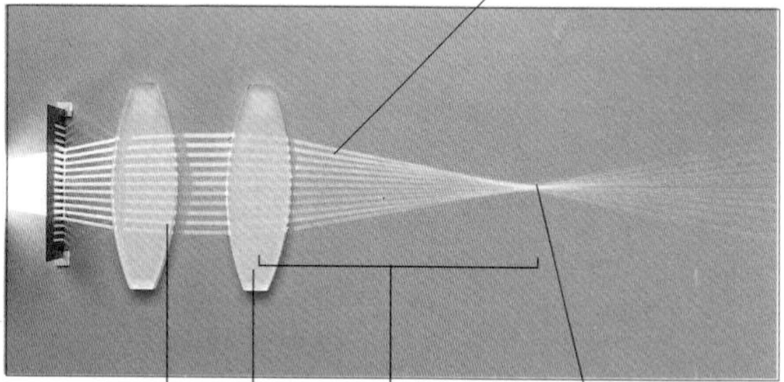

Light rays converge

First convex lens produces parallel beams | Convex lens | Focal length | Light focused to a point

CONVEX MIRROR (REFLECTS LIGHT OUTWARD)

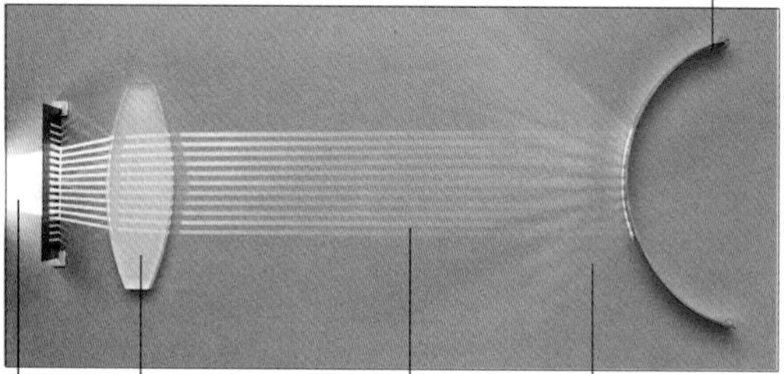

Convex mirror

Light source | Convex lens bends diverging rays into parallel beams | Parallel light rays | Light rays diverge as they reflect

CONCAVE MIRROR (REFLECTS LIGHT INWARD)

Concave mirror

Light source | Convex lens bends diverging rays into parallel beams | Light rays converge as they reflect | Focal length

LENSES

CONCAVE LENS

Regular squares

Concave lenses make objects appear smaller, and allow a larger field of vision. Objects lying within the focal length of a convex lens appear larger.

A concave lens is often fitted to the rear window of a vehicle to improve a driver's field of vision

Squares appear smaller through lens

Regular squares

CONVEX LENS

A convex lens can be used as a magnifying glass

Squares appear magnified through lens

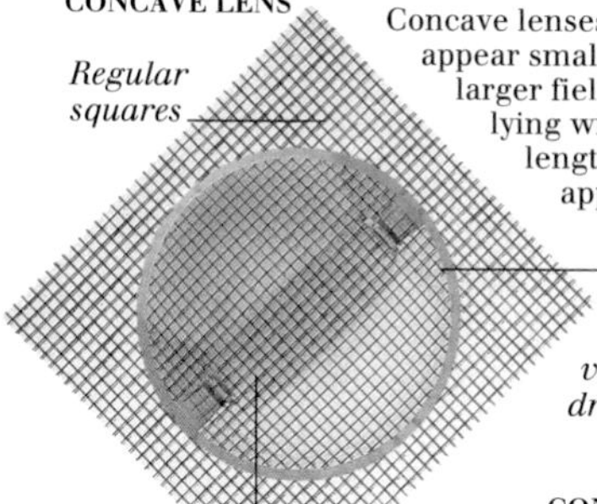

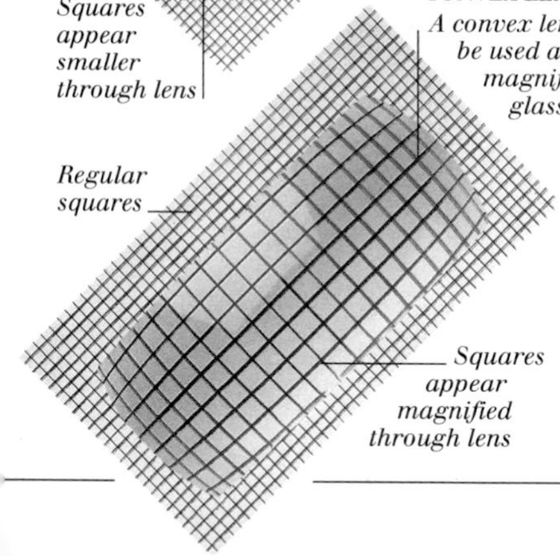

IMAGE FORMATION

Because they focus light, convex lenses can be used to project images onto a screen. The screen must be placed at a point where the rays focus in order for a clear image to be produced. Only objects that lie within a range of distances from the lens, called the **depth of field**, will be in focus at any one time.

IMAGE INVERTS

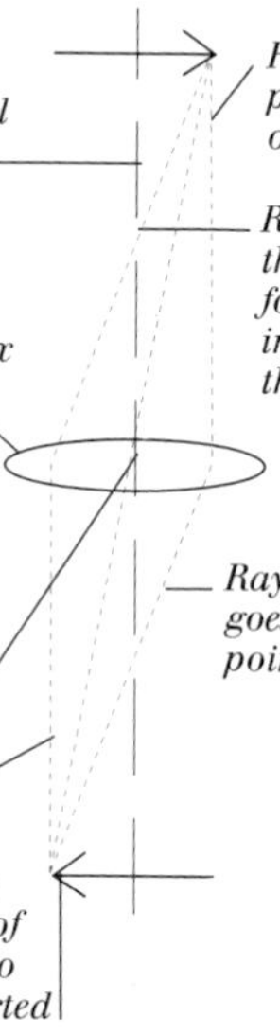

Optical axis

Ray 1 starts parallel to optical axis

Ray 3 goes through the focal point in front of the lens

Convex lens

Ray 2 goes through center of lens, so is undeviated

Ray 1 is bent and goes through focal point of lens

Ray 3 is bent parallel to the optical axis

The rays focus on the opposite side of the optical axis, so the image is inverted

PROJECTED IMAGE

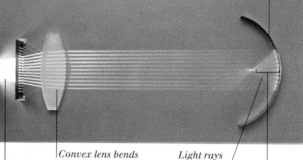

Black arrows drawn on tracing paper

Convex lens

Screen

Focused image on screen

Image is inverted vertically and horizontally

Wave behavior

ALL TYPES OF WAVES CAN COMBINE OR INTERFERE. If
two waves are in step so that the peaks coincide, the
interference results in a wave that will be larger than the
original one (**constructive interference**). If the waves are
out of step, the peak of one wave will cancel out the trough
of another (**destructive interference**). Where the waves
are equal in size, they can cancel out entirely. As waves
pass around objects or through small openings, they can
be **diffracted**, or bent. Diffraction and interference can be
observed in water waves, using a ripple tank. The colors seen
in soap bubbles are the result of some colors being removed
from the white light spectrum by destructive interference.
Light is reflected off the front and back surfaces of the film;
its interference is dependent upon the wavelength of the light
and the thickness of the film. The vibration of a light wave
is restricted to one plane by passing the light through a
polarizing filter. The resulting "polarized light" has found
many applications in the modern world, including in
liquid crystal displays (LCDs) and stress analysis.

PRINCIPLE OF SUPERPOSITION

When two waves meet, they add up or interfere, combining
their separate values. This is called the **Principle of
Superposition** and is common to all types of waves.

CONSTRUCTIVE INTERFERENCE

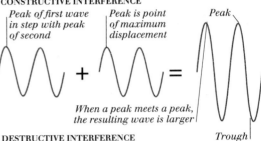

Peak of first wave
in step with peak
of second

Peak is point
of maximum
displacement

Peak

When a peak meets a peak,
the resulting wave is larger

Trough

DESTRUCTIVE INTERFERENCE

Peak of first wave is
in step with trough
of second wave

Peak

Trough is the point
of minimum
displacement

Trough

Where a peak
meets a trough,
the waves
cancel out

DIFFRACTION AND INTERFERENCE

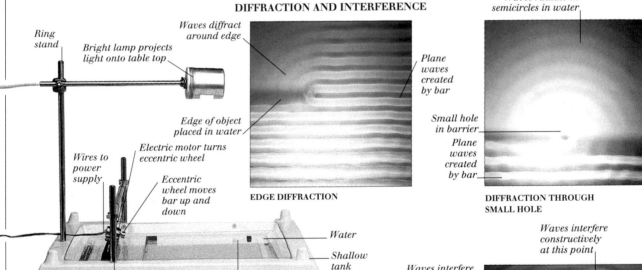

Ring
stand

Bright lamp projects
light onto table top

Waves diffract
around edge

Plane
waves
created
by bar

Edge of object
placed in water

Waves radiate in
semicircles in water

Small hole
in barrier

Plane
waves
created
by bar

EDGE DIFFRACTION

**DIFFRACTION THROUGH
SMALL HOLE**

Wires to
power
supply

Electric motor turns
eccentric wheel

Eccentric
wheel moves
bar up and
down

Water

Shallow
tank

Rubber tops
on legs stop
unwanted
vibrations
reaching
tank

Support
for bar

Oscillating bar or balls
creates waves on
surface of water

RIPPLE TANK

Diffraction and interference are probably best
observed using a ripple tank. A bar moving up
and down (oscillating) creates **plane waves** in
shallow water. These waves bend around
edges and produce semicircular waves after
passing through a small hole.

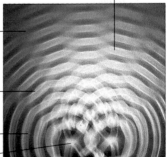

Waves interfere
constructively
at this point

Waves interfere
destructively
at this point

Circular wave
travels out in
all directions

Circular wave
produced by
oscillating ball

Oscillating ball

INTERFERENCE

THIN FILM INTERFERENCE

White light reflects off the front and back surfaces of a soap film. The two reflected beams of light interfere. Some wavelengths, and therefore some colors, will be lost from the white light by destructive interference. Which colors are lost depends on the thickness of the film.

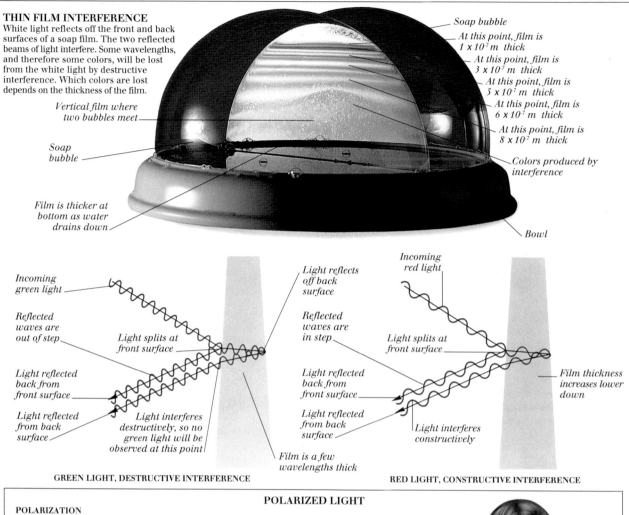

Soap bubble

At this point, film is 1×10^{-7} m thick

At this point, film is 3×10^{-7} m thick

At this point, film is 5×10^{-7} m thick

At this point, film is 6×10^{-7} m thick

At this point, film is 8×10^{-7} m thick

Colors produced by interference

Vertical film where two bubbles meet

Soap bubble

Film is thicker at bottom as water drains down

Bowl

Incoming green light

Reflected waves are out of step

Light splits at front surface

Light reflects off back surface

Reflected waves are in step

Light splits at front surface

Incoming red light

Light reflected back from front surface

Light reflected from back surface

Light interferes destructively, so no green light will be observed at this point

Light reflected back from front surface

Light reflected from back surface

Film thickness increases lower down

Light interferes constructively

Film is a few wavelengths thick

GREEN LIGHT, DESTRUCTIVE INTERFERENCE

RED LIGHT, CONSTRUCTIVE INTERFERENCE

POLARIZED LIGHT

POLARIZATION

Light is a wave motion of vibrating electric and magnetic fields. A polarizing filter only lets through light waves whose electric fields vibrate in one plane. If two polarizing filters are arranged at right angles to each other, no light at all can pass through. Certain liquid crystals can alter the direction of polarization, which is a process used in liquid crystal displays. Stresses in certain plastics can affect polarized light, and this is the basis of photoelastic stress testing.

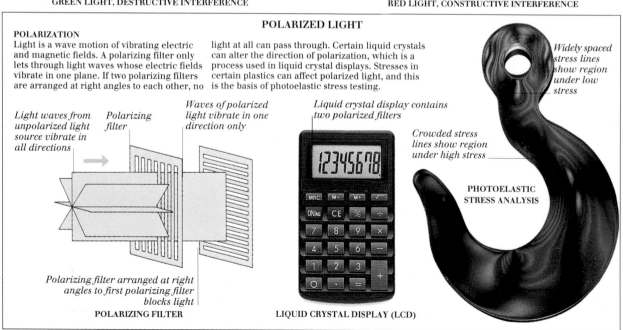

Light waves from unpolarized light source vibrate in all directions

Polarizing filter

Waves of polarized light vibrate in one direction only

Liquid crystal display contains two polarized filters

Widely spaced stress lines show region under low stress

Crowded stress lines show region under high stress

PHOTOELASTIC STRESS ANALYSIS

Polarizing filter arranged at right angles to first polarizing filter blocks light

POLARIZING FILTER

LIQUID CRYSTAL DISPLAY (LCD)

Electrons

ALL ORDINARY MATTER consists of tiny particles called **atoms** (see pp. 72-73). Each atom consists of a positively charged **nucleus** (see pp. 58-59) surrounded by negatively charged **electrons**. Electrons in the atom do not follow definite paths, as planets do, orbiting the Sun. Instead, they are said to be found in regions called **orbitals**. Electrons in orbitals close to the nucleus have less energy than those farther away and are said to be in the first electron **shell**. Electrons in the second shell have greater energy. Whenever an **excited** electron releases its energy by falling to a lower shell, the energy is emitted as electromagnetic radiation. When this radiation is visible light, this process is called luminescence, and explains "stimulated emission" – the process by which lasers produce light. In one form of luminescence, called fluorescence, certain substances glow when illuminated by ultraviolet light. Electrons can be separated from atoms in many ways. In a **cathode ray tube**, a strong electric field tears electrons away from their atoms. Free electrons in the tube are affected by **electric** and **magnetic fields**. Cathode ray tubes are used in television, where a beam of free electrons forms the picture on the screen.

ATOMIC ENERGY LEVELS

When an electron gains energy, it moves to a higher energy level. This is called excitation. As excited electrons return to their original level, the ext energy is emitted as a photon of light. This process is called luminescence

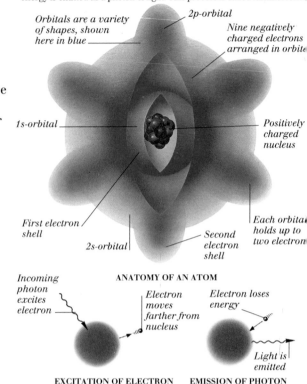

Orbitals are a variety of shapes, shown here in blue

2p-orbital

Nine negatively charged electrons arranged in orbite

1s-orbital

Positively charged nucleus

First electron shell

2s-orbital

Second electron shell

Each orbital holds up to two electron

ANATOMY OF AN ATOM

Incoming photon excites electron

Electron moves farther from nucleus

Electron loses energy

Light is emitted

EXCITATION OF ELECTRON   **EMISSION OF PHOTON**

STIMULATED EMISSION

The word "laser" stands for light amplification by stimulated emission of radiation. Laser light is generated by atoms of a substance known as the lasing medium. One type of laser uses a crystal of ruby as the lasing medium. In such a laser, an intense flash of light excites electrons to a higher energy level. Some of these electrons emit photons of light, which stimulate other excited electrons to do the same, resulting in a kind of chain reaction. The result is an intense beam of light with a precise frequency.

FLUORESCENCE

The mineral sodalite produces visible light when illuminated by invisible ultraviolet light. This is an example of a type of luminescence called fluorescence. The color of the light emitted depends upon the difference in energy between the energy levels in atoms within the sodalite.

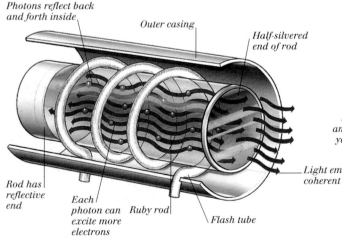

Photons reflect back and forth inside

Outer casing

Half-silvered end of rod

Rod has reflective end

Each photon can excite more electrons

Ruby rod

Flash tube

Light emitted is coherent

RUBY LASER

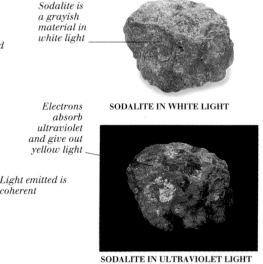

Sodalite is a grayish material in white light

SODALITE IN WHITE LIGHT

Electrons absorb ultraviolet and give out yellow light

SODALITE IN ULTRAVIOLET LIGHT

ELECTRON BEAMS

CATHODE RAY TUBE
Inside a cathode ray tube, an **electric current** heats a small filament. The heat generated gives electrons extra energy, moving them farther from their nuclei. A strong electric field then completely removes electrons from their atoms. The free electrons are attracted to the positive **anode** and pass through it as a cathode ray.

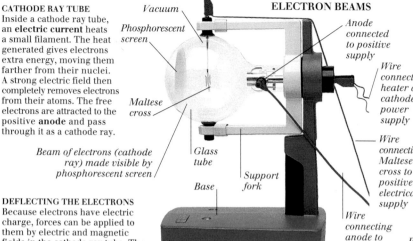

Vacuum

Phosphorescent screen

Maltese cross

Beam of electrons (cathode ray) made visible by phosphorescent screen

Glass tube

Base

Support fork

Anode connected to positive supply

Wire connecting heater and cathode to power supply

Wire connecting Maltese cross to positive electrical supply

Wire connecting anode to power supply

SIDE VIEW

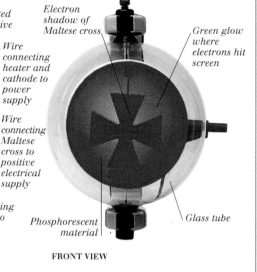

Electron shadow of Maltese cross

Green glow where electrons hit screen

Phosphorescent material

Glass tube

FRONT VIEW

DEFLECTING THE ELECTRONS
Because electrons have electric charge, forces can be applied to them by electric and magnetic fields in the cathode ray tube. The direction of the force depends upon the direction and type of the field.

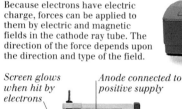

Screen glows when hit by electrons

Anode connected to positive supply

Vacuum

Glass tube

Electrons travel in straight line

Base

Wire connecting heater and cathode to power supply

Wire connecting anode to power supply

STRAIGHT CATHODE RAY IN TUBE

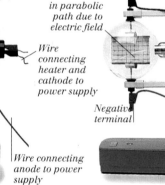

Electrons curve in parabolic path due to electric field

Positive terminal

Negative terminal

DOWNWARD DEFLECTION BY ELECTRIC FIELD

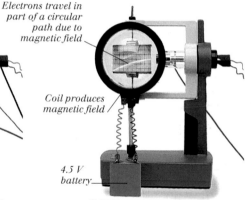

Electrons travel in part of a circular path due to magnetic field

Coil produces magnetic field

4.5 V battery

DOWNWARD DEFLECTION BY MAGNETIC FIELD

HOW A TELEVISION WORKS

DEFLECTED ELECTRON BEAMS
At the heart of most televisions is a cathode ray tube. Electron beams are produced at the back of the tube. Coils of wire around the tube create magnetic fields, which deflect the electron beams to different parts of the screen. The screen itself is coated with phosphorescent materials called **phosphors**.

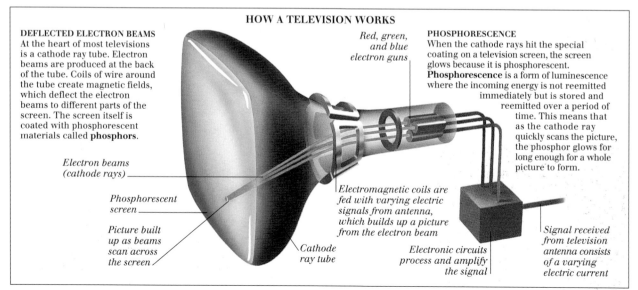

Red, green, and blue electron guns

PHOSPHORESCENCE
When the cathode rays hit the special coating on a television screen, the screen glows because it is phosphorescent. **Phosphorescence** is a form of luminescence where the incoming energy is not reemitted immediately but is stored and reemitted over a period of time. This means that as the cathode ray quickly scans the picture, the phosphor glows for long enough for a whole picture to form.

Electron beams (cathode rays)

Phosphorescent screen

Picture built up as beams scan across the screen

Cathode ray tube

Electromagnetic coils are fed with varying electric signals from antenna, which builds up a picture from the electron beam

Electronic circuits process and amplify the signal

Signal received from television antenna consists of a varying electric current

Nuclear physics

AT THE CENTER OF EVERY ATOM LIES a positively charged **nucleus**. It consists of **protons** and **neutrons**. The number of protons in the nucleus is called the **atomic number**. Because they all have the same **electric charge**, protons repel each other. The nucleus holds together despite this repulsion because of the **strong nuclear force** (see pp. 60-61). The balance between the repulsive force and the strong nuclear force determines whether a nucleus is stable or unstable. On the whole, small nuclei are more stable than larger ones, because the strong nuclear force works best over small distances. An unstable, larger nucleus can break up or decay in two main ways, **alpha decay** and **beta decay**. These produce **alpha** and **beta particles**. In each type of decay, the atomic number of the new nucleus is different from the original nucleus, because the number of protons present alters. Nuclei can also completely split into two smaller fragments, in a process called **fission**. In another **nuclear reaction** called **fusion**, small nuclei join together. Both of these reactions can release huge amounts of energy. Fusion provides most of the Sun's energy, while fission can be used in power stations to produce electricity.

FLUORINE-19 NUCLEUS
The number of protons in a nucleus defines what **element** the atom is. For example, all fluorine atoms have nine protons. Fluorine has an atomic number of . The number of neutrons can vary. Fluorine-19 has ten neutrons, while fluorine-18 has nine.

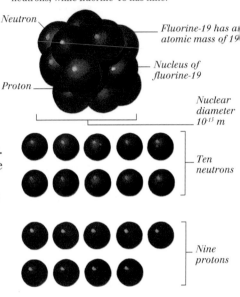

Neutron

Fluorine-19 has an atomic mass of 19

Nucleus of fluorine-19

Proton

Nuclear diameter 10⁻¹⁵ m

Ten neutrons

Nine protons

RADIOACTIVITY

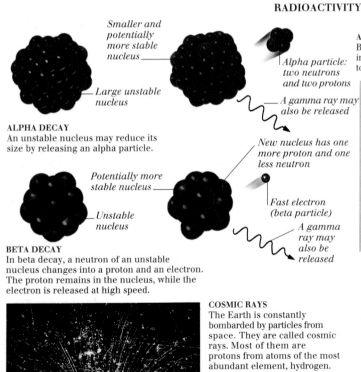

Smaller and potentially more stable nucleus

Large unstable nucleus

ALPHA DECAY
An unstable nucleus may reduce its size by releasing an alpha particle.

Alpha particle: two neutrons and two protons

A gamma ray may also be released

New nucleus has one more proton and one less neutron

Potentially more stable nucleus

Unstable nucleus

Fast electron (beta particle)

A gamma ray may also be released

BETA DECAY
In beta decay, a neutron of an unstable nucleus changes into a proton and an electron. The proton remains in the nucleus, while the electron is released at high speed.

ANALYZING RADIOACTIVITY
Because of their electric charges, alpha and beta rays will be deflec into curved paths by a strong magnetic field. Cloud chambers are to show these paths, as in the illustration below.

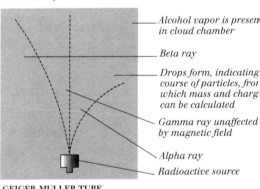

Alcohol vapor is presen in cloud chamber

Beta ray

Drops form, indicating course of particles, fro which mass and charg can be calculated

Gamma ray unaffected by magnetic field

Alpha ray

Radioactive source

GEIGER-MULLER TUBE
As they pass through the air, alpha and beta rays hit atoms, separating electrons and creating **ions**, which can be detected inside a Geiger-Müller tube.

Wire to detector

Radioactive particles enter here

Tube

Base

COSMIC RAYS
The Earth is constantly bombarded by particles from space. They are called cosmic rays. Most of them are protons from atoms of the most abundant element, hydrogen. Occasionally, the protons collide with atoms in the air, producing showers of secondary particles called secondary cosmic rays.

Tracks left by cosmic rays in a bubble chamber

NUCLEAR FISSION

A neutron hitting a large, unstable nucleus may split or fission into two smaller, more stable fragments, releasing large amounts of energy. Often, more free neutrons are produced by this fission, and these neutrons can cause other nuclei to split. The process may continue, involving many nuclei in a **chain reaction**.

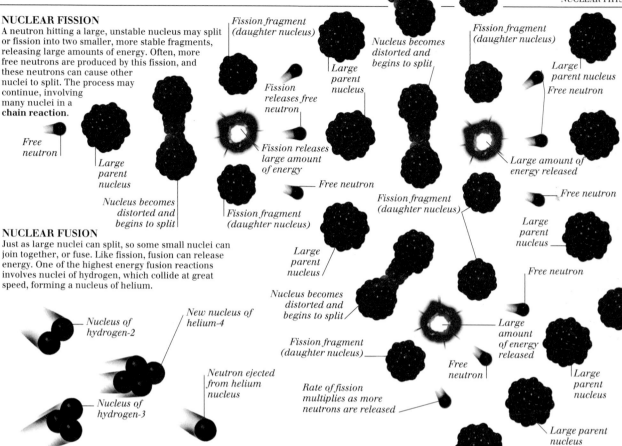

Free neutron

Large parent nucleus

Nucleus becomes distorted and begins to split

Fission fragment (daughter nucleus)

Fission releases free neutron

Large parent nucleus

Fission releases large amount of energy

Free neutron

Nucleus becomes distorted and begins to split

Fission fragment (daughter nucleus)

Nucleus becomes distorted and begins to split

Fission fragment (daughter nucleus)

Large parent nucleus

Large amount of energy released

Fission fragment (daughter nucleus)

Large parent nucleus

Large parent nucleus

Free neutron

Large parent nucleus

Free neutron

Free neutron

Large amount of energy released

Large parent nucleus

Free neutron

Fission fragment (daughter nucleus)

Rate of fission multiplies as more neutrons are released

Large parent nucleus

NUCLEAR FUSION

Just as large nuclei can split, so some small nuclei can join together, or fuse. Like fission, fusion can release energy. One of the highest energy fusion reactions involves nuclei of hydrogen, which collide at great speed, forming a nucleus of helium.

Nucleus of hydrogen-2

New nucleus of helium-4

Nucleus of hydrogen-3

Neutron ejected from helium nucleus

NUCLEAR POWER

NUCLEAR POWER STATION

A nuclear chain reaction releases huge amounts of heat. This heat can be used to generate electricity (see pp. 46-47), in a nuclear power station. The reactions occur in the nuclear reactor, and the heat produced is used to make steam.

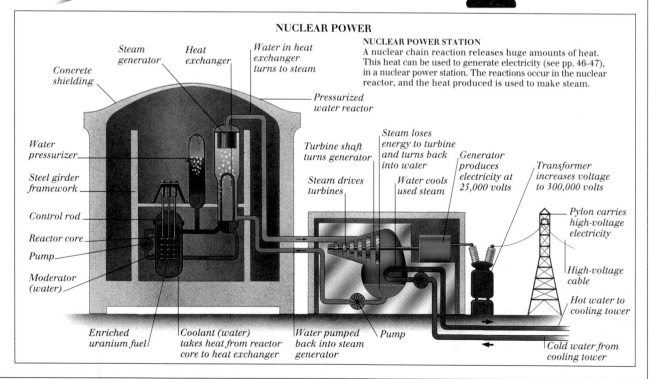

Concrete shielding

Steam generator

Heat exchanger

Water in heat exchanger turns to steam

Pressurized water reactor

Water pressurizer

Steel girder framework

Control rod

Reactor core

Pump

Moderator (water)

Turbine shaft turns generator

Steam drives turbines

Steam loses energy to turbine and turns back into water

Water cools used steam

Generator produces electricity at 25,000 volts

Transformer increases voltage to 300,000 volts

Pylon carries high-voltage electricity

High-voltage cable

Hot water to cooling tower

Enriched uranium fuel

Coolant (water) takes heat from reactor core to heat exchanger

Water pumped back into steam generator

Pump

Cold water from cooling tower

Particle physics

PARTICLE PHYSICS ATTEMPTS TO EXPLAIN matter and **force** in terms of tiny particles. The **atom**, once thought to be the smallest particle, is actually made of **protons, neutrons, and electrons**. But the proton and the neutron are themselves made up of smaller particles, known as **quarks**. There are four types of forces acting between matter, namely **gravitational force**, the **electromagnetic force**, the **strong nuclear force**, and the **weak interaction**. According to current theory, each of these forces is explained by the exchange of particles called **gauge bosons** between the particles of matter. For example, the **nucleus** holds together as a result of the exchange of particles called **mesons** (a type of gauge boson) between the protons and neutrons present. These exchanges can be visualized in Feynman diagrams, which show the particles involved in each type of force. The most important tools of particle physics are particle accelerators, which create and destroy particles in high-energy collisions. Analysis of these collisions helps to prove or disprove the latest theories about the structure of matter and the origin of forces. One of the current aims of large particle accelerators, such as the Large Hadron Collider at **CERN** (see opposite), is to prove the existence of a particle called the **Higgs boson**. It may be responsible for giving all matter mass.

PARTICLE COLLISIONS

The images below show the results of collisions between particles in particle accelerators. Particles of opposite charge curve in different directions in the strong **magnetic field** of the detector.

Spiral track of electron in the bubble chamber

Point of collision with proton

Track of antiproton

Tracks of particles created by collision

ANNIHILATION
When a particle and an antiparticle meet, they destroy each other and become energy. This energy in turn becomes new particles.

Proton

Photon does not leave a track as it has no charge

Tight spiraling electron tracks

A number particles a created in the collisi

PROTON-PHOTON COLLISION
This collision between a **photon** and a proton took place in a type of detector called a bubble chamber. The colors in this photograph have been added for clarity.

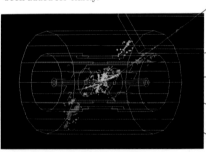

Track of a particle called a muon

Incoming electron

Point of collision

Incoming positron

Pi mesons produced by collisio

ELECTRON-POSITRON COLLISION
Here, an electron collides with its **antiparticle**, a **positron**. The detector is linked to a computer, which produces this picture of the collision.

HADRONS
Protons, neutrons, and mesons are examples of hadrons. A **hadron** is a particle consisting of quarks. There are six types of quarks, including the "up" and "down" quarks. The quarks of hadrons are held together by **gluons**.

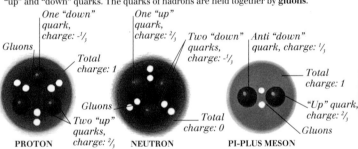

One "down" quark, charge: $-\frac{1}{3}$

One "up" quark, charge: $\frac{2}{3}$

Two "down" quarks, charge: $-\frac{1}{3}$

Anti "down" quark, charge: $\frac{1}{3}$

Gluons

Total charge: 1

Gluons

Two "up" quarks, charge: $\frac{2}{3}$

Total charge: 1

Total charge: 0

"Up" quark, charge: $\frac{2}{3}$

Gluons

PROTON   **NEUTRON**   **PI-PLUS MESON**

FEYNMAN DIAGRAMS
The diagrams below show which gauge bosons are exchanged to transfer each of the four forces. The horizontal lines represent the gauge boson, whereas the diagonal lines and the circles represent the two interacting particles.

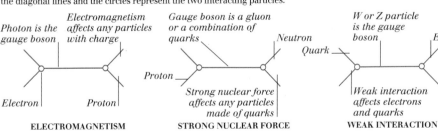

Photon is the gauge boson

Electromagnetism affects any particles with charge

Electron   Proton

ELECTROMAGNETISM

Gauge boson is a gluon or a combination of quarks

Neutron

Quark

Proton

Strong nuclear force affects any particles made of quarks

STRONG NUCLEAR FORCE

W or Z particle is the gauge boson

Electron

Weak interaction affects electrons and quarks

WEAK INTERACTION

Possible graviton as the gauge boson

Gravitatio affects all matter

Any particle

Any particle

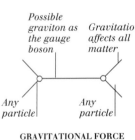

GRAVITATIONAL FORCE

THE LARGE HADRON COLLIDER

MAP OF THE SITE

The Large Hadron Collider (LHC), at CERN near Geneva, will be a huge particle accelerator, in a tunnel about 100 meters below ground. The tunnel will be a ring 27 kilometers long, which is already used for another particle accelerator, the Large Electron Positron (LEP) collider. Two beams of protons will move around in tubes at very high speed, and will be made to collide in detectors, such as the CMS (see below).

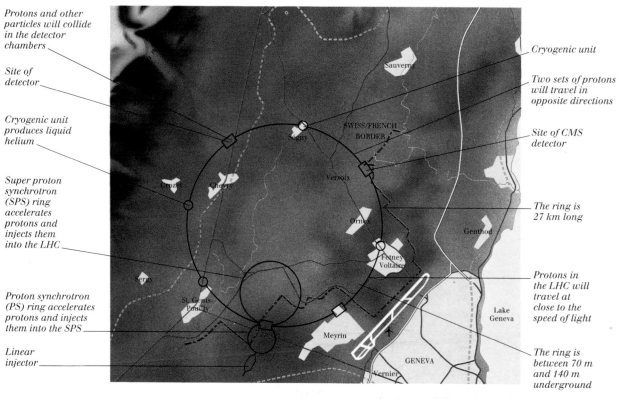

Protons and other particles will collide in the detector chambers

Site of detector

Cryogenic unit produces liquid helium

Super proton synchrotron (SPS) ring accelerates protons and injects them into the LHC

Proton synchrotron (PS) ring accelerates protons and injects them into the SPS

Linear injector

Cryogenic unit

Two sets of protons will travel in opposite directions

Site of CMS detector

The ring is 27 km long

Protons in the LHC will travel at close to the speed of light

The ring is between 70 m and 140 m underground

Sauverny · Sergy · Signy · Crozet · Cherry · Versoix · Ornex · Genthod · Ferney Voltaire · St. Genis-Pouilly · Meyrin · Vernier · GENEVA · Lake Geneva · SWISS/FRENCH BORDER

THE ACCELERATOR

In the main experiment of the LHC, protons injected into the ring will be accelerated to nearly the speed of light, traveling in opposite directions in two tubes. **Centripetal force** provided by powerful **electromagnets** keeps the protons moving in a circle.

Pipe containing liquid helium at 4.5K (-268.7°C)

Thermal shield

Radiation shield

Iron yoke prevents the magnetic field from leaking out

Electromagnets are kept extremely cold by liquid helium

Collars hold tubes in place

Tube holding proton beams

Each tube is 0.056 m in diameter

Quench discharge pipe

Pipe containing helium gas that removes heat

Support post

THE COMPACT SOLENOIDAL (CMS) DETECTOR

Several detectors will be built for detecting the particles produced by collisions in the LHC. The detectors have different parts that detect different types of particles. The hadron calorimeter, for example, can only detect hadrons.

One beam of protons enters here

Different layers of detector detect different particles

Very forward calorimeter

Collision takes place here

Hadron calorimeter

Superconducting coil

Coils of electromagnet

One beam of protons enters here

Modern physics

THE SCIENTIFIC DESCRIPTION OF FORCES, energy, and matter before 1900 is known as classical physics. Modern physics – physics since 1900 – is based on quantum theory and relativity. Quantum theory deals with the behavior of tiny **particles** and very small amounts of energy. The quantum description of the world is very different from that which our common sense would predict. For example, it was found that a small object such as an **electron** behaves both as a **wave** and as a particle. The differences between the quantum world and the world of classical physics disappear on the scale of our everyday experience. However, this leads to various paradoxes, such as the Schrödinger's-cat thought experiment, in which a cat is said to be both dead and alive at the same time. Relativity also seems to contradict common sense. It shows that measurements of distance and time are not the same for everyone – that these are relative rather than absolute quantities. There are two theories of relativity: special relativity is concerned with high-speed movement at a constant **velocity**; general relativity is an attempt to explain **gravitation** and acceleration.

ENERGY LEVELS

Energy can exist only in multiples of a basic unit, or quantum. Electrons in an atom therefore exist only at certain energy levels. **Photons** of **electromagnetic radiation** are emitted by atoms when their electrons move from one level to a lower one. The wavelength of this radiation depends upon the difference in levels.

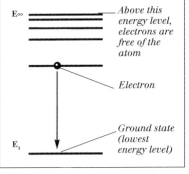

E_∞ — *Above this energy level, electrons are free of the atom*

Electron

E_1 — *Ground state (lowest energy level)*

SCHRÖDINGER'S-CAT THOUGHT EXPERIMENT

In quantum theory, a system exists in all its possible states simultaneously until it is observed to be occupying just one of these states. Austrian physicist Erwin Schrödinger (1887–1961) attempted to demonstrate this with a thought experiment in which a cat is placed inside a box with a sample of a radioactive material and a bottle of poison. If enough radioactive material decays, it triggers the release of a hammer, which then breaks the poison bottle, releasing deadly fumes. This sealed box and its contents are a system within which all possible states could be said to apply – either the cat is still alive, because not enough radioactive material has yet decayed to release the hammer, or it is dead, because sufficient material has already decayed and the poisonous fumes have done their work. The cat is therefore both dead and alive, until the box is opened and its one observable state is revealed.

PARTICLES AND WAVES

Light is a wave – it produces interference patterns (see pp. 54-55), but it is also a stream of particles called photons. Quantum theory shows that all particles have wavelike properties. In the experiment below, electrons produce an **interference pattern**. The experiment works even when electrons are sent through the apparatus individually – which indicates that they must be interfering with themselves.

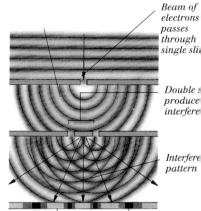

Beam of electrons passes through single sli[...]

Double s[...] produce interfere[...]

Interfere[...] pattern

Signal from Geiger counter triggers release of hammer

Hammer breaks bottle of poison

Light fringe where many electrons are detected

Dark fringe where no electr[...] are detected

DETECTING ELECTRONS

Screen detects electrons

More electrons arrive

Fringe pattern forms

Within the sealed system of the box, the cat occupies all possible states

Radioactive material

There is a 50/50 chance that the radioactive material will trigger the Geiger counter

SPECIAL RELATIVITY

TRAVELING LIGHT

The speed of light is absolute – the same for all observers. This fact has strange consequences, especially for objects traveling at close to the speed of light. Spacecraft A and B are traveling at the same speed – and are therefore stationary relative to each other. A pulse of light takes one second to pass between them. As seen from spacecraft C, the path of the light is longer. The speed of light is fixed, and the only possible conclusion from this is that time runs at a different rate for C than for A and B.

RELATIVE DISTANCE

For a meson particle traveling at close to the speed of light relative to the Earth, time runs much more slowly, and so the meson takes longer than usual to decay. Within the meson's **frame of reference**, time runs at the normal rate, but distances become distorted – so that the Earth is flattened, and the meson can reach the Earth's surface before it decays.

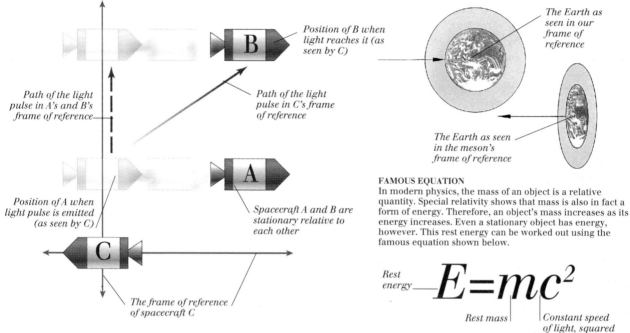

Position of B when light reaches it (as seen by C)

Path of the light pulse in A's and B's frame of reference

Path of the light pulse in C's frame of reference

Position of A when light pulse is emitted (as seen by C)

Spacecraft A and B are stationary relative to each other

The frame of reference of spacecraft C

The Earth as seen in our frame of reference

The Earth as seen in the meson's frame of reference

FAMOUS EQUATION

In modern physics, the mass of an object is a relative quantity. Special relativity shows that mass is also in fact a form of energy. Therefore, an object's mass increases as its energy increases. Even a stationary object has energy, however. This rest energy can be worked out using the famous equation shown below.

$$E=mc^2$$

Rest energy

Rest mass

Constant speed of light, squared

GENERAL RELATIVITY

SPACE-TIME DISTORTION

In relativity theory, time is treated as a dimension that, together with the three dimensions of space, forms the phenomenon of space-time. General relativity shows how massive objects distort space-time, and this gives rise to gravitational forces. The greater the mass, the greater the distortion. Even light does not travel through space in a straight line – it follows the distortions of space-time around massive objects.

GRAVITY AND ACCELERATION

In general relativity, there is no difference between gravitation and acceleration. In free space, where there is no acceleration and no gravitational force, light travels in a straight line. However, in an accelerating frame of reference, light appears bent, as it would be by gravity.

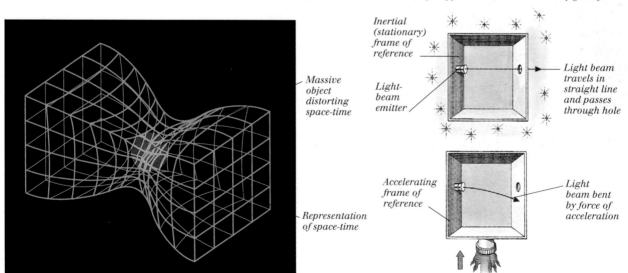

Massive object distorting space-time

Representation of space-time

Inertial (stationary) frame of reference

Light-beam emitter

Light beam travels in straight line and passes through hole

Accelerating frame of reference

Light beam bent by force of acceleration

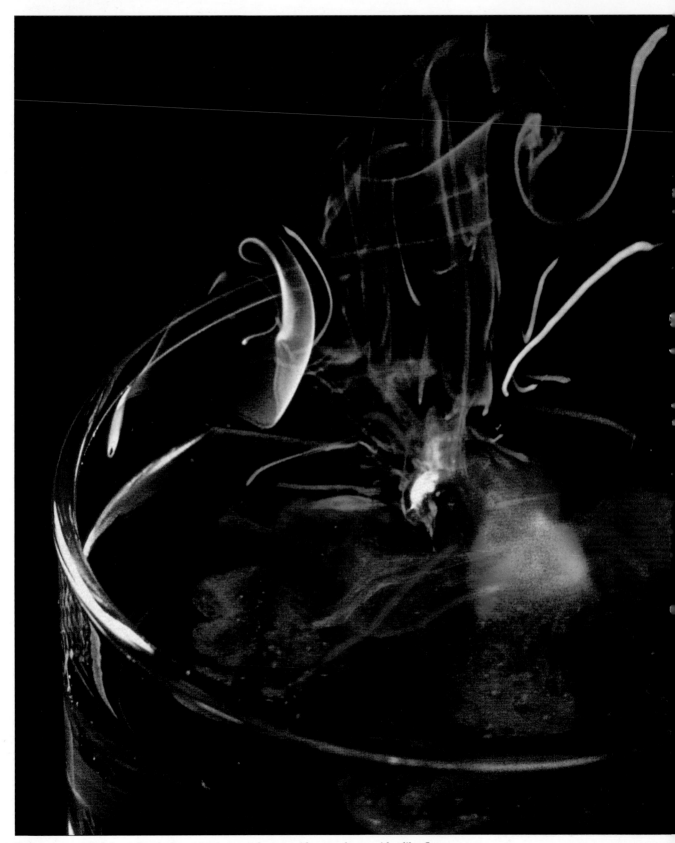

Hydrogen gas, which is produced when potassium metal reacts with water, burns with a lilac flame

CHEMISTRY

DISCOVERING CHEMISTRY 66

ELEMENTS AND COMPOUNDS 68

MIXTURES 70

ATOMS AND MOLECULES 72

PERIODIC TABLE.. 74

METALS AND NONMETALS..................................... 76

BONDS BETWEEN ATOMS 78

CHEMICAL REACTIONS 80

OXIDATION AND REDUCTION 82

ACIDS AND BASES 84

SALTS 86

CATALYSTS 88

HEAT IN CHEMISTRY 90

WATER IN CHEMISTRY 92

THE ACTIVITY SERIES 94

ELECTROCHEMISTRY 96

THE ALKALI METALS 98

THE ALKALINE EARTH METALS...........................100

TRANSITION METALS 102

CARBON, SILICON, AND TIN 104

NITROGEN AND PHOSPHORUS.............................106

OXYGEN AND SULFUR...108

THE HALOGENS..110

ORGANIC CHEMISTRY 1 112

ORGANIC CHEMISTRY 2 114

CHEMICAL ANALYSIS 116

Discovering chemistry

CHEMISTRY IS THE STUDY OF ELEMENTS and compounds, their properties, composition, and the way they react together to form new substances. Chemistry has an impact on our everyday lives in many ways – not least through the chemical industry, which is responsible for the large-scale production of artificial fertilizers, medicines, plastics, and other materials.

THE ROOTS OF CHEMISTRY

Two ideas dominated ancient Greek thinking about the nature of matter: the theory of the four elements, and the concept that matter is composed of tiny pieces, which the Greeks called atoms. The four-elements theory claimed that all matter was composed of the elements air, fire, water, and earth. Each element was a combination of the qualities hot or cold and wet or dry. Earth, for example, was cold and dry, while fire was hot and dry. Puzzling over the nature of matter in this way was important in the development of the philosophical basis of chemistry. The practical side of the science of chemistry was encouraged by activities such as metallurgy and alchemy.

ALCHEMY

The main quest of alchemy was the search for the hypothetical philosophers' stone, which would enable alchemists to change base metals (such as lead) into gold. The word "al" is Arabic for "the" and "khem" is the ancient name of Egypt. The exact origins of alchemy are unclear, though it seems to have begun in Egypt during the 6th century AD. In their search for the philosophers' stone, alchemists developed many important methods of working that were of benefit to chemists.

MEDICINE AND METALLURGY

Medicine and chemistry were first linked during the 16th century, in a combination known as iatrochemistry. The founder of iatrochemistry was **Paracelsus**. He changed the direction of alchemy toward a search for medicines. The connection between chemistry and metallurgy is not surprising, since metals are prepared from their ores by chemical reactions. Much about the nature of matter was learned by metallurgists studying metals and ores. An important figure in the development of metallurgy was Georg Bauer, also known as **Georgius Agricola**.

Paracelsus and Agricola helped enormously to put chemistry onto a firm experimental footing.

THE SCIENCE OF CHEMISTRY

The belief that all natural phenomena are explainable by physical laws became fashionable among scientists in the 17th century. As a result, mystical ideas lost much of their importance in natural philosophy during the 17th century, and chemistry became a true scientific discipline. In 1661, in his book *The Sceptical Chymist*, **Robert Boyle** attacked the four-elements theory. He defined an element as a pure substance that cannot be broken down by chemical means – the same as the modern definition. During this period, various theories sprang up to explain chemical reactions. Perhaps the most important of these was the phlogiston theory. Phlogiston was a hypothetical substance possessed by all matter. When an object burned, phlogiston was released, leaving ash behind. A major flaw in this theory was the fact that when metals burn they increase in weight. The theory was disproved when it was realized that oxygen was involved in burning. **Joseph Priestley** was the first chemist to isolate oxygen, calling it dephlogisticated air.

AIR PUMP
The air pump shown here was operated with levers, which worked two pistons. As the pistons moved, they extracted air from the glass dome, allowing experiments to be performed in an airless environment. The first artificial vacuum was demonstrated in the 1650s.

VOLTAIC PILE
Alessandro Volta noticed that when two different metals were placed in contact with each other they produced an electric current. This led him to develop the first battery, by placing layers of cardboard soaked in brine between disks of copper and zinc.

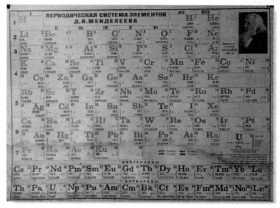

ORIGINS OF MODERN CHEMISTRY

Antoine Lavoisier found the link between the process of burning and Priestley's new gas. He did so by weighing the reactants and products of burning reactions very accurately. Such careful measurements – of mass, temperature, and other quantities – are a vital part of modern quantitative chemistry. Lavoisier discovered that the gas Priestley had called dephlogisticated air was absorbed during burning, accounting for the fact that metals gain weight as they burn. He had therefore shown the phlogiston theory to be false, and made chemistry a truly quantitative discipline. Soon after Lavoisier's discoveries, **John Dalton** restated the ancient Greek idea of atoms in a more modern sense. Dalton realized that atoms of the elements combined in definite ratios to form molecules.

ORGANIC CHEMISTRY AND ELECTROCHEMISTRY

The 19th century saw the emergence of organic chemistry and electrochemistry. It had long been believed that organic chemicals – those found in living organisms – were somehow different from inorganic ones. In the 1820s, **Friedrich Wöhler** proved that so-called organic substances could be produced from inorganic ones. At about the same time, **Humphry Davy** discovered several new metallic elements by passing electric current through various compounds – a technique called electrolysis. The importance of electricity to the formation of chemical bonds was realised later in the 19th century. **Svante Arrhenius** suggested that electrolytes – compounds or mixtures that conduct electricity – are composed of electrically charged atoms, which he named ions. The discovery of the electron, in 1897, confirmed Arrhenius' idea. It was realized that electrons are to be found in every atom, and loss or gain of an electron creates the ions that Arrhenius had predicted. The existence of electrons was also used in explanations of many chemical phenomena, including so-called oxidation and reduction (redox) reactions and acid-base reactions.

PERIODIC TABLE

Another important advance of the 19th century was spectroscopy, which allowed chemists to identify elements by the light

THE PERIODIC TABLE

Dmitri Mendeleyev noticed that elements listed in order of atomic weight showed regular, repeating (periodic) properties. In 1869 he published a list of all known elements in the form of a table based upon this periodic property. He left spaces for elements that were yet to be discovered.

they emit or absorb. Spectroscopists discovered several chemical elements by observing spectra they did not recognize. With the discovery of previously unknown elements, there was an effort to organize the known elements into some order. **Dmitri Mendeleyev** was the first to do this successfully, in 1869. He put the 63 elements known in his day into a table of rows (periods) and columns (groups), according to their properties and atomic masses. There were several gaps in the table, which Mendeleyev correctly predicted would be filled as new elements were discovered.

THE 20TH CENTURY

One of the great mysteries of chemistry during the 19th century was the way chemical bonds form between atoms. One of the triumphs of the 20th century was the explanation of bonding. The idea that the electric charges of ions held certain atoms together in crystals was generally accepted, and named ionic bonding. The covalent bond – which had previously been suggested as a simple sharing of electrons between atoms – was finally fully explained in terms of molecular orbitals in the 1930s. The 20th century has also seen a huge increase in the number of synthetic materials, including plastics. This is just one feature of the dramatic rise of the chemical industry. Biochemistry also advanced rapidly during the 20th century, and the complex chemical reactions inside living cells could finally be figured out. Another important advance was X-ray crystallography, which allowed crystallographers to figure out the structure of large molecules, including DNA.

TIMELINE OF DISCOVERIES

	3200 BC	Egyptians use fire and charcoal to obtain copper from its ores
First glassworks, in Egypt and Mesopotamia	5000 BC	
	425 BC	First comprehensive atomic theory developed in Greece by Democritus
Philosophers suggest that matter is made of four elements (in Greece) or five elements (in China)	500 BC	
	AD 180	The first work on alchemy is published in Egypt. Alchemy reaches the Arab world about 600 years later
Chinese invent gunpowder	AD 900	
	1661	Robert Boyle questions the ideas of the ancient Greeks and develops a modern definition of an element
Henry Cavendish discovers hydrogen gas	1772	
	1766	**Karl Scheele** discovers oxygen gas. He calls it "fire air." Joseph Priestley independently discovers the gas in England two years later
Antoine Lavoisier proves that mass is conserved during chemical reactions	1782	
	1785	Lavoisier shows that hydrogen burns in oxygen to produce water
Joseph Proust shows that elements are always combined in definite proportions in a compound (Proust's Law)	1799	
	1805	English chemist John Dalton proposes modern atomic theory
The elements potassium and sodium are the first to be discovered using electrolysis, by Humphry Davy	1807	
	1828	German chemist Friedrich Wöhler produces an organic compound (urea) from inorganic reactants
Robert Bunsen invents the Bunsen burner	1855	
	1860	Cesium becomes the first element to be discovered by spectroscopy, by Robert Bunsen and his colleague **Gustav Kirchhoff**
Russian chemist Dmitri Mendeleyev publishes his periodic table	1871	
	1884	Svante Arrhenius proposes his dissociation theory, which explains the formation of ions in solution
Sören Sörensen establishes the pH scale to measure acidity	1909	
	1920s	X-ray crystallography enables the deduction of crystal structures
Emilio Segrè finds technetium, the first artificial element	1937	
	1959	**Linus Pauling** produces the first comprehensive modern explanation of chemical bonding

Elements and compounds

CHEMISTRY IS THE STUDY OF MATTER. All ordinary matter consists of tiny units called **atoms** (see pp. 72-73). An **element** is a substance that contains atoms of one type only. However, pure elements are rarely found in nature – they are nearly always combined with other elements. A **compound** is a substance in which the atoms of two or more elements are combined in definite proportions. The atoms in a compound are often bound together in units called **molecules**. For example, each molecule of the compound ammonia, NH_3, consists of one atom of nitrogen, N, bound to three of hydrogen, H. Atoms interact with one another during **chemical reactions**, making or breaking bonds to form new substances. The **products** of a reaction often have very different properties to the original **reactants**. For example, iron, a magnetic element, reacts with the yellow element sulfur to produce iron(II) sulfide, which is neither magnetic nor yellow. Similarly, the compound mercury(II) oxide is an orange powder – very different from its constituent elements.

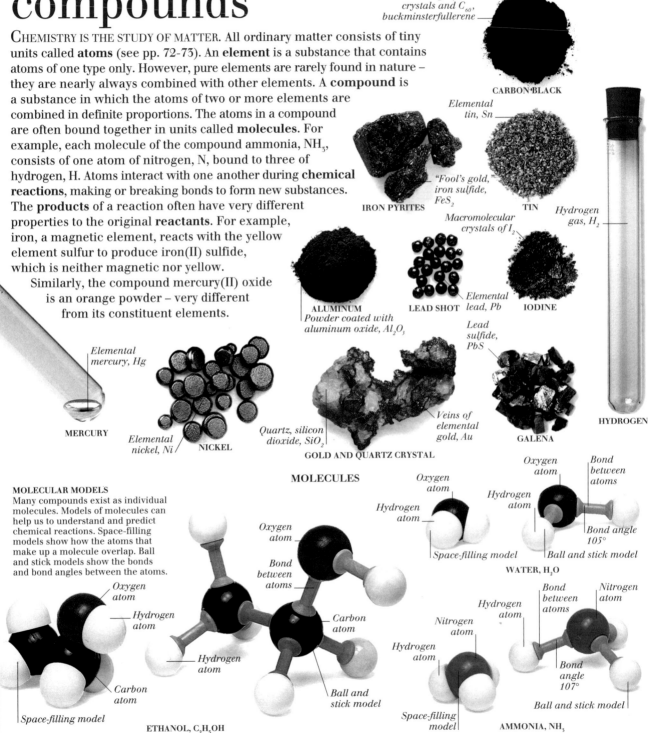

A SELECTION OF ELEMENTS AND COMPOUNDS
These pure samples of elements and compounds show the diversity of substances found in nature.

Carbon present as graphite crystals and C_{60}, buckminsterfullerene

CARBON BLACK

Elemental tin, Sn

"Fool's gold," iron sulfide, FeS_2

IRON PYRITES

TIN

Hydrogen gas, H_2

Macromolecular crystals of I_2

ALUMINUM
Powder coated with aluminum oxide, Al_2O_3

LEAD SHOT

Elemental lead, Pb

IODINE

Lead sulfide, PbS

Elemental mercury, Hg

MERCURY

Elemental nickel, Ni

NICKEL

Quartz, silicon dioxide, SiO_2

Veins of elemental gold, Au

GOLD AND QUARTZ CRYSTAL

GALENA

HYDROGEN

MOLECULES

MOLECULAR MODELS
Many compounds exist as individual molecules. Models of molecules can help us to understand and predict chemical reactions. Space-filling models show how the atoms that make up a molecule overlap. Ball and stick models show the bonds and bond angles between the atoms.

Oxygen atom

Hydrogen atom

Carbon atom

Space-filling model

ETHANOL, C_2H_5OH

Oxygen atom

Bond between atoms

Carbon atom

Hydrogen atom

Ball and stick model

Oxygen atom

Hydrogen atom

Space-filling model

Oxygen atom

Hydrogen atom

Bond between atoms

Bond angle 105°

Ball and stick model

WATER, H_2O

Hydrogen atom

Nitrogen atom

Hydrogen atom

Space-filling model

Bond between atoms

Nitrogen atom

Bond angle 107°

Ball and stick model

AMMONIA, NH_3

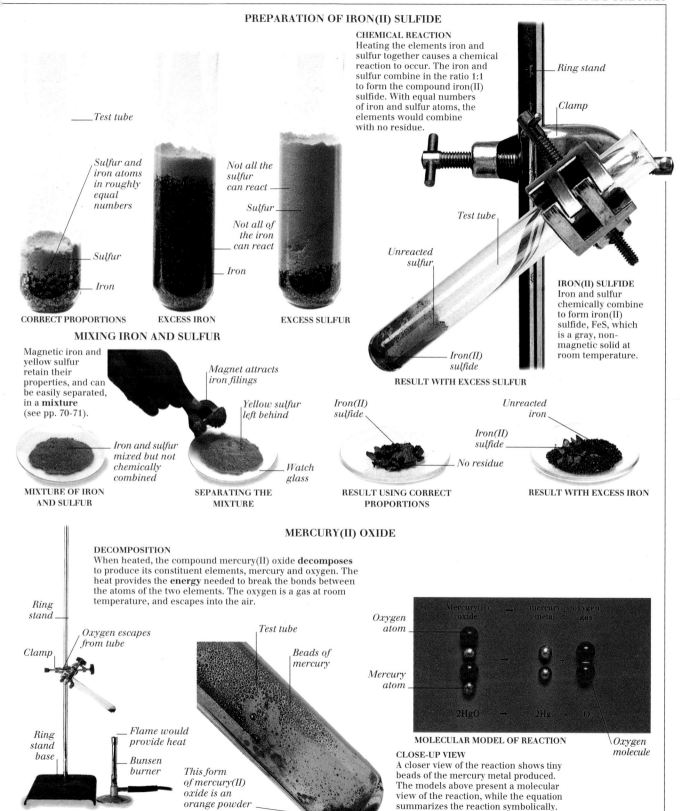

PREPARATION OF IRON(II) SULFIDE

CHEMICAL REACTION
Heating the elements iron and sulfur together causes a chemical reaction to occur. The iron and sulfur combine in the ratio 1:1 to form the compound iron(II) sulfide. With equal numbers of iron and sulfur atoms, the elements would combine with no residue.

Ring stand

Clamp

Test tube

Sulfur and iron atoms in roughly equal numbers

Not all the sulfur can react

Sulfur

Sulfur

Not all of the iron can react

Iron

Sulfur

Iron

Unreacted sulfur

Test tube

IRON(II) SULFIDE
Iron and sulfur chemically combine to form iron(II) sulfide, FeS, which is a gray, non-magnetic solid at room temperature.

Iron(II) sulfide

CORRECT PROPORTIONS

EXCESS IRON

EXCESS SULFUR

RESULT WITH EXCESS SULFUR

MIXING IRON AND SULFUR

Magnetic iron and yellow sulfur retain their properties, and can be easily separated, in a **mixture** (see pp. 70-71).

Magnet attracts iron filings

Yellow sulfur left behind

Iron(II) sulfide

Unreacted iron

Iron(II) sulfide

Iron and sulfur mixed but not chemically combined

Watch glass

No residue

MIXTURE OF IRON AND SULFUR

SEPARATING THE MIXTURE

RESULT USING CORRECT PROPORTIONS

RESULT WITH EXCESS IRON

MERCURY(II) OXIDE

DECOMPOSITION
When heated, the compound mercury(II) oxide **decomposes** to produce its constituent elements, mercury and oxygen. The heat provides the **energy** needed to break the bonds between the atoms of the two elements. The oxygen is a gas at room temperature, and escapes into the air.

Ring stand

Oxygen escapes from tube

Clamp

Test tube

Beads of mercury

Oxygen atom

Mercury(II) oxide → mercury + oxygen metal gas

Mercury atom

Ring stand base

Flame would provide heat

Bunsen burner

This form of mercury(II) oxide is an orange powder

$2HgO \rightarrow 2Hg + O_2$

Oxygen molecule

MOLECULAR MODEL OF REACTION

CLOSE-UP VIEW
A closer view of the reaction shows tiny beads of the mercury metal produced. The models above present a molecular view of the reaction, while the equation summarizes the reaction symbolically.

Mixtures

A MIXTURE CONTAINS TWO or more pure substances (**elements** or **compounds**), which may be solids, liquids, or gases. For example, air is a **mixture** of gases, cement is a mixture of solids, and seawater is a mixture of solids, liquids, and gases. A **solution** is a common type of mixture, consisting of a **solute** (often a solid) mixed evenly with a **solvent** (usually liquid). When the solvent is water, the solute particles are usually **ions**. Other types of mixtures include **colloids**, like milk, in which the dispersed particles are slightly larger than ions, and **suspensions**, in which they are larger still. Because the substances making up a mixture are not chemically combined (see pp. 78-79), they can be separated easily. **Chromatography** is used to separate mixtures for analysis, for example in Breathalyzers. A technique called **filtration** is used to separate suspensions such as muddy water. Solutions may be separated by **distillation**, in which the solvent is boiled off and collected, and the solute is left behind. If both the solute and the solvent are liquids, then a technique called fractional distillation is used (see pp. 112-113).

AIR AS A MIXTURE

The colored balls in this column represent the proportions of gases in dry air. Usually, air also contains water vapor and dust particles.

Nitrogen (white) makes up 78% of the air

Oxygen (orange) makes up 21% of the air

Argon (red) makes up 0.93% of the air

Carbon dioxide (black) makes up 0.03% of the air

SOLUTIONS

Nickel(II) nitrate is a solid at room temperature. It dissolves well in water to give a green colored **aqueous solution**.

100 ml beaker

Water (solvent)

Solid dissolves in water

Nickel(II) nitrate (solute)

Aqueous solution of nickel(II) nitrate forms

SOLUTION OF NICKEL(II) NITRATE IN WATER

Particle in solution

Water molecule

Particles break away from solid

MICROSCOPIC VIEW
When a solid dissolves in a liquid solvent such as water, the particles of the solid break away and mix evenly and thoroughly with particles of the liquid.

PAPER CHROMATOGRAPHY

Ink from a felt-tip pen is dissolved in alcohol in a glass dish. The alcohol soaks into the absorbent filter paper, carrying the ink with it. Colored ink is a mixture of several pigments, which bind to the paper to different extents. Those pigments that bind loosely move more quickly up the paper than the others, and so the ink separates into its constituent pigments.

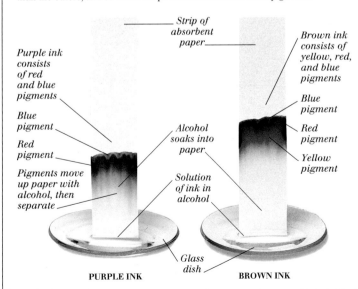

Strip of absorbent paper

Purple ink consists of red and blue pigments

Blue pigment

Red pigment

Pigments move up paper with alcohol, then separate

Alcohol soaks into paper

Solution of ink in alcohol

Brown ink consists of yellow, red, and blue pigments

Blue pigment

Red pigment

Yellow pigment

Glass dish

PURPLE INK   **BROWN INK**

GAS CHROMATOGRAPHY

The sample for analysis is vaporized and carried through a granulated solid by a moving stream of an inert gas such as helium. Different parts of the sample travel at different rates through the solid, and can be identified by a sensitive detector.

Column packed with solid

Sample introduced at this point

The sample is vaporized

Inert gas enters apparatus

Solid holds back particles of sample

Inert gas moves through column

Detector senses components of sample

Gas and vaporized sample leave column

Pen recorder produces chromatogram from detector signals

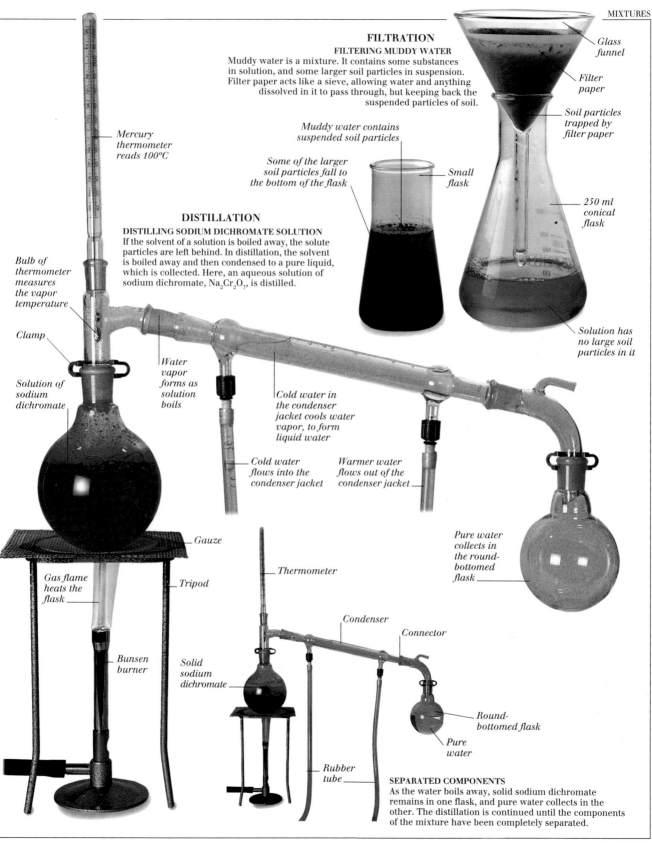

FILTRATION
FILTERING MUDDY WATER
Muddy water is a mixture. It contains some substances in solution, and some larger soil particles in suspension. Filter paper acts like a sieve, allowing water and anything dissolved in it to pass through, but keeping back the suspended particles of soil.

Glass funnel

Filter paper

Soil particles trapped by filter paper

Muddy water contains suspended soil particles

Some of the larger soil particles fall to the bottom of the flask

Small flask

250 ml conical flask

Solution has no large soil particles in it

Mercury thermometer reads 100ºC

DISTILLATION
DISTILLING SODIUM DICHROMATE SOLUTION
If the solvent of a solution is boiled away, the solute particles are left behind. In distillation, the solvent is boiled away and then condensed to a pure liquid, which is collected. Here, an aqueous solution of sodium dichromate, $Na_2Cr_2O_7$, is distilled.

Bulb of thermometer measures the vapor temperature

Clamp

Solution of sodium dichromate

Water vapor forms as solution boils

Cold water in the condenser jacket cools water vapor, to form liquid water

Cold water flows into the condenser jacket

Warmer water flows out of the condenser jacket

Pure water collects in the round-bottomed flask

Gauze

Gas flame heats the flask

Tripod

Thermometer

Condenser

Connector

Bunsen burner

Solid sodium dichromate

Round-bottomed flask

Pure water

Rubber tube

SEPARATED COMPONENTS
As the water boils away, solid sodium dichromate remains in one flask, and pure water collects in the other. The distillation is continued until the components of the mixture have been completely separated.

Atoms and molecules

EVERY ATOM CONTAINS AN equal number of **electrically charged protons** and **electrons**, and a number of uncharged **neutrons**. Neutrons and the positively charged protons are found in the central **nucleus**. The nucleus is surrounded by negatively charged electrons, which take part in chemical bonding (see pp. 78-79). Each **element** has a unique **atomic number** – the number of protons in its **atoms** – though the number of neutrons varies between different **isotopes** of the element. An atom's mass may be given simply as the total number of neutrons and protons, since these particles have nearly equal masses, far greater than that of an electron. The **relative atomic mass (RAM)** is a more precise measure, based on the accurately determined atomic mass of a carbon isotope. The sum of the RAMs of the elements making up a **compound** is called the **relative molecular mass (RMM)**. One **mole** of a substance has the same mass in grams as its RAM or RMM. The mole is a useful unit, because it specifies a fixed number of atoms, **ions**, or **molecules**.

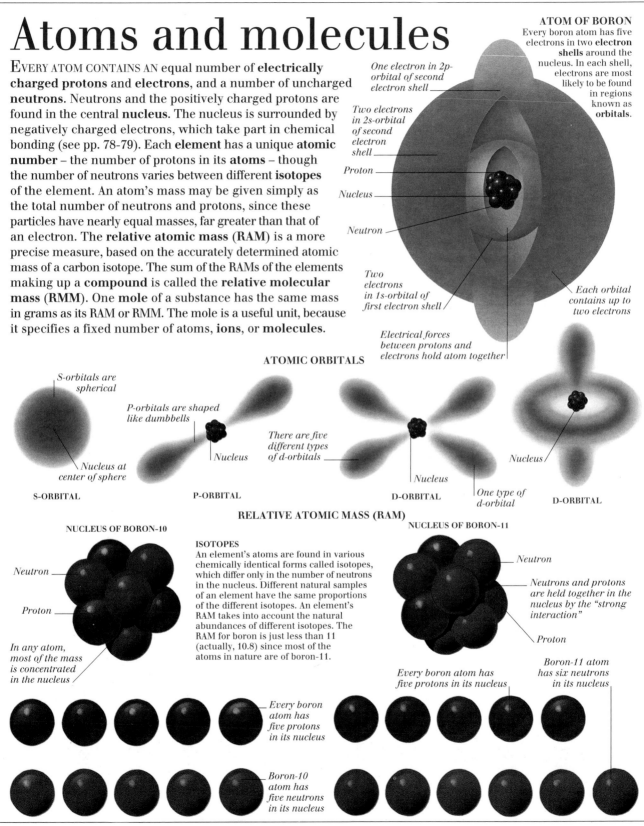

ATOM OF BORON
Every boron atom has five electrons in two **electron shells** around the nucleus. In each shell, electrons are most likely to be found in regions known as **orbitals**.

One electron in 2p-orbital of second electron shell

Two electrons in 2s-orbital of second electron shell

Proton

Nucleus

Neutron

Two electrons in 1s-orbital of first electron shell

Each orbital contains up to two electrons

Electrical forces between protons and electrons hold atom together

ATOMIC ORBITALS

S-orbitals are spherical

Nucleus at center of sphere

S-ORBITAL

P-orbitals are shaped like dumbbells

Nucleus

P-ORBITAL

There are five different types of d-orbitals

Nucleus

D-ORBITAL

One type of d-orbital

Nucleus

D-ORBITAL

RELATIVE ATOMIC MASS (RAM)

NUCLEUS OF BORON-10

Neutron

Proton

In any atom, most of the mass is concentrated in the nucleus

ISOTOPES
An element's atoms are found in various chemically identical forms called isotopes, which differ only in the number of neutrons in the nucleus. Different natural samples of an element have the same proportions of the different isotopes. An element's RAM takes into account the natural abundances of different isotopes. The RAM for boron is just less than 11 (actually, 10.8) since most of the atoms in nature are of boron-11.

NUCLEUS OF BORON-11

Neutron

Neutrons and protons are held together in the nucleus by the "strong interaction"

Proton

Boron-11 atom has six neutrons in its nucleus

Every boron atom has five protons in its nucleus

Every boron atom has five protons in its nucleus

Boron-10 atom has five neutrons in its nucleus

GAS MOLAR VOLUME

One mole of any gas at STP would fill up more than 22 of these bottles

ONE LITER BOTTLE

BOX CONTAINING ONE MOLE OF GAS

GAS VOLUME AT STP
One mole of any gas at standard temperature and pressure (STP) always occupies 22.4 liters of space. Although the number of particles (atoms or molecules) making up one mole of a gas is extremely large, each particle is very tiny. This means that the volume of a gas depends upon only the number of particles present, and not on the size of each particle. The box and the bottle (left) give an idea of the molar volume of any gas at STP.

PREPARING A 0.1 M SOLUTION OF COBALT CHLORIDE

Plastic stopper

0.1 MOLAR SOLUTION OF COBALT CHLORIDE
Enough water is mixed thoroughly with 0.1 mole of cobalt chloride (below left) to make exactly one liter of **solution**. The cobalt chloride dissolves to form a 0.1 molar (0.1M) solution. This is the **concentration** of the solution, sometimes known as its molarity.

Volumetric flask

Neck of flask is narrow so that it may be accurately filled

Etched mark on flask indicates one liter capacity

Solution of cobalt chloride

MOLAR MASSES

ONE MOLE OF COPPER
Copper has an RAM of 64.4, so the molar mass of copper is 64.4 grams. The number of atoms present is 6.02×10^{23}.

126.9 grams of iodine (one mole)

64.4 grams of copper (one mole)

Copper is a metallic element

ONE MOLE OF IODINE
The element iodine has an RAM of 126.9. The molar mass of iodine is 126.9 grams. The number of atoms, ions, or molecules in one mole of any substance is 6.02×10^{23} – a figure known as Avogadro's number.

Iodine is a violet solid at room temperature

0.1 MOLE OF COBALT CHLORIDE
The RMM of hydrated cobalt chloride, $CoCl_2.6H_2O$, is 226.9, obtained by adding the RAMs of each of the atoms making up the compound. Here, a chemical balance is used to measure accurately 0.1 mole of the substance, which has a mass of 22.69 grams.

The balance has been tared, or set to zero, with the empty beaker on the pan, so that the mass of the sample is displayed

50 ml beaker

Pan

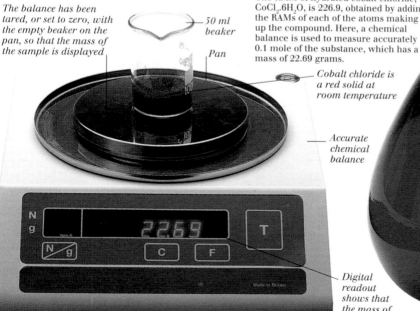

Cobalt chloride is a red solid at room temperature

Accurate chemical balance

Digital readout shows that the mass of the sample is 22.69 grams

The periodic table

THE CHEMICAL ELEMENTS CAN BE arranged according to their **atomic number** (the number of **protons** in the **nuclei** of their **atoms**) and the way in which their **electrons** are organized. The result is the periodic table. **Elements** at the beginning of each horizontal row, or period, have one electron in the outer **electron shell** of their atoms (see pp. 72-73). All of the elements in each vertical column, or group, of the table have similar chemical properties because they all have the same number of outer electrons. The elements of the last group of the table, group 18, have full outer electron shells, and are inert, or unreactive. These elements are called the **noble gases**. Moving down the table, the length of the periods increases in steps, because as the atoms become larger, more types of electron **orbitals** become available. Periods six and seven are 32 elements long, but for simplicity a series of elements from each of these periods is placed separately under the main table.

Group 1

1
H
Hydrogen
1.0

Group 2	

3	4
Li	**Be**
Lithium	Beryllium
6.9	9.0

11	12
Na	**Mg**
Sodium	Magnesium
23.0	24.3

Group 3	Group 4	Group 5	Group 6	Group 7	Group 8	Group 9
21	22	23	24	25	26	27
Sc	**Ti**	**V**	**Cr**	**Mn**	**Fe**	**Co**
Scandium	Titanium	Vanadium	Chromium	Manganese	Iron	Cobalt
45.0	47.9	50.9	52.0	54.9	55.9	58.9
39	40	41	42	43	44	45
Y	**Zr**	**Nb**	**Mo**	**Tc**	**Ru**	**Rh**
Yttrium	Zirconium	Niobium	Molybdenum	Technetium	Ruthenium	Rhodium
88.9	91.2	92.9	95.9	(99)	101.0	102.9
57-71	72	73	74	75	76	77
	Hf	**Ta**	**W**	**Re**	**Os**	**Ir**
	Hafnium	Tantalum	Tungsten	Rhenium	Osmium	Iridium
	178.5	180.9	183.9	186.2	190.2	192.2
89-103	104	105	106	107	108	109
	Unq	**Unp**	**Unh**	**Uns**	**Uno**	**Une**
	Unnilquadium	Unnilpentium	Unnilhexium	Unnilseptium	Unniloctium	Unnilennium
	(261)	(262)	(263)	(262)	(265)	(266)

Main table left columns (periods 4–7, groups 1–2):

19	20
K	**Ca**
Potassium	Calcium
39.1	40.1
37	38
Rb	**Sr**
Rubidium	Strontium
85.5	87.6
55	56
Cs	**Ba**
Cesium	Barium
132.9	137.3
87	88
Fr	**Ra**
Francium	Radium
223.0	226.0

s-block

Relative atomic mass is estimated, as element exists fleetingly *d-block*

Disputes over the discovery and naming of elements 104-109 have led to temporary systematic Latin names

KEY TO TYPES OF ELEMENTS

- ALKALI METALS
- ALKALINE EARTH METALS
- TRANSITION METALS
- LANTHANIDES (RARE EARTHS)
- NOBLE GASES
- ACTINIDES
- POOR METALS
- SEMIMETALS
- NONMETALS

57	58	59	60	61	62
La	**Ce**	**Pr**	**Nd**	**Pm**	**Sm**
Lanthanum	Cerium	Praseodymium	Neodymium	Promethium	Samarium
138.9	140.1	140.9	144.2	(145)	150.4
89	90	91	92	93	94
Ac	**Th**	**Pa**	**U**	**Np**	**Pu**
Actinium	Thorium	Protactinium	Uranium	Neptunium	Plutonium
227.0	232.0	231.0	238.0	(237)	(242)

f-block

ARTIFICIAL ELEMENTS

Uranium, atomic number 92, is the heaviest element found on Earth. Heavier elements are inherently unstable, because the nuclei of their atoms are too large to hold together. The transuranic elements, atomic numbers 93 to 109, are only produced artificially in the laboratory.

NOBLE GASES

Group 18, on the right of the table, contains elements whose atoms have filled outer electron shells. This means that they are inert elements, reacting with other substances only under extreme conditions, and so forming few **compounds**.

Group 18

2
He
Helium
4.0

Group 13 | *Group 14* | *Group 15* | *Group 16* | *Group 17*

Atomic number —
Chemical symbol —
Name of element —
Relative atomic mass —

5	6	7	8	9	10
B	**C**	**N**	**O**	**F**	**Ne**
Boron	Carbon	Nitrogen	Oxygen	Fluorine	Neon
10.8	12.0	14.0	16.0	19.0	20.2

13	14	15	16	17	18
Al	**Si**	**P**	**S**	**Cl**	**Ar**
Aluminum	Silicon	Phosphorus	Sulfur	Chlorine	Argon
27.0	28.1	31.0	32.1	35.5	40.0

Group 10 | *Group 11* | *Group 12*

28	29	30	31	32	33	34	35	36
Ni	**Cu**	**Zn**	**Ga**	**Ge**	**As**	**Se**	**Br**	**Kr**
Nickel	Copper	Zinc	Gallium	Germanium	Arsenic	Selenium	Bromine	Krypton
58.7	63.5	65.4	69.7	72.6	74.9	79.0	79.9	83.8

46	47	48	49	50	51	52	53	54
Pd	**Ag**	**Cd**	**In**	**Sn**	**Sb**	**Te**	**I**	**Xe**
Palladium	Silver	Cadmium	Indium	Tin	Antimony	Tellurium	Iodine	Xenon
106.4	107.9	112.4	114.8	118.7	121.8	127.6	126.9	131.3

78	79	80	81	82	83	84	85	86
Pt	**Au**	**Hg**	**Tl**	**Pb**	**Bi**	**Po**	**At**	**Rn**
Platinum	Gold	Mercury	Thallium	Lead	Bismuth	Polonium	Astatine	Radon
195.1	197.0	200.6	204.4	207.2	209.0	210.0	(211)	222.0

d-block

p-block

Different blocks of the periodic table contain elements whose atoms have different orbitals in their outer electron shells

Lanthanides and actinides placed separately from rest of periods six and seven

Moving to the adjacent element along a period, atomic number increases by one

63	64	65	66	67	68	69	70	71
Eu	**Gd**	**Tb**	**Dy**	**Ho**	**Er**	**Tm**	**Yb**	**Lu**
Europium	Gadolinium	Terbium	Dysprosium	Holmium	Erbium	Thulium	Ytterbium	Lutetium
152.0	157.3	158.9	162.5	164.9	167.3	168.9	173.0	175.0

95	96	97	98	99	100	101	102	103
Am	**Cm**	**Bk**	**Cf**	**Es**	**Fm**	**Md**	**No**	**Lr**
Americium	Curium	Berkelium	Californium	Einsteinium	Fermium	Mendelevium	Nobelium	Lawrencium
(243)	(247)	(247)	(251)	(254)	(253)	(256)	(254)	(257)

f-block

Metals and nonmetals

MOST OF THE ELEMENTS ARE METALS. Metals are usually lustrous (shiny), and, apart from copper and gold, are silver or gray in color. They are all good conductors of heat and electricity, and are ductile (capable of being drawn into wire) and malleable (capable of being hammered into sheets) to different extents. Found at the left-hand side of the periodic table (see pp. 74-75), metals have few outer **electrons**, which they easily lose to form **cations**. Their **compounds** generally exhibit **ionic bonding** (see pp. 78-79). Most nonmetals are gases at room temperature, and generally form **anions**. Many simple ionic compounds are formed by metal **atoms** losing electrons to nonmetals, and the resulting ions bonding to form **macromolecules**. Sodium and chlorine react in this way to form sodium chloride. In nature, most metals are found not as **elements**, but in compounds known as **ores**. Most metals easily combine with oxygen to form metal oxides, and many ores consist of metal oxides. The simple removal of oxygen is enough to extract a metal from such an ore. The more **reactive** a metal is, the more **energy** is needed for its extraction. Iron can be extracted relatively easily from iron oxide, while more reactive sodium must be extracted by a powerful electric current.

METALLIC ELEMENTS

Like many metals, tin is lustrous

TIN

A layer of gray aluminum oxide coats the particles of aluminum powder

ALUMINUM POWDER

COPPER TURNINGS

Magnesium, a typical metal, is ductile

MAGNESIUM RIBBON

CATIONS AND ANIONS

Outer electron orbitals

Nonmetal atoms have a nearly filled outer electron shell

NONMETAL ATOM

Negative ion

Gaining electrons gives a stable configuration

NONMETAL ANION

Metals have few electrons in their outer shell

Outer electron orbitals

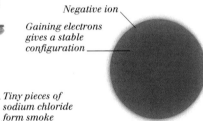

METAL ATOM

Positive ion

Losing outer electrons makes the electron configuration more stable

METAL CATION

Gas jar

FORMATION OF SODIUM CHLORIDE FROM ITS ELEMENTS

When metallic sodium, Na, is gently heated and placed in the nonmetallic gas chlorine, Cl_2, a violent **exothermic reaction** occurs. The **product** of the reaction is sodium chloride, NaCl – the familiar white **crystals** of common salt.

| sodium metal | + | chlorine gas | → | sodium chloride |

$2Na + Cl_2 \rightarrow 2NaCl$

MOLECULAR VIEW

Each chlorine **molecule** has two chlorine atoms. Two sodium atoms react with each chlorine molecule, to form sodium chloride (see p. 79). Electrons are transferred from the sodium atoms to the chlorine atoms.

Tiny pieces of sodium chloride form smoke in the jar

Sodium metal coated with a layer of sodium chloride

Heat of the reaction with chlorine ignites piece of sodium

Sodium chloride

Chlorine gas

SODIUM METAL

Like most metals, sodium is silver-gray. It is a soft metal, found in group 1 of the periodic table.

Sodium is easily cut, exposing its luster

CHLORINE GAS

Chlorine is a greenish yellow poisonous gas at room temperature. It is in group 17 of the periodic table.

SODIUM CHLORIDE

Sodium chloride is a white solid at room temperature. It consists of macromolecules.

EXTRACTION OF METALS

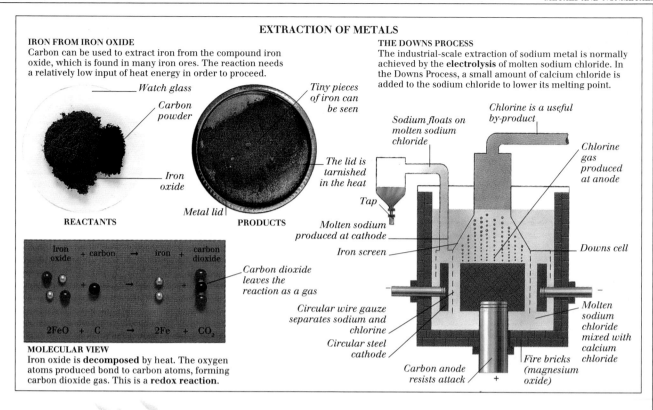

IRON FROM IRON OXIDE
Carbon can be used to extract iron from the compound iron oxide, which is found in many iron ores. The reaction needs a relatively low input of heat energy in order to proceed.

Watch glass

Carbon powder

Iron oxide

REACTANTS

Tiny pieces of iron can be seen

The lid is tarnished in the heat

Metal lid

PRODUCTS

$2FeO + C \rightarrow 2Fe + CO_2$

Iron oxide + carbon → iron + carbon dioxide

Carbon dioxide leaves the reaction as a gas

MOLECULAR VIEW
Iron oxide is **decomposed** by heat. The oxygen atoms produced bond to carbon atoms, forming carbon dioxide gas. This is a **redox reaction**.

THE DOWNS PROCESS
The industrial-scale extraction of sodium metal is normally achieved by the **electrolysis** of molten sodium chloride. In the Downs Process, a small amount of calcium chloride is added to the sodium chloride to lower its melting point.

Sodium floats on molten sodium chloride

Chlorine is a useful by-product

Chlorine gas produced at anode

Tap

Molten sodium produced at cathode

Iron screen

Circular wire gauze separates sodium and chlorine

Circular steel cathode

Carbon anode resists attack

Downs cell

Molten sodium chloride mixed with calcium chloride

Fire bricks (magnesium oxide)

METALS AND OXYGEN

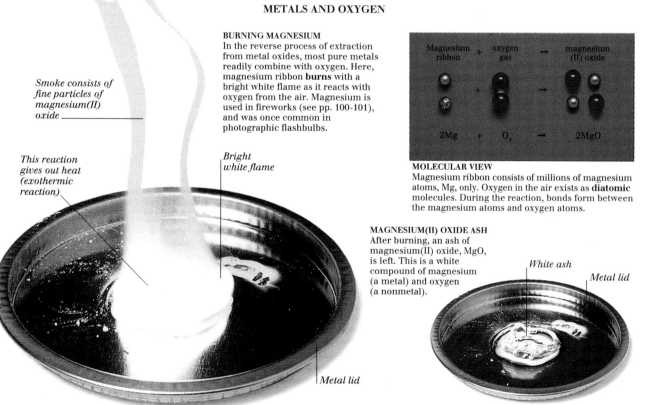

Smoke consists of fine particles of magnesium(II) oxide

BURNING MAGNESIUM
In the reverse process of extraction from metal oxides, most pure metals readily combine with oxygen. Here, magnesium ribbon **burns** with a bright white flame as it reacts with oxygen from the air. Magnesium is used in fireworks (see pp. 100-101), and was once common in photographic flashbulbs.

This reaction gives out heat (exothermic reaction)

Bright white flame

$2Mg + O_2 \rightarrow 2MgO$

Magnesium ribbon + oxygen gas → magnesium (II) oxide

MOLECULAR VIEW
Magnesium ribbon consists of millions of magnesium atoms, Mg, only. Oxygen in the air exists as **diatomic** molecules. During the reaction, bonds form between the magnesium atoms and oxygen atoms.

MAGNESIUM(II) OXIDE ASH
After burning, an ash of magnesium(II) oxide, MgO, is left. This is a white compound of magnesium (a metal) and oxygen (a nonmetal).

White ash

Metal lid

Metal lid

Bonds between atoms

ATOMS CAN JOIN – OR BOND – in many ways. Instruments called **atomic force microscopes** produce images of actual **atoms**, revealing these bonds. The two most important types of bonding are **ionic bonding** and **covalent bonding**. **Compounds** are referred to as ionic or covalent depending on the type of bonding that they exhibit. In ionic bonding, a transfer of **electrons** from one atom to another creates two **ions** with opposing **electric charge**. The transfer is generally from a metal to a nonmetal (see pp. 76-77). Electrostatic attraction between the ions of opposite charge holds them together. Ionic compounds form **macromolecules** – giant structures consisting of millions of ions. A familiar example of an ionic compound is sodium chloride (common salt). Each grain of common salt is a macromolecule. Atoms that are bound covalently share electrons in their outer **electron shells**. These shared electrons are found within regions called **molecular orbitals**. Another important type of bonding, **hydrogen bonding**, occurs between **molecules** of many hydrogen-containing compounds, and is the cause of some of the unusual properties of water.

ATOMIC FORCE MICROSCOPE IMAGE

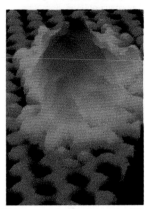

This image shows atoms of gold on a graphite surface. The colors are added to the image for clarity. The graphite atoms are joined by covalent bonds.

COVALENT AND IONIC COMPOUNDS

Flame

Gas flame

Glass

Gas burner

The mantle reaches such a high temperature in the gas flame that it glows, but still does not melt

Valve

GAS LAMP, WITH MANTLE

Candle

Wax melts and then vaporizes in the heat of the candle flame

Candle wax is quite soft, and melts easily, like many covalent compounds

RELATIVE MELTING POINTS
A covalent compound melts when the weak bonds between its molecules break. An ionic substance consists of ions held together by strong bonds in a giant macromolecule. More **energy** is needed to break these bonds, so ionic substances generally have higher melting points than covalent ones. Candle wax (covalent) melts at a lower temperature than a gas mantle (ionic), which can be heated until it glows white hot without melting.

CANDLE WAX, A COVALENT COMPOUND

AN EXAMPLE OF IONIC BONDING

1. NEUTRAL ATOMS OF LITHIUM AND FLUORINE

1s-orbital

2s-orbital holds only one electron

2p-orbital

2s-orbital

Atom of lithium, a metallic element

An atom of fluorine, a non-metallic element

Second electron shell holds seven electrons

2. ELECTRON TRANSFER

Shell now holds eight electrons and is filled

Electron transfer

1s-orbital

Lithium atom loses 2s-electron to become a lithium cation, Li+

Fluorine atom gains an electron to become a fluoride anion, F–

3. IONIC BONDING: LITHIUM FLUORIDE

Oppositely charged ions attract each other

Li+ ion

F– ion

MOLECULAR ORBITALS

The outer electron **orbitals** (see pp. 72-73) of atoms can overlap to form molecular orbitals, which make the covalent bond. Sometimes, s- and p-orbitals of an atom form combined orbitals, called **hybrid orbitals**, prior to forming molecular orbitals.

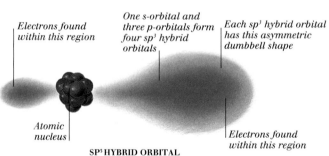

Atoms held together by attraction for shared electrons — Atomic nucleus — Electrons found within this region — π-bond

Electrons found within this region
π- (PI) ORBITAL

σ-bond — Electrons found within this region — Atomic nucleus

σ- (SIGMA) ORBITAL

Electrons found within this region — One s-orbital and three p-orbitals form four sp³ hybrid orbitals — Each sp³ hybrid orbital has this asymmetric dumbbell shape — Atomic nucleus — Electrons found within this region

SP³ HYBRID ORBITAL

HYDROGEN BONDING

Hydrogen bonds occur between some hydrogen-containing molecules, such as water. In water molecules, negatively charged electrons are concentrated around the oxygen atom, making it slightly negatively charged relative to the hydrogen atoms. Oppositely charged parts of neighboring molecules attract each other, forming hydrogen bonds.

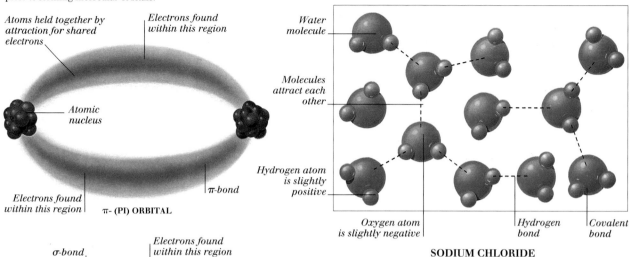

Water molecule — Molecules attract each other — Hydrogen atom is slightly positive — Oxygen atom is slightly negative — Hydrogen bond — Covalent bond

SODIUM CHLORIDE

A macromolecule of sodium chloride forms when sodium **cations** and chloride **anions** bond together. Ions are arranged in the macromolecule in a regular pattern, forming a **crystal**.

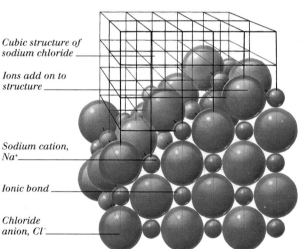

Cubic structure of sodium chloride — Ions add on to structure — Sodium cation, Na^+ — Ionic bond — Chloride anion, Cl^-

SODIUM CHLORIDE MACROMOLECULE

AN EXAMPLE OF COVALENT BONDING

1. NEUTRAL ATOMS OF HYDROGEN AND FLUORINE

1s-orbital holds only one electron — Each atomic orbital can hold up to two electrons — Hydrogen atom — 2s-orbital — 2p-orbital — Fluorine atom — 1s-orbital — 2p-orbital — Second electron shell holds seven electrons — 2p-orbital

2. HYDROGEN FLUORIDE MOLECULE

σ-orbital — Half-filled orbitals (1s- in hydrogen and 2p- in fluorine) overlap — 2p-orbital — 2p-orbital — 1s-orbital — By sharing an electron pair, both hydrogen and fluorine complete their outer electron shells — 2s-orbital

Chemical reactions

IN A CHEMICAL REACTION, THE ATOMS **or ions** of the **reactants** are rearranged to give **products** with different chemical and physical properties. For example, **solutions** of lead nitrate and potassium iodide react to produce a solid **precipitate**. Many reactions are **reversible**. Brown nitrogen dioxide gas **decomposes** at high **temperatures** to form a colorless **mixture** of oxygen and nitrogen monoxide. As the mixture cools, nitrogen dioxide forms again. The reactants and products are said to be in an **equilibrium**, the position of which depends on the temperature. Reactant and product **concentrations** may also affect the equilibrium. **Reaction rates** depend upon a number of factors, including temperature and concentration. Marble and dilute **acid** react together more rapidly if the marble is powdered to give it a greater surface area. During a **chemical reaction**, matter is neither created nor destroyed, only changed from one form to another – so the total mass of the products always equals the mass of the reactants.

EQUILIBRIUM AFFECTED BY TEMPERATURE

Glass stopper

The gas decomposes on heating

Reversible reaction symbol

Brown nitrogen dioxide gas

Colorless mixture of oxygen and nitrogen monoxide

Round-bottomed flask

As the mixture cools, nitrogen dioxide reforms

Funnel

Glass bottle

Lead nitrate solution

DOUBLE DECOMPOSITION REACTION

The reaction between solutions of lead nitrate and potassium iodide is an example of a **double decomposition** reaction. The iodide ions react with the lead ions to form a solid yellow precipitate, while potassium nitrate is left in solution. One metal **cation** of a cation-**anion** pair has been exchanged for the other metal cation.

Conical flask

MOLECULAR VIEW
In a double decomposition reaction, the metal cations in solution "swap partners." The lead ions bond to the iodide ions, while the potassium ions associate with the nitrate ions in solution.

Potassium iodide solution

Yellow precipitate of lead iodide

NITROGEN DIOXIDE, NITROGEN MONOXIDE, AND OXYGEN
The flask on the left contains nitrogen dioxide gas. At temperatures above 140°C (284°F), the gas begins to decompose, forming oxygen and nitrogen monoxide. Below this temperature, the equilibrium is pushed the other way and the reaction is reversed.

MOLECULAR VIEW
Nitrogen dioxide **molecules** are in equilibrium with **diatomic** molecules of oxygen and nitrogen monoxide.

EQUILIBRIUM AFFECTED BY CONCENTRATION

COBALT AND CHLORIDE IONS

A pink solution of a cobalt(II) salt contains cobalt ions, Co^{2+}. When concentrated hydrochloric acid is added to the solution, chloride ions, Cl^-, cluster around the cobalt ions, forming a **complex ion**, $CoCl_4^{2-}$, in a reversible reaction. The presence of this ion gives the solution a blue color. Adding more acid pushes the equilibrium position over toward the product – the complex ion. If the concentration of chloride ions is reduced by adding water, the pink color returns. The addition of water pushes the equilibrium position back toward the reactants – the simple cobalt(II) and chloride ions.

Test tube

Dropper

Adding more water reverses the reaction

Cobalt ions, Co^{2+}, give the solution a pink color

Water reduces chloride ion concentration

Concentrated hydrochloric acid added

On addition of more acid, the solution turns completely blue

Pink color returns as cobalt ions reform

Complex ions, $CoCl_4^{2-}$, turn solution blue

Complex ions begin to decompose

COBALT(II) SALT SOLUTION

ADDITION OF ACID

COMPLEX ION SOLUTION

ADDITION OF WATER

RATE OF REACTION

MARBLE CHIPS

Marble is one form of the **ionic** compound, calcium carbonate, $CaCO_3$. Relatively few of the ions making up large chips of marble (below) are found on the chip surfaces – most of the ions are within the chips.

SURFACE AREA OF REACTANT

When dilute sulfuric acid reacts with marble (right), carbon dioxide gas is produced. If powdered marble is used (far right), more ions come into contact with the acid, and the reaction proceeds more rapidly.

Dilute acid   The mixture fizzes over the beaker

250 ml beaker

Carbon dioxide gas is produced at a faster rate

Dilute acid

Marble chips

Coarse marble chips

Bubbles of carbon dioxide gas are produced slowly

Fine powder of marble

BEAKER WITH CHIPS

BEAKER WITH POWDER

CONSERVATION OF MASS

In every chemical reaction, mass is conserved. The reaction below is carried out in a sealed flask to prevent the escape of the gaseous product. An accurate chemical balance shows that there is no gain or loss of mass.

Powder of dilead(II) lead(IV) oxide, "red lead"

Air

Rubber stopper

Empty beaker

Chlorine gas and air

Dilute hydrochloric acid

Mixture of lead chlorides and water

Pan

Accurate chemical balance

Mass of products

Tare button

Mass of reactants

Oertling

182 17

Oertling

182 17

BEFORE THE REACTION

The reactants are weighed before the reaction. The balance is tared (or zeroed) with just the glassware, so that only the mass of the substances inside the glassware will be displayed.

AFTER THE REACTION

The reactants are mixed in the conical flask, and the flask is quickly sealed so that no reaction products can escape. The mass of products is identical to the mass of reactants.

Oxidation and reduction

IN MANY CHEMICAL REACTIONS (see pp. 80-81), **electrons** are transferred between the **atoms** or **ions** taking part. For example, when nitric acid reacts with copper metal, copper atoms lose electrons to become Cu^{2+} ions, while the acid gains electrons. An atom or ion that loses electrons (or gains oxygen) is said to undergo **oxidation**, while an atom or ion that gains electrons (or loses oxygen) undergoes **reduction**. Reactions that involve oxidation and reduction are called **redox reactions**. When an atom or ion is oxidized or reduced, its **oxidation number** changes by the number of electrons transferred. The oxidation number of any atom is 0 (zero), while that of an **element** in a **compound** is given by Roman numerals or by the amount of charge on its ions. For example, iron exists as iron(II) ions, Fe^{2+}, in rust, where it has an oxidation number of +2. An older definition of oxidation was combination with oxygen, as happens in **burning** reactions.

Concentrated nitric acid

Glass tap controls flow of nitric acid into the flask

Separating funnel

Gas is evolved as reaction takes place

OXIDATION OF COPPER BY NITRIC ACID

Rubber stopper

Clamp

A REDOX REACTION
When nitric acid and copper react, each copper atom loses two electrons and is oxidized to copper(II), or Cu^{2+}. Nitric acid, in which nitrogen has an oxidation number of +5, is reduced to nitrogen dioxide, NO_2, also known as nitrogen(IV) oxide, in which nitrogen has an oxidation number of +4.

Glass delivery tube

Gas jar

Round-bottomed flask

Brown nitrogen dioxide gas

Pieces of copper metal

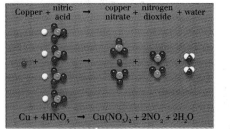

Copper + nitric acid → copper nitrate + nitrogen dioxide + water

$$Cu + 4HNO_3 \rightarrow Cu(NO_3)_2 + 2NO_2 + 2H_2O$$

MOLECULAR MODEL OF REACTION

RUSTING OF IRON

The rusting of iron is an example of a redox reaction. Iron is oxidized to iron(II), with an oxidation number of +2, when it reacts with water and oxygen. The resulting compound, known as rust, is hydrated iron oxide. The tubes below show that both water and oxygen are needed for rust to form.

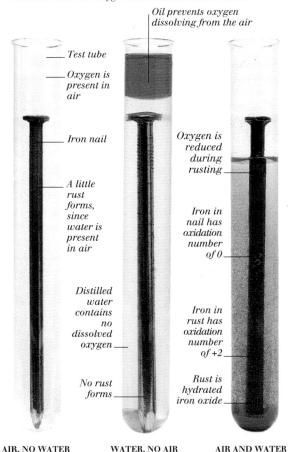

Oil prevents oxygen dissolving from the air

Test tube

Oxygen is present in air

Iron nail

A little rust forms, since water is present in air

Oxygen is reduced during rusting

Iron in nail has oxidation number of 0

Distilled water contains no dissolved oxygen

Iron in rust has oxidation number of +2

No rust forms

Rust is hydrated iron oxide

AIR, NO WATER   **WATER, NO AIR**   **AIR AND WATER**

COMBUSTION REACTION

All combustion reactions are redox reactions. Combustion, or burning, is defined as the rapid **exothermic** combination of a substance with oxygen. Candle wax is a **mixture** of **hydrocarbons**, mainly the **alkane** $C_{18}H_{38}$. Oxygen combines with the carbon atoms present to form carbon dioxide, and with the hydrogen atoms to form water.

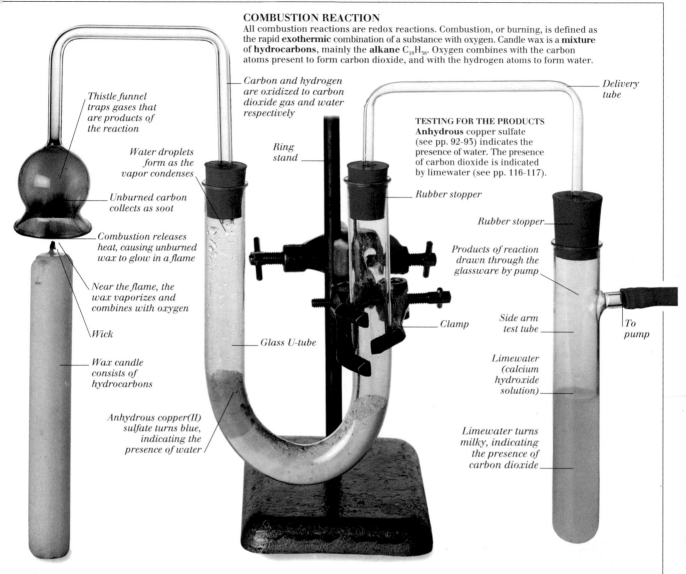

Thistle funnel traps gases that are products of the reaction

Carbon and hydrogen are oxidized to carbon dioxide gas and water respectively

Delivery tube

Water droplets form as the vapor condenses

Ring stand

TESTING FOR THE PRODUCTS
Anhydrous copper sulfate (see pp. 92-93) indicates the presence of water. The presence of carbon dioxide is indicated by limewater (see pp. 116-117).

Unburned carbon collects as soot

Rubber stopper

Rubber stopper

Combustion releases heat, causing unburned wax to glow in a flame

Products of reaction drawn through the glassware by pump

Near the flame, the wax vaporizes and combines with oxygen

Clamp

Side arm test tube

To pump

Wick

Glass U-tube

Wax candle consists of hydrocarbons

Limewater (calcium hydroxide solution)

Anhydrous copper(II) sulfate turns blue, indicating the presence of water

Limewater turns milky, indicating the presence of carbon dioxide

OXIDATION AS TRANSFER OF ELECTRONS

In many redox reactions, electrons are physically transferred from one atom to another, as shown.

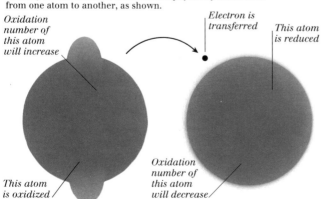

Oxidation number of this atom will increase

Electron is transferred

This atom is reduced

This atom is oxidized

Oxidation number of this atom will decrease

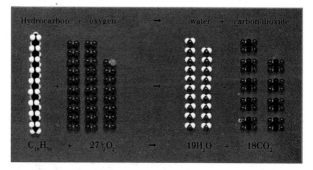

Hydrocarbon + oxygen → water + carbon dioxide

$C_{18}H_{38}$ + $27\frac{1}{2}O_2$ → $19H_2O$ + $18CO_2$

MOLECULAR MODEL OF REACTION
Two **molecules** of the hydrocarbon $C_{18}H_{38}$ react with 55 oxygen molecules, producing 38 molecules of water and 36 of carbon dioxide. Half of these amounts have been shown above.

Acids and bases

ACID IS A COMMON WORD in everyday use, but it has a precise definition in chemistry. An **acid** is defined as a **molecule** or an **ion** that can donate **protons**, or hydrogen ions, H+. A **base** is a substance, often an oxide or hydroxide, that accepts protons, and an **alkali** is a base that is water soluble. Some substances, such as water, can act as either acids or bases, depending on the other substances present. Acids and bases undergo characteristic reactions together, usually in **aqueous solution**, producing a **salt** (see pp. 86-87) and water. In **solution**, acid-base reactions involve the transfer of **hydronium ions** or hydrated protons, H_3O^+. These ions form, for example, when hydrogen chloride gas dissolves in water. The **pH scale** gives the **concentration** of hydronium ions in solution. As pH falls below 7, a solution becomes more acidic. Conversely, as pH rises above 7, the solution becomes more alkaline. The pH of a solution can be estimated using pigments called **indicators**, or measured accurately with a pH meter.

THE MEANING OF pH

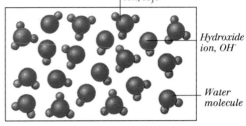

Hydronium ion, H_3O^+

Hydroxide ion, OH^-

Water molecule

PURE WATER (NEUTRAL)
Some of the molecules of liquid water break up, or dissociate, forming hydroxide ions, OH⁻, and hydrogen ions, H+, that become hydrated, H_3O^+. In one liter of pure water at 20°C, there are 10^{-7} **moles** (see pp. 72-73) of each type of ion. This gives a pH value of 7 (neutral) for pure water.

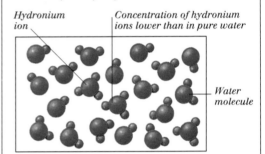

Hydronium ion

Concentration of hydronium ions lower than in pure water

Water molecule

ALKALINE SOLUTION
When an alkali is added to water, it removes protons, H+, from some of the hydronium ions, H_3O^+, present, forming more water molecules. The lower the concentration of H_3O^+, the higher the pH. Typically, a weakly alkaline solution has a pH of 10, and a strongly alkaline solution has a pH of 14.

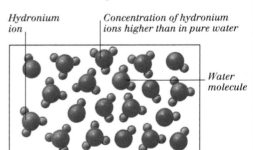

Hydronium ion

Concentration of hydronium ions higher than in pure water

Water molecule

ACIDIC SOLUTION
When an acid is dissolved in water, it donates protons, H+, to water molecules, H_2O, making more hydronium ions, H_3O^+. Water thus acts as a base. The concentration of hydronium ions increases, and the pH decreases.

UNIVERSAL INDICATOR PAPER

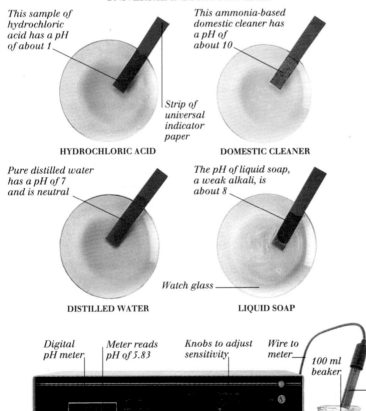

This sample of hydrochloric acid has a pH of about 1

This ammonia-based domestic cleaner has a pH of about 10

Strip of universal indicator paper

HYDROCHLORIC ACID

DOMESTIC CLEANER

Pure distilled water has a pH of 7 and is neutral

The pH of liquid soap, a weak alkali, is about 8

Watch glass

DISTILLED WATER

LIQUID SOAP

Digital pH meter

Meter reads pH of 5.83

Knobs to adjust sensitivity

Wire to meter

100 ml beaker

Electronic probe measures concentration of H_3O^+ ions

Bottle of test solution

MEASURING pH
This digital pH meter accurately measures hydronium ion concentration. Such meters are often used to find the pH of colored solutions, which could mask the true color of indicators.

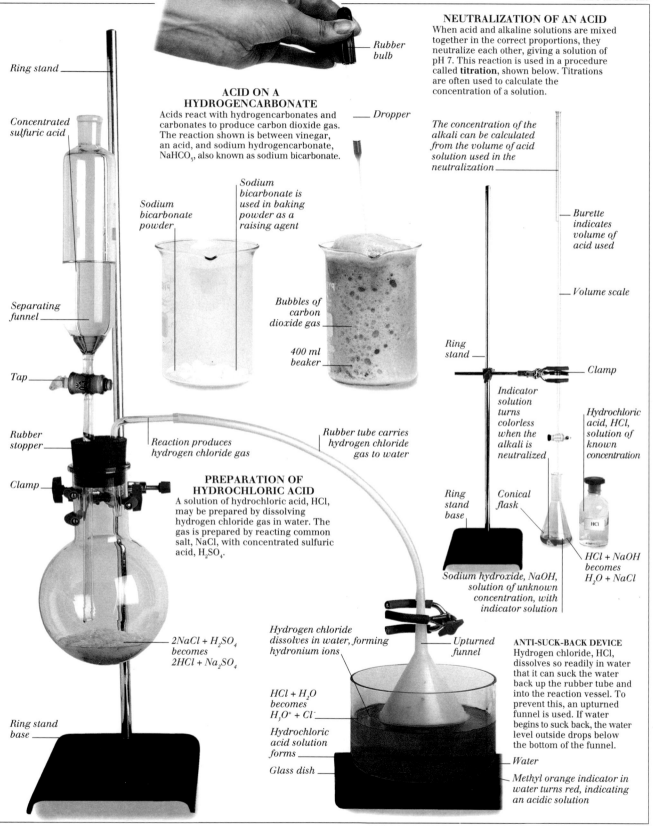

Ring stand

Concentrated
sulfuric acid

Separating
funnel

Tap

Rubber
stopper

Clamp

Ring stand
base

Rubber bulb

ACID ON A HYDROGENCARBONATE

Acids react with hydrogencarbonates and carbonates to produce carbon dioxide gas. The reaction shown is between vinegar, an acid, and sodium hydrogencarbonate, NaHCO₃, also known as sodium bicarbonate.

Dropper

Sodium
bicarbonate
powder

Sodium
bicarbonate is
used in baking
powder as a
raising agent

Bubbles of
carbon
dioxide gas

400 ml
beaker

Reaction produces
hydrogen chloride gas

Rubber tube carries
hydrogen chloride
gas to water

PREPARATION OF HYDROCHLORIC ACID

A solution of hydrochloric acid, HCl, may be prepared by dissolving hydrogen chloride gas in water. The gas is prepared by reacting common salt, NaCl, with concentrated sulfuric acid, H₂SO₄.

$2NaCl + H_2SO_4$
becomes
$2HCl + Na_2SO_4$

Hydrogen chloride
dissolves in water, forming
hydronium ions

$HCl + H_2O$
becomes
$H_3O^+ + Cl^-$

Hydrochloric
acid solution
forms

Glass dish

NEUTRALIZATION OF AN ACID

When acid and alkaline solutions are mixed together in the correct proportions, they neutralize each other, giving a solution of pH 7. This reaction is used in a procedure called **titration**, shown below. Titrations are often used to calculate the concentration of a solution.

The concentration of the alkali can be calculated from the volume of acid solution used in the neutralization

Burette
indicates
volume of
acid used

Volume scale

Ring
stand

Clamp

Indicator
solution
turns
colorless
when the
alkali is
neutralized

Hydrochloric
acid, HCl,
solution of
known
concentration

Ring
stand
base

Conical
flask

$HCl + NaOH$
becomes
$H_2O + NaCl$

Sodium hydroxide, NaOH,
solution of unknown
concentration, with
indicator solution

Upturned
funnel

ANTI-SUCK-BACK DEVICE

Hydrogen chloride, HCl, dissolves so readily in water that it can suck the water back up the rubber tube and into the reaction vessel. To prevent this, an upturned funnel is used. If water begins to suck back, the water level outside drops below the bottom of the funnel.

Water

Methyl orange indicator in
water turns red, indicating
an acidic solution

Salts

WHENEVER AN ACID AND A BASE **neutralize** each other (see pp. 84-85), the **products** of the reaction always include a **salt**. A salt is a **compound** that consists of **cations** (positive **ions**) and **anions** (negative ions). The cation is usually a metal ion, such as the sodium ion, Na^+. The anion can be a nonmetal such as the chloride ion, Cl^-, although more often it is a unit called a **radical**. This is a combination of nonmetals that remains unchanged during most reactions. So, for example, when copper(II) oxide is added to sulfuric acid, the sulfate radical (SO_4^{2-}) becomes associated with copper ions, forming the salt copper(II) sulfate, $CuSO_4$. Salts are very widespread compounds – the most familiar being sodium chloride, or common salt. Mineral water contains salts, which are formed when slightly **acidic** rainwater dissolves rocks such as limestone. Water that contains large amounts of certain dissolved salts is called hard water (see pp. 100-101). A class of salts called acid salts contains a positive hydrogen ion in addition to the usual metal cation. Acid salts can be prepared by careful **titration** of an acid and a **base**.

FORMATION OF SALTS

In the generalized equations below, an acid reacts with three typical bases – a hydroxide, an oxide, and a carbonate. A cation from the base combines with the acid's anion or negative radical, displacing the hydrogen ion to form a salt.

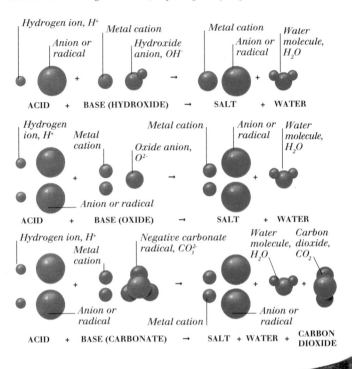

Hydrogen ion, H^+
Anion or radical
Metal cation
Hydroxide anion, OH^-
Metal cation
Anion or radical
Water molecule, H_2O

ACID + BASE (HYDROXIDE) → SALT + WATER

Hydrogen ion, H^+
Metal cation
Metal cation
Oxide anion, O^{2-}
Anion or radical
Water molecule, H_2O
Anion or radical

ACID + BASE (OXIDE) → SALT + WATER

Hydrogen ion, H^+
Metal cation
Negative carbonate radical, CO_3^{2-}
Water molecule, H_2O
Carbon dioxide, CO_2
Anion or radical
Metal cation
Anion or radical

ACID + BASE (CARBONATE) → SALT + WATER + CARBON DIOXIDE

COPPER(II) SULFATE

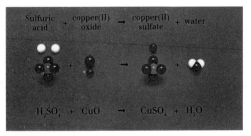

Sulfuric acid + copper(II) oxide → copper(II) sulfate + water

H_2SO_4 + CuO → $CuSO_4$ + H_2O

MOLECULAR VIEW
When the base copper(II) oxide reacts with sulfuric acid, copper(II) ions take the place of the hydrogen in the acid. The salt formed is therefore copper(II) sulfate. Water is the other product. The sulfate ion is a radical.

COPPER(II) OXIDE AND SULFURIC ACID
Copper(II) oxide, a black powder, is a base. When added to colorless dilute sulfuric acid, a neutralization reaction occurs. Hydrogen from the acid and oxygen from copper(II) oxide form water, while copper ions and the sulfate radical form the salt copper(II) sulfate.

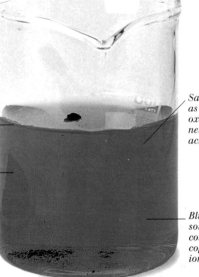

Black copper(II) oxide

Spatula

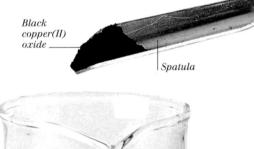

250 ml beaker

Salt forms as copper(II) oxide neutralizes acid

Dilute sulphuric acid

Blue solution contains copper ions, Cu^{2+}

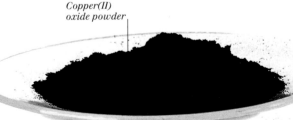

Copper(II) oxide powder

Watch glass

DISSOLVED SALTS IN MINERAL WATER

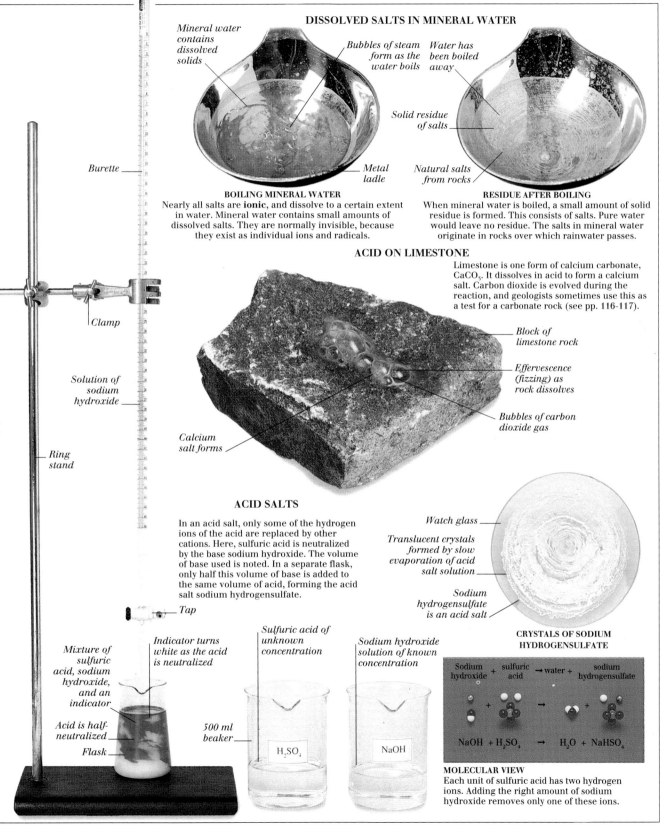

Mineral water contains dissolved solids

Bubbles of steam form as the water boils

Water has been boiled away

Solid residue of salts

Metal ladle

Natural salts from rocks

BOILING MINERAL WATER
Nearly all salts are **ionic**, and dissolve to a certain extent in water. Mineral water contains small amounts of dissolved salts. They are normally invisible, because they exist as individual ions and radicals.

RESIDUE AFTER BOILING
When mineral water is boiled, a small amount of solid residue is formed. This consists of salts. Pure water would leave no residue. The salts in mineral water originate in rocks over which rainwater passes.

ACID ON LIMESTONE

Limestone is one form of calcium carbonate, $CaCO_3$. It dissolves in acid to form a calcium salt. Carbon dioxide is evolved during the reaction, and geologists sometimes use this as a test for a carbonate rock (see pp. 116-117).

Block of limestone rock

Effervescence (fizzing) as rock dissolves

Bubbles of carbon dioxide gas

Calcium salt forms

Burette

Clamp

Solution of sodium hydroxide

Ring stand

ACID SALTS

In an acid salt, only some of the hydrogen ions of the acid are replaced by other cations. Here, sulfuric acid is neutralized by the base sodium hydroxide. The volume of base used is noted. In a separate flask, only half this volume of base is added to the same volume of acid, forming the acid salt sodium hydrogensulfate.

Watch glass

Translucent crystals formed by slow evaporation of acid salt solution

Sodium hydrogensulfate is an acid salt

CRYSTALS OF SODIUM HYDROGENSULFATE

Tap

Mixture of sulfuric acid, sodium hydroxide, and an indicator

Indicator turns white as the acid is neutralized

Sulfuric acid of unknown concentration

Sodium hydroxide solution of known concentration

Acid is half-neutralized

Flask

500 ml beaker

H₂SO₄

NaOH

Sodium hydroxide + sulfuric acid → water + sodium hydrogensulfate

$$NaOH + H_2SO_4 \rightarrow H_2O + NaHSO_4$$

MOLECULAR VIEW
Each unit of sulfuric acid has two hydrogen ions. Adding the right amount of sodium hydroxide removes only one of these ions.

Catalysts

A CATALYST IS A SUBSTANCE that increases the **rate** at which a reaction takes place but is unchanged itself at the end of the reaction. Certain **catalysts** are used up in one stage of a reaction and regenerated at a later stage. Light is sometimes considered to be a catalyst – although it is not a substance – because it speeds up certain reactions. This process is referred to as photocatalysis and is very important in photography and in **photosynthesis** (see pp. 100-101). Often, catalysts simply provide a suitable surface upon which the reaction can take place. Such surface catalysis often involves **transition metals**, such as iron or nickel. Surface catalysis occurs in catalytic converters in automobiles, which speed up reactions that change harmful pollutant gases into less harmful ones. **Enzymes** are biological catalysts and are nearly all **proteins**. They catalyze reactions in living organisms. For example, an enzyme called ptyalin in saliva helps to digest or break down starch in food to make sugars that can be readily absorbed by the body. Enzymes are also important in turning sugar into alcohol during fermentation.

CATALYSIS AT A SURFACE

Reactant A is a diatomic molecule

Reactant B approaches surface

Surface atoms of catalyst

REACTANTS APPROACH SURFACE
In this reaction, one of the **reactants** is a **diatomic molecule** that must be split before it will react.

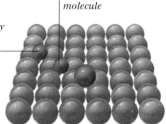

Atom of diatomic molecule

Reactant bonds weakly to surface atom

REACTANTS BOND TO SURFACE
The reactants form weak bonds with the surface atoms. As the diatomic molecule bonds, it breaks into two individual atoms.

Reactants migrate across surface

Reaction occurs at surface

REACTION TAKES PLACE
The reactants move, or migrate, across the surface. When they meet, the reaction takes place. The surface is unchanged.

Product of reaction

Catalyst surface is unchanged

PRODUCT LEAVES SURFACE
The reaction **product** leaves the surface, to which it was very weakly bonded, and the reaction is complete.

PHOTOCATALYSIS

Light can promote, or speed up, a reaction. Here, both tubes contain a yellow **precipitate** of silver bromide (see pp. 116-117). For a period of about ten minutes, one of the tubes has been left in a dark cupboard while the other has been left in the light. The light has caused silver **ions** to become **atoms** of silver. Photographic films contain tiny granules of silver halides, which produce silver on the negative wherever it is hit by light.

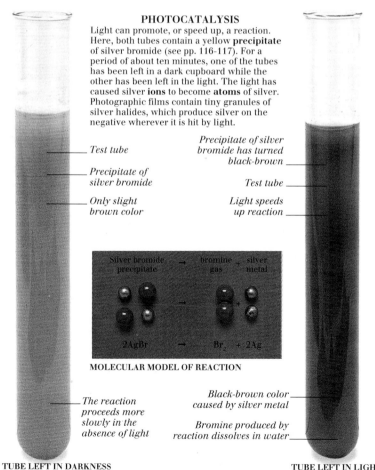

Test tube

Precipitate of silver bromide

Only slight brown color

Precipitate of silver bromide has turned black-brown

Test tube

Light speeds up reaction

Silver bromide precipitate → bromine gas + silver metal

$2AgBr \rightarrow Br_2 + 2Ag$

MOLECULAR MODEL OF REACTION

The reaction proceeds more slowly in the absence of light

Black-brown color caused by silver metal

Bromine produced by reaction dissolves in water

TUBE LEFT IN DARKNESS

TUBE LEFT IN LIGHT

EXAMPLES OF SURFACE CATALYSTS

CATALYTIC CONVERTER
Many automobiles are fitted with a catalytic converter, as part of the exhaust system. Inside is a fine honeycomb structure coated with catalysts. Harmful carbon monoxide, nitrogen oxides, and unburned **hydrocarbons** are converted into carbon dioxide and harmless water and nitrogen.

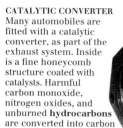

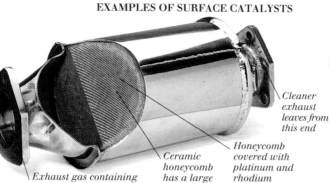

Cleaner exhaust leaves from this end

Exhaust gas containing pollutants enters here

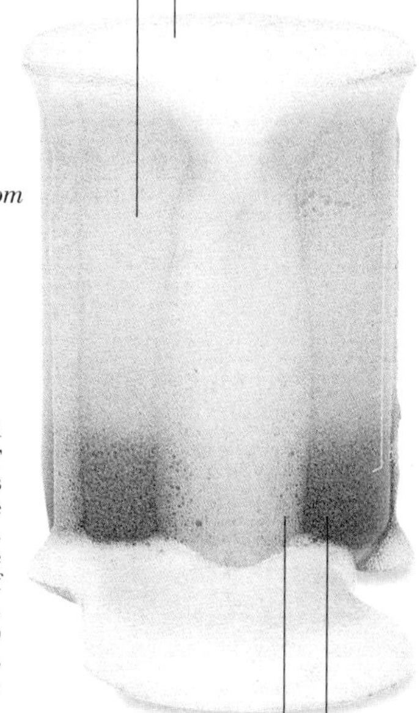

Ceramic honeycomb has a large surface area

Honeycomb covered with platinum and rhodium

250 ml beaker

Bubbles of carbon dioxide coming out of solution

SUGAR AS A SURFACE CATALYST
Carbonated drinks contain carbon dioxide gas dissolved in water. The carbon dioxide normally comes out of **solution** quite slowly. This reaction speeds up at a catalytic surface, such as that of sugar.

The reaction speeds up in the presence of sugar as a catalyst

Carbonated drink

Glass U-tube

Water prevents air from entering the reaction

Carbon dioxide gas bubbles out through water

Rubber stopper

ENZYMES

FERMENTATION
Glucose and fructose are sugars found in fruit such as grapes. These sugars are turned into alcohol (ethanol) by an enzyme called zymase in yeast. The zymase catalyzes the **decomposition** of sugars into alcohol. Carbon dioxide is also produced.

Glass bottle

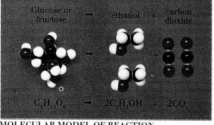

Glucose or fructose → ethanol + carbon dioxide

$C_6H_{12}O_6 \rightarrow 2C_2H_5OH + 2CO_2$

MOLECULAR MODEL OF REACTION

Powdered laundry detergent

POWDERED LAUNDRY DETERGENT
Some powdered laundry detergents contain enzymes, which catalyze the breakdown of proteins that make up stains in clothing. The enzymes are denatured, or damaged, at high **temperatures**, so these detergents only work at low temperatures.

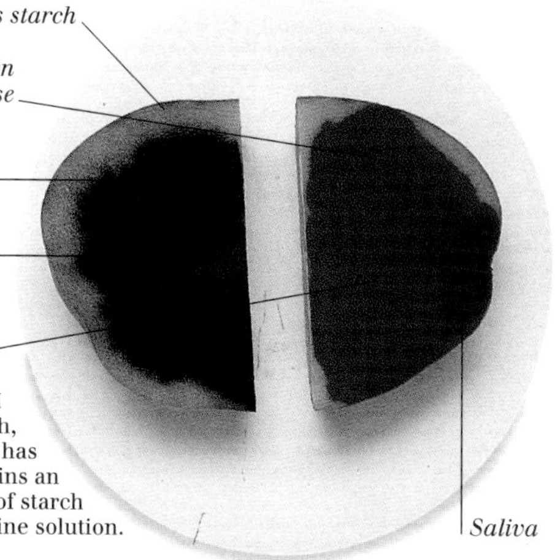

Grape juice, yeast, water, and extra sugar

Yeast contains the enzyme zymase

Alcohol is produced

Potato contains starch

Starch on this side has been broken down by amylase

Starch on this side remains

Iodine solution turns black, indicating the presence of starch

Iodine solution remains brown, indicating little starch

DIGESTION OF STARCH
Enzymes called amylases break down starch, forming sugars. Here, one side of a potato has been covered in saliva, which contains an amylase called ptyalin. The presence of starch can be indicated using an iodine solution.

Saliva

Heat in chemistry

HEAT IS A FORM OF ENERGY that a substance possesses due to the movement or vibration of its **atoms**, **molecules**, or **ions**. The **temperature** of a substance is a measure of the average heat (or **kinetic**) **energy** of its particles, and is a factor in determining whether the substance is solid, liquid, or gas. Energy changes are involved in all reactions. For example, light energy (see pp. 100-101) and electrical energy (see pp. 96-97) can make reactions occur or can be released as a result of reactions. Heat energy is taken in or released by most reactions. Some reactions, such as the **burning** of wood, need an initial input of energy, called **activation energy**, in order for them to occur. Once established, however, the burning reaction releases heat energy to the surroundings – it is an **exothermic** reaction. Other reactions take heat from their surroundings and are called **endothermic** reactions. The thermite reaction, in which aluminum metal reacts with a metal oxide, is so exothermic that the heat released can be used to weld metals.

LIQUID CHLORINE

A gas becomes a liquid if cooled below its boiling point. Here, chlorine gas has been pumped into a test tube. Heat energy is then removed from the gas by cooling the tube in dry ice.

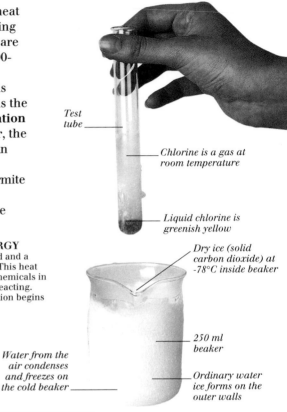

Test tube

Chlorine is a gas at room temperature

Liquid chlorine is greenish yellow

Dry ice (solid carbon dioxide) at -78°C inside beaker

250 ml beaker

Ordinary water ice forms on the outer walls

ACTIVATION ENERGY

Friction between a match head and a rough surface produces heat. This heat provides the energy that the chemicals in the match head need to start reacting. The heat released in this reaction begins the burning of the wood.

Match rubbed against rough surface

Burning wood combines with oxygen from the air

Match head contains phosphorus

Water from the air condenses and freezes on the cold beaker

Rough surface

EXOTHERMIC AND ENDOTHERMIC REACTIONS

EXOTHERMIC REACTION, $CaCl_2 \rightarrow Ca^{2+} + 2Cl^-$
Compounds contain a certain amount of energy. If the energy of the **products** of a reaction is less than that of the **reactants**, then heat will be released to the surroundings. The reaction is described as exothermic. When calcium chloride dissolves in water, an exothermic reaction takes place.

Thermometer reads 21.5°C, a few degrees above room temperature

Digital thermometer

250 ml beaker

Water, H_2O

Calcium chloride dissolves, releasing heat

Watch glass

Calcium chloride powder, $CaCl_2$

ENDOTHERMIC REACTION, $NH_4NO_3 \rightarrow NH_4^+ + NO_3^-$
If the energy of the products of a reaction is more than that of the reactants, then heat will be taken from the surroundings. The reaction is described as endothermic. An endothermic reaction occurs when ammonium nitrate is dissolved in water.

Thermometer reads 13.8°C, a few degrees below room temperature

250 ml beaker

Digital thermometer

Water, H_2O

Ammonium nitrate powder, NH_4NO_3

Watch glass

Ammonium nitrate dissolves, absorbing heat

THERMITE REACTION

REACTANTS

The thermite reaction can take place between aluminum and many different metal oxides. Here, the reactants are aluminum and iron(III) oxide.

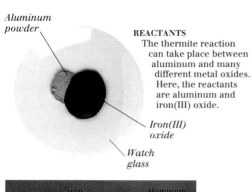

Aluminum powder

Iron(III) oxide

Watch glass

Thick smoke consists of small particles of reaction products

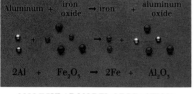

Aluminum + iron oxide → iron + aluminum oxide

2Al + Fe₂O₃ → 2Fe + Al₂O₃

$$2Al + Fe_2O_3 \rightarrow 2Fe + Al_2O_3$$

MOLECULAR MODEL OF REACTION

THERMITE WELDING

The tremendous amount of heat released by the thermite reaction is put to good use in welding railway tracks. Iron oxide is used, yielding molten iron as one of the reaction products. The molten iron helps to make the weld.

Pot containing reactants

Molten iron flows into gap to make weld

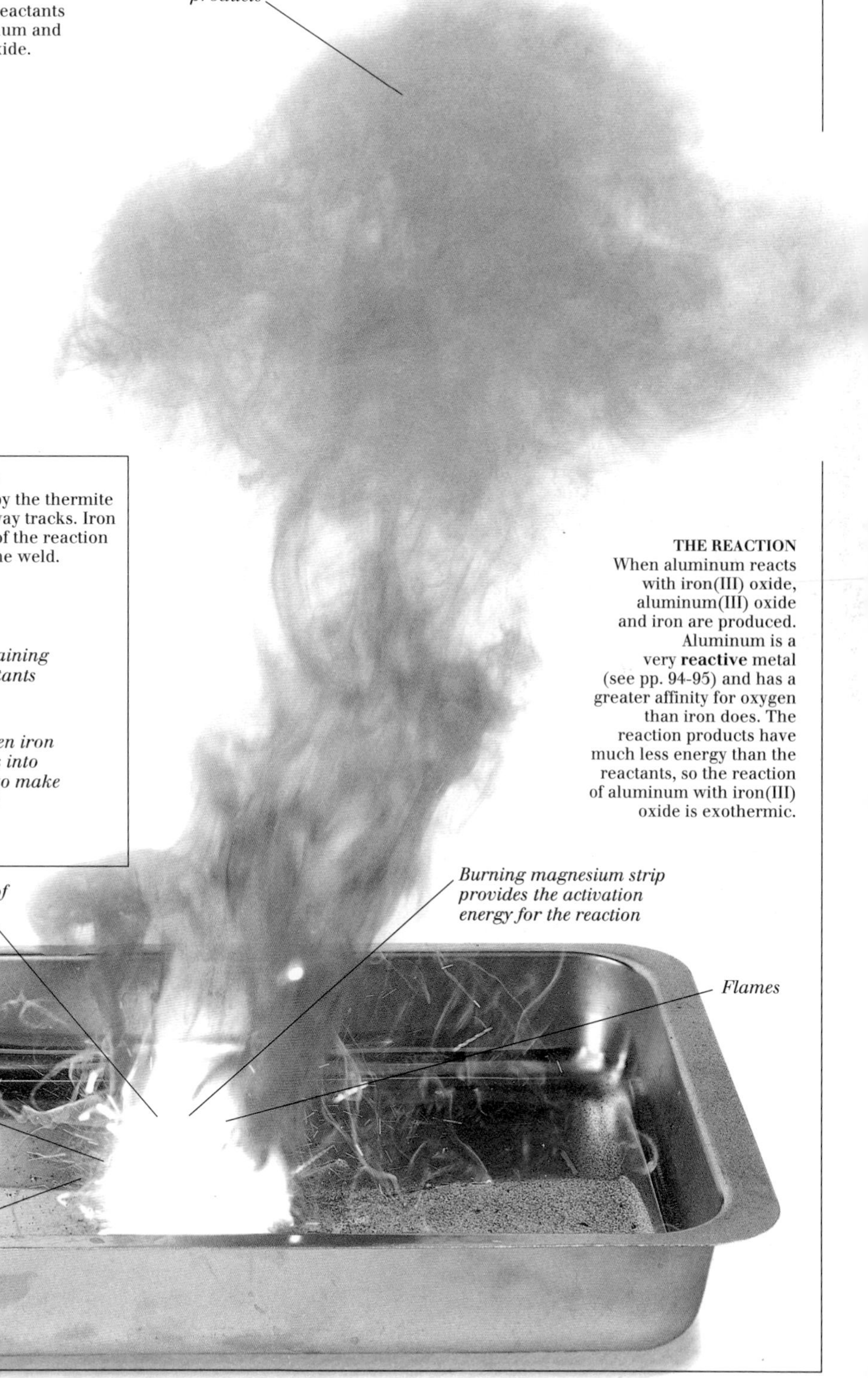

THE REACTION

When aluminum reacts with iron(III) oxide, aluminum(III) oxide and iron are produced. Aluminum is a very **reactive** metal (see pp. 94-95) and has a greater affinity for oxygen than iron does. The reaction products have much less energy than the reactants, so the reaction of aluminum with iron(III) oxide is exothermic.

Burning magnesium strip provides the activation energy for the reaction

Metal tray

A large amount of heat is released

Products of the reaction are aluminum oxide and metallic iron

Flames

Shower of sparks

Water in chemistry

EACH MOLECULE OF WATER consists of two **atoms** of hydrogen bound to an oxygen atom. Water reacts physically and chemically with a wide range of **elements** and **compounds**. Many gases dissolve in water – in particular, ammonia dissolves very readily, as demonstrated by the fountain experiment. Some compounds, called **dehydrating agents**, have such a strong affinity for water that they can remove it from other substances. Concentrated sulfuric acid is so powerful a dehydrating agent that it can remove hydrogen and oxygen from certain compounds, making water where there was none before. Water is often held in **crystals** of other substances, and is then called **water of crystallization**. A compound can lose its water of crystallization during strong heating, and is then said to be **anhydrous**. Adding water to anhydrous crystals can restore the water of crystallization. Some compounds, described as **efflorescent**, have crystals that lose their water of crystallization to the air. Conversely, **hygroscopic** compounds have crystals that absorb water from the air. Desiccators often employ such compounds to dry other substances.

WATER OF CRYSTALLIZATION

Crystals containing water of crystallization are said to be hydrated. Heating a hydrated crystal causes it to lose water.

Glass dish

Blue solution of copper(II) sulfate

Blue crystals form on evaporation

COPPER(II) SULFATE SOLUTION
Gently heating a **solution** of blue copper(II) sulfate evaporates the water, leaving behind blue crystals of hydrated copper(II) sulfate.

Strongly heated crystals dehydrate

Gauze

Tripod

Gas flame

Bunsen burner

ANHYDROUS COPPER(II) SULFATE
Strongly heating the hydrated crystals drives off the water of crystallization, leaving a white powder of anhydrous copper(II) sulfate.

SULFURIC ACID AS A DEHYDRATING AGENT
Substances known as dehydrating agents can either simply remove water from a **mixture**, or remove hydrogen and oxygen from a compound in the ratio 2:1, the ratio found in water. Concentrated sulfuric acid is a very powerful dehydrating agent (below).

H_2SO_4

CONCENTRATED SULFURIC ACID, H_2SO_4

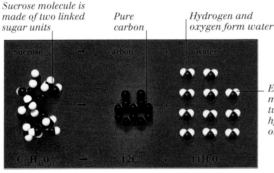

Sucrose molecule is made of two linked sugar units

Pure carbon

Hydrogen and oxygen form water

Sucrose → carbon + water

$C_{12}H_{22}O_{11}$ → $12C$ + $11H_2O$

MOLECULAR MODEL OF REACTION

Each water molecule has two atoms of hydrogen and one of oxygen

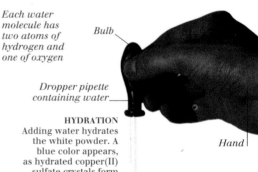

Bulb

HYDRATION
Adding water hydrates the white powder. A blue color appears, as hydrated copper(II) sulfate crystals form once more.

Dropper pipette containing water

Hand

Glass dish

Steam condenses on glass

All the hydrogen and oxygen will eventually be removed from the sucrose

Carbon

Sucrose (sugar)

DEHYDRATION OF SUCROSE
Concentrated sulfuric acid removes 22 hydrogen atoms and 11 oxygen atoms from each molecule of sucrose, leaving only black carbon behind. The reaction evolves heat, enough to boil the water produced and form steam.

Hydrated copper(II) sulfate forms

Water drop

Glass dish

AMMONIA FOUNTAIN

Water is a good solvent – even many gases dissolve in it.
Ammonia dissolves very readily in water, forming an
alkaline solution (see pp. 84-85). This fountain experiment
employs red litmus solution, an **indicator** that turns blue in
the presence of an alkali.

EFFLORESCENCE AND HYGROSCOPY

In these two processes, compounds lose or gain
water of crystallization. Efflorescent compounds lose
their water of crystallization to the air. Hygroscopic
compounds gain water from the air.

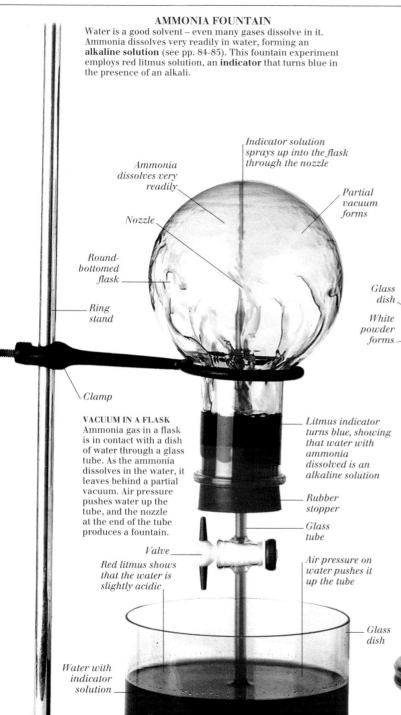

*Indicator solution
sprays up into the flask
through the nozzle*

*Ammonia
dissolves very
readily*

*Partial
vacuum
forms*

Nozzle

*Round-
bottomed
flask*

*Ring
stand*

Clamp

VACUUM IN A FLASK

Ammonia gas in a flask
is in contact with a dish
of water through a glass
tube. As the ammonia
dissolves in the water, it
leaves behind a partial
vacuum. Air pressure
pushes water up the
tube, and the nozzle
at the end of the tube
produces a fountain.

Valve

*Red litmus shows
that the water is
slightly acidic*

*Litmus indicator
turns blue, showing
that water with
ammonia
dissolved is an
alkaline solution*

*Rubber
stopper*

*Glass
tube*

*Air pressure on
water pushes it
up the tube*

*Glass
dish*

*Water with
indicator
solution*

Glass dish

*Sodium
carbonate*

SODIUM CARBONATE DECAHYDRATE

The white crystals of sodium carbonate decahydrate
(washing soda) shown here are efflorescent. Two
sodium ions and a carbonate ion are combined with
ten molecules of water of crystallization to form
sodium carbonate decahydrate, $Na_2CO_3.10H_2O$.

*Glass
dish*

*White
powder
forms*

SODIUM CARBONATE AFTER EXPOSURE TO AIR

When left in the air, the sodium carbonate
decahydrate crystals give up most of the water of
crystallization associated with them. The resulting
white powder, called a monohydrate, is visible
here on the surface of the crystals.

DESICCATOR

Some substances need to be kept free of moisture.
A desiccator is a device that removes moisture. It is
usually a glass container with a desiccant, or drying
agent, inside.

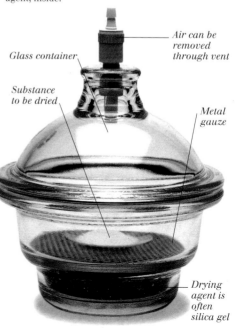

*Air can be
removed
through vent*

Glass container

*Substance
to be dried*

*Metal
gauze*

*Drying
agent is
often
silica gel*

The activity series

ALL METAL ATOMS LOSE ELECTRONS fairly easily and become positive **ions,** or **cations.** The ease with which a metal loses **electrons** is a measure of its **reactivity.** Metals in groups 1 and 2 of the periodic table (see pp. 98-101), which have one and two outer electrons respectively, are usually the most reactive. Aluminum in group 3 is a reactive metal, but less so than calcium in group 2. Metals can be arranged in order of decreasing reactivity in a series known as the activity series. In this series, zinc is placed above copper, and copper above silver. Zinc metal is more reactive than copper and can displace copper ions from a **solution.** Similarly, copper displaces silver from solution. Electrons from the more reactive metal transfer to the less reactive metal ions in solution, resulting in the **deposition** of the less reactive metal. Because electron transfer occurs in these reactions, they are classified as **redox reactions.** The reactivity of a metal may be characterized in many ways – for example, by its reactions with **acids.** The different reactivities of metals have a practical application in the prevention of corrosion in underwater pipes.

TABLE OF METAL REACTIVITY

Metal	Air or oxygen on metal	Water on metal	Acids on metal	Metals on salts of other metals
K Na Ca Mg	Burn in air or oxygen	React with cold water (with decreasing ease)	Displace hydrogen from acids that are not oxidizing agents (with decreasing ease)	Displace a metal lower in the series from a solution of one of its salts
Al Zn Fe		React with steam when heated		
Sn Pb Cu Hg	Converted into the oxide by heating in air	No reaction with water or steam	React only with oxidizing acids	
Ag Au Pt	Unaffected by air or oxygen		No reaction with acids	

ALUMINUM METAL

- Unreactive layer of aluminum oxide
- Cotton soaked in mercury(II) chloride
- Mercury(II) chloride removes aluminum's oxide layer
- Aluminum reacts with air to reform oxide layer

REMOVING THE OXIDE LAYER
Metallic aluminum, which is used to make kitchen foil and saucepans, seems unreactive. Actually, aluminum is quite high in the activity series. When pure aluminum is exposed to the air, a thin layer of unreactive aluminum oxide rapidly forms on the surfaces, preventing further reaction.

DISPLACEMENT OF COPPER(II) IONS BY ZINC METAL

A **displacement reaction** is one in which **atoms** or ions of one substance take the place of atoms or ions of another. Here, zinc loses electrons to copper ions and displaces copper from a blue solution of copper(II) sulfate. The **products** of this reaction are copper metal and colorless zinc(II) sulfate solution.

400 ml beaker

Blue copper(II) sulfate solution

Blue color caused by copper(II) ions, Cu^{2+}

Zinc is a grayish metal, and is more reactive than copper

Watch glass

ZINC METAL

COPPER(II) SULFATE SOLUTION

Zinc metal dissolves to form zinc(II) ions, Zn^{2+}

Zinc(II) sulfate solution is colorless

Red-brown copper metal forms as it is displaced from solution

ZINC(II) SULFATE SOLUTION AND METALLIC COPPER

CATHODIC PROTECTION

Sacrificial tubing of more reactive metal

Steel structure

Offshore oil rig

PROTECTION OF OIL RIGS
Many metals corrode when exposed to water and air. To prevent underwater or underground metal pipes from corroding, a more reactive metal may be placed in contact with the pipe. Being more reactive, this metal corrodes in preference to the pipe. This technique, called cathodic protection, is commonly used in oil rigs.

REACTIONS OF METALS WITH DILUTE ACIDS

Acid solutions contain hydrogen ions, H^+, in the form of **hydronium ions**, H_3O^+ (see pp. 84-85). Reactive metals in an acid solution donate electrons to hydrogen ions, producing hydrogen gas. Metal atoms become positive ions and dissolve. The more reactive the metal, the faster the reaction proceeds. Some metals are so unreactive that they will react only with hot concentrated acid, and some will not react with acids at all.

Reaction proceeds fairly rapidly

Bubbles of hydrogen gas, H_2

Zinc, Zn, is a fairly reactive metal

Magnesium, Mg, is a reactive metal

MAGNESIUM IN DILUTE ACID

ZINC IN DILUTE ACID

Test tube

Dilute sulfuric acid, H_2SO_4

Hydrogen gas is given off very slowly

Dilute sulfuric acid, H_2SO_4

Extremely slow reaction

No reaction

TIN IN DILUTE ACID

SILVER IN DILUTE ACID

PLATINUM IN DILUTE ACID

DISPLACEMENT OF SILVER(I) IONS BY COPPER METAL

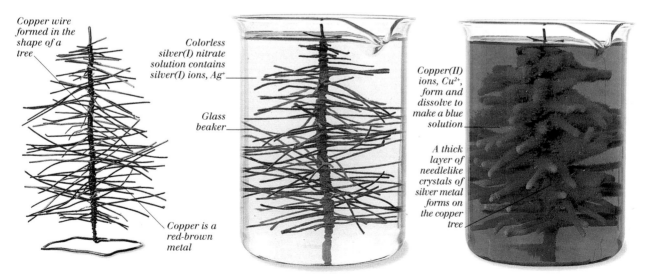

Copper wire formed in the shape of a tree

Colorless silver(I) nitrate solution contains silver(I) ions, Ag^+

Glass beaker

Copper is a red-brown metal

Copper(II) ions, Cu^{2+}, form and dissolve to make a blue solution

A thick layer of needlelike crystals of silver metal forms on the copper tree

COPPER WIRE "TREE"
Here wire made from copper is formed into the shape of a tree. This shape has a large surface area, upon which the reaction can occur.

COPPER TREE IN SILVER NITRATE SOLUTION
When the copper wire is submerged in a solution of silver(I) nitrate, the copper metal loses electrons to the silver(I) ions.

DEPOSITION OF SILVER CRYSTALS
The silver ions are displaced to form silver metal, which coats the copper tree. A blue solution of copper(II) nitrate forms.

Electrochemistry

ELECTRICITY PLAYS A PART in all **chemical reactions**, because all **atoms** consist of **electrically charged** particles (see pp. 72-73). A flow of charged particles is called a current, and is usually carried around a circuit by **electrons**, moved by an electromotive force, or voltage. In **solution**, the charge carriers are **ions**, which are also moved by a voltage. A solution containing ions that conducts current is called an **electrolyte**. There are two basic types of electrochemical systems or cells. In an electrolytic cell, two conductors called **electrodes** are dipped in an electrolyte, and connected via an external circuit to a battery or other source of voltage. Such a cell can **decompose** the electrolyte in a process called **electrolysis**. Electrolytic cells are also used in the electroplating of metals. In a voltaic cell, electrodes of two different metals are dipped in an electrolyte. The electrodes produce a voltage that can drive a current between them. Voltaic cells are the basis of common batteries. In both types of cells, the **anode** is the electrode at which **oxidation** occurs, and the **cathode** the one where **reduction** occurs. The cathode is the positive terminal of voltaic cells, but negative in electrolytic cells.

ALKALINE DRY CELL (VOLTAIC)

Electrochemistry is put to use in this **alkaline** dry cell. Powdered zinc metal forms one electrode, while manganese(IV) oxide forms the other. This cell produces electricity at 1.5 volts. Batteries producing 3, 4.5, 6, or 9 volts are made by connecting a series of these cells.

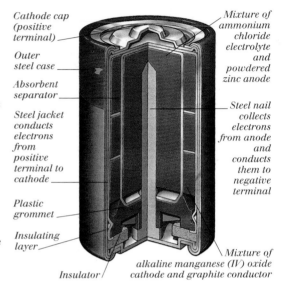

Cathode cap (positive terminal)

Outer steel case

Absorbent separator

Steel jacket conducts electrons from positive terminal to cathode

Plastic grommet

Insulating layer

Insulator

Mixture of ammonium chloride electrolyte and powdered zinc anode

Steel nail collects electrons from anode and conducts them to negative terminal

Mixture of alkaline manganese (IV) oxide cathode and graphite conductor

ELECTROLYSIS

ELECTROLYTIC DECOMPOSITION OF WATER

Passing an electric current through water decomposes it, producing the gases hydrogen and oxygen. A small amount of an **ionic compound** is dissolved in the water to make an electrolyte, into which two electrodes are dipped. The battery removes electrons, e^-, from one electrode, the anode, and pushes them toward the cathode. This is an example of an electrolytic cell.

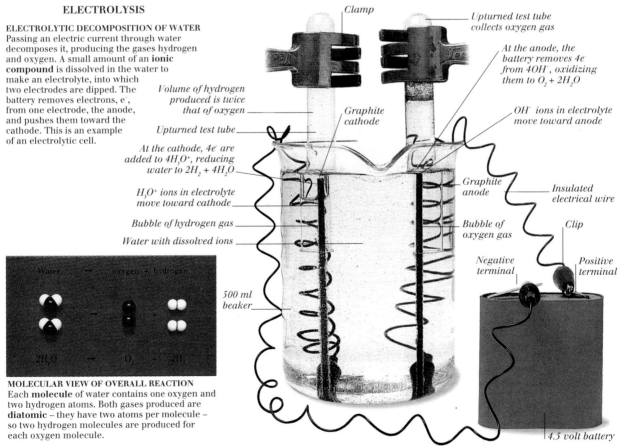

Clamp

Upturned test tube collects oxygen gas

At the anode, the battery removes $4e^-$ from $4OH^-$, oxidizing them to $O_2 + 2H_2O$

OH^- ions in electrolyte move toward anode

Volume of hydrogen produced is twice that of oxygen

Graphite cathode

Upturned test tube

At the cathode, $4e^-$ are added to $4H_3O^+$, reducing water to $2H_2 + 4H_2O$

H_3O^+ ions in electrolyte move toward cathode

Bubble of hydrogen gas

Water with dissolved ions

Graphite anode

Insulated electrical wire

Bubble of oxygen gas

Clip

Negative terminal

Positive terminal

500 ml beaker

4.5 volt battery

Water → oxygen + hydrogen

$2H_2O$ → O_2 + $2H_2$

MOLECULAR VIEW OF OVERALL REACTION

Each **molecule** of water contains one oxygen and two hydrogen atoms. Both gases produced are **diatomic** – they have two atoms per molecule – so two hydrogen molecules are produced for each oxygen molecule.

VOLTAIC CELL

PRODUCING A VOLTAGE

When two electrodes of different metals are dipped in an **acidic** solution so that they do not touch each other, an electric voltage is set up between them. This arrangement is called a voltaic cell. If the two electrodes are connected externally by a wire, the voltage causes an electric current to flow. In the voltaic cell below, zinc atoms are oxidized to zinc(II) ions at the anode. Electrons from this oxidation flow through the wire, illuminating the lightbulb, to the copper cathode, where hydrogen ions in solution are reduced to hydrogen gas.

Copper cathode (positive terminal of cell)

Clip

Bubbles of hydrogen gas produced as H⁺ ions are reduced to H_2 gas

Dilute solution of sulfuric acid, H_2SO_4

Glass dish

1.5 volt lightbulb

Bulb holder

Electric circuit

Zinc anode (negative terminal of cell)

Insulated electrical wire

Zinc electrode dissolves in acid

Some bubbles of hydrogen gas here, since zinc undergoes local reaction with acid (see p. 33)

Zinc atoms in electrode

Water molecule

Sulfate ion, SO_4^{2-}

Electron

Zinc electrode dissolves

Zinc ion, Zn^{2+}, in solution

ZINC ELECTRODE
Zinc atoms in the electrode dissolve in the acid, losing electrons to form **cations**. Oxidation occurs, so this electrode is the anode.

Water molecule

Electron

Copper atoms in electrode

Diatomic hydrogen molecule, H_2

Hydrogen ion, H^+, in solution

Sulfate ion, SO_4^{2-}

COPPER ELECTRODE
Here, at the cathode, electrons arrive from the zinc anode via the external circuit. They reduce hydrogen ions from the acid, forming hydrogen gas molecules.

ELECTROPLATING

COPPER PLATING A KEY

In electroplating, a thin layer of one metal is deposited onto the surface of another. The item to be plated is made the cathode in an electrolytic cell. The electrolyte is a solution containing ions of the other metal. Here, a brass key is plated with copper. The copper ions in solution are replenished from a copper anode.

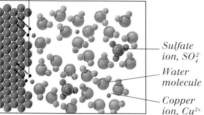

Battery removes electrons from copper atoms of anode, forming copper ions

Sulfate ion, SO_4^{2-}

Water molecule

Copper ion, Cu^{2+}

AT THE COPPER PIPE ANODE
The battery's positive terminal draws electrons from the anode, oxidizing the copper atoms to copper(II) cations. These ions dissolve and move toward the cathode.

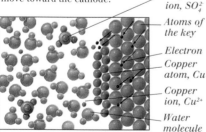

Sulfate ion, SO_4^{2-}

Atoms of the key

Electron

Copper atom, Cu

Copper ion, Cu^{2+}

Water molecule

AT THE BRASS KEY CATHODE
Copper ions that have moved to the cathode are reduced to copper atoms by electrons from the battery. These atoms build up on the surface of the brass key cathode.

BRASS KEY (BEFORE)

COPPER-PLATED KEY (AFTER)

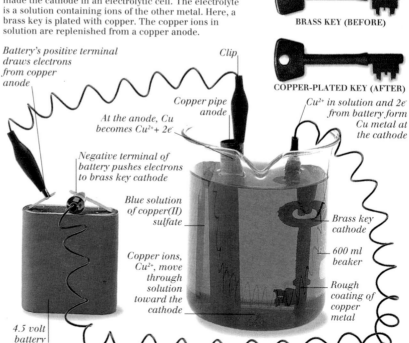

Battery's positive terminal draws electrons from copper anode

At the anode, Cu becomes $Cu^{2+} + 2e^-$

Negative terminal of battery pushes electrons to brass key cathode

Blue solution of copper(II) sulfate

Copper ions, Cu^{2+}, move through solution toward the cathode

4.5 volt battery

Clip

Copper pipe anode

Cu^{2+} in solution and $2e^-$ from battery form Cu metal at the cathode

Brass key cathode

600 ml beaker

Rough coating of copper metal

The alkali metals

THE ELEMENTS OF GROUP 1 of the periodic table (see pp. 74-75) are called the alkali metals. **Atoms** of these **elements** have one outer **electron**. This electron is easily lost, forming singly charged **cations** such as the lithium **ion**, Li⁺. As with all cations, the lithium cation is smaller than the lithium atom. All of the elements in this group are highly **reactive** metals (see pp. 76-77). They react violently with **acids**, and even react with water, to form **alkaline solutions** (see pp. 84-85) – hence their group name. The most important element in this group is sodium. Sodium forms many **compounds**, including sodium chloride, or common salt, and sodium hydrogencarbonate, which is used in baking powder. By far the most important compound of sodium in industrial use is sodium hydroxide. It is manufactured in large quantities, mainly by the **electrolysis** of brine (a solution of sodium chloride). Sodium hydroxide is a strong **base**, and it reacts with the fatty acids in fats and oils to produce soap, which is a **salt** (see pp. 86-87).

POSITION IN THE PERIODIC TABLE

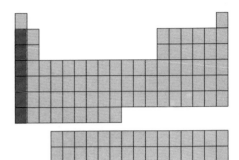

GROUP 1 ELEMENTS
The alkali metals form group 1 of the periodic table. They are (from top):
lithium (Li),
sodium (Na),
potassium (K),
rubidium (Rb),
cesium (Cs),
and francium (Fr).

Potassium is a soft, silvery metal

POTASSIUM METAL

REACTION WITH WATER

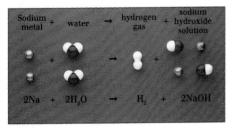

Red litmus solution

Glass bowl

The reaction evolves heat

Sodium skims across the surface on a cushion of steam and hydrogen gas

Red litmus begins to turn blue as alkaline sodium hydroxide solution forms

SODIUM IN INDICATOR SOLUTION
A piece of pure sodium metal reacts dangerously with water. Here, red litmus **indicator** is dissolved in the water. Explosive hydrogen gas is given off by the reaction, and the litmus turns blue with the resulting sodium hydroxide solution (above).

Sodium metal	+	water	→	hydrogen gas	+	sodium hydroxide solution
2Na	+	2H₂O	→	H₂	+	2NaOH

MOLECULAR VIEW
Sodium atoms lose electrons to form sodium cations, Na⁺, which dissolve in water. Water **molecules** each gain an electron and split into a hydroxide **anion**, which dissolves, and a hydrogen atom. Two atoms of hydrogen combine to form hydrogen gas, H₂.

ATOMS AND CATIONS

Atoms of the alkali metals have one electron, which is easily lost, in their outer **electron shell**. The cation formed is much smaller than the atom. Atomic and ionic diameters are given below for the first four alkali metals, measured in picometers (1 picometer, pm, is 10^{-12} m). Electron configurations of the elements are also given.

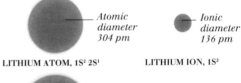

Atomic diameter 304 pm

LITHIUM ATOM, $1S^2\ 2S^1$

Ionic diameter 136 pm

LITHIUM ION, $1S^2$

Atomic diameter 370 pm

SODIUM ATOM, $1S^2\ 2S^2\ 2P^6\ 3S^1$

Ionic diameter 194 pm

SODIUM ION, $1S^2\ 2S^2\ 2P^6$

Ionic diameter 266 pm

Atomic diameter 462 pm

POTASSIUM ATOM, $1S^2\ 2S^2\ 2P^6\ 3S^2\ 3P^6\ 4S^1$

POTASSIUM ION, $1S^2\ 2S^2\ 2P^6\ 3S^2\ 3P^6$

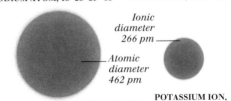
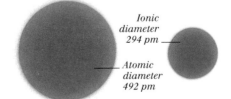

Ionic diameter 294 pm

Atomic diameter 492 pm

RUBIDIUM ATOM, $1S^2\ 2S^2\ 2P^6$ $5S^2\ 5P^6\ 5D^{10}\ 4S^2\ 4P^6\ 5S^1$

RUBIDIUM ION, $1S^2\ 2S^2\ 2P^6$ $5S^2\ 5P^6\ 5D^{10}\ 4S^2\ 4P^6$

SODIUM HYDROGENCARBONATE

Sodium hydrogencarbonate, $NaHCO_3$ – also known as sodium bicarbonate – is a weak base that **decomposes** on heating or on reaction with an acid, releasing carbon dioxide gas (see pp. 84-85). This white powder is used as a raising agent in cooking, and is an important ingredient of soda bread.

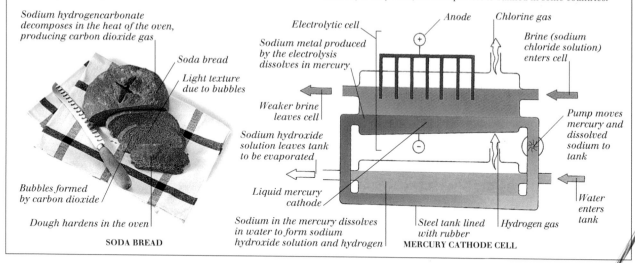

Sodium hydrogencarbonate decomposes in the heat of the oven, producing carbon dioxide gas

Soda bread

Light texture due to bubbles

Bubbles formed by carbon dioxide

Dough hardens in the oven

SODA BREAD

MANUFACTURE OF SODIUM HYDROXIDE

Much of the sodium hydroxide, NaOH, manufactured is made by the mercury cathode process. This two-stage process begins with the electrolysis of brine, NaCl, to give chlorine gas and pure sodium. The sodium then reacts with water to give sodium hydroxide solution. Mercury is very toxic, and this process is banned in some countries.

Electrolytic cell

Anode

Chlorine gas

Sodium metal produced by the electrolysis dissolves in mercury

Brine (sodium chloride solution) enters cell

Weaker brine leaves cell

Sodium hydroxide solution leaves tank to be evaporated

Pump moves mercury and dissolved sodium to tank

Liquid mercury cathode

Water enters tank

Sodium in the mercury dissolves in water to form sodium hydroxide solution and hydrogen

Steel tank lined with rubber

Hydrogen gas

MERCURY CATHODE CELL

PRODUCTION OF SOAP

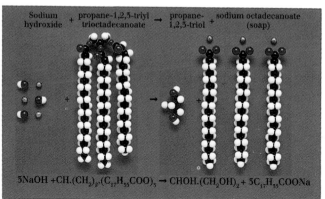

Sodium hydroxide + propane-1,2,3-triyl trioctadecanoate → propane-1,2,3-triol + sodium octadecanoate (soap)

$$5NaOH + CH.(CH_2)_2.(C_{17}H_{35}COO)_3 \rightarrow CHOH.(CH_2OH)_2 + 5C_{17}H_{35}COONa$$

MOLECULAR VIEW
The oil molecule shown consists of three long-chain fatty acids linked by propane-1,2,3-triol (glycerol). Sodium hydroxide reacts with the fatty acids from the oil to produce glycerol and the salt sodium octadecanoate.

LABORATORY PREPARATION
When fatty acids – weak acids found in fats and oils – are heated with sodium hydroxide, a strong base, they react to produce a **mixture** of salts. The main product is the salt sodium octadecanoate, $C_{17}H_{35}COONa$ (a soap). Common salt (sodium chloride) helps to separate the soap from the mixture.

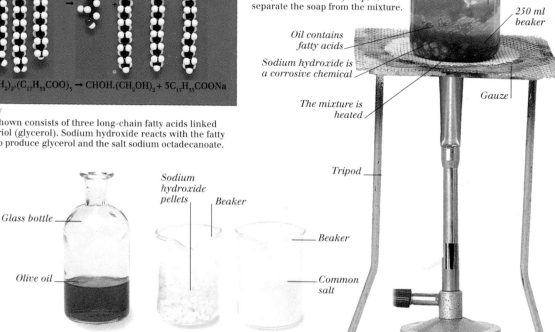

Soap forms as a layer on the top of the mixture

Glass stirrer

250 ml beaker

Oil contains fatty acids

Sodium hydroxide is a corrosive chemical

Gauze

The mixture is heated

Tripod

Glass bottle

Sodium hydroxide pellets

Beaker

Beaker

Olive oil

Common salt

The alkaline earth metals

THE ELEMENTS OF THE SECOND GROUP of the periodic table (see pp. 74-75) are called the alkaline earth metals. These **elements** are **reactive**, because their **atoms** easily lose two outer **electrons** to form doubly charged **cations**, such as the calcium **ion**, Ca^{2+}. Hard water, which contains large numbers of dissolved ions, often contains calcium ions. It is formed when slightly **acidic** water flows over rocks containing calcium **salts** such as calcium carbonate. The dissolved calcium salts can come out of **solution** from hard water, forming the scale that blocks kettles and hot water pipes. It is difficult to create a lather with soap when using hard water. In fact, a simple way to measure the hardness of water is to **titrate** it with a soap solution. Calcium **compounds** are an important constituent of mortar, which is used as a cement in bricklaying. Magnesium, another group 2 element, is found in the pigment chlorophyll, which gives green plants their color. Alkaline earth metals are commonly used in the manufacture of fireworks, and barium is used in hospitals for the production of X rays of the digestive system.

POSITION IN THE PERIODIC TABLE

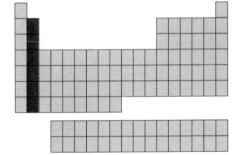

GROUP 2 ELEMENTS
The metals of group 2 of the periodic table are (from top): beryllium (Be), magnesium (Mg), calcium (Ca), strontium (Sr), barium (Ba), and radium (Ra).

MAGNESIUM IN CHLOROPHYLL

Leaf

CHLOROPHYLL IN GREEN PLANTS
Green plants contain large amounts of a vital compound called chlorophyll. It absorbs **energy** from sunlight in a process called **photosynthesis**. The energy is used to make sugars (see pp. 114-115) from carbon dioxide and water.

Green color is caused by magnesium in chlorophyll pigment

Leaf contains a store of energy built up by photosynthesis

Each cell of the leaf contains chlorophyll

Molecule head

Nitrogen atom

Magnesium atom

MOLECULE OF CHLOROPHYLL
The group 2 element magnesium plays a vital role in the chlorophyll **molecule**. Located at the center of the porphyrin ring in the head of the molecule, it absorbs light energy as part of the process of photosynthesis.

Porphyrin ring

Phytol side-chain

Carbon atom

Tail of molecule

Covalent bonds

Hydrogen atom

HARDNESS OF WATER

Burette

COMPARATIVE TITRATION
Hard water contains calcium hydrogencarbonate, $Ca(HCO_3)_2$, or other dissolved salts. These salts increase the amount of soap needed to produce a lather. The hardness of different water samples may be compared by titrating them with a soap solution of fixed **concentration**.

Ring stand

Soap solution contains a little alcohol to prevent clouding

Burette reading is noted

Clamp

TESTING HARD WATER
A solution of liquid soap in water is slowly added to a sample of hard water. The water is shaken occasionally, and the volume of soap solution is noted when a lather begins to form. Different water samples require different amounts of soap.

Flask is shaken occasionally

Conical flask

Tap

Water sample (tap water)

Water sample (bottled mineral water)

Water sample (rain-water)

ALKALINE EARTH METALS IN FIREWORKS

Red color given by strontium salts

Magnesium salts give an intense white color

CHARACTERISTIC COLOURS
Group 2 elements produce bright colors when heated in a flame (see pp. 116-117). For this reason, compounds of the elements are used in fireworks. As gunpowder in the fireworks burns, electrons in the group 2 atoms absorb heat energy and radiate it out as light of characteristic colors.

BARIUM MEAL

Large intestine

Skeleton

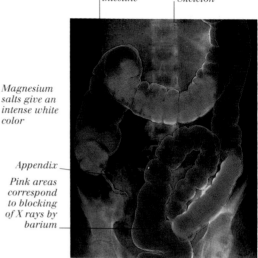

Appendix

Pink areas correspond to blocking of X rays by barium

X-RAY PHOTOGRAPH OF DIGESTIVE SYSTEM
To obtain an X ray of the digestive system, a "meal" of barium sulphate, $BaSO_4$, is administered to the patient. X rays pass through human tissue, but are stopped by atoms of barium.

CALCIUM COMPOUNDS IN MORTAR

PRODUCTION OF MORTAR
Bricklayers' mortar is calcium hydroxide – also known as slaked lime, $Ca(OH)_2$ – dissolved in water, and mixed with sand for bulk. As the mixture dries, the slaked lime **crystallizes** out of solution, and slowly reacts with carbon dioxide in the air to form hard calcium carbonate (see below).

250ml beaker

Water

Water evaporates from the mixture

Mold containing wet mortar

Mortar hardens as it reacts with carbon dioxide in air to form calcium carbonate

Sand and calcium hydroxide, $Ca(OH)_2$, mixed with water

The ingredients are mixed thoroughly

Spatula

Mortar takes the shape of the mold

MOLECULAR VIEW
Calcium ions, Ca^{2+}, and hydroxide ions, OH^-, form when slaked lime dissolves in water. Carbon dioxide, CO_2, combines with the ions as water leaves the mixture. This reaction is also the basis of a test for carbon dioxide (see pp. 116-117).

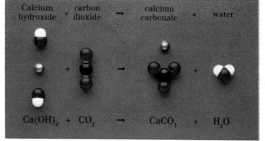

Calcium hydroxide	+	carbon dioxide	→	calcium carbonate	+	water
$Ca(OH)_2$	+	CO_2	→	$CaCO_3$	+	H_2O

Transition metals

THE TRANSITION METALS MAKE UP MOST of the periodic table (see pp. 74-75). Some of the **elements** are very familiar – for example, gold and silver are used in jewelry, copper is used in electrical wiring and water pipes, and tungsten forms the filaments of incandescent light bulbs. **Transition metals** share many properties – for example, they all have more than one **oxidation number**. In **compounds**, chromium commonly has oxidation numbers of +2, +3, or +6. Like most transition metals, it forms colored **ions** in **solution**, such as the chromate(VI) and the dichromate(VI) ions. Copper also exhibits typical transition metal behavior – it forms brightly colored compounds and **complex ions**. Perhaps the most important of the transition metals is iron. It is the most widely used of all metals, and is usually **alloyed** with precise amounts of carbon and other elements to form steel. Around 760 million tons of steel are produced per year worldwide, most of it by the basic oxygen process. Chromium is used in stainless steel alloys, and as a shiny protective plating on other metals.

POSITION IN THE PERIODIC TABLE

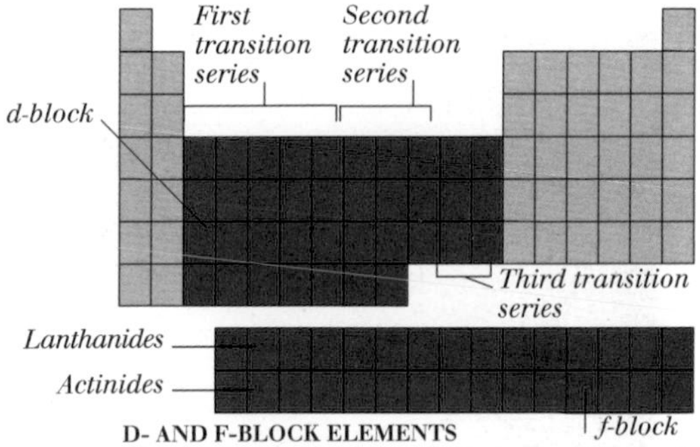

First transition series

Second transition series

d-block

Third transition series

Lanthanides

Actinides

D- AND F-BLOCK ELEMENTS
Most of the transition metals lie in the d-block of the periodic table. The lanthanides and actinides, in the f-block, are also transition metals.

f-block

THREE D-BLOCK TRANSITION METALS

Gold is very unreactive

Silver compounds are used in photographic film

Platinum is often used as a catalyst

GOLD SILVER PLATINUM

COPPER – A TRANSITION METAL

Copper(II) hydroxide can be prepared by adding a strong alkali to copper(II) salts

COPPER(II) HYDROXIDE

Copper(II) oxide, CuO, is used as a catalyst in a number of reactions

COPPER(II) OXIDE

COPPER(II) NITRATE
Copper(II) nitrate is hygroscopic, which means that it absorbs water from the air

THREE TRANSITION METAL COMPOUNDS

Like many chromium compounds, chromium(III) oxide, Cr_2O_3, is used as a pigment

CHROMIUM(III) OXIDE

COMPOUNDS OF COPPER
Like most of the transition metals, copper forms brightly colored compounds. All of the compounds shown here are of copper(II), and they all contain the ion Cu^{2+}.

Chromium(VI) oxide, CrO_3, is highly poisonous

CHROMIUM(VI) OXIDE

This form of lead(II) oxide is called litharge

LEAD(II) OXIDE

Copper(II) carbonate contains the carbonate radical, CO_3^{2-}

COPPER(II) CARBONATE

This blue-green sample of copper(II) chloride contains water of crystallization

COPPER(II) CHLORIDE

Red-brown copper turnings

Copper was one of the first metals to be used by humans

COPPER METAL

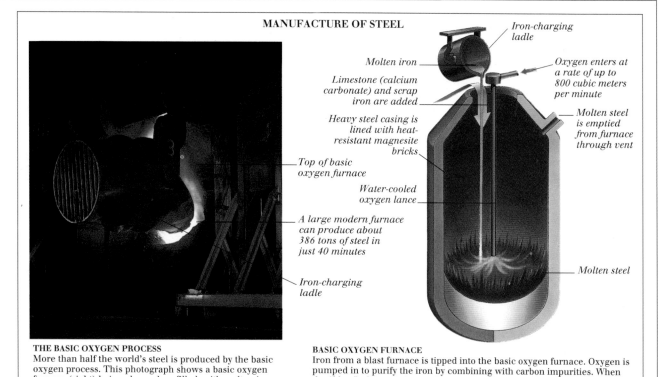

MANUFACTURE OF STEEL

Iron-charging ladle

Molten iron

Oxygen enters at a rate of up to 800 cubic meters per minute

Limestone (calcium carbonate) and scrap iron are added

Molten steel is emptied from furnace through vent

Heavy steel casing is lined with heat-resistant magnesite bricks

Top of basic oxygen furnace

Water-cooled oxygen lance

A large modern furnace can produce about 386 tons of steel in just 40 minutes

Molten steel

Iron-charging ladle

THE BASIC OXYGEN PROCESS
More than half the world's steel is produced by the basic oxygen process. This photograph shows a basic oxygen furnace (right) being charged, or filled, with molten iron.

BASIC OXYGEN FURNACE
Iron from a blast furnace is tipped into the basic oxygen furnace. Oxygen is pumped in to purify the iron by combining with carbon impurities. When the "blow" of oxygen is complete, the furnace is tilted to empty the steel.

CHROMATE IONS IN A REVERSIBLE REACTION

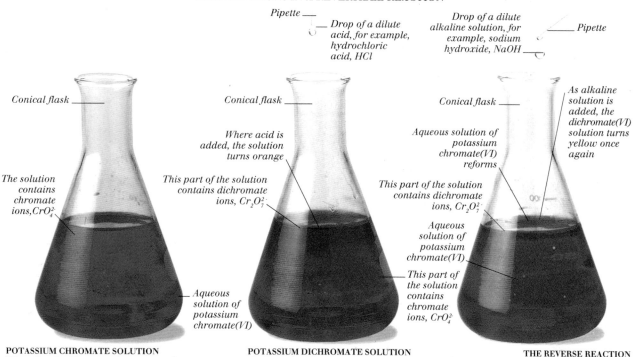

Pipette

Drop of a dilute acid, for example, hydrochloric acid, HCl

Drop of a dilute alkaline solution, for example, sodium hydroxide, NaOH

Pipette

Conical flask

The solution contains chromate ions, CrO_4^{2-}

Conical flask

Where acid is added, the solution turns orange

This part of the solution contains dichromate ions, $Cr_2O_7^{2-}$

Aqueous solution of potassium chromate(VI)

Conical flask

Aqueous solution of potassium chromate(VI) reforms

This part of the solution contains dichromate ions, $Cr_2O_7^{2-}$

Aqueous solution of potassium chromate(VI)

This part of the solution contains chromate ions, CrO_4^{2-}

As alkaline solution is added, the dichromate(VI) solution turns yellow once again

POTASSIUM CHROMATE SOLUTION
When dissolved in water, the compound potassium chromate(VI), K_2CrO_4, has a bright yellow color. Chromium in the compound has an oxidation number of +6.

POTASSIUM DICHROMATE SOLUTION
Adding an **acid** to the solution moves the position of the **equilibrium**. Two chromate(VI) ions combine to produce the dichromate(VI) ion, $Cr_2O_7^{2-}$, and water.

THE REVERSE REACTION
The addition of more water or an **alkaline** solution will push the **reversible reaction** in the direction of the original **reactants**. A yellow solution of chromate(VI) ions forms once more.

Carbon, silicon, and tin

GROUP 14 OF THE periodic table (see pp. 74-75) contains the
elements carbon, silicon, and tin. Carbon is a nonmetal that
is the basis of **organic** chemistry (see pp. 112-115). It occurs
in three distinct forms, or **allotropes**. In the most recently
discovered of these, called the fullerenes, carbon **atoms** join
together in a hollow spherical cage. The other, more familiar,
allotropes of carbon are graphite and diamond. All of the
elements in group 14 form sp **hybrid orbitals** (see p. 79). In
particular, sp^3 hybrid orbitals give a tetrahedral structure to many
of the **compounds** of these elements. Silicon is a semimetal that is
used in electronic components. It is found naturally in many types
of rocks, including quartz, which consists of silicon (IV) oxide.
Quartz is the main constituent of sand, which is used to make
glass. Tin is a metallic element. It is not very useful in its pure
form, because it is soft and weak. However, combined with other
metals, it forms useful **alloys**, such as solder and bronze.

POSITION IN THE PERIODIC TABLE

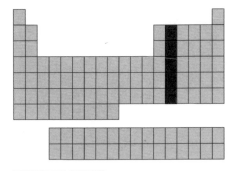

GROUP 14 ELEMENTS
Group 14 of the periodic table consists of (top to
bottom): carbon(C), silicon (Si), germanium (Ge),
tin (Sn), and lead (Pb).

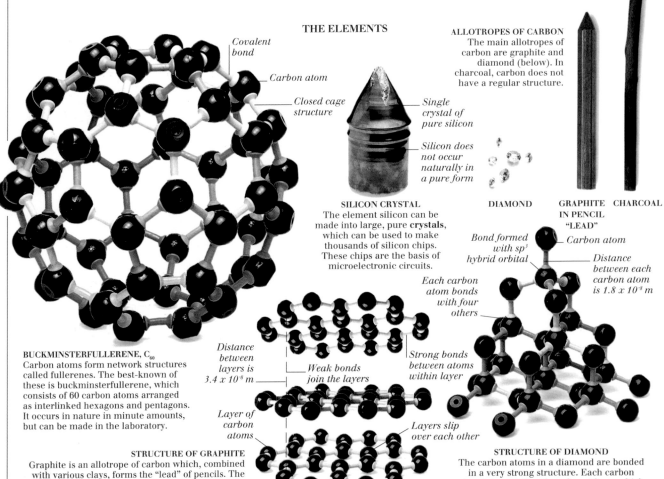

THE ELEMENTS

Covalent bond

Carbon atom

Closed cage structure

ALLOTROPES OF CARBON
The main allotropes of
carbon are graphite and
diamond (below). In
charcoal, carbon does not
have a regular structure.

Single crystal of pure silicon

Silicon does not occur naturally in a pure form

SILICON CRYSTAL
The element silicon can be
made into large, pure **crystals**,
which can be used to make
thousands of silicon chips.
These chips are the basis of
microelectronic circuits.

DIAMOND

GRAPHITE IN PENCIL "LEAD"

CHARCOAL

Bond formed with sp^3 hybrid orbital

Carbon atom

Distance between each carbon atom is 1.8×10^{-8} m

Each carbon atom bonds with four others

BUCKMINSTERFULLERENE, C_{60}
Carbon atoms form network structures
called fullerenes. The best-known of
these is buckminsterfullerene, which
consists of 60 carbon atoms arranged
as interlinked hexagons and pentagons.
It occurs in nature in minute amounts,
but can be made in the laboratory.

Distance
between
layers is
3.4×10^{-8} m

Weak bonds
join the layers

Strong bonds
between atoms
within layer

Layer of
carbon
atoms

Layers slip
over each other

STRUCTURE OF GRAPHITE
Graphite is an allotrope of carbon which, combined
with various clays, forms the "lead" of pencils. The
carbon atoms in graphite form layers that are loosely
bound together, and slip easily over each other.

STRUCTURE OF DIAMOND
The carbon atoms in a diamond are bonded
in a very strong structure. Each carbon
atom is bound directly to four others, which
sit at the corners of a tetrahedron.

SP³ HYBRIDIZATION

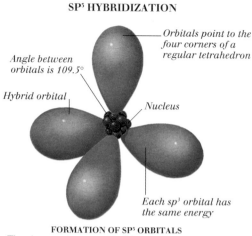

Orbitals point to the four corners of a regular tetrahedron

Angle between orbitals is 109.5°

Hybrid orbital

Nucleus

Each sp³ orbital has the same energy

FORMATION OF SP³ ORBITALS
The elements in group 14 of the periodic table have one s- and three p-orbitals in their outer **electron shells**. These combine to form four sp³ hybrid orbitals in many of the compounds of the elements.

QUARTZ AND GLASS

Quartz crystal

Pure quartz is clear

QUARTZ
Quartz is the most abundant rock type on Earth. It consists mainly of the compound silicon(IV) oxide.

GLASS
Glass is made from molten sand, which consists mainly of quartz (above). Sodium and calcium **salts** are added to lower the melting point of the sand. The glass can be colored by adding impurities such as barium carbonate and iron(III) oxide.

BROWN GLASS BOTTLE

GREEN GLASS BOTTLE

Sodium carbonate lowers the melting point of sand, but makes the glass soluble in water

Calcium carbonate lowers the melting point of sand without making the glass soluble in water

Sand consists of grains of quartz

Barium carbonate gives glass a brown color

Iron(III) oxide gives glass a green color

SODIUM CARBONATE

CALCIUM CARBONATE

SAND (MAINLY QUARTZ)

BARIUM CARBONATE

IRON(III) OXIDE

ALLOYS OF TIN

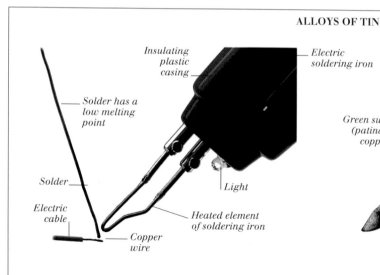

Insulating plastic casing

Electric soldering iron

Solder has a low melting point

Bronze is an alloy of copper and tin

Green surface layer (patina) forms as copper oxidizes

Solder

Light

Electric cable

Heated element of soldering iron

Copper wire

Ancient bronze statue of a horse

SOLDER
The most convenient way to connect wires and components permanently in electric circuits is to use solder. Solder is a soft alloy of tin and lead that has a low melting point (200-300°C).

BRONZE
First made about 5,000 years ago, bronze is an alloy of tin and copper (see pp. 102-103). It is easily cast when molten, but very hard-wearing when solidified.

Nitrogen and phosphorus

Nitrogen (N, uppermost) and phosphorus (P) are nonmetals that belong to group 15 of the periodic table.

NITROGEN AND PHOSPHORUS are the two most important **elements** in group 15 of the periodic table (see pp. 74-75). Phosphorus, which is solid at room temperature, occurs in two forms, or **allotropes**, called white and red phosphorus. Nitrogen is a gas at room temperature, and makes up about 78% of air (see pp. 70-71). Fairly pure nitrogen can be prepared in the laboratory by removing oxygen, water vapor, and carbon dioxide from air. By far the most important **compound** of nitrogen is ammonia (see pp. 92-93), of which over 88 million tons are produced each year worldwide. Used in the manufacture of fertilizers, explosives, and nitric acid, ammonia is produced industrially by the Haber process, for which nitrogen and hydrogen are the raw materials. Ammonia forms a positive **ion** called the ammonium ion (NH_4^+) that occurs in **salts**, where it acts like a metal **cation** (see pp. 76-77). Ammonia can be prepared in the laboratory by heating an ammonium salt with an **alkali**, such as calcium hydroxide.

Sticks of white phosphorus

Glass bowl

Water

WHITE PHOSPHORUS

White phosphorus is a white, waxy solid

White phosphorus melts at 44.1°C

Red phosphorus melts at about 600°C

ALLOTROPES OF PHOSPHORUS

There are two common allotropes of phosphorus. White phosphorus reacts violently with air, so it is kept in water, in which it does not dissolve. It changes slowly to the noncrystalline red form, which is chemically less reactive.

RED PHOSPHORUS

Watch glass

Red phosphorus is a red powder at room temperature

PREPARATION OF NITROGEN FROM AIR

Nitrogen is the most abundant gas in the air. Other gases that make up more than 1% of the air are oxygen (about 20%) and water vapor (0-4%). Air is passed through sodium hydroxide **solution**, which dissolves the small amounts of carbon dioxide present. It is then passed through concentrated sulfuric acid to remove water vapor, and, finally, over heated copper metal to remove oxygen. The result is almost pure nitrogen.

Rubber stopper

Clamp

Glass tube

Delivery tube

Nitrogen is an invisible gas at room temperature

Hot copper turnings combine with oxygen in the air to form copper(II) oxide

Turnings of copper metal

Air is pumped slowly through the apparatus from this glass tube

Gas flame heats the copper turnings

Gas sample will still contain small amounts of noble gases, such as argon

Gas displaces water from boiling tube

Almost pure nitrogen

Rubber stopper

Round-bottomed flask

Air is dried by the sulfuric acid

Solution of sodium hydroxide

Rubber stopper

Concentrated sulfuric acid

Bunsen burner

Air hole open to give hot blue flame

Bubbles of gas

Water

Delivery tube is bent

Upturned boiling tube collects gas

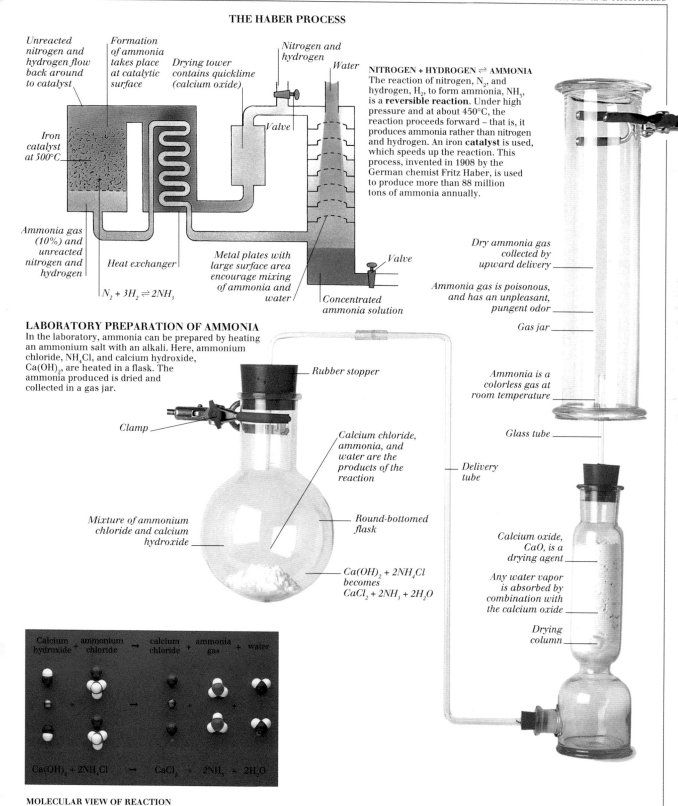

THE HABER PROCESS

Unreacted nitrogen and hydrogen flow back around to catalyst

Formation of ammonia takes place at catalytic surface

Drying tower contains quicklime (calcium oxide)

Nitrogen and hydrogen

Water

Iron catalyst at 500°C

Valve

NITROGEN + HYDROGEN ⇌ AMMONIA
The reaction of nitrogen, N_2, and hydrogen, H_2, to form ammonia, NH_3, is a **reversible reaction**. Under high pressure and at about 450°C, the reaction proceeds forward – that is, it produces ammonia rather than nitrogen and hydrogen. An iron **catalyst** is used, which speeds up the reaction. This process, invented in 1908 by the German chemist Fritz Haber, is used to produce more than 88 million tons of ammonia annually.

Ammonia gas (10%) and unreacted nitrogen and hydrogen

Heat exchanger

Metal plates with large surface area encourage mixing of ammonia and water

Valve

Concentrated ammonia solution

$$N_2 + 3H_2 \rightleftharpoons 2NH_3$$

Dry ammonia gas collected by upward delivery

Ammonia gas is poisonous, and has an unpleasant, pungent odor

Gas jar

LABORATORY PREPARATION OF AMMONIA
In the laboratory, ammonia can be prepared by heating an ammonium salt with an alkali. Here, ammonium chloride, NH_4Cl, and calcium hydroxide, $Ca(OH)_2$, are heated in a flask. The ammonia produced is dried and collected in a gas jar.

Rubber stopper

Clamp

Calcium chloride, ammonia, and water are the products of the reaction

Ammonia is a colorless gas at room temperature

Glass tube

Delivery tube

Mixture of ammonium chloride and calcium hydroxide

Round-bottomed flask

$Ca(OH)_2 + 2NH_4Cl$ becomes
$CaCl_2 + 2NH_3 + 2H_2O$

Calcium oxide, CaO, is a drying agent

Any water vapor is absorbed by combination with the calcium oxide

Drying column

Calcium hydroxide	+	ammonium chloride	→	calcium chloride	+	ammonia gas	+	water

$Ca(OH)_2 + 2NH_4Cl \rightarrow CaCl_2 + 2NH_3 + 2H_2O$

MOLECULAR VIEW OF REACTION

Oxygen and sulfur

THE TWO MOST IMPORTANT **elements** in group 16 of the periodic table are oxygen and sulfur. Oxygen, a gas at **STP**, is vital to life, and is one of the most abundant elements on Earth. It makes up 21% by volume of dry air (see pp. 70-71). In the laboratory, oxygen is easily prepared by the **decomposition** of hydrogen peroxide. Oxygen is involved in **burning** – it relights a glowing wooden splint, and this is one test for the gas. Sulfur occurs in several different structural forms, known as **allotropes**. The most stable allotrope at room temperature is rhombic sulfur, in which sulfur exists in the form of rings, each containing eight atoms. One important **compound** of sulfur is hydrogen sulfide. It has a pungent smell like that of rotten eggs, and can be prepared by reacting dilute **acids** with metal sulfides. Sodium thiosulfate is another important sulfur compound, used as a fixative in the development of photographic images.

POSITION IN THE PERIODIC TABLE

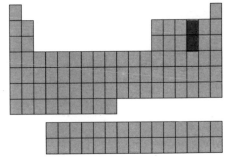

GROUP 16 ELEMENTS
Oxygen (top) and sulfur are in group 16 of the periodic table. They are both nonmetallic elements, which form a wide range of compounds.

TEST FOR OXYGEN

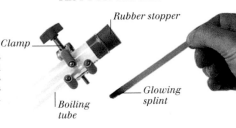

Rubber stopper

Clamp

Boiling tube

Glowing splint

OXYGEN GAS
A tube full of oxygen gas, produced in the reaction on the left, is sealed. A previously lit splint is extinguished, but left glowing.

Oxygen gas

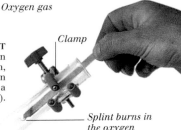

Clamp

RELIT SPLINT
The glowing splint (above) relights in the oxygen. Burning, or combustion, is defined as a rapid combination of a substance with oxygen. It is a **redox reaction** (see pp. 82-83).

Boiling tube

Splint burns in the oxygen

PREPARATION OF OXYGEN

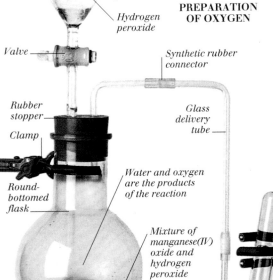

Separating funnel

Hydrogen peroxide

Valve

Rubber stopper

Clamp

Round-bottomed flask

Synthetic rubber connector

Glass delivery tube

Water and oxygen are the products of the reaction

Mixture of manganese(IV) oxide and hydrogen peroxide

Oxygen gas fills the boiling tube

Clamp

Upturned boiling tube

Glass dish

Water

CATALYTIC DECOMPOSITION OF HYDROGEN PEROXIDE
The decomposition of hydrogen peroxide to oxygen and water normally occurs very slowly. The addition of a **catalyst** of manganese(IV) oxide to hydrogen peroxide speeds up the reaction.

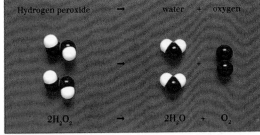

Hydrogen peroxide → water + oxygen

$2H_2O_2$ → $2H_2O$ + O_2

MOLECULAR VIEW
Hydrogen peroxide exists as **molecules**, each consisting of two hydrogen and two oxygen **atoms**. Every two molecules of hydrogen peroxide produce one molecule of oxygen. Water is the other **product**.

ALLOTROPES OF SULFUR

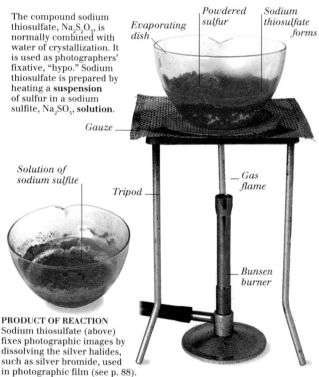

POWDERED SULFUR
In the laboratory, sulfur is usually supplied as a powder. Each grain of the powder is a crystal of rhombic sulfur (right).

Crystal of rhombic sulfur

RHOMBIC (α) SULFUR
The most stable allotrope of sulfur at room temperature is rhombic sulfur, also known as alpha (α) sulfur.

Plastic sulfur forms crystals on cooling

Watch glass

PLASTIC SULFUR
If molten sulfur is cooled by plunging it into cold water, yellow or brown plastic sulfur, which is noncrystalline, forms.

Crystals formed by rapidly cooling molten sulfur

MONOCLINIC (β) SULFUR
Needle-like crystals of monoclinic (β, or beta) sulfur slowly revert to the rhombic form at temperatures below 95.5°C (203.9°F).

Atom of sulfur

Covalent bond

SULFUR RINGS
Monoclinic and rhombic sulfur both contain crown-shaped molecules of eight sulfur atoms.

LABORATORY PREPARATION OF HYDROGEN SULFIDE

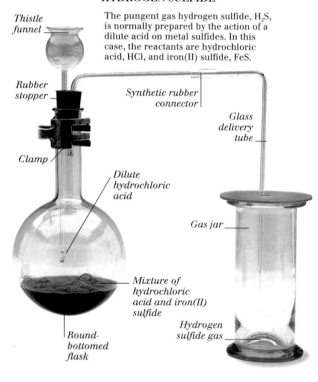

The pungent gas hydrogen sulfide, H_2S, is normally prepared by the action of a dilute acid on metal sulfides. In this case, the reactants are hydrochloric acid, HCl, and iron(II) sulfide, FeS.

Thistle funnel

Rubber stopper

Synthetic rubber connector

Clamp

Glass delivery tube

Dilute hydrochloric acid

Gas jar

Mixture of hydrochloric acid and iron(II) sulfide

Round-bottomed flask

Hydrogen sulfide gas

PREPARATION OF SODIUM THIOSULFATE

The compound sodium thiosulfate, $Na_2S_2O_3$, is normally combined with water of crystallization. It is used as photographers' fixative, "hypo." Sodium thiosulfate is prepared by heating a **suspension** of sulfur in a sodium sulfite, Na_2SO_3, **solution**.

Evaporating dish

Powdered sulfur

Sodium thiosulfate forms

Gauze

Solution of sodium sulfite

Gas flame

Tripod

Bunsen burner

PRODUCT OF REACTION
Sodium thiosulfate (above) fixes photographic images by dissolving the silver halides, such as silver bromide, used in photographic film (see p. 88).

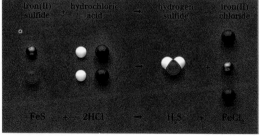

MOLECULAR VIEW
Hydrogen ions in hydrochloric acid combine with the sulfur from iron(II) sulfide. Hydrogen sulfide molecules have a similar shape to water molecules (see p. 68).

MOLECULAR VIEW
Sulfur in the sulfite ion has an **oxidation number** of +4. In the thiosulfate ion produced by the reaction above, sulfur(IV) has been **oxidized** to sulfur(VI), while elemental sulfur has been **reduced** to an oxidation state of -2.

The halogens

THE ELEMENTS OF GROUP 17 of the periodic table (see pp. 74-75) are called the halogens. **Atoms** of these **elements** are just one **electron** short of a full outer **electron shell**. Halogen atoms easily gain single electrons, forming singly charged halide **anions** such as the fluoride **ion**, F⁻. This makes the elements in this group highly **reactive** – some halogens will even react with the **noble gases** under extreme conditions. Chlorine, the most important halogen, is a greenish yellow **diatomic** gas at room temperature. Chlorine can be prepared in the laboratory by the **oxidation** of hydrochloric acid. Small amounts of chlorine are added to water in swimming pools, and to some water supplies, to kill bacteria. Simple tests may be used to measure the amount of dissolved chlorine. If the **concentration** of chlorine is too high, it can endanger human health – if it is too low, it might not be effective. One important chlorine **compound** is sodium chlorate(I), the main ingredient of domestic bleach. Other halogen compounds include **CFCs** (chlorofluorocarbons). CFCs deplete, or break down, the ozone layer in the upper atmosphere, allowing harmful radiation from the Sun to reach the Earth's surface.

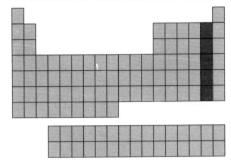

POSITION IN THE PERIODIC TABLE

GROUP 17 ELEMENTS
The halogens form group 17 of the periodic table. They are (top to bottom): fluorine (F), chlorine (Cl), bromine (Br), iodine (I), and astatine (At).

PREPARATION OF CHLORINE

Chlorine gas, Cl_2, is prepared in the laboratory by the oxidation of hydrochloric acid, HCl, using manganese(IV) oxide, MnO_2. The chlorine produced contains some water vapor, but is dried by passing it through concentrated sulfuric acid, H_2SO_4. In order to prevent this acid being sucked back into the reaction vessel, an empty dreschel bottle is placed between the acid bottle and the vessel to act as an anti-suck-back device (see p. 85). The dry gas is collected in a gas jar. Chlorine gas is poisonous.

BROMINE AND IODINE

The element bromine is a red liquid at room temperature, though it vaporizes easily, producing a brown vapor. Iodine is a violet solid at room temperature, which sublimes (turns to vapor without passing through a liquid phase) when warmed.

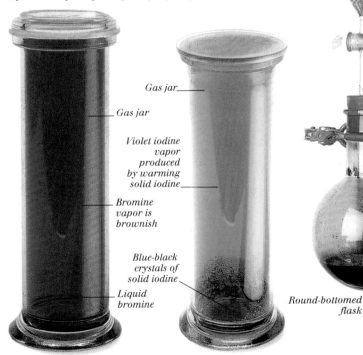

Separating funnel

Concentrated hydrochloric acid

Tap

Delivery tube

Rubber stopper

Clamp

Delivery tube

Concentrated sulfuric acid (drying agent)

Bubble of chlorine gas

Gas jar

Gas jar

Violet iodine vapor produced by warming solid iodine

Bromine vapor is brownish

Blue-black crystals of solid iodine

Liquid bromine

Round-bottomed flask

Mixture of manganese(IV) oxide and hydrochloric acid

Dreschel bottle acts as an anti-suck-back device

Dreschel bottle

BROMINE

IODINE

CHLORINE IN WATER

Scale shows that water contains about 0.6 milligrams per liter of chlorine

10 ml of the water is added to the comparitor

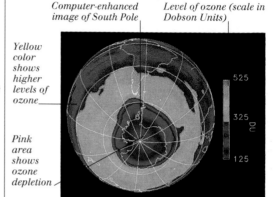

250 ml beaker

Water sample

Test kit

Color scale for comparison

Water sample becomes colored when tablet is dissolved

Clear plastic comparitor

Test tablets

CHLORINE TEST KIT
Water can be tested for its chlorine concentration using kits such as this one. Chlorine in the water forms colored **complex ions** when a tablet is added, and the intensity of the color reveals the chlorine concentration.

BLEACHING

Denim contains vegetable-based pigments that are normally blue

Sodium hypochlorite solution has begun to bleach the denim

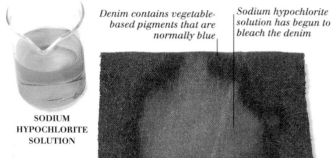

SODIUM HYPOCHLORITE SOLUTION

Gas jar

BLEACHING ACTION OF SODIUM HYPOCHLORITE
Sodium hypochlorite, NaOCl, is an industrially important chlorine compound that is a strong oxidizing agent. It bleaches pigments by giving up its oxygen to them, making them colorless.

Chlorine is a greenish yellow gas at room temperature

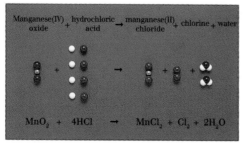

Manganese(IV) oxide + hydrochloric acid → manganese(II) chloride + chlorine + water

$$MnO_2 + 4HCl \rightarrow MnCl_2 + Cl_2 + 2H_2O$$

MOLECULAR VIEW
Four units of the hydrochloric acid are oxidized by each **molecule** of manganese(IV) oxide. The manganese(IV) is **reduced** to manganese(II).

OZONE DEPLETION REACTIONS
CFCs, synthetic **organic** compounds containing chlorine and fluorine atoms, have been used in packaging and some aerosol cans. Released into the atmosphere, CFCs lose chlorine atoms. These atoms **catalyze** reactions that damage the ozone layer, which shields the Earth from harmful solar radiation.

Computer-enhanced image of South Pole

Level of ozone (scale in Dobson Units)

Yellow color shows higher levels of ozone

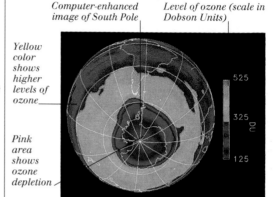

525

325

125

DU

Pink area shows ozone depletion

DEPLETION OF THE OZONE LAYER

Ozone molecule, O_3

Chlorine atom released from CFC

Ozone reacts with chlorine to form chlorine monoxide and oxygen

CHLORINE AND OZONE

Chlorine monoxide and oxygen are the products of the first reaction

Oxygen molecule, O_2

Chlorine monoxide molecule, ClO

CHLORINE MONOXIDE AND OXYGEN

Chlorine monoxide molecule, ClO, from previous reaction

Individual oxygen atoms, O, are present in the upper atmosphere

Oxygen atom reacts with the chlorine monoxide to form oxygen molecule

CHLORINE MONOXIDE AND OXYGEN

Chlorine atom left behind from chlorine monoxide molecule

Overall, chlorine atom remains unchanged and is therefore a catalyst

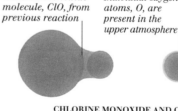

Oxygen molecule, O_2

CHLORINE AND OXYGEN

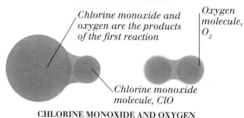

Organic chemistry 1

ORGANIC CHEMISTRY IS THE study of carbon **compounds**, although it normally excludes carbon dioxide and **salts** such as calcium carbonate (see pp. 86-87). There are more carbon-based compounds than compounds based on all the other **elements** put together. This is because carbon **atoms** easily bond to each other, forming long chains and rings that include single bonds, double bonds (see p. 79), and triple bonds. **Hydrocarbons** are **molecules** containing only carbon and hydrogen. There are three main families of hydrocarbons based on carbon chains, called **alkanes**, **alkenes**, and **alkynes** (right). Ethyne is the simplest alkyne, with two carbon atoms. Most carbon compounds occur in different structural forms, or **isomers**. For example, the hydrocarbon butene has two isomers that differ in the position of the double bond. Crude oil is a **mixture** (see pp. 70-71) of long-chain hydrocarbons, which is separated industrially in a fractionating tower, and cracked (heated with a **catalyst**) to produce more useful short-chain compounds.

Particles of soot

Ethyne burns in a flame, producing water vapor and carbon dioxide

PREPARATION OF ETHYNE

Ethyne, C_2H_2, a gas at room temperature, is the simplest alkyne. It is prepared by the **exothermic** reaction of water with calcium carbide, CaC_2. Like all hydrocarbons, ethyne **burns** to produce water and carbon dioxide. Soot (pure carbon) may be formed due to incomplete burning.

Ethyne is a colorless gas

Glass tube

Calcium carbide, CaC_2, is a brown ionic solid

Watch glass

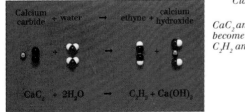

CALCIUM CARBIDE
Calcium carbide, CaC_2, is an **ionic** solid that contains the Ca^{2+} and C_2^{2-} ions. In ethyne, the **product** of the reaction, carbon and hydrogen atoms are **covalently bound**.

Rubber stopper

Ring stand

Boiling tube

Clamp

CaC_2 and H_2O become C_2H_2 and $Ca(OH)_2$

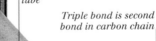

Calcium carbide + water → ethyne + calcium hydroxide

$$CaC_2 + 2H_2O \rightarrow C_2H_2 + Ca(OH)_2$$

MOLECULAR VIEW
Carbon atoms from calcium carbide combine with hydrogen atoms from water molecules to form ethyne.

FAMILIES OF HYDROCARBONS
Alkanes have only single bonds in the chain of carbon atoms. Alkenes have at least one double bond in the chain, while alkynes have a triple bond.

ALKANES

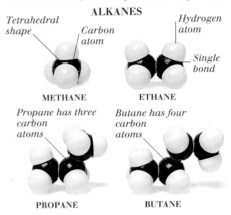

Tetrahedral shape

Carbon atom

Hydrogen atom

Single bond

METHANE   ETHANE

Propane has three carbon atoms

Butane has four carbon atoms

PROPANE   BUTANE

ALKENES

Ethene has two carbon atoms

Double bond

Propene has three carbon atoms

ETHENE   PROPENE

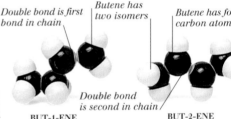

Double bond is first bond in chain

Butene has two isomers

Butene has four carbon atoms

Double bond is second in chain

BUT-1-ENE   BUT-2-ENE

ALKYNES

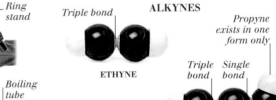

Triple bond

Propyne exists in one form only

ETHYNE

Triple bond   *Single bond*

Triple bond is second bond in carbon chain

PROPYNE

Butyne has two isomers

BUT-2-YNE

Triple bond is first bond in carbon chain

BUT-1-YNE

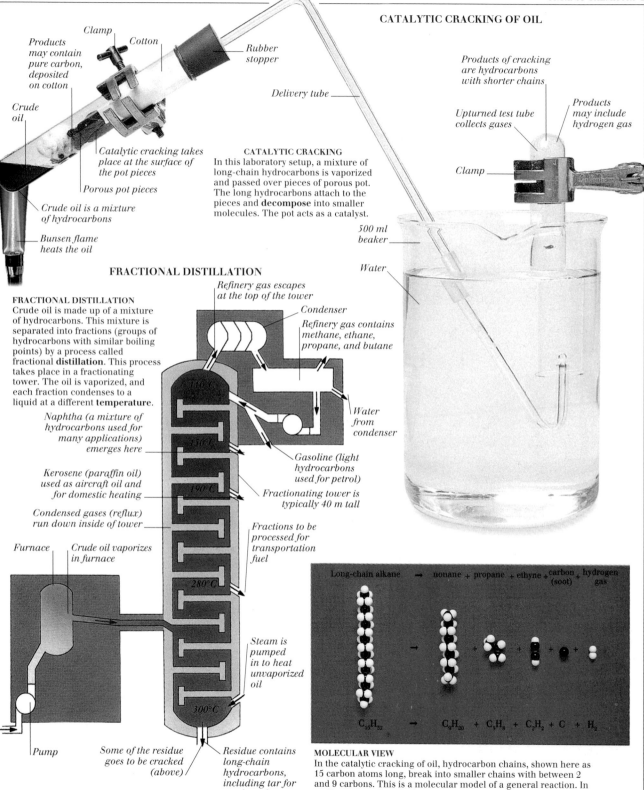

CATALYTIC CRACKING OF OIL

Products may contain pure carbon, deposited on cotton

Clamp

Cotton

Rubber stopper

Delivery tube

Crude oil

Catalytic cracking takes place at the surface of the pot pieces

Porous pot pieces

Crude oil is a mixture of hydrocarbons

Bunsen flame heats the oil

CATALYTIC CRACKING
In this laboratory setup, a mixture of long-chain hydrocarbons is vaporized and passed over pieces of porous pot. The long hydrocarbons attach to the pieces and **decompose** into smaller molecules. The pot acts as a catalyst.

Products of cracking are hydrocarbons with shorter chains

Upturned test tube collects gases

Products may include hydrogen gas

Clamp

500 ml beaker

Water

FRACTIONAL DISTILLATION

FRACTIONAL DISTILLATION
Crude oil is made up of a mixture of hydrocarbons. This mixture is separated into fractions (groups of hydrocarbons with similar boiling points) by a process called fractional **distillation**. This process takes place in a fractionating tower. The oil is vaporized, and each fraction condenses to a liquid at a different **temperature**.

Naphtha (a mixture of hydrocarbons used for many applications) emerges here

Kerosene (paraffin oil) used as aircraft oil and for domestic heating

Condensed gases (reflux) run down inside of tower

Furnace

Crude oil vaporizes in furnace

Pump

Some of the residue goes to be cracked (above)

Refinery gas escapes at the top of the tower

Condenser

Refinery gas contains methane, ethane, propane, and butane

110°C

150°C

190°C

280°C

300°C

Water from condenser

Gasoline (light hydrocarbons used for petrol)

Fractionating tower is typically 40 m tall

Fractions to be processed for transportation fuel

Steam is pumped in to heat unvaporized oil

Residue contains long-chain hydrocarbons, including tar for roads and wax for candles

Long-chain alkane → nonane + propane + ethyne + carbon (soot) + hydrogen gas

$$C_{15}H_{32} \rightarrow C_9H_{20} + C_3H_8 + C_2H_2 + C + H_2$$

MOLECULAR VIEW
In the catalytic cracking of oil, hydrocarbon chains, shown here as 15 carbon atoms long, break into smaller chains with between 2 and 9 carbons. This is a molecular model of a general reaction. In reality, many other similar reactions are also likely to occur.

Organic chemistry 2

THE CHEMISTRY OF CARBON is called **organic** chemistry. Simple organic **molecules** (see pp. 112-113) are based on chains of carbon **atoms**. Carbon atoms are very versatile at bonding, and can form very large and complicated molecules. Small organic molecules often join together to form larger ones. For example, glucose, a simple sugar or monosaccharide, is a small organic molecule. Two saccharide units join to form a disaccharide, such as sucrose. Large numbers of sugar units can join to form polysaccharides such as starch (see p. 89). The process of joining large numbers of identical molecules together is called **polymerization**. The polymers that result are commonplace both in synthetic products and in nature. Plastics, such as nylon and PVC, are polymers, and much more complicated polymers form the basis of life. Hemoglobin is a large organic molecule responsible for carrying oxygen in red blood cells. DNA is a giant molecule that holds the genetic code in all living organisms. This code is created from patterns of four small molecules called bases, which are arranged along the famous double helix structure.

SUCROSE CRYSTALS

Sugars are **carbohydrates**. Sucrose (see p. 89) is the chemical name for ordinary household sugar. In this beaker, **crystals** of sucrose have formed from an **aqueous solution** of household sugar.

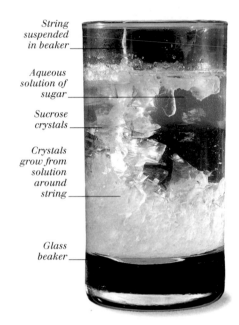

String suspended in beaker

Aqueous solution of sugar

Sucrose crystals

Crystals grow from solution around string

Glass beaker

Glass rod

Nylon drawn out as a long thread

Solution of 1,6-diaminohexane in water

250 ml beaker

Nylon forms where two solutions meet

Layers do not mix because hexane does not dissolve in water

Solution of hexanedioic acid in hexane

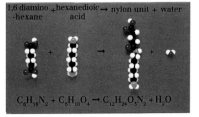

FORMATION OF NYLON

LABORATORY PREPARATION

Nylon is a polymer that is formed from two organic monomers. The form of nylon shown here is made by the synthesis (joining) of the monomers hexanedioic acid and 1,6-diaminohexane.

1,6 diamino-hexane + hexanedioic acid → nylon unit + water

$$C_6H_{16}N_2 + C_6H_{10}O_4 \rightarrow C_{12}H_{24}O_5N_2 + H_2O$$

MOLECULAR VIEW

A unit of nylon is made from one molecule of each monomer (above). Each unit reacts again with one monomer at each end, eventually forming the polymer nylon. A nylon molecule may comprise hundreds of such units.

PLASTICS

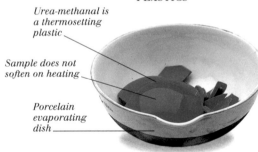

Urea-methanal is a thermosetting plastic

Sample does not soften on heating

Porcelain evaporating dish

THERMOSETTING PLASTICS

Thermosetting plastics are molded when first made, and harden upon cooling. They cannot be softened again by heating.

Polyethylene is a thermoplastic material

Sample softens on heating

Porcelain evaporating dish

THERMOPLASTICS

Some plastics soften on heating. They can be remolded while hot, then allowed to cool and harden. Polyethylene is an example of such a thermoplastic.

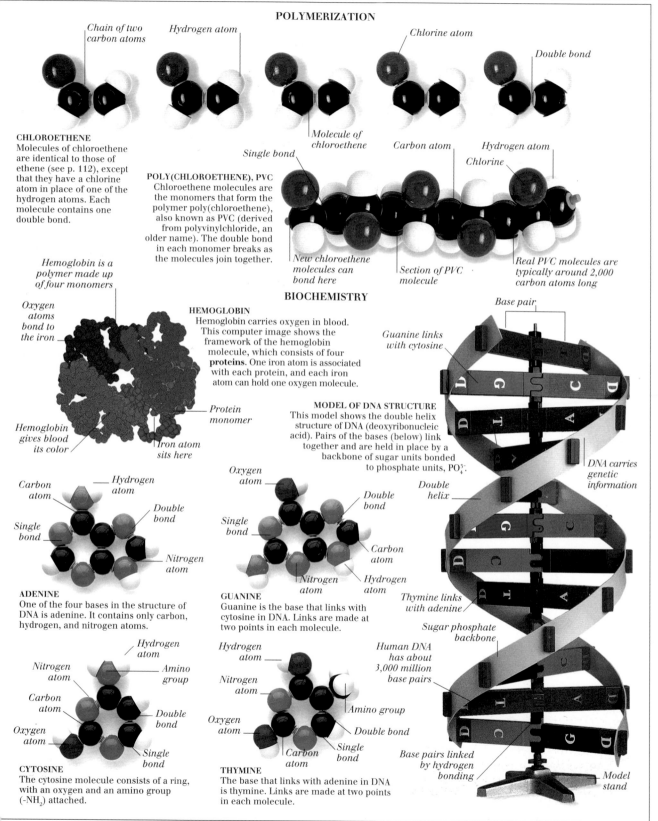

POLYMERIZATION

Chain of two carbon atoms

Hydrogen atom

Chlorine atom

Double bond

Molecule of chloroethene

Single bond

Carbon atom

Hydrogen atom

Chlorine

CHLOROETHENE
Molecules of chloroethene are identical to those of ethene (see p. 112), except that they have a chlorine atom in place of one of the hydrogen atoms. Each molecule contains one double bond.

POLY(CHLOROETHENE), PVC
Chloroethene molecules are the monomers that form the polymer poly(chloroethene), also known as PVC (derived from polyvinylchloride, an older name). The double bond in each monomer breaks as the molecules join together.

New chloroethene molecules can bond here

Section of PVC molecule

Real PVC molecules are typically around 2,000 carbon atoms long

BIOCHEMISTRY

Hemoglobin is a polymer made up of four monomers

Oxygen atoms bond to the iron

HEMOGLOBIN
Hemoglobin carries oxygen in blood. This computer image shows the framework of the hemoglobin molecule, which consists of four **proteins**. One iron atom is associated with each protein, and each iron atom can hold one oxygen molecule.

Hemoglobin gives blood its color

Protein monomer

Iron atom sits here

Base pair

Guanine links with cytosine

MODEL OF DNA STRUCTURE
This model shows the double helix structure of DNA (deoxyribonucleic acid). Pairs of the bases (below) link together and are held in place by a backbone of sugar units bonded to phosphate units, PO_4^{3-}.

Double helix

DNA carries genetic information

Carbon atom

Hydrogen atom

Single bond

Double bond

Nitrogen atom

ADENINE
One of the four bases in the structure of DNA is adenine. It contains only carbon, hydrogen, and nitrogen atoms.

Oxygen atom

Single bond

Double bond

Carbon atom

Nitrogen atom

Hydrogen atom

GUANINE
Guanine is the base that links with cytosine in DNA. Links are made at two points in each molecule.

Thymine links with adenine

Sugar phosphate backbone

Hydrogen atom

Nitrogen atom

Amino group

Carbon atom

Double bond

Oxygen atom

Single bond

CYTOSINE
The cytosine molecule consists of a ring, with an oxygen and an amino group (-NH_2) attached.

Hydrogen atom

Nitrogen atom

Oxygen atom

Amino group

Double bond

Single bond

Carbon atom

THYMINE
The base that links with adenine in DNA is thymine. Links are made at two points in each molecule.

Human DNA has about 3,000 million base pairs

Base pairs linked by hydrogen bonding

Model stand

Chemical analysis

THERE ARE MANY SITUATIONS, from geological surveys to forensic investigations, that call for the chemical analysis of unknown substances. The substances being analyzed may be present only in tiny amounts, and may be **mixtures** of many different **compounds**. Separation techniques such as **chromatography** (see pp. 70-71) are often the starting point in an analysis. Simple laboratory tests may follow – these normally identify one part of a compound at a time. For example, flame tests are used to identify **cations** of metallic **elements** in a compound, and **radicals** may be identified by heating the compound to **decompose** it, thereby releasing signifying gases. Many simple laboratory tests are performed on **aqueous solutions** of the unknown substance. The substance is crushed and dissolved in water, and other **solutions**, such as ammonium hydroxide or silver nitrate, are added. The color of any **precipitate** formed indicates the presence of a specific **ion**. In contrast, mass **spectrometry** is a highly complex but very powerful testing technique. The sample to be tested is vaporized, then ionized. The ions are separated by a strong magnetic field and identified according to their **electric charge** and mass.

FLAME TEST

A sample of an unknown compound is held on the en[...] a platinum wire in a Bunsen burner flame. Specific col[...] in the flame indicate the presence of certain metals.

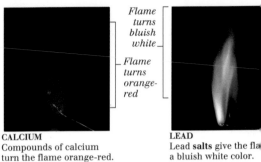

Flame turns bluish white

Flame turns orange-red

CALCIUM
Compounds of calcium turn the flame orange-red.

LEAD
Lead **salts** give the fla[...] a bluish white color.

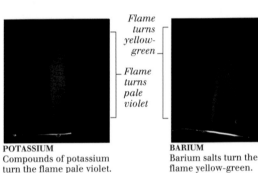

Flame turns yellow-green

Flame turns pale violet

POTASSIUM
Compounds of potassium turn the flame pale violet.

BARIUM
Barium salts turn the flame yellow-green.

TEST FOR A CARBONATE OR HYDROGENCARBONATE

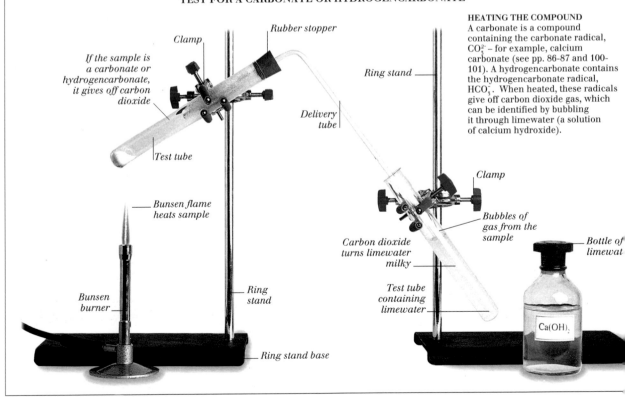

Clamp

Rubber stopper

If the sample is a carbonate or hydrogencarbonate, it gives off carbon dioxide

Test tube

Ring stand

Delivery tube

Bunsen flame heats sample

Bunsen burner

Ring stand

Ring stand base

HEATING THE COMPOUND
A carbonate is a compound containing the carbonate radical, CO_3^{2-} – for example, calcium carbonate (see pp. 86-87 and 100-101). A hydrogencarbonate contains the hydrogencarbonate radical, HCO_3^-. When heated, these radicals give off carbon dioxide gas, which can be identified by bubbling it through limewater (a solution of calcium hydroxide).

Clamp

Bubbles of gas from the sample

Bottle of limewat[...]

Carbon dioxide turns limewater milky

Test tube containing limewater

$Ca(OH)_2$

TESTING FOR CATIONS

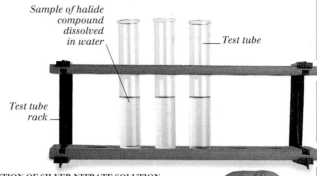

Test tube

Test tube rack

Sample of unknown compound dissolved in water

ACTION OF AMMONIUM HYDROXIDE
Many different tests are used to identify **cations** in an unknown compound. One simple test is carried out on a pure solution of the unknown compound in water. A dilute solution of ammonium hydroxide, NH_4OH, is added to the test solution. If a gelatinous precipitate forms, any cations present can often be identified by the color of the precipitate.

Dropper

Pale blue precipitate that dissolves in excess NH_4OH to give deep blue solution indicates copper(II), Cu^{2+}

Gray-green precipitate indicates iron(II), Fe^{2+}

Red-brown precipitate indicates iron(III), Fe^{3+}

White precipitate may indicate magnesium, lead, zinc, or aluminum cations

Stopper

Bottle of ammonium hydroxide solution

NH_4OH

Test tube   Test tube rack

TEST RESULTS
A few solutions have been tested, and precipitates have formed in the test tubes. From the color of the precipitates, the metal cations present in the samples have been identified.

MASS SPECTROMETER
In a mass spectrometer, the sample to be tested is vaporized, then converted into ions and shot into a curved tube. A magnetic field in the tube deflects those ions with a specific mass and charge into a detector. Changing the magnetic field strength allows a mass spectrum – an analysis of all the ions present – to be built up, from which the the test substance can be accurately identified.

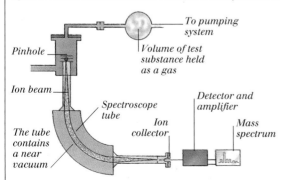

To pumping system

Volume of test substance held as a gas

Pinhole

Ion beam

Spectroscope tube

The tube contains a near vacuum

Ion collector

Detector and amplifier

Mass spectrum

TESTING FOR ANIONS

Sample of halide compound dissolved in water

Test tube

Test tube rack

ACTION OF SILVER NITRATE SOLUTION
Of the many different tests used to identify **anions** in an unknown compound, the addition of aqueous silver nitrate, $AgNO_3$, to an aqueous solution of the compound is often the first step. If halide ions – ions of the halogens (see pp. 110-111) – are present in solution, a colored precipitate forms.

Dropper

White precipitate indicates that the compound contains chloride ions

Pale yellow precipitate indicates that the compound contains bromide ions

Yellow precipitate indicates that the compound contains iodide ions

Bottle of silver nitrate solution

Stopper

$AgNO_3$

Test tube rack   Test tube

TEST RESULTS
Here, solutions of compounds containing ions of the halogens chlorine, iodine, and bromine have been tested. Salts containing ions of the halogens are called halides. Precipitates have formed in the test tubes.

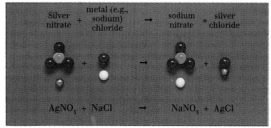

Silver nitrate + metal (e.g., sodium) chloride → sodium nitrate + silver chloride

$AgNO_3 + NaCl$ → $NaNO_3 + AgCl$

MOLECULAR VIEW OF REACTION
A **double decomposition reaction** takes place between silver nitrate and the halide salt in solution, and insoluble silver halides form. Silver halides are used in photography (see p. 88).

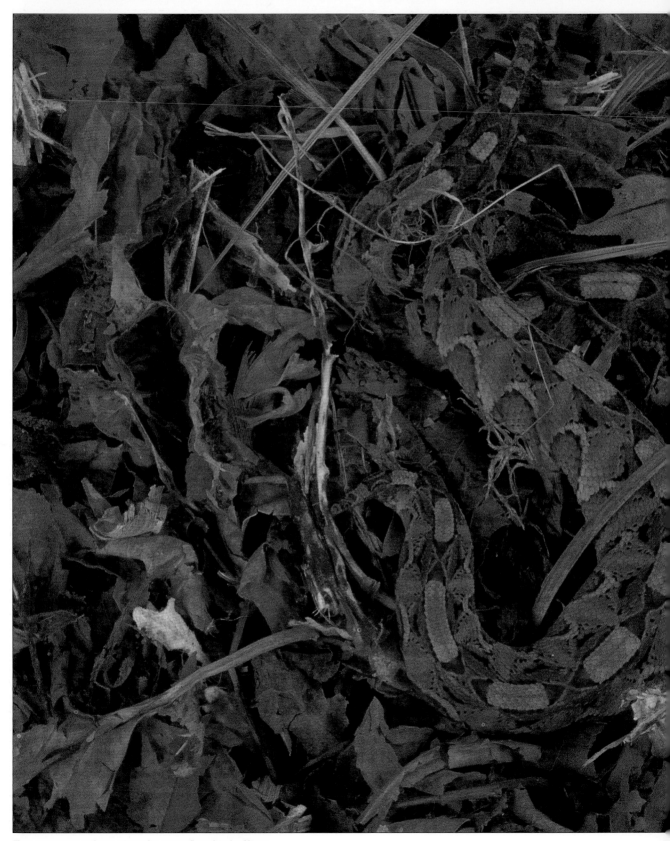

Two venomous gaboon vipers lie camouflaged in leaf litter

Life Sciences and Ecology

Discovering life sciences and ecology 120

Cells and cell structure 122

Cell functions 124

Reproduction and heredity 126

Evolution 128

Classification 1 130

Classification 2 132

Microorganisms 134

Fungi 136

Nonflowering plants 1 138

Nonflowering plants 2 140

Flowering plants 1 142

Flowering plants 2 144

Flowering-plant reproduction 146

Photosynthesis and plant-transport systems .. 148

Echinoderms, sponges, and cnidarians 150

Worms and Mollusks 152

Arthropods 1 154

Arthropods 2 156

Fish 158

Amphibians 160

Reptiles 162

Birds 164

Mammals 166

Ecology 168

Energy flow and food webs 170

Natural cycles 172

Human impact on the environment 174

Discovering life sciences and ecology

L IFE SCIENCE (ALSO CALLED BIOLOGY) is the science of living organisms. Ecology is the study of how living organisms relate to each other and to their environment, which includes nonliving matter. For most of history, the study of biology has been affected by religious or spiritual beliefs, such as the idea that matter becomes living through the influence of some kind of "living force." A more scientific approach to biology has resulted in the modern, more complex understanding of the processes of life.

EARLY STUDIES OF NATURE

Agriculture gave people practical, first-hand knowledge of plants and animals. However, there was little systematic study of living things until the rise of ancient Greece. The most influential Greek thinker was **Aristotle**. He devised a system of animal classification, while one of his pupils, **Theophrastus**, constructed a similar classification of plants. Some parts of Aristotle's work would seem crude by today's standards, but many of his ideas were advanced and played an important role in the development of the modern theory of evolution. For all their careful observation, the ancient Greeks could never have made more than clever guesses about the processes of life. Without microscopes, they could not even begin to grasp the intricacies of cell theory or be aware of the existence of microorganisms.

BIOLOGY AS A SCIENCE

During the Middle Ages, Arab scholars translated the works of Aristotle and others and added a few ideas of their own. The accumulated knowledge reached Europe around the 13th century. This period saw the rise of sciences such as zoology and botany. Comparative anatomy was advanced by Renaissance artists, who studied the muscles, bones, and internal organs of animals and human beings. During the later part of the Renaissance, a school of thought called iatrochemistry looked to chemical reactions to explain the workings of plants and animals. This was the dawn of biochemistry.

THE MICROSCOPE

Biological science was given a boost by the invention of the microscope in the early 17th century. Perhaps the best-known discovery made with a microscope was the existence of microorganisms. It was **Antony van Leeuwenhoek** who first observed single-celled organisms, in the 1670s. About ten years earlier, **Robert Hooke** had observed tiny spaces throughout a sample of cork, which he called "cells." Hooke did not realize that the cell was the basic unit of all living things. Much later, in the 20th century, the electron microscope revealed even smaller structures within cells.

ORIGIN OF SPECIES

As early as the 6th century BC, **Anaximander of Miletus** had proposed that life arose spontaneously in mud. According to Anaximander, the first animals to emerge were spiny fishes, which "transmuted" into other species. This idea remained prominent until the end of the 19th century, when several experiments began to cast doubt upon it. Two areas of study that were important in refuting the idea of spontaneous generation were classification and paleontology (the study of fossils). Modern classification is based on a system devised by **Carolus Linnaeus** during the 1730s. Comparison of species gave weight to the idea that species changed gradually and somehow adapted to their environment. The fossil record supported this idea. **Georges Cuvier** was the first naturalist to show how species change over thousands or millions of years. In the early 1800s, **Jean-Baptiste de Lamarck** suggested that organisms in one generation inherit characteristics from the previous generation. For example, giraffes have long necks because their ancestors had to stretch their necks to reach the treetops. His ideas were were shown to be mistaken by **Charles Darwin** in the 1850s.

18TH CENTURY MICROSCOPE
Microscopes began to open up the world of the miniscule from about the mid-1500s. This microscope was made in London in about 1728. It used the tilted mirror at the bottom to reflect light onto a specimen mounted above it on a glass slide.

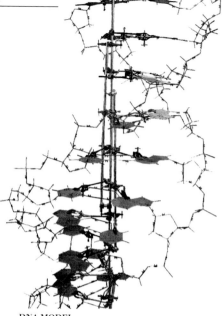

DNA MODEL
This model of DNA was made in the 1950s by
James Watson and **Francis Crick**. It comprises a
large number of repeated structures and represents
the information needed to build and maintain a
living organism, such as a human being.

EVOLUTION AND GENETICS
Darwin's great idea was natural
selection – random variations in species'
characteristics (mutation) coupled with
competition for survival. He also put
forward a more controversial idea – that
humans evolved by natural selection from
apes. For this reason, and because no one
could find a biochemical mechanism for
natural selection, Darwin's ideas were not
accepted at first. The first step to finding
the mechanism behind natural selection
was taken in the 1860s, by **Gregor Mendel**.
Through painstaking experiments,
Mendel founded the science of genetics.
He proposed a unit of heredity, which he
named the gene, and
discovered the rules
by which genes
control inherited
characteristics.
Mendel's work was
not recognized
until about 1900.
By this time, cell
biology was well

developed, but still no one could pinpoint
the biochemical reactions by which
Mendel's gene theory could work.
Biochemistry was the key to genetics.

BIOCHEMISTRY
During the 19th century, the links
between biology and chemistry became
clearer. In the 1840s and 1850s, **Claude
Bernard** laid the foundations of modern
biochemistry during experiments on the
pancreases of rabbits. Around the same
time, scientists realized that the functions
of living things depended upon the
transfer of energy by chemical reactions.
By the 1860s, scientists had realized that
life on Earth depends upon energy from
the Sun. Embryology (the study of
fertilized eggs) also played an important
role in biology during the 19th century.
A biochemical approach to embryology
led eventually to the discovery of the
chemicals involved in Mendel's genetics.
Perhaps the greatest achievement of
this approach was an understanding of
chemicals called nucleic acids, vital to
genetics and the production of proteins
within the cell. The structure of the most
famous nucleic-acid molecule, DNA,
was worked out in 1953. The genes that
Mendel had hypothesized are lengths of
DNA, which passes hereditary information
from generation to generation.

ECOLOGY AND THE ORIGIN OF LIFE
The study of how populations of plants
or animals change is central to ecology.
The factors affecting populations include
famine, disease, and – when applied to
humans – war. Ecologists today use
complicated mathematical models to
analyze populations of plants, animals,
and human beings. The term "ecology"
was coined by German zoologist **Ernst
Haeckel**. He was one of a number of
19th-century scientists who believed that
life originated simply by chance, from
chemicals present on the early Earth.
This idea was supported by several
experiments performed during the 20th
century. An example is the Miller-Urey
experiment, in which complex organic
chemicals were produced from mixtures
of simpler elements and compounds. The
origin of life on this planet remains an
unsolved mystery, as does the possibility
of life elsewhere in the universe.

DARWIN'S EQUIPMENT
Charles Darwin sailed aboard the *Beagle*
from 1832 to 1836. During this period, he
noticed many puzzling features of the
plants and animals he encountered, which
led him to formulate his theory of evolution.
Shown here is a selection of the equipment
he took with him on his voyage.

TIMELINE OF DISCOVERIES

	10,000 BC	The first farmers cultivate crops and domesticate livestock and dogs. They gain much practical knowledge about plants and animals
Anaximander considers life to have begun spontaneously from slime	520 BC	
	AD 350	Aristotle classifies about about 500 species of animals
The first compound microscopes are made. They enable important biological discoveries to be made	1609	
	1667	Antony van Leeuwenhoek observes microorganisms in pond water though his microscope
Nehemiah Grew identifies the different types of tissue in a plant	1682	
	1735	Carolus Linnaeus develops the first modern system of classification for living things
The process of photosynthesis is discovered (but not understood) by Dutch-born biologist **Jan Ingen-Housz**	1779	
	1812	Georges Cuvier attempts a classification of extinct species by studying the fossil record
The cell theory is developed. It states that all living things are made of cells	1839	
	1859	Charles Darwin publishes his theory of evolution by natural selection
Gregor Mendel discovers the laws of genetics	1860	
	1861	Viruses are discovered as a result of sophisticated filtering techniques that remove bacteria from biological samples
The work of Gregor Mendel is rediscovered by three researchers and made public	1900	
	1935	**Hans Krebs** discovers the cycle of energy production in cells. It is named the "Krebs cycle"
Electron microscopes are used for the first time to observe the cell, leading to the discovery of many new organelles (parts of the cell)	1945	
	1953	James Watson and Francis Crick discover the famous double-helix structure of the DNA molecule
Stanley Miller carries out an experiment that shows how important organic chemicals can form in a "soup" of chemicals that were found on the early Earth, indicating the possible origin of life	1954	
	1975	Genetic engineering begins, as American biologists **Seymour Cohen** and **Herbert Boyer** show how the DNA molecule can be cut and rejoined using enzymes
Genes from one animal are successfully transferred into another	1981	
	1984	Alec Jeffreys develops DNA fingerprinting, a method of identifying people from their DNA. It proves useful in forensic science
Human genome project begins in many countries. It aims to map in detail the position of all human genes (collectively known as the genome)	1990	

Cells and cell structure

ALL LIVING ORGANISMS are made of cells, self-contained units of life that require a constant supply of energy to maintain themselves. Some **organisms** consist of a single cell, others are made up of billions of cells. There are two main types of cells: eukaryotic and prokaryotic. Eukaryotic cells are found in plants, animals, fungi, and single-celled organisms called protists (see pp. 134-135). These cells have an outer membrane; a control center, called the nucleus, which contains the cell's operating instructions in the form of **DNA** (deoxyribonucleic acid); and a jellylike matrix, the cytoplasm, in which are found cell components called organelles ("little organs"). Each organelle carries out a specific task, and together organelles maintain the cell as a living entity. Prokaryotic cells, found in bacteria (see pp. 134-135), are small, simple cells that lack a nucleus and most organelles. Animal cells take in food to obtain energy to reproduce and grow (see pp. 124-125). Plant cells use structures called **chloroplasts** to make food for themselves by trapping the Sun's energy (see pp. 148-149).

TYPES OF ANIMAL CELLS

Differences in shape between types of animal cells reflect their individual functions. Thin and flattened **squamous** epithelial cells, for example, form a protective lining inside the mouth and elsewhere. Closely packed, spindle-shaped smooth-muscle cells, found in the gut wall, contract (shorten) to squeeze food along the intestines.

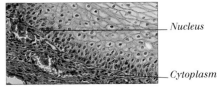

— Nucleus

— Cytoplasm

EPITHELIAL CELLS

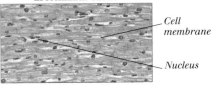

Cell membrane

— Nucleus

SMOOTH MUSCLE CELLS

STRUCTURE OF AN ANIMAL CELL

The typical cell shown below includes features common to all animal cells. The cell is surrounded by a flexible plasma membrane, through which food is taken in to provide the energy that keeps the cell alive. Within the membrane is the nucleus, which controls cell activities, and the cytoplasm, which contains organelles, each of which has a particular function. There are many different types of animal cells.

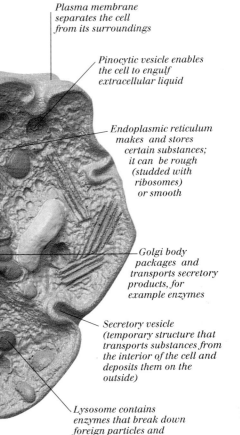

Plasma membrane separates the cell from its surroundings

Pinocytic vesicle enables the cell to engulf extracellular liquid

Mitochondrion carries out aerobic respiration to break down food and release energy

Endoplasmic reticulum makes and stores certain substances; it can be rough (studded with ribosomes) or smooth

Nucleus (control center of the cell)

Nuclear membrane

Golgi body packages and transports secretory products, for example enzymes

Glycogen granules (long term storage form of glucose)

Secretory vesicle (temporary structure that transports substances from the interior of the cell and deposits them on the outside)

Cytoplasm forms a high proportion of the cell's volume

Lysosome contains enzymes that break down foreign particles and damaged cell components

STRUCTURE OF A PLANT CELL

Plant cells share many characteristics with animal cells, but also show three main differences. Firstly, a plant cell is surrounded by a tough cell wall that gives it a definite shape, holds adjacent cells together, and helps to support the plant. Secondly, many plant cells contain organelles, called chloroplasts, which produce energy-rich food for the cell, using sunlight energy in a process called photosynthesis. Thirdly, most plant cells contain a large vacuole – a membrane-bound space filled with watery cell sap that helps cells maintain their shape. These features are illustrated in the typical plant cell shown here.

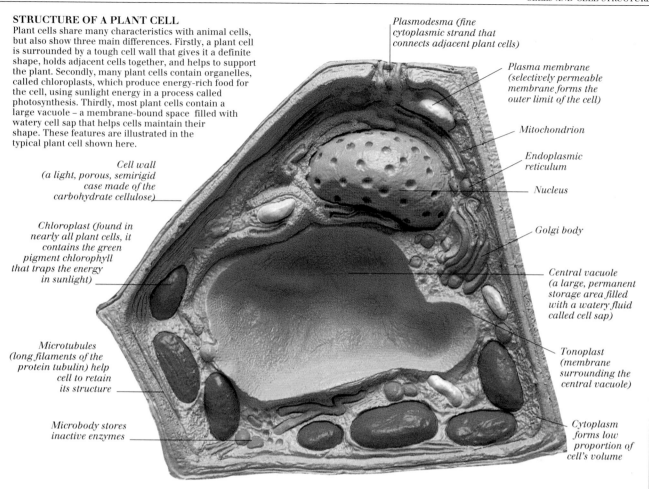

Plasmodesma (fine cytoplasmic strand that connects adjacent plant cells)

Plasma membrane (selectively permeable membrane forms the outer limit of the cell)

Mitochondrion

Endoplasmic reticulum

Nucleus

Golgi body

Central vacuole (a large, permanent storage area filled with a watery fluid called cell sap)

Tonoplast (membrane surrounding the central vacuole)

Cytoplasm forms low proportion of cell's volume

Cell wall (a light, porous, semirigid case made of the carbohydrate cellulose)

Chloroplast (found in nearly all plant cells, it contains the green pigment chlorophyll that traps the energy in sunlight)

Microtubules (long filaments of the protein tubulin) help cell to retain its structure

Microbody stores inactive enzymes

TYPES OF PLANT CELLS

Plants, like animals, contain different types of cells each with their own functions. Xylem cells are hollow, cylindrical, and dead. They carry water and mineral salts from the roots to other parts of the plant. Epidermal cells store food. The ones shown below, from the scale of an onion, store food. They lack chloroplasts because onion bulbs grow underground and do not need to photosynthesize.

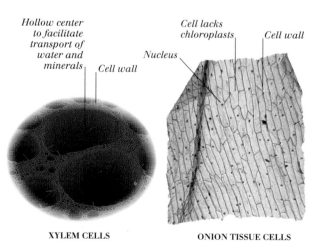

Hollow center to facilitate transport of water and minerals

Cell wall

Cell lacks chloroplasts

Nucleus

Cell wall

XYLEM CELLS

ONION TISSUE CELLS

CELL ORGANELLES

Organelles are tiny cell components. Each type of organelle performs a particular function that contributes to keeping the cell alive. Organelles are under the control of the cell's nucleus. Most are surrounded by a single or a double membrane.

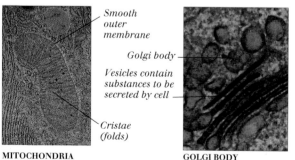

Smooth outer membrane

Golgi body

Vesicles contain substances to be secreted by cell

Cristae (folds)

MITOCHONDRIA
Mitochondria use aerobic respiration to release energy from food molecules (see pp. 124–125). This happens on the cristae – the folds of the inner of the mitochondrion's two membranes.

GOLGI BODY
The Golgi body packages substances that are destined to be secreted by the cell. Small pieces break off and release their contents at the cell's surface.

Cell functions

EVERY CELL IS A LIVING CONTAINER in which hundreds of chemical reactions – known collectively as metabolism – take place. These are accelerated and controlled by **catalysts** called **enzymes**. The activity of each enzyme depends on its shape, which is controlled by the specific sequence of **amino acids** that form its **protein structure**. The instructions that specify the order of amino acids inside each protein are found in the molecules of **DNA** (deoxyribonucleic acid) in the cell's **nucleus**. Strands of **RNA** (ribonucleic acid) copy and carry these instructions, through the nuclear envelope, to the site of protein synthesis in the **cytoplasm**. By controlling protein synthesis, DNA controls enzyme activity and thereby every aspect of cell function. Respiration releases the energy needed for protein synthesis from food and stores it as ATP (adenosine triphosphate) – a molecule that can be readily used by the cell for its energy needs.

METABOLIC REACTIONS IN A CELL

Metabolism is the sum total of all the chemical reactions taking place inside the cells of an organism. These reactions are accelerated, or catalyzed, by biological catalysts called enzymes. **Anabolic reactions** use raw materials taken in by the cell to make more complex molecules, such as the proteins and phospholipids that are used in the construction and metabolic reactions of the cell. Anabolism requires energy, released by **catabolic reactions** such as respiration, which breaks down energy-rich molecules, such as glucose, to release their energy.

ENERGY YIELD OF RESPIRATION

Aerobic respiration requires oxygen, anaerobic respiration does not, both have an initial stage called glycolysis where glucose is broken down into two molecules of **pyruvic acid**. This yields 2 ATP during anaerobic respiration and 8 ATP during aerobic respiration, with a further 30 ATP when pyruvic acid is broken down by the **Krebs cycle** inside **mitochondria**.

PROTEIN SYNTHESIS

Protein synthesis occurs in the cytoplasm, using instructions from DNA in the nucleus. DNA is divided into genes. The bases in each gene are arranged in precise order. The cell uses a genetic code that reads one codon (three bases) at a time. Each codon specifies an amino acid; the sequence of codons specifies the amino acids that make a particular protein. Protein synthesis has two stages: transcription and translation.

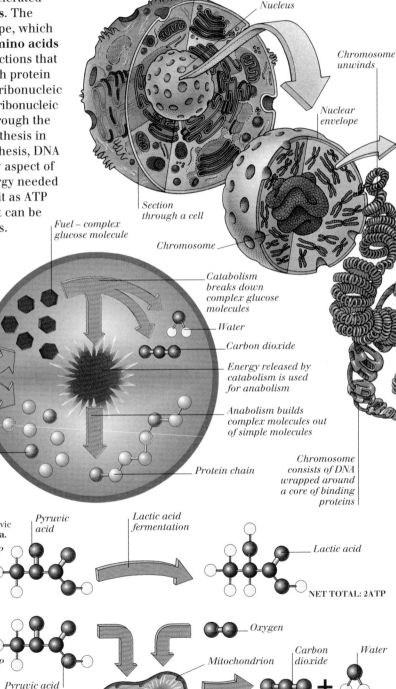

Nucleus

Chromosome unwinds

Nuclear envelope

Section through a cell

Chromosome

Fuel – complex glucose molecule

Catabolism breaks down complex glucose molecules

Water

Carbon dioxide

Energy released by catabolism is used for anabolism

Anabolism builds complex molecules out of simple molecules

Food enters cell from the outside

A single cell

Building molecule – simple amino acid

Protein chain

Chromosome consists of DNA wrapped around a core of binding proteins

Pyruvic acid

Lactic acid fermentation

Lactic acid

NET TOTAL: 2ATP

Glycolysis

2 ATP

ANAEROBIC RESPIRATION

Glucose *Glycolysis*

8 ATP

AEROBIC RESPIRATION

Pyruvic acid

Krebs cycle

Mitochondrion

30 ATP

Oxygen

Carbon dioxide *Water*

NET TOTAL: 38ATP

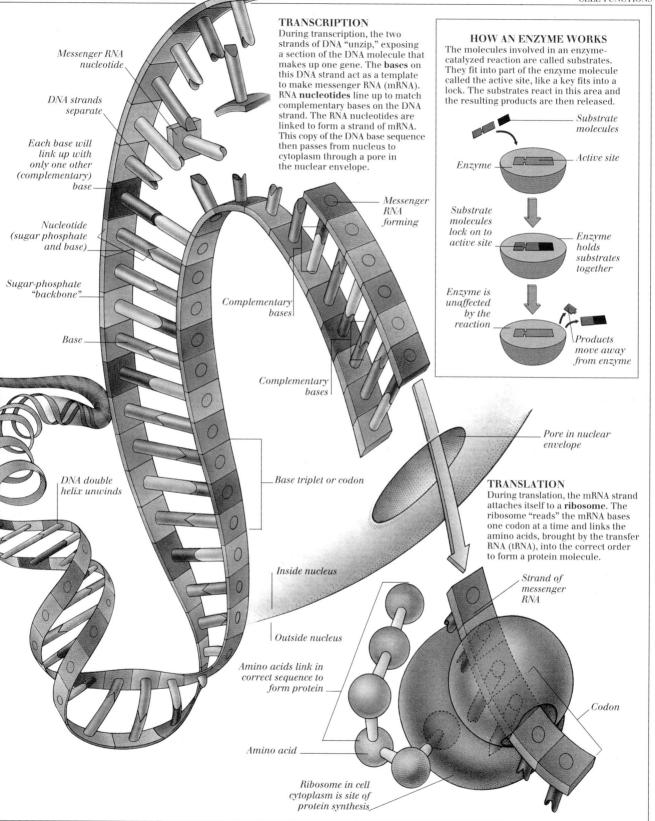

Messenger RNA
nucleotide

DNA strands
separate

Each base will
link up with
only one other
(complementary)
base

Nucleotide
(sugar phosphate
and base)

Sugar-phosphate
"backbone"

Base

DNA double
helix unwinds

TRANSCRIPTION
During transcription, the two
strands of DNA "unzip," exposing
a section of the DNA molecule that
makes up one gene. The **bases** on
this DNA strand act as a template
to make messenger RNA (mRNA).
RNA **nucleotides** line up to match
complementary bases on the DNA
strand. The RNA nucleotides are
linked to form a strand of mRNA.
This copy of the DNA base sequence
then passes from nucleus to
cytoplasm through a pore in
the nuclear envelope.

Messenger
RNA
forming

Complementary
bases

Complementary
bases

Base triplet or codon

Inside nucleus

Outside nucleus

Amino acids link in
correct sequence to
form protein

Amino acid

Ribosome in cell
cytoplasm is site of
protein synthesis

HOW AN ENZYME WORKS
The molecules involved in an enzyme-
catalyzed reaction are called substrates.
They fit into part of the enzyme molecule
called the active site, like a key fits into a
lock. The substrates react in this area and
the resulting products are then released.

Substrate
molecules

Enzyme

Active site

Substrate
molecules
lock on to
active site

Enzyme
holds
substrates
together

Enzyme is
unaffected
by the
reaction

Products
move away
from enzyme

Pore in nuclear
envelope

TRANSLATION
During translation, the mRNA strand
attaches itself to a **ribosome**. The
ribosome "reads" the mRNA bases
one codon at a time and links the
amino acids, brought by the transfer
RNA (tRNA), into the correct order
to form a protein molecule.

Strand of
messenger
RNA

Codon

Reproduction and heredity

LIVING ORGANISMS MUST REPRODUCE to ensure that their species does not die out. There are two types of reproduction: asexual reproduction, which involves a single parent and produces offspring with the same **genotype** as the parent; and sexual reproduction, which involves the fusing of **sex cells** from two parents to produce a new individual with a different genotype. Heredity explains the way that genes are passed from one generation to the next during sexual reproduction. This was first described by the Austrian monk, Gregor Mendel (1822-84). By breeding pea plants, he showed that parental traits did not blend in offspring, but remained separate, and were controlled by factors (**genes**) that occurred in pairs. There are two or more forms (alleles) of each gene: dominant alleles, which are always expressed in the offspring; and recessive alleles, which are expressed only if they occur in pairs. Mendel arrived at his conclusions by calculating the ratio of phenotypes (visible characteristics) shown by offspring of known parents.

ASEXUAL REPRODUCTION

HYDRA BUDDING
Hydra sp. is a tiny freshwater cnidarian (see pp. 150-151) that reproduces asexually by budding. A small bud grows from the side of the hydra and soon develops tentacles to catch food for itself. Within days, it pinches itself off and begins an independent existence.

— *Parent hydra with tentacles*

— *Bud attached to parent*

Adventitious bud (detachable bud with adventitious roots) drops from leaf

ADVENTITIOUS BUDS
The Mexican hat plant (*Kalanchoe daigremontiana*) reproduces asexually by producing adventitious buds, miniature plantlets, which grow from meristematic (actively dividing) tissue located on the margin of leaves. When ready, these plantlets fall to the ground, take root in the soil, and grow into new plants.

Apex of leaf

Notch in leaf margin containing meristematic (actively dividing) cells

Lamina (blade) of leaf

Leaf margin

Petiole (leaf stalk)

MITOSIS
Mitosis occurs during asexual reproduction and growth. It is a type of cell division that produces two new daughter cells that are genetically identical to the parent cell. Before division, each **chromosome** in the **nucleus** copies itself to produce two linked strands, or chromatids. These separate during mitosis, and one of each pair passes into a new daughter cell.

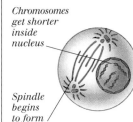

Chromosomes get shorter inside nucleus

Spindle begins to form

EARLY PROPHASE OF MITOSIS
At the beginning of mitosis, chromosomes tighten (condense), and a framework of tiny tubes (the spindle) begins to develop.

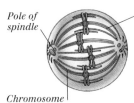

Pole of spindle

Chromosome

Nuclear envelope breaks down

METAPHASE
The chromosomes line up across the center of the spindle.

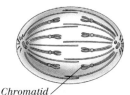

ANAPHASE
The chromatids that make up each chromosome move apart and travel to opposite ends of the spindle.

Chromatid

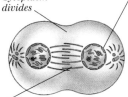

Cytoplasm divides

Nuclear envelope forms

TELOPHASE
A nuclear envelope surrounds each set of chromatids, forming a new nucleus. The **cytoplasm** then begins to divide.

Spindle begins to disappear

Nucleus

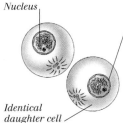

Chromosomes become longer and thinner

INTERPHASE
Once cell division is complete, the chromosomes unwind. The two new cells now have identical genetic material.

Identical daughter cell

SEXUAL REPRODUCTION AND HEREDITY

MEIOSIS

Meiosis is the type of cell division that produces **gametes** (sex cells), such as sperm and ova (eggs), which are used in sexual reproduction. Most of the cells that make up an organism are diploid – they have two sets of chromosomes in the nucleus, one from each of the organism's parents. The total number of chromosomes varies from species to species, but in every case the two sets consist of matching pairs of chromosomes, called homologous chromosomes. Meiosis consists of two divisions, during which a diploid parental cell produces four daughter cells, which are haploid – have one set of chromosomes – and are not identical to each other.

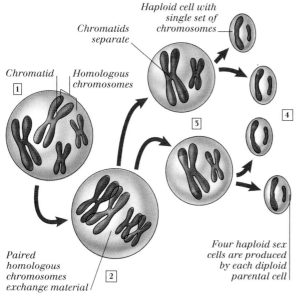

Chromatid — Homologous chromosomes

Chromatids separate

Haploid cell with single set of chromosomes

Paired homologous chromosomes exchange material

Four haploid sex cells are produced by each diploid parental cell

FIRST DIVISION
Each chromosome replicates and produces two linked chromatids (1). Homologous chromosomes swap genetic material (2), and two haploid cells are formed, each with one set of chromosomes (3).

SECOND DIVISION
The two chromatids in each chromosome separate and are pulled to opposite poles of the cells. Each cell divides to produce two daughter cells with single-stranded chromosomes (4).

MENDELIAN RATIO

Parent's genotype · Sex-cell genotype · Sex-cell genotype · Parent's genotype

RED FLOWER · WHITE FLOWER

Sex-cell genotype

Sex-cell genotype

All offspring in the first generation are red

THE FIRST GENERATION
Red-flowered parents have a genotype containing two dominant alleles (RR) for red color; white-flowered parents have two recessive alleles (rr) for white color.

RECESSIVE MASKED
After fertilization, each zygote has the same combination of flower-color alleles, Rr. All offspring are red-flowered because the dominant R allele masks the recessive r allele.

Parent's genotype · Sex-cell genotype · Sex-cell genotype · Parent's genotype · Sex-cell genotype

Sex-cell genotype

Three quarters of offspring in the second generation have red flowers

THE SECOND GENERATION
Each red-flowered parent has the same alleles for flower color, Rr. Meiosis produces sex cells that contain either the dominant allele, R, or the recessive allele, r. These cells take part in sexual reproduction.

RECESSIVE REVEALED
After fertilization, half the zygotes are Rr (red) and a quarter are RR (red). The other quarter are rr (white), as the recessive allele is revealed. The phenotype ratio is 3 red : 1 white.

FERTILIZATION

Fertilization is the fusion of a male sex cell (sperm) and a female sex cell (ovum) to form a zygote (fertilized ovum). During fertilization, several sperm surround the ovum and use enzymes to break through its outer covering – the zona pellucida. One sperm finally succeeds, and its nucleus, contained in the head of the sperm, fuses with the ovum's nucleus to form a zygote.

NATURAL VARIATION

Sexual reproduction results in offspring that are not identical to each other or to their parents. This natural variation occurs because each offspring inherits a slightly different set of genes from each of its parents. Variation can be seen most obviously in differences between external features, such as coat color in these puppies.

Tail of sperm pushes cell forward

Ovum covered by zona pellucida

Head of sperm

Mother suckling her pups

Offspring show variation in coat color

Evolution

THE THEORY OF EVOLUTION was established by English naturalist Charles Darwin (1809-82) (see pp. 120-121). Evolution is the process whereby living things change with time. Within a species there is always variation; some individuals are more successful than others in the struggle for survival and are more likely to breed and pass on their advantageous characteristics. This process is called natural selection and is the driving force of evolution. It enables species to adapt to changing **environments**, and may, in time, lead to new species appearing. Since life began on Earth, millions of new species have appeared and become **extinct. Organisms** alive today represent only a small fraction of those that have ever existed. There is much evidence for evolution, including: the **fossil** record, which reveals ancestry; the current distribution of animals and plants; and modern examples of natural selection. Although evolution is a theory widely accepted by both scientists and nonscientists, some people believe that all living things were divinely created in their present form – this theory is known as creationism.

DARWIN'S FINCHES

This group of 13 finch species is found only on the Galápagos Islands, off the coast of Ecuador. Each has its own way of life, and a beak shape related to diet. When Charles Darwin observed this, he concluded that they had all evolved from a single, ancestral, South American species. This is an example of adaptive radiation – evolution from a single ancestor of many species, each exploiting different lifestyles.

SMALL, INSECT - EATING TREE FINCH

LARGE, CACTUS-EATING GROUND FINCH

LARGE, SEED-EATING GROUND FINCH

MISSING LINK

Some fossil finds have been of great importance because they have provided a "missing link" that shows how one major group has evolved from another. One such fossil is that of *Archaeopteryx*, which, with its long, bony tail, jaws with teeth, and claws on fingers, closely resembled small dinosaurs called theropods. Like birds, it also had feathers and a forelimb adapted as a wing. It is likely, therefore, that *Archaeopteryx*, which probably glided from trees rather than flew, was a close relative of the ancestor of modern birds. The fossil also suggests that birds evolved from, and are the nearest living relatives of, the dinosaurs.

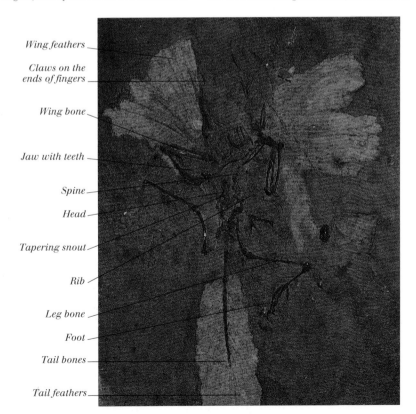

Wing feathers

Claws on the ends of fingers

Wing bone

Jaw with teeth

Spine

Head

Tapering snout

Rib

Leg bone

Foot

Tail bones

Tail feathers

NATURAL SELECTION

The peppered moth provides an example of natural selection in action. It rests on lichen-covered tree trunks, camouflaged from predatory birds by its pale color. In 19th-century industrial England, air pollution killed the lichen and blackened the tree bark with soot. Dark forms of the moth, which appeared as a result of natural variation, increased in number because they were better camouflaged against the darkened tree trunks.

Dark form of peppered moth

Pale form of peppered moth

PEPPERED MOTHS

FOSSIL EVIDENCE

Broad skull with mouth adapted to catching prey in water

Flexible backbone

Short tail

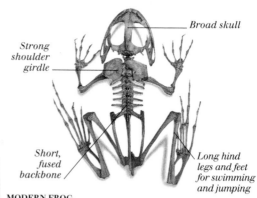

Broad skull

Strong shoulder girdle

Short, fused backbone

Long hind legs and feet for swimming and jumping

FOSSIL FROG
Fossils of early frogs reveal a newtlike animal with a flexible backbone that moved through the water with a fishlike side-to-side motion of its body and tail. They may also have kicked out with their hind legs to provide extra propulsion. Like modern frogs, they had a broad skull and a mouth adapted to catching prey in water.

MODERN FROG
During their evolution, frogs became adapted to swimming and jumping using their long hind legs and feet. As a consequence, because their tails were no longer used, these were lost and their backbones became short and rigid. Strong shoulder girdles have also developed to resist the force of landing.

LIVING EVIDENCE OF EVOLUTION
An example of living evidence that supports evolution is the pentadactyl (five-fingered) limb. All mammals share the same arrangement of bones in the four limbs, which suggests they evolved from a common ancestor. Differences between species are a result of adaptation to different lifestyles. The chimpanzee arm has the basic pentadactyl pattern. The dolphin has short, thick arm bones and splayed hand and finger bones that form a powerful flipper. The bat's hand and finger bones are long and thin, forming a light but strong framework to support a wing.

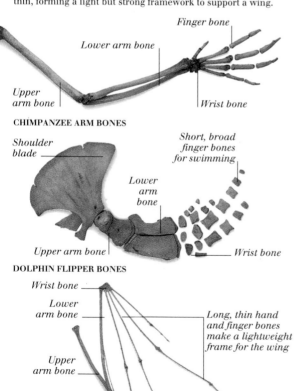

Finger bone

Lower arm bone

Upper arm bone

Wrist bone

CHIMPANZEE ARM BONES

Shoulder blade

Short, broad finger bones for swimming

Lower arm bone

Upper arm bone

Wrist bone

DOLPHIN FLIPPER BONES

Wrist bone

Lower arm bone

Upper arm bone

Long, thin hand and finger bones make a lightweight frame for the wing

BAT WING BONES

HORSE EVOLUTION
The evolution of modern horses from a dog-sized ancestor called *Hyracotherium* took over 50 million years. It did not follow a single, straight line, but branched off in many directions and included genera that are now extinct. Four ancestors of the horse are shown below. *Hyracotherium* had splayed toes and was a forest dweller, as was three-toed *Mesohippus*. *Merychippus* lived in grasslands and walked on its middle toes. *Pliohippus* was also a grazer and, like modern horses, had a single toe ending in a hoof.

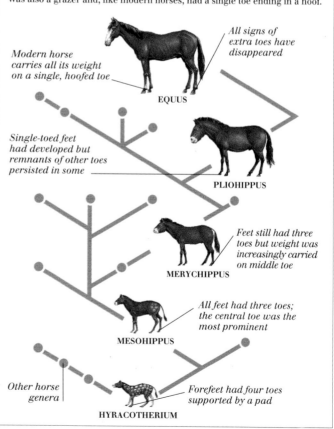

All signs of extra toes have disappeared

Modern horse carries all its weight on a single, hoofed toe

EQUUS

Single-toed feet had developed but remnants of other toes persisted in some

PLIOHIPPUS

Feet still had three toes but weight was increasingly carried on middle toe

MERYCHIPPUS

All feet had three toes; the central toe was the most prominent

MESOHIPPUS

Other horse genera

Forefeet had four toes supported by a pad

HYRACOTHERIUM

Classification 1

IN ORDER TO MAKE SENSE of the millions of **species** found on Earth, biologists classify them into a rational framework. Classification is used to identify and name individual species and to show how different species are related to each other. The Swedish naturalist Carolus Linnaeus (1707-78) (see pp. 120-121) devised the first rational system of classification, which is still used by biologists today. It groups different **organisms** together on the basis of their similarities and gives each species a Latin or latinized binomial (two-part) name. The first part identifies the genus (group of species) to which the organism belongs, and the second part identifies the species. Classification systems arrange species in groups (taxa). They are ranged in order of size from the smallest taxon – species – at the bottom, to the largest taxon – kingdom – at the top. Most systems of classification place living organisms into one of five kingdoms: monerans, protists, fungi, plants, and animals.

THE FIVE-KINGDOM SYSTEM

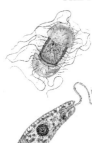

MONERA (BACTERIA)
The kingdom Monera contains bacteria, the simplest organisms on Earth. They are single-celled **prokaryotic** organisms and are found in every habitat (see pp. 134-135).

PROTISTA (PROTISTS)
The kingdom Protista is a diverse assemblage of single-celled, **eukaryotic** organisms. They include plantlike, animal-like, and fungilike organisms (see pp. 134-135).

FUNGI
Fungi are eukaryotic, mostly multicellular organisms that are typically made up of threadlike hyphae and reproduce by releasing spores from fruiting bodies (see pp. 136-137).

PLANTAE (PLANTS)
Plants are hugely diverse, multicellular, eukaryotic organisms whose cells have walls (see pp. 138-149). They make their own food by harnessing the Sun's energy during photosynthesis.

ANIMALIA (ANIMALS)
Animals are multicellular, eukaryotic organisms, whose cells lack walls (see pp. 150-167). They typically feed by ingesting food, which is then digested internally.

CLASSIFYING SPECIES

Species, such as the tiger, are classified by being placed in increasingly larger groups. The tiger is grouped into a genus (big cats); the family (cats) contains similar genera; families are grouped into an order (carnivores); related orders form a class (mammals); classes are grouped into a phylum (or division for plants) (chordates); and phyla that share broad characteristics collectively form a kingdom (animals).

KINGDOM: Animalia (animals)
Animals are multicellular organisms that move actively, respond to their surroundings, and feed by ingesting nutrients.

PHYLUM: Chordata (chordates)
Chordates are animals that have a notochord (a stiffening skeletal rod), a dorsal nerve cord, and gill slits at some stage in their life.

CLASS: Mammalia (mammals)
Mammals are chordates that are endothermic (warm-blooded), have hair or fur on their body, and suckle their young with milk.

ORDER: Carnivora (carnivores)
Carnivores are mammals that typically eat meat, are specialized for hunting, and have teeth adapted for gripping and tearing flesh.

FAMILY: Felidae (cats)
Cats are highly specialized predators. They have powerful jaws, and good vision and hearing.

GENUS: _Panthera_ (big cats)
Big cats can roar and hold their prey with their forepaws while feeding.

SPECIES: _Panthera tigris_ (tiger)
Tigers are the largest and most powerful of the big cats. Their striped coat provides camouflage.

TIGER
(*Panthera tigris*)

Chlorophyta (green algae) 70,000 species	Phaeophyta (brown algae) 1,500 species	Bryophyta (mosses) 10,000 species

Rhodophyta (red algae) 4,000 species	Hepatophyta (liverworts) 6,000 species

KEY
KINGDOM	DIVISION	CLASS

All figures given are a rough estimate of species numbers

CLASSIFYING MONERANS, PROTISTS, FUNGI, AND PLANTS

Kingdom Monera has two divisions: Archaeobacteria and Eubacteria . Kingdom Protista has 10 divisions grouped into fungilike slime and water molds (divisions Acrasiomycota, Myxomycota, Oomycota); animal-like protozoa (divisions Sarcomastigophora, Ciliophora, Sporozoa); and plantlike algae (divisions Chrysophyta, Euglenophyta, Bacillariophyta, Pyrrhophyta). The four divisions in kingdom Fungi are classified according to their means of reproduction; lichens are a **symbiotic** association between fungi and algae. There are 15 divisions of kingdom Plantae: seaweeds (divisions Chlorophyta, Rhodophyta, Phaeophyta); nonvascular, spore-producing plants (divisions Hepatophyta, Anthocerophyta); vascular, spore-producing plants (divisions Psilophyta, Lycophyta, Sphenophyta, Pterophyta); nonflowering, seed-producing plants (divisions Cycadophyta, Ginkgophyta, Gnetophyta, Coniferophyta); and flowering, seed-producing plants (division Anthophyta).

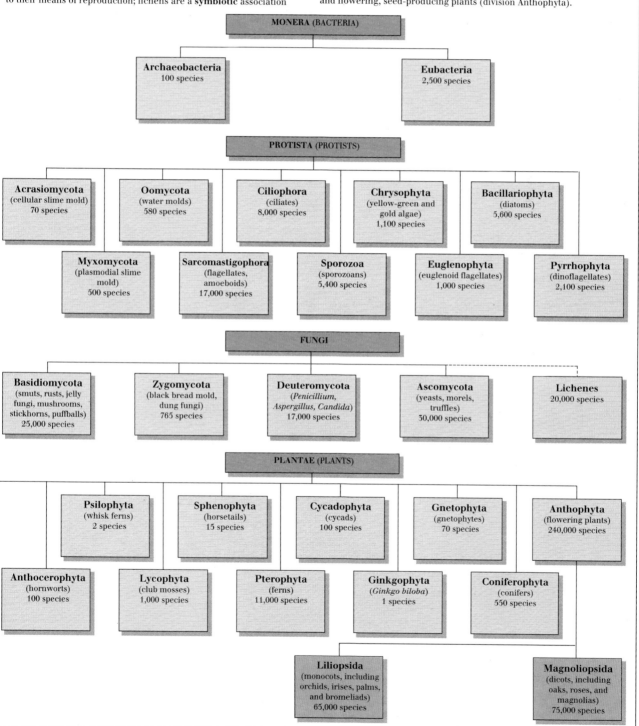

Classification 2

CLASSIFICATION ENABLES BIOLOGISTS to make sense of the bewildering array of living organisms. It identifies and names species by placing them into groups with other species that have similar characteristics. The science of classification is called taxonomy. Taxonomists – biologists that practice taxonomy – name species and trace their phylogeny – the way in which species are linked through **evolution**. They do this by looking for key **anatomical, physiological**, behavioral, or **molecular** characteristics. If different species share similarities, taxonomists may suggest that they are related through descent from a common ancestor – an extinct organism from which they have inherited their shared characteristics. Such characteristics may be ancient ancestral ones, such as the backbone in vertebrates, or more recently derived characteristics, such as modified forelimbs in bats. There are two major evolutionary classification systems in use today. Traditional systematics, used here for the animal kingdom and on pp. 130-131, groups organisms by using as many characteristics, both ancestral and derived, as possible. Cladistics groups species on the basis of shared derived characteristics alone.

ANIMALIA (ANIMALS)

Arthropoda
(arthropods)
963,000 species

Uniramia
(uniramians)
860,000 species

Porifera
(sponges)
5,000 species

Cnidaria
(cnidarians)
8,915 species

Platyhelminthes
(flatworms)
18,500 species

Nematoda
(roundworms)
12,000 species

Mollusca
(mollusks)
50,000 species

Annelida
(segmented worms)
11,600 species

Malacostraca
(lobsters, crabs, shrimps, woodlice)
22,650 species

Hydrozoa
(hydras, hydroids)
2,700 species

Cubozoa
(box jellies)
15 species

Polyplacophora
(chitons)
800 species

Bivalvia
(clams, scallops)
8,000 species

Cephalopoda
(octopuses, squid)
650 species

Scyphozoa
(jellyfish)
200 species

Anthozoa
(sea anemones, coral)
6,000 species

Gastropoda
(slugs, snails)
40,000 species

Scaphopoda
(tusk shells)
350 species

Turbellaria
(free-living flatworms)
3,000 species

Trematoda
(parasitic flukes)
11,00 species

Polychaeta
(marine worms)
8,000 species

Oligochaeta
(earthworms, freshwater worms)
3,100 species

Hirudinea
(leeches)
500 species

KEY

■ KINGDOM

□ PHYLUM

▨ SUBPHYLUM

▨ CLASS

All figures given are a rough estimate of species numbers

Monogenea
(parasitic flukes)
11,000 species

Cestoda
(tapeworms)
3,400 species

Insecta
(insects)
846,000 species

Chilopoda
(centipedes)
2,500 species

Diplopoda
(millipedes)
10,000 species

Other classes:
Symphyla (symphylans) *160 species*
Pauropoda (pauropods) *300 species*

CLASSIFYING ANIMALS

The animal kingdom is one of five kingdoms into which living things are divided. It consists of over 30 phyla, some of which are shown below, with their major classes. The phyla Arthropoda (arthropods) and Chordata (chordates) are divided into subphyla, a category of classification between phylum and class. The animal kingdom is traditionally split into invertebrates – animals without backbones, which account for most of the species – and vertebrates, animals with backbones found in the subphylum Vertebrata.

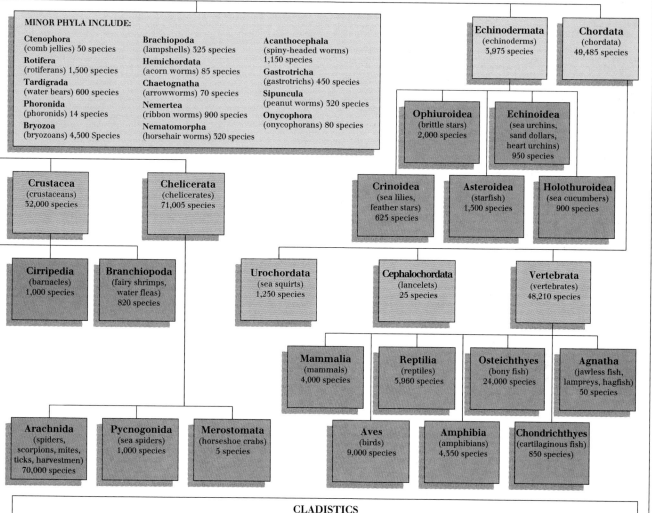

MINOR PHYLA INCLUDE:

Ctenophora
(comb jellies) 50 species
Rotifera
(rotiferans) 1,500 species
Tardigrada
(water bears) 600 species
Phoronida
(phoronids) 14 species
Bryozoa
(bryozoans) 4,500 Species

Brachiopoda
(lampshells) 325 species
Hemichordata
(acorn worms) 85 species
Chaetognatha
(arrowworms) 70 species
Nemertea
(ribbon worms) 900 species
Nematomorpha
(horsehair worms) 320 species

Acanthocephala
(spiny-headed worms)
1,150 species
Gastrotricha
(gastrotrichs) 450 species
Sipuncula
(peanut worms) 320 species
Onycophora
(onycophorans) 80 species

Echinodermata
(echinoderms)
3,975 species

Chordata
(chordata)
49,485 species

Ophiuroidea
(brittle stars)
2,000 species

Echinoidea
(sea urchins,
sand dollars,
heart urchins)
950 species

Crinoidea
(sea lilies,
feather stars)
625 species

Asteroidea
(starfish)
1,500 species

Holothuroidea
(sea cucumbers)
900 species

Crustacea
(crustaceans)
32,000 species

Chelicerata
(chelicerates)
71,005 species

Cirripedia
(barnacles)
1,000 species

Branchiopoda
(fairy shrimps,
water fleas)
820 species

Urochordata
(sea squirts)
1,250 species

Cephalochordata
(lancelets)
25 species

Vertebrata
(vertebrates)
48,210 species

Mammalia
(mammals)
4,000 species

Reptilia
(reptiles)
5,960 species

Osteichthyes
(bony fish)
24,000 species

Agnatha
(jawless fish,
lampreys, hagfish)
50 species

Arachnida
(spiders,
scorpions, mites,
ticks, harvestmen)
70,000 species

Pycnogonida
(sea spiders)
1,000 species

Merostomata
(horseshoe crabs)
5 species

Aves
(birds)
9,000 species

Amphibia
(amphibians)
4,350 species

Chondrichthyes
(cartilaginous fish)
850 species)

CLADISTICS

Cladistics is another method of classification. Species that share unique, derived characteristics are placed in a group called a clade. All species in a clade are descended from a single, common ancestor. Birds, for example, form a clade because they are descended from a common ancestor that evolved feathers. Clades are arranged into a branching diagram called a cladogram, which shows those clades that are more closely related to each other. In traditional classification, turtles, lizards and snakes, and crocodiles are grouped together as reptiles (class reptilia), this is known as a grade. Although similar to clades, species in a grade evolve from more than one ancestor.

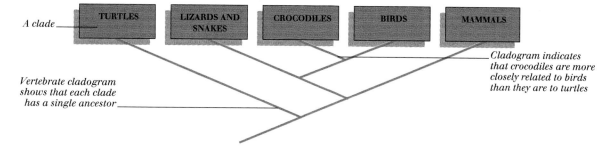

A clade

TURTLES

LIZARDS AND
SNAKES

CROCODILES

BIRDS

MAMMALS

Cladogram indicates
that crocodiles are more
closely related to birds
than they are to turtles

Vertebrate cladogram
shows that each clade
has a single ancestor

Microorganisms

LIVING THINGS THAT ARE TOO SMALL to be seen without a microscope are called microorganisms. This diverse collection of **unicellular** organisms includes bacteria, protists, and some fungi (see pp. 136-137). Bacteria (kingdom Monera or Prokaryota) are prokaryotic organisms – their cells lack a **nucleus** or any membrane-bound **organelles**. They are the most abundant and widespread organisms on Earth and include saprobes, which feed on dead material, and parasites, which feed on living organisms. Protists (kingdom Protista or Protoctista) include a wide variety of unicellular, eukaryotic organisms – their cells have a nucleus and contain membrane-bound organelles. Animal-like protists, or protozoans, are **heterotrophic** and include amoeba, ciliates, and flagellates; plantlike protists, or algae, are **autotrophic**. A third protist group includes slime and water molds. Viruses are generally included with other microorganisms but they are nonliving and must invade a living **host cell** in order to reproduce (see pp. 258-259).

STRUCTURE OF A VIRUS

A virus consists of a core of nucleic acid (either **DNA** or **RNA**) and an outer protein coat, or capsid. The length of nucleic acid forms the virus's genetic material and can be replicated only inside a host cell (see pp. 258-259). Surface proteins, called spikes, stud the outer capsid and are involved in attaching the virus to a host cell.

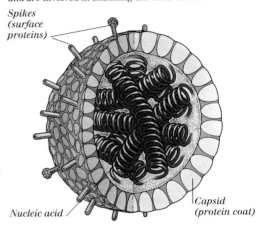

Spikes (surface proteins)

Nucleic acid

Capsid (protein coat)

BACTERIA

STRUCTURE OF A BACTERIUM

A bacterial cell is bounded by a plasma membrane and a tough cell wall. In some cases, the cell wall may be covered by a protective, gelatinous capsule. It may also have long flagella that enable it to swim, and pili that are used to attach it to other cells or food. Inside the cell, there are no membrane-bound structures. Instead of a nucleus, a circular molecule of DNA is found in a region called the nucleoid. Bacteria may be identified according to their shape: coccus (round); spiral (coiled); and bacillus (rod-shaped) (shown here).

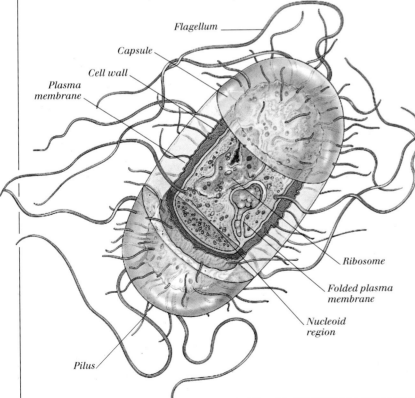

Flagellum

Capsule

Cell wall

Plasma membrane

Ribosome

Folded plasma membrane

Nucleoid region

Pilus

CYANOBACTERIA

Formerly known as blue-green algae, cyanobacteria are bacteria that can produce their own food by photosynthesis. Most cyanobacteria are found in water, and many exist as filaments of linked bacterial cells. Cyanobacteria also play an important role in nitrogen fixation (see pp. 172-173).

SOIL BACTERIA

Bacteria are found in vast numbers in the soil, and play a vital role as decomposers, helping to break down dead plant and animal material. This process of decomposition releases and recycles vital nutrients, including nitrogen and carbon, needed for plant growth.

PROTISTS

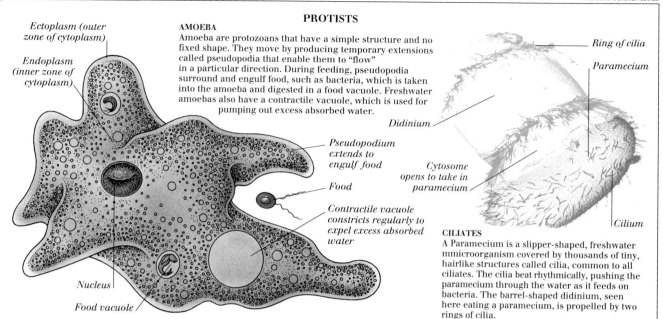

AMOEBA

Amoeba are protozoans that have a simple structure and no fixed shape. They move by producing temporary extensions called pseudopodia that enable them to "flow" in a particular direction. During feeding, pseudopodia surround and engulf food, such as bacteria, which is taken into the amoeba and digested in a food vacuole. Freshwater amoebas also have a contractile vacuole, which is used for pumping out excess absorbed water.

Ectoplasm (outer zone of cytoplasm)

Endoplasm (inner zone of cytoplasm)

Pseudopodium extends to engulf food

Food

Contractile vacuole constricts regularly to expel excess absorbed water

Nucleus

Food vacuole

Ring of cilia

Paramecium

Didinium

Cytosome opens to take in paramecium

Cilium

CILIATES

A Paramecium is a slipper-shaped, freshwater mmicroorganism covered by thousands of tiny, hairlike structures called cilia, common to all ciliates. The cilia beat rhythmically, pushing the paramecium through the water as it feeds on bacteria. The barrel-shaped didinium, seen here eating a paramecium, is propelled by two rings of cilia.

Sinus (division between two halves of cell)

Chloroplast

Silica shell

Cell wall

GREEN ALGAE

The freshwater desmid (shown here) belongs to the largest division of algae called Chlorophyta. These green algae make their own food by photosynthesis. As well as unicellular species, the division also includes the green seaweeds (see pp. 138-139).

DIATOMS

These marine and freshwater algae form an important part of the **phytoplankton**. Diatoms have a patterned shell, made of silica, consisting of two halves that fit together like a box and its lid.

Flagellum pulls euglena through water

Eyespot is sensitive to light

Paramylon (food store)

Chloroplast

Mitochondrion

Flexible, outer shell (pellicle)

Second, non-emergent, flagellum

Contractile vacuole

Golgi body

Pyrenoid

Nucleus

SLIME MOLD REPRODUCTION

Slime molds are protists that resemble amoebae. When food is plentiful, slime mold amoeba live an independent existence, feeding on bacteria and yeasts. When food is in short supply, they secrete a chemical that attracts other amoeba to form a cell mass called a slug. The slug migrates towards the light, eventually comes to rest, and extends upward to form a fruiting body. This releases spores, which disperse and germinate to form new amoeba.

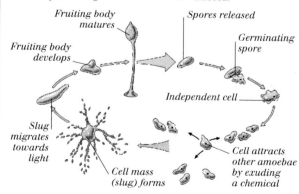

Fruiting body matures

Spores released

Fruiting body develops

Germinating spore

Independent cell

Slug migrates towards light

Cell mass (slug) forms

Cell attracts other amoebae by exuding a chemical

EUGLENOIDS

Euglenoids are freshwater protists that move using the whiplike flagellum at the anterior (front) end of their bodies. Many contain chloroplasts and make their own food by photosynthesis, using their eyespot to detect light. Others cannot photosynthesize and rely on ingesting food instead. Unlike algae, euglenoids lack a cell wall.

Fungi

FUNGI ARE A GROUP of **eukaryotic**, non**motile**, land-living organisms that includes bread molds, yeasts, mildews, mushrooms, puffballs, and smuts. Most fungi are **multicellular** and have cell walls that contain **chitin**. They consist of microscopic, threadlike filaments called hyphae, which branch profusely to form masses called mycelia. Fungi are **heterotrophic** and absorb nutrients at or near the growing tip of hyphae as they spread through food. Most fungi are saprobes, which means that they feed on dead and decaying organisms. Saprobic soil fungi, for example, recycle nutrients from dead animal and plant material. Some fungi, such as the candida fungus (see pp. 258-259) are parasites, feeding on living organisms. Others form mutually beneficial symbiotic relationships with other organisms – such as **mycorrhizae** and lichens. Fungi reproduce by releasing spores from fruiting bodies. Spore-producing structures within fruiting bodies include gills, pores, and spines, depending on the species. The spores may be dispersed actively into air currents, or passively by rain or animals.

YEAST CELLS

Yeasts are microscopic, unicellular fungi. They reproduce **asexually** by budding a "daughter" cell from the "parental" yeast cell (shown below). This then becomes detached and follows an independent existence. Some yeast species respire **anaerobically** to convert glucose into ethanol (alcohol) and carbon dioxide. This process is called fermentation. It is exploited by brewers to produce alcoholic drinks, and by bakers, who use carbon dioxide to make bread rise.

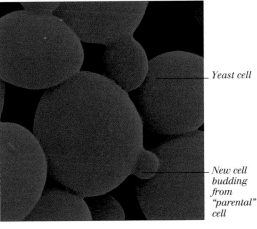

Yeast cell

New cell budding from "parental" cell

EXAMPLES OF FUNGAL FRUITING BODY SHAPES

Fungal fruiting body shapes exhibit a great variety of forms. They all support the hymenium (spore-producing tissue) and are specifically designed to aid spore dispersal. The hymenium may be exposed, as in the fluted bird's nest and common stinkhorn fungi, or concealed, as in the summer truffle and common puffball fungi. Most fungi, such as the gilled mushroom opposite, actively release their spores into the air to be dispersed by the wind. Other fungi, such as as the fluted bird's nest, rely on passive dispersal of their spores by splashing raindrops or passing animals. A few fungi, such as the stinkhorn, use scent to attract insects to disperse their spores.

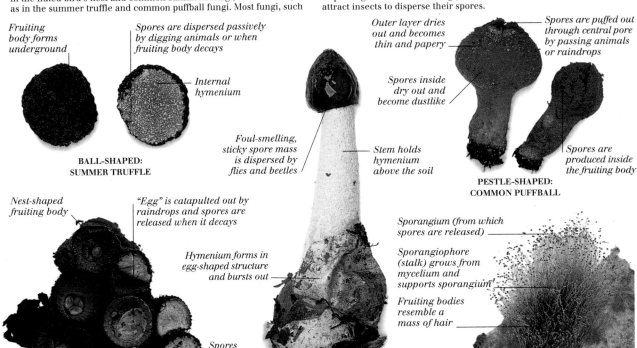

Fruiting body forms underground

Spores are dispersed passively by digging animals or when fruiting body decays

Internal hymenium

BALL-SHAPED: SUMMER TRUFFLE

Nest-shaped fruiting body

"Egg" is catapulted out by raindrops and spores are released when it decays

Hymenium forms in egg-shaped structure and bursts out

Spores develop inside "egg"

NEST-SHAPED: FLUTED BIRD'S NEST

Foul-smelling, sticky spore mass is dispersed by flies and beetles

Stem holds hymenium above the soil

PHALLUS-SHAPED: COMMON STINKHORN

Outer layer dries out and becomes thin and papery

Spores inside dry out and become dustlike

Spores are puffed out through central pore by passing animals or raindrops

Spores are produced inside the fruiting body

PESTLE-SHAPED: COMMON PUFFBALL

Sporangium (from which spores are released)

Sporangiophore (stalk) grows from mycelium and supports sporangium

Fruiting bodies resemble a mass of hair

BREAD MOLD

FEATURES OF A GILLED MUSHROOM

Mushrooms are the fruiting bodies of certain fungi belonging to division Basidiomycota. They arise from underground mycelia and consist of a compact mass of hyphae. Gilled mushrooms consist of a cap, in which spores are produced, and a stem, which lifts the cap above the ground. On the underside of the cap are vertical strips of tissue called gills, which contain spore-producing tissue. When spores are mature, they are caught by air currents as they emerge from the gills.

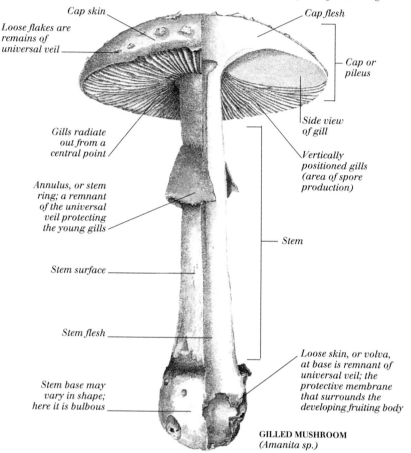

Cap skin

Loose flakes are remains of universal veil

Cap flesh

Cap or pileus

Side view of gill

Gills radiate out from a central point

Vertically positioned gills (area of spore production)

Annulus, or stem ring; a remnant of the universal veil protecting the young gills

Stem

Stem surface

Stem flesh

Stem base may vary in shape; here it is bulbous

Loose skin, or volva, at base is remnant of universal veil; the protective membrane that surrounds the developing fruiting body

GILLED MUSHROOM
(Amanita sp.)

LIFE CYCLE OF A MUSHROOM

Spores germinate when they land in a suitable location. They develop into hyphae, which branch to form a primary mycelium. Adjacent mycelia fuse to form secondary mycelia. Parts of this mass give rise to spore-producing fruiting bodies (mushrooms). Mycelia differentiate within the immature mushroom to form the cap, gills, stem, and other parts. The universal veil ruptures as the stem and cap emerge. When the mushroom matures, it releases its spores.

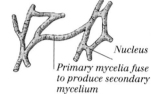

Spore

Primary mycelium develops from spore

Septum (cross wall)

Hypha

Nucleus

Primary mycelia fuse to produce secondary mycelium

SPORES GERMINATE AND PRODUCE MYCELIUM

Immature fruiting body

Mycelium

MYCELIUM FORMS FRUITING BODY

Universal veil (membrane enclosing developing fruiting body)

Pileus (cap)

Gill

Underground mycelium

Stalk

FRUITING BODY GROWS ABOVE GROUND

Expanding pileus (cap)

Partial veil (joins pileus to stalk)

Annulus (ring) being formed as partial veil breaks

Stalk

Underground mycelium

Volva (remains of universal veil)

UNIVERSAL VEIL BREAKS

LICHENS

Lichens are the result of a symbiotic (mutually beneficial) relationship between fungi and either green algae or cyanobacteria (see pp. 134-135). Fungal hyphae protect algae from environmental extremes and pass on essential minerals. Algae produce food by **photosynthesis**, which is shared with the fungus. This close relationship enables lichens to grow on bare surfaces and in extremely hostile habitats.

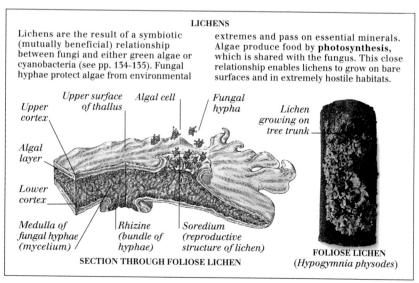

Upper cortex

Upper surface of thallus

Algal cell

Fungal hypha

Lichen growing on tree trunk

Algal layer

Lower cortex

Medulla of fungal hyphae (mycelium)

Rhizine (bundle of hyphae)

Soredium (reproductive structure of lichen)

SECTION THROUGH FOLIOSE LICHEN

FOLIOSE LICHEN
(Hypogymnia physodes)

Nonflowering plants 1

NONFLOWERING PLANTS REPRODUCE without producing flowers. The simplest of these reproduce by releasing **spores**; the more advanced produce **seeds** (see pp. 140-141). Mosses (division Bryophyta) and liverworts (division Hepatophyta) are the simplest spore-releasing plants. They are found in moist habitats; lack true leaves, stems, and roots; and have no **vascular system**. The other spore-releasers, horsetails (division Sphenophyta) and ferns (division Pterophyta), have vascular systems. The life cycle of spore-releasing plants involves two generations existing alternately. During the gametophyte generation, gametes (sex cells) are produced, which fuse to produce a **zygote**. This gives rise to the sporophyte generation, which produces spores in a sporangium. When released, these spores germinate and give rise to another gametophyte generation. In mosses and liverworts, the gametophyte is the dominant generation; in horsetails and ferns the sporophyte is the dominant generation. Although seaweeds are included as nonflowering plants here, some biologists class them as protists (see pp. 130-131).

MOSSES

These small, simple plants often grow together in clumps usually under damp conditions. They have upright "stems" and spirally arranged scalelike "leaves." In most mosses, the capsule, or sporangium, is at the end of a long seta, or stalk. When ripe, this opens to release spores.

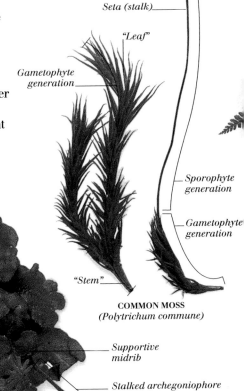

Capsule (sporangium)

Seta (stalk)

"Leaf"

Gametophyte generation

Sporophyte generation

Gametophyte generation

"Stem"

COMMON MOSS
(Polytrichum commune)

LIVERWORTS

Liverworts are simple green plants, found in damp, shaded locations, and sometimes in water. There are two types, both of which are prostrate (grow along the ground). Thalloid liverworts are flattened and ribbonlike; leafy liverworts have scalelike "leaves" arranged in rows. Both types of liverworts can reproduce sexually and asexually. Following sexual reproduction, spore-producing sporangium develops on the underside of the archegoniophore. Asexual reproduction occurs when clusters of cells, called gemmae, are splashed out of gemma cups by raindrops. They then grow into new plants.

Flattened thallus (plant body) of gametophyte

Supportive midrib

Stalked archegoniophore (female reproductive structure)

Gemma cup containing gemmae

THALLOID LIVERWORT
(Marchantia polymorpha)

SEAWEEDS

There are three types of seaweeds: brown, green, and red. They are all multicellular marine algae and are usually found in the intertidal zone of the shore or just below the low tide mark. Their color depends on the photosynthetic pigments they use to harness the Sun's energy. Typically, seaweeds have a flattened body, or thallus, that is attached to rocks or the seabed by a holdfast. Most reproduce sexually by releasing gametes into the sea. Fertilized eggs settle on rocks and grow into new seaweeds.

Fertile tip releases gametes into the sea

Supportive midrib

Crinkled margin

Unbranched, spirally twisted frond

Lamina (blade)

Lamina (blade)

Smooth margin

Holdfast

BROWN SEAWEED
(Fucus spiralis)

Holdfast attaches seaweed to mussel shell

GREEN SEAWEED
(Enteromorpha linza)

Smooth margin

Holdfast

RED SEAWEED
(Dilsea carnosa)

FERNS

The sporophyte generation in ferns is a green plant with leaves, stems, and adventitious roots that grow from an underground stem. Water and nutrients from the soil are transported around the plant by its internal vascular system. The large fronds, or leaves, are divided into many pinnae, or leaflets, each of which may be divided further into smaller pinnules. Sporangia develop on the undersides of pinnules in groups called sori and release spores into the air.

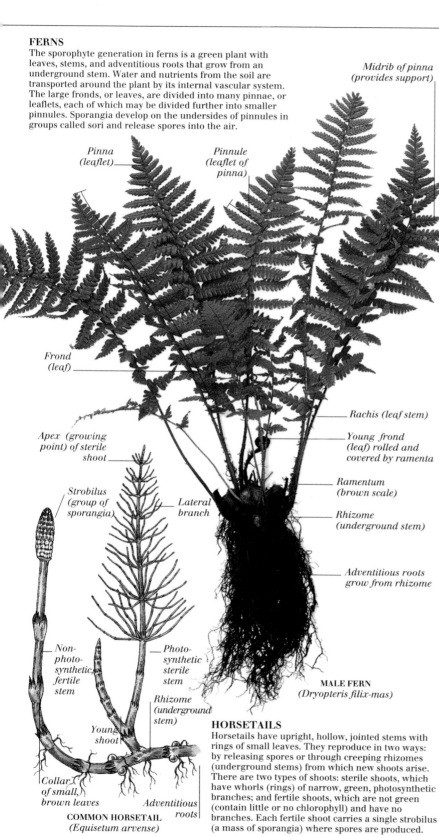

Midrib of pinna (provides support)

Pinna (leaflet)

Pinnule (leaflet of pinna)

Frond (leaf)

Rachis (leaf stem)

Young frond (leaf) rolled and covered by ramenta

Ramentum (brown scale)

Rhizome (underground stem)

Adventitious roots grow from rhizome

MALE FERN
(Dryopteris filix-mas)

Apex (growing point) of sterile shoot

Strobilus (group of sporangia)

Lateral branch

Non-photo-synthetic, fertile stem

Photo-synthetic sterile stem

Rhizome (underground stem)

Young shoot

Collar of small, brown leaves

Adventitious roots

COMMON HORSETAIL
(Equisetum arvense)

HORSETAILS

Horsetails have upright, hollow, jointed stems with rings of small leaves. They reproduce in two ways: by releasing spores or through creeping rhizomes (underground stems) from which new shoots arise. There are two types of shoots: sterile shoots, which have whorls (rings) of narrow, green, photosynthetic branches; and fertile shoots, which are not green (contain little or no chlorophyll) and have no branches. Each fertile shoot carries a single strobilus (a mass of sporangia) where spores are produced.

LIFE CYCLE OF A FERN

Spores released from sporangia germinate in damp conditions to form a simple, heart-shaped prothallus (gametophyte). This bears antheridia and archegonia, the male and female sex organs. Antheridia release mobile gametes (sex cells) called antherozoids. These swim in a film of water to an archegonium and fertilize the oosphere (egg). A new fern plant (sporophyte) develops from the fertilized oosphere.

Upper surface of pinnule (leaflet of pinna)

Sporangium (spore-producing structure)

Indusium (protecting flap of sorus)

SECTION THROUGH PINNULE

Under dry conditions, sporangium splits and releases spores

Spore

RELEASE OF SPORES

Spore germinates in damp conditions

Cells divide to produce prothallus

Rhizoid anchors prothallus

GERMINATION OF SPORE

Antheridium

Archegonium

Rhizoid

GAMETOPHYTE PRODUCES GAMETES

Antheridium

Oosphere

Antherozoid

Archegonium

FERTILIZATION

Gametophyte disintegrates as sporophyte grows

Sporophyte grows out of gametophyte

NEW SPOROPHYTE PLANT GROWS

Nonflowering plants 2

THE MORE ADVANCED PLANTS, of which there are five **divisions**, reproduce by means of **seeds**. Four divisions of seed-producing plants are nonflowering – collectively known as the gymnosperms ("naked seeds") because their seeds develop unprotected by a fruit (the fifth division is the flowering plants). Most gymnosperms are evergreen trees that have male and female reproductive structures in the form of **cones**. **Pollen** is usually blown by the wind from the male cone to the female cone, where **fertilization** takes place. The "naked" seeds then develop on the surface of **scales** in a female cone. Most gymnosperms are shrubs or trees, and many are xerophytes (adapted to living in dry conditions). The four divisions of gymnosperms are: the ginkgo, a deciduous species; cycads, found mainly in the tropics; gnetophytes, mostly trees and shrubs; and conifers, which include pines.

EXAMPLES OF GYMNOSPERMS

Petiole (leaf stalk)

Bilobed (double-lobed) leaf

Girdle scar

Stem

GINKGO
(Ginkgo biloba)

GINKGO
The only species in the division Ginkgophyta is the ginkgo, or maidenhair tree. It has fan-shaped, bilobed (double-lobed) leaves and can grow to up to 100 feet (30 meters) in height. It does not produce cones. Male and female reproductive structures are found on separate trees; the male structure resembles a catkin, and the female consists of paired ovules. After fertilization, the female tree produces seeds protected by a fleshy covering.

Pinnate leaf

Petiole (leaf stalk)

"Trunk" covered with scale leaves

Scale leaf

SAGO PALM
(Cycas revoluta)

CYCAD
Shaped like a small palm tree, cycads have a distinct "trunk" covered with woody scales, and a crown of long, divided leaves. Large cones grow in the center of the crown, with male and female cones appearing on different plants.

Needle-shaped leaf

Seed

Aril (fleshy outgrowth from seed)

Female "cone"

Stem

YEW
(Taxus baccata)

CONIFER
Conifers include pines, cypresses, redwoods, larches, cedars, and yews. Most of them are tall trees with tough, leathery, evergreen leaves that range in shape from thin needles to flat scales. Seeds typically develop within woody female cones, which are usually larger than male cones, and often grow separately on the same tree. Yews lack true cones.

GNETOPHYTE
A highly diverse gymnosperm group, the gnetophytes are mostly trees and shrubs. The desert plant welwitschia is an unusual, horizontally growing gnetophyte with two long, straplike leaves and a central, short trunk.

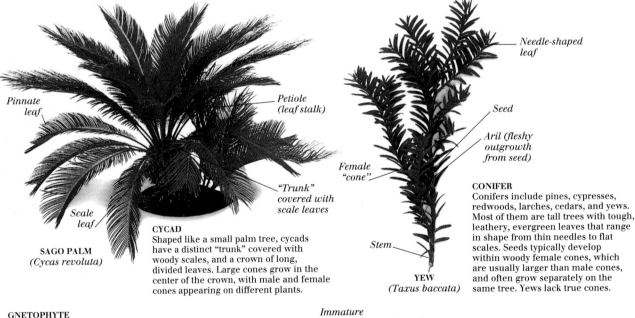

Immature cone

Continuously growing leaf

Site of cone growth

Adaxial (upper) surface of leaf

Abaxial (lower) surface of leaf

Frayed end of leaf

Scars left where cones fall away

Woody stem

WELWITSCHIA
(Welwitschia mirabilis)

FEATURES OF BISHOP PINE *(Pinus muricata)*

MICROGRAPH OF FOLIAGE LEAF (NEEDLE)
The surface of a pine needle is pitted with rows of stomata (pores). The stomata are sunken in the waterproof cuticle (outer covering) of the needle. This adaptation reduces water loss from the leaf and enables the tree to withstand the drying effect of the wind.

Upper surface

Margin

Stoma (pores through which gases enter and leave)

Needle-shaped leaf

Apical bud (point at which main growth takes place)

Dwarf shoot (bears needle-shaped leaves)

Stem

TERMINAL ZONE OF BRANCH
The apical bud at the tip of a branch is an active growing point from which the next year's growth of the branch will occur. Behind it are dwarf shoots that show limited growth and bear the needle-shaped leaves typical of all pines.

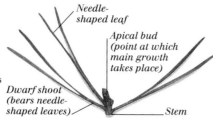

LIFE CYCLE OF SCOTS PINE *(Pinus sylvestris)*

Pollen grains, which contain male **gametes**, are released in the spring from male cones and are carried by the wind to immature (first-year) female cones. Pollination occurs when a pollen grain sticks to the micropyle – the opening to the ovule that contains the female gamete (ovum). A pollen tube grows slowly from it and carries the male gamete toward the ovum. The gametes meet, fertilization occurs, and a winged seed develops. The mature (third-year) cone opens up and releases the seed into the wind. When it reaches the soil, it germinates into a pine seedling which grows into a new plant.

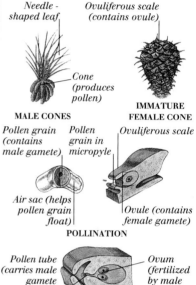

Needle-shaped leaf

Ovuliferous scale (contains ovule)

Cone (produces pollen)

MALE CONES

IMMATURE FEMALE CONE

Pollen grain (contains male gamete)

Pollen grain in micropyle

Ovuliferous scale

Air sac (helps pollen grain float)

Ovule (contains female gamete)

POLLINATION

Pollen tube (carries male gamete to ovum)

Ovum (fertilized by male gamete)

FERTILIZATION

Ovuliferous scale

Seed (forms from ovule and contains embryo plant)

Seed

Wing (aids seed dispersal)

MATURE FEMALE CONE AND WINGED SEED

Plumule (embryo shoot)

Cotyledon (seed leaf)

Young root

GERMINATION OF PINE SEEDLING

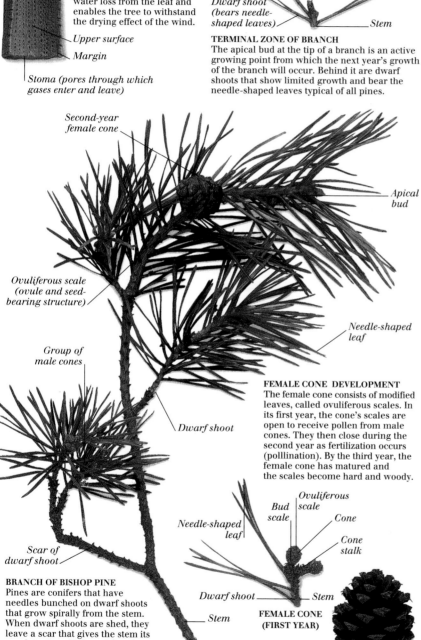

Second-year female cone

Apical bud

Ovuliferous scale (ovule and seed-bearing structure)

Needle-shaped leaf

Group of male cones

Dwarf shoot

Scar of dwarf shoot

BRANCH OF BISHOP PINE
Pines are conifers that have needles bunched on dwarf shoots that grow spirally from the stem. When dwarf shoots are shed, they leave a scar that gives the stem its rough texture. Male and female cones are borne on different branches; male cones in clusters at the tip of a branch, and female cones singly or in pairs.

FEMALE CONE DEVELOPMENT
The female cone consists of modified leaves, called ovuliferous scales. In its first year, the cone's scales are open to receive pollen from male cones. They then close during the second year as fertilization occurs (pollination). By the third year, the female cone has matured and the scales become hard and woody.

Needle-shaped leaf

Bud scale

Ovuliferous scale

Cone

Cone stalk

Dwarf shoot

Stem

FEMALE CONE (FIRST YEAR)

Stem

Woody, ovuliferous scale (open to release seed)

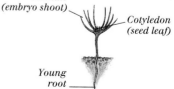

FEMALE CONE (THIRD YEAR)

Flowering plants 1

THE LARGEST AND MOST DIVERSE group of plants are the
flowering plants (division Anthophyta). These reproduce by
releasing **seeds,** which are produced by reproductive structures
called flowers. Flowers consist of sepals and petals, which protect
the flower, and male and female reproductive organs(see pp. 146-
147); many attract **pollinating** animals. There are two classes of
flowering plants: monocotyledonous plants, or monocots (class
Liliopsida), which produce seeds with a single **cotyledon**, and
dicotyledonous plants, or dicots (class Magnoliopsida), which
produce seeds with two cotyledons. Herbaceous flowering
plants have green stems and die back at the end of the
growing season. Woody flowering plants, which include
shrubs and trees, have thick, supportive stems,
reinforced with wood; these survive cold winters
above ground and may live for many years.
Most monocots are herbaceous, while dicots
include both herbaceous and woody species.

ANATOMY OF A WOODY FLOWERING PLANT

Flowering plants have a root system below ground that
anchors the plant and takes in water and nutrients from
the soil. Above ground level is a stem with leaves and
buds that arise at nodes. Leaves are borne on petioles
(leaf stalks). Buds may form at the stem apex (apical
buds) or between the stem and petiole (lateral buds).
Both types of buds may give rise to leaves or flowers.
The stem of the tree mallow is typical of most woody
flowering plants with, in the mature plant, a woody
core surrounded by a layer of protective bark.

HERBACEOUS FLOWERING PLANT

The stem of a herbaceous plant, such as this
strawberry, is green and nonwoody, dying back
at the end of each growing season. If the plant is
perennial, the underground parts survive to produce
new shoots in the next growing season. Annual
plants die completely, having first produced seeds.

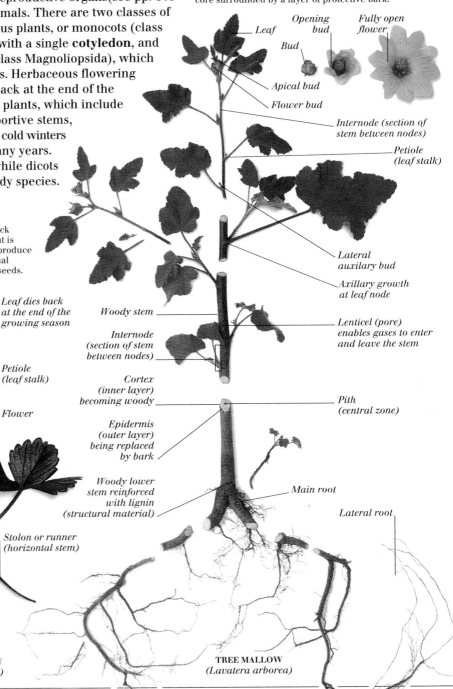

Opening bud

Leaf

Bud

Fully open flower

Apical bud

Flower bud

Internode (section of stem between nodes)

Petiole (leaf stalk)

Lateral auxilary bud

Axillary growth at leaf node

Lenticel (pore) enables gases to enter and leave the stem

Pith (central zone)

Main root

Lateral root

Leaf dies back at the end of the growing season

Woody stem

Internode (section of stem between nodes)

Cortex (inner layer) becoming woody

Epidermis (outer layer) being replaced by bark

Woody lower stem reinforced with lignin (structural material)

Petiole (leaf stalk)

Flower

Green, non-woody stem

Stolon or runner (horizontal stem)

Root system

STRAWBERRY
(Fragaria sp.)

TREE MALLOW
(Lavatera arborea)

MONOCOTYLEDONOUS AND DICOTYLEDONOUS PLANTS

VEINS OF A MONOCOT LEAF

VEINS OF A DICOT LEAF

Inner tepal
(monocot petal)

Style

Honey
guide, directs
insects into
flower

Filament

Anther

Stigma

Outer tepal
(monocot sepal)

MONOCOT FLOWER

Posterior sepal

Honey guide

Posterior
petal

False anthers
attract pollinating
insects

Anther

Anterior
petal

Anterior
sepal

Pedicel
(flower stalk)

DICOT FLOWER

MONOCOT AND DICOT LEAF STRUCTURE
Monocot and dicot leaves differ according to
the arrangement of their veins. Monocot leaves
have parallel veins that run along the long axis
of the leaf. Dicot leaves typically have a network
of veins that radiate from a central midrib.

MONOCOT AND DICOT FLOWER STRUCTURE
Monocot flowers such as the lily (shown above) have flower parts that occur in multiples
of three. The sepals and petals are typically large and indistinguishable; individually they
are called tepals. Dicot flowers, such as this larkspur (shown above), have flower parts
that occur in fours or fives. Most have small, green sepals and prominent, colorful petals.
The larkspur, however, has large, colorful sepals and smaller petals.

GENERAL FLOWER STRUCTURE

FEATURES OF A FLOWER
A flower consists of four whorls (rings) of parts
arranged around the receptacle (tip of the flower
stalk). The outermost whorl, the calyx, consists of sepals –
large and colorful in monocots, usually small and green
in dicots. The corolla is the whorl of petals; these are
prominent and colorful in animal-pollinated flowers.
The androecium (male reproductive structure) is a
whorl of stamens, each consisting of a filament and an
anther. The gynoecium (female reproductive structure)
has one or more carpels. Each carpel consists of a
stigma, style, and an ovary.

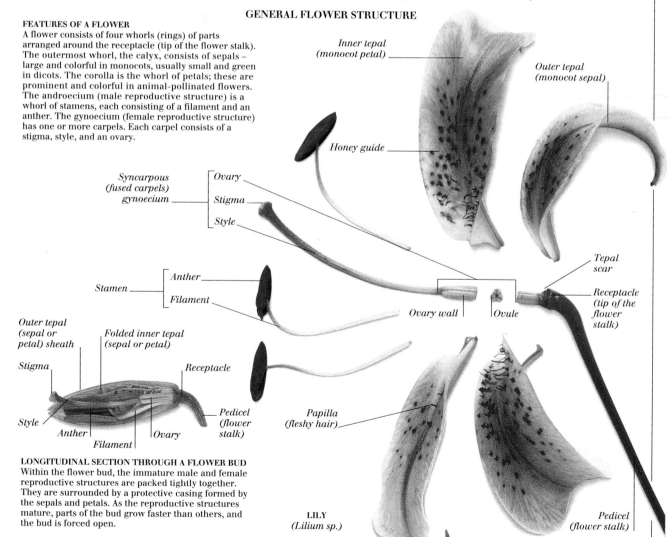

Inner tepal
(monocot petal)

Outer tepal
(monocot sepal)

Honey guide

Syncarpous
(fused carpels)
gynoecium

Ovary

Stigma

Style

Stamen

Anther

Filament

Tepal
scar

Receptacle
(tip of the
flower
stalk)

Ovary wall

Ovule

Outer tepal
(sepal or
petal) sheath

Stigma

Style

Anther

Filament

Folded inner tepal
(sepal or petal)

Receptacle

Ovary

Pedicel
(flower
stalk)

Papilla
(fleshy hair)

LONGITUDINAL SECTION THROUGH A FLOWER BUD
Within the flower bud, the immature male and female
reproductive structures are packed tightly together.
They are surrounded by a protective casing formed by
the sepals and petals. As the reproductive structures
mature, parts of the bud grow faster than others, and
the bud is forced open.

LILY
(Lilium sp.)

Pedicel
(flower stalk)

Flowering plants 2

FLOWERING PLANTS FORM a diverse group that ranges in size and form from delicate pondweeds to tall, ancient oak trees. They all consist of the same basic parts, but these show great variety. Flowers vary greatly in shape and size and have evolved to maximize the chances of **pollination** and **fertilization**. Many have large petals to attract pollinating animals; wind-pollinated flowers are small and less colorful (see pp. 146-147). Some plants have solitary flowers; others have groups of flowers. Leaves are similarly varied. All **monocots** and some **dicots** have simple leaves; other dicots have compound leaves consisting of smaller leaflets. Flowering plants have successfully exploited most of the world's **habitats,** including deserts, marshland, freshwater, and the tropics. Some are adapted to surviving in conditions that flowering plants would not normally tolerate.

EXAMPLES OF LEAF TYPE

Leaves are classified according to the form of their lamina, or blade. In simple leaves, such as the iris and sweet chestnut, the lamina is a single unit. In compound leaves, such as the black locust, the lamina is divided into separate leaflets. Leaves can be further classified by the overall shape of the lamina and whether its margin (edge) is smooth or not.

Single lamina / *Leaf margin* / *Parallel leaf veins*

SIMPLE LINEAR LEAF: IRIS

Lateral vein / *Lamina* / *Midrib* / *Lamina base* / *Leaf base* / *Petiole (leaf stalk)*

SIMPLE ELLIPTIC LEAF: SWEET CHESTNUT

Terminal leaflet / *Rachis (main axis of pinnate leaf)* / *Petiolule (leaflet stalk)* / *Petiole (leaf stalk)* / *Leaflet*

COMPOUND ODD PINNATE LEAF: BLACK LOCUST

EXAMPLES OF FLOWER TYPE

Some flowering plants, such as the glory lily, have a single flower on a pedicel (flower stalk). Others produce inflorescences (flower heads), which vary in size, shape, and number of flowers. They can be classified as, for example, spadix, spike, cyme, or umbel, according to the arrangement of flowers. Composite flowers, such as the sunflower, have an inflorescence that consists of many tiny flowers (florets) clustered together.

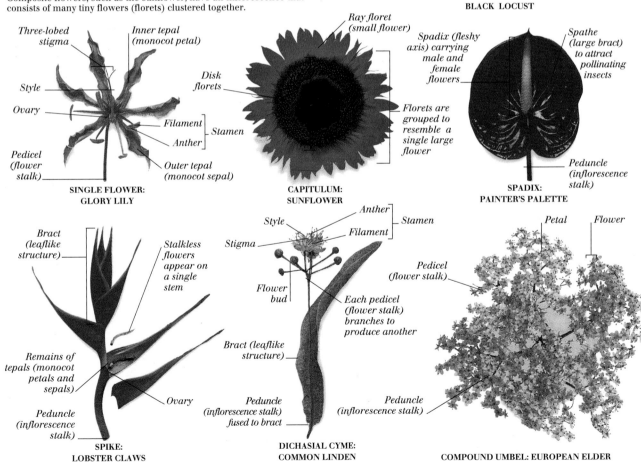

Three-lobed stigma / *Inner tepal (monocot petal)* / *Style* / *Ovary* / *Filament* / *Anther* / *Stamen* / *Pedicel (flower stalk)* / *Outer tepal (monocot sepal)*

SINGLE FLOWER: GLORY LILY

Ray floret (small flower) / *Disk florets* / *Florets are grouped to resemble a single large flower*

CAPITULUM: SUNFLOWER

Spadix (fleshy axis) carrying male and female flowers / *Spathe (large bract) to attract pollinating insects* / *Peduncle (inflorescence stalk)*

SPADIX: PAINTER'S PALETTE

Bract (leaflike structure) / *Stalkless flowers appear on a single stem* / *Remains of tepals (monocot petals and sepals)* / *Ovary* / *Peduncle (inflorescence stalk)*

SPIKE: LOBSTER CLAWS

Style / *Stigma* / *Anther* / *Filament* / *Stamen* / *Flower bud* / *Bract (leaflike structure)* / *Each pedicel (flower stalk) branches to produce another* / *Peduncle (inflorescence stalk) fused to bract*

DICHASIAL CYME: COMMON LINDEN

Petal / *Flower* / *Pedicel (flower stalk)* / *Peduncle (inflorescence stalk)*

COMPOUND UMBEL: EUROPEAN ELDER

EXAMPLES OF FLOWERING PLANT DIVERSITY

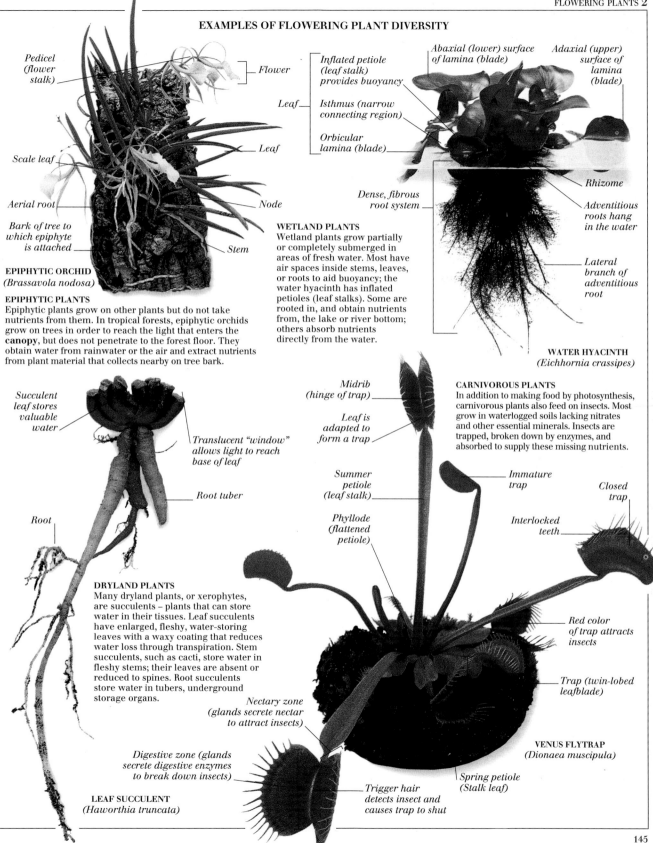

Pedicel (flower stalk)

Flower

Scale leaf

Leaf

Aerial root

Node

Bark of tree to which epiphyte is attached

Stem

EPIPHYTIC ORCHID
(*Brassavola nodosa*)

EPIPHYTIC PLANTS
Epiphytic plants grow on other plants but do not take nutrients from them. In tropical forests, epiphytic orchids grow on trees in order to reach the light that enters the **canopy**, but does not penetrate to the forest floor. They obtain water from rainwater or the air and extract nutrients from plant material that collects nearby on tree bark.

Inflated petiole (leaf stalk) provides buoyancy

Leaf

Isthmus (narrow connecting region)

Orbicular lamina (blade)

Abaxial (lower) surface of lamina (blade)

Adaxial (upper) surface of lamina (blade)

Rhizome

Dense, fibrous root system

Adventitious roots hang in the water

Lateral branch of adventitious root

WETLAND PLANTS
Wetland plants grow partially or completely submerged in areas of fresh water. Most have air spaces inside stems, leaves, or roots to aid buoyancy; the water hyacinth has inflated petioles (leaf stalks). Some are rooted in, and obtain nutrients from, the lake or river bottom; others absorb nutrients directly from the water.

WATER HYACINTH
(*Eichhornia crassipes*)

Succulent leaf stores valuable water

Translucent "window" allows light to reach base of leaf

Root tuber

Root

DRYLAND PLANTS
Many dryland plants, or xerophytes, are succulents – plants that can store water in their tissues. Leaf succulents have enlarged, fleshy, water-storing leaves with a waxy coating that reduces water loss through transpiration. Stem succulents, such as cacti, store water in fleshy stems; their leaves are absent or reduced to spines. Root succulents store water in tubers, underground storage organs.

LEAF SUCCULENT
(*Haworthia truncata*)

Midrib (hinge of trap)

Leaf is adapted to form a trap

Summer petiole (leaf stalk)

Phyllode (flattened petiole)

Nectary zone (glands secrete nectar to attract insects)

Digestive zone (glands secrete digestive enzymes to break down insects)

Trigger hair detects insect and causes trap to shut

CARNIVOROUS PLANTS
In addition to making food by photosynthesis, carnivorous plants also feed on insects. Most grow in waterlogged soils lacking nitrates and other essential minerals. Insects are trapped, broken down by enzymes, and absorbed to supply these missing nutrients.

Immature trap

Closed trap

Interlocked teeth

Red color of trap attracts insects

Trap (twin-lobed leafblade)

VENUS FLYTRAP
(*Dionaea muscipula*)

Spring petiole (Stalk leaf)

Flowering-plant reproduction

Flowers are the sites of sexual reproduction in flowering plants. In order for them to produce **seeds**, pollination and fertilization must occur. Pollination involves the transfer of **pollen**, which contains the male **gametes**, from an **anther** to a **stigma**. Most flowers contain both anthers and stigmas, but to ensure **genetic variation**, pollination usually occurs between flowers on different plants. The pollen may be carried between plants by animals, the wind, or water. When the male and female gametes meet, fertilization takes place. This happens within the ovule, which is surrounded by the ovary. The fertilized ovum – female gamete – develops into an **embryo**, which, with its food store and **testa**, forms the seed. When fully developed, seeds are dispersed (sometimes within their fruit) away from the parent plant. Under the right conditions, the seeds germinate and grow into new plants.

MICROGRAPH OF A POLLEN GRAIN

During the journey between the anther and stigma, the male gametes are protected within the thick walls of a pollen grain. The wall consists of an inner intine and a tough, external exine that, when viewed under a scanning electron microscope, is often seen to be elaborately sculptured. These patterns can be used to identify plant species.

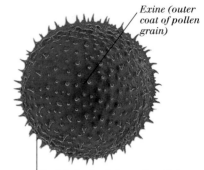

Exine (outer coat of pollen grain)

Sculpted exine helps pollen stick to insects during pollination

REPRODUCTIVE STRUCTURES IN A WIND-POLLINATED PLANT

Because they have no need to attract animal pollinators, wind-pollinated flowers are usually small, inconspicuous, dull-colored, and unscented. They are also commonly unisexual – male and female flowers are found on separate plants or on different parts of the same plant. Anthers in the male flower hang exposed at the end of long filaments and release large numbers of light, smooth pollen grains that are carried by the wind. Stigmas in the female flower are also exposed and poised to intercept any windblown pollen grains that pass near.

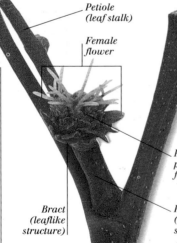

Petiole (leaf stalk)

Female flower

Bract (leaflike structure)

Prominent stigma protrudes from flower

Peduncle (inflorescence stalk)

FEMALE

Flower bud

Part of male catkin (inflorescence adapted for wind pollination)

Male flower

Peduncle (inflorescence stalk)

Filament

Anther

SWEET CHESTNUT
(*Castanea sativa*)

MALE

INSECT POLLINATION

Insects, such as bees, are attracted to flowers by their color, smell, and the sugary nectar they often contain. As the bee crawls into the flower, pollen grains are dusted onto it. When the insect visits another flower of the same species, pollen grains are transferred to the sticky stigma.

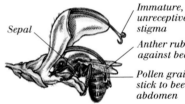

Immature, unreceptive stigma

Sepal

Anther rubs against bee

Pollen grains stick to bee's abdomen

BEE VISITS FIRST FLOWER

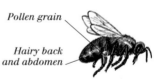

Pollen grain

Hairy back and abdomen

BEE FLIES TO SECOND FLOWER

Long style curves down when bee enters flower

Mature stigma touches abdomen and picks up pollen

BEE VISITS SECOND FLOWER

DEVELOPMENT OF A SUCCULENT FRUIT: BLACKBERRY (*Rubus fruticosus*)

The blackberry flower attracts insects to pollinate it. Once pollination and fertilization have occured, the flower parts wither. A seed develops inside each of the **carpels,** and the ovary wall surrounding the seeds swells and ripens, forming the pericarp. Together, the seed and pericarp form a fruit. Animals eat the succulent fruit and the seeds pass out, unharmed, in their droppings.

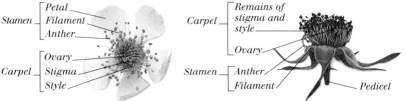

Stamen — Petal
Filament
Anther

Carpel — Ovary
Stigma
Style

FLOWER ATTRACTS POLLINATORS

Carpel — Remains of stigma and style

Ovary

Stamen — Anther
Filament

Pedicel

OVARIES SWELL, STAMENS WITHER

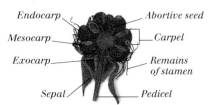

Endocarp
Mesocarp
Exocarp
Sepal

Abortive seed
Carpel
Remains of stamen
Pedicel

PERICARP FORMS

Exocarp
Fruit drupelet
Remains of stamen
Pedicel

Remains of style
Remains of sepal

DRUPELETS RIPEN FULLY

GERMINATION OF A FAVA BEAN SEED (*Vicia faba*)

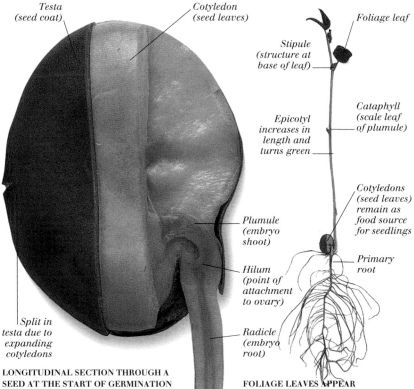

Testa (seed coat)
Cotyledon (seed leaves)

Foliage leaf

Stipule (structure at base of leaf)

Epicotyl increases in length and turns green

Cataphyll (scale leaf of plumule)

Cotyledons (seed leaves) remain as food source for seedlings

Plumule (embryo shoot)

Hilum (point of attachment to ovary)

Primary root

Split in testa due to expanding cotyledons

Radicle (embryo root)

LONGITUDINAL SECTION THROUGH A SEED AT THE START OF GERMINATION
A fava bean seed consists of an embryo plant, a food store in the form of two cotyledons (seed leaves), and a protective outer coat (testa). When conditions are right, the seed takes in water and the radicle (embryo root) swells, breaking through the testa and growing downward.

FOLIAGE LEAVES APPEAR
Fava beans exhibit hypogeal germination – the plumule (embryo shoot) grows upward from the seed and out of the soil. The energy for this is provided by the cotyledons, which remain under the soil. The first true leaves allow the plant to make food itself, by photosynthesis.

THE PROCESS OF FERTILIZATION

When a pollen grain lands on a stigma it produces a pollen tube, which grows through the style and ovary wall and enters the inner part of the ovule. The two male **gametes** from the pollen grain travel down the pollen tube. One fuses with the ovum to form the embryo. The other fuses with the **polar nuclei** to form the endosperm – the embryo's food supply.

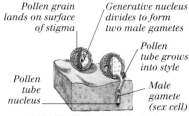

Pollen grain lands on surface of stigma

Generative nucleus divides to form two male gametes

Pollen tube grows into style

Pollen tube nucleus

Male gamete (sex cell)

POLLEN GRAIN GERMINATES

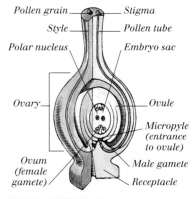

Pollen grain
Style
Polar nucleus

Ovary

Ovum (female gamete)

Stigma
Pollen tube
Embryo sac

Ovule
Micropyle (entrance to ovule)
Male gamete
Receptacle

MALE GAMETES TRAVEL TO EMBRYO SAC

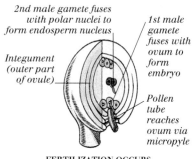

2nd male gamete fuses with polar nuclei to form endosperm nucleus

Integument (outer part of ovule)

1st male gamete fuses with ovum to form embryo

Pollen tube reaches ovum via micropyle

FERTILIZATION OCCURS

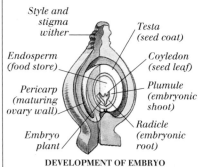

Style and stigma wither

Endosperm (food store)

Pericarp (maturing ovary wall)

Embryo plant

Testa (seed coat)
Coyledon (seed leaf)
Plumule (embryonic shoot)
Radicle (embryonic root)

DEVELOPMENT OF EMBRYO

Photosynthesis and plant-transport systems

PLANTS ARE AUTOTROPHIC – they manufacture food themselves, by photosynthesis. This is a process that converts sunlight **energy** into chemical energy, which is then used to combine carbon dioxide and water to produce complex **carbohydrates** such as glucose, sucrose, and starch – the plant's main energy store. Photosynthesis takes place inside chloroplasts – **organelles** that are found only in plant and algal cells (see pp. 122-123). Chloroplasts contain pigments, including chlorophyll, that can absorb and harness sunlight energy. Photosynthesis is of vital importance to living organisms because it "fixes" carbon by removing carbon dioxide from the air to produce carbohydrates. These feed and build plants and are also the primary food source for all **heterotrophic** organisms. Plant-transport systems carry materials to where they are needed. There are two types of vascular tissue, which consist of tubular cells: xylem carries water and minerals from the roots to other parts of the plant and also helps to support it; phloem carries nutrients from where they are made, such as carbohydrates in the leaves, to where they are required.

STRUCTURE OF A CHLOROPLAST

A chloroplast is a disk-shaped organelle that is surrounded by an inner and outer membrane. Inside the chloroplast, molecules of chlorophyll and other pigments are packed into a system of membranes. These form flattened, saclike structures called thylakoids, which are arranged in stacks called grana that provide a large surface area for trapping sunlight energy during photosynthesis. Grana are surrounded by the stroma, a liquid matrix in which trapped energy is used to manufacture sugars.

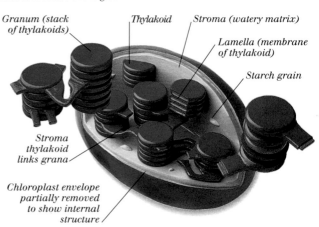

Granum (stack of thylakoids) *Thylakoid* *Stroma (watery matrix)* *Lamella (membrane of thylakoid)* *Starch grain* *Stroma thylakoid links grana* *Chloroplast envelope partially removed to show internal structure*

THE PROCESS OF PHOTOSYNTHESIS

Photosynthesis takes place inside the chloroplasts of leaf cells and of other green parts of the plant. The raw materials for photosynthesis are carbon dioxide from the air and water from the soil. There are two stages in photosynthesis. The first is light-dependent and takes place in the grana. Sunlight energy is "captured" by chlorophyll in the chloroplasts and converted into chemical energy in the form of **ATP**. This process also splits up water into oxygen and hydrogen, with oxygen being released as a waste product. The second, light-independent stage, takes place in the stroma. Carbon dioxide is combined with hydrogen, using energy from ATP to produce glucose.

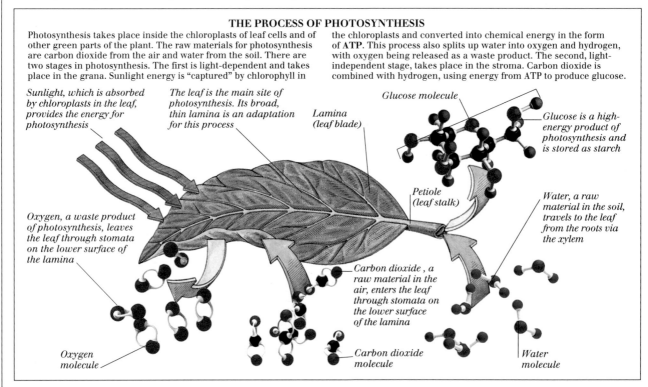

Sunlight, which is absorbed by chloroplasts in the leaf, provides the energy for photosynthesis

The leaf is the main site of photosynthesis. Its broad, thin lamina is an adaptation for this process

Lamina (leaf blade)

Glucose molecule

Glucose is a high-energy product of photosynthesis and is stored as starch

Oxygen, a waste product of photosynthesis, leaves the leaf through stomata on the lower surface of the lamina

Petiole (leaf stalk)

Water, a raw material in the soil, travels to the leaf from the roots via the xylem

Carbon dioxide , a raw material in the air, enters the leaf through stomata on the lower surface of the lamina

Oxygen molecule

Carbon dioxide molecule

Water molecule

INTERNAL PLANT ANATOMY AND TRANSPORT SYSTEMS

Leaves, shoots, and roots are all covered with an outer epidermis, which prevents water loss and protects against disease. Water vapor is constantly lost through stomata (pores) in the lower epidermis. This process, called transpiration, draws water into the leaves through the xylem of the roots and stem. Stems and shoots support the plant and carry water from the roots to the leaves, and nutrients from the leaves to other parts of the plant. Roots anchor the plant in the soil and absorb water and mineral salts from soil water.

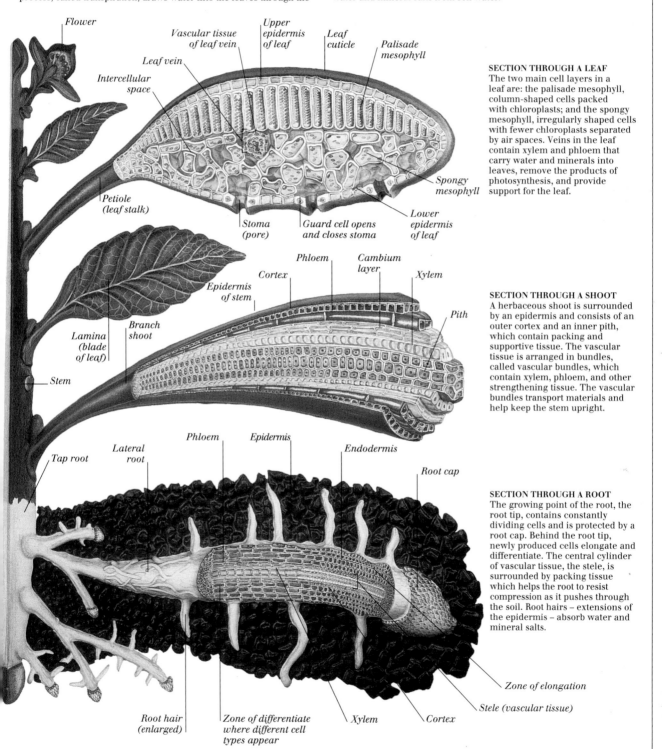

Flower

Vascular tissue of leaf vein

Upper epidermis of leaf

Leaf cuticle

Palisade mesophyll

Leaf vein

Intercellular space

Petiole (leaf stalk)

Spongy mesophyll

Stoma (pore)

Guard cell opens and closes stoma

Lower epidermis of leaf

SECTION THROUGH A LEAF
The two main cell layers in a leaf are: the palisade mesophyll, column-shaped cells packed with chloroplasts; and the spongy mesophyll, irregularly shaped cells with fewer chloroplasts separated by air spaces. Veins in the leaf contain xylem and phloem that carry water and minerals into leaves, remove the products of photosynthesis, and provide support for the leaf.

Phloem

Cambium layer

Cortex

Xylem

Epidermis of stem

Pith

Branch shoot

Lamina (blade of leaf)

Stem

SECTION THROUGH A SHOOT
A herbaceous shoot is surrounded by an epidermis and consists of an outer cortex and an inner pith, which contain packing and supportive tissue. The vascular tissue is arranged in bundles, called vascular bundles, which contain xylem, phloem, and other strengthening tissue. The vascular bundles transport materials and help keep the stem upright.

Phloem

Epidermis

Endodermis

Lateral root

Root cap

Tap root

SECTION THROUGH A ROOT
The growing point of the root, the root tip, contains constantly dividing cells and is protected by a root cap. Behind the root tip, newly produced cells elongate and differentiate. The central cylinder of vascular tissue, the stele, is surrounded by packing tissue which helps the root to resist compression as it pushes through the soil. Root hairs – extensions of the epidermis – absorb water and mineral salts.

Zone of elongation

Stele (vascular tissue)

Root hair (enlarged)

Zone of differentiate where different cell types appear

Xylem

Cortex

Sponges, cnidarians, and echinoderms

SPONGES, CNIDARIANS, AND ECHINODERMS are aquatic animals that belong to three very different **phyla**. Sponges, the simplest of all animals, are **sessile** and live firmly attached to a rock or coral reef. They extract food particles from water currents that pass through them. Cnidarians, which include hydras and corals, exhibit **radial symmetry** and are either polyps – sessile and fixed by their base to an object – or medusae – bell-shaped and free-swimming. Both forms have a single opening, the mouth, which is surrounded by tentacles armed with unique stinging cells called cnidocytes. Echinoderms, "spiny-skinned" animals, are exclusively marine. They show **pentaradiate symmetry** and have an internal skeleton made from **calcareous** ossicles (plates). They use external, **protrusible** tube feet for moving and feeding.

STRUCTURE OF A CNIDOCYTE

Cnidocytes are cells that are found in the tentacles of cnidarians. If an animal touches the cnidocil, the operculum flies open and the nematocyst (stinging structure) is discharged. The thread of the nematocyst injects a paralyzing poison, and hooks secure the prey as it is pulled toward the cnidarian's mouth.

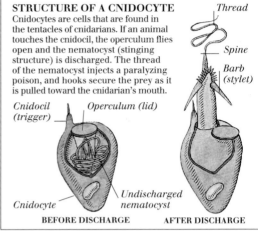

Thread
Spine
Barb (stylet)
Cnidocil (trigger)
Operculum (lid)
Undischarged nematocyst
Cnidocyte

BEFORE DISCHARGE **AFTER DISCHARGE**

INTERNAL FEATURES OF SPONGES

Sponges are supported by a mesohyal (gelatinous matrix), which contains spicules (skeletal struts) and is perforated by large numbers of pores (ostia). Water constantly passes into the atrium (interior) through the ostia and out through a large opening called the osculum. Choanocytes create a water current and filter out food particles.

Choanocyte (collar cell)
Mesohyal
Porocyte
Spicule
Atrium
Osculum (excurrent pore)
Pinacocyte (epidermal cell)
Ostium (incurrent pore)

INTERNAL FEATURES OF ANEMONES

Anemones are supported by a **hydrostatic skeleton**, against which the muscular system can act. The mouth opens through the pharynx and into the gastrovascular cavity. This is partitioned by folds, called septa, which release enzymes that digest prey taken in through the mouth.

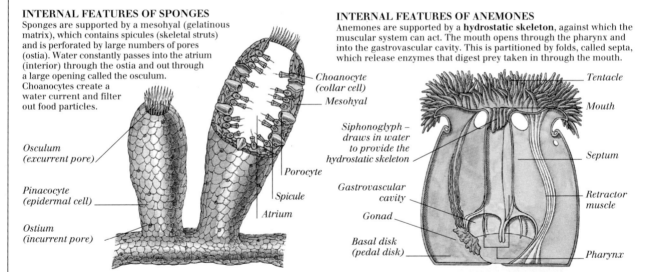

Tentacle
Mouth
Septum
Retractor muscle
Pharynx
Siphonoglyph – draws in water to provide the hydrostatic skeleton
Gastrovascular cavity
Gonad
Basal disk (pedal disk)

EXAMPLES OF CNIDARIAN TYPES

ANEMONES

Anemones are solitary, polypoid cnidarians. They have thick, column-shaped bodies with a suckerlike basal disk that is used to attach them to solid objects. Tentacles are used to catch passing prey and pull it toward the mouth. They can be retracted into the column to protect them from predators.

MEDITERRANEAN SEA ANEMONE
(*Condylactis sp.*)

GREEN SNAKELOCK ANEMONE
(*Anemonia viridis*)

BEADLET ANEMONE
(*Actinia equina*)

GHOST ANEMONE
(*Actinothoe sphyrodeta*)

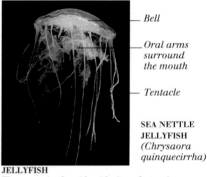

Bell
Oral arms surround the mouth
Tentacle

SEA NETTLE JELLYFISH
(*Chrysaora quinquecirrha*)

JELLYFISH

These are medusoid cnidarians that swim actively by alternately contracting and relaxing their bell-shaped body. Trailing tentacles and oral arms catch prey, such as small fish, and pull it into the mouth on the underside of the bell.

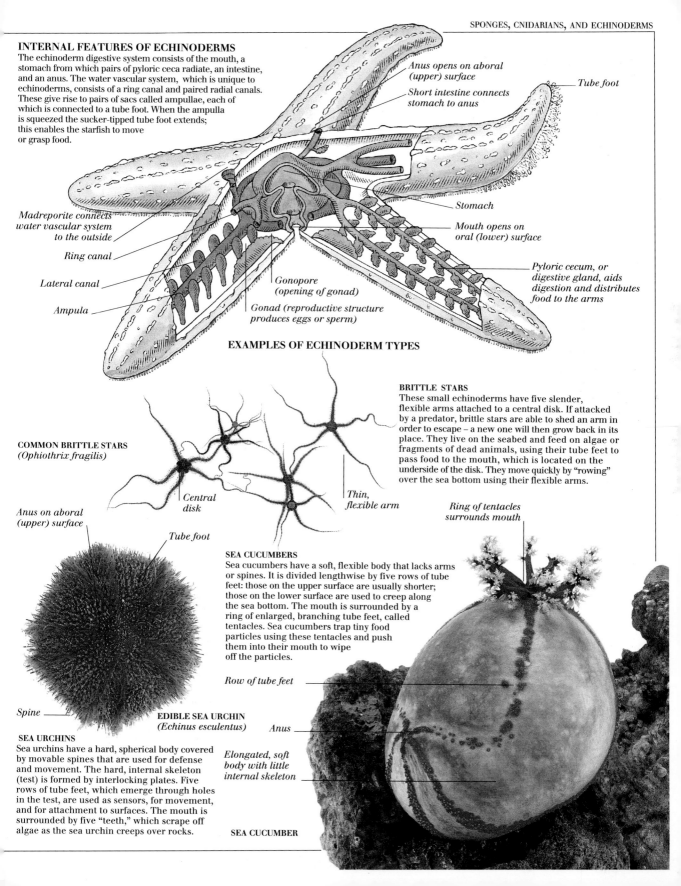

INTERNAL FEATURES OF ECHINODERMS

The echinoderm digestive system consists of the mouth, a stomach from which pairs of pyloric ceca radiate, an intestine, and an anus. The water vascular system, which is unique to echinoderms, consists of a ring canal and paired radial canals. These give rise to pairs of sacs called ampullae, each of which is connected to a tube foot. When the ampulla is squeezed the sucker-tipped tube foot extends; this enables the starfish to move or grasp food.

Anus opens on aboral (upper) surface

Short intestine connects stomach to anus

Tube foot

Stomach

Mouth opens on oral (lower) surface

Pyloric cecum, or digestive gland, aids digestion and distributes food to the arms

Madreporite connects water vascular system to the outside

Ring canal

Lateral canal

Ampula

Gonopore (opening of gonad)

Gonad (reproductive structure produces eggs or sperm)

EXAMPLES OF ECHINODERM TYPES

BRITTLE STARS

These small echinoderms have five slender, flexible arms attached to a central disk. If attacked by a predator, brittle stars are able to shed an arm in order to escape – a new one will then grow back in its place. They live on the seabed and feed on algae or fragments of dead animals, using their tube feet to pass food to the mouth, which is located on the underside of the disk. They move quickly by "rowing" over the sea bottom using their flexible arms.

COMMON BRITTLE STARS
(Ophiothrix fragilis)

Central disk

Thin, flexible arm

Ring of tentacles surrounds mouth

Anus on aboral (upper) surface

Tube foot

SEA CUCUMBERS

Sea cucumbers have a soft, flexible body that lacks arms or spines. It is divided lengthwise by five rows of tube feet: those on the upper surface are usually shorter; those on the lower surface are used to creep along the sea bottom. The mouth is surrounded by a ring of enlarged, branching tube feet, called tentacles. Sea cucumbers trap tiny food particles using these tentacles and push them into their mouth to wipe off the particles.

Row of tube feet

Spine

EDIBLE SEA URCHIN
(Echinus esculentus)

Anus

SEA URCHINS

Sea urchins have a hard, spherical body covered by movable spines that are used for defense and movement. The hard, internal skeleton (test) is formed by interlocking plates. Five rows of tube feet, which emerge through holes in the test, are used as sensors, for movement, and for attachment to surfaces. The mouth is surrounded by five "teeth," which scrape off algae as the sea urchin creeps over rocks.

Elongated, soft body with little internal skeleton

SEA CUCUMBER

Worms and mollusks

WORMS AND MOLLUSKS ARE SOFT-BODIED, **invertebrate** animals. "Worm" is a general term that includes several **phyla**. Two such phyla are: phylum Annelida (earthworms, marine worms, and leeches), which have segmented, cylindrical bodies with a body cavity (coelom) surrounding the digestive system; and phylum Platyhelminthes (flatworms, tapeworms, and flukes), which have flattened, unsegmented bodies with a single body opening. Mollusks (phylum Mollusca) typically have a head, a muscular foot used in movement, and a **visceral** hump containing most internal organs. Many mollusks secrete a **calcerous** shell from their mantle to protect their soft, moist bodies. There are three main mollusk classes: snails and slugs (class Gastropoda), which creep along on a muscular foot and feed using a rasplike **radula**; clams, scallops, and mussels (class Bivalvia), which are aquatic filter feeders; and squid, octopus, and nautilus (class Cephalopoda), which are free-swimming marine **predators**.

EARTHWORM REPRODUCTION

Earthworms are hermaphrodites – each has both male and female reproductive organs. During reproduction two worms face in opposite directions, held together by a mucus wrap that they secrete. Each worm releases sperm, which is stored by the other. After a few days, they secrete cocoons into which eggs are laid and fertilized externally by the stored sperm.

INTERNAL FEATURES OF ANNELID WORMS

Annelid worms, such as this earthworm, have a fluid-filled body cavity divided internally into segments by transverse folds called septa. The digestive system - pharynx, esophagus, crop, gizzard, and intestine - passes through the septa from the mouth to the anus. Waste is excreted by one pair of nephridia in each segment. Blood, which is pumped by pseudohearts, surrounds the esophagus and circulate along a dorsal vessel through branches in each segment before returning along the ventral vessel. The nervous system consists of a "brain" and a ventral nerve cord, with branches in each segment to coordinate movement.

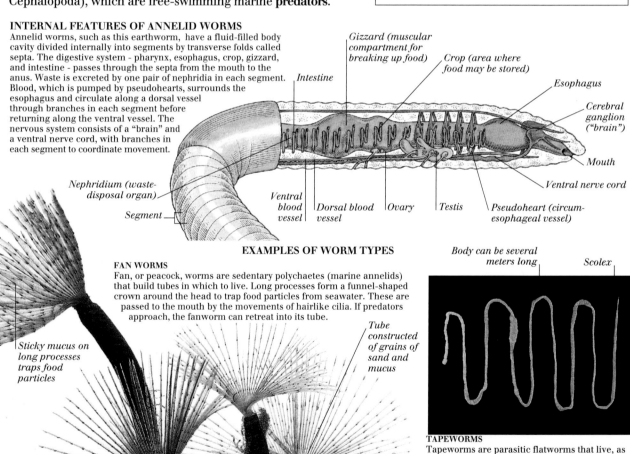

Gizzard (muscular compartment for breaking up food)

Crop (area where food may be stored)

Esophagus

Cerebral ganglion ("brain")

Intestine

Mouth

Ventral nerve cord

Nephridium (waste-disposal organ)

Segment

Ventral blood vessel

Dorsal blood vessel

Ovary

Testis

Pseudoheart (circum-esophageal vessel)

EXAMPLES OF WORM TYPES

FAN WORMS

Fan, or peacock, worms are sedentary polychaetes (marine annelids) that build tubes in which to live. Long processes form a funnel-shaped crown around the head to trap food particles from seawater. These are passed to the mouth by the movements of hairlike cilia. If predators approach, the fanworm can retreat into its tube.

Sticky mucus on long processes traps food particles

Tube constructed of grains of sand and mucus

Body can be several meters long

Scolex

FAN WORMS *(Sabella sp.)*

Funnel-shaped crown

TAPEWORMS

Tapeworms are parasitic flatworms that live, as adults, in the intestines of vertebrates. The tiny "head" (scolex) has hooks and suckers, that attach it to the host's intestinal wall. The body consists of reproductive segments (proglottids), which leave the host's body in feces when they are ripe and filled with eggs.

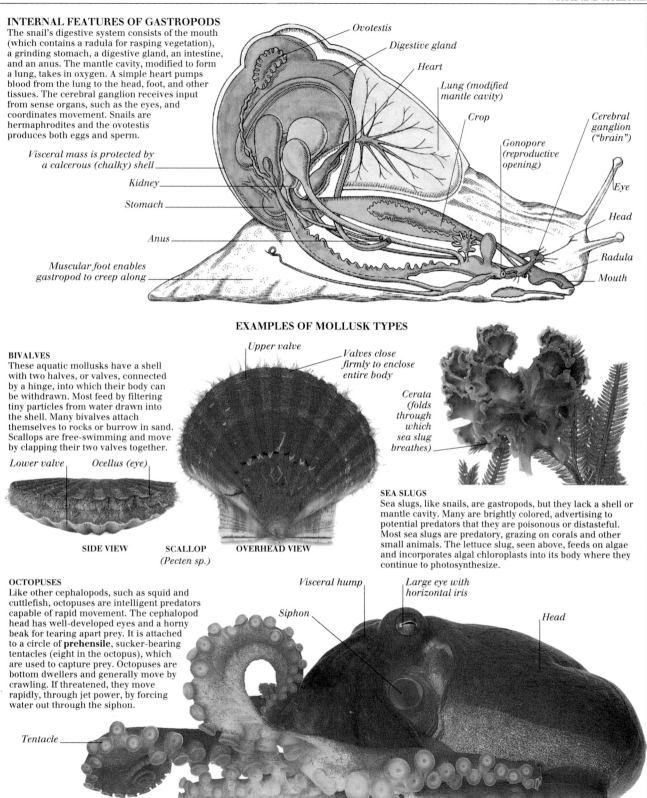

INTERNAL FEATURES OF GASTROPODS

The snail's digestive system consists of the mouth (which contains a radula for rasping vegetation), a grinding stomach, a digestive gland, an intestine, and an anus. The mantle cavity, modified to form a lung, takes in oxygen. A simple heart pumps blood from the lung to the head, foot, and other tissues. The cerebral ganglion receives input from sense organs, such as the eyes, and coordinates movement. Snails are hermaphrodites and the ovotestis produces both eggs and sperm.

Ovotestis

Digestive gland

Heart

Lung (modified mantle cavity)

Crop

Gonopore (reproductive opening)

Cerebral ganglion ("brain")

Eye

Head

Radula

Mouth

Visceral mass is protected by a calcerous (chalky) shell

Kidney

Stomach

Anus

Muscular foot enables gastropod to creep along

EXAMPLES OF MOLLUSK TYPES

BIVALVES

These aquatic mollusks have a shell with two halves, or valves, connected by a hinge, into which their body can be withdrawn. Most feed by filtering tiny particles from water drawn into the shell. Many bivalves attach themselves to rocks or burrow in sand. Scallops are free-swimming and move by clapping their two valves together.

Upper valve

Valves close firmly to enclose entire body

Cerata (folds through which sea slug breathes)

Lower valve   *Ocellus (eye)*

SIDE VIEW   **SCALLOP**
(*Pecten sp.*)   **OVERHEAD VIEW**

SEA SLUGS

Sea slugs, like snails, are gastropods, but they lack a shell or mantle cavity. Many are brightly colored, advertising to potential predators that they are poisonous or distasteful. Most sea slugs are predatory, grazing on corals and other small animals. The lettuce slug, seen above, feeds on algae and incorporates algal chloroplasts into its body where they continue to photosynthesize.

OCTOPUSES

Like other cephalopods, such as squid and cuttlefish, octopuses are intelligent predators capable of rapid movement. The cephalopod head has well-developed eyes and a horny beak for tearing apart prey. It is attached to a circle of **prehensile**, sucker-bearing tentacles (eight in the octopus), which are used to capture prey. Octopuses are bottom dwellers and generally move by crawling. If threatened, they move rapidly, through jet power, by forcing water out through the siphon.

Visceral hump

Large eye with horizontal iris

Siphon

Head

Tentacle

Arthropods 1

ARTHROPODS (PHYLUM ARTHROPODA) form the largest and most diverse animal group. An arthropod's body and limbs are completely covered by an exoskeleton (external skeleton), or cuticle, which consists of inflexible plates that meet at flexible joints. Arthropods are divided into three subgroups (subphyla) – crustaceans, chelicerates, and uniramians. Crustaceans (subphylum Crustacea) are mostly marine animals. Their bodies consist of a head, with **compound eyes** and two pairs of **antennae**, and a trunk, made up of a **thorax**, an abdomen, and several pairs of jointed appendages. The major classes include: lobsters and crabs; barnacles; and water fleas. The chelicerates (subphylum Chelicerata) have bodies divided into a cephalothorax and an abdomen. The cephalothorax bears a pair of feeding appendages (chelicerae), a pair of **pedipalps**, and four pairs of legs. The largest of the three chelicerate classes is the arachnids, which includes spiders, scorpions, harvestmen (or daddy longlegs), and ticks. The uniramians (subphylum Uniramia) include insects, millipedes, and centipedes (see pp. 156-157).

WALKING MECHANISMS OF AN ARTHROPOD

An arthropod limb consists of tubular plates connected by articular membranes, which form flexible joints. Sets of muscles attached across the joint between limb and body move the whole limb up and down, or back and forth. Opposing muscles, which cross joints within the limb, flex or extend the particular joint they cross. Collectively, the combined contractions or relaxations of muscle groups enable the animal to walk in a coordinated way.

Protractor muscle pulls limb forward

Flexor muscle pulls limb downward

Retractor muscle pulls limb backward

Extensor muscle pulls limb upward

MECHANISM IN BODY

Extensor muscle straightens joint

Articular membrane connects plates

Flexor muscle bends joint

MECHANISM IN LEG

CRUSTACEANS

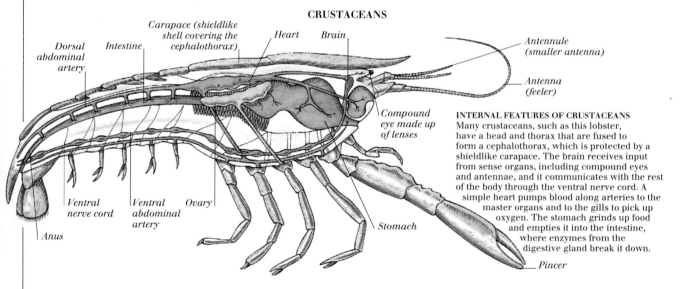

Dorsal abdominal artery

Intestine

Carapace (shieldlike shell covering the cephalothorax)

Heart

Brain

Antennule (smaller antenna)

Antenna (feeler)

Compound eye made up of lenses

Ventral nerve cord

Ventral abdominal artery

Ovary

Stomach

Anus

Pincer

INTERNAL FEATURES OF CRUSTACEANS
Many crustaceans, such as this lobster, have a head and thorax that are fused to form a cephalothorax, which is protected by a shieldlike carapace. The brain receives input from sense organs, including compound eyes and antennae, and it communicates with the rest of the body through the ventral nerve cord. A simple heart pumps blood along arteries to the master organs and to the gills to pick up oxygen. The stomach grinds up food and empties it into the intestine, where enzymes from the digestive gland break it down.

EXAMPLES OF CRUSTACEAN TYPES

Internal organs are visible through transparent carapace

WATER FLEAS
These small, freshwater crustaceans have laterally flattened, transparent bodies. Frilled appendages, attached to the trunk, are used to filter food from the water. Water fleas move by flicking their antennae.

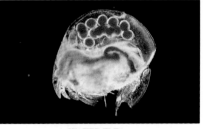

WATER FLEA
(*Turycecus lamellata*)

Tergum plate

Scutum plate

Cirri filter food particles from the water

Carina plate

STALKED BARNACLE
(*Lepas sp.*)

BARNACLES
Barnacles are sedentary, marine crustaceans that spend their lives permanently attached to rocks, boats, or even whales. Overlapping calcareous (chalky) plates form the exoskeleton, which surrounds and protects the animal.

ARACHNIDS

INTERNAL FEATURES OF ARACHNIDS
Scorpions capture their prey with pedipalps modified to form powerful claws. The prey is then torn apart by the chelicerae and soaked in digestive juices. The muscular foregut sucks in the liquefied food, the midgut completes digestion within the animal, and the hindgut expels waste. Air enters the book lungs through openings in the thorax and abdomen called spiracles. The posterior abdomen forms an arched "tail" at the tip of which is a sting; glands at the base of the sting produce venom, which is used to subdue prey.

Poison gland containing venom
Cephalothorax
Simple eye
Midgut
Heart
Hindgut
Pedipalp used to catch prey
Sting is used to paralyze prey
Brain
Intestine
Esophagus
Claw of pedipalp (chela)
"Tail" section of abdomen
Powerful muscles in pedipalp
Book lung
Foregut
Spiracle (air hole)
Ventral nerve cord

EXAMPLES OF ARACHNID TYPES

Long leg
Cephalothorax
Oval-shaped abdomen

HARVESTMAN

HARVESTMEN
Harvestmen inhabit damp, shaded areas of vegetation in tropical and temperate regions of the world. They have an oval-shaped body and long, thin legs. They feed on small invertebrates and scavenge for dead plant and animal material. Unlike other arachnids, harvestmen can ingest small food particles that are then digested in the gut.

SPIDERS
The most successful and abundant arachnids are the spiders. Their bodies consist of a distinct cephalothorax joined to the abdomen by a waistlike pedicel. They have four pairs of walking legs and a pair of leglike pedipalps, which act as sensory organs. Spiders produce silk, which is released from spinnerets at the tip of the abdomen. This may be used to produce egg cocoons, for building nests, and, in some species, to construct webs. All spiders are carnivorous, and most feed on insects. They pump digestive enzymes into paralyzed prey and then suck out the resulting juices.

Fourth walking leg
Spinneret for releasing silk
Abdomen
Pedicel
Patella
Third walking leg
Second walking leg
First walking leg
Cephalothorax
Femur
Tibia
Metatarsus
Tarsus
Claw
Simple eye
Pedipalp acts as sensory organ
Fanglike chelicera inject poison into prey to immobilize it

TARANTULA

SHEEP TICK
(Ixodes ricinus)

TICKS
Ticks are small, parasitic arachnids that live on the blood of land-living vertebrates. They puncture the host's skin, using serrated chelicerae, and work their toothed mouthparts into the wound. As they feed, their bodies expand (see above).

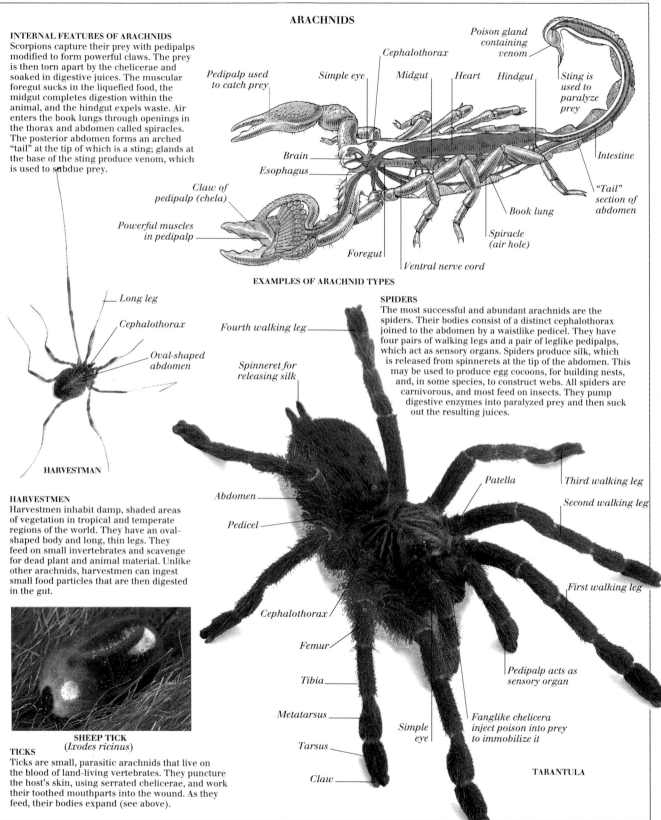

Arthropods 2

ARTHROPODS ARE INVERTEBRATES that have a segmented exoskeleton (external skeleton), or cuticle. The three main groups are: uniramians, which include insects, millipedes, and centipedes; crustaceans; and chelicerates (see pp. 154-155). Uniramians are mainly **terrestrial** and breathe air through **spiracles**. Insects (class Insecta) have bodies divided into three parts: a head; a thorax, which has three pairs of legs and typically two pairs of wings; and an abdomen. During their life cycle, insects undergo **metamorphosis**. Some, such as grasshoppers, show incomplete metamorphosis: young hatch from eggs as miniature adults, which grow and **molt** until they reach adult size. More advanced insects, such as beetles, show complete metamorphosis: young hatch from eggs as larvae, which undergo reorganization in a **pupa** and emerge as adults. Centipedes (class Chilopoda) and millipedes (class Diplopoda) have a body that consists of a head and trunk. Their cuticle lacks a waxy layer, and they are found mainly in humid habitats, such as leaf litter.

COMPOUND EYES

Most insects, and many crustaceans (see p. 154), have compound eyes, which are made up of long, cylindrical units called ommatidia. These consist of an outer, transparent lens-cornea and a crystalline cone, which focus light into the inner rhabdome. This contains light-sensitive cells, which, when stimulated by light, send nerve impulses to the brain.

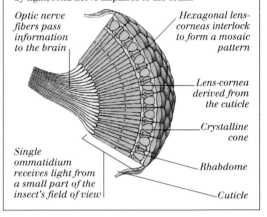

Optic nerve fibers pass information to the brain

Hexagonal lens-corneas interlock to form a mosaic pattern

Lens-cornea derived from the cuticle

Crystalline cone

Single ommatidium receives light from a small part of the insect's field of view

Rhabdome

Cuticle

ANATOMY OF INSECTS

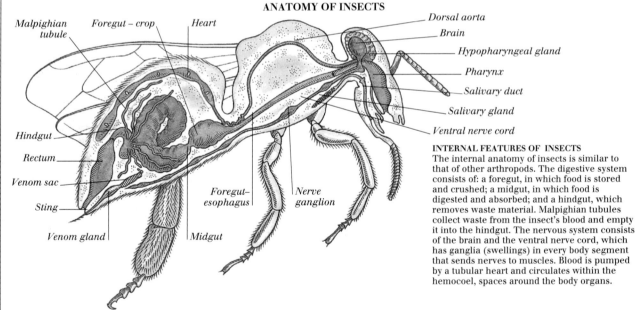

Malpighian tubule

Foregut – crop

Heart

Dorsal aorta

Brain

Hypopharyngeal gland

Pharynx

Salivary duct

Salivary gland

Ventral nerve cord

Hindgut

Rectum

Venom sac

Sting

Venom gland

Foregut–esophagus

Midgut

Nerve ganglion

INTERNAL FEATURES OF INSECTS

The internal anatomy of insects is similar to that of other arthropods. The digestive system consists of: a foregut, in which food is stored and crushed; a midgut, in which food is digested and absorbed; and a hindgut, which removes waste material. Malpighian tubules collect waste from the insect's blood and empty it into the hindgut. The nervous system consists of the brain and the ventral nerve cord, which has ganglia (swellings) in every body segment that sends nerves to muscles. Blood is pumped by a tubular heart and circulates within the hemocoel, spaces around the body organs.

INSECT WINGS

A majority of insects have wings; most have two pairs – forewings and hindwings. The insect wing consists of two thin layers of cuticle, which form the upper and lower surfaces. They are separated by veins that support the wing and supply it with blood. Wings vary greatly in size, shape, and color. Apart from flying, wings may also be used to attract a mate, act as camouflage, and to warn predators that the insect may be poisonous.

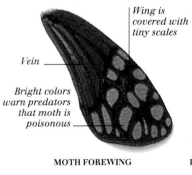

Wing is covered with tiny scales

Vein

Bright colors warn predators that moth is poisonous

MOTH FOREWING

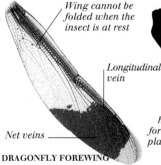

Wing cannot be folded when the insect is at rest

Longitudinal vein

Net veins

DRAGONFLY FOREWING

Forewing protects delicate hindwing and gives extra lift during flight

Wing is hardened to form a curved plate (elytron)

BEETLE FOREWING

LADYBUG METAMORPHOSIS

Like all beetles, ladybugs undergo complete metamorphosis. Eggs laid by the female hatch to produce larvae that feed on other insects. They grow rapidly, molting several times, and eventually form a pupa. The larval tissues reorganize within the pupa, and the pupal skin splits open to reveal the young, adult ladybug. Its soft wing cases harden within a few hours and, once its wings have expanded, it can fly.

Discarded egg case
Larva emerging
Larva
Pupa forming
Point of attachment to leaf
Adult ladybug can fly and reproduce
Wing cases harden within a few hours

LARVA HATCHING FROM EGG

LARVA ATTACHES ITSELF TO LEAF PRIOR TO PUPATION

ADULT LADYBUG

EXAMPLES OF INSECT TYPES

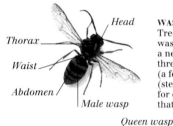

Head
Thorax
Waist
Abdomen
Male wasp

WASPS
Tree wasps, like ants, some bees, and other wasps, are social insects that live together in a nest. Within the tree wasp colony, there are three types (castes) of individuals: the queen (a fertile female) that lays eggs; workers (sterile females) that tend the nest and hunt for caterpillars to feed wasp larvae; and males that fertilize the queen.

Hairs prevent flea from falling out of fur
Laterally flattened body helps flea to move in fur
Rounded head
Stylet
Powerful hind leg enables flea to jump

Queen wasp
Worker (female) wasp
Forewings and hindwings are connected by a row of tiny hooks

TREE WASPS
(*Dolichovespula sylvestris*)

FLEAS
Fleas are small, parasitic, wingless insects that, as adults, live on the skin of birds and mammals. They feed by pushing their stylets (piercing mouthparts) through the host's skin and sucking blood. Flea larvae live in the host's nest or bedding and feed on dried blood.

CAT FLEA
(*Ctenocephalides felis*)

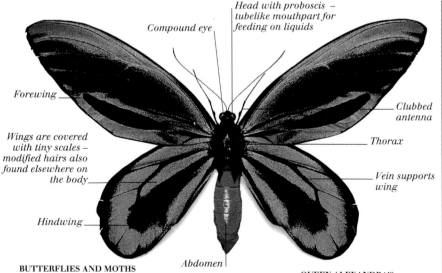

Head with proboscis – tubelike mouthpart for feeding on liquids
Compound eye
Forewing
Wings are covered with tiny scales – modified hairs also found elsewhere on the body
Hindwing
Abdomen
Clubbed antenna
Thorax
Vein supports wing

BUTTERFLIES AND MOTHS
Butterflies and moths have large, paired wings. The adults feed on liquids, particularly nectar from flowers, and the larvae, called caterpillars, feed on leaves and other plant parts. Butterflies typically have brightly colored wings, clubbed antennae, and fly by day; moths are usually duller in color, have feathery antennae, and are active at night.

QUEEN ALEXANDRA'S BIRDWING BUTTERFLY
(*Ornithoptera alexandrae*)

CENTIPEDES AND MILLIPEDES
Centipedes have a flattened body with a pair of legs on each trunk segment. They are carnivorous and kill prey using poisonous claws on the underside of their head. Millipedes have a cylindrical body with two pairs of legs on each trunk segment. They use chewing mouthparts to feed on decaying vegetation. Millipedes can roll or coil up to protect themselves against predators.

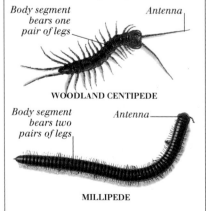

Body segment bears one pair of legs
Antenna

WOODLAND CENTIPEDE

Body segment bears two pairs of legs
Antenna

MILLIPEDE

Fish

WITH OVER 25,000 SPECIES, fish are the most successful group of vertebrates (animals with backbones) and can be found in both freshwater and saltwater habitats. They are adapted for life in water by having a streamlined head and a body typically covered with smooth, protective **scales** that are often coated with slippery **mucus**. These features reduce resistance as they propel themselves through the water. Fish also have fins, projecting structures supported by bony or **cartilaginous** rays, that are used for propulsion, steering, and stability. Respiratory organs, called **gills**, are adapted for absorbing oxygen from the water. They can be divided, on the basis of external body form and internal structure, into three main groups: the jawless fish (order Cyclostomata); the cartilaginous fish (class Chondrichthyes); and the bony fish (class Osteichthyes) to which the majority of fish belong.

HOW FISH BREATHE

Fish breathe by extracting oxygen from the water using their gills. They take in water through the mouth when the opercula (protective gill flaps) are closed. The mouth then closes and muscles in the mouth cavity contract to push water over the gills and out through the opercula. As water flows over the gills, oxygen passes through the lamellae and into the blood. Waste carbon dioxide diffuses out from the gills and into the water.

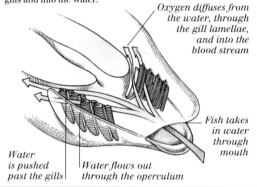

Oxygen diffuses from the water, through the gill lamellae, and into the blood stream

Fish takes in water through mouth

Water is pushed past the gills

Water flows out through the operculum

ANATOMY OF BONY FISH

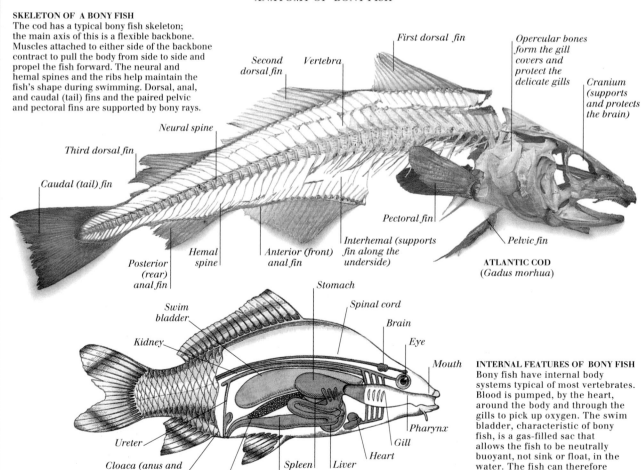

SKELETON OF A BONY FISH

The cod has a typical bony fish skeleton; the main axis of this is a flexible backbone. Muscles attached to either side of the backbone contract to pull the body from side to side and propel the fish forward. The neural and hemal spines and the ribs help maintain the fish's shape during swimming. Dorsal, anal, and caudal (tail) fins and the paired pelvic and pectoral fins are supported by bony rays.

First dorsal fin

Second dorsal fin

Vertebra

Opercular bones form the gill covers and protect the delicate gills

Cranium (supports and protects the brain)

Neural spine

Third dorsal fin

Caudal (tail) fin

Pectoral fin

Pelvic fin

ATLANTIC COD
(Gadus morhua)

Posterior (rear) anal fin

Hemal spine

Anterior (front) anal fin

Interhemal (supports fin along the underside)

Swim bladder

Kidney

Stomach

Spinal cord

Brain

Eye

Mouth

Pharynx

Gill

Heart

Liver

Spleen

Intestine

Ovary

Ureter

Cloaca (anus and urinogenital opening)

INTERNAL FEATURES OF BONY FISH

Bony fish have internal body systems typical of most vertebrates. Blood is pumped, by the heart, around the body and through the gills to pick up oxygen. The swim bladder, characteristic of bony fish, is a gas-filled sac that allows the fish to be neutrally buoyant, not sink or float, in the water. The fish can therefore maintain its position at any depth.

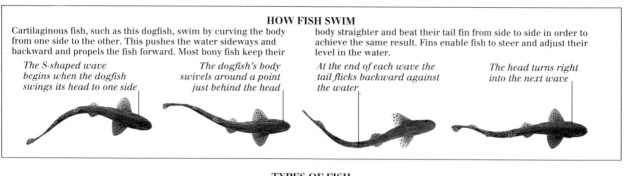

HOW FISH SWIM

Cartilaginous fish, such as this dogfish, swim by curving the body from one side to the other. This pushes the water sideways and backward and propels the fish forward. Most bony fish keep their body straighter and beat their tail fin from side to side in order to achieve the same result. Fins enable fish to steer and adjust their level in the water.

The S-shaped wave begins when the dogfish swings its head to one side

The dogfish's body swivels around a point just behind the head

At the end of each wave the tail flicks backward against the water

The head turns right into the next wave

TYPES OF FISH

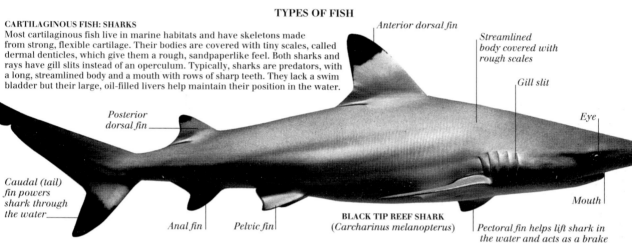

CARTILAGINOUS FISH: SHARKS

Most cartilaginous fish live in marine habitats and have skeletons made from strong, flexible cartilage. Their bodies are covered with tiny scales, called dermal denticles, which give them a rough, sandpaperlike feel. Both sharks and rays have gill slits instead of an operculum. Typically, sharks are predators, with a long, streamlined body and a mouth with rows of sharp teeth. They lack a swim bladder but their large, oil-filled livers help maintain their position in the water.

Anterior dorsal fin

Streamlined body covered with rough scales

Gill slit

Eye

Posterior dorsal fin

Caudal (tail) fin powers shark through the water

Anal fin

Pelvic fin

BLACK TIP REEF SHARK
(*Carcharinus melanopterus*)

Mouth

Pectoral fin helps lift shark in the water and acts as a brake

BONY FISH

These are the largest and most diverse group of fish and are found in both sea- and freshwater. They have a skeleton made of bone and a swim bladder to maintain buoyancy. Most have thin scales to protect their body. Their gills are covered by a flap called the operculum.

CARTILAGINOUS FISH: RAYS

Rays are cartilaginous fish with flattened bodies and enlarged, winglike pectoral fins that undulate to provide propulsion. Most rays are bottom dwellers, feeding on mollusks and crustaceans with their crushing teeth. Some, such as the large manta rays, "fly" through the water, eating plankton.

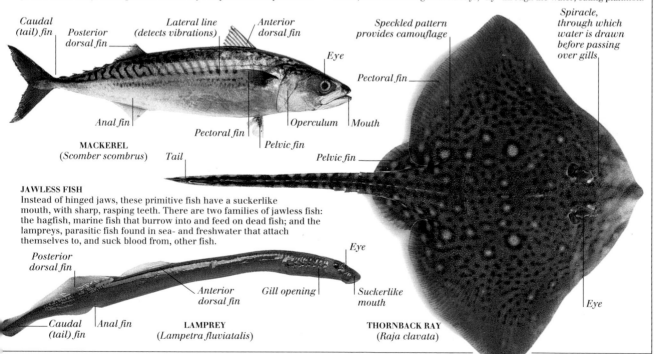

Caudal (tail) fin

Posterior dorsal fin

Lateral line (detects vibrations)

Anterior dorsal fin

Eye

Speckled pattern provides camouflage

Spiracle, through which water is drawn before passing over gills

Pectoral fin

Anal fin

Pectoral fin

Operculum

Mouth

Pelvic fin

MACKEREL
(*Scomber scombrus*)

Tail

Pelvic fin

JAWLESS FISH

Instead of hinged jaws, these primitive fish have a suckerlike mouth, with sharp, rasping teeth. There are two families of jawless fish: the hagfish, marine fish that burrow into and feed on dead fish; and the lampreys, parasitic fish found in sea- and freshwater that attach themselves to, and suck blood from, other fish.

Posterior dorsal fin

Eye

Anterior dorsal fin

Gill opening

Suckerlike mouth

Caudal (tail) fin

Anal fin

LAMPREY
(*Lampetra fluviatilis*)

Eye

THORNBACK RAY
(*Raja clavata*)

Amphibians

AMPHIBIANS ARE VERTEBRATES that typically develop in water. Female amphibians lay eggs, which are **fertilized** externally by the male. Legless larvae, called tadpoles, hatch from the fertilized eggs and undergo metamorphosis – a rapid change from larval form to an air-breathing adult with four legs. Most adults leave the water and then return to it to breed; some never leave and may spend their entire lives in water. As adults, amphibians are **carnivorous** and will eat any animal they can catch, kill, and swallow. They have moist, nonwaterproof, naked skin, and most land-living species live in damp **habitats** to help prevent the skin from drying out. All amphibians are **ectothermic** – their body temperature and activity levels vary with the external temperature. The greatest diversity of amphibians is found in tropical regions, where conditions are warm and moist, although there are also some **temperate** and desert species. There are three groups of amphibians: frogs and toads, which form the largest and most advanced group; salamanders, which includes newts, axolotls, mud-puppies, and sirens; and caecilians – wormlike, legless amphibians found in **tropical** regions.

AMPHIBIAN SKIN
Amphibian skin lacks the scales, feathers, and fur found in other vertebrates. Mucus keeps their skin damp and protects it from damage and infection. Amphibians can take in oxygen through their skin to "assist" their lungs in breathing. It is also **permeable** to water and helps to control the amount of water lost or gained by the animal.

Skin of a White's tree frog

Skin is naked, smooth, and covered with mucus

ANATOMY OF AMPHIBIANS

INTERNAL FEATURES OF AMPHIBIANS
Frogs breathe using paired, saclike lungs and by absorbing oxygen through their skin. Male frogs can amplify the sounds produced in their larynx (voice box) by inflating a vocal sac beneath their mouth. The heart has a single ventricle and two atria; a circulatory system moves the blood around the body. The testes, which produce sperm, share a common duct with the kidneys, which remove waste from the blood. This duct joins with the rectum to form a common opening called the cloaca.

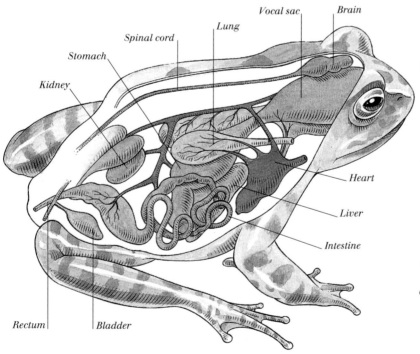

Vocal sac · Brain · Lung · Spinal cord · Stomach · Kidney · Heart · Liver · Intestine · Rectum · Bladder

FOOT ADAPTATIONS
Amphibian feet vary considerably according to habitat and lifestyle. Some amphibians are primarily aquatic and have webbed feet for swimming; others may have feet adapted for walking, climbing, gripping, or digging.

Webbed hind foot for swimming

PALMATE NEWT FOOT

Flattened foot for walking and digging

TIGER SALAMANDER FOOT

Sticky disk for gripping leaves and branches

TREE FROG FOOT

Claw for gripping slippery surfaces

Webbed foot for swimming

CLAWED TOAD FOOT

FROG METAMORPHOSIS

Frogs and toads undergo a complete change in body form during metamorphosis. When the tadpole hatches from its egg, it feeds on vegetation and breathes using gills. Six to nine weeks after hatching, the hind legs appear and the tadpole begins to eat dead animals. Gradually the front legs emerge, the tail is absorbed, and the body shape becomes froglike. Lungs develop internally, and the frog is ready for life on land.

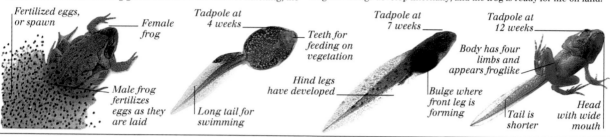

Fertilized eggs, or spawn

Female frog

Male frog fertilizes eggs as they are laid

Tadpole at 4 weeks

Teeth for feeding on vegetation

Hind legs have developed

Long tail for swimming

Tadpole at 7 weeks

Bulge where front leg is forming

Tadpole at 12 weeks

Body has four limbs and appears froglike

Tail is shorter

Head with wide mouth

TYPES OF AMPHIBIANS

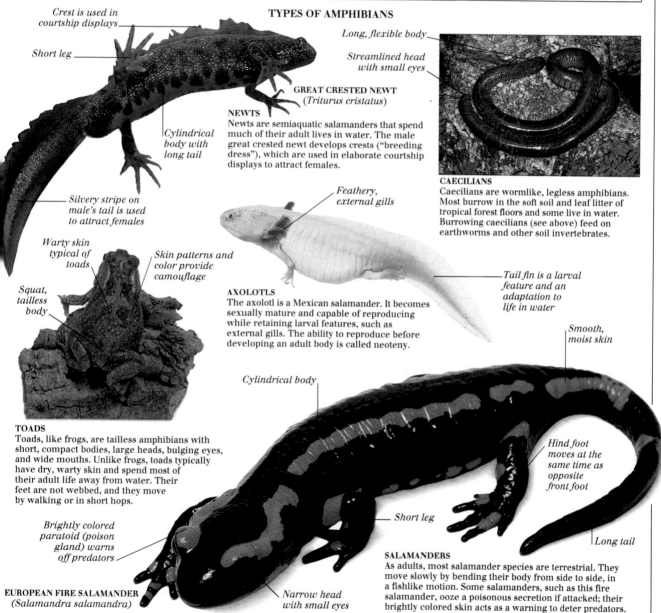

Crest is used in courtship displays

Short leg

Cylindrical body with long tail

Silvery stripe on male's tail is used to attract females

NEWTS

GREAT CRESTED NEWT
(*Triturus cristatus*)

Newts are semiaquatic salamanders that spend much of their adult lives in water. The male great crested newt develops crests ("breeding dress"), which are used in elaborate courtship displays to attract females.

Long, flexible body

Streamlined head with small eyes

CAECILIANS

Caecilians are wormlike, legless amphibians. Most burrow in the soft soil and leaf litter of tropical forest floors and some live in water. Burrowing caecilians (see above) feed on earthworms and other soil invertebrates.

Feathery, external gills

AXOLOTLS

The axolotl is a Mexican salamander. It becomes sexually mature and capable of reproducing while retaining larval features, such as external gills. The ability to reproduce before developing an adult body is called neoteny.

Tail fin is a larval feature and an adaptation to life in water

Smooth, moist skin

Warty skin typical of toads

Skin patterns and color provide camouflage

Squat, tailless body

Cylindrical body

TOADS

Toads, like frogs, are tailless amphibians with short, compact bodies, large heads, bulging eyes, and wide mouths. Unlike frogs, toads typically have dry, warty skin and spend most of their adult life away from water. Their feet are not webbed, and they move by walking or in short hops.

Brightly colored paratoid (poison gland) warns off predators

EUROPEAN FIRE SALAMANDER
(*Salamandra salamandra*)

Narrow head with small eyes

Short leg

Hind foot moves at the same time as opposite front foot

Long tail

SALAMANDERS

As adults, most salamander species are terrestrial. They move slowly by bending their body from side to side, in a fishlike motion. Some salamanders, such as this fire salamander, ooze a poisonous secretion if attacked; their brightly colored skin acts as a warning to deter predators.

Reptiles

REPTILES FORM A HIGHLY VARIED class of mainly land-living
vertebrates. There are four orders: tortoises and turtles, including
river turtles (terrapins); snakes and lizards, the largest reptile order;
the tuataras, two lizardlike species found in New Zealand; and the
crocodilians (crocodiles, alligators, caimans, and gavials). Typically,
reptiles have scaly, waterproof skin that helps them to retain water
and survive in hot, dry habitats. To permit growth, the skin is shed
periodically either as flakes, as in lizards, or in one piece, as in snakes.
Most reptiles are **oviparous** and lay eggs (on land) that are protected
by a shell. Within the egg the **embryo** is contained in a fluid-filled sac
(amnion), which prevents it drying out. Usually, female reptiles lay
their eggs and leave them, but crocodilians lay their eggs in a nest
and show **parental care** after hatching. Reptiles are **ectothermic**,
depending on external warmth to keep them active. Most live in
tropical or subtropical regions, where they bask in the morning
sun in order to raise their body temperature.

JACOBSON'S ORGAN

Snakes and some lizards use a sense organ
called the Jacobson's organ for detecting
smells. This is located in the roof of the mouth
and smells, or tastes, airborne chemicals
picked up by the continually flicking tongue.
As snakes have poor eyesight, smell is
important to find prey, taste food, detect
enemies, and find a mate.

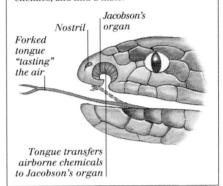

Nostril
Jacobson's organ
Forked tongue "tasting" the air
Tongue transfers airborne chemicals to Jacobson's organ

SKELETON OF A TORTOISE

Like other reptiles, tortoises
have a bony endoskeleton
(internal skeleton). They also
have a hard, protective shell,
which encloses their body and
into which the head, limbs, and
tail, can be retracted. This
consists of an inner layer of bony
plates that are fused to the ribs
and trunk vertebrae, and an
outer layer of horny shields
(scutes), which are comparable
to the scales of other reptiles.

RADIATED TORTOISE
(*Testudo radiata*)

ANATOMY OF REPTILES

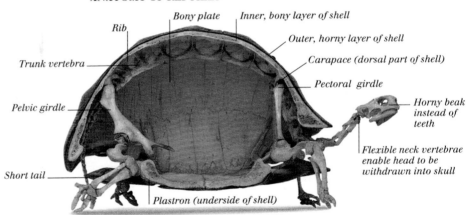

Rib
Bony plate
Inner, bony layer of shell
Trunk vertebra
Outer, horny layer of shell
Carapace (dorsal part of shell)
Pectoral girdle
Pelvic girdle
Horny beak instead of teeth
Flexible neck vertebrae enable head to be withdrawn into skull
Short tail
Plastron (underside of shell)

INTERNAL FEATURES OF REPTILES

The lizard has an internal structure similar to
most reptiles. Its brain is relatively small but
permits fairly complex behavior patterns. Food
is broken down in the digestive system prior to
absorption. The heart, with its single ventricle
and two atria, pumps the blood around the
body. Eggs are produced, after fertilization,
in the female reproductive system. A shell is
secreted around each one as it passes down
the oviduct. The digestive and reproductive
systems empty into a common cloacal chamber.

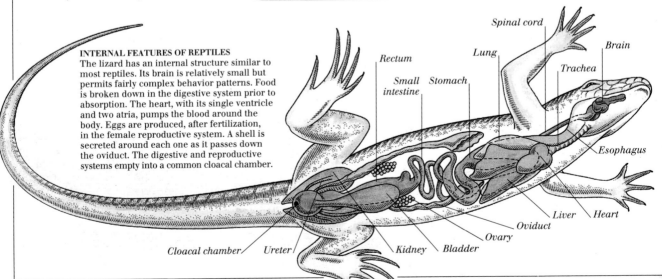

Spinal cord
Lung
Brain
Rectum
Trachea
Small intestine
Stomach
Esophagus
Liver
Heart
Oviduct
Ovary
Cloacal chamber
Ureter
Kidney
Bladder

REPTILE EGG HATCHING

Most snakes lay eggs. The female rat snake (see below) lays soft-shelled eggs in material, such as leaf litter, that releases heat as it decays. Inside the egg, the developing embryo snake absorbs nutrients from a sac containing yolk. Between 7 and 15 weeks after laying, depending on the external temperature, the young rat snake hatches. It uses a temporary "egg tooth" on the upper jaw to break through the eggshell. The hatchling, like all other young reptiles, looks like a smaller version of its parents.

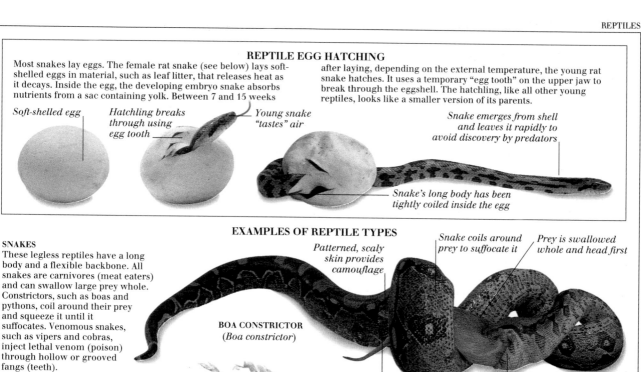

Soft-shelled egg

Hatchling breaks through using egg tooth

Young snake "tastes" air

Snake emerges from shell and leaves it rapidly to avoid discovery by predators

Snake's long body has been tightly coiled inside the egg

EXAMPLES OF REPTILE TYPES

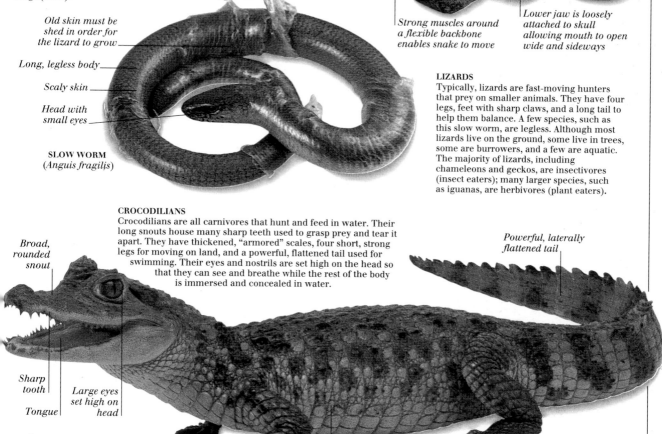

SNAKES

These legless reptiles have a long body and a flexible backbone. All snakes are carnivores (meat eaters) and can swallow large prey whole. Constrictors, such as boas and pythons, coil around their prey and squeeze it until it suffocates. Venomous snakes, such as vipers and cobras, inject lethal venom (poison) through hollow or grooved fangs (teeth).

Patterned, scaly skin provides camouflage

Snake coils around prey to suffocate it

Prey is swallowed whole and head first

BOA CONSTRICTOR
(Boa constrictor)

Strong muscles around a flexible backbone enables snake to move

Lower jaw is loosely attached to skull allowing mouth to open wide and sideways

Old skin must be shed in order for the lizard to grow

Long, legless body

Scaly skin

Head with small eyes

SLOW WORM
(Anguis fragilis)

LIZARDS

Typically, lizards are fast-moving hunters that prey on smaller animals. They have four legs, feet with sharp claws, and a long tail to help them balance. A few species, such as this slow worm, are legless. Although most lizards live on the ground, some live in trees, some are burrowers, and a few are aquatic. The majority of lizards, including chameleons and geckos, are insectivores (insect eaters); many larger species, such as iguanas, are herbivores (plant eaters).

CROCODILIANS

Crocodilians are all carnivores that hunt and feed in water. Their long snouts house many sharp teeth used to grasp prey and tear it apart. They have thickened, "armored" scales, four short, strong legs for moving on land, and a powerful, flattened tail used for swimming. Their eyes and nostrils are set high on the head so that they can see and breathe while the rest of the body is immersed and concealed in water.

Broad, rounded snout

Powerful, laterally flattened tail

Sharp tooth

Large eyes set high on head

Tongue

SPECTACLED CAIMAN
(Caiman crocodilus)

Body covered by hard scales

Partially webbed foot with sharp claws

Birds

BIRDS ARE THE ONLY ANIMALS that have feathers and, apart from bats, are the only vertebrates capable of powered flight. This has enabled them to become established all over the world, from the hottest deserts to Antarctica. Most birds, apart from the flightless species, have a uniform body plan especially adapted for flight. Modified forelimbs form wings and their bodies are covered with feathers: down feathers **insulate** the bird's body; contour feathers produce a **streamlined** shape; and flight feathers on the wings enable flight and steering. Hollow bones reduce the weight of the skeleton and a light, horny beak has replaced heavy jaws and teeth. The size and shape of the bird's beak depends on its diet. Most birds have feet with four digits and claws that vary according to lifestyle: perching birds have gripping feet, and waterbirds have webbed feet for swimming. All birds lay hard-shelled eggs; most are **incubated** in a nest until they hatch. Like mammals, birds are **endothermic**, with a body temperature of about 40° C. They also have a high **metabolic rate** that reflects the energy demands of flight.

SECTION THROUGH A CHICKEN'S EGG

A shelled egg provides a protective environment for the embryo bird to develop. Within the hard shell, a system of membranes surrounds the embryo: the amnion prevents the embryo from drying out and acts as a shock absorber; the allantois stores waste and, with the chorion, acts as a respiratory surface. Food is provided by the yolk sac.

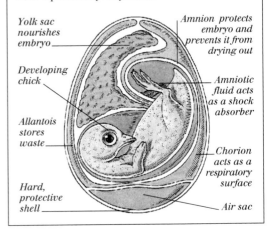

Yolk sac nourishes embryo

Developing chick

Allantois stores waste

Hard, protective shell

Amnion protects embryo and prevents it from drying out

Amniotic fluid acts as a shock absorber

Chorion acts as a respiratory surface

Air sac

ANATOMY OF BIRDS

INTERNAL FEATURES OF BIRDS
Birds have organs that are unique to their **class**. The crop is used for storing food, and a muscular bag called the gizzard grinds up food, in the absence of teeth, to a digestible pulp. Plant-eating birds swallow small stones to aid the grinding action of the gizzard. The lungs are linked to extensive air sacs that improve their efficiency and increase the uptake of the oxygen needed to release energy for flight.

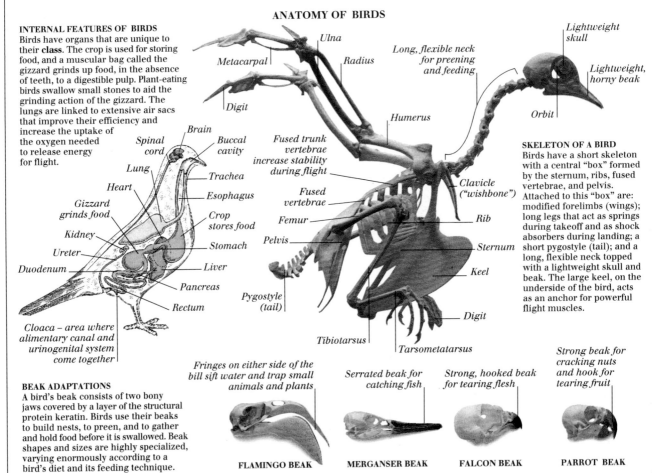

Ulna

Metacarpal

Radius

Long, flexible neck for preening and feeding

Digit

Humerus

Orbit

Lightweight skull

Lightweight, horny beak

Brain

Spinal cord

Lung

Heart

Gizzard grinds food

Kidney

Ureter

Duodenum

Buccal cavity

Trachea

Esophagus

Crop stores food

Stomach

Liver

Pancreas

Rectum

Cloaca – area where alimentary canal and urinogenital system come together

Fused trunk vertebrae increase stability during flight

Fused vertebrae

Femur

Pelvis

Pygostyle (tail)

Tibiotarsus

Clavicle ("wishbone")

Rib

Sternum

Keel

Digit

Tarsometatarsus

SKELETON OF A BIRD
Birds have a short skeleton with a central "box" formed by the sternum, ribs, fused vertebrae, and pelvis. Attached to this "box" are: modified forelimbs (wings); long legs that act as springs during takeoff and as shock absorbers during landing; a short pygostyle (tail); and a long, flexible neck topped with a lightweight skull and beak. The large keel, on the underside of the bird, acts as an anchor for powerful flight muscles.

BEAK ADAPTATIONS
A bird's beak consists of two bony jaws covered by a layer of the structural protein keratin. Birds use their beaks to build nests, to preen, and to gather and hold food before it is swallowed. Beak shapes and sizes are highly specialized, varying enormously according to a bird's diet and its feeding technique.

Fringes on either side of the bill sift water and trap small animals and plants

Serrated beak for catching fish

Strong, hooked beak for tearing flesh

Strong beak for cracking nuts and hook for tearing fruit

FLAMINGO BEAK

MERGANSER BEAK

FALCON BEAK

PARROT BEAK

HOW A BIRD FLIES

A bird's wing has an airfoil shape – a convex upper surface and concave lower surface – which naturally generates lift when air flows over it. Propulsion occurs when the wings are pulled up and down by separate sets of muscles. During the downstroke, the wing twists to push down and back, creating forward propulsion and lift. During the upstroke, the feathers separate to let air through and the wing twists in the opposite direction, fanning backward to create further propulsion.

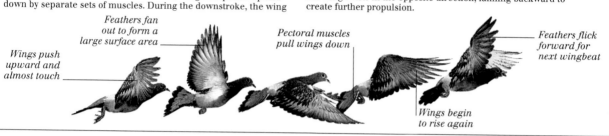

Wings push upward and almost touch

Feathers fan out to form a large surface area

Pectoral muscles pull wings down

Wings begin to rise again

Feathers flick forward for next wingbeat

EXAMPLES OF BIRD TYPES

FLIGHTLESS BIRDS

Over millions of years, some bird species, such as the ratites and penguins, have lost the power of flight. Their wings have become smaller and in some cases, have adapted to perform other functions. Penguins, for example, use their flipperlike wings to swim rapidly underwater in search of food. The ratites, including emu, ostrich, rhea, and kiwi, have relatively small wings that lack flight feathers, no keel, and long legs that enable them to run quickly to escape predators.

WADING BIRDS

Wading birds, which include herons, ibises, oystercatchers, snipes, and avocets, are well adapted for life on the edges of rivers, lakes, estuaries, and the sea. They have long, thin legs that enable them to wade through the water in search of food. The beaks of wading birds vary according to their feeding method and prey. Avocets, for example, sweep their narrow, upturned beaks from side to side through the water, in search of tiny animals.

Long, flexible neck enables head to reach food on the ground

Short, strong beak

Lighter underside camouflages bird in the sky as it hovers over prey

Secondary flight feathers

Forward-pointing eyes give kestrel clear binocular vision

Hooked beak to tear flesh

Primary flight feathers

Sharp talons to grip prey

KESTREL
(*Falcano tinnunculus*)

BIRDS OF PREY

Birds of prey are powerful hunters that seek out prey, pounce on it in a sudden attack, and carry it away to eat it. The group includes falcons, kites, harriers, kestrels, sparrowhawks, and eagles. These all use their excellent vision to locate prey, and employ their strong feet and curved talons to catch and hold it while they tear at the flesh with a sharp, curved beak.

Long, upturned beak for seeking out food in water

Webbed foot distributes the bird's weight to prevent it sinking in soft sand or mud

Long leg for wading through water

Underdeveloped wings do not allow flight

Body is covered with soft, flexible feathers

Long, powerful legs enable rhea to run very quickly

AVOCET
(*Recurvirostra avosetta*)

Thick, sturdy toe supports rhea's weight

RHEA
(*Rhea americana*)

Mammals

MAMMALS FORM A DIVERSE GROUP of **vertebrates**, which includes bats, elephants, baboons, whales, rabbits, and tigers. All female mammals produce milk with which they feed their young. This is formed in modified skin glands, called mammary glands, and plays a key role in parental care. As mammals are **endothermic**, most have a covering of fur or hair that helps insulate their bodies. They also have **dentition** that is adapted to coping with their diet. Mammals are divided into three groups according to the way they reproduce. Monotremes, found in Australasia, lay soft-shelled eggs from which young hatch. The other two groups give birth to live young. Marsupials, found in the Americas and Australasia, give birth to tiny, undeveloped young, which make their way to an abdominal pouch where they attach themselves to a **nipple** and continue their development. The largest group is the placental mammals. Their young develop inside the mother's **uterus** and are nourished through an organ called the **placenta**.

SUCKLING

Suckling is unique to mammals and is an essential part of parental care. Female mammals produce milk in mammary glands and release it through their nipples. After birth, newborn mammals instinctively seek out a nipple. Milk is released in response to the infant's sucking action. As they grow older, mammals are weaned onto solid food.

ANATOMY OF MAMMALS

SKELETON OF A MAMMAL
Mammals have a bony **endoskeleton** typical of tetrapods (four-limbed vertebrates). A backbone forms the main body axis; an anterior skull houses the brain and sense organs; and ribs surround the thorax. Considerable variations do occur, especially in the limbs. For example, monkeys and apes have long arms and hands for climbing; the forelimbs of seals are modified as flippers for swimming; fast-running horses have slender legs that end in a hoof; and moles have short, strong, spadelike forelimbs for digging.

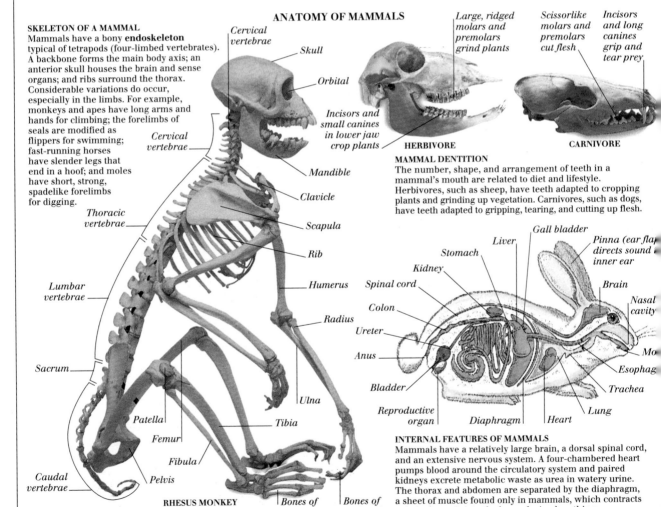

Cervical vertebrae

Skull

Orbital

Incisors and small canines in lower jaw crop plants

Large, ridged molars and premolars grind plants

Scissorlike molars and premolars cut flesh

Incisors and long canines grip and tear prey

HERBIVORE

CARNIVORE

MAMMAL DENTITION
The number, shape, and arrangement of teeth in a mammal's mouth are related to diet and lifestyle. Herbivores, such as sheep, have teeth adapted to cropping plants and grinding up vegetation. Carnivores, such as dogs, have teeth adapted to gripping, tearing, and cutting up flesh.

Cervical vertebrae

Mandible

Clavicle

Scapula

Rib

Humerus

Radius

Thoracic vertebrae

Lumbar vertebrae

Sacrum

Caudal vertebrae

Patella

Femur

Fibula

Pelvis

Tibia

Ulna

Bones of the foot

Bones of the hand

RHESUS MONKEY
(*Macaca mulatta*)

Gall bladder

Liver

Stomach

Kidney

Spinal cord

Colon

Ureter

Anus

Bladder

Reproductive organ

Diaphragm

Heart

Lung

Trachea

Esophag

Mo

Nasal cavity

Brain

Pinna (ear fla directs sound inner ear

INTERNAL FEATURES OF MAMMALS
Mammals have a relatively large brain, a dorsal spinal cord, and an extensive nervous system. A four-chambered heart pumps blood around the circulatory system and paired kidneys excrete metabolic waste as urea in watery urine. The thorax and abdomen are separated by the diaphragm, a sheet of muscle found only in mammals, which contracts to help draw air into the lungs during breathing.

HOW CHEETAHS RUN

Over short distances, cheetahs can reach speeds of up to 100 kilometers per hour. Their hind legs push off together, providing the main propulsive thrust. Nonretractable claws act like running spikes to increase grip. Cheetahs also have a streamlined body and a highly flexible backbone. As the backbone extends and flexes, it increases the stride length and overall speed.

Powerful hind legs push off together

Both forefeet come off the ground together

Flexible backbone stretches to its full extent

Backbone curves upward

Tail helps balance cheetah as it runs

Back legs come farther forward than front legs ready for next leap

TYPES OF MAMMALS

Long, delicate finger

Skin is stretched between fingers

FRUIT BAT
(*Pteropus sp.*)

PLACENTAL MAMMALS: FLYING MAMMALS
Bats (order Chiroptera) are the only mammals capable of powered flight. Their forelimbs are modified as wings; a flap of skin is stretched over elongated finger bones. There are two groups of bats: fruit bats, which use their large eyes to find food, such as fruit and nectar; and insect-eating bats, which use **echolocation**.

Dorsal fin

Streamlined body lacks hindlimbs

Smooth, hairless, rubbery skin

Forelimbs form paddlelike flippers used for steering

Tail propels dolphin through the water

PLACENTAL MAMMALS: SEA MAMMALS
There are three groups of sea mammals: whales and dolphins (order Cetacea) and dugongs and manatees (order Sirenia), which spend their entire life in water; and seals and walruses (order Pinnipedia), which come ashore in order to breed.

BOTTLENOSE DOLPHIN
(*Tursiops truncatus*)

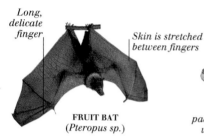

Short forelimb

Pouch where young develop

Ducklike bill is used to locate prey

Flat tail

Webbed forefoot for swimming

DUCK-BILLED PLATYPUS
(*Ornithorhynchus anatinus*)

MONOTREMES
There are three species of monotreme or egg-laying mammals (order Monotremata): the platypus and two species of echidnas. The platypus is semi-aquatic, swimming in streams and rivers. Echidnas are armed with spines and use their snout and long tongue to feed on ants.

Forward-facing eyes

Strong, muscular shoulders

Long hind legs

Thick tail provides balance

Long, powerful forearm

RED-NECKED WALLABY
(*Macropus rufogriseus*)

MARSUPIALS
Marsupials, or pouched mammals (order Marsupialia), show considerable diversity in shape, lifestyle, and habitat. They include grazing kangaroos and wallabies, tree-living koalas, **omnivorous** opossums, burrowing wombats, the marsupial mole, and the carnivorous Tasmanian devil.

PLACENTAL MAMMALS: PRIMATES
Primates (order Primates) include lemurs, tarsiers, monkeys, apes, and humans. Most are tree-dwelling, but some, such as this gorilla, are adapted for life on the ground. Primates typically have grasping hands and feet with long digits for climbing and manipulating objects.

GORILLA
(*Gorilla gorilla*)

Ecology

ECOLOGY IS THE STUDY of the relationship between living **organisms** and their **environment**. It is studied by scientists called ecologists, who analyze interrelationships such as energy flow and **food webs** (see pp. 170-171), and nutrient recycling (see pp. 172-173). In the same area or habitat, different species form a community; the community, together with its surroundings, such as vegetation, temperature, or soil type, forms an ecosystem. This can range in size, complexity, and **species** diversity, from a puddle to an ocean. In any ecosystem, individuals compete for resources, and there is a limit to the resources available to each species. This is described as the carrying capacity – the maximum size of population for which the ecosystem can provide resources. Different species in an ecosystem interact by, for example, competing for food or shelter, or by having a **predator** and prey relationship. Two species may also have a **symbiotic** relationship, such as mutualism, commensalism, or parasitism, from which one or both benefits.

GEOGRAPHICAL LIFE ZONES

Life zones, or biomes, are geographical areas of the world that have particular physical and climatic characters and distinctive vegetation and animal life. Biomes are essentialy large ecosystems. The same biomes can appear in different continents; for example tropical rainforests occur in both South America and West Africa. They have life forms that appear similar because they are adapted to the same environmental conditions.

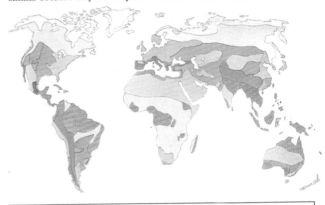

KEY				
○ Tundra	◐ Temperate forest	○ Savanna	● Temperate grassland	● Temperate rainforest
○ Boreal forest	◐ Desert	● Tropical rainforest	● Mountain	● Scrubland

HIERARCHY OF COMPLEXITY

The hierarchy of complexity describes the different levels of relationships between living organisms and their environment. At the base of the hierarchy are individual organisms. Organisms of the same species form a population, and populations that live in the same area form a community. An ecosystem, such as a pond or a woodland, is made up of a community and its surroundings – both living and non-living. The biosphere is the sum total of all Earth's ecosystems, and includes oceans, land, inland water, and the lower atmosphere.

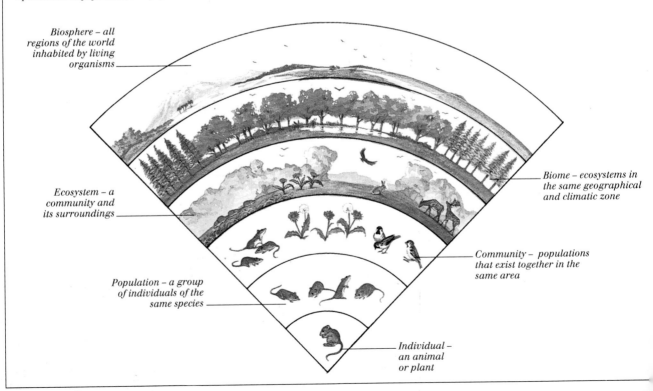

Biosphere – all regions of the world inhabited by living organisms

Ecosystem – a community and its surroundings

Population – a group of individuals of the same species

Biome – ecosystems in the same geographical and climatic zone

Community – populations that exist together in the same area

Individual – an animal or plant

REPRODUCTIVE STRATEGIES

Baby elephants are born in an advanced state of maturity

Carrying capacity

Population bust

Number of water fleas

Population boom

Water flea

Time

K STRATEGY

K is a measure of the carrying capacity of a species. K strategists are organisms that are long-lived, reproduce slowly, and produce only a small number of offspring. A population of K strategists tends to remain close to the carrying capacity for its ecosystem. Elephants are K strategists that produce one offspring at a time in an advanced state of development. They nurture the offspring to increase its chances of survival.

r STRATEGY

r is a measure of population growth speed. r strategists, such as water fleas, are organisms that exploit available resources by reproducing as quickly as possible. They are usually small, short-lived, and invest energy in reproducing frequently and prolifically. Populations can increase rapidly (boom) or decrease dramatically (bust) if environmental conditions change. The r strategy enables populations to recover quickly.

SPECIES INTERACTIONS

Threadlike stem of dodder twined around stem of host plant

COMMENSALISM

Commensalism is a form of interaction where one species benefits while the other remains unaffected by the relationship. Clownfish, for example, are small reef fish that seek protection from predators by sheltering among the poisonous tentacles of sea anemones; a mucus covering protects the clownfish from the anemone's stings.

Sea anemone

Clownfish

Cleaner wrasse picks parasites from the mouth of the sweetlip

MUTUALISM

Mutualism is a relationship where both species benefit. In the case of the sweetlip fish and the cleaner wrasse, the sweetlip remains motionless while the wrasse picks off irritating parasites from its skin, mouth, and gills. Thus the sweetlip loses its parasites and the wrasse gets food.

Micrograph of dodder haustorium penetrating stem of host

DODDER
(Cuscuta europaea)

PARASITISM

Parasitism is a relationship in which one species, the parasite, benefits at the expense of the other, the host. Dodder, for example, is a parasitic flowering plant that wraps around a host plant and forms specialized absorptive organs, called haustoria, which penetrate the host's stem and extract nutrients.

Energy flow and food webs

LIFE ON EARTH DEPENDS ON A CONSTANT input of energy from the Sun. Sunlight energy is trapped by **autotrophs** (producers), which use it to produce food for themselves. The trapped energy is passed to **herbivorous** animals (primary consumers), which eat the producers. They, in turn, are eaten by **carnivorous** animals (secondary consumers), which are themselves eaten by tertiary consumers. This pathway is called a food chain. The position each species occupies within the food chain is called a trophic (feeding) level. At each level, energy is stored as biomass, the mass of living plants or animals. Much energy is used for maintaining the organism or is lost into the environment as heat. This means that only a small percentage of the energy taken in by one trophic level is available to the next. An ecosystem, such as a woodland or coastline, can contain thousands of different species, many of which are involved in different food chains. These interconnect to form a complex food web.

MEASURING ENERGY

The amount of energy contained in a trophic level can be measured using a bomb calorimeter. An organism is weighed and then burned rapidly in a combustion chamber. The energy stored within the organism is converted to heat energy, which can be measured. This is then multiplied by the estimated mass or numbers of all the organisms in the trophic level to give its total energy content.

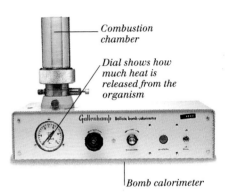

Combustion chamber

Dial shows how much heat is released from the organism

Bomb calorimeter

THE TROPHIC PYRAMID

The trophic pyramid reflects the loss of energy that occurs at each trophic level as energy flows through an ecosystem. The area of each section of the pyramid is proportional to the biomass in each trophic level – it also represents the amount of potential energy available to the next level. As only about 10 percent of the energy in each level is taken up by the level above, each level supports less biomass and fewer individuals. Because of the energy lost, the maximum number of trophic levels that can be supported in a food chain is limited to six. The trophic pyramid shown at right relates to a food chain found in a deciduous woodland.

LEVEL 4
The tawny owl is a top predator that feeds on both weasels and rodents. It has no predators, but when it dies, decomposers recycle its raw materials back into the environment.

LEVEL 3
Weasels are carnivores and secondary consumers that prey on rodents. There are fewer weasels than rodents because there is less available energy in this trophic level.

LEVEL 2
Voles and mice are primary consumers that feed on seeds and fruits. They are very active and lose much of their energy as heat.

LEVEL 1
Grasses are producers that use sunlight energy to make food for themselves. Seeds and berries are sources of stored energy.

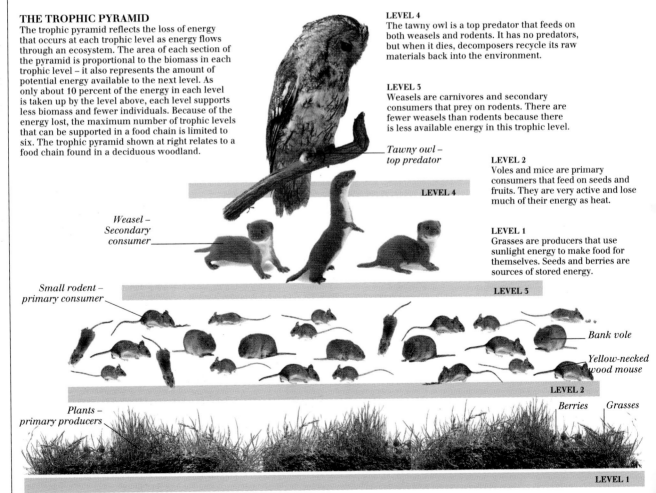

Tawny owl – top predator

LEVEL 4

Weasel – Secondary consumer

Small rodent – primary consumer

LEVEL 3

Bank vole

Yellow-necked wood mouse

LEVEL 2

Plants – primary producers

Berries   *Grasses*

LEVEL 1

COASTAL FOOD WEB

The food web below shows the feeding relationships among species that live in the sea in coastal waters. It indicates how energy enters and flows through this particular ecosystem. At the "base" of the food web are autotrophic organisms – seaweeds and phytoplankton – which use simple raw materials and sunlight energy to produce energy-rich organic compounds by photosynthesis (see pp. 148-149). The food energy they produce is passed on within a series of food chains. In each food chain the direction of the arrows indicates which species is being eaten by which, and also the direction of energy flow. Because in an ecosystem, each species is involved in different food chains, they become interconnected to form an intricate food web, within which animals may feed at different trophic levels. This coastal food web is highly simplified and shows only a few of the interlinked food chains and species involved.

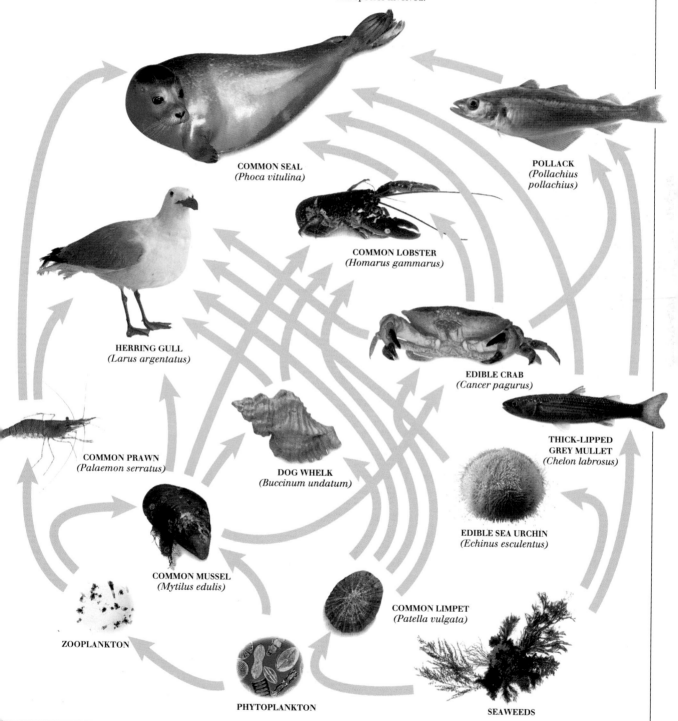

COMMON SEAL
(*Phoca vitulina*)

POLLACK
(*Pollachius pollachius*)

COMMON LOBSTER
(*Homarus gammarus*)

HERRING GULL
(*Larus argentatus*)

EDIBLE CRAB
(*Cancer pagurus*)

COMMON PRAWN
(*Palaemon serratus*)

DOG WHELK
(*Buccinum undatum*)

THICK-LIPPED
GREY MULLET
(*Chelon labrosus*)

EDIBLE SEA URCHIN
(*Echinus esculentus*)

COMMON MUSSEL
(*Mytilus edulis*)

COMMON LIMPET
(*Patella vulgata*)

ZOOPLANKTON

PHYTOPLANKTON

SEAWEEDS

171

Natural cycles

CARBON, NITROGEN, OXYGEN, WATER, and other raw materials that make up living organisms are continually recycled between the living and nonliving parts of the **biosphere**; energy from the Sun drives these natural cycles. All life is based on complex **organic molecules** that have a "skeleton" of carbon **atoms.** These are synthesized during **photosynthesis,** using carbon dioxide, water, and sunlight energy, and are passed to animals when they eat plants. Carbon dioxide is returned to the atmosphere when carbohydrates are broken down during **respiration.** Oxygen is released during photosynthesis and is used during respiration. Nitrogen is taken in by plants as nitrates and added to the carbon skeleton to form proteins, **DNA**, and other essential compounds. When organisms die, the complex molecules from which they are made are broken down by decomposing organisms to yield simple substances that can be reused. Water forms a large part of all organisms and is constantly being lost and recycled.

THE WATER CYCLE

Wind and the heat of the Sun cause water molecules to evaporate from the surface of oceans and lakes, from soil, and from living organisms. The water vapor formed rises, cools, and condenses to form water droplets, which collect as clouds. As clouds rise and move into cooler air, they become saturated with water droplets which fall as rain or snow, soaking into the soil and running into lakes, rivers, and oceans.

Sun's heat evaporates water from the Earth's surface

Water evaporates from land and water

Water vapor condenses to form clouds

Clouds rise and move into cooler air

Water returns to land, rivers, and oceans

Rain fall from the clouds

THE NITROGEN CYCLE

Nitrogen-fixing bacteria absorb nitrogen and combine it with oxygen to form nitrates, which can be absorbed by plants. Nitrogen is also fixed by lightning. Animals obtain nitrogen by eating plants. Decaying dead animals and plants release nitrogenous compounds, which are then converted by nitrifying bacteria to nitrates. These are absorbed by plants through their roots. Denitrifying bacteria also break down nitrates released from dead animals and plants and release nitrogen back into the atmosphere.

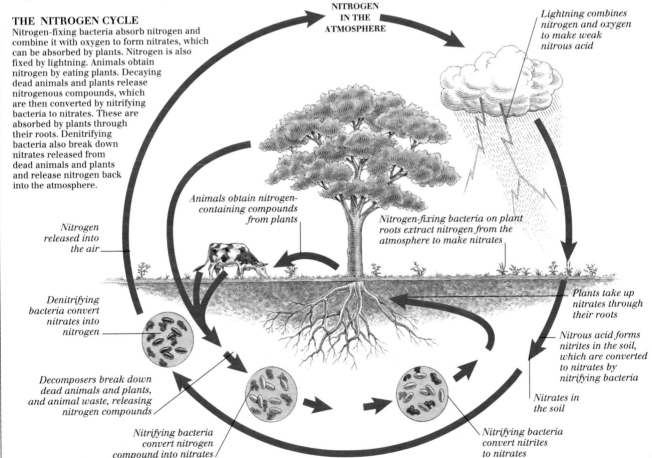

NITROGEN IN THE ATMOSPHERE

Lightning combines nitrogen and oxygen to make weak nitrous acid

Animals obtain nitrogen-containing compounds from plants

Nitrogen-fixing bacteria on plant roots extract nitrogen from the atmosphere to make nitrates

Nitrogen released into the air

Denitrifying bacteria convert nitrates into nitrogen

Plants take up nitrates through their roots

Nitrous acid forms nitrites in the soil, which are converted to nitrates by nitrifying bacteria

Decomposers break down dead animals and plants, and animal waste, releasing nitrogen compounds

Nitrates in the soil

Nitrifying bacteria convert nitrogen compound into nitrates

Nitrifying bacteria convert nitrites to nitrates

THE CARBON CYCLE

Green plants and some bacteria use carbon dioxide as a raw material in photosynthesis to make organic, carbon-containing compounds, such as carbohydrates, which are eaten by animals. Both animals and plants use carbohydrates in respiration and release waste carbon dioxide into the atmosphere. During the day, the amount of carbon dioxide consumed by plants for photosynthesis is greater than that released from respiration; at night, however, the reverse is true.

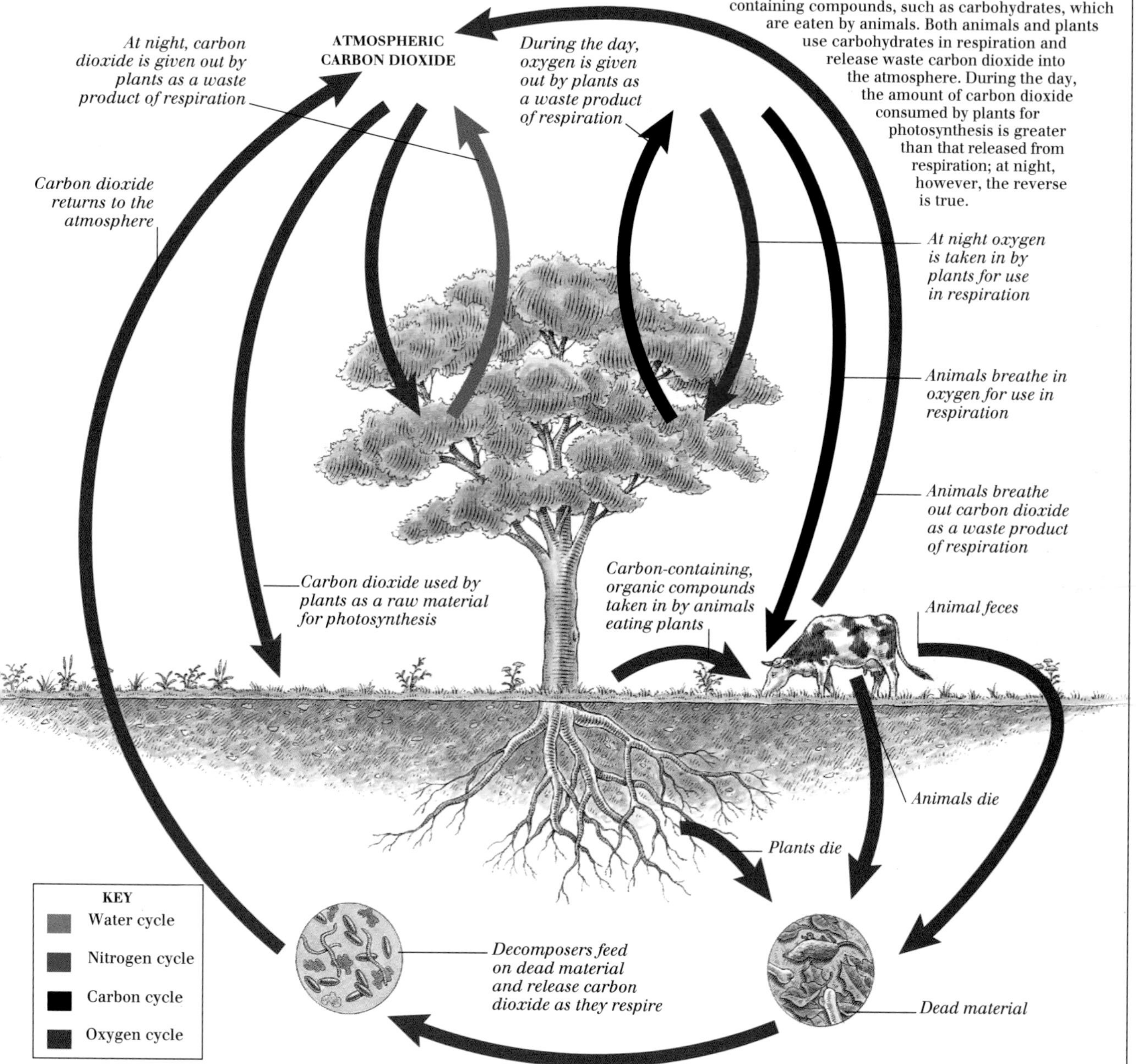

At night, carbon dioxide is given out by plants as a waste product of respiration

ATMOSPHERIC CARBON DIOXIDE

During the day, oxygen is given out by plants as a waste product of respiration

Carbon dioxide returns to the atmosphere

At night oxygen is taken in by plants for use in respiration

Animals breathe in oxygen for use in respiration

Animals breathe out carbon dioxide as a waste product of respiration

Carbon dioxide used by plants as a raw material for photosynthesis

Carbon-containing, organic compounds taken in by animals eating plants

Animal feces

Animals die

Plants die

KEY
- Water cycle
- Nitrogen cycle
- Carbon cycle
- Oxygen cycle

Decomposers feed on dead material and release carbon dioxide as they respire

Dead material

THE OXYGEN CYCLE

Animals and plants take in oxygen and use it to release energy from carbohydrates through aerobic respiration (see pp. 124-125). During the day, when sunlight energy is available, plants release oxygen as a waste product of photosynthesis. The amount of oxygen released by day from photosynthesis far exceeds oxygen consumed by the plant for respiration. At night, there is a net intake of oxygen as photosynthesis ceases but respiration continues.

DECOMPOSITION

When a living organism dies, its constituent organic compounds are broken down into simple raw materials by organisms called decomposers. During this process, carbon dioxide, nitrates, phosphates, and other essential nutrients are released. Large decomposers (detritivores), such as earthworms, break down larger pieces of dead material so that fungi and bacteria can complete the process of decomposition.

Flies lay eggs

Maggots hatch and feed on dead shrew

173

Human impact on the environment

HUMAN BEINGS HAVE HAD A GREATER IMPACT on the environment than any other species in the Earth's history. The main reason for this has been the huge increase in human population, from 2.5 billion in 1950 to over 5 billion in the 1980s, and it is estimated to reach 8.5 billion by 2025. The rising population has required more space for towns and cities and more land to produce food. The resulting **habitat** destruction has led to the **extinction** of many species and a decrease in the Earth's **biodiversity**. Modern manufacturing methods, transportation systems, and intensive agriculture consume vast amounts of energy and often nonrenewable natural resources. This frequently causes pollution, which has reduced biodiversity, affected human health, and caused global warming. Ecologists have monitored the changes to **ecosystems** caused by human impact. Such monitoring may indicate the need to slow or reverse the damage caused by conserving habitats and endangered species, cutting pollution, and reducing consumption of nonrenewable resources.

HOW GLOBAL WARMING OCCURS

The Sun's rays are reflected from the Earth's surface into space. Gases in the atmosphere, particularly carbon dioxide, act like greenhouse glass, trapping some of the Sun's heat energy. This "greenhouse effect" naturally warms the Earth enough to sustain life. This century, carbon dioxide levels have risen due to increased burning of **fossil fuels**. This has led to global warming – the retention of extra heat by the atmosphere and a rise in the Earth's average temperature.

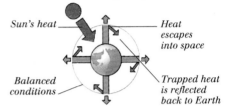

Sun's heat — Heat escapes into space

Balanced conditions — Trapped heat is reflected back to Earth

NATURAL GREENHOUSE EFFECT

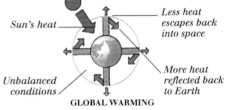

Sun's heat — Less heat escapes back into space

Unbalanced conditions — More heat reflected back to Earth

GLOBAL WARMING

POLLUTION

Pollution is the release, by humans, of agents that upset the natural balance of the living world. Vast quantities of pollutants, such as garbage, sewage, chemical waste, pesticides, and waste gases from vehicle exhausts and power plant emissions, are released every day. Pollution is now seriously affecting the environment by introducing synthetic and potentially poisonous chemicals in huge quantities.

Smog is produced mainly by vehicle exhaust fumes

MEXICO CITY, MEXICO

False-color photograph taken from space shows ozone levels

Ozone "hole" over Antarctica

OZONE LAYER

The ozone layer screens out harmful ultraviolet rays from the Sun. As a result of damage from atmospheric pollutants, particularly CFCs (chlorofluorocarbons), holes in the ozone layer appear annually over Antarctica, and the layer is also thinning elsewhere.

Acid rain removes vital minerals from soil

ACID RAIN

The burning of fossil fuels releases nitrogen and sulfur oxides into the air. These combine with water vapor in the atmosphere to form acidic droplets that fall to Earth as acid rain. This damages trees, erodes and defaces buildings, and lowers the **pH** of lakes, killing fish.

Conifers dying

Acid water runs off into lakes and rivers

Fish dying as a result of water pollution

WATER POLLUTION

Rivers, ponds, and lakes can be polluted by chemicals from industry and agriculture. Acid rain, chemical spills, and agricultural pesticides poison fish and other aquatic organisms. Fertilizers are washed into lakes where they encourage algal growth; this depletes oxygen levels and "suffocates" aquatic animals.

THREATS TO WILDLIFE

ENDANGERED SPECIES

During evolution, species naturally become extinct. However, in recent centuries the rate of extinction has accelerated enormously due to human pressures, such as pollution, loss of habitat, hunting, and the introduction of alien species. The numbers of endangered species are monitored by the World Conservation Union (IUCN – International Union for the Conservation of Nature). This chart shows the relative proportions of endangered species, in different animal groups, that are recorded in the IUCN's Red Data Book.

Relative proportions of endangered species

There are proportionately fewer endangered amphibian species

| Birds | Insects | Other invertebrates | Mammals | Fish | Reptiles | Amphibians |

Paratoid gland produces toxic secretions

Cane toad can grow up to 24cm in length

CANE TOAD
(Bufo marinus)

INTRODUCED SPECIES

In 1935, the cane toad was introduced from South America to Queensland, Australia, in order to eat the cane beetle, which was destroying the sugar-cane crop. This large toad ate not only cane beetles but also many native invertebrates and vertebrates, some of which are now threatened with extinction. The cane toad population has increased rapidly, as it has no natural predators due to the toxic secretions it produces, which kill its attackers.

MONITORING AND CONSERVING LIVING ORGANISMS

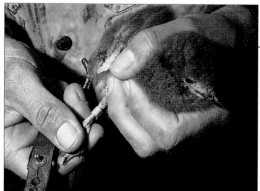

The bird is tagged with a loose fitting ring

Number of organisms are recorded

Scientist sampling species distribution on the seabed

Quadrat

MARKING AND TAGGING ANIMALS

Marking animals with a tag allows scientists to monitor their movements. The type of tag must be chosen carefully to ensure that it does not interfere with the animal's normal behavior. Birds are tagged, or banded, with a ring on the leg; fish are marked with a tag attached to a fin; and larger mammals have a radio collar that transmits a radio signal.

American bison in Yellowstone National Park, Wyoming

WILDLIFE RESERVES

Wildlife reserves are areas of habitat that are set aside, protected from human impact, and managed to ensure conservation of their natural populations of animals and plants. Yellowstone Park, seen here, was the world's first national park. Its inhabitants include bison, an animal that was hunted to near extinction in the 19th century by European settlers. Bison have since prospered in this protected area.

SAMPLING THE ENVIRONMENT

It is impossible to count all the organisms in an area, but by taking samples, the numbers and distribution of species can be calculated. One method is to use a quadrat, a square frame of known area, within which the numbers of members of species are counted. Random placement of quadrats allows scientists to look for changes in patterns of distribution.

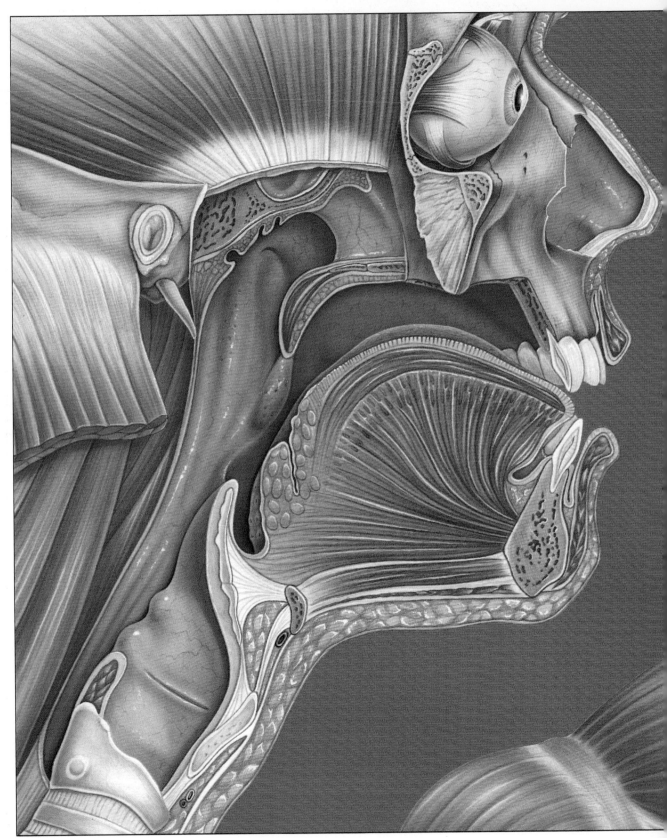

Lateral and posterior views of the head and neck

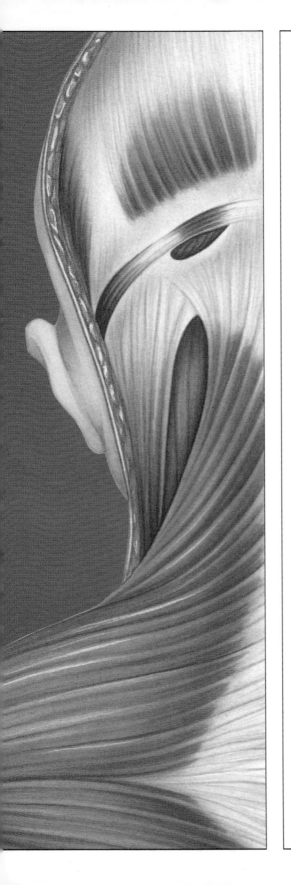

Human Anatomy

DISCOVERING HUMAN ANATOMY 178

BODY AREAS 180

SKELETON 182

MUSCLES 184

BRAIN, SPINAL CORD, AND NERVES 186

ENDOCRINE SYSTEM 188

HEART AND BLOOD VESSELS 190

LYMPHATIC SYSTEM 192

RESPIRATORY ORGANS 194

DIGESTIVE ORGANS 196

URINARY AND REPRODUCTIVE SYSTEMS...............198

HEAD AND NECK 1 200

HEAD AND NECK 2 202

HEAD AND NECK 3 204

HEAD AND NECK 4 206

TRUNK 1 208

TRUNK 2 210

THORAX 1...212

THORAX 2...214

ABDOMEN 1 216

ABDOMEN 2 218

ABDOMEN 3 220

PELVIC REGION 1 222

PELVIC REGION 2 224

SHOULDER AND UPPER ARM.............................226

FOREARM AND HAND 228

THIGH...230

LOWER LEG AND FOOT 232

Discovering human anatomy

T HE STUDY OF HUMAN ANATOMY is closely related to physiology and to medical science. Physiology is the study of how the body works, and medical science is concerned with keeping the body healthy. Since the restrictions on dissection of human bodies were lifted by the 16th century, progress in the field of anatomical research has been rapid, and modern anatomists now have a detailed understanding of the human body.

ANCIENT IDEAS
Members of early civilizations had very little experience of the internal organs of the human body, glimpsing them only when people were badly injured. Crude surgery also provided opportunities for acquiring a working knowledge of the body. Embalmists of ancient Egypt removed the organs of dead bodies while making mummies, but this was done for religious rather than scientific reasons. The human skeleton, however, was well known to the ancients, because it remains intact after death.

THE INFLUENCE OF GALEN
The quest of the ancient Greek philosophers to understand the world around them included attempts to comprehend the human body. As in other civilizations, dissection of a human being was illegal in ancient Greece. The greatest contributions to anatomy during this time were made by **Galen**. Galen performed dissection on animals and made many precise observations. During such dissections, he observed the valves in the heart, identified several nerves in the head (cranial nerves), and described muscles and bones with great accuracy. In experiments on living animals (vivisection), he demonstrated the functions of nerves in several parts of the body, by observing the effect of tying them off, or by slicing through the spinal chord between different vertebrae. He also showed that arteries carry blood, not air as had been taught previously. However, Galen made as many wrong guesses as he did accurate observations. He considered, for example, that flesh formed from blood. After Galen,

almost all anatomical research ceased until the 15th century, and until then all his ideas were accepted as correct.

THE RENAISSANCE
During the 15th and 16th centuries, restrictions on human dissection were lifted. It was then that many of the experiments that Galen described were first reproduced, and some of his claims about the human body were at last shown to be false. During this time, most artists studied anatomy to help them draw the human body. For example, the Italian artist **Leonardo da Vinci** is famous for his remarkably accurate drawings of the human body, including drawings of fetuses developing in the womb. Leonardo carried out several dissections himself, but his anatomical work remained unknown until long after his death. Interest in human anatomy was focused on Italy, in particular in Padua and Bologna. It was at Padua that a brilliant anatomist called **Andreas Vesalius** carried out most of his important work. Vesalius is known as the founder of modern human anatomy. He was one of the first to deny some of Galen's anatomical studies – he produced far more accurate ones of his own. In 1543, he published *De Humani Corporis Fabrica (On the Structure of the Human Body)*. This comprehensive work gave details of all the major systems of the human

ANATOMICAL MODEL
After restrictions on human dissection were lifted, the study of anatomy spread. Students would often use models such as this one. It is a fairly accurate anatomical model of a woman and includes the uterus (womb), containing a fetus.

SETTING BONES
Jointed models were used, from the late 16th century, to teach bonesetting to students of anatomy. This model has joints that correspond to human joints such as the shoulder, elbow, and wrist.

body, including the nervous system, reproductive system, and the blood vessels.

THE MICROSCOPE
The invention of the microscope in the 17th century was important in most of the sciences, including human anatomy. The study of anatomy on the microscopic scale is called histology. An important example of the impact of the microscope on human anatomy is the verification of the theory of blood circulation. **William Harvey** formulated the theory in the 1620s. In a set of inspired experiments, he contradicted many of Galen's ideas about blood. Whereas Galen had assumed that blood is manufactured directly from food and then becomes flesh, Harvey correctly realized that blood circulated continuously, out from the heart in arteries and back through veins. The theory had one major problem that prevented it from being widely accepted. No one could find any links between arteries and veins. Without such links, blood could not circulate as Harvey had suggested. In 1661, Marcello Malpighi observed tiny blood capillaries under his microscope. These capillaries were the missing link in Harvey's theory. Histology also added to knowledge of muscles and bones. Microscopic observations of muscle fibers led to the classification of the three types of muscle (voluntary, involuntary, and cardiac), and the realization that muscles contract due to the combined shortening of thousands of individual fibers. Clopton Havers used the microscope in his important examinations of the inner structure of bones.

18TH AND 19TH CENTURIES
During the 18th century, anatomical studies were becoming more and more detailed. In the 19th century the first comprehensive textbook on histology was published. In physiology, however, many questions remained unanswered. One such question concerned the action of nerves. Toward the end of the 18th century, **Luigi Galvani** made the legs of dead frogs move by applying electrical impulses to them. This work inspired a whole new avenue of research, known as electrophysiology, which led eventually to the modern understanding of nerve impulses. During the 19th century, there were two main advances in the study of physiology. The first was the

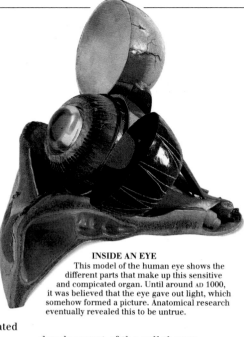

INSIDE AN EYE
This model of the human eye shows the different parts that make up this sensitive and compicated organ. Until around AD 1000, it was believed that the eye gave out light, which somehow formed a picture. Anatomical research eventually revealed this to be untrue.

development of the cell theory – the cell is the basic unit of all living things, including human beings. The second was an understanding of the chemical basis of physiology. One of the pioneers in this field was **Claude Bernard**. Among his many important discoveries was the fact that the liver breaks down a compound called glycogen into a sugar called glucose. This reaction helps to regulate the sugar content of the blood. Bernard's discovery made him begin to realize how the body's internal environment remains so nearly constant, a process known as homeostasis.

20TH CENTURY
Perhaps the most important developments in anatomy and physiology during the 20th century are studies of the endocrine system, the immune system, and the brain. The endocrine system distributes hormones, which help to carry out many of the body's vital functions. The term "hormone" was coined in 1905, and the identification and isolation of hormones such as insulin and epinephrine kept many physiologists busy throughout the century. The body's immune response was not understood until the 1950s, when the electron microscope was used to study minute structures within the cell and the structure of viruses. Other technological advances, including magnetic resonance imaging (MRI) and computer-assisted tomography (CAT) have increased understanding of the brain. MRIs and CAT scans of the living brain have helped physiologists to understand how the brain's functions are related to its structure.

TIMELINE OF DISCOVERIES

Empedocles shows that the heart is the center of the body's system of blood vessels — 450 BC

500 BC — **Alcmaeon of Croton**, probably the first person to scientifically dissect human beings, discovers the optic nerves and identifies the brain as the seat of intellect

AD 170 — Galen carries out detailed dissections, but works mainly on animals

Mondino de Luzzi publishes the first practical manual of anatomy — 1516

1545 — **Andreas Vesalius** publishes probably the most important book ever on anatomy, *On the Structure of the Human Body*

Bartolommeo Eustachio describes many human features in great detail, including the adrenal glands and the Eustachian tubes, named after him — 1552

1605 — **Heironymus Fabricius** presents a detailed study of the valves in veins

William Harvey announces his idea that blood circulates around the body, with the heart as a pump. The idea is published 12 years later — 1616

1652 — **Thomas Bartholin** discovers the lymphatic system

Francis Glisson publishes an important study of the liver — 1654

1658 — Jan Swammerdam is the first scientist to observe red blood cells

Marcello Malpighi studies the lungs and the blood capillaries under the microscope — 1660

1669 — **Richard Lower** shows that blood changes color in the lungs

Clopton Havers produces the first complete textbook of the bones of the human body — 1681

1772 — Italian anatomist Antonio Scarpa, makes an extensive study of the ear, discovering the semicircular canals and the cochlea

William Beaumont studies digestion in the open stomach of a wounded man — 1822

1830 — **Charles Bell** releases an enlarged version of his 1811 book, *The Nervous System of the Human Body*, in which he distinguishes between sensory and motor neurones (nerves)

Paul Langerhans discovers the islets of Langerhans, groups of cells that were later shown to produce insulin in the pancreas — 1869

1875 — **Camillo Golgi** devises a way to stain nervous tissue so that it can be studied under the microscope

William Bayliss and **Ernest Starling** discover the importance of hormones in the body — 1902

Body areas

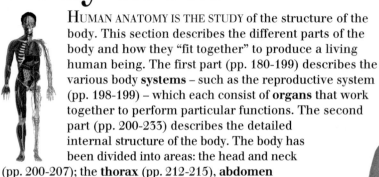

HUMAN ANATOMY IS THE STUDY of the structure of the body. This section describes the different parts of the body and how they "fit together" to produce a living human being. The first part (pp. 180-199) describes the various body **systems** – such as the reproductive system (pp. 198-199) – which each consist of **organs** that work together to perform particular functions. The second part (pp. 200-233) describes the detailed internal structure of the body. The body has been divided into areas: the head and neck (pp. 200-207); the **thorax** (pp. 212-215), **abdomen** (pp. 216-221), and **pelvic region** (pp. 222-225), which together form the **trunk** (pp. 208-211); the shoulder and upper arm (pp. 226-227); the forearm and hand (pp. 228-229); the thigh (pp. 230-231); and the lower leg and foot (pp. 232-233). Males and females have the same body areas, but their body shapes and reproductive organs differ. The entire body is covered by skin, a waterproof layer that stops the entry of **microorganisms** and acts as a **sense organ**.

ANTERIOR VIEW OF FEMALE

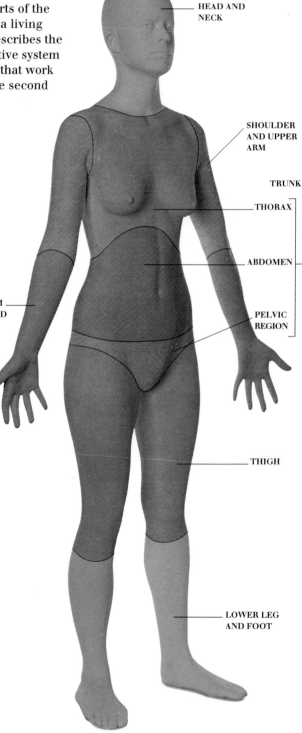

HEAD AND NECK

SHOULDER AND UPPER ARM

TRUNK

THORAX

ABDOMEN

FOREARM AND HAND

PELVIC REGION

THIGH

LOWER LEG AND FOOT

POSTERIOR VIEW OF FEMALE

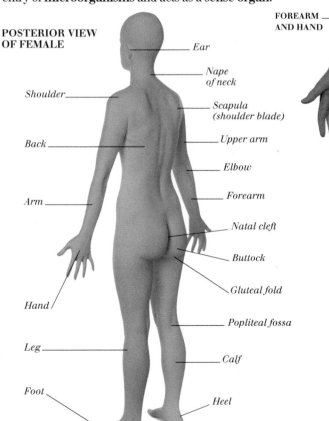

Ear

Nape of neck

Shoulder

Scapula (shoulder blade)

Back

Upper arm

Elbow

Arm

Forearm

Natal cleft

Buttock

Gluteal fold

Hand

Popliteal fossa

Leg

Calf

Foot

Heel

ANTERIOR VIEW OF MALE

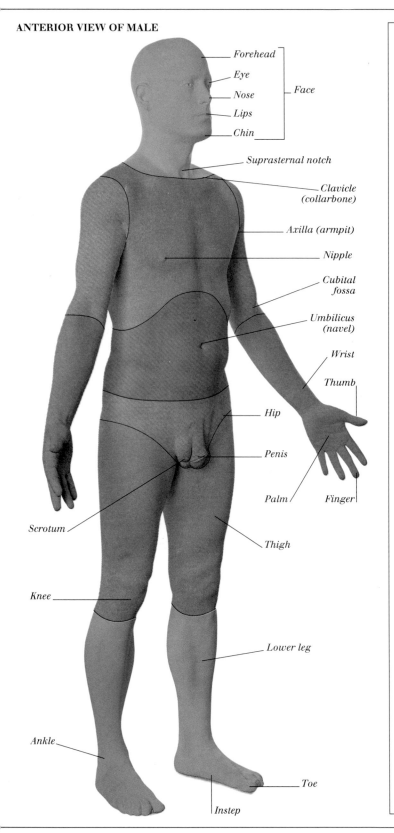

Forehead
Eye
Nose
Lips
Chin
Face
Suprasternal notch
Clavicle (collarbone)
Axilla (armpit)
Nipple
Cubital fossa
Umbilicus (navel)
Wrist
Thumb
Hip
Penis
Palm
Finger
Scrotum
Thigh
Knee
Lower leg
Ankle
Toe
Instep

SKIN, HAIR, AND NAILS

DERMIS

Skin consists of two layers, the outer epidermis and the dermis. The dermis contains nerve endings, hair follicles, and oil-producing sebaceous glands.

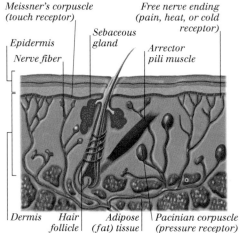

Meissner's corpuscle (touch receptor)
Free nerve ending (pain, heat, or cold receptor)
Sebaceous gland
Epidermis
Arrector pili muscle
Nerve fiber
Dermis
Hair follicle
Adipose (fat) tissue
Pacinian corpuscle (pressure receptor)

EPIDERMIS

The uppermost of the five epidermal layers consists of tough, flattened cell remnants that protect the lower layers. The upper layer is continually worn away and replaced by cells produced by the basal layer; these flatten and die as they move toward the surface.

Stratum corneum (cornified layer)
Stratum lucidum (clear layer)
Stratum granulosum (granular layer)
Stratum spinosum (prickly layer)
Stratum basale (basal layer)
Epidermal cell

NAIL STRUCTURE

Nails are plates that are derived from the epidermis. They contain keratin to make them hard. Their function is to protect the tips of the fingers and toes and to help the fingers grasp small objects. Nails grow from the matrix, where nail cells divide, lengthening the nail plate by pushing it forward over the nail bed.

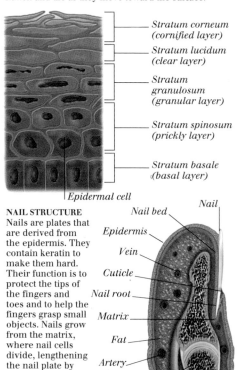

Nail
Nail bed
Epidermis
Vein
Cuticle
Nail root
Matrix
Fat
Artery
Phalanx (bone)

Skeleton

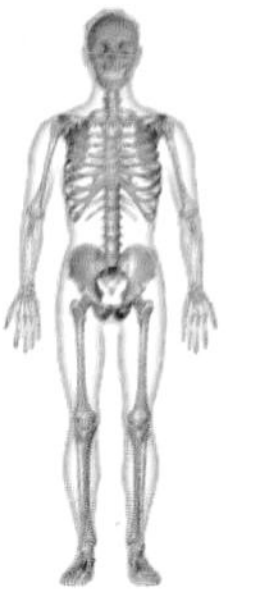

THE SKELETON IS A STRONG but lightweight framework that supports the body, protects the major **organs**, and enables movement to take place. In adults, it consists of 206 bones, and makes up 20 percent of the body's mass. Bone is a living **tissue**, supplied by blood vessels and nerves. In addition to its supportive role, it also stores **calcium** and other **minerals**, and manufactures blood cells.

The skeleton is divided into two parts. The axial skeleton forms the axis of the body trunk and consists of the skull, which protects the brain; the vertebral column, which surrounds the spinal cord; and the ribs, which encircle the heart and lungs, and assist in breathing. The appendicular skeleton consists of the bones of the arms and legs, as well as those of the pectoral (shoulder) and pelvic (hip) girdles that attach the limbs to the axial skeleton. Where two or more bones meet, a **joint** is formed. Joints are held together and stabilized by tough, straplike **ligaments**. Muscles attached to the bones on both sides of a joint produce movement when they contract.

BONES OF THE BODY

There are four basic types of bones that make up the body's internal framework: long bones, such as the femur and humerus; flat bones, such as the ribs and most skull bones; short bones, such as the carpals and tarsals; and irregular bones, such as the vertebrae.

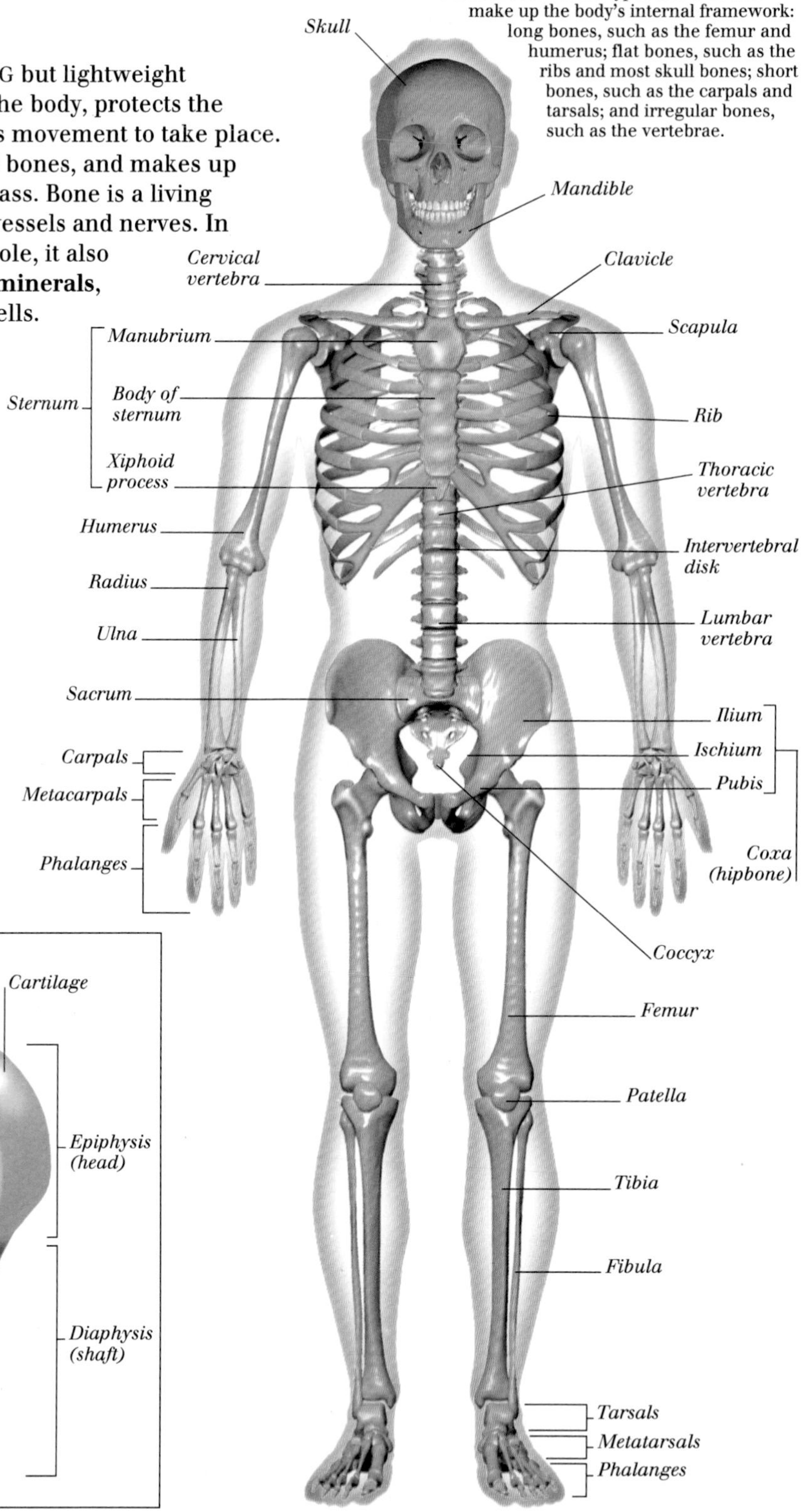

Skull

Mandible

Cervical vertebra

Clavicle

Scapula

Manubrium

Sternum

Body of sternum

Rib

Xiphoid process

Thoracic vertebra

Humerus

Intervertebral disk

Radius

Ulna

Lumbar vertebra

Sacrum

Ilium

Ischium

Carpals

Pubis

Metacarpals

Coxa (hipbone)

Phalanges

Coccyx

Femur

Patella

Tibia

Fibula

Tarsals

Metatarsals

Phalanges

BONE STRUCTURE

The combination of an outer covering of dense compact bone with an inner layer of lighter, spongy bone, makes bones both strong and light. A medullary canal, which contains marrow, runs along the length of the shaft of long bones.

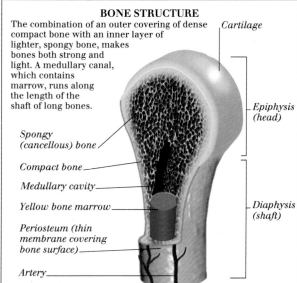

Cartilage

Epiphysis (head)

Spongy (cancellous) bone

Compact bone

Medullary cavity

Yellow bone marrow

Diaphysis (shaft)

Periosteum (thin membrane covering bone surface)

Artery

EXPLODED LATERAL VIEW OF THE SKULL

The skull surrounds and protects the brain and forms the framework of the face. It consists of 22 bones. Apart from the freely movable mandible (lower jaw), these bones are united by immovable interlocking joints called sutures.

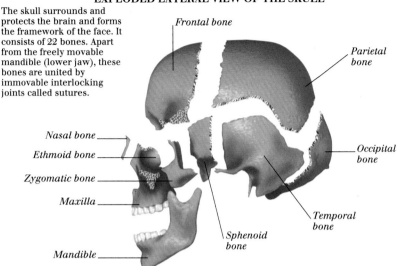

Frontal bone

Parietal bone

Nasal bone

Ethmoid bone

Zygomatic bone

Maxilla

Mandible

Occipital bone

Temporal bone

Sphenoid bone

THE SPINE (VERTEBRAL COLUMN)

The S-shaped vertebral column, which consists of 33 vertebrae, supports the head and trunk. Cartilage disks in the joints between pairs of vertebrae individually allow only limited movement, but collectively produce considerable flexibility. This allows the body to bend and twist.

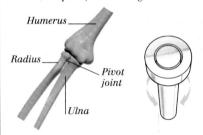

Atlas

Axis

Cervical vertebrae (7 vertebrae)

Transverse process

Thoracic vertebrae (12 vertebrae)

Transverse process

Spinous process

Lumbar vertebrae (5 vertebrae)

Intervertebral disc

Sacrum (5 fused vertebrae)

SIDE VIEW

Coccyx (4 fused vertebrae)

FRONT VIEW

EXPLODED LATERAL VIEW OF THE PELVIS

The pelvis is made up of the pelvic girdle and the sacrum. The pelvic girdle consists of two hipbones that are formed by the fusion of three bones (the ilium, ischium, and pubis) and connected at the pubic symphysis.

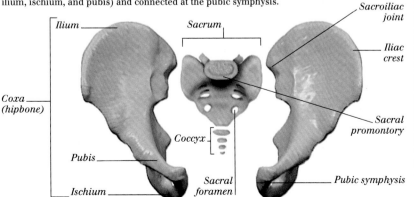

Ilium

Sacrum

Sacroiliac joint

Iliac crest

Coxa (hipbone)

Pubis

Coccyx

Ischium

Sacral foramen

Sacral promontory

Pubic symphysis

MOVABLE JOINTS

Some joints between bones show little or no movement, but most joints are freely movable. Four types of movable joints are shown below.

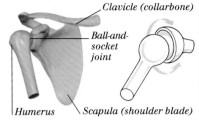

Clavicle (collarbone)

Ball-and-socket joint

Humerus

Scapula (shoulder blade)

BALL-AND-SOCKET JOINT
Both hip and shoulder are ball-and-socket joints. Here, the spherical head of one bone moves inside the cup-shaped socket of another – an arrangement that permits movement in all planes.

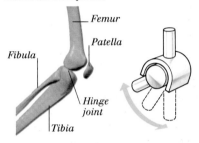

Femur

Patella

Fibula

Hinge joint

Tibia

HINGE JOINT
Hinge joints, which include the knee, elbow, and the interphalangeal joints of the finger, move in one plane, like the hinge of a door.

Humerus

Radius

Pivot joint

Ulna

PIVOT JOINT
Here, the end of one bone rotates inside a ring formed by another. The radius and ulna form a pivot joint that allows the forearm to twist.

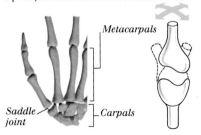

Metacarpals

Saddle joint

Carpals

SADDLE JOINT
This joint permits movement both backward and forward, and side to side, with limited rotation. It is found at the base of the thumb.

Muscles

MUSCLE IS TISSUE that can contract, or shorten, in response to a nerve impulse (message) from the central nervous system (the brain and spinal cord). Three types of muscles – skeletal, smooth, and cardiac – make up nearly 40 percent of the body's weight. Over 600 skeletal, or voluntary, muscles operate under conscious control to move the body, stabilize joints, and maintain body posture. Skeletal muscles are attached to bones by tough, fibrous cords called tendons. Typically, each muscle connects two bones by stretching across the joint between them. When the muscle contracts, one bone (the muscle's origin) remains fixed in position, while the other (the muscle's insertion) moves. Muscles lying near the skin's surface are called superficial, while those layered beneath them are called deep. Smooth, or involuntary, muscle is found in the walls of hollow organs, such as the intestine, and performs functions that are not under conscious control, such as moving partially digested food. Cardiac muscle is found only in the heart. It contracts rhythmically to pump blood around the body, but needs external nerve stimulation to accelerate or slow its pace.

TENDON

A tendon links a muscle to a bone. Tendons consist of strong connective tissue packed with tough collagen fibers. When a muscle contracts, the tendon pulls the bone, causing it to move. Most tendons are cordlike, but some, known as aponeuroses, are broad and flat.

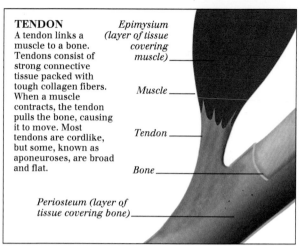

Epimysium (layer of tissue covering muscle)

Muscle

Tendon

Bone

Periosteum (layer of tissue covering bone)

NEUROMUSCULAR JUNCTION

Skeletal muscle fibers (cells) contract when stimulated by nerve impulses arriving along a motor neuron (nerve cell). A neuromuscular (nerve–muscle) junction is the site at which motor neuron and muscle fiber meet but do not touch; there is a tiny gap, or synapse, between them, across which impulses are chemically transmitted.

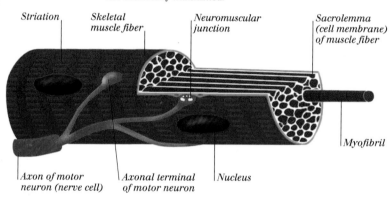

Striation

Skeletal muscle fiber

Neuromuscular junction

Sacrolemma (cell membrane) of muscle fiber

Myofibril

Axon of motor neuron (nerve cell)

Axonal terminal of motor neuron

Nucleus

TYPES OF MUSCLE

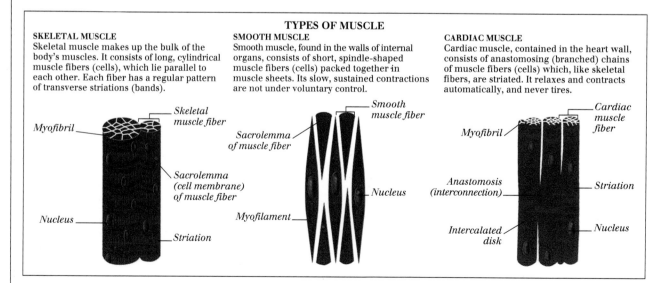

SKELETAL MUSCLE

Skeletal muscle makes up the bulk of the body's muscles. It consists of long, cylindrical muscle fibers (cells), which lie parallel to each other. Each fiber has a regular pattern of transverse striations (bands).

Myofibril

Skeletal muscle fiber

Sacrolemma (cell membrane) of muscle fiber

Nucleus

Striation

SMOOTH MUSCLE

Smooth muscle, found in the walls of internal organs, consists of short, spindle-shaped muscle fibers (cells) packed together in muscle sheets. Its slow, sustained contractions are not under voluntary control.

Smooth muscle fiber

Sacrolemma of muscle fiber

Nucleus

Myofilament

CARDIAC MUSCLE

Cardiac muscle, contained in the heart wall, consists of anastomosing (branched) chains of muscle fibers (cells) which, like skeletal fibers, are striated. It relaxes and contracts automatically, and never tires.

Cardiac muscle fiber

Myofibril

Anastomosis (interconnection)

Striation

Intercalated disk

Nucleus

MAJOR SKELETAL MUSCLES

ANTERIOR VIEW
This view shows the main superficial muscles of the front of the head, trunk, and upper and lower limbs.

POSTERIOR VIEW
This view shows the main superficial muscles of the back of the head, trunk, and upper and lower limbs.

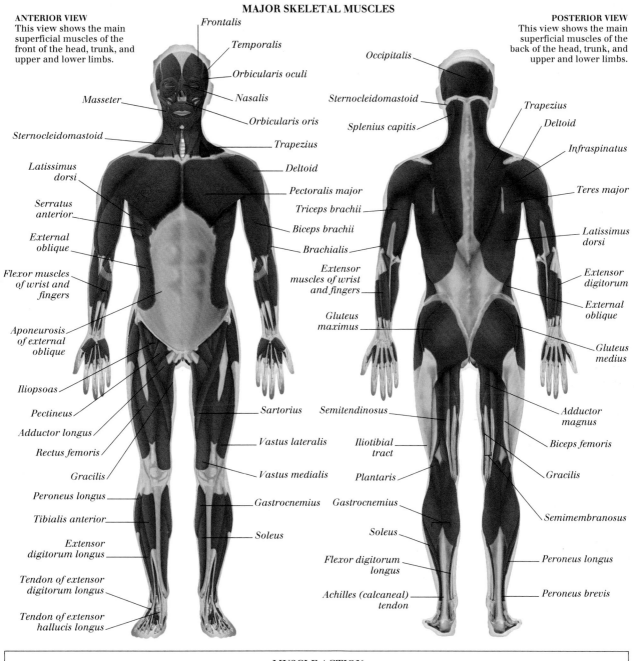

Frontalis
Temporalis
Orbicularis oculi
Nasalis
Orbicularis oris
Masseter
Sternocleidomastoid
Trapezius
Latissimus dorsi
Deltoid
Serratus anterior
Pectoralis major
External oblique
Triceps brachii
Biceps brachii
Brachialis
Flexor muscles of wrist and fingers
Extensor muscles of wrist and fingers
Aponeurosis of external oblique
Iliopsoas
Pectineus
Adductor longus
Rectus femoris
Gracilis
Peroneus longus
Tibialis anterior
Extensor digitorum longus
Tendon of extensor digitorum longus
Tendon of extensor hallucis longus
Sartorius
Vastus lateralis
Vastus medialis
Gastrocnemius
Soleus

Occipitalis
Sternocleidomastoid
Splenius capitis
Trapezius
Deltoid
Infraspinatus
Teres major
Latissimus dorsi
Extensor digitorum
External oblique
Gluteus maximus
Gluteus medius
Semitendinosus
Adductor magnus
Iliotibial tract
Biceps femoris
Plantaris
Gracilis
Gastrocnemius
Semimembranosus
Soleus
Flexor digitorum longus
Peroneus longus
Achilles (calcaneal) tendon
Peroneus brevis

MUSCLE ACTION

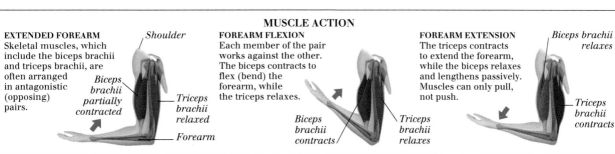

EXTENDED FOREARM
Skeletal muscles, which include the biceps brachii and triceps brachii, are often arranged in antagonistic (opposing) pairs.

Shoulder
Biceps brachii partially contracted
Triceps brachii relaxed
Forearm

FOREARM FLEXION
Each member of the pair works against the other. The biceps contracts to flex (bend) the forearm, while the triceps relaxes.

Biceps brachii contracts
Triceps brachii relaxes

FOREARM EXTENSION
The triceps contracts to extend the forearm, while the biceps relaxes and lengthens passively. Muscles can only pull, not push.

Biceps brachii relaxes
Triceps brachii contracts

Brain, spinal cord, and nerves

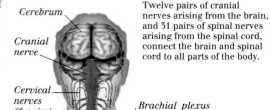

THE BRAIN, SPINAL CORD, AND NERVES together form the nervous **system**, the communication network of the body. It has two main parts: the central nervous system (CNS), which consists of the brain and spinal cord, and is the control center of the network; and the peripheral nervous system (PNS), which consists of cablelike nerves that link the CNS to the rest of the body. The nervous system contains billions of intercommunicating **neurons**, highly specialized cells capable of rapidly transmitting impulses (one-way electrochemical messages). There are three types of neurons. The first, sensory neurons, carry impulses from internal and external **sensory receptors**, such as the eye and ear, to the CNS, constantly updating it about events occurring both inside and outside the body. The second type, motor neurons, transmit impulses from the CNS to effector organs, such as muscles, instructing them to respond by contracting. Sensory and motor neurons are bundled together to form nerves. The third type, association neurons, are found only in the CNS, and link sensory and motor neurons. They form complex pathways that enable the brain to interpret incoming sensory messages, compare them with past experiences, decide on what should be done, and send out instructions in response along motor pathways to keep the body functioning properly.

THE NERVE NETWORK

Twelve pairs of cranial nerves arising from the brain, and 31 pairs of spinal nerves arising from the spinal cord, connect the brain and spinal cord to all parts of the body.

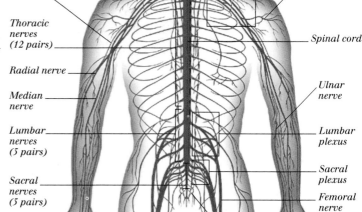

Cerebrum

Cranial nerve

Cervical nerves (8 pairs)

Brachial plexus

Axillary nerve

Musculocutaneous nerve

Thoracic nerves (12 pairs)

Spinal cord

Radial nerve

Ulnar nerve

Median nerve

Lumbar nerves (5 pairs)

Lumbar plexus

Sacral nerves (5 pairs)

Sacral plexus

Femoral nerve

Median nerve

Radial nerve

Ulnar nerve

Sciatic nerve

Coccygeal nerve

Common peroneal nerve

Tibial nerve

Medial plantar nerve

Saphenous nerve

Lateral plantar nerve

ANATOMY OF THE SPINAL CORD

The spinal cord forms a two-way information pathway between the brain and the rest of the body via the spinal nerves. It is protected by three layers of tissue called meninges and by cerebrospinal fluid circulating in the subarachnoid space.

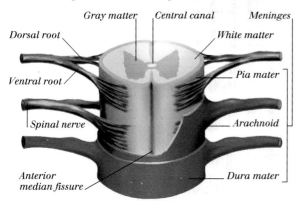

Gray matter

Central canal

Meninges

Dorsal root

White matter

Ventral root

Pia mater

Spinal nerve

Arachnoid

Anterior median fissure

Dura mater

THE BRAIN

The brain, with the spinal cord, controls and coordinates all body functions. The largest part of the brain is the cerebrum, which is divided into two halves, the left and right cerebral hemispheres. The outer, thin layer of the cerebrum (the cerebral cortex) consists of gray matter (the cell bodies of neurons); the inner part is white matter (nerve fibers). The cerebral cortex is the site of conscious behavior. Different areas of the cortex are responsible for different functions, such as movement, touch, vision, hearing, and thought. The cerebellum, the second largest part of the brain, coordinates balance and movement. The brain stem (the midbrain, pons, and medulla oblongata) regulates heartbeat, breathing, and other vital functions. The thalamus relays and sorts the nerve impulses that pass between the spinal cord and brain stem, and the cerebrum.

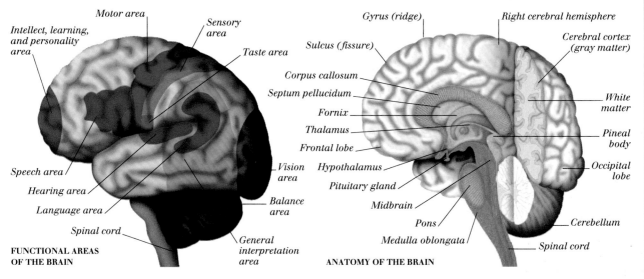

FUNCTIONAL AREAS OF THE BRAIN

ANATOMY OF THE BRAIN

NERVES AND NEURONS

Neurons are the basic structural units of the nervous system. They typically consist of a cell body, which lies in or near the central nervous system (brain and spinal cord); a single long process (the nerve fiber or axon), which carries nerve impulses; and short, multiple branches (dendrites), which carry impulses from one neuron to the next and link each neuron with many others. Nerves are long, cordlike organs that consist of bundles of the nerve fibers of both sensory and motor neurons.

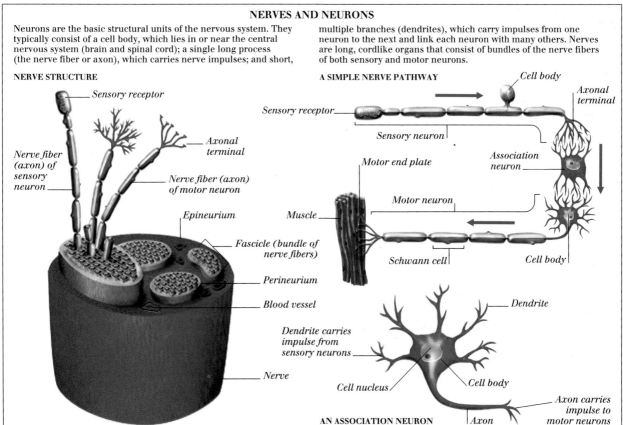

NERVE STRUCTURE

A SIMPLE NERVE PATHWAY

AN ASSOCIATION NEURON

Endocrine system

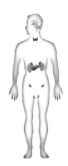

THE ENDOCRINE, OR HORMONAL, SYSTEM consists of a number of endocrine glands, which are scattered around the body. These glands manufacture chemical messengers called hormones and release them into the bloodstream. Hormones control the rate at which specific target organs or glands work. Together, the endocrine system and the nervous system (see pp. 186-187) control and coordinate all the body's activities. While the nervous system acts rapidly, with short-lived results, hormones act more slowly, and with longer-lasting effects. The endocrine glands include the pineal, which controls the daily rhythms of sleeping and waking; the parathyroids, which determine calcium levels in the blood; the thyroid, which controls metabolism (the rate at which the body uses energy); the adrenals, which release a number of hormones, including fast-acting epinephrine, which increases the heart rate under stress conditions; the pancreas, which controls the level of blood glucose (the body's energy supply); and the ovaries and testes, which release the sex hormones that produce secondary sexual characteristics, such as breasts in women and facial hair in men. Most, but not all, endocrine glands are controlled by hormones released by the pituitary gland in the brain. This, in turn, is controlled by the hypothalamus – an adjacent part of the brain.

ENDOCRINE GLANDS OF THE BRAIN

The hypothalamus plays an important part in coordinating hormone production. It sends instructions to the nearby pituitary gland, which then releases hormones that target other endocrine glands.

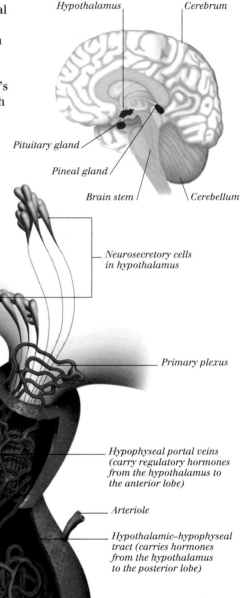

Hypothalamus

Cerebrum

Pituitary gland

Pineal gland

Brain stem

Cerebellum

Neurosecretory cells
in hypothalamus

Primary plexus

THE PITUITARY GLAND

The pituitary consists of two parts. The anterior lobe produces a number of hormones, including growth hormone and thyroid-stimulating hormone, which stimulates the thyroid gland to release hormones. The posterior lobe stores two hormones produced by the hypothalamus: oxytocin, which causes uterine contractions during labor, and antidiuretic hormone, which controls urine concentration.

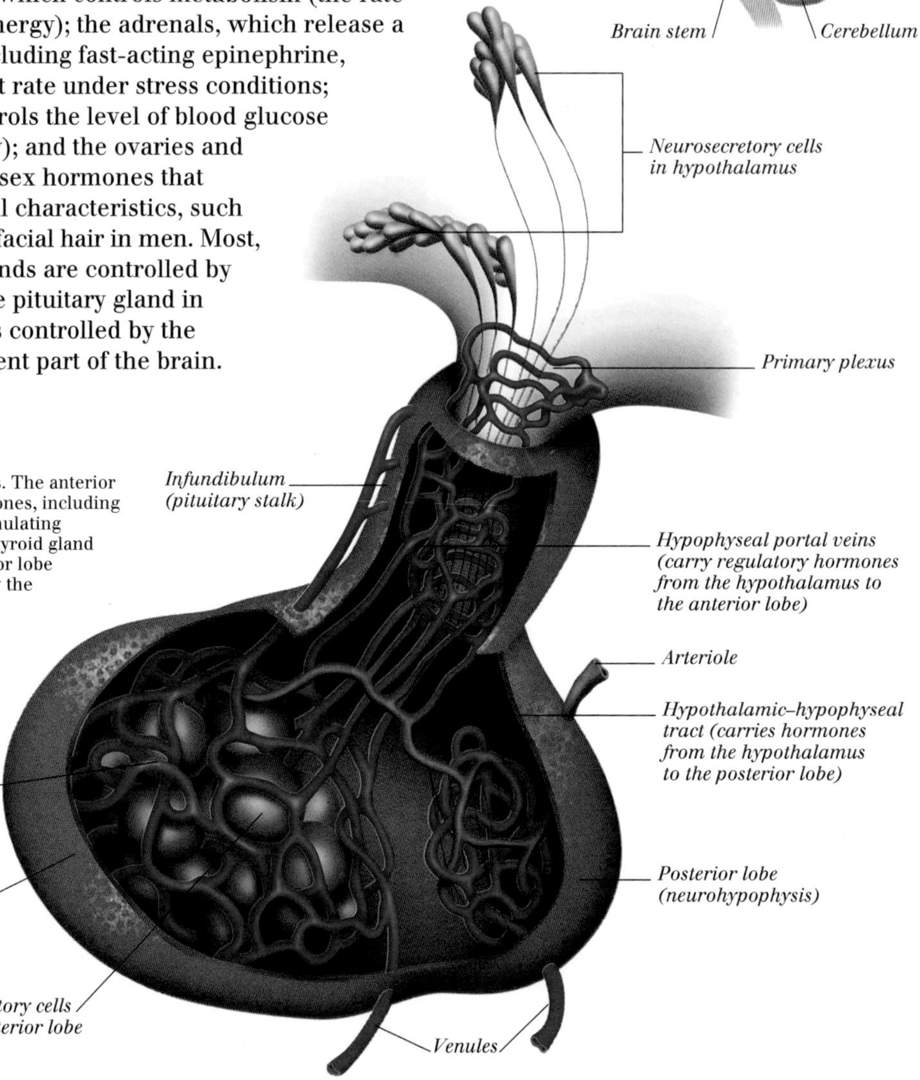

Infundibulum
(pituitary stalk)

Hypophyseal portal veins
(carry regulatory hormones
from the hypothalamus to
the anterior lobe)

Arteriole

Hypothalamic–hypophyseal
tract (carries hormones
from the hypothalamus
to the posterior lobe)

Secondary plexus

Posterior lobe
(neurohypophysis)

Anterior lobe
(adenohypophysis)

Secretory cells
of anterior lobe

Venules

HOW THE ENDOCRINE SYSTEM WORKS

Hormones manufactured by an endocrine gland are secreted into the circulatory system, and carried in the blood to specific target tissues. Here, they attach themselves to tissue cells and exert their effect.

THE RELEASE OF HORMONES INTO THE BLOODSTREAM

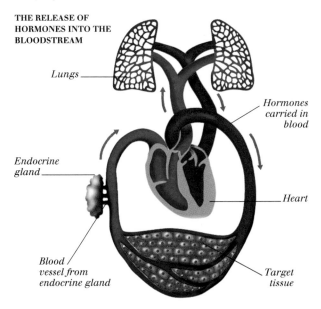

Lungs

Hormones carried in blood

Endocrine gland

Heart

Blood vessel from endocrine gland

Target tissue

ENDOCRINE GLANDS

Even though they are scattered around the body, most of the endocrine glands come under the control of the pituitary gland.

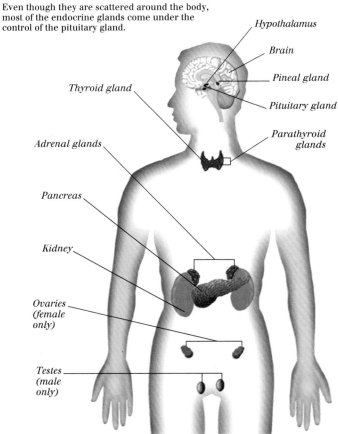

Hypothalamus

Brain

Pineal gland

Pituitary gland

Thyroid gland

Parathyroid glands

Adrenal glands

Pancreas

Kidney

Ovaries (female only)

Testes (male only)

HORMONE-PRODUCING GLANDS

The hormone-producing endocrine glands are also known as ductless glands. Unlike other glands, such as salivary glands, which release their products along ducts, endocrine glands release their products directly into the bloodstream.

POSTERIOR VIEW OF THE THYROID GLAND

The thyroid gland produces two hormones: thyroxine, which speeds up metabolism, and calcitonin, which decreases calcium levels in the blood. The parathyroids produce parathyroid hormone, which increases blood calcium levels.

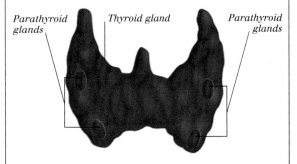

Parathyroid glands

Thyroid gland

Parathyroid glands

THE PANCREAS

The pancreas produces two hormones, insulin and glucagon, which respectively decrease and increase the level of blood glucose to keep it within set limits. The pancreas also has an exocrine (ducted) portion that produces digestive enzymes.

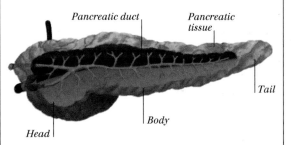

Pancreatic duct

Pancreatic tissue

Tail

Head

Body

ADRENAL GLANDS

On top of each kidney there is an adrenal gland. The outer part (cortex) produces corticosteroids, which regulate blood concentration and influence metabolism. The inner part (medulla) produces epinephrine, which prepares the body for dealing with stress or danger by increasing heart and breathing rate.

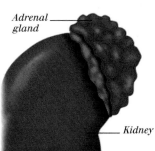

Adrenal gland

Kidney

OVARIES AND TESTES

Testes release testosterone, which controls sperm production. Ovaries release progesterone and estrogen, which prepare women's bodies for pregnancy. Secondary sexual characteristics, such as facial hair and breasts, are also produced by these hormones.

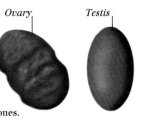

Ovary

Testis

Heart and blood vessels

THE HEART AND **BLOOD VESSELS**, together with the **blood** they contain, form the cardiovascular, or circulatory, **system**. This transports **nutrients** and **oxygen** to all body cells and removes their waste products. It also carries specialized cells that help protect against infection. The heart is a powerful muscle. It pumps blood around the circuit of blood vessels that supplies the whole body.

There are two circulatory routes: the pulmonary circulation, which carries blood through the lungs, and the systemic circulation, which carries blood through body tissues. The heart is composed of two halves, each divided into an atrium (upper chamber) and a ventricle (lower chamber). Blood returning from the body to the heart is low in oxygen. It enters the right atrium, passes into the right ventricle, and is pumped into the lungs, where it is enriched with oxygen. The oxygen-rich blood passes back into the left atrium and is pumped back into the body via the left ventricle.

THE CIRCULATORY SYSTEM
This consists of a massive network of over 100,000 km (60,000 miles) of blood vessels (arteries, veins, and capillaries). This circulates blood between the heart and all parts of the body.

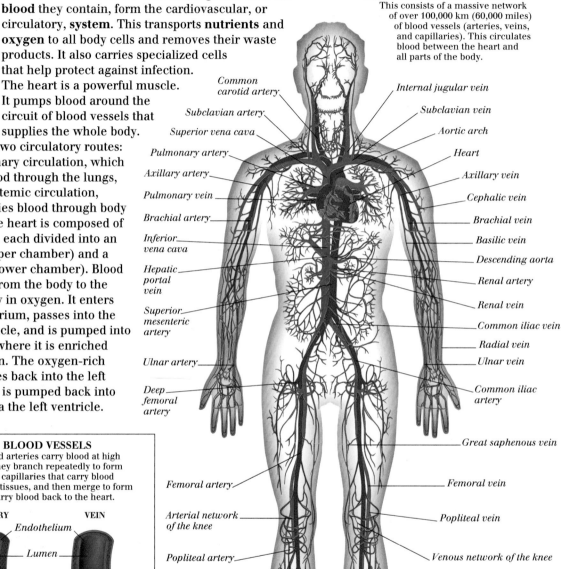

Common carotid artery
Subclavian artery
Superior vena cava
Pulmonary artery
Axillary artery
Pulmonary vein
Brachial artery
Inferior vena cava
Hepatic portal vein
Superior mesenteric artery
Ulnar artery
Deep femoral artery

Internal jugular vein
Subclavian vein
Aortic arch
Heart
Axillary vein
Cephalic vein
Brachial vein
Basilic vein
Descending aorta
Renal artery
Renal vein
Common iliac vein
Radial vein
Ulnar vein
Common iliac artery

Great saphenous vein

Femoral artery
Arterial network of the knee
Popliteal artery
Anterior tibial artery
Posterior tibial artery
Peroneal artery
Dorsal digital veins and arteries

Femoral vein
Popliteal vein
Venous network of the knee
Anterior tibial vein
Posterior tibial vein
Dorsal metatarsal arteries and veins

BLOOD VESSELS
Thick-walled arteries carry blood at high pressure. They branch repeatedly to form microscopic capillaries that carry blood through the tissues, and then merge to form veins that carry blood back to the heart.

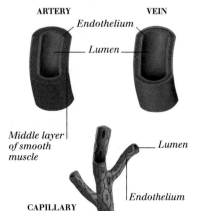

ARTERY   VEIN
Endothelium
Lumen
Middle layer of smooth muscle
Lumen
Endothelium
CAPILLARY

THE HEART

The heart is made of cardiac muscle that contracts automatically and never tires. The left pump pushes blood around the body; the right pump pushes blood into the lungs. Both sides beat together in a cycle with three stages: diastole, atrial systole, and ventricular systole.

ANTERIOR VIEW

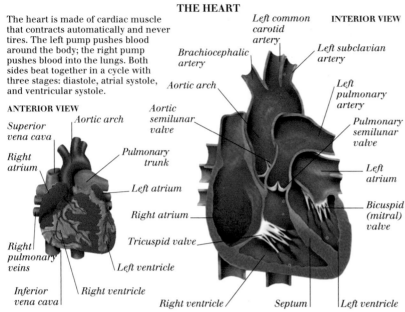

Superior vena cava
Right atrium
Right pulmonary veins
Inferior vena cava
Aortic arch
Pulmonary trunk
Left atrium
Right atrium
Tricuspid valve
Left ventricle
Right ventricle

INTERIOR VIEW

Left common carotid artery
Brachiocephalic artery
Aortic arch
Aortic semilunar valve
Left subclavian artery
Left pulmonary artery
Pulmonary semilunar valve
Left atrium
Bicuspid (mitral) valve
Right ventricle
Septum
Left ventricle

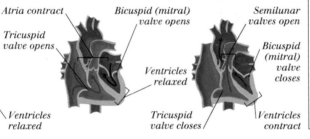

DIASTOLE
Blood returning from the body flows into the right atrium, and oxygen-rich blood flowing from the lungs flows into the left atrium.

Right and left atria relaxed
Ventricles relaxed

ATRIAL SYSTOLE
The right and left atria contract to push blood into the ventricles. The semilunar valves close to stop blood flowing back into the heart.

Atria contract
Tricuspid valve opens
Bicuspid (mitral) valve opens
Ventricles relaxed
Tricuspid valve closes

VENTRICULAR SYSTOLE
The ventricles contract to push blood out of the heart through semilunar valves. The bicuspid and tricuspid valves close to prevent backflow.

Semilunar valves open
Bicuspid (mitral) valve closes
Ventricles contract

SYSTEMIC AND PULMONARY CIRCULATIONS

The circulatory system has two parts. The systemic circulation carries oxygen-rich blood to all body tissues except the lungs, and returns oxygen-poor blood to the right atrium. The pulmonary circulation carries oxygen-poor blood from the right ventricle to the lungs, and returns oxygen-rich blood to the left atrium.

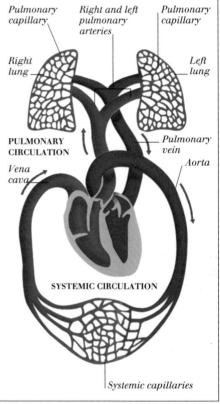

Pulmonary capillary
Right and left pulmonary arteries
Pulmonary capillary
Right lung
Left lung
PULMONARY CIRCULATION
Pulmonary vein
Vena cava
Aorta
SYSTEMIC CIRCULATION
Systemic capillaries

STRUCTURE AND FUNCTIONS OF BLOOD

Blood is a liquid tissue consisting of 55 percent plasma (a yellowish fluid that contains proteins) and 45 percent blood cells. Suspended in the plasma are red and white blood cells, and cell fragments called platelets. Blood has two main functions: transport and defense. Plasma transports nutrients and hormones to cells, and removes wastes. Erythrocytes (red blood cells) carry oxygen. Three types of white blood cells protect the body against infection: neutrophils and monocytes hunt and eat invaders; lymphocytes produce chemicals called antibodies that destroy foreign cells. Platelets help the blood clot when a wound occurs.

COMPONENTS OF BLOOD

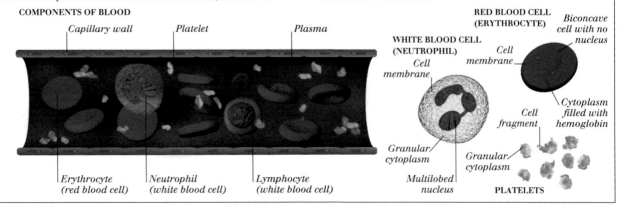

Capillary wall
Platelet
Plasma
Erythrocyte (red blood cell)
Neutrophil (white blood cell)
Lymphocyte (white blood cell)

WHITE BLOOD CELL (NEUTROPHIL)
Cell membrane
Granular cytoplasm
Multilobed nucleus

RED BLOOD CELL (ERYTHROCYTE)
Biconcave cell with no nucleus
Cell membrane
Cytoplasm filled with hemoglobin
Cell fragment
Granular cytoplasm
PLATELETS

Lymphatic system

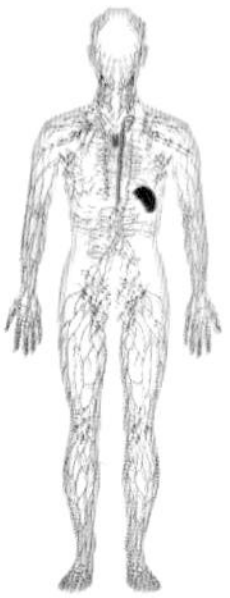

THE LYMPHATIC SYSTEM removes excess fluid from the body's tissues and returns it to the circulatory system. It also helps the body fight infection. It consists of lymphatic vessels, lymph nodes, and associated lymphoid organs, such as the spleen and tonsils. Lymph vessels form a network of tubes that reach all over the body. The smallest vessels – lymphatic capillaries – end blindly in the body's tissues. Here, they collect a liquid called lymph, which leaks out of blood capillaries and accumulates in the tissues. Once collected, lymph flows in one direction along progressively larger vessels: firstly, lymphatic vessels; secondly, lymphatic trunks; and, finally, the thoracic and right lymphatic ducts, which empty the lymph into the bloodstream. Lymph nodes are swellings along lymphatic vessels that defend the body against disease by filtering disease-causing microorganisms, such as bacteria, as lymph passes through them. There are two types of defensive cells in lymph nodes: macrophages, which engulf microorganisms, and lymphocytes, which release antibodies that target and destroy microorganisms. Lymphoid organs also contain defensive cells that destroy microorganisms found in blood or, in the case of the tonsils, air. Lymphoid organs do not filter lymph.

THE LYMPHATIC SYSTEM
Fluid lost from the blood is constantly accumulating in the body's tissues. The lymphatic network returns this excess fluid back into the bloodstream, and at the same time filters out disease-causing microorganisms.

Tonsils
Cervical nodes
Right lymphatic duct
Right subclavian vein
Right broncho-mediastinal trunk
Axillary nodes
Intercostal lymph node
Cisterna chyli
Common iliac nodes
External iliac nodes
Inguinal nodes

Internal jugular vein
Left subclavian vein
Thymus gland
Heart
Thoracic duct
Spleen
Lateral aortic nodes
Lymphatic vessel
Popliteal lymph node

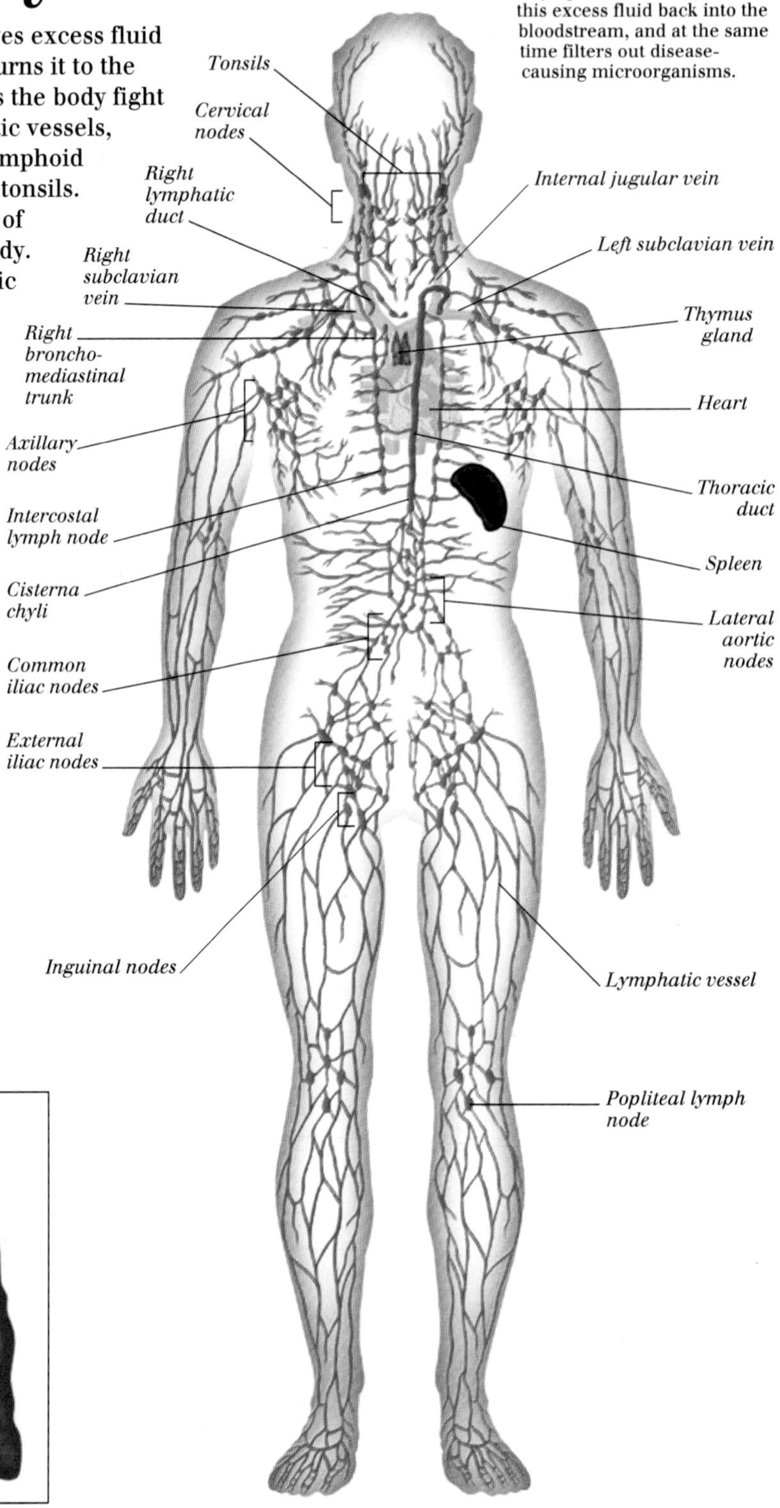

THE THYMUS GLAND

This lymphoid organ assists in the production of cells called "T lymphocytes," which target specific disease-causing micro-organisms for destruction and help defend the body against infection. The thymus is most active in children and gradually shrinks during adulthood.

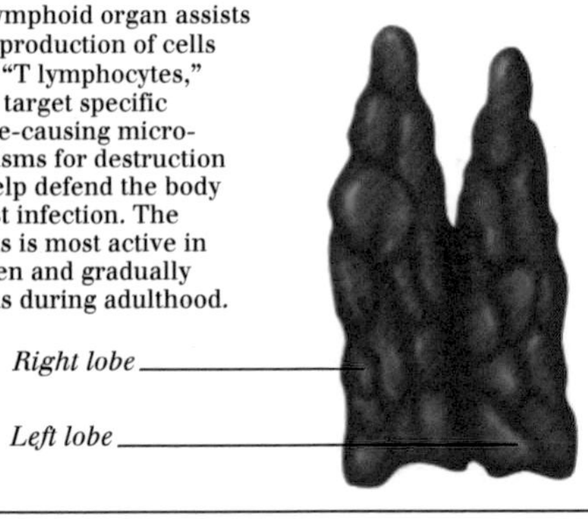

Right lobe
Left lobe

HOW THE LYMPHATIC SYSTEM WORKS

Lymph capillaries join to form larger lymphatic vessels, which transport lymph and empty it into the bloodstream.

STRUCTURE OF A LYMPH NODE

Hundreds of these small, bean-shaped organs are clustered along lymphatic vessels. Each one is surrounded by a capsule and divided into compartments by trabeculae. These compartments contain a network of fibers supporting the lymphocytes and macrophages that filter out foreign microorganisms and general debris. This process "cleans up" the lymph as it flows through the lymph node.

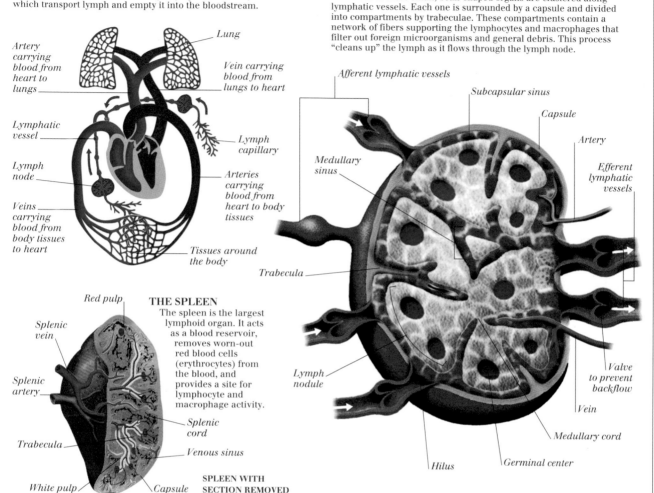

Artery carrying blood from heart to lungs

Lung

Vein carrying blood from lungs to heart

Lymphatic vessel

Lymph node

Lymph capillary

Arteries carrying blood from heart to body tissues

Veins carrying blood from body tissues to heart

Tissues around the body

Afferent lymphatic vessels

Subcapsular sinus

Capsule

Artery

Medullary sinus

Efferent lymphatic vessels

Trabecula

Lymph nodule

Valve to prevent backflow

Vein

Medullary cord

Germinal center

Hilus

THE SPLEEN

The spleen is the largest lymphoid organ. It acts as a blood reservoir, removes worn-out red blood cells (erythrocytes) from the blood, and provides a site for lymphocyte and macrophage activity.

Red pulp

Splenic vein

Splenic artery

Trabecula

White pulp

Splenic cord

Venous sinus

Capsule

SPLEEN WITH SECTION REMOVED

ANTIBODY AND CELLULAR DEFENSES

The body has two mechanisms to protect itself from infection. The antibody defense system employs lymphocytes that release killer chemicals called antibodies. When substances called antigens – located on the surface of bacteria, viruses, and other disease-causing microorganisms – are detected, the antibodies target them and either disable or destroy them. The cellular defense system employs phagocytes ("cell eaters"), which seek out invaders, engulf them, and destroy them. Lymphocytes and phagocytes are found in both lymphatic and circulatory systems, and phagocytes also wander through the tissues. One type of phagocyte is called a macrophage.

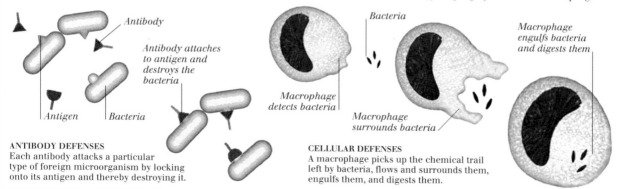

Antibody

Antibody attaches to antigen and destroys the bacteria

Antigen

Bacteria

Bacteria

Macrophage detects bacteria

Macrophage surrounds bacteria

Macrophage engulfs bacteria and digests them

ANTIBODY DEFENSES
Each antibody attacks a particular type of foreign microorganism by locking onto its antigen and thereby destroying it.

CELLULAR DEFENSES
A macrophage picks up the chemical trail left by bacteria, flows and surrounds them, engulfs them, and digests them.

Respiratory organs

THE RESPIRATORY **ORGANS** CONSIST OF THE NOSE, pharynx (throat), larynx (voice box), trachea (windpipe), the bronchi (sing. bronchus), and the lungs. Collectively, they form the respiratory **system**, which supplies the body with **oxygen** and removes waste **carbon dioxide**. Air is moved into and out of the respiratory system by breathing. During inhalation (breathing in), air is drawn in through the nose, pharynx, trachea and bronchi, and into the lungs. Inside the lungs, each bronchus divides repeatedly to form a "tree" of tubes called bronchioles, which progressively decrease in diameter and end in microscopic air sacs called alveoli (sing. alveolus). Oxygen from the air that reaches the alveoli diffuses through the alveolar walls and into the surrounding blood capillaries. This oxygen-rich blood is carried first to the heart and is then pumped to cells throughout the body. Carbon dioxide diffuses out of the blood into the alveoli and is removed from the body during exhalation (breathing out). Breathing is the result of muscular contraction. During inhalation, the **diaphragm** and **intercostal muscles** contract to enlarge the **thorax** (chest), decreasing pressure inside the thorax, so that air from the outside of the body enters the lungs. During exhalation, the muscles relax to decrease the volume of the thorax, increasing its internal pressure so that air is pushed out of the lungs.

LATERAL VIEW OF THE LARYNX

The larynx (voice box) links the pharynx with the trachea. It consists of an arrangement of nine pieces of cartilage and has two main functions. First, during swallowing, the upper cartilage (the epiglottis) covers the larynx to stop food from going into the lungs. At other times, the epiglottis is open, and the larynx provides a clear airway. Second, the larynx plays a part in voice production. Sound is produced as vocal cords vibrate in the stream of air flowing out of the body.

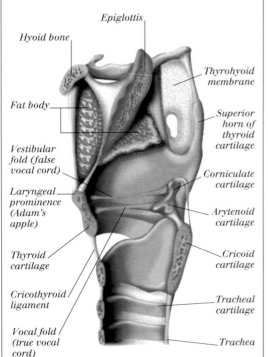

Epiglottis

Hyoid bone

Thyrohyoid membrane

Fat body

Superior horn of thyroid cartilage

Vestibular fold (false vocal cord)

Corniculate cartilage

Laryngeal prominence (Adam's apple)

Arytenoid cartilage

Thyroid cartilage

Cricoid cartilage

Cricothyroid ligament

Tracheal cartilage

Vocal fold (true vocal cord)

Trachea

THE RESPIRATORY SYSTEM

The two lungs are located on either side of the heart. The left lung has one oblique fissure, dividing it into superior and inferior lobes. The right lung has two fissures (oblique and horizontal), dividing it into superior, middle, and inferior lobes. Below the lungs, separating the thorax from the abdomen, is a muscular sheet called the diaphragm.

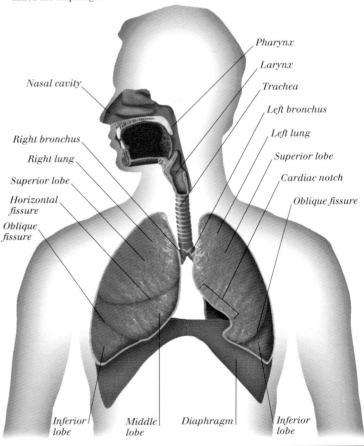

Pharynx

Larynx

Trachea

Left bronchus

Left lung

Superior lobe

Cardiac notch

Oblique fissure

Nasal cavity

Right bronchus

Right lung

Superior lobe

Horizontal fissure

Oblique fissure

Inferior lobe

Middle lobe

Diaphragm

Inferior lobe

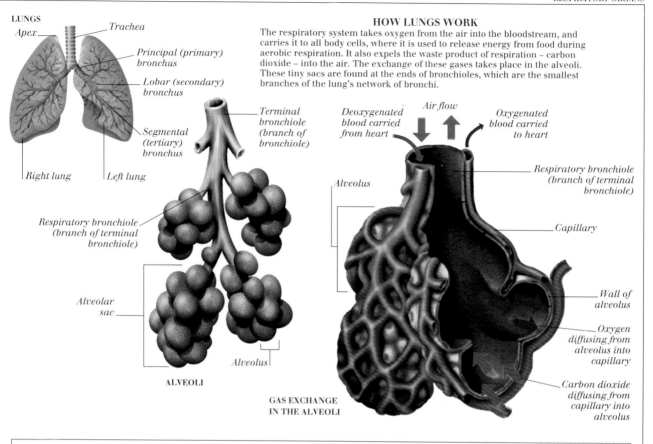

LUNGS

Apex

Trachea

Principal (primary) bronchus

Lobar (secondary) bronchus

Segmental (tertiary) bronchus

Right lung

Left lung

Terminal bronchiole (branch of bronchiole)

Respiratory bronchiole (branch of terminal bronchiole)

Alveolar sac

Alveolus

ALVEOLI

HOW LUNGS WORK

The respiratory system takes oxygen from the air into the bloodstream, and carries it to all body cells, where it is used to release energy from food during aerobic respiration. It also expels the waste product of respiration – carbon dioxide – into the air. The exchange of these gases takes place in the alveoli. These tiny sacs are found at the ends of bronchioles, which are the smallest branches of the lung's network of bronchi.

Air flow

Deoxygenated blood carried from heart

Oxygenated blood carried to heart

Alveolus

Respiratory bronchiole (branch of terminal bronchiole)

Capillary

Wall of alveolus

Oxygen diffusing from alveolus into capillary

Carbon dioxide diffusing from capillary into alveolus

GAS EXCHANGE IN THE ALVEOLI

HOW BREATHING WORKS

BREATHING IN
Breathing moves air in and out of the lungs. During breathing in (inhalation), the diaphragm contracts and flattens, increasing the volume and decreasing the pressure inside the thorax, sucking air into the lungs.

BREATHING OUT
The reverse occurs during breathing out (exhalation). The diaphragm relaxes, reducing the volume and increasing the pressure inside the thorax, forcing air out of the lungs.

RIB ACTION
The ribs also play a part in breathing. During inhalation, the intercostal muscles connecting the ribs contract. This lifts the ribs outward and upward, increasing the volume and decreasing the pressure inside the thorax.

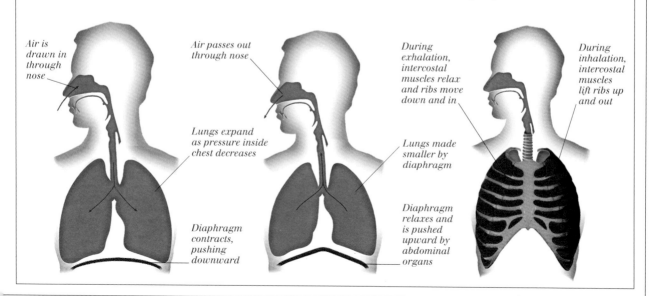

Air is drawn in through nose

Lungs expand as pressure inside chest decreases

Diaphragm contracts, pushing downward

Air passes out through nose

Lungs made smaller by diaphragm

Diaphragm relaxes and is pushed upward by abdominal organs

During exhalation, intercostal muscles relax and ribs move down and in

During inhalation, intercostal muscles lift ribs up and out

Digestive organs

THE DIGESTIVE **ORGANS** BREAK DOWN food into small **nutrient molecules** that are used to supply the body's energy needs and the raw materials that are required for growth and repair. Mechanical **digestion**, such as chewing, breaks down food by physical action; chemical digestion uses digesting agents called **enzymes** to break down food particles even further. Food ingested through the mouth is cut and ground by the teeth, lubricated with **saliva**, pushed by the tongue into the pharynx, where it is swallowed, and squeezed down the esophagus into the stomach by muscular action. Here, mechanical and chemical digestion occur, producing a souplike fluid that is released into the small intestine. The digestive process is completed here, assisted by enzyme-containing secretions from the pancreas, as well as **bile** produced in the liver. Digested food is then absorbed through the small intestine wall into the bloodstream. The large intestine absorbs most of the remaining water from undigested food, which is eliminated through the anus as feces.

SALIVARY GLANDS

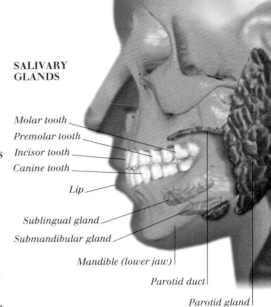

Molar tooth
Premolar tooth
Incisor tooth
Canine tooth
Lip
Sublingual gland
Submandibular gland
Mandible (lower jaw)
Parotid duct
Parotid gland

There are three pairs of salivary glands that release saliva into the mouth through ducts, especially during eating. Saliva moistens and lubricates food, and digests starch.

SWALLOWING

Swallowing, the sequence of movements that takes food from mouth to stomach, has two phases. In the first, the tongue forces the bolus (ball) of chewed-up food backward into the pharynx.

PHASE 1

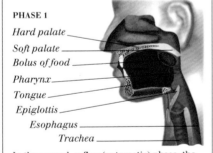

Hard palate
Soft palate
Bolus of food
Pharynx
Tongue
Epiglottis
Esophagus
Trachea

In the second, reflex (automatic) phase, the epiglottis closes to stop food going into the trachea; the soft palate blocks the entrance to the nasal cavity; and throat muscles push the food bolus into the esophagus.

PHASE 2

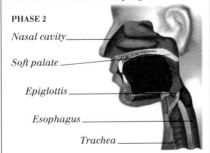

Nasal cavity
Soft palate
Epiglottis
Esophagus
Trachea

THE DIGESTIVE SYSTEM

The digestive system has two parts: the alimentary canal, formed by the mouth, pharynx (throat), esophagus, stomach, and small and large intestine; and the accessory organs, formed by the salivary glands, teeth, tongue, liver, gallbladder, and pancreas.

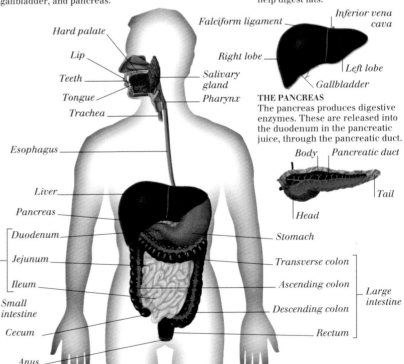

Hard palate
Lip
Teeth
Tongue
Trachea
Esophagus
Liver
Pancreas
Duodenum
Jejunum
Ileum
Small intestine
Cecum
Anus
Falciform ligament
Right lobe
Salivary gland
Pharynx
Stomach
Transverse colon
Ascending colon
Descending colon
Rectum
Large intestine

LIVER AND GALL BLADDER

The liver produces bile, which is stored in the gall bladder and emptied into the duodenum to help digest fats.

Inferior vena cava
Left lobe
Gallbladder

THE PANCREAS

The pancreas produces digestive enzymes. These are released into the duodenum in the pancreatic juice, through the pancreatic duct.

Body
Pancreatic duct
Tail
Head

TEETH

Teeth cut and crush food so that it can be swallowed and digested more easily. A tooth has an outer layer of hard enamel, overlying a layer of bonelike dentine, which encloses the pulp cavity.

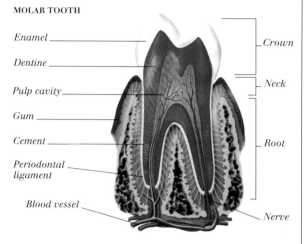

MOLAR TOOTH

Enamel
Dentine
Pulp cavity
Gum
Cement
Periodontal ligament
Blood vessel

Crown
Neck
Root
Nerve

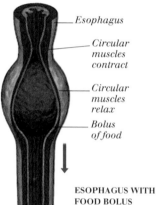

Esophagus
Circular muscles contract
Circular muscles relax
Bolus of food

ESOPHAGUS WITH FOOD BOLUS

PERISTALSIS

This is the process that moves food along the alimentary canal toward the stomach. After swallowing, for example, the circular muscle that surrounds the esophagus contracts behind the food, but relaxes in front of it. As this powerful wave of contraction moves toward the stomach, it pushes the food forward.

THE STOMACH

The stomach stores food for several hours, during which time its muscular wall contracts to churn up food, and its digestive juices work to break down proteins. This partially digests food into a souplike liquid, which is then released into the duodenum.

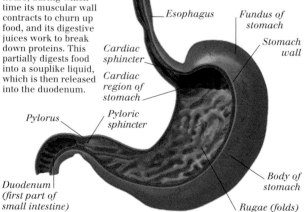

INTERIOR VIEW OF STOMACH

Esophagus
Cardiac sphincter
Cardiac region of stomach
Pylorus
Pyloric sphincter
Duodenum (first part of small intestine)

Fundus of stomach
Stomach wall
Body of stomach
Rugae (folds)

THE SMALL INTESTINE

This is the part of the alimentary canal where digestion is completed with the aid of enzymes secreted by the intestinal wall. Microscopic projections called villi give the small intestine wall a larger surface area to make the absorption of food more efficient.

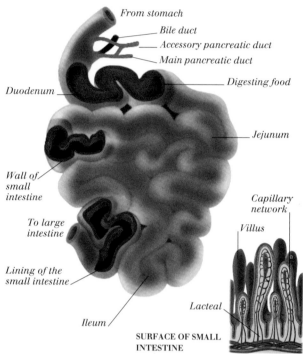

From stomach
Bile duct
Accessory pancreatic duct
Main pancreatic duct
Digesting food
Duodenum
Jejunum
Wall of small intestine
To large intestine
Lining of the small intestine
Ileum

Capillary network
Villus
Lacteal

SURFACE OF SMALL INTESTINE

THE LARGE INTESTINE

This carries undigested waste out of the body. Water is absorbed from liquid waste as it passes through the colon, leaving only solid feces. These are stored in the rectum before being released through the anus.

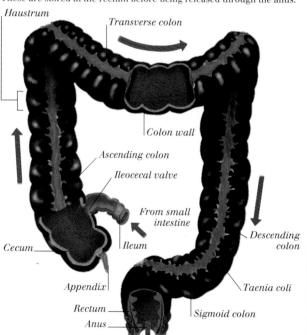

Haustrum
Transverse colon
Colon wall
Ascending colon
Ileocecal valve
From small intestine
Descending colon
Cecum
Ileum
Appendix
Taenia coli
Rectum
Sigmoid colon
Anus

Urinary and reproductive systems

THE URINARY **SYSTEM**, which consists of the urinary bladder, ureters, urethra, and kidneys, produces **urine**, a waste liquid, and transports it out of the body. Urine forms as the two kidneys remove all water and salts excess to the body's requirements, along with urea (a waste substance produced by the liver), and other poisonous wastes from the blood. It flows down the ureters to the muscular bladder which, when full, gently squeezes the urine out of the body through the urethra. The reproductive system works by generating and transporting male and female sex cells (sperm or ova) with the purpose of producing offspring. The male reproductive system consists of two sperm-producing testes, the vasa deferentia (sing. vas deferens), the urethra and **erectile** penis, and semen-producing glands, including the prostate. The female reproductive system consists of two ovaries, which alternately release one ovum (egg) each month, the fallopian tubes, the uterus, and the vagina. The male and female reproductive systems are brought together when the erect penis is placed inside the vagina during sexual intercourse. Sperm, activated by semen, are transported along the vasa deferentia and ejaculated from the penis. They then swim through the uterus and fertilize an ovum, if present, in the fallopian tubes.

THE URINARY SYSTEM

Daaily, over a million filtration units called nephrons, found in the kidney's medulla and cortex, process up to 180 liters (39.5 gallons) of fluid from blood to produce about 1.5 liters (2.6 pints) of urine. This passes down the ureter and is stored in the bladder.

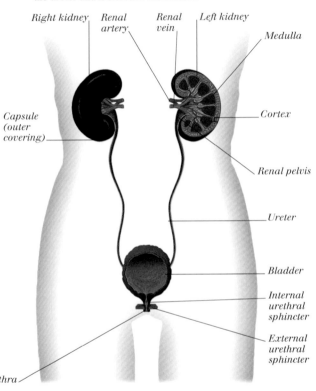

Right kidney
Renal artery
Renal vein
Left kidney
Medulla
Cortex
Capsule (outer covering)
Renal pelvis
Ureter
Bladder
Internal urethral sphincter
External urethral sphincter
Urethra

HOW KIDNEYS WORK

Tiny blood-processing units (nephrons) collect fluid from the blood through Bowman's capsules. Useful substances are reabsorbed into the blood as the fluid passes through the tubules. When it reaches the collecting duct, it contains only waste (urine).

Cortex
Arcuate vein
Arcuate artery
Collecting duct
Bowman's capsule
Distal convoluted tubule
Proximal convoluted tubule
Loop of Henle
Nephron
Medulla

THE BLADDER

As the bladder fills with urine, it expands and triggers a conscious urge to urinate. The two sphincters (muscle rings) are relaxed, the bladder contracts rhythmically, and urine is expelled along the urethra.

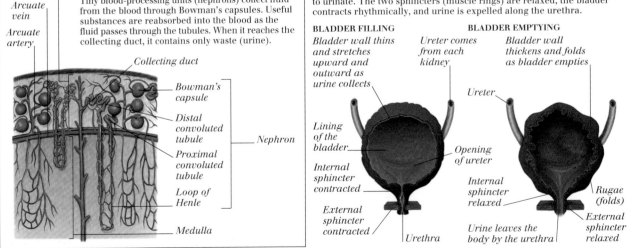

BLADDER FILLING

Bladder wall thins and stretches upward and outward as urine collects
Lining of the bladder
Internal sphincter contracted
External sphincter contracted
Urethra

BLADDER EMPTYING

Ureter comes from each kidney
Bladder wall thickens and folds as bladder empties
Ureter
Opening of ureter
Internal sphincter relaxed
Urine leaves the body by the urethra
Rugae (folds)
External sphincter relaxed

REPRODUCTIVE ORGANS

FEMALE REPRODUCTIVE ORGANS

Each month, one ovary releases an ovum and the endometrium (lining of the uterus) thickens in preparation to receive the ovum, should it be fertilized in the fallopian tube on its way to the uterus. The vagina is the canal through which sperm enter a woman's body, and through which a baby is born.

MALE REPRODUCTIVE ORGANS

The testes produce millions of sperm each day. On their way to the penis along the vasa deferentia (sing. vas deferens), sperm are mixed with fluid from the seminal vesicles and prostate gland to form semen. The penis contains spongy tissue that fills with blood before sexual intercourse, making the penis erect.

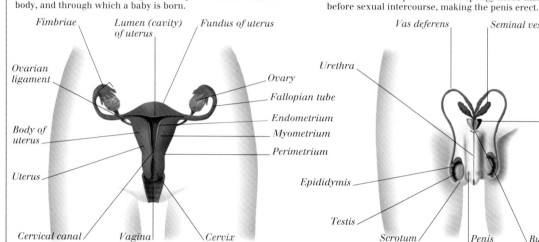

Fimbriae · Lumen (cavity) of uterus · Fundus of uterus · Ovarian ligament · Ovary · Fallopian tube · Endometrium · Myometrium · Perimetrium · Body of uterus · Uterus · Cervical canal · Vagina · Cervix

Vas deferens · Seminal vesicle · Urethra · Prostate gland · Epididymis · Testis · Scrotum · Penis · Bulbourethral gland

HOW REPRODUCTION WORKS

SEXUAL INTERCOURSE

Sexual intercourse (coitus) is the act that brings male and female sex cells into contact. When a couple becomes sexually aroused, a man puts his erect penis inside his partner's vagina. As they move together, the man ejaculates, releasing semen into the vagina. Sperm in the semen swim through the cervix, into the uterus, and up to the fallopian tubes.

FERTILIZATION OF THE OVUM

The union of the ovum with a single sperm produces a zygote (fertilized ovum) that will develop into a baby in the uterus. For fertilization to occur, sperm must reach the ovum within 24 hours of its release from the ovary.

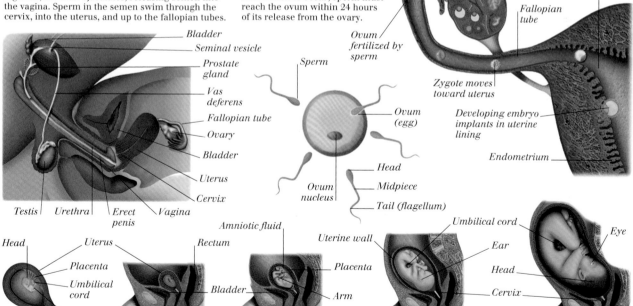

Bladder · Seminal vesicle · Prostate gland · Vas deferens · Fallopian tube · Ovary · Bladder · Uterus · Cervix · Testis · Urethra · Erect penis · Vagina

Sperm · Ovum (egg) · Head · Midpiece · Tail (flagellum) · Ovum nucleus

Release of ovum (ovulation) · Fimbria · Ovary · Uterus · Fallopian tube · Ovum fertilized by sperm · Zygote moves toward uterus · Developing embryo implants in uterine lining · Endometrium

Head · Uterus · Placenta · Umbilical cord · Tail · Amniotic fluid · Rectum · Placenta · Bladder · Uterine wall · Placenta · Arm · Umbilical cord · Ear · Head · Cervix · Vagina · Eye

SIX-WEEK-OLD EMBRYO

For its first eight weeks inside the uterus, the developing baby is called an embryo. At six weeks, the apple-seed-sized embryo has limb buds, a simple brain, and eyes. It obtains food and oxygen from its mother through the placenta and umbilical cord.

12-WEEK-OLD FETUS

At 12 weeks, the developing baby, now called a fetus, has tiny fingers and toes. Amniotic fluid protects it from external shocks.

22-WEEK-OLD FETUS

By week 22, the fetus is recognizably human, with its major body systems in place. Its kicking movements can be felt by the mother.

FULL-TERM FETUS

The fetus is fully developed and ready to be born. During the birth, the cervix widens, and the uterus muscles contract to push the baby out of the vagina.

Head and neck 1

THE HEAD CONTAINS THE BRAIN – the body's control center – and major **sense organs**. Its framework is provided by the skull, which is made up of the cranium and the facial bones. The cranium encloses and protects both the brain and the organs of hearing and balance. The facial bones form the face and provide the openings through which air and food enter the body. They also contain the organs of smell and taste, hold the teeth in place, house and protect the eyes, and provide attachment points for the **facial muscles**. The neck supports the head and provides a conduit for communication between the head and **trunk**. Blood is carried to and from the head by the carotid arteries and jugular veins. The spinal cord, which links the brain to the rest of the nervous system, runs protected within a tunnel formed by the cervical vertebrae. The trachea (windpipe) carries air between the pharynx (throat) and lungs. The esophagus transports food from the pharynx to the stomach.

SUPERFICIAL AND DEEP FACIAL MUSCLES

These muscles produce the wide range of facial expressions that communicate thoughts and emotions. These muscles include the frontalis, which wrinkles the forehead; the orbicularis oculi, which causes blinking; the risorius, which pulls the edge of the lip sideways into a smile; and the depressor labii inferioris, which pulls the lower lip downward into a pout.

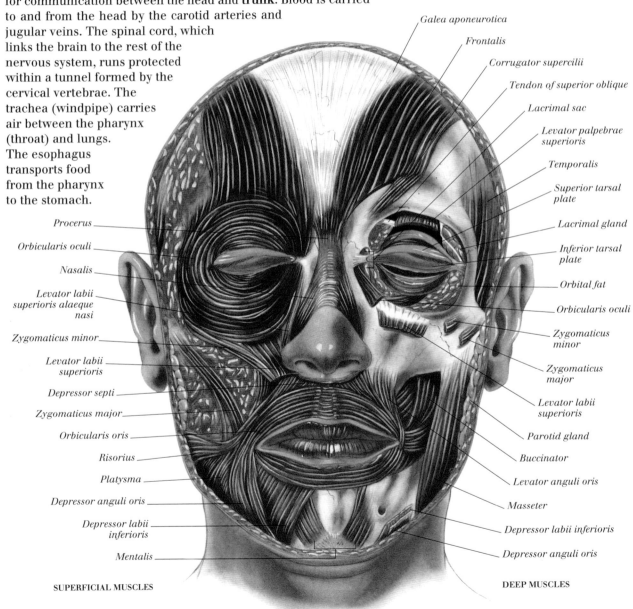

Galea aponeurotica

Frontalis

Corrugator supercilii

Tendon of superior oblique

Lacrimal sac

Levator palpebrae superioris

Temporalis

Superior tarsal plate

Lacrimal gland

Inferior tarsal plate

Orbital fat

Orbicularis oculi

Zygomaticus minor

Zygomaticus major

Levator labii superioris

Parotid gland

Buccinator

Levator anguli oris

Masseter

Depressor labii inferioris

Depressor anguli oris

Procerus

Orbicularis oculi

Nasalis

Levator labii superioris alaeque nasi

Zygomaticus minor

Levator labii superioris

Depressor septi

Zygomaticus major

Orbicularis oris

Risorius

Platysma

Depressor anguli oris

Depressor labii inferioris

Mentalis

SUPERFICIAL MUSCLES

DEEP MUSCLES

MUSCLES OF THE HEAD AND NECK

Two muscles located on each side of the head, the masseter and temporalis, close the jaw by pulling the mandible upward. The deeper buccinator (cheek muscle) keeps food between the teeth during chewing. The larger neck muscles (the sternocleidomastoid and the splenius capitis) support and move the head.

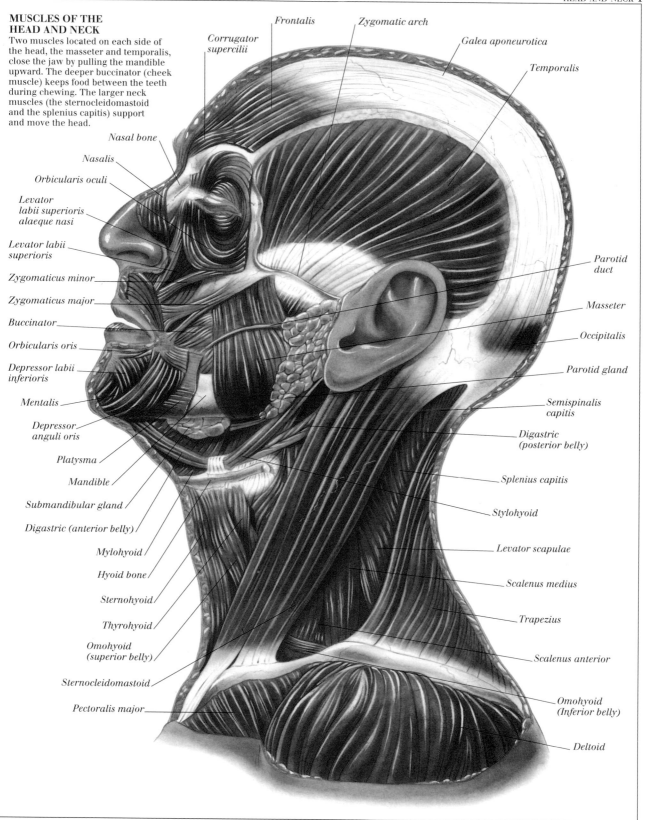

Frontalis

Zygomatic arch

Corrugator supercilii

Galea aponeurotica

Temporalis

Nasal bone

Nasalis

Orbicularis oculi

Levator labii superioris alaeque nasi

Levator labii superioris

Zygomaticus minor

Zygomaticus major

Buccinator

Orbicularis oris

Depressor labii inferioris

Mentalis

Depressor anguli oris

Platysma

Mandible

Submandibular gland

Digastric (anterior belly)

Mylohyoid

Hyoid bone

Sternohyoid

Thyrohyoid

Omohyoid (superior belly)

Sternocleidomastoid

Pectoralis major

Parotid duct

Masseter

Occipitalis

Parotid gland

Semispinalis capitis

Digastric (posterior belly)

Splenius capitis

Stylohyoid

Levator scapulae

Scalenus medius

Trapezius

Scalenus anterior

Omohyoid (Inferior belly)

Deltoid

Head and neck 2

SUPERFICIAL MUSCLES, NERVES, AND BLOOD VESSELS

Branches of the facial nerve supply the muscles of facial expression, such as the risorius. Blood is supplied to most parts of the head by branches of the external carotid arteries and internal jugular veins. These include the superficial temporal, and facial arteries and veins.

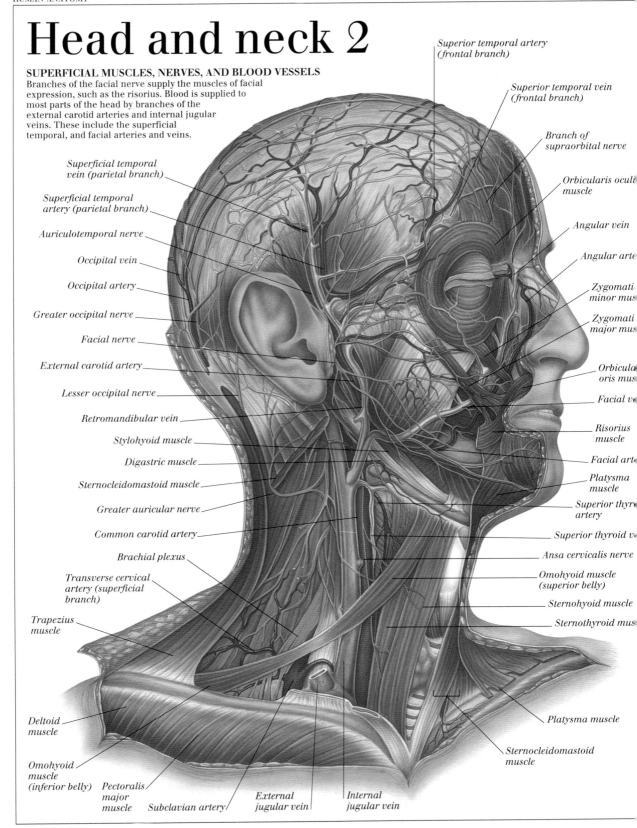

Superior temporal artery
(frontal branch)

Superior temporal vein
(frontal branch)

Branch of
supraorbital nerve

Orbicularis oculi
muscle

Angular vein

Angular arte

Zygomati
minor mus

Zygomati
major mus

Orbicula
oris mus

Facial ve

Risorius
muscle

Facial art

Platysma
muscle

Superior thyr
artery

Superior thyroid v

Ansa cervicalis nerve

Omohyoid muscle
(superior belly)

Sternohyoid muscle

Sternothyroid mus

Platysma muscle

Sternocleidomastoid
muscle

Superficial temporal
vein (parietal branch)

Superficial temporal
artery (parietal branch)

Auriculotemporal nerve

Occipital vein

Occipital artery

Greater occipital nerve

Facial nerve

External carotid artery

Lesser occipital nerve

Retromandibular vein

Stylohyoid muscle

Digastric muscle

Sternocleidomastoid muscle

Greater auricular nerve

Common carotid artery

Brachial plexus

Transverse cervical
artery (superficial
branch)

Trapezius
muscle

Deltoid
muscle

Omohyoid
muscle
(inferior belly)

Pectoralis
major
muscle

Subclavian artery

External
jugular vein

Internal
jugular vein

POSTERIOR VIEW OF THE NECK AND HEAD

The head is balanced on top of the vertebral column.
The muscles of the posterior of the neck, such as the
splenius capitis and semispinalis capitis, assisted by the
trapezius, support the head by pulling it back to
prevent it from falling forward.

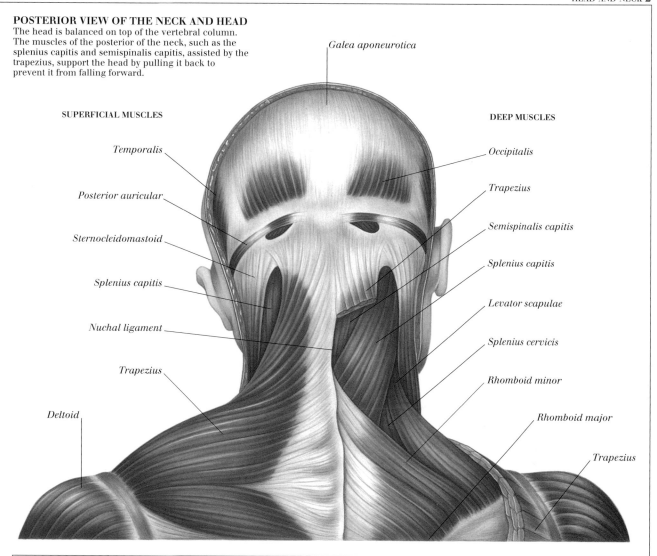

Galea aponeurotica

SUPERFICIAL MUSCLES

Temporalis

Posterior auricular

Sternocleidomastoid

Splenius capitis

Nuchal ligament

Trapezius

Deltoid

DEEP MUSCLES

Occipitalis

Trapezius

Semispinalis capitis

Splenius capitis

Levator scapulae

Splenius cervicis

Rhomboid minor

Rhomboid major

Trapezius

ANATOMY OF THE EAR, NOSE, AND EYE

EAR
The middle section of the ear is traversed by
three small bones, which carry sounds to the
cochlea, where they are converted into
nerve impulses and then carried to the brain
for interpretation.

NOSE
The framework of the external nose has a
bony part, consisting mainly of the nasal
bones, and a more flexible cartilaginous
part, consisting of the lateral, septal, and
alar cartilages.

EYE
The spherical eyeball consists of a tough
outer layer (the sclera) with a clear cornea
at the front. It is moved up and down, and
from side to side by four rectus and two
oblique muscles.

*Auricle
(pinna)*

*Tympanic membrane
(eardrum)*

Semicircular canal

*Vestibulocochlear
nerve*

Cochlea

*Lateral
cartilage*

*Greater alar
cartilage*

*External
auditory
canal*

Malleus

Incus

Stapes

Nasal bone

*Orbicularis
oculi*

*Septal
cartilage*

*Orbicularis
oris*

*Superior oblique
muscle*

Sclera

Cornea

*Superior rectus
muscle*

Optic nerve

*Lateral
rectus
muscle*

*Inferior
rectus muscle*

*Inferior
oblique
muscle*

Head and neck 3

LATERAL VIEW OF HEAD AND NECK
The removal of the skull bones reveals three sense organs: the eye, nasal cavity, and tongue. The muscles of the neck rotate the head and bend it to the side. The epiglottis closes the entrance to the trachea during swallowing to stop food from entering it.

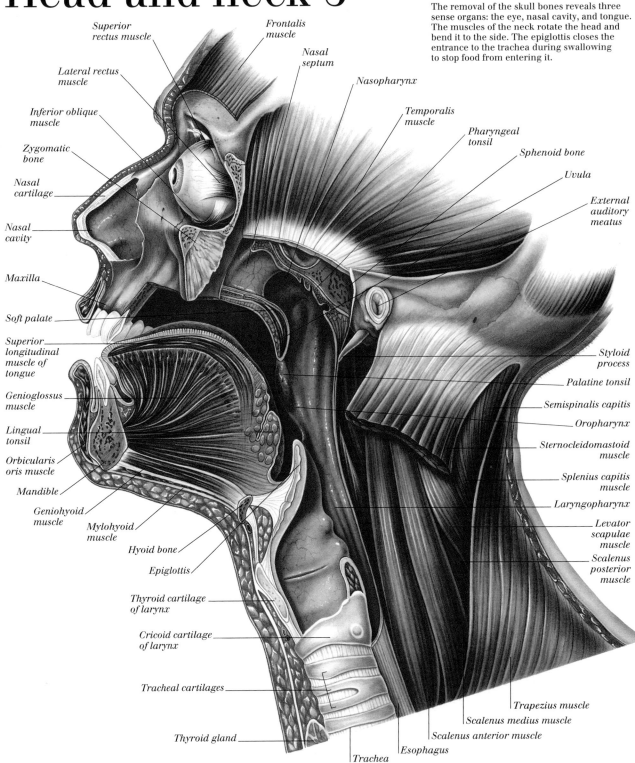

Superior rectus muscle

Frontalis muscle

Nasal septum

Nasopharynx

Lateral rectus muscle

Temporalis muscle

Pharyngeal tonsil

Inferior oblique muscle

Sphenoid bone

Zygomatic bone

Uvula

Nasal cartilage

External auditory meatus

Nasal cavity

Maxilla

Soft palate

Styloid process

Superior longitudinal muscle of tongue

Palatine tonsil

Semispinalis capitis

Genioglossus muscle

Oropharynx

Lingual tonsil

Sternocleidomastoid muscle

Orbicularis oris muscle

Splenius capitis muscle

Mandible

Laryngopharynx

Geniohyoid muscle

Levator scapulae muscle

Mylohyoid muscle

Scalenus posterior muscle

Hyoid bone

Epiglottis

Thyroid cartilage of larynx

Cricoid cartilage of larynx

Tracheal cartilages

Trapezius muscle

Scalenus medius muscle

Thyroid gland

Scalenus anterior muscle

Trachea

Esophagus

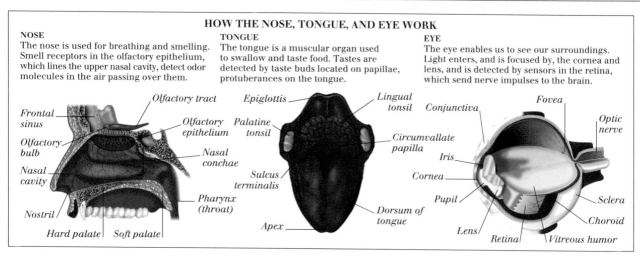

HOW THE NOSE, TONGUE, AND EYE WORK

NOSE
The nose is used for breathing and smelling. Smell receptors in the olfactory epithelium, which lines the upper nasal cavity, detect odor molecules in the air passing over them.

TONGUE
The tongue is a muscular organ used to swallow and taste food. Tastes are detected by taste buds located on papillae, protuberances on the tongue.

EYE
The eye enables us to see our surroundings. Light enters, and is focused by, the cornea and lens, and is detected by sensors in the retina, which send nerve impulses to the brain.

Olfactory tract
Frontal sinus
Olfactory epithelium
Olfactory bulb
Nasal conchae
Nasal cavity
Nostril
Pharynx (throat)
Hard palate
Soft palate

Epiglottis
Lingual tonsil
Palatine tonsil
Circumvallate papilla
Sulcus terminalis
Dorsum of tongue
Apex

Conjunctiva
Fovea
Optic nerve
Iris
Cornea
Pupil
Sclera
Choroid
Lens
Retina
Vitreous humor

ANTERIOR VIEW OF NECK
Most anterior neck muscles, including the omohyoid, sternohyoid, digastric, thyrohyoid, and mylohyoid, are involved in the movements that occur during swallowing.

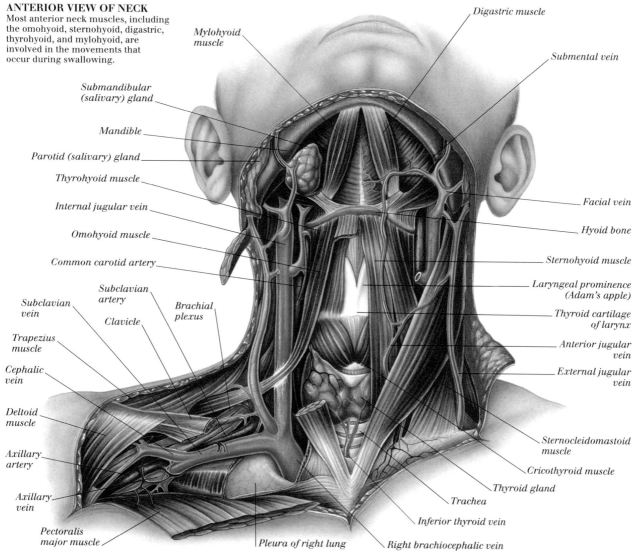

Digastric muscle
Mylohyoid muscle
Submental vein
Submandibular (salivary) gland
Mandible
Parotid (salivary) gland
Thyrohyoid muscle
Internal jugular vein
Omohyoid muscle
Common carotid artery
Subclavian artery
Subclavian vein
Clavicle
Brachial plexus
Trapezius muscle
Cephalic vein
Deltoid muscle
Axillary artery
Axillary vein
Pectoralis major muscle
Pleura of right lung
Facial vein
Hyoid bone
Sternohyoid muscle
Laryngeal prominence (Adam's apple)
Thyroid cartilage of larynx
Anterior jugular vein
External jugular vein
Sternocleidomastoid muscle
Cricothyroid muscle
Thyroid gland
Trachea
Inferior thyroid vein
Right brachiocephalic vein

Head and neck 4

ANTERIOR VIEW OF SKULL
The skull is made up of 22 bones. Cranial bones, such as the frontal bone, form the helmetlike cranium; facial bones, such as the maxilla, form the face.

POSTERIOR VIEW OF SKULL
Skull bones, apart from the mandible (lower jaw), are fused together at interlocking joints called sutures, which stop the bones from moving.

INFERIOR VIEW OF SKULL
The foramen magnum is a large hole through which the brain connects to the spinal cord. The occipital condyles form a joint with the top of the backbone.

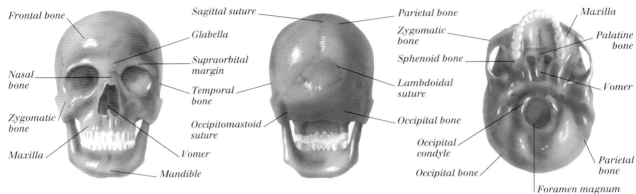

Frontal bone
Glabella
Supraorbital margin
Nasal bone
Temporal bone
Zygomatic bone
Maxilla
Vomer
Mandible

Sagittal suture
Occipitomastoid suture

Parietal bone
Zygomatic bone
Sphenoid bone
Lambdoidal suture
Occipital bone
Occipital condyle
Occipital bone
Maxilla
Palatine bone
Vomer
Parietal bone
Foramen magnum

LATERAL VIEW OF SKULL AND BRAIN
The cerebrum is the largest part of the brain. Its surface is folded into ridges called gyri (sing. gyrus) and separated by grooves called sulci (sing. sulcus). It is divided into left and right cerebral hemispheres. Deep sulci divide each hemisphere into five lobes.

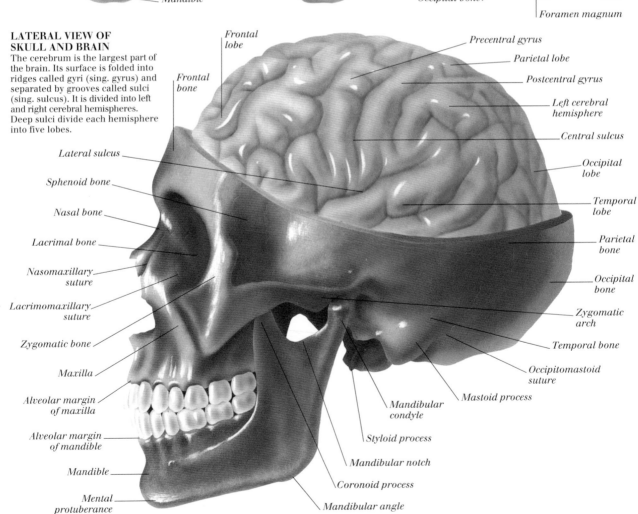

Frontal lobe
Frontal bone
Lateral sulcus
Sphenoid bone
Nasal bone
Lacrimal bone
Nasomaxillary suture
Lacrimomaxillary suture
Zygomatic bone
Maxilla
Alveolar margin of maxilla
Alveolar margin of mandible
Mandible
Mental protuberance

Precentral gyrus
Parietal lobe
Postcentral gyrus
Left cerebral hemisphere
Central sulcus
Occipital lobe
Temporal lobe
Parietal bone
Occipital bone
Zygomatic arch
Temporal bone
Occipitomastoid suture
Mastoid process
Mandibular condyle
Styloid process
Mandibular notch
Coronoid process
Mandibular angle

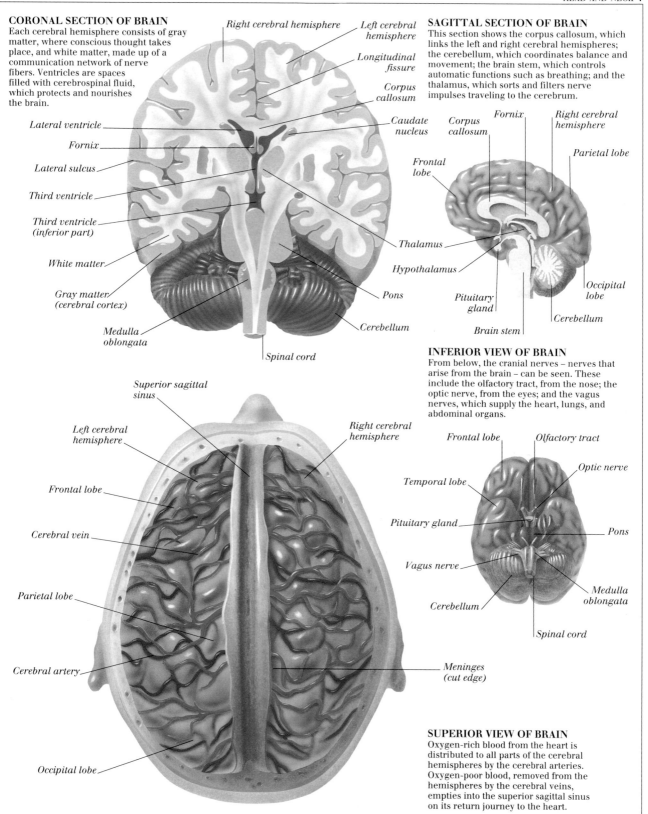

CORONAL SECTION OF BRAIN

Each cerebral hemisphere consists of gray matter, where conscious thought takes place, and white matter, made up of a communication network of nerve fibers. Ventricles are spaces filled with cerebrospinal fluid, which protects and nourishes the brain.

Right cerebral hemisphere

Left cerebral hemisphere

Longitudinal fissure

Corpus callosum

Lateral ventricle

Fornix

Lateral sulcus

Third ventricle

Third ventricle (inferior part)

White matter

Gray matter (cerebral cortex)

Medulla oblongata

Caudate nucleus

Thalamus

Pons

Cerebellum

Spinal cord

SAGITTAL SECTION OF BRAIN

This section shows the corpus callosum, which links the left and right cerebral hemispheres; the cerebellum, which coordinates balance and movement; the brain stem, which controls automatic functions such as breathing; and the thalamus, which sorts and filters nerve impulses traveling to the cerebrum.

Corpus callosum

Fornix

Right cerebral hemisphere

Frontal lobe

Parietal lobe

Thalamus

Hypothalamus

Pituitary gland

Occipital lobe

Cerebellum

Brain stem

SUPERIOR VIEW OF BRAIN — heading placement

Superior sagittal sinus

Left cerebral hemisphere

Frontal lobe

Cerebral vein

Parietal lobe

Cerebral artery

Occipital lobe

Right cerebral hemisphere

Meninges (cut edge)

INFERIOR VIEW OF BRAIN

From below, the cranial nerves – nerves that arise from the brain – can be seen. These include the olfactory tract, from the nose; the optic nerve, from the eyes; and the vagus nerves, which supply the heart, lungs, and abdominal organs.

Frontal lobe

Olfactory tract

Optic nerve

Temporal lobe

Pituitary gland

Pons

Vagus nerve

Medulla oblongata

Cerebellum

Spinal cord

SUPERIOR VIEW OF BRAIN

Oxygen-rich blood from the heart is distributed to all parts of the cerebral hemispheres by the cerebral arteries. Oxygen-poor blood, removed from the hemispheres by the cerebral veins, empties into the superior sagittal sinus on its return journey to the heart.

Trunk 1

THE TRUNK, OR TORSO, IS THE CENTRAL part of the body, to which the head, arms, and legs are attached. It is divided into an upper thorax, or chest, and a lower abdomen. Major superficial muscles of the anterior trunk include the pectoralis major, which pulls the arm forward and inward, and the external oblique, which holds in the contents of the abdomen and flexes the trunk. Major deep muscles include the external intercostals, which move the ribs upward during breathing, and the rectus abdominis, which flexes the lower back. Women have breasts – soft, fleshy domes that surround the mammary glands overlying the pectoralis major muscle. Each breast consists of lobes of milk-secreting glands, which are supported by ligaments and embedded in fat, with ducts that open out of the body through the nipple. Major superficial muscles of the posterior trunk include the trapezius, which stabilizes the shoulder, and the latissimus dorsi, which pulls the arm backward and inward. Major deep muscles include the rhomboid minor and rhomboid major, which "square the shoulders." The trunk has a bony axis, which is known as the vertebral column, or spine. Spinal nerves emerge from the spinal cord, which is protected within the spine.

LATERAL VIEW OF SUPERFICIAL MUSCLES

The lateral view of the trunk shows two powerful muscles that act as antagonists (work in opposite directions to each other): the latissimus dorsi, which extends the arm, pulling it backward, and the pectoralis major, which, assisted by the biceps brachii, flexes the arm and pulls it forward.

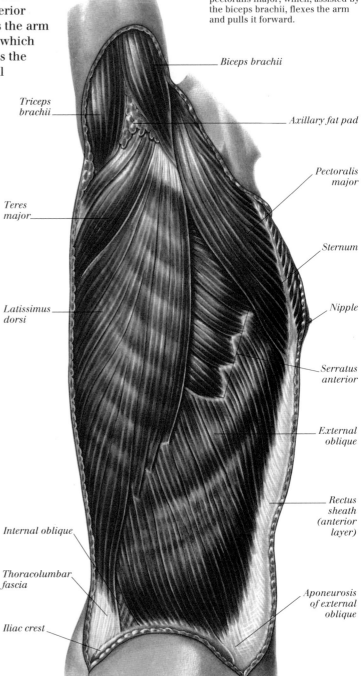

Biceps brachii

Triceps brachii

Axillary fat pad

Pectoralis major

Teres major

Sternum

Latissimus dorsi

Nipple

Serratus anterior

External oblique

Rectus sheath (anterior layer)

Internal oblique

Thoracolumbar fascia

Iliac crest

Aponeurosis of external oblique

SAGITTAL SECTION OF LEFT BREAST

After a baby is born, a woman begins to produce milk (lactate). This is produced by the glands in the lobules, and accumulates in the lactiferous sinuses. It is released from the sinuses through the lactiferous ducts when the baby sucks on the nipple.

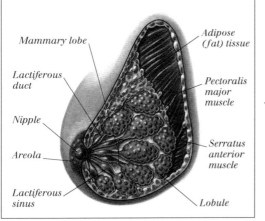

Mammary lobe

Lactiferous duct

Nipple

Areola

Lactiferous sinus

Adipose (fat) tissue

Pectoralis major muscle

Serratus anterior muscle

Lobule

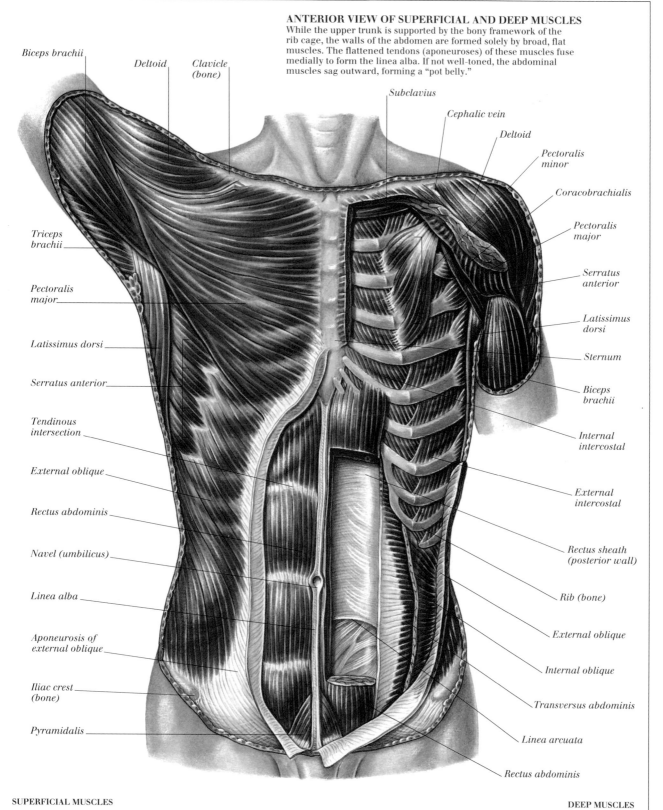

ANTERIOR VIEW OF SUPERFICIAL AND DEEP MUSCLES
While the upper trunk is supported by the bony framework of the
rib cage, the walls of the abdomen are formed solely by broad, flat
muscles. The flattened tendons (aponeuroses) of these muscles fuse
medially to form the linea alba. If not well-toned, the abdominal
muscles sag outward, forming a "pot belly."

Biceps brachii

Deltoid

*Clavicle
(bone)*

Subclavius

Cephalic vein

Deltoid

*Pectoralis
minor*

Coracobrachialis

*Pectoralis
major*

*Triceps
brachii*

*Pectoralis
major*

*Serratus
anterior*

*Latissimus
dorsi*

Latissimus dorsi

Sternum

Serratus anterior

*Biceps
brachii*

*Tendinous
intersection*

*Internal
intercostal*

External oblique

Rectus abdominis

*External
intercostal*

Navel (umbilicus)

*Rectus sheath
(posterior wall)*

Linea alba

Rib (bone)

*Aponeurosis of
external oblique*

External oblique

Internal oblique

*Iliac crest
(bone)*

Transversus abdominis

Pyramidalis

Linea arcuata

Rectus abdominis

SUPERFICIAL MUSCLES

DEEP MUSCLES

Trunk 2

POSTERIOR VIEW OF SUPERFICIAL AND DEEP MUSCLES

The superficial back muscles move the arms and shoulders. The deep erector spinae muscles act to extend (straighten) the back by pulling the trunk upward to an erect position, and to control back flexion (bending forward at the waist).

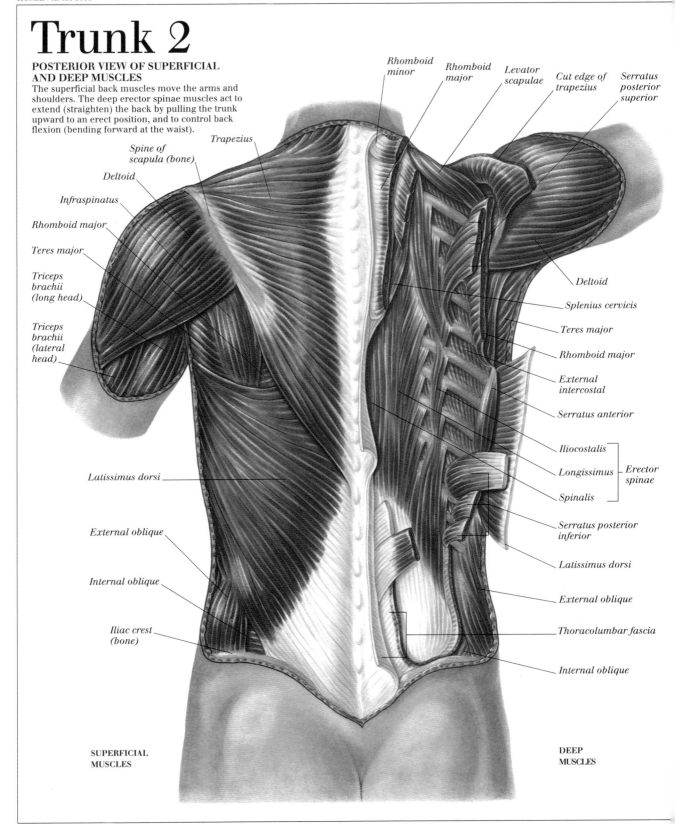

Rhomboid minor

Rhomboid major

Levator scapulae

Cut edge of trapezius

Serratus posterior superior

Trapezius

Spine of scapula (bone)

Deltoid

Infraspinatus

Rhomboid major

Teres major

Triceps brachii (long head)

Triceps brachii (lateral head)

Deltoid

Splenius cervicis

Teres major

Rhomboid major

External intercostal

Serratus anterior

Iliocostalis

Longissimus — Erector spinae

Spinalis

Serratus posterior inferior

Latissimus dorsi

Latissimus dorsi

External oblique

External oblique

Internal oblique

Thoracolumbar fascia

Iliac crest (bone)

Internal oblique

SUPERFICIAL MUSCLES

DEEP MUSCLES

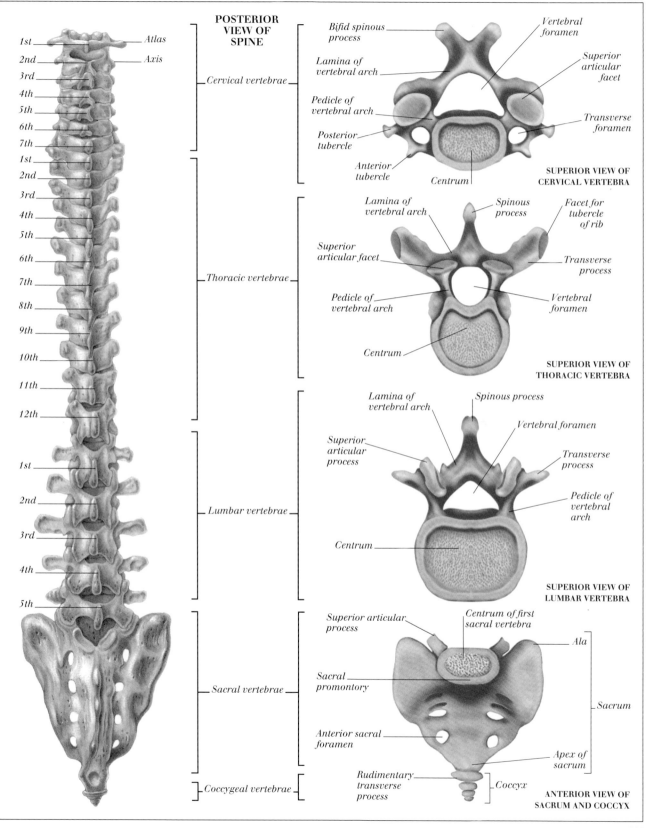

POSTERIOR VIEW OF SPINE

1st — Atlas
2nd — Axis
3rd
4th
5th
6th
7th
} Cervical vertebrae

1st
2nd
3rd
4th
5th
6th
7th
8th
9th
10th
11th
12th
} Thoracic vertebrae

1st
2nd
3rd
4th
5th
} Lumbar vertebrae

} Sacral vertebrae

} Coccygeal vertebrae

Bifid spinous process

Vertebral foramen

Lamina of vertebral arch

Superior articular facet

Pedicle of vertebral arch

Transverse foramen

Posterior tubercle

Anterior tubercle

Centrum

SUPERIOR VIEW OF CERVICAL VERTEBRA

Lamina of vertebral arch

Spinous process

Facet for tubercle of rib

Superior articular facet

Transverse process

Pedicle of vertebral arch

Vertebral foramen

Centrum

SUPERIOR VIEW OF THORACIC VERTEBRA

Lamina of vertebral arch

Spinous process

Vertebral foramen

Superior articular process

Transverse process

Pedicle of vertebral arch

Centrum

SUPERIOR VIEW OF LUMBAR VERTEBRA

Superior articular process

Centrum of first sacral vertebra

Ala

Sacral promontory

Anterior sacral foramen

Apex of sacrum

} Sacrum

Rudimentary transverse process

} Coccyx

ANTERIOR VIEW OF SACRUM AND COCCYX

Thorax 1

THE THORAX, OR CHEST, IS THE UPPER PART OF THE TRUNK, and lies below the neck and above the abdomen. The wall of the thorax – formed by the chest muscles, ribs, and intercostal muscles – surrounds the thoracic cavity. This is separated from the abdominal cavity by the diaphragm. The thoracic cavity contains the heart and major blood vessels; right and left lungs; the trachea and bronchi; and the esophagus, which connects the throat and stomach. Two thin membranes called pleurae surround the lungs, sliding over each other to prevent friction with the thoracic wall during breathing. The heart is enclosed by membranes that form a sac called the pericardium, which protects the heart and reduces friction as it beats. Blood vessels entering the heart are the inferior and superior venae cavae and the pulmonary veins. Leaving the heart, blood is carried through the aorta and the pulmonary trunk.

THE THORACIC CAVITY

The open thorax reveals the rib cage and diaphragm, which form the boundaries of the thoracic cavity, and the heart, lungs, and major blood vessels, which occupy most of the space within the cavity.

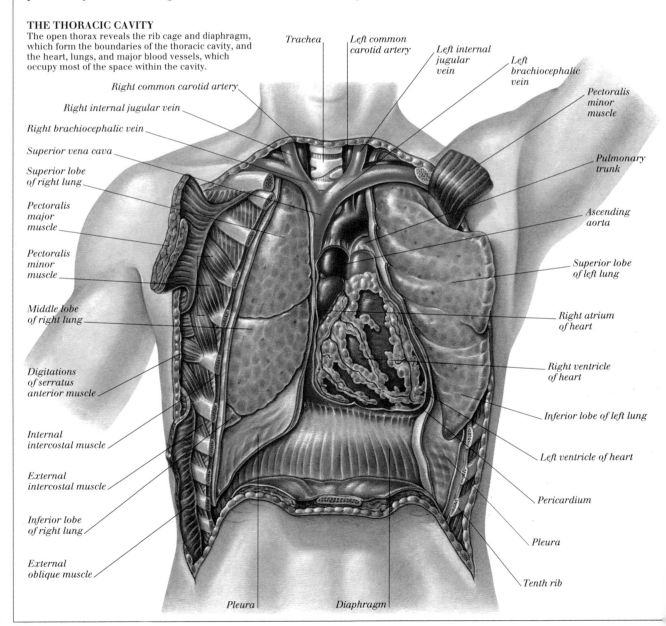

Trachea

Left common carotid artery

Left internal jugular vein

Left brachiocephalic vein

Pectoralis minor muscle

Right common carotid artery

Right internal jugular vein

Right brachiocephalic vein

Superior vena cava

Superior lobe of right lung

Pectoralis major muscle

Pectoralis minor muscle

Middle lobe of right lung

Digitations of serratus anterior muscle

Internal intercostal muscle

External intercostal muscle

Inferior lobe of right lung

External oblique muscle

Pleura

Diaphragm

Pulmonary trunk

Ascending aorta

Superior lobe of left lung

Right atrium of heart

Right ventricle of heart

Inferior lobe of left lung

Left ventricle of heart

Pericardium

Pleura

Tenth rib

THE LUNGS

Each lung consists of an air-conducting network of tubular passages, known as the bronchial tree. This consists of the principal (primary) bronchi – two branches of the trachea – which divide into lobar (secondary) bronchi. These, in turn, divide into segmental (tertiary) bronchi, which divide repeatedly to form tiny tubes called bronchioles.

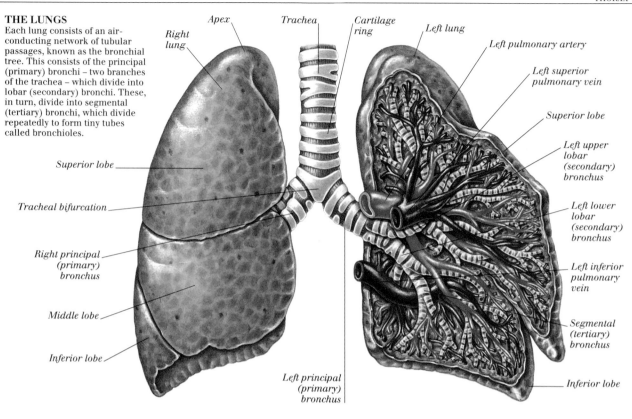

Apex

Trachea

Cartilage ring

Right lung

Left lung

Left pulmonary artery

Left superior pulmonary vein

Superior lobe

Left upper lobar (secondary) bronchus

Superior lobe

Tracheal bifurcation

Left lower lobar (secondary) bronchus

Right principal (primary) bronchus

Left inferior pulmonary vein

Middle lobe

Segmental (tertiary) bronchus

Inferior lobe

Left principal (primary) bronchus

Inferior lobe

POSTERIOR VIEW OF THE HEART

The heart's muscular walls have their own blood supply. Oxygen-rich blood is carried to the walls of the atria and ventricles by the coronary arteries; oxygen-poor blood is removed by the cardiac veins that join to form the coronary sinus.

Left subclavian artery

Descending aorta

Left pulmonary artery

Auricle of left atrium

Left pulmonary veins

Circumflex artery (branch of left coronary artery)

Left ventricle

Left common carotid artery

Brachiocephalic artery

Right brachiocephalic vein

Pericardiocophrenic artery

Superior vena cava

Azygos vein

Right pulmonary artery

Right pulmonary veins

Right atrium

Great cardiac vein

Coronary sinus

Intercostal artery

Inferior vena cava

Right ventricle

Pericardium (reflected)

RIGHT LATERAL VIEW OF THE HEART

Right subclavian artery

Right common carotid artery

Right internal jugular vein

Right subclavian vein

Right phrenic nerve

Left brachiocephalic vein

Aorta

Auricle of right atrium

Right coronary artery

Pulmonary trunk

Intercostal vein

Pericardium (reflected)

Right ventricle

Thorax 2

LUNGS PULLED BACK TO SHOW HEART
The fist-sized heart is contained within a cavity in the middle of the thorax. It is enclosed by the double-walled pericardium, which prevents friction, and is normally overlapped and partially covered by the lungs.

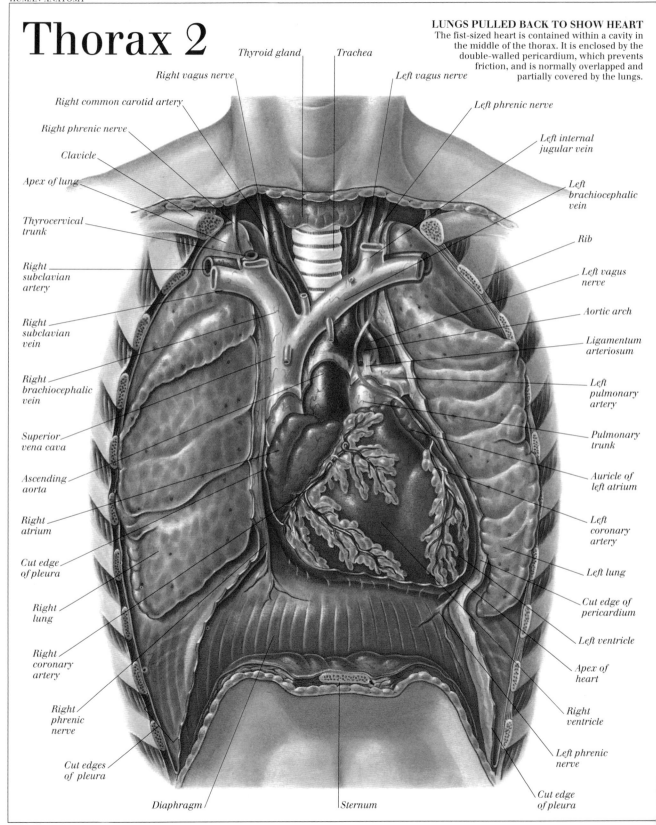

Thyroid gland
Trachea
Right vagus nerve
Left vagus nerve
Right common carotid artery
Left phrenic nerve
Right phrenic nerve
Left internal jugular vein
Clavicle
Apex of lung
Left brachiocephalic vein
Thyrocervical trunk
Rib
Right subclavian artery
Left vagus nerve
Aortic arch
Right subclavian vein
Ligamentum arteriosum
Right brachiocephalic vein
Left pulmonary artery
Superior vena cava
Pulmonary trunk
Ascending aorta
Auricle of left atrium
Right atrium
Left coronary artery
Cut edge of pleura
Left lung
Right lung
Cut edge of pericardium
Right coronary artery
Left ventricle
Apex of heart
Right phrenic nerve
Right ventricle
Cut edges of pleura
Left phrenic nerve
Diaphragm
Sternum
Cut edge of pleura

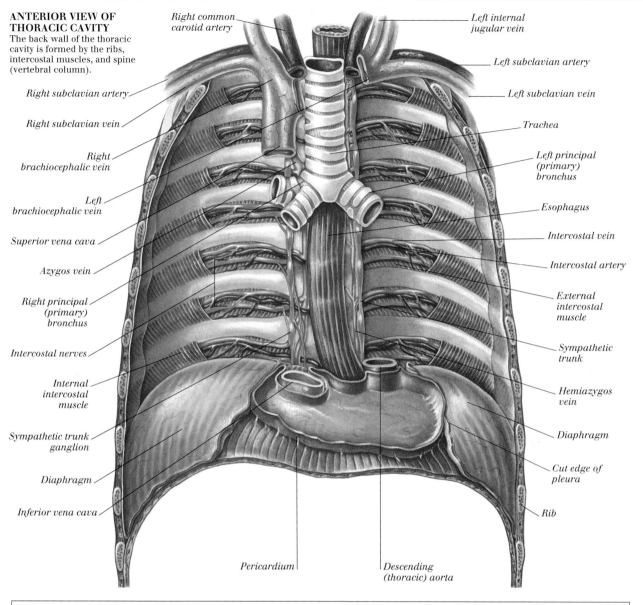

ANTERIOR VIEW OF THORACIC CAVITY
The back wall of the thoracic cavity is formed by the ribs, intercostal muscles, and spine (vertebral column).

Right common carotid artery

Left internal jugular vein

Left subclavian artery

Right subclavian artery

Left subclavian vein

Right subclavian vein

Trachea

Right brachiocephalic vein

Left principal (primary) bronchus

Left brachiocephalic vein

Esophagus

Superior vena cava

Intercostal vein

Azygos vein

Intercostal artery

Right principal (primary) bronchus

External intercostal muscle

Intercostal nerves

Sympathetic trunk

Internal intercostal muscle

Hemiazygos vein

Sympathetic trunk ganglion

Diaphragm

Diaphragm

Cut edge of pleura

Inferior vena cava

Rib

Pericardium

Descending (thoracic) aorta

SUPERIOR VIEW OF LARYNX
The vocal cords are horizontal membranes stretching between the pieces of cartilage that make up the larynx (voice box). They vibrate in the airstream to produce sounds.

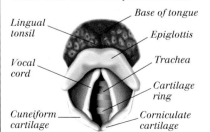

Lingual tonsil

Base of tongue

Epiglottis

Vocal cord

Trachea

Cartilage ring

Cuneiform cartilage

Corniculate cartilage

CROSS SECTION OF TRACHEA
C-shaped cartilage rings prevent the trachea from collapsing, unlike the esophagus, which remains flattened unless food passes along it.

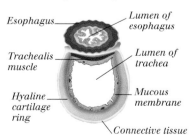

Esophagus

Lumen of esophagus

Trachealis muscle

Lumen of trachea

Hyaline cartilage ring

Mucous membrane

Connective tissue

EXPLODED VIEW OF RIB CAGE
The rib cage consists of twelve pairs of curved ribs, the vertebral column, and the sternum, to which most are attached anteriorly through the costal cartilages.

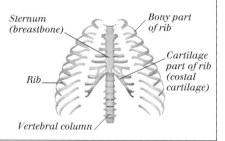

Sternum (breastbone)

Bony part of rib

Rib

Cartilage part of rib (costal cartilage)

Vertebral column

Abdomen 1

THE ABDOMEN LIES IN THE LOWER part of the trunk between the thorax and the pelvis. The wall of the abdomen surrounds the abdominal cavity (which is separated from the thoracic cavity by the diaphragm), and protects the organs contained within it. Four pairs of muscles form the abdominal wall: the external oblique, internal oblique, transversus abdominis, and rectus abdominis. Within the abdominal cavity are the stomach, and the small and large intestines, which are all digestive organs; the liver and pancreas, which are associated with the digestive system; the spleen, which forms part of the body's defenses against disease; and two kidneys, which remove waste products from the blood. A thin, continuous membrane called the peritoneum covers the abdominal organs and lines the abdominal cavity to prevent organs from sticking to each other and causing severe pain. In the lower abdomen, the dorsal aorta (the large artery that carries blood away from the heart) divides into right and left common iliac arteries, which supply the pelvic region and legs. The right and left common iliac veins join to form the inferior vena cava, a large vein that carries blood back to the heart.

THE GALLBLADDER

This muscular sac stores a greenish liquid called bile, produced by the liver. During digestion, the gallbladder contracts, squirting bile along ducts into the duodenum, where it aids the breakdown of fats.

Folds in mucous membrane

Spiral fold

Right and left hepatic duct

Muscular coat

Common hepatic duct

Cystic duct

Common bile duct

Mucous membrane

Body of gall-bladder

Fundus of gallbladder

Pancreatic duct

INTERIOR VIEW OF GALLBLADDER

SUPERFICIAL VIEW OF ABDOMINAL CAVITY

The greater omentum covers the intestines like a fatty apron. It serves to attach digestive organs to each other and to the body wall, and to protect and insulate the intestines.

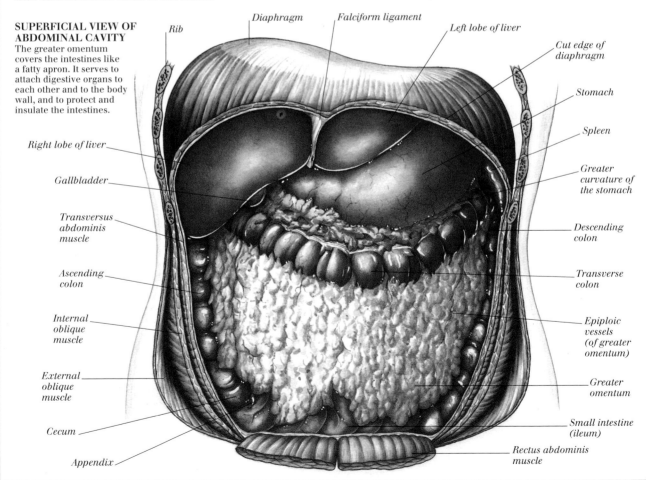

Rib

Diaphragm

Falciform ligament

Left lobe of liver

Cut edge of diaphragm

Stomach

Spleen

Right lobe of liver

Gallbladder

Transversus abdominis muscle

Ascending colon

Internal oblique muscle

External oblique muscle

Cecum

Appendix

Greater curvature of the stomach

Descending colon

Transverse colon

Epiploic vessels (of greater omentum)

Greater omentum

Small intestine (ileum)

Rectus abdominis muscle

THE ABDOMINAL CAVITY

The intestines form the longest part of the digestive system. In the small intestine, food is digested and absorbed into the bloodstream. The large intestine carries undigested material to the outside of the body, and absorbs water from this waste back into the body.

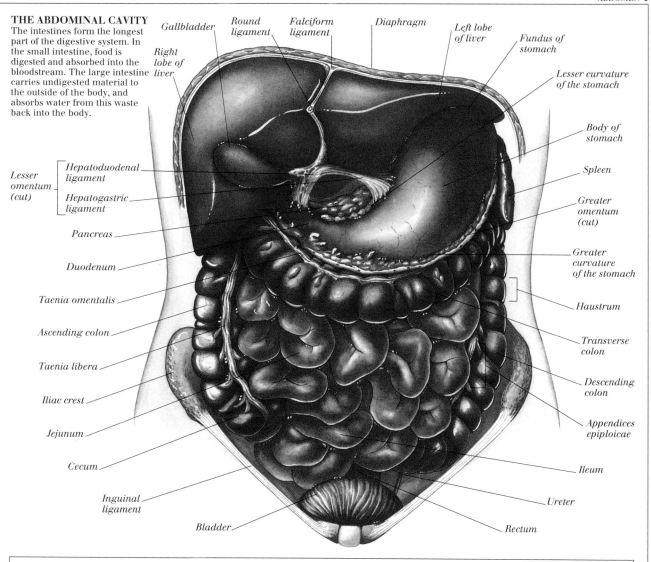

Gallbladder
Round ligament
Falciform ligament
Diaphragm
Left lobe of liver
Fundus of stomach
Right lobe of liver
Lesser curvature of the stomach
Body of stomach
Lesser omentum (cut)
Hepatoduodenal ligament
Hepatogastric ligament
Spleen
Greater omentum (cut)
Pancreas
Greater curvature of the stomach
Duodenum
Taenia omentalis
Haustrum
Ascending colon
Transverse colon
Taenia libera
Descending colon
Iliac crest
Jejunum
Appendices epiploicae
Cecum
Ileum
Inguinal ligament
Ureter
Bladder
Rectum

THE LIVER

The liver is the body's largest gland. It performs over 500 functions, which include processing the blood that arrives through the hepatic portal vein, its direct link with the digestive system (see pp. 196-197), and the hepatic artery. It controls levels of fats, amino acids, and glucose in the blood; stores vitamins A and D; removes worn-out red blood cells; removes drugs and poisons; warms the blood; and produces bile, which is used in digestion. Blood leaves the liver through the hepatic veins, which empty into the inferior vena cava.

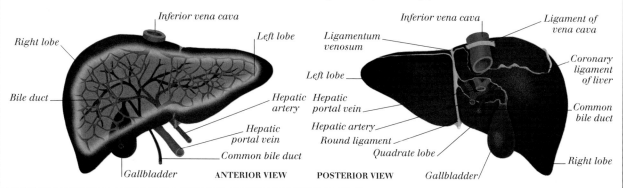

Inferior vena cava
Right lobe
Left lobe
Bile duct
Hepatic artery
Hepatic portal vein
Common bile duct
Gallbladder
ANTERIOR VIEW

Inferior vena cava
Ligamentum venosum
Ligament of vena cava
Left lobe
Coronary ligament of liver
Hepatic portal vein
Hepatic artery
Round ligament
Quadrate lobe
Common bile duct
Right lobe
Gallbladder
POSTERIOR VIEW

Abdomen 2

THE ABDOMINAL CAVITY WITH LIVER REMOVED

The removal of the liver reveals the opening in the diaphragm through which the esophagus enters the abdomen from the thorax. This carries food into the stomach and then the duodenum, which is the first, short section of the small intestine.

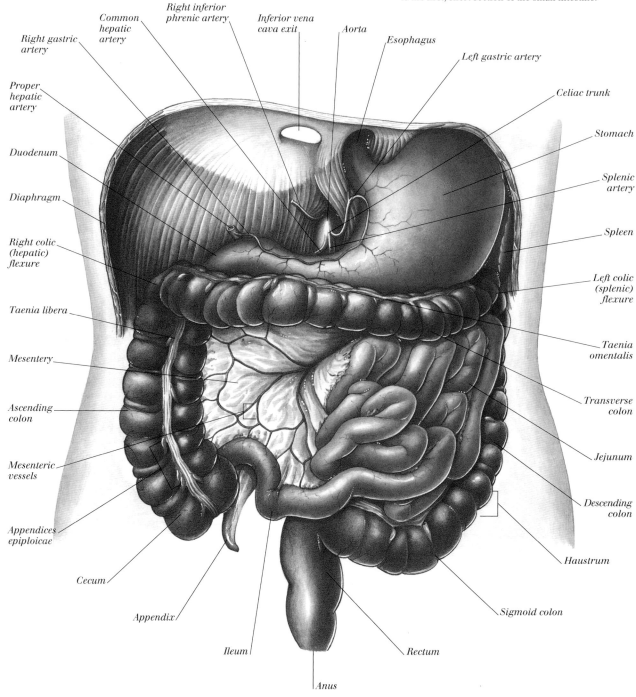

Right inferior
phrenic artery

Common
hepatic
artery

Right gastric
artery

Inferior vena
cava exit

Aorta

Esophagus

Left gastric artery

Proper
hepatic
artery

Celiac trunk

Stomach

Duodenum

Splenic
artery

Diaphragm

Spleen

Right colic
(hepatic)
flexure

Left colic
(splenic)
flexure

Taenia libera

Taenia
omentalis

Mesentery

Transverse
colon

Ascending
colon

Jejunum

Mesenteric
vessels

Descending
colon

Appendices
epiploicae

Haustrum

Cecum

Sigmoid colon

Appendix

Ileum

Rectum

Anus

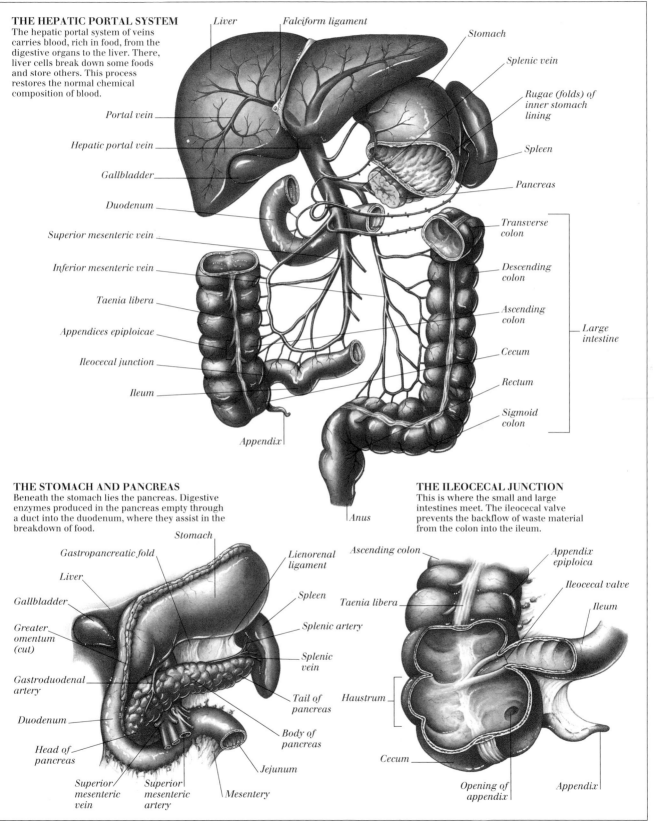

THE HEPATIC PORTAL SYSTEM
The hepatic portal system of veins carries blood, rich in food, from the digestive organs to the liver. There, liver cells break down some foods and store others. This process restores the normal chemical composition of blood.

Liver

Falciform ligament

Stomach

Splenic vein

Rugae (folds) of inner stomach lining

Portal vein

Hepatic portal vein

Spleen

Gallbladder

Pancreas

Duodenum

Transverse colon

Superior mesenteric vein

Descending colon

Inferior mesenteric vein

Ascending colon

Taenia libera

Appendices epiploicae

Large intestine

Ileocecal junction

Cecum

Ileum

Rectum

Sigmoid colon

Appendix

Anus

THE STOMACH AND PANCREAS
Beneath the stomach lies the pancreas. Digestive enzymes produced in the pancreas empty through a duct into the duodenum, where they assist in the breakdown of food.

Stomach

Gastropancreatic fold

Lienorenal ligament

Liver

Spleen

Gallbladder

Splenic artery

Greater omentum (cut)

Splenic vein

Gastroduodenal artery

Tail of pancreas

Duodenum

Head of pancreas

Body of pancreas

Superior mesenteric vein

Superior mesenteric artery

Mesentery

Jejunum

THE ILEOCECAL JUNCTION
This is where the small and large intestines meet. The ileocecal valve prevents the backflow of waste material from the colon into the ileum.

Ascending colon

Appendix epiploica

Ileocecal valve

Taenia libera

Ileum

Haustrum

Cecum

Opening of appendix

Appendix

Abdomen 3

**THE ABDOMINAL CAVITY WITH
DIGESTIVE ORGANS REMOVED**
The removal of the digestive organs reveals the two
kidneys. These remove waste products and excess
water from blood, which enters the kidneys through the
renal arteries; the waste is then passed to the bladder,
where it is stored before release from the body.

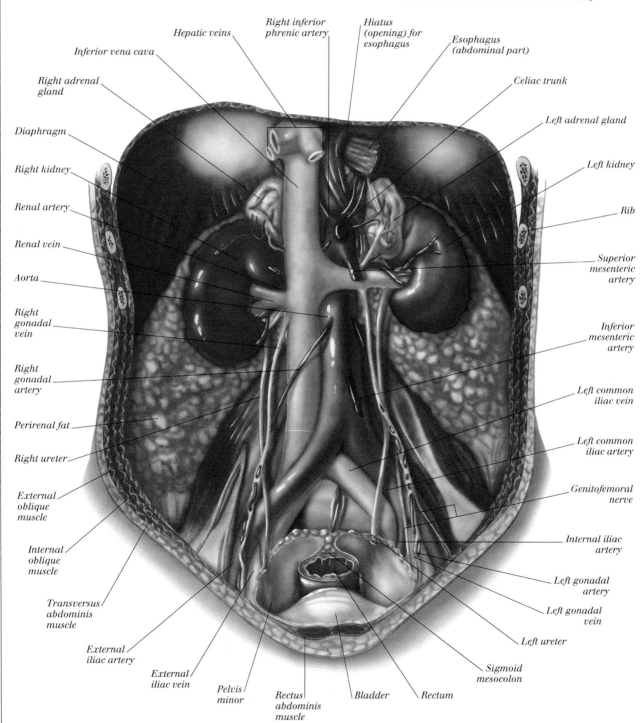

Hepatic veins

Right inferior
phrenic artery

Hiatus
(opening) for
esophagus

Esophagus
(abdominal part)

Inferior vena cava

Celiac trunk

Right adrenal
gland

Left adrenal gland

Diaphragm

Left kidney

Right kidney

Rib

Renal artery

Renal vein

Superior
mesenteric
artery

Aorta

Right
gonadal
vein

Inferior
mesenteric
artery

Right
gonadal
artery

Left common
iliac vein

Perirenal fat

Left common
iliac artery

Right ureter

Genitofemoral
nerve

External
oblique
muscle

Internal iliac
artery

Internal
oblique
muscle

Left gonadal
artery

Transversus
abdominis
muscle

Left gonadal
vein

External
iliac artery

Left ureter

External
iliac vein

Sigmoid
mesocolon

Pelvis
minor

Rectus
abdominis
muscle

Bladder

Rectum

THE POSTERIOR ABDOMINAL WALL

Major muscles of the posterior abdominal wall include the quadratus lumborum, which helps support the backbone; the iliacus and psoas major, which flex the hip and help maintain posture; and the transversus abdominis, which compresses abdominal contents.

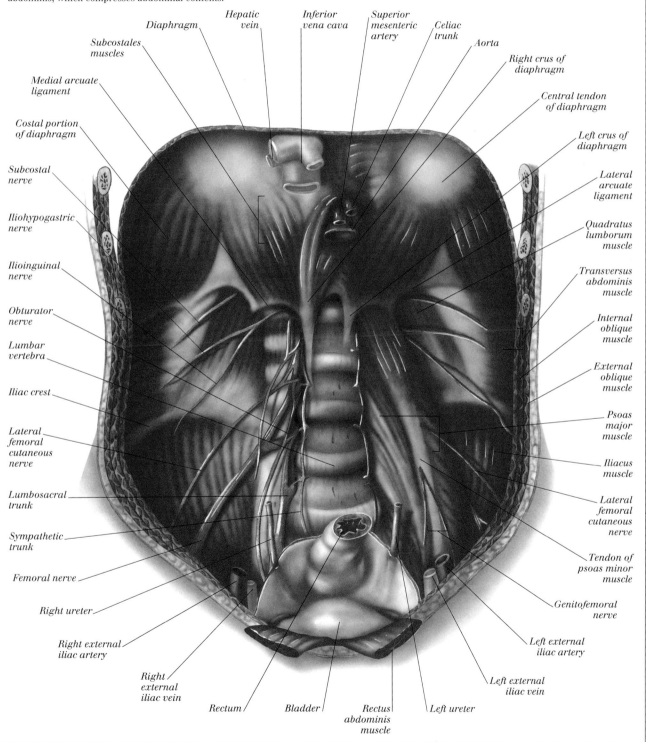

Diaphragm

Hepatic vein

Inferior vena cava

Superior mesenteric artery

Celiac trunk

Aorta

Subcostales muscles

Right crus of diaphragm

Medial arcuate ligament

Central tendon of diaphragm

Costal portion of diaphragm

Left crus of diaphragm

Subcostal nerve

Lateral arcuate ligament

Iliohypogastric nerve

Quadratus lumborum muscle

Ilioinguinal nerve

Transversus abdominis muscle

Obturator nerve

Internal oblique muscle

Lumbar vertebra

External oblique muscle

Iliac crest

Psoas major muscle

Lateral femoral cutaneous nerve

Iliacus muscle

Lumbosacral trunk

Lateral femoral cutaneous nerve

Sympathetic trunk

Tendon of psoas minor muscle

Femoral nerve

Genitofemoral nerve

Right ureter

Left external iliac artery

Right external iliac artery

Left external iliac vein

Right external iliac vein

Rectum

Bladder

Rectus abdominis muscle

Left ureter

Pelvic region 1

THE PELVIC AREA IS THE LOWEST part of the trunk. It lies below the **abdomen** and above the junction between the **trunk** and the legs. The framework of the pelvic region is formed **anteriorly** and **laterally** by the pelvic (hip) girdle, and **posteriorly** by the sacrum, which is part of the vertebral column. Together, these bones form the bowl-shaped **pelvis**, which provides attachment sites for the muscles of the legs and trunk, and surrounds and protects the organs within the pelvic cavity. The pelvic cavity is continuous with, and lies below the abdominal cavity. It contains the rectum, the terminal region of the large intestine, which opens out of the body through the anus; the bladder, which is a muscular bag that stores urine; and the internal reproductive organs of the male and female. The muscles of the pelvic floor, or pelvic diaphragm – which include the levator ani – close the lower opening of the pelvis (the pelvic outlet) and support the pelvic organs, preventing them from being forced downward by the weight of the content of the abdomen.

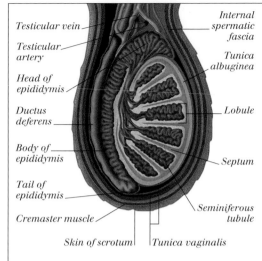

Testicular vein

Testicular artery

Head of epididymis

Ductus deferens

Body of epididymis

Tail of epididymis

Cremaster muscle

Skin of scrotum

Internal spermatic fascia

Tunica albuginea

Lobule

Septum

Seminiferous tubule

Tunica vaginalis

ANATOMY OF THE TESTIS

The testis consists of tightly coiled, sperm-producing seminiferous tubules connected through efferent ducts to the crescent-shaped epididymis. Sperm mature here before entering the ductus deferens, which carries them toward the penis.

MALE PERINEUM

The perineum overlies the pelvic floor. Its muscles include the anal sphincter, which controls the release of feces; the urinogenital diaphragm, which controls the release of urine; the bulbospongiosus, which empties the urethra of urine; and the ischiocavernosus, which helps maintain penile erection.

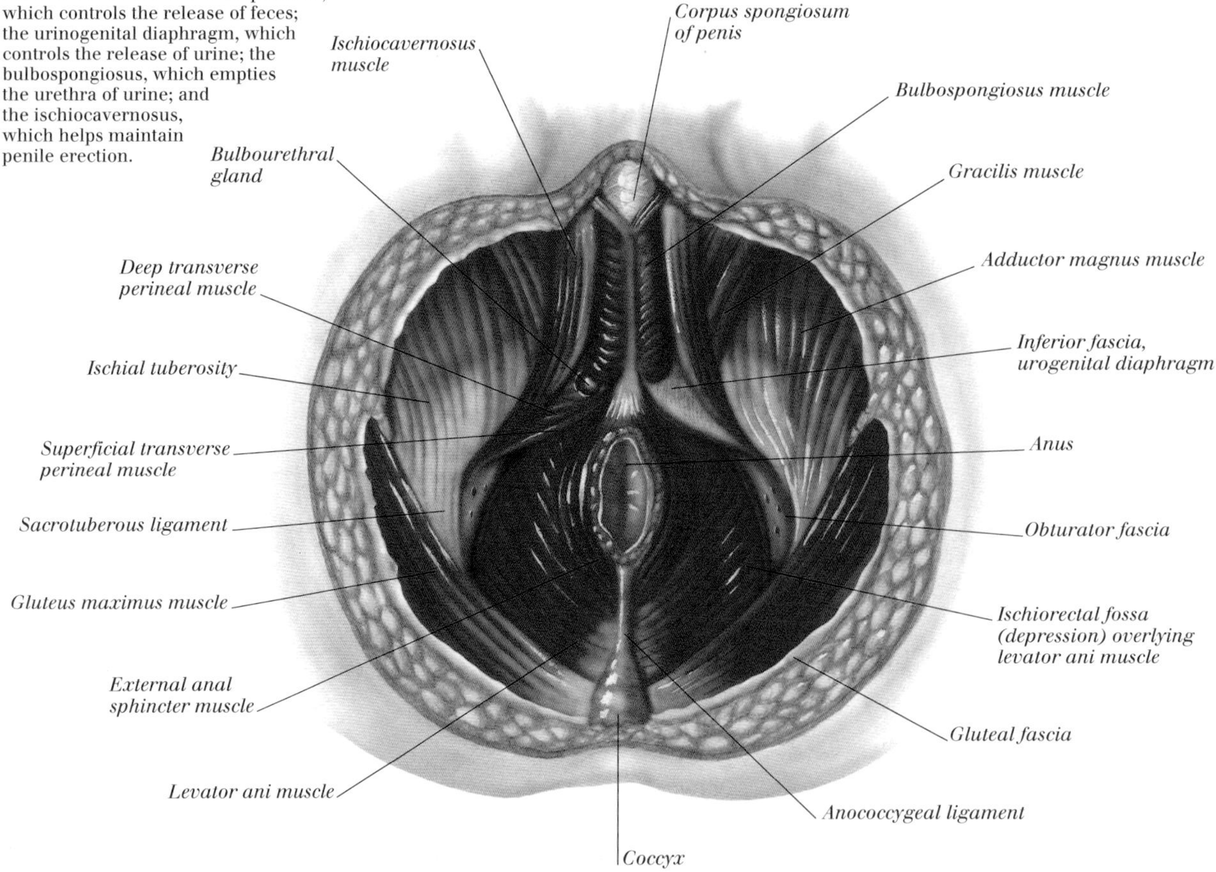

Ischiocavernosus muscle

Corpus spongiosum of penis

Bulbospongiosus muscle

Gracilis muscle

Bulbourethral gland

Deep transverse perineal muscle

Adductor magnus muscle

Inferior fascia, urogenital diaphragm

Ischial tuberosity

Superficial transverse perineal muscle

Anus

Sacrotuberous ligament

Obturator fascia

Gluteus maximus muscle

Ischiorectal fossa (depression) overlying levator ani muscle

External anal sphincter muscle

Gluteal fascia

Levator ani muscle

Anococcygeal ligament

Coccyx

MALE PELVIC CAVITY

Most of the male reproductive system lies outside the pelvic cavity. From each of the testes runs a ductus deferens that joins the urethra in the prostate gland. The urethra opens through the erectile penis.

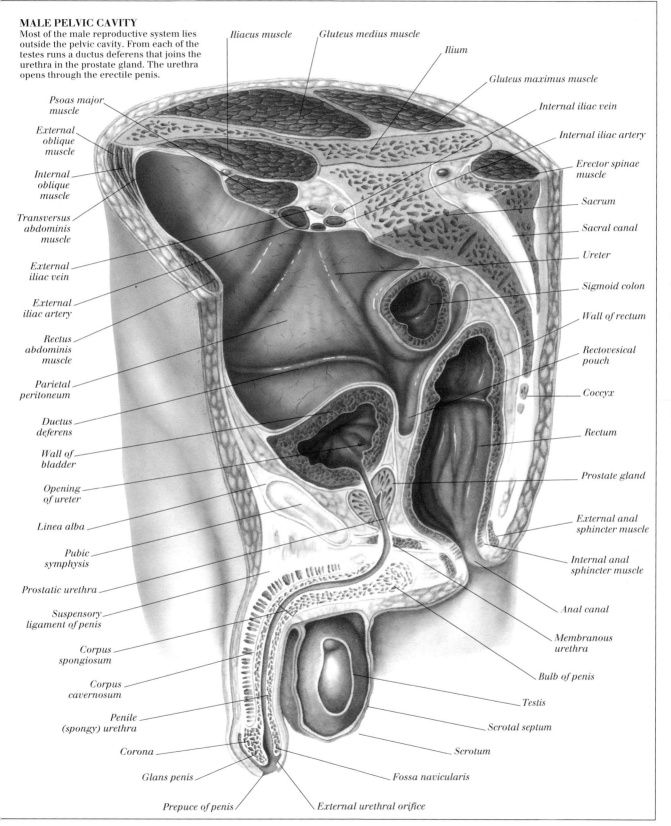

Iliacus muscle

Gluteus medius muscle

Ilium

Gluteus maximus muscle

Internal iliac vein

Internal iliac artery

Erector spinae muscle

Sacrum

Sacral canal

Ureter

Sigmoid colon

Wall of rectum

Rectovesical pouch

Coccyx

Rectum

Prostate gland

External anal sphincter muscle

Internal anal sphincter muscle

Anal canal

Membranous urethra

Bulb of penis

Testis

Scrotal septum

Scrotum

Fossa navicularis

Psoas major muscle

External oblique muscle

Internal oblique muscle

Transversus abdominis muscle

External iliac vein

External iliac artery

Rectus abdominis muscle

Parietal peritoneum

Ductus deferens

Wall of bladder

Opening of ureter

Linea alba

Pubic symphysis

Prostatic urethra

Suspensory ligament of penis

Corpus spongiosum

Corpus cavernosum

Penile (spongy) urethra

Corona

Glans penis

Prepuce of penis

External urethral orifice

Pelvic region 2

FEMALE PELVIC CAVITY
Extending from each side of the uterus is a fallopian tube, with ends that extend into fingerlike fimbriae overhanging the ovary. The uterus is connected to the vulva (external genitalia) through the vagina.

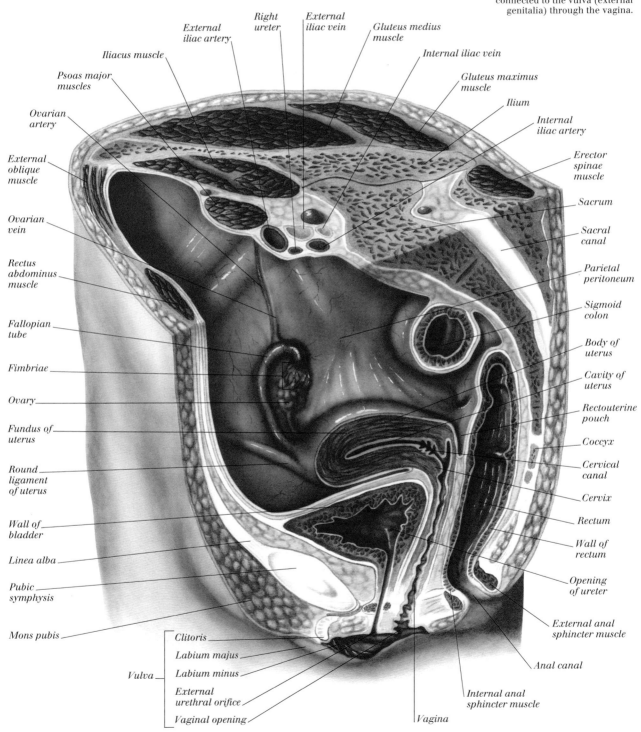

External iliac artery

Right ureter

External iliac vein

Gluteus medius muscle

Iliacus muscle

Psoas major muscles

Internal iliac vein

Gluteus maximus muscle

Ilium

Ovarian artery

Internal iliac artery

External oblique muscle

Erector spinae muscle

Sacrum

Ovarian vein

Sacral canal

Rectus abdominus muscle

Parietal peritoneum

Fallopian tube

Sigmoid colon

Fimbriae

Body of uterus

Ovary

Cavity of uterus

Fundus of uterus

Rectouterine pouch

Round ligament of uterus

Coccyx

Cervical canal

Wall of bladder

Cervix

Linea alba

Rectum

Pubic symphysis

Wall of rectum

Mons pubis

Opening of ureter

Clitoris

External anal sphincter muscle

Labium majus

Labium minus

Anal canal

Vulva

External urethral orifice

Internal anal sphincter muscle

Vaginal opening

Vagina

THE MENSTRUAL CYCLE

Throughout every month, women of reproductive age experience the menstrual cycle – a sequence of events that prepares their bodies for pregnancy. It has three phases. During the menstrual phase (also known as the "period"), the lining of the uterus breaks down and is shed with some blood through the vagina. The proliferative phase, when the uterine lining thickens once more, coincides with the ripening of a new egg (ovum) inside the ovary. After the egg is released at ovulation, around day 14, the uterine lining thickens still further during the secretory phase, in readiness to receive the egg, should it be fertilized by a sperm. If the egg is not fertilized, there is no pregnancy, so the uterine lining breaks down and is shed, and the cycle begins again.

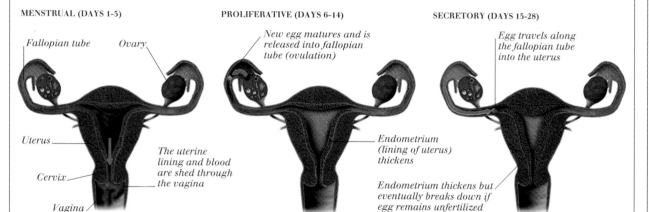

MENSTRUAL (DAYS 1-5)

Fallopian tube

Ovary

Uterus

Cervix

Vagina

The uterine lining and blood are shed through the vagina

PROLIFERATIVE (DAYS 6-14)

New egg matures and is released into fallopian tube (ovulation)

Endometrium (lining of uterus) thickens

Endometrium thickens but eventually breaks down if egg remains unfertilized

SECRETORY (DAYS 15-28)

Egg travels along the fallopian tube into the uterus

FEMALE PERINEUM

The urinogenital diaphragm and the anal sphincter control the release of urine and feces respectively. The bulbospongiosus constricts the vaginal opening; the ischiocavernosus assists in erection of the clitoris.

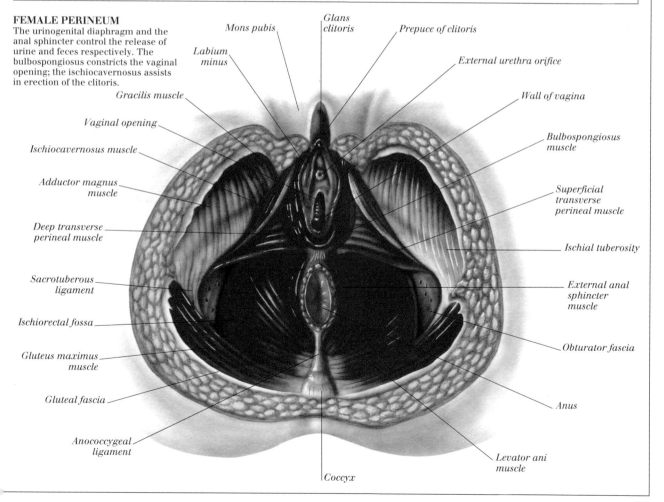

Mons pubis

Labium minus

Gracilis muscle

Vaginal opening

Ischiocavernosus muscle

Adductor magnus muscle

Deep transverse perineal muscle

Sacrotuberous ligament

Ischiorectal fossa

Gluteus maximus muscle

Gluteal fascia

Anococcygeal ligament

Glans clitoris

Prepuce of clitoris

External urethra orifice

Wall of vagina

Bulbospongiosus muscle

Superficial transverse perineal muscle

Ischial tuberosity

External anal sphincter muscle

Obturator fascia

Anus

Levator ani muscle

Coccyx

Shoulder and upper arm

THE BONY FRAMEWORK OF THE SHOULDER and upper arm is formed by the scapula (shoulder blade), clavicle (collarbone), and humerus (upper arm bone). At its upper end, the humerus forms a joint with the scapula at the shoulder, which permits movement of the upper arm in all planes. The group of muscles that cross the shoulder joint to move the humerus include the deltoid, pectoralis major, latissimus dorsi, and teres major. The supraspinatus, infraspinatus, teres minor, and subscapularis – collectively, the rotator cuff muscles – stabilize the shoulder joint, preventing its dislocation. At its lower end, the humerus forms a joint with the radius and ulna (forearm bones) at the elbow, which permits flexion (bending) and extension (straightening) only. The muscles that flex the elbow include the biceps brachii, brachioradialis, and brachialis; the muscle that extends the elbow is the triceps brachii. Blood is carried into the arm by the axillary artery (which becomes the brachial artery as it enters the upper arm), and out of the arm by the cephalic vein and the brachial and basilic veins (which join to form the axillary vein as they enter the shoulder). The main nerves supplying the upper arm include the radial, median, and ulnar nerves.

ANTERIOR VIEW OF SUPERFICIAL MUSCLES

The major anterior superficial muscles are the deltoid and pectoralis major, which pull the arm forward or backward, and the biceps ("two heads") brachii, which flexes the arm at the elbow.

ANTERIOR VIEW OF DEEP MUSCLES

The removal of superficial muscles reveals the coracobrachialis muscle. This pulls the arm forward and upward, or toward the body.

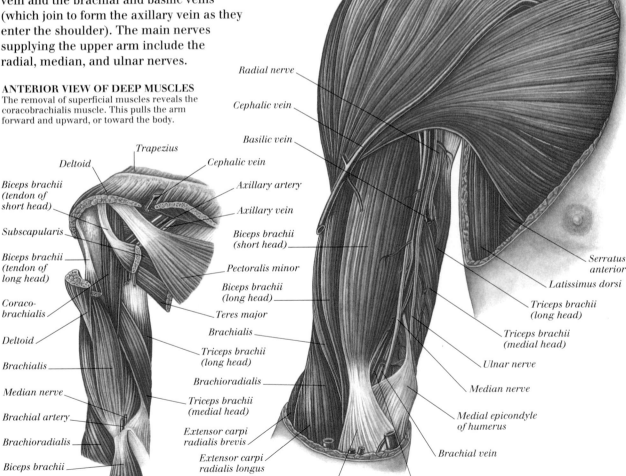

Trapezius

Pectoralis major

Deltoid

Radial nerve

Cephalic vein

Basilic vein

Biceps brachii (short head)

Serratus anterior

Latissimus dorsi

Triceps brachii (long head)

Triceps brachii (medial head)

Ulnar nerve

Median nerve

Medial epicondyle of humerus

Brachial vein

Brachial artery

Deltoid

Trapezius

Biceps brachii (tendon of short head)

Cephalic vein

Axillary artery

Axillary vein

Subscapularis

Biceps brachii (tendon of long head)

Biceps brachii (short head)

Pectoralis minor

Coraco-brachialis

Biceps brachii (long head)

Teres major

Deltoid

Brachialis

Triceps brachii (long head)

Brachialis

Brachioradialis

Median nerve

Triceps brachii (medial head)

Brachial artery

Extensor carpi radialis brevis

Brachioradialis

Extensor carpi radialis longus

Biceps brachii

Bicipital aponeurosis

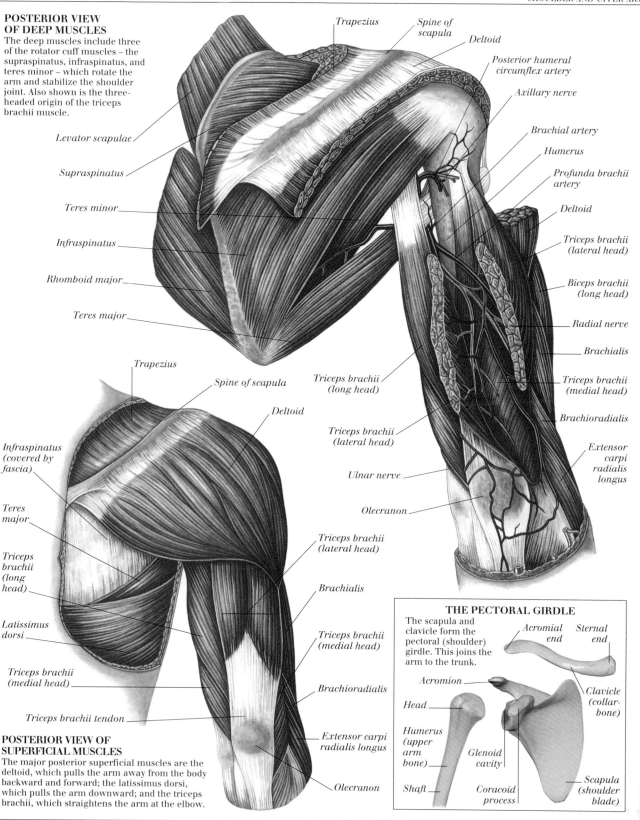

POSTERIOR VIEW OF DEEP MUSCLES

The deep muscles include three of the rotator cuff muscles – the supraspinatus, infraspinatus, and teres minor – which rotate the arm and stabilize the shoulder joint. Also shown is the three-headed origin of the triceps brachii muscle.

Levator scapulae

Supraspinatus

Teres minor

Infraspinatus

Rhomboid major

Teres major

Trapezius

Spine of scapula

Deltoid

Trapezius

Spine of scapula

Deltoid

Posterior humeral circumflex artery

Axillary nerve

Brachial artery

Humerus

Profunda brachii artery

Deltoid

Triceps brachii (lateral head)

Biceps brachii (long head)

Radial nerve

Brachialis

Triceps brachii (medial head)

Brachioradialis

Extensor carpi radialis longus

Triceps brachii (long head)

Triceps brachii (lateral head)

Ulnar nerve

Olecranon

Infraspinatus (covered by fascia)

Teres major

Triceps brachii (long head)

Latissimus dorsi

Triceps brachii (medial head)

Triceps brachii tendon

Triceps brachii (lateral head)

Brachialis

Triceps brachii (medial head)

Brachioradialis

Extensor carpi radialis longus

Olecranon

POSTERIOR VIEW OF SUPERFICIAL MUSCLES

The major posterior superficial muscles are the deltoid, which pulls the arm away from the body backward and forward; the latissimus dorsi, which pulls the arm downward; and the triceps brachii, which straightens the arm at the elbow.

THE PECTORAL GIRDLE

The scapula and clavicle form the pectoral (shoulder) girdle. This joins the arm to the trunk.

Acromial end

Sternal end

Acromion

Head

Humerus (upper arm bone)

Shaft

Glenoid cavity

Coracoid process

Clavicle (collar-bone)

Scapula (shoulder blade)

Forearm and hand

THE HAND IS CAPABLE OF A WIDE range of precise movements. It owes its flexibility and versatility to the many muscles of the forearm and hand, and to a bony framework that consists of fourteen phalanges (finger bones), five metacarpals (palm bones), and eight carpals (wrist bones), four of which articulate with the ends of the radius and ulna (forearm bones) at the wrist joint. Forearm muscles taper into long tendons that extend into the hand. These tendons, along with blood vessels and nerves, are held in place by two fibrous bands: the flexor retinaculum and the extensor retinaculum. Most muscles in the anterior (inner) part of the forearm are flexors; most in the posterior (outer) part are extensors. Wrist flexors include the flexor carpi radialis; wrist extensors include the extensor carpi ulnaris. Finger flexors include the flexor digitorum superficialis; finger extensors include the extensor digitorum. Inside the hand, the lumbrical and the interosseus muscles between the metacarpals flex the metacarpophalangeal (knuckle) joints and extend the fingers.

ANTERIOR VIEW OF SUPERFICIAL MUSCLES

The median nerve controls the action of most of the flexor muscles of the forearm, which flex the wrist, and the flexor and abductor pollicis brevis, which move the thumb.

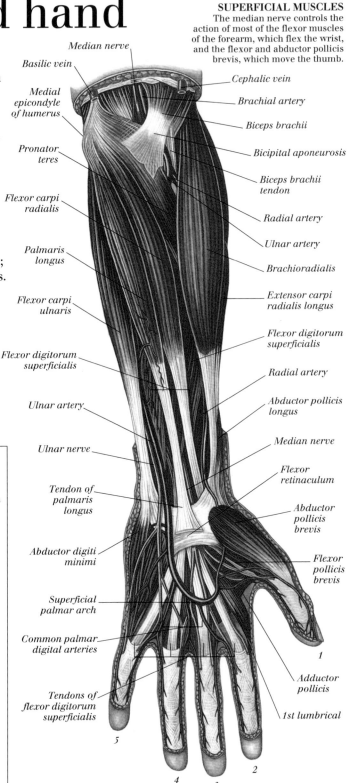

Median nerve
Basilic vein
Medial epicondyle of humerus
Pronator teres
Flexor carpi radialis
Palmaris longus
Flexor carpi ulnaris
Flexor digitorum superficialis
Ulnar artery
Ulnar nerve
Tendon of palmaris longus
Abductor digiti minimi
Superficial palmar arch
Common palmar digital arteries
Tendons of flexor digitorum superficialis

Cephalic vein
Brachial artery
Biceps brachii
Bicipital aponeurosis
Biceps brachii tendon
Radial artery
Ulnar artery
Brachioradialis
Extensor carpi radialis longus
Flexor digitorum superficialis
Radial artery
Abductor pollicis longus
Median nerve
Flexor retinaculum
Abductor pollicis brevis
Flexor pollicis brevis
Adductor pollicis
1st lumbrical

5
4
3
2
1

SUPERIOR VIEW OF BONES OF THE HAND

The long phalanges, which shape the fingers of the hand, together with the bones of the metacarpus (palm) and carpus (wrist), enable the hand to perform gripping movements. These range from the precision grip used when holding a pen to the power grip used when making a fist.

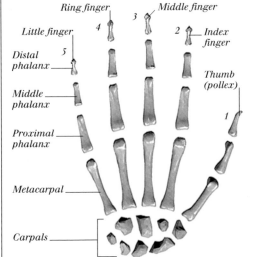

Ring finger
Middle finger
Little finger
Index finger
Distal phalanx
Thumb (pollex)
Middle phalanx
Proximal phalanx
Metacarpal
Carpals

1
2
3
4
5

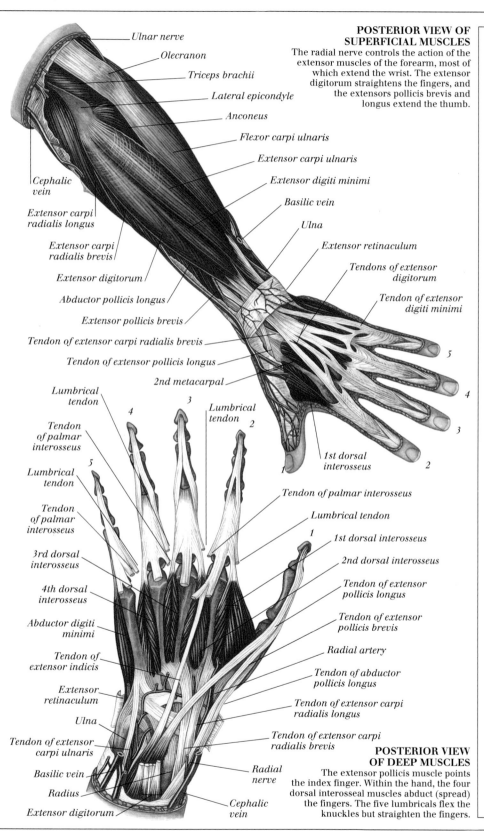

Ulnar nerve

Olecranon

Triceps brachii

Lateral epicondyle

Anconeus

Flexor carpi ulnaris

Extensor carpi ulnaris

Extensor digiti minimi

Basilic vein

Ulna

Extensor retinaculum

Tendons of extensor digitorum

Tendon of extensor digiti minimi

Cephalic vein

Extensor carpi radialis longus

Extensor carpi radialis brevis

Extensor digitorum

Abductor pollicis longus

Extensor pollicis brevis

Tendon of extensor carpi radialis brevis

Tendon of extensor pollicis longus

2nd metacarpal

1st dorsal interosseus

Lumbrical tendon

Lumbrical tendon

Tendon of palmar interosseus

Lumbrical tendon

Tendon of palmar interosseus

3rd dorsal interosseus

4th dorsal interosseus

Abductor digiti minimi

Tendon of extensor indicis

Extensor retinaculum

Ulna

Tendon of extensor carpi ulnaris

Basilic vein

Radius

Extensor digitorum

Tendon of palmar interosseus

Lumbrical tendon

1st dorsal interosseus

2nd dorsal interosseus

Tendon of extensor pollicis longus

Tendon of extensor pollicis brevis

Radial artery

Tendon of abductor pollicis longus

Tendon of extensor carpi radialis longus

Tendon of extensor carpi radialis brevis

Radial nerve

Cephalic vein

POSTERIOR VIEW OF SUPERFICIAL MUSCLES

The radial nerve controls the action of the extensor muscles of the forearm, most of which extend the wrist. The extensor digitorum straightens the fingers, and the extensors pollicis brevis and longus extend the thumb.

POSTERIOR VIEW OF DEEP MUSCLES

The extensor pollicis muscle points the index finger. Within the hand, the four dorsal interosseal muscles abduct (spread) the fingers. The five lumbricals flex the knuckles but straighten the fingers.

BONE GROWTH

NEWBORN
The cartilage framework that forms before birth is replaced by bone to form the skeleton. X rays show the presence of bone but not cartilage.

Ossified epiphysis of phalanx

Ossified diaphysis of metacarpal

4-YEAR-OLD
The diaphysis (shaft) and epiphysis (head) have become ossified (changed to bone). The cartilage plate between them continues growing.

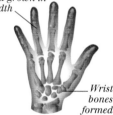

Epiphysis of metacarpal

Cartilage plate

Ossification of carpals

Diaphysis of metacarpal

11-YEAR-OLD
By late childhood, most of the wrist bones are now formed, and the palm and finger bones have become longer.

Bones have extended and grown in width

Wrist bones formed

20-YEAR-OLD
The palm, finger, and wrist bones of an adult are fully grown and ossified. Diaphyses and epiphyses have fused.

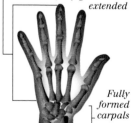

Phalanges and metacarpals are fully grown and extended

Fully formed carpals

Thigh

THE THIGH IS THE REGION OF THE LOWER LIMB between the **pelvis** and the knee. It is supported by the femur (thigh bone), which **articulates** with the **pelvis** at the hip joint to permit the thigh to move in most planes. At the knee joint, the femur articulates with the tibia to permit flexion (bending) and extension (straightening) only. The thigh muscles are used for walking, running, and climbing. **Anterior** thigh muscles are divided into two groups: the iliopsoas and sartorius, which flex the thigh at the hip; and the rectus femoris, vastus lateralis, vastus medialis, and vastus intermedius (known collectively as the quadriceps femoris), which extend the leg at the knee. The major **posterior** thigh muscles, which consist of the biceps femoris, the semitendinosus, and the semi-membranosus (known as the hamstrings) extend the thigh at the hip, and flex the leg at the knee. The gluteus maximus (buttock) muscle assists with the extension of the thigh during climbing and running. Blood is supplied to the thigh by the femoral artery, and removed by the femoral vein. The main nerves supplying the thigh muscles are the femoral and sciatic nerves.

ANTERIOR VIEW OF SUPERFICIAL MUSCLES
Most of the anterior thigh muscles straighten the leg and pull it forward during walking or running. The adductor longus and pectineus also pull the leg inward.

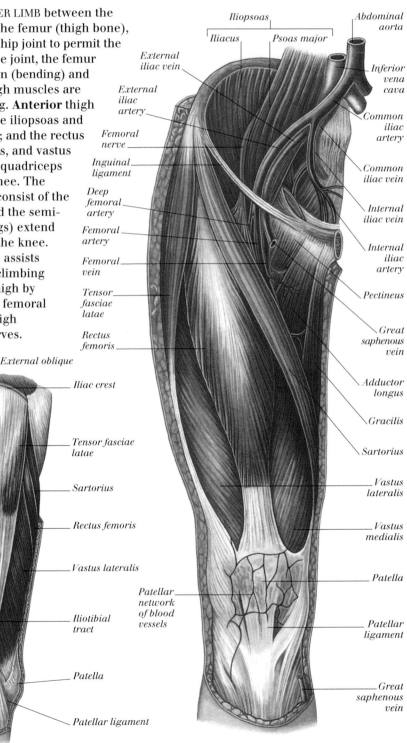

Iliopsoas
— Iliacus — Psoas major
External iliac vein
External iliac artery
Femoral nerve
Inguinal ligament
Deep femoral artery
Femoral artery
Femoral vein
Tensor fasciae latae
Rectus femoris

Abdominal aorta
Inferior vena cava
Common iliac artery
Common iliac vein
Internal iliac vein
Internal iliac artery
Pectineus
Great saphenous vein
Adductor longus
Gracilis
Sartorius
Vastus lateralis
Vastus medialis
Patella
Patellar ligament
Great saphenous vein

Patellar network of blood vessels

LATERAL VIEW OF SUPERFICIAL MUSCLES
The tensor fasciae latae muscle helps to steady the trunk on the thighs when a person is standing upright.

Gluteus maximus

Vastus lateralis
Biceps femoris (long head)
Biceps femoris (short head)
Semimembranosus
Plantaris
Gastrocnemius (lateral head)

External oblique
Iliac crest
Tensor fasciae latae
Sartorius
Rectus femoris
Vastus lateralis
Iliotibial tract
Patella
Patellar ligament

POSTERIOR VIEW OF SUPERFICIAL MUSCLES
The posterior thigh muscles produce the backswing of walking or running by bending the leg and pulling it backward. The gluteus maximus also steadies the pelvis, thus helping in the maintenance of posture.

POSTERIOR VIEW OF DEEP MUSCLES
During walking, the gluteus medius holds the pelvis parallel to the ground when one leg is in motion in order to prevent a lurching gait. The gemellus, piriformis, and obturator internus stabilize the hip joint. The adductor magnus pulls the thigh inward.

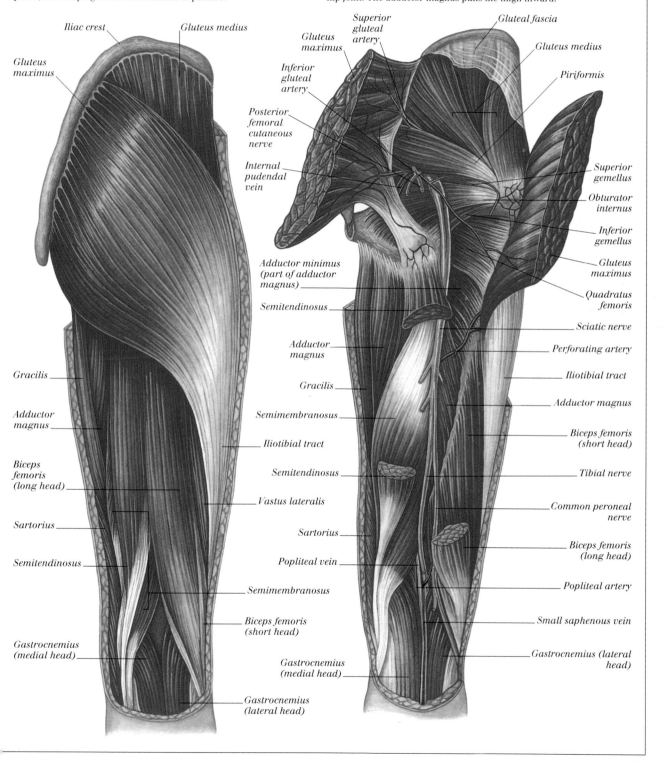

Iliac crest

Gluteus medius

Gluteus maximus

Superior gluteal artery

Gluteus maximus

Inferior gluteal artery

Posterior femoral cutaneous nerve

Internal pudendal vein

Gluteal fascia

Gluteus medius

Piriformis

Superior gemellus

Obturator internus

Inferior gemellus

Gluteus maximus

Quadratus femoris

Adductor minimus (part of adductor magnus)

Semitendinosus

Adductor magnus

Gracilis

Semimembranosus

Iliotibial tract

Semitendinosus

Sartorius

Popliteal vein

Semimembranosus

Biceps femoris (short head)

Gastrocnemius (medial head)

Gastrocnemius (lateral head)

Gracilis

Adductor magnus

Biceps femoris (long head)

Sartorius

Semitendinosus

Vastus lateralis

Gastrocnemius (medial head)

Sciatic nerve

Perforating artery

Iliotibial tract

Adductor magnus

Biceps femoris (short head)

Tibial nerve

Common peroneal nerve

Biceps femoris (long head)

Popliteal artery

Small saphenous vein

Gastrocnemius (lateral head)

Lower leg and foot

THE FOOT IS A FLEXIBLE PLATFORM that supports and moves the body. The skeleton of the foot consists of 14 phalanges (toe bones); 5 metatarsals (sole bones); and 7 tarsals (ankle bones), 2 of which articulate with the tibia and fibula (leg bones) at the ankle joint. The anterior leg muscles – which include the tibialis anterior, extensor digitorum longus, extensor hallucis longus, and peroneus tertius – primarily dorsiflex the foot (bend it upward). The two extensor muscles extend (straighten) the toes and the big toe respectively. The posterior leg muscles – which include the gastrocnemius, soleus, tibialis posterior, flexor digitorum longus, and flexor hallucis longus – primarily plantar flex the foot (straighten the ankle), providing forward thrust during walking and running. The flexor muscles flex (bend) the toes and the big toe respectively. The muscles inside the foot help move the toes and support the arches. Blood is carried to the leg and foot by the anterior and posterior tibial arteries, and the peroneal artery; it is removed by the anterior and posterior tibial veins, and the great saphenous vein. The main nerves supplying the muscles of the leg and foot are the tibial nerve, and the peroneal nerve.

ANTERIOR VIEW OF SUPERFICIAL MUSCLES
The main function of the superficial muscles is to dorsiflex the foot, preventing the toes from dragging on the ground during walking.

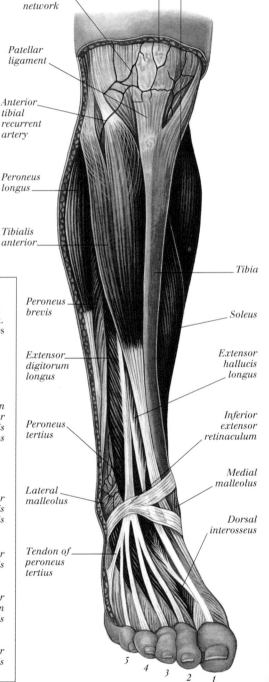

Genicular arterial network

Patella

Gastrocnemius

Patellar ligament

Anterior tibial recurrent artery

Peroneus longus

Tibialis anterior

Tibia

Peroneus brevis

Soleus

Extensor digitorum longus

Extensor hallucis longus

Peroneus tertius

Inferior extensor retinaculum

Lateral malleolus

Medial malleolus

Tendon of peroneus tertius

Dorsal interosseus

5 4 3 2 1

THE FOOT
The bones of the foot support the body on both flat and uneven surfaces, and form a springy base from which to push the body off the ground during walking, running, or climbing.

The primary actions of the muscles of the underside of the foot are to arch the foot and to stabilize it during movement. As the foot leaves the ground, the flexors bend the foot downward.

SUPERIOR VIEW OF BONES OF THE RIGHT FOOT

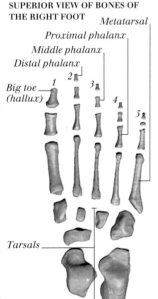

Metatarsal

Proximal phalanx

Middle phalanx

Distal phalanx

Big toe (hallux)

1
2
3
4
5

Tarsals

SUPERFICIAL MUSCLES OF THE SOLE OF THE RIGHT FOOT

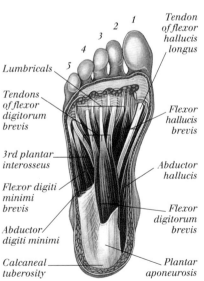

1
2
3
4
5

Tendon of flexor hallucis longus

Lumbricals

Tendons of flexor digitorum brevis

Flexor hallucis brevis

3rd plantar interosseus

Abductor hallucis

Flexor digiti minimi brevis

Flexor digitorum brevis

Abductor digiti minimi

Calcaneal tuberosity

Plantar aponeurosis

POSTERIOR VIEW OF SUPERFICIAL MUSCLES

The major superficial muscles – the gastrocnemius and soleus – act by pulling on the calcaneal (heel) bone to plantar flex the foot during walking or running.

MUSCLES AND TENDONS OF ANKLE AND FOOT

Long tendons extend into the foot from the extensor digitorum longus and extensor hallucis longus muscles. These work to straighten the toes, with the assistance of the smaller extensor muscles inside the foot.

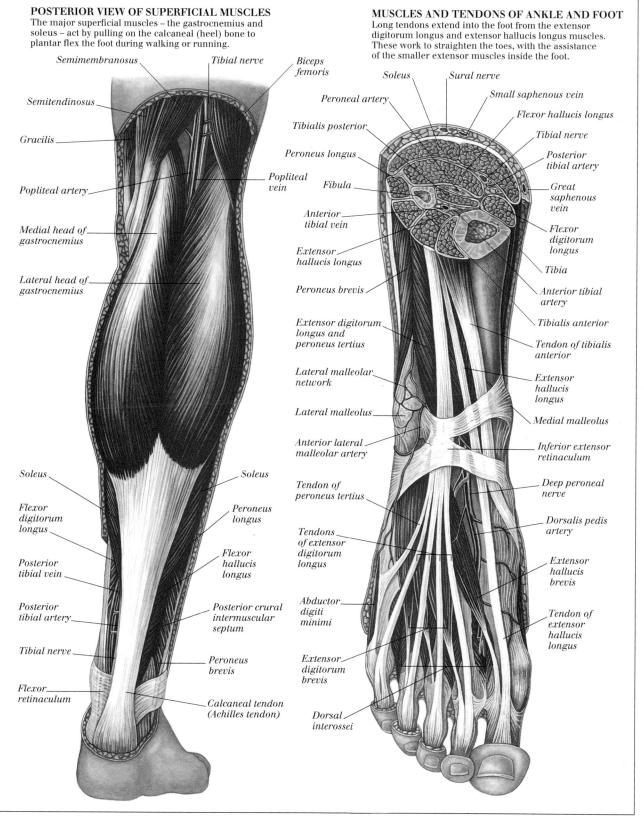

Semimembranosus

Semitendinosus

Gracilis

Popliteal artery

Medial head of gastrocnemius

Lateral head of gastrocnemius

Soleus

Flexor digitorum longus

Posterior tibial vein

Posterior tibial artery

Tibial nerve

Flexor retinaculum

Tibial nerve

Biceps femoris

Popliteal vein

Soleus

Peroneus longus

Flexor hallucis longus

Posterior crural intermuscular septum

Peroneus brevis

Calcaneal tendon (Achilles tendon)

Soleus

Peroneal artery

Tibialis posterior

Peroneus longus

Fibula

Anterior tibial vein

Extensor hallucis longus

Peroneus brevis

Extensor digitorum longus and peroneus tertius

Lateral malleolar network

Lateral malleolus

Anterior lateral malleolar artery

Tendon of peroneus tertius

Tendons of extensor digitorum longus

Abductor digiti minimi

Extensor digitorum brevis

Dorsal interossei

Sural nerve

Small saphenous vein

Flexor hallucis longus

Tibial nerve

Posterior tibial artery

Great saphenous vein

Flexor digitorum longus

Tibia

Anterior tibial artery

Tibialis anterior

Tendon of tibialis anterior

Extensor hallucis longus

Medial malleolus

Inferior extensor retinaculum

Deep peroneal nerve

Dorsalis pedis artery

Extensor hallucis brevis

Tendon of extensor hallucis longus

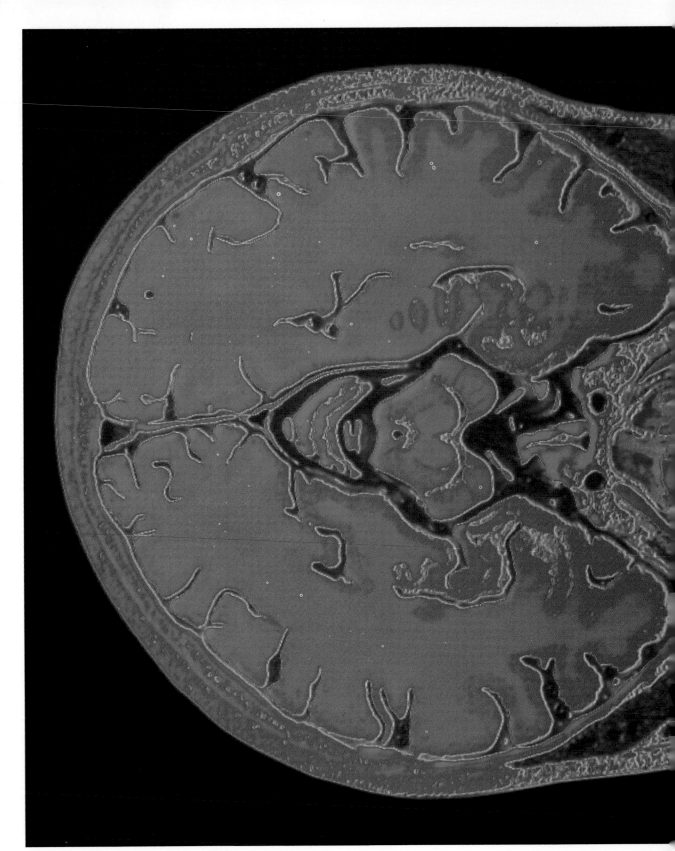

False-color Magnetic Resonance Imaging (MRI) scan of a human head

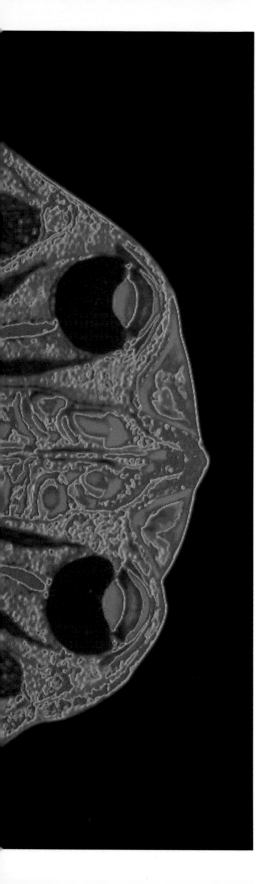

Medical Science

Discovering medical science 236

Diagnosis 238

Medical imaging 1 240

Medical imaging 2 242

Emergency care 244

Surgery 246

Minimally invasive surgery 248

Transplants 250

Artificial body parts 252

Drugs and drug delivery 254

Pregnancy and childbirth 256

Infection and disease 258

The immune system 260

Genetics and medicine 262

Discovering medical science

THE SCIENCE OF MEDICINE is the science of human health. It has always had close links with anatomy and life science, and more recently with physics and chemistry. Medical science includes areas not covered here, including dentistry (concerning teeth and gums) and psychiatry (concerning mental, emotional, and behavioral disorders). Surgery is considered to be separate from general medicine.

FOLK MEDICINE

Traditional, nonscientific medicine is usually called "folk medicine." In the folk medicine of many cultures, it is believed that illness is due to the influence of demons and other evil spirits. Despite this, even ancient folk medicine often involved the use of herbal remedies and even fairly complex surgery. An example of prehistoric surgery is the process of trepanning. This involved drilling a small hole in the skull, thus allowing "evil spirits" to leave the brain. In the ancient civilizations of India and China, medical practice was well organized, but still had little scientific basis. Physicians (doctors) carefully recorded diagnoses of a host of different symptoms, but did not understand physiology well enough to treat these symptoms effectively.

A BALANCED VIEW

In both India and China, from a few hundred years before Christ, medicine depended upon the concept of balance. The body was thought to consist of a small number of elements or "principles." An illness was caused by an imbalance of these principles. The Chinese system assumed that health depends upon the balance of two principles – "yin" and "yang." Hindu philosophers developed a similar system based on the balance of three elements. The ancient Greeks believed that the body consisted of four humors – blood, phlegm, black bile, and yellow bile – based on the four-elements theory that the Greeks applied to matter in general.

MEDICINE IN ANCIENT GREECE

There were few groundbreaking practical developments in ancient Greek medicine, although many Greek physicians were expert anatomists. Despite their expertise, they could not make successful diagnosis of, nor effectively treat, many diseases because their knowledge of anatomy was gained by examining animals such as apes and pigs. One valuable contribution that the Greeks made to medicine was the Hippocratic method. This encouraged careful observation of symptoms and a professional approach to medicine. It also included an oath, a form of which is still taken by medical doctors today.

HOSPITALS AND PUBLIC HEALTH

Great importance was attached to health throughout the Roman Empire. For example, water supplies, drainage, and public baths were features common to all large towns. The Roman Empire also had the first hospitals. During the Middle Ages, several great hospitals were developed by scholars and physicians. There was still little, however, that could truly be called medical science. There was no real understanding of how the body works, for example, and no technological aids to diagnosis. Medical science did not begin to develop until the scientific revolution of the Renaissance.

ANATOMY AND MEDICINE

Treatment of disease or injury during the Renaissance was primitive by modern standards, but the rise of the scientific method enabled anatomists and physicians to make real progress. In Italy, **Andreas Vesalius** corrected many of the inaccurate anatomical observations that had been made by earlier anatomists. This improved knowledge enabled surgeons to operate more efficiently. The knowledge that the blood circulates continuously around the body is essential to any scientific approach to medicine. **William Harvey** discovered blood circulation during the 1620s. The functions of the body's organs were slowly figured out, helped by the invention of the microscope in the 17th century. Despite rapid advances in many areas, the real causes of disease could only be speculated upon until the development of the germ theory in the 19th century.

ACUPUNCTURE
Practioners of acupuncture believe that energy flows along pathways called meridians. They insert needles at points along the meridians in the belief that it allows energy to enter, leave, or be diverted around the body. This 18th-century bronze figure acts as a guide to insertion points.

THE GERM THEORY

The development of a vaccine for the killer disease smallpox during the 18th century was a scientific breakthrough. But **Edward Jenner**, who perfected the technique in the 1790s, did not really understand why it worked. In 1840, **Friedrich Henle** published the theory that infectious diseases were caused by microscopic living organisms. Evidence in support of this "germ theory" came during the 1850s, as one species of microorganism was observed in the blood of a group of people suffering from the same disease. More and more diseases were attributed to particular microorganisms – normally either rod-shaped (bacillus) or spherical (coccus) bacteria. The work of **Paul Ehrlich** led to the development of chemotherapy. His drugs killed bacteria but left patients unharmed. The first antibiotic was penicillin, discovered in 1928 by **Alexander Fleming**. Antibiotics are substances produced by some bacteria or fungi that are harmful to pathogenic (disease-causing) bacteria or fungi in the body.

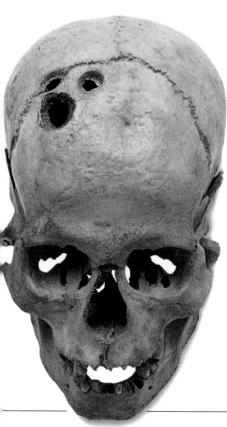

TISSUE STAINING
Some synthetic dyes will stain certain types of biological tissue but leave the host organism untouched. Paul Ehrlich discovered that he could safely treat certain conditions by "attaching" an arsenic compound to the synthetic dye molecule.

ANESTHETICS AND ANTISEPTICS

Other chemical or biological substances used in medical science include anesthetics and antiseptics. For hundreds of years, alcohol and opium were used during surgery to combat the pain of incision (cutting into the body). The first really effective anesthetic was ether, first used in 1846. In addition to pain, the other problem during surgery was infection. **Joseph Lister** applied the germ theory to the prevention of infection during operations. He introduced the first antiseptic – carbolic acid – in 1867. The discovery of blood types in 1900 made possible effective blood transfusions, which further improved surgical success rates.

20TH CENTURY

Medical science since the beginning of the 20th century has benefited from medical physics, which has provided new and better means of diagnosis and treatment. The first X-ray imaging of the human body took place in 1895.

During the late 20th century, other forms of medical imaging were developed. They include ultrasound, computerized axial tomography (CAT, 1970s), and magnetic resonance imaging (MRI, 1980s). Advances in molecular biology – the science that investigates biological processes at the molecular level – have also been important in both diagnosis and treatment. They have made possible an understanding of the immune system and genetic testing for inherited diseases. It has also led to an understanding of viruses, the cause of many diseases. Gene therapy (1980s), the treatment of diseases caused by "defective" genes, has given new hope in the fight against conditions such as the lung disease cystic fibrosis. Insertion of the "correct" gene into the patient can often give the patient a more healthy lung.

EARLY SURGERY
This skull, which dates from around 2000 BC, has three trepanned holes. These holes were made using a crude, drill-like instrument. Some people survived the process of trepanning, including this individual. This can be deduced from the signs of healing around the edges of the holes.

TIMELINE OF DISCOVERIES

2500 BC	The use of surgery is well documented in Egypt
500 BC	Indian physician **Sushruta** performs the first cataract operation
400 BC	Greek physician **Hippocrates** develops the professional outlook on medical practice, encouraging its separation from religion
50 BC	The *Ayurveda* is compiled. It is the basic Hindu medical encyclopedia for many hundreds of years
AD 20	Roman scholar **Celcus** writes an important medical encyclopedia
AD 170	Roman physician **Galen** suggests using the pulse as a diagnostic aid
1540s	French surgeon **Ambroise Paré** suggests use of soothing ointment for treatment of wounds. He also introduced ligatures (tying of blood vessels) instead of cauterization (heat treatment) after amputation
1620s	Iatrophysics and iatrochemistry gain popularity. These schools of thought see the body as a relatively simple "machine"
1628	English physician William Harvey publishes his discovery of the circulation of the blood
1770s	English surgeon **John Hunter** advances the professional nature of surgery and pioneers the art of skin grafting
1796	English surgeon Edward Jenner discovers the scientific principles of vaccination
1841	American surgeon **Charles Jackson** discovers that ether is an anesthetic
1867	English surgeon Joseph Lister publishes his results concerning the use of the first antiseptic, carbolic acid
1870s	German bacteriologist **Robert Koch** establishes the link between disease and microorganisms
1900	Austrian-born physician **Karl Landsteiner** discovers the ABO blood group system
1903	Dutch physician **Willem Einthoven** invents the electrocardiogram, a device that monitors a patient's heartbeat
1910	German bacteriologist Paul Ehrlich produces the first synthetic drug. It is Salvarsan 606 (arsphenamine) and is effective against syphilis
1928	Scottish bacteriologist Alexander Fleming discovers the antibiotic penicillin
1953	American virologist **Jonas Salk** develops the first effective vaccine for poliomyelitis
1967	The first successful heart transplant is performed by South African physician Christiaan Barnard

Diagnosis

A MEDICAL CONDITION MAY BE DIAGNOSED by the examination of a patient's signs and **symptoms**; this must be done if the correct care and treatment is to be given. Diagnosis usually begins with the family physician (general practitioner), who may carry out a series of physical or clinical tests. The doctor will start by asking the patient to describe their symptoms. They will also compile a case history that includes personal and family medical histories. Standard tests, which can be performed in the doctor's clinic, may also be carried out. The **nervous reflexes**, eyes, ears, nose, and throat can be checked, and the body temperature and blood pressure taken. The doctor may also use a stethoscope to listen to the internal noises of the body, such as heartbeat, pulse, and breathing. If necessary, a body fluid or tissue sample can be sent to a laboratory for further analysis, and the patient may be referred for further investigations, such as an endoscopic examination (see pp. 248-249) or an X ray or scan (see pp. 240-243).

LISTENING TO BODY SOUNDS

Auscultation is the diagnostic technique of listening to the internal sounds of the body, usually with a stethoscope. The diaphragm or bell-shaped part of the stethoscope is pressed against the patient. Sounds from within the body, for example in the lungs, heart, joints, and stomach, are conveyed along hollow tubes to the examiner's ears.

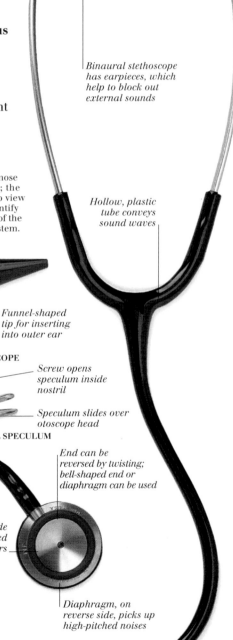

Binaural stethoscope has earpieces, which help to block out external sounds

Hollow, plastic tube conveys sound waves

VIEWING PARTS OF THE BODY

Looking into the eyes, ears, nose, mouth, and throat can reveal signs of infection and abnormalities. It can also give an indication of general health. Attachments can be clipped onto a handle that provides a light source to illuminate the area being examined. The otoscope is used to look inside the ears or nose (when the nasal speculum is attached); the laryngoscope, with attachments, is used to view the throat. The ophthalmoscope can identify eye abnormalities and give an indication of the general health of the blood circulation system.

Rotating set of magnifying lenses for examining the eye

Various head attachments screw on here

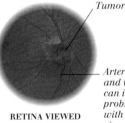

Tumor

RETINA VIEWED THROUGH AN OPHTHALMOSCOPE

Arteries and veins can indicate problems with circulation

Funnel-shaped tip for inserting into outer ear

OTOSCOPE

Screw opens speculum inside nostril

Speculum slides over otoscope head

NASAL SPECULUM

Light source tip

LARYNGOSCOPE HEAD

Flat end for pressing down tongue

TONGUE DEPRESSOR FOR LARYNGOSCOPE

End can be reversed by twisting; bell-shaped end or diaphragm can be used

Bell-shaped side picks up low-pitched sounds and murmurs

Angled mirror to reflect image

Handle containing batteries for light source

OPHTHALMOSCOPE

MIRROR HEAD

Diaphragm, on reverse side, picks up high-pitched noises

BODY FLUIDS AND TISSUE ANALYSIS

In order to establish or confirm a diagnosis, it may be necessary to remove body fluids or tissues for further analysis in a medical laboratory. The instruments below are used for obtaining cell samples. The cytology brush gently rubs cells off moist body surfaces, such as the inside of the mouth. The wooden spatula is designed to obtain cells and fluid from the cervix (neck of the womb). Most samples are immediately placed into sterile specimen tubes, labeled, and sent to the laboratory.

Bristles gently rub away cells

Blunt end for scraping off cells

Color-coded label gives patient and sample information

Chemicals stabilize or preserve sample

DISPOSABLE SPECIMEN TUBE

MEASURING TEMPERATURE

A high temperature may be an indication that the body is fighting infection, it can be monitored using a thermometer. Traditional clinical thermometers consist of a glass tube with a bulb of mercury at one end. Electronic versions have a **thermocouple** in the heat sensitive end and a digital readout, which makes them easier and safer to use.

Temperature-sensitive end

Digital temperature readout

Reset button

VISION TESTS

Abnormalities in vision can be detected using a variety of tests. Sharpness of vision may be tested by reading letters from the **Snellen chart**. The Ishahara test uses dots of related colors to test for color blindness. Here, a pattern of green dots can be seen on a background of red, orange, and yellow dots.

Readings are taken from the mercury scale

Sphygmomanometer scale, measured in millimeters of mercury (mm Hg)

Column of mercury measures air pressure in cuff, which reflects blood pressure inside artery

MEASURING BLOOD PRESSURE

This procedure measures the pressure waves produced in the arteries with each contraction of the heart. It can reveal problems with the heart and blood vessels. A cuff is inflated around the upper arm until a pulse cannot be felt in the wrist. As it is slowly deflated, the doctor listens for a pulse in the artery at the elbow. Readings are taken at systolic (maximum) pressure – when the blood is first heard to force its way through – and diastolic (minimum) pressure – when the blood flow is uninterrupted.

Stethoscope is placed over artery in the elbow to listen for blood flow sounds

Support for arm

Bulb is squeezed to inflate cuff; red button is pressed to deflate it

Cuff is inflated to stop blood flow, then slowly deflated to take systolic (maximum) and diastolic (minimum) pressures

CYTOLOGY BRUSH   SPATULA

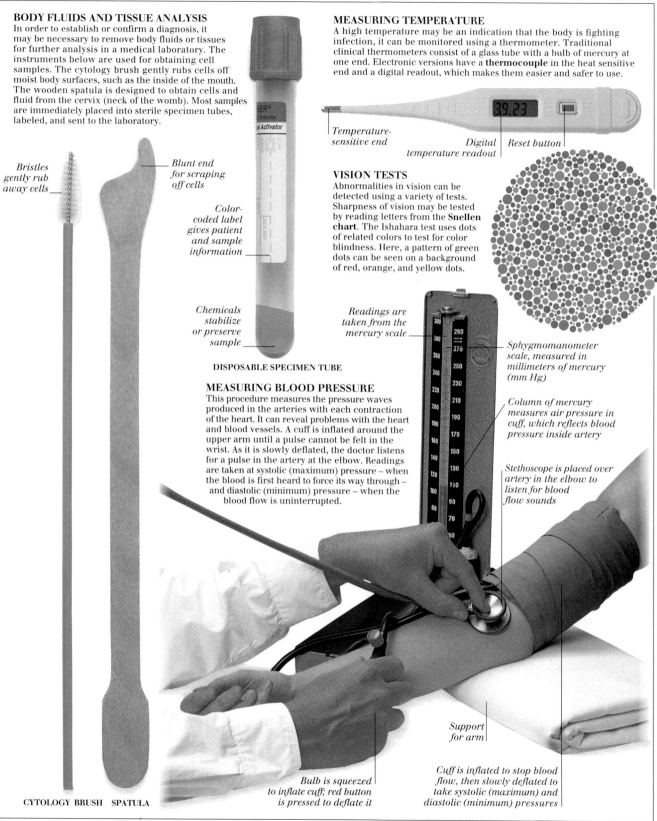

Medical imaging 1

SOUND AND ELECTROMAGNETIC RADIATION can be used to create visual images of the body's interior without the need for surgery. Medical imaging is used for **diagnostic** reasons and to check on the effects of treatment and surgery. With the development of computers, technology has advanced greatly, and there are now various techniques used to produce images. In ultrasound scanning, **high frequency sound waves** transmitted through the body are absorbed and reflected to different degrees by different body tissues. It is considered a safe method of imaging, as it does not use **radiation**. X-ray imaging is the oldest form of imaging and is still the most commonly used in most **clinical** cases. Short-wave electromagnetic rays are passed through the body and detected, making a photographic-type image. This image may be of limited use, and exposure to radiation can damage cells. Computerized tomography (CT) scanning combines the use of multiple X-ray beams and detectors, with a computer that can create more detailed cross-sectional or three dimensional images.

ULTRASOUND IN PREGNANCY

Ultrasound scanning is generally considered to be safer than certain types of X-ray imaging. For this reason, it is often used to provide images of the fetus during pregnancy. These images can reveal abnormal development and can also be used to tell if the fetus is male or female. In many countries an ultrasound scan is part of routine prenatal testing. It is usually done about 16-18 weeks into pregnancy.

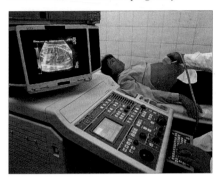

ECHOCARDIOGRAPHY

HOW ECHOCARDIOGRAPHY WORKS

Echocardiography has become an important diagnostic tool for most cardiologists (heart specialists). It uses ultrasound to visualize the internal structure of the heart and its movements. The emitter in the transducer produces pulses of ultrasound waves, which are beamed painlessly into the body. Different densities of organs or tissues absorb the waves or reflect them as echoes; these are picked up by the transducer's receiver. As the transducer is moved over the skin, the strength and time delay of the returning echoes are analyzed by a computer and an image of the heart is built up.

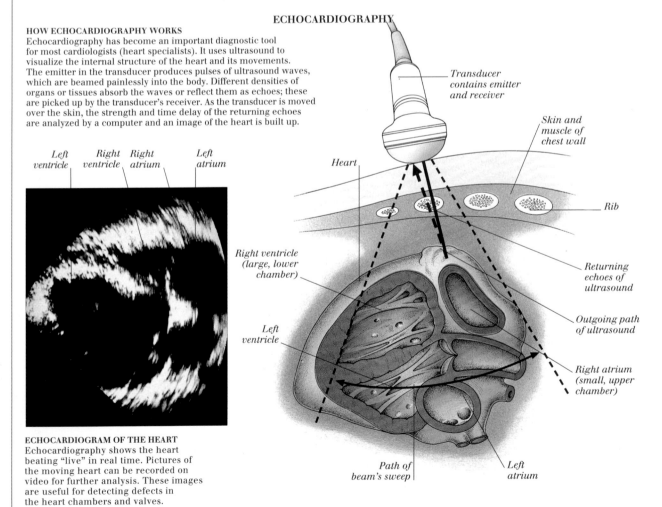

Transducer contains emitter and receiver

Skin and muscle of chest wall

Heart

Rib

Returning echoes of ultrasound

Outgoing path of ultrasound

Right atrium (small, upper chamber)

Left atrium

Path of beam's sweep

Left ventricle

Right ventricle (large, lower chamber)

Left ventricle *Right ventricle* *Right atrium* *Left atrium*

ECHOCARDIOGRAM OF THE HEART

Echocardiography shows the heart beating "live" in real time. Pictures of the moving heart can be recorded on video for further analysis. These images are useful for detecting defects in the heart chambers and valves.

X-RAY IMAGING

An X-ray image is a shadow picture showing the shape and density of body parts. Plain X rays are the simplest, and are used for diagnosing bone and joint disorders. Very dense tissue – bones and cartilage – is revealed against a background of less dense tissue. Low-power X rays distinguish between abnormal, dense tissue – tumors – and the surrounding normal, less dense tissue. In this way, mammograms are used to screen for unusual growths in breasts. Contrast X rays use a contrast medium, such as barium or iodine, which shows up well on X ray. The medium may be swallowed (barium meal) or injected into blood vessels (angiography) in order to highlight blockages, growths, or ruptures.

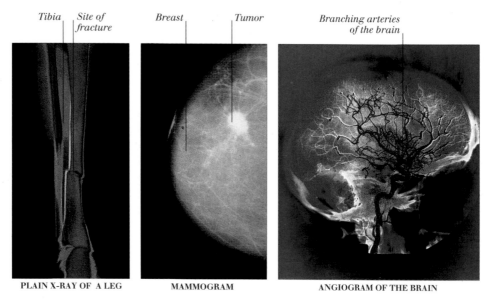

Tibia   Site of fracture

Breast   Tumor

Branching arteries of the brain

PLAIN X-RAY OF A LEG   **MAMMOGRAM**   **ANGIOGRAM OF THE BRAIN**

COMPUTERIZED TOMOGRAPHY (CT) SCANNING

HAVING A CT SCAN

A sliding table moves the person being scanned into a large, circular opening in the machine. As the person lies still on the table, the X-ray source rotates within the scanner and sends out a succession of narrow, low-power X-ray beams at different angles through the body. Detectors on the opposite side pick up the beams, which are weakened by differing amounts by the tissues they pass through, and send signals to a computer. This translates the information provided into a two-dimensional "slice" through the body, which is displayed on a screen.

Table slides through machine between scans to build up a "slice-by-slice" image of the body

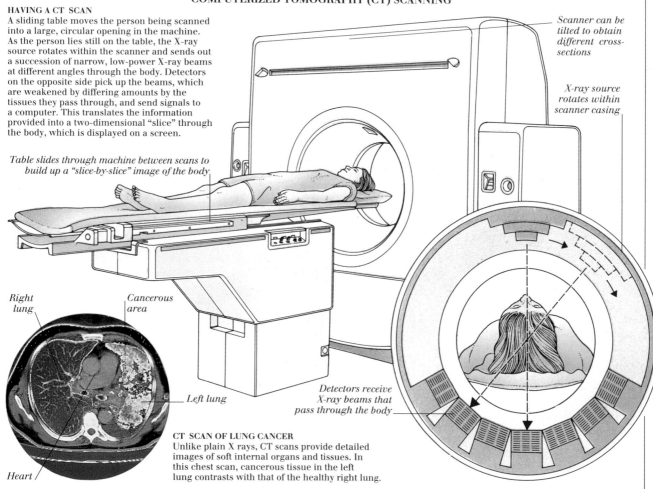

Scanner can be tilted to obtain different cross-sections

X-ray source rotates within scanner casing

Right lung

Cancerous area

Left lung

Detectors receive X-ray beams that pass through the body

Heart

CT SCAN OF LUNG CANCER

Unlike plain X rays, CT scans provide detailed images of soft internal organs and tissues. In this chest scan, cancerous tissue in the left lung contrasts with that of the healthy right lung.

Medical imaging 2

CONTINUED DEVELOPMENT OF COMPUTERS and the desire for safer, more detailed ways of imaging the body have led to scientists developing new methods of medical imaging. Magnetic resonance imaging (MRI) uses radio waves in a powerful magnetic field. This produces highly detailed images of tissues within the body, especially of those with a high fat or water content, such as the brain. It can be used to diagnose a range of diseases – including cancer – and can also enable doctors to monitor degenerative disorders of the central nervous system, such as multiple sclerosis. In radionuclide scanning, a radioactive substance is introduced into the body, and the radiation given off is detected by a special camera. Positron emission tomography (PET) is a form of radionuclide scanning that uses computers to produce images that reflect the function of tissues as well as their structure. One of the main uses of PET has been to study the brain, as it can provide valuable information about brain function in mental illnesses.

HAVING AN MRI BRAIN SCAN
A sliding table moves the patient into a large magnet where the scan takes place. The image can be viewed on the scanner's computer screen, which is shielded from the magnetic field by a partition.

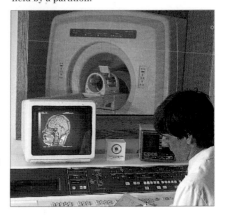

HOW MAGNETIC RESONANCE IMAGING (MRI) WORKS
Within the body's water molecules, hydrogen nuclei usually spin randomly around magnetic axes pointing in all directions. The intense magnetic field produced by the electromagnet in the MR scanner causes these nuclei to line up in the same direction as the polarity of the electromagnetic waves emitted. A pulse of radio frequency energy then knocks them out of alignment and causes them to wobble. As they realign themselves, they emit their own weak radio waves, which are picked up by detectors and analyzed by a computer.

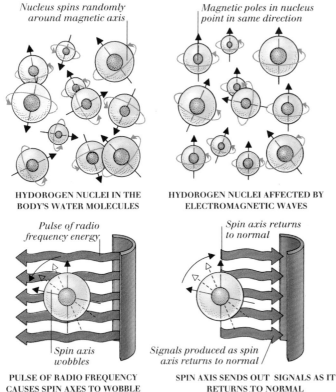

Nucleus spins randomly around magnetic axis

Magnetic poles in nucleus point in same direction

HYDOROGEN NUCLEI IN THE BODY'S WATER MOLECULES

HYDOROGEN NUCLEI AFFECTED BY ELECTROMAGNETIC WAVES

Pulse of radio frequency energy

Spin axis returns to normal

Spin axis wobbles

Signals produced as spin axis returns to normal

PULSE OF RADIO FREQUENCY CAUSES SPIN AXES TO WOBBLE

SPIN AXIS SENDS OUT SIGNALS AS IT RETURNS TO NORMAL

MRI SCAN OF THE BRAIN
MRI provides clear images of parts of the body that are surrounded by dense bone, making it particularly valuable for studying the brain and spinal cord. It is also useful for showing small details of soft tissues, such as nerves and blood vessels. It works by imaging different body tissues according to the density of their hydrogen atoms, hydrogen being present in the body's most common substance, water (H_2O), and also in many other body chemicals. Tissues with a high water content, such as fat, show up brightest on the image. This section, or slice, through the head shows the nerve tissue of the brain in great detail. The wrinkled cerebrum – where higher thought processes and consciousness are centered – can be seen at the top.

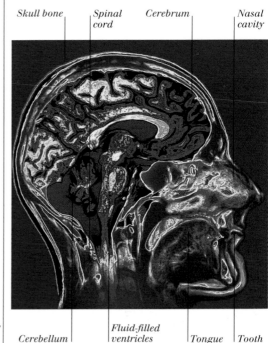

Skull bone *Spinal cord* *Cerebrum* *Nasal cavity*

Cerebellum *Fluid-filled ventricles* *Tongue* *Tooth*

RADIONUCLIDE IMAGING

HAVING A POSITRON EMISSION TOMOGRAPHY (PET) SCAN

During a PET scan, a radiation source is temporarily introduced into the body. This source is a radionuclide, called a radioisotope – a specially manufactured, radioactively tagged chemical – which can be injected, swallowed, or inhaled. Within the body, this takes part in a biochemical process, concentrating in tissues that are more metabolically active. A ring of detectors measure the radiation emitted from the radioactive particles and a cross section of the part of the body being examined is built up. The procedure is safe, as the amount of radiation involved is tiny.

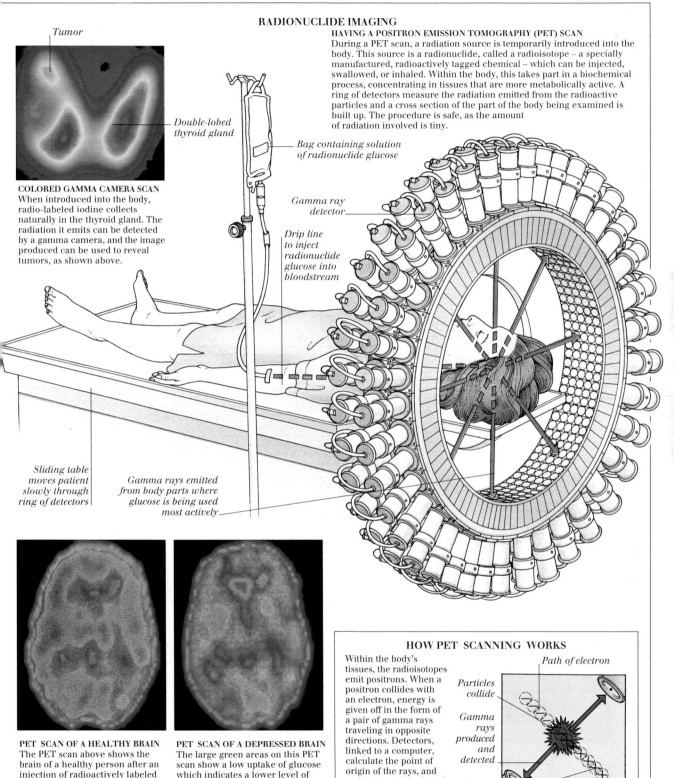

Tumor

COLORED GAMMA CAMERA SCAN
When introduced into the body, radio-labeled iodine collects naturally in the thyroid gland. The radiation it emits can be detected by a gamma camera, and the image produced can be used to reveal tumors, as shown above.

Double-lobed thyroid gland

Bag containing solution of radionuclide glucose

Gamma ray detector

Drip line to inject radionuclide glucose into bloodstream

Sliding table moves patient slowly through ring of detectors

Gamma rays emitted from body parts where glucose is being used most actively

PET SCAN OF A HEALTHY BRAIN
The PET scan above shows the brain of a healthy person after an injection of radioactively labeled glucose. The red and yellow areas show the most active parts of the brain, indicating normal glucose use.

PET SCAN OF A DEPRESSED BRAIN
The large green areas on this PET scan show a low uptake of glucose which indicates a lower level of brain activity. In order to assist interpretation, the computer has colored this scan.

HOW PET SCANNING WORKS

Within the body's tissues, the radioisotopes emit positrons. When a positron collides with an electron, energy is given off in the form of a pair of gamma rays traveling in opposite directions. Detectors, linked to a computer, calculate the point of origin of the rays, and an image can be plotted on a monitor.

Path of electron

Particles collide

Gamma rays produced and detected

Path of positron

Emergency care

PARAMEDICS AND AMBULANCE STAFF give emergency medical care at the scene of an accident and on route to the hospital. Most accidents are served by ambulances, but **paramedics** now also travel by helicopter and motorcycle. Modern ambulances are equipped to provide basic **first aid** and advanced life support. The aim of ambulance staff is to save the lives of victims and to prevent their condition from worsening. Once on scene, they evaluate the situation and follow the "ABC" of emergency care priorities – Airway, Breathing, and Circulation. Lightweight, portable equipment, such as respirators, defibrillators, and oxygen therapy kits, enable paramedics to treat and stabilize victims without moving them. Injured limbs or joints are immobilized immediately and wounds are dressed to prevent fluid loss and minimize infection. Ambulances also carry a selection of **fast-acting drugs** that can be administered by paramedics. The ambulance provides quick transportation to the hospital emergency room where doctors and medical staff take over and may refer accident victims to other departments including intensive care.

MONITORING HEART RATE

A heartbeat is essential for circulating oxygen-carrying blood around the body, especially to the brain. The portable heart monitor allows "hands-free" monitoring of the pulse, even if it is very weak. Conductor pads are stuck to the wrist and a screen display and paper trace record the heart's actions. If the heart contracts rapidly and irregularly, "paddles" (not shown) can be attached, which deliver an electric shock to defibrillate the heart into a normal rhythm.

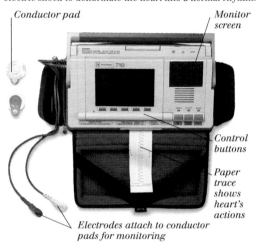

Conductor pad

Monitor screen

Control buttons

Paper trace shows heart's actions

Electrodes attach to conductor pads for monitoring

PRIMARY RESPONSE PACK

When paramedics reach the scene of an accident, they often carry a primary response pack. It is light and portable and contains a selection of basic items that are most effective in stabilizing the victim and saving life. The blood pressure monitor and stethoscope can be used to assess the person's condition (see pp. 238-239). The plastic airways and air bag and mask are used to help and, if necessary, assist breathing. Sterile dressings prevent blood loss and minimize the risk of infection.

KEEPING THE AIRWAY CLEAR

It is vital that a clear airway (mouth, nose, throat, and windpipe) is maintained so that fresh air can pass into the lungs. The portable aspirator, below, is a battery-powered pump, connected to a long catheter (flexible tube) that sucks out any blood, mucus, or vomit that may be blocking the airway.

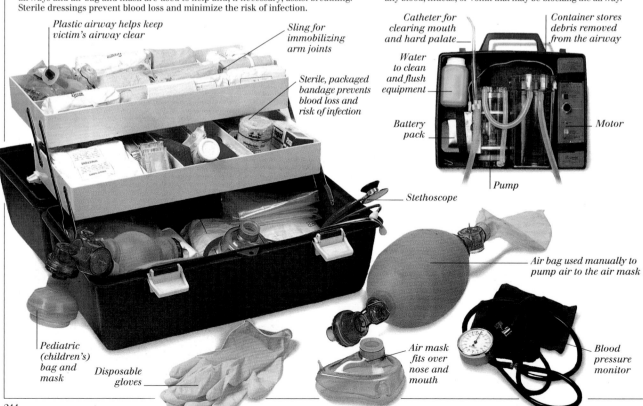

Plastic airway helps keep victim's airway clear

Sling for immobilizing arm joints

Sterile, packaged bandage prevents blood loss and risk of infection

Catheter for clearing mouth and hard palate

Container stores debris removed from the airway

Water to clean and flush equipment

Battery pack

Motor

Pump

Stethoscope

Air bag used manually to pump air to the air mask

Pediatric (children's) bag and mask

Disposable gloves

Air mask fits over nose and mouth

Blood pressure monitor

BREATHING AND OXYGEN SUPPLY

A shortage of oxygen, due to slow, weak breathing, can be harmful to the brain. When almost pure oxygen is passed into the lungs, the amount being picked up by the blood can be increased. It is supplied by a pressurized cylinder and delivered to the patient via a pressure-reducing regulator, gas tube, and a face mask or plastic airway.

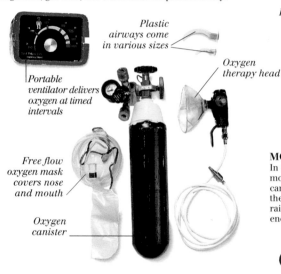

Plastic airways come in various sizes

Oxygen therapy head

Portable ventilator delivers oxygen at timed intervals

Free flow oxygen mask covers nose and mouth

Oxygen canister

EMERGENCY ROOM

When a patient arrives at the emergency room their injuries are assessed. Some are treated and discharged, others are admitted to other departments in the hospital or for surgery (see pp. 240-243). If needed, a medical cart, below, can be wheeled directly to the victim. It contains essential lifesaving equipment, such as airways, ventilation pumps, and fast-acting drugs.

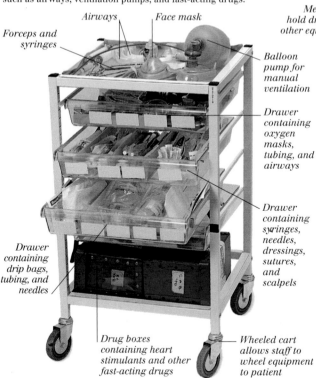

Airways

Face mask

Forceps and syringes

Balloon pump for manual ventilation

Drawer containing oxygen masks, tubing, and airways

Drawer containing syringes, needles, dressings, sutures, and scalpels

Drawer containing drip bags, tubing, and needles

Drug boxes containing heart stimulants and other fast-acting drugs

Wheeled cart allows staff to wheel equipment to patient

IMMOBILIZING JOINTS

In the event of bone, joint, or nerve damage, the affected part must be immobilized to prevent further injury or even paralysis. If possible, paramedics will do this at the scene of the accident before transportation to the emergency room. A series of specially designed, lightweight splints and braces have been developed that snap or clip into place around the injured part.

Rigid material holds limb straight

Leg or arm splint

Velcro straps secure box splint around leg

Neck braces come in various sizes

Cervical neck brace snaps together around neck

MOVING THE PATIENT

In order to minimize the effect of injuries, the patient should be moved as little as possible. Once lifted onto the hospital cart, they can be wheeled from the scene of the accident to the ambulance then straight into the emergency room. The head end can be raised or lowered for comfort, and the legs can be raised to encourage blood flow to the upper body and brain.

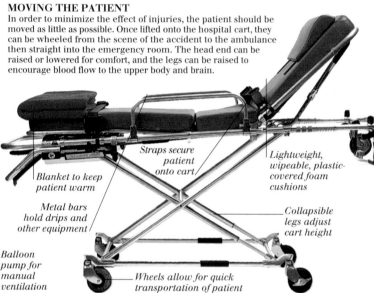

Straps secure patient onto cart

Lightweight, wipeable, plastic-covered foam cushions

Blanket to keep patient warm

Metal bars hold drips and other equipment

Collapsible legs adjust cart height

Wheels allow for quick transportation of patient

INTENSIVE CARE

Some patients may be so seriously ill that they require intensive care. Units within hospitals that provide this have a huge variety of highly technical equipment. Artificial ventilators, heart defibrillators, and intravenous tubes to deliver drugs and fluids, help keep the patient alive. Sensors and electrodes monitor breathing and heart rates, temperature, and other body variables.

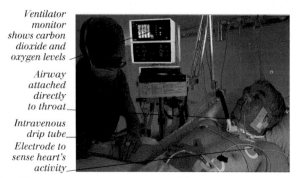

Ventilator monitor shows carbon dioxide and oxygen levels

Airway attached directly to throat

Intravenous drip tube

Electrode to sense heart's activity

Surgery

SURGERY IS THE MANUAL TREATMENT of **diseases**, injuries, or deformities. It may be elective – with an element of choice – or non-elective – when it is essential, lifesaving, and usually done in an emergency (see pp. 244-245). Minor surgery, such as the removal of skin warts, can be done, under hygienic conditions, almost anywhere. Major surgery is usually carried out in a specialized room – the operating room – with a team of staff including a chief surgeon and an anesthetist. Surgeons use equipment, such as scalpels and scissors, that has changed little over several centuries. Recent developments in anesthetics and equipment, particularly in the field of less invasive surgery (see pp. 248-249), have enabled surgeons to perform more complicated operations with far less risk to the patient. There have also been huge developments in **transplant surgery** (see pp. 250-251). The heart-lung machine, for example, has made open-heart surgery and heart transplants possible for the first time.

STANDARD SURGICAL INSTRUMENTS

Most basic, handheld surgical instruments have changed little over time. They are specialized to perform physical tasks, such as incising (cutting), probing, gripping, clamping, separating, and suturing (sewing up). The handles are shaped to fit the hand and reduce finger fatigue and sliding. The instruments are generally made of stainless steel or special metal alloys strong enough to deal with tough body tissues and bone and to withstand repeated sterilization with chemicals or steam.

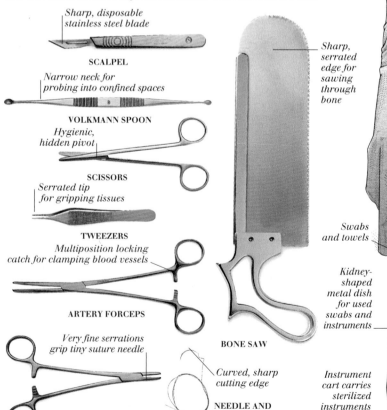

Sharp, disposable stainless steel blade

SCALPEL

Narrow neck for probing into confined spaces

VOLKMANN SPOON

Hygienic, hidden pivot

SCISSORS

Serrated tip for gripping tissues

TWEEZERS

Multiposition locking catch for clamping blood vessels

ARTERY FORCEPS

Very fine serrations grip tiny suture needle

NEEDLE HOLDER

Sharp, serrated edge for sawing through bone

BONE SAW

Curved, sharp cutting edge

NEEDLE AND SURGICAL THREAD

OPERATING ROOM

The operating room is a brightly lit, sterile environment. The air in it is filtered to remove contamination and the walls and floor are washed daily to kill bacteria. Surgeons, nurses, assistants, and the anesthetist all stand in their customary positions, surrounded by surgical and life-support equipment. This increases their efficiency and minimizes the amount that they have to move and look around. They wear sterilized clothing, disposable gloves, and face masks.

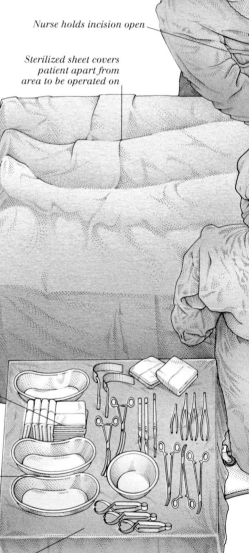

Sterilized clothing and face mask helps prevent infection

Nurse holds incision open

Sterilized sheet covers patient apart from area to be operated on

Swabs and towels

Kidney-shaped metal dish for used swabs and instruments

Instrument cart carries sterilized instruments laid out in a specific order

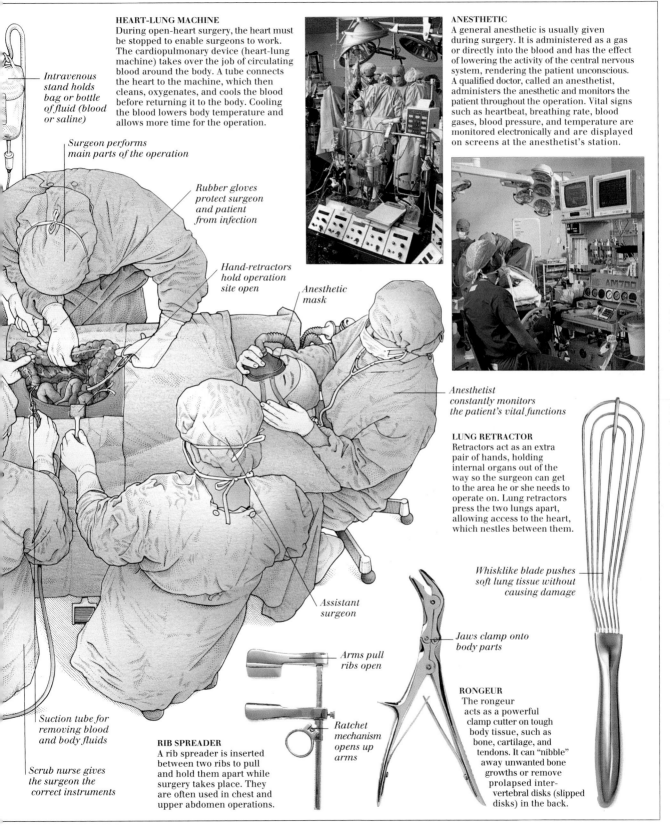

HEART-LUNG MACHINE
During open-heart surgery, the heart must be stopped to enable surgeons to work. The cardiopulmonary device (heart-lung machine) takes over the job of circulating blood around the body. A tube connects the heart to the machine, which then cleans, oxygenates, and cools the blood before returning it to the body. Cooling the blood lowers body temperature and allows more time for the operation.

Intravenous stand holds bag or bottle of fluid (blood or saline)

Surgeon performs main parts of the operation

Rubber gloves protect surgeon and patient from infection

Hand-retractors hold operation site open

Anesthetic mask

ANESTHETIC
A general anesthetic is usually given during surgery. It is administered as a gas or directly into the blood and has the effect of lowering the activity of the central nervous system, rendering the patient unconscious. A qualified doctor, called an anesthetist, administers the anesthetic and monitors the patient throughout the operation. Vital signs such as heartbeat, breathing rate, blood gases, blood pressure, and temperature are monitored electronically and are displayed on screens at the anesthetist's station.

Anesthetist constantly monitors the patient's vital functions

LUNG RETRACTOR
Retractors act as an extra pair of hands, holding internal organs out of the way so the surgeon can get to the area he or she needs to operate on. Lung retractors press the two lungs apart, allowing access to the heart, which nestles between them.

Whisklike blade pushes soft lung tissue without causing damage

Assistant surgeon

Jaws clamp onto body parts

Arms pull ribs open

Suction tube for removing blood and body fluids

Scrub nurse gives the surgeon the correct instruments

RIB SPREADER
A rib spreader is inserted between two ribs to pull and hold them apart while surgery takes place. They are often used in chest and upper abdomen operations.

Ratchet mechanism opens up arms

RONGEUR
The rongeur acts as a powerful clamp cutter on tough body tissue, such as bone, cartilage, and tendons. It can "nibble" away unwanted bone growths or remove prolapsed inter-vertebral disks (slipped disks) in the back.

Minimally invasive surgery

TRADITIONAL SURGERY IS "invasive" and "gross." The body is entered, or invaded, through speccially made **incisions** in the skin and outer layers. Surgeons work at the level of gross anatomy, that is, the scale of size visible to the unaided eye. Recent advances in technology have offered surgeons a different approach involving the least possible physical trauma to the patient. The endoscope has enabled them to view the inside of the body without having to cut it open. It is used for **diagnosis** and also in keyhole surgery to view and treat internal conditions with minimal disruption to the surrounding **tissues.** Laser technology uses light as a very precise method of cutting through tissues, destroying unwanted parts and growths, and heat-sealing raw areas. Microsurgical equipment lets the surgeon work at magnifications of up to 50 times, to manipulate and repair tiny and delicate body parts, such as hair-thin nerves and blood vessels. New technology has also helped to train surgeons in a safe way, using virtual reality instead of a live patient.

HOW AN ENDOSCOPE WORKS

Endoscopes consist of a thin plastic tube containing flexible bundles of plastic or glass fibers. A light is shone down one of the bundles to illuminate the area. The image is then reflected back up another bundle. Each fiber shows a tiny area. The whole scene is built up from smaller parts, like dots on a television screen.

Observer
Lens
Fiber-optic bundle
Repeated reflection along optic fibers
Object

ENDOSCOPY AND KEYHOLE SURGERY

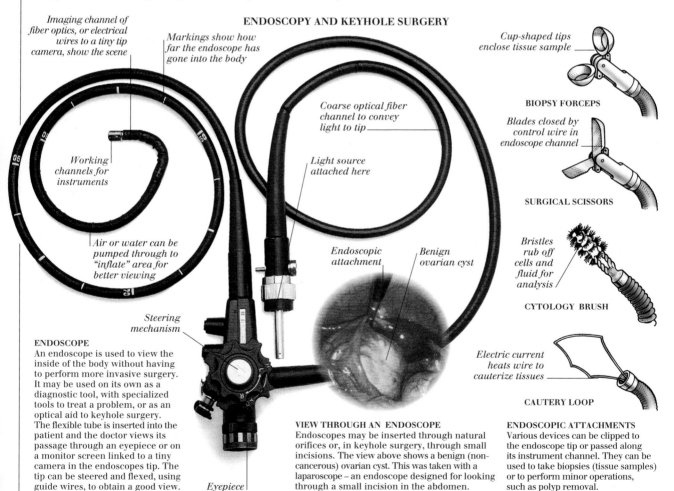

Imaging channel of fiber optics, or electrical wires to a tiny tip camera, show the scene

Markings show how far the endoscope has gone into the body

Cup-shaped tips enclose tissue sample

BIOPSY FORCEPS

Coarse optical fiber channel to convey light to tip

Blades closed by control wire in endoscope channel

Working channels for instruments

Light source attached here

SURGICAL SCISSORS

Bristles rub off cells and fluid for analysis

Air or water can be pumped through to "inflate" area for better viewing

Endoscopic attachment

Benign ovarian cyst

CYTOLOGY BRUSH

Steering mechanism

Electric current heats wire to cauterize tissues

CAUTERY LOOP

ENDOSCOPE
An endoscope is used to view the inside of the body without having to perform more invasive surgery. It may be used on its own as a diagnostic tool, with specialized tools to treat a problem, or as an optical aid to keyhole surgery. The flexible tube is inserted into the patient and the doctor views its passage through an eyepiece or on a monitor screen linked to a tiny camera in the endoscopes tip. The tip can be steered and flexed, using guide wires, to obtain a good view.

Eyepiece

VIEW THROUGH AN ENDOSCOPE
Endoscopes may be inserted through natural orifices or, in keyhole surgery, through small incisions. The view above shows a benign (non-cancerous) ovarian cyst. This was taken with a laparoscope – an endoscope designed for looking through a small incision in the abdomen.

ENDOSCOPIC ATTACHMENTS
Various devices can be clipped to the endoscope tip or passed along its instrument channel. They can be used to take biopsies (tissue samples) or to perform minor operations, such as polyp removal.

VIRTUAL REALITY SURGERY

Surgery requires great skill and many years of training. Traditionally, trainee surgeons have learned their trade by watching expert surgeons and practicing procedures on real patients. The development of virtual reality has enabled surgeons to practice on simulated situations without risk to a patient. A computer-generated image of the body part, for example the eye, is displayed on a monitor screen and viewed through a binocular microscope. The trainee surgeon manipulates a "scalpel," which is a digitized pen attached to a framework of levers. Its movements are tracked by the computer and displayed with the image. The levers give the scalpel resistance and a realistic feel to its motion.

Stereoscopic operating microscope

Image on monitor screen

Pen represents scalpel

Cut

Scalpel

VIRTUAL REALITY SURGERY IN USE

COMPUTER-GENERATED IMAGE OF THE EYE

LASER SURGERY

Laser surgery uses a very thin, high-intensity beam of light (see pp. 56-57) to cut and seal tissues. The light is conveyed from its source along optical fibers to the tip. It can be used with great precision to treat areas of abnormality without damaging the surrounding tissues. If the rays are focused some distance from the tip, they can pass harmlessly through nearer tissues and cut or cauterize further away, at their focus. The heat from the beam of light seals tiny blood vessels and nerve endings during cutting, so there is minimal bleeding and pain from the incision.

Laser light passes along tube to handle

Handle and power controls for single-handed operation

Fiber optic can be retracted while going through hard tissue, such as bone, to avoid damage

Stainless steel shaft contains optical fibers

MICROSURGERY

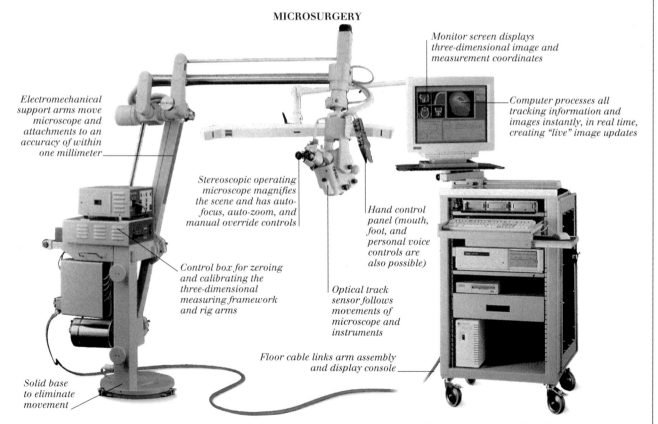

Monitor screen displays three-dimensional image and measurement coordinates

Computer processes all tracking information and images instantly, in real time, creating "live" image updates

Electromechanical support arms move microscope and attachments to an accuracy of within one millimeter

Stereoscopic operating microscope magnifies the scene and has auto-focus, auto-zoom, and manual override controls

Hand control panel (mouth, foot, and personal voice controls are also possible)

Control box for zeroing and calibrating the three-dimensional measuring framework and rig arms

Optical track sensor follows movements of microscope and instruments

Floor cable links arm assembly and display console

Solid base to eliminate movement

STEREOTACTIC MICROSURGICAL RIG

Microsurgery allows surgeons to operate on parts of the body that were previously inaccessible or too small to work on, such as the inside of the ear, the spinal cord, and the brain. Highly intricate procedures are performed using miniature precision instruments and viewed under an operating microscope. The stereotactic rig provides a framework for measuring and controlling the instruments. Using delicate, mechanical sensors in the support arm and optical-beam sensors on the operating microscope, the instruments and the area being treated are tracked and calculated to an accuracy of within one millimeter. All the information is fed into a computer, which displays the scene on a monitor screen and controls the rig's movements.

Transplants

TRANSPLANTATION IS THE IMPLANTATION of **organs** or the grafting of **tissues** from one person to another or from one part of the same body to another. Biological tissues and organs can be donated by human beings or derived from animals (see pp. 262-263). Success depends on compatibility between the donor and recipient, autografts (self-grafts) being the most successful. Transplants have become possible because of major developments in the science of **immunology**, and in the **pharmacology** of drugs capable of suppressing **immunological reactions** without causing too much danger to the patient. The success of transplantation has also required substantial developments in surgical technique and in ways of avoiding **infection** during surgery (see pp. 246-247). Initially, success in transplantation was limited to corneal and kidney grafts. Today, almost any organ in the body, outside the **nervous system**, can be successfully transplanted, as can many tissues.

T CELL

Lymphocytes are types of white blood cells that are involved in the immune system. There are two types, B cells and T cells. B cells are responsible for producing antibodies (see Transplant and Graft Rejection below), and T cells (shown here) act as recognition agents, B-cell helpers, and killers of certain cell invaders. T cells can recognize and kill cancer cells, cells infected with viruses, and cells from a different individual, for example in a transplanted organ.

T cells seek out and destroy invading cells

TRANSPLANT AND GRAFT REJECTION

All biological tissues carry chemical "flags," called antigens, which can be identified by the immune system. In most cases, except with identical twins, donated organs or tissue are immediately recognized as "foreign." This promotes a destructive reaction by T cells and the production of antibodies by B cells (see below). These reactions occur at the interface between the grafted organ and the host. Drugs such as cyclosporin have been developed to suppress the immune system and to help prevent rejection of transplanted organs and grafts.

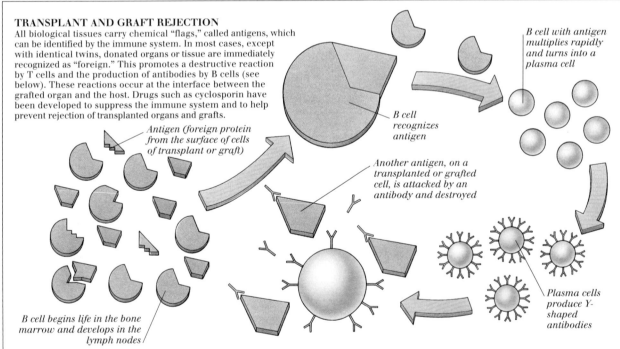

Antigen (foreign protein from the surface of cells of transplant or graft)

B cell recognizes antigen

B cell with antigen multiplies rapidly and turns into a plasma cell

Another antigen, on a transplanted or grafted cell, is attacked by an antibody and destroyed

Plasma cells produce Y-shaped antibodies

B cell begins life in the bone marrow and develops in the lymph nodes

BONE MARROW

Bone marrow is a bloodlike liquid containing stem cells – the cells from which the red and white blood cells are developed. When transplanted, these enable the recipient to make new, healthy blood cells. The bone marrow is usually taken from a pelvic bone (iliac crest) or from the breastbone (sternum). It is removed, under local or general anesthetic, by passing a strong needle through the outer plate of the bone and drawing the marrow into a syringe.

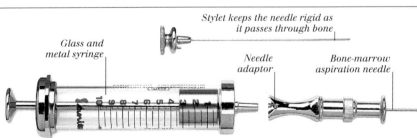

Stylet keeps the needle rigid as it passes through bone

Glass and metal syringe

Needle adaptor

Bone-marrow aspiration needle

EXAMPLES OF TRANSPLANTS

Any organ in the chest or abdomen can now be successfully transplanted. In the case of the eye, only the cornea is used, as removing the whole eye would involve cutting the optic nerve, which cannot be rejoined. Skin and bone can be transplanted only from one site to another on the same person; this is called an autograft. Many transplanted organs, such as the heart and lungs, must be inserted into the same site as the original organs. In some instances it is safer and surgically more convenient to place the organ in a different site; a transplanted kidney, for example, is always placed in the pelvis near the bladder.

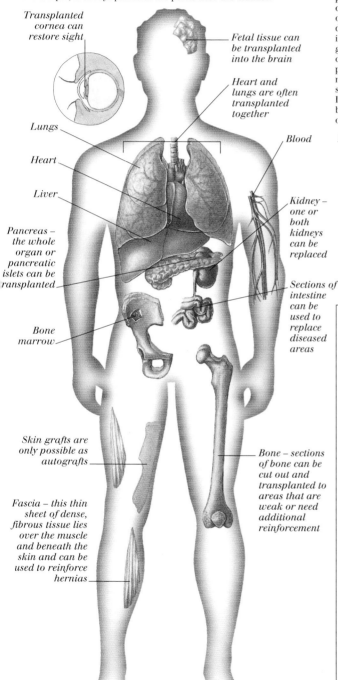

Transplanted cornea can restore sight

Fetal tissue can be transplanted into the brain

Heart and lungs are often transplanted together

Lungs

Heart

Liver

Blood

Pancreas – the whole organ or pancreatic islets can be transplanted

Kidney – one or both kidneys can be replaced

Sections of intestine can be used to replace diseased areas

Bone marrow

Skin grafts are only possible as autografts

Fascia – this thin sheet of dense, fibrous tissue lies over the muscle and beneath the skin and can be used to reinforce hernias

Bone – sections of bone can be cut out and transplanted to areas that are weak or need additional reinforcement

TISSUE TRANSPLANTS

BLOOD TRANSFUSION

Blood is the most common tissue to be transplanted. It is obtained by bleeding volunteer donors from a vein into a sterile receptacle containing a chemical that prevents the blood from clotting. About 450 ml of blood is taken. As a dangerous reaction occurs if blood of the wrong group is transfused, a test, called cross-matching, is performed. This involves mixing donor red cells with serum from the recipient. Incompatibility is shown by agglutination (clumping) of the donor red cells.

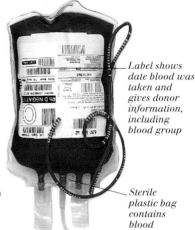

Label shows date blood was taken and gives donor information, including blood group

Sterile plastic bag contains blood

Pig-tissue valve

HEART-VALVE TRANSPLANT

Heart valves can be replaced by a bionic, mechanical valve (see pp. 252-253) or a biological valve from a human or pig donor. Pig valves are sometimes used since they are readily available, very similar to human valves, and do not cause blood clots as mechanical valves do. Unfortunately, they only have a working life of 7 to 10 years before the tissues degenerate.

KIDNEY DIALYSIS

A lack of donor organs for transplantation often means that people with total kidney failure have to wait long periods before a suitable kidney becomes available. During this time a technique called hemodialysis takes over the function of the diseased kidney. The dialysis machine consists of a system of tubes or plates made of a semiporous material and immersed in a watery solution. Blood is pumped from the patient, into the system where impurities diffuse out into the water, which is continuously renewed. The procedure is fairly simple and requires three 4–8 hour sessions a week.

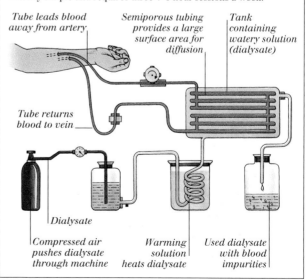

Tube leads blood away from artery

Semiporous tubing provides a large surface area for diffusion

Tank containing watery solution (dialysate)

Tube returns blood to vein

Dialysate

Compressed air pushes dialysate through machine

Warming solution heats dialysate

Used dialysate with blood impurities

Artificial body parts

THE DEVELOPMENT OF BIOENGINEERING – a discipline involving close cooperation between doctors and mechanical and electronic engineers – and advances in technology and materials science have brought about a medical revolution in the area of artificial body parts. Bionic structures have been developed, and implanted artificial body parts, such as heart pacemakers, are now used extensively. Safe implantation involves the use of materials that do not excite adverse **chemical reactions** in the **tissues**. Some metals, such as iron and copper, are dangerous when implanted into the body. Therefore alloys that remain **inert** when in contact with tissue fluids are used. Many synthetic, polymer, plastic materials have proved to be safe, and some, such as silicone rubber, even allow the **diffusion** of oxygen. In most cases, the development of the ideal design of an implantable part has involved years of trial. Modern implants are consequently very successful and reliable.

ARTIFICAL EYE LENS

An artificial lens may be implanted in order to refocus the eye after the removal of a **cataract**. The optical power of the lens is set using **ultrasound** measurements taken before the operation. The lens is centered and held within the transparent capsule of the original lens by supporting loops.

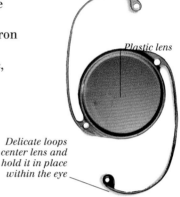

Plastic lens

Delicate loops center lens and hold it in place within the eye

HEART PACEMAKER

When a heart cannot respond normally to the demands made on it, an artificial pacemaker may be implanted. This electronic device sends a series of small electric pulses to the heart, causing it to beat regularly. Demand pacemakers work more quickly when required and can be programmed from the outside by radio signals. Pacemakers work by internal batteries that last for about 10 years.

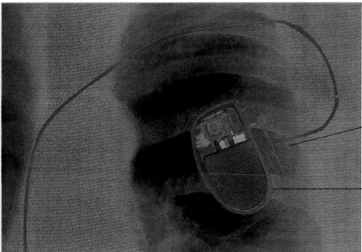

Lead connects pacemaker to heart

Electronic heart pacemaker fitted in the chest

VASCULAR GRAFTS

At the end of the 20th century, the most common cause of long-term illness and premature death has been the formation of **cholesterol plaques** in the arteries. This may cause a blockage or weaken the artery, causing its wall to bulge or split. Replacement of the diseased area with a woven-plastic arterial graft can be lifesaving. Before being sewn in place, the inert material is soaked in blood. Body cells, called **fibroblasts**, then invade the structure and eventually turn it into virtually normal body tissue.

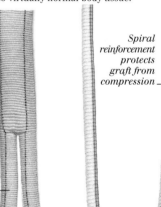

Spiral reinforcement protects graft from compression

Tough polyester material

VASCULAR GRAFT

MECHANICAL HEART VALVES

Several types of heart disease can lead to severe narrowing or leakage of the heart valves. As a result, the heart has to work more strenuously and may eventually fail. Heart valves can be replaced with biological valves (see pp. 250-251) or one of a range of reliable, mechanical valves. These are very efficient and present no rejection problems, but require long-term blood anticlotting treatment.

Ball blocks valve opening and stops blood flow

Stainless steel ball falls into cage to allow blood to flow past

OPEN

CLOSED

BIFURCATED AORTIC VASCULAR GRAFT

EXAMPLES OF ARTIFICIAL PARTS

Artificial body attachments, such as false teeth and hooks to replace lost hands, have been used for hundreds of years and predate any implanted body parts. The problem of causing a rejection reaction by the body's immune system (see pp. 250-251) has, until quite recently, prevented the implantation of such artificial body parts as pacemakers and joints. Inert materials, such as metal alloys and plastics, do not react chemically with body fluids and are strong enough to withstand repeated use. Their development has made implantation possible.

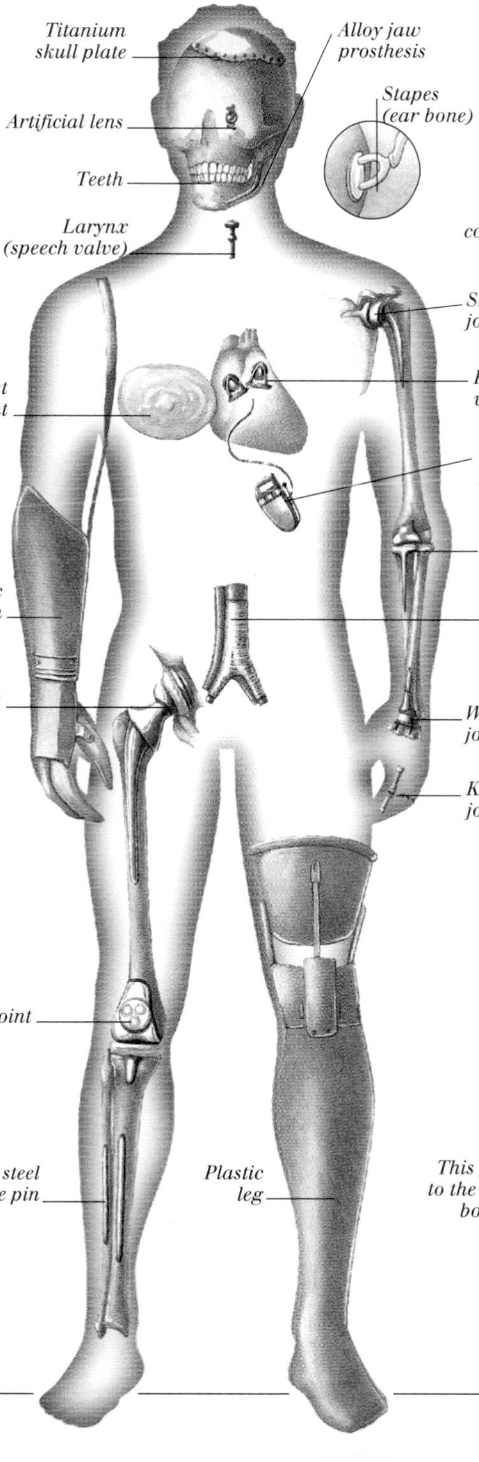

Titanium skull plate

Artificial lens

Teeth

Larynx (speech valve)

Breast implant

Myoelectric arm

Hip joint

Knee joint

Stainless steel bone pin

Plastic leg

Alloy jaw prosthesis

Stapes (ear bone)

Shoulder joint

Heart valve

Heart pacemaker

Elbow joint

Vascular graft

Wrist joint

Knuckle joint

ARTIFICAL ORTHOPEDIC PARTS

MYOELECTRIC ARM

Even after the total loss of a wrist and hand, the muscles in the forearm can still contract in an attempt to move the missing limb. Modern **transducer** technology has made it possible to sensitively detect these movements. Amplified control signals are sent to its motors and other activators to bring about the desired actions in the artificial arm. The availability of microprocessors on a single silicon chip has helped greatly in the development of these devices.

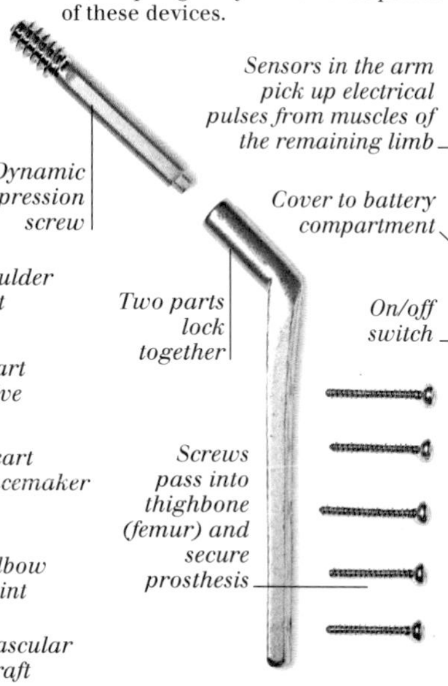

Sensors in the arm pick up electrical pulses from muscles of the remaining limb

Cover to battery compartment

On/off switch

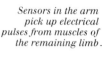

Dynamic compression screw

Two parts lock together

Screws pass into thighbone (femur) and secure prosthesis

DYNAMIC HIP SCREW

Fracture of the neck of the thigh bone (femur) is a common injury in elderly people. It can be stabilized using a dynamic hip screw. The upper part is screwed inside the fractured neck, while the lower part is fixed into the shaft of the femur.

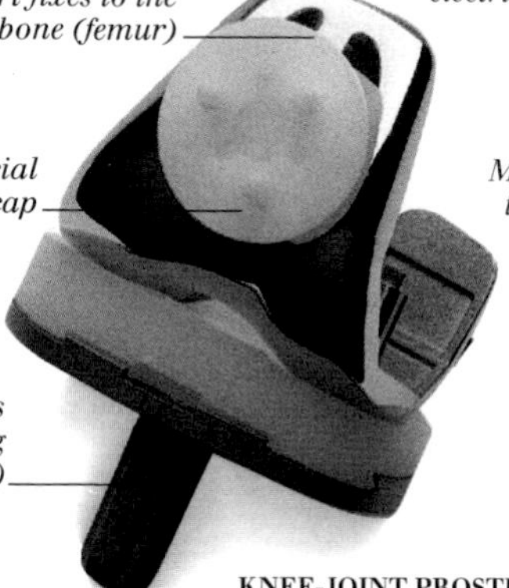

This part fixes to the thighbone (femur)

Artificial kneecap

This part fixes to the lower leg bone (tibia)

KNEE-JOINT PROSTHESIS

Knee movements are complex and involve sliding and slight rotation. These elements are incorporated into the design of modern artificial knee joints, making them highly effective prostheses.

Wrist twist

Electronic control unit

Servo (powerful electric motor)

Moving thumb

Two fingers move toward thumb to give a powerful grip

Drugs and drug delivery

A DRUG IS ANY SUBSTANCE that can affect the structure or functioning of the body. Drugs are used to prevent, **diagnose**, and treat **disease** and to relieve **symptoms**. Drug action ranges enormously; they may be used to save life in cases of dangerous infection or they may be used to relieve minor skin irritations. Pharmacology – the science of drugs and how they work – has developed into a highly sophisticated discipline. Drug action is now well understood and new drugs are designed by computer. Advances have also occurred in the pharmaceutical industry, which applies the technology that is based on pharmacology. Drugs may be administered in many different ways: including by ingestion, inhalation, injection, skin implantation, skin application, or insertion. All the drugs given in these ways require special formulation in order to ensure correct dosage, reasonable shelf life, and maximum safety.

NATURAL DRUGS

The earliest effective medical substances were largely of natural origin and derived from plants. This was the case until well into the 20th century. Such drugs included quinine, opium, cocaine, and digitalis.

Digitalis tablet

FOXGLOVE
(Digitalis purpurea)

COMPOSITION OF A TABLET

Some drugs may be formulated as a tablet. The design of a tablet involves determining the best inert substances with which to mix the active ingredient. Inert materials include binding agents, lubricants, disintegrating agents, dispersing agents, preservatives, and flavorings. Often, the weight of the active substance is only a tiny proportion of the total weight of the tablet.

Bulking agents to give volume to the tablet

Binding agents to hold ingredients together

Granulating agents to make particle size uniform

Drug

Disintegrating agents to help tablet break up and release the drug in the stomach

Coatings, such as sugar, to conceal taste

Lubricants to make tablet easier to swallow

TABLET

DRUG DEVELOPMENT

Modern methods of drug development often involve the use of computers to aid in the synthesis of new compounds by the modification of molecules of known pharmacological action. This is followed by extensive trials to establish the drug's effectiveness and safety.

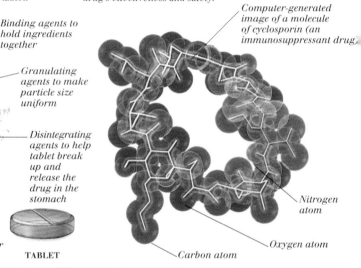

Computer-generated image of a molecule of cyclosporin (an immunosuppressant drug)

Nitrogen atom

Oxygen atom

Carbon atom

HOW DRUGS WORK

All cells have receptor sites on the outer surface of the cell membrane. Drugs are shaped to lock into these receptor sites and, as a result, effect changes within the cell. Using this method, drugs can work in two ways: they can resemble a natural body substance that normally stimulates the receptors; or they can block the receptor sites so that the natural substances cannot have their normal effect. Drugs can be designed to produce a more powerful stimulus to the cell than natural substances. They can also block the receptors for prolonged periods.

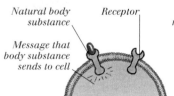

Natural body substance

Receptor

Message that body substance sends to cell

Drug reinforces message sent by body substance to the cell

DRUG REINFORCING NATURAL BODY SUBSTANCES

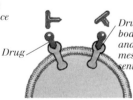

Natural body substance

Message that body substance sends to cell

Drug

Drug blocks body substance and prevents message being sent to cell

DRUG BLOCKING NATURAL BODY SUBSTANCES

SITES AND ROUTES OF DRUG ADMINISTRATION

There are a huge number of ways in which drugs can be introduced into the body. All of the body's orifices can be used, either for local application or to allow the drug to be absorbed into the bloodstream for general distribution around the body. Drugs that are required to act quickly are given by intravenous injection; drugs given by subcutaneous or intramuscular injections are absorbed at varying rates, depending on the medium in which they are dissolved or suspended. The slowest absorption and longest action is provided by depot implants and skin patches.

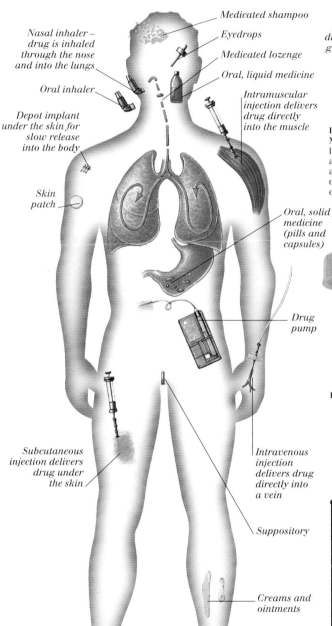

Medicated shampoo

Eyedrops

Nasal inhaler – drug is inhaled through the nose and into the lungs

Medicated lozenge

Oral, liquid medicine

Oral inhaler

Intramuscular injection delivers drug directly into the muscle

Depot implant under the skin for slow release into the body

Skin patch

Oral, solid medicine (pills and capsules)

Drug pump

Subcutaneous injection delivers drug under the skin

Intravenous injection delivers drug directly into a vein

Suppository

Creams and ointments

METHODS OF DRUG ADMINISTRATION

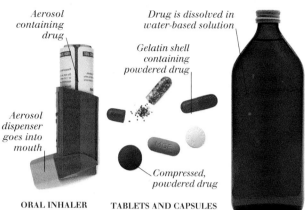

Aerosol containing drug

Drug is dissolved in water-based solution

Gelatin shell containing powdered drug

Aerosol dispenser goes into mouth

Compressed, powdered drug

ORAL INHALER

INHALED MEDICINE
Medication for certain lung disorders, chiefly asthma, is delivered by an aerosol or in a dispersed powder cloud from an inhaler.

TABLETS AND CAPSULES

ORAL MEDICINE
The majority of drugs are taken by mouth, most commonly in the form of tablets or capsules. The practice of giving drugs in the form of liquids, once the commonest vehicle, is now rare, as accurate dosage is impossible.

ELIXIR

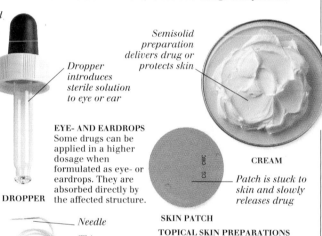

Semisolid preparation delivers drug or protects skin

Dropper introduces sterile solution to eye or ear

CREAM

EYE- AND EARDROPS
Some drugs can be applied in a higher dosage when formulated as eye- or eardrops. They are absorbed directly by the affected structure.

DROPPER

Patch is stuck to skin and slowly releases drug

SKIN PATCH

TOPICAL SKIN PREPARATIONS
Local application to a body surface is called topical, and refers mostly to the skin. Topical preparations may be lotions, creams, ointments, or skin patches. Topical drugs include antibiotics, antifungals, hormones, and protective substances. Some topical drugs are formulated to be absorbed into the skin; others have an action confined to the surface skin layers.

Needle

Thin tube

Dials control dosage and speed

Disposable syringe

Presser moves slowly along screw thread

Medicated, bullet-shaped solid dissolves at body temperature

DRUG PUMP
A mechanical drug pump can be set to deliver drugs in an exact dosage, either continuously or at precise intervals.

SUPPOSITORIES
Suppositories can be inserted into the vagina or rectum. The drug is delivered topically and it is absorbed into mucous membranes.

Pregnancy and childbirth

THE PERIOD FROM THE FERTILIZATION OF AN EGG to the birth of a young human being is known as pregnancy and takes about nine months (38 weeks). In recent decades, medical science has become involved in many stages of pregnancy and childbirth. Fertility treatments, including *in vitro* fertilization, have been developed to help people with low fertility levels. Once pregnancy has been confirmed, screening tests such as blood tests, chorionic villus sampling, and **amniocentesis** are done to check general health and test for any genetic or chromosomal abnormalities (see pp. 262-263). During labor and the delivery, monitoring equipment is used to measure contractions and the baby's heartbeat. If the birth is difficult, doctors may assist by performing a **cesarian section**, by using forceps, or by using **vacuum extraction**. Babies that are born ill or premature (early) are cared for in special baby care units, often in incubators, until they recover health and strength.

PREGNANCY TESTS

Most pregnancy tests check for the presence of **human chorionic gonadotropin** (hCG), which can be detected in urine or blood. Home tests (see below) use chemicals, on a card or dipstick, to test for hCG in the urine 14 days after the mother's first missed **menstrual period.**

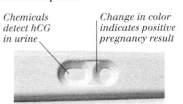

Chemicals detect hCG in urine

Change in color indicates positive pregnancy result

HOW IN VITRO FERTILIZATION (IVF) WORKS

IVF is often used in cases of infertility to increase the chances of conception. *In vitro* literally means "in glass"; children conceived this way are sometimes known as "test-tube babies." Fertility drugs are taken to stimulate eggs to mature in the woman's ovaries. They are collected with a long aspiration needle, using an ultrasound image as a guide. The ripe eggs are mixed with sperm in an incubated culture dish. The cells then divide, and at around the eight-cell stage, two or three embryos are transferred into the uterus using a catheter.

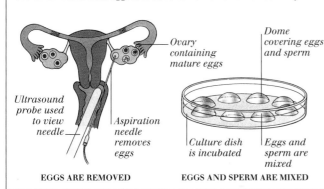

Ovary containing mature eggs

Dome covering eggs and sperm

Ultrasound probe used to view needle

Aspiration needle removes eggs

Culture dish is incubated

Eggs and sperm are mixed

EGGS ARE REMOVED

EGGS AND SPERM ARE MIXED

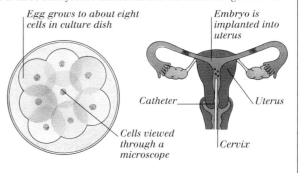

Egg grows to about eight cells in culture dish

Embryo is implanted into uterus

Catheter

Uterus

Cells viewed through a microscope

Cervix

CELLS DIVIDE

EMBRYO IS IMPLANTED

AIDING FERTILIZATION

The process of IVF (and other, similar infertility treatments) involves the chance meeting of an egg and a sperm in a petri dish. To increase the chances of fertilization, a technique has been developed whereby the male genetic material is injected directly into the female egg. The ripe egg is held steady on the end of a micropipette, and a very fine needle is used to inject the sperm cell into it. This all takes place under a high-powered microscope.

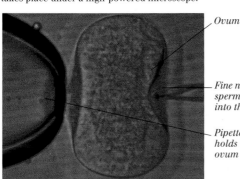

Ovum

Fine needle injects sperm directly into the ovum

Pipette holds ovum still

PRENATAL TESTS

Prenatal tests are done before the baby is born and are designed to assess the well-being of the mother and of the developing baby. Some tests are routine, such as urine and blood tests. Others, such as amniocentesis and fetal blood sampling, are performed only if the baby is considered to be at risk. Chorionic villus sampling, seen here, is used when problems such as chromosome abnormalities or inherited disorders are suspected. It involves taking blood and tissue samples from the chorionic villi and sending them for laboratory tests.

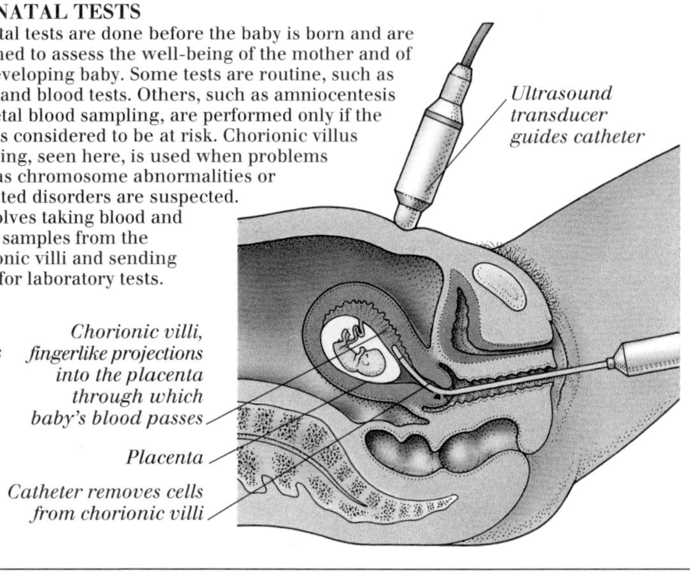

Ultrasound transducer guides catheter

Chorionic villi, fingerlike projections into the placenta through which baby's blood passes

Placenta

Catheter removes cells from chorionic villi

MONITORING THE BABY DURING LABOR

Labor is the first main stage of childbirth, when the strong uterine muscles begin to contract. It can be stressful for the baby, and electronic fetal monitoring (EFM) is sometimes used. Internal fetal monitoring involves clipping a small electrode to the baby's skin, usually the scalp. This detects the electrical signals of the baby's heartbeat, which are displayed on a monitor screen or paper strip. A catheter, inserted through the birth canal into the uterus, detects the pressure inside. If the baby's heart rate drops or the intrauterine pressure gets too high, doctors may need to intervene.

ASSISTED DELIVERY

In some instances it may be necessary for the doctor to assist with the delivery. If the baby's head is in the correct position, vacuum extraction or forceps may be used. Vacuum extraction uses a disk-shaped plastic cup, which is applied to the baby's head, and a vacuum pump. When the pump is turned on, the suction created enables the doctor to pull the baby into view. Forceps have become less commonly used. The two blades are clipped around the head and the doctor uses the handles to guide the baby's head out through the birth canal. The forceps can then be removed and the baby delivered normally.

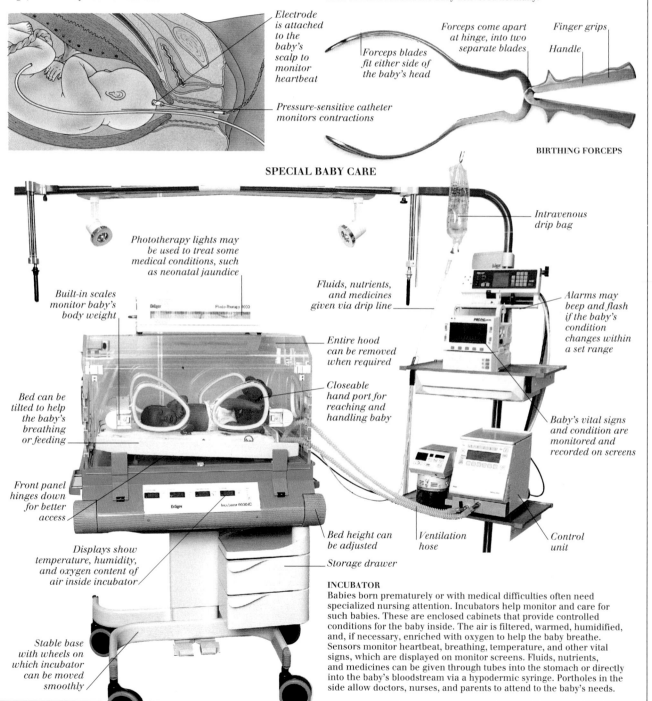

Electrode is attached to the baby's scalp to monitor heartbeat

Pressure-sensitive catheter monitors contractions

Forceps come apart at hinge, into two separate blades

Finger grips

Handle

Forceps blades fit either side of the baby's head

BIRTHING FORCEPS

SPECIAL BABY CARE

Phototherapy lights may be used to treat some medical conditions, such as neonatal jaundice

Intravenous drip bag

Built-in scales monitor baby's body weight

Fluids, nutrients, and medicines given via drip line

Alarms may beep and flash if the baby's condition changes within a set range

Entire hood can be removed when required

Bed can be tilted to help the baby's breathing or feeding

Closeable hand port for reaching and handling baby

Baby's vital signs and condition are monitored and recorded on screens

Front panel hinges down for better access

Displays show temperature, humidity, and oxygen content of air inside incubator

Bed height can be adjusted

Ventilation hose

Control unit

Storage drawer

Stable base with wheels on which incubator can be moved smoothly

INCUBATOR

Babies born prematurely or with medical difficulties often need specialized nursing attention. Incubators help monitor and care for such babies. These are enclosed cabinets that provide controlled conditions for the baby inside. The air is filtered, warmed, humidified, and, if necessary, enriched with oxygen to help the baby breathe. Sensors monitor heartbeat, breathing, temperature, and other vital signs, which are displayed on monitor screens. Fluids, nutrients, and medicines can be given through tubes into the stomach or directly into the baby's bloodstream via a hypodermic syringe. Portholes in the side allow doctors, nurses, and parents to attend to the baby's needs.

Infection and disease

INFECTION IS THE INVASION of the body by germs (microorganisms) that can cause disease. The term is also used to describe the actual disease caused by germs, a disease being a disorder, not resulting from physical injury, with a specific cause and recognizable **symptoms**. As a result of improved standards of hygiene and more effective **antibiotics** and drugs, infections are no longer the principal cause of disease in developed countries. However, they still cause much damage to the quality of life and result in many deaths. A wide range of infecting microorganisms can cause disease. These include viruses, bacteria, fungi, protozoa, and microscopic worms. Recently, a new addition to the list – the prion protein – has attracted much interest and considerable scientific research. Also of great concern are the **evolutionary** changes in many microorganisms, especially viruses and bacteria, that lead to their becoming **resistant** to previously effective antibotics.

BIOCHEMICAL RESEARCH

An important part of the war against infection is the development of new and more effective antibiotics and other drugs. Biochemical research can work out their chemical structure and change them by informed modification.

CULTURE PLATES

These dishes contain a medium, often **agar**, on which bacteria and other microorganisms will grow. They are incubated at human body temperature (37 °C). Bacterial culture is as an essential part of medical diagnosis (see pp. 238-239). Antibiotic sensitivity can be tested by placing disks of paper soaked in antibiotic solutions onto the culture plate. The largest zone of growth inhibition indicates which antibiotic will be the most effective in treating the infection.

Merged growths, or colonies, of bacteria

Colonies dripped by pipette containing antibiotics

Colonies grow in strands where smeared by spreader

GROWING A CULTURE

Healthy growth of yeast microbes

Paper disk containing anti- fungal drug

Area where drug has spread into agar and prevented yeast growth

ANTIBIOTIC SENSITIVITY

VIRAL INFECTIONS

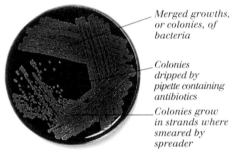

Human cell

Invading virus attaches to specific receptor site on cell wall

Replicated viral genome generates new virus particles within cell

Virus penetrates host cell and sheds protein shell

Host cell swells with virus particles and eventually bursts

Viral genome is released into host cell

HOW A VIRAL INFECTION OCCURS

Viruses can reproduce only inside living cells. The outer surface of a cell is studded with **receptor sites** to which viruses attach themselves in order to enter the cell. The virus sheds its protein coat to expose the viral **genome** – DNA or RNA – which incorporates itself into the genome of the cell. This allows the virus to reproduce many times, until the host cell bursts and releases them.

HIV

Human Immunodeficiency Virus (HIV) is a **retrovirus** with a specific attraction to cells of the helper class of T lymphocytes. It is the destruction of these cells that results in the severe damage to the function of the immune system – the Acquired Immune Deficiency Syndrome (AIDS).

Virus particles are released and subsequently infect other cells

PROTOZOAN INFECTIONS

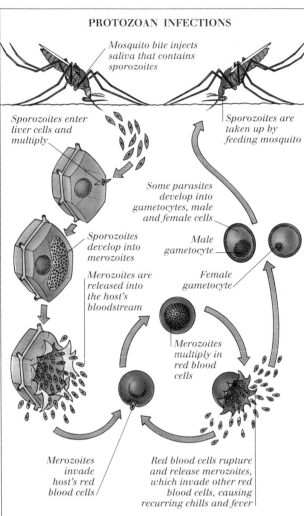

Mosquito bite injects saliva that contains sporozoites

Sporozoites are taken up by feeding mosquito

Sporozoites enter liver cells and multiply

Some parasites develop into gametocytes, male and female cells

Sporozoites develop into merozoites

Male gametocyte

Merozoites are released into the host's bloodstream

Female gametocyte

Merozoites multiply in red blood cells

Merozoites invade host's red blood cells

Red blood cells rupture and release merozoites, which invade other red blood cells, causing recurring chills and fever

HOW MALARIA OCCURS

Malaria is caused by a protozoan spread by certain mosquitoes. While feeding on a malaria sufferer, they take up blood containing malarial parasites. These multiply in the mosquito and enter its salivary glands. When it next feeds, it injects the parasites into the bloodstream of another human being. The parasites pass to the liver, where they multiply before re-entering the bloodstream and invading the red blood cells to multiply further. The release of the new parasites is associated with fever, shivering, and anemia.

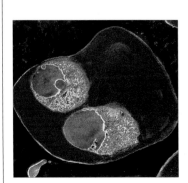

PROTOZOA

Protozoa are a class of single-celled organisms, some of which can cause disease in humans. The most important of these are the malarial parasites (shown here as two merozoites in a human blood cell) and the amoeba that causes amoebic dysentery. The group also includes the organisms that cause toxoplasmosis and sleeping sickness.

BACTERIAL INFECTIONS

Bacteria are single-celled organisms, whose shapes vary greatly (see pp. 134-135). The bacteria shown here are of part of a colony of *Legionella* organisms that cause the form of pneumonia known as Legionnaire's disease. Fortunately, antibiotics are effective against most bacteria.

LEGIONELLA **BACTERIA**

FUNGAL INFECTIONS

Fungi are organisms that scavenge on dead or rotting tissue. Some can infect human beings, causing both superficial and fatal infections. The *Candida* fungus, shown below, is the cause of one of the most common, superficial human infections and is usually confined to the skin or to the mucous membranes.

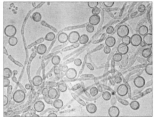

CANDIDA **FUNGUS**

PRION PROTEIN

Prion proteins are short lengths of normally harmless protein found in the human body. Research indicates that the principal prion disease – the brain disorder Creutzfeldt-Jacob disease – results from a modification of the normal prion protein. This involves a partial unfolding of helical parts of the protein **molecule** as a result of the substitution of a single **amino acid** for a different amino acid in the **protein sequence**. It can occur as a result of an inherited gene mutation, or when a slightly modified form of the normal protein enters the body and starts a chain reaction that causes the body's own prion protein in the brain to be modified.

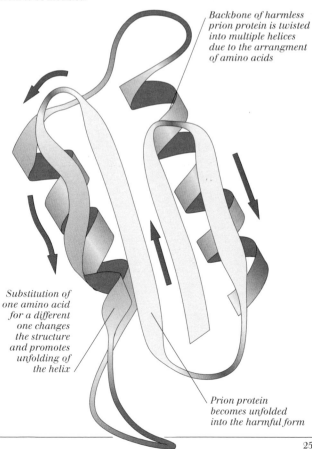

Backbone of harmless prion protein is twisted into multiple helices due to the arrangment of amino acids

Substitution of one amino acid for a different one changes the structure and promotes unfolding of the helix

Prion protein becomes unfolded into the harmful form

The immune system

THE IMMUNE SYSTEM PROTECTS the human body from infection. Unlike other systems of the body, it consists of a range of individual cells that are not joined together to form **tissues**. These cells fall into various classes including recognition cells, antibody-producing cells, killer cells, and eating or scavenging cells (phagocytes). The most important are the lymphocytes – B cells that produce **antibodies,** and T cells that assist B cells and also act as killer cells (see pp. 250-251). The main function of the immune system is to destroy invaders, such as **germs**, **parasites**, and biological tissue. They do this by the recognition of chemical groups called **antigens**. These differ from those carried by the body's own cells, so that under normal conditions the body does not turn on itself. In some instances, however, the body does attack its own cells; this is known as an autoimmune disorder. Allergies occur when the body becomes hypersensitive to certain antigens. Mast cells within the body release a cocktail of irritating substances that produce the characteristic allergic responses. The body can be artificially protected from disease by immunization.

PHAGOCYTES

These are the "eating" cells of the immune system (larger phagocytes are called macrophages). They are amoebic and perform a major cleaning-up function. When they encounter an antigen, with antibody attached, they extend pseudopodia (false feet) that surround and eventually engulf it. The phagocyte then uses **oxygen free radicals** to destroy the foreign material.

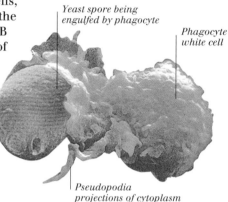

Yeast spore being engulfed by phagocyte

Phagocyte white cell

Pseudopodia projections of cytoplasm

AUTOIMMUNE DISORDERS

The immune system protects the body by recognizing and destroying foreign tissue (see pp. 250-251). Normally, it is suppressed against reacting to tissues of its own body. Sometimes, however, the regulation mechanisms that ensure this suppression fail, and the immune system is left free to attack its own tissues. The resulting disorders are called autoimmune diseases. They include rheumatoid arthritis, multiple sclerosis, and various anemias. Because antigens on certain germs so closely resemble human antigens, the antibodies to them can also attack human cells. This mechanism, involving viruses, is thought to be responsible for diabetes and is shown below. If it is caught in time and the body treated with **anti-antibodies**, the process can be halted.

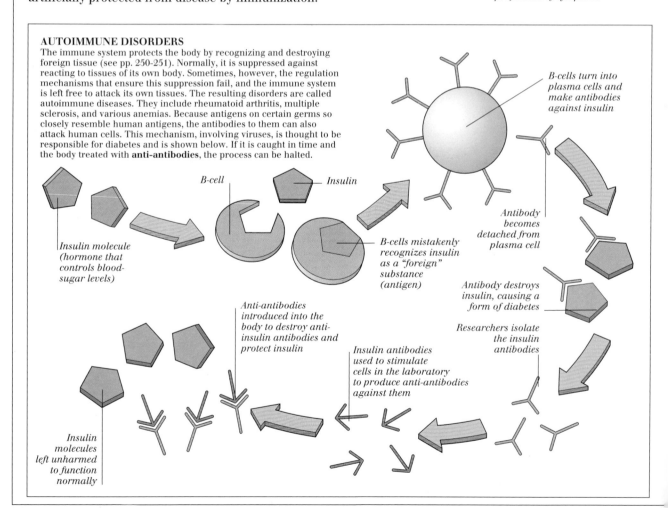

B-cell

Insulin

Insulin molecule (hormone that controls blood-sugar levels)

B-cells mistakenly recognizes insulin as a "foreign" substance (antigen)

B-cells turn into plasma cells and make antibodies against insulin

Antibody becomes detached from plasma cell

Antibody destroys insulin, causing a form of diabetes

Researchers isolate the insulin antibodies

Insulin antibodies used to stimulate cells in the laboratory to produce anti-antibodies against them

Anti-antibodies introduced into the body to destroy anti-insulin antibodies and protect insulin

Insulin molecules left unharmed to function normally

IMMUNITY

HOW IMMUNIZATION WORKS

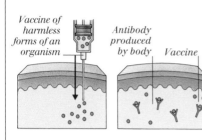

Vaccine of harmless forms of an organism

Antibody produced by body

Vaccine

Disease is recognized by antibody

Blood with antibodies is removed

Serum is injected into recipient

Antibody attacks infection

ACTIVE IMMUNIZATION
This process relies on the body's immune system producing antibodies itelf. It does so in response to the administration, usually by injection, of dead or harmless forms of an organism. These can no longer cause the actual disease but still carry the antigens by which the immune system can recognize them. As a result, the body produces protective antibodies against any future infection of the same kind.

PASSIVE IMMUNIZATION
In this form of immunization, antibodies that have been formed in another individual or animal as a result of infection or immunization, are purified and concentrated into a serum. This is given to an infected person by injection. If these ready-made antibodies are of the correct type, they will immediately attack the organisms causing the infection and usually destroy them. Passive immunization can also be used to provide a short-term form of protection against disease.

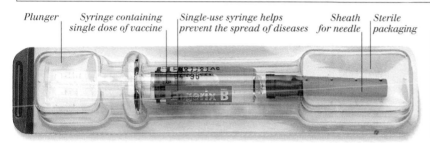

Plunger *Syringe containing single dose of vaccine* *Single-use syringe helps prevent the spread of diseases* *Sheath for needle* *Sterile packaging*

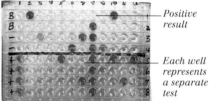

Positive result

Each well represents a separate test

INTRODUCING VACCINES
Vaccines have proved invaluable in controlling many infectious diseases, such as whooping cough, influenza, rubella, poliomyelitis, and tetanus. In the case of smallpox, they have succeeded in eradicating the disease altogether.

Some vaccines may be given as an oral solution, but most are delivered by injection. The appropriate amount may be drawn into a disposable syringe from a multidose vial, or it may come from a prepacked, single-dose syringe, like the one shown above.

ENZYME-LINKED IMMUNOSORBENT ASSAY
The ELISA test is used to diagnose disease by the presence of antibodies. When screening for HIV, a sample of blood serum is added to an enzyme in a well on the test plate. A positive result shows the presence of HIV antibodies.

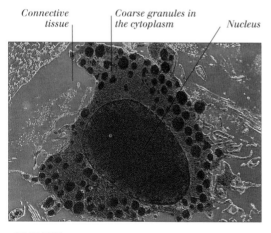

Connective tissue *Coarse granules in the cytoplasm* *Nucleus*

MAST CELL
Mast cells are present in most connective tissues. The cytoplasm is full of granules that contain heparin (a blood anticoagulant), histamine (a mediator of inflamation), and serotonin (also associated with inflamation). These are released during an allergic response, causing typical symptoms of allergy – widening of blood vessels, swelling of tissues, excessive nasal and eye secretion, and the tightening and narrowing of air passages in the lungs.

ALLERGY

Hygienic, disposable tube fits into mouthpiece of FEV meter

Patient blows hard into mouthpiece

Forced expiratory volume in 1-second measurement is displayed

Control and reset buttons

Compact, portable FEV meter can be used in doctor's surgery

MEASURING LUNG FUNCTION
Asthma is an allergic condition in which the air passages in the lungs are narrowed by the spasming of involuntary muscles and the inflammation of the mucous membrane. FEV (Forced Expiratory Volume) meters are used to check the freedom with which air can be expelled from the lungs. When blown into, they measure the rate of airflow and equate it with the peak volume passing in a given time. This can give vital information about the condition of the sufferer.

Genetics and medicine

IN THE LAST YEARS OF THE 20TH CENTURY, genetics has become the most important of the basic sciences underlying medicine. Advances in genetics, in particular the location of genes responsible for disease and the determination of the **genetic code** of large parts of the human genome – the whole genetic basis of an individual – have revolutionized modern medicine. Scientists predict that all of the human genome will be sequenced within a few years and that the location and exact detail of all the human genes – for normal characteristics and for disease – will soon be known. Genes can now be made artificially and incorporated into living cells. Any gene can be cloned to produce large numbers of perfect copies. Theoretically, such genes can be used to replace abnormal (mutant) genes to prevent or cure serious **genetic disorders**. Genetic engineering is also used to produce an ever-increasing number of **biochemicals** for use as drugs or **vaccines**. These substances are replacing medication that, because of the way it was obtained or made, could not always be relied upon to be pure and safe; for example human growth hormone, which has been implicated in the transfer of Creutzfeld-Jacob Disease (CJD) (see pp. 258-259).

GENETICALLY ENGINEERED DRUGS

Many drugs, such as insulin, are produced naturally in the body. In the past, such drugs were obtained from animals and, as a result, were often significantly different from the human version. Many of these drugs can now be produced by genetic engineering. The illustration below shows the equipment that is used to grow the microorganisms into which the human gene for the desired product has been inserted. By this method, massive culturing of the organism and large quantities of the resulting drug can be obtained.

HOW GENETIC ENGINEERING WORKS

Scientists have discovered several hundred different enzymes that can selectively cut the DNA molecule at particular points. Because the action of these enzymes results in restricted lengths of DNA, they are called restriction enzymes. Many of the DNA lengths cut out in this way are single genes that code for a particular protein, such as insulin. These genes may then be incorporated into the **plasmid** of a bacterium using certain other enzymes. The bacterium will then be capable of synthesizing the required protein. Bacteria can be cultured in enormous numbers to facilitate the production of large quantities of the protein. For a "foreign" gene to be expressed in a new host, such as an animal cell, it must be carried into the cell in a DNA molecule; bacteria plasmid DNA is commonly used for this.

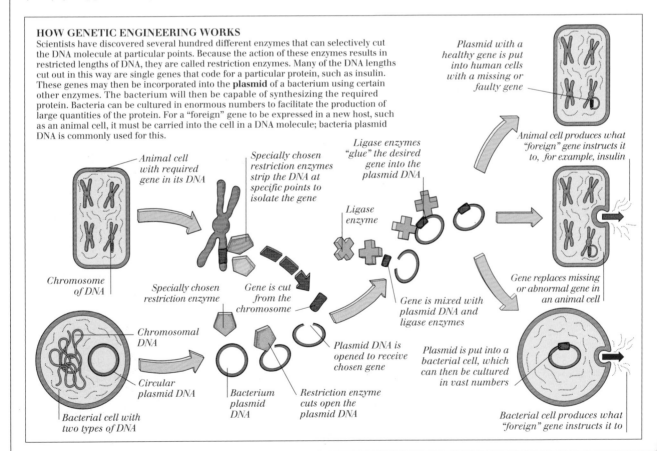

Plasmid with a healthy gene is put into human cells with a missing or faulty gene

Animal cell produces what "foreign" gene instructs it to, for example, insulin

Gene replaces missing or abnormal gene in an animal cell

Animal cell with required gene in its DNA

Specially chosen restriction enzymes strip the DNA at specific points to isolate the gene

Ligase enzymes "glue" the desired gene into the plasmid DNA

Ligase enzyme

Chromosome of DNA

Specially chosen restriction enzyme

Gene is cut from the chromosome

Gene is mixed with plasmid DNA and ligase enzymes

Chromosomal DNA

Plasmid DNA is opened to receive chosen gene

Plasmid is put into a bacterial cell, which can then be cultured in vast numbers

Circular plasmid DNA

Bacterium plasmid DNA

Restriction enzyme cuts open the plasmid DNA

Bacterial cell with two types of DNA

Bacterial cell produces what "foreign" gene instructs it to

CHROMOSOMAL ABNORMALITIES

Human karyotype has 23 pairs of chromosomes

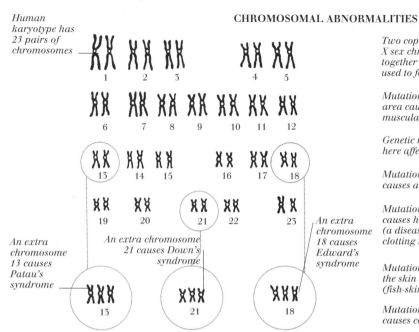

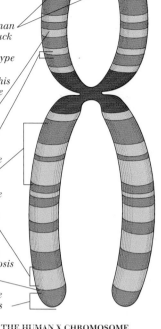

Two copies of the human X sex chromosome stuck together at the stage used to form a karyotype

Mutation in gene in this area causes Duchenne muscular distrophy

Genetic mutation here affects the eyes

Mutation in gene here causes a cleft palate

Mutation in gene here causes hemophilia (a disease that affects clotting in the blood)

Mutation here causes the skin disease icthyosis (fish-skin disease)

Mutation in gene here causes color blindness

An extra chromosome 13 causes Patau's syndrome

An extra chromosome 21 causes Down's syndrome

An extra chromosome 18 causes Edward's syndrome

EXTRA CHROMASOMES IN THE HUMAN KARYOTYPE

Healthy eggs and sperms each have 23 pairs of chromosomes. However, numerical chromosomal abnormalities can occur. These usually originate during cell division, when eggs and sperm are formed. An extra chromosome can appear as a result of abnormal separation at the stage of cell replication. This is called trisomy, and it most commonly affects chromosomes 21 (trisomy 21), 18 (trisomy 18), and 13 (trisomy 13).

GENE MUTATIONS IN THE HUMAN X CHROMOSOME

Mutations are changes in the sequence of bases in the chromosome. They occur due to deletions of bases or substitutions of the wrong base. Such changes result in abnormalities in the proteins, usually enzymes, for which the genes code. The X sex chromosome is particularly prone to genetic mutations.

GENETIC ANALYSIS

DNA FINGERPRINTING

This is a recording of a pattern of bands unique to each unrelated individual but with common features in related people. The bands, which are produced using restriction enzymes, electrical-attraction sorting, and radioactive DNA probes, correspond to regions in the DNA called core sequences. Bands are produced on photographic film by the action of radiation. DNA fingerprinting can be used for paternity testing and has great forensic significance. Only a tiny sample of blood, semen, or any body tissue is needed to provide the DNA for the procedure.

Band corresponds to core sequence in the DNA

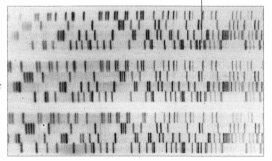

MAPPING THE HUMAN GENOME

The human genome project is one of the greatest scientific enterprises of all time. Its purpose is to discover the base sequence of the complete human DNA molecule – all the genetic information of the human organism. The development of automated machinery to carry out the sequencing has greatly sped up the project, which is now nearing completion. It has already increased knowledge of human genetics, and it is also transforming medicine.

Part of a computer screen display showing the sequence of the initial letters of the four bases (G,C, A, and T)

GENETIC CLONING

The cloning of an animal, such as Dolly the sheep (see below), involves the insertion of the whole DNA (genome) from a donor cell into the nucleus of an ovum from another animal. First, the ovum is isolated and its nucleus – which contains a complete copy of the DNA – is removed. Then, in its place is inserted the whole DNA taken from a cell from a donor animal. Because the whole genome has come from a donor, the resulting individual is a clone (identical copy) of the donor.

Satellite image of the Earth

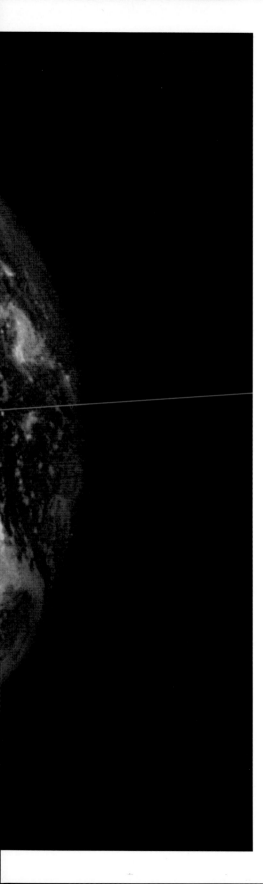

Earth Sciences

DISCOVERING EARTH SCIENCES 266

GEOLOGICAL TIME 268

THE EARTH 270

PLATE TECTONICS 272

EARTHQUAKES AND VOLCANOES 274

FAULTS AND FOLDS 276

ROCKS AND MINERALS 278

ROCKY LANDSCAPES 280

GLACIERS AND ICE SHEETS 282

RIVERS 284

COASTLINES 286

OCEANS 288

THE ATMOSPHERE 290

WEATHER 292

Discovering earth sciences

T HE EARTH SCIENCES INVOLVE THE STUDY of the Earth's rocks and minerals, water, and atmosphere. These fields include geological science, hydrological science, and atmospheric science. Geological science is the study of landforms, rocks, and minerals. Hydrological science includes the study of oceans, rivers, and glaciers. Atmospheric science deals with the study of weather (meteorology) and climate.

MEASURING ANGLES
One way in which scientists are able to identify crystals is by measuring the angle between corresponding faces of a particular mineral. They do this with a device (shown above) called a goniometer.

ANCIENT IDEAS

Ancient people put forward untested explanations for natural phenomena, such as the weather, the tides, and earthquakes and volcanoes. For example, several writers suggested that earthquakes and volcanoes are caused by hot wind that circulated underground. The occurrence of seashells on the tops of mountains was explained by hypothesizing catastrophic global floods. For all their mistaken ideas, many ancient natural philosophers made excellent observations. For example, the link between the tides and the motion of the Moon was noted around 100 BC. The study of earthquakes (seismology) began in ancient China. Astronomer and geographer Chang Heng invented a seismograph that was used to keep comprehensive records of seismic activity. Also, many people had a good knowledge of geological science. For example, some Roman architects could find locations that were likely to supply large quantities of groundwater by recognizing particular rocks and land formations. The spirit of inquiry and ingenuity that the ancient Greeks, Romans, Chinese, and Arabs possessed, and that served them so well in their investigations of natural phenomena, appears to have been lost during the Middle Ages. However, much of what they wrote survived and helped to inspire new investigations during the Renaissance period in Europe.

ROCKS AND MINERALS

Ancient civilizations were able to distinguish between common rock types. In particular, they were able to identify those ores from which they could smelt metals. After the Middle Ages, in 1546, **Georgius Agricola** produced the first scientific textbook on geological science. It included a classification of rocks and minerals. Many people gave thought to the actual origins of rocks and minerals. In 1669, **Niels Stensen** suggested that rocks are laid down in the ocean by sedimentation. His theory correctly suggested that the strata (layers) of sedimentary rocks provide a record of the Earth's history. He was also the first geologist to suggest that fossils were the remains of ancient plants and animals – this idea was crucial to Darwin's theory of evolution some 200 years later. During the 18th century, a debate raged between two rival theories of rock formation. Both theories involved Stenson's idea of sedimentation. One theory was that the Earth was originally covered with ocean and that all the rocks were laid down at the same time. The opposing theory involved a notion similar to the modern idea of the rock cycle. It claimed that the heat of the Earth forms lava, which solidifies to produce igneous rocks.

A CHINESE SEISMOGRAPH
Seismology originated in China. This seismograph is equipped with a brass ball that tumbles out from a dragon's head into a frog's mouth when the Earth is disturbed. The head from which the ball emerges points to where the earthquake has occurred.

Rain and rivers erode these igneous rocks, depositing them in the ocean, where they form sedimentary rocks. The heat of the Earth then melts the sedimentary rocks to form igneous rocks once again.

WATER CYCLE

Most ancient thinkers were aware of at least parts of the water cycle. **Aristotle** had reasoned that water becomes air as it evaporates and turns to water again in the air to form clouds. But like all philosophers of his time, he did not realize that this process transported enough water from the ocean to mountaintops to form rivers. Until the 17th century, most thinkers assumed that seawater was somehow transported to the mountains underground. It was not until scientists began making careful estimates of the weight of water at each stage of the water cycle – including measurements of the rate of evaporation – that the truth became clear. Some people, however, still disbelieved the claim that water from the oceans could form clouds. The invention of the air pump in the 17th century helped to convince them of evaporation, especially when artificial clouds were produced in laboratories by reducing the pressure of humid air to that of air at the level at which clouds form.

PLATE TECTONICS

Plate tectonics – the theory that the Earth's crust consists of several moving sections, or plates, which may be driven by convection currents in the mantle – rests

upon two main observations. In 1912, **Alfred Wegener** observed that separate continents looked as if they were once joined. He suggested that the continents had once been connected together, forming one vast landmass, which he called Pangaea. This continental drift theory accounted for many puzzling observations. For example, it had been noted that fossils of ancient animals that lived about 200 million years ago were found in Africa and Australia. The fossil records of these two landmasses are different only where they are records of later periods in the Earth's history. Living things in the two regions would have evolved differently after the continents split, explaining the inconsistency of the fossil record since then. The second observation came in 1960, when the seabed was shown to be spreading in certain places. The rate of this seabed spreading has been measured with extreme accuracy using global positioning satellites. Later, in the 1960s, Canadian geologist **John Tuzo Wilson** revived Wegener's continental drift idea, combining it with seabed spreading and his own new theory of fault formation in the Earth's crust. The result was the plate tectonics theory, which revolutionized the geological sciences during the 1970s.

METEOROLOGY

Another area of the Earth sciences that advanced rapidly during the 20th century is meteorology, the study of weather. Scientific weather prediction dates back to the invention of the mercury barometer in the 17th century. Meteorologists noticed that local atmospheric pressure rose and fell before and after changes in the weather. However, these predictions were crude. More sophisticated predictions could be made only with knowledge of wind speed and direction, and with pressure and temperature measurements taken over a wide area. In the 19th century, the invention of the telegraph enabled the coordination of measurements from weather-monitoring stations across whole continents. New technology at the disposal of meteorologists during the 20th century includes weather balloons, weather radar, airplanes, and of course, satellites.

THE CIRCUMFERENTOR

This very highly decorated circumferentor was used to compare angles and so figure out how far away distant objects were. This proved particularly useful during early mapmaking. The example shown here was made in 1676.

TIMELINE OF DISCOVERIES

	550 BC	**Anaximander of Miletus** proposes that the Earth is a cylinder
Eratosthenes assumes the Earth to be spherical and figures out a fairly accurate value for its circumference	240 BC	
	AD 132	**Chang Heng** invents the first seismograph
Neils Stensen suggests that rocks are laid down in horizontal layers	1669	
	1735	**George Hadley** formulates theory of wind circulation in the Earth's atmosphere
Horace de Saussure coins the term "geology"	1779	
	1785	**James Hutton** suggests that geological processes are slow and continuous, and that the Earth has existed for millions of years
William Smith provides evidence for "faunal succession" – different plant fossils existing in different types of rocks – which leads to the idea of geological eras	1815	
	1822	**Friedrich Mohs** introduces his scale of hardness of minerals
Jean Louis Agassiz uses the term "Ice Age" when suggesting that Europe was once covered in glaciers	1857	
	1880	**John Milne** invents the modern seismograph
Analysis of waves in a violent earthquake leads **Richard Oldham** to suggest existence of the Earth's core	1897	
	1902	**Oliver Heaviside** suggests the existence of a layer of ions (charged particles) in the atmosphere. This layer is now called the ionosphere
Vilhelm Bjerknes pioneers scientific weather forecasting	1904	
	1912	**Alfred Wegener** proposes the theory of continental drift
Charles Fabry discovers the ozone layer	1913	
	1935	The Richter scale for measuring the magnitude of earthquakes is introduced by **Charles Richter** and **Beno Gutenberg**
Harry Hess develops the theory of plate tectonics	1962	

Geological time

THE EARTH FORMED SOME 4.6 billion years ago from
a vast cloud of gas and dust. At first, it glowed red-hot,
and the Earth's surface was a seething mass of volcanoes
and smoke (see pp. 274-275). Gradually, however, the
Earth began to cool, and its **atmosphere** began to clear
as rain fell and created oceans (see pp. 288-289).
The first microscopic life forms appeared almost
3.6 billion years ago. Some 3 billion years ago, large
continents began to form. These have changed shape
and fragmented continually ever since, as the Earth's
surface has shifted, forming rocks and breaking them
down again and again (see pp. 272-273). As plantlike
organisms called **algae** evolved and multiplied,
they added oxygen to the atmosphere; this allowed,
eventually, for more complex life forms to emerge,
marking the end of the Precambrian era – the long
Dark Age of the Earth's first 4 billion years.

RADIOCARBON DATING

Geologists use a technique called radiocarbon dating – which
relies on measurements of **radioactive** decay – in order to
determine the age of organic remains. Carbon-12 and carbon-14
are present in all living things, but carbon-14 decays into
nitrogen-14 at a known rate when an organism dies. After 5,730
years, half of the carbon-14 remains; after another 5,730 years,
only a quarter remains; and so on. Geologists arrive at a figure
by measuring the ratio of carbon-14 to carbon-12.

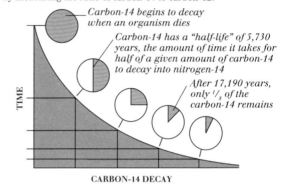

*Carbon-14 begins to decay
when an organism dies*

*Carbon-14 has a "half-life" of 5,730
years, the amount of time it takes for
half of a given amount of carbon-14
to decay into nitrogen-14*

*After 17,190 years,
only $1/8$ of the
carbon-14 remains*

TIME

CARBON-14 DECAY

FORMATION OF THE EARTH

The Earth probably formed as tiny pieces of
space debris called planetesimals gathered
together into a lump. This lump grew as more
space debris smashed into it. Among the
materials added by these impacts was water
ice, from the edge of the solar system.

EVOLUTION OF THE EARTH

Geologists know a great deal about how the
Earth, and life upon it, has changed over the
last 570 million years. They know this from
the fossilized remains of creatures buried over
time in layer upon layer of sediments. If these
sediments had remained undisturbed, it would

be possible to cut a column down through
the layers to reveal the entire sequence
right up to the present day. This sequence
is called the geological column. The illustration
below shows what the Earth would have been
like as each layer of sediment was laid down.

*The Earth formed
about 4.6 billion
years ago (bya)*

*An atmosphere formed
as the cooling Earth gave
off gases and water vapor*

*Rivers of red-hot
lava criss-cross
the Earth's surface*

*By 4 bya,
the Earth
had a crust
of solid rock*

*Surface water
appeared on
the Earth
about 3.9 bya*

PRECAMBRIAN ERA

Little is known about the first
4 billion years of the Earth's history,
but during this period the first
microscopic, single-celled life
forms appeared, then, much later,
multi-cellular, soft-bodied animals.

EARLIER PALEOZOIC ERA

Algae and **invertebrates** flourished in the oceans
and the first complex organisms appeared, followed
later by **crustaceans** and early fishlike **vertebrates**.
Around 438 mya, the continents began to
drift together slowly to form the supercontinent, Pangaea. Simple plants
began to colonize the land.

*Giant
tree fern*

*Icythyostega
(amphibian)*

*Cooksonia
(land plant)*

*Crinoid
(marine animal)*

*Single-celled
life form*

Trilobite

*PRECAMBRIAN ERA
4.6–0.5 billion years ago (bya)*

*Cambrian period
570–510 million
years ago (mya)*

*Ordovician period
510–438·mya*

*Silurian
period
438–410 my*

PALEOZOIC ERA

FOSSIL FORMATIONS

Fossils are the remains of living things preserved in rock. When a creature such as a shellfish falls onto the seafloor, its soft body tissue decays quickly, but its hard shell may be buried intact by sediments. Over millions of years, the shell may be preserved virtually unaltered. At other times, minerals forming the shell may dissolve, leaving a mold that is filled in with other minerals, thus preserving the original form.

Most fossils are of shellfish that lived in shallow seas, although many other types may be preserved

Fossils are destroyed by pressure and heat when they sink to a certain depth

Water

Soft sediment

Compacted sediment

Metamorphic rock

INDEX FOSSILS

Most fossils are of small, shelled sea creatures, because these creatures have a high chance of fossilization when their shells become buried in the seafloor. Particularly important are index fossils, which are used to date rocks because they are abundant, easy to identify, and appear only in particular time periods. Examples of index fossils include ammonites (of the Jurassic and Cretaceous periods) and trilobites (of the Cambrian period).

Trilobite fossil from the Cambrian period

The trilobite is an extinct sea creature with a hard, flexible shell divided into three parts

LATER PALAEOZOIC ERA

Arthropods appeared on land, and fish swarmed the sea. Spore-bearing plants grew as big as trees, and the first amphibians appeared. By 355 mya, vast forests flourished in river deltas, eventually forming coal deposits. By 290 mya, the first reptiles had appeared. Pangaea formed from the collision of Laurasia and Gondwana, and the world climate cooled as ocean currents were disrupted by **tectonic-plate** movement.

Homo sapiens (modern human)

Large mammal

Small mammal

Dinosaur

Marine reptile

Early conifer

vonian period –355 mya

Carboniferous period 355–290 mya

Permian period 290–250 mya

Triassic period 250–205 mya

Jurassic period 205–135 mya

Cretaceous period 135–66 mya

MESOZOIC ERA

Tertiary period 66–1.6 mya

Quaternary period 1.6 mya–now

CENOZOIC ERA

MESOZOIC ERA

The era began with the mass extinction of around 90 percent of all species. Seed-bearing plants began to dominate. The Jurassic period was the era of the dinosaurs. By the late Jurassic, *Archaeopteryx*, the first bird, had evolved. The Atlantic Ocean began to form, dividing Pangaea. After 135 mya, flowering plants and small mammals appeared, and oil and gas deposits began to form from the remains of sea creatures. The dinosaurs died out suddenly at the end of the era.

CENOZOIC ERA

Mammals began to diversify widely. Primates evolved, grasslands expanded, birds flourished, and the continents took on their present form. Habitats continued to alter with the shift of the continents and the changes in climate. Modern humans appeared toward the end of the era.

The Earth

THE EARTH IS A not-quite-perfect sphere of rock with a metal core, wrapped in a blanket of gases called the **atmosphere**. It is 12,756 kilometers in diameter and 40,075 kilometers in circumference (at the equator). It orbits the Sun once every 365.242 days, traveling 939,886,400 kilometers, and rotates on its axis once every 24 hours, spinning much faster at the equator than at the poles. The result is that the planet bulges slightly at the equator and is flattened at the poles. The Earth is the only planet in the solar system (see pp. 304-305) that is known to support life. This is because, unlike the other planets, there is an abundance of liquid water on the Earth's surface, and a significant amount of oxygen in its atmosphere.

ROCKS FROM SPACE

The Earth is made of material similar to that of meteorites (see pp. 322-323). Meteorites usually consist of silicate materials similar to those of the Earth's mantle (stony meteorites) or iron, like the Earth's core (iron meteorites).

A chondrite (a type of stony meteorite)

STRUCTURE OF THE EARTH

The Earth has four main layers. The inner and outer cores are metallic, composed mostly of iron. The mantle is made from silicate minerals. Its lower part is made from solid, closely packed crystals. Its upper part is partially molten and is the source of most of the Earth's **magma**. The crust is the thin outer layer. The interior of the Earth is hot. This heat is left over from the time of the Earth's formation and is added to by **nuclear reactions** deep inside the planet.

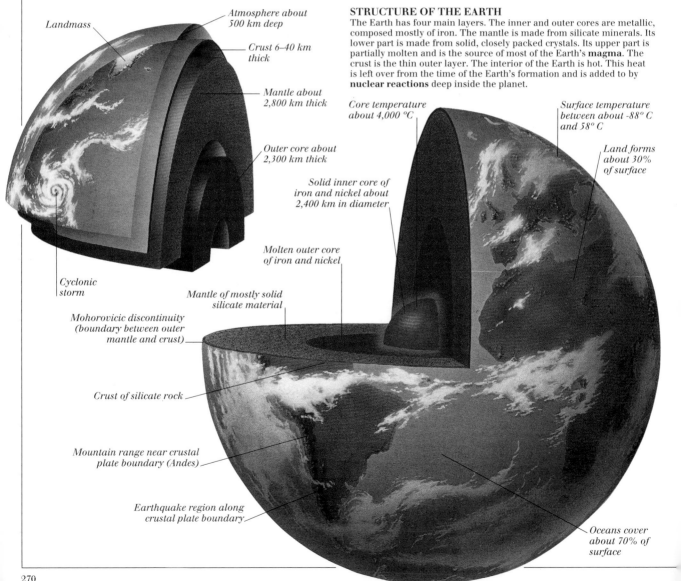

Landmass

Atmosphere about 500 km deep

Crust 6–40 km thick

Mantle about 2,800 km thick

Outer core about 2,300 km thick

Core temperature about 4,000 °C

Surface temperature between about -88° C and 58° C

Land forms about 30% of surface

Solid inner core of iron and nickel about 2,400 km in diameter

Molten outer core of iron and nickel

Cyclonic storm

Mantle of mostly solid silicate material

Mohorovicic discontinuity (boundary between outer mantle and crust)

Crust of silicate rock

Mountain range near crustal plate boundary (Andes)

Earthquake region along crustal plate boundary

Oceans cover about 70% of surface

SEASONAL CHANGE

The Earth's axis is tilted at an angle of 23.5° to the Sun. As the Earth orbits the Sun, different zones of the Earth lean in turn gradually nearer to the Sun and then farther away, creating four distinct phases, or seasons.

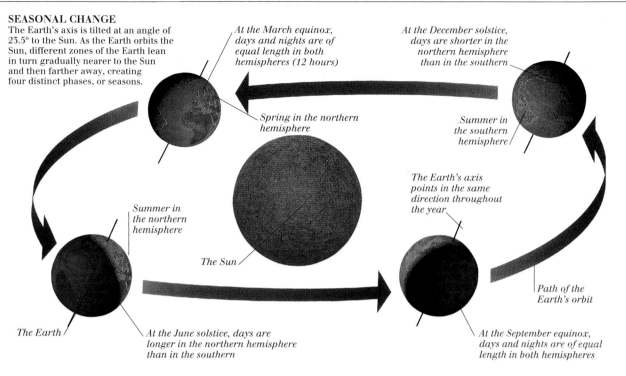

At the March equinox, days and nights are of equal length in both hemispheres (12 hours)

At the December solstice, days are shorter in the northern hemisphere than in the southern

Spring in the northern hemisphere

Summer in the southern hemisphere

The Earth's axis points in the same direction throughout the year

Summer in the northern hemisphere

The Sun

Path of the Earth's orbit

The Earth

At the June solstice, days are longer in the northern hemisphere than in the southern

At the September equinox, days and nights are of equal length in both hemispheres

THE EARTH'S MAGNETIC FIELD

THE EARTH'S MAGNETOSPHERE

The Earth's magnetic field affects electrically charged particles in a region called the magnetosphere, which extends up to 60,000 km into space. The magnetosphere is "stretched" far out into space by the solar wind, a stream of charged particles emanating from the Sun.

THE EARTH'S MAGNETIC POLES

The Earth's magnetic field is created by convection currents in the molten outer core. These are continuously cycling and create electrical currents, which turn the planet into a giant magnet. Like a bar magnet, the Earth has two magnetic poles, which are situated near to the geographic North and South Poles.

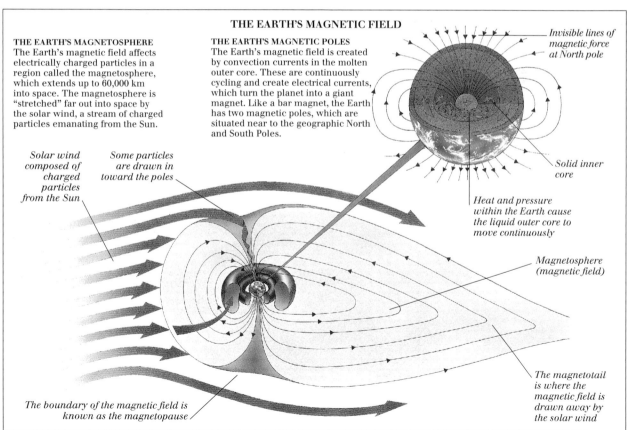

Invisible lines of magnetic force at North pole

Solid inner core

Heat and pressure within the Earth cause the liquid outer core to move continuously

Solar wind composed of charged particles from the Sun

Some particles are drawn in toward the poles

Magnetosphere (magnetic field)

The magnetotail is where the magnetic field is drawn away by the solar wind

The boundary of the magnetic field is known as the magnetopause

Plate tectonics

THE EARTH'S OUTER SHELL, or **lithosphere**, is not a single, solid piece, but is cracked, like a broken eggshell, into a number of giant fragments called tectonic plates. These are composed of crust and the upper part of the mantle. The continents are embedded in these plates, which are moving slowly but inexorably – pulling apart, smashing together, or sliding past each other. As they jostle to and fro, they split continents apart and open up new oceans – all of the world's continents were once joined in a single supercontinent called Pangaea. They can also push continents together, crumpling up layers of rock into giant mountain ranges. The interaction of the tectonic plates is also behind some of the world's most spectacular natural events, such as earthquakes, which are set off by tectonic plates rumbling past each other, and volcanic eruptions, most of which occur where one plate meets another (see pp. 274-275).

CONVECTION CURRENTS

The movement of the tectonic plates may be driven by the slow churning of the mantle. Mantle rock is constantly being driven up toward the surface by the enormous temperatures below, which generate huge convection currents that extend right through the mantle. As it nears the surface, the mantle rock then cools and sinks back down. This whole process takes place over millions of years.

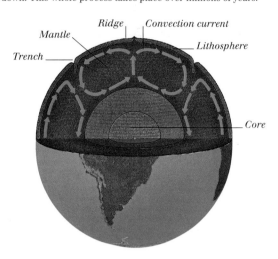

MAJOR PLATES OF THE EARTH'S CRUST

The rigid surface of the Earth is split into around eight large plates and ten or so smaller ones. The continents are formed from thick pieces of crust, which are embedded in the lithospheric plates and ride around on them as if on a raft. Oceanic crust is much thinner. The movement of these plates is very slow in human terms, but can be quite rapid in geological terms (see pp. 268-269). The gradual pulling apart of the Eurasian and North American plates is currently widening the Atlantic Ocean by around 20 mm every year.

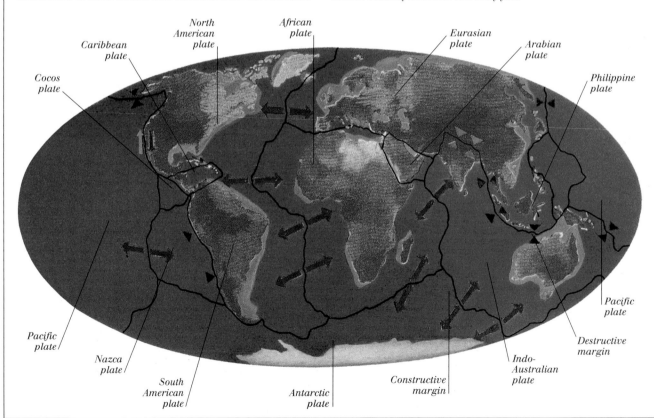

CONVERGING AND DIVERGING PLATES

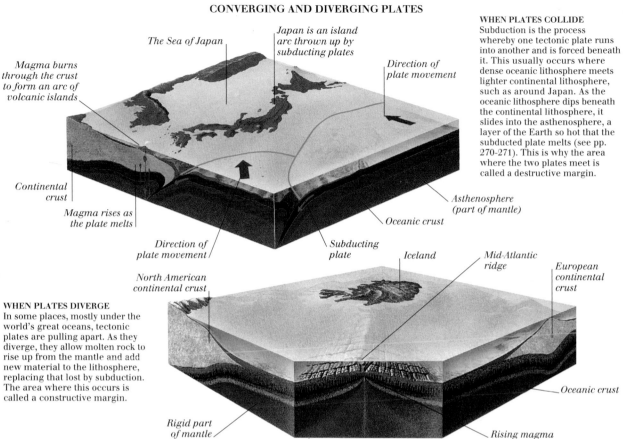

The Sea of Japan

Japan is an island arc thrown up by subducting plates

Direction of plate movement

Magma burns through the crust to form an arc of volcanic islands

Continental crust

Magma rises as the plate melts

Direction of plate movement

Subducting plate

Asthenosphere (part of mantle)

Oceanic crust

WHEN PLATES COLLIDE
Subduction is the process whereby one tectonic plate runs into another and is forced beneath it. This usually occurs where dense oceanic lithosphere meets lighter continental lithosphere, such as around Japan. As the oceanic lithosphere dips beneath the continental lithosphere, it slides into the asthenosphere, a layer of the Earth so hot that the subducted plate melts (see pp. 270-271). This is why the area where the two plates meet is called a destructive margin.

North American continental crust

Iceland

Mid-Atlantic ridge

European continental crust

WHEN PLATES DIVERGE
In some places, mostly under the world's great oceans, tectonic plates are pulling apart. As they diverge, they allow molten rock to rise up from the mantle and add new material to the lithosphere, replacing that lost by subduction. The area where this occurs is called a constructive margin.

Oceanic crust

Rigid part of mantle

Rising magma

THE DEVELOPMENT OF THE CONTINENTS

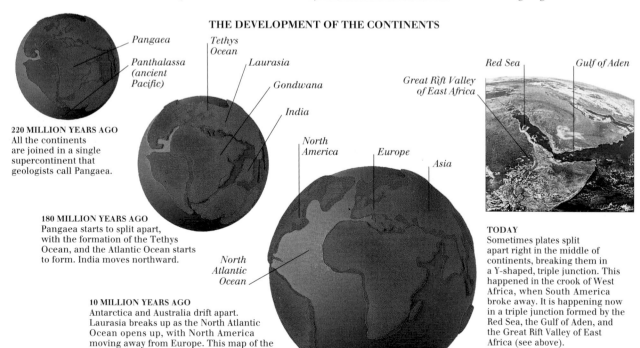

Pangaea

Panthalassa (ancient Pacific)

Tethys Ocean

Laurasia

Gondwana

India

North America

Europe

Asia

Great Rift Valley of East Africa

Red Sea

Gulf of Aden

220 MILLION YEARS AGO
All the continents are joined in a single supercontinent that geologists call Pangaea.

180 MILLION YEARS AGO
Pangaea starts to split apart, with the formation of the Tethys Ocean, and the Atlantic Ocean starts to form. India moves northward.

North Atlantic Ocean

10 MILLION YEARS AGO
Antarctica and Australia drift apart. Laurasia breaks up as the North Atlantic Ocean opens up, with North America moving away from Europe. This map of the world looks similar to the one we know today.

TODAY
Sometimes plates split apart right in the middle of continents, breaking them in a Y-shaped, triple junction. This happened in the crook of West Africa, when South America broke away. It is happening now in a triple junction formed by the Red Sea, the Gulf of Aden, and the Great Rift Valley of East Africa (see above).

Earthquakes and volcanoes

THE CONTINUAL MOVEMENT of the gigantic plates that make up the Earth's surface creates two kinds of disturbance – earthquakes and volcanoes (see pp. 274-275). Earthquakes start as the plates rumble past each other, sending shock waves radiating through the ground. There are over a million earthquakes a year around the world. Most are so small that they can hardly be felt, but a few are so violent that they can cause extensive damage over a wide area (see Richter/Mercalli Scale in Useful data). Volcanoes, too, are very variable. (A volcano is a place where molten rock from the Earth's red-hot interior forces its way to the surface.) In some places, the molten rock emerges slowly and gently. In others, it explodes onto the surface in a violent eruption.

EARTHQUAKE AND VOLCANO LOCATIONS

Most earthquake and volcano activity is concentrated along the boundaries of the Earth's tectonic plates – where the plates are crunching together, breaking apart, or rumbling past each other. The Pacific Ocean forms one large plate and its edges, known as the "ring of fire," have more earthquakes and land-based volcanoes than anywhere else in the world.

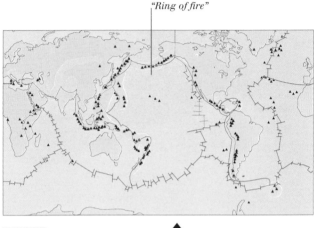

"Ring of fire"

▢ Earthquake zone   ▲ Volcanoes

STRUCTURE OF AN EARTHQUAKE

Fast-moving P- or pressure waves pass through the Earth's mantle and core

Mantle

Inner core

Outer core

Earthquake focus

Slow-moving S (secondary) waves pass only through the Earth's mantle

Plates can often jam as they slide past each other, so stress builds up until the rock cracks and the plates rumble on, sending out shock waves

P-waves are refracted by the Earth's core, creating shadow zones where no waves are received

SEISMIC WAVES

Earthquake damage occurs as the result of seismic waves at the surface of the planet. Waves that occur far below ground can travel right through the body of the Earth. Geologists record these "body" waves on seismographs stationed around the world, and have been able to build up a detailed picture of the Earth's interior by analyzing the way in which these waves are deflected.

MEASURING EARTHQUAKES

Seismometers monitor seismic waves at strategic points around the world. The information gathered is transmitted to a recording station, where it triggers a seismograph. This records changes in seismic waves, most commonly as a recorded signal.

As the shock waves travel away from the epicenter, destruction diminishes

Damage is greatest at the epicenter

Hypocenter or focus

HOW AN EARTHQUAKE WORKS

The vibrations of an earthquake radiate out from a point underground called the hypocenter, or focus, which may be anything from just a few hundred meters to around 700 km below the surface. It is only when the vibrations reach the surface that they begin to do any real damage. The surface vibrations ripple out from a point directly above the hypocenter called the epicenter.

STRUCTURE OF A VOLCANO

Many explosive volcanoes are built up into a cone by the debris of successive eruptions. Deep beneath the volcano is a reservoir of hot, molten rock, called the magma chamber. Above the chamber is a vent leading to the neck of the volcano. This vent can become clogged because the lava may solidify. Pressure on this plug of lava builds as magma wells up into the chamber, until it is finally blasted away and the magma is forced up the vent.

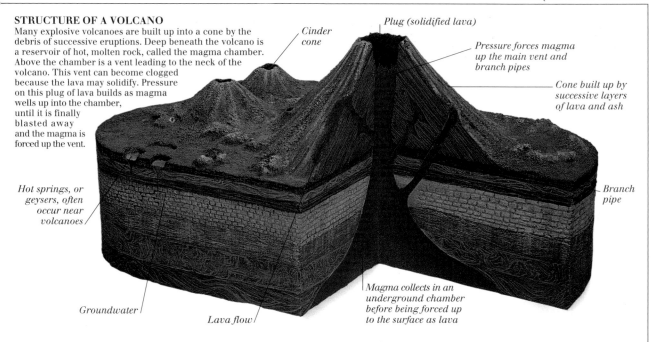

Cinder cone

Plug (solidified lava)

Pressure forces magma up the main vent and branch pipes

Cone built up by successive layers of lava and ash

Branch pipe

Hot springs, or geysers, often occur near volcanoes

Magma collects in an underground chamber before being forced up to the surface as lava

Groundwater

Lava flow

TYPES OF VOLCANOES

The shape of a volcano depends mainly on the type of lava it produces. Basaltic lava is runny because it erupts at high temperatures and contains little silica. It forms low volcanoes with gentle slopes. Acidic lava is thick because it erupts at lower temperatures and has a higher silica content. It forms steep-sided or even domed volcanoes. Many acidic lavas are explosive and so some volcanoes may be built partially of volcanic ashes.

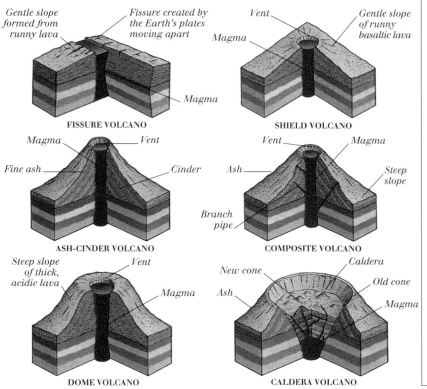

Gentle slope formed from runny lava

Fissure created by the Earth's plates moving apart

Magma

FISSURE VOLCANO

Vent

Magma

Gentle slope of runny basaltic lava

SHIELD VOLCANO

Magma

Vent

Fine ash

Cinder

ASH-CINDER VOLCANO

Vent

Magma

Ash

Steep slope

Branch pipe

COMPOSITE VOLCANO

Steep slope of thick, acidic lava

Vent

Magma

DOME VOLCANO

New cone

Ash

Caldera

Old cone

Magma

CALDERA VOLCANO

VOLCANIC FEATURES

In certain parts of the world (most notably Iceland), volcanic activity beneath the surface heats up water on and below the ground. This can create spectacular volcanic landscapes, where hot water, mud, and gases emerge from the ground.

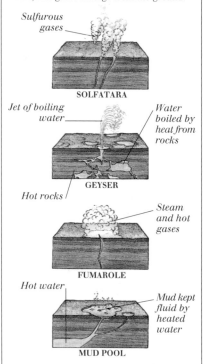

Sulfurous gases

SOLFATARA

Jet of boiling water

Water boiled by heat from rocks

Hot rocks

GEYSER

Steam and hot gases

FUMAROLE

Hot water

Mud kept fluid by heated water

MUD POOL

Faults and folds

AS THE TECTONIC PLATES (see pp. 272-273) that make up the Earth's surface move about, they can put rocks under huge strain. Sometimes the rocks crack, so that large blocks can slip past each other, producing faults that break up the landscape. In many cases, the plates crunch together, crumpling and twisting the rock **strata** into folds of all shapes and sizes, from tiny wrinkles just a few centimeters long to gigantic folds thousands of meters high. Both faulting and folding can be caused by events such as earthquakes (see pp. 274-275) or landslides, but it is **tectonic-plate** movement that is responsible for the most dramatic faults and folds. Tectonic-plate movement has created the faults that opened up the world's longest valley, the Great Rift Valley of East Africa. It has also folded rock layers to pile up the world's greatest mountain ranges, including the Himalayas, the Andes, the Rockies, and the Alps.

SAN ANDREAS FAULT
Perhaps the most famous fault in the world is the San Andreas Fault in California. This is a type of wrench fault called a transcurrent fault, which occurs when two tectonic plates slip sideways past each other.

DESCRIBING A FAULT
A fault is described in terms of the geometry of its movement – its direction, angle, and extent. The surface of the fault along which the rock slips is called the fault plane. The rock will slip only a few centimeters at a time, but the cumulative effect of numerous slips over millions of years can be that blocks are moved hundreds or even thousands of meters up or down.

Dip (angle of fault plane to the horizontal)

Fault plane

Heave (sideways shift)

Horizontal shearing across vertical fault plane

Fault block

NORMAL FAULT
A normal fault is one in which blocks of rock slip straight down. It occurs where tension in the Earth's crust fractures rock and allows blocks to slip down by gravity in line with the dip of the fault plane. This is why it is also called a dip-slip fault.

Hade (angle of the fault plane to the vertical)

WRENCH FAULT
A wrench fault, also known as a tear fault, occurs when fault blocks move horizontally past each other, with no vertical movement.

Fault scarp (huge cliff exposed as graben drops)

Graben

Horst (a block of rock thrown up between normal faults)

Reverse fault

Normal fault

RIFT VALLEY
Rift valleys probably form when a block of rock (called a graben) drops down between two facing normal faults. These eventually form cliffs, or fault **scarps**. The world's most dramatic rift valley is the Great Rift Valley of East Africa.

COMPLEX FAULT
Faults very rarely occur singly. Most occur in fault zones along plate margins. The result is often a series of faults, which tilt blocks in many different directions.

DESCRIBING A FOLD

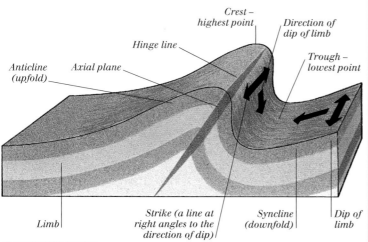

FOLD TERMINOLOGY

Geologists use many technical terms to describe the geometry and different parts of a fold. The hinge line is the "crease" of a fold. The term dip refers to the angle, in degrees, between the tilted layers of rock and the horizontal plane. Limb is the term given to the strata (layers of rock) on either side of a fold. An anticline is an arch-shaped upfold and a syncline is a bowl-shaped downfold. The axial plane is an imaginary plane halfway between the limbs of a fold.

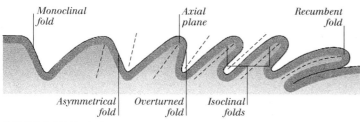

DIFFERENT TYPES OF FOLDS

Folds vary in complexity, depending on the intensity of the force causing the rock to have become deformed. As the fold becomes progressively more deformed, it may pass through the stages from a monoclinal fold to an asymmetrical fold, then an overturned fold, and finally a recumbent fold. Isoclinal folds form after repeated tight folding produces two or more parallel folds.

MOUNTAIN BUILDING

Most of the world's great mountain ranges were built by the crumpling of rock layers as tectonic plates crashed into each other at the edge of continents. This is why the great fold-mountain systems of the world lie along the edges of colliding plates. The Andes, for example, have formed where the Nazca plate (see pp. 272-273) runs into South America, and the Himalayas rise where the Indo-Australian plate runs into Asia. This demonstration, which substitutes layers of colored clay for rock strata, shows what happens when one plate is forced below another (subducted), crumpling the crustal rocks.

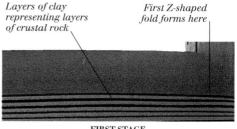

FIRST STAGE

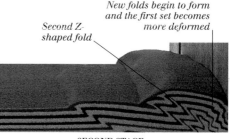

SECOND STAGE

FINAL STAGE

HEAVILY FOLDED ROCK

Where oceanic crust meets less dense continental crust, the oceanic crust is forced under the continental crust. This is then buckled by the impact, and fold mountains occur. Such buckling is clearly visible here in the face of the mountains of Picos de Vallibierna in the Pyrenees in northeast Spain.

Rocks and minerals

THE EARTH IS MADE UP OF ROCKS, and rocks are made up of minerals. Minerals have a specific chemical composition – sometimes a single **element**, but usually a chemical **compound** – and a unique **crystal** structure (see pp. 34-35). Mineral types may be distinguished by certain distinctive physical properties, such as hardness. Rocks are composed of one or more minerals, and the way in which the minerals are combined is a clue to the way in which rocks have been formed. Rocks are products of natural processes, which have created (and continue to change) the Earth and its surface. There are three main types of rocks, which are continuously recycled by the Earth. Igneous rocks are composed of interlocking crystals produced during the cooling of molten **magmas** derived from within the Earth. Sedimentary rocks are commonly formed through the accumulation of particles of many sizes, which have been eroded from other rocks exposed at the surface of the Earth. Metamorphic rocks are formed by the heat and pressure generated by tectonic-plate movement in the Earth's crust (see pp. 272-273).

STAGES IN THE ROCK CYCLE

Igneous rocks are often formed by the cooling of lavas that have erupted from volcanoes. These rocks are eroded through the actions of wind, water, and ice. The resulting particles are carried along in a variety of ways and are ultimately deposited by rivers as layers of sediment, which are then compacted under the weight of other layers of sediment to form sedimentary rocks. Metamorphic rocks are created through the heating and crushing of igneous and sedimentary rocks in the Earth's crust.

Waterfalls erode rock

Glaciers erode rock and carry the rock particles to rivers

Magma emerges as lava and solidifies to form rock

Volcano

Rising magma melts the surrounding rock

Heat and pressure change sedimentary rock into metamorphic rock

THE ROCK CYCLE

The rock cycle starts when molten magma from the Earth's interior cools and solidifies, forming igneous rocks. Sediments may be eroded from igneous rocks exposed at the surface and then compacted and cemented to form sedimentary rocks. Metamorphism occurs when existing rocks are deformed or carried down into the Earth to be remelted, forming magmas. The cooling of these magmas starts the cycle once again.

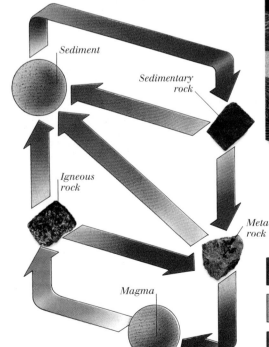

Sediment

Sedimentary rock

Igneous rock

Metamorphic rock

Magma

MELTING

CRYSTAL-LIZATION

WEATHERING

METAMORPHISM

LITHIFICATION (COMPRESSION AND CEMENTATION)

ROCK FORMATION

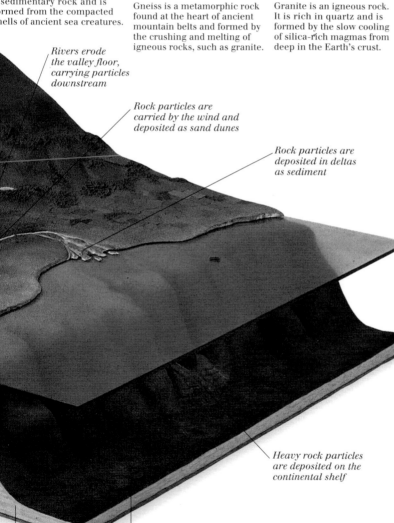

Shelly limestone

Gneiss

Granite

SEDIMENTARY ROCK
Shelly limestone is composed of one mineral – calcite. It is a sedimentary rock and is formed from the compacted shells of ancient sea creatures.

METAMORPHIC ROCK
Gneiss is a metamorphic rock found at the heart of ancient mountain belts and formed by the crushing and melting of igneous rocks, such as granite.

IGNEOUS ROCK
Granite is an igneous rock. It is rich in quartz and is formed by the slow cooling of silica-rich magmas from deep in the Earth's crust.

Rivers erode the valley floor, carrying particles downstream

Rock particles are carried by the wind and deposited as sand dunes

Rock particles are deposited in deltas as sediment

Heavy rock particles are deposited on the continental shelf

Light rock particles settle on the seabed as sediment

Sediments are compressed, forming layers of sedimentary rock

MOHS' SCALE OF HARDNESS
Mohs' scale of hardness, which is used to distinguish mineral types, depends simply on the ability of one mineral to scratch another. There are ten minerals in the scale. The hardest, diamond (at 10), will scratch all the other minerals on the scale. Quartz, with a hardness of 7, is fairly hard (it cannot be scratched by the steel of a knife blade). The softest minerals, talc (1) and gypsum (2), can both be scratched with a fingernail.

Talc (1)

Gypsum (2)

Calcite (3)

Fluorite (4)

Apatite (5)

Orthoclase (6)

Quartz (7)

Topaz (8)

Corundum (9)

Diamond (10)

Rocky landscapes

WEATHERING AND EROSION break down the geological materials of the Earth's surface, producing a range of rocky features. Physical weathering results in the mechanical breakdown of rocks. This is achieved through the expansion and growth of **crystals** of salt or ice in spaces in the rock, and by the invasive growth of plant roots. Chemical weathering results in the **decomposition** or **solution** of the minerals that form the rock (see pp. 278-279). For example, limestone is commonly dissolved by acidic **groundwaters**. Rocks composed of several minerals may be significantly weakened by the chemical decomposition of those minerals susceptible to attack. By contrast, erosion is the physical wearing away of exposed rock or soils through the action of wind, water, and ice. Erosion is common where there is little vegetation to bind and protect the land surface, such as in deserts. Here, sand held in suspension in the air actually wears down exposed surfaces and may also be deposited in sand dunes.

SAND BLASTING
The abrasive action of sand carried by the wind is a very important agent of erosion. Typically, most sand is carried in those winds close to the land surface. Continuous "sand blasting" will leave large rocks apparently balanced on a narrow neck.

FEATURES OF ROCKY LANDSCAPES
Arid landscapes are particularly susceptible to the processes of weathering and erosion, as there is little vegetation to protect the barren landscape. Physical weathering occurs as a result of the expansion and contraction of rock surfaces caused by the heat of the day and the cool of the night. This creates scree slopes, huge piles of rock fragments found at the bottom of rock faces. The abrasive action of sand carried by winds erodes weaker rocks to produce landforms such as mesas and buttes. Sands eroded from the surface may later be deposited in dunes, landforms that are continually modified by the action of the wind.

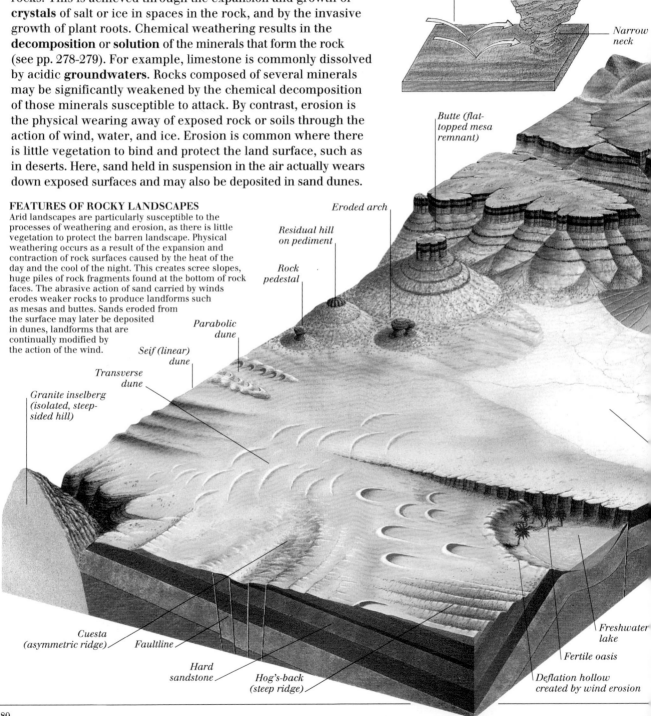

Wind-blown sand

Mushroom-shaped rock

Narrow neck

Butte (flat-topped mesa remnant)

Eroded arch

Residual hill on pediment

Rock pedestal

Parabolic dune

Seif (linear) dune

Transverse dune

Granite inselberg (isolated, steep-sided hill)

Cuesta (asymmetric ridge)

Faultline

Hard sandstone

Hog's-back (steep ridge)

Freshwater lake

Fertile oasis

Deflation hollow created by wind erosion

TORS

Rock outcrops that stand out on all sides from the surrounding slopes are known as tors. Tors are formed mostly in crystalline rocks with deep fractures or joints, such as granite. Intense chemical weathering along the joints attacks and breaks down some of the constituent minerals of the granite. Later, erosion strips away the weathered granite, leaving unweathered blocks protruding from the newly eroded surface. Eventually, these unweathered blocks will wear away, too.

Granite tor

Eroded rock

Grassy surface with boulders

GORGE FORMATION

Deep gorges are common in limestone areas. Caves develop when the limestone is dissolved by the concentrated flow of acid-rich waters. If an entire system of interlinked caves collapses, a long, rocky-walled valley (called a gorge) is created. In some big gorges, there is no evidence of rubble from the collapsed cave roofs. Some experts think these gorges were, therefore, cut by powerful rivers when the Earth's climate was wetter than it is today.

Below the surface, the stream eats away the limestone along the fault line

FIRST STAGE

Gradually the water opens up caves and caverns

SECOND STAGE

The water enlarges the caves and caverns, forming a huge cavity

THIRD STAGE

Eventually the roof falls in, creating a gorge

FINAL STAGE

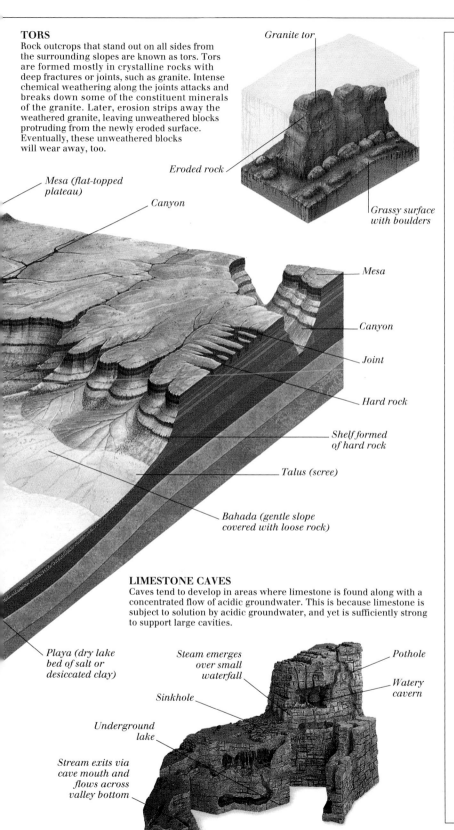

Mesa (flat-topped plateau)

Canyon

Mesa

Canyon

Joint

Hard rock

Shelf formed of hard rock

Talus (scree)

Bahada (gentle slope covered with loose rock)

LIMESTONE CAVES

Caves tend to develop in areas where limestone is found along with a concentrated flow of acidic groundwater. This is because limestone is subject to solution by acidic groundwater, and yet is sufficiently strong to support large cavities.

Playa (dry lake bed of salt or desiccated clay)

Steam emerges over small waterfall

Pothole

Watery cavern

Sinkhole

Underground lake

Stream exits via cave mouth and flows across valley bottom

Glaciers and ice sheets

GLACIERS ARE SLOW-MOVING masses of snow and ice. The most familiar are those in mountain valleys, developing from the accumulation of snow at the head of the valley, which is cooler because of its higher **altitude**. Here, successive layers of winter snow compress previous snowfalls to form granular ice, called firn, which is then finally compressed to become more dense. Such valley glaciers flow to lower altitudes at a typical rate of about two meters per day. Icebergs may be formed where the glacier flows into the sea or a lake. In high **latitudes**, close to the poles, glaciers may be extensive, covering much of the landscape. These glaciers are known as ice sheets or continental glaciers, and typical examples are seen in Antarctica and Greenland. They are domed and flow outward in all directions, replenished by fresh winter snowfalls.

RIVERS OF ICE
Glaciers often combine to form a massive, sluggish flow. For glaciers to grow, more snow must accumulate on the upper reaches than is lost by melting near the ends. This ongoing process is what drives glaciers forward.

FEATURES OF A GLACIER
Valley glaciers usually form high in the mountains from an ice-worn hollow known as a cirque, corrie, or cwm. The glaciers flow gradually down the valley to lowland areas. Variations in the rate of flow of different parts of the glacier produce deep cracks known as crevasses. As the glacier flows, it scours a new shape for the valley bottom and dumps piles of eroded sediments, called moraines.

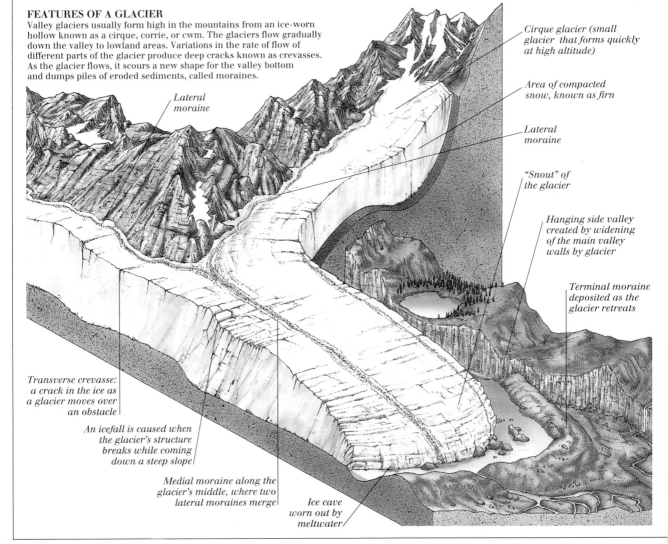

Lateral moraine

Cirque glacier (small glacier that forms quickly at high altitude)

Area of compacted snow, known as firn

Lateral moraine

"Snout" of the glacier

Hanging side valley created by widening of the main valley walls by glacier

Terminal moraine deposited as the glacier retreats

Transverse crevasse: a crack in the ice as a glacier moves over an obstacle

An icefall is caused when the glacier's structure breaks while coming down a steep slope

Medial moraine along the glacier's middle, where two lateral moraines merge

Ice cave worn out by meltwater

ICE SHEETS

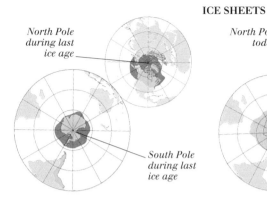

North Pole
during last
ice age

South Pole
during last
ice age

North Pole
today

South Pole
today

COURSE OF ICE AGES
Today's polar ice caps started forming
10 million years ago, probably because
of a grouping of continents in the polar
regions, which prevented the warming
effect of the oceans. Current variations in
the extent of the ice caps may be caused
by regular variations in the Earth's **axial
tilt** and **orbital** shape.

Earth's
axis today

Earth's axis
during last
ice age

CHANGES IN THE EARTH'S AXIAL TILT

THE POLES DURING THE LAST ICE AGE
During the last Ice Age, ice sheets extended
from the polar regions to the midlatitudes,
covering much of Canada and northern Europe
in the northern hemisphere, and extending
well beyond Antarctica in the southern
hemisphere.

THE POLES TODAY
Although we are still technically within an Ice
Age, major ice sheets are limited to Antarctica,
which has 90 percent of the world's ice, and
Greenland. It is possible that midlatitude ice
sheets may return over the next 10,000 years.

GLACIAL EROSION AND DEPOSITION

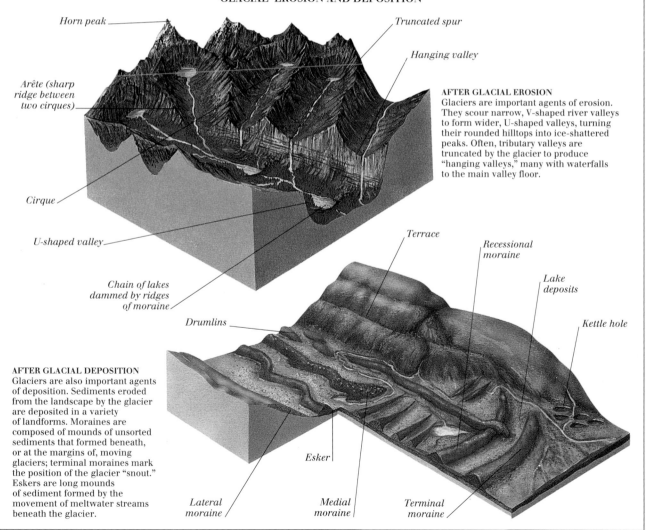

Horn peak

Truncated spur

Hanging valley

Arête (sharp
ridge between
two cirques)

AFTER GLACIAL EROSION
Glaciers are important agents of erosion.
They scour narrow, V-shaped river valleys
to form wider, U-shaped valleys, turning
their rounded hilltops into ice-shattered
peaks. Often, tributary valleys are
truncated by the glacier to produce
"hanging valleys," many with waterfalls
to the main valley floor.

Cirque

U-shaped valley

Chain of lakes
dammed by ridges
of moraine

Terrace

Recessional
moraine

Lake
deposits

Kettle hole

Drumlins

AFTER GLACIAL DEPOSITION
Glaciers are also important agents
of deposition. Sediments eroded
from the landscape by the glacier
are deposited in a variety
of landforms. Moraines are
composed of mounds of unsorted
sediments that formed beneath,
or at the margins of, moving
glaciers; terminal moraines mark
the position of the glacier "snout."
Eskers are long mounds
of sediment formed by the
movement of meltwater streams
beneath the glacier.

Esker

Lateral
moraine

Medial
moraine

Terminal
moraine

283

Rivers

RIVERS PERFORM AN IMPORTANT role in the continuous circulation of water between the land, the sea, and the **atmosphere** (see pp. 172-173). Wherever there is enough rain, rivers flow overland from the mountains down to the sea, or to a lake. The flow varies according to the **rainfall pattern**, and while some rivers are perennial (flowing year round), others, in dry areas, may be ephemeral (usually dry). Typically, a river begins as a trickle high up in the hills before growing into a **rill**, then a stream, and finally a river. Running water has considerable **erosive** power, especially when carrying sand and other debris. Because of this, the river gradually carves a channel out of the landscape, then a valley, and eventually – as it nears the sea – a broad plain. Although no one is quite sure why, all rivers have a tendency to wind, with bends in the lower reaches of the river developing into elaborate, often symmetrical, loops called meanders.

RUNNING WATER

When rain falls on the landscape, most of the water either soaks into the ground or runs off over the surface; the rest **evaporates** or is taken up by plants. Water that runs over the surface (overland flow) gathers into tiny rivulets and eventually into rivers. When the rain is heavy, the overland flow may flood across the land as a thin sheet of water (called sheetwash) before it gathers into streams and rivers. Some of the water that sinks into the ground (groundwater) will flow into rivers eventually too, emerging from lower down the hillside through springs.

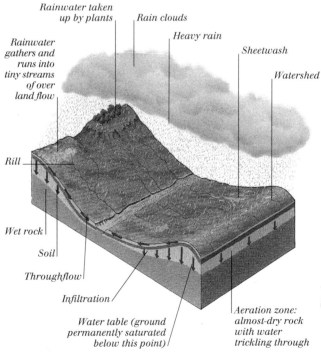

Rainwater taken up by plants

Rain clouds

Heavy rain

Sheetwash

Watershed

Rainwater gathers and runs into tiny streams of over land flow

Rill

Wet rock

Soil

Throughflow

Infiltration

Water table (ground permanently saturated below this point)

Aeration zone: almost-dry rock with water trickling through

RIVER COURSE

In its upper reaches, a river is small and typically tumbles down over rapids and waterfalls between steep valley sides. Further down, the river gets wider and begins to flow more smoothly as tributaries bring in more water. Just as tributaries bring in more water, so they bring in more silt, which is washed off the land or worn away from the river banks. As it reaches the sea, it may flow into a wide tidal estuary, or split into branches and build out a delta.

Source of spring

Plunge pool

Waterfall

V-shaped valley with steep sides

Rapids

The valley broadens as the river begins to wind

Slip-off slope on inside of meander

STORM HYDROGRAPH

In most damp areas, the seeping of water from underground keeps rivers flowing steadily throughout the year. But rainstorms provide short-lived peak flows as the ground becomes saturated and water flows overland into the river. Because overland flow takes time to reach the river, there is a delay, or lag, before the flow peaks. This peak can be shown on a graph called a storm hydrograph.

Discharge

Time (hours since storm began)

FORMATION OF A WATERFALL

Riverbeds usually slope gradually, but can drop suddenly in places. The place where this occurs is called a waterfall. Waterfalls are formed where a river flows from hard rock to softer, more easily eroded rock. The river cuts back through the soft rock, and water pours over the ledge of hard rock into a plunge pool below.

TRANSPORTATION OF LOAD

A river is capable of sweeping along considerable quantities of sediment. The greater the river's flow, the more sediment it can carry. The Yellow River in China, for example, gets its name because it carries so much silt that its waters are turned yellow. A river carries its load of sediment in three different ways: stones rolled along the riverbed (bedload); grit and sand (also called bedload) bounced along the bed (a process called saltation); and silt and other fine particles carried along in the water (suspended load). Material may also be dissolved in the water and carried in solution.

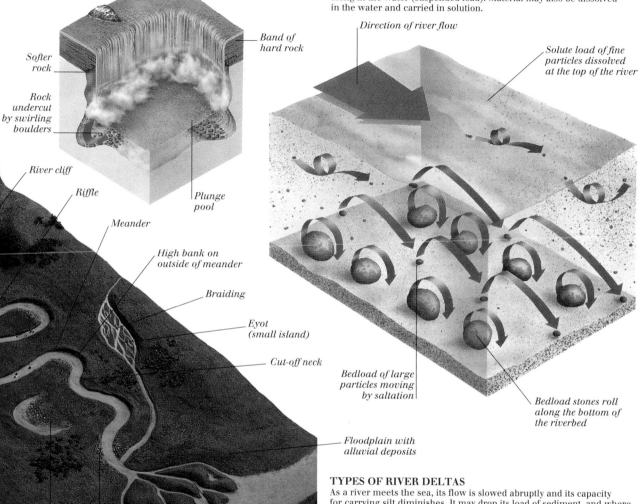

Band of hard rock

Softer rock

Rock undercut by swirling boulders

Plunge pool

River cliff

Riffle

Meander

High bank on outside of meander

Braiding

Eyot (small island)

Cut-off neck

Floodplain with alluvial deposits

Oxbow lake

Levee

Delta

Deposited sediment

Distributary

Direction of river flow

Solute load of fine particles dissolved at the top of the river

Bedload of large particles moving by saltation

Bedload stones roll along the bottom of the riverbed

TYPES OF RIVER DELTAS

As a river meets the sea, its flow is slowed abruptly and its capacity for carrying silt diminishes. It may drop its load of sediment, and where the amount dropped exceeds the amount removed by the sea, a delta forms. The shape of the delta depends upon the interaction between the river and currents in the sea. Bird's foot deltas have a ragged coast, whereas arcuate deltas have a curved coastline. Cuspate deltas are said to be kite-shaped.

MISSISSIPPI: BIRD'S FOOT DELTA

NILE: ARCUATE DELTA

NIGER: CUSPATE DELTA

Coastlines

THE BROAD REGIONS of the Earth where the land meets the sea are called coastlines. They include both the zone of shallow water, within which waves are able to move sediment, and that area of the land that is affected by waves, tides, and currents. Coastlines are a result of changes in the height of the land relative to the sea, or changes in the level of the sea relative to the land. Many were formed by changes in sea level over the last 20,000 years, since the end of the last Ice Age, when a major rise in sea levels submerged older landscapes. This produced an indented coastline of flooded valleys and created broad bays as the plains also became flooded. Many landforms are still in the process of being modified at the sea coast. There are two broad types of modification: those caused by the erosional effects of wave attack, where cliffs are undercut and collapse; and those formed by the transport and accumulation of sedimentary particles by water, building out from river mouths, or accumulating through the action of waves and currents to form mud flats or beaches.

SANDY SHORE
Constant battering by waves and seawater gives coastal regions their own unique landforms. Sand shifts, beaches are built up or washed away, cliffs crumble and fall, and even big boulders are pounded to sand as waves crash against the shore.

FEATURES OF A COASTLINE
Many coastlines were formed when sea levels rose and submerged the land. Submerged coasts are attacked by the action of the sea, which produces erosional landforms by, for example, progressively undercutting cliffs and exploiting weaknesses to form caves, arches, and then finally stacks. Long features, such as spits, form through the accumulation of sediments. Fine sediments transported by rivers accumulate in lagoons and estuaries, particularly where they are protected by beaches and spits.

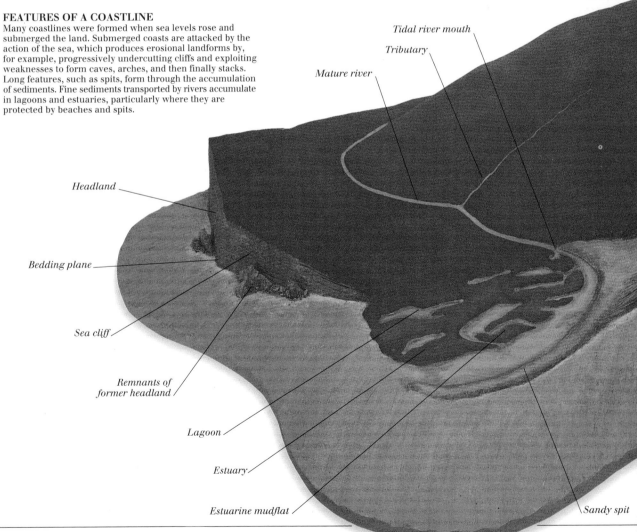

Tidal river mouth

Tributary

Mature river

Headland

Bedding plane

Sea cliff

Remnants of former headland

Lagoon

Estuary

Estuarine mudflat

Sandy spit

THE FORMATION OF WAVES

Waves are formed by the action of wind. The wind whips the water's surface up into ripples, which in turn build up into waves (if the wind is strong enough). As the waves travel through water, they cause it to move around in circles known as orbital paths. The size of a wave depends on the strength of the wind that formed it and the distance that the wind had to carry the wave before it reached the shore. Breaking, which occurs when the wave reaches the shore, is caused by the change in the orbital path of the water – from circular to elliptical – as the water becomes shallower.

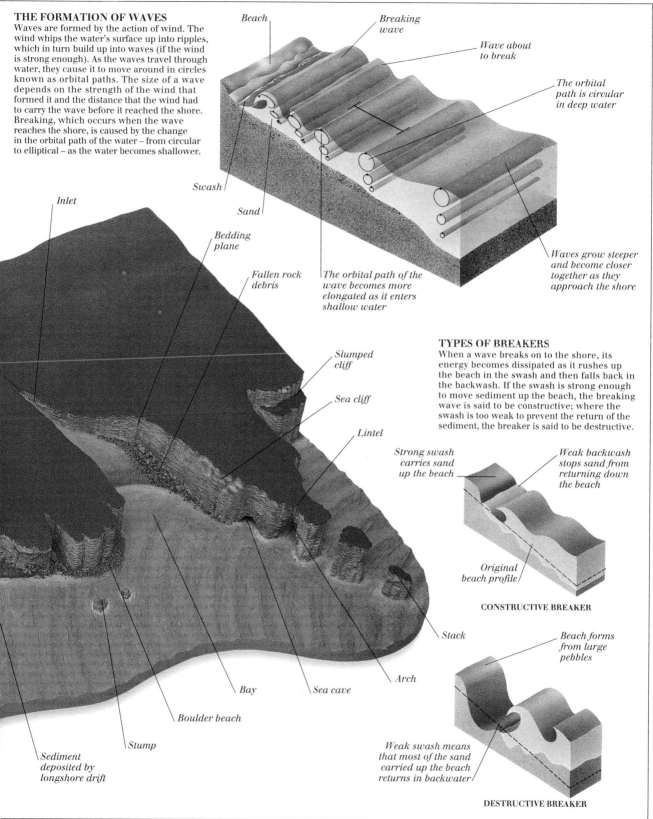

Beach

Breaking wave

Wave about to break

The orbital path is circular in deep water

Swash

Sand

Waves grow steeper and become closer together as they approach the shore

The orbital path of the wave becomes more elongated as it enters shallow water

Inlet

Bedding plane

Fallen rock debris

Slumped cliff

Sea cliff

Lintel

Stack

Arch

Sea cave

Bay

Boulder beach

Stump

Sediment deposited by longshore drift

TYPES OF BREAKERS

When a wave breaks on to the shore, its energy becomes dissipated as it rushes up the beach in the swash and then falls back in the backwash. If the swash is strong enough to move sediment up the beach, the breaking wave is said to be constructive; where the swash is too weak to prevent the return of the sediment, the breaker is said to be destructive.

Strong swash carries sand up the beach

Weak backwash stops sand from returning down the beach

Original beach profile

CONSTRUCTIVE BREAKER

Beach forms from large pebbles

Weak swash means that most of the sand carried up the beach returns in backwater

DESTRUCTIVE BREAKER

287

Oceans

ALTHOUGH IT MAKES UP 70 percent of the Earth's surface, the ocean
floor was once as much a mystery as was the surface of the Moon.
We now know that it is composed of two sections. The first is flooded
continental crust, known as the continental shelf. This is rarely deeper
than 140 meters. The amount of the continental shelf that is actually
flooded has fluctuated through time as polar ice sheets have advanced
and retreated (see pp. 282-283). There are extensive sedimentary
deposits on the continental shelf. These are brought overland by rivers
and deposited in the ocean. The second section of the ocean floor is the
deep-ocean floor, which has a depth of about 3,800 meters. Much of
the deep-ocean floor is covered by a clay, called ooze, formed from the
shells of tiny sea creatures. New ocean crust is constructed at plate
boundaries in mid-oceanic ridges, where **magma** emerges from the
Earth's crust, ultimately helping to push apart plates and drive plate
tectonics (see pp. 272-273). Old ocean crust is consumed in ocean
trenches or **subduction zones**, where one tectonic plate dives
sharply down beneath the other. Here, the descending plate melts and
the resulting magma forms a chain of volcanoes known as an island arc.
The circulation of ocean water occurs as a result of prevailing winds.

MINERAL CONTENT OF SEAWATER

Seawater is salty because it contains minerals
derived from the land over millions of years, and
brought to the sea by rivers. The most common
mineral is salt itself (sodium chloride), but other
soluble materials are also found in seawater.
Typically, seawater has a salt content of around
35 grams per liter, although this varies from one
part of the ocean to another.

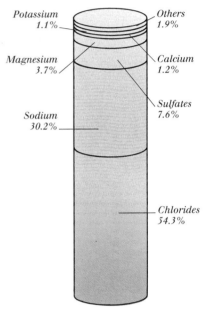

Potassium
1.1%

Others
1.9%

Magnesium
3.7%

Calcium
1.2%

Sulfates
7.6%

Sodium
30.2%

Chlorides
54.3%

OCEAN FLOOR

Echo sounding and remote sensing from
satellites have revealed that any deep-ocean
floor is divided by a system of mountain
ranges, far bigger than any on land – the mid-
ocean ridge. Here magma (molten rock) wells
up from the Earth's interior and solidifies,
widening the ocean floor. As the ocean floor
spreads, volanoes that have formed over hot
spots in the crust move away from their magma
source and become increasingly submerged
and eroded. Volcanoes eroded below sea level
remain as seamounts (underwater mountains).

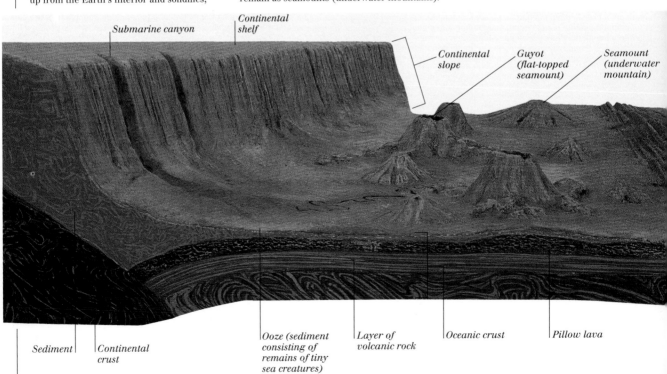

Submarine canyon

Continental
shelf

Continental
slope

Guyot
(flat-topped
seamount)

Seamount
(underwater
mountain)

Sediment

Continental
crust

Ooze (sediment
consisting of
remains of tiny
sea creatures)

Layer of
volcanic rock

Oceanic crust

Pillow lava

THE FORMATION OF AN ATOLL

An atoll is an island in the open ocean, composed of a circular chain of coral reefs surrounding a lagoon. The English naturalist Charles Darwin (1809–82) was the first scientist to consider in detail the way in which they are formed. He found that the reefs formed on the margins of a submerged volcano, or seamount. As the volcano became dormant, it cooled and subsided, and its top was eroded, lowering it to sea level. Growth of the coral reefs continued as the volcano subsided, finally producing the atoll.

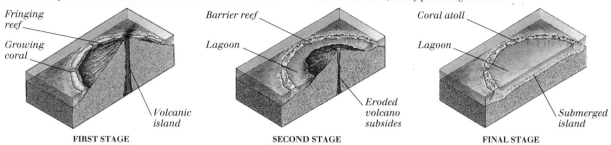

Fringing reef

Growing coral

Volcanic island

FIRST STAGE

Barrier reef

Lagoon

Eroded volcano subsides

SECOND STAGE

Coral atoll

Lagoon

Submerged island

FINAL STAGE

COLD-WATER UPWELLING

Ocean currents occur where the surface water flows in any one direction, driven by prevailing winds. In deep-coastal regions, prevailing winds may drive warm surface waters out to sea. The water removed in this way is then replaced by cooler waters, which well up from the deep ocean. These waters often bring rich nutrients with them and affect the local climate.

SEA CURRENTS

Prevailing winds blowing across the ocean surface produce currents in the upper layers of the water to a depth of about 100 meters. The Earth's rotation causes a deflection in these currents, usually at right angles to the direction of the wind. This is known as the Coriolis force, and is named after the French physicist Gaspard Coriolis (1792–1843). The currents are deflected to the right in the northern hemisphere and to the left in the southern hemisphere.

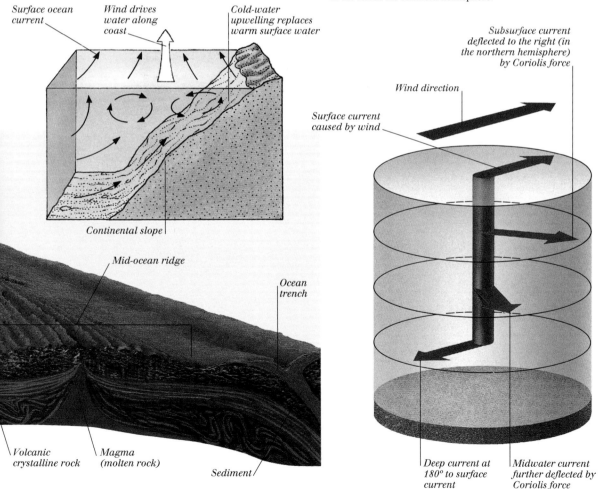

Surface ocean current

Wind drives water along coast

Cold-water upwelling replaces warm surface water

Continental slope

Mid-ocean ridge

Ocean trench

Volcanic crystalline rock

Magma (molten rock)

Sediment

Subsurface current deflected to the right (in the northern hemisphere) by Coriolis force

Wind direction

Surface current caused by wind

Deep current at 180° to surface current

Midwater current further deflected by Coriolis force

The atmosphere

THE ATMOSPHERE is an odorless, tasteless, colorless mixture of **gases**. It may seem as if it is nothing but thin air, but it actually has a surprisingly complex structure, with several distinct layers or spheres, each with its own particular characteristics – from the turbulent troposphere just above the ground to the rarefied exosphere, which merges into the black nothingness of space. The atmosphere is about 700 km deep, but there is no real boundary – it simply fades away into space as the air becomes thinner and light gas **molecules** such as hydrogen and helium float away. In comparative terms, the atmosphere is no thicker on the Earth than is the peel on an apple, but without it the Earth would be as inhospitable as the Moon (see pp. 310-311). The atmosphere gives us air to breathe and water to drink; it keeps us warm; it protects us from the Sun's harmful rays; and shields us from meteorites (see pp. 322-323).

THE FATE OF SOLAR RADIATION

Less than 47 percent of the energy from the Sun reaches the ground; the remaining 53 percent or so is absorbed by the atmosphere or is reflected back into space. Water vapor, carbon dioxide, and other gases in the atmosphere act like the panes of glass in a greenhouse, trapping some of the energy that reaches the ground as heat and preventing it from being lost into space. This heat energy is then spread through the air by a process called **convection**.

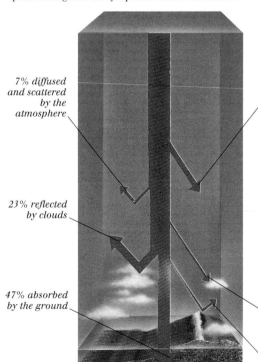

7% diffused and scattered by the atmosphere

16% absorbed by water vapor, dust, and gases in the air

23% reflected by clouds

47% absorbed by the ground

3% absorbed by clouds

4% reflected by land and oceans

LAYERS OF THE ATMOSPHERE

The atmosphere is divided into layers according to temperature variation and height. In the troposphere, which is the lowest layer, the temperature decreases with height. In the stratosphere the temperature increases with height. The mesosphere lies above the stratosphere and is a thin layer of gases where the temperature drops rapidly. Gases within the final three layers of the atmosphere – the ionosphere, thermosphere, and exosphere – get progressively thinner.

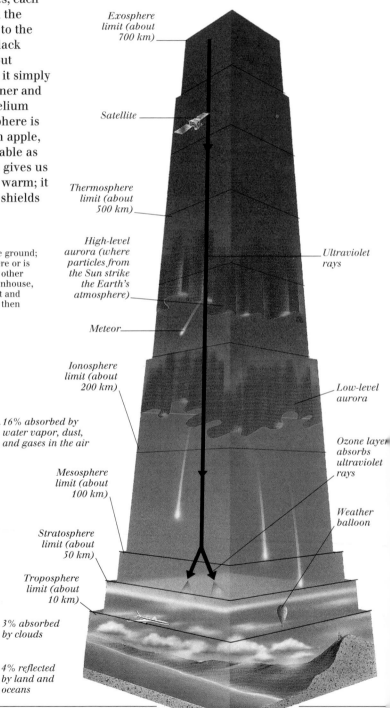

Exosphere limit (about 700 km)

Satellite

Thermosphere limit (about 500 km)

High-level aurora (where particles from the Sun strike the Earth's atmosphere)

Meteor

Ionosphere limit (about 200 km)

Mesosphere limit (about 100 km)

Stratosphere limit (about 50 km)

Troposphere limit (about 10 km)

Ultraviolet rays

Low-level aurora

Ozone layer absorbs ultraviolet rays

Weather balloon

WIND PATTERNS

GLOBAL WIND CIRCULATION

The massive difference in the amount of the Sun's warmth received by the tropics and the poles creates a very strong pattern of prevailing winds around the world. Because hot air rises at the equator (where the Sun's warmth is greatest) and sinks at the poles, there is a constant movement of air at ground level from the poles to the equator and a reverse movement higher in the atmosphere. This general circulation is split into three zones or "cells," each with its own wind pattern: dry, northeasterly and southeasterly trade winds in the tropics; warm, moist westerlies in the midlatitudes; and cold, polar easterlies in the polar regions.

North Pole (high pressure)

Rotation of the Earth

Polar cell

Polar-front jet stream

Polar easterlies

Westerlies

Northeasterly trade winds

A Rossby wave forms in the polar-front jet stream

Warm air

Cold air

Equator

The wave becomes deeper and more pronounced

Southeasterly trade winds

Warm and cold air caught in loops may become detached to form cyclones and anticyclones

Winds are deflected from north-south direction by the Earth's rotation

Westerlies

South Pole (high pressure)

Subtropical jet stream

Warm equatorial air rises and flows toward South Pole

Doldrums (low pressure)

ROSSBY WAVES

In addition to the low-altitude circulation cells that are part of the large-scale pattern of air circulation, there are also high-speed, high-altitude winds in the atmosphere. Included among these is the polar-front jet stream, which meanders around the world in four to six giant waves, each about 2,000 km long. These waves are called Rossby waves, and are caused by the Coriolis effect (the deflection of winds by the Earth's rotation). They have no fixed positions, but probably snake along the polar front, where the confrontation between warm, tropical westerly winds and cold, polar easterly winds causes continual storms.

JET STREAM

Jet streams are narrow bands of high-altitude westerly winds that were discovered by the Swedish-American meteorologist Carl-Gustaf Rossby (1898–1957). They roar around the atmosphere at speeds of up to 370 kph, driving the world's weather systems. The steadiest jet streams are the subtropical jet streams (shown right, over Egypt and the Red Sea), which lie between 20° and 30° North, and 20° and 30° South. There is also a polar-front jet stream along the polar front, an Arctic jet stream, and a polar-night jet stream, which blows only in winter during the long polar night.

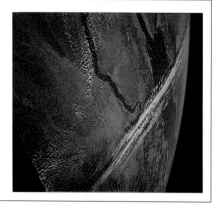

Weather

THE LOWEST LAYER of the **atmosphere** – the troposphere – is in continuous motion (see pp. 290-291), driven by pressure differences created by unequal distribution of the Sun's heat between the poles and the **equator**. This continuous motion causes the differences in weather conditions that occur across the globe. Weather conditions are usually assessed in terms of **temperature**, wind, cloud cover, and precipitation, such as rain or snow. The most important atmospheric changes influencing weather are: the way the atmosphere moves, controlling wind patterns; its temperature, helping define cold spells and warm periods; and its moisture content, influencing cloud formation and precipitation. It is the forecaster's job to record these changes and predict their effect on the weather. For example, clear weather is usually associated with high-pressure zones, where air is sinking. In contrast, cloudy, wet, and changeable weather is usually found in low-pressure zones, which have rising air. An extreme form of low-pressure area is a hurricane, which brings with it strong winds and torrential rains.

TYPES OF CLOUD

Clouds form when water vapor in the air is lifted high into the sky so that it cools down and condenses, to form either water droplets or tiny ice crystals. The ratio of ice crystals to water drops depends on how high the cloud is and how cold the air is. The highest clouds are generally all composed of ice crystals, while the lowest are composed mostly of water drops. Clouds take many forms, but there are three basic types – cirrus (wispy clouds of ice crystals), cumulus (fluffy white clouds), and stratus (vast, layered clouds). These three basic types are broken down further into 10 categories according to the **altitudes** at which they occur.

Cirrus

Cirrocumulus

Freezing level above which clouds consist of ice crystals

Altocumulus

Altostratus

Cumulus

Stratus

Cirrostratus

Cumulonimbus

Nimbus

Nimbostratus

Condensation level

LIGHTNING

Lightning is created by violent air currents inside thunderclouds, which hurl cloud particles together, making them electrically charged. Heavier, negatively charged particles sink in the cloud and positively charged particles rise. This creates a charge difference, which is equalized by a bolt of lightning flashing either within the cloud (sheet lightning) or between the cloudbase and the positively charged ground (fork lightning).

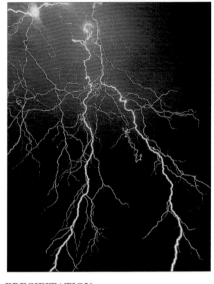

PRECIPITATION

Precipitation is a blanket term used to describe rain, snow, hail, and every other form of moisture that falls from clouds. Clouds are made of drops of water plus ice crystals that are small enough and light enough to float in air. Rain starts when a cloud is disturbed – perhaps by a strong updraft – causing the water drops to grow too large and too heavy to float in the air any longer. Raindrops grow in various ways, including colliding with other drops and growing into ice crystals.

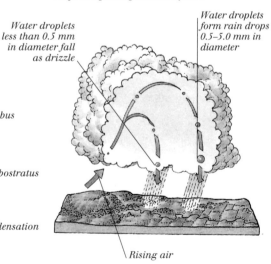

Water droplets less than 0.5 mm in diameter fall as drizzle

Water droplets form rain drops 0.5–5.0 mm in diameter

Rising air

STRUCTURE OF A HURRICANE

Hurricanes, which are also known as willy-willies, tropical cyclones, and typhoons, are violent tropical storms. They begin life as clusters of thunderstorms over warm seas. Massive banks of clouds form in a ring as winds begin to spiral around the storm center with gathering force, eventually merging into a single spiral. The very center of the storm, however, is a calm "eye." As the storm develops, it drives across the ocean, bringing torrential rain and winds that gust up to 360 kilometers per hour.

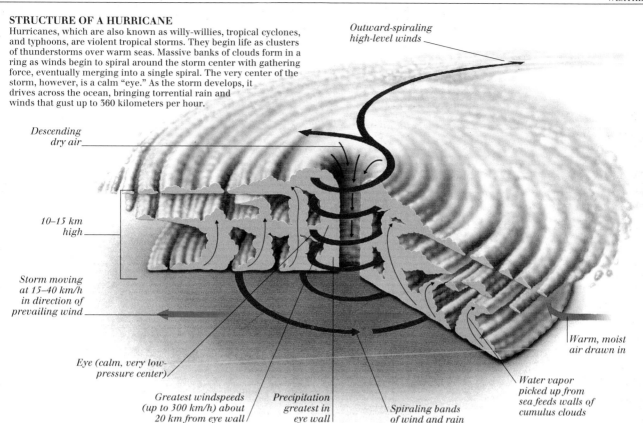

Outward-spiraling high-level winds

Descending dry air

10–15 km high

Storm moving at 15–40 km/h in direction of prevailing wind

Eye (calm, very low-pressure center)

Greatest windspeeds (up to 300 km/h) about 20 km from eye wall

Precipitation greatest in eye wall

Spiraling bands of wind and rain

Warm, moist air drawn in

Water vapor picked up from sea feeds walls of cumulus clouds

WEATHER MAP

Weather maps are a way of displaying the weather data from numerous weather stations in a single, graphic form. The contour lines on the map are isobars, lines joining points where the barometric (air) pressure is equal. Thick lines with either bumps (warm fronts) or spikes (cold fronts) indicate where air masses meet and storms are concentrated. Key-shaped symbols mark weather stations and indicate wind strength and direction.

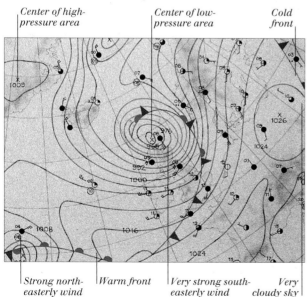

Center of high-pressure area

Center of low-pressure area

Cold front

Strong north-easterly wind

Warm front

Very strong south-easterly wind

Very cloudy sky

EVOLVING FRONTS

Warm air   Cold air

AIR MASSES COLLIDE
Cold, polar air (spikes) and warm, tropical air (bumps) collide at the polar front.

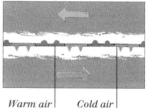

Depression caused by warm air

PUSH AND BULGE
A depression forms where the warm air bulges into the cold air at the polar front.

Spiralling air

SPLITTING IN TWO
Cold air chases the warm air in a spiral, causing the polar front to split into two arms.

Cold and warm fronts merge

OCCLUDED FRONT
The cold air catches up and merges with the warm air, forming an occluded front.

Crescents of Neptune and one of its moons – Triton, taken by Voyager 2

ASTRONOMY AND ASTROPHYSICS

DISCOVERING ASTRONOMY AND ASTROPHYSICS 296

TELESCOPES 298

OBSERVATIONAL TECHNIQUES 300

SPACE PROBES 302

THE SOLAR SYSTEM 304

THE SUN 306

PLANETARY SCIENCE 308

THE MOON 310

MERCURY AND VENUS 312

MARS 314

JUPITER 316

SATURN AND URANUS 318

NEPTUNE AND PLUTO 320

COMETS, ASTEROIDS, AND METEOROIDS 322

STARS 324

STELLAR LIFE CYCLES 326

GALAXIES 328

NEUTRON STARS AND BLACK HOLES 330

COSMOLOGY 332

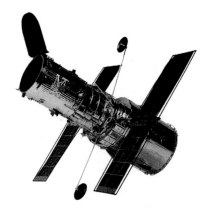

Discovering astronomy and astrophysics

THE SCOPE OF ASTRONOMY is vast. It is the most ancient of sciences – people have always studied the sky – and includes the origin and evolution of the universe, as well as the position, motion, and behavior of all the objects in space. Astrophysics is a modern branch of astronomy that deals with the physics behind cosmic processes, such as the formation and evolution of stars and galaxies.

ANCIENT ASTRONOMY

Early attempts at timekeeping made use of observations of the position of the Sun during the day and the stars at night. Before long, the Sun and stars became aids to navigation. Systematic study of the sky seems to have begun with the ancient Babylonians, who identified several constellations as early as 3000 BC. Many other early civilizations studied the sky, producing star maps that were illustrated with drawings of mythological creatures. This suggests that they had developed mystical beliefs about the stars that are no longer held.

ASTRONOMY AND MATHEMATICS

In the ancient civilizations of Greece, China, and India, astronomers used ingenious mathematical methods to predict solar and lunar eclipses. In Greece, around 400 BC, **Aristotle** presented a convincing argument that the Earth is a sphere, based on the shape of the shadow that falls on the Moon during a lunar eclipse. **Eratosthenes** – another Greek thinker – figured out a fairly accurate value for the diameter of the Earth. In the 2nd century AD, the Greek astronomer **Ptolemy** produced the first comprehensive theory of the universe. He proposed that the planets, the Sun, and the Moon exist on concentric spheres, centered on the Earth, with the fixed stars on the outermost sphere. The Ptolemaic system was laid out in *Almagest*, Ptolemy's great astronomical encyclopedia, which contained lists of constellations and the magnitude (brightness) of each of 1,022 stars. Translated into Arabic and Latin, it served as a guide to astronomy across much of the world until the 17th century.

THE SOLAR SYSTEM

Ptolemy's theory of the universe could not explain the paths of the planets. **Hipparchus** attempted to fix the theory by suggesting that the planets revolve around points that themselves move around the Earth. This system could not, however, account fully for the motions of celestial objects. In 1543, a solar, or heliocentric, system was proposed by **Nicolaus Copernicus**. His system proposed that the planets, including the Earth, orbit the Sun. It also correctly suggested that the Earth rotates on its axis as it revolves around the Sun. Support for Copernicus came from the careful observations of **Tycho Brahe**. Brahe's data was also used by **Johannes Kepler** to discover three laws of planetary motion. Kepler's laws describe orbits in terms of ellipses, and they

NEWTON'S REFLECTOR
Isaac Newton's reflecting telescope used mirrors rather than lenses to form an image. Incoming light was gathered by a large, curved mirror and then reflected by a smaller mirror into the observer's eye. The image was sharper than that obtained with earlier telescopes.

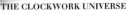

THE CLOCKWORK UNIVERSE
In the words of the poet Alexander Pope, "Nature and nature's laws lay hid in night: God said, 'Let Newton be!' and all was light." This clockwork model of the solar system, which places the Sun at the center, orbited by the Earth and the Moon, reflects Isaac Newton's view of the universe as a giant machine.

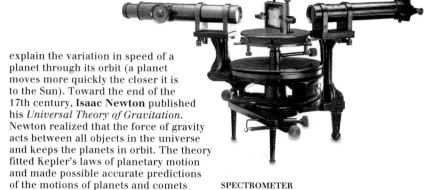

explain the variation in speed of a planet through its orbit (a planet moves more quickly the closer it is to the Sun). Toward the end of the 17th century, **Isaac Newton** published his *Universal Theory of Gravitation*. Newton realized that the force of gravity acts between all objects in the universe and keeps the planets in orbit. The theory fitted Kepler's laws of planetary motion and made possible accurate predictions of the motions of planets and comets around the Sun.

THE TELESCOPE

Isaac Newton invented the first practical reflecting telescope around 1670. (Earlier refracting telescopes of the type used by **Galileo Galilei** tended to distort the image.) By the end of the 17th century, several impressive telescopic observatories had been built. During the 18th century, **William Herschel** conducted several detailed telescopic studies of the sky. He produced a catalog of 848 double stars and, in 1781, discovered the planet Uranus, the first planet to be discovered since ancient times. In 1838, careful telescopic observations and brilliant mathematics enabled **Friedrich Bessel** to calculate the distance of a star for the first time. Telescopes equipped with prisms were used to observe in detail the spectra of stars. These spectroscopic observations meant that astronomers could begin to discover the chemical composition of stars. Combined with photography, telescopes could produce ever more revealing images of celestial objects. In 1846, the telescope was used to discover the planet Neptune. It was not until 1930 that the most distant planet, tiny Pluto, was discovered.

SPACE AND TIME

In the 1920s, **Edwin Hubble** realized that the universe is far larger than had been thought when he discovered that the Andromeda Nebula is in fact a galaxy just like our own. Hubble had discovered that our galaxy is just one of thousands of millions of galaxies in the universe. **Albert Einstein's** two theories of relativity had a profound effect on astrophysics. The special theory of relativity (1905) proposed that energy

SPECTROMETER
All atoms emit particular wavelengths of light. Spectrometers are used to investigate the light in a spectrum. Analyzing the light emitted by a distant star tells us a great deal about its composition.

has mass, and mass has energy. This idea held the key to understanding the energy source of stars. (It was **Hans Bethe** who first put forward a detailed theory of energy production in stars, in 1959.) Einstein's general theory of relativity (1915) treated gravity as the curvature of space-time and proved more accurate than Newton's theory of gravitation.

MODERN ASTRONOMY

The invention of radio astronomy and the use of space probes to explore the planets drastically changed many of the theories and practices of astronomy. Radio astronomy collects radio waves from stars, galaxies, and interstellar gas, using huge dishes called radio telescopes. It has provided many new insights into cosmic processes. Telescopes have also been built that are sensitive to infrared radiation, ultraviolet radiation, X rays, and gamma rays. In 1964, **Arno Penzias** and **Robert Wilson** discovered cosmic background radiation (CBR). This provided support for the Big Bang theory of cosmology, which suggests that the universe was created in a huge explosion of space and time some 10 to 20 billion years ago. The first successful space probe, the Russian lunar probe, *Luna 1*, was launched in 1959. Since then, a much more detailed understanding of the solar system has been built up by sending space probes to most planets, as well as some comets and asteroids. Similarly, the use of telescopes in orbit above the Earth's atmosphere has enabled astronomers to see into space with yet more clarity. The most celebrated of these is the *Hubble Space Telescope*, launched in 1990, which has provided stunning new views of the planets, as well as of distant stars, galaxies, and nebulas.

TIMELINE OF DISCOVERIES

The Egyptian calendar of 360 days (12 months of 30 days each) is drawn up based on observations of the Sun and the Moon	4000 BC	
	5000 BC	Evidence of systematic astronomical observations in Egypt, Babylonia, India, and China
Aristotle puts the Earth at the center of the universe, a belief that dominates until the 15th century	355 BC	
	250 BC	Eratosthenes suggests that the Earth moves around the Sun
Ptolemy records the positions of 1,022 stars, dividing them into 48 constellations, in his book, *Almagest*	AD 157 -145	
	1543	Nicolaus Copernicus places the Sun at the center of the universe in his book, *On the Revolutions of Celestial Objects*
Tycho Brahe publishes his great star catalog, which gives accurate positions for about 770 stars	1596	
	1608	**Hans Lippershey** invents the first telescope
Johannes Kepler establishes the elliptical motion of the planets	1609	
	1610	Galileo Galilei uses a telescope to discover four of Jupiter's moons. He also shows that Venus, like the Moon, has phases, adding support to the idea that the Sun is at the center of the universe
Isaac Newton establishes the laws of gravitation governing celestial bodies. In 1668 he invents the reflecting telescope	1667	
	1705	**Edmond Halley** predicts the return of what comes to be known as Halley's comet
William Herschel discovers Uranus	1781	
	1846	**Johann Galle** and **Heinrich D'Arrest** discover Neptune
The first photographs of stars are taken at Harvard Observatory, Boston, Massachusetts	1849	
	1907	Albert Einstein discovers mass/energy equivalence, the key to understanding the energy source of stars
The notion of an expanding universe is suggested by American astronomer **Vesto Slipher**	1919	
	1924 -50	**Georges Lemaître** formulates what comes to be known as the Big Bang theory of the origin of the universe
Edwin Hubble finds strong evidence in support of an expanding universe	1929	
	1930	Pluto is discovered by **Clyde Tombaugh**
Radio signals from the Milky Way are discovered by **Karl Jansky**	1932	
	1965	Arno Penzias and Robert Wilson discover cosmic background radiation, believed to be a remnant of the Big Bang
The first pulsar (pulsating star) is discovered by **Jocelyn Bell Burnell**	1967	
	1986	The *Giotto* space probe sends back the first images of a comet's nucleus, in this case Halley's comet
The *Hubble Space Telescope* is launched, the first large, optical telescope to be placed above the Earth's atmosphere	1990	
	1992	*COBE* (Cosmic Microwave Background Explorer) provides further evidence of the Big Bang origins of the universe
NASA's *Pathfinder* lands on Mars. Its unique rover, *Sojourner*, samples rocks and soils	1997	

Telescopes

THE HUMAN EYE HAS ONLY a small opening (aperture) to collect light, and its magnification is fixed. Optical telescopes, which collect visible light, have a much larger aperture than the eye, and so collect much more light. This means that much fainter objects can be observed, and also that features that are too close together for the eye to distinguish can be seen as separate objects (resolved). The magnification of a telescope is less important than the size of its aperture, especially when observing stars, which are so far away that they appear only as a point of light, whatever the magnification of the telescope used. The Earth's turbulent atmosphere distorts the light that reaches Earth-based telescopes. Far better images can be obtained by placing a telescope in space. The most famous space telescope is the *Hubble Space Telescope*, which has provided astronomers with exciting new insights into star formation, as well as having produced stunning photographs of objects within the solar system. Modern astronomy relies increasingly on telescopes that are sensitive to parts of the **electromagnetic spectrum** other than visible light.

REFRACTION AND REFLECTION

A refracting telescope, or refractor, produces images using only lenses (normally two of them). A reflecting telescope produces an image using a large mirror. This image is magnified by a smaller eyepiece lens, which has a short **focal length**. The degree to which the image is magnified depends upon the focal lengths of the mirror and the eyepiece lens.

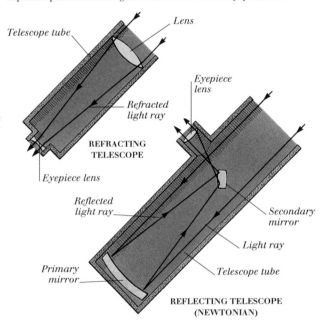

HUBBLE SPACE TELESCOPE

The *Hubble Space Telescope* (*HST*) is in orbit 600 kilometers above the Earth's surface, well away from the distorting effects of the Earth's atmosphere. Because it is above the atmosphere, the *HST*'s resolution is ten times better than that of a ground-based telescope. It is a reflecting telescope with a primary mirror 2.4 meters in diameter. Its cameras and **spectrographs** are sensitive to infrared, visible light, and ultraviolet. Images from its cameras are gathered electronically, using a charge coupled device (CCD) and beamed back to the Earth.

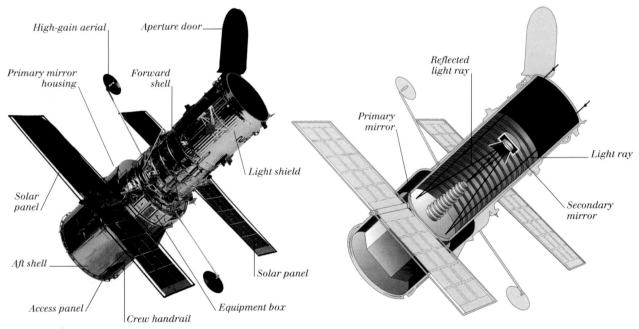

EXTERNAL FEATURES OF *HUBBLE*   **HOW *HUBBLE* WORKS**

ELECTROMAGNETIC SPECTRUM

Radio waves are not readily absorbed by any part of the atmosphere. **Infrared** radiation is absorbed by water in clouds but visible light passes through the atmosphere. **Ultraviolet** radiation and **gamma** rays are absorbed by ozone concentrated at a level higher than the clouds. For this reason, ultraviolet and gamma-ray astronomy is effectively carried out only using orbiting telescopes.

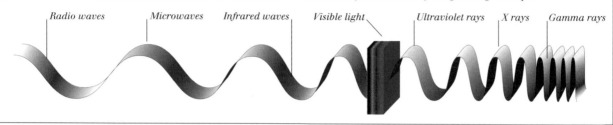

Radio waves   *Microwaves*   *Infrared waves*   *Visible light*   *Ultraviolet rays*   *X rays*   *Gamma rays*

ORBITING AND GROUND-BASED TELESCOPES

The first telescopes sensitive to parts of the electromagnetic spectrum other than light were radio telescopes. The long wavelengths of radio waves mean that huge dishes are needed if the images they produce are to resolve any detail. It is often possible to learn more about the nature of a galaxy by examining the data collected by radio telescopes than from images produced in visible light. Infrared astronomy is particularly useful for studying the Sun and the planets, while X rays and gamma rays are emitted only by very powerful galactic centers and black holes.

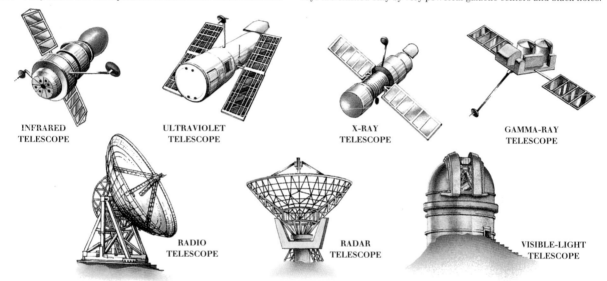

INFRARED TELESCOPE

ULTRAVIOLET TELESCOPE

X-RAY TELESCOPE

GAMMA-RAY TELESCOPE

RADIO TELESCOPE

RADAR TELESCOPE

VISIBLE-LIGHT TELESCOPE

TWO IMAGES OF OUR GALAXY

These images show our galaxy, the Milky Way Galaxy. The upper image was taken by the Infrared Astronomical Telescope (IRAS), while the lower image was produced by a gamma-ray observatory. Both are false-color images (neither infrared nor gamma radiation has any true color). The infrared image is very bright along the galactic plane (disk), where hot young stars are common. The gamma-ray image shows a contrast between the center, or nucleus, of the galaxy and the rest of the disk. Gamma rays are given out only by extremely energetic sources – there may be a massive black hole at the center of our galaxy (see pp. 330-331). This image also highlights activity above and below the galactic plane.

INFRARED IMAGE

GAMMA-RAY IMAGE

Observational techniques

ASTRONOMERS HAVE DEVISED many techniques and devices to help them make the most of their observations. For example, accurate measurement of the position in the sky of a star taken at different times of the year can lead to a determination of its distance from the Earth – making use of an effect known as parallax. The positions of stars and other astronomical objects are given as points in a coordinate system (see pp. 366-367). Astronomers imagine the sky as a hollow sphere, with the Earth at its center. Coordinates called right ascension (RA) and declination (Dec) have the same meaning for the sphere as **longitude** and **latitude** do for the Earth's surface. Astronomers measure the brightness of a star in terms of its apparent magnitude. This is not necessarily a clue to its actual **luminosity**, which is measured instead by absolute magnitude. A device called a blink comparator enables astronomers to highlight objects that change their appearance or position, including supernovas or asteroids. Analysis of the **spectrum** of a star's light can tell astronomers which chemical **elements** are present in the star, enabling stars to be categorized by their **spectral type**.

PARALLAX SHIFT
The apparent position of nearby stars is different when viewed from different points in the Earth's orbit. This difference is called parallax shift. The parallax shift of even the nearest stars is tiny, but using simple geometry it can be used to calculate the distance of a star with some accuracy.

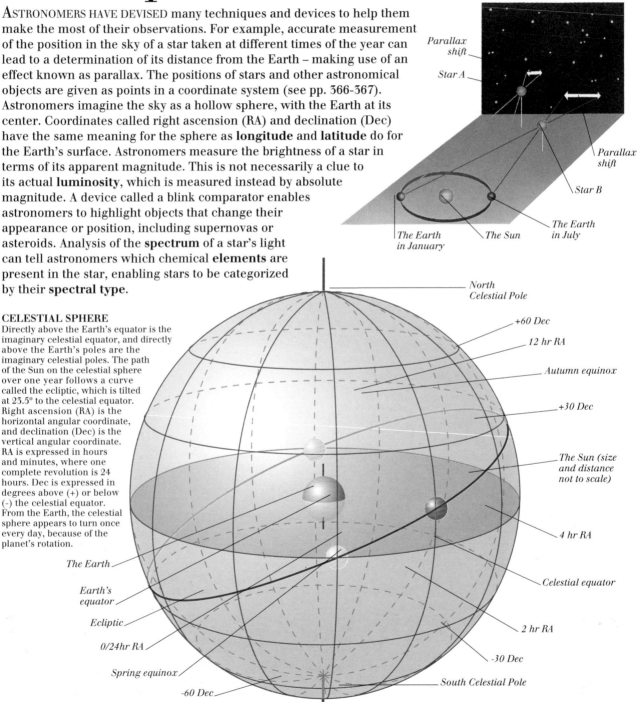

Parallax shift

Star A

Parallax shift

Star B

The Earth in January

The Sun

The Earth in July

CELESTIAL SPHERE
Directly above the Earth's equator is the imaginary celestial equator, and directly above the Earth's poles are the imaginary celestial poles. The path of the Sun on the celestial sphere over one year follows a curve called the ecliptic, which is tilted at 23.5° to the celestial equator. Right ascension (RA) is the horizontal angular coordinate, and declination (Dec) is the vertical angular coordinate. RA is expressed in hours and minutes, where one complete revolution is 24 hours. Dec is expressed in degrees above (+) or below (-) the celestial equator. From the Earth, the celestial sphere appears to turn once every day, because of the planet's rotation.

North Celestial Pole

+60 Dec

12 hr RA

Autumn equinox

+30 Dec

The Sun (size and distance not to scale)

4 hr RA

Celestial equator

2 hr RA

-30 Dec

South Celestial Pole

-60 Dec

Spring equinox

0/24hr RA

Ecliptic

Earth's equator

The Earth

STAR MAGNITUDES

The brighter a star or planet appears in the sky, the lower its apparent magnitude is said to be. The absolute magnitude of a star is the magnitude it would appear at a distance of ten parsecs (32.6 light years). The apparent magnitude of the Sun is -26.7, while its absolute magnitude is +4.8.

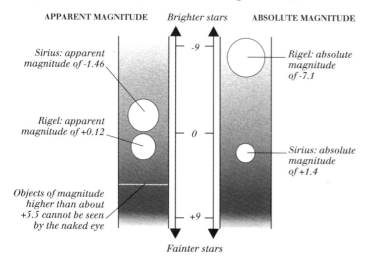

APPARENT MAGNITUDE

Brighter stars

ABSOLUTE MAGNITUDE

Sirius: apparent magnitude of -1.46

Rigel: absolute magnitude of -7.1

-9

Rigel: apparent magnitude of +0.12

0

Sirius: absolute magnitude of +1.4

Objects of magnitude higher than about +5.5 cannot be seen by the naked eye

+9

Fainter stars

BLINK COMPARATOR

Blink comparators flash up time-lapsed photographs of the same part of the sky. Any differences between the photographs – caused by objects moving against the background of "fixed" stars – are immediately apparent.

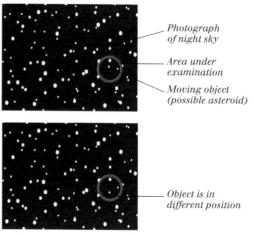

Photograph of night sky

Area under examination

Moving object (possible asteroid)

Object is in different position

RED SHIFT

Wavelengths of light (or other **electromagnetic radiation**) emitted by a star or galaxy moving rapidly away from the Earth are lengthened, an effect known as Döppler redshift. The opposite effect is called Döppler blueshift. Astronomers can figure out redshifts or blueshifts by measuring the wavelengths of known spectral lines (see below) and comparing them with the wavelengths of those lines from a stationary source. The objects moving away fastest are distant **quasars**, which have a correspondingly high degree of redshift.

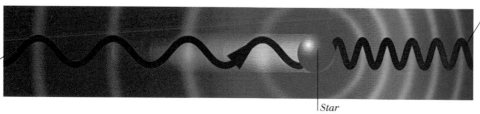

Light from a star moving away from us is shifted to the red end of the spectrum

Light from a star moving toward us is shifted to the blue end of the spectrum

Star

STELLAR SPECTRAL ABSORPTION LINES

When starlight is analyzed by being passed through a prism or a **diffraction grating** (a piece of glass with closely spaced parallel lines ruled on it), many dark lines are seen against the resulting spectrum. These lines are caused by absorption of light by **atoms** in stars and are characteristic of particular chemical elements. Stellar spectra can therefore tell astronomers much about the chemical composition of a star.

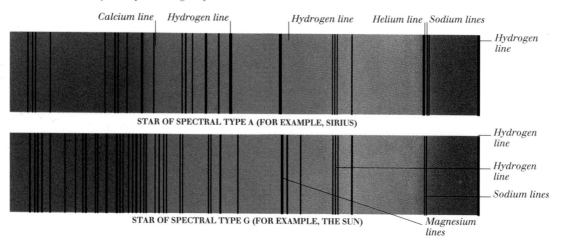

Calcium line   *Hydrogen line*   *Hydrogen line*   *Helium line*   *Sodium lines*

Hydrogen line

STAR OF SPECTRAL TYPE A (FOR EXAMPLE, SIRIUS)

Hydrogen line

Hydrogen line

Sodium lines

STAR OF SPECTRAL TYPE G (FOR EXAMPLE, THE SUN)   *Magnesium lines*

Space probes

MOST SPACE PROBES ARE SENT OUT to gather information about planets. One of the most successful space probes was *Voyager 2*. It visited four planets in total and made many important discoveries. Like most space probes, it carried other instruments as well as cameras. Information from these instruments was sent back to the Earth as radio signals, which were detected using radio telescopes (see pp. 298-299). The *Galileo* probe traveled to Jupiter (see pp. 316-317) and made extensive observations of the planet and its moons. It also sent a small descent probe into the **atmosphere** to gather data. Some probes are designed to land on planets. Landers, as these are called, have been sent to the surfaces of the Moon (see pp. 310-311) and Mars (see pp. 314-315). Space probes do not visit only planets; a few probes have visited comets and asteroids (see pp. 322-323), while others have been sent into orbit around the Sun.

INFORMATION FOR ALIENS

The American space probe *Pioneer 10* passed Jupiter in 1973, and *Pioneer 11* passed Saturn in 1974. Both probes eventually left the Solar system but it is highly unlikely that they will ever be found by some extraterrestrial life form. In case they do, however, both probes carry plaques with information about the Earth.

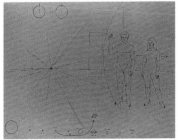

INFORMATION PLAQUE FROM PIONEER PROBES

VOYAGER 2 PROBE

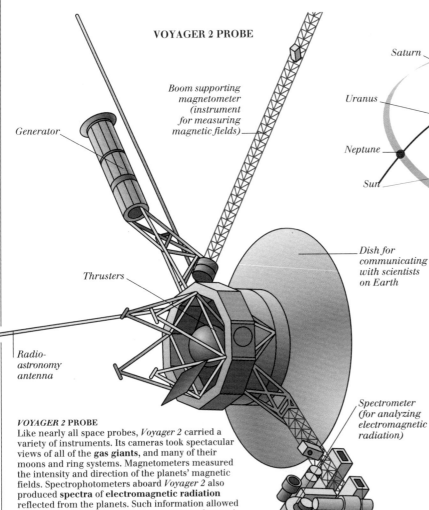

Generator

Boom supporting magnetometer (instrument for measuring magnetic fields)

Thrusters

Dish for communicating with scientists on Earth

Radio-astronomy antenna

Spectrometer (for analyzing electromagnetic radiation)

Camera

The Earth

Jupiter

Saturn

Uranus

Neptune

Sun

VOYAGER 2'S JOURNEY

Voyager 2 was probably the most successful space probe ever launched. It left the Earth in August 1977 and passed Jupiter in July 1979. It passed Saturn in August 1981, Uranus in January 1986, and Neptune in August 1989. The probe will remain operational until 2020 and will send back information about the Sun's magnetic field.

VOYAGER 2 PROBE

Like nearly all space probes, *Voyager 2* carried a variety of instruments. Its cameras took spectacular views of all of the **gas giants**, and many of their moons and ring systems. Magnetometers measured the intensity and direction of the planets' magnetic fields. Spectrophotometers aboard *Voyager 2* also produced **spectra** of **electromagnetic radiation** reflected from the planets. Such information allowed astronomers to figure out the composition of **gases** in the planets' atmospheres. The probe was also fitted with small thrusters that were used to change the alignment of the probe and its instruments.

IMAGES FROM VOYAGER 2

Voyager 2's flyby of Neptune led to the discovery of six previously unknown moons of the planet, plus three rings. It also carried out accurate measurements of the planet's magnetic field. Shown here is a *Voyager 2* image of Neptune with Triton, the largest of Neptune's moons.

THE *GALILEO* PROBE'S MISSION TO JUPITER

FLIGHT PATH

The *Galileo* probe was launched in October 1989 and reached Jupiter in the summer of 1995. The probe was assisted on its journey by the **gravitational** effect of Venus, which it passed in January 1990. In July 1994, *Galileo* observed the collision of comet Shoemaker–Levy 9 with Jupiter's atmosphere (see pp. 316-317) and on July 13 1995, an atmospheric probe was dropped into the clouds of Jupiter's upper atmosphere.

GALILEO PROBE DESCENT

The *Galileo* probe entered Jupiter's atmosphere near the equator. Two minutes after entry, a parachute slowed the probe's descent. The probe sent data back to the orbiter, which relayed the information back to the Earth. The probe made several types of measurements, including temperature, pressure, and composition of the atmosphere. After about 70 minutes, the probe was destroyed by the intense pressure of Jupiter's atmosphere.

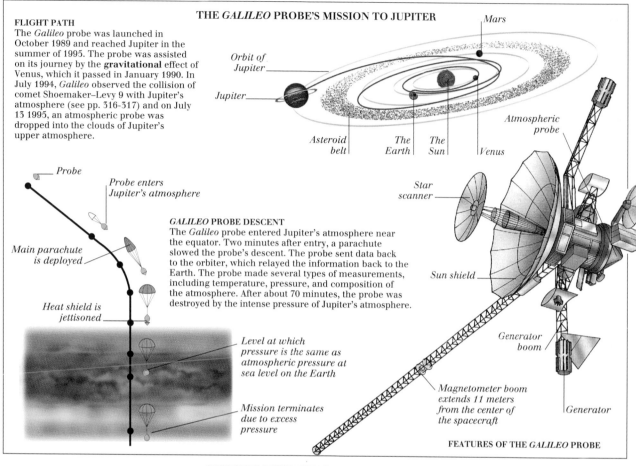

FEATURES OF THE *GALILEO* PROBE

INVESTIGATING THE SURFACE OF MARS

In the summer of 1976, two *Viking* landers were sent to Mars. Each had an orbiter that relayed signals from the lander to the Earth. The landers deployed robotic arms to collect the Martian rock and soil, and a series of chemical and biochemical tests were carried out on the samples. One set of experiments tested for signs of life on Mars, but none were found. The landers also carried instruments to study the Martian weather.

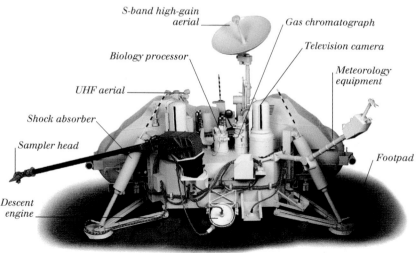

SCALE MODEL OF THE *VIKING* LANDER

IMAGES FROM THE *VIKING* LANDERS
The *Viking* landers took the first ever close-up photographs of the surface of Mars. Many of the surface features, such as dunes and boulders, are similar to those observed on the Earth.

The Solar System

THE SOLAR SYSTEM CONSISTS OF THE SUN, the nine planets and their satellites, and millions of comets, asteroids, and meteoroids (see pp. 322-323). Most of the objects that currently **orbit** the Sun probably formed millions of years ago from a rotating disk of gas and dust left over from the Sun's formation. The **mass** of the Sun is far greater than the combined masses of all the planets, and so it commands a position at the center of the solar system. All of the planets are held in orbit by **gravitational forces** (see pp. 308-309). The four inner planets are relatively small, rocky bodies. They include the Earth (see pp. 270-271) and are often referred to as the terrestrial planets. The outer planets, with the exception of Pluto, are all **gas giants** – huge planets that consist largely of gases in various forms. Pluto is unlike the other planets in many ways and may have come from the Kuiper Belt (see pp. 320-321) – a band of rocky bodies outside the main part of the Solar System.

BIRTH OF THE SOLAR SYSTEM

The Sun was created from a nebulous cloud of gas and dust around 4.6 billion years ago. The material that was left over from the solar nebula formed a flat, rotating disk. (This remaining material amounted to less than one percent of the total mass of the solar System.) Bodies called protoplanets condensed out of this disk and clumped together, under the influence of **gravity**, to become planets and asteroids.

The Sun

Ring of gas and dust

Gas and dust moving in an elliptical orbit

ORBITS OF THE INNER PLANETS

The orbits of the inner planets are nearly circular and are all very well aligned with the **ecliptic plane**. Between Mars – the outermost terrestrial planet – and Jupiter – the first of the gas giants – lies the asteroid belt. This is essentially debris left over from the formation of the solar system. Jupiter's gravity prevents this debris coming together to form a planet.

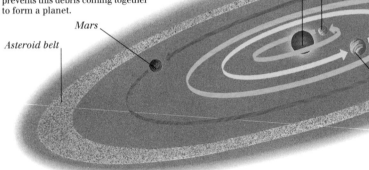

The Sun

Mercury, the closest planet to the Sun, completes each orbit in just 88 days

Mars

Asteroid belt

The Earth

Venus travels faster in its orbit than the Earth, but more slowly than Mercury

ALMOST A STAR

The gas giant Jupiter is by far the largest planet in the solar system. It has a diameter more than eleven times as great as the Earth's. The Sun is even larger, having a diameter more than one hundred times that of the Earth's.
The Sun is so massive that gravitational forces created enough heat and pressure at its core for nuclear reactions to begin. This is why the Sun is a star. If Jupiter's mass were to increase by a factor of 75, nuclear reactions would start at its core, and it too would become a star.

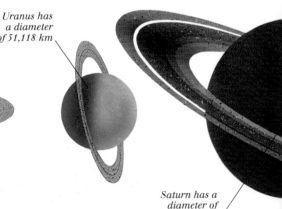

Uranus has a diameter of 51,118 km

Pluto, the smallest of the planets, has a diameter of just 2,290 km

Neptune, the outermost of the gas giants, has a diameter of 49,528 km

Saturn has a diameter of 120,536 km

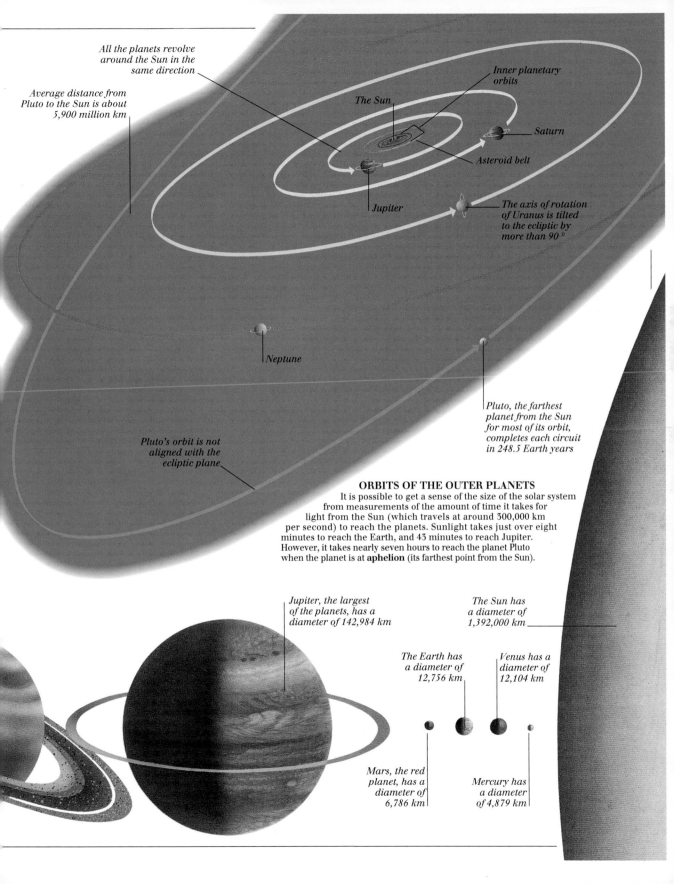

All the planets revolve around the Sun in the same direction

Average distance from Pluto to the Sun is about 5,900 million km

Inner planetary orbits

The Sun

Saturn

Asteroid belt

Jupiter

The axis of rotation of Uranus is tilted to the ecliptic by more than 90 °

Neptune

Pluto, the farthest planet from the Sun for most of its orbit, completes each circuit in 248.5 Earth years

Pluto's orbit is not aligned with the ecliptic plane

ORBITS OF THE OUTER PLANETS

It is possible to get a sense of the size of the solar system from measurements of the amount of time it takes for light from the Sun (which travels at around 300,000 km per second) to reach the planets. Sunlight takes just over eight minutes to reach the Earth, and 43 minutes to reach Jupiter. However, it takes nearly seven hours to reach the planet Pluto when the planet is at **aphelion** (its farthest point from the Sun).

Jupiter, the largest of the planets, has a diameter of 142,984 km

The Sun has a diameter of 1,392,000 km

The Earth has a diameter of 12,756 km

Venus has a diameter of 12,104 km

Mars, the red planet, has a diameter of 6,786 km

Mercury has a diameter of 4,879 km

The Sun

THE SUN IS A STAR at the center of our solar system (see pp. 304-305). It is about 1.4 million kilometers in diameter and dominates the sky during the daytime. The Sun is made almost entirely of hydrogen and helium. Nuclear **fusion** reactions at the Sun's core convert hydrogen into helium, releasing huge amounts of energy. Some of this energy reaches the Earth as sunlight. This is scattered by air **molecules** in the Earth's atmosphere, creating a blue sky. Sunlight is the source of nearly all of the energy on the Earth. This life-sustaining energy is absorbed indirectly by most living organisms, but is absorbed directly by plants in a process called **photosynthesis** (see pp. 148-149). Much can be discovered about the Sun from Earth-based observations. Projections of the Sun's image reveal surface features such as sunspots, and analysis of the solar spectrum (see pp. 300-301) tells us much about the composition of the Sun. The normally invisible outer layers of the Sun can be studied during a solar eclipse, when the Moon blocks out the Sun's light.

OBSERVING THE SUN

It is very dangerous to look directly at the Sun through a telescope or even with the naked eye. Astronomers do, however, use telescopes to observe the Sun. They do this by projecting the Sun's image on to a white surface or photographic film. Astronomers can also pass sunlight through a **spectrometer** in order to study its component colors. There are several large telescopes that are dedicated mainly to solar observations. One of the best known of these is the McNath-Pierce facility (see below) at Kitt Peak National Observatory in Arizona.

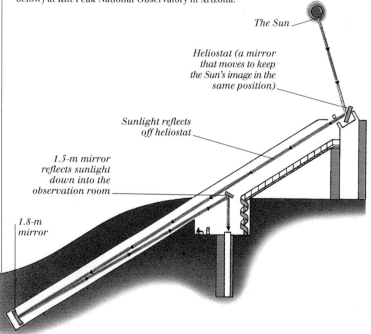

The Sun

Heliostat (a mirror that moves to keep the Sun's image in the same position)

Sunlight reflects off heliostat

1.5-m mirror reflects sunlight down into the observation room

1.8-m mirror

SUNSPOTS

Sunspots appear dark in photographs because they are cooler than the rest of the surface of the Sun. They are caused by variations in the Sun's magnetism, which prevents convection from bringing hotter gas to some parts of the surface. Observation of sunspots has revealed an eleven-year cycle of solar activity. This is referred to as the sunspot cycle, although many other signs of solar activity also vary according to the same cycle.

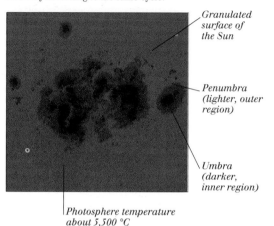

Granulated surface of the Sun

Penumbra (lighter, outer region)

Umbra (darker, inner region)

Photosphere temperature about 5,500 °C

HOW A SOLAR ECLIPSE OCCURS

Occasionally, the Moon passes directly in front of the Sun – as viewed from the Earth – and causes a solar eclipse. During an eclipse, the Moon blocks out the disk of the Sun, allowing astronomers to study the solar atmosphere. A solar eclipse can happen only at new moon, but does not occur with every new moon because the Moon's orbit is tilted slightly compared to the **ecliptic plane**.

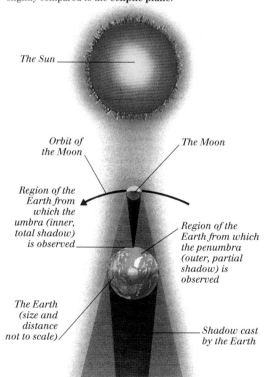

The Sun

Orbit of the Moon

The Moon

Region of the Earth from which the umbra (inner, total shadow) is observed

Region of the Earth from which the penumbra (outer, partial shadow) is observed

The Earth (size and distance not to scale)

Shadow cast by the Earth

THE STRUCTURE OF THE SUN

The hot gas of the photosphere (the Sun's visible surface) produces light by **incandescence**, and it is this light that we see from the Earth. Other features of the photosphere – such as prominences, flares, and sunspots – are all related to the Sun's magnetism. Beneath the photosphere are the convective zone (in which hot gas rises constantly to the surface), the radiative zone, and the core, which is the source of the Sun's energy.

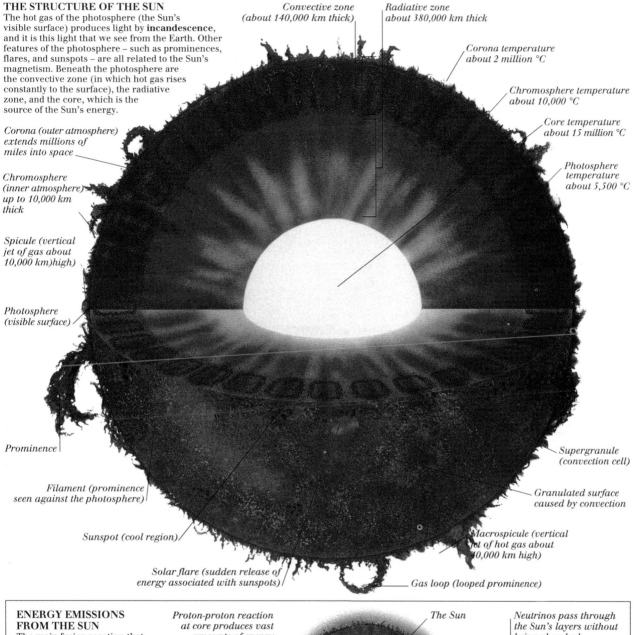

Convective zone (about 140,000 km thick)

Radiative zone about 380,000 km thick

Corona temperature about 2 million °C

Chromosphere temperature about 10,000 °C

Core temperature about 15 million °C

Photosphere temperature about 5,500 °C

Corona (outer atmosphere) extends millions of miles into space

Chromosphere (inner atmosphere) up to 10,000 km thick

Spicule (vertical jet of gas about 10,000 km) high)

Photosphere (visible surface)

Prominence

Supergranule (convection cell)

Filament (prominence seen against the photosphere)

Granulated surface caused by convection

Sunspot (cool region)

Macrospicule (vertical jet of hot gas about 40,000 km high)

Solar flare (sudden release of energy associated with sunspots)

Gas loop (looped prominence)

ENERGY EMISSIONS FROM THE SUN

The main fusion reaction that occurs at the Sun's core is called the proton-proton chain, in which protons (the nuclei of hydrogen atoms) fuse to form helium nuclei. Energy, mostly in the form of gamma radiation, interacts with matter in the radiative zone, causing heating. Heated gas then rises to the photosphere by **convection**. Some of the energy, however, is carried away by particles called neutrinos, which are a by-product of the proton-proton chain.

Proton-proton reaction at core produces vast amounts of energy

The Sun

Neutrinos pass through the Sun's layers without being absorbed

Energy produced as gamma radiation takes hundreds of thousands of years to reach the photosphere (surface of the Sun)

Radiation from the photosphere (sunlight) consists mostly of infrared, ultraviolet, and visible light

Planetary science

THE WORD "PLANET" comes from a Greek word meaning "wanderer," as planets appear to move across the sky relative to the fixed stars. All the planets of the solar system (see pp. 304-305) move around the Sun in paths called orbits. In recent years, several planets have been discovered orbiting distant stars, confirming a long-held belief that planetary systems other than our own do exist. Most of the planets have one or more natural satellites (moons) in orbit around them. In addition to moons, all of the **gas giants** – Jupiter, Saturn, Uranus, and Neptune – have ring systems. The most spectacular ring system in the solar system, that around the planet Saturn (see pp. 318-319), can be observed through a small telescope. Planetary rings are composed of millions of chunks of rock and ice, ranging in size from tiny particles to boulder-sized pieces. Craters are a feature common to the **terrestrial planets** – and to most natural satellites. They are caused by the impact of comets and meteorites (see pp. 322-333). Much of the history of a planet or satellite can be ascertained by studying its craters. Knowledge of the planets has been greatly enhanced by the use of space probes (see pp. 302-303), which have discovered new satellites and rings, and have mapped craters and sent other valuable data back to the Earth.

PLANETARY ORBIT

The shape of each of the orbits of the planets is an ellipse: a "flattened" circle. The orbits of some planets are more flattened, or **eccentric**, than others. The orbits of most of the planets lie more or less in one plane, called the **ecliptic plane**. Comets also orbit the Sun, but are not restricted to this plane.

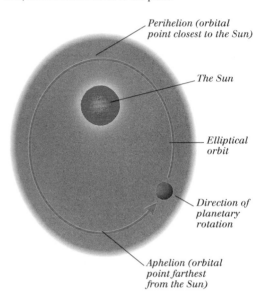

Perihelion (orbital point closest to the Sun)

The Sun

Elliptical orbit

Direction of planetary rotation

Aphelion (orbital point farthest from the Sun)

NATURAL SATELLITES

A satellite is any object in orbit around a planet. Artificial satellites form part of the telecommunications network. Natural satellites are called moons, and all the planets in the Solar System – with the exceptions of Mercury and Venus (see pp. 312-313) – have them. Moons are generally named after characters from literature or mythology. All of the 15 known moons of Uranus, for example, have Shakespearean characters' names, including Titiana and Oberon..

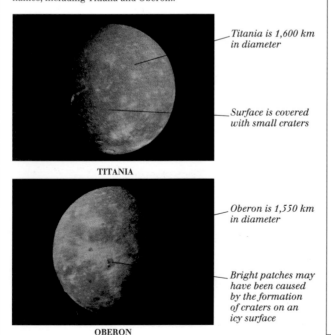

Titania is 1,600 km in diameter

Surface is covered with small craters

TITANIA

Oberon is 1,550 km in diameter

Bright patches may have been caused by the formation of craters on an icy surface

OBERON

STAR WOBBLE

Although distant planets are too far away to be seen from the Earth, astronomers have been able to discover several of them by examining their **gravitational** effects on the stars that they orbit. Each of these planets causes its star to wobble on its axis, and this can be observed from the Earth using powerful telescopes. As the star wobbles, there is a shift in the **wavelengths** of **radiation** it emits – an effect known as Döppler shift. Astronomers can calculate the **mass** of the planet from the degree of shift.

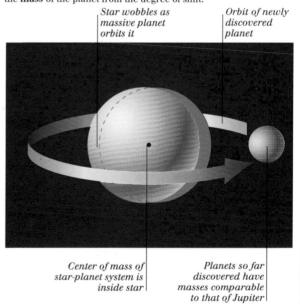

Star wobbles as massive planet orbits it

Orbit of newly discovered planet

Center of mass of star-planet system is inside star

Planets so far discovered have masses comparable to that of Jupiter

RING SYSTEMS

The ring systems of the gas giants differ slightly from one another, but most seem to consist of millions of rocky or icy particles. The smallest of these particles is perhaps the size of a grape, while the largest is the size of a boulder. The origin of the material making up the rings is uncertain. Some may be the result of debris left over from planetary formation, while others may be created from moons that have broken up.

DUST LANES

Many rings have an intricate structure. In some rings, like those around Uranus (shown below), there are dust lanes where there is little or no material. Dust lanes and gaps between rings are probably due to the complex gravitational interaction of the planets with their satellites.

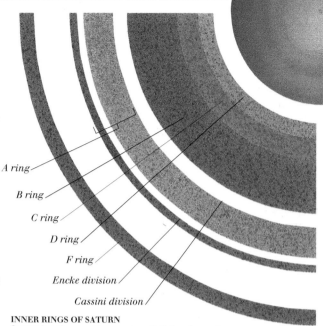

A ring
B ring
C ring
D ring
F ring
Encke division
Cassini division

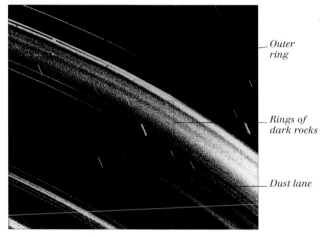

Outer ring

Rings of dark rocks

Dust lane

INNER RINGS OF SATURN

Saturn has the most impressive of all the ring systems. Until 1977, it was the only ring system known. The material of which the rings are made is more reflective than the material of other ring systems, suggesting that Saturn's rings are composed of icy rather than rocky particles. From the Earth, only two rings (A and B) and the gap between them (the Cassini division) are visible with a telescope.

FORMATION OF A RAY CRATER

Formed by the impacts of comets and meteorites (see pp. 322-323), craters are a feature of the surfaces of all known rocky bodies in the solar system. On planets or satellites that have volcanic activity, however, many of the craters are covered over as volcanic material flows over the surface. Craters are also less common on planets with a thick **atmosphere** – most small objects burn up in the atmosphere and never hit the surface. The rate of crater formation was greater when there was more debris left over from the formation of the solar system.

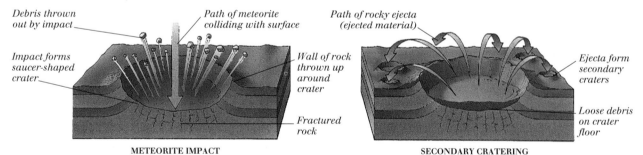

Debris thrown out by impact

Path of meteorite colliding with surface

Impact forms saucer-shaped crater

Wall of rock thrown up around crater

Fractured rock

METEORITE IMPACT

Path of rocky ejecta (ejected material)

Ejecta form secondary craters

Loose debris on crater floor

SECONDARY CRATERING

Central mountain rings form if floor of large crater recoils from meteorite impact

Wall of rock forms ring of mountains

Ray of ejecta (ejected material)

Small secondary crater

Falling debris forms ridges on side of crater wall

Loose, ejected rock

A RAY CRATER

The Moon

THE MOON IS THE SECOND BRIGHTEST object in the sky after the Sun (see pp. 306-307). It is the Earth's only natural satellite, and it is a cold, dry, and airless place. One side of the Moon – the "far side" – cannot be seen from the Earth and had never been observed before a Russian space probe took photographs of it in 1959. The Sun illuminates one half of the Moon at all times. The portion of this illuminated half that is visible from the Earth varies on a monthly cycle, giving rise to the lunar phases. When the Moon is between the Earth and the Sun, at new moon, we cannot see the illuminated side at all. At full moon, the Earth is between the Sun and the Moon, and the side of the Moon facing the Earth is fully illuminated. Occasionally, at full moon, the Moon passes through the shadow of the Earth, causing its surface to darken. This phenomenon is called a lunar eclipse. Perhaps the best known of the Moon's surface features are its craters, formed by meteorite impacts (see pp. 322-323) and dark "seas" called maria. Analysis of moon rock reveals that the Moon is made of **igneous** material, formed by the cooling of lava (see pp. 278-279).

MOON DUST

The soil that covers the Moon's surface is called regolith and consists mainly of dust and rock fragments ejected during crater formation. Tiny, glassy particles called spherules are common in the lunar regolith. They are formed by the rapid heating and cooling that occurs as a result of meteorite impacts. The spherules below are about 0.025 mm in diameter.

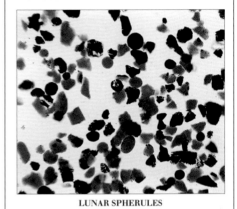

LUNAR SPHERULES

HOW A LUNAR ECLIPSE OCCURS

The total phase of a lunar eclipse, when the Moon passes through the central part of the Earth's shadow (the umbra) lasts for up to an hour. During an eclipse, the Moon is not totally black, but appears reddish brown. This is because sunlight passing through the Earth's **atmosphere** is **refracted** so that some of it strikes the Moon. Most of the blue part of the **spectrum** is scattered by the atmosphere, leaving red light to reflect off the Moon.

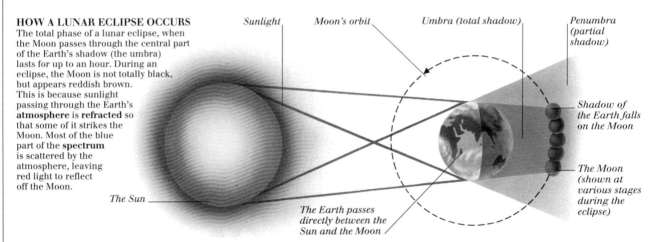

Sunlight *Moon's orbit* *Umbra (total shadow)* *Penumbra (partial shadow)*

Shadow of the Earth falls on the Moon

The Moon (shown at various stages during the eclipse)

The Sun

The Earth passes directly between the Sun and the Moon

PHASES OF THE MOON

The Moon reflects light from the Sun and is the brightest object in the night sky. The amount of light it reflects varies as seen from the Earth. Once during every cycle, it reflects no light at all and is called a new moon. A few days after new moon, the Moon's near side becomes visible, at first as a thin crescent. The proportion of the Moon's disk that we see increases (waxes) until, at full moon, the near side is completely illuminated. Over the next 14 days, the Moon's disk appears to decrease (wane), until the Moon once again lies between the Earth and the Sun.

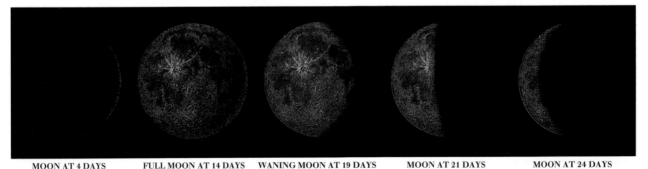

MOON AT 4 DAYS FULL MOON AT 14 DAYS WANING MOON AT 19 DAYS MOON AT 21 DAYS MOON AT 24 DAYS

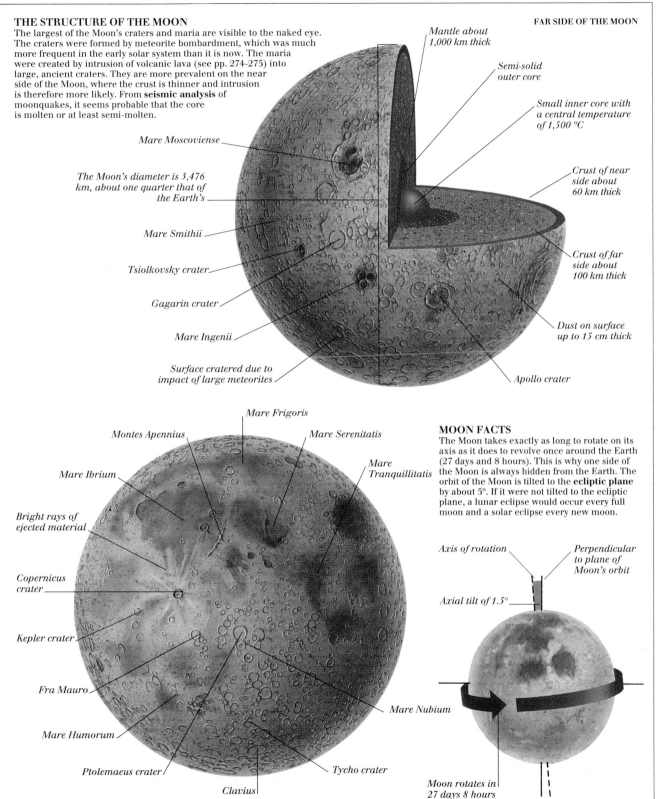

THE STRUCTURE OF THE MOON

The largest of the Moon's craters and maria are visible to the naked eye. The craters were formed by meteorite bombardment, which was much more frequent in the early solar system than it is now. The maria were created by intrusion of volcanic lava (see pp. 274-275) into large, ancient craters. They are more prevalent on the near side of the Moon, where the crust is thinner and intrusion is therefore more likely. From **seismic analysis** of moonquakes, it seems probable that the core is molten or at least semi-molten.

FAR SIDE OF THE MOON

Mantle about 1,000 km thick

Semi-solid outer core

Small inner core with a central temperature of 1,500 °C

Crust of near side about 60 km thick

Crust of far side about 100 km thick

Dust on surface up to 15 cm thick

Apollo crater

Mare Moscoviense

The Moon's diameter is 3,476 km, about one quarter that of the Earth's

Mare Smithii

Tsiolkovsky crater

Gagarin crater

Mare Ingenii

Surface cratered due to impact of large meteorites

Mare Frigoris

Montes Apennius

Mare Serenitatis

Mare Tranquillitatis

Mare Ibrium

Bright rays of ejected material

Copernicus crater

Kepler crater

Fra Mauro

Mare Humorum

Ptolemaeus crater

Clavius

Tycho crater

Mare Nubium

NEAR SIDE OF THE MOON

MOON FACTS

The Moon takes exactly as long to rotate on its axis as it does to revolve once around the Earth (27 days and 8 hours). This is why one side of the Moon is always hidden from the Earth. The orbit of the Moon is tilted to the **ecliptic plane** by about 5°. If it were not tilted to the ecliptic plane, a lunar eclipse would occur every full moon and a solar eclipse every new moon.

Axis of rotation

Perpendicular to plane of Moon's orbit

Axial tilt of 1.5°

Moon rotates in 27 days 8 hours

Mercury and Venus

MERCURY AND VENUS ARE THE TWO PLANETS closest to the Sun. Because their orbits are nearer to the Sun than the Earth's is, they exhibit **phases** like those of the Moon, when observed through an Earth-based telescope (see pp. 310-311). From the Earth, Mercury and Venus are visible only around sunrise or sunset. Venus is larger than Mercury, closer to the Earth, and usually at a greater elongation (apparent distance across the sky from the Sun). For these reasons, it is normally the brighter of the two. It is, in fact, the brightest object in the sky after the Sun and the Moon, and its prominence before sunrise or after sunset has led to it being called both the Morning Star and the Evening Star. Despite being so close in astronomical terms, Mercury and Venus are two very different worlds. The surface of Mercury is dry, rocky, and pock-marked with many craters, large and small. It is small – about the same size as the Moon – and has no **atmosphere**. Venus has a thick atmosphere and is about the same size as the Earth. Both planets have been visited by space probes (see pp. 302-303). Mercury was mapped by *Mariner 10* in 1974, while several probes have visited Venus. The most recent of these, *Magellan*, made extensive use of **radar**, allowing astronomers to penetrate its thick atmosphere and produce accurate maps of the planet's surface.

EARTH-BASED OBSERVATION

Mercury and Venus are close to the Sun in space, so they are never far from it in the sky. Each of the planets is visible to the naked eye – either just before sunrise or just after sunset – but Mercury is visible only when it is at its greatest elongation. Very occasionally, Mercury and Venus are seen to pass across the disk of the Sun, an occurrence called a transit.

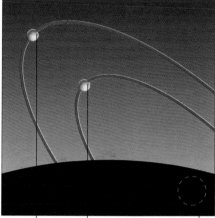

Venus | *Mercury* | *The Sun below the Earth's horizon*

THE STRUCTURE OF MERCURY

Mercury's most obvious surface features are its millions of craters. Many of these are old, indicating that there has been no recent volcanic activity – which would otherwise have filled in some of the older craters with volcanic lava. Beneath the surface, Mercury is dominated by a huge, iron core. Its diameter is about 3,700 km: more than 75 percent of the diameter of the planet as a whole. Surrounding the core are a mantle and a crust. These are made of silicates, materials that are common in the mantle and crust of the Earth.

MERCURY FACTS

Mercury is almost exactly upright with respect to the **ecliptic plane**. The planet rotates on its axis exactly three times for every two complete orbits of the Sun. The planet's orbit is very **eccentric**. This, together with the planet's slow rotation and lack of atmosphere, leads to a huge variation in surface temperatures, which range from -183 °C to 427 °C.

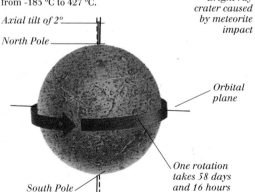

Axial tilt of 2°

North Pole

Orbital plane

One rotation takes 58 days and 16 hours

South Pole

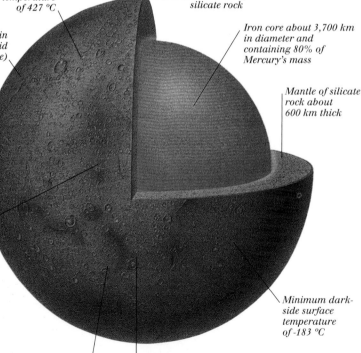

Maximum sunlit surface temperature of 427 °C

Thin crust of silicate rock

Caloris basin (asteroid impact site)

Iron core about 3,700 km in diameter and containing 80% of Mercury's mass

Mantle of silicate rock about 600 km thick

Bright ray crater caused by meteorite impact

Minimum dark-side surface temperature of -183 °C

The surface of Mercury is pitted with many old craters

Michelangelo (the craters of Mercury are named after great artists, composers, writers, and poets)

THE STRUCTURE OF VENUS

Venus and the Earth are alike in many respects. They have very similar **densities** and diameters. Volcanic activity is another common feature, and both planets have atmospheres that protect them from radiation and prevent the dramatic variations in surface temperature found on Mercury. Like the Earth, Venus has an iron core and a rocky mantle and crust. Unlike the Earth, however, the atmosphere of Venus is composed largely of carbon dioxide, with clouds of corrosive sulfuric acid. The abundance of carbon dioxide has led to a runaway **greenhouse effect**, giving rise to surface temperatures of up to 467 ºC. The atmospheric pressure at the surface of Venus is around 90 times that of the Earth's.

VENUS FACTS

The axis of rotation of Venus is almost exactly 90º to the **ecliptic**. The rotation of Venus is retrograde (east-west). Most planets rotate counterclockwise as viewed from above their North poles. The planet rotates on its axis once every 243 days, and orbits the Sun once every 225 days, making its day longer than its year.

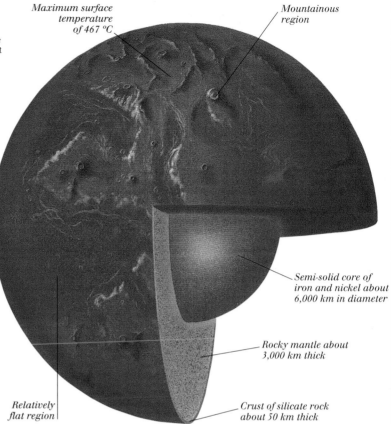

Maximum surface temperature of 467 ºC

Mountainous region

Semi-solid core of iron and nickel about 6,000 km in diameter

Rocky mantle about 3,000 km thick

Crust of silicate rock about 50 km thick

Relatively flat region

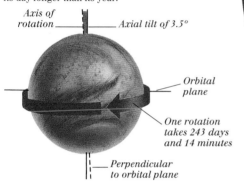

Axis of rotation

Axial tilt of 3.5º

Orbital plane

One rotation takes 243 days and 14 minutes

Perpendicular to orbital plane

RADAR MAPPING THE SURFACE OF VENUS

The principle of radar mapping is very simple: bursts of microwave radiation are transmitted from a probe and reflect off the surface of the planet. From the time delay between transmission and reception of the reflected pulse, the height of the probe in relation to the planet's surface can be worked out with great accuracy. This technique can map a planet's rocky terrain through thick clouds, and even under layers of dust. The *Magellan* probe (launched in May 1989 from the space shuttle) produced very accurate radar maps of the surface of Venus. Detailed three-dimensional computer models were created using the data gathered by the probe.

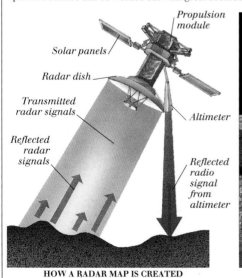

Propulsion module

Solar panels

Radar dish

Transmitted radar signals

Altimeter

Reflected radar signals

Reflected radio signal from altimeter

HOW A RADAR MAP IS CREATED

IMAGE OF THE SURFACE OF VENUS CREATED BY RADAR MAPPING

Mars

MARS IS THE FOURTH PLANET from the Sun. It is the outermost of the **terrestrial planets** and is separated from Jupiter (see pp. 316-317), the first of the **gas giants**, by the asteroid belt (see pp. 322-323). From the Earth, Mars is seen as a bright object that appears to move across the sky from night to night. Its two small moons, Phobos and Deimos, can easily be seen through a small telescope. Although the **atmosphere** on Mars is very thin by comparison with that on the Earth, dust storms are a common occurrence. The winds that cause the dust storms occur across the whole planet and change direction as the Martian seasons change. There are four seasons during the course of a Martian year, which lasts almost twice as long as a year on Earth. Mars has several enormous, extinct volcanoes, including Olympus Mons, the largest known volcano (see pp. 274-275) in the solar system. The surface is also scarred by a number of vast canyons, some of which are bigger than the Grand Canyon. The Martian surface is covered with a dust that contains a large proportion of the **compound** iron oxide, which gives the planet its distinctive red color. Beneath its surface, Mars has a cold, rocky crust and mantle, and a solid, iron core. During the 19th century, some astronomers observed what they assumed to be signs of intelligent life on the planet. These signs included canal-like markings and varying dark patches, which were thought to be areas under cultivation. It is now known that these assumptions were mistaken.

MARS FACTS

The tilt of Mars's axis is almost the same as the Earth's. As is the case on the Earth, this axial tilt is the cause of the planet's seasons. Mars rotates once on its axis every 24 hours and 37 minutes, which makes a Martian day about the same length as a day on the Earth.

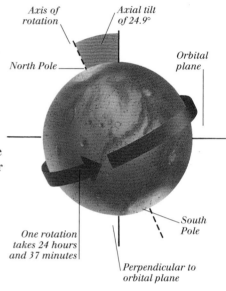

Axis of rotation

Axial tilt of 24.9°

North Pole

Orbital plane

South Pole

One rotation takes 24 hours and 37 minutes

Perpendicular to orbital plane

ORBIT OF MARS

Watched over a period of a few weeks, the apparent motion of Mars across the night sky sometimes follows several irregular loops. This is called retrograde motion and occurs, to a lesser extent, with other planets. The explanation of this phenomenon is that our vantage point, the Earth, moves more quickly through its orbit than does Mars, and therefore overtakes it.

At the time that this was first suggested, most people believed in the geocentric model of the universe (which puts a fixed Earth at the center of the universe). Observations of the actual motion of Mars helped to disprove this theory, placing the Sun at the center of the solar system.

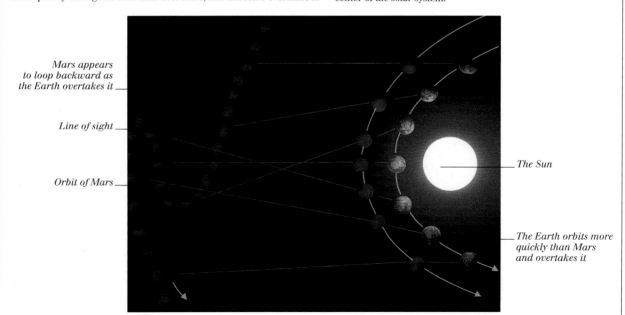

Mars appears to loop backward as the Earth overtakes it

Line of sight

Orbit of Mars

The Sun

The Earth orbits more quickly than Mars and overtakes it

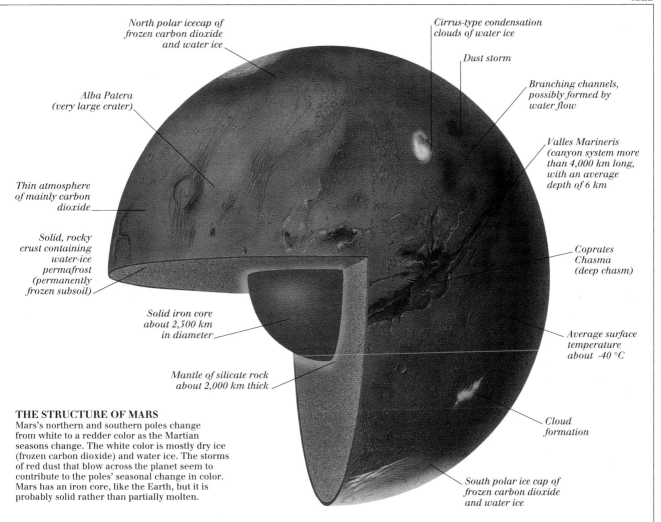

North polar icecap of frozen carbon dioxide and water ice

Cirrus-type condensation clouds of water ice

Dust storm

Alba Patera (very large crater)

Branching channels, possibly formed by water flow

Valles Marineris (canyon system more than 4,000 km long, with an average depth of 6 km)

Thin atmosphere of mainly carbon dioxide

Solid, rocky crust containing water-ice permafrost (permanently frozen subsoil)

Coprates Chasma (deep chasm)

Solid iron core about 2,500 km in diameter

Average surface temperature about -40 °C

Mantle of silicate rock about 2,000 km thick

Cloud formation

South polar ice cap of frozen carbon dioxide and water ice

THE STRUCTURE OF MARS

Mars's northern and southern poles change from white to a redder color as the Martian seasons change. The white color is mostly dry ice (frozen carbon dioxide) and water ice. The storms of red dust that blow across the planet seem to contribute to the poles' seasonal change in color. Mars has an iron core, like the Earth, but it is probably solid rather than partially molten.

SURFACE FEATURES OF MARS

Mars has a heavily cratered surface that has remained unchanged for millions of years. There seems to be evidence of the flow of liquid water at some time in the past at many locations on the surface of Mars. For example, there are huge canyons that look like river valleys. There is no plate movement (see pp. 272-273) in the Martian crust, so landscape features do not change for millions of years. The lack of plate movement also means that volcanoes on Mars are not carried away from the **magma** source. This may explain why Mars has some of the largest volcanoes in the solar system. These include Olympus Mons, which is 25 km high – three times higher than Mount Everest.

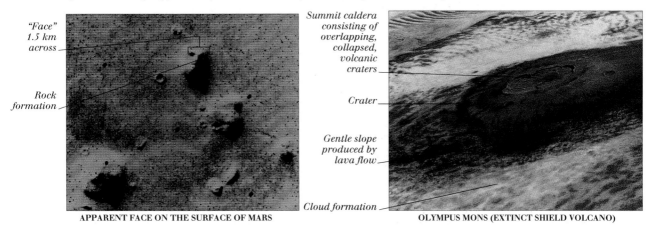

"Face" 1.5 km across

Rock formation

Summit caldera consisting of overlapping, collapsed, volcanic craters

Crater

Gentle slope produced by lava flow

Cloud formation

APPARENT FACE ON THE SURFACE OF MARS

OLYMPUS MONS (EXTINCT SHIELD VOLCANO)

Jupiter

JUPITER IS THE LARGEST PLANET in the solar system
(see pp. 304-305). Like Saturn (see pp. 318-319), Jupiter
consists nearly exclusively of the **elements** hydrogen and
helium. Its recognized diameter is more than eleven times
that of the Earth's, and its **mass** is more than 300 times
greater. Jupiter's rocky core is surrounded by metallic
hydrogen (liquid hydrogen that behaves like a metal) and
is very hot – around 30,000 °C. If the planet were about 75
times more massive, **nuclear fusion** (see pp. 58-59) would
start at its core and it would become a star. Jupiter rotates
rapidly on its axis, giving rise to a slight widening around its
middle, known as its **equatorial** bulge. The banded structure
of Jupiter's gaseous **atmosphere** is caused by this rapid
rotation, as is the Great Red Spot, a high-pressure storm
system that is more than twice the diameter of the Earth and
which has been observed for over 300 years. The outer layers
of Jupiter's atmosphere have been studied directly by the
Galileo probe (see pp. 302-303). Jupiter is normally the
fourth-brightest object in the sky – after the Sun, the Moon,
and Venus. The planet's four principal moons – known as the
Galilean moons – were the first moons, other than the
Earth's, to be discovered. In July 1994, fragments of Comet
Shoemaker–Levy 9 bombarded Jupiter in a historic series of
impacts. Later analysis of the results of these impacts has
revealed much about the planet.

TILT AND ROTATION OF JUPITER

Jupiter takes just under 10 hours to rotate once on its axis.
This is less than half the time it takes for the Earth to rotate on
its axis. Matter around the equator travels more quickly than
matter around the poles, giving rise to an equatorial bulge.

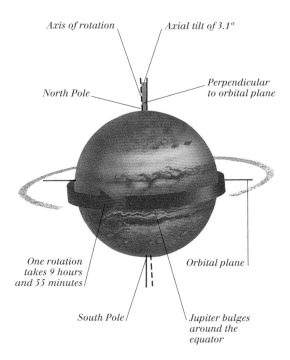

Axis of rotation

Axial tilt of 3.1°

North Pole

*Perpendicular
to orbital plane*

*One rotation
takes 9 hours
and 55 minutes*

Orbital plane

South Pole

*Jupiter bulges
around the
equator*

GREAT RED SPOT

The Great Red Spot is a huge anticyclonic storm in the southern hemisphere of
Jupiter. (White ovals are smaller, similar features of the planet's atmosphere.)
The colors of the clouds in Jupiter's atmosphere vary depending on their
altitudes. The lowest cloud layer is blue, followed by dark orange, and white.
Red clouds, like those of the Great Red Spot, are highest. The different colors
are associated with different chemical reactions in the atmosphere of the planet.

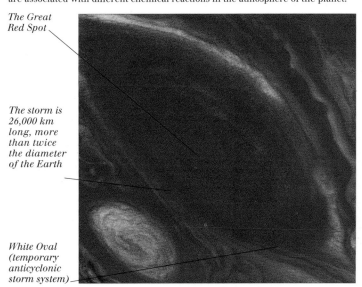

*The Great
Red Spot*

*The storm is
26,000 km
long, more
than twice
the diameter
of the Earth*

*White Oval
(temporary
anticyclonic
storm system)*

GALILEAN MOONS OF JUPITER

Jupiter has 16 known moons. Of these, four are large enough to
be seen from the Earth through a small telescope or binoculars.
These are the Galilean moons, named after their discoverer,
the Italian astronomer Galileo Galilei (see pp. 394-395). Io, the
innermost moon, is one of the few bodies in the solar system
known to have active volcanoes.

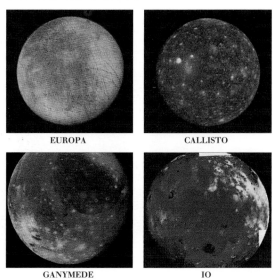

EUROPA

CALLISTO

GANYMEDE

IO

THE STRUCTURE OF JUPITER

Jupiter's rocky core is surrounded by an inner mantle of metallic hydrogen. This unusual form of hydrogen is found only in conditions of very high temperature and pressure. It is a dense "soup" of hydrogen **nuclei** and **electrons** that behaves like a metal. Jupiter's outer mantle is liquid and merges with the atmosphere.

North polar aurora

North Temperate Zone

North Temperate Belt

North Tropical Zone

North Equatorial Belt

Equatorial Zone

South Equatorial Belt

South Tropical Zone

South Temperate Belt

South Temperate Zone

Rocky core about 28,000 km in diameter

Core temperature around 30,000 °C

Inner mantle of metallic hydrogen

Outer mantle of liquid hydrogen and helium, which merges with the atmosphere

Atmosphere of mainly hydrogen and helium

Red color probably due to the presence of phosphorus

White oval (temporary anticyclonic storm system)

Cloud-top temperature about -120 °C

Great Red Spot (anticyclonic storm system)

Flash of lightning

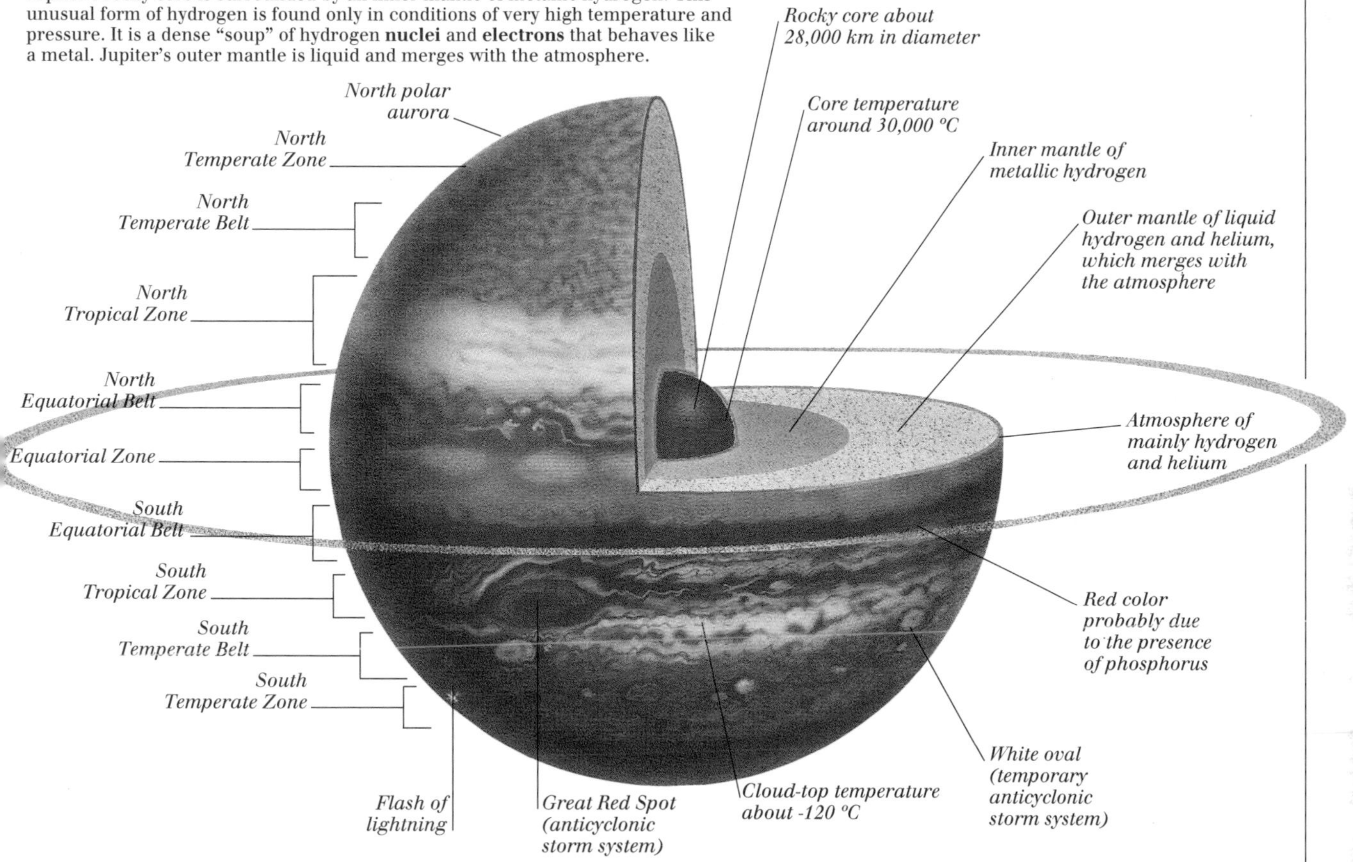

ATMOSPHERE OF JUPITER

Like all of the **gas giants**, Jupiter does not have a definite **radius**. Instead, it becomes gradually more dense with depth. Its radius is defined as the distance out from the center of the planet at which the **atmospheric pressure** is equal to atmospheric pressure at sea level on the Earth.

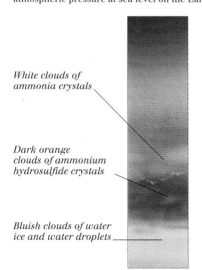

White clouds of ammonia crystals

Dark orange clouds of ammonium hydrosulfide crystals

Bluish clouds of water ice and water droplets

IMPACT OF COMET SHOEMAKER–LEVY 9 ON JUPITER

In July 1994, Comet Shoemaker–Levy 9 approached Jupiter. Tidal forces due to Jupiter's strong gravitational field broke the comet into a number of fragments. These fragments hit the planet one by one, over a period of six days. The results were spectacular, and the impacts left a series of "bruises" in the atmosphere. These were the result of violent explosions called fireballs, caused by the impacts of the cometary fragments.

Jupiter

Path of comet

Fragment G

COMET-IMPACT PATH

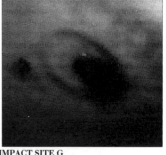

IMPACT SITE G
The dark areas in this photograph, taken by the *Hubble Space Telescope*, correspond to the presence of methane gas. The bright areas are due to sunlight reflected off other material, ejected high above the methane cloud layers by the largest impact, that of fragment G.

Saturn and Uranus

SATURN AND URANUS are the sixth and seventh planets out from the Sun. They are typical **gas giants**, consisting mainly of hydrogen and helium in liquid and gas forms. Both planets have **atmospheres** with banded structures, which are caused by rising and falling regions of gases and high winds that blow in alternate directions. These bands are barely noticeable on Uranus, largely because they are masked by the planet's uniformly blue-green upper atmosphere. Both planets have a ring system (see pp. 308-309). Saturn's ring system was first discovered in the 17th century, during early telescopic observations. It is the largest and most complex ring system of any planet in the solar system. In contrast, the rings around Uranus were discovered only as recently as 1977. Much of what we know about Saturn and Uranus was learned from data sent back by the *Voyager 2* space probe (see pp. 302-303), which visited both planets and discovered several moons. Saturn has eighteen moons – the greatest number for any planet – while Uranus has fifteen.

SATURN FACTS

Each revolution of Saturn around the Sun takes 29.5 Earth-years to complete. Saturn rotates rapidly on its axis. This rapid rotation causes an equatorial bulge similar to Jupiter's. The planet's axis of rotation is tilted with respect to the **ecliptic** by about the same angle as the Earth's is.

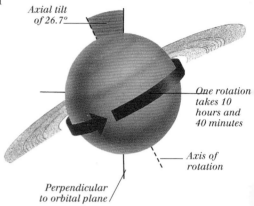

Axial tilt of 26.7°

One rotation takes 10 hours and 40 minutes

Axis of rotation

Perpendicular to orbital plane

THE STRUCTURE OF SATURN

Saturn has a core of rock and ice that is surrounded by metallic hydrogen. The rest of the planet is composed mainly of hydrogen and helium, in liquid and gaseous forms. The planet's upper atmosphere contains a good deal of ammonia and its **compounds**. The overall **density** of Saturn is the lowest of all the planets. Saturn is less dense than water and so would float on a lake – if there were one large enough. It has the best-known and most spectacular ring system of all the gas giants. Mysterious dark lines in the ring system, called radial spokes, have been observed by the *Voyager* space probes.

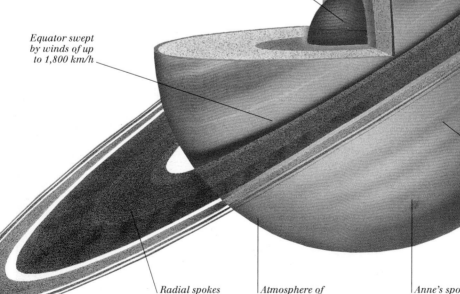

Outer mantle of liquid hydrogen

Inner mantle of liquid metallic hydrogen

Core of rock and ice about 30,000 km in diameter

Equator swept by winds of up to 1,800 km/h

Radial spokes

Atmosphere of mainly hydrogen and helium

Anne's spot (an anticyclonic storm system)

Cloud-top temperature about -180 °C

THE STRUCTURE OF URANUS

The blue-green color of the upper atmosphere of Uranus is due to a relatively high abundance of methane. (This **compound** absorbs red light, reflecting only blue and green light from the white light falling on it from the Sun.) The planet's rings were discovered during Earth-based observations of the planet as it occulted (passed in front of) a star. They are incomplete and nonuniform, which would seem to indicate that the ring system may be relatively young. (The ring system may be composed of fragments of a moon that was broken up by the gravitational influence of the planet.)

URANUS FACTS

Uranus has an 84-year orbit. It rotates as though it were on its side with respect to the **ecliptic** plane. As the planet revolves around the Sun, light shines first on to one pole, then the equator, then the other pole, then the equator once again. This is one reason why the planet shows little temperature difference throughout its atmosphere.

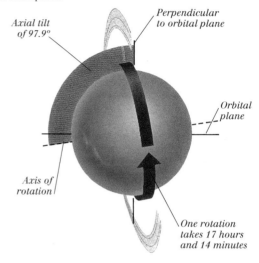

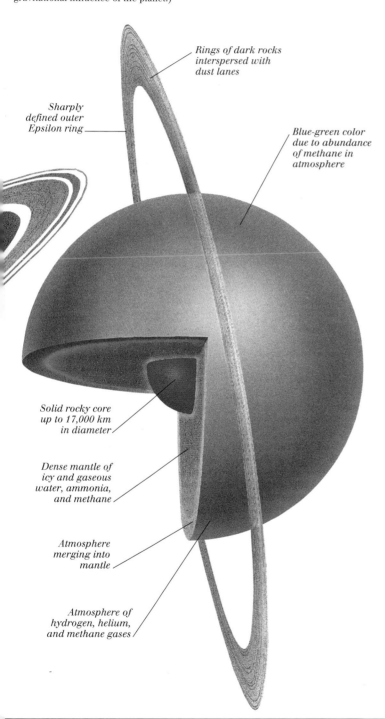

Rings of dark rocks
interspersed with
dust lanes

Sharply
defined outer
Epsilon ring

Blue-green color
due to abundance
of methane in
atmosphere

Solid rocky core
up to 17,000 km
in diameter

Dense mantle of
icy and gaseous
water, ammonia,
and methane

Atmosphere
merging into
mantle

Atmosphere of
hydrogen, helium,
and methane gases

Perpendicular
to orbital plane

Axial tilt
of 97.9°

Orbital
plane

Axis of
rotation

One rotation
takes 17 hours
and 14 minutes

TECTONIC PLATES

Miranda is the most interesting of the outer moons of Uranus and is pictured here in a photograph taken by *Voyager 2* in 1986. Miranda's diameter is about 484 km – only one seventh the diameter of our moon – and it orbits Uranus at an average distance of 129,800 km. The scarred face of Miranda is covered not only with craters, but also with valleys, faults, and highland plateaus. All of these features suggest that the surface of Miranda, like that of the Earth, is composed of tectonic plates (see pp. 272-273).

Valleys and faults
suggest tectonic activity

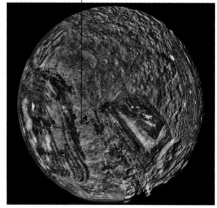

MIRANDA – A MOON OF URANUS

Neptune and Pluto

NEPTUNE IS THE OUTERMOST of the **gas giants**. Like Uranus (see pp. 318-19), its blue color is due to the presence of methane gas in its atmosphere. Neptune has eight known moons and a ring system (see pp. 308-309). Pluto is a small, rocky body with just one moon and no ring system. For most of its 248-year orbit, Pluto is the planet farthest from the Sun. However, it has a very **eccentric orbit**, which causes it to pass inside the orbit of Neptune. Pluto was discovered in 1930, after calculations based on deviations in the orbits of Uranus and Neptune prompted the search for the planet. Pluto's **mass** is not great enough to have caused these deviations, and so, after the discovery of Pluto, astronomers began a search for yet another planet. The hypothetical planet – called Planet X – was never found. Recent, more accurate, measurements of the masses of Neptune and Pluto show that the orbital deviations of Uranus and Neptune are not caused by Planet X. They are, in fact, caused by other objects of a similar size to Pluto that have been found beyond the orbit of Neptune. These objects – called Plutinos – are probably similar to asteroids (see pp. 322-323), and are found in a region of the outer solar system called the Kuiper Belt.

NEPTUNE FACTS

Neptune's orbit takes just under 165 Earth-years to complete. The planet rotates more rapidly on its axis than does the Earth. This rapid rotation, together with an axial tilt of nearly 29°, causes strong winds in Neptune's **atmosphere**. The planet's diameter is nearly four times as large as the Earth's.

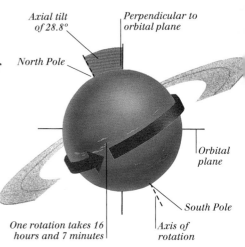

Axial tilt of 28.8°

Perpendicular to orbital plane

North Pole

Orbital plane

South Pole

One rotation takes 16 hours and 7 minutes

Axis of rotation

THE STRUCTURE OF NEPTUNE

Most of what is known about Neptune was discovered during its encounter with the space probe *Voyager 2* in August 1989. Neptune is a typical gas giant, being composed mainly of hydrogen and helium, with methane and ammonia also present. It has a rocky core and its mantle is composed largely of various types of ice, including water. The icy mantle merges gradually into the gaseous atmosphere. *Voyager 2* sent back stunning pictures of the rings of Neptune, about which little was previously known. It is still not known for certain what the rings are composed of, but they probably consist of small chunks of rock and ice.

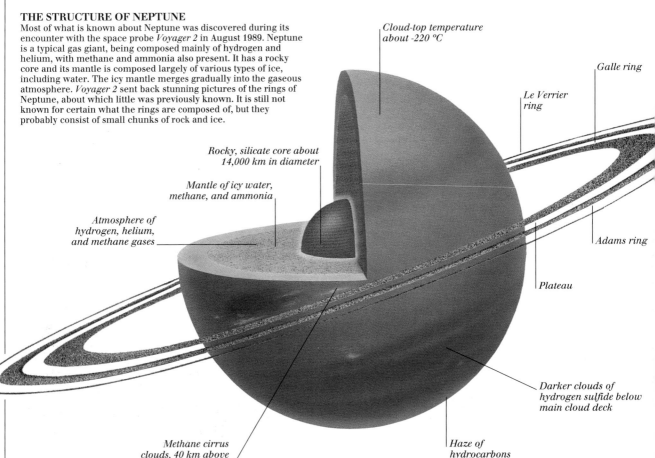

Cloud-top temperature about -220 °C

Galle ring

Le Verrier ring

Rocky, silicate core about 14,000 km in diameter

Mantle of icy water, methane, and ammonia

Atmosphere of hydrogen, helium, and methane gases

Adams ring

Plateau

Darker clouds of hydrogen sulfide below main cloud deck

Methane cirrus clouds, 40 km above main cloud deck

Haze of hydrocarbons above clouds

THE STRUCTURE OF PLUTO

The composition of Pluto is unknown. The **density** of the planet, calculated from its mass and its size, suggests that it consists largely of rock and water ice. Most of what is known of the structure of Pluto is computed from the **spectrum** of sunlight reflected off the planet. The planet appears to have a thin atmosphere, which may exist only when Pluto is near **perihelion** (its closest approach to the Sun). When the planet is farther from the Sun, its surface temperature falls, and the atmosphere probably freezes.

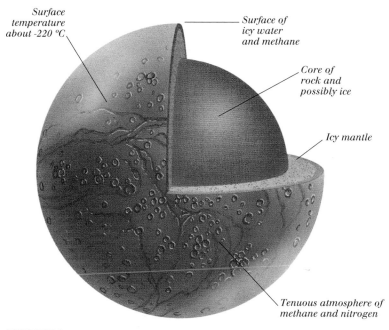

Surface temperature about -220 °C

Surface of icy water and methane

Core of rock and possibly ice

Icy mantle

Tenuous atmosphere of methane and nitrogen

PLUTINOS

Beyond the orbit of Neptune lies the Kuiper Belt, a collection of rocky bodies similar to asteroids. Some astronomers consider Pluto to be a Kuiper Belt object rather than a true planet. It takes exactly one-and-a-half times as long as Neptune to orbit the Sun (a ratio of 3 to 2). This is known as 3:2 orbital resonance, and several recently discovered Kuiper Belt objects (called Plutinos) share this property. Further weight is given to the argument that Pluto is not a true planet by the fact that Pluto's orbit is inclined steeply to the **ecliptic plane**.

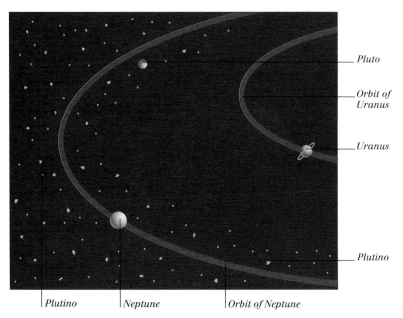

Pluto

Orbit of Uranus

Uranus

Plutino

Plutino   *Neptune*   *Orbit of Neptune*

PLUTO FACTS

Pluto orbits the Sun at an average distance of 5,900 million km. This is nearly 40 times greater than the average distance of the Earth from the Sun, or nearly 40 **astronomical units**. At this distance, Pluto must be a very cold and dark world. It is actually smaller than several of the moons orbiting some of the other planets in the solar system.

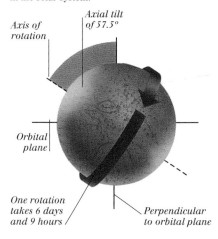

Axis of rotation

Axial tilt of 57.5°

Orbital plane

One rotation takes 6 days and 9 hours

Perpendicular to orbital plane

DOUBLE-PLANET SYSTEM

Pluto and its satellite, Charon, are often considered to be a double-planet system because their masses are so similar. Using Earth-based telescopes, it is almost impossible to figure out the relative masses of the two planets, which will not be known for certain until a space probe travels close to the system.

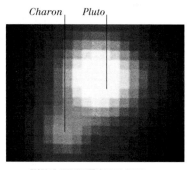

Charon   *Pluto*

USUAL VIEW FROM EARTH

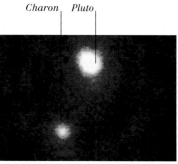

Charon   *Pluto*

***HUBBLE* TELESCOPE IMAGE**

Comets, asteroids, and meteoroids

COMETS ARE SMALL BODIES consisting mainly of dust and various ices. As a comet approaches the Sun (see pp. 306-307), it warms up, releasing huge amounts of **gas** and dust, which form long tails. Short-period comets are always within the orbits of the planets, but the majority of comets spend most of their time outside the orbit of Pluto (see pp. 320-321). Asteroids are rocky bodies up to 1,000 kilometers in diameter. Most of them are found in the asteroid belt, which lies between the orbits of Mars (see pp. 314-315) and Jupiter (pp. 316-317). Meteoroids are mostly fragments of asteroids or are debris left behind by the dust tail of a comet. As they enter the Earth's atmosphere, they heat up due to **air resistance**, appearing as bright, fast-moving streaks called meteors. Meteor showers occur when the Earth passes through the trail of dust particles left by a comet.

OBSERVING A COMET
A bright comet can be a spectacular sight, even to the naked eye. It looks like a bright, fuzzy star and has a long tail that points away from the Sun. Comets are visible to the naked eye only while they are relatively close to the Sun. A photographic exposure taken over a period of a few minutes (as shown below) allows astronomers to record the full glory of a comet.

TAILS OF A COMET
When they are near the Sun, comets have two tails: a straight gas tail and a curved dust tail. The gas tail forms as frozen material **sublimes**. A stream of fast-moving particles emitted by the Sun (the solar wind) pushes the gas tail into a straight line. As the frozen material sublimes, it releases dust from the comet's nucleus. The dust is pushed less easily by the solar wind, so it is left behind as a trail of debris along the curve of the comet's orbit.

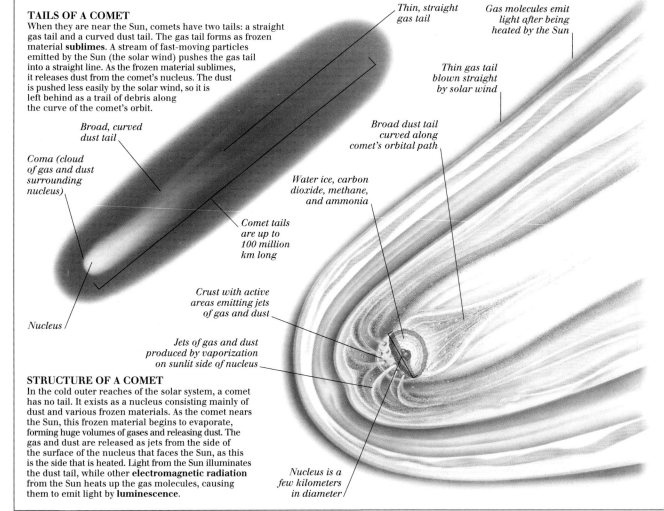

Thin, straight gas tail

Gas molecules emit light after being heated by the Sun

Thin gas tail blown straight by solar wind

Broad, curved dust tail

Broad dust tail curved along comet's orbital path

Coma (cloud of gas and dust surrounding nucleus)

Water ice, carbon dioxide, methane, and ammonia

Comet tails are up to 100 million km long

Crust with active areas emitting jets of gas and dust

Nucleus

Jets of gas and dust produced by vaporization on sunlit side of nucleus

Nucleus is a few kilometers in diameter

STRUCTURE OF A COMET
In the cold outer reaches of the solar system, a comet has no tail. It exists as a nucleus consisting mainly of dust and various frozen materials. As the comet nears the Sun, this frozen material begins to evaporate, forming huge volumes of gases and releasing dust. The gas and dust are released as jets from the side of the surface of the nucleus that faces the Sun, as this is the side that is heated. Light from the Sun illuminates the dust tail, while other **electromagnetic radiation** from the Sun heats up the gas molecules, causing them to emit light by **luminescence**.

ASTEROIDS AND THE ASTEROID BELT

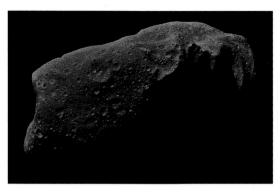

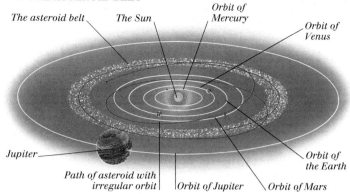

The asteroid belt

The Sun

Orbit of Mercury

Orbit of Venus

Jupiter

Path of asteroid with irregular orbit

Orbit of Jupiter

Orbit of Mars

Orbit of the Earth

ASTEROIDS
There are probably only about 200 asteroids with diameters greater than 100 km. The rest are smaller bodies, with an average diameter of about 1 km. Asteroid 243 (shown above) is a typical asteroid – small, irregularly shaped, and cratered.

THE ASTEROID BELT
The asteroid belt probably formed at the same time as the planets, and one theory suggests that it may have been a failed planet, which was prevented from forming due to the **gravitational** influence of Jupiter. Some asteroids have irregular orbits and can approach dangerously close to the Earth.

METEOROIDS AND METEOR SHOWERS

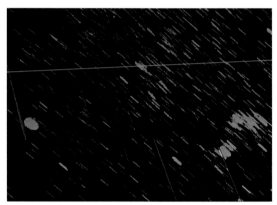

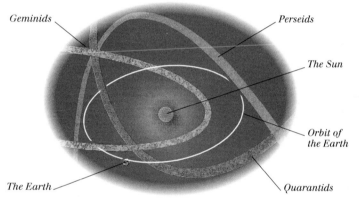

Geminids

Perseids

The Sun

Orbit of the Earth

The Earth

Quarantids

METEOROIDS
As a meteoroid encounters the Earth's atmosphere, it appears as a bright streak called a meteor. Air resistance can vaporize a small meteoroid in just a few seconds. Meteoroids that survive their journey through the atmosphere are called meteorites.

PATHS OF METEOR SHOWERS
A comet passing near to the Sun sheds dust. As the Earth passes through this dust it is "showered" with meteors. These showers occur annually and appear to radiate from particular points in the sky. For example, the Geminids meteor shower (December 7 and 16) appears to radiate from the constellation Gemini.

NO ATMOSPHERE
The Moon's surface is pitted with numerous craters, great and small. There are far more craters on the surface of the Moon than on the Earth. This is because, unlike the Earth, the Moon has no atmosphere, so even the smallest meteoroids are able to strike the surface rather than burn up before a collision occurs.

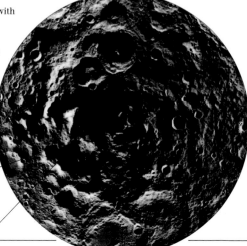

Large crater

Small crater

South polar region of the Moon

LIFE FROM MARS?
Some meteorites consist of material ejected during crater formation on other planets (see pp. 308-309). One such meteorite found on the Earth (named ALH84001) has been shown to have originated from Mars. It contained several of the chemicals vital for life to occur. Objects resembling cells were also found.

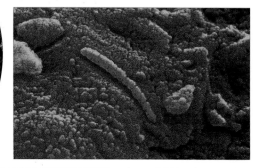

Stars

STARS ARE HUGE BALLS OF GLOWING GAS that are created in **nebulae** (see pp. 326-327). Groups of stars that are created in the same nebula form clusters. There are around 6,000 stars that are visible to the naked eye, and they all belong to the Milky Way Galaxy (see pp. 328-329). These stars are named according to the constellations in which they appear. The **absolute magnitude** of a star (see pp. 300-301) depends upon its **luminosity**, while its surface temperature can be determined from observations of its color. Absolute magnitudes and surface temperatures are plotted on a graph called the Hertzsprung–Russell diagram, and the size of a star can be estimated from its position on the diagram. Some stars have one or more companion stars relatively close by. This arrangement is called a binary system. An eclipsing-binary system is one in which a star passes in front of its brighter partner. An eclipsing binary is an example of a variable star, because its **apparent magnitude** varies periodically.

GLOBULAR CLUSTER
Globular clusters contain hundreds of thousands of stars and are held together by mutual gravitational attraction. They are nearly spherical in shape and appear as hazy blobs when viewed through a small telescope. Globular clusters are more tightly packed toward their centers and contain relatively old stars.

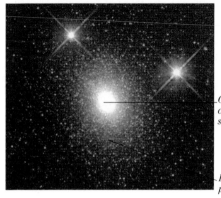

Central region containing old stars

Less densely packed region

OPEN CLUSTER
Open clusters normally contain only a few hundred stars. Most of the stars in an open cluster are hot and young and are within 10 **parsecs** (32.6 **light years**) of each other. The Pleiades (or Seven Sisters) is an open cluster that is visible to the naked eye.

Wisps of dust and hydrogen gas remaining from cloud in which stars formed

Young star in an open cluster of 300–500 stars

CONSTELLATION OF ORION
In ancient times, astronomers divided the sky into distinct groups of stars called constellations. Although stars in the same constellation appear close to each other in the sky, they are rarely close to one another in space. The main stars of the constellation of Orion, for example, are between 70 light years and 2,300 light years distant.

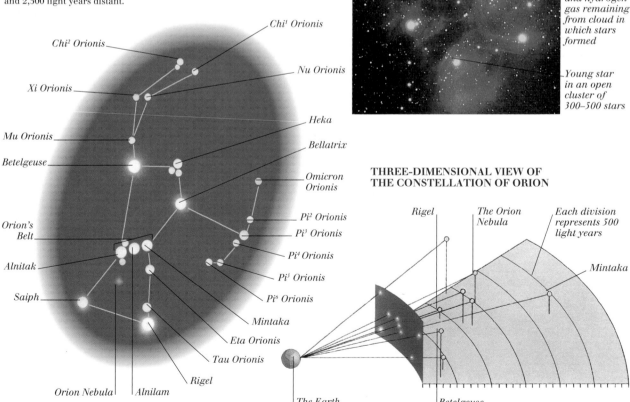

Chi² Orionis
Chi¹ Orionis
Xi Orionis
Nu Orionis
Mu Orionis
Heka
Bellatrix
Betelgeuse
Omicron Orionis
Orion's Belt
Pi² Orionis
Pi³ Orionis
Alnitak
Pi⁴ Orionis
Saiph
Pi⁵ Orionis
Pi⁶ Orionis
Mintaka
Eta Orionis
Tau Orionis
Rigel
Orion Nebula
Alnilam

THREE-DIMENSIONAL VIEW OF THE CONSTELLATION OF ORION

Rigel
The Orion Nebula
Each division represents 500 light years
Mintaka
The Earth
Betelgeuse

HERTZSPRUNG–RUSSELL DIAGRAM

It is possible to gauge the temperature of a star from its color. (The hottest stars are blue and the coolest stars are red.) Stars can be grouped into "spectral types" according to their colors and temperatures. The Hertzsprung–Russell diagram plots a star's spectral type against its absolute magnitude. The brightest stars are at the top of the diagram, and the dimmest are near the bottom. The hottest stars are to the left of the diagram and the coolest to the right. This simple relationship appears as a diagonal band across the diagram and is called the **main sequence**. Most stars spend some part of their lives in the main sequence. Giant stars are found above the main sequence and dwarf stars below.

STAR MASSES

Stars fall into specific regions of the Hertzsprung–Russell diagram according to their sizes. All stars on the main sequence – including the Sun – are called dwarf stars. Toward the end of its lifetime, a star the size of the Sun swells to become a red giant and is then found at the upper right on the diagram. Larger stars become supergiants at this stage. At a later stage, they shrink to become white dwarfs, found below and to the left of the main sequence on the Hertzsprung–Russell diagram.

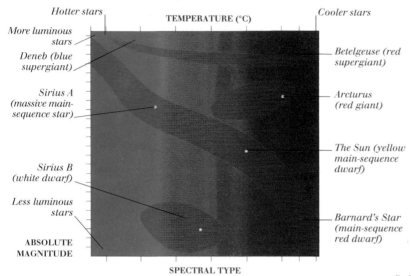

Hotter stars
More luminous stars
Deneb (blue supergiant)
Sirius A (massive main-sequence star)
Sirius B (white dwarf)
Less luminous stars
ABSOLUTE MAGNITUDE
TEMPERATURE (°C)
Cooler stars
Betelgeuse (red supergiant)
Arcturus (red giant)
The Sun (yellow main-sequence dwarf)
Barnard's Star (main-sequence red dwarf)
SPECTRAL TYPE

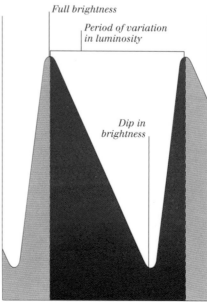

White dwarf (diameters between about 3,000 km and 50,000 km)

The Sun (main-sequence star with diameter of about 1.4 million km)

Red Giant (diameters between 15 million km and 150 million km)

VARIABLE STARS

The amount of light that reaches us from many of the stars in the night sky is variable. The periodic fluctuations in the magnitude of these variable stars can be plotted on a graph, and the resulting line is called a light curve. When two or more stars are orbiting the same center of **gravity**, they are said to form a binary or double-star system. In some cases, two stars periodically eclipse each other, as seen from the Earth. This causes characteristic dips in the light curve of the system. The fluctuations in magnitude of most variable stars are caused by real changes in the stars' luminosities. In one important class of variable stars, called Cepheid variables, a relationship exists between the period of variation of a star's light curve and the absolute magnitude of the star. Astronomers can work out a star's distance from the Earth by comparing the star's absolute magnitude to its apparent magnitude.

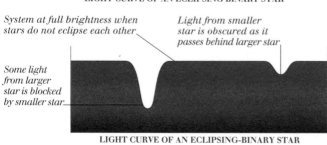

Large, bright star
Small, less bright star

LIGHT CURVE OF AN ECLIPSING BINARY STAR

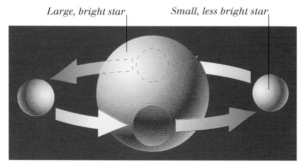

System at full brightness when stars do not eclipse each other
Light from smaller star is obscured as it passes behind larger star
Some light from larger star is blocked by smaller star

LIGHT CURVE OF AN ECLIPSING-BINARY STAR

Full brightness
Period of variation in luminosity
Dip in brightness

LIGHT CURVE OF A CEPHEID-VARIABLE STAR

Stellar life cycles

Stars exist for hundreds of millions or even billions of years. Although astronomers will never be able to observe the complete life cycle of a star, they have developed theories of stellar evolution based on observations of stars of all ages. New stars are created from gas and dust in the space between existing stars. This interstellar matter is **denser** in some regions – called **nebulae** – than in others. There are five types of nebulae: emission nebulae; reflection nebulae; dark nebulae; planetary nebulae; and supernova remnants. The first three of these are where stars are "born," initially as protostars. A protostar becomes a star when **nuclear fusion** starts making helium from the hydrogen at its core. The course and duration of a star's life cycle depends upon its **mass**. All stars shine relatively steadily until the fusion of hydrogen into helium ceases. This can take billions of years in a small star, but may last only a few million years in massive stars – where the rate of conversion is so much greater. Planetary nebulae are the result of the deaths of small stars like the Sun (see pp. 306-307). More massive stars explode in extremely energetic explosions called supernovae. Supernova remnants consist of gas thrown off during a supernova. The remaining core of a massive star may become a neutron star or a black hole (see pp. 330-331).

REGION OF STAR FORMATION IN ORION

Gravity causes the contraction of interstellar matter inside a nebula, such as this one in the constellation of Orion. The nebula heats up as it contracts, and it may glow. Dense regions within the nebula contract further to form protostars. As a protostar collapses, its temperature may rise high enough for nuclear fusion reactions to begin at its core. At this stage it becomes a true star and is said to be in its **main sequence**.

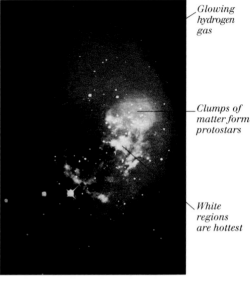

Glowing hydrogen gas

Clumps of matter form protostars

White regions are hottest

HORSEHEAD NEBULA

The Horsehead Nebula is a feature of the constellation of Orion, which contains examples of emission nebulae, reflection nebulae, and dark nebulae, as well as many bright, young stars. Emission nebulae glow as a result of the contracting gas, and protostars, contained within them.

In many regions, a nebula's gas and dust may not yet have contracted enough to begin to glow. Where this type of nebula reflects light from nearby stars, it is called a reflection nebula. If it obscures light from stars beyond it (thereby appearing as a dark patch), it is called a dark nebula.

Glowing filament of hot, ionized hydrogen gas

Alnitak, a star in Orion's Belt

Young stars are blue-white

Dark nebula

Star near southern end of Orion's Belt

Emission nebula

Horsehead Nebula

Reflection nebula

Dark nebula obscuring light from distant stars

LIFE CYCLES OF SMALL AND MASSIVE STARS

When the hydrogen "fuel" of a main-sequence star begins to run out, the production of energy at the star's core is no longer sufficient to prevent further gravitational contraction. At this point the star collapses, and its temperature rises enough for **elements** such as carbon to be "cooked" by fusion reactions. The star then becomes a red giant or red supergiant, depending on its mass. A red giant develops into a planetary nebula and eventually a cold, white dwarf. A red supergiant undergoes rapid collapse – which takes less than a second. This causes a huge explosion, called a supernova. The remnants of a supernova may include a neutron star or a black hole.

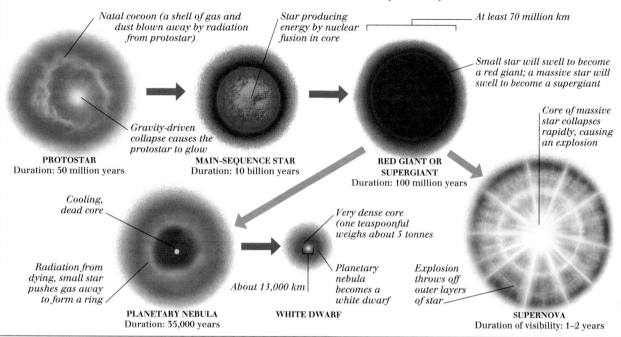

Natal cocoon (a shell of gas and dust blown away by radiation from protostar)

Star producing energy by nuclear fusion in core

At least 70 million km

Small star will swell to become a red giant; a massive star will swell to become a supergiant

Gravity-driven collapse causes the protostar to glow

Core of massive star collapses rapidly, causing an explosion

PROTOSTAR
Duration: 50 million years

MAIN-SEQUENCE STAR
Duration: 10 billion years

RED GIANT OR SUPERGIANT
Duration: 100 million years

Cooling, dead core

Very dense core (one teaspoonful weighs about 5 tonnes)

Radiation from dying, small star pushes gas away to form a ring

About 13,000 km

Planetary nebula becomes a white dwarf

Explosion throws off outer layers of star

PLANETARY NEBULA
Duration: 35,000 years

WHITE DWARF

SUPERNOVA
Duration of visibility: 1–2 years

HOURGLASS NEBULA

After about 100 million years as a red giant, a small star will collapse once more due to the force of gravity. Nuclear reactions begin again, and the star swells and pushes away its outer layers into a ring. The matter in these layers glows by **fluorescence**, as it is illuminated by **ultraviolet** light from the star.

VELA SUPERNOVA REMNANT

When the core of a supergiant undergoes gravitational collapse, it contracts rapidly before "bouncing" back, throwing off its outer layers in an explosion called a supernova. The debris is strewn around space as a type of nebula called a supernova remnant.

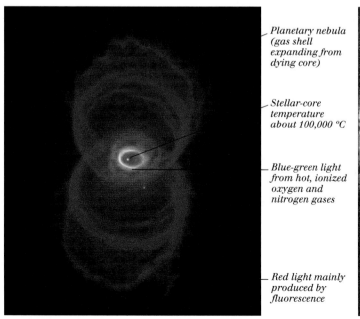

Planetary nebula (gas shell expanding from dying core)

Stellar-core temperature about 100,000 °C

Blue-green light from hot, ionized oxygen and nitrogen gases

Red light mainly produced by fluorescence

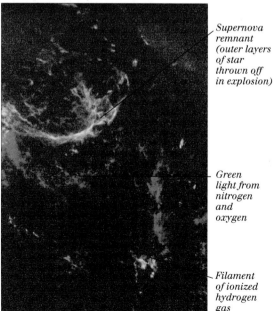

Supernova remnant (outer layers of star thrown off in explosion)

Green light from nitrogen and oxygen

Filament of ionized hydrogen gas

Galaxies

A GALAXY IS A HUGE SYSTEM of stars and interstellar gas, all of which are held together by the forces of **gravity** they exert on one another (see pp. 22-23). There are about 100 billion galaxies in the universe. They are grouped in clusters, which are themselves grouped into superclusters. Before galaxies were even recognized as such, a number of them had been listed – together with nebulae and other objects – in a catalog created by the French astronomer Charles Messier (1730-1817). Many galaxies are therefore denoted by the letter "M" followed by a number. A more comprehensive list is the New General Catalog, where all known galaxies are given an NGC number. In 1926, the American astronomer Edwin Hubble (1889-1953) categorized all of the known galaxies into four basic types – irregular, elliptical, spiral, and barred spiral – according to their shape. Another type of galaxy, called a **quasar** (the name stands for *quasi*-stell*ar* objects), was discovered in 1960. Although these galaxies are very bright, they are not well understood because they lie billions of light years from the Earth. The solar system (pp. 304-305) is situated inside one arm of a spiral galaxy called the Milky Way Galaxy.

NEIGHBORING GALAXIES

Some nearby galaxies are visible to the naked eye as fuzzy patches of light. One member of the Local Group, the Andromeda Galaxy (M31, NGC 224), is the most distant object visible to the naked eye – it is located about two million light years from the Earth – and appears to be very similar to our own Milky Way Galaxy.

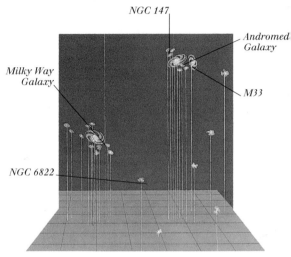

NGC 147

Andromeda Galaxy

Milky Way Galaxy

M33

NGC 6822

LOCAL GROUP

TYPES OF GALAXIES

IRREGULAR GALAXY
Galaxies with no particular form are called irregular galaxies. Some of these may appear similar in shape to spiral galaxies. About three percent of all known galaxies are irregular in shape.

ELLIPTICAL GALAXY
Through a telescope, elliptical galaxies look spherical, or like flattened spheres. Small, so-called dwarf ellipticals are the most common type of galaxy in the known universe.

SPIRAL GALAXY
Most of the bright galaxies are spiral in shape. They are huge systems, normally about 100,000 light years in diameter. The Milky Way Galaxy is thought to be a typical spiral galaxy.

BARRED-SPIRAL GALAXY
Although often similar in appearance to a spiral galaxy, the arms of a barred-spiral galaxy start at the end of a straight bar of stars, which extends in two directions from its galactic nucleus.

Vega, a white main sequence star; the fifth-brightest star in the sky

Polaris (the Pole Star), a blue-green variable binary star

Galactic plane

Pleiades (the Seven Sisters), an open star cluster

Andromeda Galaxy (a spiral galaxy 2.2 million light years away, and the most distant object visible to the naked eye)

THE MILKY WAY GALAXY

The main part of the Milky Way Galaxy is about 100,000 light years across. Astronomers think that it is a spiral galaxy, but cannot be certain of this. The spiral nature of the galaxy can be inferred only from astronomical observations because the solar system is within it. The Solar System is part of the Orion Arm (one of four arms that make up the galaxy) and rotates around the galactic center at a speed of 155 miles (250 km) per second. Traveling at this speed, the solar system takes about 220 million years to complete one lap of the galaxy. As is true of all spiral galaxies, star formation occurs mostly in the arms, while the galactic nucleus contains mainly older stars.

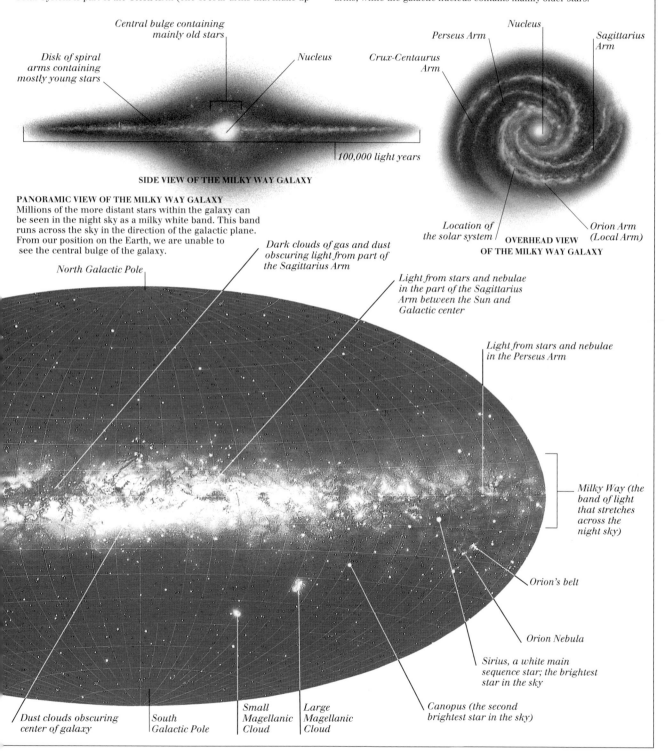

Central bulge containing mainly old stars

Nucleus

Disk of spiral arms containing mostly young stars

100,000 light years

SIDE VIEW OF THE MILKY WAY GALAXY

Nucleus

Perseus Arm

Sagittarius Arm

Crux-Centaurus Arm

Location of the solar system

Orion Arm (Local Arm)

OVERHEAD VIEW OF THE MILKY WAY GALAXY

PANORAMIC VIEW OF THE MILKY WAY GALAXY
Millions of the more distant stars within the galaxy can be seen in the night sky as a milky white band. This band runs across the sky in the direction of the galactic plane. From our position on the Earth, we are unable to see the central bulge of the galaxy.

North Galactic Pole

Dark clouds of gas and dust obscuring light from part of the Sagittarius Arm

Light from stars and nebulae in the part of the Sagittarius Arm between the Sun and Galactic center

Light from stars and nebulae in the Perseus Arm

Milky Way (the band of light that stretches across the night sky)

Orion's belt

Orion Nebula

Sirius, a white main sequence star; the brightest star in the sky

Canopus (the second brightest star in the sky)

Dust clouds obscuring center of galaxy

South Galactic Pole

Small Magellanic Cloud

Large Magellanic Cloud

Neutron stars and black holes

THE FINAL STAGES of any star's existence are determined by the extent of its **gravitational** collapse, and the core that remains after a **supernova** explosion (see pp. 326-327) may become a neutron star or, if it has enough **mass**, a black hole. Stars consist largely of **protons, neutrons,** and **electrons.** As a star shrinks, crushing the **matter** of which it is made into a smaller and smaller **volume** and thereby increasing its **density,** protons and electrons are pushed together with such force that they become neutrons. At this stage the stellar remnant is composed almost exclusively of neutrons and so is called a neutron star. Rapidly rotating neutron stars are called pulsars (*puls*ating st*ars*). The gravitational pull on anything near a neutron star is enormous, but around a black hole it is so great that even **electromagnetic radiation** cannot escape it. When a neutron star or black hole interacts with a nearby star, it can develop an **accretion disk,** which is visible as a strong **X-ray** source. The gravitational effect around a black hole is so great that it distorts **space-time,** perhaps enough to produce wormholes, hypothetical pathways to other places and times, or even other universes. It is thought that black holes exist at the centers of most galaxies, including our own.

PULSAR (ROTATING NEUTRON STAR)

Neutron stars can be detected in two ways. First, gases accelerated by its intense gravitational field emit X rays as they hit the solid surface. These X rays are then detected by X-ray telescopes. Second, because neutron stars tend to spin, they emit pulses of radio waves, which are produced as the strong **magnetic field** of the star interacts with the star's own charged particles.

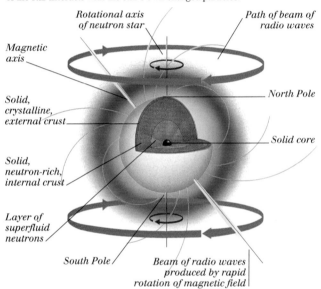

Rotational axis of neutron star

Magnetic axis

Path of beam of radio waves

North Pole

Solid, crystalline, external crust

Solid core

Solid, neutron-rich, internal crust

Layer of superfluid neutrons

South Pole

Beam of radio waves produced by rapid rotation of magnetic field

FORMATION OF A BLACK HOLE

During a supernova explosion, much of the star's mass is thrown off into space. The remaining core may become a neutron star or, if massive enough, a black hole. The stronger the gravitational pull at the surface of the stellar remnant, the higher is the speed required to escape from it.

When this escape velocity is equal to the speed of light, even electromagnetic radiation cannot escape. This is a black hole, the surface of which is called an event horizon. In theory, there is a region of infinite density, called a **singularity,** at the center of a black hole.

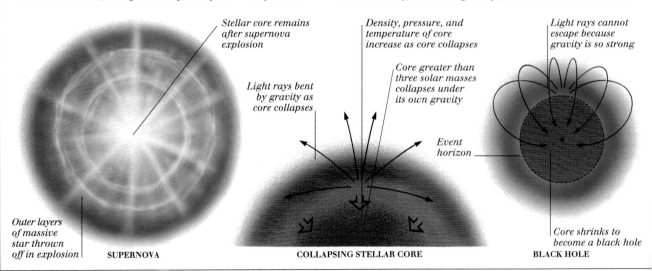

Stellar core remains after supernova explosion

Density, pressure, and temperature of core increase as core collapses

Light rays cannot escape because gravity is so strong

Light rays bent by gravity as core collapses

Core greater than three solar masses collapses under its own gravity

Event horizon

Outer layers of massive star thrown off in explosion

SUPERNOVA

COLLAPSING STELLAR CORE

Core shrinks to become a black hole

BLACK HOLE

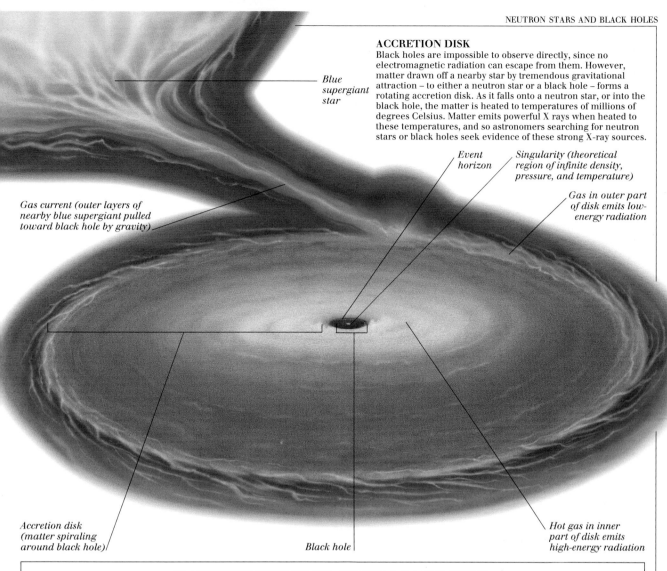

ACCRETION DISK

Black holes are impossible to observe directly, since no electromagnetic radiation can escape from them. However, matter drawn off a nearby star by tremendous gravitational attraction – to either a neutron star or a black hole – forms a rotating accretion disk. As it falls onto a neutron star, or into the black hole, the matter is heated to temperatures of millions of degrees Celsius. Matter emits powerful X rays when heated to these temperatures, and so astronomers searching for neutron stars or black holes seek evidence of these strong X-ray sources.

Blue supergiant star

Event horizon

Singularity (theoretical region of infinite density, pressure, and temperature)

Gas in outer part of disk emits low-energy radiation

Gas current (outer layers of nearby blue supergiant pulled toward black hole by gravity)

Accretion disk (matter spiraling around black hole)

Black hole

Hot gas in inner part of disk emits high-energy radiation

BLACK HOLES, WORMHOLES, AND THE GALACTIC CENTER

WORMHOLES IN SPACE-TIME

The General Theory of Relativity (see pp. 62-63) treats gravity as the distortion of space-time. It predicts that at a singularity, space-time is so distorted that it creates an open channel, or wormhole. This wormhole can exist between two black holes in the same universe, or perhaps between black holes in two different universes.

GALACTIC CENTER

In a photograph that shows up X-ray emissions, the center of the Milky Way Galaxy appears very bright. This suggests the possibility that there is a vast black hole situated there, creating an accretion disk out of interstellar gas and perhaps material from nearby stars. X-ray images of other galaxies – **quasars**, in particular – show similar results.

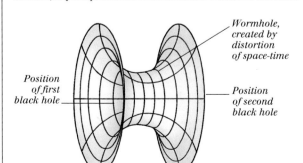

Wormhole, created by distortion of space-time

Position of first black hole

Position of second black hole

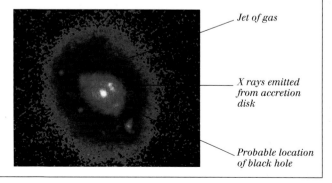

Jet of gas

X rays emitted from accretion disk

Probable location of black hole

Cosmology

THE STUDY OF THE NATURE, origins, and evolution of the universe is called cosmology. People have long wondered about the creation of space and time, and modern astrophysics seems to be moving toward an answer. The uuniverse is not infinitely old nor infinitely large – facts confirmed by a simple logical argument known as Olbers' Paradox. Instead, most astronomers believe that the universe came into existence between 10 and 20 billion years ago, in an explosion of space and time called the Big Bang. There is much evidence in support of this cosmological model. For example, galaxies are receding from the Earth in every direction, as if they all came from one point some time ago. The rate at which galaxies are moving away depends upon their distance from us – a simple relationship known as Hubble's Law. **Quasars**, the most distant observable objects in the uuniverse, are receding most quickly. More evidence comes from the **cosmic background radiation** (CBR), a remnant of the Big Bang that has been observed by radio telescopes (see pp. 298-299) to come from every direction in space. Furthermore, there are ripples in the CBR, indicating a slight irregularity in the **density** of the early universe. This would have been necessary for the formation of galaxies. Ideas concerning the fate of the universe are also part of cosmology. If the Big Bang Theory is correct, then, depending on the total amount of **mass** present, the universe may begin to contract under its own gravity, concluding in a reverse of the Big Bang, named the Big Crunch.

OLBERS' PARADOX

If you were standing in an infinitely large crowd of people, you would see people in every direction. In the same way, if the universe were infinite, we would see star light coming from every direction in the sky. However, the sky is mainly dark, and so the universe cannot be infinite. This argument is known as Olbers' Paradox, after the German astronomer, Wilhelm Olbers.

The clumps contract due to gravity and become galaxies or clusters of galaxies

THE BIG BANG AND COSMIC EXPANSION

According to the Big Bang Theory, the universe began as an incredibly dense fireball. At the time of its creation, all of the mass and **energy** of the current universe was contained in a space far smaller than an **atomic nucleus**. The energy of the Big Bang gradually became **matter**, in accordance with the equation $E = mc^2$ (see pp. 62-63), where E is energy, m is the mass of the matter produced, and c is the constant speed of light. All the time, the universe was expanding, as it is still observed to do today.

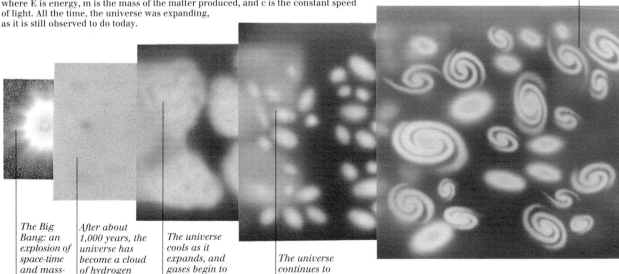

The Big Bang: an explosion of space-time and mass-energy

After about 1,000 years, the universe has become a cloud of hydrogen and helium

The universe cools as it expands, and gases begin to form clumps

The universe continues to expand

HUBBLE'S LAW

Distant galaxies appear to be moving away from us in whichever direction we look. The farther away a particular galaxy, the faster it recedes, a relationship known as Hubble's Law. This is consistent with an expanding universe, such as would have occurred after the Big Bang.

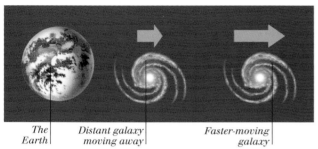

The Earth *Distant galaxy moving away* *Faster-moving galaxy*

QUASARS

Quasars are the most distant observable objects in the universe. As they move away from us, the wavelengths of the radiation they emit is increased, or **redshifted**. Their huge value of redshift indicates that some quasars may be as far as 10 billion light years away from us.

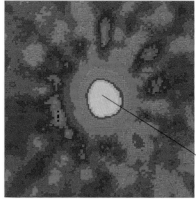

False color image of quasar

CRITICAL DENSITY

The universe contains a huge amount of mass, which is more or less uniformly distributed, over a large scale. The gravitational effect of the mass slows the apparent expansion of the universe. If there is enough mass in the universe (in other words, if the density of the universe is above some critical value) the expansion may cease altogether and become a contraction, concluding with the Big Crunch (see below).

Big Bang

The universe may not contain enough mass to begin contracting and may continue to expand for ever

At critical density, the universe expands to a certain size, then stops

Enough mass will cause the universe to contract, creating a Big Crunch

SIZE

TIME

COSMIC BACKGROUND RADIATION

The strongest evidence so far in support of the Big Bang Theory is the cosmic background radiation (CBR). If CBR was produced at the time of the Big Bang, it provides cosmologists with information about conditions in the early universe. For galaxies to form, there would need to have been slight irregularities in the density of the young universe. These irregularities have been detected, as ripples in the CBR.

False-color image of CBR

Pink areas are slightly warmer

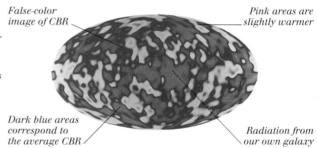

Dark blue areas correspond to the average CBR

Radiation from our own galaxy

COSMIC CONTRACTION AND THE BIG CRUNCH

In the future, if the density of the universe is high enough (see above left), the cosmic expansion may cease, due to gravitational attraction, and reverse to become a contraction. Huge black holes will form and will attract one another, increasing the rate of contraction. Eventually all of space and time will become contained in a tiny volume – as it was at the time of the Big Bang. This is the Big Crunch scenario. It is possible that another universe could then be born out of the singularity formed by the Big Crunch.

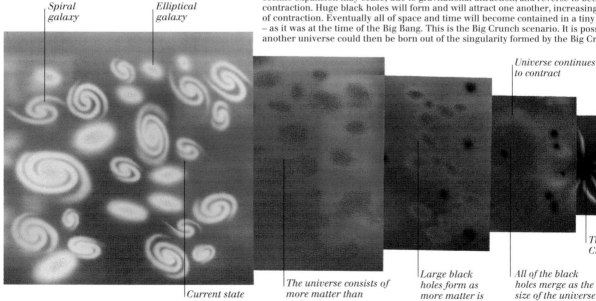

Spiral galaxy

Elliptical galaxy

Universe continues to contract

Current state of the universe

The universe consists of more matter than radiation

Large black holes form as more matter is clumped together

All of the black holes merge as the size of the universe reduces rapidly

The Big Crunch

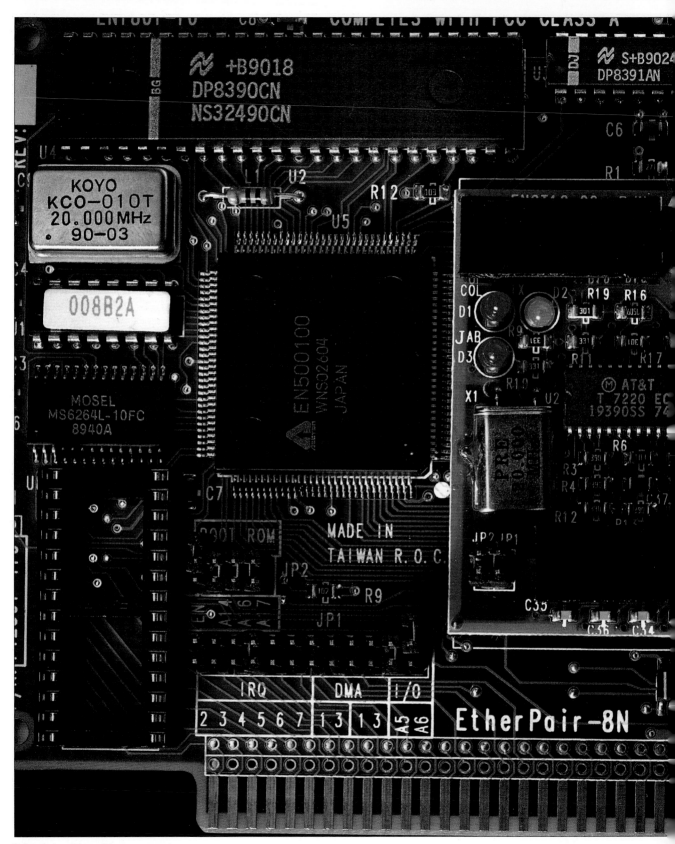

Printed circuit board from a computer

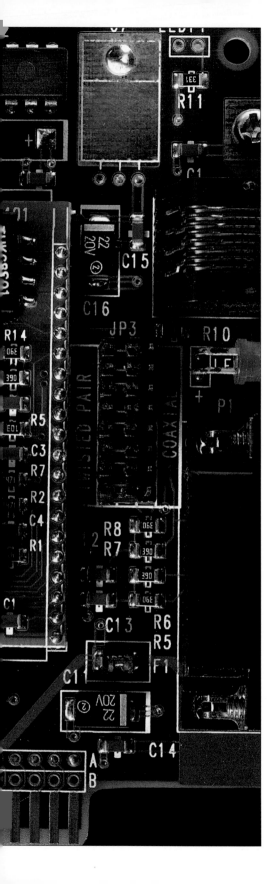

ELECTRONICS AND COMPUTER SCIENCE

DISCOVERING ELECTRONICS & COMPUTER SCIENCE .. 336

ELECTRONIC CIRCUITS 338

RESISTORS 340

CAPACITORS 342

INDUCTORS AND TRANSFORMERS 344

DIODES AND SEMICONDUCTORS 346

TRANSISTORS 348

INTEGRATED CIRCUITS 350

COMPUTERS 352

COMPUTER NETWORKS 354

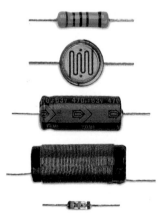

THE FIRST ELECTRONIC VALVE
John Ambrose Fleming was a British electrical engineer who adapted Edison's light bulbs by adding an extra electrode, enabling them to modify current for use in telegraph machines.

HOME-BUILT AMPLIFIER
This magnificent creation from the late 1920s is a home-built amplifier. At the time it was made, there was no large-scale industrial production of amplifiers. It has two valves to drive the loudspeaker and draws a great deal of power. In many respects, it resembles a modern amplifier.

Discovering electronics and computer science

ELECTRONICS IS A BRANCH OF PHYSICS that deals with the behavior of electrons. In practice, it involves the design of useful electric circuits. One of the fruits of the growth of electronics is computer science. The impact of electronics on the modern developed world cannot easily be overestimated, with television, radio, modern telephones, and compact disc players becoming commonplace.

THE BEGINNING OF ELECTRONICS

All electronic circuits are powered by electricity. The first power stations were built during the 1880s, and batteries were already available at that time. Without the large-scale availability of electric currents from these sources, there would have been no "electronics revolution" during the 20th century. Around the time of the first power stations, many physicists were experimenting with cathode-ray tubes (CRTs). The discovery of the electron was made using a CRT. A CRT is a glass tube that contains a vacuum, in which streams of electrons are produced by a process called thermionic emission. Heat in a metal cathode (negative electrode) supplies energy to electrons, freeing them from the metal. Electrons emitted in this way are attracted to a positive electrode (anode) as a continuous stream – a cathode ray.

THE VACUUM TUBE

The CRT, or vacuum tube, developed into several important electronic devices. For example, the X-ray tube, the klystron (a device that produces microwave radiation), and the television tube are all based on it. The vacuum tube was first used in electronic circuits by English physicist **John Ambrose Fleming**, in 1904. He called it a "valve," because it allows electric current to flow in one direction only (electrons flow from the cathode to the anode). This simple property made it useful in detecting radio signals. Its

value to the development of electronics was increased in 1906 by **Lee De Forest**, who added a metal grid between the anode and cathode. Voltages applied to the grid could control electric currents. The "triode," as De Forest's invention became known, was used in amplifier or oscillator circuits. Thanks to the development of the vacuum tube, electronics soon became a vital part of radio and sound recording.

SEMICONDUCTORS

Early radios depended on a "cat's whisker" for the detection of radio signals. This was a fine wire in contact with a crystal of germanium or other semiconductor material. Although this method of radio detection was superseded by the diode valve, scientific research into semiconductors was not carried out in vain. The semiconductor diode – made of a junction of different types of semiconductors – replaced the diode valve. Similarly, the transistor – a sandwich of three semiconductor layers – replaced De Forest's triode. This enabled electronic devices to be made much smaller and more cheaply. They also consumed less electric power. The transistor was invented in 1947, at Bell Laboratories in the United States. Transistors were used in radios and the newly invented magnetic tape recorders and televisions. Early electronic computers also benefited from the replacement of vacuum tubes by semiconductor diodes and transistors.

ELECTRONIC COMPUTERS

The idea of using a machine to carry out calculations has a long history that spans several centuries. The electronic computer, however, is a very recent invention. The basic idea behind the modern electronic computer was conceived by the American physicist **John Atanasoff** and his colleague Clifford Berry. Around 1940, they built the "Atanasoff-Berry computer," the ABC. The desire for electronic computers was enhanced by the Second World War – the design of missiles and warplanes relied upon calculations being carried out quickly and accurately. Several computers were designed by military organizations during the 1940s. Perhaps the most famous is ENIAC (Electronic Numerical Integrator and Calculator), which contained 17,468 triode and diode valves. Computers that used transistors instead of valves were faster, smaller, and used much less electric power. The "architecture" (internal organization) of the modern computer was established by Hungarian-born American mathematician **John Von Neumann** in the late 1940s. His concept of a computer that has a memory, a flexible program (set of instructions), and a central processing unit (CPU) remains the model of computers today. Inside a computer, letters, numbers, and simple instructions are held as groups of "off" or "on" electrical pulses. These pulses represent the binary digits, or bits, "0" and "1". For this reason, the computer is an example of a digital device.

MINIATURIZATION

In 1958, American electronics engineer Jack Kilby devised a way of creating several electronic components on a single slice of semiconductor. Integration, as this is known, soon enabled complicated electronic circuits to be formed on a single "chip." This led to dramatic miniaturization of electronic devices, particularly computers. In the 1960s, integration became large-scale integration (LSI), and in the 1980s, very large-scale integration (VLSI), as more and more electronic components could be formed on to a single "integrated circuit." In the late 1970s, the microprocessor was born. This is a single integrated circuit that carries out calculations or a set of instructions. Microprocessors found their way into a host of devices, including facsimile (fax) machines, compact-disc (CD) players, camcorders, and even electric toasters. The microprocessor made possible pocket calculators (1970s) and the general-purpose, personal computer (late 1970s).

THE FIRST TRANSISTOR
Although it resembles components from earlier radios, this transistor is, in fact, a form of amplifier. Two wires are connected to the surface of a germanium crystal, while a third wire connects to the base. A change of current in one wire causes a larger change in current through the other.

COMPUTER NETWORKS

Electronics today is used in countless ways: in business, scientific research, entertainment, and just about every are a of modern life. Much of the impact of electronics today is focused on computer networks – personal computers, as well as larger, "mainframe" computers and supercomputers, linked together by communications links such as fiber-optic cables. Information in digital form can be passed and shared across such networks. Individual networks can be connected to others. The Internet is just such a "network of networks." Its origins lie in the late 1960s, when the United States Defense Department set up ARPANET (Advanced Research Projects Agency Network). The strength of ARPANET was that it would be impervious to attack from hostile forces – if one part of the network was destroyed, information could be re-routed around other parts. Academics from universities across the United States were soon sending information across ARPANET, from their own networks. In 1983, several other networks joined ARPANET, and the Internet was born. In 1986, the "backbone" of the Internet was created by the American National Science Foundation. More and more networks, in other countries as well as in the USA, became connected to the Internet. By 1993, the Internet consisted of networks in 53 countries. Millions of people use the Internet every day, for the transmission of serious information and as a means of expressing opinions, as well as for entertainment or simply for keeping in touch with friends.

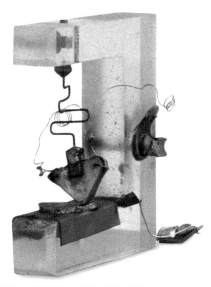

TIMELINE
OF DISCOVERIES

1642 – French mathematician **Blaise Pascal** invented a numerical calculator that could add and subtract

Gottfried Leibniz 1694 improved Pascal's device by creating a machine that could also multiply

1705 – Gottfried Leibniz shows the importance of binary (base 2) mathematics, used in all digital electronic computers

Georg Ohm discovers 1822 the mathematical relationship between electric current and voltage, known as Ohm's law

1827 – **Charles Babbage** designs general-purpose calculating machine, the analytical engine

Joseph Henry discovers 1830 self-inductance, the basis of electronic components called inductors

1854 – **George Boole** develops Boolean algebra. Microprocessors use the mathematics of Boolean algebra in their calculations

William Crookes 1879 observes cathode rays in his "Crookes tube"

1880 – **Thomas Edison** discovers the Edison effect

Electron is discovered 1997 by English physicist **Joseph Thomson** as he is studying cathode rays

1904 – English inventor John Ambrose Fleming invents the thermionic valve

Lee De Forest 1906 develops the triode valve, the forerunner of the transistor

1930s – **Claude Shannon** develops electronic circuits called logic gates – the basis of the digital electronic computer

John Von Neumann 1940s figures out the internal structure, or "architecture," of the general-purpose electronic computer

1943 – ENIAC (Electronic Numerical Integrator and Calculator), the world's first truly general-purpose, programmable computer, is built

Printed circuit boards 1945 (PCBs) are perfected

1947 – The transistor is invented at Bell Laboratories in the US

Jack Kilby develops the 1958 first integrated circuit

1971 – The first microprocessor chip, the Intel 4004, is produced

Apple launches the 1984 first Macintosh computer. It uses the first commercially available GUI (graphical user interface)

1995 – **Microsoft** launches Windows '95 software

Electronic circuits

ELECTRONIC CIRCUITS CARRY out countless different
tasks, in devices such as radios, calculators, amplifiers,
and computers (see pp. 352-353). All of these circuits work
on simple principles and consist of various electronic
components, such as resistors, capacitors, inductors, and
semiconductor devices, including transistors and integrated
circuits. These components are normally assembled on some
kind of circuit board. Most commercial electronic circuits are
built on printed circuit boards (PCBs), with copper tracks
connecting the various components. Temporary, experimental
circuits are often built on breadboards, into which the
connecting legs of the components are pushed. A circuit
diagram is a shorthand way of representing the connections
between the components. When built, the input and output
voltages and **currents** often need to be compared with
desired values. A multimeter is used to measure these
quantities. Many electronic circuits produce rapidly
alternating voltages, which cannot be measured accurately
on a multimeter. These can, however, be measured, and
displayed, with the aid of an oscilloscope.

TYPES OF CURRENTS

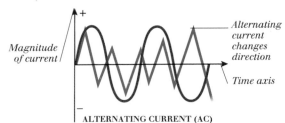

DIRECT CURRENT (DC)
The flow of electric charge in just one direction is called
direct current, even if the magnitude of the current varies.
Batteries and some power supplies produce direct current.

ALTERNATING CURRENT (AC)
Electric current that changes direction, or alternates,
many times every second is called alternating current.
Many devices, including oscillators, microphones, and
some generators, produce alternating currents.

TYPES OF CIRCUIT BOARDS

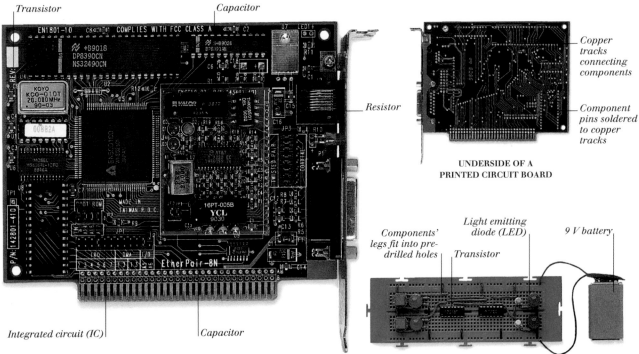

PRINTED CIRCUIT BOARDS
Several types of electronic components are visible on this printed circuit board,
which is taken from a computer. Printed circuit boards are made of insulating
materials such as ceramics, plastics, or glass fiber, coated with copper foil. The
foil is etched away by a photographic process, to leave behind tracks that are
used to connect the components together.

BREADBOARD
Many electronics engineers use a predrilled block called
a breadboard to construct temporary prototypes of their
circuits. The components' connecting legs are simply
pushed into holes in the board. Metal strips inside the
board connect the components together to form a circuit.

EXAMPLES OF CIRCUITS

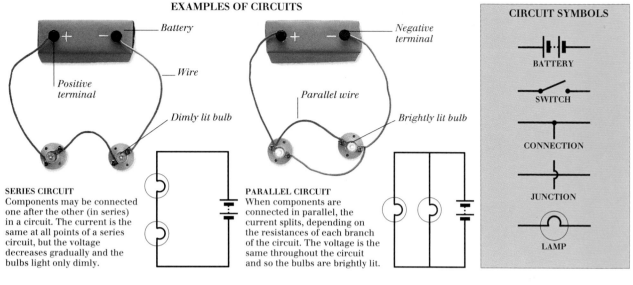

Battery

Positive terminal

Wire

Dimly lit bulb

Negative terminal

Parallel wire

Brightly lit bulb

CIRCUIT SYMBOLS

BATTERY

SWITCH

CONNECTION

JUNCTION

LAMP

SERIES CIRCUIT
Components may be connected one after the other (in series) in a circuit. The current is the same at all points of a series circuit, but the voltage decreases gradually and the bulbs light only dimly.

PARALLEL CIRCUIT
When components are connected in parallel, the current splits, depending on the resistances of each branch of the circuit. The voltage is the same throughout the circuit and so the bulbs are brightly lit.

TEST EQUIPMENT

ANALOGUE MULTIMETER
An electronics engineer will normally calculate the voltages and currents at certain points in a circuit while designing that circuit. A multimeter is then used to test these quantities once the circuit is built. Most meters can measure AC and DC, but they can also check resistances and capacitances.

Needle

Multi-purpose scale

Lead to probe

Dial selects different voltage or current ranges

Meter can be used as a battery tester

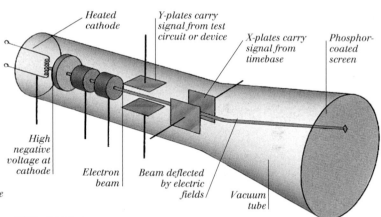

Heated cathode

Y-plates carry signal from test circuit or device

X-plates carry signal from timebase

Phosphor-coated screen

High negative voltage at cathode

Electron beam

Beam deflected by electric fields

Vacuum tube

HOW AN OSCILLOSCOPE WORKS
Inside an oscilloscope is an **electron** beam that produces a spot on the screen of a **cathode ray tube**. **Electric fields** produced by two pairs of metal plates make the spot move around the screen. The field at the X-plates causes the spot to sweep across the screen, while a signal from a circuit under test is fed to the Y-plates, so that the spot is made to move up or down depending on the voltage of the signal.

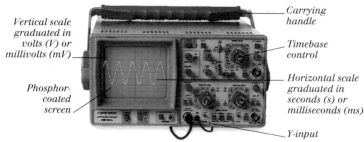

Vertical scale graduated in volts (V) or millivolts (mV)

Phosphor-coated screen

Carrying handle

Timebase control

Horizontal scale graduated in seconds (s) or milliseconds (ms)

Y-input

USING AN OSCILLOSCOPE
When using an oscilloscope, the output of a test circuit is connected to the Y-input, which controls the vertical motion of the electron beam. The time taken for the beam to sweep horizontally across the oscilloscope screen is called the timebase. This beam can combine with the vertical motion to produce a wave pattern on the screen.

Resistors

RESISTORS ARE ELECTRONIC COMPONENTS that have known resistances. Most fixed-value resistors are filled with carbon granules, and are marked with color-coded bands that denote their resistance. This is measured in ohms (Ω) or kilohms (kΩ, thousands of ohms). They are used in most electronic circuits, normally for one of two purposes – limiting **current** or controlling **voltage**. When incorporated into a circuit, resistors are often combined **in series** or **in parallel**. In addition to fixed resistors, there are several very useful types of resistors that have variable resistance. The most common of these is the potentiometer, which may be used as a volume control in mixers and other audio equipment. One important use of resistors is in voltage dividers. These consist of two or more resistors – in series – and are used to supply a desired voltage to different parts of a circuit. A voltage divider that incorporates a light-dependent resistor can be used in a light-sensitive circuit.

INSIDE A FIXED RESISTOR

Most fixed-value resistors consist of a case containing carbon granules. Another common type of resistor is formed from a ceramic tube coated with thin, metal film. End caps allow for connection to a circuit via connecting wires.

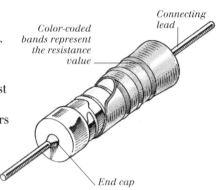

Color-coded bands represent the resistance value

Connecting lead

End cap

MEASURING RESISTANCE

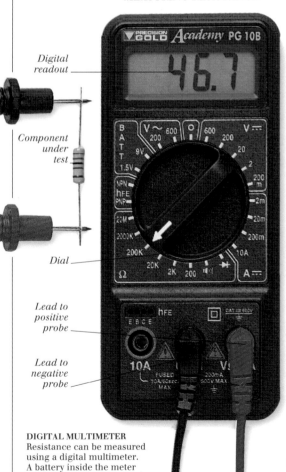

Digital readout

Component under test

Dial

Lead to positive probe

Lead to negative probe

DIGITAL MULTIMETER
Resistance can be measured using a digital multimeter. A battery inside the meter produces a voltage across the component, and measures the current flowing through it. The resistance is displayed directly.

RESISTOR NETWORKS

Combined resistance of 57 kΩ

10 kΩ resistor   *47 kΩ resistor*

RESISTORS IN SERIES
The combined resistance of two (or more) resistors connected in series is simply the sum of the individual resistances. An electronics engineer who needs a 20 kΩ resistance in part of a circuit can simply connect two 10 kΩ resistors in series.

Combined resistance of 8.25 kΩ

RESISTORS IN PARALLEL
The combined resistance of two resistors connected in parallel is less than the resistance of either of the resistances involved. (Total resistance is the product of the two resistances divided by their sum.) The total resistance in this circuit is 8.25 kilohms.

10 kΩ resistor   *47 kΩ resistor*

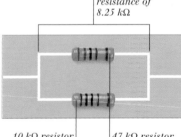

3.6 V dropped by 100 Ω resistor

5.4 V dropped by 150 Ω resistor

VOLTAGE DIVIDER
A component can be made to receive a fraction of the supplied voltage by using a pair of resistors connected together as a voltage divider. The voltage difference, or drop, between the ends of each resistor depends upon the values of the resistances involved.

9 V supply (battery)

100 Ω resistor

This point is at 5.4 V

150 Ω resistor

EXAMPLES OF RESISTORS

Potentiometers, which are a type of variable resistor, allow current or voltage to be controlled as desired, and have a wide range of applications. Potentiometers normally have a carbon track along which a slider makes contact. Thermistors contain a semiconducting material whose resistance decreases as it gets hotter. They are often used to compensate for the increase in resistance of other components that can occur at higher temperatures.

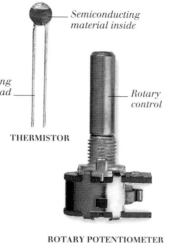

Semiconducting material inside

Connecting lead

THERMISTOR

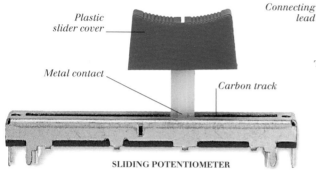

Plastic slider cover

Metal contact

Carbon track

SLIDING POTENTIOMETER

Rotary control

ROTARY POTENTIOMETER

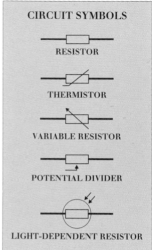

CIRCUIT SYMBOLS

RESISTOR

THERMISTOR

VARIABLE RESISTOR

POTENTIAL DIVIDER

LIGHT-DEPENDENT RESISTOR

APPLICATIONS OF VARIABLE RESISTORS

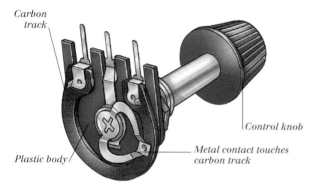

Carbon track

Plastic body

Control knob

Metal contact touches carbon track

VOLUME CONTROL
Potentiometers are used as volume controls in circuits that produce an audible output. The varying resistance of a potentiometer, determined by the position of a metal contact on its carbon track, controls the amount of current flowing through the part of the circuit that drives the loudspeaker.

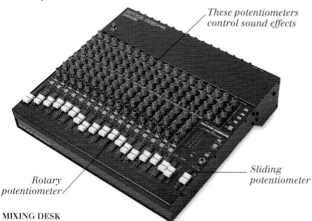

These potentiometers control sound effects

Rotary potentiometer

Sliding potentiometer

MIXING DESK
Mixing desks rely on several potentiometers, each one affecting the output of an amplifier circuit. In this way, the relative volumes of several instruments or voices can be controlled at the same time.

LIGHT-DEPENDENT RESISTOR CIRCUIT

As light falls on a light-dependent resistor (LDR), it decreases its resistance. This can be put to use in a circuit that switches on a light emitting diode (LED) when light falls upon the LDR (see below). The circuit includes two voltage dividers. The LED joins the midpoints (A and B below) of the two voltage dividers. It lights only if point A is at a lower voltage than point B. The voltage at point B is held at 3 volts. The potentiometer is adjusted so that, in the dark, point A is also at 3 volts. As points A and B are at the same voltage, the LED does not light. When light falls on the LDR its resistance drops, so that the potentiometer drops more voltage and the voltage at point A rises. The LED lights.

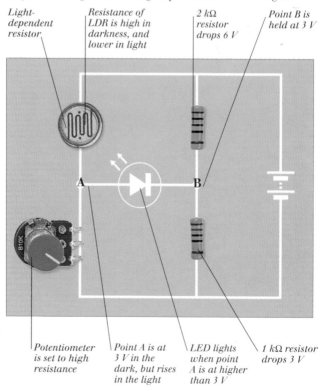

Light-dependent resistor

Resistance of LDR is high in darkness, and lower in light

2 kΩ resistor drops 6 V

Point B is held at 3 V

A

B

Potentiometer is set to high resistance

Point A is at 3 V in the dark, but rises in the light

LED lights when point A is at higher than 3 V

1 kΩ resistor drops 3 V

Capacitors

CAPACITORS STORE ELECTRIC **charge** when a **voltage** is applied across them. They can be found in almost every electronic circuit. Most capacitors have metal plates inside, separated by an insulating material called a **dielectric**. The charge stored on the plates increases as the voltage increases – the amount of charge a capacitor can store with one volt across it is called its **capacitance** and is measured in farads (F). Most capacitors are rated in millionths of a farad (microfarads, μF), or trillionths of a farad (picofarads, pF). A rapidly **alternating current** (AC) passes through a capacitor easily, while **direct current** (DC) cannot pass at all. For this reason, capacitors are often used to prevent the passage of direct current through a circuit, such as an amplifier (see pp. 348-349). In circuits that require the passage of AC, the current passing through the capacitor reaches a maximum when the voltage is at a minimum.

INSIDE A CAPACITOR

The metallized film capacitor is typical of most capacitors. Inside, plastic plates are coated with a thin layer of metal. The capacitance of such a component is increased by sandwiching several layers of plates very closely together.

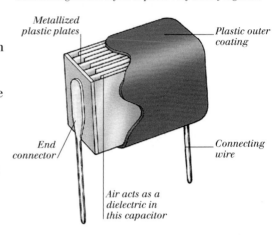

Metallized plastic plates

Plastic outer coating

End connector

Connecting wire

Air acts as a dielectric in this capacitor

CHARGING AND DISCHARGING A CAPACITOR

RESISTOR–CAPACITOR CIRCUIT

A capacitor charges up when a voltage is applied across its plates. It discharges if the voltage is removed and its ends are connected to a circuit. The rate at which a capacitor charges and discharges depends upon the resistance (R) of the circuit or circuits involved and the capacitance (C) of the capacitor. This arrangement is therefore called a resistor–capacitor circuit or, more commonly, an R–C circuit.

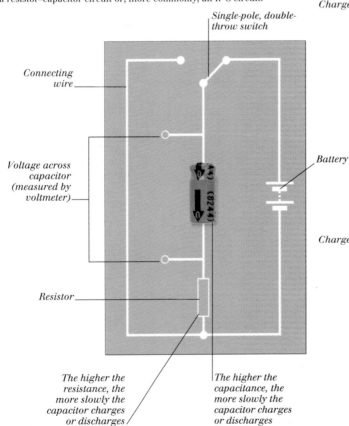

Connecting wire

Single-pole, double-throw switch

Voltage across capacitor (measured by voltmeter)

Battery

Resistor

The higher the resistance, the more slowly the capacitor charges or discharges

The higher the capacitance, the more slowly the capacitor charges or discharges

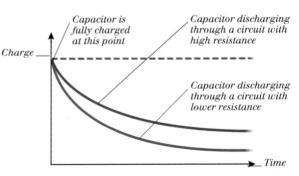

Capacitor is fully charged when this point is reached

Rate of charging falls as capacitor becomes more charged

Charge

Equivalent capacitor charging through a higher resistance

Time

CHARGING

A voltage connected across a capacitor pulls **electrons** away from one plate and forces electrons onto the other. This creates an **electric field** between the plates, which becomes strong enough to prevent any further charging. (The current flowing through the capacitor falls to zero at this point.)

Capacitor is fully charged at this point

Capacitor discharging through a circuit with high resistance

Charge

Capacitor discharging through a circuit with lower resistance

Time

DISCHARGING

When the voltage is removed and the capacitor's plates are connected together with a resistor, the capacitor forces the stored charge out once more, so a current flows in the opposite direction. The current reduces as the capacitor discharges and falls to zero when it is fully discharged.

EXAMPLES OF CAPACITORS

Different types of capacitors are used in different parts of circuits, depending on their desired function. Variable capacitors are used in the tuning circuit of most radios (see pp. 344-345). Variable capacitance can be achieved by allowing plates to move past each other. When a high capacitance is needed, an electrolytic capacitor is used. The dielectric in this type of capacitor is a very thin layer of aluminum oxide that forms on the aluminum plates.

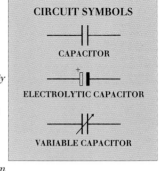

Positive terminal

Chemically treated paper separates the foil layers

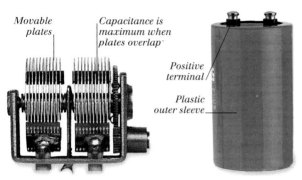

Movable plates

Capacitance is maximum when plates overlap

Positive terminal

Plastic outer sleeve

Aluminum foil

Marking indicating negative terminal

Metal legs for connection in circuit

VARIABLE CAPACITOR

ELECTROLYTIC CAPACITOR

METALLIZED FILM CAPACITOR

CAPACITOR NETWORKS

47 pF capacitor

10 pF capacitor

Combined capacitance is 8.2 pF

IN SERIES

The total capacitance of two capacitors in series is less than either of the capacitances involved. The overall capacitance (C) can be figured out by the formula $1/C = 1/C_1 + 1/C_2$ (where C_1 and C_2 are the values of the capacitances involved).

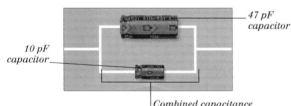

47 pF capacitor

10 pF capacitor

Combined capacitance is 57 pF

IN PARALLEL

The overall capacitance of two capacitors in parallel is equal to the sum of the capacitances involved ($C = C_1 + C_2$). Charge can be stored by one or other of the capacitors.

VOLTAGE CURRENTS IN CAPACITORS

Alternating current (AC) passes easily through a capacitor. As the voltage applied to the capacitor changes direction, the capacitor charges and discharges. The current is at a maximum when the voltage is zero (which occurs twice in each cycle).

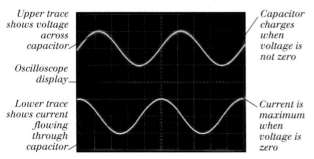

Upper trace shows voltage across capacitor

Oscilloscope display

Lower trace shows current flowing through capacitor

Capacitor charges when voltage is not zero

Current is maximum when voltage is zero

STORING CHARGE

The dome of a Van de Graaff generator (see pp. 40-41) is effectively a huge capacitor. It can store as many as 10 million volts. When the Van de Graaff generator (see below) is activated, huge sparks leap through the air, as the voltage created by the separation of charge causes a breakdown of the surrounding air into ions, and a current flows.

Metal dome stores millions of volts

Voltage multiplier

Insulated wooden stand

Inductors and transformers

ANY COIL OF WIRE can be called an inductor. An **electric current** flowing in an inductor creates a **magnetic field**. If the current changes, the field changes. This change in the magnetic field always acts to impede (resist) the change in current, so inductors resist **alternating current** (AC), while allowing **direct current** (DC) to pass unimpeded. The more rapidly the current changes, the greater the impedence, so inductors allow lower-**frequency** AC through more easily than higher-frequency AC. Inductors have many applications in electronic circuits. For example, inductors called solenoids are used to control switches called relays. Transformers, which are used to increase or decrease **voltage**, consist of two separate inductors wound around the same iron core. When AC passes through one inductor, the magnetic field it produces induces a current in the other.

INSIDE AN INDUCTOR

Most inductors are wound onto a core of iron, or more often onto a **compound** called a ferrite. The core intensifies and focuses the magnetic field produced by the inductor. Ferrite compounds have magnetic properties, but unlike iron, they do not conduct electricity.

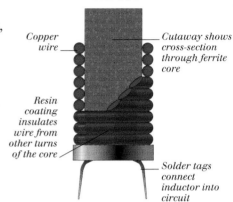

Copper wire

Cutaway shows cross-section through ferrite core

Resin coating insulates wire from other turns of the core

Solder tags connect inductor into circuit

SELF INDUCTANCE

A fluctuating magnetic field is created when an alternating current is supplied to a coil of wire. Each change in the field produces an **electromotive force** (emf) in the coil, a process known as self induction. The current produced in the coil by this emf always opposes the change in supply current. A coil that produces a high emf in this situation is said to have a high self inductance.

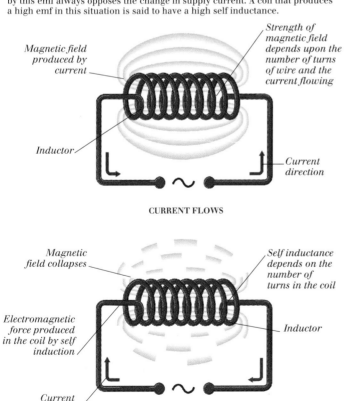

Magnetic field produced by current

Strength of magnetic field depends upon the number of turns of wire and the current flowing

Inductor

Current direction

CURRENT FLOWS

Magnetic field collapses

Self inductance depends on the number of turns in the coil

Electromagnetic force produced in the coil by self induction

Inductor

Current direction

CURRENT REVERSES

INDUCTORS IN AC CIRCUITS

Inductors allow direct current (DC) to pass unimpeded but resist the flow of alternating current (AC). As can be seen using an oscilloscope, the trace from the AC is not in step with the trace of the voltage applied to the inductor.

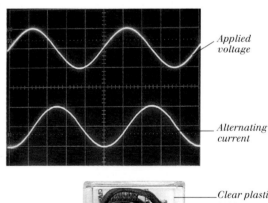

Applied voltage

Alternating current

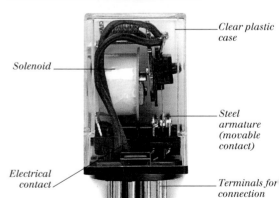

Clear plastic case

Solenoid

Steel armature (movable contact)

Electrical contact

Terminals for connection to circuit

RELAY

A relay is a type of electromechanical switch. A magnetic field is created around a solenoid when a current flows through it. This attracts a steel armature, which in turn forces a pair of electrical contacts together and completes a circuit.

EXAMPLES OF INDUCTORS AND TRANSFORMERS

There are many types of inductors, which are used for countless applications in electronic circuits. An RF choke is used in radio circuits to filter out unwanted frequencies. Transformers are used to change high voltages into the lower voltages required for domestic appliances. An audio transformer generally increases the voltage of a signal in order to drive a loudspeaker.

Output wires to low-voltage appliance

High-voltage input wires

Plastic covering

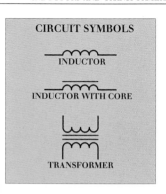

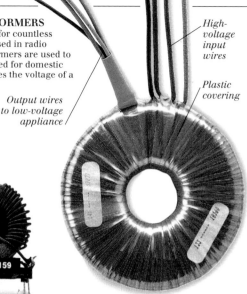

RF CHOKE

GENERAL-PURPOSE INDUCTOR

AUDIO INDUCTOR

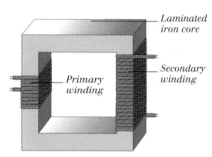

INDUCTOR FOR BLOCKING CURRENT INTERFERENCE

TOROIDAL TRANSFORMER

AUDIO TRANSFORMER

HOW TRANSFORMERS WORK

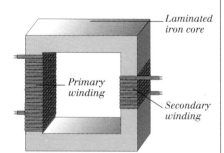

Laminated iron core

Secondary winding

Primary winding

STEP-UP TRANSFORMER
When the primary winding has fewer turns of wire than the secondary, the output voltage at the secondary is higher than the voltage supplied to the primary. Current is reduced as a consequence of the increase in voltage.

Laminated iron core

Primary winding

Secondary winding

STEP-DOWN TRANSFORMER
When the primary winding has more turns of wire than the secondary, the output voltage at the secondary is lower than the voltage supplied to the primary. Current is increased as a consequence of the decrease in voltage.

TUNED CIRCUIT

When a capacitor (pp. 342-343) and an inductor are connected, or coupled, in parallel they form a tuned circuit. The capacitor discharges through the inductor, creating a magnetic field. When the field collapses, it produces a current that charges the capacitor again. This process repeats at a rate – called the resonant frequency – that depends on the capacitance and inductance of the components in the circuit. The circuit produces a large output when supplied with an alternating current that matches its resonant frequency.

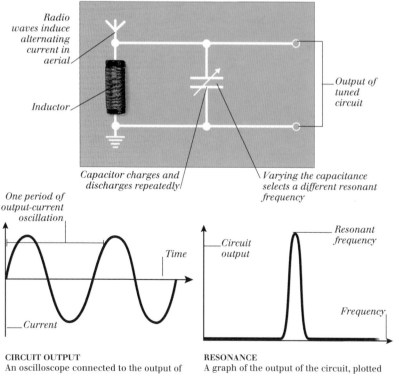

Radio waves induce alternating current in aerial

Inductor

Output of tuned circuit

Capacitor charges and discharges repeatedly

Varying the capacitance selects a different resonant frequency

One period of output-current oscillation

Time

Current

Circuit output

Resonant frequency

Frequency

CIRCUIT OUTPUT
An oscilloscope connected to the output of a tuned circuit shows current alternating at the circuit's resonant frequency.

RESONANCE
A graph of the output of the circuit, plotted over a range of frequencies, centers on the resonant frequency.

Diodes and semiconductors

DIODES ARE ELECTRONIC components that restrict the flow of **electric current** to one direction only. They are made from materials called semiconductors, most notably the **element** silicon (see pp. 104-105). The addition of small amounts of other elements to a pure semiconductor (doping) produces two new types of materials, called p-type and n-type semiconductors. A diode consists of small regions of both types, combined to form a p–n junction. This p–n junction is utilized in transistors and integrated circuits (see pp. 348-349 and 350-351), as well as in light-emitting diodes (LEDs), where current flowing across the junction produces light. Diodes are commonly used to change alternating current (AC) into direct current (DC). This operation is called rectification, and diodes or diode circuits that achieve it are called rectifiers.

INSIDE A DIODE

All semiconductor diodes consist of a p–n junction (see below). The junction is often bonded by a lead or silver strip and encased in glass. Metal wires enable connection to an electronic circuit.

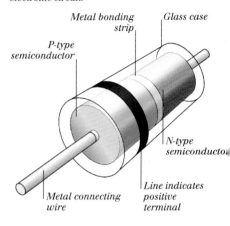

Metal bonding strip

Glass case

P-type semiconductor

N-type semiconductor

Line indicates positive terminal

Metal connecting wire

DOPING A SEMICONDUCTOR

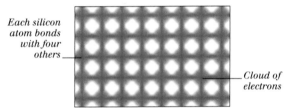

Each silicon atom bonds with four others

Cloud of electrons

PURE SILICON

A crystal of pure silicon consists of millions of silicon **atoms. Electrons** are held only loosely to the atoms, and when they are given extra energy – for example by light or heat – they become free and can flow through the crystal as an electric current.

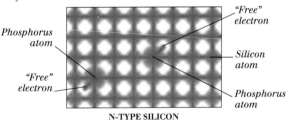

"Free" electron

Phosphorus atom

Silicon atom

"Free" electron

Phosphorus atom

N-TYPE SILICON

In n-type silicon, some electrons are free of the atoms and can move through the crystal. To produce n-type silicon, the crystal is doped with other atoms, such as those of phosphorus.

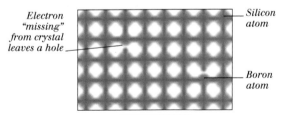

Electron "missing" from crystal leaves a hole

Silicon atom

Boron atom

P-TYPE SILICON

In p-type silicon, some positions in the crystal are unoccupied, leaving a "hole." When an electron moves into this hole, the hole effectively moves to where the electron came from and a charge is carried. P-type silicon is often produced by doping the crystal with atoms of boron.

SEMICONDUCTOR DIODE

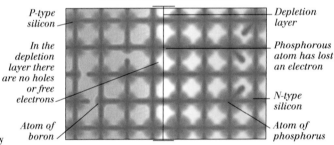

P-type silicon

In the depletion layer there are no holes or free electrons

Atom of boron

Depletion layer

Phosphorous atom has lost an electron

N-type silicon

Atom of phosphorus

P-N JUNCTION

Inside a diode, p- and n-type silicon form a p–n junction (which is often made from a single, appropriately doped crystal). At the junction boundary is the depletion layer, in which electrons from the n-type silicon have filled holes in the p-type silicon. This layer acts as a potential barrier to any further movement of charge carriers.

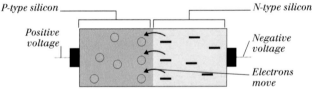

P-type silicon

Positive voltage

N-type silicon

Negative voltage

Electrons move

FORWARD BIAS

A diode conducts electricity when a voltage is applied in one direction only (forward bias). Electrons from its n-type region are attracted across the p–n junction and flow around the circuit. The barrier formed by the depletion layer is reduced, and charge flows easily through the crystal.

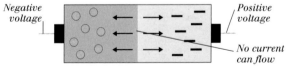

Negative voltage

Positive voltage

No current can flow

REVERSE BIAS

When the voltage is reversed, electrons are pulled away from the p–n boundary toward the positive voltage, and "holes" are pulled away from the depletion layer. This has the effect of raising the barrier, and virtually no current flows.

EXAMPLES OF DIODES

Diodes that control larger currents, such as those in power supplies, are called rectifiers. Diodes that control small voltages, such as those in telecommunications circuits, are called small-signal diodes. Light-emitting diodes (LEDs) are used as power-indicator lights and in moving-sign displays. **Infrared** LEDs produce a beam of invisible infrared radiation and are used in remote controllers. Often, LEDs in the form of strips are used in displays in calculators and alarm clocks.

Red or green LEDs are the most common

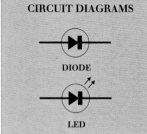

CIRCUIT DIAGRAMS

DIODE

LED

Anode (positive terminal)

LARGE DIODE

Anode lead (positive)

P–n junction is encased in colored plastic

Package contains bridge rectifier circuit

Glass body

Cathode lead (negative)

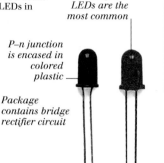

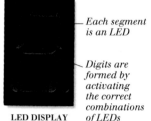

Each segment is an LED

Digits are formed by activating the correct combinations of LEDs

SMALL-SIGNAL DIODES

SMALL RECTIFIER

LEDS

LED DISPLAY

DIODE CHARACTERISTICS

VOLTAGE –CURRENT GRAPH

A diode's characteristics can be summarized on a voltage-current graph, shown here. Even when forward biased, very little current can flow through a diode until the voltage exceeds about 0.6 volts. This voltage is called the contact potential and is required to overcome the potential barrier created by the depletion layer (see left). Above 0.6 volts, the current rises steeply. To the left of the vertical axis, the voltages are negative, and the diode is reverse biased. Very little current flows until the voltage reaches about 150 volts. At this large voltage, the semiconductor crystal breaks down, and electrons are ripped from their atoms, making the whole diode conduct.

Diode "breaks down" at high reverse-bias voltages

Current rises steeply with increase in voltage

0.6 volts

Horizontal axis shows voltage (volts)

Vertical axis shows current (mA)

CONVERTING AC TO DC

Vertical axis shows current

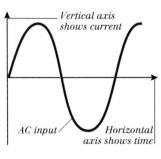

AC input

Horizontal axis shows time

AC INPUT

Mains electricity is supplied as an alternating current (AC). Many domestic appliances require direct current (DC). A rectifier circuit, which makes use of a number of diodes, converts the AC to DC.

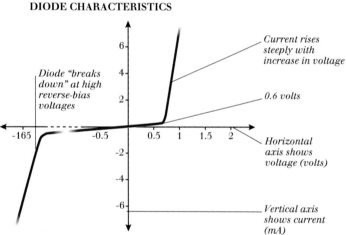

BRIDGE RECTIFIER

A four-way bridge of diodes is generally used as a rectifying circuit in AC adapters. Different sections of the bridge allow current to flow to the output circuit – in one direction only – during different stages of the supply cycle.

Vertical axis shows current

Capacitor smooths output

Rectifier produces varying DC (solid line)

Horizontal axis shows time

DC OUTPUT

A full-wave rectifier circuit has an output that rises and falls with the supply current. A capacitor, which charges when current is high and discharges as it falls, compensates for the varying DC output.

Transistors

THE WORD "TRANSISTOR" is derived from "transfer resistor"; transistors act as variable **resistors**, controlling **currents** and **voltages** in most electronic circuits. A typical transistor is made of sections of n-type and p-type semiconductors (see pp. 346-347). There are two main of types of transistors: bipolar and field-effect (FET). In a bipolar transistor, a small current flowing through the central section (the base) controls a much larger current flowing between two outer sections (the emitter and the collector). There are two main types of field-effect transistors: junction (JFET) and metal-oxide-semiconductor (MOSFET). Both work in a similar way to a bipolar transistor, except that the main current flows between two sections called the source and the drain, and is controlled by a small voltage (not current) at the third section (the gate). There are many examples of transistors, each designed for specific working conditions. Some control high-frequency alternating current, while others are designed to work with high voltages or large currents. When used as a switch (see pp. 350-351), transistors have countless applications, including computer logic gates (see pp. 370-371).

INSIDE A TRANSISTOR

In a typical bipolar transistor (shown below) a layer of n-type semiconductor is sandwiched between two layers of p-type semiconductor, making a p-n-p structure. Alternatively, an n-p-n structure can also be used.

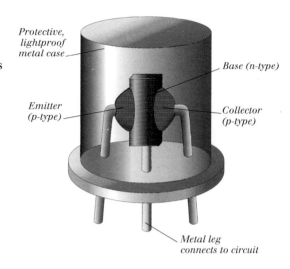

Protective, lightproof metal case

Base (n-type)

Emitter (p-type)

Collector (p-type)

Metal leg connects to circuit

HOW TRANSISTORS WORK

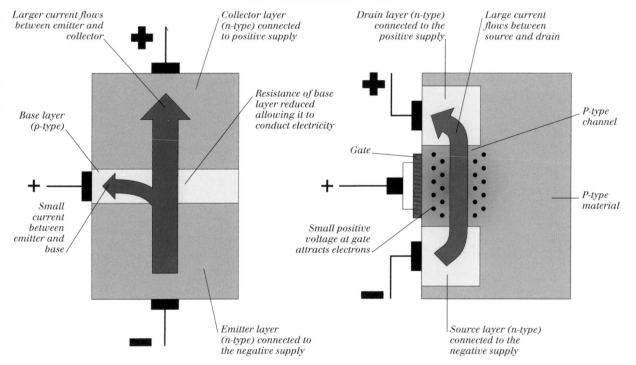

Larger current flows between emitter and collector

Collector layer (n-type) connected to positive supply

Resistance of base layer reduced allowing it to conduct electricity

Base layer (p-type)

Small current between emitter and base

Emitter layer (n-type) connected to the negative supply

Drain layer (n-type) connected to the positive supply

Large current flows between source and drain

P-type channel

Gate

P-type material

Small positive voltage at gate attracts electrons

Source layer (n-type) connected to the negative supply

CROSS-SECTION OF A BIPOLAR TRANSISTOR (NPN)
When no current flows between the base and emitter of a bipolar transistor, no current can flow between the emitter and collector. When a small current flows between the base and emitter, it brings electrons to the base. This reduces the resistance of the base layer and enables a larger current to flow between the emitter and collector.

CROSS-SECTION OF A FIELD-EFFECT TRANSISTOR (MOSFET)
A small, positive voltage at the gate attracts electrons from the p-type material to the region (known as the channel) between the source and the drain. These electrons lower the resistance of the channel and enable a current to flow between the source and drain. In a JFET, the gate is on either side of the transistor.

EXAMPLES OF TRANSISTORS

Transistors are used in a wide range of applications, but their two main uses are amplification and switching. Bipolar signal transistors are often used to amplify low-level signals. Power transistors act as switches to turn large currents on or off using safer, low-voltage inputs. Thyristors are also used as switches, but once triggered into conducting electricity, they stay switched on without further input, just like a mechanical switch.

Case is bolted to a heat sink (device that absorbs heat)

MEDIUM-VOLTAGE-CONTROL TRANSISTOR

Tag indicates emitter leg

BIPOLAR SIGNAL TRANSISTOR

Plastic case

LOW-FREQUENCY BIPOLAR TRANSISTOR

Terminal connects to circuit

HIGH-CURRENT THYRISTOR

CIRCUIT SYMBOLS

NPN TRANSISTOR

PNP TRANSISTOR

JFET TRANSISTOR

MOSFET TRANSISTOR

THE TRANSISTOR AS AN AMPLIFIER

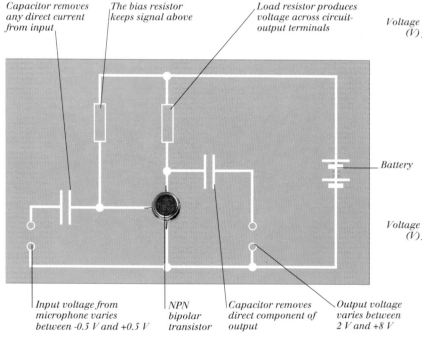

Capacitor removes any direct current from input

The bias resistor keeps signal above

Load resistor produces voltage across circuit-output terminals

Battery

Input voltage from microphone varies between -0.5 V and +0.5 V

NPN bipolar transistor

Capacitor removes direct component of output

Output voltage varies between 2 V and +8 V

SIMPLE AMPLIFIER CIRCUIT

An amplifier is a circuit or device that increases the **amplitude** of a signal. In the case of sound, this results in it being louder. In the circuit shown above, the input signal is a small, varying voltage from a microphone that produces a small, alternating current between a transistor's emitter and base. This small current allows a larger current to flow between the emitter and collector. This current flows through the load resistor and so produces a voltage across it. The voltage is an amplified copy of the input signal.

Voltage (V)

Sine wave input from microphone

Bias voltage level provided by bias resistor

Time

INPUT SIGNAL

A graph of the voltage at the base of the transistor shows that the input signal has an amplitude of about 0.5 V.

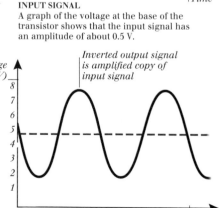

Voltage (V)

Inverted output signal is amplified copy of input signal

Time

OUTPUT SIGNAL

The circuit's output is a varying voltage that is an amplified copy of the input signal – it has an amplitude of about 6 V.

Integrated circuits

INTEGRATED CIRCUITS CONSIST of complete electronic circuits built onto a single slice of **semiconductor**, normally silicon. They can contain hundreds of thousands of linked components and yet may be as small as a fingernail. Such miniaturization has made possible personal computers, digital watches, and many other familiar electronic devices. Integrated circuits are also known as chips, microchips, or silicon chips. Electronic components, such as resistors, capacitors, diodes, and transistors, are formed within the silicon. Chips used in computers are called microprocessors and contain many transistors, which are used as switches. Transistor switches are ideal for handling the on or off electric currents that form the basis of computer logic (see pp. 370-371). The components are built up as layers of n- and p-type semiconductor (see pp. 346-347), formed within the silicon by a photographic process. The process of building layers is broken down into many stages of masking, doping, and etching. Aluminum tracks connect the many components together, just as copper tracks do on ordinary printed circuit boards (see pp. 338-339).

TYPES OF INTEGRATED CIRCUITS
The two main types of integrated circuits are digital and linear (or analog). Digital integrated circuits include microprocessors. Linear integrated circuits are often used as amplifiers, in audio equipment for example. The most common type of linear integrated circuit is the operational amplifier (op-amp).

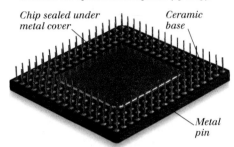

Chip sealed under metal cover
Ceramic base
Metal pin

DIGITAL INTEGRATED CIRCUIT

Plastic case
Metal connecting pin

LINEAR (ANALOG) INTEGRATED CIRCUIT

TRANSISTOR-SWITCH CIRCUIT
Microprocessors contain thousands of transistor switches. The simplified circuit shown below explains the operation of a switch using a field-effect transistor (see pp. 348-349). The input to the switch is from computer input devices or from previous digital circuits. When the input to the transistor's gate is low, there can be no current flow between the source and the drain. In this case, the output voltage will be equal to the supply voltage (high), because the load resistor drops no voltage when no current flows. When the input voltage increases above a certain level, the transistor switches on (current flows from source to drain), the load resistor drops most of the supply voltage, and so output drops to near zero.

MINIATURIZATION
Only through a microscope is it possible to see the thousands of tiny transistors and other components that can be put on one tiny slice of silicon to make a complete integrated circuit. The circuit is encased in ceramic or plastic for protection. A set of metal pins projecting from the case connects the integrated circuit to a circuit board.

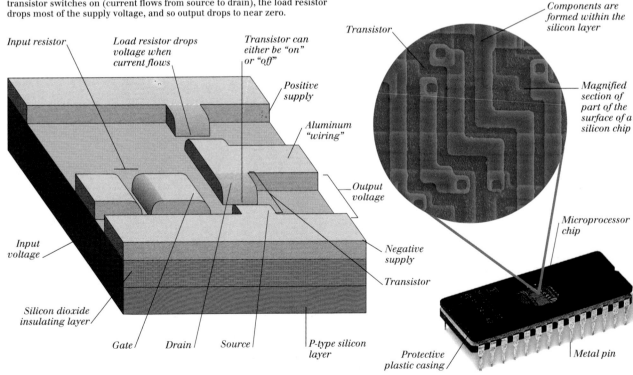

Input resistor
Load resistor drops voltage when current flows
Transistor can either be "on" or "off"
Positive supply
Aluminum "wiring"
Output voltage
Input voltage
Negative supply
Transistor
Silicon dioxide insulating layer
Gate
Drain
Source
P-type silicon layer

Transistor
Components are formed within the silicon layer
Magnified section of part of the surface of a silicon chip
Microprocessor chip
Protective plastic casing
Metal pin

MAKING AN INTEGRATED CIRCUIT

Cylinders of pure, crystalline silicon are the starting point in the production of integrated circuits, a process known as very large-scale integration (VLSI). The crystal is sliced into a large number of circular wafers, and a few hundred microchips at a time are produced from each wafer. Most of the process takes place in very clean conditions, as dust or other contaminants can ruin the chips during production. In a series of stages, n- and p-type silicon, polysilicon (a conductor), and aluminum "wiring" are laid down to form the circuit.

Designs for each layer have a different color

Transparent plastic sheet

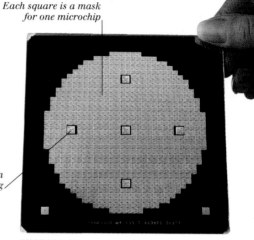

Each square is a mask for one microchip

Control pattern used for testing

CIRCUIT DESIGN
An integrated circuit is built up as a series of n- and p-type layers. Each layer must be designed separately. For more simple circuits, transparent, enlarged plans are laid on top of one another to check that each layer fits precisely with all the others.

PHOTO MASK
The designs for each layer are reduced and reproduced to form a photo mask. Ultraviolet light is shone through the photo mask on to a wafer of silicon. The wafer has an insulating layer of silicon oxide, which is broken down where ultraviolet light falls on the oxide. The exposed areas are etched away by acid, and this leaves pure silicon exposed and ready to receive the next treatment.

DIFFUSION OF IMPURITIES
Once the appropriate areas of silicon dioxide have been removed by etching, the wafer is heated in the presence of doping elements. Atoms of these doping elements diffuse into the exposed silicon, forming n- or p-type regions. Further layers are built up by more masking, etching, and doping, until the components are complete.

P-type layer formed by doping

Silicon dioxide formed by heating silicon in oxygen

Silicon dioxide insulating layer

Silicon dioxide is etched away in some parts

N-type silicon forms transistor's drain

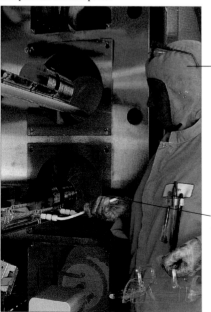

Workers operate in ultraclean rooms and wear gowns and gloves

N-type silicon forms transistor's source

Batches of wafers fed into furnace

Aluminum connection to gate

Aluminum connection to source

Aluminum connection to drain

BUILDING UP THE LAYERS
A field-effect transistor is formed on the surface of an integrated circuit by building up layers of n-and p-type silicon, polysilicon, silicon dioxide, and aluminum. The finished transistor is just one thousandth of a millimeter wide.

Computers

AT THE HEART of the personal computer (PC) are microprocessors that perform mathematical operations using numbers in binary form (see pp. 360-361). The binary system uses only two digits, 0 and 1, called binary digits, or bits. These bits are expressed inside the computer in a number of ways: voltages that may be low (for 0) or high (for 1); transistor switches that may be off or on; or tiny capacitors (see pp. 342-343) that may be uncharged or charged. Alphanumeric characters (letters and numbers), as well as simple computer instructions, are represented by groups of eight bits, called bytes (see pp. 390-391). The main processor inside a computer is the central processing unit (CPU). This is a chip that carries out huge numbers of calculations every second. Software is a set of instructions that is needed to enable it to carry these out. The software and the results of the calculations must be stored inside the computer, and this is achieved by random access memory (**RAM**) and read-only memory (**ROM**).

PERSONAL COMPUTER

PCs consist of three main parts: an input device (such as a keyboard); output device (such as a monitor); and the system unit, which houses the main electrical components.

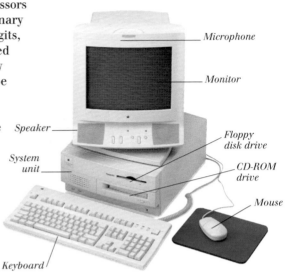

Microphone

Monitor

Speaker

System unit

Floppy disk drive

CD-ROM drive

Mouse

Keyboard

CENTRAL PROCESSING UNIT (CPU)

All computers have a chip called the CPU. The CPU is the computer's center of operations. It takes in information from a keyboard or mouse, the RAM, and the ROM. It can also send data to the monitor (or other output devices) or to be stored in the RAM, but it cannot send information to the ROM. The content of the ROM is normally fixed – it cannot be altered or removed, and can only be read.

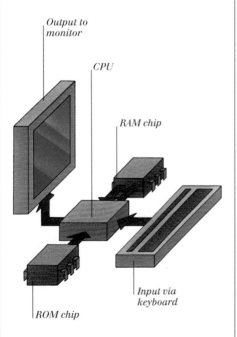

Output to monitor

CPU

RAM chip

Input via keyboard

ROM chip

HOW RANDOM ACCESS MEMORY (RAM) WORKS

Information stored in RAM is temporary; it is lost when the computer's power is switched off. Tiny capacitors on the RAM chip store binary digits. They are uncharged for bit 0, and charged for bit 1. The chip is covered with tiny crisscrossed metal tracks. Located at each intersection of these tracks is a transistor switch and a capacitor. To store information at a particular location, or address, pulses are sent along a set of tracks, called address lines. Within a particular address, there are normally 8 or 16 bits. Where a 1 is to be stored within the address, a pulse sent along a data line charges a capacitor.

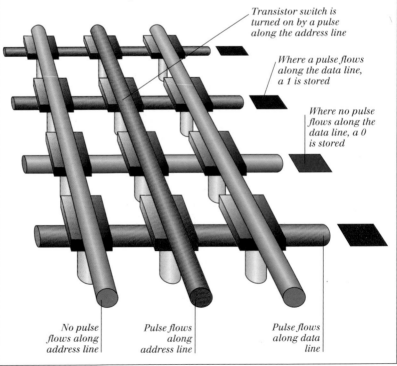

Transistor switch is turned on by a pulse along the address line

Where a pulse flows along the data line, a 1 is stored

Where no pulse flows along the data line, a 0 is stored

No pulse flows along address line

Pulse flows along address line

Pulse flows along data line

INSIDE A PERSONAL COMPUTER

The computer itself is normally housed in a hard disk unit. This has socket connections, called ports, that allow information to be input into the computer or read from it. Input and output devices, collectively known as peripherals, include keyboards, monitors, and printers.

Inside every CPU chip is an arithmetic unit, dedicated to carrying out addition and other logical operations. The rate at which these are carried out is a measure of the speed of the computer and is normally measured in megahertz (MHz, millions of calculations per second).

CD-ROM drive

Floppy disk drive

Hard disk housed in a strong protective plastic shell

HARD DISK UNIT

All of the computer's major subunits are housed in the hard disk unit. The CPU, RAM, and ROM chips are plugged into a motherboard, along with additional circuit boards, called cards, which extend the computer's capabilities. All the various cards and chips inside the unit are connected by buses. At the rear of the unit are sockets called ports. These enable the computer to be connected to input and output devices (peripherals), including the keyboard, printer, and monitor.

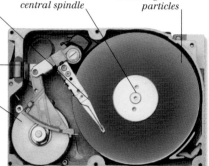

Disk rotates on central spindle

Read/write head

Ribbon connector provides link between computer and read/write head

Head actuator

Mylar disk, coated with magnetic particles

HARD DISK DRIVE

Information is stored magnetically on the surfaces of the disks inside a hard disk drive. It has read and write heads, which are positioned very close to the disk surface. The disks spin rapidly, and the heads move in and out to capture information from the disk.

Plug-in video card controls the output of the computer to monitors

CPU chip mounted on plug-in board

Heat sink

Motherboard, a piece of fiberglass that doesn't conduct electricity, on which all the components are mounted

Slots available for other plug-in boards that can extend the capabilities of the computer

Arithmetic chip provides extra processing power

ROM chips

Integrated circuits are plugged and soldered directly into the motherboard

Bus (metal strip) connects different regions of motherboard

Screw hole

Input and output ports

SCSI (Small Computer Standard Interface) port

Network connection port

Connection to keyboard and mouse

Connections to microphone and speaker

RAM expansion slots

Battery for internal clock

RAM chips

Plug-in expansion card holds RAM chips

MOTHERBOARD

Metal tracks on the surface of the motherboard, called buses, carry information between the CPU, RAM, and ROM chips. They also connect the CPU to input and output ports, located at the rear of the unit. Extra circuit boards, called cards, can be plugged into the motherboard to extend the computer's capabilities.

Computer networks

A GROUP OF COMPUTERS CONNECTED TOGETHER sharing information
is called a network. The information they share is digital, which means
that it consists of long series of binary digits, or bits (see pp. 352-353).
In addition to text and numerical information, pictures, sound, and video
can be transferred over a network. Digital information passes between
computers along cables, or in some cases through the air as **radio waves**
or **microwave radiation**. Often, some of the network links are part of
the telephone network. Most telephones are analog devices, and
most telephone signals are therefore analog. For this reason, digital
computer information is first coded (modulated) into an analog
form so that it can be sent across the telephone network. At a
computer receiving the information, it must be demodulated
back to its original digital form. A device called a modem
(modulator-demodulator) is used to link a computer to the
telephone network. Computer networks can be linked to
other computer networks, and by far the largest example
of this arrangement is the Internet.

MOBILE MULTIMEDIA

A laptop computer provides access to computer
networks from anywhere in the world via a
mobile telephone. A plug-in modem the size
of a credit card connects the computer to a
telephone for fax communications, e-mail,
and access to the World Wide Web.

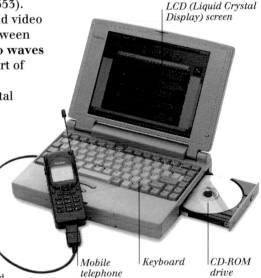

LCD (Liquid Crystal Display) screen

Mobile telephone

Keyboard

CD-ROM drive

SAMPLING

In order to digitize analog sound signals to a high quality, an electronic circuit called
an analog-to-digital converter measures (samples) the signal 44,100 times per second.
The more samples per second, the more accurate the digital representation of the sound.
Each sample is a numerical value, which is represented in **binary** form as a string of eight
or sixteen bits. Large numbers of bits are needed to encode sound – for example, ten
seconds of high-quality sound requires more than seven million bits.

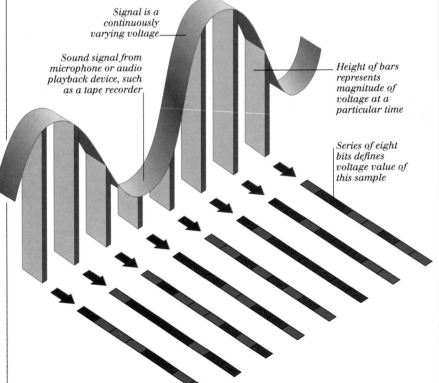

Signal is a continuously varying voltage

Sound signal from microphone or audio playback device, such as a tape recorder

Height of bars represents magnitude of voltage at a particular time

Series of eight bits defines voltage value of this sample

CABLES

Three types of cable are commonly
used to link computers across a network.
Coaxial cable consists of one wire
wrapped around another. A twisted pair
consists of two insulated wires twisted
around each other. The fastest links are
provided by fiber-optic cables, which
transmit digital information as pulses
of light or **infrared**.

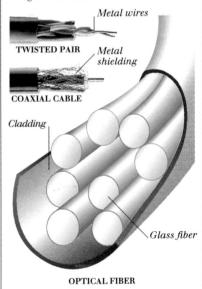

Metal wires

TWISTED PAIR

Metal shielding

COAXIAL CABLE

Cladding

Glass fiber

OPTICAL FIBER

THE INTERNET

Powerful computers, called servers, are the points of connection to the Internet. Individual personal computers connect to servers via cables within a single building, or via a telephone link using a modem. Servers enable connected users to send and receive e-mail; they may also hold "pages" of information. There is a server at the heart of every LAN (Local Area Network); groups of LANs form WANs (Wide Area Networks).

Cable physically joins computer to server

Personal computer connects to the server

Modem

Analog telephone line

Server provides Internet access

DIAL-UP CONNECTION

Most individual users of the Internet normally have a dial-up connection to an Internet service provider, via a modem. The modem converts digital information from the user's personal computer to an analog signal (see below), so that it can be sent down a telephone line. Another modem at the Internet service provider converts the information back into digital form.

High-speed cable provides fast connection to Internet backbone

SERVER

A server is a powerful computer that is constantly connected to many other computers. There is a server at the center of every computer network. Most servers are also connected to the Internet, providing access to e-mail and the World Wide Web for those connected to the network.

e-mail message on computer screen

Server or mail server

Web page accessed on personal computer

WORLD-WIDE WEB

Most servers contain information, stored electronically as "pages." This can be accessed by users of the Internet and forms a complex, interconnected "web" of information. Web pages carry a wide range of information, including news and commercial advertising.

E-MAIL

One of the most useful applications of the Internet is electronic mail, or e-mail. Anyone with access to the Internet can send and receive e-mails to and from each other. Servers called mail servers are designed to process electronic mail, ensuring that it is delivered to the correct destination.

"Firewall" restricts outside users' access to server

Server at the heart of the intranet

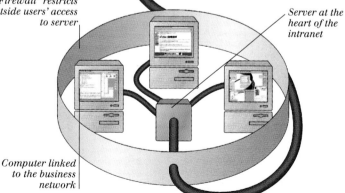

MODEMS

A modem creates a rapidly changing analog signal, which carries digital information with it. The digital information is broken into groups of two, three, or more bits ("0" or "1"). Different combinations of bits change the frequency, amplitude, or phase of the analog signal. The digital information is decoded at the other modem.

Each group affects the analog signal in a particular way

Analog signal corresponding to the group of bits "0" or "1"

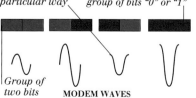

Group of two bits

MODEM WAVES

Computer linked to the business network

INTRANETS

Many large organizations have internal computer networks called intranets. Often the server at the heart of an intranet gives connected users limited access only to the Internet, such as e-mail capability only. This limited Internet access is often called a firewall.

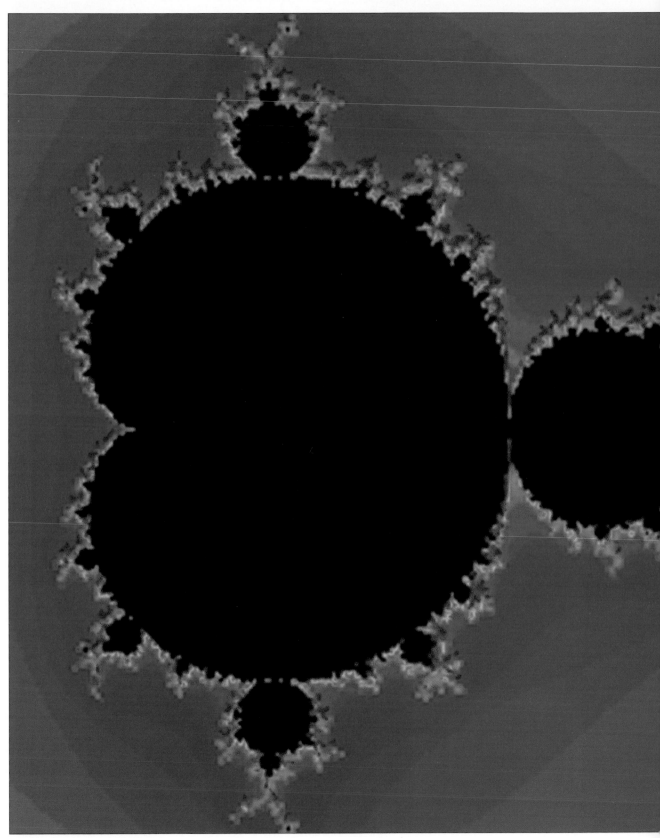

A computer-generated fractal image constructed using the Mandelbrot set of numbers

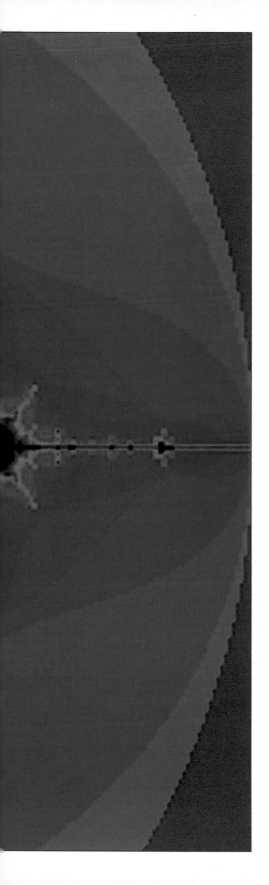

Mathematics

Discovering mathematics 358

Numbers 360

Algebra 362

Geometry 364

Coordinates and triangles 366

Probability and statistics 368

Logic and sets 370

Chaos theory and fractals 372

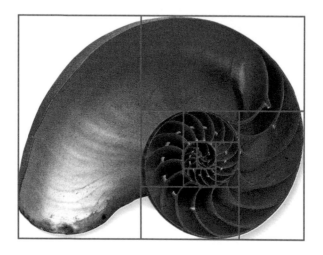

PASCAL'S CALCULATOR
Built in 1642, Pascal's calculating machine
consisted of a number of toothed wheels. The
wheels were connected to concentric rings on
which were inscribed numbers. Numbers to
be added or subtracted were dialed in, and the
answer appeared in holes to the left of the rings.

Discovering mathematics

THE STUDY OF MATHEMATICS is concerned with numbers and
geometry. Numbers are used in arithmetic, probability
theory, statistics, and in algebra. Geometry deals with shapes
and curves. Algebra and geometry are combined in a branch of
mathematics known as coordinate geometry, in which shapes
may be described in terms of numbers. Modern mathematics
includes non-Euclidean geometry, set theory, and chaos theory.

PURE AND APPLIED MATHEMATICS
Even before written language developed,
numbers were recorded as tally marks,
and simple calculations were applied to
activities such as trade and surveying.
From around 3000 BC, ancient Egyptian
scribes were applying arithmetic to the
construction of the pyramids. Being very
practical, the ancient Egyptians had no
desire to prove or to generalize their
mathematical ideas. Mathematicians in
Mesopotamia, however, were beginning
to ponder on the fundamental and rather
abstract nature of numbers and shapes –
part of what is now called pure mathematics.
The distinction between pure and applied
mathematics persists today.

MATHEMATICS IN ANCIENT GREECE
Around 600 BC, Greek philosophers,
astronomers, and mathematicians began
to produce generalized mathematical
statements (theorems). They saw the need
to take a logical approach to the subject
and to provide proofs for their theorems.
For example, what later became known
as the **Pythagorean** theorem had been
known for centuries in China, but was
first proved by the Pythagorean school in
Greece. Through their logical approach, the
Greeks developed a deeper understanding
of pure mathematics. Ancient Greek
mathematics is characterized by logic
and by its investigations of geometry.
For example, Greek astronomers estimated
the diameter of the Earth and proved that
it was round by using geometrical
techniques. Greek mathematics was built
up from basic statements called axioms, or
postulates (such as "the shortest distance
between two points is a straight line").
The Greeks arrived at their theorems
by assuming the truth of postulates and
applying logical arguments. The most
important contribution to this process
was **Euclid's** 13-volume work entitled
Elements, which was a comprehensive
collection of Greek ideas of geometry
at the time.

MIDDLE AGES
Greek mathematics survived the Dark
Ages because it was translated into
several languages. Meanwhile, Indian
and Mesopotamian mathematicians made
important contributions to arithmetic.
For example, Indian mathematicians
implemented the number zero, which
had also been discovered, but not used,
by the Maya of Central America some
centuries earlier. **Muhammad ibn-Musa
al-Khwarizmi**, the 9th-century Islamic
mathematician, wrote many books,
including *The Book of Restoring and
Balancing*. The Arabic word for
restoring is *al-jabr*, and this is the
origin of the modern term "algebra."
By the 15th century, the focus of
activity had moved to Europe, and
although Chinese, Japanese, and
Korean mathematicians made important
discoveries during this period, their
work was not known outside Eastern
Asia until the 17th century.

EUROPEAN MATHEMATICS
Latin translations of Greek and Arabic
mathematics reached Europe between
the 11th and 15th centuries. Many of the
mathematical symbols familiar today
originated in Germany in the 15th
century, while Italian artists made
important advances in geometry in
their studies of perspective during the
16th century. The 17th and 18th centuries
saw a fresh approach to much of the
mathematics that had been passed down
from the Greeks and Arabs. For example,
the ancient Greeks thought of the
number 1 as the indivisible basis of all
numbers, and therefore saw fractions
as ratios rather than numbers less than 1.
Around 1585, European mathematicians
began to write fractions as decimal
numbers, as well as common fractions
and ratios. Several fundamental branches
of modern mathematics were invented
during this period, an important example
being coordinate geometry, in which

geometrical shapes can be represented by sets of numbers called coordinates. Perhaps even more important than coordinate geometry is calculus, an immensely powerful branch of algebra developed independently by **Isaac Newton** and **Gottfried Leibniz** in the 1680s.

19TH-CENTURY MATHEMATICS

Despite the dominance of calculus, geometry was still studied extensively during the 17th and 18th centuries. Euclid had presented a set of basic postulates of geometry that were thought to be self-evident (therefore needing no proof). In the early years of the 19th century, it was discovered that the so-called parallel postulate is not self-evident and indeed is not true in all cases. This led to the development of non-Euclidean geometry – the geometry of curved spaces, such as the surface of a sphere. It has been useful in many important theories, including general relativity. Both pure and applied mathematics became more rigorous and abstract during the 19th century, and more and more powerful. During this time, mathematicians developed set theory, which is closely related to logic theory. Two important tools in set theory and logic theory

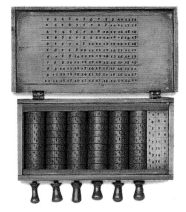

NAPIER'S BONES
In 1617, John Napier created a series of rods engraved with numbers in such a way that they could be set side by side and used to do complex calculations. The rods, which were usually made of ivory or bone, were soon known as "Napier's Bones."

were Boolean algebra and Venn diagrams. Boolean algebra is a system of notation that was important in the development of computers in the 1940s. The power of set theory and logic theory, together with a desire to understand the true nature of mathematics, led to an attempt to formulate all of mathematics using logic alone. This quest kept many of the best mathematical minds busy until around 1930, when **Kurt Gödel** published the first of his incompleteness theorems. These showed that the quest had been futile – that it was impossible to derive all of mathematics without making assumptions.

CHAOS THEORY AND FRACTALS

The second half of the 20th century saw the development of chaos theory. In the 1890s, **Jules Henri Poincaré** noted that while the orbits of two objects (such as the Sun and the Earth) could be figured out easily, adding a third orbiting object to the model could cause all three orbits to become surprisingly unpredictable. This three-body problem was the first realization of the importance of the mathematics of unpredictability – chaos theory. During the 1960s and 70s, **Benoit Mandelbrot** defined a new type of geometry, which was found to be related to chaos theory. He coined the term "fractal" – from the phrase "fractional dimension" – to describe the new geometry. The relationship between chaos theory and fractals is enabling mathematicians to gain a deeper understanding of complex and unpredictable systems, from the weather to the stock market.

ELLIPSOGRAPH
This ellipsograph is a device that was used to draw perfect ellipses. The user was required to set the two foci of the ellipse and then establish the ellipse's boundary (distance from the center point of a line between the two foci). It was made in 1817 by John Farey of London.

TIMELINE OF DISCOVERIES

	8000 BC — People in Mesopotamia use clay tablets to record numbers of animals and measures of grain
Positional notation (place-value system) is developed by the Sumerians	2400 BC
	1900 BC — Mesopotamian mathematicians produce what is now known as the Pythagorean theorem
Decimal numbers are first used, in China	1350 BC
	900 BC — The symbol for zero is first used, in India
Euclid writes *Elements*, the standard geometry textbook for the next 2,000 years	300 BC
	250 BC — **Apollonius of Perga** defines several important geometrical figures in terms of slices through a cone
Negative numbers are used for the first time, in China	100 BC
	AD 1 — Decimal fractions first used in China
Arabian mathematician Muhammad ibn-Musa al-Khwarizmi writes several works on algebra. The word "algebra" is derived from the title of one of his books	AD 800
	1000 — The decimal system of numbers is introduced into Europe by Arab mathematicians
Dutch mathematicians use the symbols "+" and "-" for the first time in their modern sense	1514
	1614 — **John Napier** introduces logarithms. They greatly improve speeds of calculation
Analytical geometry developed independently by **René Descartes** and Pierre de Fermat	1630s
	1660s — English draper John Graunt lays the foundations of statistics by analyzing birth and death records
Isaac Newton and Gottfried Leibniz develop calculus independently	1660s 70s
	1830s — Non-Euclidean geometry is developed
Georg Cantor and others develop set theory	1870s
	1960 — IBM researcher Benoit Mandelbrot develops fractal geometry, including devising the Mandelbrot Set
Chaos theory is used to analyze a number of different complex systems	1980s

Numbers

MATHEMATICIANS USE MANY types of numbers. The most basic is the class of numbers called counting numbers – **whole numbers** greater than zero. When counting, we use a number system based on the number 10, called the denary system, which evolved independently in many different cultures. Although the modern number system is based on the number 10, any number can be expressed using any **base**. Binary numbers are based on the number 2, for example. For any given number, there are always other numbers greater or less than it. Also, there are always numbers between any two numbers, however close those two particular numbers may be in value. These facts make it possible to construct a number line, which extends to infinity either side of zero. Fractions have values between those of whole numbers. They may be expressed as the ratio of two whole numbers (common fraction), as a number with a decimal point (decimal fraction), or as a percentage. Other types of number include irrational numbers, squares, and cubes.

NUMBER SYSTEMS
The digits 0-9 have evolved over many centuries (see below). The modern number system is a place-value system. This means that the value of any digit depends on its position in a number. For example (reading from left to right), in the number 333, the first three is worth 300, the second is worth 30, and the third is worth three.

$$1 \quad 2 \quad 3 \quad 4 \quad 5$$

MODERN NUMBERS

$$I \quad II \quad III \quad IV \quad V$$

ROMAN NUMERALS

BABYLONIAN NUMBERS

ARABIC NUMBERS

DENARY SYSTEM
The denary system is referred to as base ten, because it has ten symbols (0 to 9). An abacus uses beads to represent numbers in base ten – a bead on one row is worth ten times more than a bead on the row above. The abacus below shows the number 206,243 using 17 beads.

BINARY NUMBERS
Binary numbers use two digits (0 and 1). A two-state system, such as a light bulb, can be used to represent a binary number. The light bulbs represent, from left to right, eight, four, two, and one. The binary number 1010 equals ten (8+0+2+0), and 1001 equals nine (8+0+0+1).

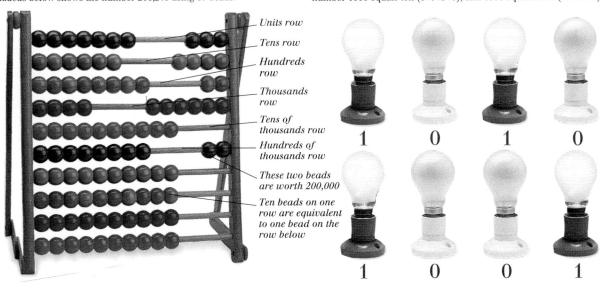

Units row

Tens row

Hundreds row

Thousands row

Tens of thousands row

Hundreds of thousands row

These two beads are worth 200,000

Ten beads on one row are equivalent to one bead on the row below

1   0   1   0

1   0   0   1

NUMBER LINE
All whole numbers greater than zero are called positive numbers. Negative numbers are those less than zero and are written with a negative sign (-). Positive and negative whole numbers are called integers. The numbers between them (non-integers) are fractions.

The number -1 is a negative integer

Zero is at the center of the number line

The number 2.4 is a fraction that lies between 2 and 3

The number 4 is a positive integer

Minus infinity

$$-\infty \quad -4 \quad -3 \quad -2 \quad -1 \quad 0 \quad 1 \quad 2 \quad 3 \quad 4 \quad \infty$$

Infinity

FRACTIONS AND PERCENTAGES

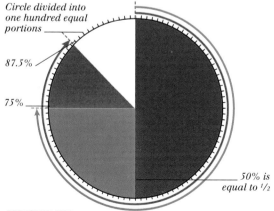

Seven eighths (⁷/₈)

Each section represents one eighth

Circle divided into halves, quarters and eighths

Three quarters (³/₄) is equivalent to six eighths (⁶/₈)

Three sixths (³/₆) is equivalent to one half (¹/₂)

Two sixths (²/₆) is equivalent to one third (¹/₃)

Each section represents one twelfth

Circle divided into thirds, sixths, and twelfths

FRACTIONS

Common fractions are written as a ratio of two numbers. For example, the number that has exactly half the value of 1 is written ¹/₂, because it is equal to 1 divided by 2. The number above the line is called the numerator, while the number below it is called the denominator.

Circle divided into one hundred equal portions

87.5%

75%

50% is equal to ¹/₂

PERCENTAGES

Fractions can also be written as decimal numbers or percentages, with each digit having a value one tenth of the digit to its left. So, the fraction 0.66 is six tenths and six hundredths. It is equivalent to ⁶⁶/₁₀₀, which can also be written as 66% (66 percent).

IRRATIONAL NUMBERS

Irrational numbers cannot be written down exactly as integers or fractions. They are important because they are needed to express certain scientific theories mathematically. An example is the golden ratio, approximately equal to 1.618:1. A rectangle having sides in this ratio is called a golden rectangle and is found commonly in nature, art, and architecture. The golden rectangle can be used to construct a logarithmic spiral (see below) in the shape of this nautilus shell.

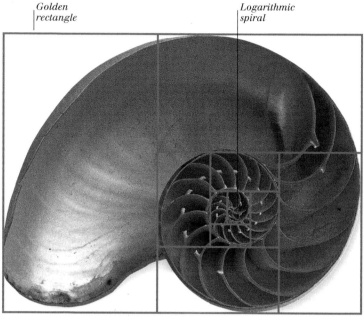

Golden rectangle

Logarithmic spiral

SQUARES AND CUBES

The square of a number is that number multiplied by itself. Similarly, the area of a square is found by multiplying the length of one side by itself. The area of the face of a cube that has sides three units long (see below) is therefore nine units. Nine is the circle of three and can be written as 3^2. A cubic number is a number that is multiplied by itself, and then by itself again. This process is called cubing because it yields the volume of a cube. The volume of the cube below is therefore twenty-seven units. Twenty-seven is the cube of 3 and can be written as 3^3.

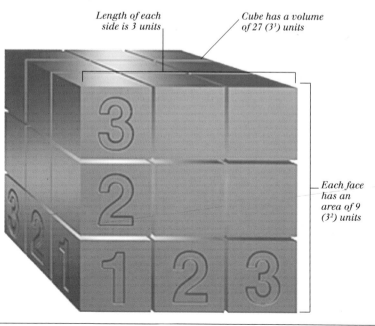

Length of each side is 3 units

Cube has a volume of 27 (3^3) units

Each face has an area of 9 (3^2) units

Algebra

THE BRANCH OF MATHEMATICS in which numbers are represented by letters or other symbols is called algebra. Algebraic expressions are normally in the form of an equation involving **constants** and **variables**. By definition, the values of both sides of an equation must be equal. Alternatively, an expression may be an inequality, such as one involving the symbol ">", which means "greater than" (see pp. 392-393). Equations that relate the values of one variable to the values of another (or several others) are called functions. Among the most useful functions are polynomials, which involve variables raised to various powers. When a number or variable is squared (see pp. 360-361), it is said to be raised to the second power; if it is cubed, it is said to be raised to the third power. Algebraic formulas are used to describe phenomena in all scientific disciplines. For example, the motion of a projectile can be summarized by a formula that relates speed, time, and distance to the rate of acceleration due to **gravity**.

ALGEBRAIC EQUATIONS

The scales below are balanced with eight eggs in one pan and a 400g mass in the other. Assuming that each egg has the same mass, then the mass of each egg must be 50 g (400 g divided by eight). In a similar way, algebraic equations can be used to find the value of unknown numbers.

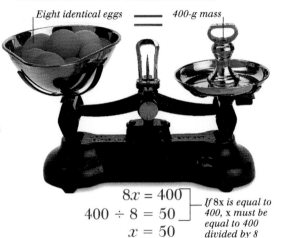

Eight identical eggs ══ *400-g mass*

$$8x = 400$$
$$400 \div 8 = 50$$
$$x = 50$$

If 8x *is equal to 400,* x *must be equal to 400 divided by 8*

CONSTANTS AND VARIABLES

Algebraic expressions involve constants (fixed numbers) and variables (which can take many different values). For example, the area of any circle is always related directly to its radius. In the equation below, *a* and *r* are variables used to denote the area and radius respectively, and π (pi) is a constant whose value is about 3.14. This equation expresses a relationship, or function, between area and radius.

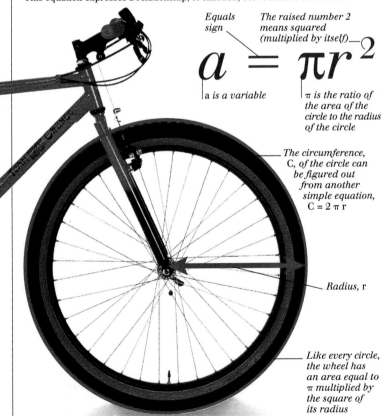

$$a = \pi r^2$$

Equals sign

The raised number 2 means squared (multiplied by itself)

a is a variable

π is the ratio of the area of the circle to the radius of the circle

The circumference, C, of the circle can be figured out from another simple equation, C = 2 π r

Radius, r

Like every circle, the wheel has an area equal to π multiplied by the square of its radius

PICTURING ALGEBRA

When several values of the function $y = 4 - x$ (see table) are plotted on **axes**, they lie in a straight line. Inequalities can also be shown on graphs. For example, the shaded area in the graph below is the region for which the following inequalities are true: $y < x$, $y < 4 - x$, $y > 0$ (> means "greater than," < means "less than").

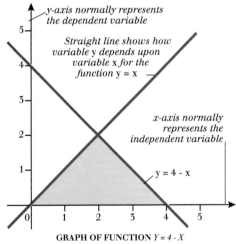

y-axis normally represents the dependent variable

Straight line shows how variable y depends upon variable x for the function y = x

x-axis normally represents the independent variable

y = 4 - x

GRAPH OF FUNCTION Y = 4 - X

Variable y is always equal to 4 - x, whatever the value of x   *When x = 1, y = 3*

x	0	1	2	3	4
$4 - x$	4	3	2	1	0

TABLE OF VALUES OF Y = 4 - X

GRAPHS OF POLYNOMIAL FUNCTIONS

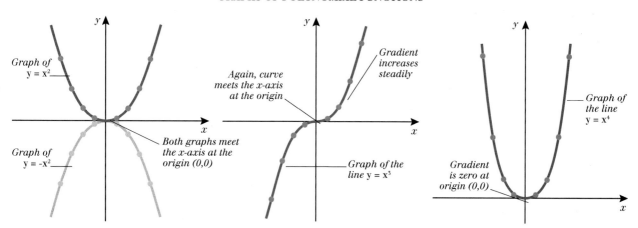

Graph of y = x²

Both graphs meet the x-axis at the origin (0,0)

Graph of y = -x²

Gradient increases steadily

Again, curve meets the x-axis at the origin

Graph of the line y = x³

Graph of the line y = x⁴

Gradient is zero at origin (0,0)

QUADRATIC CURVE
A function involving powers (see pp. 360-361) of a variable no higher than two is said to be a quadratic. Here, the two simplest quadratics are plotted: $y = x^2$ and $y = -x^2$. The resulting curves are **parabolas**.

CUBIC CURVE
A function involving the cube (see pp. 360-361) of a variable is called a cubic. The simplest cubic function is $y = x^3$. A cubic can contain terms of x^2 and x as well as x^3, but the shape of the graph is not as simple as that shown here.

BIQUADRATIC CURVE
Functions involving the fourth power of a variable (for example x^4) are called biquadratic. This is a graph of the simplest biquadratic curve, and it has a shape similar to a quadratic curve but with steeper gradients.

FORMULAS

Scientists regularly develop and use formula that describe or predict the dependence of two or more variables. Here, a ball is fired vertically upward from a truck that is moving at a constant speed. A formula figured out from the known laws of motion (see pp. 20-21) shows that the height, h, of the ball above the truck is equal to $ut - \frac{1}{2}gt^2$. (In this equation, u is the initial vertical **velocity** of the ball, g is the acceleration due to **gravity,** and t is the time elapsed after the ball is fired.) The formula is a quadratic equation (see above), and a graph of h versus t has the shape of a parabola (as does the path of the ball).

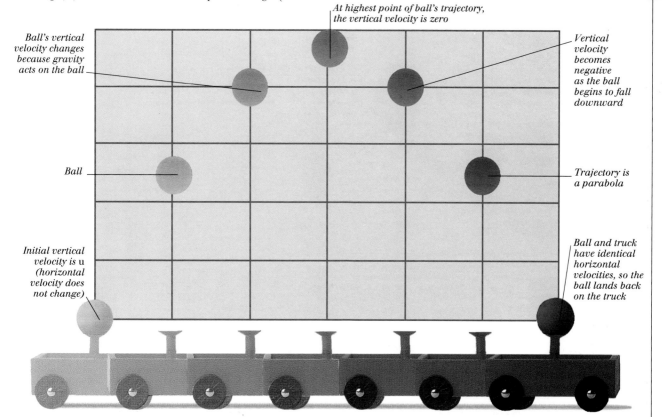

At highest point of ball's trajectory, the vertical velocity is zero

Ball's vertical velocity changes because gravity acts on the ball

Vertical velocity becomes negative as the ball begins to fall downward

Ball

Trajectory is a parabola

Initial vertical velocity is u (horizontal velocity does not change)

Ball and truck have identical horizontal velocities, so the ball lands back on the truck

Geometry

THE STUDY OF SHAPES, LINES, and the space that they inhabit, is called geometry. Two-dimensional shapes, such as circles, are said to be flat, while three-dimensional shapes are said to be solid. Among the most familiar flat shapes are simple **polygons**, which have straight sides. Solid shapes include **polyhedra**, which have a polygon at each face. Mathematicians generally refer to lines as curves, the shapes of which are described in a branch of geometry known as coordinate geometry (see pp. 366-367). In addition to the study of shapes and curves, geometry looks at the nature of space itself. The ancient Greek mathematician Euclid (see p. 295) published a set of axioms (rules) that originally applied to all shapes in space. Non-Euclidean geometry is the study of those spaces for which Euclid's axioms do not apply. For example, the theory of general relativity (see pp. 62-63), in which space is seen as curved, makes use of non-Euclidean geometry.

FLAT SHAPES

Two-dimensional shapes are called flat shapes. They include circles, squares, and triangles. Flat shapes constructed with straight sides only are called polygons, and are categorized according to the number of sides they have. For example, all polygons with three sides are triangles, and all polygons with four sides are quadrilaterals. A polygon that has sides of equal length and internal angles of equal size is said to be regular. A square, for example, is a regular quadrilateral.

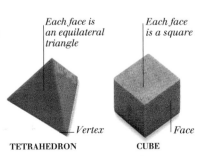

The point where two sides meet is called a vertex

The internal angles of any triangle add up to 180°

A square is a regular quadrilateral

A rectangle is a quadrilateral with pairs of equal sides

A triangle is a polygon with three sides

Circle

CIRCLE

The distance from the center of a circle to its circumference is called the radius and is equal to half the circle's diameter. Dividing a circle's circumference by its diameter results in an irrational number, (π), which is the same for every circle and is approximately equal to 3.14.

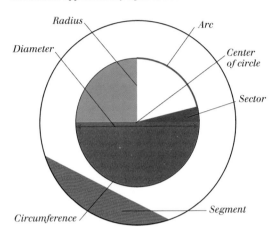

Radius

Arc

Diameter

Center of circle

Sector

Segment

Circumference

SPHERE

All points on the surface of a sphere lie at the same distance from the center. As with a circle, this distance is the radius, which is equal to half the sphere's diameter. Slicing the sphere through the diameter splits the sphere into two equal hemispheres. The flat surface of a hemisphere is a circle.

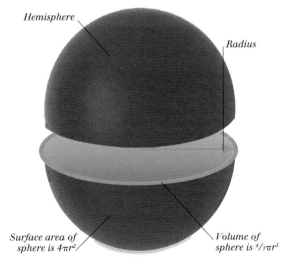

Hemisphere

Radius

Surface area of sphere is $4\pi r^2$

Volume of sphere is $\frac{4}{3}\pi r^3$

PLATONIC SOLIDS

Three-dimensional shapes are called solid shapes. They include spheres, cubes, and pyramids. Solid shapes with a polygon at each face are called polyhedra. Regular polyhedra have a regular polygon at each face. There are just five regular polyhedra, all of which are shown here.

Each face is an equilateral triangle

Each face is a square

Each face is an equilateral triangle

Each face is a pentagon

This polyhedron has 20 sides, each an equilateral triangle

Vertex

Face

Edge

TETRAHEDRON

CUBE

OCTAHEDRON

DODECAHEDRON

ICOSAHEDRON

MÖBIUS STRIP

The Möbius strip is an interesting **topological** figure. It is formed by putting a single twist in a two-sided, two-edged strip and then attaching the two ends of the strip. It has strange properties, including having only one face and one edge.

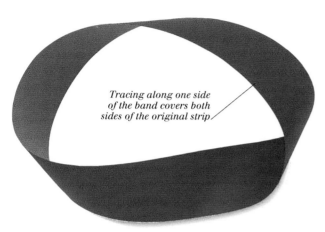

Tracing along one side of the band covers both sides of the original strip

CONIC SECTIONS

The surface of a cone is at a fixed angle to the cone's axis. This angle is called the generating angle. Slicing a cone at an angle equal to the generating angle produces a curve called a parabola. At an angle less than the generating angle, a hyperbola is produced, while an ellipse results from a slice at greater than the generating angle. Cutting a cone parallel to its base produces a circle.

Generating angle

Circle produced by slice parallel to cone's base

Axis of cone

Ellipse

Hyperbola

Surface of cone

Parabola

Base

THE GEOMETRIES OF SPACE

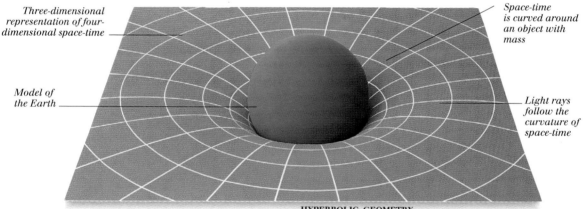

Three-dimensional representation of four-dimensional space-time

Space-time is curved around an object with mass

Model of the Earth

Light rays follow the curvature of space-time

HYPERBOLIC GEOMETRY

Hyperbolic geometry applies to surfaces that have negative curvature. On such a surface, the internal angles of a triangle add up to less than 180º. Space is negatively-curved around a massive object such as the Sun.

Triangle formed by three right angles (each 90º)

The Earth is not perfectly spherical, but it still has a positively curved surface

Internal angles of triangle add up to 270º

ELLIPTIC GEOMETRY

Elliptic geometry applies to surfaces with positive curvature. The internal angles of a triangle on a positive surface add up to more than 180º. The surface of a sphere is an example of a surface with positive curvature.

Coordinates and triangles

THE SIMPLEST COORDINATE SYSTEMS – called Cartesian coordinates – consist of lines (called axes) at right angles to each other. Lines with magnitude (size) and direction – called **vectors** – can represent various quantities, such as **velocity** or **force** (see pp. 20-21). The magnitude and direction of vectors are represented as lengths and angles in coordinate systems. It is useful to think of a vector as the longest side (the hypotenuse) of a right-angled triangle; an understanding of the properties of triangles is therefore useful when manipulating vectors. A simple rule called the Pythagorean theorem makes it possible to calculate the length of the hypotenuse of a right-angled triangle, armed only with the lengths of the other two sides of the triangle. The relationships between the sides and angles of right-angled triangles are studied in a branch of mathematics known as trigonometry.

ANGLES
An angle is formed where two lines meet or cross and is expressed as the amount of rotation needed to move one of the lines to the position of the other, keeping the crossing point fixed. The size of an angle is normally measured in degrees (°). There are 360° in one complete turn.

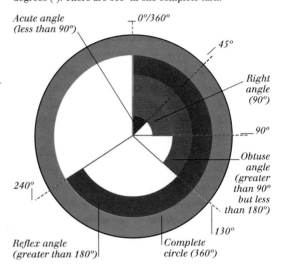

Acute angle (less than 90°)

0°/360°

45°

Right angle (90°)

90°

Obtuse angle (greater than 90° but less than 180°)

240°

130°

Reflex angle (greater than 180°)

Complete circle (360°)

CARTESIAN COORDINATES
The position of a point within a coordinate system can be defined using sets of numbers called coordinates. In a Cartesian system, coordinates are defined as lengths along axes, each of which is at right angles to all of the others. A two-dimensional Cartesian system has two axes, and so two coordinates are needed.

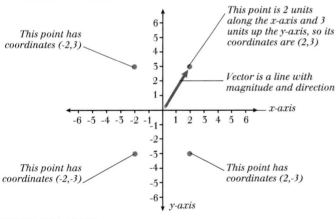

This point has coordinates (-2,3)

This point is 2 units along the x-axis and 3 units up the y-axis, so its coordinates are (2,3)

Vector is a line with magnitude and direction

x-axis

This point has coordinates (-2,-3)

This point has coordinates (2,-3)

y-axis

PYTHAGOREAN THEOREM
The square of the length of the longest side of a right-angled triangle (the hypotenuse, C, below) is equal to the sum of the squares of the other two sides ($C^2 = A^2 + B^2$).

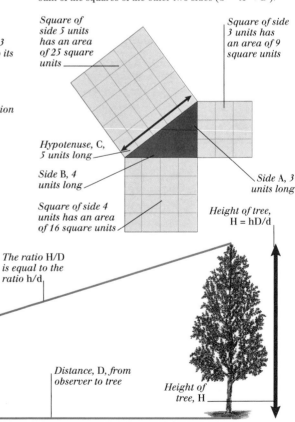

Square of side 5 units has an area of 25 square units

Square of side 3 units has an area of 9 square units

Hypotenuse, C, 5 units long

Side B, 4 units long

Side A, 3 units long

Square of side 4 units has an area of 16 square units

Height of tree, H = hD/d

HEIGHT OF A TREE
The sides of any two **similar** triangles are always in proportion. The ratios of corresponding sides of two similar triangles are therefore always the same. Here, this property of similar triangles is used to figure out the height of a tree when standing at a known distance from it. One right-angled triangle has the height of the tree as one side, and the distance to the tree as another. When a similar triangle – all of whose sides are measurable – is compared with the larger triangle, the height of the tree can easily be figured out.

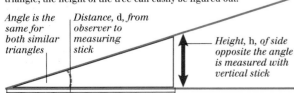

The ratio H/D is equal to the ratio h/d

Angle is the same for both similar triangles

Distance, d, from observer to measuring stick

Height, h, of side opposite the angle is measured with vertical stick

Distance, D, from observer to tree

Height of tree, H

TRIGONOMETRIC FUNCTIONS FOR RIGHT ANGLED TRIANGLES

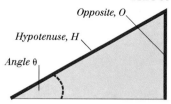

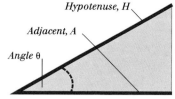

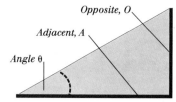

SINE (SIN) θ = O/H
The sine of angle θ is the ratio of the length of the side opposite the angle to the length of the hypotenuse. A graph of the **function** $y = \sin x$ produces a repeating curve.

COSINE (COS) θ = A/H
The cosine of angle θ is the ratio of the length of the side adjacent to the angle to the length of the hypotenuse. A graph of the function $y = \cos x$ also produces a repeating curve.

TANGENT (TAN) θ = O/A
The tangent of angle θ is the ratio of the length of the side opposite the angle to the length of the side adjacent to the angle. The function $y = \tan x$ varies between $-\infty$ and $+\infty$.

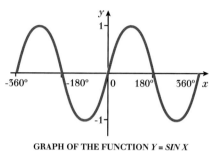

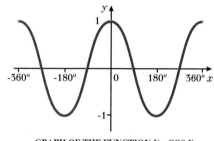

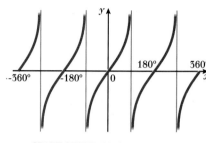

GRAPH OF THE FUNCTION Y = SIN X

GRAPH OF THE FUNCTION Y = COS X

GRAPH OF THE FUNCTION Y = TAN X

VECTOR COORDINATES

In the map shown below, a vector represents the **displacement** of point B (at 5,4) from point A (at 1,1). Its magnitude can be worked out easily, using Pythagorean theorem. The direction of the vector can be solved by trigonometry, using the tangent function. The vector is at an angle (measured from the horizontal) whose tangent is $\frac{3}{4}$, or 0.75. This is the tangent of an angle of about 37°. So, the vector has a compass bearing of 53° East (compass bearings are measured from North). Vectors have their own rules of addition. They are added head-to-tail, as shown.

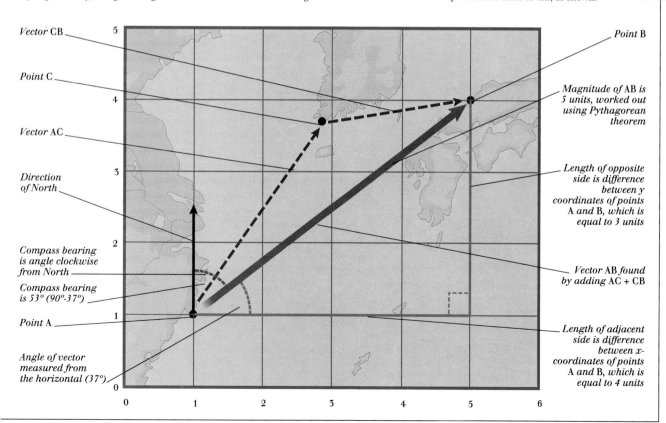

Vector CB

Point C

Vector AC

Direction of North

Compass bearing is angle clockwise from North

Compass bearing is 53° (90°-37°)

Point A

Angle of vector measured from the horizontal (37°)

Point B

Magnitude of AB is 5 units, worked out using Pythagorean theorem

Length of opposite side is difference between y coordinates of points A and B, which is equal to 3 units

Vector AB found by adding AC + CB

Length of adjacent side is difference between x-coordinates of points A and B, which is equal to 4 units

Probability and statistics

THE LIKELIHOOD THAT A CERTAIN EVENT will occur (its probability) is given as a number between zero (impossible) and one (certain). Some probabilities can be calculated quite easily – for example, those that govern the random selection from a collection of colored balls. Complex probabilities, such as the shapes of atomic **orbitals** (see pp. 160-161), however, may require the formulation of an algebraic **function** (see pp. 362-363). Probability theory is used in a branch of mathematics called statistics, which involves collecting and analyzing sets of data. Algebra is used in statistics in many ways, such as in calculating averages of a group of numbers or in finding trends in data. Statisticians use line graphs, bar charts, pie charts and scatter diagrams to visualize data. A line graph can highlight the distribution of a set of data around a particular value, called the mean. One common form of curve produced on line graphs is called the Gaussian distribution.

ATOMIC ORBITALS
The idea that an **electron** is not located at a definite distance from the **nucleus** is central to the modern understanding of the atom. Scientists think of electrons as existing in regions called orbitals, whose shapes can be calculated using probability theory. A distribution of probability is figured out as an algebraic function. As an illustration, one such function is plotted here over a diagram of an atomic orbital.

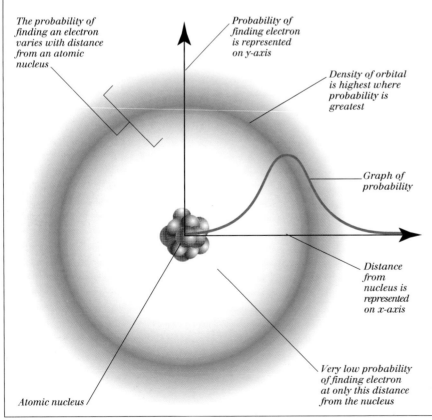

The probability of finding an electron varies with distance from an atomic nucleus

Probability of finding electron is represented on y-axis

Density of orbital is highest where probability is greatest

Graph of probability

Distance from nucleus is represented on x-axis

Very low probability of finding electron at only this distance from the nucleus

Atomic nucleus

A LOT OF BALLS IN A BEAKER
The chance of selecting a ball of a particular color is equal to the number of balls that have that color divided by the total number of balls.

Glass beaker

Balls to be selected at random

It is most likely that a red ball will be picked

INITIAL PROBABILITIES
The beaker contains 5 red balls, 3 yellow balls, and 2 green balls. The probabilities of selecting these colors are 5/10, 3/10, and 2/10 respectively.

Probability of selecting a yellow ball is now 1/3

Nine balls are left

Red ball is selected

INDIVIDUAL EVENT
The probability of removing a red ball is initially 5/10. With one red ball removed, the probability of selecting another red ball is 4/9.

A red ball is selected, followed by a yellow ball

COMBINED EVENTS
The probability of selecting a red ball and then a yellow ball is equal to the probabilities of the two individual events multiplied together ($5/10 \times 1/3$).

GRAPHS AND CHARTS

Probability and statistics are closely related. A bar chart and a pie chart are used here to visualize the probabilities of obtaining scores when throwing a pair of dice. Similar charts could have been obtained using so-called **empirical** data, collected by actually throwing a pair of dice a large number of times. A scatter diagram, which was produced from real empirical data, is also shown.

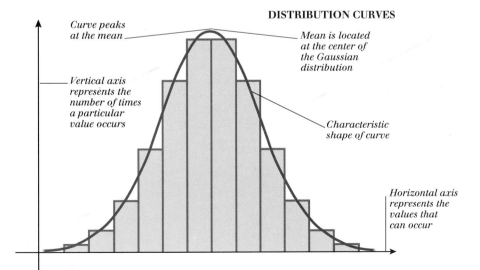

The chance of throwing a 5 and a 2 is $^2/_{36}$ ($^1/_{18}$)

DICE

BAR CHART
On a bar chart, a quantity is represented by the height of a bar. Here, the bars represent the number of possible ways of throwing a particular score related to its probability.

The chance of scoring 7 is $^1/_6$ ($^6/_{36}$)

The probability of scoring 9 is $^4/_{36}$ ($^1/_9$)

There are 36 different possible combinations with two dice

The probability of scoring 2 is $^1/_{36}$

PIE CHART
Here, the same set of data that is shown in the bar chart is illustrated using a pie chart. The number of ways of throwing a particular score is represented by the angle of each sector.

Largest sector represents probability of scoring 7

Each sector represents the probability of a particular score being obtained when a pair of dice are thrown

SCATTER DIAGRAM
A scatter graph can highlight trends, or correlations, in sets of data. Here, each cross represents the number of times a particular score was obtained (its frequency) when a pair of dice were thrown 100 times.

Frequency

General trend is that scores closer to 7 are more probable than scores closer to 2

Most crosses lie on or near best-fit line

Score

DISTRIBUTION CURVES

Curve peaks at the mean

Mean is located at the center of the Gaussian distribution

Vertical axis represents the number of times a particular value occurs

Characteristic shape of curve

Horizontal axis represents the values that can occur

GAUSSIAN CURVE
Some sets of data can be plotted on a line graph, with the vertical axis representing the frequency of the values laid out on the horizontal axis. The shape of the curve shows the distribution of values of the data. The curve is often centered on a particular value, called the **mean**. Random variation around the mean of a distribution produces a Gaussian curve.

WELL-WORN STEPS
These ancient steps are a physical example of a Gaussian, or normal, distribution. The center of each step is more worn than the outer edges. This is because that is where the greatest number of people have walked.

Logic and sets

LOGIC IS USED TO DEDUCE whether mathematical ideas are correct or not. It is based on natural reasoning powers – such as those used when solving logic puzzles. Logic theory is used in the design of computers. A computer's central processing unit (see pp. 352-353) contains circuits called logic gates, which perform simple logical operations. Logic gates are combined to form circuits called adders, which perform **binary addition** (see pp. 360-361). Perhaps the most important part of logic theory is the formulation of logical arguments. These produce a statement (the conclusion) based on other statements (premises). The theory of logic is closely related to set theory – a set is a well-defined collection of items called elements. Using the rules of logic, set theory can help to solve simple or complex mathematical problems. Sets are often represented by circles, in pictures called Venn diagrams. These diagrams can help us visualize the relationships between sets, such as areas where sets have common elements (called intersections).

TOWER OF HANOI

This logic puzzle, called the Tower of Hanoi, consists of three rings and three pins. The rings must be moved from one pin to another, one-by-one, without ever placing a large ring on top of a small one. The least number of move needed to complete the puzzle is given by the formula 2^n-1, where n is the number of rings present. So, with three rings, the puzzle can be completed in a minimum of seven moves (2^3-1).

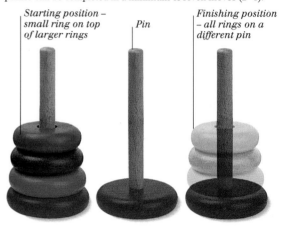

Starting position – small ring on top of larger rings

Pin

Finishing position – all rings on a different pin

EXAMPLES OF LOGIC GATES

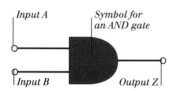

Input A

Symbol for an AND gate

Input B

Output Z

A	B	Z
0	0	0
0	1	0
1	0	0
1	1	1

AND GATE
A computer AND gate will output bit (binary digit) 1 only if both its inputs are 1s. This function, summarized in the truth table (left), is based on the logical operation AND.

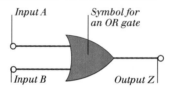

Input A

Symbol for an OR gate

Input B

Output Z

A	B	Z
0	0	0
0	1	1
1	0	1
1	1	1

OR GATE
A computer OR gate will output bit 1 if either or both its inputs are 1s. This function is based on the logical operation OR, and is summarized in the truth table (left).

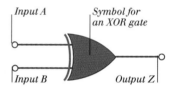

Input A

Symbol for an XOR gate

Input B

Output Z

A	B	Z
0	0	0
0	1	1
1	0	1
1	1	0

XOR GATE
A computer's XOR (exclusive OR) gate will output bit 1 only if just one of its inputs is 1. If both of its inputs are 1, or if both of its inputs are 0, then it will output a 0.

FULL ADDER

However complex a computer may seem, the only arithmetic operation it can perform is addition. Subtraction is achieved by adding a negative number; multiplication is achieved by repeated addition; and division is achieved by repeated subtraction. Addition is carried out by logic gates, which are connected together to form circuits called adders. In binary, the sum of two bits (binary digits) can be only 0 (0 + 0), 1 (0 + 1 or 1 + 0) or 10 (1 + 1). In the last of these, the 1 of the sum must be carried over to the next part of the calculation. The inputs to the adder shown here are A, B, and C. The input at C is one bit carried over from the last part of a previous calculation.

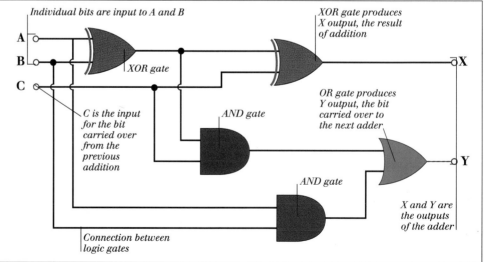

Individual bits are input to A and B

XOR gate produces X output, the result of addition

XOR gate

C is the input for the bit carried over from the previous addition

AND gate

OR gate produces Y output, the bit carried over to the next adder

AND gate

X and Y are the outputs of the adder

Connection between logic gates

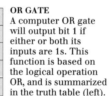

LOGICAL ARGUMENTS

Logic is based upon arguments that consist of two or more premises and a conclusion. Both premises and conclusions may be in the form of written statements, simple equations, or complex mathematical statements. The aim of the argument is to prove or disprove the truth of the conclusion. Simple arguments – of the kind shown here – are used in most logical proofs. It is the structure of these proofs that is important – not the particular statements involved. So, although the arguments presented here may seem obvious, these simple structures can be very powerful when built into complicated mathematical proofs, sometimes providing new insights into complex mathematical problems.

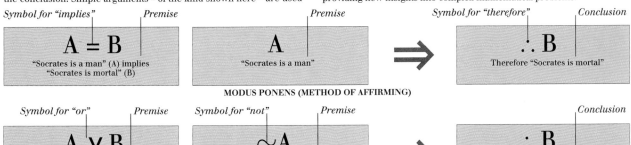

Symbol for "implies"   *Premise*   *Premise*   *Symbol for "therefore"*   *Conclusion*

$$A \Rightarrow B$$

"Socrates is a man" (A) implies "Socrates is mortal" (B)

$$A$$

"Socrates is a man"

$$\therefore B$$

Therefore "Socrates is mortal"

MODUS PONENS (METHOD OF AFFIRMING)

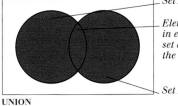

Symbol for "or"   *Premise*   *Symbol for "not"*   *Premise*   *Conclusion*

$$A \vee B$$

"Socrates is a woman" or "Socrates is a man"

$$\sim A$$

It is not true that "Socrates is a woman"

$$\therefore B$$

Therefore "Socrates is a man"

MODUS TOLLENDO PONENS (METHOD OF DENYING AND AFFIRMING)

SETS

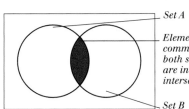

Set A
Elements common to both sets are in the intersection
Set B

Set A
Elements in either set are in the union
Set B

Set A
All elements in (sub)set A are also in set B
Set B

INTERSECTION
This is a Venn diagram. It shows the intersection of set A with set B. Intersection has the symbol ∩ and is similar to the logic function AND, since an element in the intersection is in both sets.

UNION
This Venn diagram shows the union of two sets. Union has the symbol ∪ and is similar to the logic function OR, since elements in the union may be in either set A or set B.

SUBSET
This Venn diagram shows one set as the subset of another – the elements in set A are all found in set B. The subset function has the symbol ⊂.

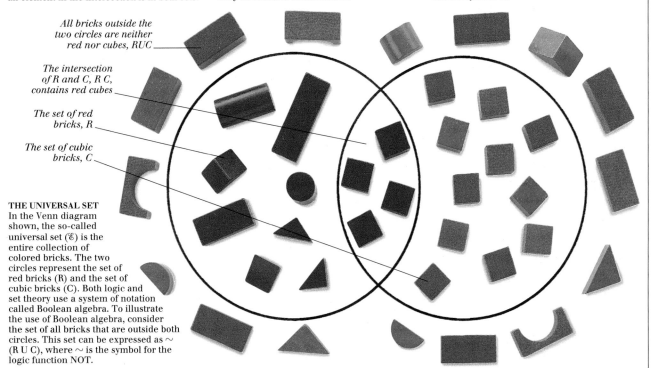

All bricks outside the two circles are neither red nor cubes, R∪C

The intersection of R and C, R∩C, contains red cubes

The set of red bricks, R

The set of cubic bricks, C

THE UNIVERSAL SET
In the Venn diagram shown, the so-called universal set (ℰ) is the entire collection of colored bricks. The two circles represent the set of red bricks (R) and the set of cubic bricks (C). Both logic and set theory use a system of notation called Boolean algebra. To illustrate the use of Boolean algebra, consider the set of all bricks that are outside both circles. This set can be expressed as ∼ (R ∪ C), where ∼ is the symbol for the logic function NOT.

Chaos theory and fractals

THE MOVEMENT OF RISING SMOKE **particles** is affected by many factors – including the immeasurable motions of millions of nearby air **molecules** – which is why it is described as a chaotic system. Chaos theory is an attempt to understand such systems. Mathematicians use graphs called simple or strange attractors to visualize the behavior of chaotic systems. Strange attractors are examples of fractals – geometrical figures that are closely related to chaos theory. Many fractals are seen in the natural world and are the result of underlying chaotic processes. These processes, which include growth and erosion, are iterated (repeated). Iteration gives rise to an important property of fractals, called self-similarity. A tiny portion of a fern frond, for example, looks similar to the entire fern. Like many natural fractals, computer-generated fractals are often stunningly beautiful.

TURBULENCE

Turbulence is easily seen in this photograph of smoke flowing upward from an extinguished candle. The lower part of the flow is smooth (laminar) and predictable. Higher up, however, there is a transition to turbulent (chaotic) flow.

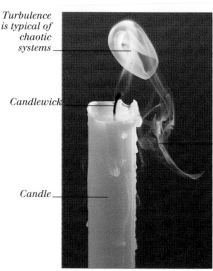

Turbulence is typical of chaotic systems

Candlewick

Candle

The motion of smoke particles is impossible to predict, even though they follow simple physical laws

ATTRACTORS

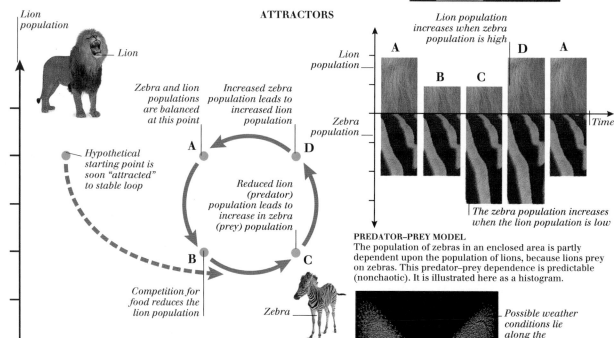

Lion population

— Lion

Zebra and lion populations are balanced at this point

Increased zebra population leads to increased lion population

A   **D**

Hypothetical starting point is soon "attracted" to stable loop

Reduced lion (predator) population leads to increase in zebra (prey) population

B   **C**

Competition for food reduces the lion population

Zebra —

Zebra population

Lion population increases when zebra population is high

A   **D**   **A**

B   **C**

Lion population

Zebra population

Time

The zebra population increases when the lion population is low

PREDATOR–PREY MODEL

The population of zebras in an enclosed area is partly dependent upon the population of lions, because lions prey on zebras. This predator–prey dependence is predictable (nonchaotic). It is illustrated here as a histogram.

Possible weather conditions lie along the attractor

STRANGE ATTRACTOR

All chaotic systems can be represented with a graph called a strange attractor. This one is associated with the intricate and unpredictable nature of weather patterns, and is called the Lorenz strange attractor after its creator, Edward Lorenz (1917–).

SIMPLE ATTRACTOR

The predator–prey model shown as a histogram (above right) can also be plotted as an attractor, to help visualize the system and formulate a model of its behavior. When the population values from the predator–prey histogram are plotted, a predictable, repeating cycle arises. It appears as a loop on the graph. This loop is called the attractor. Random factors, such as disease, may cause the predator–prey situation to become chaotic, in which case the graph would become a "strange attractor."

FRACTALS

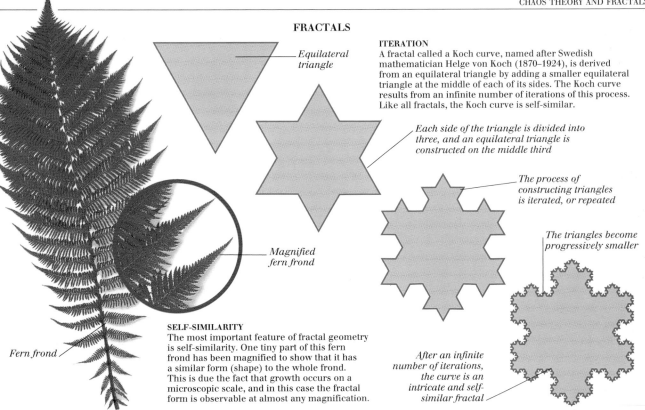

Equilateral triangle

ITERATION
A fractal called a Koch curve, named after Swedish mathematician Helge von Koch (1870–1924), is derived from an equilateral triangle by adding a smaller equilateral triangle at the middle of each of its sides. The Koch curve results from an infinite number of iterations of this process. Like all fractals, the Koch curve is self-similar.

Each side of the triangle is divided into three, and an equilateral triangle is constructed on the middle third

The process of constructing triangles is iterated, or repeated

The triangles become progressively smaller

Magnified fern frond

Fern frond

SELF-SIMILARITY
The most important feature of fractal geometry is self-similarity. One tiny part of this fern frond has been magnified to show that it has a similar form (shape) to the whole frond. This is due the fact that growth occurs on a microscopic scale, and in this case the fractal form is observable at almost any magnification.

After an infinite number of iterations, the curve is an intricate and self-similar fractal

MANDELBROT-SET FRACTALS

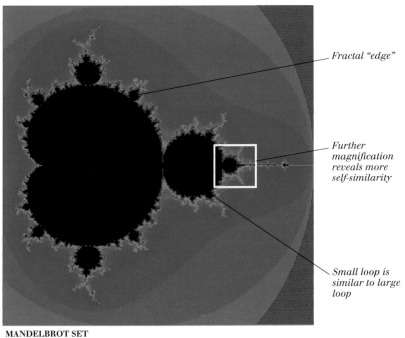

Fractal "edge"

Further magnification reveals more self-similarity

Small loop is similar to large loop

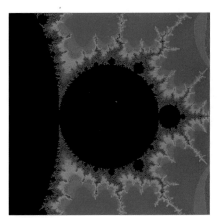

EXPLODED VIEW
Magnifying one small part of the Mandelbrot set reveals dramatic self-similarity. Parts of the Mandelbrot set are also reminiscent of natural forms that are created by chaotic processes, such as fractures in a sheet of ice.

$$z = z^2 + c$$

MANDELBROT SET
The most famous fractal is the Mandelbrot set, named after Benoit Mandelbrot (1924–). It is a purely mathematical object, created by iterating a simple equation many times for each point in the square. Different colors represent different final values of the iterated equation, which is calculated using the power of modern computers.

ITERATED EQUATION
The equation that is used to derive the Mandelbrot set is deceptively simple. Variables z and c are **complex numbers**.

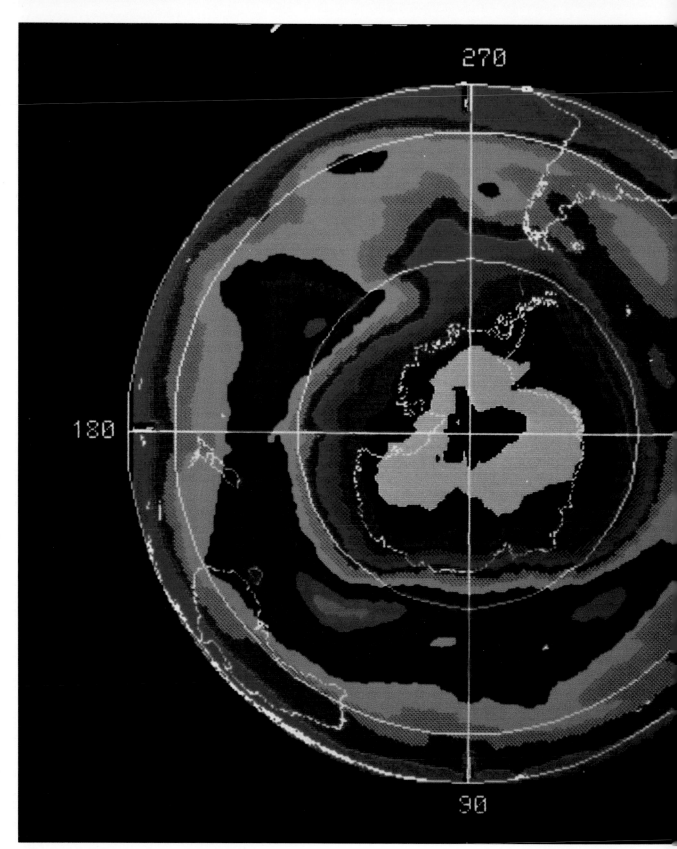

False-color satellite map of ozone levels over the South Pole

USEFUL DATA

WEIGHTS AND MEASURES 376

PHYSICS FORMULAS/CHEMISTRY DATA 378

LIFE SCIENCES AND MEDICAL SCIENCE DATA 380

EARTH SCIENCES DATA 382

ASTRONOMICAL DATA 384

STARS OF THE NORTHERN SKIES 386

STARS OF THE SOUTHERN SKIES 388

ELECTRONICS AND COMPUTING DATA 390

MATHEMATICS DATA 392

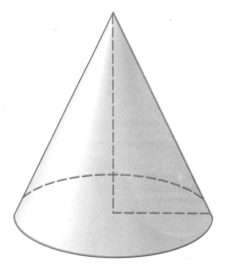

Weights and measures

UNITS OF MEASUREMENT

Imperial unit	Equivalent
Length	
1 foot (ft)	12 inches (in)
1 yard (yd)	3 feet
1 rod (rd)	5.5 yards
1 mile (mi)	1,760 yards
Mass	
1 dram (dr)	27.343 grains (gr)
1 ounce (oz)	16 drams
1 pound (lb)	16 ounces
1 hundredweight (cwt) (short)	100 pounds
1 hundredweight (cwt) (long)	112 pounds
1 short ton (US)	2,000 pounds
1 long ton (UK)	2,240 pounds
Area	
1 square foot (ft²)	144 square inches (in²)
1 square yard (yd²)	9 square feet
1 acre	4,840 square yards
1 square mile	640 acres
Volume	
1 cubic foot	1,728 cubic inches
1 cubic yard	27 cubic feet
Capacity (liquid and dry measures)	
1 fluidram (fl dr)	60 minims (min)
1 fluid ounce (fl oz)	8 fluidrams
1 gill (gi)	5 fluid ounces
1 pint (pt)	4 gills
1 quart	2 pints
1 gallon (gal)	4 quarts
1 peck (pk)	2 gallons

Metric unit	Equivalent
Length	
1 centimeter (cm)	10 millimeters (mm)
1 meter (m)	100 centimeters
1 kilometer (km)	1,000 meters
Mass	
1 kilogram (kg)	1,000 grams (g)
1 metric ton (t)	1,000 kilograms
Area	
1 square centimeter (cm²)	100 square millimeters (mm²)
1 square meter (m²)	1,000 square centimeters
1 hectare	10,000 square meters
1 square kilometer (km²)	1,000,000 square meters
Volume	
1 cubic centimeter (cc or cm³)	1 milliliter (ml)
1 liter (l)	1,000 milliliters
1 cubic meter (m³)	1,000 liters
Capacity (liquid and dry measures)	
1 centiliter (cl)	10 milliliters (ml)
1 deciliter (dl)	10 centiliters
1 liter (l)	10 deciliters
1 decaliter (dal)	10 liters
1 hectoliter (hl)	10 decaliters
1 kiloliter (kl)	10 hectoliters

NUMBER SYSTEMS

Roman	Arabic	Binary
I	1	1
II	2	10
III	3	11
IV	4	100
V	5	101
VI	6	110
VII	7	111
VIII	8	1000
IX	9	1001
X	10	1010
XI	11	1011
XII	12	1100
XIII	13	1101
XIV	14	1110
XX	20	10100
XXX	30	11110
XL	40	101000
L	50	110010
LX	60	111100
LXX	70	1000110
LXXX	80	1010000
XC	90	1011010
C	100	1100100
M	1,000	1111101000

TEMPERATURE SCALES

To convert	Into	Equation
Fahrenheit	Celsius	$C = (F - 32) \times 5 \div 9$
Celsius (C)	Fahrenheit (F)	$F = (C \times 9 \div 5) + 32$
Kelvin (K)	Fahrenheit	$F = ((K - 273) \times 9 \div 5) + 32$
Fahrenheit	Kelvin	$K = ((F - 32) \times 5 \div 9) + 273$
Celsius	Kelvin	$K = C + 273$

Fahrenheit	-4	14	32	50	68	86	104	122	140	158	176	194	212
Celsius	-20	-10	0	10	20	30	40	50	60	70	80	90	100
Kelvin	253	263	273	283	293	303	313	323	333	343	353	363	373

IMPERIAL – METRIC CONVERSIONS

To convert	Into	Multiply by
Length		
Inches	centimeters	2.5400
Feet	meters	0.3048
Miles	kilometers	1.6090
Yards	meters	0.9144
Mass		
Ounces	grams	28.3500
Pounds	kilograms	0.4536
Short tons (US)	metric tons	0.9070
Area		
Square inches	square centimeters	6.452
Square feet	square meters	0.09290
Acres	hectare	0.4047
Square miles	square kilometer	2.590
Square yards	square meters	0.8361
Volume		
Cubic inches	cubic centimeters	16.3900
Cubic feet	cubic meters	0.02852
Cubic yards	cubic meters	0.7646
Capacity (liquid)		
Pints	liters	0.5683
Gallons	liters	4.546

METRIC – IMPERIAL CONVERSIONS

To convert	Into	Multiply by
Length		
Centimeters	inches	0.3937
Meters	feet	3.2810
Kilometers	miles	0.6214
Meters	yards	1.0940
Mass		
Grams	ounces	0.03527
Kilograms	pounds	2.205
Metric tons	short tons (US)	1.1023
Area		
Square centimeters	square inches	0.1550
Square meters	square feet	10.7600
Hectares	acres	2.4710
Square kilometers	square miles	0.3861
Square meters	square yards	1.1960
Volume		
Cubic centimeters	cubic inches	0.06102
Cubic meters	cubic feet	35.31
Cubic meters	cubic yards	1.308
Capacity (liquid)		
Liters	pints	1.7600
Liters	gallons	0.2200

POWERS OF TEN

Factor	Name	Prefix	Symbol
10^{18}	quintillion	exa	E
10^{15}	quadrillion	peta	P
10^{12}	trillion	tera	T
10^{9}	billion	giga-	G
10^{6}	million	mega-	M
10^{3}	thousand	kilo-	k
10^{2}	hundred	hecto-	h
10^{1}	ten	deca-	da
10^{-1}	one tenth	deci-	d
10^{-2}	one hundredth	centi-	c
10^{-3}	one thousandth	milli-	m
10^{-6}	one millionth	micro-	μ
10^{-9}	one billionth	nano-	n
10^{-12}	one trillionth	pico-	p
10^{-15}	one quadrillionth	femto-	f
10^{-18}	one quintillionth	atto-	a

BASE SI UNITS

Physical quantity	SI unit	Symbol
Length	meter	m
Mass	kilogram	kg
Time	second	s
Electric current	ampere	A
Temperature	kelvin	K
Luminous intensity	candela	cd
Amount of substance	mole	mol
Plane angle	radian	rad
Solid angle	steradian	sr

DERIVED SI UNITS

Physical quantity	SI unit	Symbol
Frequency	hertz	Hz
Energy	joule	J
Force	newton	N
Power	watt	W
Pressure	pascal (newtons per square meter)	Pa (Nm^{-2})
Electric charge	coulomb	C
Voltage	volt	V
Electric resistance	ohm	Ω

Physics formulas

PHYSICS SYMBOLS

Symbol	Meaning	Symbol	Meaning	Symbol	Meaning
α	alpha particle	η	efficiency; viscosity	ν	frequency; neutrino
β	beta particle	λ	wavelength	ρ	density; resistivity
γ	gamma ray; photon	μ	micro-; permeability	σ	conductivity
ϵ	electromotive force			c	speed of light

WEIGHT

Weight is equal to mass multiplied by acceleration due to gravity

$$W = mg$$

W = weight
m = mass
g = acceleration due to gravity

TURNING FORCE

Turning force is equal to force multiplied by distance of applied force from pivot

$$T = Fd$$

T = turning force (moment)
F = applied force
d = distance

PRESSURE

Pressure is equal to force applied divided by area over which force acts

$$P = F/A$$

P = pressure
F = applied force
A = area over which force acts

FORCE AND MOTION

NEWTON'S SECOND LAW
Acceleration is equal to force divided by mass

$$a = F/m$$

SPEED
Speed is equal to distance divided by time

$$v = d/t$$

CONSTANT ACCELERATION
Acceleration is equal to change in speed divided by time taken for that change

$$a = (v_2 - v_1)/t$$

MOMENTUM
Momentum is equal to mass multiplied by speed

$$p = mv$$

a = acceleration
m = mass
F = applied force
v_1 = speed at the beginning of the time interval
v_2 = speed at the end of the time interval
d = distance
t = time
p = momentum

GRAVITATION

Gravitational force equals a constant multiplied by mass one, multiplied by mass two, divided by the distance between the masses squared

$$F = Gm_1 m_2/d^2$$

F = gravitational force between two objects
G = gravitational constant
m_1 = mass of object one
m_2 = mass of object two
d = distance between the two objects

FRICTION

Frictional force between two surfaces is equal to the coefficient of friction multiplied by the force acting to keep the surfaces together

$$F = \mu N$$

F = frictional force
μ = coefficient of friction; this varies with materials
N = force between two surfaces

WORK

Work is equal to force multiplied by distance

$$W = Fd$$

W = work done
F = applied force
d = distance moved in line with force

CENTRIPETAL FORCE

Force is equal to mass multiplied by the speed squared divided by the radius

$$F = mv^2/r$$

F = centripetal force
m = mass of object
v = speed of circular motion
r = radius of object's path

LIQUID PRESSURE

Pressure is equal to the liquid's density multiplied by acceleration due to gravity multiplied by height of water above point

$$P = \rho gh$$

P = pressure
ρ = liquid density
g = acceleration due to gravity
h = height of liquid above measured point

ELASTICITY

The extension of a solid is proportional to the force applied to it

$$F \propto x$$

F = applied force
x = extension of solid

GAS LAWS

BOYLE'S LAW
Volume is proportional to one divided by pressure

$$V \propto 1/P$$

CHARLES' LAW
Volume is proportional to temperature

$$V \propto T$$

PRESSURE LAW
Pressure is proportional to temperature

$$P \propto T$$

THE IDEAL-GAS EQUATION
Pressure multiplied by volume is equal to ideal-gas constant multiplied by temperature

$$PV = RT \text{ (for one mole of gas)}$$

V = volume
P = pressure
T = temperature
R = ideal-gas constant

ELECTRIC CIRCUITS

CURRENT, VOLTAGE, AND RESISTANCE
Current is equal to voltage divided by resistance

$$I = V/R$$

POWER
Power is equal to voltage multiplied by current

$$P = VI$$

I = current
V = voltage
R = resistance
P = power

IMAGE FORMATION

One divided by the focal length is equal to one divided by the object's distance from lens added to one divided by distance from the lens to the image

$$1/f = 1/u + 1/v$$

f = focal length
u = object's distance from lens
v = distance from lens to image

Chemistry data

IONS AND RADICALS

Name	Formula and charge
Hydrogen	H^+
Sodium	Na^+
Potassium	K^+
Magnesium	Mg^{2+}
Calcium	Ca^{2+}
Aluminum	Al^{3+}
Iron (II)	Fe^{2+}
Iron (III)	Fe^{3+}
Copper (I)	Cu^+
Copper (II)	Cu^{2+}
Silver (I)	Ag^+
Zinc	Zn^{2+}
Ammonium	NH_4^+
Hydronium	H_3O^+
Oxide	O^{2-}
Sulfide	S^{2-}
Fluoride	F^-
Chloride	Cl^-
Bromide	Br^-
Iodide	I^-
Hydroxide	OH^-
Carbonate	CO_3^{2-}
Hydrogen Carbonate	HCO_3^-
Nitrate (V)	NO_3^-
Sulfate (VI)	SO_4^{2-}

COMMON NAMES AND FORMULAS OF IMPORTANT COMPOUNDS

Common name	Chemical name	Formula
Water	Hydrogen oxide	H_2O
Salt	Sodium chloride	$NaCl$
Baking soda	Sodium bicarbonate	$NaHCO_3$
Washing soda	Sodium carbonate decahydrate	$Na_2CO_3.10H_2O$
Household bleach	Sodium chlorate (I)	$NaOCl$
Rubbing alcohol	Methanol	CH_3OH
Alcohol	Ethanol	C_2H_5OH
Vinegar	Ethanoic acid	$CH_3.COOH$
Vitamin C	Ascorbic acid	$C_4H_5O_4.CHOH.CH_2OH$
Aspirin	Acetylsalicylic acid	$C_6H_4.COOCH_3.COOH$
White sugar	Sucrose	$C_6H_{11}O_5.O.C_6H_{11}O_5$
Limestone/chalk	Calcium carbonate	$CaCO_3$
Plaster of Paris	Calcium sulfate hemihydrate	$CaSO_4.^1/_2H_2O$
Rust	Hydrated iron (III) oxide	$Fe_2O_3.xH_2O$

NAMES AND STRUCTURES OF COMMON PLASTICS

Common name of plastic	Proper name	Repeated unit (monomer)
Polythene	Poly(ethene)	Ethene, C_2H_4
PVC or polyvinylchloride	Poly(chloroethene)	Chloroethene, C_2H_3Cl
Polystyrene	Poly(phenylethene)	Phenylethene, $C_2H_3.C_6H_5$
Acrylic	Poly(propenonitrile)	Propenonitrile, $C_2H_2.CH_2.CN$
PTFE or Teflon®	Poly(tetrafluoroethene)	Tetrafluoroethene, C_2F_4

DISCOVERY OF ELEMENTS

Element name	Discovered*	Origin of name
Carbon, C	Known since ancient times	Latin *carbo*, charcoal
Gold, Au	Known since ancient times	Old English *geolo*, yellow; Latin *aurum*, gold
Sulfur, S	Known since ancient times	Latin *sulfur*, brimstone
Platinum, Pt	16th century	Spanish *platina*, little silver
Cobalt, Co	1735 by Georg Brandt	German *kobold*, goblin
Hydrogen, H	1766 by Henry Cavendish	Greek *hydro-* and *genes*, water-maker
Chlorine, Cl	1774 by Karl Wilhelm Scheele	Greek *chloros*, greenish-yellow
Tungsten, W	1783 by Juan José and Fausto Elhuyar	Swedish *tung*, heavy, and *sten*, stone; German *wolfram*
Chromium, Cr	1797 by Nicolas-Louis Vauquelin	Greek *chroma*, color
Bromine, Br	1826 by Antoine-Jérôme Balard	Greek *bromos*, stench
Helium, He	1868 by Pierre Janssen and Norman Lockyer	Greek *helios*, the Sun
Unnilquadium, Unq	1964 (in USSR) and 1969 (in US)	Latin for 104, the element's atomic number

* *Generally refers to when the pure substance was first isolated – its recognition as an element often came later.*

** *Because of disputes over the discovery of elements with atomic numbers 104–109, their names are yet to be finalized.*

MELTING AND BOILING POINTS OF ELEMENTS

Element	Melting point °C	°F	Boiling point °C	°F
Mercury	-39	-38	357	675
Helium	-272	-458	-269	-452
Tungsten	3,410	6,170	5,555	10,031
Nitrogen	-210	-346	-196	-321
Sodium	98	208	883	1,621
Oxygen	-219	-362	-183	-297
Bromine	-7	19	59	138
Iron	1,535	2,795	2,862	5,184
Carbon	3,550	6,420	4,827	8,720
Gold	1,063	1,945	2,970	5,379

ELEMENTS IN THE EARTH'S CRUST

Element	Mass (%)
Oxygen	49.13
Silicon	26.00
Aluminum	7.45
Iron	4.20
Calcium	3.25
Sodium	2.40
Potassium	2.35
Magnesium	2.35
Hydrogen	1.00
Others	1.87

Life sciences data

ANIMAL ENERGY REQUIREMENT

Animal	Scientific name	kJ required per day for moderate amount of acitivity
House mouse	*Mus musculus*	45.4
European robin	*Erithacus rubecula*	89.9
Peregrine falcon	*Falco peregrinus*	277
Gray squirrel	*Sciurus carolinensis*	386
Fennec fox	*Vulpes zerda*	1,067
Domestic cat	*Felis catus*	1,554
Baboon	*Papio hamadryas*	6,762
Giant anteater	*Myrmecophaga tridactyla*	7,392
Female human being	*Homo sapiens*	10,080
Male human being	*Homo sapiens*	13,713
Llama	*Lama glama*	16,128
Tiger	*Panthera tigris*	33,600
Gorilla	*Gorilla gorilla*	34,020
American black bear	*Ursus americanus*	38,556
Giraffe	*Giraffa camelopardalis*	152,754
Walrus	*Odobnus rosmarus*	159,852
Male Indian elephant	*Elephas maximus*	256,872

ANIMAL SPEED OF MOVEMENT

Animal	Scientific name	Top speed
Spine-tailed swift	*Chaetura caudacuta*	177
Mallard	*Anas platyrhynchra*	108
English hare	*Lepus timidus*	75
Racehorse, mounted	*Equus caballus*	75
Dragonfly	*Austrophlebia*	60
Human being	*Homo sapiens*	48
Fox	*Vulpes fulva*	47
Salmon	*Salmo salar*	38
Wasp	*Vespa vulgaris*	20
Adelie penguin*	*Pygoscelis adeliae*	14
Spider	*Tegenaria atrica*	2
Centipede	*Scutigera coleoptera*	1.8
Giant tortoise	*Geochelone gigantea*	0.28
Garden snail	*Helix aspersa*	0.03

* = underwater

ANIMAL LONGEVITY

Animal	Scientific name	Approximate maximum life span
Marion's tortoise	*Testudo sumerii*	152 years
Human being	*Homo sapiens*	115 years
Blue whale	*Balaenoptera musculus*	90 years
Indian elephant	*Elephas maximus*	70 years
Hippopotamus	*Hippopotamus amphibius*	54 years
Common boa	*Boa constrictor*	40 years
Giant clam	*Tridacna gigas*	30 years
Sheep	*Ovis aries*	22 years
Guinea pig	*Cavia porcellus*	13 years
House mouse	*Mus musculus*	6 years
Bedbug	*Cimex lectularius*	0.5 years
Housefly	*Musca domestica*	0.2 years

ANIMAL KINGDOM PIE CHART

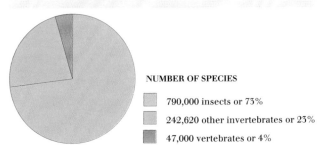

NUMBER OF SPECIES

790,000 insects or 73%

242,620 other invertebrates or 23%

47,000 vertebrates or 4%

ANIMAL HOMES

Animal	Description of home	Name of home
Squirrel	Nest of twigs	Drey
Badger	Underground chambers	Sett
Eagle	Nest of twigs	Eyrie
Rabbit	Burrow	Warren
River otter	Burrow in riverbank	Holt

ECOLOGY: PRIMARY PRODUCTION

Habitat	Primary production (grams of dry plant material per sq meter per year)
Coral reef	2,500
Tropical rainforest	2,200
Temperate rainforest	1,250
Savannah	900
Cultivated land	650
Open sea	125
Semidesert	90

GESTATION PERIODS

Animal	Scientific name	Gestation period (days)	Number of young
Virginia opossum	*Didelphis virginiana*	12	8–14
Golden hamster	*Mesocricetus auratus*	15	6–8
House mouse	*Mus musculus*	20	6–8
Red kangaroo	*Macropus rufus*	33	1
Lion	*Panthera leo*	105–108	3–4
Domestic goat	*Capra hircus*	150	1–2
Orangutan	*Pongo pygmaeus*	250	1
Human being	*Homo sapiens*	267	1
Wild cattle	*Bovidae artiodactyla*	278	1
Bottle-nosed dolphin	*Tursiops truncatus*	360	1
Indian elephant	*Elephas maximus*	660	1

Medical science data

VITAMINS TABLE

Name	Where found	Required for
Vitamin A	Liver, fish, oils, egg yolk, yellow-orange fruit and vegetables	Growth, healthy eyes and skin, fighting infection
Vitamin B1 (thiamine)	Whole grains (wholemeal bread and pasta) brown rice, liver, beans, peas, and eggs	Healthy functioning of nervous and digestive systems
Vitamin B2 (riboflavin)	Milk, liver, cheese, eggs, green vegetables, brewer's yeast, whole grains, and wheat germ	Metabolism of protein, fat, and carbohydrates; keeping tissue healthy
Vitamin B3 (niacin)	Liver, lean meats, poultry, fish, and dried beans and nuts	Production of energy and a healthy skin
Vitamin B6 (pyridoxine)	Liver, poultry, pork, fish, bananas, potatoes, dried beans, and most fruit and vegetables	Metabolism of protein and production of red blood cells
Vitamin C	Citrus fruit, strawberries, and potatoes	Healthy skin, teeth, bones, and tissues; for fighting disease
Vitamin D	Oily fish (such as salmon), liver, cod-liver oil, eggs, and cereals	The absorption of calcium and phosphates
Vitamin E	Margarine, whole-grain cereals, and nuts	The formation of new red blood cells; protection of cell linings in the lungs

BRANCHES OF MEDICINE

Name	Concerns
Cardiology	Heart and arteries
Chiropody	Feet
Dermatology	Skin
Endocrinology	Hormones
Gastroenterology	Stomach, intestines
Geriatics	Elderly people
Gynecology	Female reproductive organs
Hematology	Blood
Nephrology	Kidneys
Neurology	Brain and nerves
Ophthalmology	Eyes
Osteopathy	Manipulation of back and limbs to ease pain
Pediatrics	Children
Pharmacology	Drugs
Physiotherapy	Manipulation and massage of body to ease pain
Psychiatry	Mental illness
Obstetrics	Pregnancy and childbirth
Oncology	Growths and tumors (cancers)
Orthopedics	Bones, joints, and muscles
Pathology	Body tissues and fluids
Radiology	X rays
Radiotherapy	Use of radiation to kill unwanted cells

COMMON MEDICAL COMPLAINTS

Complaint	Description
Alzheimer's disease	Deterioration of speech, memory, and general mental faculties, due to death of brain cells
Anemia	Deficiency of hemoglobin in red blood cells
Aneurysm	Thinning and dilation of walls of artery
Angina	Tight chest pain caused by lack of oxygen, often because of narrowed arteries
Asthma	Disease of the respiratory system that causes wheezing and difficult breathing
Bronchitis	Inflammation of the bronchi
Cavities	Patches of decay and erosion of tooth enamel, and dentine by plaque
Cataracts	Cloudiness of the lens of the eye. Causes nearsightedness or blindness
Conjunctivitis	Inflammation of the conjunctiva, causing eye redness and discomfort
Eczema	Itchy skin infection, often causing blisters and scaling
Endocarditis	Infection of the heart tissue
Glaucoma	High pressure in the eye's fluid, causing pain and partial or total loss of vision
Hayfever (allergic rhinitis)	Inflammation of mucus membrane caused by allergy to pollen
Hepatitis	Inflammation of the liver caused by viral infection
Laryngitis	Inflammation of the larynx due to infection, leading to loss of voice
Meningitis	Inflammation of the meninges (outer layers of brain), bacterial and viral forms
Multiple sclerosis (MS)	Progressive disease of the central nervous system that destroys the outer coating of nerves
Muscular dystrophy	Progressive wasting of muscle fibers (an inherited illness)
Osteoporosis	Thinning and weakening of bone with age
Pneumonia	Inflammation of the lungs caused by infection
Psoriasis	Skin disorder causing red skin covered with silvery scales
Tetanus	Continuous contraction of muscle
Varicose vein	Swelling and twisting of a vein

DRUG TYPES

Name	Use
Analgesic	Provides relief from pain such as headache and stomachache
Antacid	Counteracts acid in the stomach to relieve heartburn, indigestion, etc.
Antibiotic	Treats infection by killing bacteria in the body
Antihistamine	Counteracts allergies such as hayfever
Antipyretic	Reduces fevers such as influenza
Bronchodilator	Eases breathing in diseases such as asthma
Decongestant	Common cold treatment; works by unblocking nasal passages

Earth sciences data

EARTH PROFILE

Feature	
Average distance from Sun (km)	149,600,000
Maximum distance from Sun (km)	152,100,000
Minimum distance from Sun (km)	147,100,000
Length of year (days)	365.26
Length of day (hours)	23.93
Surface temperature range (° C)	-88.3 to 58.0
Mass (billion billion metric tons)	5,976
Volume (km³)	1,083,230,000,000
Axial tilt (degrees)	23.5
Specific gravity (water = 1)	5.52
Polar diameter (km)	12,714
Equatorial diameter (km)	12,756
Polar circumference (km)	40,008
Equatorial circumference (km)	40,075
Total surface area (km²)	510,000,000
Land as % of total surface area	29.2
Water as % of total surface area	70.8
Highest point on land (m)	8,848
Lowest point on land (m below sea level)	2,538
Average height of land (m)	840
Greatest ocean depth (m)	10,924
Average ocean depth (m)	3,808
Oceanic crust thickness (km)	6
Continental crust thickness (km)	40
Mantle thickness (km)	2,800
Outer core thickness (km)	2,300
Inner core diameter (km)	2,400
Approximate age of Earth (millions of years)	4,600

DEEPEST TRENCHES

Name	Length (km)	Deepest point	Depth (m)
Mariana Trench (W. Pacific)	2,250	Challenger Deep	10,924
Tonga-Kermadec Trench (S. Pacific)	2,575	Vityaz II (Tonga)	10,800
Kuril-Kamchatka Trench (W. Pacific)	2,250	Unnamed	10,542
Philippine Trench (W. Pacific)	1,325	Galathea Deep	10,539
Soloman/New Britain Trench (S. Pacific)	640	Unnamed	8,940
Puerto Rico Trench (W. Atlantic)	800	Milwaukee Deep	8,605
Yap Trench (W. Pacific)	560	Unnamed	8,527
Japan Trench (W. Pacific)	1,600	Unnamed	8,412
South Sandwich Trench (S. Atlantic)	965	Meteor Deep	8,325

LARGEST OCEANS AND SEAS

Name	Area (km²)	Average depth (m)
Pacific Ocean	166,229,000	4,028
Atlantic Ocean	86,551,000	3,926
Indian Ocean	73,422,000	3,963
Arctic Ocean	13,223,000	1,205
South China Sea	2,975,000	1,652
Caribbean Sea	2,516,000	2,467
Mediterranean Sea	2,509,000	1,429
Bering Sea	2,261,000	1,547
Gulf of Mexico	1,508,000	1,486
Sea of Okhotsk	1,392,000	840
Sea of Japan	1,013,000	1,370
Hudson Bay	730,000	120
East China Sea	665,000	180
Black Sea	508,000	1,100
Red Sea	453,000	490

LARGEST ISLANDS

Name	Area (km²)
Greenland	2,175,219
New Guinea	792,493
Borneo	725,416
Madagascar	587,009
Baffin Island (Canada)	507,423
Sumatra	427,325
Honshu (Japan)	227,401
Great Britain	218,065
Victoria Island (Canada)	217,278
Ellesmere Island (Canada)	196,225

CONTINENTS

Name	Area (km²)	% of total surface area	% of total land area	Highest point	Height (m)	Lowest point	Below sea level (m)
Asia	44,000,000	8.6	29.5	Mt. Everest	8,848	Dead Sea	400
Africa	30,000,000	5.9	20.1	Kilimanjaro	5,895	Lac Assal	156
N. America	24,000,000	4.7	16.1	Denali (Mt. McKinley)	6,194	Death Valley	86
S. America	18,000,000	3.5	12.1	Aconcagua	6,960	Peninsular Valdez	40
Antarctica	14,000,000	2.7	9.4	Vinson Massif	5,140	Bently Trench	2,538
Europe	10,000,000	2.0	6.7	El'brus	5,642	Caspian Sea	28
Australasia	9,000,000	1.8	6.1	Mt. Wilhelm	4,884	Lake Eyre	16

WEATHER

Record	Reading	Place	Date
Highest-recorded temperature	58° C	Al' Aziziyah, Libya	September 13, 1922
Lowest-recorded temperature	-88.38° C	Vostok, Antarctica	August 24, 1960
Greatest average yearly rainfall	11,455 mm	Mt. Wai'ale'ale, Hawaii	
Greatest-recorded rainfall in any one year	26,461 mm	Cherrapunji, India	1860–61
Windiest place	320 km/h winds	Commonwealth Bay, Antarctica	
Highest-recorded windspeed	371 km/h	Mt. Washington, New Hampshire	1934

LAKES AND INLAND SEAS

Largest	Area (km²)
Caspian Sea (Asia/Europe)	370,980
Lake Superior (N. America)	82,098
Lake Victoria (Africa)	69,480
Aral Sea (Asia)	64,498
Lake Huron (N. America)	59,566
Lake Michigan (N. America)	57,754
Lake Tanganyika (Africa)	32,891
Lake Baikal (Asia)	31,498
Great Bear Lake (N. America)	31,197
Lake Nyasa (Africa)	28,877

MOUNTAINS

Highest	Height (m)
Mt. Everest (Tibet/Nepal)	8,848
K2 (Pakistan/Tibet)	8,611
Kangchenjunga (India/Nepal)	8,598
Makalu (Tibet/Nepal)	8,480
Cho Oyu (Tibet/Nepal)	8,201
Dhaulagiri (Nepal)	8,172
Nanga Parbat (India)	8,126
Annapurna (Nepal)	8,078
Gasherbrum (India)	8,068
Xixabangma Feng (Tibet)	8,013

ACTIVE VOLCANOES

Highest	Height (m)
Gualltiri (Chile)	6,060
Lascar (Chile)	5,990
Cotopaxi (Ecuador)	5,897
Tupungatito (Chile)	5,640
Ruiz (Colombia)	5,400
Sangay (Ecuador)	5,230
Purace (Colombia)	4,755
Klyuchevskaya Sopka (Russia)	4,750
Colima (Mexico)	4,268
Galeras (Colombia)	4,266

RIVERS

Longest	Length (km)
River Nile (Africa)	6,695
Amazon River (S. America)	6,437
Yangtze River/Chang Jiang (Asia)	6,379
Mississippi-Missouri River (N. America)	6,264
River Ob-Irtysh (Asia)	5,411
Yellow River/Huang He (Asia)	4,672
River Congo/Zaire (Africa)	4,667
River Amur (Asia)	4,416
River Lena (Asia)	4,400
Mackenzie-Peace River (N. America)	4,241

GLACIERS

Name	Length (km)
Lambert-Fisher Ice Passage (Antarctic)	515
Novaya Zemlya (Russia)	418
Arctic Institute Ice Passage (Antarctica)	362
Nimrod-Lennox-King Ice Passage (Antarctica)	289
Denman Glacier (Antarctica)	241
Beardmore Glacier (Antarctica)	225
Recovery Glacier (Antarctica)	225
Petermanns Glacier (Greenland)	200
Unnamed glacier (Antarctica)	193

DESERTS

Largest	Area (km²)
Sahara (Africa)	8,800,000
Gobi Desert (Asia)	1,300,000
Australian Desert (Australasia)	1,250,000
Arabian Desert (Asia)	850,000
Kalahari Desert (Africa)	580,000
Chihuahuan Desert (N. America)	370,000
Takla Makan Desert (Asia)	320,000
Kara Kum (Asia)	310,000
Namib Desert (Africa)	310,000
Thar Desert (Asia)	260,000

CAVES

Deepest	Depth (m)
Reseau Jean Bernard (France)	1,602
Shakta Pantjukhina (Georgia)	1,508
Lamrechtsofen (Austria)	1,485
Sistema del Trave (Spain)	1,441

Longest system	Length (km)
Mammoth Cave System (US)	560
Optimisticheskaya (Ukraine)	183
Hölloch (Switzerland)	137
Jewel Cave (US)	127
Ozernaya (Ukraine)	107

EARTHQUAKE MEASUREMENT

Mercalli Scale	Characteristics/possible damage
1	Not felt by people, but recorded by instruments; doors may swing slowly
2-4	Felt by people indoors and some outdoors; hanging objects may swing
5-6	Felt by most or all outdoors; buildings tremble, books fall off shelves
7-8	General alarm; branches may fall off trees and it is difficult to drive
9-10	General panic; cracks appear in roads and buildings and bridges collapse
11-12	Few buildings standing, waves are seen in the ground, rivers may change course

Richter Scale	Probable effects
1-3	Detectable only by instruments
4	Detectable within 32 km of epicenter
5	May cause slight damage
6	Moderately destructive
7	A major earthquake
8-9	A very destructive earthquake

WINDSPEED

Beaufort Scale	Description	Speed (9 km/h)	Characteristics
0	Calm	1	Smoke rises vertically
1	Light air	1-5	Smoke blown by wind
2	Light breeze	6-12	Leaves rustle
3	Gentle breeze	13-20	Extends a light flag
4	Moderate breeze	21-29	Raises dust and loose paper
5	Fresh breeze	30-39	Small trees sway
6	Strong breeze	40-50	Umbrellas are difficult to use
7	Moderate gale	51-61	Difficult to walk
8	Fresh gale	62-74	Twigs snap from trees
9	Strong gale	75-87	Slates and chimneys blown away
10	Whole gale	88-102	Trees uprooted
11	Storm	103-120	Cars overturned, trees blown away
12	Hurricane	120+	Buildings destroyed

WATERFALLS

Highest drop	Height (m)
Angel Falls (Venezuela)	979
Tugela Falls (South Africa)	948
Utgaard (Norway)	800
Mongefossen (Norway)	774
Yosemite Falls (US)	739
Mardalsfossen (Norway)	655
Cuquenen Falls (Venezuela)	610
Sutherland Falls (New Zealand)	580
Ribbon Falls (US)	491
Gavarnie (France)	425

Volume	(m³/sec)
Boyoma Falls (Zaire)	17,000
Guaira Falls (Brazil/Paraguay)	13,000
Khone Falls (Laos)	11,500
Niagara Falls (Canada/US)	6,000
Paulo Afonso Falls (Brazil)	2,800
Urubupunga Falls (Brazil)	2,700
Cataras del Iguazu Falls (Brazil/Paraguay)	1,700
Patos-Maribondo Falls (Brazil)	1,500
Victoria Falls (Zimbabwe)	1,100

Astronomical data

PLANETS OF THE SOLAR SYSTEM

	Mercury	Venus	Earth	Mars	Jupiter	Saturn	Uranus	Neptune	Pluto
Mass (Earth =1)	0.055	0.81	1	0.11	318	95.18	14.5	17.14	0.0022
Equatorial diameter (km)	4,878	12,103	12,756	6,786	142,984	120,536	51,118	49,528	2,300
Average density (g/cm³; water = 1g/cm³)	5.42	5.25	5.52	3.94	1.33	0.69	1.27	1.71	2.03
Axial tilt (degrees)	2	2	23.4	24	3.1	26.7	97.9	28.8	57.5
Rotational period (length of day) (d = Earth day, h = Earth hour)	58.65d	243.01d*	23.93h	24.62h	9.92h	10.67h	17.23h*	16.12h	6.38d*
Average surface temperature (° C)	-170 to 430	464	15	-40	-120	-180	-210	-220	-220
Maximum apparent magnitude	-1.4	-4.4	-	-2.8	-2.8	-0.3	5.5	7.8	13.6
Aphelion (million km)	69.7	109	152.1	249.1	815.7	1,507	3,004	4,537	7,375
Perihelion (million km)	45.9	107.4	147.1	206.7	740.9	1,347	2,735	4,456	4,425
Average distance from Sun (million km)	57.9	108.2	149.6	227.9	778.3	1,427	2,869.6	4,496	65,900
Orbital tilt (degrees)	7	3.39	0	1.85	1.3	2.49	0.77	1.77	17.2
Orbital period (length of year) (y = Earth year, d = Earth day)	87.97d	224.7d	365.26d	1.88y	11.86y	29.46y	84.01y	164.79y	248.54y

*denotes retrograde (backwards) spin

LOCAL GROUP OF GALAXIES

Name	Type	Distance (light years)	Luminosity (million Suns)	Diameter (light years)
Milky Way	Spiral	0	15,000	100,000
Large Magellanic Cloud	Irregular spiral	170,000	2,000	30,000
Small Magellanic Cloud	Irregular	190,000	500	20,000
Sculptor	Elliptical	300,000	1	6,000
Carina	Elliptical	300,000	0.01	3,000
Draco	Elliptical	300,000	0.1	3,000
Sextans	Elliptical	300,000	0.01	3,000
Ursa Minor	Elliptical	300,000	0.1	2,000
Fornax	Elliptical	500,000	12	6,000
Leo I	Elliptical	600,000	0.6	2,000
Leo II	Elliptical	600,000	0.4	2,000
NGC 6822	Irregular	1,800,000	90	15,000
IC 5152	Irregular	2,000,000	60	3,000
WLM	Irregular	2,000,000	90	6,000
Andromeda (M 31)	Spiral	2,200,000	40,000	150,000
Andromeda I,II,III	Elliptical	2,200,000	1	5,000
M 32 (NGC 221)	Elliptical	2,200,000	130	5,000
NGC 147	Elliptical	2,200,000	50	8,000
NGC 185	Elliptical	2,200,000	60	8,000
NGC 205	Elliptical	2,200,000	160	11,000
M 33 (Triangulum)	Spiral	2,400,000	5,000	40,000
IC 1613	Irregular	2,500,000	50	10,000
DDO 210	Irregular	3,000,000	2	5,000
Pisces	Irregular	3,000,000	0.6	2,000
GR 8	Irregular	4,000,000	2	1,500
IC 10	Irregular	4,000,000	250	6,000
Sagittarius	Irregular	4,000,000	1	4,000
Leo A	Irregular	5,000,000	20	7,000
Pegasus	Irregular	5,000,000	20	7,000

BRIGHTEST STARS

Name	Constellation	Apparent magnitude	Absolute magnitude	Distance (light years)	Star type
Sun		-26.7	4.8	0.000015*	Yellow main-sequence
Sirius A	Canis Major (The Great Dog)	-1.4	1.4	8.6	White main-sequence
Canopus	Carina (The Keel)	-0.7	-8.5	1,200	White supergiant
Alpha Centauri A	Centaurus (The Centaur)	-0.1	4.1	4.3	Yellow main-sequence
Arcturus	Boötes (The Herdsman)	-0.1	-0.3	37	Red giant
Vega	Lyra (The Lyre)	0.04	0.5	27	White main-sequence
Capella	Auriga (The Charioteer)	0.1	-0.6	45	Yellow giant
Rigel	Orion (The Huntsman)	0.1	-7.1	540-900	White supergiant
Procyon	Canis Minor (The Little Dog)	0.4	2.7	11.3	Yellow main-sequence
Achernar	Eridanus (River Eridanus)	0.5	-1.3	85	White main-sequence

* = 149,600,000 km

MOONS

Name of planet	Name of moon	diameter (km)	Distance from planet (km)
Earth	Moon	3,476	384,400
Mars	Phobos	22*	9,400
	Deimos	13*	23,500
Jupiter	Metis	40*	128,000
	Adrastea	20*	129,000
	Amalthea	200	181,300
	Thebe	100*	221,900
	Io	3,642	421,800
	Europa	3,138	670,900
	Ganymede	5,262	1,070,000
	Callisto	4,800	1,880,000
	Leda	15	11,094,000
	Himalia	170	11,480,000
	Lysithea	35	11,720,000
	Elara	70	11,737,000
	Ananke	25	21,200,000
	Carme	40	22,600,000
	Pasiphae	60	23,500,000
	Sinope	40	23,700,000
Saturn	Pan	20	133,600
	Atlas	31*	137,700
	Prometheus	102*	139,400
	Pandora	85*	141,700
	Epimetheus	117	151,400
	Janus	188*	151,500
	Mimas	397	186,000
	Enceladus	498	238,000
	Tethys	1,050	295,000
	Telesto	22*	295,000
	Calypso	24*	295,000
	Dione	1,118	377,000
	Helene	32*	377,000
	Rhea	1,528	527,000
	Titan	5,150	1,222,000
	Hyperion	286*	1,481,100
	Iapetus	1,436	3,561,300
	Phoebe	22	12,954,000
Uranus	Cordelia	26	49,700
	Ophelia	32	53,800
	Bianca	44	59,200
	Cressida	66	61,800
	Desdemona	58	62,700
	Juliet	84	64,400
	Portia	110	66,100
	Rosalind	58	69,900
	Belinda	68	75,300
	Puck	154	86,000
	Miranda	472	129,800
	Ariel	1,158	191,200
	Umbriel	1,169	266,000
	Titania	1,578	435,900
	Oberon	1,523	582,600
Neptune	Naiad	54	48,000
	Thalassa	80	50,000
	Despina	180	52,500
	Galatea	150	62,000
	Larissa	192	73,500
	Proteus	416	117,600
	Triton	2,705	354,800
	Nereid	3005	514,000
Pluto	Charon	1,200	19,600

*denotes average diameter for irregularly shaped moon

**never look directly at the Sun

THE SUN

Feature	
Approximate age (billion years)	4.6
Star type	Yellow main-sequence
Mass (Earth = 1)	332,946
Equatorial diameter (km)	1,392,000
Average density (g/cm^3; water = 1g/cm^3)	1.41
Apparent magnitude	-26.7
Absolute magnitude	4.8
Luminosity (billion billion megawatts)	390
Average surface temperature (° C)	5,500
Approximate core temperature (° C)	15,000,000
Maximum distance from Earth (km)	152,100,000
Minimum distance from Earth (km)	147,100,000
Polar rotation period (Earth days)	35
Equatorial rotation period (Earth days)	25

FAMOUS COMETS

Name	Period (years)
D'Arrest's Comet	6.6
Encke's Comet	3.3
Comet Giacobini-Zinner	6.5
Great Comet of 1811	3,000
Great Comet of 1843	512.4
Great Comet of 1844	102,050
Hale-Bopp	3,000
Halley's Comet	76.3
Holmes' Comet	6.9
Comet Kohoutek	75,000
Comet Mrkós	5.3
Pons-Winnecke Comet	6
Comet Schwassmann-Wachmann	16.2

TOTAL SOLAR ECLIPSES (UNTIL 2010)

Date	Where visible **
February 26, 1998	Mid-Pacific, Central America, North Atlantic
August 11, 1999	North Atlantic, North Europe, Western Asia, North India
June 21, 2001	South America, South Atlantic, Southern Africa, Pacific
December 4, 2002	Mid-Atlantic, Southern Africa, South Pacific, Australia
November 23, 2003	South Pacific, Antarctica
April 8, 2005	Mid-Pacific, Central America
March 29, 2006	Central Africa, Western Asia, parts of China
August 1, 2008	Arctic and Siberia
July 22, 2009	Mid-Atlantic, North America

TOTAL LUNAR ECLIPSES (UNTIL 2010)

Date	Where visible
January 21, 2000	North, South, and Central America, Southwest Europe, West Africa
July 16, 2000	Pacific, Australia, Southeast Asia
January 9, 2001	Africa, Asia, Europe
May 16, 2003	South and Central America, Antarctica
November 9, 2003	North, South, and Central America
May 4, 2004	Africa, Western Asia, India
October 28, 2004	North, South, and Central America, West Africa, southern Europe
March 3, 2007	Europe, Africa, Arctic
August 28, 2007	Southeastern tip of Australia, Pacific Ocean
February 21, 2008	North, Central, and South America, West Africa, Northwestern Europe
December 21, 2010	North and Central America, Pacific Ocean

Stars of the northern skies

MAJOR NORTHERN CONSTELLATIONS

Latin name	Alternative name
Andromeda	Andromeda
*Aquila	Eagle
Aries	Ram
Auriga	Charioteer
Boötes	Herdsman
Cancer	Crab
Canis Minor	Little Dog
Cassiopeia	Cassiopeia
Cepheus	Cepheus
Cygnus	Swan
Draco	Dragon
Gemini	Twins
Hercules	Hercules
*Hydra	Water Snake
Leo	Lion
Lyra	Lyre
Ophiuchus	Serpent Holder
Orion	Hunter
Pegasus	Pegasus
Pisces	Fishes
*Serpens	Serpent
*Sextans	Sextant
Taurus	Bull
Ursa Major	Great Bear
Ursa Minor	Little Bear
*Virgo	Virgin

*Constellations in this table are found in the northern celestial hemisphere. Those marked * lie on or near the celestial equator.*

VISIBLE STARS IN THE NORTHERN SKY

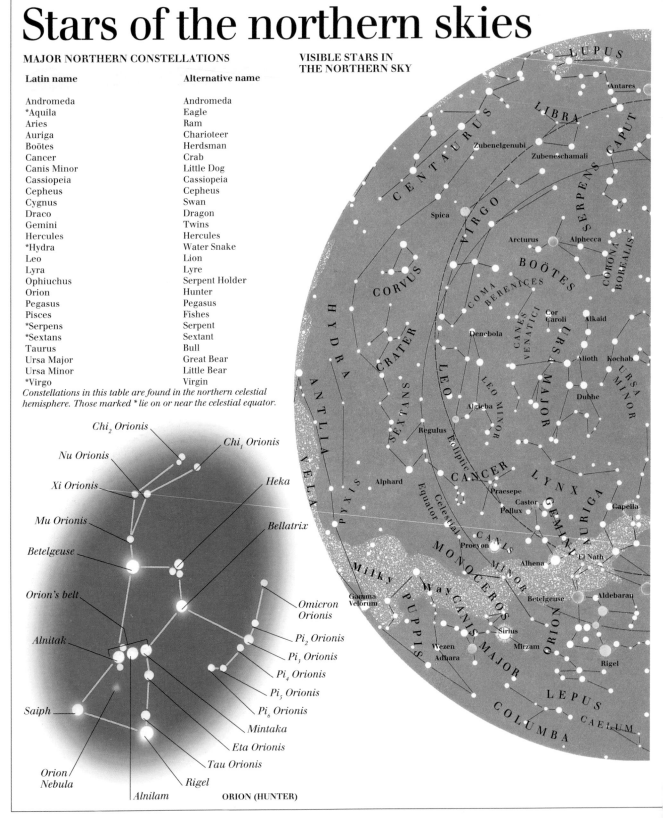

ORION (HUNTER)

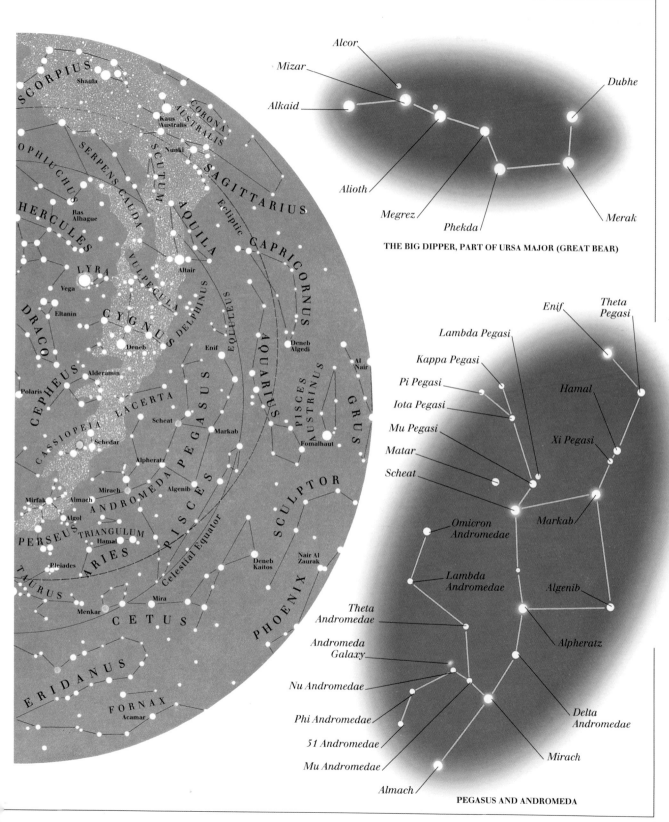

THE BIG DIPPER, PART OF URSA MAJOR (GREAT BEAR)

PEGASUS AND ANDROMEDA

Stars of the southern skies

MAJOR SOUTHERN CONSTELLATIONS

Latin name	Alternative name
Apus	Bird of Paradise
Aquarius	Water Bearer
*Aquila	Eagle
Canis Major	Great Dog
Capricornus	Sea Goat
Centaurus	Centaur
Chamaeleon	Chameleon
Columba	Dove
Corona Australis	Southern Crown
Corvus	Crow
Crater	Cup
Crux	Southern Cross
Dorado	Swordfish
Eridanus	River Eridanus
Fornax	Furnace
Grus	Crane
*Hydra	Water Snake
Lepus	Hare
Libra	Scales
Lupus	Wolf
Mensa	Table Mountain
Microscopium	Microscope
Pavo	Peacock
Phoenix	Phoenix
Pisces Austrinus	Southern Fish
Sagittarius	Archer
Scorpius	Scorpion
Sculptor	Sculptor
*Serpens	Serpent
*Sextans	Sextant
Triangulum Australe	Southern Triangle
Tucana	Toucan
Vela	Sail
*Virgo	Virgin
Volans	Flying Fish

Constellations in this table are found in the southern celestial hemisphere. Those marked * lie on or near the celestial equator.

VISIBLE STARS IN THE SOUTHERN SKY

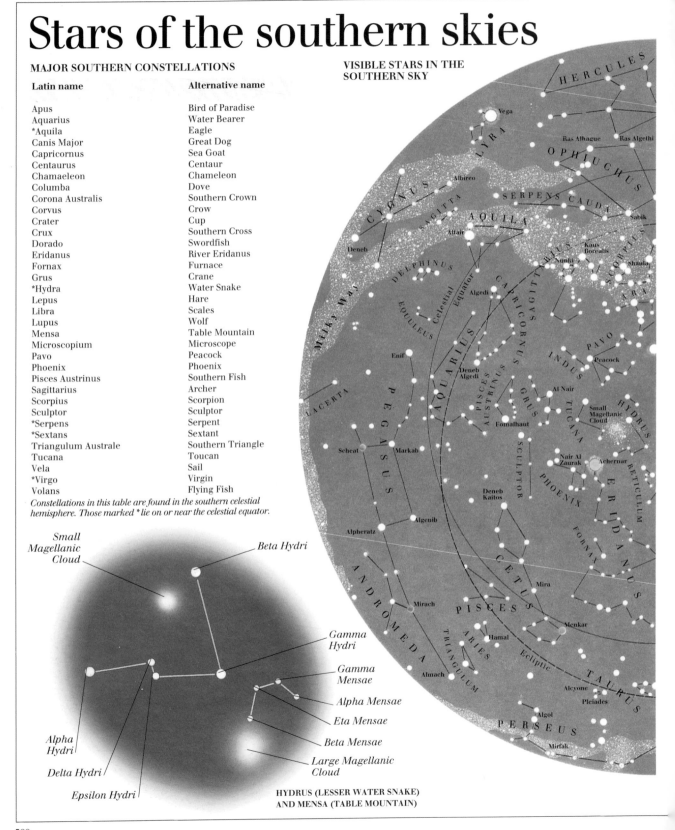

HYDRUS (LESSER WATER SNAKE) AND MENSA (TABLE MOUNTAIN)

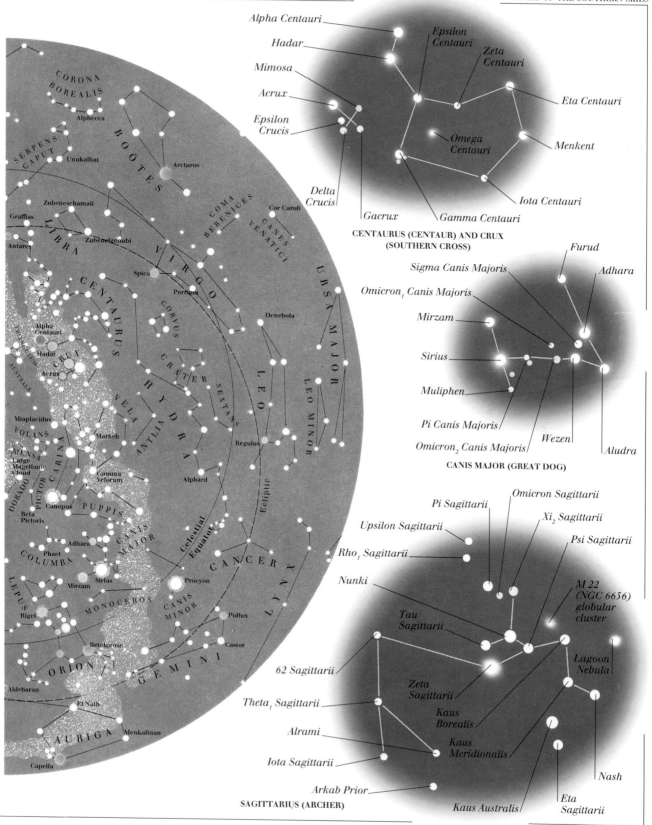

**CENTAURUS (CENTAUR) AND CRUX
(SOUTHERN CROSS)**

CANIS MAJOR (GREAT DOG)

SAGITTARIUS (ARCHER)

Electronics and computing data

ELECTRONIC CIRCUIT SYMBOLS

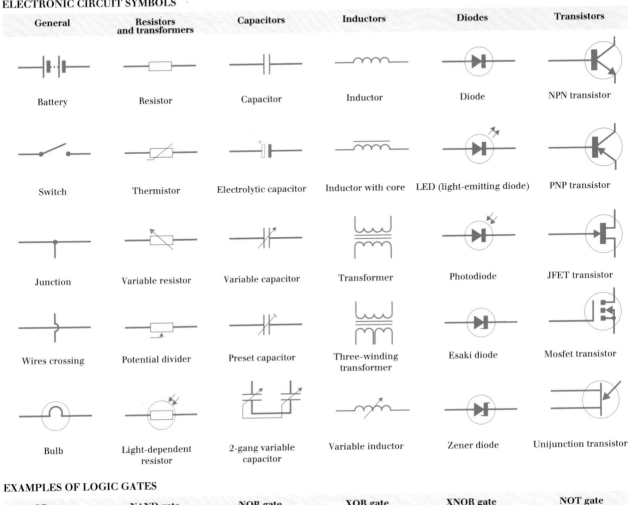

General	Resistors and transformers	Capacitors	Inductors	Diodes	Transistors
Battery	Resistor	Capacitor	Inductor	Diode	NPN transistor
Switch	Thermistor	Electrolytic capacitor	Inductor with core	LED (light-emitting diode)	PNP transistor
Junction	Variable resistor	Variable capacitor	Transformer	Photodiode	JFET transistor
Wires crossing	Potential divider	Preset capacitor	Three-winding transformer	Esaki diode	Mosfet transistor
Bulb	Light-dependent resistor	2-gang variable capacitor	Variable inductor	Zener diode	Unijunction transistor

EXAMPLES OF LOGIC GATES

OR gate	NAND gate	NOR gate	XOR gate	XNOR gate	NOT gate

The OR gate gives an output of logic 1 when any or all of its inputs are at logic 1.

This is the inverse of an AND gate. Output Q is zero only if both inputs, A and B, are 1.

This is the inverse of the OR gate. Output Q is 1 only if neither input A nor B is 1.

XOR stands for exclusive OR. Output Q is 1 only if either, but not both, inputs are 1.

XNOR stands for exclusive NOR. Output Q is zero if either, but not both, inputs are 1.

Also known as an inverter, this gate has one input. Output Q is the inverse of input A.

A	B	Q	A	B	Q	A	B	Q	A	B	Q	A	B	Q	A	Q
0	0	0	0	0	1	0	0	1	0	0	0	0	0	1	0	1
0	1	1	0	1	1	0	1	0	0	1	1	0	1	0	1	0
1	0	1	1	0	1	1	0	0	1	0	1	1	0	0		
1	1	1	1	1	0	1	1	0	1	1	0	1	1	1		

RESISTOR COLOR CODES

1st digit	2nd digit	3rd digit	Multiplier	Tolerance
0	0	0	1	
1	1	1	10	1%
2	2	2	100	2%
3	3	3	1000	
4	4	4	10000	
5	5	5	100000	
6	6	6	1000000	
7	7	7		
8	8	8	0.1	5%
9	9	9	0.01	10%

RESISTOR VALUES

Code	Value
1R2	1.2 Ω
12R	12 Ω
120R	120 Ω
1K	12 kΩ
120K	120 kΩ
1M2	1.2 MΩ
12M	12 MΩ

CIRCUIT FORMULAS

Formulas	Comments
$R = R_1 + R_2 + \ldots$	Resistors in series
$1/R = 1/R_1 + 1/R_2 + \ldots$	Resistors in parallel
$C = C_1 + C_2 + \ldots$	Capacitors in parallel
$1/C = 1/C_1 + 1/C_2 + \ldots$	Capacitors in series

ELECTRONICS AND COMPUTER ABBREVIATIONS

Abbreviation	Meaning
A	Ampere
A.C.	Alternating current
AF	Audio frequency
AM	Amplitude modulation
CD-ROM	Compact-disc read-only memory
CPU	Central processing unit
CRT	Cathode ray tube
dB	Decibel
D.C.	Direct current
DOS	Disk-operating system
DRAM	Dynamic random-access memory
e-mail	Electronic mail
e.m.f.	Electromotive force
EPROM	Erasable programmable read-only memory
F	Farad
FM	Frequency modulation
GSM	Global system mobile
hi-fi	High fidelity
I	Current
IC	Integrated circuit
k (kb, kB)	Kilobyte (1024 bytes)
kbps	Kilobits per second
LCD	Liquid crystal display
LED	Light-emitting diode
(V)LSI	(Very) large scale integration
M (Mb, MB)	Megabyte (1000 kilobytes)
Mbps	Megabits per second
OCR	Optical character recognition
P	Power
PC	Personal computer
PROM	Programmable read-only memory
R	Resistance
RAM	Random-access memory
ROM	Read-only memory
Rx	Receiver
SRAM	Station random-access memory
Tx	Transmitter
V	Volt
VDU	Visual display unit
W	Watt
Ω	Ohm

Decimal number	Binary	Hexa-decimal	ASCII code	ASCII character
0	00000000	00	00000000	NUL*
1	10000001	01	10000001	SOH*
2	10000010	02	10000010	Start of text*
9	00001001	09	00001001	HT*
10	00001010	0A	00001010	Line feed*
11	00001011	0B	10001011	VT*
12	00001100	0C	00001100	Form feed*
13	00001101	0D	10001101	Carriage return*
14	00001110	0E	10001110	SO*
15	00001111	0F	00001111	SI*
16	00010000	10	10010000	DLE*
17	00010001	11	00010001	DC1*
18	00010010	12	00010010	DC2*
32	00100000	20	10100000	SPACE
33	00100001	21	00100001	!
34	00100010	22	00100010	"
64	01000000	40	11000000	@
65	01000001	41	01000001	A
66	01000010	42	01000010	B
119	01110111	77	01110111	w
120	01111000	78	01111000	x
121	01111001	79	11111001	y
122	01111010	7A	11111010	z
123	01111011	7B	01111011	{

* control characters (nonprinting)

GENERATIONS OF COMPUTER

Generation	Dates	Characteristic
1st	1944-59	Used valves (vacuum tubes)
2nd	1959-64	Used transistors
3rd	1964-75	Large-scale Integrated Circuits (LSI)
4th	1975-	Very Large-scale Integrated Circuits (VLSI)
5th	Under development	Artificial intelligence

Mathematics data

SHAPES

Plane shapes

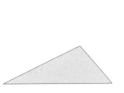

SCALENE TRIANGLE
A triangle (three-sided polygon) with no equal sides or angles.

ISOCELES TRIANGLE
A triangle with only two sides and two angles equal.

RIGHT-ANGLED TRIANGLE
A triangle with one angle as a right angle (90°).

EQUILATERAL TRIANGLE
A regular triangle. All angles are 60°.

SQUARE
A regular quadrilateral. All angles are 90°.

RHOMBUS
A quadrilateral with all sides equal and two pairs of equal angles.

RECTANGLE
A quadrilateral with four right angles and opposite sides of equal length.

PARALLELOGRAM
A quadrilateral with two pairs of parallel sides.

TRAPEZIUM
A quadrilateral with one pair of parallel sides.

PENTAGON
A five-sided polygon. A regular pentagon is shown above.

HEXAGON
A six-sided polygon. A regular hexagon is shown above.

OCTAGON
An eight-sided polygon. A regular octagon is shown above.

Solid shapes

TETRAHEDRON
A four-sided polyhedron. A regular tetrahedron is shown.

CUBE
A regular hexahedron. All sides are equal and all angles are 90°.

OCTAHEDRON
A polyhedron with eight sides.

PRISM
A polyhedron of constant cross-section in planes perpendicular to its longitudinal axis.

PYRAMID
A polygonal base and triangular sides that meet at a point.

TORUS
A doughnutlike, ring shape.

SPHERE
A round shape, as in a ball or an orange.

HEMISPHERE
Formed when a sphere is cut exactly in half.

SPHEROID
An egg-shaped object whose cross-section is a circle or an elipse.

CONE
An elliptical or circular base with sides tapering to a single point.

RIGHT CYLINDER
A tube-shaped, solid figure. A right cylinder has parallel faces.

HELIX
A twisted curve. The distance moved in one revolution is its pitch.

AREAS AND VOLUME

Plane shapes

Radius = r
Diameter = d = 2 × π r

Height = h, Base = b
Sides = a, b, c

Sides = a, b

Solid shapes

Height = h
Radius = r

Height = h
Radius = r, Side = l

Sides = a, b, c

| CIRCLE | TRIANGLE | RECTANGLE | CYLINDER | CONE | RECTANGULAR BLOCK |

Circumference =
2 × π × r

Perimeter =
a + b + c

Perimeter =
2 × (a + b)

Surface area =
2 × π × r × h
(excl. bases)

Surface area =
π × r × l + πr²

Surface area =
2 (a × b + b × c + a × c)

Area = π × r²

Area = ¹/₂ × b × h

Area = a × b

Volume = π × r² × h

Volume = ¹/₃ × π × r² × h

Volume = a × b × c

MATHEMATICAL SYMBOLS

Symbol	Explanation
+	addition
−	subtraction
×	multiplication
÷	division
=	equals
≠	does not equal
>	greater than
<	less than
≥	greater than or equal to
≤	less than or equal to
∞	infinity
Σ	summation
u,<u>u</u>	vectors
f(x)	function
!	factorial
√	square root
ℰ	universal set
A ∩ B	intersection
A ∪ B	union
A ⊂ B	subset
∅	null set

SCIENTIFIC NOTATION

Number	Number between 1 and 10	Power of ten	Scientific notation
10	1	10^1	$1 × 10^1$
150	1.5	10^2 (= 100)	$1.5 × 10^2$
274,000,000	2.74	10^8 (= 100,000,000)	$2.74 × 10^8$
0.0023	2.3	10^{-3} (= 0.001)	$2.3 × 10^{-3}$

TRIGONOMETRY

Angle A (degrees)	sin A	cos A	tan A
0	0	1	0
30	1/2	√3/2	1/√3
45	1/√2	1/√2	1
60	√3/2	1/2	√3
90	1	0	∞

RULES OF ALGEBRA

Expression	Comments	Expression becomes
$a + a$	Simple addition	$2a$
$a + b = c + d$	Subtract b from either side	$a = c + d - b$
$ab = cd$	Divide both sides by b	$a = cd/b$
$(a + b)(c + d)$	Multiplication of bracketed terms	$ac + ad + bc + bd$
$a^2 + ab$	Use parentheses	$a(a + b)$
$(a + b)^2$	Expand parentheses	$a^2 + 2ab + b^2$
$a^2 - b^2$	Difference of two squares	$(a + b)(a - b)$
$1/a + 1/b$	Find common denominator	$(a + b)/ab$
$a/b ÷ c/d$	Dividing by a fraction is the same as multiplying by its reciprocal	$a/b × d/c$

Biographies

The names featured here relate directly to the scientists highlighted in bold in the historical sections of the book.

JEAN LOUIS AGASSIZ
(1807 - 1873)
Swiss geologist and zoologist who studied the effects of ice erosion and proved that glaciers move.

GEORGIUS AGRICOLA, ALSO KNOWN AS GEORG BAUER
(1494 - 1555)
German geologist and mining engineer who was the first person to study rocks and minerals in a scientific way.

ALCMAEON OF CROTON
(c. 520 BC)
Ancient Greek physician and philosopher, generally considered to be the first anatomist.

ANAXIMANDER OF MILETUS
(c. 611 - 546 BC)
Ancient Greek natural philosopher, among whose reputed contributions to science are an accurate sundial, the earliest map of the Earth, and a primitive theory of evolution.

APOLLONIUS OF PERGA
(3RD CENTURY BC)
Ancient Greek mathematician noted for his work on an important set of curves called conic sections. He also used mathematics in attempts to account for the motions of the known planets.

ARCHIMEDES
(c. 287 - 212 BC)
Greek mathematician and engineer. He derived mathematical formulas for various geometrical shapes and discovered the principle of upthrust on an object floating in water. He also studied simple machines, in particular the screw thread.

ARISTOTLE
(384 - 322 BC)
Influential Greek philosopher and naturalist. Wrote extensively on force and motion, plant and animal classification, and many other subjects. His ideas were believed to be fact by most religious thinkers, at least until the 17th century.

HEINRICH LOUIS D'ARREST
(1822 - 1875)
German astronomer involved in the discovery of Neptune and famous for his studies of asteroids and nebulae.

SVANTE ARRHENIUS
(1859 - 1927)
Swedish chemist who won the 1903 Nobel prize for his work on the dissociation (splitting) of molecules into ions in solution.

JOHN VINCENT ATANASOFF
(BORN 1903)
American physicist and computer pioneer who, with Clifford Berry, built one of the first electronic computers.

CHARLES BABBAGE
(1792 - 1871)
English mathematician who invented a sophisticated calculating machine (the Difference Engine) that eliminated errors from tables of mathematical figures.

THOMAS BARTHOLIN
(1616 - 1680)
Danish physician (doctor) and mathematician. The first person to produce a detailed description of the human lymphatic system.

WILLIAM MADDOCK BAYLISS
(1860 - 1924)
English physiologist who, with his colleague **Ernest Starling**, first used the word "hormone," after discovering secretin in 1902.

WILLIAM BEAUMONT
(1796 - 1853)
American army surgeon who was the first person to observe and study human digestion, after working on a patient with a shotgun wound.

CHARLES BELL
(1774 - 1842)
Scottish anatomist and surgeon who discovered the distinction between sensory and motor neurons (nerves).

JOCELYN BELL BURNELL
(BORN 1943)
English radio astronomer who detected regular pulses of radio waves from outer space. The source of the radio signal was later shown to be from the first-discovered pulsar.

CLAUDE BERNARD (1813 - 1878)
French physiologist who established the concept of homeostasis, whereby the internal chemical environment of the human body resists dramatic fluctuations of temperature or composition.

FRIEDRICH WILHELM BESSEL
(1784 - 1864)
German mathematician and astronomer whose calculation of the distance of the double star, 61 Cygni, was the first scientific reckoning of stellar distance.

HANS ALBRECHT BETHE
(BORN 1906)
German physicist who figured out the role of nuclear fusion in stars.

VILHELM BJERKNES
(1862 - 1951)
Norwegian meteorologist whose theory of weather fronts (boundaries between air masses) was the foundation of modern weather forecasting.

GEORGE BOOLE
(1815 - 1864)
English mathematician whose system of mathematical logic (Boolean algebra) has had a profound influence on the development of modern electronic computers.

HERBERT WAYNE BOYER
(BORN 1936)
American biochemist. In 1973, with **Stanley Cohen**, successfully spliced two sections of DNA from a bacterium, heralding the beginning of genetic engineering.

ROBERT BOYLE
(1627 - 1691)
Irish physicist who is famous for his work on gases. He was also the first to produce a modern definition of an element.

TYCHO BRAHE
(1546 - 1601)
Danish astronomer, famous for his accurate observations. These were utilized by **Copernicus** in his heliocentric (sun-centered) theory of the Solar System.

ROBERT WILHELM BUNSEN
(1811 - 1899)
German chemist and physicist whose name is given to the gas burner he invented. With **Gustav Kirchoff**, he was also a pioneer of spectroscopy.

GEORG FERDINAND LUDWIG PHILIP CANTOR
(1845 - 1918)
German mathematician who made important contributions to set theory.

HENRY CAVENDISH
(1731 - 1810)
English scientist, most famous for his work on gases. He was the first to isolate oxygen gas, and built sensitive apparatus for determining the density of the Earth.

CELSUS
(1ST CENTURY AD)
Roman scholar and writer who wrote extensively on medical topics. His ideas were rejected by **Paracelsus**, whose self-appointed name means "against Celsus."

JOHN DOUGLAS COCKCROFT
(1897 - 1967)
English nuclear physicist who in 1924, with **Ernest Walton**, succeeded in disintegrating lithium atoms by bombarding them with high-energy protons.

SEYMOUR STANLEY COHEN
(BORN 1917)
American biochemist who, with **Herbert Boyer**, pioneered genetic engineering in the 1970s.

NICOLAUS COPERNICUS
(1473 - 1543)
Polish astronomer who founded modern astronomy by being the first to suggest that the Earth is not at the center of the Universe. His suggestion that the Earth moves around the Sun inspired **Galileo**, **Newton**, and **Kepler**.

FRANCIS HARRY COMPTON CRICK
(BORN 1916)
English molecular biologist famous for figuring out the molecular structure of DNA with his colleague, **James Watson**.

WILLIAM CROOKES (1832 - 1919)
English chemist and physicist. The Crookes tube, important in the discovery of the electron, is named after him.

GEORGES CUVIER
(1769 - 1832)
French anatomist whose work on animal classification was based on the structure of animals' bodies. He also founded paleontology (the scientific study of fossils).

JOHN DALTON
(1766 - 1844)
English scientist and originator of modern atomic theory. He discovered the law of partial pressures, known as Dalton's Law.

CHARLES ROBERT DARWIN
(1809 - 1882)
English naturalist, geologist, and physician (doctor) who developed the theory of evolution, discussed in *The Origin of Species*, while on an expedition to the Galapagos Islands aboard the ship the *HMS Beagle*.

HUMPHREY DAVY
(1778 - 1829)
English chemist, most famous for his work on electrochemistry and his invention of the miner's safety lamp.

DEMOCRITUS
(c. 460 - 370 BC)
Greek philosopher and mathematician who was the first to construct a comprehensive atomic theory.

RENE DESCARTES
(1596 - 1650)
Prolific French natural philosopher who studied many branches of science and mathematics.

THOMAS ALVA EDISON
(1847 - 1951)
American inventor, one of those responsible for the development of electric lighting.

PAUL EHRLICH
(1854 - 1915)
German biologist, a pioneer of hemotology (study of the blood), and immunology (study of the immune system). He coined the term "chemotherapy."

ALBERT EINSTEIN
(1879 - 1955)
German-born American physicist generally regarded as one of history's greatest scientists. He is most famous for his special and general theories of relativity, for which he won the Nobel Prize in 1921.

WILLEM EINTHOVEN
(1860 - 1927)
Dutch physiologist, inventor of the first electrocardiogram (ECG) machine in 1903.

EMPEDOCLES
(c. 450 BC)
Ancient Greek philosopher and poet who was one of the originators of the theory of the four elements.

ERATOSTHANES
(c. 275 - 192 BC)
Greek philosopher, mathematician, and astronomer who was the first to figure out scientifically a value for the size of the Earth.

EUCLID
(c. 500 BC)
Greek mathematician, best known for his comprehensive work on geometry.

BARTOLOMMEO EUSTACHIO
(1520 - 1574)
Italian pioneer of modern anatomy.

**HIERONYMUS FABRICIUS,
ALSO KNOWN AS
GIROLAMO FABRICI**
(1537 - 1619)
Italian anatomist who studied the valves in veins. He was a tutor of **William Harvey**.

CHARLES FABRY
(1867 - 1945)
French physicist and discoverer of the ozone layer. He was the co-inventor of the Fabry–Perot interferometer, a device that measures the wavelengths of light.

MICHAEL FARADAY
(1791 - 1867)
English experimental physicist and chemist who originated the idea of magnetic and electric fields. His work was put into mathematical form by **Maxwell**. Faraday also invented the dynamo and discovered electromagnetic induction.

ENRICO FERMI
(1901 - 1954)
Italian physicist who used the work of Lise Meitner and others to build the world's first nuclear reactor.

ALEXANDER FLEMING
(1881 - 1955)
Scottish biologist who conducted research into bacteria. He discovered the antibiotic penicillin in 1928.

JOHN AMBROSE FLEMING
(1849 - 1945)
English inventor who developed the thermionic valve, a forerunner of the modern semiconductor diode.

GALEN
(c. 129 - 199)
Greek anatomist, an expert at dissecting animals and working out muscle and bone structures.

GALILEO GALILEI
(1564 - 1642)
Italian astronomer and founder of classical physics, whose work on force and motion challenged that of **Aristotle**. In 1609, he became the first to use a telescope to observe craters on the Moon and four of the satellites of Jupiter.

JOHANN GOTTFRIED GALLE
(1812 - 1910)
German astronomer who was the first to observe the planet Neptune, working from calculations made by **Heinrich D'Arrest**.

LUIGI GALVANI
(1737 - 1798)
Italian physiologist whose studies of the relationship between nerves, muscles, and electricity were the beginning of the study of electrophysiology.

MURRAY GELL-MANN
(BORN 1929)
American theoretical physicist who was the first to hypothesize the existence of quarks.

WILLIAM GILBERT
(1540 - 1603)
English physician and experimenter who is known for his work on electricity and magnetism.

FRANCIS GLISSON
(c. 1597 - 1677)
English anatomist and physician who made a detailed study of the human liver.

KURT GÖDEL
(1906 - 1978)
Austrian-born American mathematician, famous for Gödel's theorem, which is an important part of the study of mathematical logic.

CAMILLO GOLGI
(1843 - 1926)
Italian cell biologist known for his study of the structure of the nervous system. He also discovered tiny structures within cells, called Golgi bodies.

NEHEMIAH GREW
(1641 - 1712)
English botanist and physician. He introduced the term "comparative anatomy," where the anatomy of a plant is compared with that of another plant or an animal.

BENO GUTENBERG
(1889 - 1960)
German-born American seismologist, among the first to suggest that the Earth's core is molten. Together with **Charles Richter**, he devised a scale for measuring the strength of earthquakes.

GEORGE HADLEY
(1685 - 1768)
English physicist and meteorologist who described global patterns of wind circulation, now called Hadley cells.

ERNST HEINRICH PHILIPP AUGUST HAECKEL
(1834 - 1919)
German biologist whose extensive zoological and botanical researches led him to coin the term "ecology."

OTTO HAHN
(1879 - 1968)
German physicist who, with **Fritz Strassmann**, was a co-discoverer of nuclear fission.

EDMUND HALLEY
(1656 - 1742)
English astronomer who was the first to discover the fact that some comets return on a regular basis. Halley's comet is named after him.

WILLIAM HARVEY
(1578 - 1657)
English anatomist who formulated the theory of blood circulation through arteries and veins.

OLIVER HEAVISIDE
(1850 - 1925)
English physicist who made important contributions to telegraphy and earth science. He suggested the existence of a layer of charged particles, now called the ionosphere.

FRIEDRICH GUSTAV JAKOB HENLE
(1809 - 1885)
German anatomist who discovered tubules in the kidney, named Henle's loops in his honor.

JOSEPH HENRY
(1797 - 1878)
American physicist who discovered electromagnetic induction independently of **Michael Faraday**. The unit of inductance is named after him.

WILLIAM HERSCHEL
(1758 - 1822)
German astronomer, best remembered for his discovery of the planet Uranus.

HEINRICH RUDOLF HERTZ
(1857 - 1894)
German experimental physicist. In 1888, he discovered radio waves, confirming **Maxwell's** theory of electromagnetic radiation.

HARRY HAMMOND HESS
(1906 - 1969)
American geophysicist who discovered seafloor spreading, an important factor in the theory of plate tectonics.

HIPPARCHUS
(2ND CENTURY BC)
Ancient Greek astronomer who made many important astronomical measurements, including a fairly accurate determination of the sizes of the Sun and the Moon.

HIPPOCRATES
(c. 460 - 570 BC)
Greek physician (doctor) who created the Hippocratic Oath – a code of conduct for doctors. A form of the oath is still used today.

ROBERT HOOKE
(1635 - 1703)
English physicist, chemist, and biologist who formulated Hooke's Law, relating to the extension or compression of a solid to the force applied to it. He also coined the term "cells," after observing plant cells under a microscope and likening them to rooms in a prison.

EDWIN POWELL HUBBLE
(1889 - 1953)
American astronomer who is
remembered for his calculation
of the immense distance of the
Andromeda galaxy. The *Hubble
Space Telescope* is named
after him.

JOHN HUNTER
(1728 - 1795)
Scottish anatomist and biologist
who founded experimental
medicine. He pioneered the art of
grafting tissue.

JAMES HUTTON
(1726 - 1797)
Scottish geologist who was the
first to take a scientific approach
to the subject.

JAN INGEN-HOUSZ
(1730 - 1799)
Dutch botanist who, inspired
by Joseph **Priestley's** discovery
that plants produce oxygen,
demonstrated photosynthesis.

CHARLES JACKSON
(1805 - 1880)
American doctor, chemist, and
earth scientist. He was one of the
first to use ether as an anesthetic
during surgical operations.

KARL JANSKY
(1905 - 1950)
American engineer and pioneer
of radio astronomy.

EDWARD JENNER
(1749 - 1823)
English physician (doctor), and
a pupil of **John Hunter**. Jenner
was a pioneer of vaccination.

JAMES PRESCOTT JOULE
(1818 - 1889)
English physicist whose
experiments with heat made it
possible for others to construct
the law of conservation of energy.

WILLIAM THOMSON KELVIN
(1824 - 1907)
Irish-born Scottish physicist whose
many important contributions to
physics included formulation of the
law of conservation of energy. The
Kelvin temperature scale is named
after him.

JOHANNES KEPLER
(1571 - 1630)
German astronomer, physicist, and
mathematician. He formulated
three laws of planetary motion.

**MUHAMMED IBN MUSA
AL-KHWARIZMI**
(c. 780 - 850)
Arab mathematician, geographer,
and astronomer, influential in
passing knowledge from Indian
and Arab scholars to Europe.

GUSTAV ROBERT KIRCHHOFF
(1824 - 1887)
German physicist who, with
Robert Bunsen, developed
spectroscopy, which led to
the discovery of several
new elements.

ROBERT KOCH
(1843 - 1910)
German biologist who discovered
the bacillus responsible for
cholera and produced a vaccine
against tuberculosis.

HANS ADOLF KREBS
(1900 - 1981)
German-born British biochemist,
notable for working out the
metabolic (energy) pathways
in cells, known as the Krebs cycle.

JEAN-BAPTISTE LAMARCK
(1744 - 1829)
French evolutionary biologist
whose work on the way species
change over time paved the way
for Darwin's theory of evolution.

PAUL LANGERHANS
(1847 - 1888)
German physician (doctor)
remembered for his discovery
of regions in the pancreas, called
islets of Langerhans, which are
now known to produce insulin.

ANTOINE LAVOISIER
(1743 - 1794)
French chemist often hailed
as the father of chemistry. He
discovered the role of oxygen
in the process of combustion
(burning) and the chemical
composition of water.

KARL LANDSTEINER
(1868 - 1943)
Austrian-born American
pathologist who discovered the
four major blood groups (A, O, B,
AB) in 1901 and the M and N
blood groups in 1927.

LEE DE FOREST
(1873 - 1961)
American physicist and inventor,
a pioneer of the technologies of
radio and sound recording.

ANTONY VAN LEEUWENHOEK
(1652 - 1725)
Dutch microscopist who
designed and used a powerful
single-lens microscope. He
was the first person to observe
microorganisms, calling
them animalcules.

GOTTFRIED WILHELM LEIBNIZ
(1646 - 1716)
German mathematician who
was the first to publish work on a
branch of algebra called calculus.
He also originated the idea of a
calculating machine.

GEORGES LEMAÎTRE
(1894 - 1966)
Belgian cosmologist and civil
engineer who formulated the
modern Big Bang theory of the
origin of the universe.

LEONARDO DA VINCI
(1452 - 1519)
Italian artist, architect, engineer,
and scientist. As an artist, he
produced an impressive collection
of anatomical studies.

**CAROLUS LINNAEUS, ALSO
KNOWN AS CARL VON LINNÉ**
(1707 - 1778)
Swedish biologist who introduced
the universal system of plant and
animal classification, known as
the binomial system.

HANS LIPPERSHEY
(1570 - 1619)
Dutch spectacle-maker credited
with the invention of the telescope.

JOSEPH LISTER
(1827 - 1912)
English surgeon who improved the
success rate in surgical operations
by introducing antiseptics.

RICHARD LOWER
(1631 - 1691)
English physiologist who
discovered, with **Robert Hooke**,
that blood becomes bright red in
the lungs – now known to be due
to the oxygen that dissolves there.

MARCELLO MALPIGHI
(1628 - 1694)
Italian biologist and microscopist
who discovered blood capillaries,
giving weight to the system of
blood circulation put forward by
William Harvey.

BENOIT MANDELBROT
(BORN 1924)
Polish mathematician who is a
central figure in the development
of fractal geometry.

JAMES CLERK MAXWELL
(1831 - 1879)
Scottish mathematician whose
most famous work was his theory
of electromagnetic radiation,
which he created by adapting
Faraday's ideas of electric and
magnetic fields.

GREGOR JOHANN MENDEL
(1822 - 1884)
Austrian monk and botanist, whose
studies of the heredity patterns of
plants laid foundations for the
science of genetics. His work
enabled a mechanism to be found
for Darwin's evolution.

DMITRY MENDELEYEV
(1834 - 1907)
Russian chemist who constructed
the first satisfactory periodic table
of elements.

STANLEY LLOYD MILLER
(BORN 1930)
American chemist whose most
famous work concerns the origin of
life on Earth. In 1953, he produced
some of the essential complex
chemicals necessary for life.

JOHN MILNE
(1850 - 1913)
English seismologist who
invented the modern seismograph
and saw the importance of worldwide seismological stations.

FRIEDRICH MOHS
(1773 - 1839)
German geologist and mineralogist.
The scale of mineral hardness that
he devised bears his name.

MONDINO DE LUZZI
(c. 1270 - 1326)
Italian anatomist and physician
who wrote the first book of
anatomy since ancient times.

JOHN NAPIER
(1550 - 1617)
Scottish mathematician who
was the inventor of logarithms,
which allowed faster and more
accurate calculation.

JOHN VON NEUMANN
(1903 - 1957)
Hungarian-born American
mathematician, designer of some
of the earliest electronic computers.
His theoretical approach provided a
model for the future development
of electronic computers.

ISAAC NEWTON
(1642 - 1727)
English mathematician and
physicist who is perhaps the most
famous and influential scientist of
all time. His achievements include
a universal theory of gravitation,
three laws of motion (called
Newton's laws), and the first
understanding that white light
consists of a spectrum of colors.

HANS CHRISTIAN OERSTED
(1777 - 1851)
Danish physicist who discovered
the magnetic effect of electric
current. His discovery inspired the
work of many experimenters,
most notably **Michael Faraday**.

GEORG OHM
(1789 - 1854)
German physicist who developed
a law (Ohms Law) that relates
flow of electric current to voltage.
The unit of electrical resistance
(the ohm) is named after him.

RICHARD DIXON OLDHAM
(1858 - 1836)
English geologist and seismologist
whose studies of earthquake
waves led him to realize the
existence of the Earth's core.

PARACELSUS, ALSO KNOWN AS THEOPHRASTUS VON HOHENHEIM
(1493 - 1541)
German physician (doctor) who introduced the role of chemistry in medicine. He also made important discoveries about several diseases.

AMBROISE PARÉ
(c. 1510 - 1590)
French surgeon who is the father of modern surgery. He introduced ligatures (threads for binding blood vessels) into the treatment of surgical amputation.

BLAISE PASCAL
(1623 - 1662)
French mathematician and physicist who was the first to realize that the pressure in a fluid (liquid or gas) acts in all directions. This is known as Pascal's Principle.

LINUS CARL PAULING
(1901 - 1994)
American chemist who applied quantum theory to chemistry in order to understand bonding within molecules. He used X-ray diffraction techniques to figure out molecular structures. His belief in Vitamin C helped combat many non-nutritional diseases.

ARNO ALLAN PENZIAS
(BORN 1933)
American astrophysicist born in Germany who discovered, with **Robert Wilson,** the microwave cosmic background radiation by examining emissions from the Milky Way.

MAX KARL ERNST PLANCK
(1858 - 1947)
German theoretical physicist who was the first to suggest that energy is "quantized," which means it can only take certain values. This idea led to quantum theory that revolutionized science in the early 20th century.

JULES HENRI POINCARÉ
(1854 - 1912)
Prolific French mathematician whose important contributions to mathematics included the first steps in what is now called chaos theory. He also predicted some of the results of relativity a few years before **Einstein.**

JOSEPH PRIESTLEY
(1733 - 1804)
English experimental chemist who, in 1774, discovered oxygen (also discovered independently by **Scheele**). This discovery became known to **Lavoisier,** who then realized the importance of oxygen to burning.

JOSEPH LOUIS PROUST
(1754 - 1826)
French chemist who devised the law of constant proportions – Proust's Law. This states that the proportions of elements present in a compound is always the same.

PTOLEMY, ALSO KNOWN AS CLAUDIUS PTOLEMAEUS
(c. 150)
Alexandrian astronomer and geographer whose greatest work was *Almagest*, which consisted of thirteen books that listed constellations and presented the contemporary understanding of Greek astronomers. Ptolemy's idea that the Earth is at the center of the universe was challenged by **Copernicus, Kepler,** and **Galileo.**

PYTHAGORAS
(c. 580 - 500 bc)
Greek mathematician and philosopher who believed that everything is number. The theorem that bears his name was known long before his time.

CHARLES FRANCIS RICHTER
(1900 - 1985)
American seismologist who, together with **Beno Gutenberg,** devised the Richter scale for measuring the strength of earthquakes.

WILHELM KONRAD VON RÖNTGEN
(1845 - 1923)
German physicist who discovered Xrays in 1895. He also worked on the heat conductivity of crystals and the electromagnetic rotation of polarized light.

ERNEST RUTHERFORD
(1871 - 1937)
New Zealand-born British physicist who was the first person to identify the three types of radioactive emissions and to suggest the existence of the atomic nucleus.

JONAS SALK
(BORN 1914)
American microbiologist who developed the first effective vaccine for the disease poliomyelitis.

HORACE BENÉDICT DE SAUSSURE
(1740 - 1799)
Swiss physicist and geologist who coined the term "geology." Remembered for his invention of the first hygrometer.

CARL WILHELM SCHEELE
(1742 - 1786)
Swedish chemist who discovered oxygen independently of **Joseph Priestley,** and prepared several previously unknown acids.

EMILIO GINO SEGRÉ
(1905 - 1989)
Italian-born American physicist who found traces of the first artificial element (technetium) in a discarded cyclotron in 1937 and helped develop the atomic bomb.

CLAUDE ELWOOD SHANNON
(BORN 1916)
American mathematician who originated a branch of mathematics called information theory. He applied the logic theory of **George Boole** to electronic switches, aiding modern computer development.

ERNEST THOMAS SINTON WALTON
(1903 - 1995)
Irish nuclear physicist who built the first successful particle accelerator with **John Cockcroft.** They became the first scientists to "split the atom."

VESTO MELVIN SLIPHER
(1875 - 1969)
American astronomer whose observations of spiral galaxies gave the first evidence that the universe is expanding.

WILLIAM SMITH
(1769 - 1839)
English geologist who was the first person to make accurate geological maps.

SÖREN PETER SÖRENSEN
(1868 - 1939)
Danish chemist who invented the pH scale used for measuring the concentration of acids.

ERNEST HENRY STARLING
(1866 - 1927)
English physiologist who, with his colleague **William Bayliss,** identified the first known hormone, secretin, in 1902.

NIELS STENSEN, ALSO KNOWN AS NICOLAUS STENO
(1638 - 1686)
Danish scientist who carried out important work in a number of scientific fields. In geology, he is remembered for his ideas on sedimentary rocks.

FRITZ STRASSMAN
(1902 - 1980)
German physicist who, with **Otto Hahn,** discovered nuclear fission in 1938.

SUSHRUTA
(2ND CENTURY bc)
Indian surgeon who wrote extensively on all aspects of medicine known at the time.

THEOPHRASTUS
(c. 370 - 285 bc)
Greek philosopher, often called the father of botany, who was the first person to attempt a full classification of plants.

JOSEPH JOHN THOMSON
(1856 - 1940)
English physicist who discovered the electron in 1897 while investigating Xrays.

CLYDE WILLIAM TOMBAUGH
(BORN 1906)
American astronomer who discovered the planet Pluto in 1930. He also discovered several star clusters and galaxies.

EVANGELISTA TORRICELLI
(1608 - 1647)
Italian mathematician, physicist, and inventor of the mercury barometer. His most famous contribution, the idea of atmospheric pressure, was confirmed by **Blaise Pascal.**

ANDREAS VESALIUS
(1514 - 1564)
Italian founder of modern anatomy, one of the first to prove **Galen's** ideas wrong.

ALESSANDRO VOLTA
(1745 - 1827)
Italian physicist and inventor of the electric battery. His invention made possible the discoveries of **Davy, Faraday,** and many others.

JAMES DEWEY WATSON
(BORN 1928)
American molecular biologist who, with **Francis Crick,** figured out the molecular structure of DNA in 1953.

ALFRED WEGENER
(1880 - 1930)
German meteorologist and geophysicist, originator of the theory of continental drift (the Wegener hypothesis).

JOHN TUZO WILSON
(1908 - 1993)
Canadian geologist and geophysicist remembered for his work on plate tectonics.

FRIEDRICH WÖHLER
(1800 - 1882)
German chemist who transformed the study of organic chemistry in 1828 by producing an organic substance from inorganic reagents.

ROBERT WOODROW WILSON
(BORN 1936)
American astronomer who, with **Arno Penzias,** discovered cosmic background radiation – the best evidence yet for the Big Bang theory.

Glossary

A

ABDOMEN
The lower part of the trunk, which is separated from the chest by the **diaphragm**. Contained in the abdomen are the organs of **digestion** and excretion and, in women, the uterus and **ovaries**.

ABSOLUTE MAGNITUDE
A measure of the **luminosity** of a celestial object. Absolute magnitude is taken to be the **apparent magnitude** an object would display if measured at a standard distance of 10 **parsecs**.

ABSOLUTE ZERO
The lowest possible **temperature**. Absolute zero is zero kelvin, -273.15° Celsius or -459.67° Fahrenheit.

ACCELERATION
A change in the **speed** of an object. A reduction in speed is a negative acceleration and is often called a deceleration. Acceleration is usually measured in ms^{-2} (meters per second per second, or meters per second squared).

ACCRETION DISK
A rotating, disk-shaped mass in space, which is formed by gravitational attraction.

ACHROMATIC DOUBLET
A system of two lenses that eliminates **chromatic aberration**. The two lenses are made of different types of glass.

ACID
A compound that contains hydrogen and can donate **protons** (hydrogen ions, H^+). In **aqueous solution**, the protons associate with water **molecules** to form hydronium ions, H_3O^+.

ACTIVATION ENERGY
The least **energy** required for a particular **chemical reaction** to take place. Typically, it is supplied as heat energy; for example striking a match produces heat to start the match **burning**.

ADDITIVE PROCESS
Combining light of different colors. When light of more than one color enters the eye, the resulting color is different from each of the initial colors.

ADHESIVE FORCES
The attractive **forces** between a liquid and its container, such as water and glass. The balance between adhesive and **cohesive forces** determines whether the **meniscus** of a liquid will be upward or downward.

AGAR
A seaweed extract that forms a gel on which liquid, bacteriological culture media can be solidified.

AIR RESISTANCE
A **force** acting on anything moving through the air, such as a falling object, which slows it down.

ALGAE
Unicellular or **multicellular**, chlorophyll-containing organisms that live in moist or aquatic **habitats**. Formerly thought to be plants, algae are now classified as members of the kingdom Protista.

ALKALI
A **base** that is soluble in water. When an alkali is dissolved, it produces hydroxide **ions**, OH^-.

ALKANE
A **hydrocarbon** in which the carbon **atoms** are joined only to each other or to atoms of other elements, with single bonds. An example is ethane.

ALKENE
A **hydrocarbon** that has one or more double bonds between its carbon **atoms**. An example is ethylene.

ALKYNE
A **hydrocarbon** that has one or more triple bonds between its carbon **atoms**. An example is ethylene.

ALLOTROPES
Forms of the same **element** with different crystalline structures. For example, diamond and graphite are allotropes of carbon.

ALLOY
A mixture of a metal with other metals or nonmetals, in specific proportions, prepared when they are molten. Bronze is an alloy of the metals copper and tin, while steel is an alloy of the metal iron and the nonmetal carbon.

ALPHA DECAY/ ALPHA PARTICLE
The breakup of an unstable atomic **nucleus**, resulting in the release of a **particle** consisting of two **protons** and two **neutrons** – an alpha particle. During alpha decay, the **atomic number** of the nucleus reduces by two and the **atomic mass** reduces by four. See **beta decay**.

ALTERNATING CURRENT (AC)
An **electric current** that reverses in magnitude and direction. Electricity power supply current is AC. Compare **direct current (DC)**.

ALTITUDE
Another word for height. In astronomy, it also refers to the angle of a celestial object above the horizon.

AMINO ACID
Any of a group of water-soluble **organic compounds** that have both a carboxyl (-COOH) and an amino ($-NH_2$) group joined to the same carbon **atom**. By forming peptide bonds, amino acids join together to form short chains – peptides – or longer chains – polypeptides. One or more of these chains make up a **protein**. There are about 20 commonly occurring amino acids.

AMNIOCENTESIS
The withdrawal and sampling of the amniotic fluid, which surrounds the **embryo** in the **uterus**. The amniotic fluid contains **cells** from the embryo, which can be cultured and their chromosomal patterns studied in order to detect any chromosomal abnormalities, such as Down's syndrome.

AMORPHOUS SOLID
Any noncrystalline solid. The **particles** are not regularly arranged, so over time, they can flow. Amorphous solids are often called supercooled liquids or glass.

AMPLITUDE
The maximum value of a continuously varying quantity. For a water **wave**, the amplitude is the height of the wave – half the distance from peak to trough. For a sound wave, the amplitude determines how loud the sound will be.

ANABOLIC REACTION
Any **enzyme**-mediated **chemical reaction** that occurs inside a **cell** and results in the building of complex **compounds**, particularly **proteins**. Compare **catabolic reaction**.

ANAEROBICALLY
Without oxygen. Many animals respire anaerobically.

ANATOMICAL
Relating to anatomy, the study of the parts of a living **organism**.

ANGULAR MOMENTUM
The product of a spinning object's **speed** of rotation and its moment of inertia. An

object's moment of inertia is a measure of how hard it is to get the object spinning.

ANHYDROUS
Describing a substance that has lost its **water of crystallization**. Adding water rehydrates an anhydrous substance.

ANION
An **ion** with a negative **electric charge**, for example the fluoride ion, F$^-$, and the sulfate ion, SO_4^{2-}. Anions are attracted to the **anode** during **electrolysis**.

ANODE
The electrode in an **electrochemical cell** where **oxidation** occurs. The anode is the positive terminal in an electrolytic cell, but negative in a voltaic cell.

ANTENNA
(Life Sciences and Ecology) Long, jointed, paired appendages on the head of many **arthropods**. They usually facilitate smell or touch.

ANTENNA
(Electronics) Another word for an aerial, which receives or transmits **radio waves**.

ANTERIOR
Relating to the front of an **organism**. The opposite of posterior.

ANTHER
The upper, double-lobed part of a plant **stamen**. A **pollen** sac is contained in each lobe. Inside the pollen sacs are pollen grains, which are released when the anther ruptures.

ANTIBIOTIC
A substance obtained from **microorganisms** that destroys or inhibits the growth of certain other microorganisms, particularly **disease**-producing **bacteria** and fungi. Common antibiotics include penicillin and streptomycin.

ANTIBODY
A **protein** that is made by certain white blood cells (lymphocytes), in the body, in response to the invasion of a foreign substance (**antigen**) such as **bacteria**, inhaled pollen grains and dust, and foreign **tissue** grafts.

ANTIGEN
Any substance that the body considers to be foreign and which therefore triggers an immune response.

ANTIPARTICLE
A **particle** that has the same **mass** as another particle, but has an opposite **charge** or some other opposite property.

APHELION
The farthest point from the Sun in the **orbit** of any planet, comet, or artificial satellite.

APPARENT MAGNITUDE
A measure of how bright a celestial object appears in the sky. The brighter an object, the lower its magnitude. Compare **absolute magnitude**.

AQUEOUS SOLUTION
A **solution** in which the **solvent** is water.

ARTICULATED
Describing two bones connected by a **joint**.

ARTHROPOD
Any member of Arthropoda, the largest **phylum** in animal classification. All arthropods have jointed legs and segmented bodies. Spiders, crabs, and houseflies are all arthropods.

ASEXUAL REPRODUCTION
Production of offspring that are **genetically** identical to the parent. This form of reproduction takes place without the formation of **gametes**.

ASTRONOMICAL UNIT
The average distance between the Sun and the Earth. An astronomical unit equals 149,597,870 km (499 light seconds).

ATMOSPHERE
A layer of gases that surround a planet or moon. On some planets and most moons, the **gravitational** force is not strong enough to retain an atmosphere. The Earth's atmosphere supports life and protects it from certain **radiation**; it also prevents the planet from massive fluctuations in **temperature**. See **greenhouse effect**, **atmospheric pressure**.

ATMOSPHERIC PRESSURE
The standard **pressure** of the Earth's **atmosphere** at sea level, equal to about 101 000 Nm^{-2} (101 000 pascals), or 760 mmHg (millimeters of mercury). This pressure is also equal to 1 atm (atmosphere).

ATOM
The smallest part of an **element** that retains its chemical identity. Atoms are electrically neutral. They consist of negatively charged **electrons** that surround a central, positively charged **nucleus**.

ATOMIC FORCE MICROSCOPE
A device used to produce images of **atoms**. A probe scans a solid surface, closely following the contours of its atoms. A computer converts the probe's motion into an image of the surface atoms.

ATOMIC MASS
The total **mass** of **protons** and **neutrons** in the **nucleus** of an **atom**, expressed in atomic mass units. Fluorine-19, with nine protons and ten neutrons, has an atomic mass of 19. Also known as relative atomic mass (**RAM**).

ATOMIC NUCLEUS
See **nucleus**.

ATOMIC NUMBER
The number of **protons** present in the **nucleus** of an **atom**.

ATP
Abbreviation for "adenosine triphosphate," the name of a chemical used as a carrier of chemical **energy** in the **cells** of all living things.

AUTOTROPH
Literally means "self-feeding." Any **organism** that produces food, normally by **photosynthesis**, is an autotroph. Compare **heterotroph**.

AXIAL TILT
The angle between the **axis** of a planet and the **ecliptic** plane.

AXIS
An imaginary line about which an object is symmetrical or about which it spins. In astronomy, axis is taken as axis of rotation, the line (north-south) about which plan a planet rotates.

B

BACTERIUM
Unicellular organism of the kingdom Protista. A bacterial **cell** lacks a membrane, but has a **nucleus** and a cell wall. Some bacteria are **disease**-causing **parasites**.

BASE
(Chemistry) A **compound** that can accept **protons** (hydrogen ions, H⁺) to neutralize **acids** and produce a salt and water.

BASE
(Life Sciences and Ecology) Any of the four nitrogen-containing **organic** compounds that link to the sugar phosphate chain in **DNA**. Bases are the fundamental units of the **genetic code**.

BETA DECAY/
BETA PARTICLE
The breakup of an unstable atomic **nucleus**, resulting in the release of a fast-moving **electron**. This electron is called a beta **particle**. During beta decay, the **atomic number** of the nucleus increases by one. This is because a **neutron** changes into a **proton**, releasing the electron, the **atomic mass** is unchanged. See **alpha decay**.

BILE
Also known as gall. A greenish, bitter-tasting fluid produced in the liver. It helps to digest fats.

BINARY
The number system based on the number two. It has only two digits (binary digits, or bits), "0" and "1". Binary is well suited to arithmetic and logical operations in computers. Inside a computer, binary digits are represented by electric pulses that may be "off" or "on". See **binary addition**.

BINARY ADDITION
Addition in base 2 (binary). The rules governing binary addition are the same as those for addition in base 10, except that the binary system uses only two digits, "0" and "1". In binary, *0 + 1 = 1* and *1 + 1 = 10* (number *2* in binary).

BIOCHEMICALS
A term generally used to encompass those **organic** compounds directly involved in vital processes within a living **organism**, such as **DNA** and **enzymes**.

BIODIVERSITY
A measure of the total number or variety of **species**, in a particular area. Rainforests, for example, have high biodiversity.

BIOSPHERE
The name given to the total area of the Earth's surface (including the seas) that is inhabited by living things.

BLOOD
A fluid **tissue**, which has many vital functions within animals, especially the transport of oxygen and food for **respiration**.

BLOOD CAPILLARY
The smallest type of **blood vessel**, which forms a link between arteries and veins.

BLOOD VESSEL
Any of the tubes of the **vascular system** in an animal. In humans, arteries carry blood from the heart, and veins carry blood to the heart.

BROWNIAN MOTION
The random motion of small solid objects, such as smoke **particles**, which can be observed under a microscope. It is caused by **atoms** and **molecules** of liquid or **gas** bombarding the solid objects.

BUBBLE CHAMBER
A device used to detect subatomic **particles** in collisions that take place in particle accelerators.

BURNING
The rapid combination of a substance with oxygen; it is an **exothermic** reaction. Also called combustion.

C

CESARIAN SECTION
A surgical operation which is carried out to remove a fetus (unborn young) from a **uterus**.

CALCAREOUS
Consisting of or containing calcium carbonate. In anatomy, the term is applied to any buildup of the **compound** in the body.

CALCIUM
A chemical **element** that is found in bones. It is a metallic element in group 2 of the periodic table.

CANOPY
The highest layer of a forest, formed by the branches of the tallest trees. Leaves in the canopy receive the most sunlight and are, therefore, the most successful **photosynthesisers**.

CAPACITANCE
A measure of the capability of an object to store **electric charge**. It is measured in farads (F).

CAPILLARY ACTION
The rising or falling of a liquid in a narrow tube, above or below the liquid surface, due to **surface tension**. The narrower the tube, the higher the liquid will rise or fall.

CARBOHYDRATE
An **organic compound**, such as a sugar, that only contains the **elements** carbon, hydrogen, and oxygen.

CARBON DIOXIDE
A **compound** with the formula CO_2 and a gas at room temperature. It is a waste product of **respiration** and one of the **reactants** of **photosynthesis**.

CARNIVOROUS
An animal that primarily eats meat. A few plants are described as carnivorous, although they only supplement their diet with insects. Compare **omnivorous** and **herbivorous**.

CARPEL
The female reproductive structure of a flower, typically consisting of **stigma**, **style**, and **ovary**.

CARTILAGINOUS
Fish of the class Elasmobrachii, whose skeleton is made from cartilage, a material common to all **vertebrates**. Cartilage forms the skeleton of vertebrate **embryos** and is replaced by bone as the young grow and mature.

CATABOLIC REACTION
Any **enzyme**-mediated reaction within a **cell** that results in the breakdown of complex **compounds**, with large **molecules**, into simpler chemicals, with smaller molecules. Compare **anabolic reaction**.

CATALYST
A substance that increases the rate of a **chemical reaction** but is itself unchanged at the end of the reaction. An **enzyme** is a biological catalyst.

CATARACT
A clouding of the lens of the eye, which usually occurs during old age.

CATHODE
The **electrode** in an **electrochemical cell** where **reduction** occurs. The cathode is the negative terminal in an electrolytic cell but the positive one in a voltaic cell.

CATHODE-RAY TUBE
A sealed glass tube used in the display of most televisions. Inside the tube, **electrons** leave a **cathode** and are attracted toward the high-voltage **anode**. The electrons form a beam, sometimes called a cathode ray.

CATION
An **ion** with a positive **electric charge**. Metals readily form cations, such as the copper(II) ion, Cu^{2+}. Cations are attracted to the **cathode** during **electrolysis**.

CELL
(Life Sciences and Ecology)
The basic unit of all living things. Prokaryotic cells do not have a distinct **nucleus**, whereas eukaryotic cells do. All plants and animals consist of **tissues, which** consist of eukaryotic cells.

CELL
(Chemistry) See **electrochemical cell**.

CELSIUS
A **temperature** scale on which water freezes at zero degrees and boils at 100 degrees. Each degree Celsius is equal to one degree **kelvin**. The Celsius scale was once called the Centigrade scale but was renamed in 1948.

CENTRAL NERVOUS SYSTEM
See **nervous system**.

CENTER OF GRAVITY
The point of an object at which clockwise and counter clockwise moments are equal and the object is, therefore, balanced.

CENTRIPETAL FORCE
The **force** needed to keep an object moving in a circle or an **ellipse**. In the case of circular motion, the force is always directed to the center of the circle.

CERN (CONSEIL EUROPEEN POUR LA RECHERCHE NUCLEAIRE)
The European Laboratory for Nuclear Physics based near Geneva on the Swiss-French border and run by 19 European nations.

CFC
Abbreviation for chlorofluorocarbon. Any **compound** formed by replacing some or all of the hydrogen **atoms** of a **hydrocarbon** with chlorine and fluorine atoms. CFCs released in the **atmosphere** attack the ozone layer.

CHAIN REACTION
A process, such as nuclear **fission**, in which each reaction is, in turn, the stimulus for a further reaction.

CHARGE
See **electric charge**.

CHEMICAL REACTION
A process in which **elements** or **compounds** (the **reactants**) change to form different elements or compounds (the **products**). The change may be permanent or reversible. During a chemical reaction, **electrons** are transferred or shared between the reactants.

CHITIN
A complex **carbohydrate**, similar to cellulose, that strengthens the bodies of **invertebrates**.

CHLOROPLAST
An **organelle** found in plant **cells** that undergoes **photosynthesis**. Chloroplasts contain the pigment chlorophyll.

CHOLESTEROL PLAQUE
A thickening of the arteries, which is caused by a buildup of cholesterol; it is a major cause of heart **disease**. Cholesterol plaque is also called atherosclerotic plaque.

CHROMATIC ABERRATION
A defect in a lens, caused by different wavelengths of light being refracted by different amounts as they pass through glass. The image produced by the lens has colored fringes around it. The problem can be solved by using an **achromatic doublet**.

CHROMATOGRAPHY
A technique used to separate a mixture. The various types of chromatography all use a substance, called the stationary phase, that takes up different parts of the mixture at different rates.

CHROMOSOME
A structure found in plant and animal **cells**, consisting of chromatin, which in turn consists largely of **DNA**. All of the **genes** of an **organism** are found in its chromosomes. Humans have 23 pairs of chromosomes in each cell (except **gametes**).

CIRCULATORY SYSTEM
The heart, **blood vessels**, blood, lymph, and lymphatic vessels, which transport substances around the body.

CLINICAL
Relating to the direct observation and treatment of a patient.

CLOUD CHAMBER
A device used to detect and track **particles** resulting from **radioactive** decay. **Alpha** and **beta particles** cause a vapor in the chamber to condense around them, making their tracks visible.

COHESIVE FORCES
The attractive **forces** between **atoms** or **molecules** in a liquid, such as water. Cohesive forces are responsible for **surface tension**.

COLLOID
A type of mixture, similar to a **solution**, in which **particles** of one substance are distributed evenly throughout another. Colloidal particles are larger than those in a solution but smaller than those in a **suspension**.

COMPLEX ION
A type of **ion** in which a central metallic **cation** is combined with surrounding **anions** or **molecules**. Iron and other transition metals form complex ions with water molecules.

COMPLEX NUMBER
A type of number, generally $a + ib$, consisting of a real part (a) and an imaginary part (ib). The real part is a real number, while the imaginary part is a multiple of the square root of -1, written i. An example of a complex number is $7 + 4i$.

COMPONENT
The effect of a **force** in a particular direction. A force can be thought of as a combination of two or more components.

COMPOUND
A pure substance in which **elements** are chemically combined in a definite ratio. In the compound water, H_2O, **atoms** of hydrogen and oxygen are bound together in the ratio 2:1. Compounds with **covalent bonding** generally consist of **molecules**.

COMPOUND EYE
The eye of an insect, consisting of many, individual visual units.

COMPRESSION
The action of squashing a substance so that it takes up a smaller space. When a gas is compressed, its **pressure** increases. When a solid is compressed, **reaction forces** are produced. These forces are responsible for the strength of a solid.

CONCAVE
Shaped like the inside of a bowl. Concave mirrors make parallel light rays **converge**. Concave lenses make parallel light rays **diverge**.

CONCENTRATION
The amount of a dissolved substance (solute) present in unit volume of **solution**. Molar concentration has units of **moles** per liter (mol l^{-1} or mol dm^{-3}). The units of mass concentration are kilograms per liter (kg l^{-1} or kg dm^{-3}).

CONDUCTIVE
Describes a material that allows **electric current** to flow through it easily. A material with a high conductivity allows electricity to flow easily and is called a conductor. The term can be used to describe heat flow, as well as the flow of electricity.

CONE
(Human Anatomy) A type of **cell** at the back of the human eye (the retina), which is sensitive to light in a particular color range. The cones allow for color vision. There are three types of cone cells: red-, green-, and blue-sensitive.

CONE
(Life Sciences and Ecology) A reproductive structure that is common to all gymnosperms, such as pines and ferns.

CONE
(Mathematics) A solid (three-dimensional) figure with a circular or **elliptical** base and an apex (point).

CONSTANT
A term in an algebraic equation that does not change its value. Compare **variable**.

CONSTRUCTIVE INTERFERENCE:
The combination of two **waves** where the waves are "in step" – the peaks of one wave correspond to the peaks of the other.

CONVECTION
A process by which heat is transferred within a fluid (liquid or gas), by the movement of the fluid. For example, hot air rises and is replaced by cold air; this is an important factor in determining weather patterns.

CONVERGE
To come together. For example, parallel light rays come together when they come to a point of focus.

CONVEX
Shaped like the outside of a bowl, when it is turned upside down. Convex lenses make parallel light rays **converge**. Convex mirrors make parallel light rays **diverge**.

COSMIC BACKGROUND RADIATION (CBR)
Electromagnetic radiation in the microwave region of the **spectrum** that emanates from every region of space. Also known as **microwave background radiation**. It is the strongest evidence of the Big Bang.

COTYLEDON
Part of a plant **embryo** that either stores food or grows to become the first leaves to undergo **photosynthesis**. Flowering plants are classified as **monocotyledons** or **dicotyledons**, according to whether they possess one or two cotyledons.

COVALENT BONDING
A type of chemical bonding in which **electrons** are shared between the **atoms** involved. **Compounds** that exhibit this type of bonding are called covalent compounds.

CRITICAL ANGLE
The angle at or above which light, striking the boundary between two different materials, undergoes total internal reflection.

CRUSTACEAN
Any member of the class Crustacea. This class consists of mainly marine or freshwater **arthropods**, such as crabs.

CRYOGENIC UNIT
Device used to reduce the temperature of substances to very low values, often only a few degrees above absolute zero.

CRYSTAL
A regular arrangement of **atoms**, **ions**, or **molecules** in a solid. This regular internal structure leads to a geometrically regular external shape. Sodium chloride crystals, for example, are cubic.

CRYSTAL LATTICE
A regular, repeating arrangement of **atoms** or **molecules** in a solid. See **unit cell**.

CURRENT
See **electric current**.

CYTOPLASM
A jellylike material that surrounds the **nucleus** of a **cell** and contains most of the cell's **organelles**.

D

DECOMPOSITION
Any **chemical reaction** in which a **compound** breaks down into simpler compounds or **elements**. Many compounds decompose upon heating or **electrolysis**.

DEEP MUSCLE
Any large muscle that is situated deep under the skin. Deep muscles in the back are responsible for rotation, extension, and flexion of the spine.

DEHYDRATING AGENT
Removes water from another substance in a **chemical reaction** called dehydration. Some dehydrating agents can remove hydrogen and oxygen in the ratio 2:1 to make water where there was none before.

DENSITY
A measure of the concentration of **mass** in a substance. The numerical value for density is calculated by dividing the mass of a given amount of the substance by its volume.

DENTITION
The type, number, and arrangement of teeth in an animal.

DESTRUCTIVE INTERFERENCE
The combination of two **waves** where the waves are "out of step." This means that the peaks of one wave correspond to the troughs of the other.

DIAGNOSIS
The act of identifying a **disease** or any other medical condition, by its **symptoms**.

DIAPHRAGM
A powerful muscle, which is essential to breathing, located in the **abdomen** of the mammal. When it contracts, the diaphragm causes the lungs to expand, drawing in air.

DIATOMIC
Relating to a **molecule** that is made up of two **atoms**, for example hydrogen.

E

DICOTYLEDON (DICOT)
See cotyledon.

DIELECTRIC
Any material between the plates of a capacitor (electronic component); normally chosen to increase the **capacitance** of the capacitor.

DIFFRACTION
The bending of **waves** around the edge of an object. When the rays pass through a narrow gap, they bend outward from the edges of the gap so that the light spreads out.

DIFFRACTION GRATING
A device for producing **spectra**, normally of visible light. The most common type of grating consists of a glass plate ruled with thousands of lines.

DIFFUSION
The mixing of substances, caused by the random motion of their **particles**. Diffusion is most noticeable in gases, because the movement of the particles is much faster than in liquids or solids.

DIGESTION
The process by which the large, complex **molecules** in food are broken down into simpler compounds that can be used by the body in activities such as **respiration**.

DIRECT CURRENT
An **electric current** that does not change direction, although its magnitude may vary. Compare **alternating current**.

DISEASE
Any impairment of the vital functions of an **organism**, often caused by a virus or a **parasitic bacterium**. Diseases can also be caused by a deficiency of substances, such as vitamins.

DISPLACEMENT
A movement away from, or the distance of an object from its normal position.

DISPLACEMENT REACTION
A **chemical reaction** in which one **atom**, **ion**, or **molecule** replaces another. Zinc displaces copper from a **solution** of copper(II) ions, Cu^{2+}.

DISTILLATION
Boiling a liquid to vaporize it and then condensing the vapor back into a liquid in a separate vessel. Distillation is used to separate the **solute** from the **solvent** in a **solution**. A mixture of liquids with different boiling points is separated out by fractional distillation.

DIVERGE
To move apart, as parallel light rays do when they pass through a **concave** lens.

DIVISION
The level below kingdom in the classification of plants. The names of all the divisions end in -phyta, for example Bryopyhta.

DNA
Deoxyribonucleic acid. A complex **molecule** with the shape of a double-stranded helix. DNA is found in most living **organisms** and carries the hereditary information that is used in the synthesis (formation) of **proteins**. Compare **RNA**.

DOMAIN
Tiny magnetized regions, between 0.1 and 1 mm across, which occur within magnetic materials. In an unmagnetized state, the domains cancel each other out. When a material is magnetized, the domains are made to line up with each other.

DOUBLE DECOMPOSITION
A **chemical reaction** between two salts in which **ions** or radicals are exchanged, usually in **solution**.

ECCENTRIC
Describing an **orbit** that is not circular. The difference between **aphelion** and **perihelion** is greater for planets with eccentric orbits.

ECHOLOCATION
A method used by some animals to locate objects. It involves the detection of echoes of pulsed sound that are produced by the animals themselves.

ECLIPTIC PLANE
The plane of the Earth's **orbit**. On the celestial sphere, the ecliptic plane appears as the path followed annually by the Sun in the sky.

ECTOTHERMIC
Relating to an animal that derives its body heat from external sources; reptiles are ectothermic.

ECOSYSTEM
A community of **organisms** and their physical surroundings.

EFFLORESCENT
Describing a substance that loses some or all of its **water of crystallization** to the air, forming a new, often powdery substance. If all the water is lost, the **anhydrous** form results.

ELASTICITY
The ability of a substance to regain its size and shape after being stretched by **forces** of **tension**. Forces of attraction between **atoms** within the substance are made stronger when the atoms are pulled apart. These forces are responsible for elasticity.

ELECTRIC CHARGE
A property of certain **particles** or substances that results in **electrostatic forces**. There are two types or signs of charges – positive and negative. The numbers of positive and negative charges in matter is normally balanced, giving no overall charge. See **ion**.

ELECTRIC CURRENT
The movement of **particles** with **electric charge**. Most electric currents are the result of moving **electrons**. The movement of electrons is caused by **electrostatic** or **electromagnetic forces**.

ELECTRIC FIELD
A region in which a **particle** with **electric charge** will experience an **electrostatic force**.

ELECTROCHEMICAL CELL
A **system** that consists of an **electrolyte**, two **electrodes** (a **cathode** and an **anode**), and an external electric circuit. There are two basic types of electrochemical cells: the electrolytic cell, used in electrolysis and electroplating, and the voltaic cell, found in household batteries.

ELECTRODE
A plate made from an electrical **conductor**, sometimes graphite but usually metal, that is used in **electrochemical cells**. In a cell, one electrode is the **anode**, the other is the **cathode**.

ELECTROLYSIS
A process in which a **chemical reaction** occurs as a result of an **electric current** being passed through an **electrolyte**. **Decomposition** of **compounds** can be achieved by electrolysis.

ELECTROLYTE
A paste, liquid, or **solution** containing **ions** that conducts an **electric current**. The current is carried by electrically charged **ions**, which move toward the oppositely charged **electrode**. Sodium chloride solution and molten sodium chloride are both electrolytes.

ELECTROMAGNET
A device made by winding a continuous coil of wire around an iron core. **Electric current** flowing through the wire creates magnetism that lines up the **domains** in the iron. This turns the iron into a temporary magnet.

ELECTROMAGNETIC FORCE
The **forces** on **electric charges** moving in a **magnetic field**. The size and direction of the force depends upon the **speed**, sign, and size of the charge, and on the strength and direction of the magnetic field.

ELECTROMAGNETIC RADIATION
A form of **energy** that travels through space and matter. It is associated with **electric fields** and **magnetic fields,** and behaves as a **wave** motion involving these fields. It also behaves as a stream of particles called **photons**. The many types of radiation include light waves, **radio waves**, and **X rays**.

ELECTROMAGNETIC SPECTRUM
The range of **electromagnetic radiation**. Each type of radiation is identical except for its **wavelength** and its **energy**. Radiation types with short wavelengths and high energy include **X rays** and **gamma rays**, while longer-wavelength and lower-energy radiation includes **infrared** and **radio waves**.

ELECTROMOTIVE FORCE
The **force** on a **particle** with **electric charge**. In an electric circuit, the emf is supplied by a battery or by a power pack connected to mains electricity.

ELECTRON
A particle carrying a negative **electric charge** that is found in all **atoms**. In a neutral atom, there are equal numbers of **protons** and electrons.

ELECTRON SHELL
A set of **orbitals** in an **atom**, where **electrons** may be found. The first shell, closest to the **nucleus**, holds up to two electrons in an s-orbital. The second shell has one s- and three p-orbitals, holding up to eight electrons, while the third shell, which also has five d-orbitals, can hold up to 18.

Usually shells are filled progressively from the first shell outward. Across a period, from group 1 through group 18, empty orbitals up to the current shell are filled. Moving from a group 18 element to the next (group 1) element, a new shell is begun.

ELECTROPLATING
A process in which metal **cations** from an **electrolyte** are deposited as a thin layer onto the surface of a metal object that has been used as the **cathode**. Many items, from spoons to car bodies, are electroplated.

ELECTROSCOPE
An instrument for measuring the extent of imbalanced **electric charge** in an object. The most common example is a glass box with two pieces of gold foil that are pushed apart as they are charged by **induction**.

ELECTROSTATIC FORCE
The **forces** between **electric charges**. Two charges of the same sign will push apart, or repel. Charges of different signs pull together, or attract.

ELEMENT
A substance containing **atoms** with the same atomic number. Every **element** has characteristic chemical properties. There are 91 naturally occurring elements on Earth.

ELLIPSE
A shape that looks like a flattened circle. The **orbits** of the planets are ellipses.

EMBRYO
An animal before it has hatched or been born. A human embryo is called a fetus after eight weeks of pregnancy. An embryo is also the structure in many plants that develops from the **zygote** and becomes a new plant.

EMPIRICAL
Describing a result or formula that is gained directly from observation or experiment.

ENDOTHERMIC
Describing a **chemical reaction** during which heat **energy** is taken in from the surroundings and converted into chemical energy.

ENERGY
The ability to make something happen. Energy must be expended in order to do **work**. Although the total amount of energy in the universe is constant, it can take many interchangeable forms. The two basic forms of energy are **potential energy** and **kinetic energy**.

ENVIRONMENT
The surroundings in which an **organism** live, and its chemical, physical, and biological conditions.

ENZYME
A **catalyst** that is found in, or derived from, a living **organism**. Enzymes increase the rate of **chemical reactions** and are highly specific, usually catalyzing a particular step in a long and complex chain of reactions. Nearly all enzymes are **proteins**.

EQUATOR
An imaginary line around the middle of the Earth, at equal distances from the two (geographical) poles. Other planets and the Sun also have equators. The Earth's equator is at **latitude** 0°.

EQUILIBRIUM
A stable state in a reversible **chemical reaction**. Such a reaction can be thought of as two simultaneous reactions (the forward and reverse reactions). The reactions are in equilibrium when they proceed at the same rate, so there is no overall change.

ERECTILE
Biological **tissue** that has the ability to become rigid. The penis consists largely of erectile tissue, which stiffens when blood is temporarily trapped inside it.

ERROR BAR
A vertical or horizontal line drawn on a **graph** to indicate the margin of accuracy with which a particular measurement is taken.

EROSION
Any process by which landforms are worn away. Agents of erosion include rivers, ocean waves, and glaciers.

EUKARYOTE
Any **organism** with **cells** that have their **genetic** material contained within a **nucleus**.

EVAPORATION
The loss of **atoms** or **molecules** from a liquid as they break free of the liquid to become a vapor. Evaporation takes place below the boiling **temperature** of the liquid.

EVOLUTION
The gradual process that gives rise to new **species** through adaptation to the **environment**. The adaptation of species to their environment takes place by natural selection.

EXCITED
In possession of extra **energy**. **Electrons** in **atoms** can be excited by heat or light energy. When this is so, they occupy a new position in the atom, depending on their new energy.

EXOTHERMIC
A **chemical reaction** during which chemical energy of the **reactants** is converted to heat energy and given off to the surroundings. Exothermic reactions are generally accompanied by a rise in **temperature**.

EXTENSOR
Any muscle that straightens or extends a **joint**. Compare **flexor**.

EXTINCT
A **species** whose population has declined to zero.

F

FACIAL MUSCLE
Any of the **superficial muscles** of the face. Facial muscles are controlled by certain pairs of the cranial nerves.

FAHRENHEIT
Scale of **temperature** on which water freezes at 32 degrees and boils at 212 degrees.

FAST-ACTING DRUG
A drug that is administered directly into the bloodstream.

FERTILIZATION
The process by which the **nuclei** of male and female **gamete cells** join, or fuse.

FIBROBLAST
A **cell** that produces fibers in connective **tissue**.

FILAMENT
(Physics) The fine wire in an incandescent light bulb. The filament heats up when **electric current** flows through it and at high **temperatures** it glows.

FILAMENT
(Life Sciences and Ecology) The stalk of the **stamen** within a flower.

FILTRATION
A method for separating **suspensions**. The suspension is passed through a filter, often made of paper, which is perforated by tiny holes.

FIRST AID
Emergency medical care that is administered by the first person to arrive at the scene of an accident.

FISSION
(Physics) The splitting of unstable **nuclei** of **atoms**. It may result in a **chain reaction**.

FISSION
(Life Sciences and Ecology) **Asexual reproduction** of some single-celled **organisms**, during which the single parent cell splits to form two or more daughter cells.

FLEXOR
Any muscle that bends or flexes a **joint**. Compare **extensor**.

FLUID
Any substance that flows. Liquids and gases are both fluids.

FLUORESCENCE
A type of **luminescence** in which a substance glows with visible light immediately after being **excited** by invisible **ultraviolet radiation**.

FOCAL LENGTH
The distance from a lens or curved mirror at which a parallel beam of light becomes focused.

FOOD WEB
A set of interrelationships between **organisms** in an **ecosystem**.

FORCE
A push or a pull that can cause an object to speed up, slow down, or change direction.

FOSSIL
Traces of ancient plants or animals that are preserved in geological formations, in particular **sedimentary rocks**.

FOSSIL FUEL
Coal, oil, or natural gas. These substances were formed from the remains of ancient plants or animals. See **fossil**.

FRAME OF REFERENCE
In relativity theory, a particular set of Cartesian axes, with its origin centered about the observer. Observers moving relative to each other have different frames of reference.

FREQUENCY
The regularity with which something happens. It is most often applied to a **wave** or vibration. A wave's frequency is the number of times its complete cycle occurs each second. Frequency is measured in hertz (Hz).

Higher-frequency vibrations produce higher-pitched sounds.

FULCRUM
The point about which an object turns. For example, the fulcrum of a lever is its pivot.

FUNCTION
A mathematical relationship between two or more **variables**. It may be expressed by an algebraic equation. $y = 2x$ is an example of a function involving the variables y and x.

FUSION
A joining of small **nuclei** of **atoms** to form larger nuclei. In some cases there is a release of **energy** during the process.

G

GAMETE
A sex **cell**, which may be male or female, found in an animal or plant that reproduces sexually.

GAMMA RAYS
Electromagnetic radiation with a **wavelength** of $10[^{-10}]$ to $10[^{-14}]$ m. Gamma rays are normally released during a **nuclear reaction**.

GAS
One of the states of matter, in which the **particles** (**atoms** or **molecules**) are practically free from one another.

GAS GIANT
A planet that is composed mainly of gases (methane and ammonia are most common). Compare **terrestrial planet**.

GAUGE BOSON
A **particle** exchanged between two interacting **particles**. At the submicroscopic level of the tiniest particles, the exchange is responsible for producing **forces**.

GEIGER–MULLER TUBE
A device for detecting **radioactivity**. When **alpha** or **beta particles** enter, an **electric current** flows between the wall of the tube and a metal wire at its center.

GENE
The unit of inheritance. Genes are composed of lengths of **DNA** and each length holds the **genetic code** for a single **protein**.

GENERATOR
A machine that produces an electrical **voltage** whenever its rotor is turned. The **kinetic energy** of the rotor becomes electrical energy because of the presence of coils and magnets.

GENETIC CODE
The means by which genetic information is coded in **DNA**. The information is held as a sequence of DNA **bases**.

H

GENETIC DISORDER
A disease caused by a mutation (usually inherited) in the **genetic code**.

GENETIC VARIATION
The difference between individual **organisms** within a particular species. Genetic variation is normally inherited and is due to differences in the **genotype** between indiviuals of the same **species**, for example eye color in humans.

GENOME
All the **genes** held on a single set of **chromosomes**. In sexual reproduction, each parent gives its genome to the offspring.

GENOTYPE
The entire **genetic code** of an **organism**, which is held on all the **chromosomes**.

GERM
Any **microorganism** that causes **disease**.

GILL
The part of a fish (and certain amphibians) that is involved in **respiration**. Oxygen and carbon dioxide is exchanged (between the water and the animal's blood supply) in the gills.

GLAND
A group of **cells**, in plants or animals, that releases particular substances. An example is the thyroid gland, which releases two **hormones** into the **circulatory system**.

GLUON
According to modern scientific theory, gluons are the **particles** responsible for carrying the **strong nuclear force**. See **gauge boson**.

GRAPH
A visual representation showing a set of results of an experiment. A graph will highlight any relationships between the various types of data.

GRAVITATION
See **gravity**.

GRAVITY
A **force** of attraction between all objects with **mass**. The size of the force depends upon the masses of the two objects and the distance between the objects. Some modern theorists believe that **gravity** is carried by particles known as gravitons. See **gauge boson**.

GREENHOUSE EFFECT
The mechanism that results in global warming. **Ultraviolet** and visible light pass easily through the **atmosphere**, but are re-radiated as **infrared**, which is absorbed by "greenhouse gases," such as carbon dioxide. Because the radiation cannot pass through the **atmosphere**, the **temperature** of the Earth is gradually increasing.

GROUNDWATER
Any water below ground, either held in the soil or in underground lakes and caves.

GYROSCOPE
Usually a spinning metal disk supported in a metal cage, although it can also refer to any spinning object. Gyroscopes have stability because they spin.

HABITAT
The place where an **organism** lives. An earthworm's habitat is the soil.

HADRON
Any **particle** that is composed of **quarks**. Examples are the **proton** and the pi **meson**.

HERBIVOROUS
Relating to animals that primarily eat vegetation. Compare **carnivorous** and **omnivorous**.

HETEROTROPH
Any **organism** that derives its **energy** from the intake and digestion of plants or animals. All animals are heterotrophs. Compare **autotroph**.

HIGGS BOSON
Hypothetical **particle** whose existence would link together the **electromagnetic force** and the weak interaction, explaining why particles have **mass**.

HIGH-FREQUENCY SOUND WAVE
See **Frequency**.

HOLE
A vacant **electron** position within the crystal lattice of a **semiconductor** that can be thought of as a positive **electric charge**.

HORMONE
A chemical **compound** secreted by a **gland** in the body that regulates growth or the function of an **organ**. Examples of this are insulin and follicle stimulating hormone. Hormones also promote growth in plants.

HOST
In a **parasitic** relationship between two **species**, the host is the **organism** that provides shelter or nutrition for another organism.

HUMAN CHORIONIC GONADOTROPHIN (HCG)
A **hormone** secreted by a human **embryo** and later by the **placenta**. Urine-based pregnancy tests display a positive result if they detect hCG.

HYBRIDIZATION
The formation of new bonding **orbitals** from the combination of two others. For example, diamond consists of carbon **atoms** joined to four others by sp³ hybrid orbitals, each one a combination of an s- and a p-orbital.

HYDROCARBON
A **compound** containing only the **elements** carbon and hydrogen. Hydrocarbons are classed as **organic compounds**.

HYDROGEN BONDING
Weak bonding between some **molecules** that contain hydrogen **atoms**. It is caused by the uneven distribution of **electric charge** within the molecules. Hydrogen bonding is found in water and is responsible for its relatively high boiling point.

HYDRONIUM ION
Also called a hydroxonium or oxonium ion. This is an **ion** with formula H_3O^+, which consists of a **proton** or hydrogen ion, H^+, associated with a water **molecule**, H_2O. Hydronium ions form in equal numbers with hydroxide ions, OH^-, when water splits into ions. In a **solution** of an **acid**, the concentration of H_3O^+ is higher than that of OH^-.

HYDROSTATIC SKELETON
The part of certain animals, such as earthworms, that is held rigid by fluid **pressure**.

HYGROSCOPIC
Describing a substance that absorbs water from the air.

HYPOTHALAMUS
A part of the brain (situated near the center, below the thalamus) that controls several basic body functions, including **temperature** regulation.

IJK

IGNEOUS ROCKS
One of the three main types of rocks, together with **sedimentary** and **metamorphic**. Igneous rocks form from **magma** that solidifies. Granite is an example of an igneous rock.

IMAGE
A picture formed by a lens or a curved mirror. Images cast on screens by **convex** lenses are called real images, while those seen through telescopes or microscopes, which cannot be directly projected, are called virtual images.

IMMUNOLOGICAL REACTION
The production of **antibodies** when the body is infected by foreign substances. During **vaccination**, foreign **disease**-causing substances, such as **antigens,** cause an immune response that protects the body from further, more virulent **infection**.

IMMUNOLOGY
The study of the immune system of humans and other animals.

IN PARALLEL
Describing part of an electric circuit that splits at one point and rejoins again. Two or more components in parallel receive the same **voltage**. Compare **in series**.
.

IN SERIES
Describing part of a circuit in which the components are connected one after the other. The electric **current** through each circuit component is the same, but the **voltage** across each component may be different. Compare **in parallel**.

INCISION
A cut made during a surgical operation.

INCUBATION
The process of keeping an unhatched egg warm before it hatches. Birds normally incubate their eggs by sitting on them to insulate them with their feathers.

INDICATOR
A substance, usually based on natural plant material, whose color changes according to the **acidity** or **alkalinity (pH)** of its environment. Indicators such as litmus solution and universal indicator are used in chemical analysis.

INDUCTION
The apparent charging of one object by an **electrically charged** object nearby. The charging is apparent, since it is only a shift of electric charge within the object. Induction is the magnetization of iron objects in the presence of a magnet. The **domains** inside the iron line up with the **magnetic field** of the magnet.

INERT
Relating to an unreactive chemical **compound**.

INERTIA
The resistance of an object to any change in its motion.

INFECTION
The invasion of a **host** by a **disease**-causing **parasite** such as a **bacterium**. An infection can also be a name for an affected area.

INFRARED RADIATION
A type of **electromagnetic radiation**, with a **wavelength** that is longer than visible light.

INSULATION
The covering or wrapping up of an object with a material that does not conduct heat well. Some animals are covered with insulating fur.

INTERCOSTAL MUSCLE
Muscle that lies between the ribs.

INTERFERENCE
The combination of two or more **waves**.

INVERTEBRATE
An animal without a backbone.

ION
A **particle** with **electric charge**, formed when an **atom** gains or loses **electrons**. A positive **ion** is called a **cation**, and a negative ion is an **anion**. Groups of atoms with electric charge (sometimes called radicals) may also be called ions. An example is the carbonate ion, $CO_3{}^{2-}$.

IONIC BONDING
A type of bonding in which **cations** and **anions** are held together by **forces** due to their **electric charges**. The **ions** form a **crystal** structure called a **macromolecule**.

ISOTOPE
One of the possible forms of an **element** that differ in their nuclear structure. Although all **atoms** of a particular element have the same number of **protons** in the **nucleus**, there may be different numbers of **neutrons**. Different isotopes of an element have the same chemical properties but different **RAMs**.

JOINT
The point of contact between two bones. There are three main types of joints: immovable joints; slightly movable joints; and freely movable joints.

KL

KELVIN SCALE
The absolute scale of **temperature**. The Kelvin scale begins at **absolute zero** and, unlike the **Celsius** and **Fahrenheit** scales, does not rely on fixed points.

KINETIC ENERGY
The **energy** that a **particle** or an object possesses due to its motion or vibration. The more **mass** an object has and the faster it moves, the more kinetic energy it possesses. Heat energy is the kinetic energy of the random motion of the **atoms**, **ions**, and **molecules** that make up matter.

KREBS CYCLE
A series of **chemical reactions** in plants and animals that respire aerobically. The most important yield of the Krebs cycle is **ATP** (adenosine triphosphate), which is a source of **energy** for the **cell**'s vital functions.

LATENT HEAT
Heat **energy** that melts a solid or vaporizes a liquid. Latent heat does not raise the **temperature** of the substance.

LATITUDE
With **longitude**, one of two coordinates that defines any position on the Earth's surface. Latitude ranges from 90° south (South Pole) through to 0° (**equator**), and up to 90° north (North Pole).

LENS
A curved piece of glass or other transparent material that refracts light and can form **images**.

LIGAMENT
A tough but flexible strand of **tissue** that holds two bones together at a movable **joint**.

LIGHT YEAR
The distance light travels in one year in free space, measuring approximately 9.465×10^{12} km (5.879×10^{12} miles).

M

LIMITING FRICTION
The **force** that must be overcome to start an object moving when it is in contact with a surface.

LITHOSPHERE
The Earth's outermost solid layer. Also referred to as the crust, although the liquid mantle and the core are sometimes included in the definition.

LONGITUDE
Along with **latitude**, longitude is one of two coordinates that defines any position on the Earth's surface. Longitude is an angular measure, with 0° passing through Greenwich, London.

LUMINESCENCE
The emission of light due to a decrease in the energy level of an **excited electron** within an **atom** or **molecule**. The two main types are **fluorescence** and **phosphorescence**.

LUMINOSITY
A measure of the total amount of **energy** radiated by a star. Luminosity is directly related to **absolute magnitude** and less directly related to **apparent magnitude**.

MACROMOLECULE
Any **molecule** with an **RMM** greater than about 10,000. The term is often used to refer to ionic crystals, such as those of sodium chloride.

MAGMA
Molten material found in the Earth's mantle that forms **igneous rocks** when it cools.

MAGNETIC FIELD
A field of **force** around a magnet's poles or around a wire carrying an **electric current**.

MAIN SEQUENCE
The main part of the evolution of a star. The Sun is a main sequence star. The term is related to the Hertzsprung-Russell diagram.

MASS
The measure of an object's **inertia**. Mass is also defined in terms of **gravitation**. The gravitational **force** between two objects depends upon their masses.

MATTER
The matter that inhabits space. Matter has **mass** and therefore **inertia**.

MELTING POINT
The **temperature** at which a solid substance becomes a liquid. It is dependent upon **atmospheric pressure**.

MENISCUS
The curved surface of a liquid where it meets its container. It is caused by a combination of **adhesive** and **cohesive forces**.

MENSTRUAL CYCLE
The repeating period, of about one month, during which eggs (ova) are released from the **ovaries** of primates, including human females.

MESON
A **hadron** consisting of two **quarks**. An example is the pi meson, which carries the strong nuclear **force** between **protons** and **neutrons** within the **nucleus**.

METABOLIC RATE
A measure of how quickly metabolic reactions occur within a human body. People with a high metabolic rate are more likely to be thin.

METAMORPHIC ROCK
Relating to rocks that are formed as **sedimentary** or **igneous** rocks and are subjected to high **pressures** or **temperature** in the Earth's crust. Metamorphic rocks consist of the same **minerals** but have different **crystal** structures.

METAMORPHOSIS
The transformation of the larval stage of certain amphibians and **invertebrates** into the adult stage. Metamorphosis often involves the growth of legs or wings.

MICROMETER
A device used to measure very small **displacements**.

MICROORGANISM
An **organism** that is too small to be seen without the aid of a microscope, such as a **bacterium**. Microorganisms are also known as microbes.

MICROWAVE RADIATION
Electromagnetic waves with a short **wavelength**. Microwaves are produced in a similar way to **radio waves**, but they have a higher **frequency**.

MINERAL
Any **element** or **compound**, normally occurring naturally as **crystals**. Rocks consist of two or more minerals.

MITOCHONDRION
A structure found in all plant and animal **cells** that is associated with the production of available **energy**. The **enzymes** that take place in the **Krebs cycle** are manufactured in the mitochondria.

MIXTURE
Two or more pure substances (**elements** or **compounds**) that are mixed but not chemically combined. The components of a mixture can be separated by methods such as **chromatography** and **filtration**. **Solutions** and **colloids** are two types of mixtures.

MOLE
A unit of the amount of a substance, defined in terms of the number of **particles** that are present. One mole of a substance contains 6.02×10^{23} particles and has a **mass** in grams equal to its **RAM** or **RMM** – so the mass of one mole of copper is 64.4 grams. The quantity 6.02×10^{23} mol^{-1} is Avogadro's number.

MOLECULAR
Pertaining to **molecules**.

MOLECULAR ORBITAL
A region within a **molecule** in which the **electrons** involved in **covalent bonding** are likely to be found. Molecular orbitals are formed by the overlap of the outer **orbitals** of the atoms that are bound together.

MOLECULE
The smallest unit of many **compounds**. It consists of two or more **atoms** held together by **covalent bonding**.

MOMENT
The turning effect of a **force**.

MONOCOTYLEDON (MONOCOT)
See **cotyledon**.

MOTILE
Describing a **microorganism** that can move, often using a "tail," called a *flagellum* or oscillating "hairs," called *cilia*.

MOLT
The loss of hair, feathers, or fur from birds and mammals, or the integument (outer skin) from **arthropods** or reptiles.

N

O

MUCUS
A fluid mixture that is secreted by **cells** in the respiratory system and alimentary canal.

MULTICELLULAR
An **organism** that consistis of more than one **cell**.

MYCORRHIZA
A **symbiotic** relationship between a fungus and the root of a plant.

NEBULA
A hazy object that is observed, most of them only with a telescope, in the night sky. Most nebulae are the birthplaces of stars.

NERVOUS REFLEX
An involuntary muscular action brought about by a particular stimulus.

NERVOUS SYSTEM
The brain, spinal cord (nerve cord in **invertebrates**), and all other **neurons** that carry information between sensory neurons and motor neurons.

NEURON
A long single **cell** within the body of an animal.The brain and spinal cord consist of billions of neurons.

NEUTRON
One of the **particles** in the **nucleus** of an **atom**. It is a **hadron** and has zero **electric charge**.

NEWTON METER
A device used to measure **force**. A pointer moves along a scale as a spring inside the meter extends. The extension of the spring depends upon the force that has been applied.

NIPPLE
The raised center of a mammary gland, present in female mammals, through which lactated milk is made available to newborn young.

NOBLE GAS
Any of the elements of group 18 of the periodic table. These elements are all **gases** at room **temperature** and are very unreactive because their outer **electron shells** are filled.

NUCLEAR FISSION
See **fission**.

NUCLEAR REACTION
A change, such as **fission** and **fusion**, that involves the **nuclei** of **atoms**.

NUCLEOTIDE
The monomer from which the **polymers DNA** or **RNA** are formed.

NUCLEUS
(Life Sciences and Ecology) The part of a **cell** that holds genetic information as **DNA**. **Bacterial cells** have no nucleus.

NUCLEUS
(Physics) The central, positively charged part of an **atom**, made up of **protons** and **neutrons**. The common **isotope** of hydrogen is the only type of atom that does not have neutrons in its nucleus.

NUTRIENT
A substance that gives sustenance to an **organism**.

NUTRIENT MOLECULE
Any **molecule** of the groups of **compounds** essential to a balanced diet. In humans, these groups are **carbohydrates**, **proteins**, fats and vitamins, and **minerals**.

OMNIVOROUS
Relating to animals that eat both meat and vegetation. Compare **carnivorous** and **herbivorous**.

ORBIT
The path of a planet around the Sun, or the path of a satellite around a planet. The orbit exhibits circular motion (or motion in an **ellipse**), with the centripetal **force** supplied by **gravity**.

ORBITAL
The region of space around an **atom**, an **ion**, or a **molecule** where **electrons** are likely to be found. In an atom, the simpler types of orbitals are called s-, p-, and d-orbitals. Atomic orbitals hold up to two electrons each.

ORE
A **mineral** containing metal **atoms**, normally combined with atoms of oxygen or other **elements**.

ORGAN
Any group of **cells** that carries out a specific task within the body of a plant or an animal (including humans).

ORGANELLE
A tiny object within a biological **cell** that carries out a specific function.

ORGANIC
Relating to a **compound** based on chains or rings that are formed by carbon **atoms**. These compounds are the basis of life as we know it. Organic chemistry is the study of such compounds.

ORGANIC MOLECULES
Molecules of **organic compounds**.

ORGANISM
Any living thing.

OSCILLATOR
An electric circuit that produces an alternating **electric current**, which repeatedly changes direction.

PQ

OVARY
The part of a female animal where eggs (ova) are produced. Also, the part of a **carpel** of a flower in which fertilization of the ovules takes place.

OVIPAROUS
An animal that lays eggs outside its body.

OXIDATION
The removal of **electrons** from, or the addition of oxygen to, an **atom**, an **ion**, or a **molecule**. An **element** that is oxidized increases its **oxidation number**.

OXIDATION NUMBER
A positive or negative number that indicates whether an **element** has lost or gained **electrons** during a **chemical reaction**. When copper atoms lose two electrons to form doubly charged copper(II) ions, Cu^{2+}, the oxidation number of copper (initially 0) becomes $+2$, also given by the Roman numeral II.

OXYGEN
A chemical **element** essential to most living **organisms**. It is produced by plants during **photosynthesis** but is used as a **reactant** during animal and plant **respiration**.

OXYGEN FREE RADICAL
A single, negatively charged oxygen **atom**. As with all free radicals, it is highly reactive.

PARABOLA
An important curve used as the basis of the shape of parabolic dishes. It is one of the conic sections.

PARAMEDIC
A medical professional who specializes in **first aid** and who is also trained to carry out certain other medical proceedures.

PARASITE
An **organism** in a **symbiotic** relationship that lives on or in another organism (the **host**). This is a relationship that causes harm to the host.

PARENTAL CARE
The behavior of certain animals that increases the chances of survival of their young.

PARSEC
A standard unit of distance used by astronomers. It is equal to 3.26 **light years**.

PARTICLE
Any tiny, distinct object. The term is specifically applied to **molecules**, **atoms**, and subatomic particles.

PEDIPALP
A sensory appendage in the **anatomy** of spiders and scorpions. In some spiders, the pedipalp is involved in sexual activity, often to carry sperm.

PELVIC REGION
Part of the lower **abdomen** in human **anatomy**. The pelvic girdle is a bony structure, found in all **vertebrates**, to which the posterior (back) legs or dorsal fins are attached.

PELVIS
The lower part of the human **abdomen**, generally defined by the bones of the pelvic girdle.

PENTARADIATE SYMMETRY
Fivefold radial symmetry associated with, for example, starfish.

PERIHELION
The point in an object's **orbit** when it is closest to the body it is orbiting.

PERMANENT MAGNET
Objects with a fixed magnetism. The **domains** in a permanent magnet always align to produce a **magnetic field**. Compare **electromagnet**.

PERMEABILITY
The ability of some rocks (and other substances) to allow water to pass through them.

PH SCALE
A scale that indicates whether a solution is acidic or alkaline. The scale runs from 1 (strong **acid**), through 7 (neutral), to 14 (strong **alkali**). The pH value relates directly to the **concentration** of hydrogen **ions** in the **solution**.

PHARMACOLOGY
The study of the chemical treatment of **disease**.

PHASE
(Astronomy and Astrophysics)
The shape that the illuminated surface of an astronomical object (especially the Moon) appears from Earth. The Moon's phase changes gradually in a repeating monthly cycle.

PHASE
(Electronics)
The stage reached in the cycle of a **wave** or vibration.

PHOSPHORESCENCE
A type of **luminescence** in which a substance glows with visible light some time after being **excited**. A phosphor is any substance exhibiting phosphorescence. Compare **fluorescence**.

PHOTON
A **particle** of **electromagnetic radiation**. The **energy** of a photon depends only upon the **wavelength** of the radiation. A photon can be thought of as a packet of waves.

PHOTOSYNTHESIS
A **chemical reaction** that occurs in green plants, during which the green pigment chlorophyll uses light **energy** to make **carbohydrates**.

PHYLUM
A category in the classification of **organisms**, below kingdom. Human beings are in the phylum Chordata (animals with backbones).

PHYSIOLOGICAL
The study of the vital functions of **organisms**, such as nutrition.

PHYTOPLANKTON
Tiny **autotrophic** marine **organisms** that are fundamental in ocean food webs.

PLACENTA
The **organ** that attaches an **embryo** to the wall of the **uterus**.

PLANE WAVE
A **wave** motion in which the waves are parallel to one another and perpendicular to the direction of the wave's motion.

POLAR NUCLEUS
The **nucleus** of a **cell** during the metaphase stage of meiosis. The two nuclei for the new cells formed during the process occupy opposite ends of the dividing cell and are connected by a fibrous structure called the spindle.

POLLEN
The grains inside **seed**-bearing plants that contain the male **gametes**. They are produced inside the pollen sacs in the **anther**.

POLLINATION
The process by which **pollen** is transferred from the **anther** (male part) of one flower to the **stigma** (female part) of another flower.

POLYGON
A flat shape with straight sides. Examples of polygons are triangles, squares, and pentagons.

POLYHEDRON
A solid (three-dimensional) shape with a **polygon** as each face. The plural of *polyhedron* is *polyhedra* or *polyhedrons*.

POLYMER
A large **molecule** that is formed by the joining of smaller molecules – units called monomers – in a reaction called polymerization.

POSITRON
The **antiparticle** of the **electron**. It is identical to the electron in every way, except that it has a positive **electric charge**.

POTENTIAL ENERGY
Energy that is "stored" in some way. For example, an object held in the air has potential energy by virtue of its height and the **gravitational force** pulling it downward.

PRECIPITATE
A solid substance formed by a **chemical reaction** taking place in a **solution**. Precipitates often form during **double decomposition** reactions.

PREDATOR
A **carnivorous organism** that hunts and eats other animals.

PREHENSILE
Part of the anatomy of an animal that is specially adapted for gripping. Some monkeys have prehensile tails that help them to stay balanced on tree branches.

PRESSURE
A measure of the concentration of a **force**. The pressure exerted by a force is equal to the size of the force divided by the area over which it acts. Solids, liquids, and **gases** exert pressure.

PRIMARY COLOR
Any of a set of three colors, which, when combined in the correct proportion, can produce any other color. The set of primaries for the **additive process** is different from that for the **subtractive process**.

PRINCIPLE OF SUPERPOSITION
The rules governing the **interference** of **waves**.

PRINCIPLE OF THE CONSERVATION OF ENERGY
Energy can be neither created nor destroyed; it can only change or be transferred from one form to another.

PRODUCT
An **element** or **compound** that is formed in a **chemical reaction**.

PROTEIN
An **organic polymer** that contains carbon, hydrogen, oxygen, and nitrogen. Most proteins also contain sulfur.

PROTEIN SEQUENCE
The sequence of **amino acids** that make up a **protein**. Each protein has a unique sequence that is coded for in the genes of an **organism**. See **genetic code**.

PROTEIN STRUCTURE
The structure of a protein depends on the way in which its component polypeptides are arranged. **Proteins** may be described as globular or fibrous.

PROTON
A particle with a positive **electric charge**, which is found in the **nucleus** of every **atom**. The charge on a proton is exactly the opposite of that on an **electron**.

PROTRUSIBLE
A part of an **organism** that can be made to protrude (stick out).

PUPA
The third stage in the life cycle of some insects. It is during this stage that **metamorphosis** takes place, for example when a caterpillar becomes a butterfly.

PYRUVIC ACID
An important carboxylic **acid**, which is essential in **metabolism** as it takes part in the **Krebs cycle**.

QUARK
Particles, such as **protons** and **neutrons**, that combine together to form **hadrons**. No quark has ever been detected in isolation.

QUASAR
Quasars have huge **redshifts** and are the most distant objects known, being up to 10 billion **light years** away.

R

RADAR
An acronym for *radio detection and ranging*. A technique for determining the distance and direction of an object (typically airplanes) by reflecting pulses of **radio waves** off them. It has been applied to mapping the surfaces of planets and their moons.

RADIAL SYMMETRY
A property of some shapes and some **organisms** whereby rotation through a certain angle results in the same appearance of the shape or organism. Starfish, for example, have radial symmetry.

RADIATION
In its most general sense, any transfer of **energy** that moves outward in all directions. The term is most often applied to **electromagnetic radiation** and can also be applied to the product of **radioactivity**.

RADICAL
An **ion**, normally consisting of two or more nonmetals, that generally remains unchanged during a **chemical reaction**. An example is the carbonate ion, CO_3^{2-}.

RADIOACTIVITY
The breakup (disintegration) of certain atomic **nuclei**, accompanied by the release of **alpha**, **beta**, or **gamma** radiation.

RADIO WAVES
Electromagnetic radiation, with a frequency of between 3 kHz (kilohertz) and 300 GHz (gigahertz). Radio waves are normally produced by an **antenna**.

RADIUS
Half the diameter of a circle or sphere.

RAINFALL PATTERN
The average or typical rainfall in a particular region or biome over a year. Often shown visually on a **graph**.

S

RAM
(Chemistry) Abbreviation for *relative atomic mass*. It is the mass of an **atom** of an **element** relative to $\frac{1}{12}$ of the atomic mass of the carbon isotope, carbon-12. RAMs are average values, weighted for the relative natural abundances of different **isotopes** of an element.

RAM
(Electronics) Abbreviation for *random-access memory*. The RAM is part of the computer's memory whose contents can be changed. It consists of integrated circuits, or microchips, that store the data and programs that are fed into the computer. This data can be retrieved from the RAM in any order and can be altered and added to.

RAREFACTION
The lowering of the **density** and **pressure** of a gas; the opposite of **compression**.

RATE OF REACTION
How quickly a **chemical reaction** proceeds. It depends upon various factors, including **temperature**, and may be increased by using a **catalyst**.

REACTANT
An **element** or **compound** that is the starting material of a **chemical reaction**.

REACTION
A **force** produced by an object that is equal and opposite to a force applied to the object.

REACTIVITY
A measure of the ease with which an **atom**, an **ion**, or a **molecule** reacts. **Elements** in groups 1 and 17 of the periodic table are generally the most reactive.

RECEPTOR SITE
The location of a nerve ending that is sensitive to a particular type of stimulus. For example, some painkilling drugs act by blocking pain receptors and preventing the chemicals that stimulate those sites from acting.

REDSHIFT
The apparent shift of a **spectrum** of light, or other **electromagnetic radiation**, to longer **wavelengths**. This is due to the extreme **speed** at which the source of the light is receding from Earth. Galaxies in every direction have redshift, indicating that they are all receding, and suggesting that the universe is expanding.

REDOX REACTION
Any **chemical reaction** that involves the transfer of **electrons** (**reduction** and **oxidation**). Nearly all reactions can be seen as redox reactions.

REDUCTION
The addition of **electrons** to, or the removal of oxygen from, an **atom**, an **ion**, or a **molecule**. The **oxidation number** of an **element** that is reduced decreases.

REFRACTION
The bending of light, or other **electromagnetic radiation**, as it passes from one material to another.

RESISTANCE
A measure of the opposition to the flow of **electric current**. It is the ratio of **voltage** to current.

RESISTANT
A **parasitic**, **disease**-causing **organism** that has evolved a resilience to the drugs and other treatments that would otherwise destroy it.

RESISTOR
An electronic component that has a **resistance** that is determined precisely at the factory. Variable resistors have controllable resistance and may, for example, be used as volume controls in amplifier circuits.

RESPIRATION
The process in plants and animals in which nutrients are broken down, releasing **energy** and waste products. See **aerobic**, **anaerobic**, **Krebs cycle**.

RESULTANT
The combined effect of two or more **forces**.

RETROVIRUS
A **virus** whose RNA produces **DNA** inside the **host cell**. The viral DNA then becomes incorporated into the host's DNA. This is the mechanism for many **viral** diseases.

REVERSIBLE REACTION
A **chemical reaction** in which the **products** react to form the **reactants** once again.

RIBOSOME
A small body within a **cell** that is involved in the transcription (copying) of **DNA**. A ribosome consists of **RNA** and a **protein**.

RILL
A stream or brook.

RMM
Abbreviation for relative molecular mass. RMM is the sum of the **RAMs** of the **elements** that make up a **compound**. For example, the RMM of water, H_2O, is 18, this is because the RAM of hydrogen is 1 and the RAM of oxygen is 16.

RNA
Abbreviation for ribonucleic acid. RNA is a complex chemical **compound** that is found in all **viruses** and cells during transcription (copying) of **DNA**, when **proteins** are synthesized (made).

ROM
Abbreviation for read-only memory. The ROM is part of a computer's memory whose contents cannot be changed. Once data has been recorded into the ROM chip, it cannot be removed or altered; it can only be read.

SALIVA
An alkaline fluid found in the mouth of humans and certain other animals.

SALT
An ionic **compound** that is formed whenever an **acid** and a **base** react together.

SANKEY DIAGRAM
An illustration of the **energy** changes in a process. The diagram consists of a large arrow that represents the input of energy to the process and that splits according to the energy changes that occur.

SCALES
The small horny plates that cover the bodies of reptiles. Scales are also the bony plates that cover the bodies of fish.

SCARP
A steep slope in a folded, or belted, landscape that is created by the fold and its subsequent erosion. Scarps are also known as escarpments.

SECONDARY SEXUAL CHARACTERISTIC
External features of animals that are found only in one sex. They affect reproductive behavior but are not directly involved in copulation, for example antlers on male deer.

SEDIMENTARY ROCKS
Rocks that have formed from the **compression** of sediment, such as soil, sand, and salt, over millions of years. Sandstone and limestone are examples of sedimentary rocks. See **igneous** and **metamorphic rocks**.

SEED
A structure found in certain classes of plants that contains the **embryo** and the nutritional substances required for germination. The seed develops from the ovule after **fertilization**.

SEISMIC
Concerning earthquakes. Seismology is the study of earthquakes.

SEMICONDUCTOR
A material in which the **electrons** are held only loosely to their **atoms**. Only a small input of energy is needed to free the electrons and therefore make the material **conductive**.

SEMIMETAL
An **element** that shows characteristics between those of metals and nonmetals. Semimetals are fairly good **conductors** of heat and electricity. They are also known as metalloids.

SENSE ORGAN
A part of the body of an animal that consists of a concentration of **receptor cells**. See **sensory receptor**.

SENSORY RECEPTOR
A **cell**, or group of cells, that produce nerve impulses under certain conditions. **Cone cells** are receptors that produce impulses when light of a particular range of colors falls on them.

SESSILE
Being attached to a surface. Limpets are sessile for much of their time, as they are connected to rocks.

SEX CELLS
See **gamete**.

SHELL
(Chemistry and Physics)
An energy level that is occupied by **electrons** within an **atom**. It is generally accepted that the lower the energy of electrons in the shell, the closer the shell is to the **nucleus**.

SI UNITS (SYSTEME INTERNATIONAL D'UNITES):
A system of units that is accepted by the worldwide scientific community as the standard system. Its seven base units include the kilogram and the second.

SINGULARITY
The central point of a black hole. Einstein's general relativity predicts that a singularity has infinite **density**.

SOLENOID
A long coil of wire that produces a **magnetic field** similar to that of a bar magnet. When an iron bar is inside the coil, a solenoid becomes an **electromagnet**.

SOLUBLE
A **compound** that will dissolve in another compound. Salt, for example, is soluble in water. See **solution**.

SOLUTE
The substance that dissolves in a **solvent** to form a **solution**.

SOLUTION
An even **mixture** of two or more substances in which the particles involved are **atoms**, **ions**, or **molecules**. The **solvent**, a solid, liquid, or gas, dissolves one or more other substances (the **solutes**) to form a solution.

SOLVENT
The substance that a **solute** dissolves into to for a **solution**.

SPACE-TIME
A concept that arose as a result of Einstein's special relativity theory, in which the three dimensions of space are combined with the one dimension of time.

SPECIES
The lowest level in the classification of living **organisms**. Humans are of the species *Homo sapiens*.

SPECTROGRAPH
A **spectrometer** that has a photographic plate or some other way of recording the observed **spectra**.

SPECTRAL TYPE
A classification system for stars, which is based on the **spectra** of the stars observed through a spectrometer. Spectral type is also known as spectral class.

SPECTROMETER
Every **element** or **compound** produces a unique **spectrum**, which corresponds to **energy** levels in its **atoms**, **ions**, or **molecules**. A spectrometer is an instrument that is used to analyze a spectrum during chemical analysis. Spectroscopes are spectrometers that use light. Astronomers use spectroscopes to determine the compositions and spectral types of stars. See **spectrograph**.

SPECTRUM
A distribution of some property according to a continually changing quantity. The term usually refers to the white light spectrum, in which the colors that make up white light are arranged in order of their **wavelengths**.

SPEED
The rate at which an object moves, equal to the distance moved divided by the time taken.

SPINAL NERVES
Pairs of nerves that stem from the spinal cord. Each spinal nerve consists of a sensory and a motor **neuron**.

SPIRACLES
Small openings on either side of the head of a **cartilaginous** fish.

SPORE
A **cell** that is involved in **asexual** reproduction and which can develop into an individual without **fertilization**. Compare **gamete**.

STAMEN
One of the male parts of a flower. The fertile part – the **anther** – is held up by a stalk called a filament.

STATE
The form of a substance, which can be solid, liquid, or **gas**.

STIGMA
The sticky part of the **carpel** of a flower that receives **pollen**.

STP
Abbreviation for standard **temperature** and **pressure**. STP equals 0° C (32° F) and **atmospheric pressure** (101,325 Nm^{-2}).

STRATUM
A distinct layer of **sedimentary** rock. Older strata are below younger ones because they were laid down first.

STREAMLINED
A shape that will pass through a **fluid** with little resistance. A car, for example, is designed with a shape that will reduce **air resistance**.

STRESS
Force per unit area on an object that is being **compressed** or stretched. Stress causes a deformation of the object, which is called strain.

STRONG NUCLEAR FORCE
The force between **hadrons**, which is carried by **gluons** or by combinations of **quarks** (see **gauge boson**). The strong nuclear force is responsible for holding the **nucleus** together.

STYLE
The stalk of **a carpel** that, in the female part of a flower, holds up the **stigma**.

SUBDUCTION ZONE
A region of the Earth's crust in which one **tectonic plate** is forced under another.

SUBLIMATION
The direct change from a solid to a gas.

SUBTRACTIVE PROCESS
The process by which pigments absorb parts of the visible **spectrum** of light but reflect others, making objects appear to have color.

T

SUPERCOOLED LIQUID
See **amorphous solid**.

SUPERFICIAL MUSCLE
A muscle found just under the skin. Compare **deep muscle**.

SUPERNOVA
The brightening of a star, which happens as **fusion** at the star's core. When activity in the core stops, the star collapses, and this leads to a massive explosion that throws the star's outer layer off into space.

SURFACE TENSION
The resultant **force** at the surface of a liquid that is due to the **cohesive forces** between the **particles** of the liquid.

SUSPENSION
A type of **mixture** in which **particles**, larger than those in a **colloid**, are unevenly distributed in a liquid or a **gas**. Suspensions can be separated by **filtration**. Muddy water, for example, contains soil particles in suspension.

SYMBIOSIS
A relationship between two **species**. Symbiotic relationships may have several different effects on the species involved: it may harm one of the species to the benefit of the other (parasitism); it may benefit both species (mutualism); it may not benefit either (commensalism).

SYMPTOM
Any number of physical signs that are used in the **diagnosis** of a **disease**. For example, increased body **temperature** is a symptom that is common to many diseases.

SYSTEM
A physical arrangement, used in formulating physical theories. A system is open if **energy** can enter or leave it but closed if it cannot.

TECTONIC PLATE
The large pieces of which the Earth's crust is made. Tectonic plates are constantly moving; where they meet, earthquakes and volcanoes are common. See **subduction zone**.

TEMPERATE
Describing a climate of the middle **latitudes** ($30°$ to $40°$ north or south).

TEMPERATURE
A measure of how hot or cold a substance is. The temperature of a substance is directly related to the average **kinetic energy** of its **atoms**, **ions**, or **molecules**.

TENDON
A strand or sheet of **tissue** that connects muscles to bones.

TENSION
A reaction **force** in a solid that is stretched, which pulls the **atoms** of the solid together. It is the opposite of **compression**.

TERMINAL VELOCITY
The maximum **speed** attained by an object falling through a liquid or **gas**. A parachute falling through air has a relatively low terminal velocity, while that of a ball bearing will be much greater.

TERRESTRIAL
Anything that relates to the Earth.

TERRESTRIAL PLANET
Any of the rocky planets of the inner part of the solar system: Mercury, Venus, Earth, and Mars.

TESTA
The tough or fibrous outer covering around a **seed**.

THERMAL EXPANSION
The expansion of a solid as its **temperature** increases. It is due to the increased vibration of the **atoms** and **molecules** of the solid. This increased vibration occurs at higher temperatures, due to the increased **kinetic energy** of the atoms and molecules.

THERMOCOUPLE
A pair of connected wires of different metals that produces a small **voltage**. The magnitude of the voltage depends upon **temperature**. Thermocouples are, therefore, used in thermometers, particularly at high temperatures.

THORAX
The front of the **trunk** of an animal. In **vertebrates** it contains the heart and lungs, in insects it is divided into a front prothorax, a middle mesothorax, and an anterior metathorax.

TISSUE
Any collection of **cells** of a particular type that forms a distinct part of a plant or animal. A lung, for example, is made up of different tissues from those of the heart.

TITRATION
A procedure in which a measured amount of one **solution** of known **concentration** is added to another solution, usually in order to determine the latter's concentration.

TOPOLOGICAL
Concerning topology, which is the study of the abstract properties of shape.

TOTAL INTERNAL REFLECTION
Light rays that pass through a dense substance (such as a glass block) and are reflected from its inner surface back into the substance.

TRANSDUCER
Any device that changes one form of **energy** into another. A microphone, for example, changes sound into electrical energy.

TRANSITION METAL
The elements that are found in the d- and f-blocks of the periodic table. Most metals, including iron and copper, are transition metals.

TRANSPLANT SURGERY
Surgery in which **organs** or **tissues** are transferred from one person to another, or from one part of an individual to another part of the same individual.

TROPICAL
Describing a climate typical of the tropics, the regions $23\frac{1}{2}°$ north and south of the equator.

TRUNK
The central part of the body that contains the heart, lungs, and other vital **organs**.

TURBINE
A machine in which a liquid or a **gas** causes rotation. When attached to a **generator**, the turning of the turbine helps to generate electricity.

U

ULTRASOUND
A sound of **frequency** that is too high for the human ear to perceive. It is usually taken as above 20,000 Hz.

ULTRAVIOLET (UV)
Electromagnetic radiation of **wavelength** that is shorter than visible light, in the range 400 – 200 nm.

UNICELLULAR
An **organism** that consists of just one **cell**. **Bacteria**, for example, are unicellular.

UNIT CELL
The group of **atoms** or **molecules** in a **crystal**; when repeated, it forms the crystal lattice. There are seven naturally occurring unit-cell types.

UPTHRUST
An upward **force** on an object immersed in a liquid or a **gas**. Upthrust is the resultant of the liquid or gas **pressure** acting on the object. Upthrust supports ships in the ocean and hot-air balloons in the air.

URINE
A water-based fluid that is excreted by animals. In most reptiles and mammals urine is excreted from an **organ** called the bladder.

UTERUS
The **organ** in a female mammal in which the **embryo** develops. The uterus is also known as the womb.

V

VACCINE
A liquid that contains **disease-producing microorganisms**, which, when introduced to the body, trigger the production of antibodies. These **antibodies** protect the body against the full onset of the disease.

VACUUM EXTRACTION
A method of assisted childbirth in which a suction cap is fitted onto the baby's head to enable the midwife or doctor to pull the baby through the birth canal.

VARIABLE
A term in an algebraic equation that can take a number of different values. Compare **constant**.

VASCULAR SYSTEM
The part of the **circulatory system** in animals that is involved with blood circulation in animals. It is also a system that enables the circulation of **fluids** around plants.

VECTOR
A quantity, often represented visually as an arrow, that has both magnitude and direction. **Displacement** and **velocity** are vectors.

VELOCITY
The **speed** and direction of an object's motion.

VERNIER SCALE
A scale, which is attached to an instrument such as callipers, to allow very accurate measurements to be taken.

VERTEBRATE
An animal with a backbone.

VIRUS
A tiny object that is composed of **RNA** or **DNA** and is surrounded by a **protein** coat or capsid. A virus is not capable of independent reproduction and relies on a **host cell** from a living **organism** to enable it to reproduce.

VISCERAL
Relating to the viscera, or internal **organs** that are present in the **thorax** and **abdomen** of mammals.

VOLTAGE
A measure of the **electromotive force** on particles with **electric charge**. The voltage in an electric circuit pushes **electrons** around the circuit.

VOLUME
The amount of space an object takes up. This is measured in cubic meters (m^3).

WXZ

WATER OF CRYSTALLIZATION
Water that is held in **crystals** of a **compound**.

WAVE
A transfer of **energy** that is caused by a vibration. For example, the vibrations that cause sound travel as waves.

WAVELENGTH
The distance from one **wave** peak to another. The wavelength of **electromagnetic radiation** determines the type of radiation. For example, **X rays** have a shorter wavelength than light. Light of different wavelengths causes the sensation of color.

WEAK INTERACTION
A **force** between some types of **particle**, including **electrons**. Weak interaction is also involved in the decay of **hadrons**, such as the **beta decay** of **neutrons** in the **nucleus**. The force is carried by W and Z particles. See **gauge boson**.

WEIGHT
The **force** of **gravity** on an object. It is dependent on the **mass** of the object. Weight is therefore variable under different gravitational conditions, such as on other planets.

WHOLE NUMBER
Any of the numbers ...-3, -2, -1, 0, 1, 2, 3...

WORK
The amount of **energy** involved in a particular task. For example, work is said to be done when a pulley lifts a load. The amount of work done is equal to the force acting multiplied by the distance moved.

X RAYS
Electromagnetic radiation of **wavelength** between 10^{-11} to 10^{-10} m.

ZYGOTE
A fertilized female **gamete**.

Index

A

Abacuses 360
Abbreviations
electronics and
computers 391
"ABC," emergency
care 244
Abdomen 398
crustaceans 154
human anatomy 180,
208, 212, 216-21
mammals 166
Absolute magnitude,
stars 301, 324, 325, 398
Absolute zero 32, 398
Absorption
color 50
light 52
AC see Alternating
current
Acamar 387
Acanthocephala 133
Acceleration 398
formula 378
measurement 22, 23
Newton's Laws 22, 23
terminal velocity 24
theory of relativity 62, 63
Accessory organs,
digestive system 196
Accessory pancreatic
duct 197
Accretion disks, black
holes 330, 331, 398
Acetabulum 183
Acetylsalicylic acid 379
Achernar 388
Achromatic doublets 398
Acid-base reactions 67
Acid rain 174
Acid salts 86, 87
Acidic lava 275
Acids 84-5, 398
and alkali metals 98
ammonia fountain 93
fatty acids 99
neutralization 85
pH scale 84
reaction rates 80, 81
reactive metals 94, 95
salts 86
voltaic cells 97
Aconcagua 382
Acorn worms 133
Acquired Immune
Deficiency Syndrome
(AIDS) 258
Acrasiomycota 131
Acres 376, 377
Acromion 227
Acrux 389
Acrylic, structure 379

Actinia equina 150
Actinides 102
periodic table 74-
Actinium 74
Actinothoe
sphyrodeta 150
Activation energy 90, 398
Activity series 94-5
Acupuncture 236
Acute angles 366
Adam's apple 194, 205
Adaptive radiation,
evolution 128
Adders, logic gates 370
Addition, computers 370
Additive process, color
50, 51, 398
Address lines,
computers 352
Aden, Gulf of 273
Adenine 115
Adenohypophysis 188
Adenosine triphosphate
(ATP) 398
photosynthesis 148
respiration 124
Adhara 386, 389
Adhesive forces 398
capillary action 36
liquids 36
Adipose tissue 181
Adrenal glands 188,
189, 220
Adrenaline 188, 189
discovery of 179
Advanced life support 398
Adventitious buds 126
Adventitious roots
ferns 139
flowering plants 145
Aeration zone, rocks 284
Aerial roots 145
Aerobic respiration
energy yield 124, 195
mitochondria 122, 123
oxygen cycle 173
Aerosols, CFCs 111
Afferent lymphatic
vessels 193
Africa
data 382
formation of 273
Great Rift Valley 273, 276
African plate 272
Agar 398
culture plates 258
Agassiz, Jean Louis 267, 394
Agnatha 133
Agricola, Georgius 66,
266, 394
Agriculture 120
human impact on
environment 174

AIDS see Acquired
Immune Deficiency
Syndrome
Air
diatomic molecules 77
diffusion 38
four-elements theory 66
gases 106
liquification 32
mixture 70
nitrogen 106
noble gases 106
oxygen 108
respiratory system
194, 195
soap bubbles 36
sound waves 30, 31
total internal reflection 52
upthrust 37
see also Atmosphere
Airfoils, birds' wings 165
Air masks 244
Air masses, fronts 293
Air molecules
Brownian motion 16
evaporation 16
sound waves 30, 31
Air pressure
discovery of 15
increasing pressure
with depth 37
isobars 293
sound waves 31
Air pumps 66
Air resistance 24, 398
Air sacs, birds' eggs 164
Airway, emergency
care 244
Al' Aziziyah 382
Al Nair 387, 388
Ala 211
Alarm clocks, LEDs 347
Alba Patera, Mars 315
Albireo 388
Alchemy 66
Alcmaeon of
Croton 179, 394
Alcohol
cloud chambers 58
fermentation 88, 89, 136
formula 379
paper chromatography 70
Alcor 387
Alcyone 388
Aldebaran 386, 389
Alderamin 387
Algae 134, 398
blue-green 134
classification 130, 131
diatoms 135
evolution 268
green 135
lichens 137
pollution 174
Algebra 362-3
Boolean 337, 359, 371
calculus 359
history 358

probability and
statistics 368
rules of 393
Algedi 388
Algenib 387, 388
Algieba 386
Algol 387, 388
Alhena 386
Aliens, space probes 302
Alimentary canal 196, 197
Alioth 386, 387
Alkaid 386, 387
Alkali metals 98-9
periodic table 74-5
Alkaline dry cells 96
Alkaline earth metals 100-1
periodic table 74-5
Alkalis 84, 398
ammonia fountain 93
ammonia production 106
neutralization of acids 85
pH scale 84
preparation of acid
salts 87
solutions 98
Alkanes 398
combustion 83
fractional distillation 113
hydrocarbons 112
Alkenes 398
Alkynes 398
Allantois, birds' eggs 164
Alleles 126, 127
Allergic rhinitis 381
Allergies 260
mast cells 261
Alligators 162
Allotropes 398
carbon 104
phosphorus 106
sulfur 108, 109
Alloys 398
artificial body parts
252, 253
iron 102
tin 104, 105
Alluvial deposits 285
Almach 387, 388
Alnilam 324, 386
Alnitak 324, 326, 386
Alpha Centauri 389
Alpha decay 58, 398
Alpha (‡) sulfur 109
Alphard 386, 389
Alphecca 386, 389
Alpheratz 387, 388
Alps 276
Alrami 389
Altair 387, 388
Alternating current (AC)
338, 398
capacitors 542
diodes 346, 347
inductors 344
multimeters 339
Altitude 398
Alto clouds 292
Altostratus clouds 292

Aludra 389
Aluminum
in Earth's crust 379
element 68
formula 379
integrated circuit
manufacture 351
periodic table 75
powder 76
reactivity 94
thermite reaction 90, 91
Aluminum oxide 68, 76
electrolytic capacitors 343
reactivity 94
thermite reaction 91
Alveoli 194, 195
Alzheimer's disease 381
Amanita 137
Amateur scientists 10
Amazon River 383
Ambulances 244
Ambystoma
mexicanum 161
American National
Science Foundation 337
Americium 75
Amino acids 217, 398
enzymes 124
prion proteins 259
protein synthesis 124-5
Ammeters
electric circuits 43
measuring electric
current 44
measuring resistance 42
Ammonia
in comets 322
dissolution in water 92
fountain experiment 93
Haber process 106, 107
ions 106
on Jupiter 317
laboratory production
106, 107
molecules 68
on Neptune 320
nitrogen compound 106
pH scale 84
on Saturn 318
on Uranus 319
Ammonites 269
Ammonium, formula 379
Ammonium chloride
96, 107
Ammonium
hydrosulfide, on
Jupiter 317
Ammonium hydroxide
116, 117
Ammonium ion 106
Ammonium nitrate 90
Amniocentesis 256 398
Amnion
birds' eggs 164
reptiles' eggs 162
Amniotic fluid
birds' eggs 164
human pregnancy 199

Amoebas 134
structure 135
Amoebic dysentery 259
Amoeboids,
classification 131
Amorphous solids 34
Amount of substance, SI
units 377
Amperes, SI units 377
Amphibia 133
Amphibians 160-1
classification 133
endangered species 175
evolution 269
Amplifiers
capacitors 342
integrated circuits 350
invention of 336
mixing desks 341
transistors 349
Amplitude 30, 398
Amps 42
Ampula, echinoderms 151
Amur, River 383
Amylases 89
Anabolic reactions
(anabolism) 398
metabolism 124
Anaerobic respiration,
yeasts 136
Anaerobically 398
Anal canal 223, 224
Anal fins, fish 158, 159
Anal sphincter
female pelvic region
224, 225
male pelvic region
222, 223
Analgesics 381
Analog integrated
circuits 350
Analog multimeters 339
Analog signals,
computer networks
354, 355
Analog-to-digital
converters 354
Analysis 70, 116-17
Analytical geometry 359
Anaphase, mitosis 126
Anatomical 398
Anatomy, human 176-233
history 120, 178-9
Anaximander of Miletus
120, 121, 267, 394
Anconeus 229
AND gates 370
Andes 276, 277
Androecium, flowers 143
Andromeda constellation
386, 387, 388
Andromeda galaxy 528, 387
Andromeda Nebula 297
Anemia 260, 381
Anemones (cnidarians) 150
Anemonia viridis 150
Anesthetics 247
discovery of 237

Anesthetists 246, 247
Aneurysm 381
Angel Falls 383
Angina 381
Angiography 241
Angles
  circumferentor 267
  cones 365
  crystal systems 34-5
  elliptic geometry 365
  geometry 364
  hyperbolic geometry 365
  light reflection 52
  light refraction 52
  molecular models 68
  SI units 377
  sp3 orbital 105
  total internal reflection 52
  trigonometry 366-7, 393
Anguis fragilis 163
Angular momentum
  29, 398
Anhydrous compounds
  92, 399
Anhydrous copper
  sulfate 83, 92
Animalia 130
Animals
  carbon cycle 173
  cells 122
  classification 120, 121,
    130, 132-3
  ecology 121
  endangered species 175
  energy requirements 380
  evolution 128-9
  extinction 175
  food chains 170
  gestation periods 380
  homes 380
  lifespan 380
  natural cycles 172-3
  nitrogen cycle 172
  oxygen cycle 173
  pollination 142, 144
  seed dispersal 147
  speed 380
  transplants 250
  vivisection 178
Anions 399
  chemical reactions 80
  halogens 110
  nonmetals 76
  salts 86
  testing for 117
Ankle 180, 233
Annapurna 383
Anne's spot, Saturn 318
Annual flowering
  plants 142
Annulus, gilled
  mushrooms 137
Anococcygeal ligament
  222, 225
Anodes 347, 399
  cathode-ray tubes 57, 336

Downs Process 77
  electrodes 97
  electrolytic cells 96
  electroplating 97
Antacids 381
Antarctic plate 272
Antarctica
  data 382
  ice sheet 282, 283
  ozone layer 174, 374-5
Antares 386, 389
Anteaters, energy
    requirements 380
Antennae 399
  butterflies and moths 157
  centipedes and
    millipedes 157
  crustaceans 154
  water fleas 154
Antennae, radio waves
  48, 399
Anterior 399
Anterior lobe, pituitary
  gland 188
Anterior median fissure,
  spinal cord 186
Anterior sacral
  foramen 211
Anterior superior iliac
  spine 217
Anterior tubercle 211
Anthers 143, 144, 399
  insect-pollinated
    plants 146
  pollination 146
  succulent fruit 147
  wind-pollinated
    plants 146
Anthocerophyta 131
Anthophyta 131, 142
Anthozoa 132
Anti-suck-back device
  85, 110
Antibiotics 258, 259,
  381, 399
  discovery of 237
  topical drugs 255
Antibodies 193, 260, 399
  B cells 250, 260
  in blood 191
  immunization 261
  lymphatic system 192
  transplant and graft
    rejection 250
Anticline, folds 277
Anticlockwise moment 21
Anticyclones 291
Antidiuretic hormone 188
Antifungals, topical
  drugs 255
Antigens 193, 260, 399
  immunization 261
  transplant and graft
    rejection 250
Antihistamine 381
Antimony 75
Antiparticles 399
  particle accelerators 60

Antipyretics 381
Antiseptics, discovery
  of 237
Antlia constellation 386
Anus
  annelid worms 152
  crustaceans 154
  echinoderms 151
  female pelvic region 225
  fish 158
  gastropods 153
  human anatomy 196,
    197, 218
  male pelvic region 222
  mammals 166
Aorta
  human anatomy 190, 191
  insects 156
  vascular grafts 252
Aortic hiatus 221
Aortic lymph nodes 192
Aortic semilunar valve 191
Apatite 279
Apes 166, 167
Aphelion 305, 308, 399
Apical buds
  conifers 141
  flowering plants 142
Apollo crater 311
Apollonius of Perga
  359, 394
Aponeuroses 184
  abdominal muscles 209
  external oblique
    muscle 185, 208, 209
Apparent magnitude,
  stars 301, 324, 325, 399
Appendicular skeleton 182
Appendix 197, 216, 218, 219
Appendix epiploica 217,
  218, 219
Apple Macintosh
  computers 337
Applied mathematics 358
Apus constellation 388
Aquarius constellation
  387, 388
Aqueous solutions 399
  acids and bases 84
  chemical analysis 116
  nickel nitrate 70
  sucrose 114
Aquila constellation
  386, 388
Arabian Desert 383
Arabian plate 272
Arabic numbers 560, 376
Arabs 8
  life sciences 120
  mathematics 358, 359
  physics 14
Arachnida 133
Arachnids 154, 155
Arachnoid 186
Aral Sea 383
Archaeobacteria 131
Archaeopteryx 128, 269
Archegoniophores,

liverworts 138
Archer constellation
  388, 389
Arches
  coastlines 286, 287
  erosion 280
Archimedes 15, 394
Arctic Institute Ice
  Passage 383
Arctic jet stream 291
Arctic Ocean
  size 382
Arcturus 386, 389
Arcuate deltas 285
Arcuate ligament 221
Area 393
  circles 362
  conversion tables 377
  measurements 376
Areola 208
Arètes 283
Argon
  in air 70, 106
  periodic table 75
Arguments, logical 370, 371
Aries constellation 386, 388
Aril, yew 140
Aristotle 394
  animal classification
    120, 121
  astronomy 9, 296, 297
  deduction 8
  physics 8, 14
  water cycle 267
Arithmetic 358
Arkab Prior 389
Armpit 181
Arms
  bones 182
  forearm 180
  joints 183
  mammals 166
  muscles 185, 226-7
  posterior back
    muscles 210
  prostheses 253
  upper arm 180, 226-7
ARPANET (Advanced
  Research Projects
  Agency Network) 337
Arrest, Heinrich Louis d'
  297, 394
Arrhenius, Svante 67, 394
Arrow worms,
  classification 133
Arsenic 75
Arteries 190, 193
  angular 202
  aorta 190, 191
    in abdomen 218,
    220, 221
  ascending aorta
    212, 214
  descending aorta
    213, 215
  dorsal aorta 216
  aortic arch 214
  arcuate 198

axillary 190, 205, 226
brachial 190, 226,
  227, 228
brachiocephalic 191,
  202, 205, 213
brain 241
carotid 200
  common carotid 190,
    191, 202, 205, 212, 213,
    214, 215
  external carotid 202
cerebral 207
cervical 202
circumflex 213
coronary 213, 214
crustaceans 154
digital 190
dorsal metatarsal 190
dorsalis pedis 233
facial 202, 205
femoral 190, 230
gastric 190, 218
gastroduodenal 219
genicular arterial
  network 232
gluteal 231
gonadal 220
grafts 252, 253
hepatic 217, 218
humeral circumflex 227
iliac
  common iliac 190,
    216, 220, 230
  external iliac 220, 221,
    224, 230
  internal iliac 223, 224
intercostal 213, 215
lateral malleolar 233
lingual 202
measuring blood
  pressure 239
mesenteric 218
  inferior mesenteric 220
  superior mesenteric
    190, 219, 220, 221
occipital 202
ovarian 224
palmar digital 228
perforating 251
peroneal 190, 233
phrenic 213, 218, 220
popliteal 190, 231, 233
profunda brachii 227
proper hepatic 218
pulmonary 190, 191,
  213, 214
pulmonary trunk 212,
  213, 214
radial 228, 229
renal 190, 198, 220
splenic 193, 218, 219
subclavian 190, 191,
  202, 205, 213, 214, 215
superficial temporal 202
superior temporal 202
temporal 202
thyroid 202
tibial 190, 233

tibial recurrent 232
transverse cervical 202
ulnar 190, 228
Arterioles 188
Artery forceps 246
Arthropoda 132, 133, 154
Arthropods 154-7, 399
  classification 132
  evolution 269
Articular membrane,
  arthropods 154
Articulated 399
Artificial body parts 252-3
Artificial elements,
  periodic table 75
Arytenoid cartilage 194
Ascending colon 196,
  197, 216, 217, 218, 219
Ascomycota 131
Ascorbic acid 379
Asexual reproduction
  126, 399
  liverworts 138
  yeasts 136
Ash, magnesium oxide 77
Ash-cinder volcanoes 275
Asia
  data 382
  formation of 273
  mountain building 277
Aspergillus,
  classification 131
Aspirators 244
Aspirin, formula 379
Assal, Lac 382
Association neurons
  186, 187
Astatine 75, 110
Asteroid belt 304, 314,
  322, 323
Asteroidea 133
Asteroids 322-3
  observational
    techniques 300, 301
  solar system 304
  space probes 302
Asthenosphere 273
Asthma 255, 261, 381
Astronomical units 399
Astronomy 7, 294-333
  amateur scientists 10
  comets, asteroids and
    meteoroids 322-3
  cosmology 332-3
  data 584-5
  galaxies 328-9
  history 296-7
  Moon 310-11
  neutron stars and black
    holes 330-1
  observational
    techniques 300-1
  planets 308-9, 312-21
  solar system 304-5
  space probes 302-3
  stars 324-7
  Sun 306-7
  telescopes 298-9

Astrophysics 7, 296
Asymmetrical folds 277
Atanasoff, John Vincent 337, 394
Atlantic Ocean
    formation 269, 273
    Mid-Atlantic Ridge 273
    plate tectonics 272
    size 382
Atlas vertebra 183, 211
Atmosphere 290-1, 399
    acid rain 174
    carbon cycle 173
    formation of 268
    global warming 174
    historical theories 266
    ionosphere 267
    Jupiter 316, 317
    Mars 314, 315
    meteoroids 322
    Neptune 320
    nitrogen cycle 172
    ozone layer 110, 111, 174, 267
    Pluto 321
    Saturn 318
    sunlight 306
    Uranus 318, 319
    Venus 312, 313
    water cycle 172
    weather 292
    see also Air
Atmospheric pressure 37, 399
    sound waves 31
Atolls 289
Atomic force
    microscopes 78, 399
Atomic mass 399
Atomic number 72, 399
    nuclear physics 58
    periodic table 74
Atomic orbitals 368
Atomic weight, periodic table 67
Atoms 72-3, 399
    absolute zero 32
    activity series 94-5
    alkali metals 98
    alkaline earth metals 100
    atomic diameter 98
    Avogadro's constant 73
    bonds 67, 78-9
    boron 72
    Brownian motion 16
    buckminsterfullerene 104
    carbon 104, 114
    chemical reactions 80
    compounds 68
    crystal systems 34
    discovery of 67
    displacement reactions 94-5
    doping a semiconductor 346
    electric charges 40
    electric circuits 42
    electric current 42

electrochemistry 96
electromagnetic radiation 49
electron shells 72
electrons 56-7, 72
elements 58, 68
energy levels 56
equalization of temperature 33
evaporation 16
friction 24
gas molar volume 73
gases 38
graphite 104
halogens 110
heat 90
heat energy 32
historical theories 66
ions 40, 67
matter 16
metals 76
modern chemistry 67
mole 72
molecular orbitals 78, 79
neutrons 72
nonmetals 76
nuclear physics 58-9
nucleus 72
orbitals 72
organic chemistry 112, 114
oxidation 82, 83
oxidation number 82
particle physics 60
precipitation reaction 8
probability theory 368
protons 72
quantum theory 15, 62
reduction 82
relative atomic mass (RAM) 72
relative molecular mass (RMM) 72
solar cells 47
solids 34
solids under tension 35
solutions 16
spectral absorption lines 301
thermal expansion 34
water 92
ATP see Adenosine triphosphate
Atrial systole 191
Atrium, heart 190, 191, 212, 213, 214
    echocardiography 240
Atrium, sponges 150
Attractors, chaos theory 372
Audio transformers 345
Auditory meatus (canal) 203, 204, 206
Auricle, atrium of heart 213, 214
Auricle, ear 203
Auriculotemporal nerve 202
Auriga constellation

386, 389
Aurora 290
Auscultation 238
Australasia, data 382
Australian Desert 383
Autoimmune
    disorders 260
Autografts 250, 251
Autotrophs 399
    algae 134
    energy flows 170
    plants 148
Autumn 271
Autumn equinox 271, 300
Aves 133
Avocet 165
Avogadro's number 73
Axe, wedge 26
Axes
    algebra 362
    Cartesian coordinates 366
Axial plane, folds 277
Axial skeleton 182
Axial tilt 399
Axilla 181
Axillary fat pad 208
Axillary lymph nodes 192
Axillary nerve 186, 227
Axioms, mathematics 358
Axis 399
    gyroscopes 29
Axis vertebra 183, 211
Axles
    ball bearings 25
    wheels 27
Axolotls 160, 161
Axonal terminal 184, 187
Axons
    association neuron 187
    motor neuron 184
    sensory neuron 187
Ayurveda 257

B

B cells, immune system 250, 260
Babbage, Charles 337, 394
Babies, pregnancy and childbirth 256-7
Baboons 166
    energy requirements 380
Babylonians
    astronomy 296, 297
    numbers 360
Bacillariophyta 131
Bacillus 134, 237
Back 180
    muscles 210
Backbone see Spine;
    Vertebral column
Backwash, waves 287
Bacteria 134, 400
    antibiotics 237
    antibodies 193
    carbon cycle 173
    chlorination of water 110
    classification 130, 131

culture plates 258
decomposition 173
genetic engineering 262
germ theory 237
infections 258, 259
lymphatic system 192
nitrogen cycle 172
prokaryotic cells 122
structure 134
Badgers, homes 380
Baffin Island 382
Bahada 281
Baikal, Lake 383
Baking powder 98
Balard, Antoine-Jérôme 379
Ball-and-socket joints 183
Ball and stick models 68
Ball bearings 25
Balloons
    hot air 39
    weather 290
Bandages 244
Bank vole 170
Bar charts 368, 369
Barbs, cnidocytes 150
Barium
    contrast X rays 100, 101, 241
    flame tests 116
    periodic table 74, 100
Barium carbonate 105
Barium sulfate 101
Bark 142
Barnacles 154
    classification 133
Barnard, Christiaan 237
Barnard's Star 325
Barometric pressure 293
Barrages, tidal power 47
Barred spiral galaxies 328
Bartholin, Thomas 179, 394
Basal disks, anemones 150
Basal layer, epidermis 78
Basaltic lava 275
Bases 84, 400
    alkalis 84
    numbers 360
    salts 86
    sodium hydroxide 98
Bases, genetics 400
    DNA 114, 115
    protein synthesis 124
    transcription 125
    translation 125
Basic oxygen process, manufacture of steel 102, 103
Basidiomycota 131, 137
Basioccipital bone 206
Bats 166, 167
    wings 129
Batteries
    alkaline dry cells 96
    cars 17
    circuit symbol 339
    direct current 338
    electric circuit 43
    electric current 42

history 336
    invention of 15, 66
    voltaic cells 96, 97
Bayliss, William Maddock 179, 394
Bays, coastlines 286, 287
Beaches 286, 287
Beadlet anemone 150
Beaks
    birds 164
    evolution 128
    octopuses 153
    tortoises 162
    wading birds 165
Beardmore Glacier 383
Bearings
    ball bearings 25
    gyroscopes 29
Bears, energy requirements 380
Beaufort scale, winds 383
Beaumont, William 179, 394
Bedbugs, lifespan 380
Bedding plane 286, 287
Bedload, rivers 285
Bees, pollination 146
Beetles
    metamorphosis 156, 157
    wings 156
Bell, Charles 179, 394
Bell Laboratories 336, 337
Bellatrix 324, 386
Bently Trench 382
Bering Sea, size 382
Berkelium 75
Bernard, Claude 121, 179, 394
Berries, food chains 170
Berry, Clifford 337
Beryllium 100
    neutron detectors 15
    periodic table 74
Bessel, Friedrich Wilhelm 296, 394
Beta decay 58, 400
Beta Pictoris 389
Betelgeuse 324, 325, 386, 389
Bethe, Hans Albrecht 297, 394
Big Dipper constellation 385
Bicipital aponeurosis 226, 228
Bicuspid valve 191
Bicycles 27
Big Bang 297, 332-3
Big Crunch 332, 333
Big toe 252
Bile 400
    digestion 196, 216, 217
    "humors" 236
Bile duct 197, 216, 217
Billion 377
Bills
    duck-billed platypus 167
    see also Beaks

Binary 400
Binary addition 400
Binary numbers 360, 376
    computer networks 354
    computers 337, 352
    logic gates 370
Binary stars 324, 325
Binding agents, tablets 254
Binoculars
    lenses 52
    total internal reflection 52
Binomial classification 11
Biochemicals 400
    genetic engineering 262
    research 258
Biochemistry 115
    history 67, 120, 121
Biodiversity 174, 400
Bioengineering 252-3
Biology 120-67
    history 120-1
Biomass 170
Biomes 168
Bionic body parts 252-3
Biopsy forceps 248
Biosphere 168, 400
    natural cycles 172-3
Bipolar transistors 348, 349
Biquadratic curves 363
Bird of Paradise constellation 388
Birds 164-5
    birds of prey 165
    cladistics 133
    classification 133
    endangered species 175
    evolution 128, 269
    food webs 171
    tagging 175
Bird's foot deltas 285
Birth 257
Bishop pine 141
Bismuth 75
Bison 175
Bits
    computer networks 354
    computers 352
Bitumen 113
Bivalves 153
Bivalvia 132, 152
Bjerknes, Vilhelm 267, 394
Black bile, "humors" 236
Black bread mold, classification 131
Black holes 330-1
    Big Crunch 333
    formation 326, 327, 330
    telescopes 299
    wormholes 331
Black Sea 382
Blackberries 147
Bladder
    amphibians 160
    female 199, 224
    human body 198, 217, 220, 221
    lizards 162
    male 199, 222, 223

mammals 166
Blast furnaces 103
Bleach
  formula 379
  sodium chlorate 110, 111
Blind spot, eyes 205
Blink comparators 300, 301
Block and tackle 26
Blood 400
  amphibians 160
  annelid worms 152
  blood groups 237
  cross-matching 251
  crustaceans 154
  DNA fingerprinting 263
  functions 191
  hemoglobin 115
  hemophilia 263
  heart-lung machines 247
  "humors" 236
  immunization 261
  insects 156
  liver and 217
  lizards 162
  malaria 259
  mammals 166
  manufacture of blood
    cells 182
  red blood cells 114, 191
  structure 191
  transfusions 237, 251
  white blood cells 191, 250
  see also Circulatory
    system
Blood pressure,
  measuring 239, 244
Blood tests, pregnancy 256
Blood vessels 190-1, 400
  magnetic resonance
    imaging (MRI) 242
  mast cells 261
  microsurgery 248
  vascular grafts 252, 253
Blue-green algae 134
Blue light
  additive process 51
  color vision 50
  photons 48
  subtractive process 51
  white light spectrum 49
Blue pigments, paper
  chromatography 70
Blueshift, Dippler 301
Boa constrictors 163
  lifespan 380
Body fluids, diagnosis 239
Body parts, artificial 252-3
Body temperature
  amphibians 160
  birds 164
  mammals 166
  measuring 239
  reptiles 162
Bohr, Niels 15
Boiling point 32, 379
Boj Bulok 383
Bolus of food 196, 197
Bomb calorimeters 170

Bonds
  angles 68
  atoms 67, 78-9
  carbon atoms 114
  covalent 78-9
  hydrocarbons 112
  hydrogen bonding 78, 79
  ionic 78
  molecular models 68
  organic chemistry 112
  surface catalysis 88
Bone marrow 182
  transplants 250, 251
Bone saws 246
  bonesetting 178
Bones 49, 182-3
  ear 203
  emergency care 245
  female pelvic region
    224, 225
  foot 232
  fossils 128, 129
  grafts 251
  hand 228, 229
  joints 183
  lower leg 232, 233
  male pelvic region
    222, 223
  muscles 184
  neck 204
  nose 205
  pectoral girdle 227
  pinning 253
  shoulder 226, 227
  skull 204, 206
  spine 211
  structure 182
  surgery 247
  thigh 230
  thorax 212, 215
  see also Skeleton
Bony fish 159
  anatomy 158
  classification 133
  sharks 159
Book lungs, arachnids 155
Boole, George 337, 394
Boolean algebra 337,
  359, 371
Boîtes constellation 386, 389
Boreal forest, life zones 168
Borneo 382
Boron
  atoms 72
  doping a semiconductor
    346
  periodic table 75
Bosons, particle physics 60
Botany, history 120
Bottlenose dolphin 167
Boulder beaches 287
Bourdon gauge 39
Bowman's capsule 198
Box jellies,
  classification 132
Boyer, Herbert Wayne
  121, 394
Boyle, Robert 67, 394

The Sceptical Chymist 66
Boyle's Law 38
  formula 378
Boyoma Falls 383
Braces, immobilizing
  joints 245
Brachial plexus 186, 202,
  205, 226
Brachiopoda 133
Bracts, flowers 144
Brahe, Tycho 296, 297, 394
Braiding, rivers 285
Brain
  amphibians 160
  angiography 241
  arachnids 155
  birds 164
  coronal section 207
  Creutzfeld-Jacob
    disease 259, 262
  crustaceans 154
  fetal tissue transplants 251
  fish 158
  human body 186-7, 200
  inferior view 207
  insects 156
  lateral view 206
  lizards 162
  magnetic resonance
    imaging (MRI) 242
  mammals 166
  microsurgery 249
  positron emission
    tomography (PET)
    242, 243
  research 179
  sagittal section 207
  superior view 207
  trepanning 236
Brain stem 187, 188, 207
Brakes
  cars 17
  friction 25
Branchiopoda 133
Brandt, Georg 379
Brass, electroplating 97
Brassavola nodosa 145
Bread
  raising agents 99
  yeasts 136
Bread molds 136
Breadboards, printed
  circuit boards 338
Breakers, waves 287
Breastbone see Sternum
Breasts 180
  breast-feeding 208
  implants 253
  mammograms 241
Breathalyzers 70
Breathing
  amphibians 160
  crocodilians 163
  emergency care 245
  fish 158
  mammals 166
  medical diagnosis 238
  respiratory organs 194-5

Bridge rectifiers 347
Bright filament lamps 50
Brine 98, 99
Brittle stars 151
  classification 133
Bromide, formula 379
Bromine 110
  diffusion 38
  discovery of 379
  mass spectrometry 117
  melting and boiling
    points 379
  periodic table 75, 110
  photocatalysis 88
Bronchi 194, 212
  left lower lobar
    (secondary) bronchus
    213
  left principal (primary)
    bronchus 213, 215
  left upper lobar
    (secondary)
    bronchus 213
  right principal
    (primary) bronchus
    213, 215
  segmental (tertiary)
    bronchus 195, 213
Bronchial tree 213
Bronchioles 194, 195, 213
Bronchitis 381
Bronchodilators 381
Bronchomediastinal
  lymphatic trunk 192
Bronchus see Bronchi
Bronze 104, 105
Brown algae,
  classification 130
Brown seaweeds 138
Brownian motion 16, 400
Bryophyta 130, 138
Bryozoa 133
  classification 133
Bubble chambers 400
  cosmic rays 58
  particle accelerators 60
Bubbles
  colors 54, 55
  surface tension 36
Buccal cavity, birds 164
Buccinum undatum 171
Buckminsterfullerene
  68, 104
Budding, asexual
  reproduction 126
Buds
  adventitious 126
  apical 141, 142
  flowering plants 142, 143
Bufo marinus 175
Buildings 21
Bulb of penis 223
Bulbourethral gland
  199, 222
Bulking agents, tablets 254
Bull constellation 386
Bunsen, Robert Wilhelm
  67, 394

Bunsen burners, flame
  tests 116
Burnell, Jocelyn Bell
  297, 394
Burning 32, 400
  activation energy 90
  chemical reaction 83
  hydrocarbons 112
  magnesium 77
  oxidation 82
  oxygen 66, 67, 108
Buses, computers 353
Bushels 376
But-1-ene 112
But-1-yne 112
But-2-ene 112
But-2-yne 112
Butane
  atoms 112
  fractional distillation 113
Butene, isomers 112
Butterflies 157
Buttes 280
Butyne, isomers 112
Bytes, computers 352

C

Cables, computer
  networks 354
Cacti 145
Cadmium 75
Caecilia tentaculata 161
Caecilians 160, 161
Caelum constellation 386
Cecum 196, 197, 216,
  217, 218
  iliocecal junction 219
Cesarean section 256, 400
Cesium 98
  discovery of 67
  periodic table 74
Caiman crocodilus 163
Caimans 162
  spectacled 163
Calcaneal tuberosity 232
Calcareous 400
Calcareous ossicles,
  echinoderms 150
Calcareous shells,
  mollusks 152
Calcite 279
Calcitonin 189
Calcium 400
  compounds 100
  in Earth's crust 379
  flame tests 116
  formula 379
  glass 105
  hard water 100
  ions 100
  mortar 101
  periodic table 74, 100
  reactivity 94
  sea water 288
  spectral absorption
    lines 301
Calcium carbide 112

Calcium carbonate
  formula 379
  glass 105
  hard water 100
  limestone 87
  manufacture of steel 103
  marble 81
  mortar 101
Calcium chloride 77, 90
Calcium
  hydrogencarbonate 100
Calcium hydroxide
  ammonia production
    106, 107
  mortar 101
  preparation of ethyne 112
  testing for carbon
    dioxide 83
  testing for carbonates 116
Calcium oxide 107
Calcium sulfate
  hemihydrate 379
Calculators
  invention of 337, 358
  LEDs 347
Calculus 359
Caldera volcanoes 275
Calf muscles 180
California, San Andreas
  Fault 276
Californium 75
Caliper units 25
Callisto 316
Caloric 14
Calorimeters 170
Caloris basin, Mercury 312
Calyx, flowers 143
Cambium layer 149
Cambrian period 268, 269
Camcorders 337
Camouflage
  birds 165
  peppered moth
    evolution 128
  rays (fish) 159
  snakes 163
  toads 161
Canada, ice sheets 283
Cancellous bone 182
Cancer
  computerized
    tomography 241
  magnetic resonance
    imaging (MRI) 242
  T cells and 250
Cancer constellation
  386, 389
Cancer pagurus 171
Candela, SI units 377
Candida fungi 136
  classification 131
  infections 259
Candle wax
  combustion 83
  fractional distillation 113
  melting point 78
Cane beetle 175
Cane toad 175

Canes Venatici
  constellation 386, 389
Canine teeth
  carnivores 166
  herbivores 166
  human 196
Canis Major
  constellation 388, 389
Canis Minor
  constellation 386, 389
Canopus 329, 389
Canopy 400
Cantor, Georg Ferdinand
  Ludwig Philip 359, 394
Canyons 281
  on Mars 314, 315
  submarine 288
Capacitance 400
  capacitors 342
  multimeters 339
Capacitors 342-3
  computers 352
  electronic circuits 338
  integrated circuits 350
  rectifiers 347
  tuned circuits 345
Capacity
  conversion tables 377
  measurements 376
Capella 386, 389
Capillaries 190, 400
  bone 182
  discovery of 179
  lungs 194, 195
  lymphatic 192, 193
  pulmonary
    circulation 191
  small intestine 197
  systemic circulation 191
Capillary action 36, 400
Capitulum flowers 144
Capricorn constellation 387
Capricornus
  constellation 388
Caps, gilled
  mushrooms 137
Capsid, viruses 134
Capsules
  drugs 255
  kidney 198
  lymph nodes 193
  mosses 138
  spleen 193
Caput constellation 386
Carapace
  crustaceans 154
  tortoises 162
Carbohydrates 400
  carbon cycle 173
  organic chemistry 114
  oxygen cycle 173
  photosynthesis 148
Carbolic acid 237
Carbon 104
  allotropes 104
  alloys 102
  atoms 114
  carbon cycle 173

catalytic cracking
  of oil 113
combustion 83
compounds 68
decomposition 134
dehydration of sucrose 92
discovery of 379
DNA 115
ethanol 68
extraction of iron 77
fatty acids 99
fractional distillation 113
fullerenes 104
hydrocarbons 112
melting and boiling
  points 379
molecular structure of
  diamond 104
organic chemistry 104,
  112, 114
periodic table 75, 104
photosynthesis 148
radiocarbon dating 268
stellar life cycles 327
Carbon dioxide 400
  acid on a
    hydrogencarbonate 85
  acid on limestone 87
  atmosphere 290
  carbon cycle 173
  carbonated drinks 89
  catalytic converters 89
  chemical reactions 81
  and combustion 83
  in comets 322
  decomposition 173
  dry ice 90
  extraction of iron 77
  fermentation 89, 136
  gills 158
  global warming 174
  on Mars 315
  and mortar 101
  photosynthesis 100, 148
  respiration 124
  respiratory system
    194, 195
  sodium
    hydrogencarbonate 99
  testing for carbonates 116
  on Venus 313
Carbon granules,
  resistors 340
Carbon monoxide 89
Carbonated drinks 89
Carbonates 85
  formula 379
  rocks 87
  salts 86
  testing for 116
Carboniferous period 269
Carcharinus
  melanopterus 159
Cardia of stomach 220
Cardiac notch 194
Cardiac sphincter 197
Cardiologists 240
Cardiology 381

Cardiovascular system
  190-1
Cards, computers 353
Caribbean plate 272
Caribbean Sea, size 382
Caries 381
Carina 213
Carnivora 130
Carnivorous 400
  amphibians 160
  classification 130
  crocodilians 163
  energy flow 170
  food chains 170
  plants 145
  snakes 163
  teeth 166
Carpals 182, 228
  bone growth 229
  joints 183
Carpels 400
  flowers 143
  succulent fruits 147
Carpus 228
Carrying capacity,
  ecosystems 168, 169
Cars
  brakes 17
  catalytic converters 88, 89
  energy transfer 17
  engines 22
Cartesian coordinates 366
Cartilage
  fish 158
  hands 229
  human skeleton 182
  intervertebral discs 183
  larynx 194, 215
  nose 203
  ribs 215
  surgery 247
  trachea 204, 213, 215
  X-ray imaging 241
Cartilaginous fish 158,
  159, 400
  classification 133
Caspian Sea 382, 383
Cassini division 308
Cassiopeia
  constellation 386
Castanea sativa 146
Castor 386, 389
Casualties, emergency
  care 244-5
Cat fleas 157
Catabolic reactions
  (catabolism) 124, 400
Catalysts 88-9, 400
  catalytic cracking
    of oil 113
  cell functions 124
  CFCs 111
  copper oxide 102
  decomposition of
    hydrogen peroxide 108
  Haber process 107
  hydrocarbons 112
Catalytic converters 88, 89

Cataphyll 147
Cataracts, eyes 237, 252,
  381, 400
Cataras del Iguazu
  Falls 383
Caterpillars 157
Catheters, aspirators 244
Cathode-ray tubes
  (CRTs) 400
  electrons 56, 57
  history 336
  oscillographs 31
  oscilloscopes 339
  television 56, 57
Cathodes 400
  Downs Process 77
  electrolytic cells 96
  electroplating 97
Cathodic protection 95
Cations 400
  acid salts 87
  activity series 94
  alkali metals 98
  alkaline earth metals 100
  ammonium ion 106
  chemical reactions 80
  electrodes 97
  flame tests 116
  metals 76
  salts 86
  testing for 117
Catkins 146
Cats
  classification 130
  energy requirements 380
"Cat's whiskers," radio 336
Cattle, gestation period 380
Caudal fins, fish 158, 159
Caudal vertebrae,
  mammals 166
Caudate nucleus 207
Cautery loops,
  endoscopes 248
Cavendish, Henry 67,
  379, 394
Caverns 281
Caves
  ice 282
  limestone 281
  sea 286, 287
  sizes 383
CBR see Cosmic
  background radiation
Cedars 140
Celcus 237
Celestial sphere 300
Celiac trunk 218,
  220, 221
Cell, unit (crystals) 34
Cell membrane
  blood cells 191
  cell functions 124
  receptor sites 254
Cells 401
  animal 122
  biochemistry 121
  blood 191
  chromosome
    abnormalities 263

cnidocytes 150
discovery of 120, 179
division 126-7, 263
energy 122
epidermis 181
eukaryotic 122, 134
functions 124-5
fungi 136
genetic cloning 263
immune system 260-1
Krebs cycle 121
meiosis 127
microorganisms 134-5
mitosis 126
organelles 123
plant 122, 123
prokaryotic 122, 134
red blood cells 114
respiratory system 195
sex 126, 199
structure 122-3
viral infections 258
walls 123, 134
see also
  Electrochemical cells
Cellulose, plant cells 123
Celsius scale 32, 376, 401
Celsus 394
Cement
  mixture 70
  mortar 100
  teeth 197
Cenozoic era 269
Centaur constellation
  388, 389
Centaurus constellation
  386, 388, 389
Centigrade scale see
  Celsius scale
Centiliters 376
Centimeters 376, 377
Centipedes 154, 156, 157
  classification 132
  speed 380
Central nervous system
  184, 186-7, 401
  anesthetics 247
  magnetic resonance
    imaging (MRI) 242
Central processing units
  (CPUs), 352, 353
  logic gates 370
Center of gravity 401
  point of suspension 21
Centripetal force 28-9, 401
  formula 378
  particle accelerators 61
Centrum, vertebrae 211
Cephalochordata 133
Cephalopoda 132, 152
Cephalopods 153
Cephalothorax
  arachnids 155
  chelicerates 154
  crustaceans 154
Cepheid variable stars 325
Cepheus constellation 386
Cerata, lettuce slugs 153

Cerebellum 187, 188, 207
  magnetic resonance
    imaging (MRI) 242
Cerebral cortex 187, 207
Cerebral ganglion
  annelid worms 152
  gastropods 153
Cerebral hemispheres
  187, 206, 207
Cerebrospinal fluid
  186, 207
Cerebrum 186, 187,
  188, 206
  magnetic resonance
    imaging (MRI) 242
Cerium 74
CERN (Conseil European
  pour la Récherche
  Nucleaire) 401
  Large Hadron Collider
    60, 61
Cervical canal 199, 224
Cervical lymph nodes 192
Cervical nerves 186
Cervical plexus 186, 202
Cervical vertebrae
  human anatomy 182,
    183, 200, 211
  mammals 166
Cervix 199, 224, 225
  diagnosis 239
Cestoda 132
Cetacea 167
Cetus constellation
  387, 388
CFCs
  (chlorofluorocarbons)
    401
  and ozone layer 110,
    111, 174
Chaetognatha 133
Chain reactions 59, 401
Chainwheel 27
Chalk, formula 379
Challenger Deep 382
Chamaeleon
  constellation 388
Chameleons 163
Chang Heng 266, 267
Chang Jiang River 383
Chaos theory 15, 358,
  359, 372-3
Charcoal 104
Charge see Electric
  charge
Charged atoms 40
Charged particles
  current 96
  lightning 292
  magnetosphere 271
  pulsars 330
Charging capacitors 342
Charioteer constellation
  386
Charles' Law 38
  experiment 39
  formula 378
Charon 321

Charts, statistics 368, 369
Cheetahs 167
Chela, arachnids 155
Chelicera, spiders 155
Chelicerae
  arachnids 155
  chelicerates 154
Chelicerata 133, 154
Chelicerates 154, 156
  classification 133
Chelon labrosus 171
Chemical analysis
  70, 116-17
Chemical balances 73
Chemical energy 17
Chemical reactions
  80-1, 401
  acid-base 84
  atoms 68
  catalysts 88-9
  combustion 83, 108
  conservation of mass 81
  decomposition 69, 80
  displacement 94-5
  electrochemistry 96
  endothermic 90
  energy changes 90
  exothermic 76, 77, 83, 90
  extraction of metals 77
  iron sulfide 69
  metabolism 124
  oxidation 82-3
  phlogiston theory 66, 67
  reaction rates 80, 81
  redox 77, 82-3
  reduction 82-3
  reversible 103, 107
  thermite 91
  titration 85
Chemical weathering
  280, 281
Chemicals
  pollution 174
  symbols 75
Chemistry 6, 64-117
  acids and bases 84-5
  activity series 94-5
  alkali metals 98-9
  alkaline earth
    metals 100-1
  atoms and molecules 72-3
  bonds between
    atoms 78-9
  carbon, silicon
    and tin 104-5
  catalysts 88-9
  chemical analysis 116-17
  data 379
  electrochemistry 96-7
  elements and
    compounds 68-9
  halogens 110-11
  heat 90-1
  history 66-7
  laboratories 10
  metals and nonmetals
    76-7
  mixtures 70-1

nitrogen and
  phosphorus 106-7
organic chemistry 112-15
oxidation and
  reduction 82-3
oxygen and sulfur 108-9
periodic table 74-5
reactions 80-1
salts 86-7
transition metals 102-3
water 92-3
Chemotherapy 237
Cherrapunji 382
Chest see Thorax
Chestnut, sweet 144, 146
Chickens, eggs 164
Chicks 164
Chihuahuan Desert 383
Childbirth 257
Chilopoda 132
Chimpanzees, limbs 129
China
  astronomy 296, 297
  chemistry 67
  mathematics 358, 359
  medicine 236
  rivers 285
  seismology 266
Chips see Integrated
  circuits
Chiropody 381
Chiroptera 167
Chitin 136, 401
Chitons, classification 132
Chloride
  chemical reactions 81
  formation of sodium
    chloride 79
  formula 379
  salts 86
  sea water 288
Chlorine
  bleaching 111
  CFCs 111
  characteristics 76
  chloroethene 115
  compounds 110
  concentrations 110
  discovery of 379
  Downs Process 77
  gas 90, 110
  halogen 110
  macromolecules 76
  mass spectrometry 117
  periodic table 75, 110
  preparation 110
  sodium hydroxide 99
  in water 110, 111
Chlorine monoxide 111
Chlorofluorocarbons see
  CFCs
Chlorophyll 100
  chloroplasts 123
  photosynthesis 148
Chlorophyta 130, 135
Chloroplasts 123, 401
  euglenoids 135
  lettuce slugs 153

photosynthesis 122, 148
  structure 148
Cho Oyu 383
Choanocytes, sponges 150
Cholesterol plaque 252, 401
Chondrichthyes 133, 158
Chondrites 270
Chordata 130, 133
Chorion, birds' eggs 164
Chorionic villus
  sampling 256
Chromate ion 103
Chromatic aberration 401
Chromatids 126, 127
Chromatography 116, 401
  gas chromatography 70
  paper chromatography 70
  separating mixtures 70
Chromium
  alloys 102
  discovery of 379
  oxidation number
    102, 103
  oxides 102
  periodic table 74
Chromosomes 401
  abnormalities 263
  antenatal screening 256
  cell functions 124
  genetic engineering 262
  meiosis 127
  mitosis 126
Chromosphere, Sun 307
Chrysaora quinquecirrha
  150
Chrysophyta 131
Cilia
  ciliates 135
  fan worms 152
Ciliates 134, 135
  classification 131
Ciliophora 131
Cinder cones,
  volcanoes 275
Circles
  algebra 362
  area and volume 393
  cones 365
  geometry 364
  hemispheres 365
  set theory 370
Circuit boards 338
Circuit breakers 46
Circuit diagrams 338
Circuits
  electronic 338-9
  integrated 350-1
  logic gates 370
  see also Electric
    circuits
Circular motion 28-9
Circular waves 54
Circulatory system 401
  human body 190-1
  mammals 166
  research 179
Circumference,
  circles 364

Circumferentor 267
Circumvallate papilla 205
Cirques 282, 283
Cirripedia 133
Cirrocumulus clouds 292
Cirrostratus clouds 292
Cirrus clouds 292
Cisterna chyli 192
CJD see Creutzfeld-
  Jacob disease
Clades, classification 133
Cladistics 132, 133
Cladograms 133
Clams
  classification 132
  lifespan 380
Classes, classification
  130, 133
Classical physics 62
Classification 130-3
  history of 120
  scientific names 11
  species 130-3
Clavicle
  birds 164
  human body 180, 182,
    205, 209, 214, 226
  joints 183
  mammals 166
  pectoral girdle 227
Clavius, Moon 311
Clawed toad 160
Claws
  birds 164
  cheetahs 167
  crocodilians 163
  lizards 163
  spiders 155
Cleaner wrasse 169
Cleft palate 263
Cliffs 286, 287
Climate
  atmospheric science 266
  geological time 269
  global warming 174
  ocean currents 288, 289
Clinical 401
Clinical thermometers 239
Clitoris 224, 225
Cloaca
  amphibians 160
  birds 164
  fish 158
  lizards 162
Clocks
  LEDs 347
  pendulums 14
Clockwise moment 21
Clones, genes 262
Cloning 263
Cloud chambers 58, 401
Clouds
  hurricanes 293
  on Jupiter 316, 317
  on Mars 315
  precipitation 292
  solar energy
    reflection 290

types of 292
water cycle 172, 267
Clownfish 169
Club mosses,
  classification 131
Clusters
  galaxies 328
  stars 324
CMS detectors 61
Cnidaria 132
Cnidarians 150
  classification 132
  reproduction 126
Cnidocil 150
Cnidocytes 150
Coal
  formation of 269
  power stations 46
Coastal food webs 171
Coastlines 286-7
Coatings, tablets 254
Coaxial cables 354
Cobalt
  chemical reactions 81
  discovery of 379
  periodic table 74
Cobalt chloride 73
COBE (Cosmic
  Microwave Background
  Explorer) 297
Cobras 163
Cocaine 254
Coccus bacteria 134
Coccygeal nerve 186
Coccygeal vertebrae 211
Coccyx 182, 183
  female pelvic region
    224, 225
  male pelvic region
    222, 223
  vertebrae 211
Cochlea 179, 203
Cockcroft, John Douglas
  15, 394
Cockroaches, spiders 155
Cocoons, spiders 155
Cocos plate 272
Cod, Atlantic 158
Codons, genes 124, 125
Coelom, worms 152
Cohen, Seymour Stanley
  121, 394
Cohesive forces 36, 401
Coils
  electric motors 45
  electromagnets 44, 45
  generators 46
  inductors 344
  solenoids 45
  televisions 57
Coitus 199
Cold 32
  four-elements theory 66
  receptors 181
Cold fronts 293
Colic flexure 218
Colima 383
Collagen, tendons 184
Collar bone see Clavicle

Collectors, transistors 348
Collisions 60
Colloids 70, 401
Colon
  ascending colon 196,
    197, 216, 217, 218, 219
  descending colon 196,
    197, 216, 217, 218, 219
  function 197
  mammals 166
  sigmoid colon 197, 218,
    219, 220, 223, 224
  transverse colon 196,
    197, 216, 217, 218, 219
Colonies, tree wasps 157
Color 50-1
  additive process 50, 51
  alkaline earth metals 101
  bleaching 111
  chemical analysis 117
  chlorine test kit 111
  destructive
    interference 55
  fireworks 101
  flame tests 116
  fluorescence 56
  glass 105
  insect wings 156
  metals 76
  paper chromatography 70
  primary colors 50
  secondary colors 51
  soap bubbles 54, 55
  stars 325
  subtractive process 51
  transition metals 102
Color blindness 263
  tests 239
Columba constellation
  386, 388, 389
Coma Berenices
  constellation 386, 389
Comb jellies,
  classification 133
Combustion reaction 83
  hydrocarbons 112
  oxygen 108
Comet Shoemaker-Levy
  303, 316, 317
Comets 322-3
  data 385
  impact craters 308, 309
  solar system 304
  space probes 302
Commensalism 16
Common fractions 360, 361
Common peroneal
  nerve 186
Commonwealth Bay 382
Communication,
  scientific ideas 11
Communities, ecology 168
Commutator 45
Compact bone 182
Compact discs (CDs) 337
Comparitors 111
Compasses
  electromagnetism

affecting needle 44
magnetism 41
Complex ions 401
chlorine in water 111
reactions 81
Complex numbers 401
Component, weight 20
Components 401
Composite flowers 144
Composite volcanoes 275
Compound eyes 156, 401
Compound leaves 144
Compounds 68-9, 70, 401
anhydrous 92
bonds 78
calcium 100
chemical analysis 116
chlorine 110
copper 102
decomposition 69
dehydrating agents 92
efflorescent 92, 93
exothermic reactions 90
formulae 379
hygroscopic 92, 93
macromolecules 76
metals 76
minerals 278
nitrogen 106
organic chemistry 112
oxidation number 82
relative molecular
mass (RMM) 72
salts 86
sodium 98
sp3 hybrid orbitals 104
sulfur 108
transition metals 102
water and 92
Compression 401
solids 34
sound waves 31
springs 30
Computer-assisted
tomography (CAT)
179, 237, 240, 241
Computers 7, 352-3
data 390-1
drug development 254
fractals 372
generations 391
history 336-7
integrated circuits 350
logic theory 370
medical imaging 240, 242
microsurgery 249
networks 354-5
printed circuit boards 338
supercomputers 8
virtual-reality surgery 249
Concave 401
lenses 53
mirrors 53
Concentrations 72, 401
chemical reactions 80, 81
chlorine 110
solutions 73
titration 85

Concha 205
Conclusions, logic 371
Condensation 32
clouds 292
fractional
distillation 113
Condenser jackets 71
Conduction 32
Conductive 401
Conductors
electric circuits 42
electrochemistry 96
metal 76
Condylactis 150
Cones (botany) 402
conifers 140, 141
cycads 140
gnetophytes 140
gymnosperms 140
Cones (eyes) 402
color vision 50
Cones (mathematics) 402
area and volume 393
geometry 365, 392
Cones, volcanoes 275
Congo, River 383
Coniferophyta 131
Conifers 140, 269
acid rain 174
classification 131
Conjunctiva 205
Conjunctivitis 381
Connections, circuit
symbol 359
Connective tissue
mast cells 261
tendons 184
trachea 215
Conservation,
endangered animals
175
Conservation of energy 17
Conservation of mass 81
Constants 402
algebra 362
Constellations 324
history of astronomy 296
Northern sky 386-7
Southern sky 388-9
Constrictors 163
Constructive breakers 287
Constructive
interference 54, 402
Constructive margins,
plate tectonics 273
Contact lenses 239
Contact potential, diodes
347
Continental crust 288
fold mountains 277
Continental drift 267
Continental glaciers 282
Continental shelf 279, 288
Continental slope 288
Continents
data 582
formation of 268, 273
ice ages 283

plate tectonics 267,
272-3
Contour feathers 164
Contractile vacuoles
amoebas 135
euglenoids 135
Contractions, childbirth
256, 257
Contrast X rays 241
Convection 402
atmosphere 290
Convection currents,
plate tectonics 272
Convective zone, Sun
307
Conventional current 42
Converge 402
light rays 52
Convex 402
lenses 52
mirrors 53
Cooksonia 268
Cooling towers 59
Coordinate geometry
358-9, 364, 366-7
Coordinates, astronomy
300
Copernicus, Nicolaus 9,
296, 297, 394
Copernicus crater, Moon
311
Copper 76
bronze 105
compounds 102
discovery of 67
displacement reactions
94-5
electrodes 97
electroplating 97
formula 379
molar mass 73
oxidation 82
periodic table 75
preparation of nitrogen
106
printed circuit boards
338
reactivity 94
transition metals 102
Copper carbonate 102
Copper chloride 102
Copper hydroxide 102
Copper nitrate 95, 102
Copper oxide 86, 102
Copper sulfate
anhydrous 83
displacement reactions
94
formation 86
water of crystallization
92
Coprates Chasma, Mars
315
Cor Caroli 386, 389
Coracoid process 227
Coral reefs
atolls 289
primary production 380

Corals 150
classification 132
Core
Earth 270, 271
Mars 314
Moon 311
Neptune 320
Sun 307
Venus 313
Coriolis, Gaspard 289
Coriolis effect 289, 291
Corkscrews 26
Cornea 203, 205
transplants 250, 251
Corners 29
Corniculate cartilage
194, 215
Cornified layer 181
Corolla, flowers 143
Corona, penis 223
Corona, Sun 307
Corona Australis
constellation 387, 388
Corona Borealis
constellation 389
Coronary ligament of
liver 217
Coronary sinus 213
Coronoid process 206
Corpus callosum 187, 207
Corpus cavernosum 223
Corpus spongiosum 222,
223
Corries 282
Corrosion 94, 95
Cortex
adrenal glands 189
cerebral 187, 207
herbaceous shoots 149
kidneys 198
roots 149
woody flowering plants
142
Cortical sinus, lymph
nodes 193
Corundum 279
Corvus constellation
386, 388
Cosine, trigonometry 367
Cosmic background
radiation (CBR) 402
Big Bang 297, 332, 333
ripples 333
Cosmic rays 58
Cosmology 352-3
Big Bang theory 297
Costadiaphragmatic
recess 220
Costal cartilage 215
Costs of science 10-11
Cotopaxi 383
Cotyledons 147, 402
conifers 141
Coulombs 377
Counting numbers 360
Courtship, newts 161
Covalent bonds 78-9, 402
discovery of 67

ethyne 112
Coxa 182, 183
Crab constellation 386
Crabs 154
classification 132, 133
food webs 171
Cracking, hydrocarbons
112, 113
Crane constellation 388
Cranial bones 206
Cranial nerves 186, 207
Cranium
fish 158
human skeleton 200,
206
Crater constellation 386,
388
Craters
on asteroids 323
on Mars 315
on Mercury 312
on Moon 310, 311, 323
planets 308, 309
Creams, drugs 255
Creation myths 8
Creationism 128
Cremasteric fascia 222
Crest, folds 277
Cretaceous period 269
Creutzfeld-Jacob disease
(CJD) 259, 262
Crevasses 282
Crick, Francis 121, 394
Cricoid cartilage 194, 204
Cricothyroid ligament 194
Cricotracheal ligament
194
Crinoid 268
Crinoidea 133
Critical angle, total
internal reflection 52,
402
Crocodile clips 19
Crocodiles 162
cladistics 133
Crocodilians 162, 163
Crookes, William 337, 394
"Crookes tube" 337
Crop
annelid worms 152
birds 164
gastropods 153
Cross-sectional area 35
Crow constellation 388
Crown, teeth 197
Crown wheels 17
Crude oil 112, 113
Crust
Mars 314
Moon 311
Venus 313
Crust (Earth's) 270
earthquakes and
volcanoes 274-5
elements 379
faults and folds 276-7
plate tectonics 272-3
Crustacea 133, 154

Crustaceans 154, 156, 402
classification 133
evolution 268
Crux-Centaurus Arm,
Milky Way Galaxy 329
Crux constellation 388,
389
Cryogenic units 402
Crystal lattices 34, 402
Crystallization, states of
matter 16, 32
Crystals 402
cubic system 34
external features 34
hexagonal system 35
identification 266
macromolecules 79
minerals 278
monoclinic system 35
orthorhombic system 34
particles 16
rhombic sulfur 109
semiconductors 346
silicon 104
solids 34
sucrose 114
tetragonal system 34
triclinic system 35
trigonal system 35
unit cells 34
water of crystallization
92, 93
X-ray crystallography 67
CT scanning see
Computerized
tomography scanning
Ctenocephalides felis 157
Ctenophora 133
Cubes, geometry 364, 392
Cubic curves 363
Cubic numbers 360, 361
algebra 362
Cubic system, solids 34
Cubital fossa 180
Cubozoa 132
Cuesta 280
Cultivated land, primary
production 380
Culture plates 258
Cumulonimbus clouds
292
Cumulus clouds 292
Cuneiform cartilage 215
Cup constellation 388
Cuquenen Falls 383
Curium 75
Current see Electric
current
Currents, ocean 289
coastlines 286
plate tectonics 272
Curves
distribution 368, 369
elliptic geometry 365
geometry 364
hyperbolic geometry 365
polynomial functions 363
Cuscuta europaea 169

Cuspate deltas 285
Cuticle
  arthropods 154, 156
  insect wings 156
  leaves 149
  nails 181
  pine needles 141
Cuttlefish 153
Cuvier, Georges 120, 121, 394
Cwms 282
Cyan 51
Cyanobacteria 134
  lichens 137
Cycadophyta 131
Cycads 140
  classification 131
Cycas revoluta 140
Cyclones 291
  tropical 293
Cyclosporin 250, 254
Cyclostomata 158
Cygnus constellation 386, 388
Cylinders
  area and volume 393
  geometry 392
Cypresses 140
Cystic duct 216
Cystic fibrosis 237
Cysts, ovarian 248
Cytology brushes 239
  endoscopes 248
Cytoplasm 402
  amoebas 135
  animal cells 122
  mast cells 261
  mitosis 126
  phagocytes 260
  plant cells 123
  protein synthesis 124
Cytosine 115
Cytosome 135

D

D-block, periodic table 102
D-orbitals 72
Dalton, John 15, 67, 394
Dark nebulae 326
Darwin, Charles 120-1, 128, 266, 289, 394
Data 374-95
  graphs 18
  interpreting 19
Dating, radiocarbon 268
Daughter cells
  asexual reproduction 136
  meiosis 127
  mitosis 126
Daughter nucleus, nuclear fission 59
Davy, Humphrey 67, 394
DC see Direct current
De Forest, Lee 336, 337, 396
Dead Sea 382

Death Valley 382
Decaliters 376
Decay
  alpha decay 58
  beta decay 58
December solstice 271
Deciliters 376
Decimal fractions 360
Decimal numbers 361
  mathematics 358, 359
Declination, astronomy 300
Decomposition 402
  carbon cycle 173
  catalytic cracking of oil 113
  chemical reaction 80
  double decomposition reaction 117
  electrolytic 96
  fermentation 89
  flame tests 116
  mercury oxide 69
  natural cycles 173
  nitrogen cycle 172
  preparation of oxygen 108
  sodium hydrogencarbonate 99
  soil bacteria 134
Decongestants 381
Deduction 8
Deep muscles 184, 402
  forearm and hand 229
  head and neck 200, 203
  shoulder and upper arm 226, 227
  thighs 231
  trunk 209, 210
Defibrillators 244
Deflation hollows, erosion 280
Deflection 57
Degree Celsius 32
Degree Fahrenheit 32
Degree Kelvin 32
Degrees, angles 366
Dehydrating agents 92, 402
Deimos 314
Delphinus constellation 387, 388
Deltas 279, 284, 285
Democritus 15, 67, 395
Denali 382
Denary system, numbers 360
Dendrites 187
Deneb 325, 387, 388
Deneb Algedi 387, 388
Deneb Kaitos 387, 388
Denebola 386, 389
Denitrifying bacteria 172
Denman Glacier 383
Denominator 361
Density 402
  neutron stars 330
  solids 54
  universe 332, 333
Dentine 197
Dentition 402

see also Teeth
Deoxyribonucleic acid (DNA) 114, 115
Depletion layer, semiconductors 346, 347
Deposition
  glacial 283
  reactivity 94
Depot implants, drugs 255
Depressions, weather 293
Depth 37
Depth of field 53
Derived SI units 377
Dermal denticles, fish 159
Dermatology 381
Dermis 181
Descartes, René 14, 359, 395
Descending colon 196, 197, 216, 217, 218, 219
Deserts
  erosion 280
  life zones 168
  primary production 380
  sizes 383
Desiccators 92, 93
Desmid 135
Destructive breakers 287
Destructive interference 54, 402
Destructive margins, plate tectonics 273
Detrivores 173
Deuteromycota 131
Devonian period 269
Dhaulagiri 383
Diabetes 260
Diagnosis 238-9, 402
  endoscopes 248
  medical imaging 240-3
Diagrams
  circuit 338
  scatter 368, 369
  Venn 370, 371
Dialysis, kidney 251
Diameter
  circles 364
  spheres 365
1,6-diaminohexane 114
Diamond
  carbon atoms 104
  hardness 279
Diaphragm 212, 214, 215, 216, 217, 218, 220, 402
  breathing 194, 195
  central tendon 221
  costal portion 221
  left crus 221
  mammals 166
  right crus 221
  stethoscopes 238
Diaphragm, pelvic 222
Diaphragm, urogenital 222, 225
Diaphysis

bone 182
  metacarpals 229
Diastole 191
Diastolic pressure, blood pressure 239
Diatomic molecules 402
  electrolytic decomposition of water 96
  gases 110
  nitrogen monoxide 80
  oxygen 77, 80
  surface catalysis 88
Diatoms 135
  classification 131
Dichasial cyme flowers 144
Dicotyledonous plants (dicots) 142
  classification 131
  leaves 143, 144
Didinium 135
Dielectric, capacitors 342, 343, 403
Diffraction 403
  electromagnetic radiation 48
  waves 54
Diffraction gratings 301, 403
Diffusion 403
  gases 38
Digestion 403
  amoebas 135
  annelid worms 152
  arachnids 155
  birds 164
  carnivorous plants 145
  crustaceans 154
  echinoderms 151
  enzymes 189
  gastropods 153
  insects 156
  lizards 162
  organs 196-7, 216
  starch 89
  X rays 100, 101
Digital integrated circuits 350
Digital multimeters 340
Digital signals, computer networks 354, 355
Digital thermometers 19
Digitalis 254
Digitalis purpurea 254
Dilsea carnosa 138
Dim filament lamp 50
Dinoflagellates, classification 131
Dinosaurs 269
  evolution of birds 128
  extinction 269
Diodes 346-7
  integrated circuits 350
  semiconductors 336
Dionaea muscipula 145
Dioxides, silicon 68
Dip, folds 277
Dip-slip faults 276

Diplopoda 132
Direct current (DC) 338, 403
  capacitors 342
  diodes 346, 347
  inductors 344
  multimeters 339
Disaccharides 114
Disk brakes 25
Discharging capacitors 342
Disks, intervertebral 182, 183
Diseases 258-9, 381, 403
  autoimmune disorders 260
  germ theory 237
  immunization 261
Disintegrating agents, tablets 254
Displacement 403
  oscillation 30
Displacement reactions 94-5, 403
Dissection, anatomical 178
Dissociation theory 67
Dissolving 16
Distal convoluted tubule 198
Distal phalanx 228, 232
Distance
  measurement 18
  speed 23
  theory of relativity 62, 63
Distillation 403
  fractional 113
  solutions 70, 71
Distilled water 84
Distributaries, rivers 285
Distribution curves 368, 369
Diverge 403
  light rays 52
Division, computers 370
Division, classification 403
DNA (deoxyribonucleic acid) 121, 403
  bacteria 134
  bases 114
  cell nucleus 122
  cloning 263
  DNA fingerprinting 121, 263
  genetic engineering 262
  human genome 263
  protein synthesis 124
  structure 115
  transcription 125
  viruses 134, 258
Dobson Units 111
Doctors
  diagnosis 238
  emergency care 244
  history 236
Dodder 169
Dodecahedrons 364
Dog whelk 171
Dogfish 159

Dogs 166
Doldrums 291
Dolichovespula sylvestris 157
Dolphins 167
  flippers 129
  gestation period 380
Domains, magnetism 40, 41, 403
Dome volcanoes 275
Dominant alleles 126, 127
Doping
  integrated circuit manufacture 351
  semiconductors 346
Döppler blueshift 301, 308
Döppler redshift 301, 308
Dorado constellation 388, 389
Dorsal fins
  dolphins 167
  fish 158, 159
Dorsal root, spinal cord 186
Dorsal tarsometatarsal ligament 233
Double bonds, organic chemistry 112
Double decomposition 80, 117, 403
Double-planet systems 321
Double pulleys 27
Double-star systems 325
Dove constellation 388
Down feathers 164
Down quarks 60
Downs process, sodium production 77
Down's syndrome 263
Downward meniscus 36
Draco constellation 386
Dragon constellation 386
Dragonflies
  speed 380
  wings 156
Drawing pins 21
Dreschel bottles 110
Drugs 254-5, 381
  discovery of 237
  emergency care 244
  fertility treatment 256
  genetic engineering 262
  infection and disease 258
  and transplant surgery 250
Drumlins 283
Drupelets 147
Dry, four-elements theory 66
Dry cells 96
Dry ice 90
Drying agents 93, 110
Drying towers 107
Dryland plants 145
Dryopteris filix-mas 139
Dubhe 386, 387
Duchenne muscular

dystrophy 263
Ductility, metals 76
Ductless glands see
  Endocrine system
Ductus deferens see Vas
  deferens
Dugongs 167
Dunes 279, 280
Dung fungi,
  classification 131
Duodenum
  birds 164
  human anatomy 217, 218
Dura mater 186
Dust, Moon 310
Dust lanes, planetary
  rings 308
Dwarf stars 325
Dyes, tissue staining 237
Dysentery 259
Dysprosium 75

E

E-mail (electronic mail)
  11, 354, 355
Eagle constellation
  386, 388
Eagles 165
  homes 380
Eardrum 203
Ears 180, 203
  diagnosis 238
  ear drops 255
  implants 253
  mammals 166
  microsurgery 249
Earth metals
  alkaline 100-1
  periodic table 74-5
Earth sciences 7, 264-93
  age of Earth 267
  in ancient cosmology 9
  atmosphere 290-1, 306
  axial tilt 285
  biosphere 168
  celestial sphere 300
  centripetal force 28
  circumference 267
  coastlines 286-7
  Copernicus's theory 9
  cosmic rays 58
  crust 379
  data 382-3, 384
  diameter 296, 358
  earthquakes and
    volcanoes 274-5
  faults and folds 276-7
  formation of 268
  four-elements theory 66
  geological time 268-9
  geothermal power 47
  glaciers and ice
    sheets 282-3
  global warming 174
  global wind
    circulation 291
  gravity 18, 22, 23

history of Earth
  sciences 266-7
  life zones 168
  magnetic field 41, 271
  Moon 310
  oceans 288-9
  orbit 270, 271, 304
  ozone layer 110, 111
  plate tectonics 272-3
  rivers 284-5
  rocks and
    minerals 278-9
  rocky landscapes 280-1
  seasonal change 271
  size 305
  structure 270
  temperature 32
  weather 292-3
Earthquakes 274
  faults and folds 276
  historical theories 266
  measurement 383
  on the Moon 311
  plate tectonics 272
  Richter scale 267
Earthworms 152
  classification 132
  and decomposition 173
East China Sea 382
Easterly winds 291
Eccentric 403
Eccentric orbits,
  planets 308
Echidnas 167
Echinodermata 133
Echinoderms 150, 151
  classification 133
Echinoidea 133
Echinus esculentus
  151, 171
Echocardiography 240
Echolocation 403
  bats 167
Eclipses
  lunar 296, 310, 311, 385
  solar 306, 311, 385
Eclipsing-binary stars
  324, 325
Ecliptic plane 403
  celestial sphere 300
  Mercury's orbit 312
  Moon's orbit 311
  planetary orbits 304, 308
  solar eclipses 306
Ecology 6, 168-75
  energy flow and food
    webs 170-1
  history 121
  human impact on
    environment 174-5
  natural cycles 172-3
  primary production 380
Ecosystems 168, 403
  food chains 170
  human impact on
    environment 174
  ocean currents 288
Ectoplasm, amoebas 135

Ectothermic 403
  amphibians 160
  reptiles 162
Eczema 263
Edible crab 171
Edible sea urchin 151
Edison, Thomas Alva 395
  Edison effect 337
  light bulbs 336
Edward's syndrome 263
Efflorescent 92, 93, 403
Effort 26
  levers 27
EFM see Electronic fetal
  monitoring
"Egg tooth," snakes 163
Eggs (ovum) 198
  amphibians 160
  birds 164
  chromosomes 263
  earthworms 152
  fertility treatment 256
  fertilization 127, 199
  flowers 146
  frog spawn 161
  gastropods 153
  genetic cloning 263
  human 198
  insects 157
  lizards 162
  meiosis 127
  menstrual cycle 225
  monotremes 166
  reptiles 162
  snakes 163
Egypt
  alchemy 66
  astronomy 297
  chemistry 67
  jet streams 291
  mathematics 358
  medicine 237
Ehrlich, Paul 237, 395
Eichhornia crassipes 145
Einstein, Albert 11, 395
  theories of relativity
    15, 297
Einsteinium 75
Einthoven, Willem
  237, 395
Ejaculation 198, 199
Ejaculatory duct 223
El Nath 386, 389
Elasticity 403
  formula 378
  solids 34
  solids under tension 35
Elbows 180
  artificial joints 253
  joint 183, 226
El'brus 382
Elder, European 144
Electric charge 40, 403
  atoms 72, 86
  electromagnetic
    radiation 48
  ionic bonding 78
  mass spectrometry 116

nuclear physics 58
  SI units 377
Electric circuits 42-3
  formula 378
  resistance 42
  solder 105
Electric current 96, 97,
  338, 403
  cathode-ray tubes 57
  circuits 42-3
  diodes 346-7
  electromagnetism 44
  electronic circuits 338
  formula 378
  inductors 344
  Ohm's Law 42
  potentiometers 341
  resistors 340
  SI units 377
  solar cells 47
  transistors 348, 349
  Van de Graaff
    generators 41
Electric fields 403
  capacitors 342
  cathode-ray tubes 56, 57
  electrostatic forces 40
  radio waves 48
Electric motors
  electromagnetism 44, 45
  energy transfer 17
  kinetic energy 17
Electric resistance, SI
  units 377
Electricity 40-1
  batteries 66
  car batteries 17
  chemical reactions 90
  conductors 76
  energy 15, 16
  history 336
  lightning 292
  loudspeakers 31
  nuclear physics 58
  oscilloscopes 31
  photovoltaic cells 17
  static 40
  superconductors 15
  Van de Graaff
    generators 41
Electricity generation 46-7
  geothermal power 47, 446
  nuclear power stations 59
  renewable sources 46-7
  solar energy 47
  water power 46
  wind power 47
Electrochemical cells
  96-7, 403
Electrochemistry 67, 96-7
Electrodes 403
  batteries 42
  cathode-ray tubes 336
  electrolytic cells 96
  electronic fetal
    monitoring 257
  voltaic cells 97
Electrolysis 67, 96, 403

Downs Process 77
  sodium hydroxide 98, 99
Electrolytes 96, 403
  electroplating 97
  ions 67
Electrolytic capacitors 343
Electrolytic cells 96
Electromotive force
  20, 404
  particle physics 60
Electromagnetic
  radiation 48-9, 404
  black holes 330, 331
  discovery of 15
  Döppler shift 301
  light 52
  quantum physics 15
  quantum theory 62
  Sun 17
Electromagnetic
  spectrum 48-9,
    299, 404
  telescopes 298
  visible light 50
Electromagnetism
  44-5, 404
  compass needles 44
  discovery of 15
  electric motors 45
  electricity generation 46
  electromagnets 45
  freefall experiment 19
  history 15
  loudspeakers 31
  magnetic resonance
    imaging (MRI) 242
  particle accelerators 61
  particle physics 60
  solenoids 45
Electromotive force
  (emf) 96, 404
  self inductance 344
Electron guns 57
Electron microscopes
  120, 121
Electron shells 72, 404
  alkali metals 98
  covalent bonding 78
  discovery of 15
  halogens 110
  periodic table 74
Electronic circuits 338-9
  capacitors 342-3
  formula 391
  resistors 340
  symbols 390
Electronic fetal
  monitoring (EFM) 257
Electronic mail (e-mail)
  11, 354, 355
Electronic
  thermometers 239
Electronics 7, 335-55
  capacitors 342-3
  computers 352-3
  data 390-1
  diodes and
    semiconductors 346

history 336-7
  inductors and
    transformers 344-5
  integrated circuits 350-1
  resistors 340-1
  silicon 104
  and society 10
  transistors 348-9
Electrons 56-7, 404
  activity series 94
  alkali metals 98
  alkaline earth metals
    100, 101
  atoms 72
  batteries 42
  capacitors 342
  cathode-ray tubes 57, 336
  current 96
  discovery of 15, 67
  doping a
    semiconductor 346
  electric circuits 42
  electric current 42
  electromagnetic
    radiation 48, 49
  excitation 56
  fluorescence 56
  halogens 110
  interference pattern 62
  ionic bonding 78
  isotopes 72
  light bulbs 43
  metals 76
  negative electric
    charge 40
  nuclear physics 58
  orbitals 56, 72
  oxidation 82, 83
  particle physics 60
  periodic table 74
  positron emission
    tomography (PET) 243
  probability theory 368
  quantum physics 15
  quantum theory 9, 62
  reduction 82
  sodium lamps 50
  solar cells 47
  in stars 330
  static electricity 40
  Van de Graaff
    generators 41
  X rays 49
Electrophysiology 179
Electroplating 97, 404
Electroscopes 40, 404
Electrostatic force 404
  attraction 78
  electric charges 40
  electric circuits 42
Elements 68-9, 404
  alkali metals 98
  alkaline earth metals 100
  ancient medicine 236
  atomic number 72
  atoms 56
  boiling points 379
  compounds 68

discovery of 67, 379
Earth's crust 379
flame tests 116
halogens 110
historical theories 66
isotopes 72
melting points 379
metals 76-7
minerals 278
mixtures 70
nitrogen 106
nonmetals 76
organic chemistry 112
oxidation number 82
oxygen 108
periodic table 67, 74-5
phosphorus 106
protons 58
Proust's Law 67
spectral absorption
  lines 301
in stars 300
sulfur 108
transition metals 102
water and 92
Elements, set theory 370
Elephants 166
energy requirements 380
gestation period 380
lifespan 380
reproductive strategy 169
Elhuyar, Fausto 379
Elhuyar, Juan José 379
Elixirs, drugs 255
Ellesmere Island 382
Ellipses 404
cones 365
planetary orbits 29
Ellipsographs 359
Elliptic geometry 365
Elliptical galaxies
  328, 333
Eltanin 387
Elytrons 156
Embalming 178
Embryology 121
Embryos (animals) 404
birds 164
human 199
in-vitro fertilization 256
reptiles 162, 163
Embryos (plants) 404
flowering plants 146
seed fertilization 147
Emergency medical
  care 244-5
emf see
  Electromotive force
Emission nebulae 326
Emitters, transistors 548
Empedocles 179, 395
Empirical 404
Empirical data,
  charts 369
Empiricism 9
Emu 165
Enamel, teeth 197
Endangered species 175

Endocarditis 381
Endocarp, succulent
  fruit 147
Endocrine system
  179, 188-9
Endocrinology 381
Endodermis, roots 149
Endometrium 199, 225
Endoplasm, amoebas 135
Endoplasmic reticulum
  122, 123
Endoscopes 248
Endoskeleton
  mammals 166
  tortoises 162
Endosperm 147
Endothelium 190
Endothermic animals
  birds 164
  mammals 166
Endothermic reactions
  90, 404
Energy 16-17, 404
activation energy 90
acupuncture 236
animal requirements 380
Big Bang 332
biochemistry 121
catabolic reactions 124
cathode-ray tubes 57
cells 122
conduction 32
decomposition 69
ecology 168
electricity generation 46-7
electromagnetic
  radiation 48
electrons 56
energy flow and food
  webs 170-1
extracting metals from
  ores 76
fireworks 101
food webs 171
heat 32-3, 90-1
human impact on
  environment 174
kinetic 16, 90
Krebs cycle 121, 124
latent heat 33
melting points 78
nuclear fission 58, 59
nuclear fusion 58, 59
nuclear power
  stations 59
ocean waves 287
oxygen cycle 173
particle physics 60
phosphorescence 57
photosynthesis 100,
  123, 148
Principle of the
  Conservation of
  Energy 17
quantum theory 62
respiration 124
scientific history 15
SI units 377

Sun 17, 290, 306, 307
theory of relativity 63
transfers 17
waves 30
work 26
Engineering,
  bioengineering 252-3
ENIAC (Electronic
  Numerical Integrator
  and Calculator) 337
Enif 387, 388
Enteromorpha linza 138
Environment 404
ecology 168-9
energy flows and food
  webs 170-1
human impact 174-5
natural cycles 172-3
natural selection 128
Enzyme-linked
  immunosorbent assay
  (ELISA test) 261
Enzymes 404
arachnids 155
biological washing
  powder 89
carnivorous plants 145
catalysts 88
cell functions 124, 125
crustaceans 154
digestion of starch 89
digestive system 189,
  196, 197, 219
DNA fingerprinting 263
fermentation 89
genetic engineering 262
genetic mutations 263
Golgi body 122
Epicenter, earthquakes 274
Epicotyl 147
Epidermal cells
  plants 123
  skin 181
Epidermis
  plant anatomy 149
  skin 181
Epididymis 199, 222
Epiglottis 204, 205, 215
  swallowing 194, 196
Epimysium 184
Epineurium 187
Epiphysis
  bone 182
  phalanx 229
Epiphytic orchids 145
Epiploic vessels 216
Epithelial cells 122
Equalization of
  temperature 33
Equations
algebra 362
fractals 372
logic 371
Equator 270, 404
celestial 300
global wind
  circulation 291
Equilateral triangles 392

fractals 372
Equilibrium 20, 404
chemical reactions
  80, 81
oscillation 30
Equinoxes 271, 300
Equisetum arvense 139
Equuleus constellation
  387, 388
Equus 129
Eras, geological 267
Eratosthenes 267, 296,
  297, 395
Erbium 75
Erectile 404
Eridanus constellation
  387, 388
Erosion 404
coastlines 286
glacial 283
rivers 284
rock cycle 278
rocky landscapes 280-1
Error bar 404
Erythrocytes 191
Escape velocity, black
  holes 330
Eskers 283
Esophagus
annelid worms 152
arachnids 155
birds 164
hiatus 220
human anatomy 200,
  204, 212, 215, 218
insects 156
lizards 162
mammals 166
peristalsis 197
swallowing 196
Estrogen 189
Estuaries 284, 286
Ethane 112, 113
Ethanoic acid 379
Ethanol 379
  fermentation 136
Ether 237
Ethmoid bone 183, 206
Ethyne 112, 113
Eubacteria 131
Euclid 359, 364, 395
  Elements 358, 359
Euglenoid flagellates 135
  classification 131
Euglenophyta 131
Eukaryotes 122, 404
  fungi 136
  protists 134
Eurasian plate 272
Europa 316
Europe
  data 382
  formation of 273
  ice sheets 283
Europium 75
Eustachian tubes 179
Eustachio, Bartolommeo
  179, 395

Evaporation 404
states of matter 16, 32
Evening Star 312
Event horizon, black
  holes 330, 331
Everest, Mount 382, 383
Evolution 128-9, 404
discovery of 120-1
fossils and 266
microorganisms 258
phylogeny 132
Excited 56, 404
Exhalation 194, 195
Exine, pollen grains 146
Exocarp, succulent
  fruit 147
Exoskeleton, arthropods
  154, 156
Exosphere 290
Exothermic reactions 404
burning 77, 85, 90
formation of sodium
  chloride 76
preparation of ethyne 112
Expansion
  solids 35
  thermal 34
Expansion joints 34
Experiments 9, 14, 18-19
Explosives 106
Expansion
Extensors 404
  arthropods 154
External auditory
  meatus (canal) 203,
  204, 206
Extinction 128, 404
human impact on
  environment 174, 175
  mass 269
Extraction, metals 76, 77
Extraterrestrial life,
  space probes 302
"Eye," hurricanes 293
Eye spot, euglenoids 135
Eyeball 203, 204
Eyes
anatomy 203
arachnids 155
artificial lenses 252, 253
birds 165
cataracts 237, 252
color blindness 263
color vision 50
compound 156
corneal transplants 251
crocodilians 163
crustaceans 154
diagnosis 238
eye drops 255
fish 158, 159
gastropods 153
genetic mutations 263
glass 253
human 181
octopuses 153
optic nerve 207
research 179
seeing by reflected

light 52
spiders 155
virtual-reality
  surgery 249
vision 205
vision tests 239
Eyots 285
Eyre, Lake 382

F

F see Farads
F-block, periodic table 102
Fabricius, Hieronymus
  179, 395
Fabrics, bleaching 111
Fabry, Charles 267, 395
Face 181
bones 200, 206
muscles 200, 405
Facial nerve 202
Fahrenheit scale 32,
  376, 405
Fairy shrimps,
  classification 133
Falcano tinnunculus 165
Falciform ligament 196,
  216, 217, 219
Falcons 164, 165
Falling 19
Fallopian tubes 198, 224
fertilization of ovum 199
menstrual cycle 225
False vocal cords 194
Family, classification 130
Fan worms 152
Fangs, snakes 163
Faraday, Michael 15, 395
Farads (F) 342
Farey, John 359
Fascia, transplants 251
Fascicle 187
Fast-acting drugs 405
Fats
adipose tissue 181
digestion 196, 216, 217
production of soap 99
Fatty acids 98, 99
Fault plane 276
Faults, plate tectonics 276
Fava beans 147
Fax machines 337, 354
Feather stars,
  classification 133
Feathers 164
flight 165
fossil 128
Feces 196, 197, 222, 225
Feet
amphibians 160
birds 164, 165
bones 232
crocodilians 163
duck-billed platypus 167
gastropods 153
human anatomy 180
mammals 166
muscles 232-3

tendons 253
toenails 181
Feet, unit of
  measurement 376, 377
Felidae 130
Femoral cutaneous
  nerve 221, 231
Femoral nerve 186,
  221, 230
Femur
  birds 164
  dynamic hip screws 253
  human anatomy 182
  joints 183
  mammals 166
  spiders 155
Fennec fox, energy
  requirements 380
Fermat, Pierre de 359
Fermentation
  enzymes 88, 89
  yeasts 136
Fermi, Enrico 15, 395
Fermium 75
Ferns 138, 139
  classification 131
  fractals 372
Ferrite, inductors 344
Fertility treatments 256
Fertilization 127, 405
  amphibians 160
  conifers 141
  flowering plants 144, 146
  gymnosperms 140
  human body 199, 225
  seeds 147
Fertilizers
  nitrogen 106
  pollution 174
Fetus
  blood sampling 256
  ultrasound scanning 240
FEV meters see
  Forced Expiratory
  Volume meters
Feynman diagram 60
Fiber-optic cables 337
  computer networks 354
  endoscopes 248
  laser surgery 249
Fibroblasts 405
  vascular grafts 252
Fibula
  human anatomy 182,
  183, 230, 233
  joint 183
  mammals 166
Field-effect transistors
  (FET) 548
  integrated circuits
  350, 351
Field laboratories 10
Field of vision 53
Filaments (life
  sciences) 405
  flowers 143, 144
  succulent fruit 147
Filaments (physics) 405

cathode-ray tubes 57
light bulbs 43, 50
Sun 307
Film, thin film
  interference 55
Films, photographic 109
Filter paper 70, 71
Filters
  color 51
  polarizing 54, 55
Filtration 405
  mixtures 70
  muddy water 71
Fimbriae 199, 224
Finches, evolution 128
Fingers 180
  bones 228
  muscles 185, 229
  myoelectric arms 253
  nails 181
Fins
  dolphins 167
  fish 158, 159
Fire, four-elements
  theory 66
Fire bricks 77
Firewalls, computer
  networks 355
Fireworks 100, 101
Firn 282
First aid 405
  ambulances 244
Fish 158-9
  acid rain 174
  classification 133
  endangered species 175
  evolution 269
  food webs 171
  species interactions 169
  tagging 175
Fish-skin disease 263
Fishes constellation 386
Fission (life sciences) 405
Fission, nuclear physics
  15, 58, 59, 405
Fissure volcanoes 275
Fissures, lungs 194
Fixed resistors 340
Fixer, sodium
  thiosulfate 109
Flagella
  bacteria 134
  euglenoids 135
Flagellates 134
  classification 131
Flame tests 116
Flamingo 164
Flares, Sun 307
Flat shapes, geometry 364
Flatworms 152
  classification 132
Fleas 157
Fleming, Alexander
  237, 395
Fleming, John Ambrose
  336, 337, 395
Flexors 405
  arthropods 154

Flies
  and decomposition 173
  lifespan 380
Flight
  bats 167
  birds 164, 165
Flight feathers 164
Flightless birds 165
Flippers
  evolution 129
  seals 166
Floating 36, 37
Floodplains 285
Florets, flowers 144
Flotation principle 15
Flowering plants 142-7
  classification 131
  reproduction 146-7
Flowers 142
  pollination 144
  structure 143
  types 144
  wind-pollinated
  plants 146
Fluid ounces 376
Fluidram 376
Fluids 405
  lubrication 24, 25
Flukes 152
  classification 132
Fluorescence 56, 405
  nebulae 327
Fluorescent lamps 50
Fluoride, ions 110
Fluorine
  atomic number 58
  CFCs 111
  covalent bonding 79
  ionic bonding 78
  periodic table 75, 110
Fluorite 279
Fluted bird's nest fungi 136
Flying Fish
  constellation 388
Flying mammals 167
Focal length 405
  concave mirrors 53
  convex lenses 53
  telescopes 298
Focusing an image 53
Folds, plate
  tectonics 276-7
Foliose lichen 137
Folk medicine 236
Follicles, hair 181
Fomalhaut 387, 388
Food chains 170
  food webs 171
Food webs 168, 170,
  171, 405
Fool's gold 68
Foot see Feet
Foramen magnum 206
Foramina, perineal 222
Force 20-3, 405
  adhesive 36
  atomic 72
  centripetal 28-9

cohesive 36
compression 34
electric fields 40
electromagnetism 10
electrostatic 40
equilibrium 20
formula 378
friction 24-5
gravity 20, 23
magnetism 41
Newton's Laws 14, 22-3
oscillation 30
particle physics 60-1
pressure 21
reaction 20
resultant 20
SI units 377
simple machines 26
tension 34, 35
turning 21
upthrust 37
work 26
Force lines 44
Forced Expiratory
  Volume (FEV)
  meters 261
Forceps
  artery 246
  biopsy 248
  childbirth 256, 257
Forearm 180
  joint 183
  muscles 185, 228-9
Forecasts, weather 292
Foregut
  arachnids 155
  insects 156
Forehead 181
Forensic medicine, DNA
  fingerprinting 263
Forests, life zones 168
Forewings, insects 156
Fork lightning 292
Formulas
  algebra 362, 363
  chemical 379
  circuits 591
  physics 378
Fornax constellation
  387, 388
Fornix 187, 207
Fossa navicularis 223
Fossil fuels 405
  acid rain 174
  global warming 174
Fossils 266, 405
  and evolution 128-9
  evolution of
  the Earth 268
  formation 269
  geological eras 267
  palaeontology 120
  plate tectonics 267
Foundations 21
Fountain experiment,
  ammonia 93
Four-elements theory 66
Fovea 205

Foxes, speed 380
Foxgloves 254
Fra Mauro, Moon 311
Fractals 359, 372-3
Fractional distillation
  70, 113
Fractionating towers
  112, 113
Fractions, mathematics
  358, 360, 361
Fractures
  bones 49
  X ray imaging 241
Fragaria 142
Frame of reference,
  theory of relativity
  63, 405
Francis turbine 46
Francium 74, 98
Free radicals,
  phagocytes 260
Freefall experiment 19
Freezing points
  mercury 32
  states of matter 32
  water 32
Frequency 405
  SI units 377
  sound waves 31
Friction 24-5
  activation energy 90
  centripetal force 29
  formula 378
  limiting 24
Frogs
  anatomy 160
  evolution 129
  fossils 129
  metamorphosis 161
Frontal bone 183, 206
Frontal lobe, brain 187,
  206, 207
Frontal sinus 205
Fronts, weather 293
Fructose 89
Fruit
  succulent fruits 147
  sugars 89
Fruit bats 167
Fruiting bodies
  fungi 136, 137
  slime molds 135
Fucus spiralis 138
Fulcrum 405
  levers 27
  scales 18
Full moon 310
Fullerenes 104
Fumaroles 275
Functions 405
  algebra 362
  probabilities 368
Funding 10-11
Fundus
  gall bladder 216
  stomach 197, 217
  uterus 199, 224
Fungi 136-7

cells 122
classification 130, 131
decomposition 173
infections 258, 259
microorganisms 134
symbiosis 137
Fungiform papilla 205
Fur, mammals 166
Furnace constellation 388
Furnaces
  fractional distillation 113
  manufacture of steel 103
Furud 389
Fusion, nuclear physics
  58, 59, 326, 405

G

Gacrux 389
Gadolinium 75
Gadus morhua 158
Gagarin crater, Moon 311
Galapagos Islands 128
Galathea Deep 382
Galaxies 328-9
  Big Bang 352-3
  black holes 330
  centers 299
  data 384
  Döppler shift 301
  history of astronomy 297
  Hubble's Law 333
  images of 299
  radio telescopes 299
Galen 178, 179, 237, 395
Galena 68
Galeras 383
Galilean moons, Jupiter
  316
Galileo Galilei 15, 395
  clocks 31
  Galilean moons 316
  telescopes 297
Galileo space probe 302,
  303, 316
Gall bladder
  bile 196
  human anatomy 216,
  217, 219
  mammals 166
Galle, Johann Gottfried
  297, 395
Gallium 75
Gallons 376, 377
Galvani, Luigi 179, 395
Gametes 405
  conifers 141
  fertilization 147
  meiosis 127
  nonflowering plants 138
  pollination 146
Gametophyte
  generation 138
Gamma rays 405
  astronomy 299
  discovery of 15
  electromagnetic
  spectrum 48, 49, 299

positron emission tomography (PET) 243
radioactivity 58
Sun 307
Gamma Velorum 386, 389
Ganymede 316
Gas chromatography 70
Gas exchange, alveoli 195
Gas giants 304, 405
  Neptune and Pluto 320-1
  rings 308, 309
  Saturn and Uranus 318-19
Gas laws, formulas 378
Gas loops, Sun 307
Gas mantles 78
Gases 38-9, 405
  air 70, 106
  atmosphere 290-1
  Boyle's Law 38
  Charles' Law 39
  chlorine 76, 110
  diffusion 38
  evaporation 16
  as liquids 90
  mixtures 70
  molar volume 73
  natural gas 32, 269
  nitrogen 106
  nonmetals 76
  oxygen 108
  particles 32
  periodic table 74
  pressure 38-9
  Pressure Law 39
  temperature 32, 38-9
  water and 92
Gasherbrum 383
Gasoline
  car engines 17
  fractional distillation 113
Gastroenterology 381
Gastropancreatic fold 219
Gastropoda 132, 152
Gastropods 153
Gastrotricha 133
Gastrovascular cavity, anemones 150
Gauge bosons 60, 405
Gaussian distribution curves 368, 369
Gavarnie 383
Gears
  electric motors 17
  wind turbines 47
Geckos 163
Geiger-Muller tubes 58, 405
Gell-Mann, Murray 15, 395
Gemini constellation 323, 386, 389
Geminids meteor shower 323
Gemmae, liverworts 138
Genera see Genus
General anaesthetics 247
General practitioners 238

Generating angle, cones 365
Generators 405
  alternating current 338
  electricity generation 46-7
  hydroelectricity 46
  nuclear power stations 59
  Van de Graaff 41, 343
  wind power 47
Genes and genetics 262-3, 405
  analysis 263
  cloning 263
  gene therapy 237
  heredity 126, 127
  history 121
  human genome project 10, 121
  mitosis 126
  mutations 263
  pollination 146
  prenatal screening 256
  protein synthesis 124
  viruses 134
Genetic code 405
  DNA 114, 115
  genetic engineering 262
Genetic disorders 262, 406
Genetic engineering 262
Genetic variation 406
Genitofemoral nerve 220, 221
Genome 406
  human genome project 10, 121, 262, 263
  viruses 258
Genotypes 406
  asexual reproduction 126
Genus, classification 130
Geocentric model, universe 314
Geological column 268
Geological eras 267
Geological time 268-9
Geology 266
  coastlines 286-7
  earthquakes and volcanoes 274-5
  Earth's structure 270
  faults and folds 276-7
  glaciers and ice sheets 282-3
  plate tectonics 272-3
  rivers 284-5
  rocks and minerals 278-9
Geometry 364-5
  coordinate 358-9, 364, 366-7
  data 392-3
  fractals 359, 372
  history 358, 359
  non-Euclidean 358, 359, 364
Geothermal power 46, 47
Geriatrics 381
Germ theory 237
Germanium 75, 104
Germany, mathematics 358

Germinal center, lymph nodes 193
Germination
  conifers 141
  seeds 147
Germs 406
  immune system 260
  infection and disease 258-9
Gestation periods 380
Geysers 275
Gharials 162
Ghost anemone 150
Gilbert, William 15, 395
Gill, unit of measurement 376
Gill slits, fish 159
Gills 406
  axolotls 161
  crustaceans 154
  fish 158, 159
  fungi 136
  gilled mushrooms 137
  tadpoles 161
Ginkgo 140
  classification 131
Ginkgo biloba 140
Ginkgophyta 131, 140
Giotto space probe 297
Giraffes 120
  energy requirements 380
Gizzard
  annelid worms 152
  birds 164
Glabella 206
Glaciers 282-3
  erosion 278
  hydrological science 266
  sizes 383
Glands 406
  adrenal 188, 189, 220
  bulbourethral 199, 222
  endocrine system 188-9
  lacrimal 200
  mammary 208
  ovaries 188, 189, 198, 199
  pancreas 188, 189
  parathyroid 188, 189
  parotid 196, 200, 201, 205
  pineal 187, 188, 189
  pituitary 187, 188, 189, 207
  prostate 198, 199, 223
  salivary 189, 196, 201, 205
  sebaceous 181
  testes 188, 189, 198, 199
  thymus 192
  thyroid 188, 189, 204, 205, 214
Glans
  clitoris 225
  penis 223
Glass 105
  capillary action 36
  discovery of 67
  flow 32
  prisms 49
  quartz 104, 105
  refraction 52

total internal reflection 52
Glasses, vision tests 239
Glaucoma 381
Glenoid cavity 227
Glisson, Francis 179, 395
Global warming 174
Globular clusters, stars 324
Glucagon 189
Glucose
  fermentation 89, 136
  glycolysis 124
  liver and 179
  organic chemistry 114
  photosynthesis 148
  positron emission tomography (PET) 243
Gluons 60, 406
Gluteal fascia 222, 225, 231
Gluteal fold 180
Glycerol, fatty acids 99
Glycogen
  in cells 122
  liver and 179
Glycolysis, respiration 124
Gneiss 279
Gnetophyta 131
Gnetophytes 140
  classification 131
Goats, gestation period 380
Gobi Desert 383
Gödel, Kurt 359, 395
Gold
  alchemy 66
  atoms 78
  discovery of 379
  element 68
  melting and boiling points 379
  periodic table 75
  reactivity 94
  transition metals 102
Gold algae, classification 131
Gold leaf
  electroscopes 40
Golden ratio 361
Golden rectangle 361
Golgi, Camillo 179, 395
Golgi body
  animal cells 122
  euglenoids 135
  plant cells 123
Gonads
  anemones 150
  echinoderms 151
Gondwana 269, 273
Goniometers 266
Gonopores
  echinoderms 151
  gastropods 153
Gorges 281
Gorilla gorilla 167
Gorillas 167
  energy requirements 380
Graben, rift valleys 276
Grades, classification 133
Graffias 389

Grafts, surgery 250, 251, 252
Grain, unit of measurement 376
Grams 376, 377
Grana, chloroplasts 148
Grand Canyon 314
Grand unified theory (GUT) 15
Granite
  formation 279
  inselbergs 280
  tors 281
Grants, scientific funding 11
Granulating agents, tablets 254
Graphite 68
  atoms 78, 104
Graphs 18, 406
  algebra 362
  chaos theory 372
  freefall experiment 19
  statistics 368, 369
Grasses 170
Grasshoppers, metamorphosis 156
Grasslands
  geological time 269
  life zones 168
Graunt, John 359
Gravity 406
  asteroid belt 323
  Big Crunch 332, 333
  centripetal force 28
  force 20
  formula 378
  freefall experiment 19
  galaxies 328
  globular clusters 324
  gyroscopes 29
  neutron stars and black holes 330, 331
  Newton's theory of 14
  oscillation 30
  particle physics 60
  planetary rings 309
  planets 29, 308
  solar system 22, 23, 304
  stars 326, 327
  theory of relativity 62, 63
  tidal power 47
  turning force 21
  universe 333
  weight 18
  wormholes 331
Gray matter 186, 187, 207
Gray mullet, thick lipped 171
Great alar cartilage, nose 203
Great Bear constellation 386, 387
Great Bear Lake 383
Great Britain, size 382
Great Dog constellation 388, 389
Great Red Spot, Jupiter

316, 317
Great Rift Valley 273, 276
Greater auricular nerve 202
Greater omentum 216, 217, 219
Greece, ancient 8, 9
  anatomical research 178
  astronomy 296
  life sciences 120
  mathematics 358
  medicine 236
  physics 14
  theories of matter 66
Green algae 135
  classification 130
  symbiosis 137
Green light
  additive process 51
  color vision 50
  destructive interference 55
  LEDs (light-emitting diodes) 50
  subtractive process 51
  white light spectrum 49
Green seaweeds 138
Greenhouse effect 174, 290, 406
  on Venus 313
Greenland
  ice sheet 282, 283
  size 382
Grew, Nehemiah 121, 395
Groundwater 406
  limestone caves 281
  rivers 284
  water table 284
  weathering 280
Growth hormone 188, 262
Grus constellation 387, 388
Guaira Falls 383
Gualltiri 383
Guanine 115
Guinea pigs, lifespan 380
Gums 196, 197
Gunpowder
  discovery of 67
  fireworks 101
Gutenberg, Beno 267, 395
Guyots 288
Gynecology 381
Gynoecium, flowers 143
Gypsum 279
Gyroscopes 406
  angular momentum 29
  centripetal force 28
Gyrus 187, 206

H

Haber, Fritz 107
Haber process, ammonia production 106, 107
Habitats 406
  amphibians 160
  ecology 168
  flowering plants 144

human impact on environment 174
Hadar 389
Hade, faults 276
Hadley, George 267, 395
Hadrons 60, 406
  particle accelerators 61
Haeckel, Ernst Heinrich Philipp August 121, 395
Hafnium 74
Hagfish 159
  classification 133
Hahn, Otto 15, 395
Hail 292
Hair, mammals 166
Hair follicles 181
Halide ions 110, 117
Halley, Edmond 297, 395
Halley's comet 297
Hallux 232
Halogens 110-11
  chemical analysis 117
Hamal 387, 388
Hammer thrower 28
Hamsters, gestation period 380
Hands 180
  artificial 253
  bones 228, 229
  joints 183
  mammals 166
  muscles 228-9
  myoelectric arms 253
Hanging valleys 282, 283
Haploid cells, meiosis 127
Harbey, William 179
Hard disks, computers 353
Hard palate 196, 205
Hard water 86, 100
Hardness
  minerals 278
  Mohs' scale 279
Hare constellation 388
Hares, speed 380
Harriers (birds) 165
Harvard Observatory 297
Harvestmen 154, 155
  classification 133
Harvey, William 236, 237, 395
Hatching, snake eggs 163
Haustoria 169
Haustrum 197, 217, 218, 219
Havers, Clopton 179
Haworthia truncata 145
Hay fever 381
hCG see Human chorionic gonadotrophin
Head, human 176, 180, 200-7
  anterior view 205
  blood vessels 202
  bones 206
  brain 207
  ears 203

eyes 203, 205
facial muscles 200
  lateral view 204
magnetic resonance imaging 234-5
muscles 200-3
nerves 202
nose 203, 205
skull 206
Headlamps 17
Headlands 286
Heart
  amphibians 160
  birds 164
  cardiac muscle 184
  crustaceans 154
  echocardiography 240
  fish 158
  gastropods 153
  human anatomy 182, 190-1, 214
  insects 156
  lizards 162
  mammals 166
  measuring blood pressure 239
  monitoring heart rate 244
  open-heart surgery 246, 247
  pacemakers 252, 253
  posterior view 213
  research 179
  transplants 237, 246, 251
Heart-lung machines 246, 247
Heart urchins, classification 133
Heart valves
  mechanical 252, 253
  transplants 251
Heartbeat 238
Heat 90-1
  cars 17
  conductivity 52
  conductors 76
  decomposition 69
  electromagnetic radiation 49
  endothermic reactions 90
  energy 15, 16, 32-3
  equalization of temperature 33
  exothermic reactions 90
  extraction of metals 77
  fireworks 101
  four-elements theory 66
  global warming 174
  greenhouse effect 174, 290
  heating 33
  historical theories 14-15
  latent 32
  nuclear power stations 59
  radiation 32
  receptors 181
  thermite reaction 91
  see also Temperature
Heaviside, Oliver 267, 395

Hectares 376, 377
Hectoliters 376
Heels 180
Heka 324, 386
Heliostats 306
Helium
  atmosphere 290
  Big Bang 332
  discovery of 379
  gas chromatography 70
  on Jupiter 316, 317
  melting and boiling points 379
  on Neptune 320
  nuclear fusion 59
  particle accelerators 61
  periodic table 75
  on Saturn 318
  spectral absorption lines 301
  in stars 326
  Sun 306, 307
  on Uranus 318, 319
Helix, geometry 392
Hemichordata 133
Hemal spines, fish 158
Hematology 381
Hemocoel, insects 156
Hemodialysis 251
Hemoglobin 114, 115, 191
Hemophilia 263
Hemispheres
  cerebral 187, 206, 207
  geometry 365, 392
Henle, Friedrich Gustav Jakob 237, 395
Henle, loop of 198
Henry, Joseph 337, 395
Heparin 261
Hepatic duct 216
Hepatic flexure 218
Hepatic portal system 219
Hepatitis 261, 381
Hepatoduodenal ligament 217
Hepatogastric ligament 217
Hepatophyta 130, 138
Herbaceous flowering plants 142
Herbaceous shoots 149
Herbal remedies 236
Herbivores 406
  energy flow 170
  lizards 163
  teeth 166
Hercules constellation 386, 388
Herdsman constellation 386
Heredity 121, 126-7
Hermaphrodites
  earthworms 152
  gastropods 153
Hernias 251
Herons 165
Herring gull 171
Herschel, William 15, 297, 395

Hertz 31, 377
Hertz, Heinrich Rudolf 15, 395
Hertzsprung-Russell diagram, stars 324, 325
Hess, Harry Hammond 267, 395
Heterotrophs 406
  fungi 136
  and photosynthesis 148
  protists 134
Hexagonal system, crystals 35
Hexagons, geometry 392
Hexane 114
Hexanedioic acid 114
Hiatus
  aortic 221
  esophagus 220
Hierarchy of complexity, ecology 168
Higgs bosons 60, 406
High frequency sound waves, ultrasound scanning 240
High pressure
  compression 31
  weather 292
Hilum 147
Hilus 193
Himalayas 276, 277
Hindgut
  arachnids 155
  insects 156
Hindu medicine 236, 237
Hindwings, insects 156
Hinge joints 183
Hinge line, folds 277
Hipparchus 296, 395
Hippocrates 237, 395
Hippocratic Method 236
Hippopotamuses, lifespan 380
Hips 181, 182, 183
  artificial joints 253
  dynamic hip screws 253
  hip girdle 222
  joint 183
  muscles 221
Hirudinea 132
Histamine 261
Histograms 372
Histology 179
History of science 8-9
  astronomy and astrophysics 296-7
  chemistry 66-7
  earth sciences 266-7
  electronics and computer science 336-7
  human anatomy 178-9
  mathematics 358-9
  medical science 236-7
  physics 14-15
HIV see Human Immunodeficiency Virus (HIV)
Hog's-back, rocky

landscapes 280
Holdfast, seaweeds 138
Hole (electronics) 406
Hölloch 383
Holmium 75
Holothuroidea 133
Homarus gammarus 171
Homeostasis, human body 179
Homo sapiens 269
Homologous chromosomes 127
Honey guide, flowers 143
Honshu 382
Hooke, Robert 120, 395
Hooves, horses 129, 166
Horizontal fissure, lungs 194
Hormones 188-9, 406
  genetic engineering 262
  research 179
  topical drugs 255
Horn peaks 283
Hornworts, classification 131
Horsehair worms, classification 133
Horsehead Nebula 326
Horses 166
  evolution 129
  speed 380
Horseshoe crabs, classification 133
Horsetails 138, 139
  classification 131
Horst, faults 276
Hospitals
  emergency care 244-5
  history 236
  surgery 246-7
Hosts 406
  viruses 134
Hot, four-elements theory 66
Hot-air balloons 59
Hot objects 49
Hot springs 275
Hourglass Nebula 327
House mice
  energy requirements 380
  gestation period 380
  lifespan 380
Houseflies, lifespan 380
HST see Hubble Space Telescope
Hubble, Edwin Powell 297, 328, 396
Hubble Space Telescope (HST) 10, 297, 298
Hubble's Law 332, 333
Hudson Bay 382
Human body 6, 176-233
  abdomen 216-21
  brain, spinal cord and nerves 186-7
  digestive organs 196-7
  endocrine system 188-9
  energy requirements 380

forearm and hand 228-9
gestation period 380
head and neck 200-7
heart and blood vessels 190-1
history 178-9
human genome project 10, 121, 262, 263
immune system 260-1
lifespan 380
lower leg and foot 252-3
lymphatic system 192-3
muscles 184-5
pelvic region 222-5
pregnancy and childbirth 256-7
reproductive system 198-9
respiratory organs 194-5
shoulder and upper arm 226-7
skeleton 182-3
skin, hair and nails 181
speed 380
thigh 230-1
thorax 212-15
trunk 208-11
urinary system 198
Human chorionic gonadotrophin (hCG) 256, 406
Human Immunodeficiency Virus (HIV) 258
  ELISA test 261
Human impact, environment 174-5
Humerus
  birds 164
  human anatomy 182, 226, 227
  joint 183
  mammals 166
Humors, ancient medicine 236
Hundred 377
Hundredweights 376
Hunter, John 237, 396
Hunter constellation 386
Huron, Lake 383
Hurricanes 292, 293
Hutton, James 267, 396
Hyaline cartilage 215
Hyaline cartilage 215
Hybrid orbitals 79, 104, 105
Hybridization 120, 406
Hydra constellation 386, 388
Hydras 150
  classification 132
  reproduction 126
Hydrated cobalt chloride 73
Hydrated crystals 92
Hydrated iron oxide 379
Hydrocarbons 406
  bonds 112
  catalytic converters 89
  combustion 83
  cracking 112, 113

fractional distillation 113
organic chemistry 112
Hydrochloric acid
chemical reactions 81
pH scale 84
preparation of 85
preparation of
chlorine 110
preparation of
hydrogen sulphide 109
Hydroelectric power 46
Hydrogen
acid salts 86, 87
acids 84
ammonia 68, 106, 107
atmosphere 290
Big Bang 332
bonding 78, 79, 406
and combustion 83
cosmic rays 58
covalent bonding 79
dehydrating agents 92
discovery of 67, 379
DNA 115
in Earth's crust 379
electrolytic
decomposition of
water 96
ethanol 68
fatty acids 99
formula 379
hydrocarbons 112
on Jupiter 316, 317
magnetic resonance
imaging (MRI) 242
on Neptune 320
nuclear fusion 59
periodic table 74
pH scale 84
photosynthesis 148
reaction of sodium with
water 98
reactivity of metals 95
on Saturn 318
spectral absorption
lines 301
in stars 326, 327
Sun 306, 307
on Uranus 318, 319
voltaic cells 97
water 68, 92
Hydrogen chloride 84, 85
Hydrogen fluoride 79
Hydrogen oxide,
formula 379
Hydrogen peroxide 108
Hydrogen sulfide 108
on Neptune 320
preparation of 109
Hydrogencarbonates
acid on 85
formula 379
testing for 116
Hydrographs, storm 284
Hydroids, classification 132
Hydrological science 266
Hydronium
formula 379

ions 84, 95, 406
Hydrostatic skeletons 406
sea anemones 150
Hydroxide
anions 98
bases 84
ions 84
salts 86
Hydrozoa 132
Hydrus constellation 388
Hygiene, operating
rooms 246
Hygroscopic 406
compounds 92, 93
Hymenium, fungi 136
Hyoid bone 194, 201,
204, 205
Hyperbolas, cones 365
Hyperbolic geometry 365
Hyphae
fungi 136
lichens 137
mushrooms 137
Hypo 109
Hypocenters,
earthquakes 274
Hypogeal germination 147
Hypogymnia physodes 137
Hypopharyngeal gland,
insects 156
Hypotenuse 366-7
Hypothalamic
hypophyseal tract 188
Hypothalamus 187,
207, 406
endocrine system
188, 189
Hypotheses 9
Hyracotherium 129

I

Iatrochemistry 66,
120, 237
Iatrophysics 237
Ibises 165
Ice
caves 282
clouds 292
comets 322
erosion 280
glaciers 282
on Mars 315
on Neptune 320
planetary rings 308, 309
on Pluto 321
rock cycle 278
Ice ages 267
coastlines 286
polar ice sheets 283
Ice sheets 282-3
continental shelf 288
Icebergs 282
Icefalls 282
Iceland
plate tectonics 273
volcanoes 275
Icosahedrons 364

Icthyosis 263
Icthyostega 268
Ideal-Gas Equation 378
Igneous rocks 407
formation 278-9
historical theories 266-7
Moon 310
Iguanas 163
Ileocecal junction 219
Ileocecal valve 197, 219
Ileum 196, 197, 216, 217,
218, 219
Iliac crest 183, 208, 209,
210, 221, 230, 231
bone marrow 250
Iliac lymph nodes 192
Iliac spine 217
Iliohypogastric nerve 221
Ilioinguinal nerve 221
Iliotibial tract 230, 231
Ilium 182, 183, 223, 224
Images 407
convex lenses 53
formula 378
Imaging, medical 240-3
Immersed objects 37
Immune system 260-1
Acquired Immune
Deficiency Syndrome
(AIDS) 258
and artificial body
parts 253
lymphocytes 250
research 179
transplant and graft
rejection 250
Immunization 261
allergies 260
Immunological
reactions 407
transplants 250
Immunosuppressant
drugs 254
Impedance, inductors 344
Imperial units 376-7
"Impetus" theory 14
Implants
artificial body
parts 252-3
drugs 255
In parallel 407
In series 407
In vitro fertilization
(IVF) 256
Incandescence, Sun 307
Inches 376, 377
Incisions, surgery 248, 407
Incisor teeth
carnivores 166
herbivores 166
human anatomy 196, 204
Inclined plane 26
Incomplete
metamorphosis 156
Incompleteness
theorems 359
Incubation, eggs 164, 407
Incubators, babies 256, 257

Incus 203
Index finger 228, 229
Index fossils 269
India
astronomy 296, 297
continental formation 273
mathematics 358
medicine 236
Indian Ocean, size 382
Indicators, pH scale 84, 407
Indium 75
Indo-Australian plate
272, 277
Induction 407
charged atoms 40
Inductors 338, 344-5
Indus constellation 388
Inert 74, 407
Inertia 22, 407
Infection 258-9, 407
antiseptics 237
body temperature 239
diagnosis 238
transplant surgery 250
Inferior tarsus
ligament 200
Infinity 360
Inflammation, mast
cells 261
Inflorescences,
flowers 144
Influenza vaccine 261
Information, computer
networks 354-5
Infraorbital foramen 206
Infrared Astronomical
Telescope (IRAS) 299
Infrared radiation 407
astronomy 299
computer networks 354
discovery of 15
electromagnetic
spectrum 48, 299
hot objects 49
*Hubble Space
Telescope* 298
light-emitting diodes
(LEDs) 347
Sun 307
transfer of heat 33
Infratrochlear nerve 202
Infundibulum 188
Ingen-Housz, Jan 121, 396
Inguinal ligament
217, 230
Inguinal lymph nodes 192
Inhalers, drugs 255
Injections
drugs 255
vaccines 261
Injuries
emergency care 244
surgery 246
Ink, paper
chromatography 70
Inlets, coastlines 287
Input signal, amplifiers 349
Insect-eating bats 167

Insecta 132
Insectivores, lizards 163
Insects 154
anatomy 156
carnivorous plants 145
classification 132
endangered species 175
pollination 146
types 157
Inselbergs 280
Instep 181
Instruments, surgical 246
Insulation 407
birds 164
mammals 166
Insulin
diabetes 260
discovery of 179
genetic engineering 262
pancreas 189
Integers 360
Integrated circuits
337, 350-1
computers 353
diodes 346
electronic circuits 338
silicon 104
Integument 147
Intensive care,
hospitals 245
Intercostal lymph
nodes 192
Intercostal muscles 407
Intercostal nerves 215
Intercourse, sexual
198, 199
Interference 407
constructive 54
destructive 54
electromagnetic
radiation 48
interference pattern 62
wave behaviour 54-5
International Union for
the Conservation of
Nature (IUCN) 175
Internet 337, 354, 355
Internodes, flowering
plants 142
Interphase, mitosis 126
Interpreting data 19
Intersections, set theory
370, 371
Intervertebral disks
182, 183, 247
Intestines
amphibians 160
annelid worms 152
arachnids 155
cells 122
crustaceans 154
digestion 199
echinoderms 151
fish 158
gastropods 153
human anatomy 196,
197, 216, 219, 222
ileocecal junction 219

lizards 162
parasites 152
transplants 251
Intine, pollen grains 146
Intramuscular
injections, drugs 255
Intranets, computer
networks 355
Intravenous injections,
drugs 255
Introduced species 175
Invertebrates 407
arthropods 154-7
classification 133
endangered species 175
evolution 268
worms and
mollusks 152-3
Inverted images 53
Io 316
Iodide, formula 379
Iodine 68, 110
contrast X rays 241
mass spectrometry 117
molar mass 73
periodic table 75, 110
positron emission
tomography (PET) 243
starch indicator 89
Ionic bonding 67, 78, 407
lithium fluoride 78
metals 76
Ionosphere 267, 290
Ions 40, 67, 407
acids 84
activity series 94
alkali metals 98
alkaline earth
metals 100
ammonia 106
chemical analysis 116
chemical reactions 80
chlorine in water 111
complex ions 81
displacement
reactions 94-5
electrochemistry 96
formula 379
halogens 110
heat 90
hydronium 84
ionic diameter 98
macromolecules 76, 79
mass spectrometry
116, 117
mole 72
oxidation 82
reduction 82
salts 86, 87
solutions 70
transition metals 102
Van de Graaff
generators 41, 343
Iridium 74
Iris 144, 205
Iron
alloys 102
catalysts 88, 107

chemical reactions 69
Earth's composition 270, 379
Earth's magnetic field 41
electromagnetism 44, 45
extraction 76, 77
formula 379
hemoglobin 115
inductors 344
iron and sulphur mixture 69
iron sulfide 68
magnetism 40, 41
on Mars 315
melting and boiling points 32, 379
meteorites 270
ores 77
oxidation number 82
periodic table 74
pyrites 68
reactivity 68, 94
rusting 82
steel manufacture 103
thermite reaction 91
transition metals 102
Iron oxide
extraction of iron 76, 77
glass 105
on Mars 314
thermite reaction 91
Iron sulfide 69, 109
Irrational numbers 360, 361
Irregular bones 182
Irregular galaxies 328
Isahara test, color blindness 239
Ischial tuberosity 222, 225
Ischiorectal fossa 225
Ischium 182, 183
Islands
atolls 289
eyots 285
island arcs 288
sizes 382
volcanic 273, 288
Islets of Langerhans 179
Isobars 293
Isoceles triangles 392
Isoclinal folds 277
Isomers, carbon compounds 112
Isotopes 407
atomic number 72
Italy, mathematics 358
Iteration, fractals 372, 373
IVF see In-vitro fertilization
Ixodes ricinus 155

JK

Jackson, Charles 237, 396
Jacobson's organ,
reptiles 162
Jansky, Karl 297, 396
Janssen, Pierre 379
Japan
mathematics 358
plate tectonics 273
Japan, Sea of 382
Japan Trench 382
Jaundice 257
Jawless fish 158, 159
classification 133
Jaws
human anatomy 183, 196, 206
prostheses 253
snakes 163
Jeffreys, Alec 121
Jejunum 196, 197, 217, 218, 219
Jelly fungi, classification 131
Jellyfish 150
classification 132
Jenner, Edward 237, 396
Jet streams 291
Jewel Cave 383
Joints 182, 407
arthropods 154
ball-and-socket 183
cartilage 182
emergency care 245
hinge 183
pivot 183
saddle 183
skull 183
X-ray imaging 241
Joule, James Prescott 15, 396
Joules 16, 377
Journals, scientific 10, 11
Junction field-effect transistors (JFET) 348
Junctions, circuit symbol 339
June solstice 271
Jupiter 316-17
asteroid belt 304, 314, 323
data 384
moons 385
rings 308
size 304, 305
space probes 302, 303, 312
Jurassic period 269
K strategy, reproduction 169
K2 383
Kalahari Desert 383
Kalanchoe daigremontiana 126
Kangaroos 167
gestation period 380
Kangchenjunga 383
Kara Kum Desert 383
Karyotype, human 263
Kaus Australis 387, 389
Kaus Borealis 388, 389

Kaus Meridionalis 389
Keel, birds 164
Kelvin, SI units 377
Kelvin, William Thomson 15, 396
Kelvin scale 32, 376, 407
Kepler, Johannes 296-7, 396
Kepler crater, Moon 311
Keratin
beaks 164
nails 181
Kerosine, fractional distillation 113
Kestrel 165
Kettle holes 283
Keyboards, computers 352, 353
Keyhole surgery 248
Khone Falls 383
al-Khwarizmi, Muhammed ibn Musa 358, 359, 396
The Book of Restoring and Balancing 358
Kidneys
amphibians 160
birds 164
dialysis 251
fish 158
gastropods 153
human anatomy 216, 220
lizards 162
mammals 166
transplants 250, 251
urinary system 198
Kilby, Jack 337
Kilimanjaro 382
Killer cells, immune system 260
Kilogram meters per second 23
Kilograms 18, 376, 377
Kilohms, resistors 340
Kiloliters 376
Kilometers 376, 377
Kinetic energy 16, 407
brakes 25
energy transfer 17
generators 46
heat 32, 90
heat transfer 33
solids 34
X rays 49
Kirchhoff, Gustav Robert 67, 396
Kites (birds) 165
Kitt Peak National Observatory 306
Kiwi 165
Klystrons 336
Klyuchevskaya Sopka 383
Knees 181
artificial joints 253
joint 183
Knuckles 228, 229
artificial joints 253

Koalas 167
Koch, Helge von 372
Koch, Robert 237, 396
Koch curves 372
Kochab 386
Korea, mathematics 358
Krebs, Hans Adolf 121, 396
Krebs cycle 121, 124, 407
Krypton 75
Kuiper Belt 304, 320, 321
Kuril-Kamchatka Trench 382

L

Labium majus 224
Labium minus 224, 225
Laboratories 10, 11
chemical analysis 116
medical diagnosis 239
Labor, childbirth 257
Lacerta constellation 387, 388
Lacrimal bone 206
Lacrimal glands 200
Lacrimal sac 200
Lacrimomaxillary suture 206
Lactation 208
Lacteal 197
Lactic acid 124
Lactiferous ducts 208
Lactiferous sinuses 208
Ladybugs, metamorphosis 157
Lagoon Nebula 389
Lagoons
atolls 289
coastlines 286
Lakes 280-1
acid rain 174
glacial erosion 283
pollution 174
sizes 383
water cycle 172
Lamarck, Jean-Baptiste de 120, 396
Lambdoidal suture 206
Lambert-Fisher Ice Passage 383
Lamellae
chloroplasts 148
fish 158
Lamina
leaves 144, 145, 148
seaweeds 138
Lamina of vertebral arch 211
Lampetra fluviatilis 159
Lampreys 159
classification 133
Lamps 50
circuit symbol 339
Lampshells, classification 133
Lamrechtsofen 383
Lancelets, classification 133
Landers, space probes

302, 303
Landforms, geological science 266
Landscapes, rocky 280-1
Landslides 276
Landsteiner, Karl 237, 396
Langerhans, Paul 179, 396
LANs (Local Area Networks) 355
Lanthanides, periodic table 74-5, 102
Lanthanum 74
Laparoscopes 248
Laptop computers 354
Larches 140
Large Electron Positron (LEP) collider 61
Large Hadron Collider (LHC) 60, 61
Large intestine 196, 197, 216, 219, 222
Large Magellanic Cloud 329, 388, 389
Large-scale integration (LSI) 337
Larkspur 143
Larus argentatus 171
Larvae
amphibians 160
metamorphosis 156, 157
Laryngeal prominence 194, 205
Laryngitis 381
Laryngopharynx 204
Laryngoscopes 238
Larynx (voice box)
amphibians 160
artificial 253
cartilage 204, 205
human anatomy 194, 215
Lascar 383
Lasers 56
surgery 248, 249
Lasing medium 56
Latent heat 407
melting a substance 32, 33
Lateral buds, flowering plants 142
Lateral cartilage, nose 203
Lateral epicondyle 229
Lateral line, fish 159
Lateral malleolar network 232, 233
Lateral moraine 282, 283
Lateral plantar nerve 186
Lateral roots 149
Lateral sulcus 206, 207
Lateral ventricle, brain 207
Lather, soap 100
Latin names 130
Latitude 407
Laurasia 269, 273
Lava
igneous rocks 278
Moon 310, 311
oceanic crust 288

volcanoes 275
Lavatera arborea 142
Lavoisier, Antoine 67, 396
Lawrencium 75
Laws
natural 9
scientific 9
LCDs see Liquid crystal displays
LDRs see Light-dependent resistors
Lead 32
flame tests 116
lead shot 68
periodic table 75, 104
reactivity 94
solder 105
Lead iodide 80
precipitation reaction 8
Lead nitrate 80
precipitation reaction 8
Lead oxide 81, 102
Lead pencils 104
Lead sulfide 68
Leaf succulents 145
Leafy liverworts 138
Leaves
carnivorous plants 145
conifers 140
cotyledons 147
cycads 140
dicots 143
ferns 139
flowering plants 142, 144
ginkgo 140
gnetophytes 140
herbaceous flowering plants 142
horsetails 139
internal anatomy 149
monocots 143
photosynthesis 100, 148
pine trees 141
plant-transport systems 148, 149
succulents 145
types 144
LEDs see Light-emitting diodes
Leeches 152
classification 132
Leeuwenhoek, Antony van 120, 121, 396
Legionella 259
Legionnaire's disease 259
Legs
arachnids 155
arthropods 154
birds 164, 165
bones 182
cheetahs 167
crocodilians 163
human anatomy 180
joints 183
lower leg 232-3
mammals 166
muscles 185, 230-3
prostheses 253

tadpoles 161
thighs 181, 230-1
Leibniz, Gottfried
    Wilhelm 337, 359, 396
Lemaâtre, Georges
    297, 396
Lemurs 167
Lena, River 383
Length
    conversion tables 377
    measurements 18, 376
    SI units 377
Lens-cornea, compound
    eyes 156
Lenses 52-3, 407
    artificial eye lenses
        252, 253
    binoculars 52
    endoscopes 248
    eyes 52, 205
    telescopes 298
Lenticels, flowering
    plants 142
Leo constellation 386, 389
Leonardo da Vinci 178, 396
Lepas 154
Lepus constellation 386,
    388, 389
Lesser occipital
    nerve 202
Lesser omentum 217
Lesser Water Snake
    constellation 388
Lettuce slug 153
Levées 285
Levers, three classes 27
Libra constellation 386,
    388, 389
Lichens
    classification 131
    structure 137
    symbiosis 136, 137
Lienorenal ligament 219
Life 270
    creation of 268
    creationism 128
    evolution 128-9
    on Mars 303, 314, 323
    Miller-Urey experiment
        121
    origins of 121
    polymers 114
Life science 6, 118-67
    amphibians 160-1
    arthropods 154-7
    birds 164-5
    cell functions 124-5
    cells and cell structure
        122-3
    classification 130-3
    data 380
    evolution 128-9
    fish 158-9
    flowering plants 142-7
    fungi 136-7
    history 120-1
    mammals 166-7
    microorganisms 134-5

nonflowering plants
    138-41
photosynthesis and
    plant-transport
    systems 148-9
reproduction and
    heredity 126-7
reptiles 162-3
sponges, cnidarians
    and echinoderms 150-1
worms and
    mollusks 152-3
Life support systems,
    ambulances 244
Life zones 168
Lifespan, animals 380
Lift, birds' flight 165
Ligament of vena
    cava 217
Ligaments 182, 407
Ligamentum
    arteriosum 214
Ligamentum venosum 217
Ligase enzymes 262
Light
    additive process 51
    as a catalyst 88
    color 50
    constructive
        interference 55
    destructive
        interference 54, 55
    Döppler shift 301
    electromagnetic
        radiation 48
    electromagnetic
        spectrum 49, 299
    electrons 56
    energy 15, 16, 90
    fireworks 101
    fluorescence 56
    laser surgery 249
    lasers 56
    lenses 53
    mirrors 53
    Newton's theories 14
    photons 62
    photosynthesis 100
    phototherapy 257
    polarized 54, 55
    quantum physics 15, 62
    radiation from hot
        objects 49
    reflection 52-3
    refraction 52
    space-time distortions 63
    spectrometers 297
    speed of 52
    subtractive process 51
    Sun 307
    telescopes 298
    theory of relativity 63
    wave theory 14
    see also Sunlight
Light bulbs 43
    color 50
    electric circuits 43
Light curve, variable

stars 325
Light-dependent resistors
    (LDRs) 340, 341
Light-emitting diodes
    (LEDs)
    color 50
    digital thermometer 19
    diodes 346, 347
    light-dependent
        resistors 341
Light years 407
Lightning 292
    lightning conductors 47
    nitrogen cycle 172
    temperature 32
Lignin, woody flowering
    plants 142
Lilies 143
    glory lily 144
Liliopsida 131, 142
Limbs
    arthropods 154
    evolution 129
    mammals 166
Limbs (geological), folds
    277
Lime, slaked 101
Lime tree, common 144
Limestone
    acid on 87
    caves 281
    formation 279
    formula 379
    gorges 281
    mineral water 86
    steel manufacture 103
    weathering 280
Limewater 83, 116
Limiting friction 24, 408
Limpets 171
Line graphs 368
Linea alba 209, 223, 224
Linea arcuata 209
Linear integrated
    circuits 350
Lines, geometry 364-5
Lingual tonsils 204, 205,
    215
Linnaeus, Carolus 396
    classification 120, 121,
        130
Lintels, coastlines 287
Lion constellation 386
Lions, gestation period
    380
Lippershey, Hans 297, 396
Lips 181, 196
Liquid crystal displays
    (LCDs) 54, 55
Liquid pressure, formula
    378
Liquids 36-7
    capillary action 36
    crystallization 16
    dissolving 16
    distillation 70, 71
    drops and bubbles 36
    evaporation 16

gases as 90
meniscus 36
mixtures 70
particles 32
pressure 36, 37
supercooled 32
temperature 32
upthrust 37
Liquification 32
Lister, Joseph 237, 396
Litharge 102
Lithification 278
Lithium
    atomic diameter 98
    cation 98
    ionic bonding 78
    ionic diameter 98
    periodic table 74, 98
Lithium fluoride 78
Lithosphere 272-3, 408
Litmus paper
    ammonia fountain 93
    reaction of sodium with
        water 98
Liters 376, 377
Little Bear constellation
    386
Little Dog constellation
    386
Little finger 228
Liver
    amphibians 160
    bile 196, 216, 217
    birds 164
    coronary ligament 217
    fish 158, 159
    functions 217
    hepatic portal system
        219
    human anatomy 216, 217
    lizards 162
    malaria 259
    mammals 166
    research 179
    structure 217
    transplants 251
Liverworts 138
    classification 130
Lizards 163
    anatomy 162
    cladistics 133
Llamas, energy
    requirements 380
Load 26
    levers 27
Lobes, lungs 194, 213
Lobster claws (flower)
    144
Lobsters
    anatomy 154
    classification 132
    food webs 171
Lobules
    breasts 208
    testes 222
Local Group 328
    data 384
Lockyer, Norman 379

Locusts, black 144
Logarithmic spirals,
    golden rectangle 361
Logarithms 359
Logic 370-1
    deduction 8
    mathematics 358, 359
Logic gates 337, 370, 390
Long bones 182
Long-wave radio 48
Longevity, animals 380
Longitude 408
Longitudinal fissure,
    brain 207
Longitudinal waves 30
Longshore drift 287
Loop of Henle 198
Lorenz, Edward 372
Lorenz strange attractor
    372
Loudspeakers 31
    transformers 345
Low pressure
    rarefactions 31
    weather 292
Lower, Richard 179, 396
Lozenges, drugs 255
Lubricants, tablets 254
Lubrication 24, 25
Lumbar nerves 186
Lumbar plexus 186
Lumbar vertebrae
    human anatomy 182,
        183, 211, 221
    mammals 166
Lumbosacral joint 211
Lumen
    blood vessels 190
    esophagus 215
    trachea 215
    uterus 199
Luminescence 408
    comets 322
    electrons 56
    fluorescence 56
    phosphorescence 57
Luminosity 408
    stars 300, 324, 325
Luminous intensity, SI
    units 377
Luna 1 297
Lunar eclipses 296, 310,
    311, 385
Lunar phases 310
Lungs
    allergies 261
    amphibians 160
    arachnids 155
    birds 164
    computerized
        tomography 241
    cystic fibrosis 237
    drug inhalers 255
    gastropods 153
    heart-lung machines 247
    human anatomy 182,
        200, 213, 214
    lizards 162

mammals 166
    measuring lung
        function 261
    pleurae 212
    pulmonary circulation
        190, 191
    respiratory system 194-5
    retractors 247
    thoracic cavity 212
    transplants 251
Lupus constellation 386,
    388
Luster, metals 76
Lutetium 75
Lycophyta 131
Lymph 192, 193
Lymph nodes 192
    B cells 250
    structure 193
Lymphatic capillaries
    192, 193
Lymphatic ducts 192
Lymphatic system 192-3
    discovery of 179
Lymphatic trunks 192
Lymphatic vessels 192,
    193
Lymphocytes
    antibodies 191, 193
    B cells 250
    Human
        Immunodeficiency
        Virus (HIV) 258
    immune system 193, 260
    lymphatic system 192
    T cells 250
    transplant and graft
        rejection 250
Lynx constellation 386,
    389
Lyra constellation 386,
    388
Lyre constellation 386
Lysosomes 122

M

Macaca mulatta 166
Machines 26-7
Mackenzie-Peace River
    383
Mackerel 159
McKinley, Mount 382
McNath-Pierce facility 306
Macromolecules 408
    crystals 79
    ionic bonding 76, 78
Macrophages
    immune system 193,
        260
    lymphatic system 192
Macropus rufogriseus 167
Macrospicules, Sun 307
Madagascar 382
Madreporites,
    echinoderms 151
Magellan space probe
    312, 313

Magellanic Clouds 329
Magenta
    additive process 51
    subtractive process 51
Maggots 173
Magma 270, 408
    mid-oceanic ridges 288,
        289
    rock cycle 278
    volcanic islands 273
    volcanoes 275
Magnesite bricks 103
Magnesium
    atoms 77
    burning 77
    in chlorophyll 100
    ductility 76
    in Earth's crust 379
    fireworks 101
    formula 379
    periodic table 74, 100
    reactivity 94
    reactivity with dilute
        acids 95
    sea water 288
    spectral absorption
        lines 301
    thermite reaction 91
Magnesium oxide 77
    cathode-ray tubes 56, 57
    force lines 44
    mass spectrometry 117
    particle accelerators 60
    radio waves 48
    solenoids 45
Magnetic fields 408
    cathode-ray tubes 56, 57
    Earth's 271
    force lines 44
    inductors 344
    mass spectrometry 117
    particle accelerators 60
    pulsars 330
    radio waves 48
    solenoids 45
    tuned circuits 345
Magnetic resonance
    imaging (MRI) 242
    brain scans 234-5, 242
    invention of 179, 237
Magnetism 40-1
    electromagnetic
        radiation 48-9
    electromagnetism 44-5
    energy 15
    Sun 307
    sunspots 306
Magnetometers, space
    probes 302, 303
Magnetopause 271
Magnetosphere 271
Magnetotail 271
Magnets
    compasses 41, 44
    electricity generation 46
    electromagnets 45
    loudspeakers 31
    separating iron from

sulfur 69
Magnification
    magnifying glasses 53
    telescopes 298
Magnitude, stars 300,
    301, 324, 325
Magnoliopsida 131, 142
Maidenhair tree 140
Main-sequence stars
    325, 326, 327, 408
Mains transformers 345
Major alar cartilage,
    nose 203
Makalu 383
Malacostraca 132
Malaria 259
Mallard, speed 380
Malleability, metals 76
Malleus 203
Mallow, tree 142
Malpighi, Marcello 179,
    396
Malpighian tubules,
    insects 156
Mammalia 130, 133
Mammals 166-7
    cladistics 133
    classification 130, 133
    endangered species 175
    evolution 129, 269
    tagging 175
Mammary glands 166, 208
Mammograms 241
Mammoth Cave System
    383
Manatees 167
Mandelbrot, Benoit 359,
    372, 396
Mandelbrot set 356-7,
    359, 372
Mandibles 196
    human skeleton 182,
        183, 206
    mammals 166
    muscles 201, 204, 205
Mandibular angle 206
Mandibular condyle 206
Mandibular notch 206
Manganese
    periodic table 74
    preparation of oxygen
        108
Manganese chloride 111
Manganese oxide
    alkaline dry cells 96
    bleaching 111
    preparation of chlorine
        110
Manta rays 159
Mantle
    earthquakes 274
    Earth 270
    Jupiter 317
    Mars 314
    Moon 311
    Neptune 320
    plate tectonics 272-3
    Venus 313

Mantle cavity,
    gastropods 153
Manubrium 182
Maps
    radar mapping 313
    weather maps 293
Marble 80, 81
March equinox 271
Marchantia
    polymorpha 138
Mardalsfossen 383
Mare Frigoris 311
Mare Humorum 311
Mare Ibrium 311
Mare Ingenii 311
Mare Moscoviense 311
Mare Nubium 311
Mare Serenitatis 311
Mare Smithii 311
Mare Tranquillitatis 311
Maria, Moon 310, 311
Mariana Trench 382
Marine worms 152
    classification 132
Mariner 10 space
    probe 312
Markab 387, 388
Markeb 389
Marking animals,
    conservation 175
Marrow see
    Bone marrow
Mars 314-15
    data 384
    life on 313, 314, 323
    moons 385
    size 305
    space probes 10,
        297, 302, 303
Marsupial mole 167
Marsupialia 167
Marsupials 166, 167
Mass 408
    Avogadro's number 73
    centripetal force 28
    chemical reactions 80, 81
    conservation of 81
    conversion tables 377
    lifting with pulleys 27
    measurement 18, 376
    molar mass 73
    momentum 23
    Newton's Laws 22
    oscillation 30
    particle physics 60
    relative atomic mass
        (RAM) 72
    relative molecular
        mass (RMM) 72
    SI units 377
    theory of relativity 63
    Universe 332, 333
Mass spectrometry 116, 117
Mast cells 260, 261
Mastoid process 206
Matar 387
Matches, activation
    energy 90

Mathematics 7, 356-73
    algebra 362-3
    chaos theory and
        fractals 372-3
    coordinates and
        triangles 366-7
    data 392-3
    geometry 364-5
    history 358-9
    history of astronomy 296
    logic and sets 370-1
    numbers 360-1
    probability and
        statistics 368-9
    symbols 393
Matrix, nail 181
Matter 16-17, 408
    atoms 56-7
    Big Bang 332
    Brownian motion 16
    crystallization 16
    dissolving 16
    evaporation 16
    heat energy 32
    historical theories 66
    mass 18
    particle physics 60-1
    phlogiston theory 66
    states of 32
    temperature 32
Maxilla 183, 204, 206
Maxwell, James Clerk
    15, 396
Maya, mathematics 358
Mean, statistics 368, 369
Meanders 284, 285
Measurement 18-19, 376-7
    acceleration 22, 23
    distance 18
    electric current 42
    force 20
    frequency 31
    gas pressure 39
    heat 18
    length 18
    limiting friction 24
    liquid pressure 37
    mass 18
    momentum 23
    pressure 21
    radioactivity 58
    speed 22, 23
    temperature 32
    thermal expansion 34
    time 18
    turning force 21
    weight 18
    width 18
Mechanical advantage 26
Mechanical energy 17
"Mechanical"
    ("mechanistic")
    philosophy 14
Mechanics, history 14
Medial arcuate
    ligament 221
Medial epicondyle of
    humerus 226, 228

Medial moraine 282, 283
Medial plantar nerve 186
Median nerve 186, 226, 228
Medical imaging 240-3
Medical photography 49
Medical science 7,
    178, 234-63
    data 381
    history 66, 236-7
Mediterranean Sea,
    size 382
Medium-voltage-control
    transistors 349
Medium-wave radio 48
Medulla
    adrenal glands 189
    kidneys 198
Medulla oblongata
    187, 207
Medullary cavity,
    bone 182
Medullary cord, lymph
    nodes 193
Medullary sinus, lymph
    nodes 193
Medusae 150
Megrez 387
Meiosis 127
Meissner's corpuscle 181
Melting
    states of matter 32
    melting points 33, 78,
        379, 408
Meltwater, ice caves 282
Membrane, cell 122
Membraneous urethra 223
Memory
    brain 187
    computers 352
Mendel, Gregor Johann
    121, 126, 396
Mendelevium 75
Mendeleyev, Dmitri 396
    periodic table 15, 67
Mendelian ratio 127
Meninges 186
Meningitis 381
Meniscus 36, 408
    downward 30
    upward 36
Menkalinan 389
Menkar 387, 388
Menkent 389
Mensa constellation
    388, 389
Menstrual cycle 225, 408
Menstrual periods 256
Menstrual phase 225
Mental foramen 206
Mental protuberance 206
Merak 387
Mercalli scale,
    earthquakes 383
Mercury (element) 68
    melting and boiling
        points 379
    meniscus 36
    periodic table 75

    reactivity 94
    sphygmomanometer 239
    thermometers 19, 71, 239
Mercury (planet) 312
    data 384
    orbit 304
    size 305
    space probes 312
Mercury cathode
    process, sodium
    hydroxide 99
Mercury oxide 68, 69
Merganser 164
Meridians,
    acupuncture 236
Meristematic tissue 126
Merostomata 133
Merozoites 259
Merychippus 129
Mesas 280, 281
Mesentery 218, 219
Mesocarp, succulent
    fruit 147
Mesohippus 129
Mesohyal, sponges 150
Mesons 408
    particle physics 60
    theory of relativity 63
Mesophyll 149
Mesopotamia
    glassworks 67
    mathematics 358, 359
Mesosphere 290
Mesozoic era 269
Messenger RNA
    (mRNA) 125
Messier, Charles 328
Metabolic rate 408
    birds 164
Metabolism 124
Metacarpals
    birds 164
    human skeleton 182,
        228, 229
    joints 183
Metacarpophalangeal
    joints 228
Metacarpus 228
Metal-oxide field-
    effect transistors
    (MOSFET) 348
Metallized film
    capacitors 543
Metallurgy, history 66
Metals 76-7
    activity series 94-5
    alchemy 66
    alkali metals 98-9
    alkaline earth
        metals 100-1
    artificial body parts
        252, 253
    atoms 76
    catalysts 88
    cations 76
    characteristics 76
    color 76
    compounds 76

corrosion 94, 95
electric circuits 42
electrodes 97
electrolysis 67
electromagnetic
  radiation 49
electrons 76
electroplating 96, 97
extraction 77
flame tests 116
macromolecules 76
ores 76
oxides 76
and oxygen 77
periodic table 74-5
reactive metals 76
salts 86
thermite reaction 90, 91
transition metals 102-3
welding 32, 90, 91
Metamorphic rocks 408
formation 278-9
fossils 269
Metamorphosis 408
amphibians 160
frogs 161
insects 156, 157
Metaphase, mitosis 126
Metatarsal bones 182, 232
Metatarsus, spiders 155
Meteor Deep 382
Meteor showers 322, 323
Meteorites 323
atmosphere and 290
impact craters 308, 309,
  310, 311
materials 270
Meteoroids 304, 322-3
Meteorology, history 267
Meteors 290, 322, 323
Methane
atomic structure 112
in comets 322
fractional distillation 113
on Jupiter 317
on Neptune 320
on Uranus 319
Methanol 379
Methyl orange
indicators 85
Meters 18, 376, 377
Meters per second 22, 23
Meters per second per
  second 22, 23
Metric tons 376, 377
Metric units 376-7
Mexican hat plant 126
Mexico, Gulf of 382
mF see Microfarads
Miaplacidus 389
Mice
energy requirements 380
gestation period 380
lifespan 380
trophic pyramid 170
Michelangelo crater,
  Mercury 312
Michigan, Lake 383

Microbody, plant cells 123
Microchips see
  Integrated circuits
Microfarads (mF) 342
Micrometers 408
measuring thermal
  expansion 34
Microorganisms 154-5,
  408
discovery of 120
genetic engineering 262
germ theory 237
infection and disease
  258-9
Microphones 31
alternating current 338
amplifiers 549
Microphyle, conifers 141
Microprocessors
integrated circuits 350
invention of 337
myoelectric arms 253
personal computers 352
Micropyle 147
Microscope constellation
  388
Microscopes
atomic force 78
electron 120, 121
invention of 120,
  121, 179
traveling 18
Microscopium
  constellation 388
Microsoft 337
Microsurgery 248, 249
Microtubules,
  plant cells 123
Microwave radiation
  48, 408
computer networks 354
electromagnetic
  spectrum 299
klystrons 336
radar mapping 313
Mid-Atlantic Ridge 273
Mid-ocean ridges 288, 289
Midbrain 187
Middle Ages 8-9
life sciences 120
mathematics 358
medicine 236
physics 14
Middle finger 228
Middle phalanx 228, 232
Midgut
arachnids 155
insects 156
Mildews 136
Miles 376, 377
Milk
colloid 70
mammals 166
milk-secreting
  glands 208
Milky Way Galaxy 324
center of 331
images of 299, 329

radio astronomy 297
spiral galaxy 328
Miller, Stanley Lloyd
  121, 396
Miller-Urey experiment
  121
Milliliters 376
Millimeters 376
Million 377
Millipedes 154, 156, 157
classification 132
Milne, John 267, 396
Milwaukee Deep 382
Mimosa 389
Mineral water 86, 87
Minerals 278-9, 408
Mohs' scale of hardness
  267, 279
sea water 288
Miniaturization,
  electronics 337, 350
Minimally invasive
  surgery 248-9
Minims 376
Mintaka 324, 386
Mira 387, 388
Mirach 387, 388
Miranda 319
Mirfak 387, 388
Mirrors
laryngoscopes 238
reflection and
  refraction 52, 53
telescopes 296, 298
Mirzam 386, 389
"Missing link", fossils 128
Mississippi-Missouri
  River 285, 383
Mites, classification 133
Mitochondria 408
animal cells 122
euglenoids 135
Krebs cycle 124
plant cells 123
Mitosis 126
Mitral valves 191
Mixing desks,
  potentiometers 541
Mixtures 70-1, 408
chemical analysis 116
colloids 70
decomposition 80
dehydrating agents 92
distillation 71
filtration 70, 71
hydrocarbons 112
iron and sulfur 69
solutions 70
suspensions 70
Mizar 387
Möbius strip 365
Models, molecular 68
Modems, computer
  networks 354, 555
Modern physics 15, 62-3
Modus tollendo ponens
  371
Mohorovicic

discontinuity 270
Mohs, Friedrich 267, 396
Mohs' scale of hardness
  267, 279
Molarity 73
Molars
carnivores 166
herbivores 166
human anatomy 196, 197
Molecular 408
Molecular orbitals 408
covalent bonds 79
electron shells 78
Molecules 72-3, 408
absolute zero 32
acids 84
anabolism 124
bonding 78
Brownian motion 16
capillary action 36
carbon 114
chaos theory 372
chloroethene 115
chlorophyll 100
compounds 68
diatomic 77, 80
drug development 254
evaporation 16
extraction of metals 77
gas molar volume 73
gases 58
heat 32, 90
induction 40
macromolecules 76
matter 16
models 68
moles 72
polymerization 114
precipitation reaction 8
relative molecular
  mass (RMM) 72
surface catalysis 88
water 92
Moles (animals) 166
Moles (measurement) 408
Avogadro's number 73
gas molar volume 73
molar mass 73
molar solutions 73
SI units 72, 377
Mollusca 132, 152
Mollusks 152-3
classification 132
Molten sulphur 109
Molybdenum 74
Moment, turning force
  21, 408
Momentum 14, 23
angular 29
formula 378
oscillation 30
Mondino de Luzzi 179,
  396
Monera 130
Monerans, classification
  131
Mongefossen 383
Monitoring childbirth 257

Monitors, computers
  352, 353
Monkeys 166, 167
Monoceros constellation
  386, 389
Monoclinal folds 277
Monoclinic (·) sulphur 109
Monoclinic system,
  crystals 35
Monocotyledonous
  plants (monocots) 408
classification 131
flowers 143
leaves 143, 144
Monocytes 191
Monogenea 132
Monohydrates 93
Monomers 115
Monosaccharides 114
Monotremata 167
Monotremes 166, 167
Mons pubis 224, 225
Montes Apennius, Moon
  311
Moon 310-11
craters 310, 311, 323
gravity 22, 23
historical theories 266
history of astronomy 296
lunar eclipses 296, 385
moonquakes 311
solar eclipses 306
space probes 302
tidal power 47
Moons 308
data 385
Jupiter 316
Mars 314
Neptune 320
Pluto 320, 321
Saturn 318
Uranus 318, 319
Moraine 282, 283
Morels, classification 131
Morning Star 312
Mortar 100, 101
Mosquitoes, malaria 259
Mosses 138
classification 130
Motherboards,
  computers 553
Moths 157
natural selection 128
wings 156
Motile 408
Motion
amoebas 135
Brownian 16
circular 28-9
energy 15, 17
formula 378
friction 24
gas particles 38
Laws of 14
Newton's Laws 22-3
oscillation 30
precession 29
swimming 159

Motor neurons 184, 186,
  187
Motorcycles
brakes 25
centripetal force 28, 29
Molds 134, 135
classification 131
Molting 408
metamorphosis 156
Mountains
formation of 277
glaciers 282
highest 383
historical theories 266
life zones 168
ocean floor 288
plate tectonics 272, 276
Mouse, computers 352
Mouse (animal) see
  Mice
Mouths
annelid worms 152
cells lining 122
cnidarians 150
diagnosis 238
echinoderms 151
fish 158, 159
gastropods 153
jawless fish 159
mammals 166
Movable joints 183
Movement see Motion
MRI see Magnetic
  resonance imaging
Mucous membranes
asthma 261
suppositories 255
trachea 215
Mucus 409
amphibians 160
fish 158
Mud flats 286
Mud pools 275
Muddy water, filtration 71
Mudpuppies 160
Muliphen 389
Multicellular 409
Multimeters 338, 339, 340
Multiple sclerosis (MS)
autoimmune disease
  260
magnetic resonance
  imaging (MRI)
  scanning 242
symptoms 381
Multiplication,
  computers 370
Mummies 178
Muscles 184-5
abductor digiti minimi
  228, 229, 232, 233
abductor hallucis 232
abductor pollicis brevis
  228
abductor pollicis
  longus 228, 229
adductor longus 185, 230
adductor magnus 185,

222, 225, 231
adductor minimus 231
adductor pollicis 228
anastomosis, cardiac 184
ansa cervicalis 202
anterior scalene 201
arrector pili 181
arthropods 154
biceps brachii 185, 208, 209, 228
 long head 226, 227
 short head 226
biceps femoris 185, 230, 231, 233
birds 164, 165
brachialis 185, 226, 227
brachioradialis 226, 227, 228
buccinator 200, 201
bulbospongiosus 222, 225
cardiac 184, 191
cells 122
coracobrachialis 226
cremasteric 222
cricothyroid 205
deltoid 185, 201, 202, 203, 205, 209, 210, 226, 227
depressor anguli oris 200, 201
depressor labii inferioris 200, 201
depressor septi 200
digastric 201, 202, 205
dorsal interosseus
 foot 232, 233
 hand 229
drug injections 255
extensor 185
extensor carpi ulnaris 228, 229
extensor digiti minimi 229
extensor digitorum brevis 232
extensor digitorum longus 232, 233
extensor hallucis brevis 232, 233
extensor hallucis longus 232, 233
extensor pollicis brevis 229
extensor retinaculum
 ankle 232, 233
 wrist 228, 229
external intercostal 208, 209, 210, 212, 215
external oblique 185, 208, 209, 210, 212, 216, 220, 221, 223, 224, 230
fish 158
flexor 185
flexor carpi radialis 228
flexor carpi ulnaris 228, 229

flexor digiti minimi brevis 252
flexor digitorum brevis 232
flexor digitorum longus 185, 233
flexor digitorum superficialis 228
flexor hallucis longus 233
flexor pollicis brevis 228
flexor retinaculum 228, 233
frontalis 185, 200, 201, 204
galea aponeurotica 200, 201, 203
gastrocnemius 185, 230, 231, 232, 233
gemellus 231
genioglossus 204
geniohyoid 204
gluteus maximus 185, 222, 223, 224, 225, 230, 231
gluteus medius 185, 223, 224, 231
gracilis 185, 222, 225, 230, 231, 233
iliacus 221, 230
 female pelvic region 224
 male pelvic region 222
iliocostalis 210
iliopsoas 185, 230
inferior gemellus 231
inferior oblique 203, 204
inferior rectus 203
infraspinatus 185, 210, 226, 227
insects 156
intercostal
 breathing 194, 195
 external intercostal 205, 208, 209, 210, 212, 215
 internal intercostal 209, 212, 215
internal oblique 208, 209, 210, 216, 220, 221, 223, 224
interosseus 184
 foot 232, 233
 hand 228, 229
 plantar 232
involuntary 184
ischiocavernosus 222, 225
lateral malleolus 232, 233
lateral rectus 203, 204
latissimus dorsi 185, 208, 209, 210, 226, 227
levator anguli oris 200
levator ani 222, 225
levator labii superioris 200, 201
levator labii superioris

alaeque nasi 200, 201
levator palpebrae superioris 200
levator scapulae 201, 203, 204, 210, 227
longissimus 210
masseter 185, 200, 201
medial malleolus 232, 233
mentalis 200, 201
middle scalene 201
mylohyoid 201, 204, 205
nasalis 185, 200, 201
obturator internus 231
occipitalis 185, 201, 203
omohyoid 201, 202, 205
orbicularis oculi 185, 200, 201, 202, 203
orbicularis oris 185, 200, 201, 202, 203, 204
palmaris longus 228
pectineus 185, 230
pectoralis major 185, 201, 202, 205, 208, 209, 212, 226
pectoralis minor 209, 212, 226
perineus 225
peroneus brevis 185, 232, 233
peroneus longus 185, 232, 233
piriformis 231
plantar interosseus 232
plantaris 185
platysma 185, 200, 201, 202
posterior auricular 203
posterior scalene 201
procerus 200
pronator teres 228
psoas major 221, 223, 224, 230
pyramidalis 209
quadratus femoris 231
quadratus lumborum 221
rectus abdominis 208, 209, 212, 216, 220, 221, 223, 224
rectus femoris 185, 230
research 179
rhomboid major 203, 208, 210, 227
rhomboid minor 203, 208, 210
risorius 200, 202
rotator cuff 226, 227
sartorius 185, 230, 231
scalene 201
scalenus anterior 204
scalenus medius 204
scalenus posterior 204
semimembranosus 185, 230, 231, 233
semispinalis capitis 185, 201, 203, 204
semitendinosus 185, 231, 233

serratus anterior 185, 208, 209, 210, 212, 226
serratus posterior inferior 210
serratus posterior superior 210
skeletal 184, 185
smooth 184
snakes 163
soleus 185, 232, 233
spinalis 210
splenius capitis 185, 201, 203, 204
splenius cervicis 203, 210
sternocleidomastoid 185, 201, 202, 203, 204, 205
sternohyoid 201, 202, 205
sternothyroid 201, 202
stylohyoid 201
subclavius 209
subcostales 221
subscapularis 226
superior gemellus 231
superior longitudinal of the tongue 204
superior oblique of the eye 203
superior rectus 203, 204
supraspinatus 226, 227
temporalis 185, 200, 201, 203, 204
tensor fasciae latae 230
teres major 185, 208, 210, 226, 227
teres minor 185, 208, 210, 226, 227
thyrohyoid 201, 205
tibialis anterior 185, 232, 233
tibialis posterior 233
trachealis 215
transverse perineus 222, 225
transversus abdominis 209, 216, 220, 221, 223, 224
trapezius 185, 201, 202, 203, 204, 205, 208, 210, 226, 227
triceps brachii 185, 208, 209, 229
 lateral head 210, 227
 long head 210, 226, 227
 medial head 226, 227
vastus lateralis 185, 230, 231
vastus medialis 185, 230
voluntary 184
zygomaticus major 200, 201, 202
zygomaticus minor 200, 201, 202
Muscular dystrophy 263, 381
Musculocutaneous nerve 186
Mushrooms 136

classification 131
life cycle 137
structure 137
Muslims 14
Mussels 152
 food webs 171
Mutations, genetic 263
Mutualism 168, 169
Mycelium
 fungi 136
 lichens 137
 mushrooms 137
Mycorrhiza 409
 symbiosis 136
Myelin sheath 187
Myoelectric arms 253
Myofibrils 184
Myofilaments 184
Myometrium 199
Mythical world view 8
Mytilus edulis 171
Myxomycota 131

N

N-type semiconductors 346
 integrated circuits 350, 351
 transistors 348
Nail bed 181
Nail matrix 181
Nails 181
Nair Al Zaurak 387, 388
Names, scientific 11, 130
Namib Desert 383
NAND gate 390
Nanga Parbat 383
Naphtha, fractional distillation 113
Naphthalene 33
Napier, John 359, 396
Napier's Bones 359
NASA, Pathfinder space probe 297
Nasal bone 183, 201, 203, 206
Nasal cartilage 204
Nasal cavity
 human anatomy 194, 196, 204, 205
 mammals 166
Nasal inhalers, drugs 255
Nasal septum 204
Nasal speculum 238
Nash 389
Nasomaxillary suture 206
Nasopharynx 204
Natal cocoons, star formation 527
Natural cycles 172-3
Natural drugs 254
Natural forces 14-15
Natural gas 32
Natural laws 9
Natural philosophy 14, 66
Natural sciences 8
Natural selection 121, 128

Natural variation, heredity 127
Nautilus 152
Navel 180, 209
Navigation 41
Nazca plate 272, 277
Nebulae 324, 326, 327, 409
Neck, birds 164, 165
Neck (human body) 176, 180
 anterior view 205
 lateral view 204
 muscles 201-5
 nape of 180
Neck, teeth 197
Nectar, insect-pollinated plants 146
Nectaries, carnivorous plants 145
Needle holders 246
Needles, pine trees 141
Needles, surgical 246
Negative electric charge 40, 42
Negative numbers 359, 360
Nematocysts, cnidocytes 150
Nematoda 132
Nemertea 133
Neodymium 74
Neon 75
Neon lamps 50
Neonatal jaundice 257
Neoteny, axolotls 161
Nephridium, annelid worms 152
Nephrology 381
Nephrons 198
Neptune 294-5, 320
 data 384
 discovery of 297
 moons 385
 rings 308, 320
 size 304
 space probes 302, 320
Neptunium 74
Nervous reflexes 409
Nervous system 186-7, 409
 anesthetics 247
 annelid worms 152
 arachnids 155
 crustaceans 154
 emergency care 245
 endocrine system and 188
 head and neck 200
 insects 156
 magnetic resonance imaging (MRI) 242
 mammals 166
 microsurgery 248
 nerve endings 181
 nerve fibers 181, 187
 neuromuscular junction 184
 research 179
 teeth 197

Nests
  birds 164
  crocodilians 162
  spiders 155
Networks
  capacitors 343
  computers 337, 354-5
  fullerenes 104
Neumann, John von
    337, 396
Neural spines, fish 158
Neurohypophysis 188
Neuromuscular
    junction 184
Neurons 186-7, 409
  association 186, 187
  motor 184, 186, 187
  sensory 186, 187
Neurosecretory cells,
    hypothalamus 188
Neutralization of acids 85
Neutrinos, Sun 307
Neutron stars 326, 327, 330
Neutrons 72, 409
  boron 72
  isotopes 72
  neutron detectors 15
  nuclear fission 59
  nuclear physics 58
  particle physics 60
  relative atomic mass
    (RAM) 72
  in stars 330
Neutrophils 191
New General Catalog,
    galaxies 328
New Guinea 382
New moon 310
Newton, Isaac 11, 396
  calculus 359
  Mathematical
    Principles 15
  Newton's Laws 14, 22-3
  telescope 296, 297
  Universal Theory of
    Gravitation 297
  on the universe 296
Newton meters 9, 409
  measuring force 20
  measuring limiting
    friction 24
  measuring turning
    force 21
  measuring weight 18
Newton metres 21
Newtonian physics 14, 15
Newtonian telescopes 298
Newtons 377
  measuring force 20
  measuring weight 18
Newtons per square
    meter 21
Newts 160, 161
  great crested 161
Niacin 381
Niagara Falls 383
Nickel
  catalysts 88

  in Earth's core 270
  element 68
  periodic table 75
Nickel nitrate 70
Niger, River 285
Nile, River 285, 383
Nimbostratus clouds 292
Nimbus clouds 292
Nimrod-Lennox-King Ice
    Passage 383
Niobium 74
Nipples 409
  human body 180, 208
  mammals 166
  marsupials 166
Nitrates
  carnivorous plants 145
  decomposition 173
  formula 379
  nitrogen cycle 172
Nitric acid 82, 106
Nitrites, nitrogen
    cycle 172
Nitrogen 106-7
  acid rain 174
  in air 70
  ammonia 68, 106, 107
  catalytic converters 89
  chlorophyll 100
  compounds 106
  decomposition 134
  DNA 115
  melting and boiling
    points 379
  nitric acid 82
  nitrogen cycle 172
  periodic table 75, 106
  preparation 106
  radiocarbon dating 268
Nitrogen dioxide
  decomposition 80
  oxidation number 82
  preparation 82
Nitrogen monoxide 80
Nitrogen oxides 80, 82, 89
Nitrous acid, nitrogen
    cycle 172
Nobel Prizes 11
Nobelium 75
Noble gases 409
  in air 106
  periodic table 74, 75
  reactions with
    halogens 110
Nodes, flowering
    plants 142
Non-Euclidean geometry
    358, 359, 364
Nonflowering plants
    138-41
Nonmetals
  atoms 76
  carbon 104
  characteristics 76
  periodic table 74-5
  salts 86
Nonane, fractional
    distillation 113

NOR gate 390
North America
  data 382
  formation of 273
North American plate 272
North Celestial Pole 300
North Galactic Pole 329
North Pole
  ice sheet 283
  magnetic pole 271
  winds 291
North Sea 382
North seeking pole 41
Nose
  breathing 195
  diagnosis 238
  human anatomy 181,
    203, 205
  olfactory tract 207
  respiratory system 194-5
Nostrils
  crocodilians 163
  human anatomy 205
NOT gate 390
Notation, scientific 393
Notochord 130
Novaya Zemlya 383
Nuchal ligament 203
Nuclear fission see
    Fission
Nuclear fusion see Fusion
Nuclear membrane 122
Nuclear physics 58-9
Nuclear power stations 59
Nuclear reactions 409
  in Earth's core 270
  in stars 326, 327
  Sun 17, 304, 306, 307
Nucleic acids 121
  viruses 134
Nucleoid, bacteria 134
Nucleotides 409
  RNA 125
Nucleus (atoms) 56,
    72, 409
  atomic number 74
  boron 72
  discovery of 15
  electron shells 72
  particle physics 60
Nucleus (life
    sciences) 409
  cells 122, 123
  euglenoids 135
  mushroom cells 137
  prokaryotic
    organisms 134
Numbers 360-1, 376
  algebra 362-3
  calculators 358
  computers 352
  mathematics 358
Numerator 361
Nunki 387, 388, 389
Nurses, operating
    rooms 246
Nutrient molecules 409
Nutrients 409

  decomposition 134
  recycling 168
Nyasa, Lake 383
Nylon
  formation of 114
  polymers 114

O

Oak trees 144
Oases 280
Ob-Irtysh, River 383
Oberon 308
Objective lenses,
    binoculars 52
Oblique fissure,
    lungs 194
Observation
  astronomy 300-1
  empiricism 9
Obstetrics 381
Obturator fascia 222, 225
Obturator foramen 183
Obturator nerve 221
Obtuse angles 366
Occipital bone 183, 206
Occipital condyle 206
Occipital lobe, brain 187,
    206, 207
Occipital nerve 202
Occipitomastoid suture 206
Occluded fronts 293
Ocean-floor
    spreading 267
Oceanic crust, fold
    mountains 277
Oceans 270, 288-9
  coastlines 286-7
  food webs 171
  formation of 268
  hydrological science 266
  plate tectonics 272-3
  primary production 380
  river deltas 285
  sizes 382
  tidal power 47
  trenches 382
  water cycle 172, 267
Octagons, geometry 392
Octahedrons 364, 392
Octopus vulgaris 153
Octopuses 152, 153
  classification 132
Oersted, Hans Christian
    15, 396
Ohm, Georg 337, 396
Ohms 377
  electric circuits 42
  resistors 340
Ohm's Law 42, 337
Oil
  catalytic cracking 113
  electricity generation 46
  formation 269
  fractional distillation 113
  hydrocarbons 112
  lubrication 25
Oils, production

  of soap 99
Ointments 255
Olbers, Wilhelm 332
Olbers' Paradox 332
Oldham, Richard Dixon
    267, 396
Olecranon 229
Olfactory bulb 205
Olfactory epithelium 205
Olfactory nerve 205
Olfactory tract 205, 207
Oligochaeta 132
Olympus Mons, Mars
    314, 315
Omentum
  greater 216, 217, 219
  lesser 217
Ommatidia, compound
    eyes 156
Omnivorous 409
Oncology 381
Onions 123
Onycophora 133
Onycophorans,
    classification 133
Oomycota 131
Ooze, ocean floor 288
Open clusters, stars 324
Open heart surgery
    246, 247
Operating theatres 246-7
Operational amplifiers
    (op-amps) 350
Operculum
  cnidocytes 150
  fish 158, 159
Ophiothrix fragilis 151
Ophiuchus constellation
    386, 388
Ophiuroidea 133
Ophthalmoscopes 238
Opium 237, 254
Opossums 167
  gestation period 380
Optic nerve
  compound eyes 156
  human anatomy 203,
    205, 207, 251
Optical brighteners 56
Optical fibers
  computer networks
    337, 354
  endoscopes 248
  laser surgery 249
Optics
  binoculars 52
  history 14
  Newton's theories 14
  telescopes 298
Optimisticheskaya 383
OR gate 390
Oral medicines 255
Orangutans, gestation
    period 380
Orange light
  neon lamps 50
  sodium lamps 50
  white light spectrum 49

Orbital septum 200
Orbitals 409
  electrons 56, 72
  hybrid 79, 104, 105
  molecular 78, 79
  periodic table 74
  probability 368
Orbits 409
  centripetal force 28
  comets 322
  Earth 270, 271, 304
  Jupiter 316
  Mars 314
  Mercury 312
  Moon 311
  Neptune 320
  planets 29, 304-5, 308
  Pluto 320, 321
  Saturn 318
  Uranus 319
  Venus 29, 304, 313
Orbits (skull)
  birds 164
  mammals 166
Ordovician period 268
Ores 76, 409
  iron 77
Organelles 123, 409
  animal cells 122
  chloroplasts 123, 148
  prokaryotic
    organisms 134
Organic 409
Organic chemistry
    67, 112-15
  carbon 104
Organic molecules 409
Organisms 409
  cells 122
  classification 130-3
  evolution 128
  microorganisms 134
Organs 409
  transplants 250-1
Orion Arm, Milky Way
    Galaxy 329
Orion constellation 324,
    386, 389
Orion Nebula 324, 326,
    329
Orion's Belt 324,
    326, 329
Ornithoptera
    alexandrae 157
Ornithorhynchus
    anatinus 167
Oropharynx 204
Orthoclase 279
Orthopaedics 381
  artificial parts 253
Orthorhombic system,
    crystals 54
Oscillation 30-1
  electromagnetic
    radiation 48
  wave behavior 54
Oscillators 409
Oscilloscopes 31, 339

alternating current 338
inductors 344
tuned circuits 345
Osculum, sponges 150
Osmium 74
Ossification, hand
bones 229
Osteichthyes 133, 158
Osteopathy 381
Osteoporosis 381
Ostia, sponges 150
Ostrich 165
Othotsk, Sea of 382
Otoscopes 238
Otters, homes 380
Ounces 376, 377
Output signal,
amplifiers 349
Ova see Eggs
Ovarian ligament 199
Ovaries 410
annelid worms 152
cysts 248
endocrine system
188, 189
fertility treatment 256
fish 158
flowers 143, 144
human body 198, 224
lizards 162
menstrual cycle 225
ovulation 199, 225
seed fertilization 147
succulent fruits 147
Overturned folds 277
Oviducts, lizards 162
Oviparous 410
reptiles 162
Ovotestis, gastropods 153
Ovulation 199, 225
Ovules
conifers 141
fertilization 146, 147
flowers 143
Ovuliferous scales 141
Ovum see Eggs
Owls, food chains 170
Oxidation 67, 82-3, 410
bleaching 111
electrolytic cells 96
preparation of
chlorine 110
transition metals 102
voltaic cells 97
Oxidation number 82, 410
Oxides
bases 84
formula 379
iron 77
metals 76
salts 86
thermite reaction 90, 91
Oxonium ions 84
Oxygen 108, 410
aerobic respiration 124
in air 70, 106, 108
carbon cycle 173
combustion 77, 83, 108

dehydrating agents 92
diatomic molecules 77, 80
discovery of 66, 67
in Earth's crust 379
electrolytic
decomposition of
water 96
emergency care 245
ethanol 68
extraction of iron 77
fatty acids 99
formation of Earth's
atmosphere 268
free radical 410
gills 158
hemoglobin 114, 115
hydrogen bonding 79
laboratory
preparation 108
melting and boiling
points 379
mercury oxide 69
metal oxides 76
metals and 77
monitoring heart
rate 244
nitrogen cycle 172
nitrogen dioxide 80
oxidation 82
oxygen cycle 173
ozone depletion
reactions 111
periodic table 75, 108
photosynthesis 148
reactivity 94
rusting of iron 82
test for 108
therapy 244
thermite reaction 91
water 68, 92
Oxytocin 188
Oystercatchers 165
Ozernaya 383
Ozone layer 290
CFCs and 110, 111
discovery of 267
over South Pole 374-5
telescopes and 299
thinning 111, 174

P

P-n junctions, diodes 546
P-orbitals 72
covalent bonding 79
hybrid orbitals 79, 105
ionic bonding 78
P-type semiconductors
doping 346
integrated circuits
350, 351
transistors 348
P waves, earthquakes 274
Pacemakers, heart 252, 253
Pacific Ocean
earthquakes and
volcanoes 274
size 382

Pacific plate 272
Pacinian corpuscles 181
Pain receptors 181
Painter's palette 144
Palaemon serratus 171
Palate 196, 204, 205
cleft 263
Palatine bone 206
Palatine tonsil 204
Paleontology 120
Paleozoic era 268, 269
Palisade mesophyll 149
Palladium 75
Palm, hand 180, 228
Palmar arch 228
Palmate newt 160
Pancreas
birds 164
endocrine system 188
functions 189, 196, 219
human body 216, 217
structure 189
transplants 251
Pancreatic duct 196,
197, 216
Pangaea 267, 268, 269,
272, 273
Panthalassa 273
Panthera 130
Panthera tigris 130
Paper
burning 32
filters 70, 71
induction in 40
Paper chromatography 70
Papilla, flowers 143
Papillae, tongue 205
Parabolas 410
algebra 363
cones 365
Parabolic dunes 280
Paracelsus 66, 397
Paraffin oil, fractional
distillation 113
Parallax shift 300
Parallel circuits 539
capacitors 343
resistors 340
Parallel postulate 359
Parallelograms,
geometry 392
Paramecium 135
Paramedics 244, 410
Parasites 134, 410
fleas 157
fungi 136
immune system 260
lampreys 159
malaria 259
parasitism 168, 169
tapeworms 152
ticks 155
Parathyroid gland 188, 189
Parathyroid hormone 189
Paré, Ambroise 237, 397
Parent nucleus, nuclear
fission 59
Parental care 410

crocodilians 162
mammals 166
Parietal bone 183, 206
Parietal lobe 206, 207
Parietal peritoneum
223, 224
Parotid duct 196, 201
Parotid glands 196, 200,
201, 205
Parotid plexus 202
Parrots 164
Parsecs 410
Particle accelerators
15, 60-1
Particles 15, 60-1, 410
atoms 56-7
Brownian motion 16
chaos theory 372
colloids 70
crystallization 16
dissolving 16
distillation 71
electromagnetic
radiation 48
evaporation 16
filtration 71
gas molar volume 73
gases 32, 38
heat 90
kinetic energy 33
liquids 32, 36
matter 16
melting 33
mixtures 70
Newtonian physics 14
nuclear physics 58
quantum theory 62
solids 32
solutions 70
supercooled liquid 32
suspensions 70
temperature 32
Pascal, Blaise 337,
358, 397
Pascals 377
Passive immunization
261
Patau's syndrome 263
Patella
blood vessels 230
human skeleton 182,
230, 232
joint 183
mammals 166
Patella vulgata 171
Patellar ligament
230, 232
Paternity testing 263
Pathfinder space
probe 297
Pathology 381
Patients
emergency care 244-5
operating theatres 246-7
Patina, bronze 105
Patos-Maribondo Falls 383
Pauling, Linus Carl 67, 397

Paulo Afonso Falls 383
Pauropoda 132
Pavo constellation 388
PCBs see Printed
circuit boards
Peacock constellation 388
Peacock worms 152
Peanut worms,
classification 133
Pebbles, beaches 287
Pecks 376
Pecten 153
Pectoral fins, fish 158, 159
Pectoral girdle
human body 182, 227
tortoises 162
Pectoral muscles, birds 165
Pedals 27
Pediatrics 381
Pedicels, flowers 143,
144, 145
Pedicels, spiders 155
Pedicle of vertebral
arch 211
Pedipalps 410
arachnids 155
chelicerates 154
spiders 155
Peduncles, flowers 144
Pegasus constellation
386, 387, 388
Pellicle, euglenoids 135
Pelvic cavity 222
Pelvic diaphragm
(floor) 222
Pelvic fins, fish 158, 159
Pelvic girdle
human skeleton 182,
183, 222
tortoises 162
Pelvic region 180, 410
female 224-5
male 222-3
Pelvis 410
birds 164
bone marrow 250
human body 183, 222
mammals 166
Pelvis minor 220
Pencil "lead" 104
Pendulums 30
clocks 14
Penguins 165
speed 380
Penicillin, discovery of 237
Penicillium,
classification 131
Penile urethra 223
Peninsular Valdez 382
Penis 181, 198, 199,
222, 223
Penstock 46
Pentadactyl limbs 129
Pentagons, geometry 392
Pentaradiate symmetry 410
echinoderms 150
Penumbra 306, 310
Penzias, Arno Allan

297, 397
Peppered moth, natural
selection 128
Percentages 360, 361
Perching birds 164
Peregrine falcons, energy
requirements 380
Perennial flowering
plants 142
Pericardium 212, 213,
214, 215
Pericarp, succulent
fruits 147
Perihelion 308, 410
Perimetrium 199
Perineal blood vessels 222
Perineal nerves 222
Perineum
female 225
male 222
Periodic table 67, 74-5
alkali metals 98
alkaline earth
metals 100
carbon 104
halogens 110
nitrogen 106
oxygen 108
phosphorus 106
silicon 104
sulfur 108
tin 104
transition metals 102
Periodontal ligament 197
Periods (menstruation) 225
Periosteum 182, 184
Peripheral nervous
system 186-7
Perirenal fat 220
Peristalsis 197
Peritoneum 216
Permafrost, on Mars 315
Permanent magnets 410
loudspeakers 31
Permeability 410
Permian period 269
Peroneal nerve 231, 233
Perseid meteor
shower 323
Perseus Arm, Milky Way
Galaxy 329
Perseus constellation
387, 388
Personal computers
(PCs) 352-3
Perspective 358
Perspex 24
Pesticides 174
PET see Positron
emission tomography
Petals 142, 143, 144, 147
Petermanns Glacier 383
Petioles
cycads 140
flowering plants 142,
144, 145
ginkgo 140
herbaceous flowering

plants 142
Petiolules 144
pF see Picofarads
pH scale 84, 410
  acid rain 174
  discovery of 67
Phaeophyta 130
Phaet 389
Phagocytes 193, 260
Phalanges (phalanx)
  181, 182, 228, 232
  growth of 229
Pharmacology 254-5,
  381, 410
Pharyngeal tonsil 204
Pharynx
  anemones 150
  annelid worms 152
  fish 158
  human anatomy 194,
  196, 200, 205
  insects 156
Phase (astronomy) 410
  Mercury 312
  Moon 310
  Venus 312
Phase (electronics) 410
Phekda 387
Phenotypes, heredity
  126, 127
Philippine plate 272
Philippine Trench 382
Philosophers' stone 66
Philosophy 14
Phlegm, "humors" 236
Phloem, plant-transport
  systems 148, 149
Phlogiston theory 66, 67
Phobos 314
Phoca vitulina 171
Phoenix constellation
  387, 388
Phoronida 133
Phoronids,
  classification 133
Phosphates
  decomposition 173
  DNA 115
Phospholipids 124
Phosphor
  fluorescent lamps 50
  television screens 57
Phosphorescence 410
  cathode-ray tubes 57
Phosphorus 106
  activation energy 90
  allotropes 106
  doping semiconductors
  346
  on Jupiter 317
  periodic table 75, 106
Photo masks, integrated
  circuit manufacture 351
Photocatalysis 88
Photoelastic stress
  testing 55
Photography
  catalysts 88

sodium thiosulphate
  108, 109
X rays 49
Photons 410
  electromagnetic
  radiation 48
  lasers 56
  luminescence 56
  particle accelerators 60
  particle physics 60
  quantum theory 62
Photosphere, Sun 307
Photosynthesis 148, 410
  algae 135, 137
  carbon cycle 173
  catalysts 88
  chlorophyll 100
  chloroplasts 123
  cyanobacteria 134
  euglenoids 135
  food webs 171
  lettuce slugs 153
  oxygen cycle 173
  seaweeds 138
  sunlight 306
Phototherapy 257
Photovoltaic cells 17
Phrenic nerve 213, 214
Phyla, classification 133
Phyllodes, carnivorous
  plants 145
Phyllodes, ferns 139
Pith
  herbaceous shoots 149
  woody flowering
  plants 142
Pituitary gland 187, 207
  functions 188, 189
  structure 188
Pivot, turning forces 21
Pivot joints 183
Place-value systems,
Pilli, bacterium 134
Pillow lava 288
Pills, drugs 255
Pinacocytes, sponges 150
Pine trees 140, 141
Pineal gland 187,
  188, 189
Pinna
  human anatomy 203
  mammals 166
Pinnae, ferns 139
Pinnate leaves 144
Pinnipedia 167
Pinnules, ferns 139
Pinocytic vesicles 122
Pints 376, 377
Pinus sylvestris 141
Pioneer 10 space
  probe 302
Pioneer 11 space
  probe 302
Pisces Austrinus
  constellation 388
Pisces constellation
  386, 388
Pistons
  air pumps 66
  motorcycle brakes 25
Phylogeny 132
Phylum 410
  classification 130
Physical sciences 8
Physical weathering 280
Physicians, diagnosis 238
Physics 6, 12-63
  astrophysics 296
  circular motion 28-9
  color 50-1
  electric circuits 42-3
  electricity and
  magnetism 40-1
  electromagnetic
  radiation 48-9
  electromagnetism 44-5
  electrons 56-7
  forces 20-3
  formulas 378
  friction 24-5
  gases 38-9
  generating electricity 46-7
  heat and
  temperature 32-3
  history 14-15
  liquids 36-7
  matter and energy 16-17
  measurement and
  experiment 18-19
  medical physics 237
  modern physics 15, 62-3
  Newtonian physics 14, 15
  nuclear physics 58-9
  particle physics 60-1
  reflection and
  refraction 52-3
  simple machines 26-7

solids 34-5
  wave behavior 54-5
  waves and
  oscillations 30-1
Physiological 410
Physiology 178, 179
Physiotherapy 381
Phytol 100
Phytoplankton 410
  diatoms 135
  food webs 171
Pi, circles 364
Pi mesons 60
Pia mater 186
Picofarads (pF) 342
Picometers 98
Pie charts 368, 369
Pigments
  bleaching 111
  chlorophyll 148
  color 50
  paper chromatography 70
  pH scale 84
  subtractive process 51
  transition metals 102
Pigs, heart-valve
  transplants 251
Pileus, gilled
  mushrooms 137

numbers 360
Placenta 410
  chorionic villus
  sampling 256
  human body 199
Placental mammals
  166, 167
Plains 284, 285
Planck, Max Karl Ernst
  15, 397
Plane, inclined 26
Plane angles, SI units 377
Plane shapes,
  geometry 392
Plane wave 410
  wave behaviour 54
Planet X 320
Planetary nebulae 326, 327
Planetismals 268
Planets 308-9
  asteroid belt 323
  centripetal force 28
  data 384
  gravity 29
  history of astronomy 296-7
  infrared astronomy 299
  Jupiter 316-17
  Mars 314-15
  Mercury 312
  Neptune 320
  orbits 29, 304-5, 308
  Pluto 320-1
  rings 309
  Saturn 318
  solar system 304-5
  space probes 297, 302-
  3, 308
  Uranus 318-19
  Venus 312-13
Plankton
  food webs 171
  phytoplankton 135
Plantae 130, 131
Plantar aponeurosis 232
Plants
  asexual reproduction 126
  carbon cycle 173
  cells 122, 123
  chlorophyll 100
  classification 120, 130-1
  drugs 254
  ecology 121
  evolution 128, 268, 269
  flowering 142-7
  food chains 170
  internal anatomy 149
  natural cycles 172-3
  nitrogen cycle 172
  nonflowering 138-41
  oxygen cycle 173
  parasitism 169
  photosynthesis 88, 100,
  121, 123, 148, 306
  transport systems 148, 149
  weathering and
  erosion 280
Plasma (blood) 191
  antibodies 250

Plasma membrane
  animal cells 122
  bacteria 134
  plant cells 123
Plasmid, genetic
  engineering 262
Plasmodesma 123
Plasmodial slime mold,
  classification 131
Plaster of Paris,
  formula 379
Plastic sulfur 109
Plastics 114
  artificial body parts
  252, 253
  discovery of 67
  structures 379
  thermoplastics 114
  thermosetting 114
Plastron, tortoises 162
Plate tectonics 267, 272-3
  earthquakes and
  volcanoes 274-5
  faults and folds 276-7
  on Mars 315
  metamorphic rocks 278
  mid-oceanic ridges 288
  on Miranda 319
  mountain building 277
  ocean currents 269
Platelets 191
Platinum
  catalytic converters 89
  discovery of 379
  flame tests 116
  periodic table 75
  reactivity 94
  reactivity with dilute
  acids 95
  transition metal 102
Platonic solids,
  geometry 364
Platyhelminthes 132, 152
Platypus, duck-billed 167
Playas 281
Pleiades 324, 328,
  387, 388
Pleura 205, 212, 214, 215
Pliohippus 129
Plugs, volcanoes 275
Plumules
  conifers 141
  fava beans 147
Plunge pools 284, 285
Plutinos 320, 321
Pluto 304, 320-1
  data 384
  discovery of 297
  moons 385
  orbit 305
Plutonium 74
Pneumonia 259, 381
Poincaré, Jules Henri
  359, 397
Point of suspension 21
Poisons
  cnidocytes 150
  salamanders 161

scorpions 155
snakes 163
spiders 155
Polar-front jet
  stream 291
Polar-night jet
  stream 291
Polar nucleus 410
  seed fertilization 147
Polaris (Pole Star) 328, 387
Polarized light 54, 55
Pole Star (Polaris) 328, 387
Poles
  celestial 300
  Earth 270, 271
  magnets 41
Poliomyelitis vaccine
  237, 261
Pollachius pollachius 171
Pollack 171
Pollen 410
  conifers 141
  gymnosperms 140
  structure 146
  see also Pollination
Pollen tubes
  conifers 141
  fertilization 147
Pollex 228
Pollination 410
  conifers 141
  flowering plants 142,
  144, 146, 147
  insect-pollinated
  plants 146
  wind-pollinated
  plants 146
Pollution 174
  acid rain 174
  catalytic converters 88, 89
  electricity generation 46
Pollux 386, 389
Polonium 75
Polychaeta 132
Polychaetes 152
Poly(chloroethene)
  (PVC) 114, 115
  structure 379
Polygons 411
  geometry 364
Polyhedrons
  (polyhedra) 411
  geometry 364
Polymerization 114, 115
Polymers 114, 411
  artificial body parts 252
Polynomials, algebra
  362, 363
Polyplacophora 132
Polyps 150
Polysaccharides 114
Polystyrene, structure 379
Polythene 114
  static electricity 40
  structure 379
Polytrichum commune 138
Polyvinylchloride (PVC),
  structure 379

Ponds, pollution 174
Pondweeds 144
Pons 187, 207
Pools, plunge 284, 285
Poor metals, periodic table 74-5
Pope, Alexander 296
Popliteal fossa 180
Popliteal lymph nodes 192
Population growth, humans 174
Populations, species 168
Pores
  fungi 136
  sponges 150
Porifera 152
Porocytes, sponges 150
Porphyrin ring, chlorophyll 100
Porrima 389
Ports, computers 353
Positive electric charge 40, 42
Positive ions 41
Positive numbers 360
Positron emission tomography (PET) 242, 243
Positrons 411
  particle accelerators 60
Post-central gyrus 206
Posterior crural intermuscular septum 233
Posterior lobe, pituitary gland 188
Posterior tubercle, vertebrae 211
Postulates, mathematics 358, 359
Potassium
  atomic diameter 98
  discovery of 67
  in Earth's crust 379
  flame tests 116
  formula 379
  ionic diameter 98
  periodic table 74, 98
  reactivity 94
  sea water 288
Potassium chromate 103
Potassium dichromate 103
Potassium iodide 80
Potassium nitrate 80
Potassium permanganate
  crystallization 16
  dissolving 16
Potatoes, digestion of starch 89
Potential energy 16, 17, 411
  cars 17
  hydroelectricity 46
Potentiometers 340, 341
Potholes 281
Pouches, marsupials 167
Pounds 376, 377
Powdered laundry

detergent 89
Power
  formula 378
  SI units 377
  see also Energy
Power stations
  generators 46
  history 336
  hydroelectricity 46
  nuclear power 58, 59
Power transistors 349
Powers of ten 377
Praesepe 386
Praseodymium 74
Prawns 171
Precambrian era 268
Precentral gyrus 206
Precession 29
Precipitates 411
  chemical analysis 116
  chemical reactions 8, 80
Precipitation, weather 292
Predators 411
  birds of prey 165
  chaos theory 372
  ecosystems 168
  food chains 170
  sharks 159
Pregnancy 225, 256-7
  hormones 189
  ultrasound scanning 240
Prehensile 411
Premature babies 256, 257
Premises, logic 370, 371
Premolars
  carnivores 166
  herbivores 166
  human 196
Prenatal tests 256
Prepuce
  clitoris 225
  penis 223
Pressure 21, 411
  blood pressure 239
  Boyle's Law 38
  Charles Law 39
  formula 378
  gases 38-9
  liquids 36, 37
  SI units 377
  standard temperature and pressure (STP) 73
Pressure Law 38, 39
  formula 378
Pressure receptors 181
Prevailing winds 291
Priestley, Joseph 66, 67, 397
Primary colors 411
  additive process 51
  vision 50
Primary plexus, pituitary gland 188
Primary response packs, paramedics 244
Primates 167
  evolution 269
Principle of the

Conservation of Energy 16, 411
Principle of Superposition 54, 411
Printed circuit boards (PCBs) 337, 338
Printers, computers 353
Prion proteins 258, 259
Prisms
  binoculars 52
  geometry 392
  white light spectrum 49
Prizes 11
Probability 358, 368-9
Product, chemical reactions 80, 411
Progesterone 189
Proglottids, tapeworms 152
Prokaryotic cells 122, 134
Proliferative phase, menstrual cycle 225
Promethium 74
Prominences, Sun 307
Proofs, logic 371
Propane 112, 113
Propene 112
Properties, chemical reactions 68, 69, 80
Prophase, mitosis 126
Propyne 112
Prostate gland 198, 199, 223
Prostatic urethra 223
Prostheses 253
Protactinium 74
Proteins 411
  enzymes 88, 124
  genetic mutations 263
  hemoglobin 115
  prions 258, 259
  sequence 411
  structure 411
  synthesis 124
  viruses 134
Protista 130, 131
Protists 134
  cells 122
  classification 130, 131
  structure 135
Proton-proton chain, Sun 307
Proton synchroton (PS) ring 61
Protons 72, 411
  acids 84
  atomic number 72, 74
  bases 84
  boron 72
  cosmic rays 58
  electromagnetic radiation 49
  isotopes 72
  neutron detectors 15
  nuclear physics 58
  particle accelerators 60, 61
  particle physics 60

positive electric charge 40
relative atomic mass (RAM) 72
  in stars 330
Protoplanets 304
Protostars 326, 327
Protozoans 134
  amoebas 135
  infections 258, 259
Protractor muscle, arthropods 154
Protrusible 411
  tube feet 150
Proust, Joseph Louis 67, 397
Proust's Law 67
Proximal convoluted tubule 198
Proximal phalanx 228, 232
Pseudohearts, annelid worms 152
Pseudopodia
  amoebae 135
  phagocytes 260
Psilophyta 131
Psoriasis 381
Psychiatry 381
Pterophyta 131, 138
Pteropus 167
PTFE, structure 379
Ptolemy 296, 297, 397
  Almagest 296
Ptolemaeus crater, Moon 311
Ptyalin 88, 89
Pubic symphysis 183
Pubis 182, 183
Public health 236
Public understanding of science 11
Puerto Rico Trench 382
Puffballs 136
  classification 131
Pull 20
Pulleys 26, 27
Pulmonary capillaries 191
Pulmonary circulation 190, 191
Pulmonary semilunar valve 191
Pulp cavity, teeth 197
Pulsars 330
  discovery of 297
Pulse
  measuring blood pressure 239
  medical diagnosis 238
Pumps
  drugs 255
  nuclear power stations 59
Pupae 411
  metamorphosis 156, 157
Pupils, eyes 205
Puppis constellation 386, 389
Purace 383

Pure mathematics 358
Push 12
PVC 114, 115
  structure 379
Pycngonida 133
Pygostyles, birds 164
Pylons, electricity 59
Pyloric cecum, echinoderms 151
Pyloric sphincter 197
Pylorus 197
Pyramids, geometry 364, 392
Pyrenees 277
Pyrenoid, euglenoids 135
Pyridoxine 381
Pyrites, iron 68
Pyrrhophyta 131
Pyruvic acid 124, 411
Pythagoras 397
Pythagorean theorem 358, 359, 366, 367
Pythons 163
Pyxis constellation 386

QR

Quadrate lobe, liver 217
Quadratic curves 363
Quadrats 8, 175
Quadrilaterals, geometry 364
Quadrillion 377
Quadruple pulleys 27
Quantum theory 9, 15, 62
Quarantid meteor shower 323
Quarks 60, 411
  discovery of 15
Quarts 376
Quartz
  crystals 68
  formation 279
  glass 105
  silicon 104, 105
Quasars 328, 333, 411
  Big Bang 332
  black holes 331
  Döppler shift 301, 333
Quaternary period 269
Queen Alexandra's birdwing butterfly 157
Queens, tree wasps 157
Quicklime 107
Quinine 254
Quintillion 377
R strategy, reproduction 169
RA see Right ascension
Rabbits 166
  homes 380
Rachis
  ferns 139
  leaves 144
Radar 411
  mapping 313
  space probes 312, 313
  telescopes 299

Radial nerve 186, 226, 227, 229
Radial symmetry 411
  cnidarians 150
Radian, SI units 377
Radiated tortoise 162
Radiation 411
  cosmic background radiation (CBR) 332, 333
  electromagnetic 17, 48-9
  heat transfer 32
  ozone layer 110, 111
  Sun 307
  X-ray imaging 240
Radiative zone, Sun 307
Radicals 411
  flame tests 116
  formula 379
  salts 86, 87
Radicles, seeds 147
Radio astronomy 297
  cosmic background radiation (CBR) 332
  space probes 302
  telescopes 299
Radio waves 48, 411
  computer networks 354
  discovery of 15, 336
  electromagnetic spectrum 299
  magnetic resonance imaging (MRI) 242
  pulsars 330
  RF chokes 345
  tuned circuits 345
  variable capacitors 343
Radioactivity 411
  analyzing 58
  geothermal power 47
  nuclear physics 58
  radionuclide scanning 242, 243
Radiocarbon dating 268
Radioisotopes, positron emission tomography (PET) 243
Radiology 381
Radionuclide scanning 242, 243
Radiotherapy 381
Radium 74, 100
Radius
  circles 362, 364
  spheres 365
Radius bone 411
  birds 164
  human skeleton 182, 226, 228, 229
  joint 183
  mammals 166
Radon 75
Radula, gastropods 152, 155
Rails 34
Rain 292
  acid rain 174
  hurricanes 293

rainfall patterns 411
rainwater 86, 87
rivers 284
  storm hydrographs 284
  water cycle 172, 267
Rainforests
  life zones 168
  primary production 380
Raja clavata 159
RAM see Random access
  memory; Relative
  atomic mass
Ram constellation 386
Ramenta, ferns 139
Random access memory
  (RAM), computers 352,
  353, 412
Rapids, rivers 284
Rare earth metals,
  periodic table 74-5
Rarefaction 412
  sound waves 31
  springs 30
Ras Algethi 388
Ras Alhague 387, 388
Rat snake 163
Rate of reaction 412
Ratios
  common fractions 361
  golden ratio 361
  mathematics 358
  trigonometry 366-7
Ratites 165
Ray craters 308
Rays (fish) 159
R-C circuits 542
Reactants 80, 412
  conservation of
    mass 81
  surface area 81
Reaction 20, 412
  Newton's Laws 22
  see also Chemical
    reactions
Reactivity 412
  activity series 94-5
  halogens 110
  metals 76
Reactors 59
Read-only memory
  (ROM), computers
  352, 353, 412
Receptacles, flowers 143
Receptor sites 412
  viruses 258
Receptors 187
  cold 181
  heat 181
  pain 181
  pressure 181
  touch 181
Recessive alleles 126, 127
Recognition cells,
  immune system 260
Recovery Glacier 383
Rectangles
  area and volume 393
  geometry 392

golden rectangle 361
Rectification, diodes 346
Rectifiers 346, 347
Rectouterine pouch 224
Rectovesical pouch 223
Rectum
  amphibians 160
  birds 164
  functions 197
  human body 196, 217,
    218, 219, 220, 221, 222,
    223, 224
  insects 156
  lizards 162
  suppositories 255
Rectus sheath 208, 209
Recumbent folds 277
Recurvirostra avosetta 165
Recycling nutrients 168
Red algae,
  classification 130
Red blood cells
  blood transfusions 251
  discovery of 179
  functions 191
  hemoglobin 114
  malaria 259
  manufacture 182
  stem cells 250
Red dwarf stars 325
Red giant stars 325, 327
Red lead 81
Red light
  additive process 51
  color vision 50
  constructive
    interference 55
  photons 48
  subtractive process 51
  white light spectrum 49
Red phosphorus 106
Red pigments, paper
  chromatography 70
Red pulp, spleen 193
Red Sea 273, 291, 382
Red seaweeds 138
Redox reactions 67,
  82-3, 412
  combustion 108
  electrolytic cells 96
  extraction of metals 77
  reactivity 94
Redshift 301, 412
  quasars 333
Reduction 82-3, 412
Redwoods 140
Reef shark, black tip 159
Reefs, coral 289
Refineries, oil 113
Reflection
  color 50
  light 52-3
  telescopes 298
  total internal
    reflection 52
Reflection nebulae 326
Reflex angles 366
Reflexes, medical

diagnosis 238
Refraction 412
  telescopes 298
Regoliths 310
Regular polygons 364
Regular polyhedra 364
Regulus 386, 389
Relative atomic mass
  (RAM) 72, 412
  copper 73
  iodine 73
  periodic table 75
Relative molecular mass
  (RMM) 72, 412
Relativity 62, 297
  Einstein's theories 15
  General Theory of
    62, 331
  non-Euclidean
    geometry 364
  Special Theory of 62, 63
Relays, solenoids 544
Remote controllers,
  infrared LEDs 547
Renaissance 9
  anatomical research
    178-9
  earth sciences 266
  life sciences 120
  medical science 236
  physics 14
Renal pelvis 198
Reproduction 126-7
  amphibians 160
  conifers 141
  earthworms 152
  flowering plants
    142, 146-7
  fungi 136
  gymnosperms 140
  human body 198-9
  liverworts 138
  lizards 162
  mammals 166
  nonflowering
    plants 138
  seaweeds 138
  slime molds 135
  snakes 163
  strategies 169
Reproductive system 198-9
  female pelvic
    region 224-5
  male pelvic region 222-3
Reptiles 162-3
  classification 133
  endangered species 175
  evolution 269
Reptilia 133
Research, costs 10-11
Reseau Jean Bernard 383
Reserves, wildlife 175
Resistance, to
  antibiotics 258
Resistance (electrical) 412
  capacitors 542
  formula 378
  multimeters 339

Resistant 412
Resistor-capacitor
  circuits (R-C circuits) 342
Resistors 340-1, 412
  colour codes 391
  electronic circuits 338
  integrated circuits 350
  transistors 348
  values 391
Resonant frequency,
  tuned circuits 345
Respiration 412
  carbon cycle 173
  energy yield 124
  fish 158
  human body 194-5
  oxygen cycle 173
  and protein synthesis 124
Respiratory
  bronchioles 195
Restriction enzymes,
  genetic engineering 262
Resultant 412
Reticulum
  constellation 388
Retina 205
  ophthalmoscopic
    view 238
Retractor muscles
  anemones 150
  arthropods 154
Retractors, surgical 247
Retrograde motion,
  Martian orbit 314
Retroviruses 258, 412
Reversible reactions
  80, 412
  ammonia production 107
  chromate ions 103
RF chokes 345
Rhabdomes, compound
  eyes 156
Rhea 165
Rhea americana 165
Rhenium 74
Rhesus monkey 166
Rheumatoid arthritis 260
Rhizine, lichens 137
Rhizomes
  ferns 139
  flowering plants 145
  horsetails 139
Rhodium
  catalytic converters 89
  periodic table 74
Rhodophyta 130
Rhombic sulphur 108, 109
Rhombus, geometry 392
Rib spreaders 247
Ribbon Falls 383
Ribbon worms,
  classification 133
Ribcage 209
  exploded view 215
Riboflavin 381
Ribosomes 412
  animal cells 122
  bacteria 134

protein synthesis 125
Ribs
  birds 164
  breathing 195, 208
  fish 158
  human skeleton 182,
    209, 212, 214, 215,
    216, 220
  mammals 166
  tortoises 162
Richter, Charles Francis
  267, 397
Richter scale,
  earthquakes 267, 385
Riffles 285
Rift valleys 276
Rigel 324
  magnitude 301
  star maps 386, 389
Right-angled
  triangles 392
Right angles 366
Right ascension (RA),
  astronomy 300
Rills 284, 412
Ring finger 228
"Ring of fire" 274
Rings
  planets 308, 309, 318-19
  sulphur 108, 109
River Eridanus
  constellation 388
River turtles 162
Rivers 284-5
  coastlines 286
  deltas 279, 284, 285
  hydrological science 266
  longest 383
  pollution 174
  rock cycle 278-9
  water cycle 172, 267
RMM see Relative
  molecular mass
RNA 412
  protein synthesis 124
  transcription 125
  viruses 134, 258
Robins, energy
  requirements 380
Rockies 276
Rocks 278-9
  carbonate 87
  evolution of
    the Earth 268
  faults and folds 276-7
  fossils 269
  geological science 266
  geothermal power 47
  historical theories 266-7
  igneous 266-7, 278-9
  on Mars 303
  metamorphic 269, 278-9
  on Moon 310
  planetary rings 308, 309
  plate tectonics 272-3
  quartz 104, 105
  rock cycle 278
  sedimentary 266,

267, 278-9
  strata 276
Rocky landscapes 280-1
Rod, unit of
  measurement 376
Rodents, food chains 170
Rollers
  ball bearings 25
  reducing friction 24, 25
ROM see Read-only
  memory
Roman Catholic Church 14
Roman Empire
  earth sciences 266
  medicine 236
Roman numerals 360, 376
Rongeurs 247
Röntgen, Wilhelm
  Konrad von 15, 397
Root succulents 145
Roots
  aerial 145
  ferns 139
  flowering plants 142, 145
  internal anatomy 149
  root cap 149
  root hairs 149
  root tip 149
  weathering and
    erosion 280
Roots, teeth 197
Rossby, Carl-Gustaf 291
Rossby waves 291
Rotifera 133
Rotiferans,
  classification 133
Rotors
  electric motors 45
  generators 46
Round ligament 217, 224
Roundworms,
  classification 132
Rubber 35
Rubbing alcohol
  formula 379
Rubella vaccine 261
Rubidium
  atomic diameter 98
  ionic diameter 98
  periodic table 74, 98
Rubus fruticosus 147
Ruby lasers 56
Rudimentary transverse
  process 211
Rugae
  bladder 198
  stomach 197, 219
Ruiz 383
Runners, herbaceous
  flowering plants 142
Rust 82
  formula 379
Rusts (fungi),
  classification 131
Ruthenium 74
Rutherford, Ernest 15,
  379, 397
Rutherfordium 379

S

S-orbitals 72
  covalent bonding 79
  hybrid orbitals 79, 105
  ionic bonding 78
S waves, earthquakes 274
Sabella 152
Sabik 388
Saccharides 114
Sacral canal 223, 224
Sacral foramen 183
Sacral nerves 186
Sacral plexus 186
Sacral promontory 183, 211
Sacral vertebrae 211
Sacroiliac joint 182
Sacrolemma 184
Sacrotuberous ligament
  222, 225
Sacrum 182, 183
  female pelvic region 224
  male pelvic region
  222, 223
  mammals 166
  vertebrae 211
Saddle joints 183
Sagitta constellation 388
Sagittal suture 206
Sagittarius Arm, Milky
  Way Galaxy 329
Sagittarius constellation
  387, 388, 389
Sago palm 140
Sahara Desert 383
Sail constellation 388
Saiph 324, 386
Salamanders 160
  European fire 161
Salamandra
  salamandra 161
Saliva 196, 412
  enzymes 88, 89
Salivary glands
  human body 189, 196,
  201, 205
  insects 156
Salk, Jonas 237, 397
Salmon, speed 380
Salt (common) 86, 98
  erosion 280
  formation of 76
  formula 379
  hydrogen chloride gas 85
  ionic bonding 78
  production of soap 99
  sea water 288
Saltation, rivers 285
Salts 86-7, 412
  acid salts 84, 87
  ammonium ions 106
  hard water 100
  production of soap 99
  reactivity 94
Salvarsan 237
Samarium 74
Sampling, computer
  networks 354

San Andreas Fault 276
Sand
  dunes 279, 280
  erosion 280
  glass 105
  mortar 101
  quartz 104
  in rivers 285
  sandy shores 286
  spits 286
Sand dollars,
  classification 133
Sandpaper 24
Sandstone 280
Sangay 383
Sankey diagrams 17, 412
Sap, plant cells 123
Saphenous nerve 186
Saprobes 134, 136
Sarcomastigophora 131
Satellites, artificial
  290, 308
Satellites, natural see
  Moons
Saturn 318
  data 384
  moons 385
  rings 308, 318
  size 304
  space probes 302, 318
Saussure, Horace
  Bénédict de 267, 397
Sauveur, Joseph 15
Savannah
  life zones 168
  primary production 380
Saws, bone 246
Scale, calcium salts 100
Scale leaves 145
Scalene triangles 392
Scales 412
  crocodilians 163
  fish 158, 159
Scales, weighing with 18
Scales constellation 388
Scallops 153
  classification 132
Scalpels 246
Scandium 74
Scanning
  medical diagnosis 240-1
  pregnancy 256
Scaphopoda 132
Scapula (shoulder blade)
  human skeleton 180,
  182, 226
  joint 183
  mammals 166
  pectoral girdle 227
  spine of 210
Scarpa, Antonio 179
Scarps 412
  rift valleys 276
Scatter diagrams 368, 369
Scheat 387, 388
Schedar 387
Scheele, Carl Wilhelm
  67, 379, 397

Schrödinger, Erwin 62
Schrödinger's cat
  thought experiment 62
Schwann cells 187
Sciatic nerve 186, 231
Science
  history 8-9
  the practice of
  science 10-11
  scientific laws 9
  and technology 8
  what is science 8-9
Scientific Revolution 8-9
Scientists 10, 11
Scissors, surgical 246, 248
Sclera 203, 205
Scolex, tapeworms 152
Scomber scombrus 159
Scorpion constellation 388
Scorpions 154
  classification 133
  internal features 155
Scorpius constellation
  387, 388
Scots pine 141
Scrapyard
  electromagnets 45
Scree slopes 280, 281
Screening, pregnancy 256
Screens
  cathode-ray tubes 57
  computers 352, 353
  projecting images onto 53
  television 57
Screws 26
Scrotal septum 223
Scrotum 181, 199,
  222, 223
Scrubland, life zones 168
Sculptor constellation
  387, 388
Scutes, tortoises 162
Scyphozoa 132
Sea anemones 169
  classification 132
  Mediterranean 150
Sea caves 286, 287
Sea cucumbers 151
  classification 133
Sea-floor spreading 267
Sea Goat constellation 388
Sea lilies, classification 133
Sea mammals 167
Sea nettle jellyfish 150
Sea slugs 153
Sea spiders,
  classification 133
Sea squirts,
  classification 133
Sea urchins 151
  classification 133
  food webs 171
Sea water 70
  mineral content 288
Seals 166, 167
  food webs 171
Seamounts 288, 289
Seas see Oceans

Seasons
  Earth's axis 271
  on Mars 314
Seaweeds
  classification 138
  food chains 171
  food webs 171
  green seaweeds 135
Sebaceous glands 181
Second World War,
  computers 337
Secondary colors 51
Secondary plexus,
  pituitary gland 188
Secondary sexual
  characteristics 412
Seconds, SI units 18, 377
Secretory cells, pituitary
  gland 188
Secretory phase,
  menstrual cycle 225
Secretory vesicles 122
Sedimentary rocks 266, 267
  formation 278-9
Sediments 412
  coastlines 286
  deltas 285
  fossil remains 268, 269
  glacial deposition 283
  moraine 282
  ocean deposits 288
  rivers 285
  waves 287
Seed leaves 147
Seeds 412
  conifers 141
  fertilization 147
  flowering plants
  142, 146-7
  food chains 170
  germination 146, 147
  gymnosperms 140
  nonflowering plants 138
  succulent fruits 147
Segmental bronchus 213
Segmented worms,
  classification 132
Segrä, Emilio Gino 67, 397
Seif dunes 280
Seismic 413
Seismic waves 274
Seismographs 266, 274
Seismology 266
Selenium 75
Self inductance,
  inductors 344
Self-similarity, fractals
  372, 373
Semen 198, 199
  DNA fingerprinting 263
Semicircular canals,
  ears 179, 203
Semiconductors 346, 413
  computers 337
  electronic circuits 338
  history 336
  integrated circuits 350
  LEDs (light-emitting

diodes) 50
  solar cells 46, 47
  thermistors 341
  transistors 348
Semilunar fold 219
Semilunar valve 191
Semimetals 413
  periodic table 74-5
Seminal vesicles 199, 223
Seminiferous tubules 222
Sense organs 413
  mammals 166
  smell 162, 205
  taste 162, 205
  touch 181, 187
  see also Ears; Eyes
Sensory neurons 186, 187
Sensory receptors 187, 413
Sepals 142, 143, 147
Septa, annelid worms 152
Septal cartilage, nose 203
September equinox 271
Septum
  anemones 150
  heart 191
Septum pellucidum 187
Series circuits 339
  capacitors 343
  resistors 340
Serotonin 261
Serpens Caput
  constellation 389
Serpens Cauda
  constellation 388
Serpens constellation
  386, 388
Serpent constellation
  386, 388
Serpent Holder
  constellation 386
Serum, immunization 261
Servers, Internet 355
Sessile 413
  sponges 150
Seta, mosses 138
Sets 358, 359, 370-1
Seven Sisters 324, 528
Sex cells 126
  fertilization 127
  human body 198, 199
  meiosis 127
  nonflowering plants 138
Sex chromosomes,
  genetic mutations 263
Sex hormones 188
Sextans constellation
  386, 388, 389
Sextant constellation
  386, 388
Sexual intercourse 198, 199
Sexual reproduction 126
  flowering plants 146-7
  humans 198-9
  liverworts 138
  seaweeds 138
Shakta Pantjukhina 383
Shampoo, medicated 255
Shannon, Claude

Elwood 337, 397
Shapes, geometry
  364-5, 392
Sharks 159
Shaula 387, 388
Sheep 166
  cloning 263
  lifespan 380
Sheep ticks 155
Sheet lightning 292
Sheetwash 284
Shellfish, fossils 269
Shells
  birds' eggs 164
  bivalves 153
  diatoms 135
  mollusks 152
  reptile eggs 162, 163
  tortoises 162
Shells, electrons 56, 413
Shelly limestone 279
Shield volcanoes 275, 315
Ships 37
Shoots
  horsetails 139
  internal anatomy 149
Shores 286-7
Short-wave radio 48
Shoulder blade (scapula)
  human skeleton 180,
  182, 226
  joint 183
  mammals 166
  pectoral girdle 227
  spine of 210
Shoulders 180
  artificial joints 253
  bones 182
  joint 183
  muscles 185, 208, 226-7
  pectoral girdle 227
Shrews 173
Shrimps, classification 132
Shrubs
  flowering plants 142
  gymnosperms 140
SI (Systéme
  Internationale) units
  11, 18, 377, 413
Sight 205
Sigmoid colon 197, 218,
  219, 220, 223, 224
Signals, amplifiers 349
Silica, lava 275
Silica gel, desiccators 93
Silicates
  Earth's composition 270
  on Mars 315
  on Mercury 312
  meteorites 270
Silicon
  crystals 104
  diodes 346
  in Earth's crust 379
  integrated circuits
  350, 351
  periodic table 75, 104
  solar cells 47

Silicon chips see
  Integrated circuits
Silicon dioxide 68
  integrated circuit
  manufacture 351
Silicon oxide 104, 105
Silicone rubber, artificial
  body parts 252
Silk, spiders 155
Silt, rivers 284, 285
Silurian period 268
Silver
  displacement reactions 95
  formula 379
  periodic table 75
  reactivity 94
  reactivity with dilute
  acids 95
  transition metals 102
Silver bromide,
  photographic films
  88, 109
Silver halides 117
  photographic films
  88, 109
Silver nitrate
  chemical analysis
  116, 117
  reactivity 95
Simple attractors, chaos
  theory 372
Simple machines 26-7
Simple pulleys 27
Sine, trigonometry 367
Single bonds, organic
  chemistry 112
Singularity, black holes
  330, 331, 413
  Big Crunch 333
Sinkholes 281
Siphonoglyph,
  anemones 150
Siphons, octopuses 153
Sipuncula 133
Sirenia 167
Sirens (amphibians) 160
Sirius 329
  Hertzsprung-Russell
  diagram 325
  magnitude 301
  spectral absorption
  lines 301
  star maps 386, 389
Sistema del Trave 383
Skeleton
  birds 164
  bony fish 158, 159
  cartilaginous fish 159
  mammals 166
  tortoises 162
  X-ray imaging 241
  see also Bones;
  Exoskeleton
Skin
  amphibians 160
  dolphins 167
  drug injections 255
  grafts 251

human body 181
  reptiles 162
  salamanders 161
  snakes 163
  toads 161
  topical drugs 255
Skin patches, drugs 255
Skull
  birds 164
  human skeleton 182,
  183, 200, 206
  mammals 166
  titanium plates 253
  trepanning 236, 237
Sky, color 306
Slaked lime 101
Sleeping sickness 259
Slessor Glacier 383
Slime molds 134
  classification 131
  reproduction 135
Slipher, Vesto Melvin
  297, 397
Slipped disks 247
Slopes, forces 20
Slow worm 163
Slugs 152
  classification 132
Slugs, slime molds 135
Slumped cliffs 287
Small intestine 196, 197,
  216, 219
Small Magellanic Cloud
  329, 388
Small-signal diodes 347
Smallpox vaccine 237, 261
Smell, sense of 205
  Jacobson's organ 162
Smith, William 267, 397
Smoke particles 16
Smooth muscle cells 122
Smuts 136
  classification 131
Snails 152
  classification 132
  internal features 153
  speed 380
Snakelock anemone,
  green 150
Snakes 162, 163
  cladistics 133
  eggs 163
  Jacobson's organ 162
  venom 163
Snellen chart, vision
  tests 239
Snipe 165
"Snout", glacier 282, 283
Snow 292
  glaciers 282
  water cycle 172
Soap
  hard water 100
  lather 100
  pH scale 84
  production of 98, 99
Soap bubbles
  colours 54, 55

surface tension 36
Societies, scientific 10
Soda bread 99
Sodalite 56
Sodium
  atomic diameter 98
  characteristics 76
  compounds 98
  discovery of 67
  Downs Process 76, 77
  in Earth's crust 379
  formation of sodium
  chloride 79
  formula 379
  glass 105
  ionic diameter 98
  lamps 50
  macromolecules 76
  melting and boiling
  points 379
  periodic table 74, 98
  reaction with water 98
  reactivity 94
  salts 86
  sodium hydroxide 99
  spectral absorption
  lines 301
Sodium bicarbonate
  decomposition 99
  formula 379
  reactions 85
Sodium carbonate 105
Sodium carbonate
  decahydrate 93, 379
Sodium chlorate
  bleaching 110, 111
  formula 379
Sodium chloride 86, 98
  characteristics 76
  Downs Process 77
  formation of 76
  formula 379
  ionic bonding 78
  macromolecules 79
  sea water 288
Sodium dichromate 71
Sodium
  hydrogencarbonate 98
  decomposition 99
  formula 379
  reaction with acid 85
Sodium
  hydrogensulfate 87
Sodium hydroxide
  manufacture 98, 99
  neutralization of acid
  85, 87
  preparation of
  nitrogen 106
  production of soap 99
Sodium octadecanoate 99
Sodium sulfite 109
Sodium thiosulfate
  108, 109
Soft palate 196, 204
Software, computers 352
Soil
  bacteria 134

erosion 280
  filtering muddy
  water 71
  fungi 136
  nitrogen cycle 172
  water cycle 172
Solar cells 17
  electricity generation
  46, 47
Solar eclipses 306,
  311, 385
Solar energy 17, 46, 47
Solar flares 307
solar system 304-5
  comets, asteroids, and
  meteorites 322
  data 384
  gravity 29
  history of
  astronomy 296-7
  planets 308-21
  position in Milky Way
  Galaxy 328, 329
  space probes 302
  Sun 306
Solar wind
  comets 322
  magnetosphere 271
Solder 104, 105
Soldering irons 105
Solenoids 45, 413
  relays 344
Solfatara 275
Solid angles, SI units 377
Solid shapes, geometry
  364, 392
Solids 34-5
  amorphous 34
  crystals 16, 34-5
  dissolving 16
  electromagnetic
  radiation 49
  melting 32
  mixtures 70
  particles 32
  temperature 32
  tension 34, 35
  thermal expansion 34
Solomon/New Britain
  Trench 382
Solstices 271
Soluble 413
Solutes 413
  distillation 70, 71
  mixtures 70
Solutions 413
  acids and bases 84
  alkaline 98
  calcium salts 100
  chemical analysis 116
  chemical reactions 80
  concentration 73
  dissolving 16
  distillation 70, 71
  electric charge
  carriers 96
  filtration 71
  mixtures 70

molar 73
  pH scale 84
  reactivity 94
  sucrose 114
  titration 85
Solvents 413
  distillation 70, 71
  mixtures 70
  water 93
Soot 83, 112
Soredium, lichens 137
Sörensen, Sören Peter
  67, 397
Sound waves
  energy 15, 17
  frequency 31
  ultrasound scanning 240
  vibrations 30, 31
  wavelength 31
  waves 30, 31
Sounds (body), medical
  diagnosis 238
South America
  data 382
  formation of 273
  mountain building 277
South American plate 272
South Celestial Pole 300
South China Sea, size 382
South Galactic Pole 329
South Pole
  ice sheet 283
  magnetic pole 271
  ozone layer 111, 374-5
  winds 291
South Sandwich
  Trench 382
South seeking pole 41
Southern Cross
  constellation 388, 389
Southern Crown
  constellation 388
Southern Fish
  constellation 388
Southern Triangle
  constellation 388
Sp hybrid orbitals
  104, 105
Space
  geometry 364, 365
  see also universe
Space-filling models 68
Space probes 297,
  302-3, 308
  asteroids 302
  comets 302
  costs 10
  Jupiter 302, 303, 312
  Mars 10, 297, 302, 303
  Mercury 312
  Moon 302
  Neptune 302, 320
  Saturn 302, 318
  Sun 302
  Uranus 302, 318, 319
  Venus 303, 312
Space shuttle 313
Space telescopes 298

Space-time 413
  black holes 330
  geometry 365
  theory of relativity
  63, 331
  wormholes 351
Spadix flowers 144
Spain, fold
  mountains 277
Sparrowhawk 165
Spathes, flowers 144
Spatulas, medical
  diagnosis 239
Spawn 161
Special care baby units
  256, 257
Species 413
  classification 120, 130-3
  communities 168
  ecosystems 168
  endangered species 175
  evolution 128
  extinction 128, 174, 175
  food chains 170
  interactions 169
  introduced species 175
  natural selection 121
  populations 168
Specimen tubes 239
Spectral absorption
  lines, stars 301
Spectral type, stars 413
Spectrographs 413
  Hubble Space Telescope
  298
Spectrometers 413
  mass spectrometry
  116, 117
  observing the Sun 306
  stars 297
Spectrophotometers,
  space probes 302
Spectroscopy 67
Spectrum 413
  colors 50
  electromagnetic 48-9
  stars 300
  white light 49
Speculum, nasal 238
Speech, brain 187
Speed 23, 413
  acceleration 22, 23
  air resistance 24
  animals 380
  centripetal force 28
  cheetahs 167
  formula 378
  of light 52
  measurement 22, 23
  velocity 22
  winds 383
Sperm
  amphibians 160
  chromosomes 263
  earthworms 152
  fertility treatment 256
  fertilization 127
  gastropods 153

human body 189, 198, 199, 222, 225
meiosis 127
Sphenofrontal suture 206
Sphenoid bone 183, 204, 206
Sphenophyta 131, 138
Sphenosquamosal suture 206
Sphenozygomatic suture 206
Sphere, celestial 300
Spheres
elliptic geometry 365
geometry 364, 365, 392
Spheroids, geometry 392
Spherules 310
Sphincters
anal 222, 223, 224, 225
bladder 198
cardiac 197
pyloric 197
Sphygmomanometer 239
Spica 386, 389
Spicules, sponges 150
Spicules, Sun 307
Spiders 154, 155
classification 133
speed 380
Spike flowers 144
Spinal cord
amphibians 160
birds 164
foramen magnum 206
human body 182, 184, 186, 207
lizards 162
magnetic resonance imaging (MRI) 242
mammals 166
microsurgery 249
vertebrae 200, 208
Spinal nerves 208, 413
Spine
cheetahs 167
fish 158
human skeleton 183, 208
mammals 166
posterior view 211
slipped disks 247
snakes 163
see also Vertebrae; Vertebral column
Spines
cacti 145
fungi 136
sea urchins 151
Spinnerets, spiders 155
Spinning objects, gyroscopes 28, 29
Spinous process 183, 211
Spiny-headed worms, classification 133
Spiracles 413
arachnids 155
fish 159
uniramians 156

Spiral bacteria 134
Spiral galaxies 328, 329, 333
Spits, coastlines 286
Spleen 216, 217, 218, 219
functions 193
lymphatic system 192
Splenic cord 193
Splenic flexure 218
Splints, emergency care 245
Sponges 150
classification 132
internal features 150
Spongy bone 182
Spongy mesophyll 149
Sporangia
ferns 139
fungi 136
horsetails 139
liverworts 138
mosses 138
nonflowering plants 138
Sporangiophores 136
Spores 413
ferns 139
fungi 136
gilled mushrooms 137
horsetails 139
liverworts 138
nonflowering plants 138
slime molds 135
Sporophyte generation 138
ferns 139
Sporozoa 131
Sporozoans, classification 131
Sporozoites 259
Spring (season) 271
Spring equinox 271, 300
Springs, waves and oscillations 30
Springs (water) 284
hot springs 275
Squamosal suture 206
Squamous epithelial cells 122
Squared numbers 360, 361
algebra 362
Pythagorean theorem 366
Squares, geometry 364, 392
Squid 152, 153
classification 132
Squirrels
energy requirements 380
homes 380
Stability 29
Stacks, coastlines 286, 287
Stainless steel 102
Stamens 143, 144, 147, 413
Standard temperature and pressure (STP) 73, 413
Stapes 203

artificial 253
Starch
digestion of 89
molecules 114
photosynthesis 148
Starfish, classification 133
Starling, Ernest Henry 179, 397
Stars 324-5
constellations 324, 386-9
data 384
Döppler shift 301
galaxies 328-9
history of astronomy 296, 297
life cycles 326-7
magnitude 300, 301, 324, 325
neutron stars 330
observational techniques 300
planets 308
spectral absorption lines 301
spectrum 297
Sun 306-7
telescopes 298
Statements, logical 370
States of matter 413
gases 32
liquids 32
solids 32
supercooled liquids 32
and temperature 32
Static electricity 40
Statistics 368-9
history 358, 359
Stator 46
Steam
electricity generation 46
geothermal power 47
nuclear power stations 59
Steel
alloys 102
cathodic protection 95
expansion 54
manufacture 103
radiation from hot objects 49
Stele, roots 149
Stem cells 250
Stem succulents 145
Stems
gilled mushrooms 137
herbaceous flowering plants 142
woody flowering plants 142
Stensen, Niels 266, 267, 397
Step-down transformers 545
Step-up transformers 545
Steradian, SI units 377
Stereotactic microsurgical rig 249
Sternum
birds 164

bone marrow 250
human skeleton 182, 208, 209, 215
Stethoscopes 244
listening to body sounds 238
measuring blood pressure 239
Stickhorns, classification 131
Stigma 143, 144 413
insect-pollinated plants 146
pollination 146, 147
wind-pollinated plants 146
Stimulated emission 56
Stings
insects 156
scorpions 155
Stinkhorn 136
Stipules 147
Stolons, herbaceous flowering plants 142
Stomach
amphibians 160
birds 164
cardia of 220
crustaceans 154
echinoderms 151
fish 158
functions 197
gastropods 153
human body 196, 197, 216, 217, 218, 219
lizards 162
mammals 166
Stomata
leaves 148, 149
pine needles 141
Storms
hurricanes 293
hydrographs 284
on Jupiter 316, 317
lightning 292
on Mars 314, 315
STP see Standard temperature and pressure
Strange attractors, chaos theory 372
Strassmann, Fritz 15, 397
Stratocumulus clouds 292
Stratosphere 290
Stratum, rocks 276, 413
Stratum basale 181
Stratum corneum 181
Stratum granulosum 181
Stratum lucidum 181
Stratum spinosum 181
Stratus clouds 292
Strawberries 142
Streamlined 413
birds 164
Streams 284
limestone caves 281
Stress 413
Stress analysis, polarized

light 54, 55
Striations, muscle fibers 184
Strike, folds 277
Strobilus, horsetails 139
Stroma, chloroplasts 148
Strong nuclear force 413
grand unified theory 15
nuclear physics 58
particle physics 60
Strontium
fireworks 101
periodic table 74, 100
Structure, solids 16
Stump, coastlines 287
Styles 143, 144, 413
fertilization 147
insect-pollinated plants 146
Stylets, fleas 157
Styloid process 204, 206
Subarachnoid space 186
Subatomic particles
discovery of 15
particle physics 60-1
Subcapsular sinus, lymph nodes 193
Subcostal nerve 221
Subcutaneous injections, drugs 255
Subduction zone 273, 413
mid-oceanic ridges 288
Sublimation 32, 110, 413
Sublingual gland 196
Submandibular gland 196, 201, 205
Subphyla, classification 133
Subsets, set theory 371
Substances, state of matter 32
Substrates, enzymes 125
Subtraction, computers 370
Subtractive process, color 50, 413
filters 51
Subtropical jet streams 291
Succulents 145
Suckers, octopuses 153
Suckling, mammals 166
Sucrose
crystals 114
dehydration 92
formula 379
photosynthesis 148
Sugars
digestion of starch 89
DNA 115
fermentation 88, 89
formula 379
liver and 179
molecules 114
photosynthesis 100, 148
sucrose 114
sugar cane 175
surface catalysis 89
Sulcus 187, 206
Sulcus terminalis 205
Sulphates

formula 379
salts 86
sea water 288
Sulfides
formula 379
hydrogen sulfide 108
Sulfur 108-9
allotropes 108, 109
chemical reactions 69
compounds 108
discovery of 379
iron and sulfur mixture 69
iron sulfide 68
periodic table 75, 108
rings 108, 109
sodium thiosulphate 109
solfataras 275
Sulfur oxides, acid rain 174
Sulfuric acid
dehydrating agent 92
hydrogen chloride gas 85
neutralization 87
preparation of chlorine 110
preparation of nitrogen 106
rate of reaction 81
salts 86
on Venus 313
Sumatra 382
Sumerians, mathematics 359
Summer 271
Sun 306-7, 325
celestial sphere 300
Copernicus's theory 9
data 385
and Earth's atmosphere 290
Earth's seasons 271
eclipses 306, 311, 385
energy flow 170
flares 307
global warming 174
gravity 22, 23
history of astronomy 296
infrared astronomy 299
and the Moon 310
natural cycles 172-3
nuclear physics 58
orbit of planets 29
radiation 110, 111
size 304, 305
solar power 17, 46, 47
solar system 304-5
solar wind 271
space probes 302
spectral absorption lines 301, 306
sunspots 306, 307
temperature 32
transits 312
water cycle 172
Sunflower 144
Sunlight 306
oxygen cycle 173

photosynthesis 100, 123, 148
Super proton synchroton (SPS) ring 61
Superclusters, galaxies 328
Supercomputers 8
Superconductors 15
Supercooled liquids, particles 32
Superficial muscles 184, 185, 414
forearm and hand 228, 229
head and neck 200, 202, 203
lower leg and foot 232, 233
shoulder and upper arm 226, 227
thighs 230, 231
trunk 209, 210
Superficial palmar arch 228
Supergiant stars 325, 327, 331
Supergranules, Sun 307
Superior, Lake 383
Superior articular facet 211
Superior articular process 211
Superior sagittal sinus 207
Superior tarsus ligament 200
Supernovae 330, 414
observational techniques 300
remnants 326, 327
stellar life cycles 326, 327
Suppositories 255
Supramarginal gyrus 206
Supraorbital foramen 206
Supraorbital nerve 202
Suprasternal notch 181
Sural nerve 233
Surface catalysis 88-9
Surface tension 414
bubbles 36
cohesive forces 36
Surfaces 24
Surgeons 246-7
training 249
Surgery 246-7
anesthetics 237
artificial body parts 252-3
cesarian section 256
history 178
minimally invasive 248-9
prehistoric 236, 237
transplants 246, 250-1
Sushruta 237, 397
Suspended load, rivers 285
Suspension, mixtures 70, 414

filtration 70
Suspension, turning forces 21
Suspensory ligament of penis 223
Sutures, skull 183, 206
Sutherland Falls 383
Swammerdam, Jan 179
Swan constellation 386
Swash, waves 287
Sweetlip fish 169
Swifts, speed 380
Swim bladder, fish 158, 159
Swimming
birds 164
fish 159
Switch gear 46
Switches
circuit symbol 339
computers 352
electric circuits 43
integrated circuits 350
relays 344
transistors 349
Swordfish constellation 388
Symbiosis 168, 414
fungi 136
lichens 136, 137
parasitism 169
Symbols
electronic circuits 339, 341, 343, 345, 347, 390
mathematics 393
periodic table 75-6
physics 378
transistors 349
Symmetry
cnidarians 150
echinoderms 150
Sympathetic trunk 215, 221
Sympathetic trunk ganglion 215
Symphyla 132
Symphysis pubis 225, 224
Symptoms 238, 258, 414
Synapses 184
Syncline, folds 277
Syringes, vaccines 261
Systemic circulation 190, 191
Systems 414
Systolic pressure, blood pressure 239

T

T cells
Human Immunodeficiency Virus (HIV) 258
immune system 260
thymus gland 192
and transplants 250
Table Mountain constellation 388

Tablets, drugs 254, 255
Tadpoles 160, 161
Taenia coli 197
Taenia libera 217, 218, 219
Taenia omentalis 217, 218
Tagging animals, conservation 175
Tailraces, hydroelectric power stations 46
Tails
amphibians 161
birds 164
cheetahs 167
comets 322
crocodilians 163
dolphins 167
fish 158, 159
lizards 163
tadpoles 161
tortoises 162
Takla Makan Desert 383
Talc 279
Talons, birds 165
Talus 281
Tanganyika, Lake 383
Tangents, trigonometry 367
Tantalum 74
Tap roots 149
Tapeworms 152
classification 132
Tarantula 155
Tardigrada 133
Tarsal bones 182, 232
Tarsiers 167
Tarsometatarsus, birds 164
Tarsus, spiders 155
Tasmanian devil 167
Taste
Jacobson's organ 162
taste buds 205
Taurus constellation 386, 388
Tawny owl 170
Taxonomy 130, 132
Taxus baccata 140
Tear faults 276
Technetium
discovery of 67
periodic table 74
Technology 8
Tectonic plates 267, 272-3, 414
earthquakes and volcanoes 274-5
faults and folds 276-7
on Mars 315
metamorphic rocks 278
mid-oceanic ridges 288
on Miranda 319
mountain building 277
ocean currents 269
Teeth
crocodilians 163
false 253
human body 196, 197, 200

jawless fish 159
mammals 166
sharks 159
snakes 163
Teflon, structure 379
Telegraph 267
Telephones, computer networks 354, 355
Telescopes 297, 298-9
Galileo's 297
history of astronomy 297
Newton's 296, 297
observing the Sun 306
Television 57
cathode-ray tubes 56, 57, 336
Tellurium 75
Telophase, mitosis 126
Temperate 414
forests 168
grasslands 168
rainforests 168, 380
Temperature 32-3, 414
atmosphere 290
Boyle's Law 38
Charles' Law 39
chemical reactions 80
decomposition 80
electromagnetic radiation 49
equalization of 33
filament lamps 50
gases 38-9
heat 90
historical theories 14-15
measurement 32
melting and boiling points 379
Pressure Law 39
scales 376
SI units 377
solids 34
standard temperature and pressure (STP) 73
stars 324, 325
on Venus 313
weather 292
weather fronts 293
see also Body temperature
Temporal bone 183, 206
Temporal lobe 206, 207
Ten 377
powers of 377
Tendinous intersection 209
Tendons 184, 414
abductor pollicis longus 229
achilles 185, 233
biceps brachii 226, 228
calcaneal 185, 233
extensor carpi radialis brevis 229
extensor carpi radialis longus 229
extensor carpi ulnaris 229
extensor digiti minimi 229
extensor digitorum 229

extensor digitorum brevis 233
extensor digitorum longus 185, 232, 233
extensor hallucis 233
extensor hallucis longus 185, 232
extensor indicis 229
extensor pollicis brevis 229
extensor pollicis longus 229
flexor digitorum brevis 232
flexor digitorum superficialis 228
flexor hallucis brevis 232
flexor hallucis longus 252
lumbrical 229
palmar interosseus 229
palmaris longus 228
peroneus tertius 232, 233
surgery 247
tibialis anterior 232, 233
triceps brachii 227
Tension 414
centripetal force 28
oscillation 30
solids 34, 35
surface 36
Tension force, inclined planes 26
Tentacles
cnidarians 150
octopuses 153
Tepals, flowers 143, 144
Terbium 75
Terminal bronchioles 195
Terminal moraine 282, 283
Terminal velocity 24, 414
Terraces, glacial erosion 283
Terrapins 162
Terrestrial 414
Terrestrial planets 304, 308
Mars 314
Mercury 312
Venus 312-13
Tertiary bronchus 213
Tertiary period 269
Testa, seeds 146, 147, 414
Testes
amphibians 160
annelid worms 152
functions 199
human body 198, 222, 223
sex hormones 188, 189
Testosterone 189
Tests
chemical analysis 116
chlorine in water 111

flame tests 116
gas chromatography 70
medical diagnosis 238-9
paper chromatography 70
pregnancy 256
Testudo radiata 162
Tetanus 381
vaccine 261
Tethys Ocean 273
Tetragonal system, crystals 34
Tetrahedrons 364, 392
Tetrapods 166
Thalamus 187, 207
Thallium 75
Thalloid liverworts 138
Thallus
lichens 137
liverworts 138
seaweeds 138
Thar Desert 383
Theophrastus 120, 397
Theorems 358
Pythagorean theorem 358, 359, 366, 367
Theories 9, 18
Thermal expansion 34, 414
Thermionic emission, cathode-ray tubes 336
Thermistors 341
Thermite reaction 90, 91
Thermocouples 414
electronic thermometers 239
Thermometers 71
body temperature 239
digital 19
measuring heat 18
mercury 19
Thermoplastics 114
Thermosetting plastics 114
Thermosphere 290
Theropods 128
Thiamine 381
Thighs 181
muscles 230-1
Thin film interference 55
Thistle funnels 83
Thomson, Joseph John 15, 337, 397
Thoracic cavity 212, 215, 216
Thoracic lymphatic duct 192
Thoracic nerves 186
Thoracic vertebrae
human skeleton 182, 183, 211
mammals 166
Thoracolumbar fascia 208, 210
Thorax 414
crustaceans 154
human body 180, 194-5, 208, 212-15
mammals 166
Thorium 74
Thornback ray 159

Thousand 377
Thread, surgical 246
Three-dimensional
  shapes, geometry 364
Throat 200, 205
  diagnosis 238
  digestive system 196
  respiratory system 194
Thulium 75
Thumbs 180
  bones 228
  joint 183
  muscles 228
  myoelectric arms 253
Thunderstorms 292, 293
Thylakoids 148
Thymine 115
Thymus gland 192
Thyristors 349
Thyrocervical trunk 214
Thyrohyoid ligament 194
Thyroid cartilage 194,
  204, 205
Thyroid gland 189, 204,
  205, 214
  functions 188, 189
  positron emission
    tomography (PET) 243
Thyroid-stimulating
  hormone 188
Thyroxine 189
Tibia
  fractures 241
  human skeleton 182,
    252, 253
  joint 183
  mammals 166
  spiders 155
Tibial nerve 186, 231, 233
Tibiotarsus, birds 164
Ticks 154, 155
  classification 133
Tides
  coastlines 286
  estuaries 284
  historical theories 266
  tidal power 47
Tiger salamander 160
Tigers 166
  classification 130
  energy requirements 380
Time
  Big Bang 332
  black holes 330, 331
  freefall experiment 19
  geological 268-9
  measurement 18
  SI units 377
  theory of relativity 62, 63
Tin 104
  alloys 104, 105
  bronze 105
  element 68, 76
  periodic table 75, 104
  reactivity 94
  reactivity with dilute
    acids 95
  solder 105

Tissue 414
  analysis 237, 239
  transplants 250-1
Titania 308
Titanium 74
Titration 414
  acid salts 86
  hardness of water 100
  neutralization of an
    acid 85
Toads 160, 161
  feet 160
  metamorphosis 161
Toes
  birds 165
  bones 232
  human body 181
  nails 181
Tombaugh, Clyde
  William 297, 397
Tonga-Kermadec
  Trench 382
Tongue
  human body 205, 215
  muscles 204
  reptiles 162
  swallowing 196
Tonoplast membrane 123
Tons 376, 377
Tonsils 192
  lingual tonsil 204,
    205, 215
  palatine tonsil 204
  pharyngeal tonsil 204
Topaz 279
Topical skin
  preparations 255
Topological 414
Topology 365
Toroidal transformers 345
Torricelli, Evangelista
  15, 397
Tors 281
Torso see Trunk
Tortoises
  lifespan 380
  skeleton 162
  speed 380
Torus, geometry 392
Total internal reflection
  52, 414
  binoculars 52
Toucan constellation 398
Touch 187
  receptors 181
Tower of Hanoi 370
Toxoplasmosis 259
Trabecula
  lymph nodes 193
  spleen 193
Trachea
  birds 164
  breathing 195
  cartilage 204, 213, 215
  cross section 215
  human body 194, 196,
    200, 204, 205, 212, 214
  larynx 194

lizards 162
lungs 213
mammals 166
Tracheal bifurcation 213
"Trade" winds 291
Traditional systematics,
  classification 132
Transcription, protein
  synthesis 124, 125
Transcurrent faults 276
Transducers 414
  echocardiography 240
  myoelectric arms 253
Transfer of energy 17
Transformers 344-5
  hydroelectricity 46
  nuclear power stations 59
Transfusions, blood 237
Transistors 348-9
  computers 337, 352
  diodes 346
  electronic circuits 338
  history 337
  integrated circuits 350
  semiconductors 336
Transition metals
  102-3, 414
  catalysts 88
  periodic table 74-5
Transits, planetary 312
Translation, protein
  synthesis 124, 125
Transmission 52
Transpiration, leaves 149
Transplant surgery 246,
  250-1, 414
  heart 237, 246
  rejection 250
Transuranic elements 75
Transverse colon 196,
  197, 216, 217, 218, 219
Transverse crevasses 282
Transverse dunes 280
Transverse fascia 209
Transverse foramen 211
Transverse line,
  sacrum 211
Transverse process,
  vertebrae 183, 211
Transverse waves 30
Trapezium, geometry 392
Traveling microscopes 18
Tree ferns 268
Tree frogs 160
Tree wasps 157
Trees
  acid rain 174
  epiphytes 145
  flowering 142
  gymnosperms 140
  weathering and
    erosion 280
Trematoda 132
Trenches, ocean 288,
  289, 382
Trepanning 236, 237
Triangles
  area and volume 393

elliptic geometry 365
fractals 372
geometry 364
hyperbolic geometry 365
mathematics 366-7, 392
Triangulum Australe
  constellation 388, 389
Triangulum
  constellation 387, 388
Triassic period 269
Tributaries, rivers 284
Triclinic system, crystals 35
Tricuspid valves 191
Trigger hairs,
  carnivorous plants 145
Trigonal system, crystals 35
Trigonometry 366-7, 393
Trillion 377
Trilobites 268, 269
Triodes 336
Triple bonds, organic
  chemistry 112
Trisomy, chromosome
  abnormalities 263
Triton 302
Triturus cristatus 161
Trolleys, emergency
  care 245
Trophic levels, food
  chains 170
Trophic pyramid, food
  chains 170
Tropical 414
Tropical cyclones 293
Tropical rainforests
  life zones 168
  primary production 380
Tropics 291
Troposphere 290, 292
Troughs, folds 277
True vocal cords 194
Truffles
  classification 131
  summer truffle 136
Trunk 414
  human body 180, 208-11
Tsiolkovsky crater,
  Moon 311
Tuataras 162
Tube feet,
  echinoderms 151
Tubercle of rib 211
Tubers, succulents 145
Tubes, liquids in 36
Tubules, kidneys 198
Tucana constellation 388
Tugela Falls 383
Tumors
  positron emission
    tomography (PET) 243
  X-ray imaging 241
Tundra, life zones 168
Tuned circuits 345
Tungsten
  discovery of 379
  melting and boiling
    points 379
  periodic table 74

transition metals 102
Tunica albuginea 222
Tunica vaginalis 222
Tuning fork 31
Tupungatito 383
Turbellaria 132
Turbines 414
  geothermal power 47
  hydroelectricity 46
  nuclear power stations 59
  tidal power 47
  wind power 47
Turbulence, chaos
  theory 372
Turning forces 21
  formula 378
  rollers 24, 25
  screws 26
Tursiops truncatus 167
Turtles 162
  cladistics 133
Turycecus lamellata 154
Tusk shells,
  classification 132
Tweezers 246
Twins constellation 386
Two-dimensional
  shapes, geometry 364
Tycho crater, Moon 311
Tympanic membrane 203
Typhoons 293

U

U-shaped valleys 283
Ulna
  birds 164
  human skeleton 182,
    226, 228, 229
  joint 183
Ulnar nerve 186, 226,
  227, 228, 229
Ultrasound 415
  echocardiography 240
  medical imaging 237, 240
Ultraviolet (UV) 415
  astronomy 299
  atmosphere 290
  electromagnetic
    spectrum 49, 299
  fluorescence 56-7
  Hubble Space Telescope
    298
  integrated circuit
    manufacture 351
  nebulae 327
  ozone layer 174, 290
  Sun 307
Umbel, flowers 144
Umbilical cord 199
Umbilicus 180, 209
Umbra 306, 310
Unconsciousness,
  general anaesthetics 247
Unicellular 134, 415
Union, set theory 371
Uniramia 132, 154
Uniramians 154, 156

classification 132
Unit cells 34, 415
United States Defense
  Department 337
Units of temperature 32
Universal indicator
  paper 84
Universal set, set
  theory 371
Universe
  Big Bang theory
    297, 332
  cosmology 332-3
  creation myths 8
  galaxies 328-9
  geocentric model 314
  history of astronomy 296
  wormholes 331
Universities 11, 14
Unnilennium 74
Unnilhexium 74
Unniloctium 74
Unnilpentium 74
Unnilquadium 74
Unnilseptium 74
Unreactive elements 74
Unukalhai 389
Upquarks 60
Upthrust 415
  hot-air balloons 39
  immersed objects 36, 37
Upward meniscus 36
Uranium
  instability 75
  nuclear power 59
  periodic table 74
Uranus 318-19
  data 384
  discovery of 297
  moons 308, 385
  rings 308, 318, 319
  size 304
  space probes 302,
    318, 319
Urea
  discovery of 67
  mammals 166
Urea-methanal 114
Ureters
  birds 164
  female 224
  human body 198, 217,
    220, 221
  lizards 162
  male 223
  mammals 166
Urethras 198, 199, 222
  external orifice 223,
    224, 225
  membraneous 223
  penile 223
  prostatic 223
Urinary bladder see
  Bladder
Urinary system 198
Urine 415
  human body 188, 198,
    222, 225

mammals 166
pregnancy tests 256
Urochordata 133
Urogenital diaphragm 222, 225
Ursa Major constellation 386, 387, 389
Ursa Minor constellation 386
Urubupunga Falls 383
Uterus (womb) 166, 198, 415
childbirth 257
fundus 224
in-vitro fertilization 256
menstrual cycle 225
pregnancy 199
Utgaard 383
Uvula 204

V

Vaccines 261, 415
development of 237
genetic engineering 262
Vacuoles
amoebas 135
plant cells 123
Vacuums
air pumps 66
ammonia fountain 93
cathode-ray tubes 57, 336
Ventouse extraction, childbirth 256, 257, 415
Vagina 198, 224, 225
birth 199
sexual intercourse 199
suppositories 255
vaginal opening 224, 225
Vagus nerve 207, 214
Valles Marineris, Mars 315
Valleys
erosion 279, 283
glaciers 282, 283
hanging 282, 283
rivers 284
Valves, electronic 336
Valves (heart) 191
mechanical 252, 253
transplants 251
Valves, lymph nodes 193
Van de Graaff generators 40-1, 343
Vanadium 74
Vaporization
bromine 110
fractional distillation 113
gas chromatography 70
iodine 110
Variable capacitors 343
Variable resistors 44, 341
Variable stars 325
Variables, algebra 362-3, 415
Variation
evolution 128

heredity 127
Varicose veins 381
Vas deferens 198, 199, 222, 223
Vascular grafts 252, 253
Vascular system 415
echinoderms 151
ferns 139
human body 190-1
nonflowering plants 138
plant-transport systems 148, 149
Vauquelin, Nicolas-Louis 379
Vectors 415
Cartesian coordinates 366
vector coordinates 367
Vega 328, 387, 388
Veins 190, 193, 202
angular 202
arcuate 198
axillary 190, 205, 226
azygos 213, 215
basilic 226, 228, 229
brachial 190, 226
brachiocephalic 205, 212, 213, 214, 215
cardiac 213
cephalic 190, 205, 209, 226, 228, 229
cerebral 207
dorsal digital 190
dorsal metatarsal 190
facial 202, 205
femoral 190, 230
gonadal 220
greater occipital 202
hemiazygos 215
hepatic 196, 217, 220, 221
hepatic portal 190, 217, 219
hypophyseal portal 188
iliac
common iliac 190, 216, 220, 230
external iliac 220, 221, 224, 230
internal iliac 223, 224
inferior vena cava see vena cava
insect wings 156
intercostal 213, 215
jugular 200
external jugular 202, 205
internal jugular 190, 192, 202, 205, 212, 213, 214, 215
lymph nodes 193
mesenteric 218
inferior mesenteric 219
superior mesenteric 219
occipital 202
ovarian 224
popliteal 190, 231, 233
portal 219
pulmonary 190, 191,

212, 213
radial 190
renal 190, 198, 220
retromandibular 202
saphenous 190, 230, 233
great saphenous 233
small saphenous 231, 233
splenic 193, 219
subclavian 190, 192, 205, 213, 214, 215
submental 205
superficial temporal 202
superior mesenteric 219
superior temporal 202
superior vena cava see vena cava
thyroid 202, 205
tibial 190, 233
ulnar 190
vena cava 191
inferior vena cava 190, 215, 216, 217, 218, 220, 221, 230
superior vena cava 190, 212, 213, 214, 215
Veins, leaves 143, 149
Vela constellation 386, 388
Vela Supernova Remnant 327
Velocity 22, 415
momentum 23
terminal 24
theory of relativity 62
Venn diagrams 359, 370, 371
Venom
insects 156
scorpions 155
snakes 163
Venous sinus, spleen 193
Ventilators, intensive care units 245
Ventral nerve cord, insects 156
Ventral root, spinal cord 186
Ventricles
brain 207
echocardiography 240
heart 190, 191, 212, 213, 214
Ventricular systole 191
Vents, volcanoes 275
Venules, pituitary gland 188
Venus 312-13
data 384
orbit 29, 304, 313
size 305
space probes 303, 312
Venus flytrap 145
Vernier callipers 18
Vernier scale 415
Vertebrae
birds 164
cervical 182, 183, 200, 211

coccygeal 182, 183, 200, 211
fish 158
human skeleton 182, 183, 211
lumbar 182, 183, 211, 221
mammals 166
sacral 182, 183, 200, 211
thoracic 182, 183, 211
tortoises 162
Vertebral column 182, 183, 203, 208, 215
see also Coccyx; Sacrum
Vertebral foramen 211
Vertebrata 133
Vertebrates 415
amphibians 160
birds 164
classification 133
evolution 268
fish 158
mammals 166
reptiles 162
Vertex, geometry 364
Very high frequency (VHF) radio 48
Very large-scale integration (VLSI) 337, 351
Vesalius, Andreas 178, 236, 397
De Humani Corporis Fabrica 178-9
Vestibulocochlear nerve 203
Vibration
electromagnetic radiation 49
frequency 31
oscillation 30
sound 30, 31
thermal expansion 34
Vicia faba 147
Victoria, Lake 383
Victoria Falls 383
Victoria Island 382
Video cards, computers 553
Viking landers, Mars 303
Villi 197
Vinegar
formula 379
reaction with sodium hydrogencarbonate 85
Vinson Massif 382
Violet light 49
Vipers 163
Virgin constellation 386, 388
Virgo constellation 386, 388, 389
Virtual reality surgery 248, 249
Viruses 11, 134, 415
discovery of 121

diseases 258
structure 134
T cells and 250
Visceral 415
Vision
color 50
seeing by reflected light 52
tests 239
Vitamin A 381
Vitamin B1 381
Vitamin B2 381
Vitamin B3 381
Vitamin B6 381
Vitamin C 381
formula 379
Vitamin D 381
Vitamin E 381
Vitreous humor 205
Vityaz II 382
Vivisection 178
Vocal cords 194, 215
Vocal sacs, frogs 160
Voice box see Larynx
Voice coil 31
Volans constellation 388, 389
Volcanoes 274-5
active 383
atolls 289
formation of Earth 268
historical theories 266
igneous rocks 278
on Io 316
island arcs 273, 288
on Mars 314, 315
on Moon 311
plate tectonics 272
seamounts 288
on Venus 313
Voles 170
Volkmann spoons 246
Volta, Alessandro 15, 66, 397
Voltage 415
capacitors 342, 343
computers 552
diodes 346, 347
electric circuits 42
electrochemistry 96, 97
electronic circuits 338, 339
formula 378
generators 46
Ohm's Law 42
potentiometers 341
resistors 340
SI units 377
transformers 344, 345
transistors 348, 349
wind power 47
Voltage dividers 340
Voltaic cells 96, 97
Voltmeters, electric circuits 43
Volts 42, 377
Volume 415
Charles' Law 39

conversion tables 377
data 393
gas molar 73
gases 38-9
measurements 376
Volume controls, potentiometers 341
Volva, gilled mushrooms 137
Vomer 206
Vostok 382
Voyager 2 space probe 302, 318, 319, 320
Vulpecula constellation 387
Vulva 180, 224

W

W particles 60
Wading birds 165
Wai'ale'ale, Mount 382
Walking, arthropods 154
Wallaby, red-necked 167
Walruses 167
energy requirements 380
Walton, Ernest Thomas Sinton 15, 397
WANs (Wide Area Networks) 355
Warm fronts 293
Washing soda
efflorescence 93
formula 379
Washington, Mount 382
Wasps 157
speed 380
Water
as acid 84
and alkali metals 98
amphibians 160
atmosphere 290
as base 84
boiling point 32
capillary action 36
catalytic converters 89
in chemistry 92-3
chlorination 110, 111
clouds 292
coastlines 286-7
and combustion 83
concentrations 81
dehydrating agents 92
digestive system 196, 197
distillation 71
electricity generation 46
electrolytic decomposition 96
erosion 280
evaporation 16
exothermic reactions 90
fish 158
formation of Earth 268
formula 379
four-elements theory 66
freezing point 32
geothermal power 47

hard water 86, 100
hurricanes 293
hydrogen bonding 78, 79
hydrological science 266
kidneys 220
limestone caves 281
magnetic resonance
  imaging (MRI) 242
meniscus 36
mineral water 86, 87
as mixture 70
molecular model 68
on Neptune 320
nuclear power stations 59
oceans 288-9
pH scale 84
photosynthesis 100, 148
pollution 174
preparation of
  chlorine 110
preparation of
  oxygen 108
pressure 37
reaction with sodium 98
reactivity 94
respiration 124
rivers 284-5
rock cycle 278-9
rusting of iron 82
salts 86, 87
sea water 288
solutions 16, 70
as a solvent 93
storm hydrographs 284
succulents 145
surface tension 36
tidal power 47
transpiration 149
upthrust 37
urinary system 198
vapor 106
water cycle 172, 267
water table 284
wave behaviour 54
waves 287
Water bears,
  classification 133
Water birds 164
Water Carrier
  constellation 388
Water of crystallization
  92, 415
copper chloride 102
efflorescence 93
hygroscopy 93
monohydrates 93

sodium thiosulfate 109
Water fleas 154
  classification 133
  reproductive strategy 169
Water hyacinth 145
Water molds 134
  classification 131
Water Snake
  constellation 386, 388
Water vascular system,
  echinoderms 151
Waterfalls 284
  formation of 285
  hanging valleys 283
  highest 383
  rock cycle 278
Watersheds 284
Watson, James Dewey
  121, 397
Watts 377
Wavelengths 30, 415
  colours 50
  electromagnetic
    radiation 48-9
  sound waves 31
  white light spectrum 49
Waves 30-1, 415
  behavior 54-5
  electromagnetic
    radiation 48
  interference 54
  light 55
  oscilloscopes 339
  plane 54
Principle of
  Superposition 54
  quantum theory 62
  sound 30
  in springs 30
Waves (water)
  coastlines 286
  oceans 287
Wax
  candle wax 78, 83
  fractional distillation 113
Weak interaction 15,
  60, 415
Weasels 170
Weather 292-3
  atmospheric science 266
  balloons 290
  chaos theory 372
  historical theories 266
  maps 293
  meteorology 267
  records 382
  winds 291

Weathering
  rock cycle 278
  rocky landscapes 280-1
Web pages, computer
  networks 355
Webbed feet
  amphibians 160
  duck-billed platypus 167
  wading birds 165
  water birds 164
Webs, spiders 155
Wedges 26
Wegener, Alfred 267, 397
Weight 415
  air resistance 24
  component 20
  formula 378
  lifting with pulleys 27
  measurement 18
  resultant force 20
  upthrust 37
Weights and
  measures 376-7
Welding metals
  32, 90, 91
Welwitschia mirabilis 11,
  140
Westerly winds 291
Wet, four-elements
  theory 66
Wetland plants 145
Wezen 386, 389
Whales 166, 167
  lifespan 380
Wheels
  axles 27
  ball bearings 25
Whelks 171
Whisk ferns,
  classification 131
White blood cells
  functions 191
  lymphocytes 250
  stem cells 250
White dwarf stars
  325, 327
White light
  additive process 51
  color vision 50
  destructive
    interference 54-5
  radiation from hot
    objects 49
  spectrum 49
White matter 186,
  187, 207
White Oval, Jupiter

316, 317
White phosphorus 106
White pulp, spleen 193
Whole numbers 360, 415
Whooping cough
  vaccine 261
Width 18
Wildlife reserves 175
Wilhelm, Mount 382
Wilson, John Tuzo
  267, 397
Wilson, Robert Woodrow
  297, 397
Wind pollination 146
  flowering plants 144
  pine trees 141
Windpipe see Trachea
Winds
  erosion 280
  global circulation 291
  hurricanes 293
  on Mars 314
  ocean currents 288, 289
  rock cycle 278
  speed 383
  water cycle 172
  waves 287
  wind farms 47
  wind power 46-7
Winged seeds,
  conifers 141
Wings
  bats 167
  birds 164, 165
  butterflies and moths 157
  evolution 129
  insects 156
Winter 271
Wire
  electricity generation 46
  electromagnetism 44-5
Wishbone, birds 164
Wöhler, Friedrich 67,
  397
Wolf constellation 388
Womb see Uterus
Wombats 167
Wood
  burning 32
  woody flowering
    plants 142
Wood mouse, yellow-
  necked 170
Woodlands, food
  chains 170
Woodlice, classification 132
Work 415

formula 378
simple machines 26
Workers, tree wasps 157
World Conservation
  Union 175
World Wide Web 354, 355
Worm gear 17
Wormholes 330, 331
Worms 152
  classification 132, 133
  infections 258
Wounds, emergency
  care 244
Wrasses 169
Wrench faults 276
Wrist 180
  artificial joints 253
  bones 228, 229
  muscles 185, 228

XYZ

X-plates,
  oscilloscopes 339
X rays 49, 415
  astronomy 299
  barium meals 100, 101
  black holes 330, 331
  cathode-ray tubes 336
  computerized
    tomography 241
  crystallography 67
  discovery of 15
  electromagnetic
    radiation 48
  electromagnetic
    spectrum 49, 299
  medical diagnosis 49,
    237, 240, 241
Xenon 75
Xerophytes 145
  gymnosperms 140
Xiphoid process 182
Xixabangma Feng 383
XNOR gate 390
XOR gate 370, 390
Xylem cells, plant-
  transport systems 123,
  148, 149
Y-plates,
  oscilloscopes 339
Yangtze River 383
Yap Trench 382
Yard, unit of
  measurement 376, 377
Yeasts 136
  classification 131

fermentation 89
Yellow bile,
  "humors" 236
Yellow-green algae,
  classification 131
Yellow light
  additive process 51
  sodalite 56
  subtractive process 51
  white light spectrum 49
Yellow pigments 70
Yellow River 285, 383
Yellowstone Park 175
Yew 140
Yin and yang 236
Yolk sac, birds' eggs 164
Yosemite Falls 383
Ytterbium 75
Yttrium 74
Z particles 60
Zaire, River 383
Zero 358, 359, 360
Zinc
  alkaline dry cells 96
  displacement reactions 94
  formula 379
  periodic table 75
  reactivity 94
  reactivity with dilute
    acids 95
  voltaic cells 97
Zinc sulphate 94
Zirconium 74
Zona pellucida 127
Zoology, history 120
Zooplankton 171
Zubenelgenubi 386, 389
Zubeneschamali 386, 389
Zygomatic arch 201, 206
Zygomatic bone 183,
  204, 206
Zygomycota 131
Zygotes 415
  fertilization 127
  heredity 127
  human reproduction 199
  nonflowering plants 138
Zymase 89

Acknowledgments

DK Publishing would like to thank:
DK Publishing would like to say a special thank you to Lara Maiklem for efforts way above and beyond the call of duty: at times editor, project editor, and senior editor in one.

Physics
Griffin and George, Loughborough (scientific equipment); University College, London (glassware); Maplin electronics, Hammersmith; Kensington Park School, Kensington

Chemistry
The Hall School, South Hampstead and Imperial College, London for use of their laboratories); University College, London; Kensington Park School, Kensington

Life Sciences and Ecology
Philip Harris Education, Staffordshire (loan of models and advice); Diana Miller; Lawrie Springate; Karen Sidwell; Chris Thody; Michelle End; Susan Barnes and Chris Jones at the EMU Unit of the Natural History Museum, London; Jenny Evans at Kew Gardens, Surrey; Kate Biggs at the Royal Horticultural Gardens, Surrey; Spike Walker of Microworld Services; Neil Fletcher; John Bryant of Bedgebury Pinetum, Kent; Dean Franklin; Clare Roe; Roy Flooks; David Manning's Animal Ark; Intellectual Animals; Howletts Zoo, Canterbury; John Dunlop; Alexander O'Donnel; Sue Evans at the Royal Veterinary College, London; Dr Geoff Potts and Fred Frettsome at the Marine Biological Association of the United Kingdom, Plymouth; Jeremy Adams at the Booth Museum of Natural History, Brighton; Derek Telling at the Department of Anatomy, University of Bristrol; the Natural History Museum, London; Andy Highfield at the Tortoise Trust; Brian Harris at the Aquarium, London Zoo; the Invertebrate Department, London Zoo; Dr. Harold McClure at the Yerkes Regional Primate Center, Emory University, Atlanta, Georgia; Neilson Lausen at the Harvard Medical School; New England Regional Primates Research Center, Southborough, Massachusetts; Dr. Paul Hopwood at the Department of Veterinary Anatomy, University of Sydney

Human Anatomy
Richard Greenland, DK Multimedia

Medical Science
Dr. Sarah Metcalf (bone plate and hip bone replacement); Draeger Medical, Hertfordshire; Carl Zeiss Ltd., Hertfordshire; John Bell and Croyden, London (surgical and medical instruments); Porter Nash, London (bone marrow needle and syringe); Impra (UK) Ltd., Worcestershire (vascular grafts); Dan Humphreys and Richard Walker at the London Ambulance Service for advice and the loan of ambulance equipment

Earth Sciences
Dr. John Nudds, The Manchester Museum, Manchester; Dr. Alan Wooley and Dr. Andrew Clark, The Natural History Museum, London; Graham Bartlett, National Meteorological Library and Archive, Bracknell; Tony Drake, BP Exploration, Uxbridge; Jane Davies, Royal Society of Chemistry, Cambridge; Dr. Tony Waltham, Nottingham Trent University, Nottingham; Staff at the Smithsonian Institute, Washington, D.C.; June Duller; Staff at the United States Geological Survey, Washington, D.C.; Staff at the National Geographic Society, Washington, D.C.; Staff at Edward Lawrence Associates (Export Ltd.), Midhurst; David Lambert

Astronomy and Astrophysics
John Becklake; the Memorial Museum of Cosmonautics, Moscow; the Cosmos Pavilion, Moscow; the US Space and Rocket Center, Alabama; Broadhurst, Clarkson, and Fuller Ltd.; Susannah Massey; Tatyana Alekseyevna

PHOTOGRAPHY:
Dean Belcher, Peter Chadwick, Andy Crawford, Geoff Dann, Bob Gathany, Steve Gorton, Anna Hodgson, Dave King, Tim Ridley

ADDITIONAL PHOTOGRAPHY:
Jane Burton, Judith Harrington, Bob Langrish, Cyril Laubscher, Matthew Ward, Jerry Young

ILLUSTRATORS:
Julian Baum, Rick Blakely, Alison Brown, Joanna Cameron, Kuo Kang Chen, Simone End, Roy Flooks, Mark Franklin, Mick Gillah, Andrew Green, David Hopkins, Selwyn Hutchinson, Nick Loates, Chris Lyon, Janos Marffy, Charles Metz, Claire Naylor, Sandra Pond, Colin Rose, John Temperton, Richard Tibbits, Hali Verrinder, Gareth Wild, Philip Wilson, John Woodcock

MODEL MAKERS:
Simon Murrel, Claire Naylor, Bruce Streater

ADDITIONAL DESIGN ASSISTANCE:
Stephen Croucher

ADDITIONAL EDITORIAL ASSISTANCE:
Julie Oughton, Mukul Patel, Will Hodgkinson

PROOFREADERS:
Fred Gill, Will Hodgkinson

DK Publishing would like to say a special thank you in memory of Fred Gill for all the work he did for DK over the years

INDEX:
Hilary Bird

Some pages in this book previously appeared in the *Visual Dictionary* Series, published by DK Publishing.

Picture credits:

The publisher wishes to thank the following for their kind permission to reproduce their photograph:

c=center; b=bottom; l=left; r=right; t=top

Biofotos Associates: 258cr British Geological Survey: 274crb British Petroleum Co. Plc: 95tl British Steel: 103tl Bruce Coleman Ltd: Gerald Cubitt 286tr; Paul van Gaalen 282tr; Kim Taylor 154br; Bill Wood 152bl Steven J. Cooling: 277bl, 284br, 284br Department of Clinical Radiology, Salisbury District Hospital: 252cl Galaxy Picture Library: Michael Stecker 324cr, 326b Robert Harding Picture Library: C.Deli 47cr Philip Harris: 126clb The Image Bank: 292tr; Mel Digiacomo 55crb Leonard Lessin/ Peter Arnold Inc: 115cl Lund Observatory: 328-9 Microworld Services: 135cl NASA: 264-5c, 291br, 294, 310tr, 313br, 315bl, 315br, 324tr, 326tr, 327tl, 333cr Goddard Space Flight Centre: 331br H. Hammel/MIT: 317br JPL: 308clb, 308bl, 316bl, 316cb, 316crb, 316bc, 316br, 319br, 322tr, 332cr, 355c Raghvenda Sahai and John Trauger (JPL), the WFPC2 Science Team: 327tr Space Telescope Science Institute: 317bc National Maritime Museum: 399bl National Medical Slide Bank: 258c Natural History Museum: 129bl

Downe House 120-1 NHPA: Stephen Dalton 171br; Jany Sauvanet 161cra Newage International Ltd: 46tc NOAO: 328cb Oxford Scientific Film: Breck P. Kent 150cl London Scientific Films: 155tr Oxford University Museum: 129tl Pictor International: 101tl Premaphotos Wildlife: K.G. Preston-Mafham 152tr Press Association, Roslin Institute, Edinburgh: 263br Des Reid: 91cl Marion Tully: 34tr Science Museum: 14l, 15bl, 15tc, 66l, 66br, 67tc, 120l, 121tl, 178l, 178br, 179tl, 236l, 237bl, 237tc, 248bl, 252bl, 266tl, 267, 296-7bc, 297tc, 336tl, 336bl, 337tc, 339tl, 339tc, 351tr, 398l, 399tc Science Photo Library: 240bl, 241tl Lawrence Berkeley Laboratory: 60t Biology Media: 260tr BMDO/NRL/LLNL: 323bc Dr. Jeremy Burgess: 134br, 137tr CERN: 58bl, 60br, Charing Cross Hospital, Department of Nuclear Medicine: 243tl Prof. S. Ciniti/CNRI: 261bl CNRI: 101tr, 259bl Custom Medical Stock Photo/ Z. Binor: 248cb Barry Dowsett: 259tc Malcom Fielding/The BOC Group: 245br Simon Fraser: 47tr, 241bl Department of Neuroradiology, Newcastle General Hospital: 243tr Carlos Goldin: 240tr Hale Observatories: 306tr George Haling: 252tr Dr. William C. Keel: 328cb King's College School of Medicine, Department of Surgery: 241t Prof. E. Lorentz/Peter Arnold Inc: 372br, Dennis Milon:

323cla Hank Morgan: 249tr, 249ca, 256bl, 261cr, 262tr NASA: 111tr, 273br, 320crb, 320br, 323tl NIBSC: 258crb Omikron: 12-3c, 60cr David Parker: 49tc, 276tr, 345br, 351bl Paul Parker: 238cl Alfred Pasieka: 253br, 254cr, 350br D.Phillips: 127bl Phillippe Plailly: 78tr, 263bc Chris Priest: 247tr Royal Observatory, Edinburgh: 328clb David Scharf: 250tr Dr. Rudolph Schild: 328bl Blair Seitz: 258tr Sinclair Stammers: 134cr Stammers/Thompson: 49bc Geoff Tomkinson: 242br Alexander Tsiaras 247tc U.S. National Institute of Health: 243bl X-Ray Astronomy Group, Leicester University: 333tr The Stock Market Photo Agency: 39bc, 45cl, 47c, 351tl Simon Warner: 369br C. James Webb: 259tr

Oxford University Museum: back cover cl. Science Photo Library: Dr Jeremy Burgess back cover c; David Parker back cover crb. Southampton Oceanography Centre: front cover cb.

Every effort has been made to trace the copyright holders. DK Publishing apologises for any unintentional omissions and would be pleased, in any such cases, to add an acknowledgment in future editions.

Contributors to this series include:

Project Art Editors:
Simon Murrel, Paul Greenleaf

Additional design assistance:
Carla De Abreu, Anthea Forle, Laura Owen

Project Editors:
Philippa Colvin, Kirstie Hills, Peter Jones, Mukul Patel

Editor:
Des Reid

Additional editorial assistance:
Jo Evans, Caroline Hunt, Leah Kennedy, Jane Mason, Jane Sarlius, Roger Tritton

Senior Art Editor:
Tracey Hambleton-Miles

Senior Editor:
Louise Candlish

Picture Researchers:
Anna Lord, Sharon Southren,

Production:
Meryl Silbert, Stephen Stuart